D1455379

THE NEW INTERPRETER'S® BIBLE
IN TWELVE VOLUMES

VOLUME EIGHT

GENERAL ARTICLES ON
THE NEW TESTAMENT

THE GOSPEL OF
MATTHEW

THE GOSPEL OF
MARK

EDITORIAL BOARD

THE NEW INTERPRETER'S® BIBLE

GENERAL ARTICLES
&
INTRODUCTION, COMMENTARY, & REFLECTIONS
FOR EACH BOOK OF THE BIBLE
INCLUDING
THE APOCRYPHAL / DEUTEROCANONICAL BOOKS
IN
TWELVE VOLUMES

VOLUME
VIII

ABINGDON PRESS
Nashville

THE NEW INTERPRETER'S BIBLE
VOLUME VIII

Copyright © 1995 by Abingdon Press

This book is printed on recycled, acid-free paper.

Library of Congress Cataloging-in-Publication Data

The New Interpreter's Bible: general articles & introduction,
    commentary, & reflections for each book of the Bible, including the
Apocryphal/Deuterocanonical books.
        p. cm.
    Full texts and critical notes of the New International Version and
the New Revised Standard Version of the Bible in parallel columns.
    Includes bibliographical references.
    ISBN 0-687-27821-X (v. 8: alk. paper)
    1. Bible—Commentaries. I. Abingdon Press. II. Bible. English.
New International. 1994. III. Bible. English. New Revised
Standard. 1994.
BS491.2.N484   1994
220.7'7   94-21092
                                                                                      CIP

The Hebraica® and Graeca® fonts used to print this work are available from Linguist's Software, Inc., P.O. Box 580, Edmonds, WA 98020-0580 tel. (206) 775-1130.

PUBLICATION STAFF
President and Publisher: Robert K. Feaster
Editorial Director: Neil M. Alexander
Managing Editor: Michael E. Lawrence
Project Director: Jack A. Keller, Jr.
Assistant Editor: Eli D. Fisher, Jr.
Production Editor: Linda S. Allen
Art Director: Nancy R. Bozeman
Designer: J. S. Laughbaum
Copy Processing Manager: Sylvia S. Marlow
Composition Specialist: Kathy M. Harding
Publishing Systems Analyst: Glenn R. Hinton
Prepress Manager: William E. Gentry
Prepress Systems Technician: Thomas E. Mullins
Production Coordinator: James E. Leath
Scheduling: Laurene M. Brazzell
                Helen M. Pouliot
Print Procurement Coordinator: David M. Sanders

98 99 00 01 02 03 04—10 9 8 7 6 5 4 3

MANUFACTURED IN THE UNITED STATES OF AMERICA

CONSULTANTS

NEIL M. ALEXANDER
Vice President/Editorial Director
Abingdon Press
Nashville, Tennessee

OWEN F. CAMPION
Associate Publisher
Our Sunday Visitor
Huntington, Indiana

MINERVA G. CARCAÑO
Minister-in-Charge
South Valley Cooperative Ministry
Albuquerque, New Mexico

V. L. DAUGHTERY, JR.
Pastor
Park Avenue United Methodist Church
Valdosta, Georgia

SHARON NEUFER EMSWILER
Pastor
First United Methodist Church
Rock Island, Illinois

JUAN G. FELICIANO
Pastor
Iglesia Metodista "Juan Wesley"
Arecibo, Puerto Rico

CELIA BREWER MARSHALL
Lecturer
University of North Carolina at Charlotte
Charlotte, North Carolina

NANCY C. MILLER-HERRON
Attorney and clergy member of the
Tennessee Conference
The United Methodist Church
Dresden, Tennessee

ROBERT C. SCHNASE
Pastor
First United Methodist Church
McAllen, Texas

BILL SHERMAN
Pastor
Woodmont Baptist Church
Nashville, Tennessee

RODNEY T. SMOTHERS
Pastor
Central United Methodist Church
Atlanta, Georgia

WILLIAM D. WATLEY
Pastor
St. James African Methodist Episcopal Church
Newark, New Jersey

TALLULAH FISHER WILLIAMS
Pastor
Trinity United Methodist Church
Mt. Prospect, Illinois

SUK-CHONG YU
Pastor
San Francisco Korean United Methodist Church
San Francisco, California

CONTRIBUTORS

ELIZABETH ACHTEMEIER
Adjunct Professor of Bible and Homiletics
Union Theological Seminary in Virginia
Richmond, Virginia
(Presbyterian Church [U.S.A.])
Joel

LESLIE C. ALLEN
Professor of Old Testament
Fuller Theological Seminary
Pasadena, California
(Baptist)
1 & 2 Chronicles

GARY A. ANDERSON
Associate Professor of Religious Studies
University of Virginia
Charlottesville, Virginia
(The Roman Catholic Church)
Introduction to Israelite Religion

DAVID L. BARTLETT
Lantz Professor of Preaching and
Communication
The Divinity School
Yale University
New Haven, Connecticut
(American Baptist Churches in the U.S.A.)
1 Peter

ROBERT A. BENNETT
Professor of Old Testament
Episcopal Divinity School
Cambridge, Massachusetts
(The Episcopal Church)
Zephaniah

ADELE BERLIN
Professor of Hebrew and East Asian
Languages and Literature
University of Maryland
College Park, Maryland
Introduction to Hebrew Poetry

BRUCE C. BIRCH
Professor of Old Testament
Wesley Theological Seminary
Washington, DC
(The United Methodist Church)
1 & 2 Samuel

PHYLLIS A. BIRD
Associate Professor of Old Testament
Interpretation
Garrett-Evangelical Theological Seminary
Evanston, Illinois
(The United Methodist Church)
The Authority of the Bible

C. CLIFTON BLACK
Associate Professor of New Testament
Perkins School of Theology
Southern Methodist University
Dallas, Texas
(The United Methodist Church)
1, 2, & 3 John

JOSEPH BLENKINSOPP
John A. O'Brien Professor of Biblical Studies
Department of Theology
University of Notre Dame
Notre Dame, Indiana
(The Roman Catholic Church)
Introduction to the Pentateuch

M. EUGENE BORING
I. Wylie and Elizabeth M. Briscoe Professor of
New Testament
Brite Divinity School
Texas Christian University
Fort Worth, Texas
(Christian Church [Disciples of Christ])
Matthew

WALTER BRUEGGEMANN
William Marcellus McPheeters Professor of Old
    Testament
Columbia Theological Seminary
Decatur, Georgia
(United Church of Christ)
    Exodus

DAVID G. BUTTRICK
Professor of Homiletics and Liturgics
The Divinity School
Vanderbilt University
Nashville, Tennessee
(United Church of Christ)
    The Use of the Bible in Preaching

RONALD E. CLEMENTS
Samuel Davidson Professor of Old Testament
King's College
University of London
London, England
(Baptist Union of Great Britain and Ireland)
    Deuteronomy

RICHARD J. CLIFFORD
Professor of Old Testament
Weston School of Theology
Cambridge, Massachusetts
(The Roman Catholic Church)
    Introduction to Wisdom Literature

JOHN J. COLLINS
Professor of Hebrew Bible
The Divinity School
University of Chicago
Chicago, Illinois
(The Roman Catholic Church)
    Introduction to Early Jewish Religion

ROBERT B. COOTE
Professor of Old Testament
San Francisco Theological Seminary
San Anselmo, California
(Presbyterian Church [U.S.A.])
    Joshua

FRED B. CRADDOCK
Bandy Distinguished Professor of Preaching
    and New Testament, Emeritus
Candler School of Theology
Emory University
Atlanta, Georgia
(Christian Church [Disciples of Christ])
    Hebrews

TONI CRAVEN
Professor of Hebrew Bible
Brite Divinity School
Texas Christian University
Fort Worth, Texas
(The Roman Catholic Church)
    Introduction to Narrative Literature

JAMES L. CRENSHAW
Robert L. Flowers Professor of Old Testament
The Divinity School
Duke University
Durham, North Carolina
(Baptist)
    Sirach

KEITH R. CRIM
Pastor
New Concord Presbyterian Church
Concord, Virginia
(Presbyterian Church [U.S.A.])
    Modern English Versions of the Bible

R. ALAN CULPEPPER
Dean
The School of Theology
Mercer University
Atlanta, Georgia
(Southern Baptist Convention)
    Luke

KATHERYN PFISTERER DARR
Associate Professor of Hebrew Bible
The School of Theology
Boston University
Boston, Massachusetts
(The United Methodist Church)
    Ezekiel

ROBERT DORAN
Professor of Religion
Amherst College
Amherst, Massachusetts
    1 & 2 Maccabees

THOMAS B. DOZEMAN
Professor of Old Testament
United Theological Seminary
Dayton, Ohio
(Presbyterian Church [U.S.A.])
    Numbers

JAMES D. G. DUNN
Lightfoot Professor of Divinity
Department of Theology
University of Durham
Durham, England
(The Methodist Church [Great Britain])
1 & 2 Timothy; Titus

ELDON JAY EPP
Harkness Professor of Biblical Literature
and Chairman of the Department of Religion
Case Western Reserve University
Cleveland, Ohio
(The Episcopal Church)
*Ancient Texts and Versions of the New
Testament*

KATHLEEN ROBERTSON FARMER
Professor of Old Testament
United Theological Seminary
Dayton, Ohio
(The United Methodist Church)
Ruth

CAIN HOPE FELDER
Professor of New Testament Language
and Literature
The School of Divinity
Howard University
Washington, DC
(The United Methodist Church)
Philemon

TERENCE E. FRETHEIM
Professor of Old Testament
Luther Seminary
Saint Paul, Minnesota
(Evangelical Lutheran Church in America)
Genesis

FRANCISCO O. GARCÍA-TRETO
Professor of Religion and Chairman of the
Department of Religion
Trinity University
San Antonio, Texas
(Presbyterian Church [U.S.A.])
Nahum

CATHERINE GUNSALUS GONZÁLEZ
Professor of Church History
Columbia Theological Seminary
Decatur, Georgia
(Presbyterian Church [U.S.A.])
*The Use of the Bible in Hymns, Liturgy,
and Education*

JUSTO L. GONZÁLEZ
Adjunct Professor of Church History
Columbia Theological Seminary
Decatur, Georgia
(The United Methodist Church)
*How the Bible Has Been Interpreted in
Christian Tradition*

DONALD E. GOWAN
Robert Cleveland Holland Professor of Old
Testament
Pittsburgh Theological Seminary
Pittsburgh, Pennsylvania
(Presbyterian Church [U.S.A.])
Amos

JUDITH MARIE GUNDRY-VOLF
Assistant Professor of New Testament
Fuller Theological Seminary
Pasadena, California
(Presbyterian Church [U.S.A.])
Ephesians

DANIEL J. HARRINGTON
Professor of New Testament
Weston School of Theology
Cambridge, Massachusetts
(The Roman Catholic Church)
Introduction to the Canon

RICHARD B. HAYS
Associate Professor of New Testament
The Divinity School
Duke University
Durham, North Carolina
(The United Methodist Church)
Galatians

THEODORE HIEBERT
Professor of Hebrew Bible
McCormick Theological Seminary
Chicago, Illinois
(Mennonite Church)
Habakkuk

CARL R. HOLLADAY
Professor of New Testament
Candler School of Theology
Emory University
Atlanta, Georgia
*Contemporary Methods of Reading the
Bible*

MORNA D. HOOKER
Lady Margaret's Professor of Divinity
The Divinity School
University of Cambridge
Cambridge, England
(The Methodist Church [Great Britain])
Philippians

DAVID C. HOPKINS
Professor of Old Testament
Wesley Theological Seminary
Washington, DC
(United Church of Christ)
Life in Ancient Palestine

DENISE DOMBKOWSKI HOPKINS
Professor of Old Testament
Wesley Theological Seminary
Washington, DC
(United Church of Christ)
Judith

LUKE T. JOHNSON
Robert W. Woodruff Professor of New
Testament and Christian Origins
Candler School of Theology
Emory University
Atlanta, Georgia
(The Roman Catholic Church)
James

WALTER C. KAISER, JR.
Colman Mockler Distinguished Professor
of Old Testament
Gordon-Conwell Theological Seminary
South Hamilton, Massachusetts
(The Evangelical Free Church of America)
Leviticus

LEANDER E. KECK
Winkley Professor of Biblical Theology
The Divinity School
Yale University
New Haven, Connecticut
(Christian Church [Disciples of Christ])
Introduction to The New Interpreter's Bible

CHAN-HIE KIM
Professor of New Testament and Director of
Korean Studies
The School of Theology at Claremont
Claremont, California
(The United Methodist Church)
Reading the Bible as Asian Americans

RALPH W. KLEIN
Dean and Christ Seminary-Seminex Professor of
Old Testament
Lutheran School of Theology at Chicago
Chicago, Illinois
(Evangelical Lutheran Church in America)
Ezra; Nehemiah

MICHAEL KOLARCIK
Assistant Professor
Regis College
Toronto, Ontario
Canada
(The Roman Catholic Church)
Book of Wisdom

WILLIAM L. LANE
Paul T. Walls Professor of Wesleyan
and Biblical Studies
Department of Religion
Seattle Pacific University
Seattle, Washington
(Free Methodist Church of North America)
2 Corinthians

ANDREW T. LINCOLN
Department of Biblical Studies
University of Sheffield
Sheffield, England
(The Church of England)
Colossians

J. CLINTON McCANN
Assistant Professor of Old Testament
Eden Theological Seminary
St. Louis, Missouri
(Presbyterian Church [U.S.A.])
Psalms

ABRAHAM J. MALHERBE
Buckingham Professor of New Testament
Criticism and Interpretation, Emeritus
The Divinity School
Yale University
New Haven, Connecticut
(Church of Christ)
*The Cultural Context of the New Testament:
The Greco-Roman World*

W. EUGENE MARCH
Arnold Black Rhodes Professor of Old
Testament
Louisville Presbyterian Theological Seminary
Louisville, Kentucky
(Presbyterian Church [U.S.A.])
Haggai

JAMES EARL MASSEY
Dean Emeritus and Distiniguished
Professor-at-Large
The School of Theology
Anderson University
(Church of God [Anderson, Ind.])
*Reading the Bible from Particular Social
Locations: An Introduction;
Reading the Bible as African Americans*

J. MAXWELL MILLER
Professor of Old Testament
Candler School of Theology
Emory University
Atlanta, Georgia
(The United Methodist Church)
Introduction to the History of Ancient Israel

PATRICK D. MILLER
Charles T. Haley Professor of Old Testament
Theology
Princeton Theological Seminary
Princeton, New Jersey
(Presbyterian Church [U.S.A.])
Jeremiah

FREDERICK J. MURPHY
Associate Professor and Chair of the
Department of Religious Studies
College of the Holy Cross
Worcester, Massachusetts
(The Roman Catholic Church)
Introduction to Apocalyptic Literature

CAROL A. NEWSOM
Associate Professor of Old Testament
Candler School of Theology
Emory University
Atlanta, Georgia
(The Episcopal Church)
Job

GEORGE W. E. NICKELSBURG
Professor of Christian Origins and Early Judaism
School of Religion
University of Iowa
Iowa City, Iowa
(Evangelical Lutheran Church in America)
*The Jewish Context of the New
Testament*

IRENE NOWELL
Associate Professor of Religious Studies
Benedictine College
Atchison, Kansas
(The Roman Catholic Church)
Tobit

KATHLEEN M. O'CONNOR
Associate Professor of Biblical Studies
Maryknoll School of Theology
Maryknoll, New York
(The Roman Catholic Church)
Lamentations

GAIL R. O'DAY
Almar H. Shatford Associate Professor
of Homiletics
Candler School of Theology
Emory University
Atlanta, Georgia
(United Church of Christ)
John

BEN C. OLLENBURGER
Associate Professor of Old Testament
Associated Mennonite Biblical Seminaries
Elkhart, Indiana
(Mennonite Church)
Zechariah

DENNIS T. OLSON
Assistant Professor of Old Testament
Princeton Theological Seminary
Princeton, New Jersey
(Evangelical Lutheran Church in America)
Judges

CAROLYN OSIEK
Professor of New Testament
Department of Biblical Languages
and Literature
Catholic Theological Union
Chicago, Illinois
(The Roman Catholic Church)
Reading the Bible as Women

SAMUEL PAGÁN
  Regional Translation Coordinator for the United
    Bible Societies
  Miami, Florida
  (Christian Church [Disciples of Christ])
    Obadiah

SIMON B. PARKER
  Associate Professor of Hebrew Bible and
    Harrell F. Beck Scholar in Hebrew Scripture
  The School of Theology
  Boston University
  Boston, Massachusetts
  (The United Methodist Church)
    *The Ancient Near Eastern Literary
      Background of the Old Testament*

PHEME PERKINS
  Professor of New Testament
  Boston College
  Chestnut Hill, Massachusetts
  (The Roman Catholic Church)
    Mark

DAVID L. PETERSEN
  Professor of Old Testament
  The Iliff School of Theology
  Denver, Colorado
  (Presbyterian Church [U.S.A.])
    Introduction to Prophetic Literature

CHRISTOPHER C. ROWLAND
  Dean Ireland's Professor of the Exegesis
    of Holy Scripture
  The Queen's College
  Oxford, England
  (The Church of England)
    Revelation

ANTHONY J. SALDARINI
  Professor of Biblical Studies
  Boston College
  Chestnut Hill, Massachusetts
  (The Roman Catholic Church)
    Baruch; Letter of Jeremiah

J. PAUL SAMPLEY
  Professor of New Testament and
    Christian Origins
  The School of Theology and The Graduate Division
  Boston University
  Boston, Massachusetts
  (The United Methodist Church)
    1 Corinthians

JUDITH E. SANDERSON
  Assistant Professor of Hebrew Bible
  Department of Theology and Religious Studies
  Seattle University
  Seattle, Washington
    *Ancient Texts and Versions of the Old
      Testament*

EILEEN M. SCHULLER, O.S.U.
  Associate Professor
  Department of Religious Studies
  McMaster University
  Hamilton, Ontario
  Canada
  (The Roman Catholic Church)
    Malachi

FERNANDO F. SEGOVIA
  Associate Professor of New Testament
    and Early Christianity
  The Divinity School
  Vanderbilt University
  Nashville, Tennessee
  (The Roman Catholic Church)
    Reading the Bible as Hispanic Americans

CHRISTOPHER R. SEITZ
  Associate Professor of Old Testament
  The Divinity School
  Yale University
  New Haven, Connecticut
  (The Episcopal Church)
    Isaiah 40–66

CHOON-LEONG SEOW
  Henry Snyder Gehman Professor of
    Old Testament Language and Literature
  Princeton Theological Seminary
  Princeton, New Jersey
  (Presbyterian Church [U.S.A.])
    1 & 2 Kings

MICHAEL A. SIGNER
  Abrams Professor of Jewish Thought and
    Culture
  Department of Theology
  University of Notre Dame
  Notre Dame, Indiana
    *How the Bible Has Been Interpreted in
      Jewish Tradition*

MOISÉS SILVA
Professor of New Testament
Westminster Theological Seminary
Philadelphia, Pennsylvania
(The Orthodox Presbyterian Church)
*Contemporary Theories of Biblical
Interpretation*

DANIEL J. SIMUNDSON
Professor of Old Testament
Luther Seminary
Saint Paul, Minnesota
(Evangelical Lutheran Church in America)
Micah

ABRAHAM SMITH
Assistant Professor of New Testament
and Christian Origins
The School of Theology
Boston University
Boston, Massachusetts
(The National Baptist Convention, USA, Inc.)
1 & 2 Thessalonians

DANIEL L. SMITH-CHRISTOPHER
Associate Professor of Theological Studies
Department of Theology
Loyola Marymount University
Los Angeles, California
(The Society of Friends [Quaker])
*Daniel; Bel and the Dragon; Prayer of
Azariah; Susannah*

MARION L. SOARDS
Professor of New Testament Studies
Louisville Presbyterian Theological Seminary
Louisville, Kentucky
(Presbyterian Church [U.S.A.])
Acts

ROBERT C. TANNEHILL
Academic Dean and Harold B. Williams
Professor of Biblical Studies
Methodist Theological School in Ohio
Delaware, Ohio
(The United Methodist Church)
The Gospels and Narrative Literature

GEORGE E. TINKER
Associate Professor of Cross-Cultural Ministries
The Iliff School of Theology
Denver, Colorado
(Evangelical Lutheran Church in America)
Reading the Bible as Native Americans

W. SIBLEY TOWNER
The Reverend Archibald McFadyen Professor of
Biblical Interpretation
Union Theological Seminary in Virginia
Richmond, Virginia
(Presbyterian Church [U.S.A.])
Ecclesiastes

PHYLLIS TRIBLE
Baldwin Professor of Sacred Literature
Union Theological Seminary
New York, New York
Jonah

GENE M. TUCKER
Professor of Old Testament, Emeritus
Candler School of Theology
Emory University
Atlanta, Georgia
(The United Methodist Church)
Isaiah 1–39

CHRISTOPHER M. TUCKETT
Rylands Professor of Biblical Criticism
and Exegesis
Faculty of Theology
University of Manchester
Manchester, England
(The Church of England)
Jesus and the Gospels

RAYMOND C. VAN LEEUWEN
Professor of Religion and Theology
Eastern College
Saint Davids, Pennsylvania
(Christian Reformed Church in North America)
Proverbs

ROBERT W. WALL
Professor of Biblical Studies
Department of Religion
Seattle Pacific University
Seattle, Washington
(Free Methodist Church of North America)
Introduction to Epistolary Literature

DUANE F. WATSON
Associate Professor of New Testament Studies
Department of Religion and Philosophy
Malone College
Canton, Ohio
(The United Methodist Church)
2 Peter; Jude

RENITA J. WEEMS
Associate Professor of Hebrew Bible
The Divinity School
Vanderbilt University
Nashville, Tennessee
(African Methodist Episcopal Church)
Song of Songs

SIDNIE A. WHITE
Associate Professor of Religious Studies
Department of Religion
Albright College
Reading, Pennsylvania
(The Episcopal Church)
Esther; Additions to Esther

VINCENT L. WIMBUSH
Professor of New Testament and
    Christian Origins
Union Theological Seminary
New York, New York
(Progressive National Baptist Convention, Inc.)
*The Ecclesiastical Context of the New
    Testament*

N. THOMAS WRIGHT
Lecturer in New Testament Studies
Fellow, Tutor, and Chaplain
Worcester College
Oxford, England
(The Church of England)
Romans

GALE A. YEE
Associate Professor of Old Testament
Department of Theology
University of Saint Thomas
Saint Paul, Minnesota
(The Roman Catholic Church)
Hosea

FEATURES OF
THE NEW INTERPRETER'S® BIBLE

The general aim of *The New Interpreter's Bible* is to bring the best in contemporary biblical scholarship into the service of the church to enhance preaching, teaching, and study of the Scriptures. To accomplish that general aim, the design of *The New Interpreter's Bible* has been shaped by two controlling principles: (1) form serves function, and (2) maximize ease of use.

General articles provide the reader with concise, up-to-date, balanced introductions and assessments of selected topics. In most cases, a brief bibliography points the way to further exploration of a topic. Many of the general articles are placed in volumes 1 and 8, at the beginning of the coverage of the Old and New Testaments, respectively. Others have been inserted in those volumes where the reader will encounter the corresponding type of literature (e.g., "Introduction to Prophetic Literature" appears in Volume 6 alongside several of the prophetic books).

Coverage of each biblical book begins with an "Introduction" that acquaints the reader with the essential historical, sociocultural, literary, and theological issues necessary to understand the biblical book. A short bibliography and an outline of the biblical book are found at the end of each Introduction. The introductory sections are the only material in *The New Interpreter's Bible* printed in a single wide-column format.

The biblical text is divided into coherent and manageable primary units, which are located within larger sections of Scripture. At the opening discussion of any large section of Scripture, readers will often find material identified as "Overview," which includes remarks applicable to the large section of text. The primary unit of text may be as short as a few verses or as long as a chapter or more. This is the point at which the biblical text itself is reprinted in *The New Interpreter's Bible*. Dealing with Scripture in terms of these primary units allows discussion of important issues that are overlooked in a verse-by-verse treatment. Each scriptural unit is identified by text citation and a short title.

The full texts and critical notes of the New International Version and the New Revised Standard Version of the Bible are presented in parallel columns for quick reference. Since every translation is to some extent an interpretation as well, the inclusion of these two widely known and influential modern translations provides an easy comparison that in many cases will lead to a better understanding of a passage. Biblical passages are set in two-column format and placed in green tint-blocks to make it easy to recognize them at a glance. The NIV and NRSV material is clearly identified on each page on which the text appears.

Immediately following each biblical text is a section marked "Commentary," which provides an exegetical analysis informed by linguistic, text-critical, historical-critical, literary, social-scientific, and theological methods. The Commentary serves as a reliable, judicious guide through the text, pointing out the critical problems as well as key interpretive issues.

The exegetical approach is "text-centered." That is, the commentators focus primarily on the text in its final form rather than on (a) a meticulous rehearsal of problems of scholarship associated with a text, (b) a thorough reconstruction of the pre-history of the text, or (c) an exhaustive rehearsal of the text's interpretive history. Of course, some attention to scholarly problems, to the pre-history of a text, and to historic interpretations that have shaped streams of tradition is important in particular cases precisely in order to illumine the several levels of meaning in the final form of the text. But the *primary* focus is on the canonical text itself. Moreover, the Commentary not only describes pertinent aspects of the text, but also teaches the reader what to look for in the text so as to develop the reader's own capacity to analyze and interpret the text.

Commentary material runs serially for a few paragraphs or a few pages, depending on what is required by the biblical passage under discussion.

Commentary material is set in a two-column format. Occasional subheads appear in a bold green font. The next level of subdivisions appears as bold black fonts and a third level as black italic fonts. Footnotes are placed at the bottom of the column in which the superscripts appear.

Key words in Hebrew, Aramaic, or Greek are printed in the original-language font, accompanied by a transliteration and a translation or explanation.

Immediately following the Commentary, in most cases, is the section called "Reflections." A detailed exposition growing directly out of the discussion and issues dealt with in the Commentary, Reflections are geared specifically toward helping those who interpret Scripture in the life of the church by providing "handles" for grasping the significance of Scripture for faith and life today. Recognizing that the text has the capacity to shape the life of the Christian community, this section presents multiple possibilities for preaching and teaching in light of each biblical text. That is, instead of providing the preacher or teacher full illustrations, poems, outlines, and the like, the Reflections offer *several* trajectories of possible interpretation that connect with the situation of the contemporary listeners. Recognizing the power of Scripture to speak anew to diverse situations, not all of the suggested trajectories could be appropriated on any one occasion. Preachers and teachers want some specificity about the implications of the text, but not so much specificity that the work is done for them. The ideas in the Reflections are meant to stimulate the thought of preachers and teachers, not to replace it.

Three-quarter width columns distinguish Reflections materials from biblical text and Commentary.

Occasional excursuses have been inserted in some volumes to address topics of special importance that are best treated apart from the flow of Commentary and Reflections on specific passages. Set in three-quarter width columns, excursuses are identified graphically by a green color bar that runs down the outside margin of the page.

Occasional maps, charts, and illustrations appear throughout the volumes at points where they are most likely to be immediately useful to the reader.

CONTENTS

VOLUME VIII

ANCIENT TEXTS AND VERSIONS OF THE NEW TESTAMENT

ELDON JAY EPP

THE RELEVANCE AND NATURE OF NEW TESTAMENT TEXTUAL CRITICISM

Basic to interpreting the New Testament is a grasp of the earliest forms of the NT text, which, in turn, requires (1) knowledge of the MSS that preserve these texts and of the early versions that made the Christian writings accessible in non-Greek speaking areas and (2) acquaintance with the scribal habits that influenced the transmission process. Hence, "textual criticism," which treats these matters, is designated "lower criticism," for it refers to basic or foundational approaches that attempt to establish the "original" text written by the various NT authors, or—failing that goal—to reconstruct the earliest attainable form of the NT text. Textual criticism, logically at least, precedes "higher criticism," which comprises the whole range of philological, historical, social, philosophical, and literary approaches to the interpretation of biblical literature (though neither the term "lower criticism" nor "higher criticism" is much used anymore).

Ideally, then, an interpreter of a NT passage first establishes the most likely original text and only then proceeds with further studies or interpretations of that text. After all, if one is seeking to grasp what a NT author said or meant (the author's intention), it would be foolish to exegete a text that did not exist

during that author's time. Understandably, however, the process is not as simple as this might imply. For one thing, most interpreters—including critical scholars—do not themselves attempt to establish the text but rely on critical editions of the Greek NT or on other specialized studies that present the results of text-critical analyses. The most popular and useful of these aids are (1) the *Novum Testamentum Graece,* originally edited by Eberhard Nestle, later by Erwin Nestle, and most recently by Kurt and Barbara Aland;[1] and (2) with an identical Greek text but a differing apparatus, the United Bible Societies' *Greek New Testament,* edited originally by K. Aland, M. Black, C. M. Martini, B. M. Metzger, and A. Wikgren;[2] along with (3) the companion volume to the latter, *A Textual Commentary on the Greek New Testament,*[3] which provides text-critical discussions and assessments of the 1,440 sets of variant readings in the *UBSGNT's* critical apparatus and of 600 additional variation units of textual or

1. Barbara and Kurt Aland, eds., *Novum Testamentum Graece post Eberhard Nestle et Erwin Nestle,* 27th ed. (Stuttgart: Deutsche Bibelgesellschaft, 1993). Generally referred to as Nestle-Aland[27].

2. Barbara Aland, Kurt Aland, Johannes Karavidopoulos, Carlo M. Martini, and Bruce M. Metzger, eds., *The Greek New Testament,* 4th ed. (Stuttgart: Deutsche Bibelgesellschaft/United Bible Societies, 1993). Referred to as *UBSGNT*[4].

3. Bruce M. Metzger, ed., *A Textual Commentary on the Greek New Testament: A Companion Volume to the United Bible Societies' Greek New Testament (Third Edition)* (New York: United Bible Societies, 1971).

exegetical importance, providing reasons in each case why the committee selected certain variants for its NT text. The introductory sections of these three volumes assist the user in understanding the materials and methods of NT textual criticism, though for this purpose handbooks, such as those by Metzger, K. and B. Aland, Vaganay and Amphoux, and others will be essential for a fuller grasp of the discipline.[4]

Moreover, it is no simple matter to establish the "original" text of any NT writing, and often it cannot be done easily for a given passage. This is due not so much to a lack of ancient MSS or NT quotations in early church writers, but to difficulties in and differences of opinion about *methodology* for determining the original or earliest text forms. These difficulties and differences arise, in part, from the fact that textual criticism is not simply a "science"— if that is defined in empirical or "objective" terms— but is also an "art." Certainly, textual criticism has its "scientific" aspects, including statistical assessments and quantitative measurements of MS relationships, but more prominent are "subjective" judgments and qualitative decisions that have their basis in expert knowledge of the textual transmission process, including close acquaintance with scribal habits and experience with the phenomena of textual variation in general. Thus textual criticism is best described as the science and art of assessing the transmission of the NT text, identifying its variations, alterations, and distortions, and then attempting its restoration. Of course, the establishment of the most likely original text does not exhaust the tasks of textual criticism, for it seeks also to place variants within the history and ideology of the early church, not only to assess the age, character, and motivation of variants but also to extract from them some knowledge of the development of early Christian theology and ecclesiology.

4. Bruce M. Metzger, *The Text of the New Testament: Its Transmission, Corruption, and Restoration,* 3rd ed. (New York: Oxford University Press, 1992; 1st ed., 1964; 2nd ed., 1968); Kurt Aland and Barbara Aland, *The Text of the New Testament: An Introduction to the Critical Editions and to the Theory and Practice of Modern Textual Criticism,* 2nd rev. ed. (Grand Rapids: Eerdmans; Leiden: Brill, 1989; 1st ed., 1987); and Leon Vaganay and Christian-Bernard Amphoux, *An Introduction to New Testament Textual Criticism,* 2nd ed. (Cambridge: Cambridge University Press, 1991).

THE TEXTUAL TRANSMISSION PROCESS

New Testament textual criticism is occasioned directly by the nature of the textual transmission process—how the NT text has been passed down to us. Ancient writings, of course, are not preserved in their autographs, but through copies of copies of copies. The NT is no exception, although its contents have been preserved in far more numerous and much earlier copies than is generally the case with classical and other ancient literature. Among the many NT MSS in an array of languages, no two are exactly alike, and the most likely original text must be reconstructed from MSS of widely differing quality, age, and geographical origin. Perhaps some 300,000 variant readings exist among these NT MSS, and textual critics must devise procedures for sorting them and methods for evaluating their relative worth. This entails a long, complex story, whose beginnings can be documented in patristic writers as early as the third century and whose satisfactory resolution even now is not surely within reach. Understanding this story requires acquaintance with ancient writing materials, handwriting or paleography, scribal habits, scriptoria (monastery rooms set aside for copying, writing, or illuminating MSS), and ways that MSS were carried from place to place, as well as knowledge of the NT MSS and its versions themselves, judgments about the criteria for the originality of readings, and a grasp of how to form a critical edition of the NT text.

The transmission process, though not easily reconstructed for the early centuries, is understandable enough in its broad outlines. For example, it is obvious (or at least assumed) that in the early decades of Christianity an apostolic letter or, slightly later, portions of a Gospel would be read in a worship service and that, now and again, visiting Christians would carry copies to their own congregations, or writings would be shared in some other way among Christian churches—sometimes at the request of the writer (see Col 4:16). Soon some churches would possess several of these early Christian writings and small collections of gospels and/or apostolic letters and other writings would emerge, perhaps even through a conscious effort, for example, by a zealous follower of Paul. Beyond this sort of historical imagination, we know very little about such transmission processes, though we do know that the earliest NT

MSS (as well as OT writings copied for Christian use) were in codex form—i.e., like our book form as opposed to the rolls or scrolls that constitute the format used for Jewish and secular literature prior to Christianity. Indeed, it is likely that Christians invented the codex for use and preservation of their writings or, at very least, capitalized on this recently invented medium as a convenient and space-saving format.

We know also that NT writings circulated in certain rather regular combinations rather than individually; the four Gospels, for example, most often circulated together in a single codex, as did the Pauline letters; Acts might join either group, or it and the General Epistles might form another group—and there were other possible combinations, including some sixty extant codices containing the entire NT.

The various documents just described are *continuous-text* MSS, containing at least one NT writing in continuous fashion from beginning to end. In addition, yet later, *lectionary* MSS were created, to bring together those portions of Scripture that were appointed to be read in services. These MSS are not in canonical order, but are arranged either according to the church year—from Easter to Easter, containing readings for Saturdays, Sundays, and weekdays (and known as the synaxarion)—or according to the calendar year—beginning September 1 and containing "lessons" for feast days, saints' days, and other special church occasions (and called the menologion). Often an introductory phrase (*incipit*) had to be added to adapt the selected portion to liturgical use (e.g., "Jesus said . . . " or "In those days . . .").

Regardless of their form or the ways in which MSS were grouped, the early NT writings were transmitted and preserved in various collections, combinations, and formulations that facilitated their use in the worship and life of the church. As these codices were used and reused, they were copied and recopied in the churches and (later) in scriptoria, leaving for us a legacy of considerably more than 5,000 Greek MSS (both continuous-text and lectionaries), plus thousands of versional MSS and quotations of NT passages in patristic writings. These constitute the materials of NT textual criticism, to be discussed in more detail below.

The role of the scribes, or copyists, who produced copies of NT writings prior to the invention of movable type in the mid-fifteenth century—and

beyond—is crucial in the whole transmission process, for their inadvertent errors and quite conscious "improvements" have created the vast array of textual variants that now must be analyzed and judged. Certainly the copying of MSS was by nature and self-evidently a conservative process, with a very high percentage of a writing being copied accurately. Yet, even the most diligent and slavish scribe had inattentive moments and failures of communication between eye and hand, or were unconsciously influenced by parallel passages, to which they conformed the text they were producing. Then there were "thinking" scribes who considered the sense and sensibleness of the text they were copying and dared to "correct" it or to insert material known to them from other contexts or MSS or even from marginal notes in MSS. In these ways our considerable body of variant readings arose.

Scribal alterations usually are divided into the two categories intimated above. First, there are *unintentional scribal errors,* comprising what are often characterized as errors of the eye, of the ear (if copying by dictation), and of the memory or (unthinking) judgment. These include such errors as (1) confusion of letters or letter combinations having similar appearance (or sound); (2) mistaken word division (since uncial MSS were written without spaces or punctuation); (3) misread abbreviations or contractions; (4) interchanges in the order of letters or words (metathesis); (5) substitution of a more familiar word for a less familiar one, or use of a synonym when the meaning but not the exact word is in the copyist's mind; (6) omission of a word when it occurred twice, or skipping material between two similar words or letter groups (haplography); (7) repetition of a letter, word, or passage when, in copying, the eye falls on already copied text (dittography); (8) careless spelling and failure to correct such errors; and (9) unconscious assimilation to similar wording in a parallel passage or lection (sometimes this may be intentional), or harmonization with wording in the immediate context.

The other category is *intentional scribal alterations,* inevitably made in good faith to correct or otherwise improve the text in accordance with what the scribe believed to be its original (or intended) form or meaning—or even a meaning more relevant to the scribe's present ecclesiastical context. At times, therefore—though still with worthy motives as far as the scribe was concerned—changes were made to promote a doctrinal or ideological view not in the text being copied. The latter are usually subtle in nature and modest in scope, though they have more potential for shaping the transmission process than do accidental alterations. Intentional changes include (1) changes in grammar, spelling (often proper names), and style; (2) conscious harmonization with parallel passages (often in the Synoptic Gospels, in OT quotations, or in lectionaries); (3) clarification of geographical or historical points (e.g., time, place, authorship of OT quotations); (4) conflation of differing readings in two or more MSS known to the copyist; (5) addition of seemingly appropriate material (such as expanding "Jesus" to "Jesus Christ" or to the "Lord Jesus Christ"); and (6) theological or ideological alterations, often small changes in the interest of the virgin birth, the Trinity, asceticism, etc., or longer additions such as found in MSS of the "Western" textual tradition, where anti-Judaic, anti-feminist, pro-apostle, and other tendencies have been detected. The Greek MSS that resulted from this scribal process—whether produced informally and privately in a church (as we might imagine) or formally in the scriptoria that developed around 200 CE—number between 5,000 and 5,500 and constitute the primary sources for establishing the NT text. The same phenomena occur, of course, in the transmission of versional MSS.

THE SOURCE MATERIAL AND NEED FOR TEXTUAL CRITICISM

The nature and quantity of the NT texts preserved for us from antiquity accentuate the need for NT textual criticism. If, as in the case of numerous Greek and Latin authors, only a small number of MSS preserved the NT or its various parts, stemmata (or family trees) could be constructed and a critical edition of an early form of the NT text could be produced—though perhaps only with the help of extensive textual emendation. However, the mass of extant witnesses, including many that are early and extensive, provides both the opportunity and the problem of the NT text, for it is assumed—no doubt correctly—that hidden somewhere among our MSS and their thousands upon thousands of variants are *all* of the original readings of the NT writings, but this sheer quantity of witnesses and variant readings hinders the process of isolating those most likely original readings. For one thing, use of the genealogical method (establishing stemmata) does not work for the earlier periods because of extensive textual mixture among MSS. Rather, more complex and more subjective methods must be applied to the vast array of witnesses in efforts to group them and to establish time frames for the groups, and, concurrently, criteria must be defined by which individual readings can be judged according to their likely originality. As these methods were evolving over three hundred years and more, new MS discoveries—especially of earlier documents—were made, which constantly affected the developing methods.

The basic source materials are NT MSS, the ancient versions, and patristic quotations in various languages.

Greek Manuscripts. Greek MSS of the NT come in two forms and are written on three kinds of material in two kinds of handwriting. The two forms define at least two differing functions served by the MSS: continuous-text MSS, preserving the text of at least one NT book from beginning to end (even if now only partially extant), were probably designed for reading and study, while lectionaries, containing short portions of a text, were designed for liturgical use, notably for "lessons" in church services.

With respect to writing materials, some ninety-four different MSS (less than 2 percent of all NT MSS) were written on papyrus, which was used into the eighth century. Nearly 4,100 (almost 75 percent) of NT MSS were written on parchment or vellum from the eighth century to the fourteenth or fifteenth, and paper MSS number about 1,300 (to make up the remaining 24 percent), produced from the twelfth to the nineteenth centuries. Papyrus MSS are all continuous-text MSS, while parchment MSS include both continuous-text MSS (about 2,400) and lectionaries (about 1,700).

Paleographically, NT MSS were written in large, unconnected letters (uncials) until the tenth century, on both papyrus and parchment. From the ninth century on, cursive ("running") or connected letters were used, written on parchment and paper. Of the surviving MSS, those written in uncials comprise nearly 12 percent (some 630 MSS, including around 270 lectionaries), with the remaining 88 percent written in minuscule hand (some 4,800 MSS, including some 2,000 lectionaries).

Although continuous-text MSS were written on papyrus, parchment, or paper in uncial or in minuscule handwriting, textual critics cut across the categories and choose three terms to classify Greek continuous-text MSS: *papyri, uncials,* and *minuscules.* Counted according to these categories, there are currently ninety-four different "papyri," more than 260 different "uncials," and more than 2,800 "minuscules." When the nearly 2,300 "lectionaries" are added, the total number of NT MSS is around 5,450. Some of these, however, have been forever lost, and others doubtless will prove to be portions of other, separately catalogued MSS, as have two papyri and some thirty uncials to date—which accounts for some of the disparity in various sets of statistics. For example, $\mathfrak{P}^{33}$ and $\mathfrak{P}^{58}$ are from the same MS, as are $\mathfrak{P}^{64}$ and $\mathfrak{P}^{67}$, and ten uncial fragments actually belong to one MS (070). The safest statement, therefore, is that more than 5,000 different Greek NT MSS are presently extant.

To add to the confusion, the papyri are written in uncial script (but are not counted among the uncials!), and lectionaries are written in both uncial (around 270) and minuscule hands, though their form and function are sufficiently different from continuous-text MSS to require a separate category. In text-critical discussions, therefore, the term *papyri* describes all MSS written on papyrus; *uncial* means only non-papyrus continuous-text MSS written in uncial hand (and not the lectionaries so written); *minuscules* are only continuous-text MSS written in cursive hand (and not the many lectionaries so written); and *lectionaries* are portions for liturgical use, regardless of the script or writing material employed.

Methodologically—once it was agreed that early MSS, though fewer, are generally preferred to the agreement of a larger number of later MSS—the papyri and early uncials assume the position of prominence among NT MSS. Two groups stand out in importance: the forty-three oldest papyri, plus the four oldest uncials, all of which date prior to the early fourth century; and the great uncial MSS of the fourth century, primarily Codices Sinaiticus (‎א), Alexandrinus (A), and Vaticanus (B), but also Codex Bezae (D) of the late fourth/early fifth century and Codex Washingtonianus (W) of the early fifth. The papyri—with several important exceptions—and the very earliest uncials are highly fragmentary, while the stately fourth/fifth century codices ‎א, A,

and B contain all or most of the NT, although W has only the four Gospels and D contains the Gospels and Acts. The standard handbooks describe these MSS and many others of importance.

Some minuscules (perhaps 10 percent) may be important in establishing the original NT text, but about 80 percent of them are solid representatives of the Majority text (also known as the Byzantine or Koine text), a text-type that developed in the fourth century and beyond to become the official ecclesiastical text of the Byzantine Church. Although this text-type contains some early readings, it is a full or conflate text that gathered to itself many expansive and harmonizing variants, which over time coalesced as a whole into a smooth and refined text that was much used and highly respected in the church and, accordingly, was preserved in hundreds upon hundreds of (mostly late) MSS.

Likewise, lectionaries, though numerous, are not of primary importance in the search for the most likely original text, for to a very high degree they also represent the Byzantine text-type. By their very nature, however, lectionary texts are likely to have been preserved with a high degree of conservatism, for they had an official function in church services and would tend to preserve carefully texts much older than their own generally late dates. Yet, they are helpful mainly in studying the development of the NT text and in showing the source of readings that were introduced into the continuous-text MSS (especially when there is an accompanying *incipit*) by monk-copyists out of their daily and weekly familiarity with lections.

Versions. Textual criticism would be much simpler—but also much poorer—if the NT text were preserved only in Greek MSS. However, the expansion of the Greek text through translation into several ancient languages began very early in the history of Christianity, though the actual origins and early history of these versions remain obscure. Clearly, however, the Latin, Syriac, and Coptic versions were written earliest (though not necessarily in that order) and retain the greatest importance. The Gospels may first have been translated into Syriac for Tatian's *Diatessaron* (170 CE; the original language of this combination of the four Gospels is debated), or perhaps the Gospels were first put into Latin by missionaries to the Latin-speaking portions of the Roman Empire in the late second century. What is much clearer is that Latin, Syriac, and Coptic versions of the Gospels and other parts of the NT were widely circulated in the third century—though the earliest extant MSS date only in the fourth, and late in that century for Latin and Syriac MSS.

Nor is it a simple matter to use these and other versions as witnesses to the Greek NT text, for no language mechanically reproduces another. For instance, Syriac has no comparative or superlative; Syriac and Coptic have no case endings, and the latter employs strict word order to show subject, object, indirect object, etc.; Gothic has no future form; and even Latin—generally a fine medium for translating Greek—has a number of minor differences, including an inability to distinguish between the aorist and perfect tenses and the lack of a definite article. Factors such as these often make it difficult to ascertain the exact Greek text that lies behind the versions. In addition, some translations are secondary—that is, not translated directly from the Greek text, but from another translation. For example, the Armenian and Georgian versions could have been based on the Greek, but more likely the Armenian stems from Syriac and the Georgian from either Armenian or Syriac or both jointly. In spite of these hindrances, the ancient versions are significant in the search for the most likely original NT text, especially the three earliest ones.

The *Latin versions* constitute the largest tradition of any NT version, comprising more than 8,000 MSS. More than fifty of these (dating from the fourth to the thirteenth cents.) represent the Old Latin version, known from the earliest period in both North Africa and in Europe, and perhaps originating in North Africa in the late second century—though these matters are highly debated. The Old Latin was rough, and no unitary form of text existed. The latter was recognized already by Jerome, who was asked by Pope Damasus to prepare a revision of these diverse texts (including the OT), and Jerome and others completed the task in 383. This "common" version was known as the Vulgate (Vg), which developed into the dominant biblical text in the Roman Catholic Church and was designated the standard liturgical text by the Council of Trent in 1546. Old Latin MSS continued to be used, however, long after Jerome's time (as evidenced by MSS going into the thirteenth cent.), and a first task in Latin NT textual criticism is to identify the Old Latin readings preserved in the Vulgate, for it is primarily these Old Latin texts that are useful in the quest for

the most likely original Greek NT text. Yet, this is no easy task, as evidenced by the *Itala* (1954–72) and *Vetus Latina* (1956–) projects, which have occupied scholars for many years.

The *Syriac versions,* like the Latin, have an earlier phase followed by a "common" revision. An Old Syriac form survives in continuous-text MSS for the Gospels (in two versions in one MS each: the Curetonian and the Sinaitic), but virtually only in patristic quotations for the Acts and Paul's epistles (the limits of the canon in the early Syriac church). Again, Tatian's *Diatessaron* is a point of controversy: Did the Gospels first appear in Syriac in this combined form, or was the *Diatessaron* constructed from the four separate Gospels? A related issue is the date of origin of the Old Syriac version; opinions vary from the end of the second to the mid-fourth century.

What is much clearer is that early in the fifth century a common, or "simple," version, called the Peshitta, replaced both the *Diatessaron* and the Old Syriac; the Peshitta is preserved in some 350 MSS in a tight textual tradition. About the same time, a Palestinian Syriac (Aramaic) version appeared, apparently an independent translation from the Greek, and was followed early in the sixth century by the Philoxenian version, which in 616 was either reissued with marginal notes or revised (or more probably both) by Thomas of Harkel, producing a version known as the Harclean.

Third-century Egypt has furnished us with *Coptic versions* in several Coptic dialects: in Sahidic, the language of Upper (southern) Egypt; in Bohairic from the Delta region of Lower (northern) Egypt; and in lesser dialects, such as the Achmimic, sub-Achmimic, Middle Egyptian, and Fayyumic. The MSS are largely fragmentary or late, though a few extensive MSS from the fourth to the fifth centuries are extant for Matthew, John, and Acts.

Other early versions of significance include the *Armenian,* probably made in the early fifth century (curiously, more Armenian NT MSS exist than for any other version except the Latin, though none dates prior to the ninth cent.); the *Georgian,* closely akin to the Armenian in origin and character, though the Georgian MSS reveal an early and a later stage in the textual tradition for the Gospels; and the *Ethiopic,* perhaps stemming from the late fifth or early sixth century, though the extant MSS are from around the thirteenth century. Less important ancient versions are in *Arabic, Nubian,* and *Sogdian*

(Middle Iranian) in the East and in *Gothic, Old Church Slavonic,* and *Old High German* in the West.

Patristic Quotations. A final body of source material for establishing the NT text—and an important source if properly used—is composed of NT quotations found in church writings of the first several centuries, not only in Greek, but in all relevant languages as well. Their significance lies in the fact that they provide closely dated and geographically located textual readings—thus indicating the form a text had at a rather definite place and time—and a comparison with similar readings in continuous-text MSS enables us to specify the antiquity of such readings in the textual tradition and, though less clearly, the possible provenance of the MSS containing them. Hence, patristic quotations are especially useful in establishing text-types (see below).

Regrettably, however, the use of patristic quotations is not a simple matter. For one thing, the entire text-critical process must first be applied to each of these church writings to establish the text actually written, and modern critical editions remain to be done for some authors. Even the best critical editions, however, do not solve the further problems. Is the writer (a) quoting the text of a NT book directly and precisely as it occurs in the biblical text being used (a *citation*); or (b) paraphrasing the text by adapting it slightly to the discussion or to the writer's own syntax while generally maintaining verbal correspondence to the Greek text being used (an *adaptation*); or (c) merely alluding to a text's content but without substantial verbal correspondence (an *allusion*)? These questions must be answered to discover each writer's citing habits in each writing, as well as to determine the type of citation in each separate case. Only then can a patristic quotation be used as evidence for the NT text—taking into proper account, of course, the levels of citation/adaptation/allusion. As a rough rule, it is more likely that long quotations were copied from a MS than cited from memory, but it cannot be assumed that short or incomplete quotations mean that the text cited left out the missing portions of a NT text. Ideally, when a writer quotes the NT often (e.g., Origen), that writer's NT text should be reconstructed using all cases of citation, adaptation, and allusion.[5]

5. Lists of patristic writings cited in critical editions of the NT can be found in Nestle-Aland[27] and *UBSGNT*[4].

THE HISTORY AND METHOD OF NEW TESTAMENT TEXTUAL CRITICISM

The richness of the source material, along with the difficulties in sorting it out and in knowing exactly how to use it, have dominated the long history of NT textual criticism and its methodological considerations. During most of this history, the number of MSS supporting a given text or reading was determinative. Hence, we speak of the long period of the *textus receptus*—the "text received by all" as Elzevir put it in 1633—when the Byzantine text (found in the overwhelming majority of MSS) dominated; it was the Greek NT text printed in the critical editions and also formed the basis for major translations, such as the King James Version. Only when scholars began to "weigh" MSS rather than to count them—to consider their age and antiquity and their quality—was the tyranny of the *textus receptus* broken.

This was a long process, prepared for by such notables as John Mill (1707), Richard Bentley (1720), J. A. Bengel (1734), J. J. Wettstein (1751–52), and J. J. Griesbach (1775–1807), but the first clear and decisive break with the *textus receptus* came with the work of Karl Lachmann (1831). His procedure in establishing the text of the Greek NT was to give no consideration to the "received readings" (i.e., the *textus receptus*) but only to the most ancient MSS known to him, such as the oldest Greek uncials (though no minuscules), the Old Latin and Vulgate, and some early patristic writers, such as Origen, Irenaeus, and Cyprian.

This triumph over the *textus receptus* combined with striking new MS discoveries in the decades following Lachmann to bring textual criticism into its distinctly modern phase. Constantin von Tischendorf discovered Codex Sinaiticus and published nearly two dozen volumes of new MSS and eight editions of the Greek NT (1841–72), employing the basic principle—akin to Lachmann's—that MSS "that excel in antiquity prevail in authority." Tischendorf's 8th edition, containing C. R. Gregory's "Prolegomena" (1869–94), stands as a monument of both textual data and method. S. P. Tregelles had announced similar principles in 1854 and applied them to his edition of the NT (1857–72), but the major advance came in 1881–82 with the audaciously titled *The Greek New Testament in the Original Greek* by B. F. Westcott and F. J. A. Hort.

Westcott-Hort placed on solid ground the general principle that their predecessors had adopted largely on the basis of common sense: that the text of the NT should be determined from its *oldest* witnesses. They provide a near demonstration by employing two arguments: (1) The Greek and Latin patristic writers up to the mid-third century support one or another of the texts prior to the Byzantine (which they called Syrian) but do not support distinctive Byzantine readings; and (2) the Byzantine text is a later text, formed, in part, by conflation of readings from the earlier Neutral and Western texts. However, Westcott-Hort modified the simple principle of basing the NT text on the oldest MSS by adding "and *best* MSS." This determination of the "best" MSS was necessary in their scheme because of their conclusion that the Neutral and Western text-types had equally early origins—in the second century— but that (as they saw it) the uncontaminated "Neutral" text (hence the name) was to be preferred, on internal grounds, to the rough, paraphrastic, and often corrupt "Western" text. An exception was the so-called "Western non-interpolations," those several passages in the Gospels where the shorter Western readings were more likely original than their longer "Neutral" counterparts.

In their quest for the best (i.e., the purest) MSS, Westcott-Hort accredited most highly Codex Vaticanus (B), along with Codex Sinaiticus (א), both from the fourth century. They did so on the basis of their well-known internal or subjective principles. First is the internal evidence of *readings,* which assesses individual readings in terms of (a) intrinsic probability (what the *author* most likely wrote), and (b) transcriptional probability (what the *scribe* most likely wrote). If both assessments agree on one reading, high probability obtains; if they differ, transcriptional probability is decisive. The second principle involves the internal evidence of *documents,* which considers the groups of readings that make up a MS, yielding knowledge of a MS's general quality and reliability. This second guideline would come into play when the internal evidence of individual readings is unclear, and it results in the isolation of MSS that are generally superior in quality. Finally, a third principle is applied: that of the internal evidence of *groups of* MSS, which assesses MS groupings as to their overall character as bearers of

generally reliable documents when compared with other groups. It was by this more detailed process that the "Neutral" group, led by Codices B and א, rose (in Westcott-Hort's view) to a position above both the early but rough and corrupt "Western" group and the smooth but late and conflate Byzantine group—whose readings, in addition, were unable to explain the origin of the other readings. Since the *textus receptus* is roughly equivalent to the Byzantine text, the work of Westcott-Hort was the final, definitive triumph over the *textus receptus.*

The decades following Westcott-Hort were filled with excitement as textual critics began to test, refine, and build upon these challenging achievements. A few detractors (notably J. W. Burgon in the last two decades of the nineteenth cent.) attempted, without success, to discredit the "Neutral" MSS in favor of the now deposed Byzantine; recent followers of Burgon, equally without success, have tried to defend the "Majority Text" as original. More productive were those who argued that the "Western" text was not so much corrupt as it was rough— a sign of its early and perhaps more primitive text, especially in the Gospels and Acts—and that Westcott-Hort's "Western" category actually encompassed two types of text: the "Western" (which was also Eastern, hence the quotation marks around "Western") and "Caesarean" (embodied in the newly found Codices Washingtonianus [W] and Koridethi [Θ] and other MSS and versions). Rather quickly, however, this Caesarean text was divided into two phases, a primitive or pre-Caesarean text (exemplified in $\mathfrak{P}^{45}$, discovered in 1930–31) and a recensional phase, the Caesarean text proper. This view, widely supported for almost fifty years, more recently has been seriously questioned, leaving in its wake a $\mathfrak{P}^{45}$-W group that goes no farther and a disintegrating later group in which Codices W and Θ seem to be more closely related to other groups than to each other, calling into question the existence of both a "pre-Caesarean" and a "Caesarean" text in general.

Westcott-Hort's two earliest text forms were bolstered by additional MS discoveries, notably the Oxyrhynchus papyri (1898ff.), the Chester Beatty papyri (1930–31), and the Bodmer papyri (1956ff.), which provided very early and occasionally extensive portions of NT writings. For example, $\mathfrak{P}^{75}$ (third cent.) is extraordinarily similar in text to Codex B, putting to rest the older view that B represents a fourth-century scholarly revision; $\mathfrak{P}^{66}$ (c. 200 CE) is also a strong, though secondary, witness to the "Neutral" text [now called Egyptian or Alexandrian]; and $\mathfrak{P}^{29}$, $\mathfrak{P}^{48}$, and $\mathfrak{P}^{38}$ (third/fourth cents.), though fragmentary, attest a "Western" form. The various newly found papyri, especially the forty or so that date up to the third/fourth centuries plus four uncials of similar date, became the focus of text-critical work in the twentieth century, attracting the attention of every editor of a critical edition and virtually every text-critical theorist. It is the conviction of most that the papyri remain the key for unlocking the methodological mysteries and ambiguities surrounding NT textual criticism, particularly the clarification of the *text-types* that existed in the early periods of textual transmission.

Most (though not all) textual critics acknowledge the existence of four NT text-types: the Egyptian (or Alexandrian), the so-called "Western," the (former) Caesarean, and the Byzantine. Historically and currently, these designations are problematic, and it might be better to call them the *A-text* ("accepted" = Byzantine); the *B-text* (Codex B = the $\mathfrak{P}^{75}$-B, or Egyptian); the *C-text* (textually between B and D = the $\mathfrak{P}^{45}$-Codex W text [formerly Caesarean]); and the *D-text* (for its later representative, Codex D, or "Western"). Everyone acknowledges that the A-text (Byzantine) existed from the fourth century on; in addition, though still debated, it would appear that around 200 CE the other three text-types (B, C, and D) were in existence. Basic to this conclusion is the fact that one or more early papyri can be connected with each text-type by virtue of a clear relationship with an early major uncial MS in that text-type that possesses a similar textual complexion.

Method and theory of NT textual criticism for a very long time followed the lines broadly sketched above: a combination, on the one hand, of documentary evidence (primarily emphasis on the oldest MSS and on the multiple witness of early MSS of varying groups or geographical locations) and, on the other hand, of internal considerations employed to isolate the readings most likely to have been written by a given NT author or by a scribe. The criteria (or "canons of criticism") included in this twofold approach might be summarized as follows, with each criterion phrased in such a way that, if it accurately describes a textual variant (other things being equal), that variant would be regarded as the most likely original reading:

A. Criteria related to external evidence.
   1. A variant's support by the earliest MSS, or by MSS assuredly preserving the earliest texts.
   2. A variant's support by the "best-quality" MSS.
   3. A variant's support by MSS with the widest geographical distribution.
   4. A variant's support by one or more established groups of MSS of recognized antiquity, character, and perhaps location—i.e., of recognized best quality.
B. Criteria related to internal evidence.
   1. A variant's status as the shorter/shortest reading in the variation-unit.
   2. A variant's status as the harder/hardest reading in the variation-unit.
   3. A variant's fitness to account for the origin, development, or presence of all other readings in the variation-unit.
   4. A variant's conformity to the author's style and vocabulary.
   5. A variant's conformity to the author's theology or ideology.
   6. A variant's conformity to Koine (rather than Attic) Greek.
   7. A variant's conformity to Semitic forms of expression.
   8. A variant's lack of conformity to parallel passages or to extraneous items in the context generally.
   9. A variant's lack of conformity to OT passages.
   10. A variant's lack of conformity to liturgical forms and usages.
   11. A variant's lack of conformity to extrinsic doctrinal views.

These criteria are employed with various degrees of decisiveness and in varying combinations in all current methodologies in NT textual criticism. Those who employ them will recognize, however, that their use is highly complicated and that, in the final analysis, determinations are made on the basis of a "balance of probabilities." For example, often the criteria will compete with one another: one or more will accredit a reading while others discredit the same reading; or different criteria at the same time will accredit two or more competing readings; or external criteria may support one reading, while internal criteria support another, etc. Moreover, the "shorter reading" and the Koine vs. Attic Greek criteria have been called into question recently, and it is clear that not all carry the same weight. As Tischendorf noted long ago, the only criterion that can clearly claim priority is number 3 under B above: The preferred reading is the one that best explains the origin of all other readings in the variation-unit.

Three basic methods related to these criteria are current today. First is the *historical-documentary approach,* which emphasizes the external criteria, including the age and provenance of a document as well as the general quality of its text and its scribe. Ideally, this method attempts to reconstruct the history of the NT text by tracing the lines of transmission back through the extant MSS to the earliest stages and then selecting the reading that represents the earliest attainable level of the textual tradition. Thus the earliest papyri and uncials—that group prior to the fourth century—play the dominant role, followed by the great uncials of the fourth and fifth centuries. Also prominent in this method is the quantitative measurement of MS relationships, which assesses the total agreement and disagreement between and among a sizable number of MSS so that textually related MSS can be identified and used in this historical reconstruction. This method, however, remains more of an ideal than an actuality, for the history of our MS tradition cannot yet be worked out in all its details.

The second method is the *rigorous eclectic method* (also known as "rational criticism" or "thoroughgoing eclecticism" by its proponents—chiefly G. D. Kilpatrick and J. K. Elliott), in which the internal criteria receive almost exclusive emphasis. In practice, the variant selected is the one that best suits the context of the passage, the author's style and vocabulary, or the author's theology, while taking into account additional factors, such as scribal habits, including items B. 6–11 in the list above. Internal criteria of these kinds take precedence over the external—sometimes to the virtual exclusion of the latter—and each reading is judged on its intrinsic merits and not on its MS support.

The third basic method is *reasoned eclecticism,* which is a genuine eclecticism, for it combines these two approaches and relies on the balance of probabilities arising from the application of all relevant criteria—external and internal. Thus in any variation-unit, the reading would be chosen that appears to be in the earliest MS or group and that makes the best sense when the internal criteria are applied. This method admits that no single criterion or invariable combination of criteria will resolve all cases of textual variation, so it applies all of them as evenly as possible and without prejudice.

This method is presently employed by the vast majority of NT textual critics, and it was the method used, in general, to form the text common to Nestle-Aland[27] and *UBSGNT*[4]. Judging from its use there, it may be fair to generalize that external criteria have a slight edge among practitioners of this method, though—as always—the variant that can explain all the others in a variation-unit would possess the highest priority wherever such a variant clearly can be identified. Indeed, in actual practice, readings that find their way into our current critical editions are very often those that are attested by the Egyptian or B-text. Time and again such readings emerge as the earliest documented variants and also as superior on internal grounds. Although this result is not to be attributed to the same rationale as in Westcott-Hort, it is striking that the common text of Nestle-Aland[27] and *UBSGNT*[4] is closely similar to that of Westcott-Hort. Still, the nagging question remains regarding the claims to originality of numerous D-text readings, suggesting that the debate over the details of our most likely original NT text will continue to require our diligent attention for some time to come.

BIBLIOGRAPHY

Aland, Barbara, and Kurt Aland, eds. *Novum Testamentum Graece post Eberhard Nestle et Erwin Nestle.* 27th ed. Stuttgart: Deutsche Bibelgesellschaft, 1993. Known as Nestle-Aland[27], its additional editors were Johannes Karavidopoulos, Carlo M. Martini, and Bruce M. Metzger. The editors for the 26th edition (1979–91) were K. Aland, Matthew Black, C. M. Martini, B. M. Metzger, and Allen Wikgren. Both editions were produced in cooperation with the Institute for New Testament Textual Research, Münster/Westphalia.

Aland, Kurt, and Barbara Aland. *The Text of the New Testament: An Introduction to the Critical Editions and to the Theory and Practice of Modern Textual Criticism.* 2nd ed. Grand Rapids: Eerdmans, 1989. (1st English ed., 1987; German original, 1982). The latest and most reliable source for data on NT MSS.

Aland, Barbara, Kurt Aland, Johannes Karavidopoulos, Carlo M. Martini, and Bruce M. Metzger, eds. *The Greek New Testament.* 4th ed. Stuttgart: Deutsche Bibelgesellschaft/United Bible Societies, 1993. Known as *UBSGNT*[4] or *UBS*[4], it contains the same text as Nestle-Aland[27]. The editors for the first three editions were K. Aland, Matthew Black, C. M. Martini, B. M. Metzger, and Allen Wikgren. All editions were produced in cooperation with the Institute for New Testament Textual Research, Münster/Westphalia.

Birdsall, J. Neville. "The New Testament Text." In *From the Beginnings to Jerome.* Vol. 1 of *The Cambridge History of the Bible.* Edited by P. R. Ackroyd and C. F. Evans. Cambridge: Cambridge University Press, 1970.

Birdsall, J. Neville. "The Recent History of New Testament Textual Criticism (From Westcott and Hort, 1881, to the Present)," *ANRW* (1992) II:26.1: 99-197.

Epp, Eldon Jay. "Textual Criticism: New Testament." In *ABD*, 6:412-35.

———, and Gordon D. Fee. *Studies in the Theory and Method of New Testament Textual Criticism*. Grand Rapids: Eerdmans, 1993. Seventeen essays on the history of the NT text and on various text-critical methodologies. Chapters 2, 7, 8, 12, 13, 14, and 17 are the most relevant to this article.

Metzger, Bruce M. *The Early Versions of the New Testament: Their Origin, Transmission, and Limitations*. New York: Oxford University Press, 1977. A comprehensive work. The treatment of each version concludes with a statement, by a noted expert, on that version's "limitations in representing Greek."

———. *The Text of the New Testament: Its Transmission, Corruption, and Restoration*. 3rd ed. New York: Oxford University Press, 1992; 1st ed., 1964; 2nd ed., 1968. The standard manual in English. The appendix in the first two editions listing Greek papyri has been replaced by a chapter on advances in the field from 1964 to 1990.

———, ed. *A Textual Commentary on the Greek New Testament: A Companion Volume to the United Bible Societies' Greek New Testament (third edition)*. London: United Bible Societies, 1971. A report of the reasons for the adoption/rejection of readings in the *UBSGNT*[3] text; it covers that edition's 1,440 sets of variants plus some 600 others, many in Acts.

Vaganay, Leon, and Christian-Bernard Amphoux. *An Introduction to New Testament Textual Criticism*. 2nd ed. Cambridge: Cambridge University Press, 1991. A brief manual, now brought up to date.

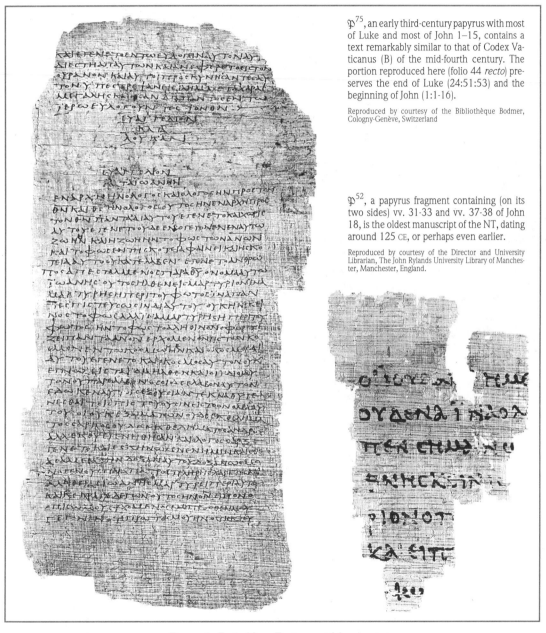

𝔓[75], an early third-century papyrus with most of Luke and most of John 1–15, contains a text remarkably similar to that of Codex Vaticanus (B) of the mid-fourth century. The portion reproduced here (folio 44 *recto*) preserves the end of Luke (24:51:53) and the beginning of John (1:1-16).

Reproduced by courtesy of the Bibliothèque Bodmer, Cologny-Genève, Switzerland

𝔓[52], a papyrus fragment containing (on its two sides) vv. 31-33 and vv. 37-38 of John 18, is the oldest manuscript of the NT, dating around 125 CE, or perhaps even earlier.

Reproduced by courtesy of the Director and University Librarian, The John Rylands University Library of Manchester, Manchester, England.

Figure 1: Early New Testament Manuscripts

THE CULTURAL CONTEXT OF THE NEW TESTAMENT: THE GRECO-ROMAN WORLD

ABRAHAM J. MALHERBE

The relationship between early Christianity and its environment has been viewed in a number of ways. From the earliest centuries, some have held that God prepared the world for the gospel, so that in "the fullness of time" (Gal 4:4) humanity was ready to receive redemption. In modern times, the relationship has frequently been thought of as one of influence, with Christianity influenced by its Jewish and pagan antecedents. Thus the "history of religions school" of interpretation in the nineteenth century described a Christianity that was strongly susceptible to such influences, and in the twentieth century scholars continue to give greater precision to the relationship viewed in this way. Another approach is to take note of the ancient world, but to relegate it to "background," which may have the potential to illuminate various aspects of the New Testament, but seldom does so in practice.

This article assumes that, to paraphrase Alfred, Lord Tennyson's "Ulysses," early Christians, like us, were part of all they had met, and that to understand them as fully as we can, we shall do well to learn as much as possible about their world. In what follows, then, we do not describe the relationship between Christians and their environment theologically, nor explain it in terms of influence or derivation, nor merely sketch a background whose relevance may not be clear. Rather, our interest will be to touch on some features of everyday life that will help us discern how Christians lived and expressed themselves in their world. Our interest is to illuminate the New Testament, and that goal will determine what we select for discussion. In taking this approach, we shall have to be on guard against two temptations, sometimes related: to see the ancient world from a Christian perspective and thus really not to understand it in its own terms, and to generalize on the basis of the very limited samplings we shall take.

THE SOCIAL WORLD

Travel and Communication. One of the first things to strike one about the Roman world is its mobility. Probably not many people traveled as much as the Phrygian merchant whose epitaph claims that he had visited Rome seventy-two times, but travel was not at all unusual, especially for merchants and artisans who followed their business and trade.[1] Travel by sea had become relatively safe

1. G. La Faye, ed., *Inscriptiones Graecae ad res Romanas pertinentes*, 4 vols. (Paris: Leroux, 1927) 4:290-91 (no. 841). See also W. M. Ramsay, "Roads and Travel in the New Testament," *HDB* 5:375-402; Lionel Casson, *Travel in the Ancient World* (Toronto: Hakkert, 1974).

and regular, but since sailing virtually ceased between mid-November and mid-March, the highways carried most of the traffic. The Roman system of highways, originally constructed to serve the needs of the military, brought people to Rome in such numbers that Roman critics became alarmed.[2] The Christian tentmakers Aquila and Priscilla, variously located in Pontius, Rome, Corinth (Acts 18:1-3), Ephesus (Acts 18:18, 26; 1 Cor 16:19), and Rome again (Rom 16:3), fit this picture well, as do the more than two dozen people Paul greets in Romans 16, whom he had evidently known in the eastern Mediterranean, but who at the time of writing had found their way to Rome.

As other religions spread along the highways, so did Judaism and Christianity.[3] For the most part, in the first century, particularly outside Palestine, Christianity took root in major cities, frequently provincial capitals, on the main routes. Its rapid spread was facilitated by a number of factors. People could communicate in the common (*koine*) Greek (see Acts 21:37), which had developed with the spread of Greek culture three centuries earlier during Alexander the Great's conquests. Latin was the official language, but local languages and dialects continued to be spoken (see John 19:20; Acts 14:11). The well constructed and drained highways, marked by milestones showing the distance to Rome, made it possible to cover about fifteen miles per day by foot, about twice as far by cart. Maps and guidebooks informed travelers of the sights and accommodations along the way. The latter consisted of inns located at convenient places on the highways, around public squares, and near important buildings in the cities. The conditions in the inns were not of high quality,[4] so, wherever possible, Jews, Christians, and well-off pagans availed themselves of private hospitality (see Acts 21:4-16).

These features associated with mobility affected people's lives and practices. Christians, for example, wrote in Greek, and it is of special importance that letters became a favorite means by which people separated from each other kept in touch as well as gave and received instruction.[5] It is no accident that most of the NT writings are letters or have epistolary

features and that letters are found in other writings (e.g., Acts 15:23-29; 23:26-30; Revelation 2–3).

Despite the abuse to which it was subject, hospitality remained a virtue among some pagans.[6] Among Christians it became a concrete expression of love for the church (Rom 12:9-13; Heb 13:1-2; 1 Pet 4:7-11; 3 John 6–8). The Christian practice of providing food and lodging to travelers and of "sending" or "speeding" them on their way—i.e., to pay their traveling expenses—invited abuse. Some became freeloaders,[7] while others took advantage of Christian hospitality to spread heresy (see 2 John; cf. 1 John 4:1-3). In order to assist travelers in securing aid while exercising some control, a special type of letter, in which the writer recommended the bearer to friends or associates, had been developed.[8] Some Christians also wrote such letters (e.g., Acts 18:27; Rom 16:1-2), and some churches evidently demanded them of travelers (2 Cor 3:1).

Life in the City. Despite a tendency among the well to do to romanticize country life, the vitality of society was in the cities, and that is where Christianity flourished.[9] To the cities were drawn purveyors of goods, proclaimers of new divinities holding out promises of salvation, and moral reformers of every stripe. Merchants and artisans tended to settle in their own neighborhoods, so that customers knew where to shop for what (e.g., 1 Cor 10:25, "in the meat market"). As diverse as the propagandists were, so were their methods of recruitment. Devotees of the Egyptian goddess Isis paraded in procession through the streets of Corinth on the way to the sea, but their initiations and other rites were performed in secret.[10] A huckster like Alexander of Abonoteichos founded his own cult by attracting public attention through his colorful behavior and playing on the credulity of the masses.[11] Philosophers taught in their own schools and the salons of the rich or wherever they were invited to speak, and some of the more unscrupulous posted themselves

2. E.g., Juvenal *Satires* 3.62: "The Syrian Orontes has long since poured into the Tiber."

3. See A. D. Nock, *Conversion* (Oxford: Oxford University Press, 1933) 48-98, for a description of how ancient cults spread.

4. See Horace *Satires* 1.5; *Acts of John* 60.

5. E. g., Seneca's *Moral Epistles*.

6. See Dio Chrysostom, *Oration* 7.

7. *Didache* 11.

8. See, e.g., Cicero *Letters to His Friends*, Book 13.

9. For a dated but still useful description of one city, see Jerome Carocopino, *Daily Life in Ancient Rome* (New Haven: Yale University Press, 1940); for social attitudes of urban and rural folk, see Ramsay MacMullen, *Roman Social Relations, 50 B.C. to A.D. 284* (New Haven: Yale University Press, 1974); and for a description of urban churches, see Wayne A. Meeks, *The First Urban Christians: The Social World of the Apostle Paul* (New Haven: Yale University Press, 1983), and John E. Stambaugh and David L. Balch, *The New Testament in Its Social Environment* (Philadelphia: Westminster, 1986) 59-82.

10. Apuleius *Metamorphoses* Book 11.

11. Lucian *Alexander the False Prophet*.

on streetcorners or shouted in the marketplace, finding their way to wherever people gathered.[12] The picture that we have, often from writers who decried it, is of an openness to new teaching,[13] a phenomenon well known to Luke (see Acts 17:18-20).

There is very little evidence that Christians in the first century proclaimed their message in so public a manner. The major exceptions are Paul's preaching in Lystra (Acts 14:8-18) and Athens, but even in the latter instance, after the initial contact in the marketplace, Paul was taken to the relative seclusion of the Areopagus, where he delivered his sermon (Acts 17:17-21). Christianity may at times have been in the public mind, but it was not in the public eye.[14] The book of Acts describes Paul as first preaching in the synagogues and then moving his base of operation to private homes (e.g., Acts 18:4-8; cf. 17:1-6), and we frequently read of churches meeting in individuals' homes (e.g., Rom 16:5, 23; Philemon 2).[15]

Most people in the cities lived in crowded quarters, some in houses on narrow streets, but more in apartments, which concentrated the population and severely limited privacy. In the hot Mediterranean climate, much of life was spent outdoors, making use of such facilities as public baths and sometimes toilets, buying meat from the market (1 Cor 10:25), hot water from the tavern on the corner, having a dispute settled by a block organization, or shopping in the stores along the main roads or surrounding the central open square where official business was also transacted. Workers labored in small shops or workrooms, which might be part of houses (Acts 18:2-3; 1 Thess 2:9); organized themselves into guilds; and entertained themselves by going out to dinner in a temple restaurant (cf. 1 Cor 8:10) or in private homes (cf. 1 Cor 10:27) or by attending plays, the races, or political speeches. Pressure could easily build up in the crowded neighborhoods, sometimes in response to mere rumor, especially when self-interest was at stake, and might result in stoning (cf. Acts 14:5, 19), something that children learned at play.[16] Then confused mobs would pour out of the alleys and streets into the stadium or forum where demagogues would work on them (cf. Acts 17:5-9; 19:23-41).

Social Groups. An important feature of city life during the early empire was the existence of large numbers of organized groups, formed to serve a variety of purposes.[17] Some of them were professional clubs (*collegia*) or guilds whose aim was not so much to improve the economic status of the craftsmen or tradesmen who organized them as to provide opportunities for social life. On occasion they engaged in political activities, and one of their major responsibilities was to bury their members. Few were completely secular; some were named after particular gods, whose names were carried on their clubhouses—for example, the "hall [*schola*] of the goddess Minerva." Sometimes these facilities were named after a club's patron; it is possible that the hall of Tyrannus, to which Paul moved his activities in Corinth, was such a clubhouse.[18] In organization they resembled their political and social contexts, so that their members enjoyed a sense of order and a certainty of how they might advance in the organization. In addition to these clubs, other organizations, such as schools of various sorts, served similar if not entirely the same purposes; and religious groups, including at times Jewish synagogues, were accommodated politically, and must in any case have looked to outsiders like *collegia*.[19]

Like the Christians, these groups often met in the homes of patrons (see Rom 16:2, 23), who thereby incurred legal responsibility for them (see Acts 17:5-9).[20] This type of extended household appears to have formed the social context for churches in the first century, and with important consequences. Some social and ethnic diversity was to be found in the pagan associations, but diversity was more common and pronounced in the churches, which therefore had to give serious attention to relations between their members. Such issues as the social stratification

---

12. See Dio Chrysostom *Oration* 32:7-11; cf. *Oration* 9.

13. E.g., Juvenal *Satires* 3.58-66, 109-25.

14. Nock, *Conversion,* 192. See also Stanley K. Stowers, "Social Status, Public Speaking and Private Teaching: The Circumstances of Paul's Preaching Activity," *NovT* 26 (1984) 59-82.

15. The fact that Paul's preaching in the synagogue is not simply a creation by Luke is indicated by 1 Cor 9:20; 2 Cor 11:24, 26; cf. Rom 1:16.

16. See MacMullen, *Roman Social Relations,* 66.

17. See Meeks, *The First Urban Christians,* 75-84, for the different groups as analogies for the Christian congregations.

18. See Abraham J. Malherbe, *Social Aspects of Early Christianity,* 2nd rev. ed. (Philadelphia: Augsburg Fortress, 1983) 89-90. The NRSV rendering of the Greek *scholē* (σχολή) into "lecture hall" is an interpretation that is almost certainly wrong.

19. Tertullian (*Apology* 38-39) would later demand that Christian groups be treated as legal associations. See Robert L. Wilken, "Collegia, Philosophical Schools, and Theology," in S. Benko and J. J. O'Rourke, eds., *The Catacombs and the Colosseum* (Valley Forge, Pa.: Judson, 1971) 279-86.

20. For the material and literary evidence of the physical space in which Jews, Mithraists, and Christians met, see L. Michael White, *The Social Origins of Christian Architecture,* 2 vols. (Minneapolis: Augsburg Fortress, 1993).

of the church and its accompanying social attitudes (e.g., 1 Cor 11:17-34); the responsibilities of members of a family (e.g., Col 3:18–4:1) and a church (e.g., Titus 2:1-10); and how Christians' social practices and religious observances should or should not influence their relations with each other (e.g., Rom 14:1–15:7) required constant attention.

The more groups looked inward and focused on their peculiar identities, the more they were viewed with suspicion by the larger society. This was so, for instance, in the cases of the Epicureans and the Jews, who were each accused of atheism because they refused to worship the traditional gods and of misanthropy because they were thought to disdain people who did not belong to their own groups.[21]

Christians met with similar responses. Knowing that they could not escape the society in which they lived (1 Cor 5:9-10; 1 Thess 4:11-12), they were sensitive to how they were to respond to "outsiders" with whom they mixed socially (1 Cor 10:27-29a), who thought their worship sometimes crazy (1 Cor 14:23), who badmouthed them (1 Pet 3:9; 4:3-4, 14), who accused them falsely of crimes (1 Pet 2:12), or who challenged their beliefs (1 Pet 3:13-16), which were thought strange or new (Acts 17:9-21).[22] In the century with which we are primarily concerned, then, the issues touching these groups were mainly social criticism and ostracism.

Political Status. Roman authorities tolerated such groups as long as they were not socially subversive or did not upset the political order. When that did happen, the authorities acted with force, as they had acted against the Bacchanalians two centuries earlier[23] and would act again against the devotees of Isis[24] and the Druids.[25] Of particular interest for our purposes is the Roman governmental attitude toward the Jews, for initially Christians were thought of as Jews (see Acts 18:12-15).[26] The Roman attitude differed from place to place and time to time, but was more positive than the local frictions, especially in Alexandria, and the popular slanders might lead one to expect. The Romans held

in high regard the Jewish claim to venerable traditions and customs, and granted the Jews, at various times, such concessions as not requiring them to appear in court and allowing them to meet for worship on the Sabbath and to collect the Temple tax.

As Christianity became distinct from Judaism, it constantly had to fend off attacks, for it enjoyed no official recognition. These persecutions, however, were always local and in response to local circumstances until the Emperor Decius (249–51), in order to secure the goodwill of the gods, required everybody in the empire to sacrifice to the ancestral gods.[27] Decius's decree was not aimed specifically at Christians, but its practical effect was that Christianity was legally proscribed by imperial decree. Before Decius's decree, action was taken against Christians because they were charged with committing crimes (cf. 1 Pet 4:15) or causing disorder (cf. Acts 17:6-7; 24:5), accusations that became associated with the name *Christian* even in the absence of proven guilt. But uncertainty about the status of Christians persisted for some time. So, for example, around 112 CE, Pliny, the Roman governor of Bithynia, even after attending a trial of a Christian, was still uncertain whether Christians should be punished simply for bearing the name or for the crimes that had evidently come to be associated with that name.[28] It need not surprise us that charges against Christians were made out of motivations ranging from economic (e.g., Acts 19:23-41) to religious competition (e.g., Acts 13:48-50; 17:4-8). As Tertullian observes, after demanding that Christian churches be allowed the same rights as *collegia,* it was easy to lay blame at their door: "If the Tiber rises as high as the city walls, if the Nile does not send its waters up over the fields, if the heavens give no more rain, if there is an earthquake, if there is famine or pestilence, straightway the cry is, 'Away with the Christians to the lions.' "[29]

More complicated was the veneration thought due the emperors and Christian reaction to it. The Roman attitude had its antecedent in Greek views. The Greeks did not distinguish sharply between the gods and extraordinary human beings, who, because of exceptional endowments and benefits they had

---

21. For attitudes toward the Jews, see Menachem Stern, *Greek and Latin Authors on Jews and Judaism,* 3 vols. (Jerusalem: Israel Academy of Sciences and Humanities, 1976–1984); for the Epicureans, see Plutarch *That Epicurus Actually Makes a Pleasant Life Impossible: Reply to Colotes* and *Is 'Live Unknown' a Wise Precept?*
22. See Robert L. Wilken, *The Christians as the Romans Saw Them* (New Haven: Yale University Press, 1984).
23. Livy 39.8-18.
24. Tacitus *Annals* 2.85
25. Ibid., 14.30.
26. Cf. Tacitus *Histories* Fragment 5.

27. See G. E. M. de Ste. Croix, "Why Were the Early Christians Persecuted?" *Past and Present* 26 (1963) 6-38; and A. N. Sherwin-White, *Past and Present* 27 (1964) 23-33.
28. Pliny *Epistles* 10.96, 97.
29. Tertullian *Apology* 40.1.

rendered, achieved after death the status of heroes. They were considered semi-divine beings who were worshiped in the locations with which they had been associated in life. The stress on virtue as their divine quality suggested the possibility that by possessing virtue in this life, such a person, particularly a ruler, was worthy of veneration. When such veneration was associated with the ruler of a domain as extensive and rich in diversity as the Roman Empire, complications were created for the ruler's subjects.[30]

Emperors in the first century differed on how they thought about their own divination and about what veneration they required or permitted. Tiberius (Luke 3:1; 20:20-26) resisted all veneration of himself, but Caligula (Gaius) proposed that Tiberius be deified and demanded that he himself, and later his sister Drusilla (Acts 24:26-27), be worshiped. His successor, Claudius (Acts 11:28; 18:2), refused such worship of himself, and rejected a request from the Alexandrians to appoint priests and establish temples in his honor. Nero, however, deified Claudius after his death and laid personal claim to many honorifics, such as acclamations of himself as god, savior, and lord. By the time of Vespasian and Titus, deification of the imperial family had become a common practice. Domitian, who exercised imperial power to the full in all aspects, insisted that he be treated as divine, and one's failure to do so resulted in punishment.

Throughout this period, more enthusiasm for the imperial cult was shown in the provinces than in Rome. There, prominent officials played major roles in the cult, so that it is difficult to be sure that participation in the cult was an expression of popular religious sentiment and not mere political expediency, as a way of currying favor with the emperor. Asia was a major center of the imperial cult after Augustus, and under Domitian venerated the emperor in a manner that called forth the description in Revelation 13.[31]

Education and Literary Culture. It is not possible to determine the level of literacy in antiquity with certainty, but perhaps half of the population of the Roman Empire could read.[32] Since it was the custom to read out loud, however, even when by oneself (cf. Acts 8:27-30), the written word did not remain a mystery to people who could not read.[33] So the illiterate person could listen as someone read the Epicurean teaching inscribed on a long wall by Diogenes of Oenoanda or hear philosophers preaching on the street corners or declaiming in large public spaces to which they had been officially invited. The theaters further introduced the masses to drama, and professional orators were always ready to speak for a fee on a large stock of topics. The Greco-Roman world was highly oral, and that exercised a profound influence on education.[34]

Education progressed through three stages. In the first, pupils were given elementary instruction in reading and writing; in the second, they learned more about grammar and, in addition, language and literature; and in the third, which was more diverse, they could specialize according to their professional interests by placing themselves under the tutelage of a philosopher, a physician, or a lawyer. Professional philosophers and rhetoricians competed for the same audiences and scathingly denounced each other, but in the schools pupils received instruction in both rhetoric and philosophy, with rhetoric gradually coming to dominate the curriculum. Education made extensive use of handbooks, such as those summarizing philosophers' teachings[35] and collections from dramatists, especially Euripides and Menander, whose works were thought to be morally valuable.[36]

Very little explicit comment is made in the NT about the educational level of Christians. The description of the disciples of Jesus as unschooled and ordinary (Acts 4:13; cf. John 7:15) means that they had not received traditional and formal religious instruction. On the other hand, Paul's development

---

30. See Donald L. Jones, "Christianity and the Roman Imperial Cult," in W. Haase and H. Temporini, eds., *Aufstieg und Niedergang der römischen Welt* (Berlin: De Gruyter, 1980) 2.23.2, 1023-54.

31. Irenaeus (*Against Heresies* 5.30.3) dated John's banishment to Patmos, and thus the book of Revelation, to the reign of Domitian.

32. William V. Harris, *Ancient Literacy* (Cambridge, Mass.: Harvard University Press, 1989), the major study in the field, is very conservative in its estimate. Attempts to correct Harris are made by contributors to the collection, J. H. Humphrey, ed., *Literacy in the Roman World, Journal of Roman Archaeology* Supplement Series 3 (Ann Arbor: University of Michigan Press, 1991).

33. See Paul J. Achtemeier, "*Omne verbum sonat:* The New Testament and the Oral Environmental of Late Western Antiquity," *JBL* 109 (1990) 3:27.

34. See H. I. Marrou, *A History of Education in Antiquity* (New York: New American Library, 1964), for Greece and Rome, and for concentration on the latter, Stanley F. Bonner, *Education in Ancient Rome: From the Elder Cato to the Younger Pliny* (Berkeley: University of California Press, 1977).

35. See pseudo-Plutarch *The Education of Children* 8C.

36. See Dio Chrysostom *Oration* 18.6-7.

is described in Acts 22:3 in the traditional three categories, and he is represented as quoting from precisely the kinds of sources that students learned in tertiary education.[37] In 1 Cor 15:33 Paul himself quotes Menander, and in Titus 1:12 Epimenides, representing the same level of literary culture, is quoted. In the final analysis, however, the NT writings themselves constitute the main evidence of the literary culture of their authors. As one would expect, they differ considerably. Paul's letters reveal him as a creative writer knowledgeable of, but not bound by, the literary conventions, rhetorical methods, and philosophical instruction of his day. Matthew and Mark wrote in a Greek that must have struck their Gentile readers as strange, but the Greek of the book of Hebrews is excellent, as is that of those sections in Luke and Acts where the author does not reflect the style of his sources.

PHILOSOPHY AND PHILOSOPHERS

The Philosophical Koine. Philosophy quickly rose in importance and changed in character in the generations immediately after Aristotle.[38] The conquests of Aristotle's pupil, Alexander the Great, contributed substantially to this development. Greeks, who now increasingly found themselves abroad, separated from their city states in Greece where traditional religion provided emotional security, were faced with the whims of arbitrary fortune. Traditional religion had already come under severe criticism in the fourth century, especially by the dramatists, and philosophy would take its place. This confidence in philosophy was later expressed by Juvenal: "Great indeed is philosophy, conqueror of Fortune, and sacred are the precepts of her book."[39] The Hellenization of the east further generated an interest in Greek philosophy among non-Greeks, many of whom were drawn to Athens, which was still thought of as the intellectual center of the world. They contributed immensely to the new character of philosophy.

Philosophy became more clearly integrated systems of thought that described the universe and

people's place in it. Philosophy was commonly divided into three parts: logic, physics, and ethics,[40] which provided a framework for the description of the systems and drew attention to what the different systems shared. The fact that people looked to philosophy for the practical benefits it conferred abetted an eclectic tendency—that is, to choose from different philosophies what appeared true or valuable. This eclecticism, plus the fact that philosophy was taught with the aid of handbooks that provided summaries of philosophical claims, meant that the differences in nuance between the different philosophies, even in apparently similar matters, were lost. The result was the birth of what has been described as a philosophical *koine*. There is an element of truth in this perception that the different philosophies had much in common, but the stress on commonality should not be overdone, for the schools continued to polemicize vehemently against each other, and even members of the same school disagreed about central doctrines.

In addition to being eclectic, philosophy had a strong religious character, the classic example of which is the prayer of Cleanthes the Stoic:

Lead me, O Mentor of the lofty heavens,
My Father, withersoever thou shalt wish.
I shall not falter, but obey with speed.
And though I would not, I shall go, and suffer,
In sin and sorrow what I might have done
in noble virtue. Aye, the willing soul
Fate leads, but the unwilling drags along.[41]

Justin Martyr said that, before his conversion to Christianity, his study of Platonism and contemplation of its ideas furnished his mind with wings, and he expected to see God, for that was the end of Platonism.[42] Even Epicurus, erroneously charged with atheism, in urging Menoeceus to study philosophy, says that he must begin by believing "that God is a living being immortal and blessed."[43]

Another important characteristic of philosophy in this period was its interest in the moral life. Philosophers disagreed about how severely the human condition had been corrupted by ignorance and over the human capacity to grow to moral maturity, but, with the exception of the Skeptics,[44] most thought

---

37. See W. C. van Unnik, *Tarsus or Jerusalem: The City of Paul's Youth* (London: Epworth, 1962); and Martin Hengel, *The Pre-Christian Paul* (Philadelphia: Trinity Press International, 1991) 18-39 for Paul, and Malherbe, *Social Aspects,* 29-58, for a broader view.

38. See A. A. Long and D. N. Sedley, *The Hellenistic Philosophies,* 2 vols. (London: Cambridge University Press, 1987), for the most important texts, commentary, and bibliography.

39. Juvenal *Satire* 13.22.

40. Cf. Diogenes Laertius *Lives of Eminent Philosophers* 1.18.

41. Seneca *Moral Epistle* 107.11.

42. Justin *Dialogue with Trypho* 2.5.

43. Diogenes Laertius *Lives of Eminent Philosophers* 10.123.

44. Cf. Sextus Empiricus *Outlines of Pyrrhonism* 3.235-238.

of philosophy as a moral educator.[45] The kind of philosophy they had in mind was practical and not confined to lecture halls and the salons of the rich or to the imperial court, but could be heard in the public speeches of invited philosophers, and even on the street corners. It was also taught in schools, where the task was "to make philosophy as it were the head and front of all education," for philosophy taught "what is honorable and what is shameful, what is just and what is unjust," and how we are to conduct ourselves in our relationships with the gods and all members of society.[46] Clearly, philosophy had been democratized; furthermore, its interest in what was obviously useful led to a high evaluation of the common coin of moral philosophy.

Epicureanism. The followers of Epicurus organized themselves into groups of friends, including women, who sought to find fulfillment within their conventicles. They claimed to be indifferent to society and its values, including those of education, and to pursue the serenity that comes from abandoning political and social ambition on the one hand, and, on the other, the fear that the gods as they were popularly perceived interfere in human affairs and in the process terrorize people. The Epicureans thought the goal of this withdrawal from society and its values and perceptions to be pleasure, which to them was quite different from the popular view then of pleasure as the pursuit of sensation. Opposition to the Epicureans was vehement and consistent. They were accused of atheism, ignorance, social irresponsibility, and sexual immorality. The very word *epicurean* became an insult, and in a transliterated form became for the rabbis a name for a heretic. Paul, who is brought into contact with Epicureans in Acts 17:18, himself uses anti-Epicurean invective when he describes the Ephesian hedonists as beasts he had fought (1 Cor 15:32).

The same charges were also applied to Christians, and sometimes the two groups were uncritically lumped together by their critics.[47] There were, indeed, striking similarities between them. Both held to the importance of the group for the development of the individual. Epicurus had begun developing procedures whereby members of the group cared for each other in an almost pastoral manner, and

those techniques were highly refined by the time Paul established his churches and used the same methods.[48] Just as Epicureans held friendship to be the basis for the common life, so also Christians, who thought of their churches in kinship terms, held "love of the brethren" to provide the framework for social behavior (see Rom 12:10; Heb 13:1; 2 Pet 1:7). Paul was aware of the similarities and was careful to warn his readers not to choose the Epicurean options, for example, to show disdain for society's opinion of the church (1 Thess 4:9-12).[49]

Cynicism. Cynicism originated as a rejection of convention and an insistence on the independence of the wise.[50] More a way of life than a system of thought,[51] Cynicism's stress on individualism was exemplified by Diogenes. Cynics had no time for logic or physics, but concentrated completely on ethics, holding to the goal of living in accord with nature.

Dependent on no one, the Cynic was free and self-sufficient. Because Cynics felt that they had attained moral freedom, they thought it their duty to improve others by speaking frankly about the human condition and impressing on their listeners the need to change their lives by adopting reason rather than convention and its values as their guide. Cynics made a deep impression on their society with their stark way of life and their insistence on the profound distinction between vice and virtue. There was a renewal of Cynicism in the first century, and it was so widespread by the second century that Cynics became the favorite target of satirists like Lucian, who delighted in criticizing all humbug.[52] Not bound by any dogma, Cynics soon differed among themselves on many matters, but they retained their stress on the individual and their insistence that the practical life of the Cynic was a shortcut to virtue.[53]

The sharp edge of Cynicism made it a useful foil for satire, but also served a Stoic like Epictetus in his description of the true philosopher, whom he calls "the Cynic."[54] Many similarities have been identi-

---

45. See Abraham J. Malherbe, *Moral Exhortation: A Greco-Roman Sourcebook* (Philadelphia: Westminster, 1986).

46. Pseudo-Plutarch *The Education of Children* 7DE.

47. E.g., Lucian *Alexander the False Prophet* 25, 38.

48. See Abraham J. Malherbe, *Paul and the Thessalonians: The Philosophical Tradition of Pastoral Care* (Philadelphia: Fortress, 1987).

49. See ibid., 95-107, for the philosophical views with which Paul had to contend when instructing recent converts in social ethics.

50. For a brief introduction to Cynicism, see Abraham J. Malherbe, "Cynics," in *IDBSup* 201-3.

51. Diogenes Laertius *Lives of Eminent Philosophers* 6.103.

52. E.g., Lucian *The Runaways*.

53. Diogenes Laertius *Lives of Eminent Philosophers* 6.104.

54. Epictetus *Discourse* 3.22.

fied between Christians and the Cynic depiction in this discourse. For example, like the Christian apostle, Epictetus's Cynic is sent by God as a herald to preach to people and oversee them. The hardships he suffers as a result of his mission show his superiority and remind one of Paul's hardships (e.g., 2 Cor 11:21-28); like Paul (Phil 4:11), the Cynic is self-sufficient or content, and he also speaks with boldness or frank criticism (e.g., 2 Cor 3:12; 7:4). There are sharp differences, however, the major one being that Paul always refers to God, whereas the true Cynic has no reference beyond self. Paul's hardships do not demonstrate his strength but his weakness; the power belongs to God and Christ (2 Cor 12:9-10). Paul is content, not because of his own accomplishments or because he is totally in control of himself, but because of the strength that is given to him (Phil 4:13). If he speaks boldly out of freedom, it is not a freedom attained through reason and self-discipline, but a freedom that comes from the Spirit and the Lord (2 Cor 3:17).

To the eye of the beholder on the outside, nevertheless, there was much that Christians and Cynics did have in common. It is quite natural that Lucian should bring the Cynic Peregrinus in contact with Christians.[55] On the Christian side, there is a venerable tradition that Justin Martyr and Crescens the Cynic had engaged in public debate and that Justin won decisively, as a result of which Crescens engineered Justin's arrest and ultimate death. The truth may be somewhat different, but it is significant that it was not thought incongruous to bring together these two men, each wearing the short cloak of the philosopher.[56] The NT does not explicitly mention Cynics, but there is little doubt that some writers, especially Paul, were aware of those Cynic elements that had become part of the common discourse.[57]

Stoicism. Stoicism had become the dominant philosophy by the time Paul is said to have encountered Stoics in Athens (Acts 17:18). Stoicism sprang from Cynicism. Its founder, Zeno, was a disciple of the Cynic Crates, and took from him the basic Cynic tenet that virtue is the only good. Soon, however,

Stoics developed a system that differed markedly from Cynicism. They still accepted a sharp distinction between virtue and vice, but introduced a class of indifferent things, which were further divided into things truly indifferent, things indifferent but to be preferred, and things indifferent but to be rejected.

In their ethical speculation, like the Cynics, the Stoics' rule was to live according to nature, but they thought of nature as the physical universe permeated by the divine reason, or Logos. This natural theology had implications for their ethics. Human beings, as part of the universe, shared in this reason. Born with a capacity to think rationally, they were to develop that reason throughout their lives and thus develop the knowledge that would enable them to live morally. As they lived rationally, they would be able to perceive that their individual and social lives would be lived well if they conformed to the ordered cosmos.[58] Such perception required training in logic and physics, which formed the basis for Stoic ethics. The intricate theoretical Stoic system that developed differed conspicuously from the simple Cynicism from which it had originated, but it retained Cynicism's strict moralism and continued to share many of its values and practices.

Some features of Stoic natural theology were present in Hellenistic Judaism, and probably came to Paul from writings like the Wisdom of Solomon, which discusses the making of religious images and the knowledge of God (Wisdom of Solomon 13). These same topics also belonged together for the Stoics, as can be seen from Dio Chrysostom.[59] In considering the nature and validity of religious images, Dio argues that such images are an expression of human yearning for the divine and are, therefore, to be viewed positively. In arguing this, he details at some length the various sources of human knowledge, which is at least potentially present in all people at birth and develops as their reason is developed. Paul uses the same Stoic categories in Romans 1, but stands the argument on its head by utilizing Jewish anti-idol polemic (Isaiah 44; Wisdom of Solomon 14).[60] Paul does not think that our knowledge of God develops slowly as we gradually become more rational. Rather, he begins his argument with a theological declaration: "For the wrath

55. Lucian *The Passing of Peregrinus* 11–13.

56. For the tradition, see Justin *2 Apology* 3; Tatian *Address to the Greeks* 19; Eusebius *Church History* 4.16; Jerome *Illustrious Men* 23; see also W. H. C. Frend, *Martyrdom and Persecution in the Early Church* (New York: New York University Press, 1967) 201-4.

57. See Abraham J. Malherbe, *Paul and the Popular Philosophers* (Philadelphia: Fortress, 1989). For a maximalist interpretation of the evidence, see F. Gerald Downing, *Cynics and Christian Origins* (Edinburgh: T. & T. Clark, 1992).

58. See Dio Chrysostom *Oration* 48.14-16; cf. *1 Clement* 20.

59. Dio Chrysostom *Discourse* 12.

60. See G. Bornkamm, "The Revelation of God's Wrath," in *Early Christian Experience* (New York: Harper & Row, 1969) 47-70.

of God is revealed from heaven against all ungodliness and wickedness of those who by their wickedness suppress the truth. For what can be known about God is plain to them, because God has shown it to them" (Rom 1:18-19 NRSV). Thus it is not human ignorance that is responsible for immorality, but their refusal to retain the knowledge of God and, instead, turning to idols (1:23, 25). Because of their actions, therefore, God gave them up to a depraved mind (1:28; cf. vv. 24, 26). Paul is not concerned with the development of human cognition, as the Stoics were in their natural theology; he uses Stoic natural theology to indict Gentiles (1:20; 2:1) and to so demonstrate their need for the gospel (1:16; cf. 3:9).

Stoic natural theology is also present in Paul's speech in Athens (Acts 17:16-31), but there the attitude is more positive. Religious objects of worship are viewed as testimony to the religiosity of the Athenians (17:22-23). Nevertheless, in good philosophical manner Paul maintains that God does not dwell in handmade temples (17:24, 29),[61] nor does he need anything (17:25).[62] All people yearn and seek for God, yet he is not far from us, for we live in him; as the pagan writers said, we are his offspring (17:27-29).[63] Seneca illustrates the Stoic mood: "God is near you, he is with you, he is within you."[64] Where Stoicism comes to a screeching halt is when Paul announces Christ's resurrection and the judgment of the world (17:31).

The Stoic picture of the wise man appealed to many people. The person with the correct perception of reality, Stoics held, is permitted all things, for the wise man "alone is free and bad men are slaves, for freedom is the right [ἐξουσία *exousia*] to act independently, and slavery is the depravation of independent action."[65] Some of Paul's converts in Corinth, impressed by their own knowledge (e.g., 1 Cor 8:1-3), asserted their right to live as they wished and justified themselves by quoting a Stoic slogan, "Everything is permissible to me" (1 Cor 6:12; 10:23). Paul took great pains to counter their view (1 Cor 6:12-21; 8:1–10:38), but evidently was unsuccessful, for he had to return to the subject in 2 Corinthians, where there are indications that some Corinthians still described themselves in Stoic terms. Stoics, for example, expressed the wise man's intellectual security in military terms. The perfect person, Seneca says, is:

full of virtues human and divine, can lose nothing. His goods are girt by strong and insurmountable defenses. . . . The walls which guard the wise man are safe from both flame and assault, they provide no means of entrance, are lofty, impregnable, godlike.[66]

Some of Paul's opponents thought they had such a fortification. Paul countered, however, that such a citadel of intellect, armed against the knowledge of God, is successfully laid under siege with the divine weaponry available to him (2 Cor 10:4-6).

Stoics gave wide currency to techniques of exhortation and instruction that they had not invented but refined. The Cynics were probably the first to develop a style of speech that would come to be known as a diatribe, but Paul's adaptation of the style has most in common with Epictetus.[67] Lists of vices and virtues were not used by Stoics alone, but they contributed significantly to their use to characterize certain types of persons (see Gal 5:19-23).[68] The construction of a pattern according to which responsibilities of various members of a household were specified did not originate with the Stoics, but they did add a cast to some of the lists in the NT (e.g., Col 3:16–4:1).[69]

Conclusion. The philosophies to which attention has been drawn were the most popular in antiquity and have also received the most attention from modern scholarship. Other philosophies have in recent decades begun to attract attention and will help us to understand more fully the intellectual context of early Christianity.

One of these philosophies is Middle Platonism, a form of Platonism that had developed its own peculiar characteristics by the first and second centuries. The writings of second-century Christian authors have already been illuminated as our knowledge of contemporary Platonism has increased, and the

61. Cf. pseudo-Heraclitus *Epistle* 4.2; Plutarch *On the Tranquility of Soul* 477C.

62. Cf. pseudo-Aristotle *On the Cosmos* 6.398B; Diogenes Laertius *Lives of Eminent Philosophers* 6.104.

63. Dio Chrysostom *Oration* 12.27-28.

64. Seneca *Moral Epistle* 41.1.

65. Diogenes Laertius *Lives of Eminent Philosophers* 7.121.

66. Seneca *On the Firmness of the Wise Man* 6.8.

67. On the diatribe, see Stanley K. Stowers, *The Diatribe and Paul's Letter to the Romans*, SBLDS 57 (Chico, Calif.: Scholars Press, 1981); on Paul and Epictetus, see Malherbe, *Paul and the Popular Philosophers*, 25-33.

68. Cf. Dio Chrysostom *Oration* 4.83-96.

69. See David L. Balch, "Household Codes," in David E. Aune, ed., *Greco-Roman Literature and the New Testament*, SBLDS 21 (Atlanta: Scholars Press, 1988) 25-50.

same may happen for some NT writings, Hebrews in particular. In the past, Philo, who was heavily indebted to Platonism, has been appealed to for assistance in clarification of elements in Hebrews that some commentators have thought Platonic, but there is no reason why Middle Platonism, unfiltered through Philo, should not be brought into the discussion.[70] Peripatetics and Neopythagoreans have also proved to be more relevant to our understanding of the social responsibilities itemized in the household codes than had been thought.[71]

People in antiquity recognized the affinity between the ethical teaching of Christians and their philosophical contemporaries. Justin Martyr claimed that whatever had been correctly said by anybody was Christian property.[72] Christianity's great opponent, Celsus, testified to the same fact when he chided Christians that there was nothing impressive or new about their system of morals.[73] Origen, who responded to Celsus's attacks, was more precise when he judged that, while Plato benefited the educated, Epictetus benefited all people who wanted a better life.[74] What is significant about Origen's statement is the recognition, widely shared by the early church, that Stoic philosophy had some affinities with the moral teaching of the NT, despite their respective differences.[75]

The NT refers to philosophy only in Col 2:8, which is not a blanket condemnation of philosophy as such, but is probably a reflection of the Colossian heretics' self-description of their much vaunted wisdom as philosophy.[76] We have noticed that Stoic traditions are quoted with approval in Acts 17:27, so the affinity is explicitly recognized also in the NT. It is true that statements in the NT distinguish sharply between pagan and Christian morality (e.g., 1 Cor 6:9-11). It is equally true that the NT frequently urges Christian behavior that would evoke favorable response from pagans, thus assuming at least some agreement with pagan moral standards

70. A beginning has been made by James W. Thompson, *The Beginnings of Christian Philosophy: The Epistle to the Hebrews*, CBQMS 13 (Washington: Catholic Biblical Association of America, 1982).

71. See David L. Balch, "Household Codes" and "Neopythagorean Moralists and the New Testament Household Codes," in Haase and Temporini, *Aufstieg und Niedergang*, 2.26.1, 380-411.

72. Justin *2 Apology* 13.4.

73. Origen, *Against Celsus* 1.4.

74. Ibid., 6.2.

75. See Abraham J. Malherbe, "Hellenistic Moralists and the New Testament," in Haase and Temporini, *Aufstieg und Niedergang*, 267-333; cf. M. L. Colish, "Stoicism and the New Testament," in ibid., 334-79.

76. See Peter T. O'Brien, *Colossians, Philemon*, WBC 44 (Waco, Tex.: Word, 1982) 198.

(e.g., 1 Thess 4:12; 1 Pet 2:12). Often, it is at those points of contact that philosophy is visible.

RELIGION

Introduction. It is impossible to speak of religion in the Roman Empire in brief compass without making certain generalizations.[77] When we do so, however, we must be aware of the complexities that existed as well as the factors that contributed to them. Once more, we cannot escape the significance of Alexander the Great. Foreign influences on Greek life predated Alexander's campaigns, but as long as the Greek city states remained self-contained and gave official status to the traditional views of the gods and the old religious observances, it was unlikely that foreign influence on Greek religion would be significant and widespread. When the citizens of the city states found themselves far from home and citizens of a society no longer structured according to ancestral beliefs and practices, they had to act as individuals, and did so with major consequences, as we shall see.

It should also be observed that even during the Roman Empire, the spirit of the non-Jewish and non-Christian religion we encounter in the NT was Greek. Some Roman practices continued, and some developed with new vigor, and local practices and traditions continued to have lives of their own, but in general the Greek element predominated in religion as it did in much else of culture in the empire.

A basic assumption of Greek religion had been that the world was governed by a pantheon of gods who ruled with a recognizable sense of justice, and who in general rewarded the good and punished the bad. In the Hellenistic period, the distinct impression arose that something was amiss and some strange power was disturbing the world. This power was arbitrary Tyche (Chance or Fortune), who became a goddess like all the rest, with whom one had to come to terms in order to live securely and happily. Philosophy was only one means by which one could do so.

The Hellenistic age took the concept of power very seriously. Power permeated everything—human beings, animals, stones, plants, metals—giving them the potency to do good or ill to people if used effectively. So great was the concentration on power

77. See the judicious summary in Everett Ferguson, *Backgrounds of Early Christianity*, 2nd ed. (Grand Rapids: Eerdmans, 1993), 161-65.

that under the empire much of religion was directed to divine power rather than to divine personalities. So Aelius Aristides said of the god Serapis:

Who he is and what nature he has, Egyptian priests and prophets may be left to say. We shall praise him sufficiently for the moment if we tell of the many and great benefits to men of which he is revealed to be the author. At the same time, his nature can be seen through these very facts. If we have said what he can do and what he gives, we have found who he is and what nature he has.[78]

The celebration of the gods' power frequently took the form of acclamations of the gods and dedications to them that celebrated the gods' deeds and virtues (ἀρεταί *aretai*; e.g., Acts 19:34).

The emphasis on power rather than personality explains why Roman paganism was not exclusivistic in its attitude toward other gods. One of the main characteristics of Hellenistic religion was its syncretism, a tendency to combine elements of different religions and to identify different deities, the Greek Zeus becoming the Roman Jupiter, for example, or Artemis being identified with Diana.[79]

Superstition. Historians of Greek religion have frequently described the Hellenistic period as being characterized by superstition, a period when there was "an intensifying of certain spiritual emotions; an increase of sensitiveness, a failure of nerve."[80] Superstition, it is thought, grew naturally in a society in which there seemed to be no correlation between people's fortunes and their merits and efforts. This may seem too pejorative a description of an entire period; after all, it is too easy to describe someone else's religion as superstition. The Greeks themselves, however, did give close attention to the phenomenon they called *deisidaimonia* (δεισιδαιμονία), by which they meant "religiosity" (see Acts 17:22, where the adjective *religious* is used) or "superstition," depending on taste. Two philosophers who wrote on the subject help us to understand this feature of Hellenistic religion.

Theophrastus (c. 370–276 CE), in a series of descriptive sketches of various character types, describes the superstitious man. He begins his description with a definition: "Superstitiousness, it is scarcely necessary to say, seems to be a kind of cowardice [δειλία *deilia*] with respect to the divine."[81] Theophrastus then vividly characterizes the life of someone who is surrounded by supernatural powers with which he must negotiate his well-being. From morning to night, there is hardly a moment when he does not sprinkle himself, eat a bay leaf, anoint himself, throw a stone across the street to break a spell, or utter formulas to protect himself from the surrounding evil. Religious sensitivity has spread to every aspect of his life, and he lives in fear.

Some five hundred years later, someone writing in the name of Plutarch took up the same subject in a short treatise *On Superstition*. The writer claimed that ignorance and blindness in regard to the gods take two forms, atheism and superstition, and that both are due to emotion that unsettles reason. Superstition "is an emotional idea and an assumption productive of fear which utterly humbles and crushes a man, for he thinks that there are gods, but that they are the cause of pain and injury."[82] The Pastoral Epistles criticize this attitude: "God did not give us a spirit of cowardice [*deilia*], but rather a spirit of power and of love and of self-discipline" (2 Tim 1:7 NRSV; cf. 3:5). It is out of this fear that people do the strangest things. For example, the Jews, "fast bound in the toils of superstition as in one great net," refused to defend their city on the Sabbath.[83] The Romans similarly called Christianity a superstition.[84]

Magic. People may have been highly sensitive to the power that dominated their world, but their response was not entirely passive. Through the use of magic they sought to bring that power into the service of their own interests. The difference between magic and religion has been thought to reside in one's attitude toward some superior being, magic seeking to compel that being to act in accord with one's own interests, religion seeking an end by

---

78. Aelius Aristides, *Oration* 8, in A. D. Nock, *Essays on Religion and the Ancient World*, Zeph Stewart, ed., 2 vols. (Cambridge, Mass.: Harvard University Press) 1:35. See further on the subject, Robert M. Grant, *Gods and the One God* (Philadelphia: Westminster, 1986) 54-57; M. P. Nilsson, *Greek Piety* (Oxford: Clarendon, 1948) 103-10.

79. The phenomenon of syncretism has attracted considerable scholarly attention in recent years as greater precision has been sought. See the account of research in Abraham J. Malherbe, "Greco-Roman Religion and Philosophy and the New Testament," in Eldon Jay Epp and George W. MacRae, S.J., eds., *The New Testament and Its Modern Interpreters* (Atlanta: Scholars Press, 1989) 5-6.

80. Gilbert Murray, *Five Stages of Greek Religion* (Garden City, N.Y.: Doubleday, 1955) 119, cf. 127.

81. Theophrastus *Characters* 16.

82. Plutarch *On Superstition* 165B.

83. Ibid., 169C.

84. See Pliny *Epistle* 10.96; Tacitus *Annals* 15.44; Suetonius *Nero* 16; and for discussion, Wilken, *The Christians as the Romans Saw Them*, 48-67.

requesting the power to do what is needed.[85] That, however, is a modern distinction. What is characteristic of magic is that the power of some being is harnessed through the use of certain techniques or formulas known to the magician, for purposes of good or ill. Magic performed with malevolent purpose was outlawed. The masses were susceptible to the appeal of magic,[86] but so were some aristocrats, including Vespasian himself.[87] The satirists, on the other hand, found in magicians a delicious target.[88] The Romans liked to associate magic with foreigners, Jews included, and the latter, rather than shying away from it, claimed that Jewish magic was superior, since it was derived from the wisdom given to Solomon.[89]

The conceptual framework that supported magical practices differed from person to person, but they shared the notion that power permeated the universe and that by acting on it at one place, one might effect a result in some other place to which one directed it. The Stoic idea of cosmic sympathy proved useful in rationalizing magic. According to Stoic theory, the universe is an essential unity in which human beings are the microcosm of the universal macrocosm. This fundamental unity explained how certain objects, such as parts of the body, could be used in a magical rite to affect a person. Others thought of a pantheistic spirit that pervades the entire cosmos, which one influences through rites, acclamations, or prayers to do one's bidding. Then there were the numberless *daimones* (δαίμονες), intermediate beings between the human and the divine. Some of them were noble, others malevolent, and they could be summoned through a ritual or the invocation of their names. A particularly forceful demonstration of magical power was exorcism, by which an evil spirit was driven out of a possessed person.[90]

The ancient preoccupation with magic is reflected in its appearance in NT vice lists (e.g., Gal 5:20; Rev 9:21; 21:8; 22:15). The Gospels record charges that Jesus exorcized demons by the power of Satan (e.g., Matt 12:22-32), and it is to be expected that Christians would encounter the same charge. Indeed, the book of Acts shows a special interest in magic.[91] Three major panels in the book's depiction of the spread of the faith begin with the Christian evangelists' encountering opposition from magicians. In Samaria, Simon the Magician is acclaimed by everyone with the words, "This man is the power of God that is called Great" (Acts 8:10 NRSV). The true magician even after his conversion, Simon saw the Christians performing wondrous deeds (8:13) and that the Holy Spirit was conferred by the laying on of hands, so he tried to buy that power from the apostles, only to be enjoined to repent (8:17-34). Luke again makes the case that magic is impotent before the gospel when early in the first missionary journey Paul blinds the Jewish magician Elymas (Bar-jesus) when he attempts to turn the proconsul away from the faith (Acts 13:6-12).

Just as philosophy was associated in the ancient world with Athens, so also magic was associated with Ephesus, and it was there that Paul dramatically bests the magicians, this time "seven sons of a Jewish high priest named Sceva" (Acts 19:11-20). Using the name of Jesus as a formula with which to exorcize, they succeeded in doing so, only to be attacked by the evil spirit, thus showing that their magical power was very limited. The result, according to Luke, was that many people were converted, including many magicians, who burned their magical books as proof of their conversion. "So the word of the Lord grew mightily and prevailed" (19:20 NRSV).

Divination. The human desire to receive direct divine guidance was fulfilled by divination, the prediction by supernatural means of future events and the interpretation of past occurrences. Cicero, our most important source for divination, divided it into two major classes: natural and artificial divination.[92]

Natural divination may involve dreams, which will receive further attention below. Incubation was a special kind of divination that entailed dreaming under controlled conditions and then interpreting the dreams. A particular kind of incubation was iatromancy, sleeping in a health shrine, like that of Asclepius. Extremely important to Greeks was prophecy. It was thought that the prophet became the mouthpiece of a divine power that took posses-

---

85. For discussion and a selection of texts, see Georg Luck, *Arcana Mundi* (Baltimore: The Johns Hopkins University Press, 1985) 1-131.

86. See Lucian *Alexander the False Prophet.*

87. Tacitus *History* 4.81; Suetonius *Vespasian* 7.2.

88. See Lucian *The Lover of Lies.*

89. E.g., Josephus *Antiquities of the Jews* 8.42-49.

90. See Lucian *The Lover of Lies* 15-17.

91. See, in general, David E. Aune, "Magic in Early Christianity," in Haase and Temporini, *Aufstieg und Niedergang*, 2.23.2, 1507-57; and on Acts, Susan R. Garrett, *The Demise of the Devil: Magic and the Demonic in Luke's Writings* (Minneapolis: Fortress, 1989).

92. Cicero *On Divination* 1.11, 2.26. See also Luck, *Arcana Mundi,* 228-305, for some ancient texts on divination and for discussion.

sion of the prophet and spoke through him or her. This possession the Greeks spoke of as inspiration,[93] which required the prophet to create the right disposition before receiving the prophetic spirit. This was achieved when the soul threw "aside the caution that human intelligence lays upon it, and thus often diverts and quenches the spirit."[94] When the prophetic faculty was not properly attuned to the spirit, the consequences could be fatal to the prophet.[95]

The term *oracle* was applied to this kind of divination and could refer to the response of a god to a question, thus an oracular saying; to the prophet, for example, the oracle at Delphi; or to the shrine where the prophesying took place. The most important shrines were those of Zeus at Dodona in Epirus and that of Apollo at Delphi. Situated at what Greeks thought was the center (or navel) of the earth,[96] the Oracle of Delphi was for some time the supreme authority in religious matters, and, since Delphi was also the central meeting place for citizens from the isolated city states, it was also socially and politically important. By the time Plutarch wrote, early in the second century, however, prophecy had declined.

Another type of oracle that became important was that associated with the name *Sibyl*. The word was first used of one prophetess, then of many who wandered around Greece, some becoming attached to certain shrines. The proper name became generic and referred to prophecy of an ecstatic kind. The prophecies were written down in Greek hexameter and collected, but the collection was destroyed when the Roman capitol burned in 83 BCE. New collections were made later, partly by Jews and Christians who found this particular oracular tradition convenient for their own propaganda.[97]

In artificial divination use was made of animate and inanimate objects to predict the future. Of things animate, birds have always been important, indicating by their number, species, and behavior what the future might hold. This type of divination was called augury; that based on the examination of animals' entrails was called haruspicy.[98] In addition to animals, the involuntary movements of humans, such as twitching or sneezing, were viewed as divine communications. Inanimate objects—like incense, flour, egg shells, or parts of animals, especially their shoulder blades—were thought potent when placed on a sacrificial fire. Lots were cast extensively (cf. Acts 1:26), and astrology became a major means by which the future was divined.

The Greeks proposed a rational framework for divination. Cicero speaks in *On Divination* of three ways in which the Stoics made a case for divination. First, they argued that the gods' love for human beings required that they tell in advance what the future would be.[99] Second, the doctrine of fate, with its inexorable succession of cause and effect, lays the future open to the diviner, who is able to see how one thing leads to another.[100] Third, nature itself provides the signs, as it does the stars and other heavenly bodies, whose mysteries are laid bare by astrology.[101] Cicero himself remained skeptical about divination, as did some philosophical schools, like the Epicureans and the Skeptics.[102] So also did satirists, who tended to see this type of thing as peculiarly Oriental, once the Oracle of Delphi had all but fallen silent.[103]

The NT does not show any great interest in divination, but according to Acts 16:16-18, at the beginning of Paul's mission in Europe, in Philippi, he encountered a slave girl with a very special kind of oracular power. Luke's description of her as having, literally, a "python spirit," is just enough to let us know that she was thought to be inspired by Apollo, who used such mouthpieces in a way ventriloquists use their props.[104] For the rest, however, Luke polemicizes against divination by treating Paul's action as straightforward exorcism of an evil spirit and accusing her owners of using her for their own mercenary purposes.

Dreams. Tertullian expressed the opinion of many when he said, "It is to dreams that the majority of people owe their knowledge of God."[105] Our major sources for the study of dreams in antiquity are Aelius Aristides and Artemidorus. The fact that they both lived in the second century and hailed

93. Cicero, *On Divination* 1.114.
94. Plutarch *On the Obsolescence of the Oracles* 432EF.
95. See ibid., 438AB; Lucan *Pharsalia* 5.130-200.
96. See Strabo *Geography* 9.3.5.
97. See J. J. Collins, "Sibylline Oracles (Second Century B.C.–First Century A.D.)," in James H. Charlesworth, ed., *The Old Testament Pseudepigrapha* (Garden City, N.Y.: Doubleday, 1993) 1:317-472.
98. Cicero *On Divination* 1.119-20.

99. Ibid., 1.82.
100. Ibid., 1.125-26.
101. Ibid., 1.129-30.
102. Ibid., 2.150.
103. See Juvenal *Satire* 6.548-91.
104. See Plutarch *On the Obsolescence of the Oracles* 414E; and further on the type, E. R. Dodds, *The Greeks and the Irrational* (Boston: Beacon, 1957) 71-72.
105. Tertullian *On the Soul* 47.2.

from the same province raises the question of whether they were representative of other places and other times. Aristides, a hypochondriac who in his dreams received orders directly from Asclepius, provides us with a picture of someone who seeks the constant companionship of the god. Perhaps the intensity of his preoccupation with dreams was unusual, but the phenomenon itself was not extraordinary.[106] Artemidorus made an extensive collection of dreams and wrote a treatise on their interpretation in which he used a system of classification that had been developing for centuries.[107] In such classifications, a distinction was made between predictive and non-predictive dreams, and each of these was still further classified. While the interpretation of dreams had a venerable history, it also had its critics, among whom were Theophrastus and Cicero, who thought of it as superstition.[108]

It is difficult to classify the dreams in the NT according to the ancient categories; indeed, it is hard to decide how dreams are related to such trance visions as those found in Acts 10:10-15.[109] One type of dream, the *chrē matismos* (χρηματισμός), a dream oracle in which a god or some other significant personage appears to give directions or predict the future, does appear with some frequency (e.g., Matt 1:20-21; 2:12-13, 19, 22; Acts 16:9-10; 18:9, etc.) In all these cases, either the Lord or a divine messenger, whether an angel or a man, appears and without ambiguity tells the dreamer what will happen or what he or she must do. There is, therefore, no need for interpretation; God makes the divine will known clearly. There is none of the inquisitiveness or egocentrism that characterizes divination. The dreams in the NT come involuntarily, and they have God at their center and can, therefore, fulfill the apologetic function that they frequently have in the NT narratives.

The Mysteries. The Mysteries were secret cults in which the uninitiated were not permitted to participate.[110] It is particularly hazardous to gener-

alize about the Mysteries because we still know so little about them. The vow of silence that initiates took was very effective, and reliable literary sources that can inform us about the Mysteries are very few. We are left to make what we can of statues, friezes, inscriptions, paintings, and the like, that represent aspects of one Mystery or another. In the face of the paucity of information, the natural tendency is to emphasize perceived commonalities and to create a composite Mystery of which particular cults are then seen as variants. This is especially tempting when two of the Mysteries about which we know most— that associated with Eleusis and the cult of the Egyptian goddess Isis—are made to supply the major constituents of a protean Mystery cult.[111]

Despite these qualifications, certain things are generally thought to have characterized the Mysteries, in addition to their secrecy. They promised salvation in the world to come, which consists of the liberation from the control of fate, the cosmic powers, and death; a passage through the underworld without fear; and eternal happy communion with the gods. This salvation was guaranteed by a series of activities, beginning with a preparatory washing and ending with a principal rite that aimed at the immortalization of the initiate. This was attained when the initiate participated in the fate of the god as it was known through the myth that gave meaning to the cult. The rite itself involved speaking certain phrases, showing things, and performing certain actions. But what all this referred to has remained a mystery. Fellowship meals were also associated with the cults.

New Testament scholars' interest in the Mysteries has waned in recent years, as it has become clear that the Mysteries may not have been as significant a factor in the first century as had been thought, and that the study of the phenomenon is fraught with methodological difficulties.[112] The Mysteries were very important from the second century on, and Christian writers then had to come to terms with them. The Mysteries are an invaluable witness to a certain type of religiosity that shared some things with Christianity. The eleventh book of Apuleius's *The Golden Ass* is one of the few extensive texts we have that provides a glimpse of the initiation into

106. For different assessments, but both of which regard the second century as an important time in pagan religiosity, see A. J. Festugière, *Personal Religion Among the Greeks* (Berkeley: University of California Press, 1954) 85-104; E. R. Dodds, *Pagan and Christian in an Age of Anxiety* (Cambridge: Cambridge University Press, 1965) 38-53.

107. See C. A. Behr, *Aelius Aristides and the Sacred Tales* (Chicago: Argonaut, 1968) 171-95, on the classification of dreams.

108. Theophrastus *Characters* 16; Cicero *On Divination* 2.124-50.

109. See J. S. Hanson, "Dreams and Visions in the Graeco-Roman World and Early Christianity," in Haase and Temporini, *Augstieg und Niedergang* 2.23.2, 1395-1427.

110. See Marvin W. Meyer, ed., *The Ancient Mysteries: A Sourcebook* (San Francisco: Harper & Row, 1987), for an optimistic account of what can be known about the Mysteries.

111. For an assessment of twentieth-century scholarship on the Mysteries, see Malherbe, "Greco-Roman Philosophy and Religion," 11-13.

112. For a thorough assessment of the issues, see Hugo Rahner, "Christian Mystery and the Pagan Mysteries," in Joseph Campbell, ed., *Pagan and Christian Mysteries* (New York: Harper, 1963) 148-78.

a Mystery, in this case, that of Isis. Such things as a ritual washing, the language of salvation and rebirth, and the spiritual paternity of Isis's priest, all present in this book, have been thought by some scholars to be similar to Christian baptism and theological language.

directly and in new ways, and at others they availed themselves of Judaism and its traditions. Always they acted with an awareness that, although they were part of their world, their true identity was to be shaped by the values they had learned through their Christian faith.

CONCLUSION

The study of the first-century Greco-Roman world can be approached from many different vantage points. The one adopted in this article—viewing that world from the perspective of a Christian interest— is no less valid than others. Christians had to come to terms with the reality of their world, and we have observed how they did so in various circumstances and ways that defy generalization. Sometimes they accommodated themselves to circumstances, and at other times they resisted; sometimes they responded

BIBLIOGRAPHY

Burkert, Walter. *Greek Religion.* Cambridge, Mass.: Harvard University Press, 1985.

Ferguson, Everett. *Backgrounds of Early Christianity.* 2nd ed. Grand Rapids: Eerdmans, 1993.

Friedlaender, Ludwig. *Roman Life and Morals Under the Early Empire.* London: Routledge, 1909.

Koester, Helmut. *Introduction to the New Testament.* Vol. 1 of *History, Culture, and Religion of the Hellenistic Age.* Philadelphia: Fortress; New York: De Gruyter, 1982.

Long, A. A. *Hellenistic Philosophy.* London: Duckworth, 1986.

Meeks, Wayne A. *The First Urban Christians: The Social World of the Apostle Paul.* New Haven: Yale University Press, 1983.

Nock, A. D. *Conversion: The Old and the New in Religion from Alexander the Great the Augustine of Hippo.* Oxford: Clarendon, 1933.

THE JEWISH CONTEXT
OF THE NEW TESTAMENT

GEORGE W. E. NICKELSBURG

INTRODUCTION

Christianity arose as one of many religions in the first-century Mediterranean world, and as such it shared much with its Greco-Roman environment. In particular, the groups that constituted the early church sprang from the matrix of Palestinian Judaism and continued to relate to Jewish communities of the diaspora. The first Christians understood themselves to be Jews, or Israelites, and outsiders viewed them as one of a number of Jewish religious sects. Thus the study of the first-century church should be informed by an understanding of contemporary Judaism and its religious, cultural, and social institutions.

Unfortunately, much of the nineteenth- and twentieth-century description of Judaism in the Greco-Roman period has been shaped by Christian categories and governed by the stereotypes of Christian apologetic and polemical agendas.[1] This article sketches a profile of first-century Judaism that should permit a more empathic understanding and appreciation of Judaism and early Christianity in their similarities and differences. The focus is on Judaism, but with appropriate reference to some implications for the study of the New Testament and early Christianity.

A discussion of first-century Judaism should oscillate between the poles of unity and diversity. Jews

of the first century had things in common with one another that distinguished them from other peoples of the Mediterranean world: a historical heritage, written and oral traditions that preserved that heritage in memory, and institutions that embodied the Jews' self-understanding and enabled them to interact with their heritage and traditions. These points of unity, however, were expressed in a cultural, intellectual, social, and religious pluralism rather than a single, monolithic normative Judaism.[2] The rich data that have accumulated since the discovery of the Dead Sea Scrolls have made this point indisputable. In order to do justice to this complex situation, we shall discuss the institutions and thought world of first-century Jews with a view toward identifying differences and discovering commonalities. As part of this exposition, we shall indicate how early Christians opted for one or another of available options.

THE PEOPLE OF GOD

Central to the Jews' self-identity was their belief that the one true God had chosen them and accepted them into a relationship of reciprocal fidelity. In our post-modern, secularized age, nations, peoples, and

---

1. See C. Klein, *Anti-Judaism in Christian Theology* (Philadelphia: Fortress, 1978).

2. Jacob Neusner even suggests that we speak of "Judaisms" rather than "Judaism"; see J. Neusner, W. S. Green, and E. Frerichs, *Judaisms and Their Messiahs and the Turn of the Christian Era* (Cambridge: Cambridge University Press, 1987) xii-xiii.

groups find their respective unity in a wide range of myths and symbols. The Jewish people of the first century, like the many peoples and nations contemporary with them, expressed their identity and interpreted their experience with reference to a divine realm. Different from many of their contemporaries, the Jews believed that there was one supreme Deity to whom they were uniquely related. Many writings of the Hebrew Bible (HB), especially Deuteronomy and texts that followed in its tradition, focused on this relationship, which they referred to as the covenant. The term *covenant* appears much less frequently in the post-biblical Jewish writings of the Greco-Roman period than a reader of the Hebrew Bible might expect; however, the components of the covenantal scheme are almost universally present.[3] The Jews are God's chosen people, who are to love and trust in that God and to worship and serve that God by living according to the divine laws and commands. In turn they expect their God will reward (or bless) them for their fidelity and punish (or curse) them when they sin.

Individual and corporate Jewish experience in the centuries around the turn of the era often contradicted this worldview. People who thought that they were faithful to God's law and just in their relationships with their fellow human beings experienced the troubles and sufferings that the Deuteronomic tradition identified as the curses of the covenant. Conversely, persons whom they considered to be sinners and unjust might prosper. On a broader scale, Israel as a nation experienced defeat, subjugation, and suffering at the hand of the Gentiles, who by definition were *not* God's chosen people.

In this article we shall attempt to imagine aspects of the world of first-century Jews. What institutions preserved and expressed their Jewishness? How did the people explain and deal with their experience when it contradicted their self-identity as faithful Israelites and children of God? How did they view and interrelate with non-Jews?

SCRIPTURE AND ITS INTERPRETATION

A Developing and Fluctuating Canon. By the first century, a growing collection of sacred texts was developing canonical authority in the Jewish communities of Palestine and the diaspora. The books of Moses and the Former and Latter Prophets (Joshua; Judges; 1–2 Samuel; 1–2 Kings; Isaiah; Jeremiah; Ezekiel; and the Twelve Minor Prophets) constituted the first two divisions of this corpus, and a third group of "Writings" was gaining recognition and authority (Psalms; Job; Proverbs; Ruth; Song of Songs; Ecclesiastes; Lamentations; Esther; Daniel; Ezra; Nehemiah; and 1–2 Chronicles).

The precise boundaries of the canon, and even the text of the biblical books, fluctuated from community to community and would not be fixed until the establishment of Rabbinic Judaism in the second century CE. The canon of the Greek translation of the Bible that developed in Alexandria included a number of works that were either translated from Hebrew or Aramaic or were composed in Greek (known in Christian circles as the apocryphal or deuterocanonical books). At Qumran the pseudepigraphal *Jubilees* and the collection known as *1 Enoch* were authoritative. The biblical manuscripts from Qumran also indicate that in the first century CE different versions of the Hebrew text of some biblical books were in circulation in the same place; the consonantal text of the Masoretic Text (MT) was not yet standardized.

Some of these textual variations were part of a broader process of interpretation that read the ancient texts with an eye toward interpreting them for new times. Narratives were revised and expanded; texts were read in the light of other texts; the original Hebrew was translated for people who understood only Greek or Aramaic (the Targums). Jewish communities of the diaspora considered the Greek text of the Septuagint (LXX) rather than the Hebrew text to be authoritative Scripture. By the middle of the first century CE, large segments of the Christian church employed this Greek translation as their Bible, as writings like Matthew, the epistles of Paul (notably Romans and Galatians), and the Epistle to the Hebrews attest.[4] Indeed, in depicting Jesus reading from a Hebrew scroll, Luke's Greek narrative in 4:18-19 uses the wording of the LXX rather than a fresh translation of the Hebrew text.[5]

---

3. This point is made by E. P. Sanders in his *Paul and Palestinian Judaism* (Philadelphia: Fortress, 1977), although his approach overlooks important differences of emphasis and expression in the texts.

4. For a discussion of the biblical quotations in Matthew and especially their relationship to the HB and the LXX, see Krister Stendahl, *The School of St. Matthew and Its Use of the Old Testament*, 2nd ed. (Philadelphia: Fortress, 1968); see also R. H. Gundry, *The Use of the Old Testament in St. Matthew's Gospel with Special Reference to the Messianic Hope* (Leiden: Brill, 1967). On Paul, see R. Hays, *Echoes of Scripture in the Letters of Paul* (New Haven: Yale University Press, 1989).

5. It is unlikely that Jesus used Greek extensively in his teaching. See J. A. Fitzmyer, "Did Jesus Speak Greek?" *BAR* (Sept.-Oct., 1992) 58-63, 76-77.

The Interpretation of Israel's History. The Jews memorialized their past in a variety of ways. The recounting of their history was a source of identity. The annual recitation of the Passover haggadah reminded them that they were God's people, chosen at the time of the exodus, and pointed them toward future deliverance. The Temple liturgy celebrated the events of Israel's history. Psalm 136 cites God's activity in creation and the exodus as evidence of God's ongoing covenantal love and as cause for thanksgiving.

Stories about Israel's past were also retold and reinterpreted, and the origin of the process antedates the canonical authority of some texts. The books of Chronicles retell events in 1–2 Samuel and 1–2 Kings with a focus on the rise and fall of the Davidic dynasty. A similar form of interpretation that goes back well into the Hellenistic period recasts patriarchal stories with an emphasis on the vices and virtues of the main characters. Stories preserved in such writings as *Jubilees,* the *Testaments of the Twelve Patriarchs,*[6] and the *Testament of Job* were a prism through which first-century Jews and Christians read about the ancient narratives. *Jubilees* 11–12 contains stories about Abram's conversion from idolatry and astrology that continued to play a role in first-century Jewish missionary preaching. James's interpretation of the sacrifice of Isaac (2:21-24) draws on the tradition preserved in *Jub.* 17:15–18:13; Sir 44:20; and 1 Macc 2:52; and his reference to Job's patience (5:11) reflects the story in the *Testament of Job* rather than the canonical book.

The events of Israel's past also provided a setting for *new* stories that were created to speak to situations of difficulty or crisis. The tale of Tobit's suffering, set in the Eastern dispersion, calls on its readers to accept God's chastisement of their sins and to await God's mercy. The book of Judith deals with faith and apostasy in the Maccabean period by fabricating an outrageously fictitious story set in the early post-exilic period. The authors of Daniel 1–6; Susanna; and Bel and the Dragon employ the exile as a setting for their exhortations to be faithful to the Torah. A fairly narrow sectarian setting may lie behind the tale of Isaiah's death in the *Martyrdom of Isaiah*; the author of Hebrews alludes to the story, to a similar one about Jeremiah, to Daniel 6, and to

6. Although it is debated whether the *Testaments of the Twelve Patriarchs* is a Christian or Jewish composition, it clearly contains traditions paralleled elsewhere in texts that are certainly Jewish.

other stories about Maccabean times (e.g., 2 Maccabees 7) as part of his exhortation to faith (Heb 11:33-38). The Jewish author of 4 Maccabees makes a similar use of the tradition. Thus Israel's past was made relevant to the present through a process of interpretation that focused on the virtues and vices of the forebears. For Jews and Christians, history was often understood as example (see 1 Cor 10:6-11).

Other narrative enhancements of the Bible served the purposes of eschatology; primordial events would have a counterpart in the final days. *First Enoch* 6–11 preserves the fountainhead of a tradition that depicted the flood as the prototype of the final judgment (Matt 24:37; Luke 17:26; 2 Pet 3:5-7).

The process of interpreting sacred tradition by enhancing old stories and creating new ones left its mark on early Christian traditions about Jesus. As a comparison of the synoptic Gospels indicates, stories in one text were revised and expanded in another to make the author's point. In addition, we can detect behind the written Gospels a haggadic tendency to create or shape stories about Jesus that expressed the storyteller's christology, often with reference to biblical traditions (Matthew 1–2; Luke 1–2; 7:11-17). Expressing the truth through story rather than by propositional statements was a thoroughly Jewish technique that is not surprising to find in the early church.

Interpretations of the Prophets. By 200 BCE, the oracles of the Latter Prophets were an integral part of the collection of Israel's sacred Scriptures (Sir 48:22–49:10). Since many of these oracles promised a glorious post-exilic restoration that had not been realized, and because God was believed to be faithful to these promises, the fulfillment of these prophecies was projected into the future (Sir 36:15-16; Tob 14:5).

This notion of prediction and fulfillment was given a special twist by persons and groups who believed that they were living in the last days. The authors of the Qumran commentaries quoted extensive passages from the prophetic books (including Psalms) and demonstrated in great detail how the prophecies were being realized in their own time and with reference to their own group. The author of Daniel 9 interpreted Jeremiah's prediction of seventy years' desolation (Jer 25:11-12) to refer to seventy weeks of years and thus awaited fulfillment in the not too distant future (Dan 9:2, 24). Interpretation of the Bible in terms of prediction and fulfillment is also a major feature in many NT texts (e.g., Matt 1:22-23; 2:5-6, 17-18; 3:3; 4:14-16; 12:17-21; 13:14-15, 35; 15:7-9; 21:4-5; 27:9-10; Luke 4:18-21; John 19:36-37; Rom 15:8-12; Heb 8:8-12; 10:15-17).

Deuteronomy 28–32 was especially fertile ground for Jewish speculation about the end time. The Deuteronomist's scheme of sin/punishment/repentance/restoration shaped many expositions of Israel's history (e.g., *Jub.* 1:7-18; 23:11-31). The *Testament of Moses* retells the events predicted in Deuteronomy 30–34, depicting Israel's future in two cycles of sin/punishment/repentance/salvation.[7] The latter cycle recounts events from the time of Antiochus Epiphanes in considerable detail, thus showing how Moses' prophecy at the end of Deuteronomy is superlatively fulfilled in the author's time, which immediately precedes the great judgment and Israel's exaltation to the heavens. An author of the early first century CE interpolated chap. 7 in order to update the text, so that it would predict the coming of the end in his own time.

Alongside the Davidic oracles and Deuteronomy, the songs of the Servant of Yahweh in Isa 42:1-4; 49:1-13; 50:4-9; and 52:13–53:12 were a special source for Jewish speculation. Interpretations varied widely, and one should not reduce them to a simple scheme of predication and fulfillment. Originally a symbol for the nation, the servant came to be understood as a type or model for a variety of individuals, usually persons of rank, and especially teachers. Daniel 12:3 predicts the heavenly exaltation of the wise, the teachers who brought many to righteousness during the days of Antiochus Epiphanes. The Wisdom of Solomon 2 and 4–5 recounts the career of the righteous one, who chides the wicked for their sins, is put to death for this activity, and is exalted as their judge. A similar pattern shapes the story of the seven brothers and their mother in 2 Maccabees 7. Their future resurrection will vindicate their obedient death for the Torah. In the Qumran Hymn Scroll (1QH 6:10), one teacher describes his activity with reference to Isaiah 50:4. An idiosyncratic interpretation of the Servant Songs appears in the Parables of Enoch (*1 Enoch* 37–71), which conflates material from the Davidic oracles in Isaiah 11 and Psalm 2, the son of man vision in Daniel 7, and the servant songs in Isaiah 49 and 52–53 into a composite portrait of a heavenly savior who is champion of the righteous and chosen and the judge of their enemies, the kings and the mighty.[8]

The texts that we have cited, from the second century BCE to the first century CE, demonstrate how Jews in this period believed that they were living in the last days and saw or expected the fulfillment of the ancient prophetic oracles in their own time. This common viewpoint was expressed, however, in a variety of ways. Other Jews at this time read prophetic scriptures in different ways that were not governed by an eschatological perspective and the expectation of an imminent judgment.

Early Christian interpretation of Scripture, however, was thoroughly eschatological. As the citation formulas in the Gospels (especially Matthew) indicate, Jesus and the events connected with his life were seen as fulfillments of the prophetic Scripture. This pertains especially to the belief that Jesus was the Lord's anointed one, the Son of Man, and the Servant of Yahweh.

The Study of the Torah. Central to the notion of covenant was the obligation that God's people live in accordance with the Torah. Few aspects of early Jewish religion have been as misunderstood as the nature and role of Torah. This obscuring of the historical facts is, in large part, a result of the Protestant dichotomy of law and gospel that resulted from Reformation polemics against medieval Catholicism. The ancient texts present a very different picture of the nature and role of the Torah.

Because Christian attitudes about the Torah have been so heavily influenced by polemic, several facts must be clarified. First, the imperative to obey the Torah stood within the framework of a covenant that God initiated by sheer grace. Obedience to the Torah was a response to God's election of Israel as the covenant people. Second, the meaning of *Torah* is often wrongly reduced to "law," because Torah was usually translated νόμος (*nomos*) in the LXX, whence it was taken over into the NT. In fact, *torah* means "instruction," and the largest part of the Pentateuch consists of narrative (almost all of Genesis and Numbers, much of Exodus, and part of Deuteronomy) and of instruction not cast in the form of commandments and ordinances (the sermon-like

---

7. *Testament of Moses* 2; 3:1-4; 3:5–4:4; 4:5-9; and 5:1–6:1; 8; 9; 10.

8. G. W. E. Nickelsburg, "Salvation Without and with a Messiah," in Neusner et al., *Judaisms and Their Messiahs,* 49-68.

addresses in Deuteronomy). For Jews *the whole* of this section of the Bible was divine "instruction" revealed by God and written by Moses. Third, these facts notwithstanding, the Torah contains many commandments and requirements for the conduct of human life, and the prophetic corpus is filled with exhortations to conduct one's life according to God's will. The desire to reverse the damage done by anti-Jewish polemics should not obscure the fact that Jews were called upon to live according to the laws and commandments of the Torah. Nor is this surprising, since law is a necessary institution in every society. Finally, the claim is made that Judaism was a legalistic religion governed by the attempt to attain divine rewards for one's deeds. This misunderstanding is based on a wrong and anachronistic reading of texts like the Mishnah, and it ignores the fact that the HB itself associates obedience and disobedience with covenantal rewards and punishments.

A closer look at the pious and righteous life according to the Torah and an analysis of the notion of reward and punishment will occupy us below. Here we focus on Torah as Scripture and on the interpretive processes. By the first century, the study of Torah was developing into a major institution in Judaism; after the destruction of the Temple, it would rise to greater prominence.

The study and exposition of Torah took two major forms in the first century, both rooted in the practice of previous centuries. The first of these was the precursor of the detailed halakhic interpretation that lies behind the Mishnah and the Talmud and is worked out in the halakhic commentaries of the Tannaitic period.[9] Individual commandments in the Torah were fine-tuned and interpreted with respect to a variety of specific situations. Pre-Christian evidence of this kind of interpretation appears in the Qumran texts, notably in the ordinances attached to the *Damascus Document* (CD 9-16) and in the *Temple Scroll.* A special case is found in *Jubilees,* which exegetically derives commandments from the narrative text of Genesis and Exodus.

The dynamic for such halakhic exegesis was twofold. First, as with every law code, new situations not mentioned or envisioned in the original codes elicited new and more specific interpretations. Second, events in the post-exilic period led

to the belief that God's people were experiencing the covenantal curses that resulted from disobedience of the Torah. It followed that one should study the Torah to ascertain God's will—what God's people should do in order to receive the covenantal blessings. *Jubilees* 23:11-31 describes the sequence of disobedience and curse, the process of repentance, and the anticipated results. Verse 26 is pivotal:

> But in those days the children will begin to study the law,
> and search the commandments,
> and return to the path of righteousness.
>
> (author's trans.)

The original Hebrew verb in line one or two was doubtless *darash* (דרש) the root from which was derived the term *midrash* (מדרש); both the verb and the noun were becoming technical terms for the process of searching the Scriptures to find the specifics of God's will in the Torah and the manner in which God would fulfill the predictions of the prophets.[10]

The same technical vocabulary appears in Ben Sira's description of the work of the scribe (Sir 39:1-8), a passage that opens a window into the world of Israel's sages. They arose early in the morning and prayed; they studied the Torah, the Prophets, and the Wisdom writings; they believed that their interpretations were inspired by God.

A second form of Torah exposition is present in the wisdom literature. Here the sage is interested not in spelling out the particulars of Torah obedience in a given situation, but in exhorting his audience to *be* obedient. The motivation is the nexus between action and consequence, between obedience and reward, or between disobedience and punishment. His instrument of persuasion is the poetic form of the proverb, whose parallel structure allows one to juxtapose action and consequence. The parallelism may also emphasize the parity between a deed and its appropriate result:

> Do not turn your face away from any poor man,
> and the face of the Lord will not be turned away from you. (Tob 4:7, author's trans.)

Behind this proverb lie the biblical commands and prophetic exhortations to care for the needy. The

---

9. See the discussion of Mishnah, Talmud, and halakhic interpretation in Michael A. Signer, "How the Bible Has Been Interpreted in Jewish Tradition," *NIB* (Nashville: Abingdon, 1994) 1:65-82.

10. See the discussion of midrash in ibid.

proverb does not spell out the details, but emphasizes the imperative and the result of obeying it. A lengthy example of such interpretation appears in Sir 5:1-16, which plays out a set of variations on the commandment in Exod 20:12 with scarcely a reference to what constitutes honoring one's parents.

These texts and others like them offer a picture of the study and exposition of Torah in first-century Judaism. Scholars mined the law codes and sought to apply the commandments to present or conceivable situations. This activity would be epitomized in the Mishnah and Talmud, but these collections should not be read as evidence of a legalistic, nit-picking Judaism to which Jesus and first-century Christianity were foils—for three reasons. First, the Mishnah and Talmud are archives in a sense, collections of opinions and discussions held over several centuries. Second, these texts were assembled after the rise of Christianity. Third, texts from the turn of the era also depict sages and scribes in a different role, teaching and exhorting right behavior and admonishing God's people to be mindful of the consequences of their behavior. While Ben Sira does not claim to *be* a prophet, he likens his exposition of the Torah to prophecy (Sir 24:32-34). (We shall turn to other forms of prophet-like wisdom instruction below.)

THE PIOUS AND RIGHTEOUS LIFE

The Centrality of Torah. The passage from *Jubilees* 23 quoted above emphasizes the connection between the study of the Torah and the obedient life that follows from it. One *studies* the commandments and then *walks* in the path of righteousness. The theme recurs in some Jewish-sounding words ascribed to Jesus: "Blessed rather are those who *hear* the word of God and *obey* it" (Luke 11:28 NRSV, italics added; cf. Matt 7:24-27). Thus at the heart of Judaism lies the imperative to live by the Torah. Different from Christianity as it has evolved over the centuries with its substantial theological and christological emphasis, the HB and later Jewish literature focus on human conduct and God's response, to bless or curse, to reward or punish.

Contrary to Christian stereotypes that obedience to the Torah was a burden borne grudgingly, many Jewish texts describe it as an obligation freely accepted. The saying of Jesus in Matt 11:28-30, far from implying a contrast to Torah obedience, is a veritable paraphrase of the Jewish sage Ben Sira, who invites his readers to submit joyfully to the Torah:

> Put your neck under her yoke,
>   and let your souls receive instruction
>
> . . . .
> May your soul rejoice in God's mercy,
>   and may you never be ashamed when
>   to praise him.
>
>   (Sir 51:26, 29 NRSV)

Writings related to the Maccabean period attest the willingness of a significant number of Jews to die on behalf of the Torah (1, 2, 4 Maccabees; the *Testament of Moses*; Daniel). Moreover, these narratives reveal the inseparability of faith and obedience (wrenched apart in some Christian interpretations of the apostle Paul). The aforementioned texts demonstrate how one enacts faith in God precisely in willing obedience to the Torah (Dan 3:17-18; 1 Macc 2:49-64).

Israelites thought of themselves as "a holy nation" (Exod 19:6), a people set apart for their God in all aspects of their lives (cf. 1 Pet 2:9). The righteous and pious life and the Torah pertaining to it covered one's public relationships to other people, one's personal and private activity, and one's worship of God and acts of atonement when one did not abide by the Torah.

A Life of Justice to Others. The majority of the commandments in the Decalogue treat one's responsibilities toward one's neighbors (Exod 20:1-17). Obligations to others and social justice run like a thread through the Pentateuch and the preaching of the prophets. Most of the law code in Exod 20:22–23:33 is devoted to the topic. Of special importance is the obligation to help the needy and the weak. In this spirit, the author of Tobit sees generosity, almsgiving, and the burial of murder victims as the epitome of the righteous life (1:16-18). This and other wisdom texts warn against stinginess and the abuse of wealth.

A Life of Personal Purity. Alongside this public, social aspect of the Torah and the righteous life, one finds considerable emphasis on personal purity and uncleanness. Again, the basic issues are laid out in the Bible, especially in Leviticus 11–15; 17–18. The meat of some animals is ritually unclean. Animal blood may not be consumed. The birth of a child renders its mother unclean. The effusion of sexually related bodily fluids creates uncleanness, and forbidden sexual relationships defile the land. Contagious skin diseases are especially dangerous. As personal as anything is the commandment that every Israelite male must be circumcised. Although this is not an issue of purity, the penalty for disobedience is excommunication (Gen 17:14).

Maintaining One's Relationship to God. The Prohibition of Idolatry. Fundamental to the Torah was each person's relationship to the God of Israel. Because Yahweh had claimed Israel as the covenant people, one was to worship God exclusively (Exod 20:2-3) and to fear, love, and trust God with all of one's being (Deut 6:4-5). Thus, as the biblical authors repeatedly emphasize, idolatry was strictly forbidden. Jewish texts of the Greco-Roman period reemphasize the point.[11] Similar strictures against idolatry were a regular part of early Christian preaching and teaching (1 Cor 10:14, 20-21; 1 Thess 1:9-11; Rev 2:14).

Specific Obligations to God. Other, positive obligations to God are focal. The command to "remember the Sabbath day and keep it holy" is basic in this respect. Not only is it the longest and most detailed of the Ten Commandments (Exod 20:8-11), but in the Greco-Roman period it is the subject of detailed, casuistic interpretation as well (*Jub.* 50:6-13; CD 10:14–11:18; Mark 2:23–3:6).

The command to offer first fruits and tithes of one's produce was a second obligation to God (Deut 12:5-14; 14:22-29; 26:1-19), although the gift to God also took the form of a gift to persons in need. For the author of Tobit, these offerings were a special sign of piety, although not all Israelites fulfilled the obligation (1:5-7).

The celebration of religious festivals was an act of worship by which one remembered God's gracious activity in Israel's past history: Passover (the exodus); Weeks or Pentecost (the giving of the Torah); Booths (the time in the wilderness).[12] The feast of Hanukkah celebrated the reconsecration of the Temple by Judas Maccabeus in 165 BCE.

An important way in which Jews made connection with the Temple was through the annual half-shekel temple tax that was obligatory for every male Jew. It recognized the central role that the temple cult played in the life of the people.

Temple and Cult. Although many Jews in Palestine and the diaspora never saw the Temple,

the worship of God centered there. Mount Zion was thought to be the center of the earth, and the Temple the place where the heavenly God was especially present. Isaiah envisioned the Temple standing in a polar relationship with God's heavenly temple and throne, so that the train of God's garment rested in the holy of holies (Isa 6:1). Jerusalem and its Temple drew pilgrims from Palestine and the diaspora to commemorate the cycle of festivals.

Central to the Temple cult was the offering of sacrifices that varied widely in type and function. Each morning and evening a whole lamb was burnt on the altar, together with a cereal offering and a libation. This continual burnt offering (עלה התמיד *'ōlah hattāmîd*), symbolizing the ongoing relationship between Israel and its God, was so essential to Israel's religious life that its disruption by Antiochus Epiphanes and during the Jewish War was viewed with great dismay.[13] The other major sacrifice of universal significance took place each year on Yom Kippur, the Day of Atonement (Leviticus 16), when the sacrifice offering of one goat and the freeing of another symbolized God's forgiveness of the people's sins. Other sacrifices were offered by individuals as means to purify uncleanness or to atone for sins, although we do not know how many Palestinian Jews from outlying areas (e.g., Galilee or Perea) journeyed to Jerusalem for such purposes. In any case, it was necessary that animals be available in Jerusalem for purchase by pilgrims, and this situation created the backdrop for the story recounted in Mark 11:15-17 par.[14]

In addition to the offering of sacrifices, the Temple cult included the singing of songs contained in the book of Psalms. Although this collection was recognized as Scripture by the first century, it also functioned as a Temple hymnbook, and its contents were appropriate to the different festivals of the Jewish religious calendar.

Finally, the Temple was a place where the Israelite priests carried out specific commandments of the Torah, those related to the conduct of the sacrificial cult and the purification of uncleanness (see Leviticus 1–17). Perhaps Sir 24:10 refers to this when it identifies Zion as the place where Wisdom took root. It may also refer to priests who served

---

11. See, e.g., *1 Enoch* 99:6-8; *Jub.* 20:7-9; 22:16-18; Bel and the Dragon; *Apocalypse of Abraham; Joseph and Aseneth.*

12. See the discussion in Gary A. Anderson, "Introduction to Israelite Religion," *NIB*, 1:272-83.

13. See Dan 8:11; Josephus *Antiquities of the Jews* 6.2.1.

14. See E. P. Sanders, *Judaism: Practice and Belief, 63 B.C.E.–66 C.E.* (Philadelphia: Trinity Press International, 1992) 103-18.

as teachers of the Torah; the *Testament of Levi* emphasizes the teaching role of the priests (chap. 13), and Luke 2:46-47 depicts the young Jesus in the Temple engaged in discussion with teachers of the Torah.[15]

For all of these reasons, one can hardly overestimate the the Temple's significance for first-century Jews. Its destruction in 70 CE was a massively traumatic event, as can be seen in the post-70 CE apocalypses that compare it to the destruction of the first Temple and the beginning of the Babylonian Exile (see 2 Esdras; 2–3 Baruch; cf. also *Apocalypse of Abraham*). Christian sources also emphasize the significance of the event; the Gospels interpret it as punishment for the Jews' rejection of Jesus, and the book of Revelation awaits the descent of a new Jerusalem, albeit without a temple (chap. 21).

The high estimation of the Temple notwithstanding, all Jews did not find it indispensable. Several temples existed outside of Jerusalem at various times—in Transjordanian Tyre (modern-day 'Araq-el-Emir), and in Egypt at Leontopolis and Elephantine. Although the Qumran community valued Jerusalem and its Temple, they believed that the priesthood was polluted (CD 5:6-15) and saw themselves as a spiritual temple and priesthood, offering atonement for the Land (1QS 8:1-10). A negative view of the Hasmonean priesthood appears also in *Pss. Sol.* 2:2-4; 8:11-13, and a more long-standing criticism of the temple and the priesthood is reflected in *1 Enoch* 12–16; 89:72–90:29; 93:8-10 + 91:11-13. While we cannot be certain where, to what extent, and among whom such viewpoints had currency in the first century, NT texts like Mark 11:15-17; the Epistle to the Hebrews; Eph 2:14-22; and 1 Pet 2:4-6 draw on the kind of anti-Temple traditions attested in the aforementioned Jewish texts.

Alternative Means of Atonement. The biblical law codes emphasize sacrifice as a means of atoning for breaches of the Torah. However, the destruction of the Temple in 587 BCE and the Jews' exile in Babylon, as well as the distance many Palestinian Jews lived from Jerusalem and simple economics, would have made it impossible for sacrifice to have been an all-encompassing means of atonement. Jewish literature of the Greco-Roman period identifies other means of making reparation for sin and cleansing from impurity.

According to one view, suffering was a means by which God scourged, disciplined, or chastised the nation, or even the righteous, for their sins. The book of Tobit contrasts such scourging with God's eventual mercy (11:15; 13:2, 5, 9). According to 2 Macc 6:12-17, God does not withdraw covenantal mercy, but disciplines Israel, teaching the people to change their ways. For the *Psalms of Solomon,* the suffering of the righteous purifies sin and wipes away transgressions (10:1-2; 13:10); both expressions are appropriate to the sacrificial cult. Martyrdom for Torah could also propitiate for the sins of the people, and 4 Macc 17:20-22 employs a cluster of cultic terms to describe the process. A similar use of one of these words, "expiation" or "sacrifice of atonement" (ἱλαστήριον *hilastērion*), appears in the pre-Pauline tradition preserved in Rom 3:24-26.[16]

Righteous deeds of either a personal or a social nature could also atone. According to *Pss. Sol.* 3:8, the righteous one expiates for sins of ignorance through fasting and humiliation, and thereby God cleanses the pious one's household. Actions directed toward others could effect atonement. Almsgiving rescues from death and purges sin (Tob 12:9-10). Ben Sira also singles out almsgiving in a context that employs cultic language to describe the function of Torah obedience (Sir 35[32]:1-2). In short, one could atone for breaches of the Torah through corresponding acts of obedience, notably deeds of kindness to others in need of them.

Finally, prayers in which the nation or an individual confesses sin become ritualized as a means of expressing the change of heart that is constitutive of the repentance that changes God's wrath to mercy. Such prayers appear in Psalm 52; Ezra 9:6-15; Neh 9:6-37; Bar 1:1–3:8; Dan 9:4-19; the Prayer of Azariah, the Prayer of Manasseh, and the Qumran *Words of the Heavenly Lights.* While these prayers are not means of atonement in themselves, they appear to be components of more extensive rituals of atonement. Taken together with fasting and almsgiving, they constitute a triad that appears in Jesus' teaching about the Torah in the Sermon on the Mount (Matt 6:1-21).

Synagogues as Places of Worship. We cannot be certain precisely when the institution known

---

15. On the teaching functions of priests, see J. C. Greenfield and M. E. Stone, "Remarks on the Aramaic Testament of Levi from the Geniza," *RB* 86 (1979) 223-24. See also the discussion of the role of Joseph in the *Testament of Levi,* in Harm W. Hollander, *Joseph as an Ethical Model in the Testaments of the Twelve Patriarchs,* SVTP 6 (Leiden: Brill, 1981) 57-62.

16. S. K. Williams, *Jesus' Death as Saving Event: The Background and Origin of a Concept,* HSR 2 (Missoula: Scholars Press, 1975).

as the synagogue came into existence. It is likely that the destruction of the Temple in 587/586 BCE and the exile in Babylon created the occasion for Jews to gather in order to reflect on their situation and religious status, to offer penitential prayer, and to worship God (see Jer 29:12-14). Such assemblies would have convened in people's houses. The continued dispersion of many Jews created the ongoing need for an institution like the synagogue, and there is some inscriptional and literary evidence that buildings existed for that purpose during the first century.[17] The book of Acts depicts the apostle Paul regularly making use of synagogues as a base for his mission work (e.g., 13:5, 14-15; 14:1; 17:1-2). His epistles, however, lack any evidence for such a locus of his preaching and teaching.

Because the Temple was rebuilt, it is not to be taken for granted that synagogue buildings existed in Palestine in the Greco-Roman period. However, stories in the synoptic Gospels set the preaching of Jesus in places called synagogues (e.g., Mark 1:21, 39; 3:1; 6:2) and archaeological evidence from Gamla in Galilee and the Herodian fortresses of Masada and Herodium attest the existence of such places.[18]

Literary evidence provides some indication of what occurred in the synagogues. According to Josephus, Alexandrian Jews gathered each week to listen to the Torah and its exposition.[19] Luke 4:16-22 suggests that the sabbath was the occasion for synagogue gatherings in which the prophets were read and expounded. If we can trust the *Psalms of Solomon* to reflect first-century BCE practice that was more widespread than in the circles of the "synagogues of the pious" (συναγωγαί ὁσίων *synagōgai hosiōn*), religious assemblies of the Jews were the occasion for prayer and the praise of God (10:5-7; 17:16). Indeed, this collection of prayers and psalms, as well as the Qumran Hymn Scroll, attest the creation of texts for communal and individual devotion.

The Righteous and the Sinners. Faithfulness to the Torah was, in the final analysis, the hallmark of a true Jew. One's birth and one's place in the covenant were affirmed through obedience to the stipulations of the covenant. A broad range of texts

dealing with the time of Antiochus Epiphanes indicate that flagrant infractions of the Torah (e.g., violations of the sabbath, reversal of one's circumcision, eating of pork, and participation in the cult of a foreign God) were widely considered to place one outside the covenant. Such persons chose to make a covenant with the Gentiles (1 Macc 1:11). These obvious issues aside, however, it is important to clarify what constituted the righteous life.

The terms *righteous* and *sinner* hold the key to such a clarification. The use of this word pair in the Gospels has led many Christian interpreters to claim that many Jews, especially the Pharisees, considered themselves qualitatively superior in a religious sense from others. In this view, the definition of oneself as righteous implied something close to sinlessness. *Psalms of Solomon* 3 offers a different picture in its contrast between the righteous and the sinner. The righteous are not sinless, but recognize God's chastening of their sins, make atonement for those sins, and receive God's blessing. The sinners, by contrast, pile up sins, ignore their religious obligations, and are ultimately punished by God. A similar view of the righteous appears in Tob 3:1-6, where the self-defined righteous one (Tob 1:3) confesses his sin, and in 2 Maccabees 7, where seven brothers who are about to die for the Torah confess their sins in solidarity with the nation. Thus righteousness does not involve a simple reckoning of good deeds; it reflects reverence for God and concern to abide by the Torah, which includes reparation for sin.

INTERPRETING EXPERIENCE: JUSTIFYING THE WAYS OF GOD

The Rise of Eschatology. Because it was axiomatic in Deuteronomic theology and the ruminations of the wisdom teachers that God rewarded obedience to the Torah and punished disobedience, it became increasingly important in the post-exilic period to explain the evidence to the contrary and to posit and try to catalyze a reversal of present conditions. Two approaches to the problem prevailed. Both admitted that the present situation was due to Israel's sin, but their solutions differed. The author of Isaiah 56–66 believed that the Jews were divided into two groups: the chosen, who were God's servants, and the sinners. In short order, God would appear to execute judgment on all humanity and divide between the chosen and the sinners. God

17. See E. M. Myers, "Synagogue: Introductory Survey," *ABD,* 6:253.
18. Ibid., 253-55.
19. Josephus *Against Apion* 2.1.17.

would create a new heaven and a new earth, and the chosen would live long, blessed lives in a new Jerusalem (Isaiah 65–66). These texts attest a genuine eschatology, which posited an *end* to the old order and a new *beginning* initiated by a new creation that would reprise the world's and humanity's first beginning.

A second approach worked with the Deuteronomic scheme of sin/punishment/repentance/salvation and blessing. The exile had been God's punishment for Israel's sins, but the return did not bring a restoration of God's blessing because the curses of the covenant were still clinging to a people who were still sinful and needed to effect the repentance that would turn curse to blessing. The use of the Deuteronomic scheme and language (sometimes combined with the idiom of Jeremiah) runs like a thread through post-exilic literature (in Malachi, the prayers of Ezra and Nehemiah and others like them mentioned above; *Jubilees* 1; 23; the *Testament of Moses*; 2 Maccabees; and *Psalms of Solomon* 2; 8; 17).

From these two general approaches, Jews of the post-exilic period saw various means toward the solution of their present situation. The righteous could await God's intervention. Through acts of representative repentance, they could act on behalf of the nation to bring a turn toward blessing. The nation as a whole could repent. Similarly, the renewal of blessing could take a variety of forms, ranging from a violent catastrophe followed by a new creation to the gradual improvement of the present world. Through all of this the future reversal was often seen as the fulfillment of God's promises through the prophets, notably Second and Third Isaiah, and oracles about the Davidic dynasty in the Prophets and the Psalms.

Agents of Divine Deliverance. Speculation about the agent of God's coming salvation differed widely.[20] Some awaited a restoration of the Davidic dynasty, collecting and appealing to the oracles in 2 Samuel 7; Isaiah 9; 11; Ezekiel 34; and Psalms 2; 45; and 89. *Psalms of Solomon* 17 and 18 and a few Qumran texts indicate such an expectation. However, even during the exile and the early post-exilic period, the hope of a Davidic restoration was not universal. Second Isaiah transfers material from Davidic oracles to the mysterious figure of the Servant of Yahweh, who bears the characteristics of

king, prophet, and perhaps priest. The Servant is both Israel and a figure apart from the nation. Third Isaiah pluralizes the Servant and chosen one to denote the righteous of the nation. Later texts following in the tradition of Second and Third Isaiah make almost no reference to a Davidic restoration. For the authors of Tobit, Baruch, and a number of post-biblical hymns about Zion, a glorified New Jerusalem does not require a king.[21] The *Parables of Enoch,* which also working within the Deutero-Isaianic tradition, posit a heavenly savior figure who combines traits traditionally ascribed to the Davidic king, Second Isaiah's Servant of Yahweh, and the "one like a Son of Man" in Daniel 7. Such a transcendental savior appears in other forms. In *1 Enoch* 10, salvation is effected by four high angels: Sariel, Raphael, Gabriel, and Michael, the latter depicted in part as a heavenly high priest who will purify the polluted earth. In *T. Mos.* 10:2, a repetition of the Sinai theophany will be preceded by the appearance of the angelic high priest. Daniel 7 and 12 expect similar angelic intervention by Michael, and the Qumran *Melchizedek* text identifies the priest of Genesis 14 as such an angel and heavenly high priest (11QMelch).[22] Finally, some people who believed the temple cult to be polluted awaited the arrival of a new high priest, who would set things right and who might, or might not, rule alongside a Davidic king. The *Testament of Levi* 12–18 awaits such an eschatological priest who will have characteristics traditionally ascribed to the Davidic king.[23] Some Qumran texts envision a triad of eschatological figures: the priest, the king, and the prophet mentioned in Deuteronomy (4QTestim; 1QS 9:11).

Resurrection, Immortality, and Eternal Life. The gravest injustice that Jews in the Greco-Roman period experienced was death on behalf of the Torah. People died because they were faithful to the covenant, while apostasy from the Torah saved others from such a fate. Texts like Dan 12:2

---

20. For Jewish and NT texts that exemplify the spectrum of belief about agents of deliverance, see G. W. E. Nickelsburg and M. E. Stone, *Faith and Piety in Early Judaism* (Philadelphia: Fortress, 1983) 161-201.

21. For examples of such hymns, see Tobit 13; Sir 36:1-17; 11QPs[a] 22:1-15.

22. Clearly the references to Melchizedek in Hebrews 5–7 know a developed speculation about this figure, but there is much debate about the relationship between Hebrews and 11QMelch, the story about Melchizedek's birth in *2 Enoch* 71–72, and the gnostic *Melchizedek* text found at Nag Hammadi. See F. L. Horton, *The Melchizedek Tradition: A Critical Examination of the Sources to the Fifth Century* A.D. *and in the Epistle to the Hebrews,* SNTSMS 30 (Cambridge: Cambridge University Press, 1976); P. J. Kobelski, *Melchizedek and Melchiresa',* CBQMS 10 (Washington, D.C.: Catholic Biblical Association, 1981); B. A. Pearson, *Nag Hammadi Codices IX and X,* NHS 15 (Leiden: Brill, 1981) 28-40.

23. See Nickelsburg and Stone, *Faith and Piety in Early Judaism,* 168-70, 199nn. 1-2.

and 2 Maccabees 7 posited resurrection as God's way of reversing an unjust death. Whatever its precise origin, such belief was tied to an interpretation of the prophetic Scripture. The story of the seven brothers and their mother is a narrative interpretation of passages in Second Isaiah that describe the vindication of the Servant of Yahweh, the return of the children of Mother Zion, and God's promise to redeem what God has created. This story and Dan 12:3 see the Servant realized in the teachers of the Maccabean period, who encouraged the people in the way of righteousness and thus earned special glory—according to Dan 12:3, among the stars.

Beliefs in post-mortem vindication varied widely in the first century, ranging from resurrection of the body (2 Maccabees 7) and resurrection of the spirit (*1 Enoch* 102:4–104:8), to the assumption of the spirit to heaven at death (*Jub.* 23:22), to the belief that one already was participating in eternal life (1QH 3:19-23; 11:3-14). Heavily Hellenized texts like the Wisdom of Solomon (2:23–3:4; 8:19-20), 4 Maccabees (7:3; 9:22; 14:5-6; 16:13; 17:12), and *Joseph and Aseneth* (16:16) employ the Greek terminology of immortality and incorruptibility. The NT attests a growing tendency to posit resurrection of the body, with reference to both Jesus and believers.[24]

The Locus of Future Divine Blessing. More often than not, the restoration of God's blessing was expected to take place on earth. This followed the viewpoint of Deuteronomy 28–29, which enumerated these blessings as fertility of the land, large families, long lives, and good health. Even a mythically shaped text like Isaiah 65–66 depicts the righteous living long lives in a newly created Jerusalem on a newly created earth. Apocalyptic texts derived from this tradition present a similar view (*1 Enoch* 10–11; Revelation 20–21). There are exceptions to this. *Testament of Moses* 10:9 envisions Israel's exaltation to the stars, and Dan 12:3 promises this as a prerogative of the righteous teachers. New Testament texts present both alternatives (Matt 5:4; Luke 1:68-79; John 14:2-3).

The Absence of Viable Eschatology. Although there is ample evidence of a widespread eschatological consciousness in first-century Palestinian Judaism, this evidence has been preserved in texts that were transmitted in communities governed by such a persuasion—mainly the early church and the Qumran community. To what extent these texts represent the larger picture of first-century Judaism is questionable, and there is some counterindicative evidence. We may consider the hymn to Simon the high priest in 1 Maccabees 14 to be eschatologically oriented, but it reflects the belief of the people in power that they were the fulfillers of prophecy. If deprivation led to hope for the future, the rich and mighty could feel that they were enjoying the blessings of the covenant (*1 Enoch* 103:5-6). For such persons and, evidently, the Sadducees, one need not postulate a resurrection of the dead at the end of a good life. While Ben Sira preserves a traditional hymn for the restoration of Zion and the fulfillment of ancient prophecies (Sir 36:1-17), most of his book of wisdom focuses on the responsibilities of everyday life, as does the *Letter of Aristeas.*

APOCALYPTICISM: RADICAL DUALISM AND NEW REVELATION

Apocalypticists viewed their world at the intersection of three kinds of dualism.[25] A spatial dualism contrasted an earth that was often bereft of divine justice with a heavenly world where divine justice was done or with the outer reaches of the universe, where the pits of destruction awaited the wicked. A temporal dualism contrasted the present evil time with a primordial past, where an angelic revolt brought into existence a horde of evil demons whose activity creates havoc now. This dualism also contrasted the present time with a future time, when God's judgment would set things right, eradicating evil, punishing the wicked, and rewarding the righteous (cf. Rom 8:18-25; 1 Cor 7:31; 10:11; Gal 1:4). An ontological dualism distinguished human beings from God and God's angels and also made human beings victims of demonic activity.

This triple dualism converged to portray a world that was spatially distant from God's presence, temporally distant from God's judgment, and the locus of injustice and demonic victimization. The dualism, however, was mitigated by the claim that the apocalypticist—said to be a figure of the past—had visited the hidden places of the cosmos, had seen into the

---

24. See G. W. E. Nickelsburg, "Resurrection," in *Anchor Bible Dictionary* (Garden City, N.Y.: Doubleday, 1992) 5:684-91.

25. Ibid., "The Apocalyptic Construction of Reality of *1 Enoch*," in J. J. Collins and J. H. Charlesworth, eds., *Mysteries and Revelations: Apocalyptic Studies Since the Uppsala Colloquium*, JSP Supplement Series 9 (Sheffield: Sheffield Academic Press, 1991) 51-64.

hidden future, and had left the faithful a message that promised divine intervention and the universal, eternal triumph of God's justice, thus encouraging them to endure in a threatening world. The revelation, allegedly received in the course of heavenly journeys and dream visions, claims to be very old, prior to Moses and the prophets. In fact, it is new, created on the brink of what the authors claim to be the end time.

This apocalypticism originated among the sages and scribes of the so-called wisdom tradition, persons whose responsibility included the preservation and interpretation of the Torah and the Prophets. Such persons, as noted above, were not merely adding secondary interpretation to canonical tradition. They saw their teaching as analogous to prophecy and inspired by God's Spirit (Sir 24:32-34; 39:1-8), and they engaged in speculation about the time of the fulfillment of prophecy (Tob 14:4). The saturation of texts like *1 Enoch,* Daniel, and, later, *2 Baruch* with language and concepts at home in the wisdom tradition and their common interest in Torah—however that might be construed—indicate that the authors of these revelations worked within a tradition that had much in common with that of scribes like Ben Sira, though their emphases and special interests differed significantly. Where the apocalypticists appear to have taken a special turn is in their claims to special revelation, said to be older than the prophets, but in fact, originating after the biblical prophets. Even here, the evidence is complex. *Testament of Moses* and *Jubilees* claim to be real Mosaic revelation, the former the true interpretation of Deuteronomy, and Daniel 9 puts forth a new interpretation of Jeremiah, claiming to have received it through an angelophany. Other historical reviews may reflect scriptural interpretation, but they present their calculations as pure revelation. Complicating the picture is the Qumranic Teacher of Righteousness, who claims a revealed interpretation of the Torah and true insight into the time when God would fulfill Habakkuk's prophecy (1QpHab 7:4-5).

If this material is placed next to the references and accounts of eschatological prophetic figures found in Flavius Josephus and the NT, the complexity of the issue emerges.[26] How did John the Baptist, Jesus, or the early apostles arrive at their eschato-

logical consciousness? Where did they fit on the eschatological and apocalyptic landscape? The answers are not easy, but two facts are clear. First, we are dealing with many points on a continuum; terms like *prophecy, wisdom,* and *apocalyptic* must be used with caution, and facile distinctions among them should be avoided. Second, whatever the complexities of its origins, the birth and early life of the Christian movement took place within the eschatological sector of Judaism, which we have been describing. Parallels in *1 Enoch,* Daniel, and the Qumran literature indicate this ambience, but they also warn us not to pinpoint the place of Christian origins too precisely on a complex social and religious map of which we have only fragments.

THE RISE OF RELIGIOUS GROUPS AND SECTS

Torah Observance. The history of the religious groups and sects in Second Temple Judaism is obscure, and the social map of such groups was more complicated than the schemes suggested by Philo, Josephus, and the NT.[27] Here we touch only on matters that enhance our understanding of the NT.

Faithfulness to the Torah was a major factor that precipitated the development of religious and social division in Palestinian Judaism. Phrases like "the congregation(s) of the pious" reflect a self-understanding that contrasts one with others who are not (so) pious. It is unclear if and when these expressions came to denote social groups with specific structures and codes for living. Texts as diverse as Psalm 149; 11QPs[a] 18:1-20; 22:1-15, 1 Macc 2:42; 7:13; 2 Macc 14:6; and the *Psalms of Solomon* doubtless refer to different social entities. The Hasidim in 1 and 2 Maccabees are mentioned for their opposition to grossly Hellenizing Jews. The other texts emphasizing the role of worship in the life of the pious may indicate small gatherings for this purpose. Whatever distinctions existed among these groups, the terminology in the texts indicates a tendency toward a common religious self-definition and may suggest some social organization.

The most developed form of such a tendency is attested in the writings of Qumran. The *Rule of the Community* employs terminology previously used

---

26. See R. A. Horsley and J. S. Hanson, *Bandits, Prophets, and Messiahs* (Minneapolis: Winston, 1985).

27. John J. Collins, "Introduction to Early Jewish Religion," *NIB,* 1:284-91.

of the nation to define a particular group as exclusively the people of God (Israel, 1QS 5:22; the Chosen, 8:6) and equates admission to the group with entrance into the covenant (5:7-11). The Hymn Scroll contrasts right and wrong teachers of the Torah (1QH 4:5-32) and depicts entrance to the community as resurrection from the dead (3:19-23; 11:10-14). The defining characteristic of this group is their possession of the revealed interpretation of the Torah, obedience to which alone can bring God's blessing (1QS 5:7-11; cf. CD 6:2-11). Several Qumran texts make polemical references to "slippery interpreters," whose facile exposition of the Torah does not meet the group's strict standards and leads many astray (4QpNah 2:2,8; cf. 4QpPss[a] 1:18-19). Two older pseudepigraphal works found at Qumran express a similar viewpoint. *Jubilees* claims to present the true Mosaic Torah, rediscovered through a process of "searching" the ancient texts; its strict halakoth parallel some of the Qumranic laws. The last chapters of *1 Enoch* criticize false teachers for perverting the Torah and leading many astray with their writings (98:14-99:2). These texts reflect a sectarianism that defines one's group as the true and exclusive people of God. The Qumran *Rule of the Community* attests strict social organization around a set of community rules (1QS 6:8-7:25).

Somewhere in this spectrum were the Pharisees of the first century. They did not consider themselves to be exclusively the people of God, and one must be cautious of the polemical descriptions of them in the Gospels. Nonetheless, they appear to have organized themselves into groups that were bound to special interpretations of the sabbath law, fasting beyond the letter of the biblical law, and purity obligations that excluded certain other Jews from their table fellowship. How they related to other contemporary groups of pious Jews is uncertain. However, comparison with *Jubilees* and some Qumran texts indicates that the Pharisaic interpretation of the Torah was less strict than Christian stereotypes allow, and many interpreters identify the Pharisees as the "facile interpreters" mentioned in the Qumran Scrolls. The Gospel polemics suggest that Torah observance was a source of considerable friction between the Pharisees and some communities of Christian Jews, if not between the Pharisees and Jesus himself. A comparison with texts about the pious, such as Psalm 148 and 11QPs[a] 18:1-20; 22:1-15 may also be useful. While we should not assume that Pharisaic assemblies did not engage in the praise and worship that are focal in these texts, the lack of reference to these matters highlights the Gospels' emphasis on the dispute over Torah observance.

Eschatology. A sense that the end was imminent was a constitutive factor for some religious groups, alongside their emphasis on (a particular) interpretation and observance of the Torah. In its present form, *1 Enoch* claims to be a revelation intended for the righteous and chosen of the end time. Its content includes detailed torah about the proper calendar (chaps. 72–82), and it refers to other disputes about correct torah (98:11–99:2). Along with these concerns and other concerns that relate to the failure of social justice are two historical reviews. Allegedly based on Enoch's dream vision (*1 Enoch* 85–90) and his reading of the heavenly tablets (93:1-10 + 91:11-18), they fix the time of the end as coinciding with the publication of Enoch's revelations (104:12–105:2). While the book of Daniel does not appear to have been written for a particular religious group, its author's concern for faithful Torah obedience is complemented by the claim that the wise knew the time of the end, which was very soon. At Qumran one of the claims about the Teacher of Righteousness was his knowledge of the time when Habakkuk's prophecies would be fulfilled. In short, religious teachers built their messages around exhortations to observe the Torah and claims that this was important because the closeness of the end time had been revealed to them. To differing decrees, these twin issues might constitute audiences into closed groups. This was the case at Qumran, where the members of the community were admonished not to share their secrets with outsiders (1QS 5:15-16; 10:24-25). *First Enoch* presents a different model and anticipates the time when Enoch's revelations and admonitions, given first to the chosen, will be proclaimed to "all humanity" (10:21; 100:6; 104:12–105:1).

Early Christianity as a Jewish Eschatological Sect. Early Christianity arose as an eschatological sect within Judaism. The sayings ascribed to John the Baptist express a view close to some Qumran texts, although this need not indicate that he was schooled at Qumran. The heart of the church's message, attested in early creeds, the letters of Paul, and the Gospels, lay in the claim that the eschaton had begun with the crucifixion, resurrection, and exaltation of Jesus of Nazareth, who was the fulfill-ment or embodiment of any one of a variety of eschatological figures awaited by the Jews. Many of the teachings associated with Jesus, in all major strata of the synoptic Gospels, have a similar cast, and parallels with Jewish texts abound. Like the authors of *1 Enoch,* the church's claims were pre-sented as a revealed message that had the power to constitute the eschatological community of the cho-sen, who would soon be the beneficiaries of God's blessing.

What is not clear is the extent to which the earliest Christians posited obedience to the Torah as necessary to pass muster at the final judgment. Clearly, there was a variety of opinion on this subject, which was in part related to the rapid movement of Christianity into a Gentile world. As we shall see below, Jewish opinion on Gentile observance of the Torah was not monolithic.

The Varied Jewish Responses to Early Christianity. The variety in early Judaism, which has been traced through this article, bears on the reasons why Christianity did and did not catch on among first-century Jews. However, before one draws quick conclusions about the "disbelief" of the majority of Jews who did not adopt the Christian confession, three facts must be considered. First, one would not expect the Christian eschatological proc-lamation to attract Jews who were not eschatologi-cally oriented. Second, eschatologies differed widely, and a transcendent messianism that drew on Son of Man theologies and that was premised on Jesus' resurrection would have difficulty among Davidic messianists and persons whose view of the future did not include a resurrection. Third, the liberal attitudes toward the Torah that characterized much of early Christianity had an inherent handicap among Jews, who had been brought up all their lives to believe that observance of the Torah (however one specifically construed it) was *sine qua non* for inclusion in the covenant.

JEWS AND GENTILES

The dispersion of several million Jews in Meso-potamia and the lands around the Mediterranean was a major component of first-century Judaism. Living as a minority in a non-Jewish environment and culture, diaspora Jews developed institutions, a life-style, and a literature that enabled them to interact with their neighbors, while maintaining their historic identity. The diaspora was, in turn, an important component in the Jewish context of early Christianity because by the end of the first century CE the membership of the church was primarily Gentile and its communities were located mainly outside of Palestine. What factors in what kind of Judaism made its Christian form especially attractive to Gentiles?

Palestinian and Hellenistic Judaism: A False Dichotomy. As we have noted, features typical of Palestinian Jewish eschatology and apoca-lypticism were essential to early Christian creeds, the preaching of Paul, and the Gospels. The resur-rection and exaltation of Jesus, the anticipated parousia, the resurrection and judgment of human-ity, and the hope of eternal life all have their roots in the eschatological thought that is at home in apocalypses like *1 Enoch* and Daniel. In this respect, the evidence contradicts a clean distinction between Palestinian and diaspora manifestations of Judaism and Christianity.

By the same token, we should not equate Helle-nistic forms of Judaism and Christianity with the religion of the dispersion. Palestinian Judaism was deeply affected by Hellenistic culture long before the beginning of the common era, and early Palestinian Christianity was marked by Hellenistic features as well as by characteristics of native Jewish tradition. What were the positive interactions between Juda-ism and Hellenism—the points at which Hellenistic Judaism adopted aspects of Hellenistic culture or made concessions to the people for whom such culture was native? What were the negative inter-actions, where Judaism drew boundaries between Jews and Gentiles? The complex data resist simpli-fication and again attest a wide variety in Judaism.

The Hellenization of Judaism and Its Christian Developments. Here we shall identify three features of Hellenization that made both non-Christian and Christian forms of Judaism amenable to Gentiles. The first was the use of the Greek language and the translation of the HB into Greek. The Jewish use of Greek began in order to meet needs within the *Jewish* community. Jews living in the dispersion spoke and read Greek because it was necessary for their daily lives and relationships with their Gentile neighbors. However they may have existed as ethnic communities, Jews of the disper-sion had to be employed and needed to interact with Gentile authorities and economic institutions. The use of the Greek language became increasingly natural for successive generations of diaspora Jews, and in this context translating the Bible into Greek was inevitable. Once these linguistic phenomena occurred, religious discourse could happen between Jews and Gentiles; subsequently, Christians had a tool to demonstrate that their proclamation was grounded in the religion of Israel.

A second salient feature of Hellenistic Judaism was its adoption of the idiom and forms of Greek moral discourse. Although diaspora Jews observed the Torah, expressed their piety through the annual payment of the half-shekel temple tax, and made pilgrimages to the religious festivals in Jerusalem, one also finds typically Hellenistic features in the ethical teaching of Palestinian and diaspora Jewish authors. The recounting of Israelite history increasingly focused on the good or bad examples of major figures whose qualities were explicated as abstract vices and virtues. Heroes like Abraham, Job, and Joseph were presented as spiritual athletes running with endurance the race of virtue.[28] Paul and the author to the Hebrews picked up on this idiom (1 Cor 9:24-27; Heb 11:1–12:2; cf. 1 Tim 4:7-8). As the Wisdom of Solomon and 4 Maccabees demonstrate, Jewish authors could also employ with skill the conceptions, technical terminology, and literary forms of Hellenistic philosophy. Thus NT writers like James and especially Christian apologists of the second century CE were not breaking new ground in their interaction with Greek culture.

A third relevant feature of Hellenistic Judaism was a use of Greek myth that would affect the manner in which first- and second-century Christians embodied their christological speculations. The story of the sons of God and daughters of men (*1 Enoch* 6–11) inverts the claims of Hellenistic kings that they were sons of the gods. Luke 1:35 employs imagery at home in Greek stories of gods and women in a positive way, even if Luke does not envision a quasi-physical act of intercourse. Employing other forms of Hellenistic religious and philosophical myth, Sirach 24; Bar 3:9–4:4; the Wisdom of Solomon; and Philo of Alexandria develop models for the mediation between heaven and earth that synthesize older Jewish wisdom speculation and Hellenistic notions of the *Logos*. According to Sirach and Baruch, heavenly wisdom has become embodied in

the Mosaic Torah. For the author of Wisdom, the heavenly figure is identified with the Spirit of the Lord and the *Logos* and functions as God's witness in creation (1:1-11), God's presence in the righteous (6:12–9:18), and the divine agent of deliverance in Israel's history (10–19). In Philo's extensive middle Platonic interpretations of Israelite tradition, the *Logos* is regularly seen as a mediator of God's presence and activity on earth. Christologies that present Jesus as the incarnation of a pre-existent heavenly figure move in this same orbit, even if we cannot trace precise points of influence (John 1; Phil 2:6-11; Hebrews).[29]

Obedience to the Torah and the Salvation of the Gentiles. Since obedience to the Torah was integral to the covenantal relationship and a hallmark of the distinction between Jews and Gentiles, it might seem problematic that both non-Christian and Christian manifestations of Judaism would be friendly to the notion that Gentiles could find divine favor. The Bible itself is divided on the issue. Sources as diverse as the Pentateuch, Second Isaiah, Ruth, and Jonah offer a positive answer to this question, while the Deuteronomic history, Ezekiel, and Ezra–Nehemiah take a dismal view of the Gentiles and oppose or restrict relationships with them.

Post-biblical Jewish texts also reflect a division of the house. *Jubilees* sees observance of the Torah as a hallmark of the covenantal people and forbids intermarriage. Third Maccabees, an Alexandrian text of the first century BCE, follows the book of Esther, emphasizing the distinctiveness of Jewish custom and depicting Gentile hostility. The book of Tobit places its hero in a hostile environment and commands marriage within the community in order to preserve Israelite identity. On the other side of the coin, the second-century BCE Alexandrian *Letter of Aristeas* encourages cordial relations between Jews and their Gentile neighbors. Surely the experience of these authors affected their viewpoints, though in unpredictable ways. Gentile hostility to the Jews would, of course, generate a negative assessment. However, peaceful relations between Jews and Gentiles might lead an author to warn against intermarriage.

Early Christian authors and Jews before them

---

28. *Jubilees* 17–18; *Testament of Job*; *Testament of Joseph*.

29. For a recent discussion of the relationship of John's prologue to the varieties of Jewish speculation about Wisdom and for a bibliography on the topic, see Norman R. Petersen, *The Gospel of John and the Sociology of Light* (Valley Forge: Trinity Press International, 1993) 110-32, 156-59.

were divided on the issue of Torah obedience and the salvation of the Gentiles. Jewish synagogues of the diaspora accepted as proselytes Gentiles who observed the Torah, including the rite of circumcision for males. Nonetheless, inscriptional evidence and texts like the *Letter of Aristeas* and Book 3 of the *Sibylline Oracles* promise God's favor for Gentiles who avoid the gross sins of idolatry, murder, and sexual immorality (cf. Acts 15:29).[30] However, such persons are not considered Israelites.

Once he had put his Pharisaism behind him, Paul adopted a viewpoint similar to that of *Aristeas* and the *Sibylline Oracles,* but with one major difference. As Paul argues in Galatians, Gentiles who believe in Jesus as Messiah are heirs of Abraham's promise, even though they do not observe Jewish ritual law. Their rejection of idolatry is taken for granted (see 1 Thess 1:9), and their final salvation is related to a righteous life that, while related to commandments of the Torah, is spelled out in the tradition of Jewish two-ways theology expressed in the language of Hellenistic Jewish moral exhortation (Gal 5:16-24). The Epistle of James takes a similar viewpoint, evidently with respect to the Jews. Writing to the tribes of the dispersion (1:1), James reverses and rephrases Paul's formulation, stating that one is justified by faith and works. But these are not deeds of the law, though they fulfill it (2:8); they are expounded again in the language of Hellenistic moral exhortation (chap. 1). In a related way, the author of Hebrews argues that Jesus' sacrifice has abrogated the need for the Temple, the priesthood, and the sacrificial system.

The aforementioned cases notwithstanding, early Christian attitudes about the responsibility of Christian Jews to observe the Torah varied widely. The details are obscure because the evidence is embodied in documents directed, largely, to Gentiles. An early stratum in Mark reflects debates with the Pharisees over the viability of the Torah (see 2:15–3:6; 7:1-23). Matthew insists on the ongoing validity of "the least of these commandments" (see 5:17-19), although circumcision is never mentioned. Second-century evidence refers to Ebionite Christians who observed the Torah.

Whatever the details of the debate over Torah among Christian Jews and between Christian and non-Christian Jews, the final split between Christians and Jews resulted from a pair of considerations. Increasingly, the church was composed of Gentile converts who did not observe the Torah and whose defining characteristic was their belief that Jesus was God's unique agent of salvation, by whatever Jewish or non-Jewish terms one named him. Thus Christianity, which arose as an eschatological Jewish sect, defined itself as the true Israel, and it excluded from the realm of salvation those who did not make a christological confession, although they followed well-established tradition by identifying Torah obedience as the defining characteristic of the covenant people. Although the church's christology and the Torah were both rooted in Israelite religion, their respective presence and absence created the separation between Christians and Jews that remains to this day.

BIBLIOGRAPHY

Detailed surveys of the history, institutions, and literature of first-century Judaism can be found in:

Nickelsburg, G. W. E. *Jewish Literature Between the Bible and the Mishnah.* Philadelphia: Fortress, 1981.

Safrai, S., M. Stern, et al. *The Jewish People in the First Century.* 2 vols. CRINT. Philadelphia: Fortress, 1974–76.

Schuerer, E. *The History of the Jewish People in the Age of Jesus Christ.* 3 vols. Revised and edited by G. Vermes, M. Black, et al. Edinburgh: T. & T. Clark, 1983–87.

Stone, M. E., ed. *Jewish Writings of the Second Temple Period.* CRINT. Philadelphia: Fortress, 1984.

For a more popular treatment:

Murphy, F. J. *The Religious World of Jesus.* Nashville: Abingdon, 1991.

For a collection of texts representing the spectrum of Jewish belief on such matters as temple and cult, piety, the future life, and agents of divine deliverance:

Nickelsburg, G. W. E., and M. E. Stone. *Faith and Piety in Early Judaism: Texts and Documents.* Philadelphia: Fortress, 1983.

---

30. See J. J. Collins, "A Symbol of Otherness: Circumcision and Salvation in the First Century," in J. Neusner and E. S. Frerichs, *"To See Ourselves as Others See Us": Christians, Jews, and "Others" in Late Antiquity* (Chico: Scholars Press, 1985) 163-86.

THE ECCLESIASTICAL CONTEXT OF THE NEW TESTAMENT

VINCENT L. WIMBUSH

The twenty-seven documents collectively known as the New Testament are the products of ancient Christian communities. It was not the case that the documents created the ancient communities.[1] Rather, these documents and other such writings were written out of and addressed to these communities; hence they reflect some of the important dynamics of the communities' internal developments and shifts as well as their relations with outsiders. Thus a reading of these documents must respect communal or ecclesiastical contexts and the dynamics and challenges of these contexts. Lack of respect for such contexts is likely to lead to a premature narrowing of perspective on the documents and a tendency to focus on abstract ideas, religious claims, and theological arguments. Given the complexity and diversity of the world of early Christianity, such an emphasis simply can no longer be justified.

Every ecclesiastical context is a historical context. Each is subject to the limitations and challenges of history, of particular social locations, and of power dynamics. Thus respect for the ecclesiastical contexts of the documents that constitute the NT requires that the reader pay consistent attention to socioeconomic and sociopolitical dynamics and

challenges, which reflect different communities' attempts to define their understandings of themselves and of their ethoses and orientations in and often over against the reality that was understood to constitute the "world."

WORLDS OF DIFFERENCE: DIVERSIFICATION OF EARLY CHRISTIANITY

Respect for the ecclesiastical contexts that produced early Christian documents should inspire the reader to raise questions about *how* the different fledgling communities struggled to define themselves and the degrees to which such struggles are chronicled (or covered up) in the extant literature, canonical and noncanonical. We now know enough about ourselves and the communities to which we belong and about the history of religious communities, ancient and modern, to lead us to think that the development of ancient Christian communities was complex, explosive, and messy. Some voices have been extinguished; others have assumed exaggerated importance. Some ideas and secondary social formations are forever lost to history and to our critical consideration.

The canonical literature should be engaged to sort out and account for the different *ancient Christiani-*

1. The reverse can be said to have been the case only among successive generations—namely, at a point in the development of Christianity in which a literary tradition had become well established.

ties—the different and often conflicting ancient Christian self-understandings and orientations to the world. Although it is now clear that no simple development of earliest Christianity was the historical reality, and that no effort to reconstruct such a development is justified, it may be possible to chart the trajectories—the historical explosions—of different ancient Christianities. These different Christianities will of necessity be historical communities, interacting with other communities and being challenged by them. Together the different social formations constitute the different ecclesiastical contexts, or "worlds," of earliest Christianity.

In determining some of the immediate contexts of earliest Christianity, a number of factors are important for consideration. No one factor alone is decisive, but a variety of elements is significant in the context of the Greco-Roman world. Physical location—urban or rural—is important. Place affects what type of action, what type of discourse, is possible and to what extent. Political structures, military forces, the various free associations, and social networks from the outside provide models and limitations for the possibilities for organization, governance, and orientation among small communities. The form of organization or governance should be studied. The language world is important as well—perhaps, the most important factor. Language is certainly a product of community and is a necessary component in community construction and maintenance.

The different contexts for the making of the NT and early Christianity, then, are those different small groups within and over against certain physical, social, and political worlds in Greco-Roman antiquity that struggled to find meaning as followers of Jesus. Their struggles can be discerned in particular rhetorics and discourses, reflected primarily in the NT and other early Christian literature.

Because of the striking gaps in the extant literary sources and because of the otherwise obvious host of interpretive difficulties inherent in them, only summary discussions of necessarily synthetic or complex contexts for the NT and earliest Christianity follow. Notwithstanding the demarcations that follow, each context is assumed to have been dynamic, to have undergone change and development; no one context is thought to have been either static or without influence or challenge from other contexts. In short, no linear development of the history

of Christianity is to be told. Very early multiple communities in different settings were the reality for the phenomenon that became known as Christianity. Although scholars envision this complexity in various ways, the recognition of vitality and variety in early Christianity is universal.

Some of the situations that can be isolated as ecclesiastical contexts for the NT and early Christianity include the beginnings of the Jesus movement in Jerusalem and Palestinian villages; Hellenistic Jewish missionary movements in Syrian cities; Paul's Gentile mission in Asia Minor, Greece, and Rome; the development and consolidation of Jesus movements in Palestine and Syria; stabilization and institutionalization of movements across the Mediterranean; and submerged voices and orientation across the Mediterranean.

IN THE LAST DAYS: BEGINNINGS OF THE JESUS MOVEMENT IN JERUSALEM AND PALESTINE/SYRIA

In the wake of the death of Jesus, his followers—mainly Galileans—were left in Jerusalem and its environs to decide what should be the legacy of their leader. Accepting their Jewish ethnic and religious roots and orientations—observing temple piety, practicing circumcision, etc.—they nonetheless began early on to define themselves as a Jewish reform movement in the spirit of their leader. This loosely organized movement, led by Peter, James, and John (Gal 2:9), soon attempted to challenge other Jews and to distinguish itself from other Jewish groups by making claims about Jesus as Messiah and about the presence of the Spirit. The presence of the Spirit, poured out among members of the movement, was understood as a sign of the end time, of vindication for Jesus, and of the movement's special role in God's actions in the end times.

The movement established its identity among Jews in Jerusalem and its vicinity in two important ways: (1) by adopting a certain discourse about its special relationship with Jesus the Messiah that reflected its claim to have special insight into God's plan for Israel and the world in the last days, and (2) by establishing such rituals as baptism and the common meal that became the Lord's Supper, through which communal relationship with Jesus as

Lord and the anticipation of his return were sustained.

The first community did not produce any identifiable literature. Given the shock that the community experienced in the death of Jesus—manifested in, among other things, its heightened consciousness of living in the end times—it had little interest in producing literature. Of utmost importance was a constant state of readiness for Jesus' return, the end of history, and vindication of the faithful.

The fact that this first community did not itself produce literature does not mean it did not *inspire* literature. Although the documents called "Gospels" in the NT were not written by members of this first community, it is clear that some traditions from these persons were handed down to the Gospel writers. For example, the book of Acts—the second part of the work ascribed to Luke—represents an attempt to tell the story of this first community. Although there can be no doubt that the author of Acts intends more than a reporting of the facts, and although it is clear that this agenda is very much different from the orientation of the first community in Jerusalem, it is nevertheless striking that heightened consciousness of the end times is seen as a defining characteristic of this first community. Such consciousness was a belief with which successive generations of followers of Jesus had to wrestle; the same is true for all subsequent interpretations of the NT and early Christianity.

"NEITHER JEW NOR GREEK . . .": HELLENISTIC JEWISH CHRISTIAN MISSIONARY MOVEMENTS IN JERUSALEM AND SYRIAN CITIES

Very early in its history in Jerusalem and its environs, the movement attracted Jews from all over the Mediterranean world. These Jews were Hellenistic (Greek-speaking) and were either more subjected to the influence of or were more open to Greek culture than were their Palestinian counterparts. They were Jews who, on account of wider social and cultural influences, could not avoid seeing the world, including the challenges of Jewish religious life, differently. Yet they were not necessarily less Jewish than Palestinian Jews. On the contrary, some seemed to have been more interested in missions—in winning converts to Judaism—because of their openness to cultural exchange.

One of the attractions of the Jesus movement to such Jews was its rhetoric, which was heard and understood as prophetic and reformist. (How otherwise would the preaching about a messiah of peasant stock from Galilee have been heard?) There is no little irony that such Jews, with their cultural accommodation and reformist orientation, found themselves at odds with the small band of Galilean followers of Jesus (and with the Jewish establishment!) over issues having to do with the interpretation of and adherence to tradition—specifically the continuing validity of the temple cultus and the Law of Moses, as well as with matters of internal governance.

Acts 6–8 records the controversies that led to the beginnings of a separate movement of Jesus' followers in the more culturally mixed and challenging urban areas to the north in Syria. Stephen, who spoke for some of those Greek-speaking Jews who joined the Jesus movement, makes the case for the reform of the dominant Jewish religious traditions of the times, especially the temple cult in Jerusalem. The older community of Galilean followers of Jesus found the searing critique and reformist impulses of the Greek-speaking Jews, represented by Stephen, too radical insofar as the validity of the temple cult and the Laws of Moses were questioned. This difference very likely accounts for the internal conflict relayed in Acts 6. It is probable that the story of the distribution of the common goods and table service (διακονία *diakonia*), although much edited by Luke for specific purposes, stems from older traditions and reflects the intensity of the conflict in that situation.

At any rate, it is certain that the conflict led to the persecution of Greek-speaking Jews who had joined the movement. Thought of as agitators and blasphemers, some were expelled, and others fled Jerusalem. Dispersed to areas north and south—in Syria and Cilicia to the north, other cities and villages in Palestine and Egypt to the south[2]—these Greek-speaking Jewish followers of Jesus then began to form communities devoted to aggressive missionary efforts, advancing their conviction that following Jesus no longer necessarily entailed acknowledging the validity of the temple cult in Jerusalem and adhering to the Laws of Moses.

2. Clear evidence for the establishment and earliest development of such communities is lacking. See Helmut Koester, *Introduction to the New Testament: History and Literature of Early Christianity,* vol. 2 (New York: Walter de Gruyter, 1982) 93-94, 219-40.

These same communities established traditions that must to this day be engaged if Christianity, whether rejected or embraced, is to be understood. The idea and proclamation of Jesus (Χριστός *Christos,* or Ἰησοῦς Χριστός *Iēsous Christos* in predominantly Greek-speaking areas) as the martyr raised from the dead was and is fundamental. And the two major rituals became in the context of the gathered communities powerful and arresting confirmations of membership in the new community (baptism) and of the continuing presence of Jesus within the community (the Lord's Supper; see 1 Corinthians 11; 15).

These, then, were the communities that left the legacy of the first struggles to define devotion to Jesus (Christianity) apart from being a devout Jew—i.e., apart from strict adherence to Jewish laws, especially circumcision and dietary proscriptions. In a very important sense almost all of ancient Christian literature was inspired by the struggles and debates of these communities. Nothing less than establishing boundary markers, defining what the movement was or should be about, apart from obvious and acknowledged Jewish origins, was at stake. But the literary reflection upon these struggles and debates would await the full explosion of the Gentile mission, which was surely seen as the next necessary, God-ordained development in the unfolding end-of-the-world drama. All of the literary genres reflect the influence of these communities. The letters of Paul can be read as pastoral reflections upon community debates and challenges, or as sources (even though they are highly problematic because they are highly prejudiced) for the debates inspired by the earlier communities. Elements of the ideas, proclamations, traditions, and rituals established and handed down by these earlier communities are evidenced throughout Paul's letters. The Gospels can be read as edited and reformulated proclamations of various traditions, including those from Hellenistic Jewish Christian communities. These Gospels cannot be understood without presupposing the basic perspectives and traditions of Hellenistic Jewish Christian movements, whose perspectives and traditions guided engagements of other traditions as well.

IN THE WORLD AS THOUGH NOT: THE GENTILE MISSION AND PAULINE CHRISTIANITY

With its emphasis on membership within the Jewish movement apart from Jewish law, the Helle-

nistic Jewish Christian mission led early (by the first half of the first century) and logically to aggressive, far-reaching missionary campaigns to non-Jews (Gentiles), from the eastern Mediterranean all the way to Rome, seat of the empire. Paul was not only a product of the Hellenistic Jewish Christian mission, but he became as well the most successful and most controversial of all Hellenistic Jewish Christian missionaries to the Gentiles. Paul owed a clear debt to Hellenistic Jewish Christian missions in terms of traditions inherited and the missionary zeal to reach the Gentiles. It is important that Paul is seen first as a vital member of a movement into which he was recruited. Then it is important to understand that his astounding success within this movement gave birth to another movement of which he is the founding figure.

This new movement, often called Pauline Christianity, is distinguishable by its consistent articulation of the principle of freedom from the Law for all followers of Jesus. But after a period of notable success, in response to opposition from some Jewish Christians, this preaching became more emotional and principled, and more audience oriented, intending to capture the imagination and to alleviate the anxieties (especially regarding circumcision) of non-Jews.

Paul's missionary activity apparently began immediately after his conversion (mid 30s), under the influence of Hellenistic Jewish Christians headquartered in Antioch. He worked first—alone or in concert with others—in the regions of Arabia and Cilicia/Syria. After the Jerusalem Council (c. 48), at which agreement with the predominantly Aramaic-speaking Jewish Christians from Jerusalem and Palestine was reached regarding the legitimacy of the Gentile mission and of Christianity apart from the Law, Paul as apostle to the Gentiles cultivated the regions of Asia Minor, Greece, and Rome independently of the movement headquartered in Antioch. He died in Rome as a martyr (c. 60).

The Pauline mission was in fact an elaborate operation with many co-workers running well-organized campaigns in the cities of the eastern Mediterranean. Paul focused on cities because he was himself a product of the city and because he thought that cities, centers of Greek and Roman culture, could function as bases from which preaching about Jesus could be disseminated throughout neighboring villages, the countryside, and entire regions. This strategy worked, as Paul himself, with only a bit of hyperbole, states (Rom 15:19). But in any discussion of the different contexts for the NT and early Christianity, it is important to recognize that Paul's strategy created a radically different movement from that with which the first Palestinian followers of Jesus were associated. Place was important. The Christianity of Paul's mission was urban. This meant that the social constitution, the social and political orientations—the worldview—of the communities established by Paul were urban. Persons who joined the movement were not required to be male, free, or of high social status. Neither were they required to undergo the Jewish rite of circumcision nor to observe Jewish dietary laws. In short, the movement was in principle open to all the different groups that constituted the city. As regards social and political orientations, it was apparently recognized very early in the mission that the city, with its higher population density and its greater mix of social and economic statuses and racial and ethnic groups, would prove to be a difficult and hostile environment for a radically separatist ethic.

Thus Pauline Christianity represented critique and renewal of the city, but also some accommodation to it. The city was clearly not understood to be identical to the reign of God. The rhetoric of the Pauline Christians testifies strongly to the consensus about the shortcomings of the cities. But the city was also the culture that, with its mixed social statuses, the Pauline churches were called to imitate. Most important, although there was no practical reformation agenda among the Pauline churches, there was no exhortation to flee the city; in it were the potential converts whose transformation would result eventually in the salvation of the world. Thus the world—the city—had to be engaged, even though with the qualification, "as if not" (see 1 Cor 7:29-31).

The issue of the manner and the degree to which the world should be engaged exercised the Pauline churches during Paul's lifetime and beyond. Likewise the responses to such an issue inspired the literary form—the letter—that is now the hallmark of Paul's missionary career. The occasion for the writing of a letter was usually a community's failure to understand and apply practically Paul's teachings or older traditions. Given the different worldly statuses, backgrounds, capacities, and sensibilities represented in a Pauline church, what criteria should be used to settle honest differences?

The letter was an appropriate and powerful instrument through which communication remained open, Paul's pastoral offices could be exercised, and his authority safeguarded. With the potential for long-distance travel and ease of communication that the empire had made possible, the letter was a practical way to achieve those purposes. Further, whether the authors of these letters—Paul, other individuals, or groups in particular churches—sincerely wanted it or not, the letter's ad hoc nature, the practical matters that generally occasioned it, and the discursive practices that it required seemed always to invite further discussion.

SEEK THOSE THINGS THAT ARE ABOVE: PAULINE CHRISTIANITY AFTER PAUL IN ASIA MINOR, GREECE, AND ROME

After Paul's death, documents addressing controversies in the Pauline churches continued to appear. These documents—some genuine letters, most others treatises, sermons, church orders, etc.—sought to continue Paul's legacy into the second century as missionary, as teacher, and as pastor, as it was understood primarily by his more conservative parties and students in the communities in which he was a revered figure. Continuing the Pauline legacy was understood to include the composition of literature that imitated the Pauline letter form, including some of its basic elements (especially openings and closings), some of its rhetorical formulations, and even the broaching of some of the issues and problems common in the days of Paul's missionary works.

But what raises questions about the relationship of these "letters" to the historical Paul, and to the beginnings of Pauline Christianity, is the manner in which these letters address and—from the perspective of the writers—attempt to resolve common issues and problems. It is not simply that the issues that continue to spark controversy are now resolved in a way that is decidedly different from the way Paul—in the undisputed letters—had attempted to resolve them. Some positions remain fairly consistent among the letters, but seem less complicated in those about which Pauline authorship is in question.

The "Paul" of these letters is generally more prolix, using some words and phrases that appear in the other letters, but also many other words and phrases that appear in no other documents in the NT. This "Paul" is seemingly move conversant with popular philosophy and rhetoric and employs them without ironic apology. Since this "Paul" also appears to be more conservative and more decisive on issues that in the undisputed letters are dealt with in a compromising manner, he often appears to be more uncompromising, more pedantic, and less charismatic.

Whatever the issue or challenge, the effort to change Paul's image is most revealing in terms of a determination regarding context. In the disputed documents, Paul's image has changed from a rather charismatic figure who in his arguments and judgments had to balance his own awareness of being spiritually gifted with the gifts or capacities of the majority of persons in his churches. He has changed from being a prophetic figure with some eschatologically inspired ambivalence about the world to one who without qualification encourages embracing the world and provides an actual status-specific code of behavior for members of his churches.

These changes represent efforts to simplify what was undoubtedly a very complex situation among the Pauline churches in the two or three generations after Paul. From Colossians and Ephesians in the next generation after Paul, to the Pastoral Epistles in the next two to three generations, the agenda on the part of writers (and associates) was conservative: to establish and consolidate in respectable circles in Asia Minor and beyond the churches under Paul's influence. This entailed projecting Paul as a straightforward teacher and pastor who focused on the welfare of his churches in the world. It meant that Paul had to speak authoritatively and unequivocally on important issues, so as not to give any ground whatsoever to opponents.

The chief mark of the change in situation from Paul to the generations after him is that in some documents there is a consistent narrowing of his image as teacher and church leader and of the range of possible appropriate behaviors and "true" teachings in the Pauline circles. Opponents are characterized in such a way as to suggest that diversity of views and behaviors is itself the most serious problem in the churches. Sharp disagreements and arguments are registered in the undisputed letters of Paul, but with few exceptions Paul attempts to be persuasive; he does not generally vilify those who disagree with him. However, many of the disputed letters leave no room for differences of opinion; opponents are considered immoral or profligate, even though most are accused of practicing extreme renunciations. These changes suggest that the disputed letters were produced in situations different from Paul's own. Such a turn was not imaginable, not even wise, in Paul's time and situation. Given the social constitution of Paul's churches and the dynamic circumstances in which they were founded, some fluidity and equivocation in governance in response to the world and discourse were required. But each generation that followed Paul seemed to require more and more clarity in terms of definition, governance, and appropriate behavior. It became increasingly important to be able to determine who was in and who was out of membership in the Pauline community.

As the Pauline communities found themselves attracting converts of higher and higher social status, they would naturally have begun to be noticed as a social phenomenon. Public attention likely brought with it increased pressures for the communities to be socially respectable by conforming to certain socially acceptable mores and orientations. Notice also brought with it some scorn and criticism. Who were these motley people ranting about an obscure Galilean prophet? What were their origins? Were they Jews? If so, why were they rejected and scorned by so many local Jews? What authority did they have to interpret Jewish traditions? What traditions did they represent? What did they contribute to the social order or the common good? What of their antisocial rhetoric? Their antisocial behaviors? Their renunciations and denunciations?

The emphasis placed on the legitimate handing on of (Pauline) tradition and on correct teaching and behavior expresses the heightened sensitivities to questions such as those raised above among some within the Pauline communities after Paul. Some of the members of high social status thought that it was no longer enough simply to be against the world; it was wise to consider, as with the traditions among some philosophical schools and moralists, how to respond appropriately to the world in the light of certain firmly held ideas.

Thus came the appearance of a new discourse for Christians: the discourse of rapprochement, or accommodation. One of the controversial features of the Pauline discourse of this period was the controversial church order materials (*Haustafeln*) and church order documents (e.g., Pastoral Epistles) and their exhortations and polemic.[3] Being "in Christ" came to be understood as being in the world in a certain way, including communicating within a certain rhetorical frame of reference that reflected—in odd combination—both the ethos of the middle class of the cities of the Greco-Roman world and the oppositional stance that membership in a new social formation, which proclaimed the near end of the world, suggested.

Membership in a community with such strange features required, according to those in the "middle"—respectable status outside the new community—a very careful balancing act indeed. Status-specific behavioral prescriptions or codes were offered. All ranks or roles (e.g., slave, child, female, free male) that were recognized in the world should, according to the perspectives of church writers of this period, be recognized within the Pauline communities. Persons would relate to one another as being "in Christ," the meaning of which had to do with attitudes, not structures or institutions. Slaves must remain slaves in the new community, but could expect the master who was a member of the new community to be more humane toward them. Slave masters who became members of one of these communities could, according to this ethos, continue to own slaves, albeit being gentler masters, and could actually expect better and more consistent service from converted slaves.

These prescriptions were intended to reflect the compatibility of membership in the Pauline communities with respectable citizenship and behavior in Greco-Roman cities. It was an effort to demonstrate the social benignity, if not utility, of the Pauline churches. This stance reflected a legitimate interpretation of one aspect of the teachings of Paul.[4]

3. First Timothy in particular is often thought of as a church order document.

4. For useful discussions about the interpretations of Paul among his followers, see Elaine H. Pagels, *The Gnostic Paul* (Philadelphia: Fortress, 1979); Dennis R. MacDonald, *The Legend and the Apostle: The Battle for Paul in Story and Canon* (Philadelphia: Westminster, 1983); and Margaret Y. MacDonald, *The Pauline Churches: A Socio-historical Study of Institutionalization in the Pauline and Deutero-Pauline Writings* (New York: Cambridge University Press, 1988).

THE REIGN OF GOD IS AT HAND: DEVELOPMENT AND CONSOLIDATION OF JESUS TRADITIONS IN PALESTINE AND SYRIA

It bears repeating that what gave birth to the NT was a number of different, complex movements; different dynamics and developments were unfolding in different contexts at the same time. So it should not be forgotten that as the Hellenistic Jewish Christian mission was giving birth to the Gentile mission and as Pauline Christianity was developing in Asia Minor, Greece, and Rome, developments equally as dramatic were unfolding among followers of Jesus in Palestine and Syria. Beyond the first community left in Jerusalem after the death of Jesus, other communities were established very early in other cities and villages in Palestine and Syria (and Egypt to the south) in a development apart from that associated with the Hellenistic Jewish Christian mission headquartered in Antioch. These communities represent a second wave in the development of Christianity. Their imagination obviously seized by the teachings (sayings) of Jesus, they were characterized by their consistent and respectful preservation of these teachings and their imaginative creation and development of like sayings.

The particular memories of Jesus preserved by each of these communities reflect their self-understandings, interests, and orientations. Jesus as prophet and as teacher of wisdom may well reflect the self-definition of these groups as communities of prophets and wisdom teachers.

Of course, variations and nuances did exist among the various local communities that developed sayings of Jesus. Given the nature of the extant sources, it is impossible to determine how many communities are relevant to this discussion, where these communities were located, or how they related to each other. It is not apparent that there was anything like an overarching or umbrella organization of such communities. For obvious reasons, as long as there was a community in place there, Jerusalem probably remained an unofficial and sentimental center. We know only that Jesus' teachings remained alive in loosely organized, loosely defined communities that retained vivid memories of him, especially memories of his prophetic and wise sayings.

The sources are not unproblematic. Only strands of traditions from certain of the earliest (up to 70 CE) communities in Palestine and Syria are preserved, and what complicates the matter further is that we owe the literary preservation of such strands not to these communities but to later writers and communities—Gospel writers and their corresponding communities—that had relationships with these earlier traditions, the nature of which is not always clear. Such communities are not lost to history, and it is possible to discern some variations among these communities. But the conditions under which these variations are made evident should not be forgotten, so that it is never assumed that the full variety of Jesus traditions in Palestine and Syria is recoverable. Through form-critical studies, there is now near consensus in scholarship that most of the sayings attributed to Jesus in the Gospels are in fact older material—some oral, some written—from the early Christian communities of Palestine and Syria. These older materials are embedded within documents that do not always share the presuppositions and agenda of the sayings as an independent complex of material. Whether because of or in spite of this difference in presuppositions and agenda, the older material that is included in the Gospels is something of a patchwork, reflecting diversity.

One discernible strand of tradition about Jesus is found in the prophetic sayings, called "Q" (standing for *Quelle,* "source," in German) in scholarly literature. Jesus is here characterized as the Son of Man, the end-time figure expected to return shortly to redeem the faithful (see Daniel 7). Importance is attached to a collective psychic state, a readiness on the part of the faithful for such a return, and the radical reversals of the world—the social and political orders, including religious authorities and traditions—that it symbolized and was understood to effect. Readiness was understood to require separation from the world and radical renunciations—of family and material possessions and of traditional worldly networks and involvements (again, including Jewish religious traditions). The Jewish law has little or no role in these communities.

Devotees, thinking of themselves as communities of prophets of a type after Jesus, felt it incumbent to proclaim among themselves and to others the end of the present order and the dawn of something new. They did this in the form of sayings purporting to have their origins with Jesus. There was no emphasis on Jesus' passion or his resurrection, the very hallmarks of the proclamation associated with Paul and the Gentile mission. Jesus was, according to these communities of prophets, the great proclaimer of wiser and prophetic words.

The words or sayings of Jesus were remembered, and they helped to create communities. As a collection and tradition, these sayings are complex. They seem to have developed from general wisdom sayings and prophecies to eschatological sayings, thus reflecting development within and between the different communities, development toward heightened conviction about the imminence of the end of history. This conviction in turn reflects a greater sense of anxiety about, and alienation from, the surrounding world. Perhaps it was the case that these far-flung communities found little acceptance in the surrounding world, including the Jewish camps of the area. It remains unclear exactly what was the nature of the relationship these Jesus communities enjoyed with other Jewish eschatological groups, such as the Essenes.

The inspirations for the collection and actual writing down of such sayings may have been the felt needs to provide a greater rhetorical arsenal in a polemic against detractors, to provide some comfort and assurance of the right course taken for converts, and to seek to unite small, far-flung, but like-minded, communities. What united these communities was the memory of Jesus, which they kept alive and brought to speech in a certain key.

Another discernible strand of tradition among the early followers of Jesus in Palestine and Syria can be seen in a different type of saying: the parable. As was the case with the Q material, the parables, as collected and preserved in Mark 4, reflect no interest in Jesus' passion and resurrection. But they differ from the Q material in that they make no reference at all to the Son of Man in the articulation of eschatological expectation. Here Jesus is simply the proclaimer of the imminent reign of God. Although still eschatological, its expectation represents a different strand of tradition. It does not appear that Jesus as Son of Man was a casual reference among the Q communities; and it does not appear that the collected parables in Mark 4—with the conspicuous absence of such a reference—can be easily collapsed into traditions associated with Q. Again, there clearly was a relationship between the two traditions. But it remains unclear just what was the nature of that relationship.

The parables are at once simple and unfathomable. They focus on the mystery that is the reign of God. They tell some truths about the reign of God by relating it to some simple aspect of, or simple experience within, agrarian or village life. But the very simplicity of the situation or the experience within the story is found to be difficult, elusive, and mysterious. Whereas the wisdom and prophetic sayings of Q focus on Jesus as the agent of redemption, the parables focus on the nature of the reign of God. Jesus is in the background in the parables; it is never clear exactly how he relates to God's reign, beyond pointing to it, proclaiming its imminence, and declaring the radical demands it places upon all. The reign of God, Jesus' stories proclaim, will appear suddenly and—herein is the mystery—without the help of human beings. Its coming will be more subtle, more akin to certain things that happen in and around the simple household in a Palestinian village, yet more powerful and with cosmic effect, ushering in the end of history. Devotees need not concern themselves with membership in other groups in which great store was placed on certain forms of piety, political intrigue, or violent overthrow of oppressors. Total trust was to be placed in God to bring history and the world as it is known to an end—and to usher in a radically new order.

The absence of the Son of Man reference notwithstanding, the community that defined itself by reference to these parables was similar to the Q communities in that it was an eschatological community. It also defined itself on the margins of the larger society, alienated, highly critical of the status quo. The difference was in the nuancing of the critique. A relationship between the two traditions or movements cannot be established.

Yet another strand in the development of Jesus traditions in Palestine and Syria can be seen in the sayings collected in Mark 13. Often referred to as the "Synoptic Apocalypse," the chapter contains sayings—again dependent upon Daniel 7—that refer to Jesus as the Son of Man. In this respect, this strand of the Palestinian and Syrian Jesus traditions does not differ from that of the Q communities. What is different is the greater emphasis it places on the crisis that is to be experienced by the faithful at the approach of the end, describing persecutions that will be or actually were being experienced.

Such descriptions suggest a community close to or already in a crisis situation. In this community the call to readiness seems not to require mere renunciations or correct ethical and moral comportment in the light of intense, though vague, expectation that the end may come at any time, but a willingness to suffer persecution because of the recognition that the end has in fact already begun. The preserved texts suggest that this community, clearly related to the others discussed above, thought itself to be much closer to a major confrontation, which would be the end of history. False prophets abounded, seeking to destroy the faithful. Willingness to meet the crisis was the challenge of the sayings preserved in Mark 13.

Other strands of Jesus tradition existed in Palestinian and Syrian contexts (and beyond, in Egypt) in the period before the writing of the Gospels (c. 70 CE). For a number of reasons, these other strands were not registered in the NT. Some of them attached more importance to Jesus as a wisdom figure than as an eschatological-prophetic figure. And within such strands there were many nuances and developments. Recognition that voices and orientations were left out—even lost—is always in order.

The next and more decisive stage in the development of Jesus traditions began around 70 CE. It was a decisive stage because in it are preserved the sources for the recovery of earlier stages. It involved the consolidation and domestication in written form of certain disparate strands of traditions. The Gospel writers did not necessarily agree with the presuppositions and orientations of the older strands of the traditions, but these traditions were nonetheless deemed important; they were, after all, part of the oldest strands of the traditions about Jesus.

Each of the four documents in the NT that are classified (according to tradition) as Gospels was written within and as a response to a particular context. Scholarly consensus holds Mark to have been the first of the four to have been written. It also holds that Mark directly influenced—in terms of sources and narrative superstructure—the writers of at least two other Gospels (Matthew and Luke), and possibly all three. In the attempt to establish and account for the general context and impetus for the writing of a "gospel" as a type of literature, it is sufficient, then, to focus on Mark.

Mark's interest in some of the disparate strands of the Jesus traditions is evident in the manner in which different types of sayings (wisdom, apocalyptic) and narrative materials (exorcisms, miracle stories, the passion story)—representing different early Christian contexts and self-understandings—were collected and edited. The pre-Markan origins of some of the material is evident, given Mark's clumsy editorial framework, since the patchwork signals are often easy to detect (see Mark 4). By composing (for the first time) an extended narrative framework, the writer of Mark articulated and imposed a new message on the older materials. Mark's narrative framework, in which the passion narrative is the most extensive and carefully nuanced part, suggests the primary importance of the imagining and remembrance of Jesus as the martyr, the innocent one who nonetheless must be humiliated, suffer, and die.

An emphasis on the suffering and death of Jesus reflects the influence of the Hellenistic Jewish Christian mission, perhaps even the Pauline/Gentile mission, upon Mark. It is important to note again how little interest was placed on Jesus' death (and resurrection) in the Palestinian and Syrian Jesus traditions. It is also important to note that such an emphasis was primary within the Hellenistic Jewish Christian and Pauline/Gentile missions, as Jesus' sayings seemed to recede into the background. In focusing on the suffering and death of Jesus in the extended narrative, and in nevertheless including some of the older traditions that did not share such an interest, Mark boldly attempts to bring disparate traditions into conversation.

So what does the use of such traditions suggest about the context in which Mark was composed? It is fairly clear that the traditions—including the views of Jesus that they represent—that Mark brings into the larger narrative are criticized. According to Mark, none of them (wisdom sayings, prophetic sayings, miracle stories, etc.) alone was thought to represent the appropriate image or memory of Jesus; nor was any of them alone thought to represent the appropriate form of discipleship or response to the world, especially in a time of crisis. *Crisis* appears to be the appropriate word to use for the Markan mentality. Jesus is from beginning to end persecuted. Thus the disciples are warned about persecutions to come. There appears to be some correspondence between the Markan emphasis on Jesus as the Suffering Servant and the perception that the followers of Jesus also suffer, are persecuted, and may yet be martyred. Markan discipleship, therefore, called for an ethic of endurance, a closing of ranks of the faithful against the cruel world in expectation of the end.

Mark 13 suggests that the Gospel was written at a time in which the military conflicts with the Romans were underway or had been recently experienced. Followers of Jesus associated with Mark were apparently traumatized by these events. They understood such events as the most dramatic sign that the end of history had begun. The Gospel can be understood as having been written in response to this crisis, to help hearers and readers through the trauma associated with it. This was done by remembering, reimaging, and reproclaiming Jesus, in the form of a narrative, as the one who had gone before the associates of "Mark" as victim. The reproclamation of such a Jesus functioned to comfort those who thought themselves victims under siege.

Given such an agenda on the part of "Mark," hypothesizing a context either in Jerusalem or very near Jerusalem would seem reasonable. Mark's inclusion of the earlier strands in the Jesus traditions would seem to lend further support to this hypothesis. On the one hand, the development of various strands in Palestine and Syria, and the importance attached to a type of rapprochement with several strands in the Jesus tradition, suggest that "Mark" was situated in Palestine or Syria. On the other hand, the fact that rapprochement with earlier Jesus traditions sought to subsume the reimaging and reproclamation under the ethos and teachings influenced by the Hellenistic Jewish Christian and Gentile mission suggests a context that was more urban. In terms of accounting for influence and establishing a context for the writing of Mark, proximity to the communities in which Jesus traditions developed and to the Hellenistic Jewish Christian mission needs to be considered. Antioch fits the bill nicely, notwithstanding the traditional association of Mark with Rome.

This leads to the further suggestion that the writing of the other, later documents that have come to be known as Gospels assumes the continuing influence of developing Jesus traditions in communities in Palestine and Syria. The influence of these traditions was felt either (1) in terms of providing authoritative, but dynamic, resources for addressing community identity, challenges, or crises or (2) in terms of serving as a history of Christian origins.

In sum, the writing of a Gospel assumes general contexts in which there is enough layered history, enough stories to tell about Jesus and about the Jesus movement to allow other stories to be told in different ways and that are meaningful for different reasons to different communities. The canonical documents presuppose not only the development of diverse, sometimes conflicting, traditions, but also that such traditions can and must be consolidated under one overarching vision and formulation.

NOT OF THIS WORLD: SUBMERGED VOICES AND MOVEMENTS AROUND THE MEDITERRANEAN

In terms of self-representation, there are missing voices and movements in the NT. It is ironic that most of the documents in the NT were greatly exorcised over these voices and movements. So, although there is in later, extra-canonical material much evidence for these voices and movements, we know about them primarily through the polemic contained in the canonical documents, or through the obvious gaps in the editorial patterning in the canonical documents of the first and second centuries.

These missing voices and movements were not homogeneous. They did not constitute one single group with one agenda. The scholarly attempt to sort out and name the different voices (Jewish Christian, Jewish Christian syncretists, Gnostics, enthusiasts, etc.) continues unabated. While the diversity and complexity of these voices and movements must always be acknowledged, intellectual honesty leads us to acknowledge that we do not have the evidence required to isolate, name, and characterize particular voices and movements.

Most of the rubrics used to characterize some of these voices and movements are not helpful because they tend to proliferate with little control; they are too easily divisible into numerous anachronistic mini-denominations, absent of clear criteria for the determination of boundary markers. Above all, they give the impression that all early Christians were scrappy, heady theologians divided into camps delimited by schoolish or scholarly jargon.

But astute students of religion know that the rifts among religious people are seldom over doctrinal issues; they are almost always more viscerally felt. To attempt to account for rifts among the religious by dividing them into theological camps (or "isms") is to treat the dynamics of religious life superficially. Ethos and worldview, not mere differences over doctrinal matters, account for major shifts and dynamics in religious life. The voices and movements missing in the NT should be discussed in terms of the dynamics involved in world creation and world maintenance.

In the documents that reflect the sentiment of some within the Pauline communities after Paul, the character of the polemical rhetoric lends evidence of the alternate and missing voices and movements. We may begin to account for some of the missing voices by paying more attention to the character of the language of opposition. As important as it is to name opponents, very few such names or rubrics of the type that appear in modern scholarly writings appear in the primary ancient literature. Opponents were understood to be those who either did not understand what was required for appropriate behavior in the world or were not considered morally and ethically equipped to respond in the right manner. They were not simply wrongheaded; they were ignorant and immoral, even though the larger, substantive criticism that occasioned these documents generally belies this characterization.

The opponents' most serious problem—from the perspectives of the writers of the canonical documents—was that they did not share the proper sensitivities about the importance of making some accommodation to respectable society; they did not orient themselves in the world in such a way as to elicit positive reactions from the right sectors of society.

The eschatological and prophetic teachings and traditions that were handed down from Paul had captured the imagination of some in a way that made sensitivity to respectable society onerous. Nothing could be the same again. The self and the world were to be forever defined in radically new and different terms. The world—including all of respectable society—was now seen as a reflection or symbol of all that lies under God's judgment and that is shortly to pass away. How could it be accommodated?

Such individuals seemed peculiarly receptive to the proclamations about the end of the world. Perhaps they already thought themselves enough on the margins in their worlds in sociological-psychological terms that such rhetoric only confirmed their sense of pessimism. Perhaps, the promise of a new start, of being part of a new order without the delimitations of heredity, social status, and gender, the promise of having access to a type of social bond and power long denied them, was very attractive. There is much evidence in the polemic, especially in the Pastoral Epistles, that many women found membership in the new communities appealing precisely because of the promise that all the normal and traditional societal expectations and responsibilities would shortly be done away with (see 1 Tim 2:12; 4:3, 7; 2 Tim 3:6-7).

Whatever the explanation for people's initial attraction to the movement, clearly the acceptance of the truth claims about Jesus required an uncompromising stance and struggle against the world as a reflection of God's judgment against the world. This struggle took several forms, most of which should be seen as types of renunciation, of refusal to participate in the things of the world (see 1 Cor 7:29-31).

The new Jesus communities, then, were understood by some of the missing voices of the NT as alternate communities or worlds. This was understood to be fundamental, the very reason for the creation of new communities. How, then, could the new world be other than oppositional? How, then, could devotees be other than uncompromising in their life-style? What was the point of reaching some accommodation to the world that was passing away? On what basis could compromise be reached?

In the region of Palestine/Syria, the Jesus movement began and developed along lines such that some of Jesus' sayings and some of the stories about him were consolidated to produce the Gospels as literature. But not all stories and proclamations about Jesus in the Palestine/Syria region were easily accommodated by the writers and communities that produced what became the canonical Gospel literature.

Jewish Christianity of the type that continued to require adherence to Jewish laws and traditions, that did not accommodate itself to the ethoses of the Hellenistic Jewish Christian or Gentile missions, did not flourish among the communities that dominate the NT. The destruction of the Temple in Jerusalem, the adaptability and creativity, thus the attractiveness of, diaspora Judaism, and the great success of the Gentile mission, all put such a movement on the defensive. Although it had on its side the weight of the Jewish origins of the Jesus movement, it seemed unable to articulate what, particularly in the wake of the destruction of the Temple, was the power of its vision of discipleship for all. In the literature that became the NT, it was caricatured and stereotyped; it became either part of the primitive and innocent phase of the history of Christianity (Luke–Acts) or an aspect of the larger movement that was thought to need to be arrested in development.

Gnosticism, a general rubric in reference to very complex and still not adequately understood phenomena of late antiquity, is scarcely represented in NT documents. It is clear that as a still awkward reference to an ethos, a spirit, a worldview, or a community, gnosticism was not easily accommodated among communities in Palestine/Syria in the first and second centuries. It is best to characterize the gnostic worldview that is in evidence in first-century Palestine/Syria as highly imaginative, elitist, intellectual, pneumatic, and radically critical of and alienated from the world.

Elitism is a major characteristic of gnosticism, and it proved to be its special burden. There is little doubt that claims to have special, exclusive insight into the truth about the self and the world were not well received by others who had already been told that membership in the community carried with it certain special insights about the self and the world. The tendency to create myths or to take up mythic elements as a touting of the special claims was criticized. It was thought an abandonment of what was considered the myth about Jesus, and the claiming of license to behave as one saw fit. Although such behavior was very likely not profligate and immoral, the fact that a different authority was revered registered concern.

Although not completely lost to the critical study of early Christianity, the phenomena discussed above are among the lost voices and contexts in the NT in terms of direct, unbiased representation. Caution and qualification are always in order, therefore, lest the NT continue to be discussed as though it reflected full representation of early Christianity. These phenomena do not necessarily represent different contexts, but they do represent the greater complexity of the contexts of the NT and early Christianity. The latter should not be interpreted without reference to these and other voices.

To interpret the NT and early Christianity without reference to voices and movements not fully or directly represented is not simply to fail to be inclusive and comprehensive; it is to fail to be self-critical and intellectually honest about what the whole enterprise of interpretation, including the historical work that is Christian origins, is really all about. It is certainly about far more than historical reconstruction; among many things, in the West in general and in the United States in particular, it is part of each generation's effort to form and define itself and to understand those influences on the formation of its identity and ways of being in the world.

BIBLIOGRAPHY

The chief inspirations for this article are:

Koester, Helmut. *Introduction to the New Testament: History and Literature of Early Christianity.* 2 vols. New York: Walter de Gruyter, 1982.

Robinson, James M., and Helmut Koester. *Trajectories Through Early Christianity.* Philadelphia: Fortress, 1971.

For markedly different assessments of the evidence, see:

Dunn, James D. G. *The Evidence for Jesus.* Louisville: Westminster/John Knox, 1985.

Wright, N. T. *The New Testament and the People of God.* Volume 1 of *Christian Origins and the Question of God.* Minneapolis: Fortress, 1992.

Still other interpretations of earliest Christianity and the origins of early Christian literature within that context are offered by:

Keck, Leander E. *The New Testament Experience of Faith.* St. Louis: CBP, 1976.

Kee, Howard Clark. *Christian Origins in Sociological Perspective.* Philadelphia: Westminster, 1980.

Stambaugh, John E., and David L. Balch. *The New Testament in Its Social Environment.* Volume 2 of Library of Early Christianity. Edited by Wayne A. Meeks. Philadelphia: Westminster, 1986.

THE GOSPELS AND NARRATIVE LITERATURE

ROBERT C. TANNEHILL

The Gospels and narrative literature can be studied on several levels, e.g., the level of complete Gospels and the level of the short narrative episodes that they contain. These episodes follow recognizable patterns, and those that follow the same pattern may be classed as examples of the same literary type. This article will first examine types of short narratives in the Gospels and then will discuss the Gospels themselves as extended narratives containing these short narrative forms.

TYPES OF NARRATIVE IN THE GOSPELS

Certain stable patterns of short narrative are found within the Gospels and the surrounding culture. The repetition of these patterns is evidence that they were found to be effective and worthy of imitation. Within first-century Mediterranean culture, the development of literary skill consisted, in part, in the mastery of these narrative patterns. The patterns were seldom used rigidly; they could be adapted to the content of the story, and skillful storytellers could employ these patterns creatively.

Patterns of short narrative may be studied by form critics, who will ask about the function of each type within a community's life; by rhetorical critics, who will ask how each type is able to affect an audience; and by literary critics, who will ask how these short patterns enrich the larger narrative, helping to create a complex communication that deepens our experience of humanness.[1]

Short narrative types include pronouncement stories, parables, wonder stories, and promise and commission epiphanies. Before considering complete Gospels as narratives, one needs to note several longer narrative sequences within the Gospels in which scenes are linked by clear plot developments. These represent narrative at an intermediate level between the short episode and a complete Gospel.

Pronouncement Stories. Within the Gospels are a number of short narratives in which Jesus responds to a person or situation, and this response is the main point of the narrative. These narratives may be called pronouncement stories. Matthew 18:21-22 provides an example:

Then Peter came and said to him, "Lord, if another member of the church sins against me, how often should I forgive? As many as seven times?" Jesus said to him, "Not seven times, but, I tell you, seventy-seven times."

A pronouncement story is a brief narrative in which the climactic (and often final) element is a pronouncement that is presented as a particular person's response to something said or observed on

---

1. See Carl R. Holladay, "Contemporary Methods of Reading the Bible" in *NIB* (Nashville: Abingdon, 1994–) 1:125-49.

a past occasion. Pronouncement stories have two main parts: the pronouncement and its setting—i.e., the response and the situation provoking that response.[2] In some cases an expressive action, making a point without speech, or a response combining speech and action may substitute for the pronouncement.

The pronouncement story is closely related to a form widely used in the Greco-Roman world, the *chreia*. An ancient educational textbook, Theon's *Progymnasmata,* defines the *chreia* as "a concise statement or action which is attributed with aptness to some specified character or to something analogous to a character."[3] Although a *chreia* may sometimes simply indicate the person who is the source of the statement or action, it often provides a brief setting, presenting the statement or action as a response in a particular situation. It is then equivalent to a pronouncement story. One of Theon's examples shows how concise a *chreia* can be: "Alexander the Macedonian king, on being asked by someone where he had his treasures, pointed to his friends and said: 'In these.' "[4] Most examples of pronouncement stories in the Gospels are significantly longer, yet retain the same basic structure. Furthermore, Theon required his students in their exercises to take a concise *chreia* and expand it.[5] Thus there is some flexibility in the length and amount of detail among them.

The pronouncement story is generally equivalent to Rudolf Bultmann's *apothegms* and overlaps to some extent Martin Dibelius's *paradigms.*[6] The pronouncement story is very selective in what it presents; it is not to be confused with a full report of a dialogue. Where there are two parties in the scene, they are generally not given equal attention. The scene is rhetorically shaped so that the concluding response makes the chief impression, due to its climactic position, and often due to the forceful language used in the pronouncement. Thus the little scene serves to display the wit and wisdom of a particular person, whose pronouncement or significant action is presented for admiration and often

for emulation. When these stories present persons and highlight values that represent the cultural heritage, they maintain cultural continuity. Yet pronouncement stories may also have a sharply critical edge, undermining confidence in accepted values and seeking to replace them.

The pronouncement stories in the Gospels often present two contrasting attitudes to a situation, one in the setting and the other in the response. As the brief scene unfolds, there is a sharp shift from one attitude to the other. The setting, by expressing one attitude, makes it available for challenge. The hearer or reader is invited to make the shift traced in the scene or, at least, to reaffirm a previous decision of this kind. It is easy for persons of a different time and culture to lose a sense of the challenge in many of these pronouncements, since we may not have an investment in or attraction to the position being challenged. Yet the reason for emphasizing the climactic pronouncement and contrasting it with an initial attitude is best understood when we recognize that a significant shift in attitudes and values is being advocated.[7]

The pronouncements featured in these stories seem designed to be provocative and memorable rather than to present reasoned arguments for a position. Nevertheless, a response may include a rationale (a brief supporting reason, attached with "for" or "because"). Furthermore, there are some scenes, especially controversy scenes, in which arguments are developed. Burton Mack has studied an ancient school exercise called the "elaboration" of the *chreia* (a prescribed way of developing arguments in defense of a *chreia*), and he and Vernon Robbins have found traces of similar argumentative patterns within some Gospel pronouncement stories.[8]

Pronouncement stories are numerous in the synoptic Gospels, and they contribute much to the impression of Jesus and his message that we receive there. In spite of their brevity, many of these scenes have a dramatic quality, as Jesus interacts with other parties. The dramatic setting helps to make the climactic saying of Jesus impressive and forceful.

The nature of the dramatic interaction can be clarified by dividing pronouncement stories into

---

2. See Robert C. Tannehill, "Introduction: The Pronouncement Story and Its Types," *Semeia* 20 (1981) 1.

3. See Ronald F. Hock and Edward N. O'Neil, *The Chreia in Ancient Rhetoric, vol. 1 The Progymnasmata* (Atlanta: Scholars Press, 1986) 83.

4. Ibid., 91-93.

5. Ibid., 101-3.

6. See Rudolf Bultmann, *The History of the Synoptic Tradition,* rev. ed. (New York: Harper & Row, 1976) 11-69, and Martin Dibelius, *From Tradition to Gospel* (New York: Charles Scribner's Sons, 1934) 37-69.

7. See Robert C. Tannehill, "Attitudinal Shift in Synoptic Pronouncement Stories," in *Orientation by Disorientation,* ed. Richard A. Spencer (Pittsburgh: Pickwick, 1980) 183-97.

8. See Burton L. Mack and Vernon K. Robbins, *Patterns of Persuasion in the Gospels* (Sonoma: Polebridge, 1989).

subtypes. Below I present a typology of pronouncement stories based on the relation between their two essential parts, the setting and the response. Viewed from this perspective, there seem to be five subtypes of Gospel pronouncement stories.[9]

1. Correction Stories. In the dialogue between Peter and Jesus quoted above, Peter proposes that he might forgive up to seven times and Jesus corrects him by saying, "Not seven times, but . . . seventy-seven times" (Matt 18:21-22). In correction stories, the response corrects the views or conduct of another party. The response may be prompted by something observed, or it may be caused by a statement, request, or question. In the case of requests or questions, the response does not grant the request or answer the question but corrects an assumption on which the request or question was based, turning the encounter in a new direction. By word or action the person encountering Jesus has taken a position, and Jesus responds with a correction. Among the other correction stories in the synoptic Gospels are Matt 8:19-20 par. (the homeless Son of Man); 8:21-22 par. (let the dead bury the dead); Mark 9:33-37 par. (who is greatest?); 9:38-40 par. (the strange exorcist); 10:35-45 par. (request of James and John); 13:1-2 par. (the great temple buildings); Luke 9:61-62 (plowing and looking back); 11:27-28 (blessing of Jesus' mother); 14:7-11 (places at table); 17:20-21 (God's reign among you).

There is always tension in a correction story. This tension does not appear until the corrective response, for the person who encounters Jesus is neither criticizing nor testing him, and the attitude expressed in the setting may seem quite acceptable. The corrective response introduces tension and opens up distance. The response challenges commonly accepted thought and invites change. These stories are useful where crucial decisions are being ignored and where there is a tendency to reduce the vision of Jesus to the ordinary.

Discussion of Gospel pronouncement stories has been strongly influenced by controversy dialogues (called "objection stories" below), in which Jesus responds to critics. The correction stories,

however, are equally important, and they are addressed not primarily to critics but to Jesus' followers and other persons attracted to him.

2. Commendation Stories. Commendations are similar to corrections, except that Jesus responds by commending what he has seen or heard. Pure commendation stories are rare in the synoptic Gospels, but in Matthew, Peter's confession has been turned into a commendation story, for the emphasis now falls on Jesus' laudatory response to him (Matt 16:13-20).

As in correction stories, often there is an element of tension in commendation stories. There may be a surprise in the commendation, for Jesus may praise someone or something commonly ignored or despised. The tension with another standard of judgment may be dramatized in the story by introducing a third character (who may be an individual or a group) whose words or actions express a contrasting view. The result is a "hybrid" story in which the response will probably have a double function: to commend one party and correct another, or to commend one party and respond to the objection of another. This feature of the stories expresses tension with other views in the social context. Thus there is an indication that these stories, too, attempt to cause or reinforce a shift of attitude on the part of hearers or readers. An example of a hybrid story is Mark 10:13-16—Jesus' blessing of the children—in which Jesus both corrects the disciples and commends the children by associating the reign of God with them. In this case Jesus' affirmation of the children is expressed both in words and in action. Other examples of hybrid correction-commendation stories are Mark 3:31-35 par. (Jesus' true family); 12:41-44 par. (the poor widow); and 14:3-9 par. (the woman who anoints Jesus). Hybrid objection-commendation stories are found in Matt 21:14-16 (the children's praise) and Luke 10:38-42 (Mary and Martha).

Many Gospel pronouncement stories indirectly praise Jesus, since they present his responses for admiration. Commendation stories show, however, that Jesus is not the only representative of positive values. The neglected and despised people praised by Jesus also represent positive values. Thus these people function as models for the hearer or reader.

3. Objection Stories. In a number of stories, Jesus must answer an objection. These stories frequently have three parts, moving from description

9. For further discussion and examples, see Robert C. Tannehill, "Introduction: The Pronouncement Story and Its Types" and "Varieties of Synoptic Pronouncement Stories," *Semeia* 20 (1981) 1-13, 101-19; idem, "Types and Functions of Apophthegms in the Synoptic Gospels," in *Aufstieg und Niedergang der Römischen Welt,* eds. Hildegard Temporini and Wolfgang Haase, vol. II.25.2 (Berlin: Walter de Gruyter, 1984) 1792-1829.

of an action to an objection to that action, and then to the response. The first element, however, may appear only in the objection itself. In Mark 2:15-17 the three elements appear in sequence: the meal with tax collectors and sinners is described, the scribes object, and Jesus responds with sayings that first draw an analogy with a physician and then disclose the fundamental principle that guides his ministry.

The objection is often expressed as a demand for justification, using a question beginning with "Why?" In these scenes, which are often called "controversy dialogues," tension is introduced not by Jesus (as in correction stories) but by the party expressing the objection. Here the tension focuses on Jesus, for he is being challenged. (This is true even if the disciples are addressed, for the teacher is responsible for his disciples.) The response may consist of a rhetorical question, an analogy, or a fundamental statement of principle.

Although disciples may sometimes object, as in Mark 8:31-33, many of the objections come from the scribes and Pharisees. The formation and transmission of these stories doubtless reflect the need of the early church to defend the distinctive practices and perspectives of the Jesus movement within its historical context. The apologetic needs of the church are probably reflected in a tendency to expand Jesus' response into a series of arguments. This does not mean that these stories function only to support the early church against outside critics. Followers of Jesus would seldom be as clear and deeply committed to a position as Jesus is in these stories. They continue to be a challenge to Jesus' followers to clarify and deepen their commitment.

Some additional objection stories in the synoptic Gospels are Mark 2:18-22 par. (question about fasting); 2:23-28 par. (plucking grain on the sabbath); 3:20-30 par. (the Beelzebul controversy); 7:1-15 par. (eating with defiled hands); and Luke 2:41-51 (the boy Jesus in the Temple).

There is an overlap of objection stories with wonder stories (discussed below) in the sabbath healing stories. The objection-response sequence is primary when the story ends with Jesus' response to the objection, as in Luke 13:10-17 and 14:1-6. It may still be very important when the scene ends with the healing, as in the story of the man with a withered hand (Mark 3:1-6 par.), where the healing is part of Jesus' response to the implied objection of the opponents.

4. Quest Stories. These stories tend to be longer and more complex than most pronouncement stories and may include features of the other types. Jesus responds to an issue raised in the scene, but now this response is part of a story in which someone is in quest of something important for human well-being. This quest is sufficiently important that we are told its outcome. In other words, the scene does not end simply with Jesus' impressive response, as in many pronouncement stories. There is some resolution, positive or negative, to the other person's quest. As a result, the person coming to Jesus receives more attention in the narrative than in many pronouncement stories. In a sense it is this person's story, for the scene is shaped by his or her desire, expressed at the beginning, and ends when this desire succeeds or fails. Since we are asked to look at events in the light of this person's need and desire, sympathy for him or her is encouraged, although the social standing of the person may hinder this.

An obstacle, sometimes expressed as an objection or a difficult condition, may surface within the scene, and Jesus' response will be crucial at this point. The objections that may occur in quest stories make them similar to the objection stories just discussed, but here the objection functions as an obstacle within a quest. Several of these stories involve healing or exorcism and are similar to other wonder stories. If we simply group them with wonder stories, however, we will ignore their structural similarity with quest stories that lack healing or exorcism. An interesting example of a quest story that includes both an objection and an exorcism is that of the Syrophoenician woman (Mark 7:24-30), who seeks the exorcism of an unclean spirit from her daughter. The exorcism itself is reported very briefly, however. The main emphasis is on the dialogue between the woman and Jesus. The story is unusual in that Jesus himself objects to the woman's quest and even more unusual because the woman is able to change the mind of Jesus, who normally is viewed as the final authority. The woman's daring rejoinder enables the quest to move to a successful conclusion. The prominent role she plays and the way in which the quest shapes the whole story show that this is something more than an objection story. It is a quest story.

The social status of the questers is a significant factor in quest stories. The one quester who fails is from high social rank (Mark 10:17-22 par.), while successful questers—like the Syrophoenician woman, the centurion (Matt 8:5-13 par.), the sinful woman in the Pharisee's house (Luke 7:36-50), the Samaritan leper (Luke 17:12-19), Zacchaeus (Luke 19:1-10), and the crucified criminal (Luke 23:39-43)—are aliens and outcasts. Thus these stories reverse social judgments and undermine prejudices; they both invite the outcasts and help to create openness for them in the community.

5. Inquiry Stories. These scenes move from a question or request for instruction to the answer. Questions may also be found in other types of pronouncement stories, but the inquiry story lacks the distinctive characteristics of the other types. The responder does not correct an assumption behind the question, as in a correction story, nor does the question express an objection, as in an objection story. There is a straightforward movement from question to answer, which means that attention tends to focus almost entirely on the content of the answer. Examples are Luke 11:1-4 (the Lord's Prayer); 13:22-30 (enter through the narrow door); and 17:5-6 (increase our faith). There is generally less dramatic tension in these scenes than in other pronouncement stories.

There is dramatic tension, however, in one sub-group, the testing inquiries, for in these scenes Jesus is being tested by a hostile or skeptical party. The tension focuses on Jesus, who is put in a difficult situation. Failure to give an impressive answer would result in loss of influence and might be dangerous in other ways. On the other hand, an impressive answer is all the more impressive in a situation of risk. Matthew 22:34-40 (the greatest commandment); Mark 11:27-33 par. (by what authority?); and 12:13-17 par. (paying taxes to Caesar) are examples of testing inquiries.

Parables. Parables are figurative language. They are imaginative narratives composed in order to illuminate a subject that lies beyond the literal subject matter of the story. Scholars commonly distinguish three subtypes: the similitude, the parable proper, and the example story.[10] We may speak of the first two as metaphorical narratives, for they

refer indirectly to a sphere of meaning that is normally distinct from the literal content of the story, suggesting a connection between the two. The similitude (e.g., the mustard seed, Mark 4:30-32) is brief and focuses on an event that happens repeatedly, such as the growth of seed. Even so, it has the basic components of a narrative: events happening to one or more participants in a setting. The parable proper (e.g., the prodigal son, Luke 15:11-32) is a more fully developed story that narrates a unique and sometimes surprising sequence of events. It may have several scenes and tends to have a larger number of characters. The example story (e.g., the rich fool, Luke 12:16-21) is different in that the second level of meaning does not pertain to another sphere (as in metaphor) but to the sphere of meaning of which the story itself is a part. The example story still works as a trope; it suggests much more than its literal meaning. But the trope is not metaphor but synecdoche, in which the story is a part standing for a larger whole that must be imagined.

Metaphors often have bundles of associations and, therefore, are capable of complex development. Just as a poem may draw repeatedly from the image field suggested by a root metaphor, so also a parable may develop the image field of a metaphor through narrative. Thus linking a mustard seed metaphorically to the reign of God may lead to a narrative development from sowing to growth of the seed to the mature bush, all in some way suggestive of God's reign. In a similitude the brief narrative recalls what everyone would expect in the situation. The new element arises from the metaphorical transfer of meaning to a different sphere. In the parable proper the course of the narrative is not predictable at the beginning; indeed, some surprising things happen. Yet these stories make use of stereotypical associations, which bring with them an initial set of expectations and identifications. Thus first-century hearers would expect that a king (Matt 18:23), a father (Luke 15:11), or a landowner (Matt 20:1) might represent God. This sort of identification need not be an allegorical misreading of the parable. Stereotypical associations establish a set of expectations that the parable can use. Hearers, having made the initial identifications, discover that the parable is using traditional associations to produce unexpected results. The parable can set the traditional associations in motion, in part by reinserting them into the human sphere from which they were drawn

10. In the Gospels the term for "parable" (παραβολή *parabolē*) is used more broadly, being applied even to short aphorisms. My discussion is confined to narratives.

and using fresh human experience to reimagine how God as father or owner might act.

The parables inhabit a different narrative level from that of other stories being discussed in this article. The narrator is Jesus, a participant in the events of the larger narrative. Thus we are dealing with embedded narrative, an act of narration that occurs within the narrative world being constructed by the Gospel narrator. Techniques of narrative analysis are useful at both levels.

Narrative analysis is especially helpful in interpreting parables that are more complex. It is useful to ask whether the parable builds up to a climax at which a decisive event or crucial decision takes place. Then the prior narrative will prepare for this climax, and anything that follows will clarify its results. If the parable story can be understood according to this or some other pattern, it can be apprehended as a whole, and the function of each part within the whole becomes clear. This approach guards against the tendency to isolate an element of the story in order to derive some special meaning from it. Interpretation must concentrate on the climax of the story, to which the rest of the story contributes, if it is to do justice to the parable as a whole. Thus an interpretation of the parable of the vineyard workers (Matt 20:1-16) as primarily a call to missionary work in God's vineyard would be inadequate because it ignores the climax of the parable, which focuses on the unusual way in which the wages were paid.

The parable of the vineyard workers also exemplifies a common narrative technique: the narration of a series of events in parallel form, with a difference that will prove to be significant. The parallelism makes the difference stand out so that its significance can be considered. In the case of the vineyard workers, we have parallel accounts of hiring workers. Those hired at midday fade out of the story at the time of payment so that the story can concentrate on those showing the greatest difference, the workers hired at the beginning of the day and those hired one hour before the end. The parables avoid unnecessary descriptive detail. This encourages the comparison of persons who are essentially alike except for one characteristic, which is thereby isolated for consideration.

Through construction of such contrasts, the narrator controls the issues that are brought to the hearer's attention. In a story of a man with two sons,

we may guess at the beginning that the two sons will differ in some way that will be important to the story. Such is the case in the parable of the prodigal son (Luke 15:11-32), but this parable also presents two contrasting responses to the younger brother's homecoming. Here the contrast is between the father and the older brother, who remain in conflict at the end of the story. The development of two major contrasts adds to the complexity of this parable.

There are other ways in which the narrator guides the hearer's focus of attention. For instance, a moment of crucial decision may be emphasized by reporting a person's deliberation as internal speech (cf. Luke 16:3-4 in the parable of the dishonest steward). Here the progress of the narrative has slowed in order to give detailed attention to this moment. In other cases expansion of direct discourse between two parties may highlight a central issue. In the parable of the talents the expanded dialogue between the third servant and the master is where the main issue is clarified and resolved (cf. Matt 25:24-30).

The parables are attractive and interesting as stories, which serves their goal of persuasion. Some parables explicitly ask for a verdict from the hearer, as in the ones that begin "Which one of you . . . ?" (e.g., the lost sheep, Luke 15:4-7). In other cases Jesus is depicted as rendering a verdict himself (e.g., the parable of the Pharisee and the tax collector; cf. Luke 18:14). Some parables are open-ended because there is an unresolved conflict at the end (e.g., the prodigal son, Luke 15:11-32). Nevertheless, the story makes clear where the narrator's sympathies lie. The parables may be even-handed in allowing conflicting perspectives expression within the story. This does not mean, however, that these views are given equal value. The workers who labor all day in the sun express their objection strongly, but the owner of the vineyard has the last word (Matt 20:11-15).

Although in the Gospel of John parables are not characteristic of Jesus' teaching, as they are in the synoptic Gospels, John does contain some related forms. We find, for instance, the short simile of the grain of wheat that dies but is fruitful (John 12:24). In John 10:1-5, Jesus speaks figuratively of the shepherd, the sheepfold, and sheep. This is called a *paroimia* (παροιμία), a "figure of speech" (10:6). It describes customary activities, like the synoptic similes, yet a greater variety of details appears. The figurative language is then interpreted, and Jesus specifically identifies himself with the gate of the sheepfold and the shepherd (10:7-18). This section of John is rather similar to the parable of the sower (Mark 4:3-8, 14-20) in its movement from figurative language to allegorical interpretation.

Wonder Stories. Although these scenes are usually called miracle stories, the term *miracle* is best avoided because it means to many an act of God that violates the laws of nature. Nature itself was understood differently by those who told the Gospel wonder stories, for it was widely assumed at that time that the physical world was open to the operation of divine and demonic powers. Nevertheless, there was a strong sense, then as now, of the difference between the usual and the wonderful. The indications of amazement at the end of many of these stories attest to that difference. The wonder stories tell of occasions when God's power surprises people whose expectations are limited to normal human experience. In the Gospels the wonder is almost always a gracious act of help from God, although wonders of punishment are also possible (see Mark 11:12-14, 20-21; Acts 5:1-11). Thus the wonder stories attest to the belief that, unusual as it may be, God's grace is available even for bodily needs and dangers.

In the synoptic Gospels these wonders are sometimes called *dynameis* (δυνάμεις), literally "powers"—i.e., manifestations of divine power or "mighty acts" (cf. Matt 11:20-23; Mark 6:2, 5). The Fourth Gospel prefers to speak of Jesus' "signs" (σημεῖα *sēmeia*; see John 2:11; 12:37).

In the early Gospel tradition, Jesus' wonders were an integral part of the outburst of hope for overcoming evil associated with the coming of God's reign. Jesus' healing ministry is summarized in words that recall scriptural prophecies of salvation (Matt 11:5 par.; cf. Isa 35:5-6; 61:1), and the continuation of that ministry through the disciples is associated with the approach of God's reign (Luke 10:9). Jesus' exorcisms, especially, reveal the conquest of evil power through the appearance of God's reign (Matt 12:28-29 par.).

Most Gospel wonder stories can be divided into six types (although some of the stories have affinities with more than one type).[11] Discussion of these six

types will help us to recognize common patterns and themes, although the point of emphasis will vary among stories of the same type.

1. Exorcism Stories. In this type of wonder story, Jesus encounters a person possessed by a demon and forces the demon to leave, enabling the person to return to a normal life. The demon is evil, but the possessed person is not, for the demon is an alien force that can be expelled. When the exorcism takes place, the story focuses on the interaction between Jesus and the demon (or unclean spirit). It is the demon who speaks with Jesus; the possessed person is so controlled by the demon as to be incapable of independent thought or action. Jesus addresses the demon directly and powerfully, forcing it to submit and depart.

The exorcism in the Capernaum synagogue (Mark 1:21-28 par.) presents such an encounter in brief form. The exorcism of the Gerasene demoniac (Mark 5:1-20 par.) and of the possessed boy (Mark 9:14-29 par.) are more complex examples of this type. In the former, Jesus' interaction with the demons goes through several steps. There is also considerable interest in depicting the original condition of the possessed man and the change that takes place in him. In the latter story, the father of the boy assumes a major role, especially in the Markan version. The father requests help, and his faith is important; both features draw this story close to healing stories, which will be discussed next. However, the workings of the evil spirit and Jesus' command for it to depart are also vividly depicted. Perhaps we should speak of the story of the possessed boy as a mixed form. It is distinctly different from the story of the Syrophoenician woman (Mark 7:24-30 par.), where, even though the woman's daughter is possessed by an unclean spirit, no attention is given to Jesus' confrontation with the spirit. Therefore, the Syrophoenician woman's story should not be included among the exorcisms.

2. Healing Stories. In this type of wonder story, Jesus responds to the bodily need of another person, and the principal interaction is between Jesus as healer and the person in need (in some cases also the representative of this person, such as a mother or father). Normally the healing story presents an encounter with Jesus, together with indications of the type of illness or disability a person suffers (sometimes with emphasis on its severity), then reports the healing itself. This is often followed

---

11. This typology is my adaptation of Gerd Theissen, *The Miracle Stories of the Early Christian Tradition* (Philadelphia: Fortress, 1983) 85-112.

by an action demonstrating that the healing has taken place or a response of amazement or praise from witnesses. Frequently the action begins when persons address Jesus with a request for healing, either for themselves (blind Bartimaeus, Mark 10:46-52 par.) or for another (Jairus's daughter, Mark 5:21-24, 35-43 par.). In some episodes, however, Jesus takes the initiative. This is the case in two of the four Johannine healing stories (John 5:2-9; 9:1-7). Also in the raising of the widow's son (Luke 7:11-17) there is no request for Jesus' help; rather, Jesus' action is due to his compassion (7:13). The healing stories are the largest group of wonder stories in the Gospels.

In the story of the hemorrhaging woman (Mark 5:25-34), the cure takes place relatively early in the scene (v. 29). This is a sign that a physical cure is not the sole concern. The story continues for five more verses as Jesus searches for the woman and the woman reveals herself with fear and trembling. How will Jesus respond to an unclean woman who has violated purity laws by touching him? The healing (which responds to her social isolation as well as to her physical need) is not complete unless she is free of social condemnation for violating religious taboos.

Jesus does not condemn her but commends her for her faith (Mark 5:34). Faith is an important theme in the healing stories. Sometimes Jesus asks for faith from those who come for healing (Matt 9:28-29; Mark 5:36 par.; John 4:48-50). Most striking are the cases in which Jesus commends someone's faith. These people become models of the faith that others should show in similar situations. Such people persist in reaching out to Jesus for help when blocked by the crowd or separated by a social barrier (e.g., the hemorrhaging woman; blind Bartimaeus, who is at first rebuked by the crowd, Mark 10:46-52 par.). The same kinds of people demonstrate faith in quest stories involving healing (e.g., the centurion, Matt 8:5-13 par.; the Canaanite woman, Matt 15:21-28; the Samaritan leper, Luke 17:12-19). These stories, however, differ from healing wonders in that the questing persons raise problems other than their physical afflictions that Jesus must resolve with an authoritative pronouncement. Faith is presented in these healing and quest stories as resolute action that, in spite of society and its taboos, reaches out to Jesus as the source of help. It is the opposite of resigned acceptance of suffering.[12]

---

12. A point emphasized by Antoinette Clark Wire, "The Structure of the Gospel Miracle Stories and Their Tellers," *Semeia* 11 (1978) 106-8.

Healing stories, as well as other types of wonders, may take on symbolic meaning. This is especially characteristic of the Gospel of John (note that John 9 begins with the healing of a blind man and ends with climactic statements about spiritual sight and blindness), but it is also true of some scenes in the other Gospels. For instance, it is significant that healings of a deaf man and a blind man surround Jesus' harsh words about the disciples' deafness and blindness in Mark (see 7:31-37; 8:18, 22-26).

3. Provision Stories. Some wonder stories can be called provision stories because Jesus provides food or drink for a crowd in a surprising way. In the Gospels we find not only stories of Jesus feeding crowds in the wilderness (Mark 6:34-44 par.; 8:1-10 par.), but also stories of Jesus providing wine for a wedding (John 2:1-11) and great catches of fish (Luke 5:4-7; John 21:1-14). The great catches of fish in Luke and John are elements within commissioning stories focusing on Simon Peter. The provision stories tend to attract symbolic significance. Thus the feeding stories recall the feeding of Israel with manna in the wilderness and suggest the formation of a new people under God's care. When the great catch of fish in Luke 5:4-7 is followed by Jesus' call to share his work of "catching people," the catch of fish becomes a symbolic promise of success in the future mission. The imagery of wedding and abundant wine in John 2:1-11 suggests the new time of fulfillment that is replacing the old order.

There are three provision stories in John (2:1-11; 6:1-15; 21:1-14) but only four healing stories and no exorcisms.

4. Controversy Wonders. Stories of this type are actually a mixed form, for they follow the pattern of pronouncement stories involving controversy (called "objection stories" above) as well as wonder stories. The emphasis may not fall on the wonder. In two sabbath healing stories special to Luke (the bent woman, 13:10-17; the man with dropsy, 14:1-6), Jesus' principal pronouncement follows the healing, taking climactic position. In the case of the bent woman, the cure takes place early in the scene and is the cause of the controversy, a subordinate position. I would classify these two stories as objection stories, not wonder stories. Even in the stories of the paralyzed man (Mark 2:1-12 par.) and the man with the withered hand (Mark 3:1-6 par.), which do end with a healing, Jesus' interaction with his critics is very important, and the point being scored has more to do with Jesus' authority and insight into God's will than with his power to heal. In these two stories the wonder is significant not only for the person healed and as a disclosure of the power of the healer but also because it speaks to the issue of controversy. The healing is itself part of Jesus' answer to his opponents.

Classification of literary types is not an end in itself. It is a means of calling attention to various patterns in stories so that we can understand each story better. When a story does not fit easily into a single category, it is useful to compare it to several types, for this may show that several important developments are taking place at the same time.

The story of the paralyzed man is a case in point. It has features of healing stories, quest stories, and objection stories. The ending is typical of a healing story, but this story is more complex than most healings. The striking action of digging through the roof shows a determination that makes the paralyzed man's party stand out as remarkable people, giving them the importance typical of quest stories, and the controversy over forgiveness functions like the obstacle that appears in other quest stories. But the controversy with the scribes is also like objection stories, and the proclamation that "the Son of Man has authority on earth to forgive sins" (Mark 2:10 NRSV) is clearly a central feature of this scene. Thus this scene is both the story of a successful quest, which involves healing, and a revelation of Jesus' authority within a controversy wonder. The tension of desire in the quest and the tension of challenge in the objection are resolved at the same point, for Jesus' answer to the objection requires both words and healing action (2:9-12). Classification of the story is less important than recognizing both of these developments.

In John 5 and 9 also, Jesus' healings are connected with controversy, but John develops the controversies not within the healing scene but through lengthy dialogue and monologue following it.

5. Rescue Wonders. These relate how someone in danger (especially from a storm at sea or imprisonment) is rescued through altering natural forces or physical objects, such as the wind, chains, or prison doors (see Acts 12:1-11). Probably the stilling of the storm in Mark 4:35-41 par. belongs in this category, although Jesus addresses the sea as if

he were exorcising a demon, and the concluding question ("Who then is this?") suggests that the scene is also an epiphany. Rescue wonders encourage the belief that God's power can intervene in situations of danger.

6. Epiphany Wonders. These are stories in which the wonder primarily demonstrates Jesus' divine power and authority. This can be an aspect of the other wonder stories, but I will reserve this term for stories in which epiphany is the primary concern, for exorcism, healing, provision, controversy, and rescue are absent or secondary. The transfiguration story is a clear example (Mark 9:2-8 par.). We should probably also include Jesus' walking on the water, for the rescue of the disciples from the wind is secondary to the revelation concerning Jesus, at least in Mark 6:45-52 and John 6:16-21.

We should not assume that each type of wonder story has a single function. Even brief stories are often more complex than that, and their functions may shift with social setting. Perhaps we may say, however, that the wonder stories were told to elicit the praise of God and wonder at Jesus' power, often depicted at their end. Through presenting Jesus as the mediator of God's saving power, these stories could both call new people to trust Jesus as healer and rescuer and reinforce such faith within the church. In particular, these stories encourage belief that God's saving power extends to those who are suffering physically and those who are socially excluded because of demonic possession and uncleanness. These stories call people out of resigned acceptance of their physical and social limits by providing examples of liberation from evil powers and models of daring faith—a faith that goes beyond expected behavior in order to reach out to the power that saves.

Promise and Commission Epiphanies. In addition to the wonder stories of Jesus' earthly ministry, there are stories that report the surprising appearance of God or a messenger of God (in the Gospels, an angel or the risen Christ) who brings a message containing a promise or a commission (or both). The promise and commission will refer to events beyond the scene itself. The best examples in the Gospels are the annunciation scenes in the birth narratives and some of the resurrection appearances.

Benjamin Hubbard has called attention to a series

of "commissioning stories" in the Hebrew Bible and the New Testament.[13] In discussing some of the same stories, I have chosen a longer title in order (a) to limit consideration to stories that report an epiphany and (b) to call attention to the fact that the message may contain a promise as well as authorization and instruction to do something (a commission). Thus in the Lord's appearance to Isaac in Gen 26:23-25 (a brief example of the form) the message consists entirely of reassurance and promise. The message for the future concerns what God will do rather than commanding Isaac to do something. In some cases the message announces the future birth of a child. Raymond Brown has called attention to the precedents in the Hebrew Bible for the Gospel annunciations of birth.[14] These scenes are a subtype of the promise and commission epiphanies.

Hubbard has analyzed the commissioning stories into seven components: the *introduction,* which sets the scene; the *confrontation* (God or God's messenger appears); the *reaction,* in which the person addressed responds, often expressing fear or unworthiness; the *commission* (the core of the message, which, as I explained above, may emphasize the divine promise as much as or more than the human task); the *protest* (the person addressed may claim that the promise or commission is impossible); the *reassurance,* which may occur after the reaction of fear, the commission, or the protest; and the *conclusion,* which rounds off the scene.[15] Not all components are found in every example. The appearance of God's messenger and the message delivered are the essential elements.

The annunciations of birth in Luke 1:5-38 are examples of the full form. Following the introductions, we are told of the confrontation with the angel (vv. 11, 28), Zechariah's and Mary's disturbed reactions (vv. 12, 29), the angel's reassurance ("Do not be afraid," vv. 13, 30), the promise and commissioning (vv. 13-17, 31-33), and the protest (vv. 18, 34), followed by reassurance (or reinforcement) through additional signs of divine power (vv. 19-20, 35-37). The annunciation in Matt 1:18-25 lacks a reaction and protest from Joseph, but the situation and con-

tent of the message closely resemble other examples of the birth announcement subtype.[16]

Many of the Gospel resurrection scenes follow a similar format. In Mark's depiction of the empty tomb (16:1-8), the story moves from introduction (vv. 1-4) to confrontation with the messenger (v. 5); reaction ("They were alarmed," v. 5); reassurance ("Do not be alarmed," v. 6); message, including commission and promise (vv. 6-7); and conclusion (v. 8). Matthew's version of this scene is followed by an encounter with Jesus in which the sequence of confrontation, reaction, reassurance, commission, and promise is quickly repeated (Matt 28:9-10). The final scene in Matthew (28:16-20) concentrates on Jesus' speech, but the following elements are still clear: introduction, confrontation ("When they saw him," v. 17), reaction (v. 17), reassurance (v. 18),[17] commission, and promise (vv. 19-20).

Not only Matthew but also Luke and John contain appearances of the risen Jesus to groups of disciples, and these scenes follow the same basic pattern. In Luke 24:33-49 the reassurance following the disciples' fear is greatly expanded, so that we have these divisions: confrontation (v. 36), reaction of fear (v. 37), reassurance (vv. 38-43), commission, and promise (vv. 46-49). In John 20:19-23 the confrontation is described at the end of v. 19. The repeated "Peace be with you" probably functions as reassurance, not just greeting, and Jesus' showing of his hands and side has a similar function. The reaction of the disciples is joyous, not fearful, in this scene. The scene ends with the commission (vv. 21b-23).[18]

These stories present the holy God and the risen Christ as the source of the promise and mission that guide the church. They also seek to suggest the awesomeness of human encounters with this transcendent source. Borrowing the Hebrew Bible's pattern of epiphany scenes serves to support this sense of awe. The focus of the scenes is on the message of promise and commission that is delivered.

Longer Narrative Sequences. Despite the episodic quality of much of the Gospel material,

---

13. Benjamin J. Hubbard, *The Matthean Redaction of a Primitive Apostolic Commissioning: An Exegesis of Matthew 28:16-20* (Missoula: Scholar's Press, 1974); idem, "Commissioning Stories in Luke–Acts: A Study of their Antecedents, Form and Content," *Semeia* 8 (1977) 103-26.

14. Raymond E. Brown, *The Birth of the Messiah* (Garden City, N.Y.: Doubleday, 1979) 156-59.

15. Hubbard, "Commissioning Stories," 104-5.

16. See Brown, *Birth of the Messiah,* 156.

17. Also in Luke 1:19 the speaker emphasizes his authority in order to reassure someone who is doubtful.

18. Jerome H. Neyrey understands John 20:24-29 as the protest and reassurance that commonly follow a commission. These are presented, however, as a separate scene. See Neyrey, *The Resurrection Stories* (Wilmington: Michael Glazier, 1988), 27, 76-78.

there are portions of the Gospels in which we find clear plot developments through a series of interrelated scenes. These narratives are significantly longer than the small units we have discussed to this point and represent an intermediate level between the short episode and a complete Gospel narrative. As examples I will briefly discuss the Markan passion narrative, the Lukan birth narrative, and the Samaritan narrative in John.

Although some parts of Mark 14–15 might be told as separate stories, the significance of each scene is enhanced by its place within the larger narrative, and there are a number of indications of careful literary construction binding the sections of these chapters together.

There are at least two complementary approaches to the literary study of the Markan passion narrative (Mark 14–15). First, one may seek to understand this story as a representative of a story genre with a relatively fixed plot and set of characters. Thus one can discuss the Markan passion narrative as a variation on Jewish stories of the persecuted righteous one or of the wise person who is the object of a conspiracy but is vindicated.[19] This approach may help us to sense some of the echoes of familiar stories of the endangered Joseph, Esther, Daniel, etc., that first-century readers might have heard in the passion account and also help us to understand some of the significant points of difference from the common pattern. Second, one may study the literary composition of the Markan narrative itself, seeking to understand its plot lines, characterization, and rhetoric. I will briefly discuss the Markan passion narrative from the second perspective.

The Gospel of Mark, like other narratives, can be studied in the light of its overall plot. Such study would show that the passion narrative is the climax of Mark because each of three important plot lines is brought to a dramatic point of decision, as three continuing participants interact with one another.[20] I am referring to the plot lines centering on (1) Jesus, who has received a commission from God and must fulfill that commission; (2) the disciples, who have received a commission from Jesus and should fulfill

that commission; and (3) Jesus' opponents, who want to destroy him. From one perspective, the passion story is a narrative of how Jesus' opponents succeed in carrying out their desire to shame and kill him. From another perspective, it is a narrative of Jesus' fulfilling his commission from God, which since 8:31 is known to include rejection and death. From a third perspective, it is a narrative of the disciples who have been called to follow Jesus, taking up their own crosses and losing their lives (8:34-35), but who instead desert Jesus in order to save their lives. Each of these plot lines is prepared in Mark 1–13, and each is carefully developed in the passion story, resulting in significant characterization of all three parties.

The narrative's rhetorical shape begins to appear when we note the techniques used to highlight certain events so that they will make a strong impression on readers. Jesus predicts his betrayal by Judas (Mark 14:18-21), the flight of the disciples (14:27), and Peter's denial (14:30), thus calling readers' attention to these events before they happen. This is part of a strong emphasis on the disciples' failure in the passion story. The narrative also reinforces Jesus' experience of rejection by repeated mocking scenes (14:65; 15:16-20, 29-32), placed after each of the main events following Jesus' arrest (the Sanhedrin trial, the Pilate trial, and the crucifixion). These mocking scenes are also important because they contain ironic testimony to Jesus' true status. The narrative also contrasts Jesus' bold confession, which leads to his death, and Peter's denial by inserting Jesus' interrogation by the Sanhedrin into the story of Peter's denial (14:53-72).

Furthermore, dramatic moments are used for significant disclosures about Jesus. The Sanhedrin trial builds to a climax with the high priest's direct question about Jesus as Messiah. In this setting of official interrogation, Jesus publicly reveals the messianic secret, even though it costs him his life (Mark 14:61-62). At an equally dramatic moment, Jesus, approaching death, cries out, "My God, why have you forsaken me?" (15:34). This cry epitomizes the meaning of the passion events for Jesus. He has been rejected by the leaders of Israel and deserted by his own disciples. Rejection by humans raises sharply the question of divine abandonment, since with his death Jesus' mission comes to nothing. This cry, of course, also seeks an answer from God, which comes not as rescue from death but as resurrection.

---

19. See George W. E. Nickelsburg, "The Genre and Function of the Markan Passion Narrative," *HTR* 73 (1980) 153-84, for comparisons of Mark's passion narrative to Jewish literature; see also Burton L. Mack, *A Myth of Innocence: Mark and Christian Origins* (Philadelphia: Fortress, 1988) 249-69.

20. See Robert C. Tannehill, "The Gospel of Mark as Narrative Christology," *Semeia* 16 (1979) 60-62, 76-77.

The Lukan birth narrative (Luke 1:5–2:40) also shows signs of careful literary construction. We find, for instance, balanced scenes and motifs used in connection with John the Baptist, on the one hand, and Jesus, on the other (note especially the parallels between the two annunciation scenes in 1:5-25 and 26-38). The angelic announcements in these scenes share connecting themes with the prophetic hymns that follow (1:46-55, 68-79; 2:29-32; see also 2:10-14). These announcements and hymns gradually disclose the Lukan understanding of the purpose of God to be realized through John and Jesus, providing a basis for interpreting the rest of the Gospel narrative. Full understanding comes only through considering these revelatory scenes together. They come to a climax with the presentation of Jesus in the Temple, where Simeon's oracle (2:29-32) announces God's salvation in its full scope (encompassing both Israel and the Gentiles), and where his warning to Mary (2:34-35) provides the first indication of the resistance that Jesus must face.

The Lukan birth narrative, especially through the angelic announcements and prophetic hymns, interprets the future work of John and Jesus in the context of the divine purpose, providing a preview of the later narrative and a basis for understanding its importance. Other peoples will share in the salvation, but the birth narrative emphasizes the fulfillment of promises of salvation for Israel. Because of this emphasis, the rest of the narrative is not a simple story of success, for the expectations aroused at the beginning are not fully realized. Much of Israel, in fact, rejects salvation through Jesus, creating tension between the hopes and expectations aroused at the beginning and the actual course of the narrative. This twist in the plot carries a tragic effect.[21]

The Samaritan narrative in John 4:1-42 is a unified dramatic dialogue in which persons other than Jesus have important roles and in which each section contributes to a significant development, leading to a conclusion. Thus it is useful to analyze the statements of participants as actions within a plot and as disclosures of character. Setting is also important, for the location in Samaria is appropriate to the dialogue, and Jacob's well provides the initial topic (water) for the conversation.

To be sure, this narrative, like other sections of John, contains some shifts that, at first, are puzzling. Part of the time Jesus is talking with the Samaritan woman; part of the time with his disciples. The conversation begins with the subject of water (4:7-15), then shifts to the woman's husbands (4:16-18), to worship (4:20-24), to food (4:31-34), and to the harvest (4:35-38). Yet each part contributes to the forward movement of the narrative. To some extent the woman and the disciples balance each other as Jesus' conversation partners. While one occupies the foreground, the other is in the background. Nevertheless, we are made aware of the absent party's activity. The woman struggles to understand the water that Jesus offers; the disciples struggle to understand the food that Jesus is eating. All are led through a revelatory process that begins with ironic misunderstanding. The woman comes to recognize who Jesus is, and Jesus teaches the disciples about his mission and their place within it. This teaching includes helping the disciples to understand and accept Jesus' mission among the Samaritans, for the brief discourse about the harvest (4:35-38) is a commentary on Jesus' encounter with the Samaritan woman and the people of her town.

On the one hand, the narrative portrays a revelatory process in which Jesus carries out the mission to which he refers in 4:34 and discloses to the disciples their role in it. On the other hand, the narrative portrays the Samaritan's coming to faith, with each stage of dialogue and movement making its contribution. The Samaritan woman not only comes to faith (her progress indicated by her reactions to Jesus) but also becomes Jesus' witness, the founding missionary for her community. Through the indirect language of symbolism and irony, and through the text's narrative form, we are invited to participate in a "revelatory dynamic." It is the text as narrative that presents revelation as dynamic process. Thus the narrative form of the text is not an accidental feature that can be ignored.[22]

Even when the Samaritans come to Jesus, the narrative of this process is not quite ended. The narrative quickly draws a distinction between second-

---

21. See Robert C. Tannehill, *The Narrative Unity of Luke–Acts: A Literary Interpretation*, vol. 1, *The Gospel According to Luke* (Philadelphia: Fortress, 1986) 15-44; and "Israel in Luke–Acts: A Tragic Story," *JBL* 104 (1985) 69-85.

22. See Gail R. O'Day, *Revelation in the Fourth Gospel: Narrative Mode and Theological Claim* (Philadelphia: Fortress, 1986) 89-96; see also 49-89.

hand faith, based on the woman's testimony, and firsthand faith, based on encounter with Jesus himself. Then the narrative sequence closes with a confession of faith suitable to the missionary breakthrough that it presents.

THE GOSPELS AS NARRATIVES

Form criticism is accustomed to study a small unit of tradition apart from its Gospel context, and the liturgical reading of the Gospels also conditions us to focus on isolated units within the Gospels. Yet these small narrative units are found within a larger narrative frame, consisting of the Gospel itself. Compared to modern narrative, the synoptic Gospels seem very episodic, consisting, in part, of short scenes placed in a sequence with few connecting threads of plot. Nevertheless, attentive reading of a Gospel as a unitary narrative can help us to understand the functions of the parts within the whole.

In studying the Gospels as wholes, it is also appropriate to ask whether they belong to a larger literary genre. Much of the material within the Gospels conforms to generic types. Is this true also of the Gospels themselves? Until recently it was the conviction of many scholars that the Gospels are a unique kind of literature. In part this was due to the belief that they, as "popular" writings, could not be compared with contemporary Greco-Roman literature. This belief has been waning, and now a number of scholars argue that the Gospels belong within the genre of ancient biography.[23]

The Gospels share with ancient biography some general similarities of content, form, and function. In content, they focus on the life of one person, especially that person's public career. In form, they fit, to various degrees, the pattern of ancient biographies that frame a person's public career with narratives of origin and youth, at the beginning, and death, at the end. In between, biographical presentation could be chronological, but not necessarily so. The subject's words and deeds were used to illustrate character, and various short genres, such as the pronouncement story, were incorporated into the biography for this purpose. In function, many ancient biographies were concerned with praising

their subject as an exemplar of the virtues to be honored and emulated in the community. The Gospels have a similar function for the Christian community, while serving other functions as well.

The genre of the Gospels continues to be a subject of debate. Adela Yarbro Collins, for instance, denies that Mark is a biography. Although it may be concerned with the identity of Jesus and presents him as a model, these are not its main purposes. Basically, it records events that changed the world—eschatological events. Thus she classifies it as apocalyptic history.[24]

Luke, too, might be regarded as history, for it is part of a two-volume work that includes Acts. This could make some difference in our understanding of Luke, for biography presents a person's deeds and words as illustrations of character, while history is interested in a person's achievements in so far as they had consequences for society. Yet "during the late Hellenistic period history and biography moved closer together with the increasing emphasis on character in historiography. Biography and history became more and more difficult to distinguish."[25] The fact that one genre can be embedded in another might also suggest that Luke can be regarded as a biography even if Acts, and Luke–Acts as a whole, is placed in another category.

Narrative criticism of the Gospels frequently distinguishes between a Gospel as story (the basic events and characters that provide the content of a narrative) and as discourse (the particular perspective from which this story is told and the rhetorical means of expressing that perspective). As Seymour Chatman writes, "The story is the *what* in a narrative . . . discourse the *how*."[26] This distinction calls attention to a narrative's discourse. We are encouraged to recognize that a narrative is always being told from some perspective and that particular techniques are being used to shape it to that perspective. In other words, the distinction encourages us to consider a narrative's rhetoric.

Studying how a story is told calls attention to the voice telling the story, the voice of the narrator. The Gospel narrators seldom speak in the first person, choosing to efface themselves in order to focus

---

23. See, e.g., David E. Aune, *The New Testament in Its Literary Environment* (Philadelphia: Westminster, 1987) 17-67. The following paragraph is also based on Aune's work.

24. Adela Yarbro Collins, *The Beginning of the Gospel: Probings of Mark in Context* (Minneapolis: Fortress, 1992) 1-38.

25. Aune, *The New Testament*, 30.

26. Seymour Chatman, *Story and Discourse: Narrative Structure in Fiction and Film* (Ithaca, N.Y.: Cornell University Press, 1978) 19.

attention on their story. Yet the narrator of a Gospel is the voice through which a particular set of interests, norms, and values is presented.

The interpretive role of the narrator is most obvious when the narrator provides explanations in narrative "asides" and gives "inside views" of the characters. The narrator assumes the privilege of interpreting the inner working of human hearts and making judgments about them, as when the narrator of Mark, following the disciples' encounter with Jesus walking on the sea, states that the disciples' "hearts were hardened" (6:52). An interpretive perspective shapes the narrative in many other ways. Someone has decided which character is most important, deserving to be put in the center of the narrative. Furthermore, certain characters are presented as trustworthy and insightful. They are "reliable characters" in the sense that they become spokespersons for the perspective that is being expressed by the writing as a whole. In the Gospels, of course, Jesus is not only given central importance but also functions as the most reliable character. The underlying perspective of the narrative need not be fully and directly expressed by the narrator because it can be conveyed through Jesus' words and actions. Jesus can provide commentary on the narrative, including norms for judging persons and events, through his parables, for instance.[27]

The small narrative units discussed above are placed in a sequence in the Gospels. As a result, one scene influences our understanding of another. One factor in this process is the "primacy effect," which suggests that material placed early in the narrative takes on special importance.[28] We need to orient ourselves at the beginning of a narrative. The perspective established there will continue to influence our understanding of characters until we are told something that indicates a change in them or requires us to change our opinion of them. This observation should help us to recognize the importance of the promise and commission epiphanies (annunciation scenes) in the birth narratives of Matthew and Luke. They serve to connect Jesus to the purpose of God, provide initial statements of that

purpose, and disclose the commission from God that Jesus must fulfill. The narrative that follows is to be interpreted in the light of these initial disclosures. We are guided in interpreting Jesus' ministry not only by the birth narratives in Matthew and Luke but also by such key scenes as Jesus' announcement in the Nazareth synagogue (Luke 4:16-19). We should expect complications to develop, for the beginning of a narrative will not disclose everything. In the Gospels, Jesus encounters hardened hearts and deaf ears, not only in other religious leaders but also in his own disciples. Such conflict adds suspense to the narrative and raises the question of how Jesus' commission can still be fulfilled. The conflict leads to a crisis in the passion story. In this and other ways individual units of tradition become part of a developing plot that moves through conflict to a crisis and its results.

Thus the order of events in a Gospel is important. A Gospel's narrative rhetoric, however, also appears in variations of frequency and duration.[29] Repetition (an increase in frequency) and extended duration (a slowing of narration to give greater attention to a scene) indicate emphasis. When an event is emphasized in these ways, we must seek to understand how it is being understood and why it is important. Some types of repetition provide stability to the story by contributing, for instance, to characterization. If a person does something once, we may take note but reserve conclusions about the person. If the person does it twice or more, we conclude that it is characteristic of this person. Thus we are told twice that the disciples have failed to understand about the loaves (Mark 6:52; 8:17-21) in boat scenes following the two feedings of multitudes. This repetition suggests that the problem is not minor and temporary but arises from the basic character of the disciples.

The narrator may repeat the same type of event, as in the example above, or may repeatedly refer to a single event. We may be told about an event in advance (a preview), told about it as it happens, and then be reminded of it later (a review). In Luke, Jesus begins to announce his coming rejection and death in 9:22. The repeated previews lead up to the passion story itself. Then the messengers at the tomb and the risen Jesus remind his followers of his words and

---

27. See Mary Ann Tolbert, *Sowing the Gospel: Mark's World in Literary-Historical Perspective* (Minneapolis: Fortress, 1989) 148-59, 233-39. Mary Ann Tolbert has studied the implications of the parable of the sower (Mark 4:3-9, 14-20) and the parable of the wicked tenants (Mark 12:1-12) when understood as commentary on Mark's narrative as a whole.

28. On the primacy effect, see Menakhem Perry, "Literary Dynamics: How the Order of a Text Creates Its Meanings," *Poetics Today* 1 (1979) 53-58.

29. Gérard Genette discusses narrative time in terms of order, duration, and frequency. See his *Narrative Discourse: An Essay in Method* (Ithaca, N.Y.: Cornell University Press, 1980) 33-160.

their fulfillment because they have not been properly understood (24:6-7, 25-27, 44-46). The emphasis on this theme through repetition not only indicates its importance but also prods the reader to consider why Jesus' death was "necessary" (24:26) and how it fulfills Scripture (24:27, 44-46).

Although they have not been discussed in this article, it should be noted that the sayings of Jesus—and the extensive discourses that may be composed of these sayings—are part of the narrative. To speak is a narrative action, and what Jesus says may be studied for what it reveals about him, for the norms that it establishes in judging the behavior of others, and for its intended and actual effect on later events in the narrative.

Studying the Gospels as narratives (a literary approach) does not conflict with an interest in their historical and social settings. A narrative not only creates a narrative world, but it also depends on and comments on a preexisting social world. Our understanding of how a text functioned within a past social context can make an important difference in our view of that text's significance.

Scholars attempt to reconstruct the social contexts of the Gospel tradition, thereby providing additional contexts for the sayings and stories beyond the literary context of a Gospel. As a result, important issues may emerge. If, as Burton Mack has argued, some of the pronouncement stories arose from the disappointing experience of a group of Jesus' followers who had sought to bring synagogues to faith in Jesus, an early function of these stories may have been to justify the Christian side of a bitter conflict, reinforcing a negative stereotype of scribes and Pharisees in the process.[30] We should note the hypothetical character of such historical reconstructions and the fact that the Gospel traditions passed through several stages of use, during which their functions may have changed. Even at a particular time and place, a tradition may have had multiple functions. Nevertheless, such historical re-

constructions are valuable, not because they specify, once for all, the significance the material must have, but because they suggest ways in which the material might have been employed and help us consider whether it should be used in the same way today.

Telling the stories of Jesus did and will have a function within a social context, producing results that are good or evil. Retelling and interpreting these stories is an act for which we must take ethical and religious responsibility, with as much awareness of the consequences as possible. The Gospels reveal their original social contexts only in a general way. Through intense labor and some guesswork, scholars attempt to be more specific, with results that force us to think in new ways. Nevertheless, the fact that the Gospels themselves do not specify these social settings may, if we choose, be viewed as a gift. Thereby the Gospels free themselves, and the stories they contain, to function in various ways in different historical and social contexts. This is not to say that any narrative unit will fit any situation; rather, many texts have more possibilities of social significance than is commonly recognized. Furthermore, it is right to remember that in reading the Gospel narratives we are reading about another time and place. While we may affirm the continuing relevance of these words, a story about the past does not decide for us how it is relevant to the present. That involves ethical and religious decisions for which we must take responsibility.

BIBLIOGRAPHY

Bultmann, Rudolf. *The History of the Synoptic Tradition.* Rev. ed. New York: Harper & Row, 1976. Bultmann's discussion of the forms of synoptic tradition continues to be influential.

Rhoads, David, and Donald Michie. *Mark as Story: An Introduction to the Narrative of a Gospel.* Philadelphia: Fortress, 1982. An accessible guide to studying a whole Gospel as a narrative.

Robbins, Vernon K., comp. and ed. *Ancient Quotes and Anecdotes.* Sonoma: Polebridge, 1989. A large collection of pronouncement stories from the ancient Mediterranean world.

Scott, Bernard Brandon. *Hear Then the Parable: A Commentary on the Parables of Jesus.* Minneapolis: Fortress, 1989. The extensive introduction discusses the nature of parables.

Theissen, Gerd. *The Miracle Stories of the Early Christian Tradition.* Philadelphia: Fortress, 1983. A detailed study of miracle stories, including their motifs and types.

---

30. Mack, *Myth of Innocence,* 192-207.

JESUS AND THE GOSPELS

CHRISTOPHER M. TUCKETT

THE NATURE OF THE GOSPELS

The four books in the New Testament that now bear the title *Gospel* are clearly similar at one level. They all purport to give an account of events in the life of Jesus of Nazareth; further, they all give a detailed narrative of the course of events leading to his death by crucifixion, and they all conclude with some account of Jesus' tomb being found empty and/or Jesus appearing again alive after his death to some of his followers. As such, then, our Gospels are clearly different from, say, the book of Acts, which gives an account of the life of the later Christian community, and from the letters of the New Testament, which act as communications between individuals and various groups in the first-century Christian communities. By contrast, our Gospels appear to be, at least on the surface, "lives of Jesus"; hence, it has been assumed by many that they provide our primary source of information about the life of Jesus; indeed, they can and should be used in a relatively straightforward way to provide such information.

Such claims, however, need to be treated with some care. Few would doubt that our Gospels provide us with our primary sources of information about Jesus. On the other hand, we should not ignore contributions that other sources, both inside and outside the New Testament, may make in giving us knowledge about Jesus. Further, and perhaps more important, we must be aware that our Gospels do not provide us with information about Jesus in a straightforward way. Moreover, we should not forget that using the Gospels to provide information about Jesus is not the only way in which they may be read with profit today. The purpose of this article is to bring out some aspects of the many ways in which scholars today seek to come to grips with the phenomenon of "Jesus and the Gospels."

On almost any showing, our Gospels are highly unusual literary documents. We regularly label them as "Gospels," though even that name is strange in many ways; and the process that led to their having this name is by no means clear. Some have sought to establish that these writings were first called "Gospels" very early; however, "very early" in this context cannot be much before the end of the first century or the early part of the second century. It is unlikely that the evangelists themselves regarded their own literary works as "Gospels." Rather, in the first century, "gospel" was something proclaimed, heard, and believed (cf. Mark 1:14; 1 Cor 15:3); it was not something written or read. It was, moreover, unique; there was one and only one gospel (cf. Gal 1:6), which, for someone like Paul, was supremely concerned with the significance of the death and resurrection of Jesus but, as far as we can tell from Paul's few references, had little to do with the life and teaching of Jesus prior to his crucifixion. The use of the word *gospel* as the general term of a literary text describing the life of Jesus thus represents a very large semantic shift.

Further, it is clear now that our Gospels were not the only texts in early Christianity claiming to be "gospels." We now know of several texts that call themselves "gospels." Some of these texts are available to us, especially since the discovery of the Nag Hammadi library.[1] These include the *Gospel of Thomas,* the *Gospel of Philip,* the *Gospel of Truth,* and others. We know of the existence of other texts because they are quoted by early Christian writers, even though we do not ourselves have the full texts. For example, Jerome cites a passage from the *Gospel of the Hebrews,* giving an account of an appearance of the risen Jesus to James; yet we possess no copy of this gospel. One suspects that other texts were in existence about which we now know nothing. Eventually, of course, the church excluded these other gospels from its canon of Scripture and included only the four Gospels of Matthew, Mark, Luke, and John. We need not go into the details of canonization here, but the question of how far these non-canonical texts are important for giving us information about Jesus will be considered later. We should, however, note that many of these non-canonical gospels are rather different from our four canonical ones. The *Gospel of Thomas* is a string of over a hundred sayings of Jesus with virtually no narrative at all and certainly no account of Jesus' death or resurrection appearances. The *Gospel of Truth* is an extended meditation on aspects of God and the world with scarcely any mention of Jesus explicitly (though with a number of possible allusions to traditions of Jesus' sayings). Thus the assumption that a literary text called a "gospel" is a document giving a connected narrative of the life and death of Jesus is not justified by these other so-called gospels. Nevertheless, such an assumption does apply to the canonical Gospels, and these will be our primary focus.

Genre. If one does restrict attention to the canonical Gospels, then the question arises, What *kind* of documents are they? To what literary category, or "genre" (to use the technical term), do they belong?

The problem of classifying the genre of the Gospels has been much debated in critical scholarship

over the years. In one way it is easier to say what the Gospels are not: They are not letters; they are not plays; they are not (probably) apocalypses. In fact, the Gospels are in many ways *unlike* almost anything else in ancient literature. Thus for many years, the Gospels were said to be *sui generis*—i.e., of a genre peculiar to themselves—indeed, many today would still argue that this is the case.

As others have pointed out, however, such a claim is extremely odd in literary terms. Some understanding of the genre of a text is essential if the text is to be understood at all. We have to know that a text is a poem or a play or a detective story or an obituary if we are to be in any position to understand it. Indeed, a writer could scarcely write a text without some prior notion of the kind of writing he or she was attempting to produce. Hence the idea that a text is *sui generis* is, in literary terms, an extremely odd claim.

Therefore, in recent years there has been a number of attempts to place the Gospels within the context of other literary products of the ancient world, above all within the category of a "biography." It is recognized that the Gospels are not biographies in any modern sense of the word. Above all, there is nothing in them about Jesus' childhood and origins (at least in what is probably the earliest Gospel—namely, Mark; see below), nor about Jesus' psychological development (see below on form criticism and Jesus). Nevertheless, it is now becoming clear that such features did not always characterize ancient biography, which is now seen as a very broad literary category, so that it is possible that the NT Gospels could be placed within the wide parameters that accommodate ancient biographies. Such a procedure would resolve the problems, from a literary point of view, of asserting that the Gospels are *sui generis.* But the very breadth of the category of biography in turn means that simply calling a Gospel a "biography" does not necessarily help very much in interpreting the text.

The Gospels as Christian Texts. The unusual nature of the gospels—and their fascination—arises in part from the fact of their being written by people who were not neutral about the person they were describing and whose life they were purportedly reporting. The gospel writers were all "supporters" of Jesus; they were all Christians. Indeed, we have very little literature anywhere near contemporary

---

1. In 1945 a cache of thirteen ancient books (codices) written in Coptic was discovered just across the Nile River east of Nag Hammadi, Egypt. The codices, which date to the fourth century CE, reflect a combination of Christian and gnostic influences.

with Jesus from someone who was either neutral or hostile to Jesus.

Further, the gospel writers shared the belief, held throughout the Christian church, that the Jesus about whom they were writing had in some way or other triumphed over death. Hence, Jesus' death on the cross was not the end of his story; Jesus had been raised by God from death to a new form of life. Jesus was thus now alive again from the dead and, as such, was present in and with his community. Therefore, he continued to speak to and to guide the community in the period after his death on the cross. This guidance could be described in different ways by different people. Some could speak of Jesus' being directly with his people (cf. Matt 28:20); others could use the language of the "Holy Spirit's" directing and guiding the church (Luke; John); others, such as Paul, could speak of Christians' being "in Christ" in some sense. But there was a common belief that the presence and influence of Jesus was not confined to a period in the past and terminated by his crucifixion. Hence, any teaching ascribed to Jesus was not regarded as necessarily *only* that of a figure in the past, not perhaps even primarily that. Rather, it was above all the teaching of one who was now alive and guiding the Christian community as its Lord. Thus any sharp distinction that we might wish to make between a pre-Easter and a post-Easter situation would probably have been rather unreal for first-century Christians, including the gospel writers. For them, the teaching of Jesus was that of the person who had lived and taught and died in Palestine around 30 CE, but who was now alive and reigning at God's right hand, leading and guiding his followers in the present.

The net result was that Christians felt free to adapt and change the teaching of Jesus as it had come down in the tradition in order to apply it to their own situations. What was important about Jesus' teaching was that it was applicable in the present, not merely a relic from the past. Some traditions may have been preserved simply because they were from a revered past; but one assumes that the bulk of the tradition was preserved because it was believed to be relevant to the needs of the present. Certainly, we see this in the case of Paul, who occasionally refers to Jesus' teaching precisely because it is relevant to the situation he addresses. Thus in 1 Cor 7:10, he cites Jesus' teaching on divorce when discussing divorce in Corinth; in 1 Cor 9:14, Paul refers to Jesus' teaching on support for missionaries in his own discussion about the rights of apostles to receive financial backing. Moreover, Paul evidently felt quite free in relation to this teaching. For example, in the latter case he claims the right to be able to ignore Jesus' teaching in this respect (see 1 Cor 9:15). In part this may arise from Paul's own claim to be an apostle and hence to be in a peculiar position of authority; however, at least in Paul's eyes, the basis for his authority derives from his possession of the Holy Spirit (see 1 Cor 7:40), and this was common to all Christians.

This freedom to adapt the teachings of Jesus, no doubt conditioned above all by the church's resurrection belief that Jesus was still alive and speaking to his followers, leads to the peculiar problems our Gospels provide in relation to the issue of "Jesus and the Gospels." The precise extent to which this freedom was felt by early Christians is debated. However, the fact remains that, on any showing, the Gospels are not identical. They report incidents in the life (and death) of Jesus that do not agree. At times these reports appear to clearly refer to what is a single incident in the life of Jesus. Yet the fact that the reports differ indicates that someone somewhere has changed things to a certain extent. Thus the *differences,* or perhaps better the combination of similarities *and* differences, among the Gospels give rise to many of the problems faced by critical scholarship.

Differences Among the Gospels. Among the canonical Gospels, the most obvious differences exist between John's Gospel and the other three. Matthew, Mark, and Luke are in many respects very close to one another. They recount many similar incidents, often in the same order—indeed, they are so similar that it is both possible and often profitable to view them alongside one another in parallel and look at them together—i.e., "synoptically." (The Greek preposition *syn* means "with"; *optic* has to do with seeing and looking; hence, *synoptic* means looking at each Gospel with the others.) Hence, the designation of these three Gospels as the synoptic Gospels.

John's Gospel differs famously at many levels from the Synoptics. In terms of time and space, according to John, Jesus has a longer ministry (three years), spending much time in Jerusalem as well as Galilee; in the Synoptics his ministry appears to last for only one year, with Jesus spending only one final week in Jerusalem. Apparently similar stories appear differently: Jesus' action in the Temple, driving out those buying and selling, takes place very early in John (2:13-22), but a few days before Jesus' death in the Synoptics (Mark 11:15-19). Some important events are missing in John; for example, there is no institution of the Eucharist in John's account of the last supper. Conversely, other equally important events recorded in John are not mentioned in the Synoptics (e.g., the raising of Lazarus from the dead). So, too, the categories and methods used by Jesus in his teaching differ. In the Synoptics, Jesus teaches mostly in small units, focusing on the kingdom of God, using parables extensively and saying little about himself directly; in John, Jesus teaches in long discourses, focusing on such themes as eternal life and, at times, speaking quite explicitly about his own identity (cf. the great "I am" sayings).

These differences have, of course, been noted for a long time. In the days prior to critical scholarship, attempts were made regularly to harmonize the different Gospel accounts. One way to do this was to argue that, if two different accounts appear in our Gospels, then they must reflect two different incidents in the life of Jesus. Hence, for example, the different accounts of Jesus' action in the Temple show that Jesus drove people out of the Temple twice; two different accounts of Jesus' teaching about the double love command (Mark 12:28-34; Luke 10:25-28) reflect two different events in Jesus' ministry. Jesus, like any good teacher, may have sought to get his message across by raising important aspects on more than one occasion. Other differences between John and the Synoptics might be explained by differences in the audience: Jesus chose to teach the crowds in ways other than the methods he used to speak to the disciples.

It is now widely recognized that such attempts at harmonization can solve the problems raised by differences among our Gospels only in a very superficial way. Doubling up incidents in the life of Jesus may solve things occasionally (Jesus may have discussed the importance of the double love command on more than one occasion), but in the end the process becomes absurd. Are we to believe that Jesus entered Jerusalem on a donkey three or four times in almost (but not quite) identical circumstances and each evangelist recorded a different occasion accurately? And such an idea becomes even more ludicrous with other events; we cannot really have two

last suppers (one with an "institution" of a eucharist, as in the Synoptics, and one without, as in John), let alone three separate last suppers with similar, but slightly different, forms of institution at each one with each accurately recorded in one of the three synoptic Gospels! Least of all can we have Jesus dying more than once! Much more plausible, then, is the view that these different accounts in our Gospels represent different reports of the *same* incident, and the differences may reveal something more about the way in which a tradition was told and used later.

As far as the problem of Jesus and the Gospels is concerned, it is widely agreed that our primary evidence for recovering information about Jesus' own life and teaching is to be found in the synoptic Gospels, rather than in John. This is not to deny that John may preserve valuable historical data at times, and some of that we shall consider later. But for the most part, the considerably developed presentation of John, with the greatly heightened christology, is thought to reflect primarily a remolding of the Jesus tradition by a later Christian writer. Such remolding undoubtedly reveals the work of a Christian writer of extraordinary depth and profundity. But it is primarily the evangelist's own grasp of the truth of the Christian claims about Jesus that we see reflected in the Fourth Gospel and not so much the teaching of the pre-Easter Jesus. For the latter, we must turn to the Synoptics.

When we do so, however, we rapidly discover that the phenomenon of disagreements is not confined to a comparison between John and the Synoptics. The synoptic Gospels themselves display a pattern of agreement and disagreement. I have already referred to the extraordinary measure of agreement among the Synoptics—so great, indeed, that they are called "Synoptic." Nevertheless, the Gospels also exhibit considerable disagreement. Some items I have already noted in passing or by implication; e.g., the different versions of the story of the double love command in Mark 12 and Luke 10, or the three similar, but different, versions of the institution of the eucharist by Jesus in Matthew 26, Mark 14, and Luke 22. Many of the differences among the Synoptics are minor; they involve small differences in wording and less difference in substance. Yet the smallness of the differences is significant precisely because it makes it correspondingly difficult to ascribe them to separate events in the life of Jesus. Jesus would then need to have been repeating himself in triplicate constantly!

The nature of the agreements among the Gospels raises the possibility that these agreements might be explained by the existence of common sources used by the evangelists. Much effort has been devoted to this area of gospel studies, which is usually known as source criticism.

SOURCE CRITICISM

The close relationship among the synoptic Gospels and the rather more distant relationship between John and the Synoptics makes it sensible to consider the synoptic Gospels separately in this context. We shall, therefore, consider first the problem of the sources and the relationships of the synoptic Gospels, a problem usually referred to as the "Synoptic Problem."

The Synoptic Problem. The agreements among the synoptic Gospels are so extensive that it is now widely believed that the three Gospels are in some kind of *literary* relationship with one another. It is sometimes argued that the agreements among these Gospels could be based on common dependence on oral tradition, or on underlying Aramaic traditions, but the close verbal agreement between the Greek texts of our present Gospels—an agreement that is at times almost verbatim (cf. Matt 3:7-10/Luke 3:7-9) and that goes far beyond what one would normally expect from common oral tradition—makes this unlikely. For example, in Mark 2:10, there is a grammatical break in the narrative, as Mark has Jesus turn from talking to the crowds to address the paralyzed man. Precisely the same switch occurs in exactly the same way at exactly the same point in Matthew and Luke in their parallel accounts. Agreements of this nature and this detail are scarcely what one would expect from common dependence on oral tradition alone. The evidence thus demands a literary relationship at the level of our Greek texts: Either one Gospel has been used by the writers of the others as a source, or the evangelists have had access to common sources.

The most widely accepted solution to the synoptic problem today is the so-called "two-source theory." This theory argues that the earliest synoptic Gospel is Mark and that it was used as a source for Matthew and Luke; this, then, accounts for the agreements among all three Gospels in the material they have in common. Matthew and Luke in addition share a further body of material that, in the two-source theory, is explained by both writers' having access to another source or body of source material that is no longer extant but is usually known as "Q."[2] Matthew and Luke also have access to material that is peculiar to each, and this is usually known as "M" and "L" material, respectively (whether M and L constitute separate "sources" is less clear).

There is not enough space here to discuss the synoptic problem in detail or to offer a full defense of the two-source theory. Some loose ends in the theory remain. For example, the precise nature and extent of Q remain unclear. Was Q a single document? Was it available to Matthew and Luke in precisely the same form? How far are M and L separate sources? There is also a potentially embarrassing number of places where Matthew and Luke must have changed Mark in identical ways (the so-called minor agreements), a fact that is rather surprising on the two-source theory if Matthew and Luke did not know each other. Thus the whole theory has been questioned by some. For example, a strongly held minority view today has sought to revive an older solution to the synoptic problem associated with the nineteenth-century scholar J. J. Griesbach, who argued that Matthew's Gospel came first; that Luke wrote second, using Matthew; and that Mark wrote last, using both Matthew and Luke as sources. Others have argued for different modifications of the two-source theory; for example, some accept the priority of Mark but question whether one needs a lost Q source to explain the Matthew-Luke agreements, arguing that the latter can be fully explained by Luke's direct dependence on Matthew. Still others have pleaded for more complex solutions to the problem, postulating a number of intervening stages in the growth of our Gospels with intermediate stages.

Full discussion of these issues can be found elsewhere. Certainly the contemporary debate has highlighted the weak and inconclusive nature of some of the arguments in the past that have been used to promote the two-source theory. This applies especially to some of the more "formal" arguments, referring to global patterns in the overall set of agreements and disagreements. For example, in arguing for Markan priority, some have appealed to

2. Q stands for *Quelle,* the German term for "source."

the fact that nearly all of Mark is paralleled in Matthew or Luke or both. Yet all this shows is that some literary relationship exists; it does not prove that the only possibility is that Mark's Gospel was the *source* of Matthew and Luke. Similarly, the much discussed appeal to the failure of Matthew and Luke ever (or hardly ever) to agree against Mark in order and wording does not prove that Matthew and Luke independently used Mark as a source; it only shows that Mark is some kind of a "middle term" between the other two in any pattern of relationships.

Probably the most important kind of arguments are based on concrete comparison of individual texts, asking which way the tradition is most likely to have developed. For example, the words of Peter's confession at the scene at Caesarea Philippi are recorded by Mark as "You are the Christ" (8:29 NIV) and by Matthew as "You are the Christ, the Son of the living God" (16:16 NIV). It seems more likely that Matthew has expanded Mark's shorter version in a way that is characteristic of Matthew by adding a reference to Jesus as Son of God, than that Mark has abbreviated Matthew's longer version. It would be entirely in keeping with Matthew's interests and christological concerns if Matthew has added a reference to Jesus as Son of God here. However, Matthew's reference to Jesus as Son of God would have been very congenial to Mark had he known it, since Mark too has a keen interest in Jesus as Son of God; hence it is less likely that Mark omitted the phrase if it had been in a source available to him at this point. Thus Markan priority seems to account for the development of the tradition here better than any theory that makes Mark dependent on Matthew.

In the case of the Q tradition, advocates of the two-source theory would claim that neither Matthew nor Luke consistently gives the earlier form of a tradition they share in common. Sometimes Matthew is more original, sometimes Luke. For example, Matthew is probably more original in his version of the woe about cleansing the inside and outside of cups, where Luke suddenly and extraneously brings in an exhortation to "give alms" (Matt 23:26; Luke 11:41). But Luke is probably more original in his version of the Beatitudes in having Jesus say that the "poor" and the "hungry" are blessed, rather than the "poor in spirit" and those "hungering after righteousness" as in Matthew (Matt 5:3, 6; Luke

6:20, 21). Such examples would have to be multiplied many times over to make a fully convincing case for any one theory, and the reader is referred elsewhere for such treatments (see the bibliography below).

Great stress is laid by some, especially supporters of the Griesbach hypothesis, on the value of patristic statements about the Gospels. It is true that these are often discounted by advocates of the two-source theory, and they certainly give little (if any) support to a theory of Markan priority, asserting almost uniformly that Matthew was the first Gospel to be written. However, it is uncertain how reliable this evidence is. Much of it is relatively late, and it all may go back to one early (i.e., 2nd cent.) statement of Papias. Further, the antiquity of this statement does not establish its reliability. Hence the majority of modern scholars would prefer to rely on the evidence of the Gospel materials themselves to establish the nature of the relationship among them.

Sources of John. The problem of the sources used by John is a more difficult one in some respects. Several scholars have argued that John is using source material, especially in the miracle stories. John may have had access to a so-called Signs Source ("sign" [σημεῖον *sēmeion*] is the word used regularly in John to refer to Jesus' miracles). In this respect, scholars refer to the numbering of the first two miracles in John as the "first sign" (John 2:11) and the "second sign" (John 4:54), and also the reference in 20:31 to the "many other signs which Jesus did." Some, too, have sought to distinguish between the viewpoint of the miracle stories themselves (where Jesus' miracles are seen as stupendous feats) and the rest of the Gospel (where what is crucial is faith in Jesus himself). Nevertheless, the theory has been criticized by some, and the issue is a very open one in contemporary Johannine scholarship.

There is also the problem of the relationship between John and the synoptic Gospels. Despite the differences between them, John does share a number of features with the Synoptics, including at times some striking verbal agreements (e.g., the common mention of a sum of 200 denarii in the story of the feeding of the 5,000 in Mark 6:37 and John 6:7). At one time it was thought that John was quite independent of the Synoptics, but in recent years there has been a strong revival of support for the view that John may have known and used one or more of the synoptic Gospels. If he did, he must have exercised considerably more freedom than say Matthew and Luke did with Mark. Furthermore, there is considerably more material in John that cannot have been derived from the Synoptics, so that any theory of John's dependence on the Synoptics may have only limited use.

Source Criticism and the Quest for the Historical Jesus. In relation to the problem of discovering information about Jesus, it should be clear that a solution to the synoptic problem may be an important step in the process. Given three parallel (but not identical) versions of a saying of Jesus in our synoptic Gospels, the likelihood is that these are not three independent witnesses; rather, they represent one tradition subsequently used by the other two Gospel writers. Thus the secondary versions do not tell us anything about Jesus: rather, the earliest version must be our primary source. Assuming the two-source theory, then, Mark's Gospel will normally give us a more accurate account of Jesus' teaching than either Matthew or Luke when all three are parallel. Thus when Mark 9:1 has Jesus predict that some persons standing by him will not taste death "until they see that the kingdom of God has come with power," and Matt 16:28 has "[until] they see the Son of Man coming in his kingdom," the two-source theory would suggest that Matthew's version is secondary to Mark's and so Jesus did not refer to the Son of Man at this point. Any theories about the (very complex) problem of what *Jesus* meant by the term *Son of Man* could not then use this verse in Matthew as part of the evidence.

Yet while Mark's Gospel may be more accurate than Matthew's and Luke's, we must beware of proceeding too far too fast and deducing too much from the evidence. It would be tempting to assume (as some have!) that since Mark and Q are the earliest sources, they should provide the primary evidence about Jesus. We cannot, however, assume that M and L material is ipso facto less useful in this respect. An M tradition may well be as early as a Markan (or Q) tradition. For example, the M tradition in Matt 16:17-19, where Jesus pronounces the famous blessing on Peter, may well be very ancient (even if it may not have originally belonged in its present context of Peter's confession). So, too, many of the best-known parables of Jesus appear in the L tradition of Luke—yet that does not of itself make them less valuable as sources for discovering Jesus' teaching.

Despite these caveats, it remains true that Mark and Q (on the two-source theory) still provide sources that are earlier than the present Gospels of Matthew and Luke. Nevertheless, we cannot simply assume that Mark and Q, although perhaps more reliable as sources of the life of Jesus than Matthew and Luke, are necessarily absolutely reliable. We cannot simply take Mark's Gospel, say, as an accurate transcript of the life of Jesus. On most conventional datings of the Gospels, Mark was probably written at some point in the decade 65–75 CE. (There is considerable debate about whether Mark was written before or after the fall of Jerusalem in 70 CE.) The date of Q is very uncertain, though most would probably date the "final" version of Q (if it is indeed appropriate to talk in such terms) not much earlier than the mid 50s.

Matthew and Luke are, of course, later still. Nearly all scholars would agree that verses such as Matt 22:7 and Luke 21:20 clearly presuppose the fall of Jerusalem in 70 CE. Hence, between the end of Jesus' life (c. 30 CE) and the writing of our Gospels there is a period of probably more than 35 years, and between the end of Jesus' life and Q there is a gap of 25 years or more. Further, it is now becoming more and more clear that the earliest Gospel sources, Mark and Q, are just as much influenced by post-Easter Christian ideas as are the later Gospel writings of Matthew and Luke. The process of changing and adapting the Gospel traditions about Jesus in the light of subsequent events is not confined to Matthew and Luke. W. Wrede's work on secrecy in Mark's Gospel in 1901 has made scholars aware of this in relation to Mark; and recent studies of Q have shown how much Q has its own characteristic and distinctive features in handing on traditions about Jesus. Thus in order to discover reliable information about Jesus, we must try to reach back behind the Gospel accounts to try to bridge the gap of a generation or more over a period when the Gospel tradition was probably being handed on primarily in oral form. This attempt is usually known in scholarly circles as form criticism.

FORM CRITICISM

Forms and Setting. Form criticism (the standard English "translation" of the German word *Formgeschichte*) has many aspects. Its name (*form* criticism) derives in part from one aspect of its activity that seeks to identify the common "forms" of individual units of the tradition. One of the basic assumptions of much contemporary Gospel study is that the individual stories (pericopes) of the tradition are the basic units; the evangelists worked as editors to put these individual stories into a connected sequence. Hence, in order to reach back behind the evangelists, one needs to look at the individual units. Further, several of these units seem to display a common structural pattern, or form, in the way the stories are told. Moreover, it was believed that, on the basis of such common forms, one might be able to deduce the kind of situation, or setting, in which stories were told in such a way. It was assumed that similar settings would give rise to stories being told in similar ways or forms. In turn, given common forms, one might be able to deduce the settings in which such stories circulated. (The technical phrase used for such a setting is the German *Sitz im Leben.*)

Early New Testament form critics devoted considerable time and effort to such classification of the units of the gospel tradition. There was by no means universal agreement, either in the categories or forms identified, or in the proposed *Sitz im Leben* for each form. Some (such as Dibelius) thought of quite broad categories with a correspondingly general *Sitz im Leben.* Others (such as Bultmann) attempted far greater precision in the proposed forms, with many different categories and hence a correspondingly more precise proposal for the *Sitz im Leben* of each category. So, too, the way in which a *Sitz im Leben* was assigned to each form varied. Dibelius thought in general terms, with somewhat preconceived ideas about what such settings might be (e.g., preaching, teaching, the cult). Bultmann was far more specific, very often deducing the setting from the story itself; for example, controversy stories about debates between Jesus and the Jewish authorities were seen as reflecting similar debates between Christians and their contemporaries. Both approaches are open to criticism. The detailed suggestions of Bultmann are in danger of producing rather circular arguments: Do we know that Christians were involved in debates of the same nature as Jesus, apart from the Gospel evidence? The more general approach of Dibelius is open to the charge of producing rather preconceived ideas of what the activity of the early church was, as well as being very general. (Was preaching central to the life of the early church? What did preaching consti-

tute?) Further, the whole approach may be questioned if it is assumed that a single form could arise from one and only one setting. One *Sitz im Leben* may have given rise to a variety of forms. Conversely, one story in a single form may have been used in a variety of settings. Hence the attempt to correlate form and setting in a neat one-to-one relationship may not be satisfactory.

This is, however, not the only or the most significant aspect of form criticism. Form criticism, at least as practiced by German scholars, has always been regarded as a more wide-ranging exercise. In part this is reflected in the German word for the discipline: *Formgeschichte. Geschichte* is one of the German words for "history," and so *Formgeschichte* has been seen as including not only the analysis of the "forms" of the units of the tradition, but also an attempt to analyze their history.

Tradition History/Criticism. This aspect of form criticism tries to determine how the tradition developed in time and also to say something about its ultimate origin. The concern is thus with the tradition-history of the material, and this whole approach is sometimes referred to as "tradition criticism." In this respect, form criticism has often had rather bad press in some quarters, since many form critics are regarded as having been extremely skeptical about the historicity of much of the tradition. For some this is regarded as straying outside the proper boundaries of form criticism, since questions of form and *Sitz im Leben,* on the one hand, and historical reliability or authenticity, on the other, are separate.

On the one hand, this distinction is valid, and certainly the two aspects should not be confused. To assign a particular *Sitz im Leben* to a tradition—i.e., to make suggestions about where or how a tradition was handed on within the life of the early church, is quite separate from the question of its historical authenticity. To claim that Gospel stories of Jesus' debating sabbath observance with the Pharisees reflect early church debates about whether Christians should observe sabbath is really quite independent of whether these stories are authentic. Christians could have invented them to justify their own behavior; equally, the stories could reflect real conflicts in which Jesus was involved with the same issues continuing into the post-Easter situation.

On the other hand, to raise the question of authenticity is not in itself illegitimate, and it is not an illegitimate part of form criticism if the latter is understood as *Formgeschichte.* How skeptical some of the form critics actually were is another matter. Whatever the results proposed, the questions posed by form critics are valid and indeed vital for anyone concerned with the phenomenon of Jesus and the Gospels.

Authenticity. The validity of raising questions of authenticity would be denied by few scholars today. Very few would claim that every tradition about Jesus in all the Gospels is as it stands an authentic transcript of an event in the life of Jesus. We have already seen this in relation to parallel accounts in the Gospels themselves. Parallel, but not identical, versions in two or more Gospels do not represent accurate reports of multiple events in the life of Jesus but rather, in part at least, later Christian adaptations of earlier traditions.

Moreover, the process is unlikely to have started only when Matthew and Luke used Mark (and Q). Within Mark's Gospel itself, some traditions probably reflect later Christian adaptations of earlier traditions. A classic example is to be found in Mark 2:18-22 (esp. v. 20). Jesus is asked about the legitimacy of fasting (v. 18) and replies in vv. 19*a* and 21-22 in terms that appear to suggest that fasting is quite inappropriate in the new situation of the present, which is in radical discontinuity with the past; a new situation has arisen comparable to a wedding where one does not fast (v. 19); and the new and old situations seem to be quite separate (cf. the imagery of the patch and the garment and wine and wineskins in vv. 21-22). But v. 20 introduces a quite different note: The period of non-fasting will be only temporary, for the time will come when the bridegroom will be taken away from them and fasting will be reintroduced. Verse 20 seems somewhat out of place in the context and looks very much like a later Christian attempt to adapt the teaching of Jesus in the light of Christian practice of fasting again.

In other instances in Mark's Gospel too it seems most likely that a Christian (Mark or a pre-Markan editor) has rewritten and adapted the tradition in the light of subsequent events. For example, the very detailed passion prediction in Mark 10:32-33, which corresponds so precisely to the events of Jesus' passion (a Jewish trial with a death sentence followed by a Gentile trial and mockings, spitting, and scourging) is implausible on the lips of Jesus in quite such detail. (If Jesus had really predicted everything in such detail, why were the disciples apparently so overwhelmed with surprise when it all happened?) More plausibly, a Christian has written up the prediction in the light of subsequent events, though perhaps adopting a more general prediction of coming suffering and death (as, e.g., in Mark 9:31) that came from Jesus himself.

In both these instances, we may have examples of Christians taking up authentic sayings of Jesus and adapting and expanding them in the light of later events. How far Christians actually *created* sayings of Jesus *de novo* is hard to say (though any distinction between "adapting" and "creating" is at best a thin one). Few NT scholars would deny that it never happened. For example, the saying in Matt 18:20 ("where two or three are gathered in my name, I am there among them" [NRSV]) presupposes an ongoing presence of Jesus in the post-Easter community, together with a position ascribed to Jesus comparable to that of the Shekinah of God (cf. the well-known Jewish parallel in *m.'Abot* 3:2, which talks of God's Shekinah being present whenever two or three meet to study the Law). Both factors make it hard to ascribe the saying to Jesus himself in the pre-Easter situation. It is, therefore, probably a "creation" of the early church. Similarly, the saying three verses earlier in Matt 18:17 ("if the offender refuses to listen even to the church, let such a one be to you as a Gentile and a tax collector" [NRSV]) puts on the lips of Jesus a command for exclusion from the community, which seems incompatible with Jesus' general openness to all; it also uses terms presupposing that "Gentiles" and "tax collectors" are archetypes of people beyond the pale, which again hardly squares with Jesus' well-attested openness and welcome to tax collectors. (Jesus' attitude toward Gentiles is more difficult to assess, though it is hard to see his attitude as anything other than, at least in principle, one of equal openness.) Thus the saying in Matt 18:17 is hard to credit to the historical Jesus. Hence at times it is clear that sayings that are not authentic have been attributed to Jesus by later Christians.

Criteria of Authenticity. How, then, can we distinguish authentic from inauthentic sayings? A number of possible criteria have been proposed, and these have been discussed extensively. In part, the whole exercise depends on one's starting point and where one thinks any "burden of proof" lies. Is a tradition to be assumed authentic until it is shown to be otherwise? Or is a tradition to be assumed a Christian creation until it is shown to be authentic? For many more "skeptical" critics (i.e., those who would answer yes to the second question), a very important criterion is that known as the "criterion of dissimilarity." This argues that a tradition about Jesus is authentic if it shows Jesus to be dissimilar to both Judaism and the early church. This criterion is perhaps the one that has aroused the fiercest and most intensive debate. Few would deny that, insofar as it allows anything through its net, this criterion does establish authentic Jesus traditions; traditions not derived from Judaism, and not creations of the early church, are as likely as anything to be genuine sayings of Jesus.

However, the criterion has been heavily criticized. It is in danger of producing a very distorted picture of Jesus. (Was Jesus always "dissimilar" to the early church? Or to Judaism?) It also presupposes that our knowledge of both "Judaism" and "the early church" is sufficiently comprehensive for us to be able to determine what is "dissimilar" to either entity; and it is now quite clear how fragmentary our knowledge of both Judaism and early Christianity really is. Hence, on its own this criterion cannot be the only one used.

Other criteria will be dealt with only briefly here, and the reader is referred to fuller discussions elsewhere. Criteria have been proposed appealing to "coherence"; what coheres with material established as authentic by other means could be accepted. But good fiction is "coherent" as well! Some scholars appeal extensively to Aramaic idioms, or to Semitic or Palestinian presuppositions, in individual traditions as indicating authentic material. For example, the use of the passive voice in the Beatitudes probably reflects a Semitic "divine passive," avoiding mentioning God. Other sayings are constructed in parallelism, perhaps reflecting a Semitic idiom. Elements of the parables presuppose social structures that place the tradition firmly within Palestinian society. All this has value. However, the problem with all such arguments is that, while such considerations may show that a tradition reflects the Aramaic language and/or a Palestinian environment, Jesus was not the only person to live in Palestine and speak Aramaic! Thus the fact that a tradition reflects a Semitic milieu may only show that the tradition is to be traced back to an Aramaic-speaking, or Palestinian, community.

Some, too, have appealed to a criterion of "multiple attestation," claiming that a tradition attested in more than one of the major strands of the Gospels (Mark, Q, M, L) or in several different forms may be authentic. Again this has value, but the criterion is less useful in practice since so few of the individual traditions are multiply attested. Nevertheless, such a criterion does have value in relation to general themes of the tradition.

It is probably fair to say that none of the criteria proposed is foolproof. None should probably be considered in isolation. Very often, too, they point in different directions. For example, Jesus' use of the double love command is not dissimilar to Judaism (it is drawn from Jewish Scripture!) nor to the early church (cf. Rom 13:9); yet it is quite consistent and coherent with his radical openness to all members of his society and his apparent disregard for other parts of the Jewish law in the interest of love. Hence it could be authentic. Each tradition has to be considered on its merits, with a judicious and careful assessment of all the factors and criteria involved. A radical skepticism about the historicity of the tradition is probably out of place. Few would argue that nothing of the historical Jesus is preserved in the Gospels. Several facets of Jesus' teaching in broad terms are in some respects unlike Jewish teaching of the time and also are not carried forward in early church teaching (e.g., preaching about the kingdom of God). Conversely, many facets of the life of the early church are *not* read back into the Gospels: The widespread confession of Jesus as "Lord" is rare in the earliest gospel traditions; the debates about circumcision, which were so pressing in the Judaizing disputes in Pauline communities, are not reflected in the Gospels at all; language about Christians' possessing the Holy Spirit is also rare in the gospel tradition. Hence a radical skepticism about the authenticity of the tradition as a whole is probably out of place. Nevertheless, one cannot deny that some degree of Christian adaptation of Jesus traditions has taken place in the Gospels, and so the question of authenticity is a very real one.

Form Criticism and the Quest for the Historical Jesus. Where do the results of form criticism leave us in any search for the historical Jesus? The basic presupposition of form criticism—that the individual pericopes are the basic building blocks of the tradition, and the activity of putting them into a connected narrative is due to a later editor—means that the detailed ordering of the material in the Gospels cannot tell us anything about the chronology of the life of Jesus. The evidence is simply not available to us to reconstruct an exact sequence of events. Hence we cannot distinguish stories that belong to an early part of Jesus' ministry from those stemming from a later part, and we cannot trace any chronological development in the life of Jesus. Thus older-style "lives of Jesus" (very prevalent in the 19th cent.) written on this basis are simply non-starters in the light of form criticism. (One exception may be provided by the passion narrative where in any case an ordered chronological sequence is in part demanded by the nature of the events concerned; the sequence arrest-trial-death-resurrection appearances could not occur sensibly in any other order!)

Nevertheless, most scholars today would agree that a total skepticism about recovering information about Jesus would be far too one-sided. Even if we cannot put the events of the ministry of Jesus into a connected series, there are still a number of general themes that one can with confidence trace back to Jesus' own ministry. These would include Jesus' preaching about the kingdom of God; his use of parables in his teaching; his openness to the outcasts of religious society, including tax collectors and "sinners"; his arguments with Jewish leaders, including probably the Pharisees; and perhaps his use of the term *Son of Man* (although this is a much-debated issue). In the case of any one individual tradition, there will be doubts and arguments about its authenticity. But few would deny that in broad terms, important facets of the life and ministry of Jesus are available to us through critical use of the NT synoptic Gospels.

NON-SYNOPTIC EVIDENCE FOR JESUS

So far I have considered primarily the synoptic Gospels in discussing the problem of seeking to recover reliable information about the pre-Easter ministry of Jesus. What of other possible sources?

John. One obvious candidate to consider here is the Fourth Gospel. As we saw earlier, most scholars today would regard the Fourth Gospel as primarily evidence of the beliefs and thought of the evangelist we call John and not very easily usable for giving us

information about the historical Jesus. This assessment is, of course, a large generalization. Many have argued that John does preserve elements of tradition that may be historical. These vary in nature. They include features such as the fact that Jesus may have had a ministry longer than the single year implied by the Synoptics, and that he worked in Jerusalem for more than one final hectic week; moreover, it is possible that Jesus may have worked alongside John the Baptist, perhaps even baptizing people (John 4:1). John's dating of the last supper and the crucifixion as all taking place on the eve of Passover (rather than Passover itself, as implied by the Synoptics) has had its defenders. So, too, some sayings embedded in the Fourth Gospel may be authentic sayings of Jesus, albeit now elaborated and developed by the evangelist in the discourses in which they are placed: for example, the saying in John 5:19 ("the Son can do nothing on his own, but only what he sees the Father doing" [NRSV]) may reflect an earlier, perhaps less christologically developed, parabolic saying of Jesus himself about ordinary sons learning from their fathers.

Despite all these possibilities, however, it is questionable how much independent value John provides in giving information about Jesus. The question of chronology may be important (though, as we saw above, scholars today would not wish in the light of form criticism to place much weight on any synoptic chronology; and, in any case, many of John's chronological time references may be heavily theologically charged and influenced). Further, the value of possibly authentic sayings of Jesus being preserved in John is unlikely to enhance our actual knowledge of Jesus himself very significantly. Those who argue for the possibility of such traditions in John usually do so because the saying in John is similar to the sayings tradition in the Synoptics. Sayings in John that offer a radically different presentation of Jesus from the synoptic picture are, precisely because they are so different, rejected as being inauthentic. Hence the result of such research will inevitably produce merely a few more sayings that basically support the picture of Jesus already established from the Synoptics. Thus the overall picture obtained is unlikely to be significantly altered by the addition of a few Johannine sayings. A synoptic Jesus, with a few synoptic-like sayings from John added, will still be a synoptic Jesus! Certainly there may be elements in John that do significantly change our picture of Jesus, or perhaps fill what would otherwise be puzzling gaps. (For example, the possibility that Jesus worked alongside John the Baptist, perhaps baptizing as well, might explain better the extraordinarily privileged position given to John the Baptist in the Synoptics, and also explain why a water baptism rite was adopted in the early Christian church, apparently without any discussion at all.) Overall the evidence provided by John is unlikely to alter our picture of Jesus from the Synoptics significantly. Generally the Fourth Gospel gives us primary insight into the beliefs of the great Christian writer behind it, rather than direct information about Jesus himself.

Paul. For other sources of information about Jesus, one should not forget the letters of Paul in the New Testament. Paul rarely cites the teaching of Jesus but does so occasionally, notably in 1 Corinthians 7, 9, 11 on divorce, financial support, and the Eucharist respectively. There is also possibly an appeal to the teaching of Jesus in the "word of the Lord," cited in 1 Thess 4:15 (though it is not entirely clear that Paul is referring here to a saying that he knows as that of the pre-Easter Jesus). Other possible allusions to Jesus traditions occur elsewhere in Paul, although there is no explicit reference to Jesus (e.g., Rom 12:14: "Bless those who persecute you; bless and do not curse them" [NRSV]; cf. Matt 5:44; Luke 6:28). The amount of data is very limited. Nevertheless, its date should not be forgotten. Paul wrote his letters in the mid-50s, whereas the Gospels all date from at least 10 to 15 years later. Paul is thus our earliest witness to Jesus. Thus in seeking to find Jesus' original teaching on, say, the issue of divorce, we should not confine attention to the sayings in the Gospels (Mark 10:11-12 and par.) but must take seriously the evidence of 1 Cor 7:10-11 as well. And the somewhat freer attitude reflected in the latter (e.g., in v. 11*a*, especially if this is to be regarded as part of the quotation Paul is actually citing here and not, as it is often taken, Paul's own comment) may then throw a different slant on Jesus' attitude to divorce. However, as already noted, the extent of the data we can extract from Paul is very limited, since Paul (for whatever reason) cites the teaching of Jesus so rarely.

Non-Canonical Evidence. The question of the value of other evidence for Jesus is much disputed today. As I noted earlier, several other documents calling themselves Gospels purport to give information about Jesus. None of these, of course, is now part of our New Testament. That does not of itself necessarily negate their value in possibly providing information about Jesus. Thus the question needs to be asked: Can our knowledge of Jesus be extended by these writings?

For the most part, the majority view is that these non-canonical texts are not very useful for providing information about Jesus. For the historian of early Christianity, they are of immense interest in letting us see how later writers responded to the events of Jesus' life and how traditions about Jesus developed. But for the most part these gospels are probably to be dated much later than our canonical texts and are not of great historical value in preserving reliable traditions about Jesus. This cannot, however, be taken as a cast-iron rule. In particular, one or two of the non-canonical gospels may be early, or if not themselves early, may preserve very primitive traditions. For example, the *Gospel of Peter* exists in fragmentary form, the extant text giving us an account of the passion of Jesus. Some have argued that this gospel may preserve a very primitive early account of the passion (even if in its present form the *Gospel of Peter* is relatively late). Others would argue that the entire gospel is late and simply represents a legendary rewriting of the passion narratives of all our present canonical Gospels.

The one non-canonical text in which the issue of possibile authentic Jesus traditions is most keenly debated today is the *Gospel of Thomas.* This gospel, known in fragments for the last one hundred years, is now available to us in full in Coptic as one of the texts discovered in 1945 in the Nag Hammadi library. This "gospel," as already noted, does not conform to the genre of the canonical Gospels: It contains no narrative, no account of the passion or resurrection, but simply has a list of over one hundred sayings of Jesus loosely strung together and introduced by the very brief note "Jesus said. . . ." Some of the sayings are very similar to sayings preserved in the synoptic Gospels; others are very different. Ever since its discovery, there has been much debate about whether the sayings in *Thomas* represent a line of tradition independent of the Synoptics and so provide an independent source for the teaching of Jesus, or whether *Thomas* depends on our Gospels and thus is primarily a witness to the development of the synoptic tradition after the time of the writing of the canonical Gospels. There is no scholarly unanimity at present, and very different views are held. For some, the fact that *Thomas* presents its synoptic-like sayings in an order that seems to bear no correlation at all to the order in which these sayings come in our synoptic Gospels suggests strongly that *Thomas* is independent of our Gospels. Moreover, many would claim that the synoptic-like sayings in *Thomas* show none of the redactional features (i.e., elements attributed to the final editor of the Gospels) that the parallels in the synoptic Gospels have. Hence the sayings in *Thomas* go back to a stage at least as early as, if not earlier than, our present Gospels. Other scholars have argued that the *Gospel of Thomas* does show some features that are redactional in the canonical Gospels and, hence, presupposes the synoptic Gospels in their finished form, so that *Thomas* is post-synoptic and primarily a witness to the post-synoptic development of the tradition. It is probably fair to say that the issue of *Thomas* and the synoptics is hotly debated with scholarly opinion evenly divided on the matter.

Yet, as with the Fourth Gospel, it is uncertain how far the evidence of *Thomas* will radically alter our picture of Jesus. Almost all students of *Thomas* would agree that not *all* the sayings in that document can be traced back to Jesus. Some of the sayings reflect secondary expansions of the Jesus tradition in a quasi-"gnostic" direction. (The question of whether the *Gospel of Thomas* itself is gnostic is hotly debated, but few would deny that, at least in its present form, it reflects tendencies that are on the road to later Gnosticism.) As with John, the criterion often implicitly used to distinguish early from late sayings in *Thomas* is related to their similarity to the synoptic picture; synoptic-like sayings are more likely to be early than others. Thus the picture of Jesus that emerges is likely simply to reinforce the synoptic picture already available. It is true that some details may change; indeed, the fact that *Thomas* at times offers versions of sayings that are closely parallel to synoptic traditions may then provide us with extremely valuable information in assessing the detailed wording of individual traditions (*if*, of course, *Thomas* is judged to be independent of the synoptics). But the very similarity between these sayings implies that the overall portrait of Jesus emerging from *Thomas* will probably simply reinforce the synoptic picture rather than radically change it.

It thus appears likely that our primary source of evidence for information about the historical Jesus remains the synoptic Gospels. Other sources may provide some ancillary evidence and important snippets of information regarding details, but the prime source remains the synoptic tradition.

REDACTION CRITICISM

So far I have considered the subject of Jesus and the Gospels with the question of the historical Jesus very much to the fore, looking at the ways in which the Gospels (and other evidence) can be used to provide information about Jesus. However, this is not the only purpose for which the Gospels may be used. As with any historical text, a gospel can tell us just as much (sometimes more) about the person who has written it as about the events purportedly being described. We have seen this already in passing in relation to form criticism and in relation to the Fourth Gospel. Form criticism (in part) seeks to discover something about the early Christian groups who preserved and handed on the individual stories in the Gospels. And critical study of the Fourth Gospel is aimed primarily at discovering something about the thought and situation of the evangelist. Such an approach, which has dominated study of the Fourth Gospel ever since the rise of critical scholarship, is now being increasingly applied to the synoptic Gospels. This branch of study is usually known as "redaction criticism."

Redaction criticism as a self-conscious discipline applied to the synoptic Gospels was first developed after the last World War in the works of such scholars as G. Bornkamm on Matthew and H. Conzelmann on Luke. Earlier form critics had held a rather "low" view of the synoptic evangelists themselves. Attention had been focused on the earlier stages in the development of the tradition, and the evangelists themselves were seen as simply collectors, "scissors-and-paste" editors, putting the units of the tradition together in a relatively unstructured way. Such a view of the evangelists' work has changed in more recent study, and the evangelists are now seen as much more purposeful agents in their use of the traditions available to them. Hence the focus of attention has been much more on what the Gospels may tell us about the evangelists themselves, the communities for which they were writing, the situations and conflicts they were engaged in, etc., quite as much as anything to do with the history they are describing.

In the early days of such study, attention was focused primarily on the changes that one evangelist had made to the tradition. In the case of Matthew and Luke, the situation was (in part) relatively straightforward. On the assumption of Markan priority, one of the sources used by Matthew and Luke is directly available to us: the Gospel of Mark. Hence it is possible to look at Matthew and Luke alongside Mark and identify the ways in which the secondary evangelist has changed Mark. (The technical word for this changing is *redacting,* hence the name "redaction criticism.") Thus, for example, by looking at the ways in which Matthew has introduced a number of changes into Mark's story of the stilling of the storm, G. Bornkamm was able to show how Matthew has introduced some distinctive, characteristic ideas into the story; the account of the disciples in a boat during a storm becomes an account of Christians in the church facing turbulent times in their own day.

Such a procedure is relatively easy with Matthew and Luke using Mark, simply because Mark is directly available to us. In the case of the Q tradition, the procedure is more complex, since Q is not extant and hence the reconstruction of the Q tradition and the consequent identification of changes made by Matthew/Luke to Q is a rather more delicate operation. Nevertheless, it is not impossible. For example, it seems likely that the Q version of the Beatitudes pronounced Jesus' blessing on the "poor" and the "hungry" (Luke 6:20-21). Matthew has probably "spiritualized" these by changing the "poor" to "poor in spirit" and the "hungry" to those "hungering after righteousness" (Matt 5:3, 6). Certainly the last change reveals Matthew's own concern for "righteousness," which is a key concept in Matthew's Gospel and one that he is very keen to promote. Thus a redaction-critical approach shows us something of the evangelists' own ideas and the issues they wished to highlight and to emphasize for their communities.

Redaction criticism in general terms, in the sense of seeking to discover the concerns of the authors of the Gospel texts, has come to dominate modern gospel studies. Yet one should also note that within the broad rubric of redaction criticism, the method of approach has changed somewhat over the years. In the early days, attention was focused very much on the actual changes made by a Gospel writer to the source used. (Hence the name *redaction* criticism.) Places where the tradition was left unaltered tended to be ignored. Such an approach, however, is in danger of giving a rather lopsided, or skewed, impression of an evangelist's concerns. It may well be that there were times when an evangelist agreed strongly with a tradition and so preserved it unaltered. Indeed, the very fact that a tradition has been preserved and repeated by a later writer implies a strong measure of agreement on the part of the latter. (If a writer disapproves of a tradition, there is always the option of simply leaving it out—an option sometimes exercised by Matthew and Luke [cf. Mark 7:31-37 and 8:22-26, which are not present in the later Gospels.]) Hence, if redaction criticism is aimed primarily at rediscovering something of the characteristic ideas and concerns of an evangelist, one must take seriously the *whole* of the evangelist's work, the whole Gospel, and not merely focus on redactional changes made by a gospel writer to an earlier source.

Thus in recent years there has been a trend to move away from an exclusive, narrow focus on the changes, or emendations, made by an evangelist (sometimes called "emendation criticism") and to look quite as much at the Gospel as a whole, as a unified literary work, to see what that may tell us about an evangelist. Thus as well as looking at detailed changes in wording made by an author to the tradition, one may wish to look at the way in which the whole narrative is now structured and the way in which different parts of the narrative relate to other parts. Such an approach has been variously called "composition criticism" or "literary criticism" or "narrative criticism" (though each of these probably represents different nuances and approaches).

Thus, for example, as well as looking at detailed changes in wording by Matthew on his sources (e.g., adding a reference to "righteousness" in Matt 5:6), one can take seriously the way in which Matthew appears to have structured and arranged the material into five great "blocks," starting with the Sermon on the Mount in Matthew 5–7 and ending with the eschatological teaching in chaps. 24–25. The precise significance of such an arrangement is much disputed. (Are the five blocks meant to correspond in some way to the five books of the Torah?) But at the very least, the arrangement highlights the importance of Jesus' teaching for Matthew and shows Matthew's concern (evidenced elsewhere, cf. Matt 28:19-20) to stress the abiding validity of Jesus' teaching for the post-Easter Christian community, a concern that makes Matthew different from, say, Paul (who very rarely cites Jesus' actual teaching) and perhaps even Mark (for whom the question of *who* Jesus is may be more important than *what* Jesus actually teaches).

In recent years, some scholars have gone even further along these lines and have adopted an even more rigorously "literary" approach, bracketing off the question of sources and redactional changes completely. On this view, the text of one Gospel is to be taken as the author's own work in its entirety and is to be analyzed on its own, independently of the history of its traditions. The problem of the extent to which the history of the tradition is relevant to the interpretation of a Gospel is much disputed. Most scholars today would probably take a middle path and not want to bracket off an older type of emendation criticism completely. But the more recent literary approaches have convinced everyone of their intrinsic value. Moreover, in the case of the Gospels of Mark and John, where the identification of possible prior sources used by the evangelists is much more difficult (simply because there is no independent attestation for such sources), a more "unitary" approach, taking the Gospel text as a whole, is to a certain extent essential in the light of the available evidence. Thus in order to discover something about one evangelist, one must take the whole of the Gospel into account (and, of course, in the case of Luke, the book of Acts as well).

CONCLUDING REFLECTIONS

For some the approach of redaction criticism (however defined) is a worrisome development and seems prejudicial to what is regarded as the most "obvious" and "straightforward," indeed the theologically most valuable, way of reading the Gospels—i.e., to obtain information about the life of Jesus. The aim of this article has been in part to place some severe question marks against such claims, although there is more than one issue at stake here.

Simply at the level of facts, such a way of reading the Gospels is certainly not a straightforward exercise. The Gospels do not give us simple transcripts of the life of Jesus. Our four canonical Gospels are very different and give four different presentations of the life of Jesus. Discovering the historical Jesus from these sources (and bearing in mind other possible evidence as well) is a complex business. We have to account for the differences between John and the Synoptics, for those between the Synoptics themselves, and then use any theories and results in these areas to discriminate within our Gospels between what can confidently be traced back to the pre-Easter Jesus and what represents later Christian editing and activity. And one must bear in mind that any such later editorial activity took place within the context of the common Christian belief that the Jesus who had taught and worked in Galilee and died in Jerusalem was now alive in a new way, raised by God from the dead, and was guiding and still speaking to his church in the present. Any distinction that we might wish to make between authentic Jesus tradition and later Christian editing would have probably been totally unreal to a first-century Christian; the later Christian editing would no doubt have been assumed to be voice of the risen Jesus speaking to his church, and this risen Jesus was precisely the same person who had taught and worked in Galilee. All this indicates that the use of the Gospels to recover information about the pre-Easter Jesus is by no means straightforward.

More important, one should note that such a use of the Gospels is not necessarily the only one with any theological value. Undoubtedly for Christians, the person of Jesus has central theological significance. But equally, responses to the whole Christ-event by Christians also have theological significance. And this is especially the case in relation to the earliest responses to Jesus: Precisely because they are the first responses, they stand as the fountainhead of all subsequent Christian tradition and directly influence all later Christian theologizing. Hence the importance of a figure like Paul. (Such a significance is, of course, closely related to, but not quite identical with, any ideas we might wish to hold of biblical authority.) The evangelists and their Gospels fall into this role as well. If at times we regard their Gospels less as sourcebooks giving us direct information about Jesus, and more as sources enabling us to see early Christians struggling to come to terms with their convictions about Jesus and to make these relevant to their own day, this will for some positively enhance, rather than detract from, their theological significance.

For Christians, the primary theological task is

undoubtedly the same as that of the Gospel writers: to make beliefs and traditions about Jesus relevant to the present and to the situations we all face. Part of this process will, of course, involve the constant effort to ensure that the "Jesus" who is central to Christian faith is none other than the historical Jesus of Nazareth; hence the crucial importance of the critical effort to recover, and constantly check the accuracy of, information about Jesus that the available sources afford us. But the hermeneutical task is no less vital, and in this respect the Gospels also have much to teach us. If in some ways of studying the Gospels and considering the phenomenon of Jesus and the Gospels we see less of "Jesus" and more of the "gospels," their authors and their communities, that is no loss but a profound gain as we see, and seek to learn from, Christians engaged in struggles that are very similar to our own.

BIBLIOGRAPHY

General:

Holladay, Carl R. "Contemporary Methods of Reading the Bible." In *NIB*. Nashville: Abingdon, 1994. 1:125-49.

Marshall, I. H., ed. *New Testament Interpretation*. Exeter: Paternoster, 1977. A collection of essays covering many of the topics treated in this essay.

Sanders, E. P., and M. Davies. *Studying the Synoptic Gospels*. Philadelphia: Trinity Press International, 1989. More detailed analysis devoted to the Synoptics.

Stanton, G. N. *The Gospels and Jesus*. Oxford: Oxford University Press, 1989. Good introduction to all the major critical problems associated with modern study of the Gospels and Jesus.

Tuckett, C. M. *Reading the New Testament*. Philadelphia: Fortress, 1987; London: SPCK, 1987. A study of methods.

Genre:

Aune, D. E. *The New Testament in Its Literary Environment*. Philadelphia: Westminster, 1987. A discussion of the variety of literary forms in the NT.

Burridge, R. A. *What Are the Gospels? A Comparison with Greco-Roman Biography*. Cambridge: Cambridge University Press, 1992. A full defense of the view that the Gospels are generically similar to ancient biographies.

Source Criticism:
Synoptic Problem:

Bellinzoni, A., ed. *The Two Source Hypothesis*. Macon: Mercer University Press, 1985. Contains a collection of important essays and abstracts of many key contributions to the debate.

Farmer, W. R. *The Synoptic Problem*. 2nd ed. New York: Macmillan, 1976. Inaugurated the contemporary revival of the Griesbach Hypothesis.

Fitzmyer, J. A. "The Priority of Mark and the 'Q' Source in Luke." In *Jesus and Man's Hope*. Vol. 1. Pittsburgh: Pittsburgh Theological Seminary, 1970. A powerful modern restatement of the case for the two-source theory in the light of the contemporary debate.

Streeter, B. H. *The Four Gospels*. London: Macmillan, 1924. The classic statement of the case for the two-source theory in English.

John:

Fortna, R. *The Fourth Gospel and Its Predecessor*. Philadelphia: Fortress, 1988. A recent attempt to explain the problems on John on source-critical lines.

Lindars, B. *Behind the Fourth Gospel*. London: SPCK, 1971. A brief but valuable critical evaluation of some source-critical proposals.

Smith, D. M. *Johannine Christianity*. Columbia: University of South Carolina Press, 1984. An invaluable collection of essays on many aspects of Johannine studies from a renowned expert.

Form Criticism:

Barbour, R. S. *Traditio-Historical Criticism of the Gospels*. London: SPCK, 1972. Brief but invaluable as an introduction to many of the critical issues concerned.

Bultmann, R. *The History of the Synoptic Tradition*. Oxford: Blackwells, 1968. One of the classics in the field.

Dibelius, M. *From Tradition to Gospel*. New York: Scribners, 1934. The other classic study in form criticism.

McKnight, E. V. *What Is Form Criticism?* Philadelphia: Fortress, 1969. Probably the most readable introduction currently available.

Non-Synoptic Evidence:

Koester, H. *Ancient Christian Gospels*. Philadelphia: Trinity Press International, 1990. Full and detailed analysis of a full range of non-canonical evidence with a powerful plea for its value.

Redaction Criticism:

Perrin, N. *What Is Redaction Criticism?* Philadelphia: Fortress, 1969.

Petersen, N. R. *Literary Criticism for New Testament Critics*. Philadelphia: Fortress, 1978.

Powell, M. A. *What Is Narrative Criticism?* Minneapolis: Augsburg Fortress, 1990.

THE GOSPEL OF MATTHEW

INTRODUCTION, COMMENTARY, AND REFLECTIONS
BY
M. EUGENE BORING

THE GOSPEL OF
MATTHEW

INTRODUCTION

T he gospel was a message before it became a book. *Gospel* (εὐαγγέλιον *euaggelion*) is the term used by the early church for the good news of the saving act of God in Jesus Christ. The books called "Gospels" are in the New Testament canon because they mediate this saving message and because, with the rest of the canonical books, they are the norm for its continuing proclamation and interpretation.

Matthew was the "favorite" Gospel of early catholic Christianity. Although New Testament books, including the Gospels, were arranged in a variety of orders in the early manuscripts, Matthew was always first, just as it was the most-quoted by the Church Fathers. The modern reader can readily understand the several reasons for this favored position. Matthew is carefully structured to facilitate memory. Even today, it is likely that Christian readers acquainted with the location of key texts that occur in more than one Gospel (e.g., the beatitudes, the Lord's Prayer, Peter's confession, parables) will know the *Matthean* location. Moreover, it was believed that Matthew was written first and, unlike Mark and Luke, that it was written by an apostolic eyewitness. Besides, Matthew begins with a genealogy—distancing and forbidding to many modern readers—which served the ancient reader as a bridge connecting the Gospel with the story of salvation in the Hebrew Bible.

Responsible interpretation of the Gospel must correspond to the nature of the Gospel itself. The Gospel of Matthew, like all the New Testament Gospels, was composed as a *literary* work to interpret the *theological* meaning of a concrete *historical* event to people in a particular historical situation. An appropriate interpretation of the Gospels in the church will, therefore, be at once historical, literary, and theological. These approaches are not mutually exclusive, but correspond to the nature of the Gospel.

MATTHEW IN HISTORICAL PERSPECTIVE

Historical Criticism: Interpreting a Stratified Text. The Gospels are historical documents in the sense that each was concerned to interpret the theological meaning of a particular historical figure and was composed to address a concrete historical situation. The specific contours of Matthew's historical context will be discussed below, and the historical reliability of sayings and events narrated in the Gospel will sometimes be discussed in the Commentary. The concern here is to remind the contemporary reader that the Gospels were not written as a collection of general timeless truths, and that they were not written to us, but were directed to another historical situation in another time and place.

The historical nature of the Gospel means that authentic interpretation should be concerned with the meaning of the text in its original setting. Matthew, like all NT documents, should first be allowed to speak to the people of its own time in their conceptual framework, addressing their concerns. Then, if found also to speak to our concerns—and this is the conviction of the church in all ages and the reason for biblical study and preaching in the church—it will be the authentic word of the Bible speaking to us, not the reflection of our own desires, ideologies, and concerns. The subjective element in all interpretation prohibits any absolute distinction between the ancient meaning of the text and its contemporary meaning. Yet the quest for "what it meant" cannot be ignored in any responsible effort to discover "what it means" for our own time and place.

The Christian reader's concern to hear and understand the specific word of Matthew to his situation is a by-product of the particularity of the Christ-event. Just as Jesus of Nazareth was not humanity in general but a specific, time-conditioned historical individual, an Aramaic-speaking Jew of first-century Palestine, so also all of the canonical documents that mediate the meaning of this event are specific, time-conditioned historical documents. This fact is not to be lamented, but celebrated. While the doctrine of the advent of the Messiah affirms, to be sure, a christological truth about Jesus, it also makes an affirmation about the world and human life—namely, that God is present not only in the eternal absolutes of the transcendent world, but is manifest also in the historical ambiguities of this world and this life.

Historical interpretation is appropriate to a historical revelation, a historical Jesus, and a historical Bible. This means that every interpretation is finite, fragmentary, and inevitably involved in the relativities of history and human finitude. We interpreters are always involved in making finite judgments, and "probably" is often the best we can do. Historical study does not traffic in absolutes. This, too, is not to be lamented as a necessary evil; it is to be celebrated as the way the Word of God is mediated by a historical revelation in historical documents by historical interpreters. The following sections deal with particular dimensions of historical interpretation in the case of Matthew.

The Text of Matthew. Every student of Matthew reads a text that has been reconstructed because the original manuscript, like that of all New Testament documents, has been lost.[1] However, text critics have been able to establish the best text of Matthew (the one closest to the original text) with a great, but not absolute, degree of certainty. The two most widely used editions of the Greek New Testament have the same set of editors and hence the same text.[2] The critical apparatus for *The Greek New Testament*[4] (*UBSGNT*) gives data for 160 sets of variant readings in Matthew, selecting only those deemed most important for translation into other languages, while *Novum Testamentum Graece*[27] ("Nestle-Aland[27]") gives data for more than a thousand variant readings in Matthew, likewise only a selection of the variations considered most important for exegesis. The reconstruction of the text in Matthew by Heinrich Greeven differs from that of *UBSGNT*[4] and *Nestle-Aland*[27] in 160 places.[3] This means that about six times per chapter, two of our standard editions of the Greek text of Matthew disagree as to the original wording of the Gospel. The NRSV is based on the standard *UBSGNT*[4]/*Nestle-Aland*[27] text, departing from it only very rarely, while the NIV is based on an eclectic text constructed by the translators. Thus the differences between the NIV and the NRSV are not necessarily variant translations, but reflections of the translators' differing judgment on the wording of the original Greek text.

Source Analysis. Sometimes still called "literary criticism," this approach attempts to determine which sources were used by the author, their nature and extent. During the nineteenth and early twentieth centuries, a scholarly consensus emerged that Matthew used Mark as a major source, along with a collection of sayings of Jesus (with a minimum of narrative) called "Q." This majority viewpoint has recently been challenged, and the whole question has been thoroughly re-examined in the last three decades.[4] There is less unanimity and dogmatism than previously, and simplistic solutions are now avoided, but the opinion of the great majority of scholars continues to be that Matthew used Q (in a

1. The oldest preserved fragment of Matthew is papyrus $\mathfrak{P}^{64/67}$ in Barcelona and Oxford, from about 200 CE, which contains fragments of chapters 3, 5, and 26. Sixteen other papyri contain parts of Matthew, but most are only a few lines. The most extensive papyrus fragment of Matthew is the third-century $\mathfrak{P}^{45}$ in the Chester Beatty collection in Dublin, containing a total of 55 verses from chapters 20–26. The oldest complete Greek text of Matthew is found in the great majuscule ("uppercase") codices of the fourth century, Sinaiticus (א) in the British Museum in London, and Vaticanus (B) in the Vatican Library in Rome. The complete Greek text of Matthew is found in an additional 13 majuscules from the fifth to the tenth centuries, and in 99 later minuscules (MSS written in lowercase, cursive letters) from the ninth to the sixteenth centuries, as well as in fragmentary form in hundreds of other manuscripts, mostly late minuscules. In addition, Matthew is represented in hundreds of MSS of ancient versions, lectionaries, and quotations in the Church Fathers.

2. See Kurt Aland et al., *The Greek New Testament,* 4th ed. (Stuttgart: United Bible Societies, 1993); Kurt Aland et al., *Novum Testamentum Graece,* 27th ed. (Stuttgart: Deutsche Bibelgesellschaft, 1993).

3. See Heinrich Greeven, *Synopsis of the First Three Gospels with the Addition of the Johannine Parallels,* 13 ed. (Tübingen: J. C. B. Mohr [Paul Siebeck], 1981). Cf. Franz Neirynck, "Greeven's Texts of the Synoptic Gospels," in *Evangelica II: 1982–1991 Collected Essays,* ed. F. Van Segbroeck, BETL 99 (Leuven: Leuven University Press, 1991) 377-88.

4. For a discussion of the synoptic problem and issues raised below about form criticism, redaction criticism, and tradition criticism, see Christopher Tuckett, "Jesus and the Gospels," in this volume.

slightly different form from the version used by Luke) and Mark (perhaps in a slightly revised form from canonical Mark) as his major sources, along with materials peculiar to his own stream of tradition ("M"). This Commentary is written from the perspective that the two-source hypothesis, so understood, remains the best working hypothesis for study of the synoptic Gospels.

Form Criticism. Matthew's written sources depended on living oral tradition. For some decades after the Easter events, the materials from and about Jesus were transmitted orally in the life of the Christian community as individual stories and sayings, and collections of the same. During this period, each story or saying was communicated and heard not as part of a "life of Jesus," but as a witness to the meaning of the Christ-event as a whole in the church's preaching, teaching, worship, conflicts, and clarification of its own understanding of the meaning of Christ and the Christian life. Each unit of the tradition was thus a theological witness to the meaning of the Christian faith and was subject to continual expansion, modification, and reinterpretation in order to communicate the meaning of the faith to changing situations.

As the church passed on the traditions from and about Jesus, the individual units of tradition assumed a number of forms, which the church had adopted and adapted from its Jewish and Hellenistic environment. The following list, based on the work of Rudolf Bultmann, supplemented with recent developments, shows the major types of materials, many of which have subtypes:

I.   The Sayings Material
  A.   *Apothegms* (pithy sayings of Jesus that serve as the "punch line" for a brief narrative context; also called "pronouncement stories" and paradigms). The *chreia* is a related form with even less narrative framework.
  B.   *Dominical Sayings* (sayings of Jesus that circulated independently in the tradition—i.e., without a narrative framework).
      1.   *Logia,* also called "proverbs" or "wisdom sayings" (Matt 6:27-28; 7:6; 10:10*b*).
      2.   Prophetic and apocalyptic sayings (Matt 5:3-9; 10:32-33; 11:21-24; 16:28).
      3.   Legal sayings and church rules (Matt 6:2-4, 5-6, 16-18)
      4.   "I" sayings (Matt 5:17)
      5.   Similitudes and parables (Matt 13:3-9; Mark 4:3-9)
II.   The Narrative Material
  A.   Miracles Stories (Matt 8:23-27; 9:1-8).
  B.   Historical Stories and Legends (Matt 3:13-17; Mark 1:9-11)[5]

Form criticism studies the form, setting, function, and meaning of these individual units of tradition during the period of oral transmission. Since the form of the material is inseparably bound to both its function and its meaning, determining the form of a passage

5. See Rudolf Bultmann, *History of the Synoptic Tradition,* trans. John Marsh (New York: Harper & Row, 1963; German ed., 1931).

and perceiving how it functioned in its early-church setting is one of the steps of sound exegesis. Form-critical studies give the contemporary interpreter a sense of the dynamism of the early Christian community, which both maintained continuity with the past by faithfully handing on the traditions and creatively modified them to address new situations. This perspective is particularly appropriate to Matthew's theological perspective, in which the living Christ accompanies his church through history as its Teacher (see on 1:23; 18:20; 28:20).

Redaction Criticism. The study of how the authors of the Gospels selected, arranged, modified, and added to the tradition in the composition of the Gospels is called redaction criticism. In the case of Matthew, this means especially attending to how he has incorporated and sometimes rewritten Q and Mark. As source analysis had concentrated on the sources behind our present Gospels, and form criticism had concentrated on the individual units of tradition behind all our sources, redaction criticism returned to a concern for the meaning of the final form of the whole document. Special attention was paid to the theological tendencies of the evangelist, seen in the additions, omissions, and modifications in the sources. As the evangelists were increasingly recognized to be composers and not merely editors, this discipline was sometimes called "composition criticism," and tended to modulate into the kind of literary criticism discussed below.

Tradition Criticism and the "Three Levels" of Historical Gospel Study. Although for the sake of a clearer understanding it will sometimes be important to consider what a particular story or saying might have meant in its pre-Matthean setting, whether in the life of Jesus or the life of the church prior to Matthew, this Commentary will be devoted to disclosing the meaning of the text as Matthew composed it for his own time and place. The distinction between the pre-Easter life of Jesus and the post-Easter meaning in Matthew's church is especially important in this regard.

However, perceiving the sweep of tradition from Jesus to the written Gospels is important for understanding the nature and meaning of the final form of the canonical text. "Tradition criticism" is often used as an umbrella term for studying the whole course of the tradition from Jesus to the completed Gospels. This should be thought of as a dynamic process, as the stories and sayings from and about Jesus were preached, reinterpreted, and handed on in the various streams of early Christianity.

Of every saying or story represented by a Gospel pericope, one may ask three sets of historical questions: (1) Does this unit of tradition tell us something about the actual life of Jesus of Nazareth? If so, what did it mean in that setting? (2) Was this unit of tradition transmitted by the church between the time of Jesus and the time the Gospels were compiled orally, in written sources, or both? If so, what changes did it experience in that period, and what did it mean in that setting? (3) What contribution did the evangelist make in composing the final form of the text, and what is the meaning of this text in the evangelist's context?

In practice, historical method requires that one begin with the final form of the text, work backward through the layers to the historical Jesus, and then forward again through the history of the tradition to the final form of the text in the Gospels. Assuming that Jesus' ministry can be dated about 30 CE and that Matthew was written about 90 CE, this means that in every Matthean text the historical interpreter should try to distinguish the 30 CE Jesus meaning(s), the 30–90 CE church meaning(s), and the 90 CE meaning(s) in Matthew's own text and situation.

But such analysis should not be misunderstood as though the only "authentic" materials are those that "go back to Jesus." Matthew, like the other evangelists and those prior to him who handed on the oral tradition, interpreted by retelling, modifying, omitting and expanding, including the creation of new stories and sayings. Matthew stands in a long biblical and Jewish tradition in which such creative midrashic retelling was the legitimate means of reinterpretation, as illustrated, e.g., by Deuteronomy's retelling of the exodus story, or the Chronicler's retelling of the David story, in each case with modifications and expansions, including the creation of new sayings and speeches for the characters in the story.[6]

Despite the value of such historical study of the developing tradition "behind" the text, the object and norm of the church's study, teaching, and proclamation is the text of the Bible in its present canonical form. All of Matthew is to be taken seriously as the church's Scripture, not simply, or even particularly, the relatively more "historical" elements, for the text as a whole mediates the church's message of the meaning of the Christ-event.

Matthew's Reinterpretation of Sacred Documents and Traditions. Although Matthew was influenced by and makes use of religious ideas that were in the air in the Hellenistic world, his Gospel reflects no direct literary influence from pagan writings. His reading seems to have been limited exclusively to Jewish and Christian religious documents.

Jewish Sources. The one set of documents that we may be certain was present in Matthew's community and exercised a profound influence on the composition of his Gospel is the LXX. Matthew's tensions with the Jewish community did not result in any lessening of his interest in the Jewish Scriptures. On the contrary, he was concerned to show that the Jewish Scriptures find their fulfillment in Jesus and the church. (The Excursus "Matthew as Interpreter of Scripture," 151-54 discusses the content, language, and textual form of the biblical texts available in Matthew's time, and Matthew's purpose and methods in using the Scripture.)

Matthew contains no direct quotations from the apocryphal/deutero-canonical books or any other literature outside the Hebrew canon. The fact that Matthew was acquainted with many of the ideas and phrases used in both the deutero-canonical and pseudepigraphal

---

6. *Midrash* is the term used for the rabbinic type of exposition of biblical texts. Halakhic midrashim were expositions of legal texts, while haggadic midrashim were commentaries on narrative texts. The hermeneutical method of the latter often involved creative retelling of the biblical story.

writings seems to be clear, however, from the fact that the Gospel has 78 allusions to them (58 to the apocrypha, 20 to other extra-canonical texts, such as 4 Maccabees and *1 Enoch*).[7]

Christian Sources. *Pauline Letters and Traditions?* It has sometimes been suggested that Matthew is responding directly to Paul or Pauline Christianity (e.g., in 5:19), or even that Matthew had read Paul's letters and was influenced by them.[8] While the Gospel seems to have been written in Antioch or its environs (see below) where Paul had been active (Gal 2:11; cf. Acts 13:1; 14:26; 15:22), Paul's lasting influence in Antioch seems to have been minimal, hardly affecting the Matthean stream of Christianity. There are no indications of direct literary influence from the Pauline corpus.

The Sayings-collection Q. From the early history of the Matthean church, probably from the time of its founding, Q had been a revered document of the community's sacred tradition. Presumably, it was often read in the worship of the Matthean congregation(s), and shaped and expressed the ethos of Matthean Christianity. Q was not merely a source for the evangelist Matthew; it was a part of the history of the community of which he was a part. Q assumed the continuing validity of the law characteristic of early Jewish Christianity (cf. Q 16:17 = Matt 5:18).[9] Matthew's respect for Q may be seen in the fact that when Mark and Q overlap, Matthew often prefers the older and more rigorous Q version (see 10:10 = Luke 10:4; cf. Mark 6:8-9). Matthew set forth a major reinterpretation of Q not only by the (relatively minor) modifications he made in this document, which was part of the sacred tradition of his church, but also primarily by incorporating it within the narrative structure of the Gospel of Mark. In its original form, Q tended to be a growing, unstable document, too readily amenable to expansion by new "sayings of the risen Jesus" spoken by Christian prophets. By inserting it into the pre-resurrection framework of Mark's narrative, Matthew was able both to preserve the continuing address of Jesus to his church through Q and to prohibit its continued expansion by grounding it in the history of the pre-Easter Jesus.[10]

The Gospel of Mark. Some time after 70 CE the Gospel of Mark arrived in the Matthean community, was accepted as part of the community's own sacred tradition, and was used in its life and worship. Mark had been written in and for a Gentile Christian community no longer living under the rule of Torah (Mark 7:1-23). Matthew's Jewish-Christian community carried on a mission to Gentiles and was open to the insights of Gentile Christianity. The narrative of Mark became a fundamental part of the Matthean church's way of telling the Jesus-story, along with its characteristic emphases: Jesus the miracle worker, Jesus the crucified and risen one, Jesus the inaugurator of the Gentile mission. If the Gospel of Mark was already associated with Peter, this strengthened the emphasis on Peter as the leading apostle, already present in the Matthean stream of tradition, and

---

7. These figures are derived from the indexes of Aland et al., *Novum Testamentum Graece,* 769-75.

8. See Maurice Goulder, *Midrash and Lection in Matthew* (London: SPCK, 1974) 144.

9. This commentary follows the convention of citing Q texts by Lukan versification. Cf. John Kloppenborg, *Q Parallels: Synopsis, Critical Notes, & Concordance* (Sonoma, Calif.: Polebridge, 1988) xv and *passim.*

10. For elaboration of this point and evidence for it, see M. Eugene Boring, *The Continuing Voice of Jesus: Christian Prophecy and the Gospel Tradition* (Louisville: Westminster/John Knox, 1991) 191-234, 242-46, 255-56.

facilitated Mark's acceptance as a normative Christian text for Matthew's church. Matthew did not merely "combine" Q and Mark. He made the Markan narrative basic, inserting his Q and M materials into the Markan story line, to which they were subordinated. Matthew is an elaboration and new interpretation of the Markan narrative, not of the Q sayings collection.

The Special Matthean Materials and Traditions ("M"). In addition to Q and Mark, Matthew followed traditions and materials peculiar to his own community. "M" was not a separate document, but represents the body of peculiarly Matthean traditions. Since these traditions were formed or handed down by the local churches that also helped form Matthew's own theological perspective, it is at times difficult to distinguish M tradition from Matthew's redaction. M may have contained collections of Scripture quotations particularly relevant to Matthean theology, (*testimonia*), Christian scribal interpretations of such quotations, midrashic comments and developments of Q and Markan texts and other items of Christian tradition, as well as sayings and stories from and about Jesus unique to the Matthean tradition. Although a few of these materials could have been written down prior to Matthew, most, if not all, were handed on orally for a generation or more prior to Matthew. It is often the case that they had already been adapted, modified, and expanded to address new situations; sometimes they preserved earlier forms of the tradition with remarkable fidelity, especially traditions affirming earlier Jewish Christianity's adherence to the Torah.

Matthew and His Community's Use of This Sacred Tradition. Matthew, steeped in all of his community's sacred texts and traditions, treated them all with great seriousness and respect without being slavishly bound to any of them. Just as Matthew was familiar enough with the Jewish Scriptures to make scores of allusions to it without specifically calling attention to it (see Excursus "Matthew as Interpreter of Scripture," 151-54), so also Q, Mark, and M formed part of the warp and woof of his mind. His use of Q and Mark is at the farthest pole from a "cut-and-paste" use of them as "sources." Matthew's mind is so saturated with Q and Mark that he can allude to them even in sections where he is not "using" them. Markan phrases creep into a Q passage, and vice versa. A phrase from Q becomes a favorite "Matthean" phrase, used repeatedly in non-Q passages.[11] It is important to note that these texts had been used for decades in Matthew's church, and not only Matthew himself, but also his intended hearers/readers were intimately familiar with them.[12] Matthew does not write for naive readers.

Redaction criticism's careful attention to the interpretative changes Matthew made in his sacred tradition represented by Q and Mark is not merely a modern academic exercise, but represents the experience of the hearers/readers of the Matthean community who were already familiar with Q, Mark, and M, and who needed a new way to read them in

---

11. For example, "little faith" (ὀλιγόπιστος *oligopistos*) occurs once in Q 12:28 = Matt 6:30, but is added to Markan contexts in Matt 8:26; 14:31; 16:8; cf. 17:20.

12. See Sir John Hawkins, *Horae Synopticae: Contributions to the Study of the Synoptic Problem,* 2nd ed. (Oxford: Clarendon, 1909) 170-71. He lists nineteen passages where Matthew reproduces phrases derived from his sources but used in a different context. Nils Dahl, *Jesus in the Memory of the Early Church* (Minneapolis: Augsburg, 1976) 40, gives data from the passion story, showing that both author and intended reader presupposed familiarity with Mark.

a changed situation. Like the Chronicler's retelling/ interpretation of the story of Samuel and the monarchy in 1–2 Chronicles, Matthew retells the familiar story with respect, skill, and midrashic imagination.

This reinterpretation did not happen in a vacuum. Thus one must determine the settings—social, political, religious, ecclesiastical—within which the Gospel of Matthew emerged.

Matthew's Christian Community. The Gospel of Matthew is not the product of an isolated author, but reflects the life and concerns of a particular Christian community. Matthew has long been known as the most ecclesiastical Gospel, the only Gospel to use the word *church* to describe the community of believers (16:18; 18:17). Matthew's church has obviously been involved in an intense relationship with the surrounding dominant Jewish community, and it cannot be defined, as it did not define itself, apart from that relationship.

Relation to the Jewish Community. *Matthew as a "Jewish" Gospel.* The Gospel of Matthew has traditionally and popularly been known as the Jewish Gospel, sometimes over against Luke or John as the Gentile Gospel. Matthew does, of course, have interests that are distinctively Jewish (e.g., concern for the law, Sabbath, Temple). He feels no need to explain Jewish customs, as did his Markan source (cf. Matt 15:1 to Mark 7:1-4). Matthew's Gospel contains texts that suggest that his community is still subject to the disciplinary measures of the synagogue authorities (10:17-23; 23:2), and perhaps that it still keeps the sabbath (24:20). And Matthew does sometimes make *Gentiles* synonymous with *pagan* (5:47; 6:7, 32; 18:17; 20:25). But some features traditionally designated "Jewish" are manifested in the other "Gentile" Gospels (e.g., genealogy, fulfillment of the Scriptures). In particular, it must be pointed out that Matthew's interest in the Scripture, including his allusions to it, which assumes that his readers were biblically literate, does not establish the "Jewishness" of Matthew, since, e.g., the Gospel of Luke and Paul's Letter to the Romans display a similar use of Scripture, and since all our Gospels preserve traditions from Jewish Christianity and manifest varying degrees of Jewishness.

Jewish Christianity was not a monolith, but a spectrum of groups with a variety of stances toward the law. It is thus somewhat simplistic to think of Matthew as *the* Jewish Gospel, particularly since it has considerable elements that reflect an alienation from Judaism. We may mention, for example, references to "their" synagogues (4:23; 9:35; 10:17; 12:9; 13:54; 23:34),[13] to "their" scribes (7:29), and a final reference to "the Jews" as though they were another group (28:15; cf. Commentary on 16:1). There are also instances where Matthew has a *less* Jewish version of a saying than its Lukan parallel (Matt 10:37// Luke 14:26; Matt 10:28//Luke 12:4-5; Matt 5:18//Luke 16:17). In Matt 18:15-20, problems of discipline come before the church, not before the synagogue. Furthermore, Matthew has some (strong!) pro-Gentile tendencies, not only Jewish ones

---

13. This contrast is not only in passages where the narrator is speaking. In 10:17 Jesus speaks of "their" synagogues (cf. 16:18 "my" church).

(e.g., 28:18-20, and see Commentary on 1:2-17; 2:1-12; 4:15; 8:5-13; 12:18-21; 21:43).[14] Thus Matthew is "both deeply Jewish and painfully anti-Jewish."[15]

Matthew's church saw itself as the messianic community, the eschatological people of God, distinct from all—Jew or Gentile—who did not believe in Jesus as the Messiah. Matthew continued the Jewish practice of using *Gentile* in the sense of "outsider." Thus both his anti-Jewishness and his anti-Gentile bias are, in effect, expressions of his sense of belonging to the Christian community distinct from the non-Christian world, both Jewish and Gentile. The Gospel draws the line between believers and non-believers in Christ; it is Christ, not Jewishness, that divides people (10:21-22, 32-39). But even this division, though affirmed, is also transcended (see 25:31-46). Designations of one Gospel as "Jewish" and another as "Gentile" or "universal" are misleading and should be abandoned.

Ambiguity of Data About Judaism. Our data for assessing Matthew's relation to Judaism is not clear. There was no monolithic Judaism of Matthew's time that can serve as a fixed point of comparison. Like early Christianity, Judaism in the late first century was itself in a process of flux and development, seeking its way forward after the catastrophic war of 66–70 CE. Neither is there any unambiguous contemporary source. Pharisaic and developing Rabbinic Judaism of Matthew's time must be reconstructed from later Jewish sources, which tend to reflect later issues and situations. Thus, on the one hand, we lack a clear picture of "the" Judaism of Matthew's time.

On the other hand, the Gospel contains traditions from various periods and situations, so that it is not always clear what represents Matthew's own situation and what represents a time when the pre-Matthean community may have been more rigorously Jewish than Matthew's own church had become.[16] Thus some data in the Gospel can be interpreted in opposite ways. For example, Matthew is not concerned with the issue of circumcision for Gentile converts, which we know was important for the first-generation Gentile mission (see Acts 13–15; Galatians 1–4). In theory, this datum could mean either that Matthew's church was still within a thoroughly Jewish context where circumcision was assumed, or that the church had become so thoroughly oriented to the Gentile mission that circumcision was no longer an issue. (The latter is taken to be the case in this commentary.)

This means that the traditional way of posing the question of whether Matthew's church was still "Jewish" and "in" the synagogue or "Gentile" and already "out" of the synagogue is no longer adequate. Rather than representing Judaism and the synagogue as static entities, with a post-70 "council" of Jamnia making decrees for an established Judaism, we should think rather of an extended period after the 66–70 war, stretching to the time of the

14. The 1947 article by Kenneth W. Clark, "The Gentile Bias in Matthew," *JBL* 66 (1947) 165-72, is still classic. More recently, see Georg Strecker, *Der Weg der Gerechtigkeit,* FRLANT 82 (Göttingen: Vandenhoeck & Ruprecht, 1962); and John P. Meier, *The Vision of Matthew: Christ, Church, and Morality in the First Gospel* (New York: Paulist, 1979) 17-25.

15. Daniel Patte, *The Gospel According to Matthew: A Structural Commentary on Matthew's Faith* (Philadelphia: Fortress, 1987) xi.

16. In addition, Matthew himself may not have been consistently clear, but retained an uncomfortable tension in his own thought, so that our own inability to derive unambiguous results may itself be an accurate interpretation of the text. See R. T. France, *Matthew,* Tyndale New Testament Commentaries (Grand Rapids: Eerdmans, 1985) 19.

codification of the Mishnah (about 200 CE) as the period of "formative Judaism." During this time, the pre-70 Pharisaic party, although now dominant, still competed with other Jewish groups that had survived the war (priestly, scribal, apocalyptic, Christian, to some minor extent even Sadducean and Zealot) and finally established itself as the definitive element in that kind of Rabbinic Judaism that became "normative."[17] Within this mix, the Matthean community was apparently a movement still related to formative Judaism, a group that regarded itself as the authentic people of God, experiencing itself as a persecuted minority at the hands of the dominant Pharisaic leadership (see, e.g., 5:13-16; 10:23, 32-33, 40-42; 25:31-46). Historically, although there were instances of Jewish persecution of some early Christians—i.e., of Jewish Christians who were still within the synagogue structure and subject to its discipline—there was no extensive or systematic persecution by Jews of Christians as such. Jewish persecution of early Christians should neither be magnified as fuel for anti-Semitism nor denied altogether in the interest of contemporary Jewish-Christian relations. Such instances of Jewish persecution of Christians were not a matter of one religion or race oppressing another, not a matter of outsiders interfering in the religious practices of another group (and not at all like the later Christian pogroms against the Jewish community). Such texts as 10:17 and 23:34 reflect an internal struggle of Jew vs. Jew, analogous to the internal conflicts among Christians in the Reformation period.

Results: Clear Affirmations and Continuing Questions. As a result of recent studies, we may make the following clear affirmations as a basis for further interpretation of the Gospel of Matthew:

The Gospel of Matthew does not understand itself to represent a new religion, Christianity, over against a different religion, Judaism. Nor does it regard the church as the "new Israel" that replaces the "old" Israel. Matthew regards the Christian community of Jews and Gentiles as the continuation of the people of God, to come to eschatological fulfillment at the time when "the twelve tribes of Israel" are regathered. Both Israel and the church must undergo the judgment of the Son of Man (see Commentary on 19:28).

Matthew does, however, see those Jews who had rejected Jesus as the Messiah, especially their leadership (scribes, Pharisees, Sadducees, high priests), as having forfeited their claim as the people of God (21:43). Thus in Matthew's view empirical Israel is henceforth one nation among others, called along with them to constitute the continuing people of God by confessing Jesus as the Messiah and living by his teaching (10:32-33; 28:18-20).

The Jewish elements in the Gospel do not mean that it was written for the Jews in the sense that it was directed to Jewish outsiders to convince them that Jesus is the Messiah.

17. For a variety of perspectives on this complex history, see Jacob Neusner, "The Formation of Rabbinic Judaism: Javneh (Jamnia) from A.D. 70 to 100," *ANRW* 11.19.2.3-42; E. P. Sanders, ed., *Jewish and Christian Self-definition,* vol. 2, *Aspects of Jewish Self-definition in the Greco-Roman Period* (Philadelphia: Fortress, 1981); J. Andrew Overman, *Matthew's Gospel and Formative Judaism: The Social World of the Matthean Community* (Minneapolis: Fortress, 1990); David L. Balch, ed., *Social History of the Matthean Community* (Minneapolis: Fortress, 1991), esp. the chaps. by Anthony J. Saldarini, "The Gospel of Matthew and Jewish Christian Conflict," 38-61, and L. Michael White, "Crisis Management and Boundary Maintenance: The Social Location of the Matthean Community," 211-47. Anthony J. Saldarini, *Matthew's Christian-Jewish Community* (Chicago: University of Chicago Press, 1994); Graham Stanton, *A Gospel for a New People* (Edinburgh: T. & T. Clark, 1992), chapter 5, "Synagogue and Church" 113-145.

Matthew wrote his Gospel for members of his own community to instruct them in their own faith and to clarify it over against misunderstandings, not as an evangelistic or apologetic writing directed to outsiders.

Matthew was in some kind of continuity, intense dialogue, and debate with formative Judaism. Developments in contemporary formative Judaism, including especially what was going on at Jamnia and its effects in the synagogues in Matthew's own environs, are of deep concern to him. He had the developing Pharisaic leadership and its program for all Judaism in view as the chief opponents and alternatives to his own understanding of the way forward for the people of God. His Gospel includes traditional Jewish-Christian materials that are in some sense superseded, but were important enough for him to include, and in some sense to affirm (see Commentary on 5:17-20; 10:5-6; 23:1-3). While such texts as 10:16-25 express Christians' alienation from "their" synagogues, the fact that Christians could be beaten in these synagogues and brought before local Jewish courts (sanhedrins) indicates that the victims of such abuse were still in some sense considered within the Jewish community. In this sense, Matthew's church was "Jewish."

Although Matthew's church and/or the Q community from which it sprang had previously carried on an unsuccessful mission to the Jewish people, it now abandoned a specifically Jewish mission, no longer seeing itself as a renewal movement in Judaism, and engaged in a mission to the Gentiles—i.e., the "nations," of which Israel is now one (28:18-20). Matthew understood the present and future of his church to be oriented to the Gentiles, and thus regarded developing non-Christian Judaism only as a competitor and opponent. In this sense, Matthew's church was "Gentile."

Questions remain. In particular, the question of the "Birkath ha-Minim" ("Blessing [Curse] Against the Heretics") is unresolved. At the newly founded academy and rabbinic court at Jamnia, which was assuming leadership in the reconstitution of Judaism after the 66–70 war, one of the synagogue prayers was reformulated to include a curse against the "minim" (separatists, heretics). The later Church Fathers understood this to be directed against Christians, and thus claimed that Christians were cursed in the Jewish synagogues.[18] It has sometimes been argued that this prayer served as a tool in ferreting out Christians in the synagogue (who, of course, could not participate in this part of the liturgy) in order to force them out of the synagogue.[19] The wording of the prayer changed over time, in part due to fear of Christian reprisals, so that the original wording is disputed. It is not clear that it originally included a reference to Christians, but may have been directed against any group considered heretical by the Jamnian leaders.[20] Nor is it clear that in Matthew's time the Jamnian leadership had authority to regulate the synagogue liturgy.

18. Justin *Dialogue with Trypho* 16, 47, 96, 137; Origen *Homilies on Jeremiah* 10.8.2; Epiphanius *Panarion* 29.9.1; Jerome *Epistula ad Augustanum* 112.13.

19. See W. D. Davies, *The Setting of the Sermon on the Mount* (Cambridge: Cambridge University Press, 1966) 275-77.

20. See Reuven Kimelman, "Birkath ha-Minim and the Lack of Evidence for an Anti-Christian Jewish Prayer in Late Antiquity," in Sanders, ed. *Jewish and Christian Self-definition,* 2:245-68; Klaus Berger, M. Eugene Boring, Carsten Colpe, *Hellenistic Commentary to the New Testament* (Nashville: Abingdon, 1995), on John 16:2 for the text of this "blessing" and notes on its history and interpretation.

It is thus an oversimplification to regard the Birkath ha-Minim as proof that Matthew and his community had been officially excluded from formative Judaism, and to regard Matthew's Gospel primarily as the response of an excommunicated group to Jamnia. Thus the Birkath ha-Minim cannot be made the basis of an interpretation of Matthew's situation. Nonetheless, the evidence is clear that there were deep tensions between developing Judaism and Matthew's church, which had its own sense of identity, structures, and procedures for excommunication and promulgating new authoritative teachings (see Commentary on 18:15-20) over against formative Judaism.

Was Matthew's church a sect? Certainly not in the sense that Qumran was, a community that withdrew from the rest of society, for Matthew's church did not passively withdraw and turn inward, but carried on an active mission to the world. Yet there are sectarian features of Matthew's church,[21] in that it claimed to be the true people of God, appropriating the traditions of the parent body as its own and claiming itself as the sole legitimate heir (cf. 10:16; but this attitude had already developed in the Q community).

Is the Gospel of Matthew anti-Semitic? In view of the use of certain Matthean texts through the centuries in support of racism and anti-Semitic statements and actions (especially 21:43 and 27:25), this question must be faced honestly, especially by Christians who wish to take Matthew seriously as canonical Scripture. To pose the question in terms of anti-Semitism, however, is anachronistic, for the issue in Matthew is not racial prejudice, but religious conflict.[22] The historical situation from which the Gospel of Matthew emerged was filled with tensions not only between Jews and Gentiles, but also with internal strife among various Jewish groups (of which the Matthean church was one). The Matthean Christian community, itself partly or even predominantly Jewish, felt itself to be persecuted by the Jewish leadership.[23] In the conflict, sharp words were exchanged, so that from Matthew's side negative caricatures of Jewish leadership and religious practice were presented as a part of the polemic (see 21:43; 23:1-36; 27:24-26).[24] While it is absurd to accuse Matthew of anti-Semitism—he pictured Jesus and the disciples as Jewish, was himself a Jew, and wrote for a church with a Jewish tradition and membership—lamentably, it is true that the sayings and imagery deriving from the conflict of Matthew's church and the Jewish leadership have been used to fuel the fires of anti-Semitism. Just as modern interpreters must be on guard that Matthean texts not be used to encourage anti-Semitism, so also legitimate modern sensitivities about anti-Semitism must not obscure a historical understanding of Matthew's negative and polemical stance toward the formative Judaism of his own time.[25]

21. See Graham Stanton, *Gospel for a New People* (Edinburgh: T. & T. Clark, 1992) 85-168.

22. See Shaye J. D. Cohen, *From the Maccabees to the Mishnah* (Philadelphia: Westminster, 1987) 46-49.

23. This did not, however, make Matthew superficially pro-Gentile. He portrayed critical, negative pictures of Gentiles as well as of Jews. In 24:9, he adds "the Gentiles" to Mark's "hated by all." In 25:32, at the last judgment "all the Gentiles" will be separated into saved and condemned. In 20:19, the high priests and scribes will hand Jesus over to the Gentiles, and in 27:1-56, it is the Gentile governor and Roman soldiers who actually condemn and kill Jesus.

24. See Luke T. Johnson, "The New Testament's Anti-Jewish Slander and the Conventions of Ancient Polemic," *JBL* 108 (1989) 419-41.

25. For a more negative view of Matthew's anti-Judaism than that presented in this commentary, see Fred W. Burnett, "Exposing the Anti-Jewish Ideology of Matthew's Implied Author: The Characterization of God as Father," *Semeia* 59 (1992) 155-92.

Change and Development. We may picture Matthew himself and numbers of his community as Jews who had grown up before the war of 66–70 with the synagogue as their spiritual home. Prior to the destruction of the Temple, they had encountered early missionaries of the "Jesus movement," probably related to or identical with the missionary prophets of the Q community, with their eschatological message of Jesus' return as Son of Man. They had been converted to faith in Jesus as the Son of Man, the fulfillment of their hopes for the coming Messiah, without ever dreaming that this would eventually alienate them from their religious and cultural home in Judaism. Then tensions developed, and those who had become disciples of Jesus found themselves an isolated group within the synagogue. Following the beginnings of the reformation of Judaism at Jamnia, Matthew's group found not only itself but the synagogue as well in the process of change, and tensions increased. When the Gospel was written, Matthew and his community were alienated from these developing structures. They refer to their own gathering as the "church" (ἐκκλησία *ekklēsia;* the word is found only in Matthew in the Gospels [16:18; 18:17]; 18:15, 21 in the NRSV are translations of *adelphoi* [ἀδελφοί], usually translated "brothers and sisters"). In some ways they now found themselves more oriented to the Gentile world than to the emerging shape of Judaism, while continuing to affirm their Jewish past, of which they considered themselves the legitimate heirs. Matthew and his church had lived through a period of rapid change; the Gospel of Matthew has much to say to a community experiencing social change to which it wants to adapt while being faithful to its Scripture and tradition.

Structure and Leadership. Since the plotted story line of Matthew extends from Jesus' birth to his resurrection appearance to his disciples, but does not continue into the post-Easter period of the church, Matthew's characterization of church life is communicated indirectly, in two ways. (1) The pre-Easter Jesus predicts and describes the situation of the post-Easter church, and (2) the story of Jesus and his disciples is narrated at two levels simultaneously, so that the pre-Easter narrative framework sometimes intentionally becomes transparent to the situation of the post-Easter church and its faith in Jesus as the risen and exalted Lord.

Peter, Apostles, Disciples. The disciples are often transparently addressed as the post-Easter Christian community (e.g., 10:17-42; 18:15-20). Matthew thought of the disciples as the whole group of those who had committed themselves to follow Jesus (8:21; 9:14; 10:25, 42; 12:49; 27:57; 28:19). Within this group was a central, symbolic core of twelve who represent the present leaders and future judges of the people of God (19:28). *Apostle* is not an important word for Matthew; he uses it only once (10:2), as a synonym for *disciple* (10:1). Except for 10:2, Matthew always refers to this central group as "the twelve disciples" (10:1; 11:1; 20:17) or simply "the twelve" (10:5; 26:14, 20, 47).

Within this group of twelve, Peter plays a distinct, symbolic role. Matthew modifies and adds to his tradition to emphasize the special role of Peter (10:2; 14:22-33; 15:15; 16:16-19; 17:24-27). Just as Peter is representative of the Twelve, so also the Twelve are representative of the larger body of disciples, and there are many times when the picture becomes transparent to the whole body of post-Easter disciples, so that the reader may identify with Peter and the other disciples. Yet Peter's significance in Matthew cannot be reduced to that of a cipher for the twelve or for the church as a whole. He is called first and is designated as the "first," (10:2, added to Mark). He plays a unique role in the founding and maintenance of the Christian community, and receives a special christological revelation from God, a unique pronouncement of blessing by Jesus, and a special (and unrepeatable) responsibility in the founding of the church (see Commentary on 16:17-19). Peter had himself been in Antioch (Gal 2:11), the probable provenance of the Gospel, and in later tradition was considered the patron apostle of the church in that city and then its first bishop.[26] Petrine traditions and Petrine Christians may have played a role early in the history of Matthew's community, which may have regarded some of the M traditions as deriving from Peter or being especially associated with him. If the Gospel of Mark was already associated with Peter when it was accepted by the Matthean community, this would have both facilitated its reception and strengthened the prominence of Peter. In Matthew's stream of tradition, Peter was looked upon as the representative apostolic figure, as was Paul in the Deutero-Pauline stream, the Beloved Disciple in the Johannine stream, and James in yet other circles. The Matthean church was "Petrine" rather than "Pauline" or "Johannine" or "Jacobite."[27] (Matthew is distant from Pauline and Johannine Christianity, and James the brother of Jesus plays no role at all in Matthew's story.) Later Petrine Christianity as represented in the *Apocalypse of Peter* from Nag Hammadi appeals to Matthew as its authority, and uses Matthean vocabulary to describe itself ("little ones").

"Official" Order of Ministry? It may seem surprising that the "most ecclesiastical" Gospel has no references, direct or indirect, to formal ministerial structures. There is no mention of a bishop or deacons, which is particularly surprising if the Gospel was written in Antioch or its environs, since only a few years later Ignatius of Antioch made a strong case for the monarchical episcopate as the norm of church government, and apparently stood in the Matthean tradition and used the Gospel of Matthew (Ign. *Eph.* 19:1-3; Ign. *Smyrn.* 1:1 = Matt 3:15; Ign. *Phld.* 3:1 = Matt 15:13; Ign. *Pol.* 2:2). Likewise the *Didache,* also in the Matthean tradition, reflects the transition from earlier charismatic ministry to the formal structures of bishops and deacons. Matthew seems to be earlier in the same historical trajectory that led to Ignatius and the *Didache,* but prior to the development of formal ecclesiastical offices. The fact that some members of Matthew's community were beginning to claim the offices and titles that formative Judaism was beginning to use and invest with more formal authority than before ("rabbi," "father," "instructor,") seems clear from the Gospel's protest against such tendencies (23:8-12).

Leadership in the Matthean Church. The Matthean community seems to have

---

26. Pseudo-Clementine *Homilies* 20:23; *Recognitions* 10:68-71; Origen "Homily on Luke 6" (GCS Origen IX, 32).

27. This is not to say that, for Matthew, Peter was only a local patron saint. Unlike the Beloved Disciple or even Paul, Peter had significance as an ecumenical symbol. In the appended chap. 21 of the Gospel of John, Peter becomes such a symbol for the Johannine community, depite the predominance of the Beloved Disciple in chaps. 1–20.

had prophets among its leadership, probably as its principal leaders, as in the earlier days of the community reflected in the *Didache* (cf. Matt 5:12 to Luke 6:23; Matt 10:41; 23:34; even 7:21-22 presupposes there were "good" prophets in the community). These prophets were charismatic figures who received and transmitted revelations from the exalted Lord, and who had other leadership roles. They were at home in the life of the community, but some of them also made missionary journeys (10:41). Matthew valued such prophets and saw them as a model for all church leadership and the Christian life as such (5:12), but also saw the danger of such charismatic leadership (7:15, 21-22; 24:11, 24).

Matthew also understood the risen Lord to have sent sages and scribes to function as leaders in the church (13:52; 23:34). The exact functions of these ministers is not clear, but they apparently served in roles analogous to surrounding Judaism. Sages would have transmitted and interpreted the wisdom traditions of the community, but differently than in Judaism, since Matthew not only understood Jesus to be the messenger of Wisdom, but also utilized the figure of transcendent Wisdom as a christological category for understanding the status of the risen and exalted Christ.[28] Scribes not only would have worked over and transmitted biblical materials and provided midrashic interpretations and fulfillment quotations, but presumably would have done the same with the other sacred traditions of the community as well—namely, Q, Mark, and some of Matthew's special materials. This means that Matthew has some Q and Markan traditions that already had received Christian scribal interpretation. Matthew himself might have been such a Christian scribe who brought out of his accumulated traditional treasure both old and new things for the edification of the community (13:52). Sages and scribes (like prophets) no doubt participated in the teaching ministry within the community, but the exact roles and how they were related to each other can no longer be determined.

Matthew also used the terms *righteous* and *little ones* to designate members of his community (10:41-42; 13:17, 49; 18:6, 10, 14). It has been suggested that both are semi-technical terms for church leaders. "Righteous" or "Just" was the title given the leader of the Jerusalem church, "James the Just," so it is sometimes supposed that leaders in Matthew's church were called "righteous." "Little ones" is sometimes thought to be a special name for wandering missionaries. However, since Matthew does not use a specific title such as "Christian" to designate the members of his community, it is probably better to understand both "righteous" and "little ones" as general names for all authentic members of the community (like "brothers and sisters," "sons of God," "servants," "slaves," "disciples"), for those who were neither prophets, sages, nor scribes.

Social Status. Matthew seems to reflect a relatively wealthy urban community. The "poor" and "hungry" in the Q beatitudes become in Matthew "poor in spirit" and those who "hunger and thirst for righteousness" (Matt 5:3, 6// Luke 6:20-21). References to small-denomination copper coins are replaced by references to gold and larger-denomina-

---

28. Cf. Matt 11:18-19, 25-30; 23:34 vs. Luke 11:49. See also M. Jack Suggs, *Wisdom, Christology, and Law in Matthew's Gospel* (Cambridge, Mass.: Harvard University Press, 1970).

tion coins (Mark 6:8// Matt 10:9; Luke 19:11-27//Matt 25:14-30), and stories are told of high finance (e.g., 18:23-35) and lavish dinner parties (22:1-14). Matthew specifically adds to Mark the fact that Joseph of Arimathea, who buried Jesus, was both a disciple and a wealthy man (27:57).

Place of Origin. Several locations for the Matthean community have been argued: Palestine (Galilee, Caesarea, Jerusalem), Syria (Tyre or Sidon, Antioch), Egypt (Alexandria), Transjordan (Pella). The majority of scholars favor Antioch, for the following reasons: (1) Internal evidence of the Gospel points to some Greek-speaking urban area where Jews and Christians were in intense interaction. Greek was the dominant language of Antioch, which probably had the largest Jewish population in Syria. Matthew seems to breathe a more urbane air than either Q or Mark. Whereas Mark refers to cities eight times and villages seven times, Matthew has twenty-six references to cities and only four references to villages. (2) Peter is prominent in both Matthew and in Antiochene tradition, which made him the first bishop of Antioch. After the encounter between Paul and Peter in Antioch (Galatians 2), Paul seems to have lost popularity there. (3) Jerusalem seems out of the question, since James plays no role. (4) Matthew introduces "Syria" into his sources (4:24), perhaps as a pointer to his own church and to ground it in the saving history. (5) The contacts with Ignatius of Antioch and with the *Didache* point to this area as the origin of the Gospel of Matthew. (6) Only in Antioch did a stater equal exactly two didrachmas (17:24-27). (7) Situating Matthew in Antioch fits the situation described in Acts, where Palestinian Christians started the Antiochene church, which then developed a Gentile mission, not without tensions. (8) The early and widespread acceptance of the Gospel implies "sponsorship" by a major church. There is no evidence for Rome or Ephesus as the sponsor; Antioch is the best remaining possibility.

Date. Matthew's community stretched over an extended period, developing and changing as it confronted and adapted to new situations. But the Gospel itself represents a cross-section of this growing tradition at a particular time, a "freezing" of it in the theological composition of one particular scribal leader of the community at a specific moment in its history. Since the Gospel contains no specific chronological data to identify its time of composition, that date cannot be pinpointed, but there are indications of a general period.

(1) On the two-source hypothesis, Matthew must have been written after Q and Mark. There are good reasons for dating Mark a few years either side of 70 CE, so Matthew must be enough later for Mark to have become the sacred tradition of the community.

(2) The war of 66–70, and the consequent destruction of Jerusalem, is almost certainly reflected in 22:7. Yet Matthew does not seem to be overwhelmed by the catastrophe, which seems some distance away in both space and time.

(3) Matthew seems to be intensely concerned with the developments in formative Judaism in the generation after 70. It is difficult to determine whether he reflects the

specificity of the Birkath ha-Minim, which was apparently promulgated in the 80s (see above).

(4) Matthew, and not merely Matthean tradition, seems to have been used by both the *Didache* and Ignatius (see above). The *Didache* is difficult to date, but Ignatius wrote c. 110. Thus it seems that the Gospel of Matthew was composed in the period 80–100, for which 90 may serve as a good symbolic figure.

Authorship. Two of our oldest and best MSS (א, B) entitle the document simply "according to Matthew" (ΚΑΤΑ ΜΑΘΘΑΙΟΝ *KATA MATHTHAION*). Later MSS have "The Gospel According to Matthew," "The Holy Gospel According to Matthew," and other minor variations. Since the oldest MSS of the other Gospels also have the simple form "according to Mark," "according to Luke," "according to John," these titles apparently were added to the Gospels at the same time, with the common title "Gospel" uniting them all. The titles of our earliest MSS thus derive from the period when the fourfold Gospel canon was formed about the middle of the second century CE.[29]

The form and content of these titles is the church's testimony that there is only one gospel, the good news of Jesus Christ, but "according to" four different evangelists. It was important to early Christianity to attach apostolic names to its key documents, not as a matter of consciously falsifying history, but as a way of claiming theological adequacy and legitimacy for their contents, for which some kind of normative status was claimed. Thus most canonical and non-canonical documents for which some normative status was claimed received secondary apostolic titles (e.g., *Gospel of Thomas, Gospel of Philip, Gospel of Bartholomew*). In the case of the canonical Gospels, the value and significance of such titles is that they express the church's claim that these writings represent legitimate and authentic interpretation of the meaning of the Christ-event. It is also possible that in some cases the titles may transmit some authentic tradition with regard to the actual author.

Matthew itself, like the other NT Gospels, is anonymous. The issue is whether the title in this case, in addition to its primary theological function, also has historical value. Uncritical interpreters have always simply taken the tradition at face value, but a few recent critical scholars have also argued for apostolic authorship by the eyewitness Matthew.[30] Practically all critical scholars consider the evidence against apostolic authorship to be overwhelming: (1) The Gospel itself is anonymous. Apostolic authorship is a claim made for the book, not a claim made by the book itself. The case is thus different from the Deutero-Pauline letters. (2) The use of Mark and Q as sources undercuts its claim to eyewitness testimony. (3) The Greek language in which the Gospel was composed was the native language of the author and is of higher quality than the relatively unpolished

---

29. This is the majority scholarly view. For a more conservative evaluation of the historical value of the titles and arguments for their earlier date, see Martin Hengel, *Studies in the Gospel of Mark* (Philadelphia: Fortress, 1980).

30. Robert H. Gundry, *Matthew: A Commentary on His Literary and Theological Art* (Grand Rapids: Eerdmans, 1982) 609-22, argues for Matthean authorship, even though he believes the eyewitness Matthew relied on the secondary Mark for much of his structure and content, including the account of his own call in Matt 9:9 (Mark 2:14).

Greek of Mark. Given the author's setting and background, he may have known enough Hebrew and Aramaic to work with texts, but there is no evidence that he was fluent in these languages. (4) The claim to apostolic authority, implicit in the title, is sufficiently accounted for by the historical and theological factors discussed above. (5) Evidence used to support authorship by the publican Matthew—e.g., the numerical patterns of the narrative, supposedly pointing to a tax collector's facility with figures—are fanciful and unconvincing. Rather, the real points of contact are with Haggadic and scribal composition. The argument that Matthew was a relatively minor character in the story and would not have been chosen as the purported author if he had not actually written the Gospel runs aground on the fact that practically every character in early Christianity, major and minor, had Gospels attributed to him, as the long lists of Gospels in the NT Apocrypha make clear.[31] The apostle Matthew conceivably may have been associated with Q or some of the M materials, so that there would be a genuine historical connection between Matthew and the Gospel, however indirect. More likely, the ascription to Matthew was made on the basis of the shift from "Levi" in Mark 2:14 to "Matthew" in Matt 9:9 and the consequent identification of the Matthew of Mark 3:18 as "the publican" in Matt 10:3.

For convenience, I will continue to use the traditional name "Matthew" to refer to the anonymous author of the Gospel of Matthew. Although we do not know the author's name, from the document he has given us we can surmise that he was of Jewish background, but must have grown up in a Hellenistic city (presumably Antioch) and spoke Greek.[32] The Septuagint (LXX) was his standard Bible. He may have been able to handle Hebrew well enough to facilitate biblical study, and enough Aramaic for informal communication. He knew the traditions and methods of the synagogue, but had never had the formal training that was becoming standard for scribes in formative Judaism. He was likely some kind of teacher for his community, although it is difficult to describe in "official" terms what kind of teacher that was. He may have drawn a cameo self-portrait in 13:52 of the "scribe who has been trained for the kingdom of heaven," but *scribe* is not intended in the technical sense here.

MATTHEW IN LITERARY PERSPECTIVE

Literary Criticism. The Gospel of Matthew is neither a record made by a reporter nor a collection assembled by an editor, but a narrative composed by an author. Thus literary criticism in biblical studies today connotes something more comprehensive than analysis of language and style—namely, the study of the rhetorical techniques used by the

31. See Wilhelm Schneemelcher, *New Testament Apocrypha: Gospels and Related Writings* (Louisville: Westminster/John Knox, 1990). His table of contents lists 63 titles, several of which are attributed to characters more "minor" than Matthew (e.g., Thomas, Philip, Matthias, Gamaliel).

32. A significant minority of scholars understand the strong Gentile orientation of the Gospel to mean that the author himself must have been a Gentile, attributing the Jewish elements in the Gospel to the evangelist's tradition rather than his redaction. See Strecker, *Weg;* John Meier, *Matthew,* New Testament Message 3 (Collegeville, Minn.: Liturgical Press, 1990; reprint of Wilmington, Del.: Michael Glazier, 1980).

author in composing the narrative.[33] Matthew did not compose *ex nihilo,* but certainly used sources and traditions grounded in the actual events of the life of Jesus and the early Christian movement. Yet the final composition is the literary creation of an author, who made authorial decisions about (1) which literary genre to adopt or adapt for his composition (see below); (2) where and how to begin and end the story (see Commentary on 1:1, 18; 28:18-20); (3) how to structure the narrative so that its movement communicated the meaning he wanted to evoke (see below); (4) what kind of narrator would tell this story;[34] (5) from what point of view the story would be told;[35] (6) how the narrative was to be plotted; (7) who the characters would be and how they would be characterized; and (8) the implied reader—i.e., the ideal reader presupposed by the way the document is written, the intended readers in Matthew's church, who may or may not correspond to actual readers.[36] The interrelations of these dynamics make a story communicate meaning. The analysis of how meaning is communicated through its literary forms is the concern of a number of related and overlapping disciplines, which may all be considered aspects of literary criticism: narrative criticism (narratology), rhetorical criticism, and reader-response criticism.

Just as source criticism dominated Gospel studies of the late nineteenth and early twentieth centuries, so also form criticism prevailed in the period between the two World Wars, and redaction criticism became foremost during the 1950s and 1960s. So in the last two decades literary criticism, without replacing the other approaches, became a prominent and indispensable method of Gospel interpretation. Instead of attempting to reconstruct sources and earlier forms of the text in order to look through it as a window to the events that lay behind it, current literary criticism strives to look at the final form of the text as a whole, to enter into the story world it creates, and to be addressed by the message of the story itself. While the redaction-critical approach permitted the interpreter to state the message of the Gospel in a series of abstract statements summarizing the main points of the "theology of the evangelist," illustrated by the redactional changes he had made, literary criticism insisted on the inseparability of the message and the story form in which it is embodied, which is not a disposable container for the "message" or "theology" of the evangelist. Literary criticism reminds us that the Gospel form, the story about Jesus,

33. From the recent bibliographical explosion on this subject, the following provide readable introductions related to interpreting the Gospel of Matthew, and further bibliography: Norman R. Peterson, *Literary Criticism for New Testament Critics* (Philadelphia: Fortress, 1978); Mark Allan Powell, *What Is Narrative Criticism?* (Philadelphia: Fortress, 1990). See esp. Jack Dean Kingsbury, *Matthew as Story,* 2nd ed. (Philadelphia: Fortress, 1988); and the essays in *Interpretation* 46 (1992).

34. The Matthean narrator is omnipresent and omniscient in relation to the world of the story, allowing the reader to stand with the narrator as the silent observer of every scene. Temporally, the narrator is located after the resurrection but prior to the parousia, during the time of the church's duress in this world. The story world constructed by the author and communicated by the narrator is limited in time and space, however, not extending to the transcendent world of God or the demons or to pre-creation or post-parousia time.

35. The narrator's point of view corresponds to that of the main character, Jesus, whose point of view is identical with that of God. The reader thus sees and hears everything from God's point of view, to which the characters in the story are not privy.

36. For a concise discussion of all these aspects of literary criticism, see Kingsbury, *Matthew as Story,* 30-42.

is in continuity with the form of communication used by Jesus himself: the parable. In the Gospel, the teller of stories becomes himself the principal character in a story.

Genre. The issue of literary genre is a fundamental and indispensable *hermeneutical* concern. What kind of document one supposes one is reading is decisive for the question of meaning. Theoretically, one could think of Matthew as biography, history, fiction, midrash, lectionary, and other genres, or some hybrid of two or more of these. While a case can be made for each of the above, indicating that the Gospel genre has elements of and resemblances to more than one genre, recent scholarly debate has centered on whether the Gospel should be interpreted as a type of Hellenistic biography of Jesus, or whether the Gospel genre was an original form of narrative devised by the early church to communicate its faith in Jesus.[37] The present commentary is written from the perspective that the Gospel genre, while not utterly discontinuous from the available genres of literature, is a distinctive new departure fashioned to express in narrative form the christological convictions of early Christianity.

The following points are important for considering the genre of Matthew:

(1) Matthew is a narrative whole. It is neither a collection of individual stories nor a series of discourses with appended narrative sections. As a story, its mode of communication is indirect. Thus Matthew as a whole is to be interpreted as a story is interpreted, with the perspectives and tools of literary criticism.

(2) Because Matthew adapted and modified Mark, without a fundamental change in genre, the Gospel of Matthew is whatever Mark was. Two features distinguish Matthew (and Mark) from Hellenistic biography: (a) The Gospel is a community narrative, not an individualistic writing. The material for the story comes from the community tradition, a tradition that is already theologically charged. The story itself is intended for reading (aloud) in community worship and study, not for private, individual reading. Oral traits abound. (b) The narrative is permeated by christology. It is not only christological narrative, but it is christology in narrative form as well. Although it is the story of a historical figure who appears in almost every scene, and although it uses historical (and other) materials, the Gospel's purpose is not biographical but christological. (Especially in the case of Matthew, this means that it is also ecclesiological, since there is no christology without a corresponding understanding of discipleship.)

Three essential features characterize the narrative christology of the Gospels. (1) The story holds together in one narrative portrayals of the Christ that reveal both the transcendent power of God and the weakness of the fully human Jesus. The Gospel genre narrates the earthly career of a recent historical figure who is now the exalted and present Lord who continues to act and speak.[38] Within the narrative, Jesus is portrayed both as

---

37. During the period when form and redaction criticism of the Gospels was dominant (c. 1920–60), most NT scholars thought of the Gospel as a unique literary genre devised by the evangelists, as in the work of Rudolf Bultmann. More recently, scholarly opinion has tended toward "Hellenistic Biography," as argued most recently by Richard A. Burridge, *What Are the Gospels,* SNTSMS 70 (Cambridge: Cambridge University Press, 1992).

38. I have elaborated each of these points in Boring, *Truly Human/Truly Divine: Christological Language and the Gospel Form* (St. Louis: Christian Board of Publication, 1984) and in *Continuing Voice of Jesus: Christian Prophecy and the Gospel Tradition* (Louisville: Westminster/John Knox, 1991).

divine Lord and as truly human servant who suffers and dies. Prior to Mark, these two christologies struggled against each other. Mark saw the value of both and devised a way of presenting them together in one narrative, with the "messianic secret" as a primary literary-theological device. Matthew adopted Mark's product, but no longer needed the messianic secret, which he minimizes and includes in only a vestigial manner.

(2) The "life of Jesus" is portrayed as the definitive segment of the line of redemptive history. That is, the story of Jesus is not related as complete in itself. The narrative world of the Gospel is much larger than the plotted narrative, stretching from creation to eschaton. The story of the Christ is not the whole story of God's saving acts, but it is the definitive segment of that story. Within history, within one life, the meaning of the whole of history is disclosed, an advance picture of the eschatological victory of the kingdom of God. This is fundamental to the confession "Jesus is the Christ." The kind of narrative appropriate to this confession is the Gospel.

(3) The central figure of the narrative is at once the there-and-then Jesus of Nazareth as a figure of past history and the risen Lord who continues to speak and act in his church of the readers' present. Faith in the resurrection of Jesus is fundamental to this double perspective. As christology has implications for ecclesiology throughout, so here too the simultaneous double perspective on Jesus includes a double perspective on the other actors in the story. The disciples are not only the pre-Easter followers of Jesus, but are transparent to the Christian readers of Matthew's own time. The Pharisees are not only figures in a story about what happened to the historical Jesus, but represent the opposition to the church in Matthew's time.

The Gospels are different from Hellenistic biographies in that they presuppose and mediate a christological understanding of their central character that is different from the Hellenistic heroes and gods. This perspective on the nature of the Gospels is important for interpretation, whether or not one considers the Gospel genre unique.

Structure. Meaning and Structure. Meaning is communicated not only by what is said, but also by the strategy of communication built into the text as its rhetorical structure. We must, therefore, distinguish between outlines imposed upon the material by the modern reader and the document's own rhetorical structure built into it by the author and discovered by the interpreter. Matthew himself calls attention to the structural features of his opening section 1:1-17, from which it is clear that he is an author of considerable literary skill who does not compose randomly or casually. There are many indications of structural patterns that may be clues to the overall structure of the book.

Structural Patterns. *Chronology.* The Gospel is a narrative in chronological order, from Jesus' ancestry and birth through his baptism, ministry in Galilee, final journey to Jerusalem, conflict, arrest, crucifixion, resurrection, and concluding commissioning of the disciples. Matthew tightens the chronological connections of his sources, making many of Mark's paratactic connections (clauses that are parallel instead of each subordinated to the other) with "and" (καί *kai*) or "next" (εὐθύς *euthys*) more explicitly into a chronological narrative. This results in a more tightly knit story. Yet, it is clear that the historical chronology of Jesus' life is not Matthew's structuring principle, since he does not hesitate to rearrange the chronology of his sources and shows no interest in integrating the narrative into the chronology of the history external to the story world (cf. Luke 3:1-2), with the result that the reader is unable to designate the date or duration of the events portrayed in the narrative.

Geography. As in Mark, "Galilee" and "Judea" play important structural roles in the composition. Prior to the beginning of Jesus' ministry, he is something of a wanderer, the story line proceeding from Bethlehem to Egypt, back to Nazareth, then to the Jordan to be baptized, into the wilderness to be tempted (which involves trips back to Jerusalem and to a "very high mountain"), then back to Nazareth before finally settling in Capernaum as "his own city" (4:12-13; cf. 9:1). Matthew pointedly locates the beginning of Jesus' ministry in "Galilee of the Gentiles," underscoring the location with one of his formula quotations (4:14-16; on formula quotations, see Excursus "Matthew as Interpreter of Scripture," 151-54). Although Jesus makes journeys across the lake of Galilee and into Tyre and Sidon, Matthew seems to picture all of Jesus' ministry as being in Galilee until 19:1. From this point on, Matthew thinks of Jesus as being in Judea, including the territory on the east bank of the Jordan (Perea, Transjordan). Geographically, one could think of three sections of the narrative:

I. Pre-Galilean Preparation (1:1–4:16)
II. Galilean Ministry (4:17–18:35)
III. Judean Conflicts, Death, Resurrection, Return to Galilee (19:1–28:20)

Summaries. Q had no narrative summaries, and Mark had only two that picture Jesus traveling and that summarize an extended period of preaching and healing (Mark 1:14-15; 6:6 *b*). In addition, Mark had a number of summary statements that picture Jesus healing and teaching on individual occasions, without narrating the details (Mark 1:32-34; 3:7-12; 6:32-33, 53-56; 10:1). Matthew takes over all of the Markan summaries, uses them as transitions, and even elaborates them. Mark 3:7-12 and 6:6 *b* are used in Matt 4:23-25 and 9:35 as important structural brackets for a key Matthean unit. Otherwise, however, the summaries do not play major structural roles in Matthew's composition.

Speeches. Five times Matthew concludes a major speech of Jesus with almost identical formulae, "Now when Jesus had finished saying these things" (7:28 NRSV; cf. 11:1; 13:53; 19:1; 26:1). The formula acts not merely as a conclusion, but as a transition, pointing back to the completed speech and forward to the continuing narrative, relating Jesus' words to his deeds and binding speech and narrative together. Although perhaps derived from the transitional statement in Q (Luke 7:1), they are all redactional, representing part of Matthew's own structural pattern. The outline of the speeches, and their location in the narrative, represent Matthew's own compositional decisions (see the Outline below). Each speech represents a major theme of the Gospel: (1) The Sermon on the Mount (5:1–7:29) presents the authoritative teaching of the Messiah, who has come not to destroy the Law but to fulfill it. (2) The Missionary Discourse, 10:5b-42, is Christ's address to his disciples, who are sent forth in mission as representatives of Christ and with his authority. (3) The parable collection, 13:1-52, portrays the hiddenness of the kingdom of God in the present, in conflict with the evil kingdom of this age, but ultimately triumphing over it. (4) The discourse of 18:1-35 concerns the internal life of the church, addressing its need of both rigorous discipline and profound forgiveness if its members are to live together as Christ's disciples. (5) The concluding Judgment Discourse, 23:1–25:46, corresponds to the initial paradigmatic Sermon on the Mount, placing the life called for there in a specific eschatological context of universal judgment and triumph of God's kingdom.

Already in the second century Matthew was regarded as structuring his Gospel in five "books" in imitation of the Pentateuch and as an alternative to the Jewish understanding of Law.[39] This view was made popular by B. W. Bacon in the early twentieth century and has since been adopted with variations by several leading Matthean scholars.[40] The speeches are an important structuring device, but the Gospel should not be regarded as a structure of five speeches with a narrative framework. The narrative is primary with the speeches inserted into it.

Repeated Formulae and Framing Devices. Two examples of repeated formulae as structural markers are:

1. "From that time Jesus began to . . . [ἀπὸ τότε ἤρξατο ὁ Ἰησοῦς + infinitive, *apo tote ērxato ho Iēsous*]" (4:17/16:21). The first occurrence of the formula introduces Jesus' public proclamation of the kingdom of God, leading to conflict and rejection. The recurrence of the formula in 16:21 introduces the period of Jesus' private instruction of his disciples concerning his suffering, death, and resurrection. If these are considered the primary structural markers, the following outline results:

I. The Presentation of Jesus (1:1–4:16)
II. The Ministry of Jesus to Israel and Israel's Repudiation of Jesus (4:17–16:20)
III. Jesus' Journey to Jerusalem and His Suffering, Death, and Resurrection (16:21–28:20)[41]

2. The Sermon on the Mount and the following collection of miracle and discipleship stories are bracketed with almost identical summary formulae (4:23/ 9:35). The fact that the reader is encouraged to think of chapters 5–9 as a unit, "the messianic teaching and the messianic acts of power," seems to be clear from the narrator's reference to the collection of miracle stories in chapters 8–9 as "what Christ was doing" (11:2 NIV) and

---

39. See the discussion of an unidentified Greek fragment from the second century CE in Peter F. Ellis, *Matthew: His Mind and His Message* (Collegeville, Minn.: Liturgical Press, 1974) 10.

40. Bacon's view was set forth in his *Studies in Matthew* (New York: Henry Holt, 1930).

41. See Jack Dean Kingsbury, *Matthew as Story,* 2nd ed. (Philadelphia: Fortress, 1988) 40; David R. Bauer, *The Structure of Matthew's Gospel: A Study in Literary Design,* JSNTSup 31 (Sheffield: Almond, 1988).

from Jesus' statement that follows in 11:4, "Go and tell John what you hear [chaps. 5–7] and see [chaps. 8–9]" (NRSV). Matthew has altered Q at 11:4 in order to get this pair.

Chiastic Structures. Chiasm is an elaboration of this framing technique in which pairs of units are arranged to form a series of corresponding frames arranged around a central focus—e.g., in the pattern ABCBA. This rhetorical pattern was fairly common in the ancient world. Both Peter F. Ellis and C. H. Lohr[42] see the entire Gospel arranged according to this chiastic structure, an arrangement correlated to the "five-books" scheme discussed above:

A 1–4 Birth and beginnings		Narrative
B 5–7 Blessings, entering the kingdom		Discourse
C 8–9 Authority and invitation		Narrative
D 10 Mission discourse		Discourse
E 11–12 Rejection by this generation		Narrative
F 13 Parables of the kingdom		Discourse
E' 14–17 Acknowledgment by disciples		Narrative
D' 18 Community discourse		Discourse
C' 19–22 Authority and invitation		Narrative
B' 23–25 Woes, coming of the kingdom		Discourse
A' 26–28 Death and rebirth		Narrative

Chiastic structure is clearly a part of Matthew's technique and represents one of his favorite structuring devices, especially in 1:1–12:21, where Matthew is most freely creating his own structure. The neatness of such charts is beguiling, however, and fitting the whole Gospel into a single chiastic pattern requires some forcing.

Triadic Patterns. Matthew's tendency to compose in triads has often been noted, most recently in the work of W. D. Davies and Dale C. Allison, Jr.[43] Matthew himself calls attention to his triadic structure of the initial unit, the genealogy (1:2-17). There are numerous other triadic constructions (e.g., three temptations in 4:1-11), especially in the early part of the Gospel, where Matthew is creatively composing. However, this pattern disappears as soon as Matthew begins to follow the Markan order at Matthew 12:22/Mark 3:22 (see detailed sectional outlines in the Commentary). Triadic composition as a Matthean feature seems to be confirmed by the fact that the Matthean additions to the Markan speeches are consistently triadic, while the material adopted from Mark is not.

A Single, Comprehensive, Mono-Level Outline? Some of the patterns noted above coincide and reinforce each other. For instance, the geographical turning point at the beginning of the "Galilee" section coincides with the "from that time Jesus began . . .

42. Ellis, *Matthew,* 10-13; C. H. Lohr, "Oral Techniques in the Gospel of Matthew," *CBQ* 23 (1961) 404-27.

43. W. D. Davies and Dale C. Allison, Jr., *A Critical and Exegetical Commentary on the Gospel According to Saint Matthew,* ICC 2 vols. (Edinburgh: T. & T. Clark, 1988–91) 1:66-68. Already W. C. Allen, *A Critical and Exegetical Commentary on the Gospel According to St. Matthew,* ICC (New York: Scribners, 1910) lxv, gives a long list of Matthean triads.

[infinitive]" formulae of 4:17 and 16:21. Other patterns seem to be independent of each other. Some patterns may have belonged to Matthew's sources rather than reflecting his own composition. This means that it is not possible to integrate all of the structural patterns that can be observed in Matthew into one flat-surface, one-dimensional linear outline that the reader can see as *the* outline of Matthew. The structure of Matthew should be thought of in a more dynamic, interactive way, as a complex of interlocking structures with more than one movement present in the text at the same time, as though there were multiple layers of outline; as a result, any one element may be involved in the dynamics of more than one movement. That the "outline" is not neat and obvious may not necessarily mean that Matthew is casual or spontaneous, but that the writer was somewhat constrained by his materials. It may also be that Matthew the writer excelled at storytelling and that, therefore, he kept the outline inconspicuous, not allowing it to intrude in such a way that the story can be "summarized." The outline below is an effort to attend to and respect the different levels of structural dynamics in Matthew's story, yet present a linear, flat-surface outline to help the reader grasp the Gospel as a whole.

Matthew's Sacred Tradition (Mark and Q) as the Key to His Structure. Matthew was deeply influenced by the structures of both of his major sources. Although he rearranged several items in order to get similar material together, he maintained the rough outline of both Q and Mark, following Q more closely in the earlier chapters and Mark more closely from 12:22 on. Since both Matthew and his intended readers were thoroughly familiar with the story line of Mark, Matthew made the Markan narrative fundamental for the structure of his own story. After extracting material from later sections of Mark for his creative structure of 1:12–12:21, he never deviated from the Markan order of pericopes from Matt 12:22//Mark 3:22 to the end of the Gospel. In the first part of the Gospel, the original readers would recognize Markan and Q materials, but rearranged and amplified to produce an entirely new story world. From 12:22 (Mark 3:22) on, the reader would be in familiar territory, but would have been given a new framework within which to interpret it. In Matthew's restructuring of the story, the kingdom of God became the key theme of the whole. Matthew's Gospel should thus be thought of as being structured in two main parts oriented to his treatment of Mark, with the kingdom of God as the comprehensive theme uniting the whole.

The Structure of Part One, "The Conflict of Kingdoms Initiated and Defined" (Matthew 1:1–12:21). Matthew chose the conflict scene in Mark 3:22-30 as the key point at which to join his own composition to the Markan story line (Matt 12:22). Matthew's choice seems to have been influenced by the fact that this scene is one of the few that appears in both of his sources (for Q, see Matt 12:22-24//Luke 11:14-15). The primary reason for choosing this section where his two sources converge, however, is the conflict it pictures between the kingdom of Satan and the advent of the kingdom of God proclaimed by Jesus. This conflict between the evil of the present world represented by the "kingdom of Satan" and the coming kingdom of God already present in Jesus is fundamental to understanding both the plot and the theology of the Gospel of Matthew.

The explosive conflict in this scene is ignited by the charge that Jesus has Beelzebul—i.e., that he is in league with Satan and works by Satan's power (12:24, 26). This accusation, attributed by Matthew specifically to the Pharisees (Mark 4:22, "scribes"; Luke 11:15 "some") was very important to Matthew. Members of his own community, and perhaps he himself, had faced this charge from the emergent Pharisaic leadership (cf. 10:25). Matthew had obviously reflected deeply on this theological indictment, found in both his major sources, and made it central to the own structure of his work.

With his eye on this scene in the Markan narrative, and using materials from Q, Mark, and the traditions of his own community, Matthew composed an extensive section, the entire first part of his narrative, that builds toward this key scene of conflict in Mark. Already this is a clue that conflict is key to the plot of Matthew's story.[44] The story begins with the announcement of the advent of a new "King of the Jews" (1:1-25). But this proclamation is made in a setting where a king already represents the ruling power of that age. In the conflict that necessarily results, the Jewish leaders side with the earthly ruler, while the king sent from God is worshiped by Gentiles (2:1-23). John the Baptist appears with the message of the near advent of God's kingdom, and Jesus begins his ministry only after being baptized by John (3:1–4:17). Jesus then calls disciples (4:18-22), who are witnesses to the word and works of the messianic king (4:23–9:35). The disciples are called to follow Jesus, who empowers and equips them for their mission to represent him, but they still live in this age and are tempted to waver (9:36–11:1), as is John the Baptist himself (11:2-19). Thus the conflict continues (11:20–12:14), even though the new king is a servant figure who, when the Jews reject him, will fulfill Scripture by bringing salvation to the Gentiles (12:15-21). Using a chiastic pattern, Matthew has carefully arranged, rewritten, and expanded his traditional materials into the following structured narrative.

A Jesus as Messianic King, Son of David and Son of God 1:2-25
 B Conflict with the Kingdom of This Age 2:1-23
  C The Ministry of Jesus in Relation to John the Baptist 3:1–4:17
   D The Disciples Called 4:18-22
    E The Authority of the Messiah
     in Word and Deed 4:23–9:35
   D' The Disciples Authorized and Sent 9:36–11:1
  C' The Ministry of Jesus in Relation to John the Baptist 11:2-19
 B' Conflict with the Kingdom of This Age 11:20–12:14
A' The Servant King 12:15-21

This chiastic structure is formed "from the inside out"; thus it may be thought of as a series of concentric circles (see Fig. 2). The section 4:23–9:35 is clearly marked off by Matthew himself, by more than one signal: (1) 4:23 is a bracket with 9:35; (2) 11:2, "what the

44. See Mark Allan Powell, "The Plot and Subplots of Matthew's Gospel," *NTS* 38 (1992) 187-204.

Messiah was doing" (NRSV), points back to chapters 8–9, continued by the disciples in chapter 10; (3) 11:4, "hear and see," refers to chapters 5–7 ("hear") and 8–9 ("see"); and (4) 11:4b-5 describes the content of chapters 5–9. Thus "the Messiah in word and deed" as the central defining core is surrounded by discipleship sections: 4:18-22, the disciples called, and 9:36–11:1, the disciples authorized and sent. The Messiah is not thought of as an individual (a "great man"), but as the generator of the messianic community. So 4:18–11:1 embrace the Messiah/disciples. There are clear structural markers at these two points in the narrative.

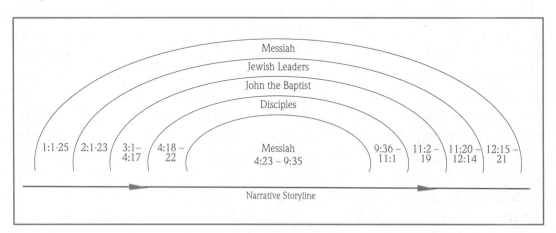

Figure 2: The Structure of Matthew 1:1–12:21

The next concentric circle comprises the sections presenting John the Baptist. John is located between "the disciples" and "the opponents." On the one hand, he is honored as a true prophet of God, the greatest "among those born of women" (11:11 NRSV), whose message anticipates and is identical with Jesus' (3:2/4:17) and whose ministry marks the turning point of the ages (11:12). On the other hand, he never becomes a disciple, nor do his disciples transfer their allegiance to Jesus but continue as an independent group (9:14); after 3:17 the logic of Matthew's theology and story requires that they should do so. Matthew's story comes to terms with this historical reality by locating John and his disciples as neither disciples nor opponents, though they play important roles in God's saving plan on the border between disciples and opponents; therefore, they are allied with Jesus.

The next circle is represented by the Jewish leadership, who are portrayed as flat characters consistently opposed to Jesus, antithetical to the kingdom proclaimed and made present by him. They are, in fact, the representatives of the kingdom of Satan. They struggle with Jesus for allegiance of "the crowds" and finally win them over (27:20-25).

The outermost bracket surrounding the whole, as well as the central core, is filled by Jesus, the king who redefines kingship. The lines that indicate the correlated sections are not intended to separate them as though they were discontinuous with each other, just as the diagram that distinguishes Part One from Part Two (Fig. 3) is not intended to divide the book into two discontinuous halves. The book as a whole is a continuous narrative, in which each section both builds on the preceding and prepares for the next. In particular, Matthew's creative Part One is not discontinuous from Part Two, but prepares the reader for it and leads in to it.

In this framework, Jesus himself as messianic king is central, filling not only pivotal central section 4:23–9:35 (E), but the beginning and ending units that frame the entire section as well (A, A'). Note that the conflict is not ultimately between Jesus and the Jewish leaders; the narrative unfolds as the earthly, historical segment of a cosmic story (see Commentary on 4:1-11; 12:22-32; 13:36-39). The this-worldly conflict with which the narrative is concerned has a cosmic, mythological backdrop and points beyond itself. Thus God is the hidden actor in the story throughout, and Satan is the hidden opponent. The conflict with Satan is woven into the structure throughout as an underlying theme (exorcism stories); thus it is not to be localized only in the "temptation" passage (4:1-11), which is only one incident among others, not a major turning point in the outline. The repeated charge of collusion with Beelzebul in 9:32-34 and 10:25 keeps the conflict alive in an ironic way, and prepares the reader to rejoin the Markan story line at 12:22 (= Mark 3:22) on the note of conflict with Israel. The reader now knows that Satan, though already defeated by Jesus, is in the background of this conflict. The original readers were aware from their own experience that the conflict continues through the narrative and into the reader's own time, even among Jesus' disciples (16:23).

Figure 3: The Structure of the Gospel of Matthew

The Structure of Part Two, "The Conflict of Kingdoms Developed and Resolved." This narrative picks up the Markan story line at 12:22 (= Mark 3:22), and the conflict continues. Matthew's church, previous hearers/readers of Mark's Gospel and Q, have now been given a new framework for interpreting their sacred tradition. From 12:22 on, the narrative sections simply follow the Markan outline and order. Matthew imposes his own stamp on it by inserting his own traditions and compositions into the narrative sections and by developing the Markan speeches into major compositional units to correspond to the Sermon on the Mount and the Missionary Discourse in Part One. The resulting series of five speeches thus forms the interlocking structure between Parts One and Two.[45]

The structure of the Gospel may thus be visualized as shown in Figure 3.

MATTHEW IN THEOLOGICAL PERSPECTIVE

The Gospel of Matthew is a theological document. The subject matter is God's saving act in Christ, with Jesus appearing in almost every scene. Thus while Matthew may also be used as a source from which to glean historical and sociological data about early Judaism and Christianity, the Gospel itself is a theological document that must be understood theologically. This means, in the first place, one needs to make an effort to apprehend the Gospel in Matthew's theological categories: God, kingdom of God (vs. kingdom of Satan), christology, church, history, fulfillment and eschatology, ethics, law, and discipleship. This is the theological minimum, necessary even to describe Matthew historically. For the contemporary interpreter who approaches the Gospel as canonical Scripture, theological interpretation also involves the hermeneutical task of translating Matthew's theological affirmations into categories meaningful to one's own age.

Although the Gospels were not originally written to us, there is another, equally valid, sense in which it is true and important to say that they were written to us. The Gospels were all addressed to the church to help the Christian community understand, clarify, and share its faith in Jesus as the Christ. The contemporary church is in historical, organic, theological unity with the Christian communities to which the Gospels were originally addressed. The life of the church through the centuries is the living theological link through which the Gospels have been transmitted and continually reinterpreted to the present day. The fact that the New Testament is the church's book means that the interpretative task already under way in the composition of the Gospels continues in the hermeneutical task of making theological sense of the Gospels' message in our time and place. The original message must first be heard in its own context and categories. To become a live option and address of the Word of God to us, it must then be translated into contemporary theological categories. The interpreter's task is not only to uncover the theology of the

45. For a more detailed rationale for the structure here proposed, see M. Eugene Boring, "The Convergence of Source Analysis, Social History and Literary Structures in the Gospel of Matthew," *JBL Seminar Papers* (Atlanta: Scholars Press, 1994) 587-611.

ancient writer in his terms, but to make it hearable in contemporary terms as well. Commentary on a canonical text and construction of a systematic statement of Matthew's theology are different tasks. No attempt will be given here to summarize Matthew's theology, which is integrated into his narrative and explicated in the commentary itself. This commentary attempts to help the modern reader interpret the ancient text with a view to its translation into contemporary meaning.

Historical study of the Gospel of Matthew is an ally in this task. Matthew was himself an interpreter, standing in the living streams of tradition, interpreting the meaning of the Old Testament into the new situation by looking back on the advent of the Christ, his ministry, crucifixion, and resurrection. In particular, Matthew stands in a Christian hermeneutical stream interpreting the sacred texts of Christian tradition revered in his church (namely, Q and Mark) and the M traditions unique to the Matthean community. Matthew's own interpretation represented in the Gospel of Matthew then entered into the living stream and has been the object of interpretation in the church for nineteen centuries. The contemporary interpreter stands with Matthew in this continuing stream, heir to Matthew's Bible and his Christian traditions (Q, Mark, M), the Gospel of Matthew itself, and the church's continuing interpretation of them all. Matthew is not the passive object of our interpretive work. He is a fellow interpreter who speaks not only to us, but also with us.

BIBLIOGRAPHY

Davies, W. D., and Dale C. Allison, Jr. *A Critical and Exegetical Commentary on the Gospel According to Saint Matthew.* 2 vols. ICC. Edinburgh: T. & T. Clark, 1988, 1991. Detailed analytical study emphasizing historical criticism, cataloguing the range of interpretation on each pericope.

France, R. T. *Matthew: Evangelist and Teacher.* Grand Rapids: Zondervan, 1989. An evangelical, moderately critical introduction to Matthew, emphasizing the historicity of the narrative and traditional conclusions. Theologically insightful.

Hagner, Donald. *Matthew 1–13.* WBC 33a. Dallas: Word Books, 1993. Detailed historical exegesis and theological interpretation from critical evangelical perspective.

———. *Matthew 14–28.* WBC 33b. Dallas: Word Books, 1995. Companion to above.

Kingsbury, Jack Dean. *Matthew as Story.* 2nd ed. Philadelphia: Fortress, 1988. Excellent example of a contemporary literary-critical approach.

Luz, Ulrich. *Matthew 1–7: A Commentary.* Minneapolis: Augsburg, 1989. The first in a projected four-volume English translation of *Das Evangelium nach Matthäus. Evangelisch-Katholischer Kommentar zum Neuen Testament.* Benziger Verlag & Neukirchener Verlag, 1985–. Emphasizes redaction criticism, history of interpretation, and hermeneutics. Further volumes to appear in *Hermeneia* series, Fortress Press.

Meier, John. *Matthew.* Volume 3 of the New Testament Message series. Collegeville, Minn.: Liturgical Press, 1980. Readable brief commentary.

Works About Matthew's Use of the Old Testament:

Gundry, Robert H. *The Use of the Old Testament in St. Matthew's Gospel.* Leiden: E. J. Brill, 1967.

McCasland, S. Vernon. "Matthew Twists the Scripture," *JBL* 80 (1961) 143-48, responded to by James A.

Sanders, "The Gospels and the Canonical Process." In William O. Walker, Jr., ed. *The Relationships Among the Gospels: An Interdisciplinary Dialogue.* San Antonio: Trinity University Press, 1978.

Soares-Prabhu, G. M. *The Formula Quotations in the Infancy Narrative of Matthew.* AnBib 63. Rome: Biblical Institute, 1976.

Stendahl, Krister. *The School of St. Matthew and Its Use of the Old Testament.* ASNU 20. Lund: C. W. K. Gleerup, 1954; reprinted with a new Introduction by the author, Philadelphia: Fortress, 1968.

Works About the Sermon on the Mount:

Augustine, "Our Lord's Sermon on the Mount." In volume 8 of *The Nicene and Post-Nicene Fathers.* Grand Rapids: Eerdmans, 1979.

Barth, Karl. *Church Dogmatics.* Edinburgh: T. & T. Clark, 1957. II.2.686-99.

Bonhoeffer, Dietrich. *The Cost of Discipleship.* New York: Macmillan, 1963.

Calvin, John. *Matthew, Mark, and Luke.* Volume 1 of *Calvin's Commentaries.* Edited by D. W. Torrance and T. F. Torrance. Grand Rapids: Eerdmans, 1972.

Guelich, Robert. *The Sermon on the Mount.* Waco, Tex.: Word Books, 1982.

Luther, Martin. "The Sermon on the Mount." In volume 21 of *Luther's Works.* Edited by Jaroslav Pelikan. St. Louis: Concordia, 1956.

Strecker, Georg. *The Sermon on the Mount: An Exegetical Commentary.* Nashville: Abingdon, 1988.

Works About the Kingdom of God:

Chilton, Bruce, ed. *The Kingdom of God in the Teaching of Jesus.* IRT 5. Philadelphia: Fortress, 1984.

Kingsbury, Jack Dean. "Matthew's View of the Son of God and the Kingdom of Heaven." In *Matthew: Structure, Christology, Kingdom.* Philadelphia: Fortress, 1975.

Ladd, George Eldon. *The Presence of the Future.* Grand Rapids: Eerdmans, 1974.

Perrin, Norman. *Jesus and the Language of the Kingdom: Symbol and Metaphor in New Testament Interpretation.* Philadelphia: Fortress, 1976.

Willis, Wendell, ed. *The Kingdom of God in 20th-Century Interpretation.* Peabody, Mass.: Hendrickson, 1987.

OUTLINE OF MATTHEW

I. Matthew 1:1–12:21, The Conflict of Kingdoms Initiated and Defined

   A. 1:1, A Title for the Whole Gospel

   B. 1:2-25, Jesus as Messianic King: Son of David and Son of God
         1:2-17, Genealogical Summary
         1:18-25, Joseph's Obedience

   C. 2:1-23, Conflict with the Kingdom of This Age
         2:1-12, Jewish Opposition and Gentile Worship
         2:13-23, Exile in Egypt, and Nazareth as Fulfillment

   D. 3:1–4:17, Jesus in Relation to John the Baptist
         3:1-12, John the Baptist

MATTHEW 1:1–12:21

THE CONFLICT OF KINGDOMS INITIATED AND DEFINED

OVERVIEW

Part One of the Gospel of Matthew comprises 1:1–12:21 (see Introduction). In this part, Matthew sets forth the conflict that results from the incursion of the eschatological kingdom of God into this world in the advent of the messianic King, Jesus of Nazareth. The omnipotent power of God's kingdom is represented by Jesus, whose kingship is characterized by non-retaliation and meekness (11:29; 21:5), and whose greatest command is love (22:34-40). The kingship of this world is the opposite of this King—i.e., it is the "normal" human concept of kingship that functions by violence, intimidation, and selfishness. In Matthew's apocalyptic, dualistic view, the "nor-

mal" administration of this world is portrayed as a kingship exercised by demonic power. When the Jewish leaders resist the kingship of God represented by Jesus, Matthew regards them as agents of Satan's domination of this world. Part One ends with the religious leadership's decision to kill Jesus (12:14), who does not retaliate, but withdraws (12:15-21). In Part Two, 12:22–28:20, the conflict between the two kingdoms is developed and resolved. The religious leaders succeed in their plot to kill Jesus, but precisely in Jesus' seeming defeat, the saving power of God is manifest both in the death of Jesus and in God's affirmation and reversal of it in the resurrection.

MATTHEW 1:1, A TITLE FOR THE WHOLE GOSPEL

NIV	NRSV
1 A record of the genealogy of Jesus Christ the son of David, the son of Abraham:	**1** An account of the genealogy[a] of Jesus the Messiah,[b] the son of David, the son of Abraham. [a] Or *birth* [b] Or *Jesus Christ*

COMMENTARY

Matthew 1:1 is composed by Matthew himself as a title for the whole Gospel.[46] The first two words, which literally mean "book of genesis" (βίβλος

γενέσεως *biblos geneseōs*), are an evocative phrase, rich in allusions, but inexact and difficult to restrict to one meaning. "Genesis" carries the overtones of Matthew's Bible rather than its usual Greek meaning, and seems perfectly suited to what Matthew is doing in his "book." The first word, *biblos* (βίβλος), occurs ten times in the New Testament (but

46. The title now prefixed to the document, various forms of "(The Gospel) According to Matthew," was added by the church in the second century (see Introduction). Others see 1:1 as introducing only the genealogy or birth story, as in both the NRSV and the NIV. Any translation embodies an interpretation here.

only here in Matthew), always elsewhere referring to a document as a whole, mostly to a book of Scripture. More important, in 41 of the 43 times *biblos*) occurs in the LXX—Matthew's Bible—it means "book," usually a book of Scripture, most often by Moses. This suggests that 1:1 does not designate merely the genealogy, or Jesus' birth story, but is Matthew's title for his whole work.

The word *genesis* has four connotations:

(1) *Genesis* connotes "story." In the LXX of Gen 2:4 and 5:1, the Greek for "genesis" (γένεσις *genesis*) translates as "generations" (תולדות *tōlēdôt*), in the sense of "history, continuing story" (cf. Tob 1:1; 1QS 1:1; 1QM 1:1). When applied to a person, *genesis* in this biblical sense can mean "account of a person and his or her continuing story" (never "ancestry"). In Gen 37:2, *tōlēdôt* is translated by the LXX as *genesis,* properly rendered in the NRSV as "This is the story. . . . " With Matt 1:1 as the title to the whole Gospel, the story itself begins at 1:2. This means that the genealogy is not a prefixed list of Jesus' ancestors, but is itself part of the story Matthew tells. Matthew's story begins not with the birth of Jesus, but with Abraham. The story of Jesus is a continuation and fulfillment of the story of 1:2-17, with no major break between 1:17 and 1:18. This means that the title can be read "The Book of the Story of Jesus Christ, 'Son of David' and 'Son of Abraham.' "

(2) *Genesis* connotes "continuing life and presence." In the Old Testament, this was by successive "generations," as the subject lived on in his or her descendants. In Matthew, Jesus' story continues not in his "descendants," but by his own continuing presence (see Commentary on 1:23).

(3) *Genesis* has the connotation of "origins," "beginnings," as well as "birth" (as in 1:18). The story of Jesus that Matthew tells is the beginning segment of the continuing story of Christ in the church. In Matthew's theology, Christ continues to be experienced as a present reality in the church (18:18-20; 28:20). Matthew's Gospel narrates the origin of that christological reality.

(4) *Genesis* connotes the first book of Moses, the first book of Matthew's Bible. Just as Matthew's Bible began with a book already called "Genesis" in his time, so also Matthew's book of the eschatological event of the Christ—which will culminate in the new creation, the "renewal of all things" (19:28; παλιγγενεσία, *paliggenesia*)—has a title that connotes "Genesis." And just as Genesis was the first of the five Books of Moses, so also Matthew's story of Jesus has many features that remind one of the biblical story of Moses. Matthew will immediately give a genealogy, which summarizes the biblical story and brings it into his own time. Matthew did not see himself as a writer of canonical Scripture; that became the perspective of the later church. But Matthew did see himself as writing in that tradition, a witness to the continuation of the biblical story of salvation (*Heilsgeschichte*) and its climax, definitive segment, and fulfillment in Jesus Christ.

Although the Greek genitive can be taken either way, "Son of Abraham" describes Jesus, not David. The title does not trace Jesus' ancestry back through David to Abraham, but characterizes Jesus as "Christ," the one who is "Son of David" and "son of Abraham." "Christ" is the key title for Jesus, not a part of his name. "Christ" (NIV) is the Greek and "Messiah" (NRSV) the Hebrew for the English word *anointed.*[47] "Son of David" is likewise a messianic title, not merely a reference to Jesus' ancestry. (For both titles, see Excursus "Matthean Christology," 353-61.) "Son of Abraham" is not a messianic title, but characterizes Jesus as being the authentic heir to whom the promises God made to Abraham apply (as in Luke 19:9; cf. Matt 3:9/ Luke 3:8). Abraham was not only the ancestor of the Israelite peoples, but he was also a Gentile when called by God, and was promised that through him all the families of the earth would be blessed, and that he would be the "father" (ancestor) of many nations (Gen 12:1-3; 17:5). Every reference to Abraham in Matthew relates him to the promises of God to all humanity, not exclusively to the Jews (3:9; 8:11; 22:32).

The title is Matthew's composition, his creative rewriting of the Markan title. Mark begins his Gospel with his sole reference to "Jesus Christ"; Matthew begins with the identical phrase, found only here and in 1:18 (the parallel is obscured by the NRSV's use of "Messiah" instead of "Christ" here). Mark also has an initial reference to Jesus as "Son of God." Matthew, too, affirms Jesus as Son of God, as he will shortly make clear (2:15;

---

47. The NRSV always translates *christos* (χριστός) in the Gospels as "Messiah" (excepting only Mark 1:1, 9:41; John 1:17; 4:25; 17:3), and translates it elsewhere in the NT as "Christ."

3:17; cf. Excursus "Matthean Christology," 353-61), but considers it theologically important to begin by referring to Jesus as the son of David and son of Abraham. In Mark, the phrase "son of David" has negative connotations and is applied to Jesus only ambiguously at best (see Commentary on Matt 20:30-31// Mark 10:47-48; Matt 22:41-44(45) //

Mark 12:35-37). For Matthew, "Son of David" is a key christological title with positive content, transformed and reinterpreted. Along with the declaration that he is the Messiah, this is the first affirmation made about Jesus, and it dominates the genealogy and birth story, which follow.

MATTHEW 1:2-25, JESUS AS MESSIANIC KING: SON OF DAVID AND SON OF GOD

Matthew 1:2-17, Genealogical Summary

NIV

²Abraham was the father of Isaac,
Isaac the father of Jacob,
Jacob the father of Judah and his brothers,
³Judah the father of Perez and Zerah, whose mother was Tamar,
Perez the father of Hezron,
Hezron the father of Ram,
⁴Ram the father of Amminadab,
Amminadab the father of Nahshon,
Nahshon the father of Salmon,
⁵Salmon the father of Boaz, whose mother was Rahab,
Boaz the father of Obed, whose mother was Ruth,
Obed the father of Jesse,
⁶and Jesse the father of King David.

David was the father of Solomon, whose mother had been Uriah's wife,
⁷Solomon the father of Rehoboam,
Rehoboam the father of Abijah,
Abijah the father of Asa,
⁸Asa the father of Jehoshaphat,
Jehoshaphat the father of Jehoram,
Jehoram the father of Uzziah,
⁹Uzziah the father of Jotham,
Jotham the father of Ahaz,
Ahaz the father of Hezekiah,
¹⁰Hezekiah the father of Manasseh,
Manasseh the father of Amon,
Amon the father of Josiah,

NRSV

²Abraham was the father of Isaac, and Isaac the father of Jacob, and Jacob the father of Judah and his brothers, ³and Judah the father of Perez and Zerah by Tamar, and Perez the father of Hezron, and Hezron the father of Aram, ⁴and Aram the father of Aminadab, and Aminadab the father of Nahshon, and Nahshon the father of Salmon, ⁵and Salmon the father of Boaz by Rahab, and Boaz the father of Obed by Ruth, and Obed the father of Jesse, ⁶and Jesse the father of King David.

And David was the father of Solomon by the wife of Uriah, ⁷and Solomon the father of Rehoboam, and Rehoboam the father of Abijah, and Abijah the father of Asaph,ᵃ ⁸and Asaphᵃ the father of Jehoshaphat, and Jehoshaphat the father of Joram, and Joram the father of Uzziah, ⁹and Uzziah the father of Jotham, and Jotham the father of Ahaz, and Ahaz the father of Hezekiah, ¹⁰and Hezekiah the father of Manasseh, and Manasseh the father of Amos,ᵇ and Amosᵇ the father of Josiah, ¹¹and Josiah the father of Jechoniah and his brothers, at the time of the deportation to Babylon.

¹²And after the deportation to Babylon: Jechoniah was the father of Salathiel, and Salathiel the father of Zerubbabel, ¹³and Zerubbabel the father of Abiud, and Abiud the father of Eliakim, and Eliakim the father of Azor, ¹⁴and Azor the father of Zadok, and Zadok the father of Achim,

ᵃOther ancient authorities read *Asa* ᵇOther ancient authorities read *Amon*

NIV

¹¹and Josiah the father of Jeconiah*ᵃ* and his brothers at the time of the exile to Babylon.

¹²After the exile to Babylon:

Jeconiah was the father of Shealtiel,
Shealtiel the father of Zerubbabel,
¹³Zerubbabel the father of Abiud,
Abiud the father of Eliakim,
Eliakim the father of Azor,
¹⁴Azor the father of Zadok,
Zadok the father of Akim,
Akim the father of Eliud,
¹⁵Eliud the father of Eleazar,
Eleazar the father of Matthan,
Matthan the father of Jacob,
¹⁶and Jacob the father of Joseph, the husband of Mary, of whom was born Jesus, who is called Christ.

¹⁷Thus there were fourteen generations in all from Abraham to David, fourteen from David to the exile to Babylon, and fourteen from the exile to the Christ.*ᵇ*

ᵃ11 That is, Jehoiachin; also in verse 12   *ᵇ17* Or *Messiah.* "The Christ" (Greek) and "the Messiah" (Hebrew) both mean "the Anointed One."

NRSV

and Achim the father of Eliud, ¹⁵and Eliud the father of Eleazar, and Eleazar the father of Matthan, and Matthan the father of Jacob, ¹⁶and Jacob the father of Joseph the husband of Mary, of whom Jesus was born, who is called the Messiah.*ᵃ*

¹⁷So all the generations from Abraham to David are fourteen generations; and from David to the deportation to Babylon, fourteen generations; and from the deportation to Babylon to the Messiah,*ᵃ* fourteen generations.

ᵃ Or the *Christ*

COMMENTARY

The purpose of the genealogy is not to give accurate history, but to set the story of Jesus into the context of the ongoing story of God's acts in history that will eventuate in the coming of God's kingdom, and of the one who is himself God with us. The genealogy is not the result of a biographical effort to discover genealogical data, but a literary-theological construction by Matthew himself, from his Bible, and (perhaps) from traditional genealogies circulating in Jewish Christianity. The list of thirty names from Abraham through Zerubbabel (1:2-12) can be reconstructed from the LXX of 1 Chr 1:28-42; 3:5-24; and Ruth 4:12-22. The nine names from Abiud through Jacob in 1:13-15 all occur in the LXX, but not in any relation to each other, so for this section Matthew will have depended on traditional material or constructed it himself from biblical names.

There is no common source lying behind either Matthew's or Luke's genealogy (Luke 3:23-38), as their differing form and content make clear. Matthew's is a narrative, a series of subjects and verbs that begins with Abraham and comes forward to Jesus. Luke's is not a narrative, but a series of genitive nouns that begins with Jesus and goes backward to Adam and God. In addition, the conflicts between Matthew and Luke where their genealogies overlap (see below) and the domination of the artificial and distinctively Matthean structure and theological concerns indicate that the Matthean genealogy is not a traditional list that goes back very early in the life of the church or to the family of Jesus. Except in priestly families, detailed genealogical records were rarely available. Many genealogies were tangled, and even some religious leaders could not trace their own genealogy. Some rabbis taught that clarification would occur in the messianic times when Elijah appeared. Occasionally genealogies were produced by imaginative puns on the words involved rather than from history or tradition. Joshua and Jonah were provided with genealogies by imaginative midrashic exegesis, as were famous rabbis. Thus the speculative, novelistic picture of Matthew or some other early Christian researching the genealogical archives of Bethlehem or interviewing members of Jesus' family should be abandoned as a fundamental misunderstanding of the historical reality of the times and of the gospel genre.

Matthew follows the biblical pattern of incorporating genealogical material into the narrative as a constituent element of the story, adopting the pattern found in Ruth 4:18-22: "A begot B." The very rigidity of the form makes the brief interruptions that mention the five women all the more striking. Thus the genealogy in Matthew is not a list, but a series of short sentences leading from Abraham to Jesus, the first narrative unit of the larger story that follows.

Like the title, the genealogical narrative is structured into three units. Matthew structures the genealogical story-summary around the Davidic kingship, the turning points being the accession of David and the loss of Davidic kingship at the exile. Israel had other kings after the exile, but they were not of the Davidic line. The artificiality of this arrangement becomes clear when it is noticed that several names must be omitted in order to achieve three periods of fourteen generations. This pattern, therefore, must have been theologically important to Matthew, who calls attention to it himself (1:17).

Dividing history into periods of fourteen appears elsewhere in Jewish tradition; e.g., world history is divided into fourteen periods from Adam to the Messiah in the pseudepigraphical book *2 Baruch* 53–74, and rabbinic interpretation counted exactly fourteen links in the chain of tradition between Moses and the final link in the last of the "pairs."[48] In such lists, the number fourteen was retained even when different names were included. The tradition already manifest in 1 Chronicles 1–2 of counting fourteen generations

from Abraham to David is reflected in other Jewish sources, and is reinforced by the fact that the numerical value of David's name in Hebrew (דוד *DWD*) is fourteen (ד, 4; ו, 6; ד, 4), who was thus "the fourteenth" in both senses. The rabbis loved such numerical word associations (*gematria*), so this is probably a significant factor in Matthew's structuring. The fact that fourteen is a multiple of seven may also have been a factor here, since Luke's genealogy, different as it is in other respects, is also structured in septads, with 56 names from Abraham to Jesus, with 42 names from David to Jesus, and contains a total of 77 names.

The genealogical story begins with Abraham, to whom the promise of blessing to all nations was made (Gen 12:1-3), and proceeds to David, the chosen king through whom the promise seemed destined to be fulfilled, who stands at the apex of the Israelite story. But David, the anointed king, was not the one to bring in God's kingdom, for Israel and David broke the covenant and the story of Israel began a sharp decline, resulting in the destruction of the holy city and the Temple and the exile of God's people to a Gentile land. It seemed that the Abrahamic promise and Davidic hope had been extinguished. But once again, things were not what they seemed. The story goes on, to arrive at the true "son of David," who will save his people. This is the meaning of the present shape of the genealogical story.

1:2. (See Genesis 12–37.) The mention of "brothers" here and in 1:11 may both accentuate the divine election of the son chosen to continue the line of redemptive history and serve as a reminder that the genealogy is not merely a list of individuals but the story of a community.

1:3. Tamar was the Canaanite wife of Judah's eldest son, Er, who died prematurely (Gen 38:1-7). When the patriarch Judah refused her normal considerations of remarriage, she tricked him into fathering her son, who then was incorporated into what was to become the messianic line (Gen 38:8-30). Judah declares her "righteous" (Gen 38:26), a key term in the Matthean story of Jesus' birth (cf. 1:19).

1:4. Ram (NIV) or Aram (NRSV) is the only name to appear in the genealogy for a span of approximately 400 years of the biblical story.

1:5. Matthew is the first, so far as we know,

48. Hillel/Shammai ('*Abot* 1:1ff).

to insert Rahab into the Davidic line, for there is no indication of this in the Old Testament, extant Jewish sources, or other early Christian sources. The importance of Rahab is that she, like Tamar, was a Gentile. Again, the generations are compressed. In the Old Testament chronology, Rahab belongs to the time of the conquest (Joshua 2–6), while Boaz lived almost 200 years later (Ruth 2–4).

Ruth was a Gentile from Moab. Moabites were specifically excluded from the Israelite community, even after ten generations (cf. Deut 23:3; Neh 13:1).

1:6-13. In this list of kings, the family line is traced through David's son Solomon, and constitutes the royal line of Judah. In v. 8, three kings are omitted (Ahaziah, 2 Kgs 8:25; Jehoash, 2 Kgs 11:1-4, 21; and Amaziah, 2 Kgs 14:1), along with Queen Athaliah (2 Kgs 9:27; 11:1), in order to conform to Matthew's structure of three sets of fourteen generations.

1:6. The "wife of Uriah" was an Israelite, but her marriage to a Hittite would cause her to be considered Gentile by later rabbinic law.

1:7-8. In 1 Kings 15:9-24, the Judean king is Asa. Asaph was a collector (the meaning of the name) of the Psalms, to whom certain psalms are attributed (Psalms 50; 73–83; cf. 2 Chr 29:30; 35:15; Matt 13:35 attributes Psalm 78 to Asaph the "prophet," in accord with his view that the Scripture as a whole is prophetic). The NRSV follows the best manuscript evidence,[49] while the NIV follows the mass of later MSS in harmonizing Matthew with the Hebrew Bible.

1:10. Similarly, the Judean king was Amon (NIV; cf. 2 Kgs 21:19-26), while Amos (NRSV) was the prophet. The manuscript tradition is divided. Although Amon/Amos and Asa/Asaph are possibly only Greek orthographical variations, it is more likely that Matthew originally wrote "Asaph" and "Amos" for theological reasons, pointing to Jesus as the fulfillment of the whole of Scripture—including the Psalms and Prophets—as well as the royal line. Later scribes then "corrected" some MSS to harmonize with the Old Testament, thus creating the variations in extant MSS.

1:11-12. Jechoniah, also called Coniah (Jer 22:24) is another name for Jehoiachin. His father

was Jehoiachim, not Josiah, who was his grandfather (2 Kgs 23:34–24:12), so either a generation is skipped here or the two similar names are confused. Jechoniah stands in the genealogy of the Messiah, despite Jeremiah's declaration (22:24-30) that he will be considered childless and that none of his descendants shall inherit the Davidic throne. Matthew inserts "brothers" for theological reasons (cf. 1:2), since Jehoiachin had only one brother (1 Chr 3:15).

1:13. Abiud is not found among the sons of Zerubbabel in 1 Chr 3:19-20. At this point Matthew's genealogy no longer depends on the Old Testament.

1:15-16. Luke 3:23 identifies Joseph's father as Heli. Since Joseph in Matthew's story seems to be typologically prefigured by his biblical namesake, whose father was Jacob (Genesis 37–50; cf. esp. revelation through dreams; a chaste and righteous person; a saving trip to Egypt; a forgiving attitude), theology rather than history may already be at work in the assignment of genealogical names two generations from Jesus.

The texts of the oldest, best, and vast majority of Greek MSS were followed by practically all modern English translations, to read as in the NIV and the NRSV. (Moffatt's translation is an exception in following the Old Syriac, see below.) One group of Greek MSS (Θ and f^{13}) and some Old Latin MSS have "Joseph, to whom the betrothed virgin Mary bore Jesus called the Christ," which could be understood and translated in such a way as to make Joseph the biological father of Jesus. It is more likely, however, that later scribes made this change to emphasize the (perpetual) virginity of Mary, since the older reading had called Joseph the "husband" of Mary. There are other variations in the MSS tradition, but only one MS, the Old Syriac (Sinaitic) reads "Joseph, to whom the virgin Mary was betrothed, begot Jesus." While it is utterly unlikely that this was the original reading in Matthew's Gospel, it is remotely possible that this was the original reading of a pre-Matthean form of the genealogy, which Matthew then changed. Matthew clearly understands Joseph to be the legal adoptive father of Jesus, not his biological father, and gives Joseph's genealogy in order to place Jesus in the legal line as the heir to Davidic kingship.

1:17. The first two segments of the genealogy

---

49. This includes $\mathfrak{P}^1$, ℵ, B, C, f^1, f^{13}, and several ancient versions.

have fourteen names each; the third has only thirteen.

The above comments have pointed to a number of inconsistencies between Matthew and the Old Testament. A comparison with Luke's genealogy of Jesus (Luke 3:23-38) reveals additional disagreements. Matthew declares that there are 42 generations between Abraham and Jesus (but he gives onlly 41), while Luke lists 56, with 42 generations from David to Jesus (for which Matthew has 27, claiming 28). Further, Matthew traces the line of Jesus from David through Solomon, so that names following David represent the royal line, the actual kings of Judah, while Luke's genealogy traces the line through David's son Nathan, resulting in a non-royal line. In Luke's list, most of the names from David on are different, making contact only at the names Salathiel, Zerubbabel, Eliakim, Amos, Eleazar, and Matthan, with all of these being in a different order except for the Salathiel/Zerubbabel pair. Matthew and Luke even give different names for Joseph's father (Matt 1:16, Jacob; Luke 3:23, Heli).

Various attempts have been made to harmonize the two genealogies. (1) One attempt to reconcile the discrepancies understands Luke to give Mary's genealogy and Matthew to give Joseph's, against the explicit statement of Luke 3:23.[50] In addition, Luke presents Mary as being related to the Leviti-

cal family of Zechariah and Elizabeth, not as belonging to the tribe of Judah and the line of David (Luke 1:5, 36). (2) Beginning with Julius Africanus in the early third century,[51] attempts have been made to harmonize some points in the two genealogies by postulating levirite marriages or adoptions in cases where Matthew and Luke present different names (cf. Deut 25:5-10). But even if this theory (for which no evidence is offered) were to be accepted as resolving some problems, many others remain. One such is the length of the generations posited by the genealogy. The four-hundred-year period from David to the deportation to Babylon, for which we have reasonably accurate records, was eighteen generations (Matthew gives fourteen)—i.e., one generation for every twenty-two years, which is historically plausible. For the remaining twenty-eight generations, covering 1,350 years, the average would be forty-eight years. The artificiality of the scheme is obvious, and Matthew's genealogy appears not to be factually correct. Detailed studies of biblical genealogies indicate their fluidity and that their function was not to reflect ancient history but to express and support a contemporary domestic, political, or religious point.[52]

50. John Calvin offered an extensive refutation of this view in his *A Harmony of the Gospels Matthew, Mark, and Luke* (Grand Rapids: Eerdmans, 1972) 52-55.

51. Eusebius *Historia Ecclesiastica* I. 7:1-10.

52. See Marshall D. Johnson, *The Purpose of the Biblical Genealogies,* SNTSMS (Cambridge: Cambridge University Press, 1969) 81; R. R. Wilson, *Genealogy and History in the Biblical World* (New Haven: Yale University Press, 1977).

REFLECTIONS

What does this text ask us to believe? Matthew is not interested in biology or genetics, but in making a theological claim, which may be summarized in the following four points.[53]

1. Jesus is the fulfillment of Israel's purpose and hopes. The theme of Matthew 1 is the identity of Jesus. But this is not expressed by describing Jesus as merely a spectacular individual. His story is part (the central, definitive part) of the story of God's saving activity, which began with Abraham and Sarah (really, as the story later makes clear, the story began with the creation) and extends to the eschaton. By definition, the Messiah does not wander onto the stage of history as an impressive newcomer to the drama, but in continuity with God's saving history in the past. Jesus, as Messiah, is saving history's goal, fulfillment, and definitive segment. Matthew has arranged the genealogy to express the threefold movement that began with Abraham, moved to David the Jewish king at the apex, then down to apparent defeat in the dissolution of David's kingdom; but then, in a surprising reversal, up again to Jesus Christ, the

53. Matthew's witness is obscured by attempting to combine it with Luke's birth story, which has its own message and theological integrity.

greater "Son of David." Despite Israel's sin in breaking the covenant, God held fast to the divine promises and directed history toward its fulfillment in Christ.

For some, this pericope is good news because of its claim that the fulfillment of the meaning of history has appeared in Christ. For others, however, the issue is whether there is any meaning in history to be fulfilled, by Christ or anyone else. Matthew is true to his Jewish faith in affirming God as the creator who will not let go of the creation, but will lead it to fulfillment even when there seems to be no meaning in history as a whole or in our own little lives. This is not an abstract idea, but is embodied in the series of particular names representing the persons, small and great, known and unknown, through whom God has already worked to bring the Messiah into this world. The ultimate meaning of what was going on was not obvious, but this list of names is Matthew's testimony that God works through the nitty gritty of ordinary human beings to bring the divine purposes to fulfillment.

2. The messianic story is inclusive, extending to women and men of all nations. *Inclusiveness* is not merely a contemporary buzzword. It is a deep note sounded in the first paragraph of the New Testament, a paragraph that sums up the story of the Old Testament, binding together the two books of the covenant (*testament* means "covenant" in both Hebrew and Greek) into one book of the story of God's saving acts in history. God's purpose is to include all. The story of redemption, the story of God's reuniting of divided and scattered humanity after the judgment of the flood and the fragmentation and alienation of the tower of Babel (Genesis 6–11) began with God's act of calling Abraham and Sarah and the promise of blessings for all peoples through them (Gen 12:1-3). As "son of Abraham," Jesus is declared to be the fulfillment of God's promises to the Gentiles.[54]

This inaugural note of inclusiveness corresponds to the inclusiveness of the whole genealogy, which names five women: Tamar, Rahab, Ruth, "the wife of Uriah," and Mary. Since ancestry and inheritance were traced through the father's line, reference to women in a genealogy was uncommon, but not unheard of.[55] Since all of the women mentioned are involved in some sort of questionable sexual behavior, it has often been suggested that this was Matthew's apologetic response to non-believers' insulting versions of the story of Jesus' birth from the virgin Mary. It could well be that, while not apologetic, Matthew is interested in affirming that the plan of God has often been fulfilled in history in unanticipated and "irregular" ways, as was the case in the birth of Jesus from Mary, and that Matthew is interested in showing that God worked through irregular, even scandalous ways, and through women who took initiative, like Tamar and Ruth. Yet the main reason for Matthew's inclusion of these women corresponds to one of the Gospel's primary themes: the inclusion of the Gentiles in the plan of God from the beginning. All of the men in Jesus' genealogy are necessarily Jewish. But the four women mentioned, with the exception of Mary, are "outsiders," Gentiles, or considered to be such in Jewish tradition. Just as the following story shows Jesus to be the fulfillment of both Jewish and Gentile hopes, so also the genealogy shows that the Messiah comes from a Jewish line that already includes Gentiles.

3. Jesus is the royal Messiah, the Son of David. "Son of David" is extremely important in Matthew's identification of Jesus (see Excursus "Matthean Christology," 353-61). Thus begins a royal motif that will be developed in the story of Jesus' birth and infancy in 1:18–2:23, which is a story of royalty. Kingship is central not only in Jesus' message of the kingdom of God, but also in the identification of his person. For Matthew, as "Son of David" Jesus is the royal heir to the throne. The first David was also "inclusive," in that he conquered other peoples and brought them within the orbit of Israel's sovereignty as conquered subjects. In the Gospel

---

54. The word for "nation" and "Gentile" is the same in Matthew's Greek. Jews understand Israel not to be a "nation," but a "people." "People of God" and "the nations/Gentiles" stand over against each other in Matthew's Jewish thought world.
55. Four women occur in the genealogy of 1 Chr 1:1–2:4.

story, Jesus, "King of the Jews," will redefine the meaning not only of inclusiveness, but also of kingship itself. Since kings and kingdoms are passé in our time, we must interpret Matthew's imagery, but dare not simply reject it, for it is the vehicle of the message he expresses.

4. God is the hidden actor. God is active in the whole story from Abraham to Jesus, from promise to fulfillment, not only in the extraordinary last item.[56] The list of "begats" in the long genealogy is not merely a dull preface to the exciting event of the virginal conception at the end of the series. God is the one who can create "children of Abraham" from stones (3:9), but who, in fact, works through the ordinary lives of ordinary people to bring into being the people of Israel represented by the descendants of Abraham, listed in the genealogy. God acted in an extraordinary manner to create Jesus as Son of God, and likewise God acted in "ordinary" ways to place Jesus in the promised line as a "son of Abraham." The same God is acting, whether in ordinary or extraordinary ways.

56. Cf. Daniel Patte, *The Gospel According to Matthew: A Structural Commentary on Matthew's Faith* (Philadelphia: Fortress, 1987) 20.

Matthew 1:18-25, Joseph's Obedience

NIV

[18]This is how the birth of Jesus Christ came about: His mother Mary was pledged to be married to Joseph, but before they came together, she was found to be with child through the Holy Spirit. [19]Because Joseph her husband was a righteous man and did not want to expose her to public disgrace, he had in mind to divorce her quietly.

[20]But after he had considered this, an angel of the Lord appeared to him in a dream and said, "Joseph son of David, do not be afraid to take Mary home as your wife, because what is conceived in her is from the Holy Spirit. [21]She will give birth to a son, and you are to give him the name Jesus,[a] because he will save his people from their sins."

[22]All this took place to fulfill what the Lord had said through the prophet: [23]"The virgin will be with child and will give birth to a son, and they will call him Immanuel"[b]—which means, "God with us."

[24]When Joseph woke up, he did what the angel of the Lord had commanded him and took Mary home as his wife. [25]But he had no union with her until she gave birth to a son. And he gave him the name Jesus.

a21 Jesus is the Greek form of Joshua, which means the LORD saves.
b23 Isaiah 7:14

NRSV

18Now the birth of Jesus the Messiah[a] took place in this way. When his mother Mary had been engaged to Joseph, but before they lived together, she was found to be with child from the Holy Spirit. [19]Her husband Joseph, being a righteous man and unwilling to expose her to public disgrace, planned to dismiss her quietly. [20]But just when he had resolved to do this, an angel of the Lord appeared to him in a dream and said, "Joseph, son of David, do not be afraid to take Mary as your wife, for the child conceived in her is from the Holy Spirit. [21]She will bear a son, and you are to name him Jesus, for he will save his people from their sins." [22]All this took place to fulfill what had been spoken by the Lord through the prophet:

[23] "Look, the virgin shall conceive and bear a son,
    and they shall name him Emmanuel,"

which means, "God is with us." [24]When Joseph awoke from sleep, he did as the angel of the Lord commanded him; he took her as his wife, [25]but had no marital relations with her until she had borne a son;[b] and he named him Jesus.

aOr Jesus Christ   bOther ancient authorities read her firstborn son

COMMENTARY

Within the thematic structure outlined above, chapter 1 presents Jesus as the royal Son of David and Son of God, whose advent immediately initiates the conflict of kingdoms developed in chapter 2. Even as a baby, the new king does not retaliate, but flees, finding safety among the Gentiles of Egypt (2:1-12). When he returns to the "land of Israel," he can no longer live in his own city, but becomes an exile in his own land, making a new home in "Galilee of the Gentiles" (2:13-23; cf. 4:15). Like all else in the Gospel narrative, every story is seen and interpreted from the narrator's post-Easter perspective so that the "infancy story" is an expression of the meaning of the whole Christ-event.

Matthew 1:18-25 is the opening scene in the Gospel, composed of five elements.

1:18a. Providing a transition to the main story, 1:18 resumes the story announced in 1:1 (the conjunction ["now" (δέ *de*) in the NRSV, not translated in the NIV] is resumptive), forming an inclusion by repeating the key words of 1:1.

1:18b-20a. This sets the narrative stage for the opening scene. When the narrative curtain opens, the reader learns from the narrator that some things have already occurred: (a) Mary and Joseph are already engaged. This was a binding arrangement between people already legally considered husband (v. 19) and wife (v. 20), so that unfaithfulness was considered adultery, and could be dissolved only by death or divorce (1:19). (b) Mary is already pregnant. The reader learns in v. 18 that conception is from the Holy Spirit; Joseph does not learn of it until v. 20, from the angel. "Found" in v. 18 does not have the tone of an exposé, but simply means "was." There are no novelistic dimensions to the story, the action of which has not yet begun. The narrator is bringing the reader up to date on the situation that obtained when the action of the story begins in v. 20. (c) Joseph has already become aware of Mary's pregnancy, but does not know its divine source. Matthew does not write for readers who know the Lukan story of the annunciation to Mary (Luke 1:26-38). The Law of Moses required capital punishment in such cases (Deut 22:23-27). By Matthew's time, this had been mitigated by rab-

binic practice, but the penalty was still severe and humiliating. The first and only thing said about Joseph's character is that he is "righteous" (δίκαιος *dikaios*), a key word in Matthew's theology, which can also be translated "just." In Matthew's setting, to be *dikaios* means to live by the law, God's revealed will. (d) Joseph, contrary to the behavior expected of one who is *dikaios*, had already decided not to go by the letter of the law, but chose out of consideration for Mary to divorce her quietly.

1:20b-21. Here the focus is on the angel's (God's) action. All of the above had already transpired by the time the story opens. After Joseph had decided on his course of action, the first action plotted in the story occurs, and it is an act of God, who sends an angel to speak to Joseph in a dream.

The angel's only action is to speak. The first words uttered are typical of angelic revelations, "Do not be afraid" (v. 20; cf. Gen 21:17; Matt 28:5; Luke 1:13, 30; 2:10; Rev 1:17). The divine message is, in effect, "Do not hesitate to take Mary as your wife." The angel gives an explanation for Mary's pregnancy, announcing the divine act that has already occurred. Based on this, a command follows: "*You* shall name the child, accepting him as your own and adopting him into the Davidic line as an authentic 'son of David.'"

The child is to be named Jesus (Ἰησοῦς *Iēsous*), Matthew's Greek for *Yēšûa* (ישוע), a shortened form of *Yĕhôšūa* (יהושע). These are all forms of the English name *Joshua*, which appeared as Ἰησοῦς (*Iēsous*, "Jesus") in Matthew's LXX. This Joshua/Yeshua/Jesus was the successor to Moses' authority (Num 27:12-23; Deut 31:7-23; Josh 1:5-9). The fact that Jesus inherits and fulfills Moses' role will be an important theme of Matthew's story. The repeated refrain in the story of Joshua, "I [God] will be with you" (e.g., Josh 1:9), is also an important Matthean motif that relates the biblical Joshua/Yeshua to his New Testament namesake (cf. 1:23).

The importance attached by Matthew to the name *Jesus* is clear from the fact that he inserted it eighty times into his sources. This name was popular in the first century (see Col 4:11; a person named Jesus is included in Jesus' genealogy by Luke [3:29]; Josephus knows of 20 different persons named Jesus). Thus the Savior receives a common human name, a sign that unites him with the human beings of this world rather than separating him from them. Yeshua/Jesus actually means "Yahweh helps." Matthew follows the popular etymology of the name, "Yahweh saves" (cf. Sir 46:1 with reference to Joshua). The Messiah is not an individualistic concept, not a "great man," but the eschatological deliverer of the people of God. Here and always in Matthew, Christ and church, christology and ecclesiology, are inseparable. Matthew declares that the deliverance Jesus will bring to "his people" will be from their sins, and he is silent about their earthly troubles and political exploitation by the Romans. The identity of "his people" is not specified. The reader would suppose the reference is to Israel, but as the plot develops the identity of the Messiah's people, the people of God, will be one of the points of conflict (21:43; 27:25).

1:22-23. This is the first formula quotation (see Excursus "Matthew as Interpreter of Scripture," 151-54). The direct address of the angel to Joseph, overheard by the reader, becomes again the direct address of the narrator to the reader, this time in an editorializing addition to the narrative, the first of the ten "formula quotations," five of which are found in the birth story of chaps. 1–2. In its original context, Isa 7:14 refers to the promise that Judah would be delivered from the threat of the Syro-Ephraimitic War before the child of a young woman who was already pregnant would reach the age of moral discernment. The child would be given a symbolic name, a short Hebrew sentence "God is with us" (עמנו אל *Immānû-ēl*) corresponding to other symbolic names in the Isaiah story. In Isa 8:8, "Immanuel" is addressed as already present. It is thus clear from both the context and the meaning of the word translated "young woman" (עלמה *'almâ*)[57] that the Isaiah passage neither referred to a virginal conception nor predicted an event in the long-range future, but was directed to Isaiah's own time. Matthew, however, understands Jesus to be a fulfillment of the whole of Scripture, and can illustrate and augment the Jesus story

with affirmations from his Bible, irrespective of their original meaning.

The selection of this passage is not arbitrary, however. Matthew is drawn to it by four things that made it appropriate: (1) The original oracle was addressed to the "House of David" (Isa 7:2, 13). (2) Matthew's faith affirms that Jesus is the one in whom the promised deliverance is realized, in and through whom "God is with us." (3) Since the LXX had translated *'almâ* with *parthenos* (παρθένος), which means primarily "virgin" but can also mean "young woman," this provided another point of contact with Matthew's story of Jesus. It is clear that Matthew already knew the story of Jesus' virginal conception, which he now understands in the light of this Scripture as its fulfillment. (4) The LXX had employed the future tense (the tense of the Hebrew is ambiguous and can mean that the young woman is already pregnant or will become pregnant). The LXX translators may have had the virgin Israel specifically in mind (cf. Amos 5:2), who by God's help would bring forth the Messiah. Matthew changes the LXX's second-person singular, "you shall call," to third-person plural, "they shall call." This does not refer to what "the people" of v. 21 will call him, for which "Jesus" (who saves from sins) would be more appropriate. Since the third plural is one of the Jewish circumlocutions to avoid pronouncing the sacred name of God,[58] and since naming in a Jewish context has to do with essential being and not merely labeling, Matthew's meaning is probably "God will constitute him the one who represents the continuing divine presence among the people of God."

1:24-25. Joseph's first act in the plotted narrative is to obey the command of God. By naming the child, he effectively adopts Jesus into the Davidic line. Matthew, and the Bible generally, invests great power in declarations and naming. By being named by Joseph, Jesus becomes part of the Davidic line.

Joseph does even more than the angel commanded in that he has no sexual relations with Mary until the child is born. The omniscient narrator, who knows the most intimate details of people's lives and makes the reader privy to them

---

57. Another word, בתולה (*bĕtûlâ*), means specifically "virgin."

58. Cf. Luke 12:20, 48; Rev 10:11; 12:6; Joachim Jeremias, *New Testament Theology: The Proclamation of Jesus* (New York: Charles Scribner's Sons, 1971) 9.

(see, e.g., 9:2-4; 26:39, 42), here he makes doubly certain that the reader understands that Joseph was not the biological father of the child. "Until" (ἕως *heōs*) in 1:25 implies that after Jesus' birth Mary and Joseph had a normal marital relationship and that the "brothers and sisters" of Jesus (13:55-56) are their children. It is possible to understand the phrase in such a way that allows for the view of Mary's perpetual virginity, developed in later tradition, but today even leading Roman Catholic exegetes question that this was Matthew's intended meaning.[59]

In all this, only the narrator and the angel speak. Joseph and Mary have no speaking parts, and Mary has no active part at all (cf. Luke 1:26-56). The only action is that of the angel, representing the divine initiative, and Joseph's obedient response. Matthew saved this action to be the end of this unit, the point to which he has been building: the naming of Jesus by Joseph, which incorporated him into the Davidic line.

59. See John P. Meier, "The Brothers and Sisters of Jesus in Ecumenical Perspective," *CBQ* 54 (1992) 1-28.

REFLECTIONS

1. As modern readers ponder the opening scene of Matthew's story, some may be struck by the similarity between Joseph's quandary and their own. We want to "do the right thing," and we believe that somehow it is revealed in the Bible. We may belong to a church that claims to accept the Bible as the norm for its faith and practice and, yet, sense that the "Christian thing to do" does not follow the letter of the Bible. There are some biblical commands that many churches, in all good conscience and with reverence for the Bible as the Word of God, simply do not obey. This is not only in such matters as the washing of feet (John 13:12-17) and holy kisses (1 Cor 16:20), but in more basic directions concerning divorce (Mark 10:2-12) and household structure and lines of authority (1 Pet 3:1-6). Matthew writes for such a church. As Jewish Christians who had always reverenced the Law, they sometimes found themselves torn between strict adherence to the letter of the Torah and the supreme demand of love to which their new faith called them (22:39-40). If they neglected the Law, they were accused by others, and perhaps by themselves, of rejecting Bible and tradition as the "unrighteous." But Joseph is pictured as "righteous," even though he had decided to act out of care for another person's dignity rather than strictly adhere to the Law. As it turned out, Joseph did not have to carry through on his decision, but the point is made: Matthew wants to instruct his church in being "righteous" (just, committed to justice) in a way that respects both the Law of the Bible and the Christian orientation to love, even if it seems to violate the Law. *How* this can be done, Matthew does not here tell us, but the first story has made contact with a live issue in Matthew's church and ours, and readers of Matthew will have their eyes open for further light (see Commentary on 5:17-48; 20:1-16; 22:34-40). Thus Matthew's meaning for this story cannot be appropriated until one has worked through the Sermon on the Mount, indeed until one has worked through the Gospel as a whole. (And this is true for every pericope in Matthew!)

Thus Joseph stands, at the beginning of Matthew's Gospel, as a model of what Matthew hopes for all disciples—indeed, for each reader of the Gospel. Joseph is already facing the "you-have-heard-that-it-was-said-but-I-say-to-you" tension that will be displayed in the Sermon on the Mount (5:21-48)—the tension between the prevailing understanding of God's commandments and the new thing that God is doing in Jesus. By Joseph's decision to obey the startling and unexpected command of God, he is already living the heart of the law and not its letter, already living out the new and higher righteousness of the kingdom (5:20). In a difficult moral situation, he attends to the voice of God, and he is willing to set aside his previous understanding of God's will in favor of this word from the living and saving God.

2. The first miracle in the New Testament is not the story of something Jesus did. It describes the act of God. In the birth story, as in the passion story, Jesus is passive and God is the actor. This is the nature of the Gospel as such. It is not the story of amazing things done by Jesus, but of what God has done for humanity in the event of Jesus Christ.

What is the particular theological meaning inherent in the Matthean story?

The birth of Jesus is important as a human birth, and not just as a miracle. While Matthew's theology does not explicitly oppose docetism (the view that the humanity and suffering of Jesus Christ were only apparent, not real), the birth story as such is inherently anti-docetic, as recognized by Ignatius, bishop of Antioch in the temporal and geographical neighborhood of Matthew. By picturing Jesus as a baby and a child who is passive and vulnerable, as he will be again in the passion story, Matthew begins and ends his story with the fragile human life of Jesus surrounded by God, who is the hidden actor throughout. Matthew tells the story in such a way that no one could mistake Jesus for a baby God (cf. the later apocryphal gospels).

While Matthew relates the miraculous virginal birth as a literal historical event, he does not base major theological claims on it. The virginal conception is not the proof, or even the meaning, of the Christian claim that Jesus is the "Son of God." The miraculous birth is never referred to again, not even in the rest of the "infancy narrative" (although Matthew does not forget it; see 2:13, 20). Verses 18-25 could drop out of the story without affecting the development of the narrative's plot or its essential message.

Yet, the claim that the Messiah was supernaturally conceived is not incidental to Matthew. It is one of several ways Matthew has of confessing his faith that Jesus is the Son of God; the fact that Matthew has other ways of so affirming Jesus means that Matthew does not bind faith in Jesus as the Son of God exclusively to one way of confessing it. When Peter later confesses the fundamental Christian faith that Jesus is "the Christ, the Son of the living God" (16:16), there is no indication that Matthew intends any reference to the extraordinary birth story. Matthew juxtaposes this way of picturing Jesus as the Son of God with other ways—e.g., Jesus' descent from David. Thus christological truth is communicated through narrative, which can hold together a variety of pictorial affirmations that logic finds difficult or impossible.

Matthew has no interest in relating the story of the virginal conception to later views of the sinfulness of sex as such from which the Messiah must be preserved, or from the taint of original sin, thought to be transmitted biologically.

The modern interpreter needs to know what Matthew and all his readers surely knew, that there were many stories of heroes and special personages who were "sons" or "daughters" of God through miraculous conception.[60] In parallel to this, Judaism had apparently already developed traditions suggesting that great figures such as Isaac and Moses had been supernaturally conceived, so that Jesus' supernatural conception is a part of Matthew's Moses typology.[61] There is a sense in which the pre-Matthean tradition of the virginal conception, adopted and interpreted by Matthew, uses this Hellenistic idea, already adopted by Hellenistic Judaism, as a means of interpreting Jesus' divine sonship. Yet there are great differences as well. In the New Testament birth stories, God does not assume the male role in the conception, but the Holy Spirit, the divine power, works in Mary to conceive a child without a human father. Jesus is not pictured as a hybrid product of divinity and humanity, and could never utter the self-description attributed by Pausanias to one of the Sibyls, born of one divine and one human parent:

---

60. For illustrative texts, see David R. Cartlidge and David L. Dungan, *Documents for the Study of the Gospels* (Philadelphia: Fortress, 1980), 129-136 (Plato, Alexander the Great, Augustus, Pythagoras, Hercules); and Klaus Berger, M. Eugene Boring, and Carsten Colpe, *Hellenistic Commentary to the New Testament* (Nashville: Abingdon, 1995) on Matt 1:18-25.

61. For Isaac typology, see 26:36; for Moses typology, see 5:1. For Isaac as having been miraculously conceived, see *Jub.* 16:12; for Moses' miraculous birth, see Philo *De Cherubim* 12–15; for Enoch's miraculous conception, see *2 Enoch* 71ff. None of these references is explicit; all are subject to other interpretations.

"I am by birth half mortal, half divine;
An immortal nymph was my mother, my father an eater of corn."[62]

In the story of Jesus, as in the Jewish traditions that had developed about Isaac and Moses, the point of the miraculous conception is not the divine nature of the child (neither Isaac nor Moses becomes a "son of God" by virtue of their special birth). It is, rather, the special role he will play in God's saving plan.[63]

3. It is clear from this opening scene that, for Matthew, the story of Jesus is a way of talking about God. In Jesus and his story, God is with us. This motif is prominent throughout Matthew: 10:40: those who receive Jesus' disciples receive him, and those who receive him, receive God; 13:37: Jesus himself (the exalted Son of Man) is the one who is active in the preaching of the gospel throughout the world; 16:18: the exalted Christ continues to build the church; 18:5 and 25:40: Christ is met in the encounter with little children and other needy persons; 18:20: Christ is present when the church convenes "in his name." And the Gospel concludes not with an ascension in which Christ departs, but with the promise of the resurrected Christ to be with his disciples until the end of the age (28:20), making a perfect literary and theological bracket with this opening scene.

4. Not only the modern reader who is more sensitive to feminist concerns, but also any careful reader will be struck by the modest role assigned to Mary in Matthew's story, in contrast to the Lukan birth story (Luke 1–2). However, the fact that the story is told from Joseph's point of view, and in such a way that Mary barely appears, is not merely the reflection of the patriarchal culture in which Matthew lived. Matthew's testimony to the role of women in the Messiah's appearance has already been documented by the striking inclusion of five women, including Mary, in the genealogy (see Reflections on 1:2-17). Here, the modest role assigned to Mary shows that the narrative of 1:18-25 is not a "birth story" at all, but an illustration of a central problem in Matthew's community, the relation of keeping the letter of the Law and being accepted by God as a righteous person. Yet Mary does play the essential human role in the advent of the Messiah, who comes at the divine initiative but not without a human mother. Joseph's obedience allows Jesus to be adopted as a true Son of David; it is Mary's role that allows Jesus to be born Son of God.[64]

---

62. Pausanias *Description of Greece* 10.12.2.
63. An excellent example of honest exegetical and historical-critical reflection on the meaning of the texts and the historicity of the virginal conception by a scholarly Roman Catholic who considers it a historical event is Raymond E. Brown's *The Birth of the Messiah: A Commentary on the Infancy Narratives of Matthew and Luke,* rev. ed. (Garden City, N.Y.: Doubleday, 1993). For an interpretation by a liberal Protestant who is skeptical about the literal historicity of the miraculous conception and considers it theologically important that Jesus was not literally born of a virgin, but who nonetheless regards the New Testament's birth stories of great theological value and importance, see J. A. T. Robinson, *The Human Face of God* (Philadelphia: Westminster, 1973) 36-66.
64. For an interpretation "against the grain of the narrative," see Elaine Mary Wainwright, *Towards a Feminist Critical Reading of the Gospel According to Matthew,* BZNW 60 (Berlin: Walter de Gruyter, 1991) 69-75, 171-75.

MATTHEW 2:1-23, CONFLICT WITH THE KINGDOM OF THIS AGE

OVERVIEW

Matthew tells the story of Jesus' birth as an anticipatory summary of the meaning of Jesus' life, death, and resurrection—as a prefiguration of Jesus' rejection by the Jewish leadership and his acceptance by seeking Gentiles. Casting the Jewish king, chief priests, and scribes in a negative light is not a matter of anti-Semitism (see Introduction) but reflects both the history of Jesus and the experience and interpretation of Matthew's Jewish-Christian community.

A king is born, but a king is already here; and there is room for only one king. The birth of Jesus, the messianic king, precipitates a conflict with the kingship already present in this world. The conflict drives Jesus from his native Judea to exile in "Galilee of the Gentiles." Thus the experience of Matthew's church is reflected in the way the story is composed. Just as 1:2-25 dealt with the question of Jesus' identity (who he is), so also 2:1-23 deals with the question of location (where he is

from), in each case from the point of view of christological expectation. If 1:2-25 can be labeled "From Abraham to Jesus," 2:1-23 can be designated "From Bethlehem to Nazareth." In the Gospel as a whole, the pattern is Galilee (3–18)/Judea (19–28), while in the birth story the pattern is Judea/Galilee, the two locations of the birth story thus forming a chiasm with the two locations of the ministry: Judea/Galilee//Galilee/Judea. Exiled from his native Judea, Jesus will return only to die. The risen Christ then returns to Galilee to begin the mission to all nations (28:16-20).

Matthew 2:1-12, Jewish Opposition and Gentile Worship

NIV

2 After Jesus was born in Bethlehem in Judea, during the time of King Herod, Magi[a] from the east came to Jerusalem [2]and asked, "Where is the one who has been born king of the Jews? We saw his star in the east[b] and have come to worship him."

[3]When King Herod heard this he was disturbed, and all Jerusalem with him. [4]When he had called together all the people's chief priests and teachers of the law, he asked them where the Christ[c] was to be born. [5]"In Bethlehem in Judea," they replied, "for this is what the prophet has written:

[6]"'But you, Bethlehem, in the land of Judah,

are by no means least among the rulers of Judah;

for out of you will come a ruler

who will be the shepherd of my people Israel.'[d]"

[7]Then Herod called the Magi secretly and found out from them the exact time the star had appeared. [8]He sent them to Bethlehem and said, "Go and make a careful search for the child. As soon as you find him, report to me, so that I too may go and worship him."

[9]After they had heard the king, they went on their way, and the star they had seen in the east[b] went ahead of them until it stopped over the place where the child was. [10]When they saw the star,

NRSV

2 In the time of King Herod, after Jesus was born in Bethlehem of Judea, wise men[a] from the East came to Jerusalem, [2]asking, "Where is the child who has been born king of the Jews? For we observed his star at its rising,[b] and have come to pay him homage." [3]When King Herod heard this, he was frightened, and all Jerusalem with him; [4]and calling together all the chief priests and scribes of the people, he inquired of them where the Messiah[c] was to be born. [5]They told him, "In Bethlehem of Judea; for so it has been written by the prophet:

[6] 'And you, Bethlehem, in the land of Judah,

are by no means least among the rulers of Judah;

for from you shall come a ruler

who is to shepherd[d] my people Israel.'"

[7]Then Herod secretly called for the wise men[a] and learned from them the exact time when the star had appeared. [8]Then he sent them to Bethlehem, saying, "Go and search diligently for the child; and when you have found him, bring me word so that I may also go and pay him homage." [9]When they had heard the king, they set out; and there, ahead of them, went the star that they had seen at its rising,[b] until it stopped over the place where the child was. [10]When they saw that the star had stopped,[e] they were overwhelmed with

l Traditionally *Wise Men*   *b*2, 9 Or *star when it rose*   *c*4 Or *Messiah*   *d*6 Micah 5:2

*a*Or *astrologers;* Gk *magi*   *b*Or *in the East*   *c*Or *the Christ*   *d*Or *rule*   *e*Gk *saw the star*

NIV	NRSV
they were overjoyed. [11]On coming to the house, they saw the child with his mother Mary, and they bowed down and worshiped him. Then they opened their treasures and presented him with gifts of gold and of incense and of myrrh. [12]And having been warned in a dream not to go back to Herod, they returned to their country by another route.	joy. [11]On entering the house, they saw the child with Mary his mother; and they knelt down and paid him homage. Then, opening their treasure chests, they offered him gifts of gold, frankincense, and myrrh. [12]And having been warned in a dream not to return to Herod, they left for their own country by another road.

COMMENTARY

The story of the magi and Herod has no relation or points of contact with the Lukan birth story, with which it is impossible to harmonize. With its setting among royalty, chief priests, and wealthy foreigners, it moves in a different world from the manger and shepherds, which form the ambiance of Luke's birth narrative. Efforts to combine the stories miss the message of both.

The story of the magi and King Herod in its present form is from Matthew, who composed it from traditional materials, inserting his own concerns and recasting it in his own style.

2:1a. A transitional note from the narrator sets the stage. Thus far in Matthew, the reader has had no indication of time or place. In chapter 1, Matthew has been concerned to relate the story of Jesus to the ongoing story of God, from Abraham through David to Jesus. Now, in a retrospective aside, the story is given a geographical and temporal setting in the contemporary world, as place (Bethlehem) and time (the days of Herod the king) are revealed.[65] Both where and when will be inquiries from characters in the story who are not yet privy to information disclosed by the narrator to the reader.

2:1b-2. The magi come to worship and inquire of the new king in Jerusalem. Their first word, which is also the first word of any human character in the Gospel of Matthew, asks "Where?"—which is also King Herod's first question (v. 4). The question must, therefore, have been of more than incidental importance to Matthew's theological purpose. One of the Jewish objections to the Christian claim that Jesus is the Messiah was that

according to Scripture the Messiah is to be born in Bethlehem (cf. John 7:42), while Jesus came from unbiblical Nazareth. In response, this chapter begins by declaring that Jesus was indeed born in Bethlehem and concludes by affirming that the Scripture does promise that the Messiah will be from Nazareth (see 2:23). It could well be that Jesus was in fact born in Nazareth,[66] and that Christian scribes provided Jesus with a Davidic genealogy and a Davidic birthplace based on their conviction that Jesus is the Christ and their interpretation of Scripture (see Excursus "Matthew as Interpreter of Scripture," 151-54).

The magis' inquiry about the "King of the Jews" is both a reminder that Jesus is the royal heir of the Davidic promises and an anticipation of his ministry proclaiming the kingdom of God and especially of the passion story in which he will be crucified as "King of the Jews" (27:11, 29, 37). The announcement—made by Gentiles —triggers the conflict of two kingdoms, which dominates the Gospel.

Magi is the transliteration of Greek μάγοι, which can also be translated "wise men," "astrologers" (NEB), or, as in the only other New Testament occurrence (Acts 13:6, 8) "magician" or "sorcerer." The word has nothing to do with "kings" (which comes from the later application of Ps 72:10-11 and Isa 60:3 to the Christmas story), but designates a priestly class of Persian or Babylonian experts in the occult, such as astrology

---

65. Matthew's dating is very general; Herod ruled 37–4 BCE.

66. Cf. the conclusion of John P. Meier, Roman Catholic biblical scholar whose book has the imprimatur, at the end of a judicious weighing of all the evidence: "During the reign of Herod the Great, and probably toward its end (c. 7–4 BC), Jesus was born in the hill town of Nazareth in Lower Galilee" (*A Marginal Jew: Rethinking the Historical Jesus* [Garden City, N.Y.: Doubleday, 1991] 350).

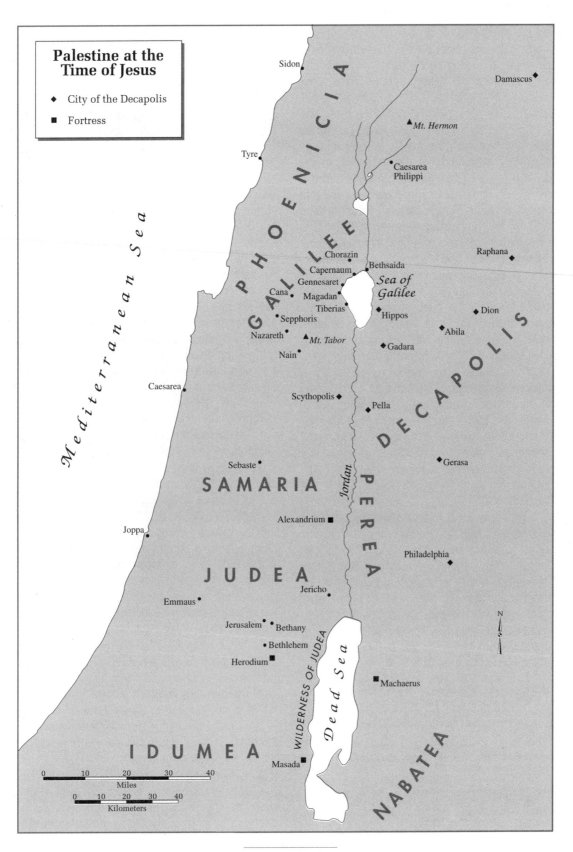

Palestine at the Time of Jesus

◆ City of the Decapolis

■ Fortress

Mediterranean Sea

Sidon

Damascus

PHOENICIA

Mt. Hermon

Tyre

Caesarea
Philippi

GALILEE

Chorazin

Raphana

Capernaum

Bethsaida

Gennesaret

Sea of
Galilee

Cana

Magadan

Tiberias

Hippos

Dion

Sepphoris

Abila

Nazareth

Mt. Tabor

Gadara

Nain

DECAPOLIS

Caesarea

Scythopolis

Pella

Sebaste

Gerasa

SAMARIA

Jordan

PEREA

Joppa

Alexandrium

Philadelphia

JUDEA

Jericho

Emmaus

Jerusalem

Bethany

Dead Sea

Bethlehem

Herodium

WILDERNESS OF JUDEA

Machaerus

N

IDUMEA

NABATEA

Masada

0   10   20   30   40
Miles

0   10   20   30   40
Kilometers

and the interpretation of dreams. They represent pagans (Gentiles) who, though they do not have the special revelation of the Torah, come to Jerusalem following the light they have seen. Their goal is to "worship" or to "pay homage" to the new king.[67]

They have seen a star "at its rising" (or "in the east"; the Greek phrase may have either meaning).[68] The magi, and not the star, were in the east and followed the star in the western sky to Bethlehem. Various attempts have been made to relate the star to natural phenomena thought to have occurred about this time—from comets, to the supposed conjunction of Jupiter and Saturn, or even to UFOs. But Matthew is clearly describing a miraculous phenomenon directed behind the scenes by God, for the star remains stationary while they are in Jerusalem, then leads them not only to Bethlehem, but to the precise location of Jesus, where it "stood still" to mark the designated spot (v. 9). The westward, then southwestward movement of the star excludes a (misunderstood) natural phenomenon—due to the rotation of the earth, all natural heavenly bodies (appear to) move east to west. Pagan beliefs associated the birth of a new ruler with astral phenomena,[69] and a broad stream of Jewish tradition related the hope for the Messiah to the "star out of Jacob" (Num 24:17; cf. 1QM 11:6). The traditional association of "Messiah" and "star" is illustrated by the nickname given the messianic claimant in Judea who led the final disastrous war against the Romans 132–35 CE, Simeon ben Kosibah, "Bar Cochba" ("Son of the Star," "Star Man"). The star thus forms something of a hermeneutical bridge, binding together pagan astrological hopes and Jewish biblical promises.

2:3-8. The historical Herod the Great was an Idumean who, backed by Rome, had established himself as king by military conquest of his "own" people. The populace, who wanted a king with Jewish blood who was not beholden to the Romans, resented his rule. Herod's architectural and cultural achievements were indeed great, the renovation and enlargement of the Jerusalem Temple into a building of splendid proportions being only one of his extravagant projects.

It is not the historical Herod with whom Matthew is concerned, however, but with Herod as a character in the story, who serves as a foil for the kingdom of God. When this Herod hears of the birth of the new king, he is "troubled" (RSV). Matthew is not describing Herod's psychology but the clash of two claims to kingship that occurs in the advent of Jesus. Herod represents the resistance of this world to the divine kingship represented by Jesus. When "all Jerusalem" is troubled with him, this is not mere sympathy with or fear of Herod. Matthew is again looking ahead to the passion story and implicating Judaism's capital city as a whole, not only its king, in the rejection of Jesus' messianic claim (cf. 21:5, 10; 23:37-38; 27:15-23). When Herod repeats the initial question "Where?" the occasion is provided to bring on the religious leaders, the other opponents of the kingdom of God, represented by Jesus.

2:4. "Chief priests" and "scribes" or "teachers of the law" appear for the first time, again reflecting in advance Jesus' opponents in the passion story (16:21; 20:18; 21:15; 27:41). Chief priests are the priestly ruling class associated with the Temple. Scribes are not mere secretaries, but are a professional class of experts in the religious/civil law of the Bible and Jewish tradition. The chief priests were associated with the Sadducean party. Many scribes belonged to the Pharisees, but the groups were not identical.

Matthew is careful to call the scribes the "scribes of the people." Jesus is to save his people (1:21). In this second occurrence of "the people," it is not clear whether they join their scribes' opposition, or whether only the leaders oppose Jesus. As the plot of the Gospel develops, there will be something of a struggle between Jesus and the religious leaders for the allegiance of the people.

2:5. The magi have been obedient, following the light. In the older, pre-Matthean form of the story, the star leads them to Bethlehem and is adequate on its own. By adding the Scripture text

67. Προσκυνέω *proskyneō* can be translated either way. From the magis' human point of view, they wanted to honor and subject themselves to the new ruler (so the NRSV); from Matthew's post-Easter perspective on what was really happening, they had come to worship their Lord (so the NIV).

68. The shift from the plural "east" of v. 1 to singular in v. 2 is decisive for "at its rising." It was important for astrological method to note the exact time a star appeared above the horizon.

69. On the night of Alexander the Great's birth, magi prophesied from a brilliant constellation that the destoyer of Asia had been born. Cf. Cicero *De Divinationi* 1.47; and W. C. Allen, *A Critical and Exegetical Commentary on the Gospel According to St. Matthew*, ICC (New York: Scribners, 1910) 12.

(a combination of Mic 5:2 and 2 Sam 5:2[70]), Matthew pictures the quest of the magi as being guided not only by pagan astrology but also by Jewish Scripture. In the present form of the story, Scripture reveals what pagan astrologers look for in the stars. The quotation is not, however, to be numbered among Matthew's ten "formula quotations," all of which are from the narrator to the reader (cf. Excursus "Matthew as Interpreter of Scripture," 151-54). Matthew here places the citation in the mouth of characters in the story. He attributes the reference to the scribes for three reasons:

(1) In Matthew's time, it was a scribal objection that Jesus could not be the Messiah, because he was from Nazareth, not Bethlehem (cf. John 7:42).

(2) Micah 5:2 was indeed interpreted messianically in Jewish scribal exegesis, in contrast to most of Matthew's own formula quotations.[71] (3) Early in the story, Matthew wants to portray the Jewish religious leaders as hypocrites who "say, but do not do." They know scriptural data, but do not act on their knowledge (23:3; cf. 7:24-27).

Likewise, when Herod asks the magi the chronological question "When?" to determine the time of Jesus' birth (like v. 4, making contact with 2:1), he acts hypocritically, claiming that he too wants to worship, but with murder in his heart. Matthew will later consider hypocrisy the chief sin of Jewish leadership (see 23:1-33), already present in this initial encounter. In all of this we again note the omniscient narrator, who knows the thoughts of Herod's heart and can report conversations in his conferences with the magi and the chief priests and scribes.

2:9-12. The story line comes back to the magis' quest; they continue to be obedient, following both the star (making a literary bracket with 2:1) and Scripture to Bethlehem. Revelation outside Scripture motivates them to obey the one God; yet, they do not find their way to Jesus without Scripture.[72] In contrast to the Jewish leaders, the magi act rather than merely hear (cf. 7:24-27). Like the merchant in search of fine pearls in Jesus' story (13:45) and the women at the tomb on Easter morning (28:8), they are filled with joy. The star guides them to the exact house in Bethlehem, the residence of Mary and Joseph. Mary is mentioned but plays no role; Joseph does not appear in this story at all. Not only is gold an appropriate gift for royalty, but, less obvious to the modern reader, so are frankincense and myrrh (both of which are expensive aromatic gum resins, not native to Palestine, with a variety of religious and medical connotations). There is no indication that the later allegorical interpretation was intended by Matthew (gold, for Jesus as king; frankincense, for Jesus as divine, since it was used in worship; myrrh, for Jesus' dying, since it was used in embalming; cf. John 19:39). The later tradition of three magi derives from the number of the gifts they bring.

Warned (by God) through a dream, the magi, who had accepted Herod's hypocritical promise at face value, disobey Herod's command to report to him and return to their Gentile land by a different route. The dream motif, which occurs six times in Matthew (1:20; 2:12, 13, 19, 22; 27:19) and elsewhere in the New Testament only in the citation of Joel in Acts 2:17, is a Matthean trademark that connects this story with the rest of the birth narrative. Like the star motif, the dream motif portrays God, who is not mentioned in the story, as being active unobtrusively and ambiguously behind the scenes.

---

70. Matthew adds the citation from 2 Sam 5:2 to relate Jesus to David, since the Micah text has no Davidic connections. Matthew also modifies the Micah text to make it fit the fulfillment more closely (cf. Excursus "Matthew as Interpreter of Scripture," 151-54).

71. Cf. Targum on Mic 5:1-2 and John 7:40-43.

72. Cf. Daniel Patte, *The Gospel According to Matthew: A Structural Commentary on Matthew's Faith* (Philadelphia: Fortress, 1987) 35.

REFLECTIONS

1. For the original readers of Matthew, the story that began in their Bible became contemporary. Chapter 1 and its genealogical summary move in continuity with the Old Testament story. Chapter 2 has the effect of locating the present fulfillment of this story in the world of the reader. This movement is the dynamic of every biblical sermon, merging the horizons of the biblical world and our own, and it may begin from either side.

Matthew began with the promises to Abraham and David, and shows how their movement through history is the fulfillment of the hopes of those who had never heard of the God who had been at work in the stories of Abraham and Sarah, David and Bathsheba. Matthew could have begun with the magi of his own time, who expressed their hopes for the meaning of things in quite unbiblical and anti-biblical ways (astrology!), and showed how their search led to the God of the Bible, whose definitive revelation is found not in the stars, but in the story that goes through Ur to Egypt to Jerusalem and to Bethlehem. The modern sermon or lesson may begin with either the biblical story or contemporary experience, but both must be there. The contemporary teacher and preacher can learn from Matthew a strategy of communication that weaves together into one fabric ancient canonical text and present life expressed in its own terms.

2. For Matthew, the story of Jesus is at once the story of the fulfillment of God's promises to Israel through Abraham, David, and the prophets, and the fulfillment of the longing of all human hope for salvation. This story shows that, although Jesus comes as the Jewish Messiah, the advent of the Christ is the fulfillment of Gentile hopes as well. Even those who do not have the Bible and the tradition to know what they are looking for are still in quest of authentic life and human community, here pictured as the incursion of God's kingship into this world in the person of Jesus. There is a subtle polemic against astrology here: What astrologers are looking for is actually found in Christ; at Bethlehem, astrology surrenders to Bible and Christ. Even this "most Jewish" of the Gospels is aware, from its first page onward, that it is not necessary first to have the biblical and Jewish hope before one can come to the Messiah and accept him as Lord. In following the light they have, the magi find the goal of their quest in bowing before the Jewish Messiah. The task of the church is often to discern the ultimate quest that is expressed in non-biblical and non-theistic ways in contemporary life, and continue Matthew's witness that the yearnings even of those who do not know fully what they seek are met in the act of God at Bethlehem. "The hopes and fears of all the years . . . "

3. Jewish tradition had not, by and large, consigned the Gentiles to eternal condemnation, but expected a pilgrimage of the nations to the God of Israel as part of the eschatological events (Isa 2:2-4; 60:1-6; cf. the rabbinic commentary on Gen 49:10: "All the nations of the world shall in the future bring a gift to the Son of David"). Matthew sees this as already happening in the response of the magi, an anticipation of the conclusion of the Gospel in 28:18-20.

Matthew is a thoroughly eschatological Gospel. The eschatological hope is not confined to the final discourse (23:1–25:46), but is integrated into the portrayal of Jesus' life and message as a whole, from the initial summary of his preaching (4:17) and the opening words of the first discourse (the Sermon on the Mount, 5:3-12), throughout his teaching (e.g., 7:15-23; 10:32-33; 13:24-30, 36-43; 16:24-28). Yet for Matthew eschatology is not a matter of speculation about the future, but the basis for action in the present. The final inclusion of all nations in God's saving plan is not to be left to the end of time, to God and the angels at the last day, but the vision of the goal of history sets the agenda for action in the present. Matthew's church has resisted those who believe that "someday" this grand vision would be implemented by God, and dares to act in the light of the eschatological reality already present in Jesus. The Christ was the one who was expected to come at the end and establish God's kingdom. Matthew knows that to confess that Jesus of Nazareth is the Christ is to confess that the eschatological reality has already invaded the present, and it calls for action. In the arrival of the magi, the eschatological purpose of God to include all nations is already being realized.

4. Traditional preaching on the magi has often been moralizing, treating the magi as object lessons: they acted on the light they had; they went to Bethlehem while the scribes who knew the Bible did not; they gave precious gifts to Jesus. Matthew would not minimize their actions, for they did not simply admire or study the star, but followed it, even to the point of resisting the enthroned powers that be. Yet their action is a response to the divine initiative. Here as elsewhere, God's grace precedes human action. Although Matthew is very concerned with Torah and right living (see Commentary on the Sermon on the Mount), he is at the farthest pole from "works righteousness."

5. The traditional use of this text as a reading for the Epiphany of the Lord underscores the truth that Jesus is God's revelation to the whole world. The magi are Gentiles in the extreme, characters who could not be more remote from the Jewish citizens of Jerusalem in heritage and worldview. Even at the very beginning of Jesus' life, then, we see the dividing walls between races and cultures breaking down. Even here, at the beginning of the Gospel, the mission to all nations, which will close the Gospel (28:19), is anticipated.

Matthew 2:13-23, Exile in Egypt, and Nazareth as Fulfillment

NIV

13When they had gone, an angel of the Lord appeared to Joseph in a dream. "Get up," he said, "take the child and his mother and escape to Egypt. Stay there until I tell you, for Herod is going to search for the child to kill him."

14So he got up, took the child and his mother during the night and left for Egypt, 15where he stayed until the death of Herod. And so was fulfilled what the Lord had said through the prophet: "Out of Egypt I called my son."[a]

16When Herod realized that he had been outwitted by the Magi, he was furious, and he gave orders to kill all the boys in Bethlehem and its vicinity who were two years old and under, in accordance with the time he had learned from the Magi. 17Then what was said through the prophet Jeremiah was fulfilled:

18"A voice is heard in Ramah,
      weeping and great mourning,
   Rachel weeping for her children
      and refusing to be comforted,
   because they are no more."[b]

19After Herod died, an angel of the Lord appeared in a dream to Joseph in Egypt 20and said, "Get up, take the child and his mother and go to the land of Israel, for those who were trying to take the child's life are dead."

21So he got up, took the child and his mother and went to the land of Israel. 22But when he heard that Archelaus was reigning in Judea in place of his father Herod, he was afraid to go

[a]15 Hosea 11:1   [b]18 Jer. 31:15

NRSV

13Now after they had left, an angel of the Lord appeared to Joseph in a dream and said, "Get up, take the child and his mother, and flee to Egypt, and remain there until I tell you; for Herod is about to search for the child, to destroy him." 14Then Joseph[a] got up, took the child and his mother by night, and went to Egypt, 15and remained there until the death of Herod. This was to fulfill what had been spoken by the Lord through the prophet, "Out of Egypt I have called my son."

16When Herod saw that he had been tricked by the wise men,[b] he was infuriated, and he sent and killed all the children in and around Bethlehem who were two years old or under, according to the time that he had learned from the wise men.[b] 17Then was fulfilled what had been spoken through the prophet Jeremiah:

18 "A voice was heard in Ramah,
      wailing and loud lamentation,
   Rachel weeping for her children;
      she refused to be consoled, because they are
         no more."

19When Herod died, an angel of the Lord suddenly appeared in a dream to Joseph in Egypt and said, 20"Get up, take the child and his mother, and go to the land of Israel, for those who were seeking the child's life are dead." 21Then Joseph[a] got up, took the child and his mother, and went to the land of Israel. 22But when he heard that Archelaus was ruling over Judea in place of his

[a]Gk he   [b]Or astrologers; Gk magi

NIV	NRSV
there. Having been warned in a dream, he withdrew to the district of Galilee, 23and he went and lived in a town called Nazareth. So was fulfilled what was said through the prophets: "He will be called a Nazarene."	father Herod, he was afraid to go there. And after being warned in a dream, he went away to the district of Galilee. 23There he made his home in a town called Nazareth, so that what had been spoken through the prophets might be fulfilled, "He will be called a Nazorean."

COMMENTARY

The movement and structure of this story closely resemble that of the previous story, reflecting Matthew's compositional hand at work in both. Just as in 2:1-12, the story of the obedient magi who accept the new king had the picture of rebellious Herod inserted into its midst (magi/Herod/magi), so also here the story of obedient Joseph surrounds the picture of evil Herod (Joseph/Herod/Joseph). The magi repeatedly follow the star and receive their final warning against the evil king in a dream (2:1, 9, 12), and Joseph repeatedly follows revelation from an angel, receiving his final warning against the evil king (a different one) in a dream (2:13, 19, 22).

2:13-15. As in 2:20, Matthew is careful not to call Jesus the son of Joseph.

Joseph moves his family to Egypt the same night. As elsewhere (1:25; 2:21), Joseph's obedience is described as the mirror image of the divine command.

No novelistic or biographical details of the stay in Egypt are given. In Matthew's theological perspective, the sojourn occurred to fulfill Scripture and to provide another parallel to Moses. Matthew's second formula quotation, Hos 11:1, originally was not a prophecy of the Messiah but referred to Israel as God's son, and was never understood in Judaism as a messianic text (see Excursus "Matthew as Interpreter of Scripture," 151-54). In Matthew's hermeneutic the application of the title to the Messiah is not completely arbitrary, since Jesus is pictured as fulfilling in his own experience the story of Israel:

Israel	Jesus
To Egypt and back	To Egypt and back
Red Sea	Baptism
Testing in wilderness	Testing in wilderness
Failure in the vocation to be God's servant to the nations	Faithful servant ministry

2:16. Herod's slaughter of the innocents is in character with the historical Herod the Great, who was ruthless in maintaining his grasp on power. There is no record of such an act among the detailed records of Herod's numerous atrocities (if it had occurred it would hardly have been considered a major event of his reign), nor is it reflected elsewhere in or out of the New Testament. The story is part of Matthew's Moses typology, with Herod cast in the role of Pharaoh (see Exod 1:22–2:10). The two-stage progression of the story, which allows the child Jesus to escape, resembles the typical folkloristic legend in which a royal child escapes attempts on his life only to return and rule in power.[73] The plot demands that Herod's troops appear in Bethlehem after the magi and the holy family have left. The historical Herod would not have been so easily foiled, but would have sent murderers with or after the magi!

Matthew does not sentimentalize the tragedy of the innocent victims or speculate on how the other mothers and fathers of Bethlehem might have interpreted the divine decision to warn one family. His attention is fixed on this event as a fulfillment of Scripture. Matthew does alter his usual formula in such citations of Scripture from his usual "in order that" (ἵνα hina), and thus avoids saying that the murders happened for the purpose of fulfilling Scripture. The interpreter still has the problem of God's warning only one family of Herod's attack (see Reflections below on confessional language).

2:17-18. Matthew's third formula quotation (see Excursus "Matthew as Interpreter of Scrip-

---

73. The list to whom this pattern was applied includes not only mythological and legendary figures, such as Apollo, Romulus and Remus, and Hercules, but also historical ones, such as Cyrus, John the Baptist (not in the New Testament, but in later Christian legends, cf. *Protevangelium of James* 22–23), Augustus, and, of course, Moses.

ture," 151-54) is from Jer 31:15. In the New Testament only Matthew explicitly mentions Jeremiah (here, 16:14 added to the Markan story; 27:9 in the M story of Judas's death). Jeremiah 31:15 pictures Rachel, matriarch of the tribes of Benjamin and Ephraim (but not of Judah) weeping at Ramah for her "children," the Israelites, as they are led away captive to Babylon in Jeremiah's time.[74] Ramah (in the area of Benjamin, five miles north of Jerusalem) was chosen by Jeremiah because one tradition locates Rachel's tomb there, at the site where Nebuchadnezzar's troops assembled captives for deportation (Jer 40:1). Another tradition locates Rachel's tomb at Bethlehem. Matthew combines these traditions to achieve the desired effect. The Jeremiah passage is in a context of hope; it is not clear whether Matthew interprets contextually or whether lamentation is the only note to be heard in this text. In any case, the child Jesus recapitulates the experience of Israel.

2:19-22. Divine intervention saves the child Jesus. Joseph's obedience is once again the mirror image of the angel's command. Herod's death in 4 BCE was the signal for them to return from refuge among the Gentiles to the "land of Israel."[75] But Herod's son Archelaus "reigned" (RSV) in Judea.[76] Mary and Joseph are thus forced from their home in Bethlehem into a divinely guided exile in Galilee of the Gentiles (cf. 4:15). The picture of the holy family as displaced persons reflects the experience of some Christians in the Matthean church after the 66–70 war. Joseph and Mary experience persecution, displacement, and exile because of Jesus, just as had the Matthean community. It is likely that some Christians who had become refugees during the war had resettled in Matthew's church, bringing their traditions with them, and had since suffered estrangement from their own Jewish communities (see Introduction).

2:23. This segment of the story reaches its goal in Nazareth. In Matthew, Jesus does not *return* to Nazareth, but the story that began in Bethlehem now reaches Nazareth for the first time. In Matthew's view, the fact that the Messiah came from Nazareth is not just chance, but is guided by a nocturnal revelation from God and was already spoken of in Scripture. This fourth formula quotation is not found in the Old Testament, either in the Masoretic Text (MT) or the LXX (note Matthew's vague "the prophets"). Matthew may have been thinking of one or both of the following: (1) The Messianic king promised in Isa 11:1-16, a text with several points of contact with this story, is called the "branch" that will spring up from the (apparently dead) Davidic line. The Hebrew for "branch" is נצר (*nēzer*), which sounds somewhat like "Nazareth." The Targum interprets the "branch" messianically. (2) Matthew's major source refers to Jesus as "the holy one of God," which is parallel with "Jesus of Nazareth" (Mark 1:24). Since "holy one" is used in the Old Testament as a synonym for "Nazirite," which sounds somewhat like "Nazareth," Matthew may have in mind passages such as Judg 13:5 and 16:7, which refer to Nazirites (although Jesus' life-style was the opposite of the Nazirites; cf. 11:19). As supporting evidence for this view, it is sometimes pointed out that "Nazorean" or "Nazarene"—the word is also spelled differently in other New Testament passages—was not related linguistically to Nazareth, but could be the name by which the Jewish sectarian group begun by Jesus was known, the "Nazarees" (parallel to "Pharisees" and "Sadducees").[77] Then Jesus would be the "holy one" who began a movement of "holy ones," an early Palestinian predecessor of the later church, which included among its self-designations "the holy ones/saints."

In all of this, and in contrast to later apocryphal gospels (e.g., *Protevangelium of James, Infancy Gospel of Thomas*), the infant Jesus is entirely passive. "Despite his supernatural conception, the child is here portrayed with great restraint."[78]

---

74. Since Rachel was a matriarch of the Northern Kingdom (mother of Joseph and Benjamin; see Genesis 30), this could be thought of as her lament for the Assyrian deportation of the northern tribes. But Jer 40:1, 4 shows Ramah as an assembly point for the Babylonian deportation of Judeans in Jeremiah's time, and that Rachel was already thought of as an ancestor for all Israel.

75. Matthew thinks of "Israel" as greater than Judea. This statement prepares for the actual settlement in Galilee.

76. Although it is historical that Archelaus succeeded Herod the Great in Judea, Matthew's terminology is not precisely historical, since Archelaus was an ethnarch (a quasi-royal title granted to a dependent monarch), not a king, and was soon deposed by the Romans, who placed Judea under direct Roman rule. Matthew portrays the story as a conflict of kingdoms.

77. George Foote Moore opposed this explanation and argued that it is linguistically possible to relate "Nazorean" and "Nazareth." See "Nazarene and Nazareth," in *The Beginnings of Christianity,* eds. K. Lake and R. J. Foakes-Jackson, 5 vols. (London: Macmillan, 1920–1933; reprint Grand Rapids: Baker, 1979) 1:426-32.

78. Douglas R. A. Hare, *Matthew,* Interpretation (Louisville: Westminster/John Knox, 1993).

REFLECTIONS

1. "The Other Babies of Bethlehem": A Story. Susanna and Jehoiachim were young parents, both twenty-three years old, just getting started in life together. They had one child, little Davey, who at eighteen months had learned to walk and was getting into everything, was putting sentences together in strange ways, his soft, high-pitched little voice giving a musical lilt even to the Aramaic gutturals. A healthy, happy child, he was the delight of their life. They named him David because they lived in the "city of David," as their village was called, located a few miles south of Jerusalem.

Late one night while everyone was sleeping, the king's soldiers surrounded the village, and at first light they came into town. They ordered all parents with small children into the village square, made a search to ensure that none remained, and without a word killed every boy younger than two years old. "Orders," they said.

After the horror of that day had receded enough for the villagers to take account, they discovered that twenty-one children had been killed.

It is a cruel world, and such things happen. In our time thousands of babies have been napalmed, gassed, starved, and shot down by the order or permission of unfeeling governments. But human beings are resilient creatures, and after periods of numbness, anger, bitterness, and acceptance, Jehoiachim and Susanna were able to pick up the pieces of their life and go on. Without hostility or condescension, they rejected the "explanations" of the tragedy from well-meaning neighbor-theologians, having no answer to the question articulated for them in their own Bible-prayer book, "My God, my God, why?" (Ps 22:1 NRSV). They even began to find new meaning in synagogue worship.

Until one day when they discovered that on the crucial night before the slaughter of the baby boys an angel had come from God to warn one family to flee. It turns out that God had arranged for Mary, Joseph, and the baby Jesus to escape and that they had been secure in Egypt. The little boy Jesus was alive and well, but not their little Davey.

This is the story of a miracle, of divine intervention in the normal course of events. It calls for reflection. When told in the above manner, the story raises questions not only of history (Did/Could such things actually happen?), but also of ethics (Should such things happen?). If God works in such a way that angels may warn persons of impending danger, is it right that only one family be warned? Which of us, with such information and the ability to save, would share it with one family and withhold it from twenty-one? Not only this story, but every other miracle story as well, raises such questions. The story of the healing of a blind person is wonderful, unless it is heard from the perspective of all those blind persons in the world who were not healed.

When the story of the "slaughter of the innocents" is presented in the above manner, it may evoke two types of response: (1) Those who think that the biblical narratives of miraculous events are being "attacked" feel obliged to defend and offer explanations for them. "If God had warned all the parents in Bethlehem, Herod would have grown suspicious and perhaps killed everyone in the village. He was that kind of person. So, although what happened was bad, it was not as bad as it might have been if God had worked the miracle for everyone." Or "God was speaking to everyone in the village, but only Mary and Joseph were sensitive enough to hear God's voice." None of this is biblical, of course. (2) Others see the inherent problem with all belief in miracles and all language about miracles, and claim these problems to be sufficient reason to dispense with miracle stories altogether.

Although these two responses may seem to be polar opposites, they have one thing in common: They take the language of miracle stories as objective, "reporter" language that, if it is "true," is subject to the same kind of inferences as any other objective language. They suppose that all true language is objectifying reporter language. The retelling of the story from the point of view of Jehoiachim and Susanna may help us to see the fallacy of this assumption. As retold above, Matthew's story does indeed have deep ethical problems. What kind of deity warns only one family of impending disaster and allows other innocent children to be killed? The careful reader will even note that Herod's anger, which resulted in the killing of all the babies of Bethlehem (not his original plan, 2:8), was *caused* by the miraculous warning given the magi in 2:12 (cf. 2:16). Thus in the biblical story it is precisely the divine intervention that saves Jesus, taken as an objective datum, that results in the needless death of the babies of Bethlehem.

Interpreters of this and all miracle stories need to be sensitive to the fundamental nature of its language, and not assume that all truth is communicated in the same kind of language.[79] The above retelling, although presenting the same "facts," transposes the biblical form of confessional language into a mode that is no longer the insider language of confession, but the spectator language of objective reporting. The present form of the biblical story of the flight to Egypt and the slaughter of the innocents functions as confessional language, *the church's confession that God was active in preserving the infant Jesus for his future mission.* This is its "point," the truth function of the story. Such language becomes problematic if it is objectified as though it reported a literal event that a spectator could observe and from which logical inferences could be drawn. The issue is not whether miracles happen, but the nature of confessional language that takes the form of a miracle story. The real issue is whether this story is to be read as if it were a report of an actual event or whether as "insider" language of confession it serves only one purpose, to confess the church's faith that God was already active in the birth and preservation of the Messiah. The truth function of such language is that it serves to confess authentic faith, but cannot legitimately be made a link in a chain of inferences in the objective world. Preaching and teaching from this passage can engender and strengthen faith that God was active in the birth and preservation of the child Jesus so that he could fulfill his messianic mission. It can give us a language of confession to give thanks to God for mighty acts in our own life. It can also serve as an occasion for reflection on the nature of the various kinds of biblical language, and how in their different ways they testify to the truth of God's act in Christ. (For further, see Excursus "Interpreting the Miracle Stories in Matthew," 241-51.)

2. Matthew looks back on the Christ-event as a whole, from his birth through his ministry, crucifixion, resurrection, and the launching of the church and its mission in the world. From Matthew's post-resurrection perspective, the Christ-event involved a threefold movement of divine act, human response, and God's sovereign counterresponse. The meaning of the whole saving drama is anticipated in his presentation of the advent, rejection and the divine reaffirmation of the infant Jesus.

(a) The messianic king, the royal Son of God, comes as the fulfillment of Israel's history, the son of David and son of Abraham, to proclaim and live out God's sovereignty over the world (1:1-25). (b) Jesus was rejected by his own people, Israel, acting through their leaders (2:1-12). (c) The divine protection and reaffirmation of Jesus is anticipated in the story of the flight to Egypt, return to Israel, and relocation in Galilee (2:13-23; cf. 28:16-20, after the rejection in Judea, the Gentile mission begins in Galilee).

As an aspect of his proclamation of the kingdom of God, Jesus had taught that the response to rejection was not to retaliate but to absorb evil at the hands of others (5:38-39; cf. 10:23; 26:53). At the crucial moment of his career, to which Matthew's story builds, the representative

---

79. On the language of prayer, see Reflections for 6:15.

of God's kingship responds to the death plot by withdrawing (see 12:15-21). And the revelatory procession of the king into Jerusalem, in which the king is "meek, humble" (πραΰς *praus*), is in fulfillment of the Scripture (cf. 21:5). In the birth story, the plot against Jesus' life is met not by divine retaliation against Herod, but by the family's withdrawal to Egypt.[80] But just as the murder of Jesus by those he came to save was not the end of Jesus, who was vindicated by God at the resurrection, so also here the child Jesus is protected and vindicated, and God's purpose continues. In all of this Jesus is passive and God is the hidden actor.

In Exod 4:2-23, when Pharaoh, who had tried to kill Moses, will not let Israel go, God kills the son of Pharaoh and the sons of the Egyptians. The liberation of Israel is led by Moses, who had killed an Egyptian and had led the Israelites through the Red Sea, spelling death for Pharaoh's armies. The new kingdom of David in the promised land is established by violence (see 1 Samuel 9–1 Kings 5). In the Gospel of Matthew, neither Herod nor his sons are killed, but continue in power. God sends his Son to die as the innocent one for the sins of others, prefigured by the death of the innocent babies of Bethlehem.[81] Just as God did not prevent the crucifixion, so also God sends no angelic armies to prevent the slaughter of the boy babies. Violence against the innocent of this world is the polar opposite of God's will, but God does not intervene to stop violence (cf. Matthew's addition to the story at 26:51-53). Here is a new paradigm for how God's saving purpose in history will finally work and a redefinition of messiahship and God's kingdom at the outset of the story of Jesus.

3. Although it is not apparent on the surface of the story, one is struck by the impression that Matt 1:18–2:23 is the story of God's activity. Since the story is "about" a baby, the infant Jesus cannot be pictured as doing mighty saving deeds himself. Nor is it a story of Mary's or Joseph's heroic deeds. They are obedient, and the story as told could not take place without them, but the initiative is with God, whose saving activity represents divine sovereignty and choice, not a response to prayer or human action. The child is born, guided, protected, and taken to his home in Galilee of the Gentiles by divine direction; yet that direction is unobtrusive and ambiguous. Only later, when Jesus comes for baptism and hears the heavenly voice declare him to be God's Son, does the reader understand that this infant could not have been just anyone, but represents the initiative of God in calling one who was born and preserved as the Son of God.

4. There may well be a place in the tableaux and pageantry of Christian celebrations of Advent and Christmas to assemble into one grand scene all the stories and images of Jesus' birth from biblical and later traditions. But if this is done in exegesis, the meaning of the text is lost or smothered. Matthew, who has no view of pre-existence (and thus no view of incarnation) cannot be combined exegetically with John, which has no birth story. Like others before us, we must reflect on the full meaning of Christ, but we must also remember that the combination of pre-existence/birth story does not occur in the New Testament. Nor can Matthew and Luke be combined. The Matthean story begins in Bethlehem, the home of Mary and Joseph, and progresses to Nazareth; Luke has the opposite movement, with the story beginning in Nazareth and progressing to Bethlehem and back. Luke has no place for the trip to Egypt; Matthew has no place for the presentation of Jesus in the Temple. Matthew's baby is royal, talked about in the king's palace, visited by important foreigners who bring him rich gifts. The baby in Luke's story is born in a stable, is visited by poor shepherds, and his mother takes the poverty-clause at his dedication (Luke 2:24; cf. Lev 12:8). To understand Matthew, the reader must steadfastly refuse to read Luke or John between the lines and vice versa. Each

---

80. Jesus' "meekness/humility" is another expression of the Moses typology, for Moses too was "meek/humble" (Num 12:3; cf. Philo *Vita Mos* 2.279; W. D. Davies and Dale C. Allison, Jr., *A Critical and Exegetical Commentary on the Gospel According to Saint Matthew*, 2 vols., ICC (Edinburgh: T. & T. Clark, 1988–91) 2:272, 290.

81. This is not a justification for the death of the boy babies of Bethlehem as a literal event; see below.

christological affirmation of each evangelist has its own meaning and integrity, which must not be lost by attempts at exegetical conglomeration.

❖   ❖   ❖   ❖

EXCURSUS: MATTHEW AS INTERPRETER OF SCRIPTURE

IMPORTANCE OF SCRIPTURE FOR MATTHEW

Matthew directly quotes the Scripture forty times with an explicit indication, such as "it is written" (e.g., Matt 4:4 = Deut 8:3). Matthew also contains several other direct citations not explicitly so identified (e.g., 27:46 = Ps 22:1; their exact number depends on how strictly one distinguishes between quotation and allusion). The current edition of the Nestle-Aland Greek New Testament identifies twenty-one such quotations, making a total of sixty-one direct quotations in twenty-eight chapters. In addition to direct quotations, Matthew's text contains a plethora of biblical paraphrases, allusions, and imagery, the exact number again depending on how strictly one determines the criteria for identifying an allusion. The count of such allusions varies from 294 in the Nestle-Aland Greek New Testament to thirty in the list provided for translators by the American Bible Society.[82] On any analysis, Matthew's mind and text are thoroughly steeped in the Scriptures, containing considerably more such quotations and allusions than any of the other Gospels.

DISTRIBUTION

Of the sixty-one quotations, twenty-four are taken over from Mark and nine from Q. Twenty-eight quotations, however, are peculiar to Matthew. Ten of these quotations are Matthean additions to Markan contexts, three are added to Q contexts, and fifteen are in peculiarly Matthean material. Thus Matthew introduces almost as many quotations as he takes over from his sources, and often adds quotations to his sources. Matthew never omits a biblical quotation from the Markan or Q material he incorporates, and he preserves most of the allusions as well.

Practically all of the direct citations belong to two categories: either Jesus quotes the Scripture to other characters in the story (43 times), or the narrator quotes the Scripture to the reader (13 times). The remaining quotations are divided among the high priests and scribes (2:5-6), the Sadducees (22:24), the devil (4:6), and the crowds (21:9), with one quotation being shared by the scribes, the disciples, and Jesus (17:10-11). Neither the disciples nor the Pharisees ever quote the Scripture directly.

The following books from the Hebrew Bible are quoted. The first figure indicates the number of quotations distinctive to Matthew; the second figure indicates the total number of quotations from the book: Genesis 0/3; Exodus 3/5; Leviticus 2/3; Numbers 0/1; Deuteronomy 2/8; Psalms 4/12; Isaiah 5/10; Jeremiah 2/2; Daniel 2/5; Hosea 3/3; Jonah 1/1; Micah 1/2; Zechariah 2/3 (cited as "Jeremiah" in 27:9); Malachi 0/2; and the unknown reference cited in 2:23. As in the other Gospels and the New Testament as a whole, Matthew cites most often the Psalms, Isaiah, and Deuteronomy. No direct citations are taken from apocryphal and pseudepigraphical books, but there may be allusions to them

---

82. Kurt Aland et al., *Novum Testamentum Graece*, 27th ed. (Stuttgart: Deutsche Bibelsellschaft, 1993) Appendix IV, 770-806; Robert G. Bratcher, *Old Testament Quotations in the New Testament* (New York: United Bible Societies, 1961) 1-11.

(e.g., Matt 11:29/ Sirach 6:24-25, 28-30; Matt 27:43/ Wis 2:13, 18-20; Matt 5:5/ *1 Enoch* 5:7; Matt 25:31/ *1 Enoch* 61:8; 62:2-3).

In Matthew's time the text of the Bible was in the process of standardization by the rabbinic/scribal leadership emanating from Jamnia. This is dramatically illustrated by the difference in the biblical texts from Qumran (hidden 70 CE), which manifest great variety, and those from the time of the Second Revolt in 132–135 CE, found in the Wadi Muraba' at, which are uniformly of the Masoretic type, indicating that the standardization of the text was effectively accomplished during that period. Since in Matthew's time the text had not yet been standardized, a variety of text forms in both Hebrew and Greek existed in the Judaism of Matthew's day.

The OT citations in Mark are consistently from the LXX, and the few direct quotations in Q are almost as consistently from the LXX. Matthew's incorporation of Mark and Q material retained their citations in LXX form, sometimes even adjusting them slightly to make them closer to the LXX. Some of the quotations peculiar to Matthew, or introduced by him into Markan or Q contexts, also are of the LXX type. The LXX was thus a familiar and respected translation in Matthew's community; it seems to have been the primary version of the Bible used by Matthew himself. Sometimes the point of the quotation is absent from the Hebrew text and depends on the Greek translation, including quotations placed in Jesus' mouth (e.g., 21:16 = Ps 8:3 LXX).

THE FORMULA QUOTATIONS

A special category is formed by ten "formula quotations," sometimes called "reflection citations" (*Reflexionszitaten*) or "fulfillment quotations" (see 1:22-23; 2:15; 2:17-18; 2:23; 4:14*b*-16; 8:17; 12:18-21; 13:35; 21:4-5; 27:9-10). All are introduced by Matthew into their contexts. Except for the four formula quotations in the birth narrative, all are triggered by a Markan context. Apart from the citation of Zech 9:9 in Matt 21:4-5, none are cited elsewhere in the New Testament. They thus seem not to belong to a standard repertoire of early Christian proof texts, but exclusively to Matthew and/or his own tradition. They are distinguished from the other quotations, including the others peculiar to Matthew, (a) by their introductory formula identifying an event in Jesus' life as the fulfillment of Scripture; (b) by the fact that all are spoken not by a character in the story to other characters, but by the narrator to the reader; and (c) by their text type. The full introductory formula is found in the first quotation, "All this took place to fulfill what had been spoken by the Lord through the prophet" (1:22), and is repeated with minor variations in all the others.[83] "To fulfill" translates ἵνα πληρωθῇ (*hina plērōthē*), which may mean "result" rather than "purpose." While Matthew generally follows the LXX, these ten quotations are distinctive in that they diverge from the LXX and from all other known text types. It is debated whether this means that they represent a lost text type, or are the products of a Matthean Christian scribal exegetical "school," or represent Matthew's own hermeneutical work on the text. In any case, they seem to represent the result of a kind of Christian scribal activity. They are not as arbitrarily placed as they may seem to us, but within the first-century Jewish context represent a sophisticated and subtle approach to Scripture. This form of interpretation, which adapts the text to fit more closely the presupposed fulfillment, was practiced in other streams of first-century Judaism, and bears some resemblance to the *pesher* mode of interpretation practiced at Qumran. It has sometimes been argued that the fulfillment quotations represent a pre-Matthean Christian collection of proof texts, or testimonia, but this is unlikely since they are all integrated into their contexts and can hardly be thought

---

83. Four additional citations are sometimes included in this group: 2:6; 3:3; 13:14-15; 26:56. Although 14 is a significant number for Matthew (1:2-17), the additional four do not meet the above criteria and are all of a different text type.

to have existed as a collection apart from their present contexts. Since they reflect Matthean themes, they seem to be the product of the same school within which the Gospel was formulated or, more likely, to have been arranged by Matthew himself. (See the Commentary on each of the above texts for details.)

MATTHEW'S THEOLOGY OF FULFILLMENT

It has often been thought that Matthew's use of Scripture is apologetic, that he is concerned to prove the messiahship of Jesus to the Jews using their own Scripture. This is a mistaken notion for two reasons: (1) The Gospel of Matthew is not directed to outsiders in order to convert them, but to insiders to express, clarify, and strengthen their faith. In particular, Matthew is not directed to Jews outside the Christian community—though Matthew's church has a strong Jewish-Christian element and a long tradition within Judaism. (2) As "proof," Matthew's use of Scripture is not convincing. If he is thought to be assembling scriptural evidence for Jesus' messiahship, his Christian interpretation of the texts in contrast with their obvious original meaning, along with the changes he makes in the text itself, make him subject to the charge of manipulating the evidence in a way that would be unconvincing to outsiders (cf. Commentary on 1:2-17).

What Matthew's use of Scripture reflects is not apologetics directed to outsiders, but confession directed to insiders. The conviction that Jesus is the Christ is the presupposition of his use of Scripture, not the result of it. From the earliest times, the idea that the Christ is the fulfillment of Scripture was the universal conviction of early Christianity. At first this was a general conviction, without specific elaboration, as in the early Christian creed cited by Paul in 1 Cor 15:3-5. The traditions that came to Matthew were already permeated with this conviction, illustrated by specific OT texts. In particular, Mark had repeatedly referred to specific events in Jesus' life as unfolding in accordance with Scripture (but without the fulfillment formula), and at the end of the story Mark has Jesus say, "But let the scriptures be fulfilled" (Mark 14:49). Matthew seems to have taken up this Markan hint and elaborated it into his ten fulfillment citations. (Cf. his emphatic rewriting of Mark 14:49 in Matt 26:56.) It is Matthew's conviction that, as the Messiah, Jesus is the fulfillment of the Scripture as a whole is expressed in his interpretation of individual texts.

Given Matthew's presupposition that the Christ is the fulfillment of Scripture, and his view that the Scripture as a whole (esp. the Prophets) predicted the eschatological times, which Matthew saw as dawning with the advent of Christ, it is understandable that he uses Scripture to add details to his story of Jesus. We can see this happening also in non-canonical documents, such as Justin Martyr's version of the story of Jesus' triumphal entry into Jerusalem, in which the colt on which Jesus rode was found "bound to a vine."[84] This detail is not found in any early Christian story, but comes from Gen 49:10-11, which Justin took to be a prophecy of Christ. Likewise, in Matt 27:42-43, the words of the chief priests, scribes, and elders at the cross are taken from Mark 15:32 and then augmented with the words of Ps 22:8. Since we can observe the growth of the tradition on the basis of Christian exegesis of the Old Testament in passages we can check, the question arises whether, in those places where we have no direct control, the Matthean scribal community, and Matthew himself, created narrative elements or even whole narrative units as an expression of their faith that the Scripture was fulfilled in Jesus. It may well be that the correspondence of "prediction" and "fulfillment," from Matthew's point of view, fits so well because elements of the narrative were generated by hermeneutical interaction with the scriptural text.

---

84. Justin *Apology* 32.

This hermeneutical phenomenon went both ways. The fact that Jesus came from Nazareth generated a "prediction" in 2:23. This would also explain why many modern interpreters have difficulty seeing the OT as a "prediction" in the first place, since they no longer share Matthew's hermeneutical presuppositions and methods. The hermeneutical task for the contemporary interpreter of the Gospels is to share Matthew's conviction that the Christ came as the fulfillment of Scripture, expressed in his theology and illustrated and communicated by his own interpretative techniques. Contemporary readers may take seriously and appropriate Matthew's theology, without being bound to adopt Matthew's hermeneutical methods as our own. An aspect of the historical conditionedness of biblical revelation is that Matthew interpreted Scripture in a way appropriate to his own time. We do not belong to that time, and so we must interpret Scripture using the methods appropriate to our own time. It is precisely our own historical method that allows us to see and appreciate Matthew's interpretation, to understand his witness to Christ in his own terms, and to be challenged to share his faith. (See Bibliography on pages 119-20.)

❖   ❖   ❖   ❖

MATTHEW 3:1–4:17, JESUS IN RELATION TO JOHN THE BAPTIST

OVERVIEW

A new subsection begins at 3:1. This is signaled by the disjunctive particle—"now," "but," etc. (δέ *de*; left untranslated by both the NRSV and the NIV)—by the passing of considerable time between 2:23 and 3:1; by the appearance of John the Baptist without preparation or warning; by the solemn, biblical-sounding "In those days"; and by the fact that both of Matthew's major sources (Q and Mark; cf. Introduction) begin at this point.

This section, which begins with the appearance of John, extends through the pericope 4:12-17, narrates the arrest of John, signaling the beginning of Jesus' own ministry. The opening scene of this section pictures John preaching, "Repent, for the kingdom of heaven has come near." It concludes, after noting the arrest of John, with Jesus preaching this identical message (3:2; 4:17). Thus 3:1–4:17 forms a unit of Matthew's story bracketed by references to John the Baptist and preaching of the kingdom, in which the significance of Jesus' ministry is presented in relation to John. This section forms a chiastic structural counterpart to 11:2-19 (see Introduction). John's announcement of "the coming one" (3:11) corresponds to his question in 11:3, "Are you the one who is to come?" In chapter 3, the Baptist is the primary speaker, and the reader receives the Baptist's view of Jesus and himself. In chapter 11, John is offstage, Jesus is the primary speaker, and the reader receives Jesus' view of the Baptist and himself.[85]

85. Cf. John P. Meier, "John the Baptist in Matthew's Gospel," *JBL* 99 (1980) 387.

Matthew 3:1-12, John the Baptist

NIV

3 In those days John the Baptist came, preaching in the Desert of Judea [2]and saying, "Repent, for the kingdom of heaven is near." [3]This is he who was spoken of through the prophet Isaiah:

"A voice of one calling in the desert,
'Prepare the way for the Lord,
    make straight paths for him.'"[a]

[4]John's clothes were made of camel's hair, and he had a leather belt around his waist. His food was locusts and wild honey. [5]People went out to him from Jerusalem and all Judea and the whole region of the Jordan. [6]Confessing their sins, they were baptized by him in the Jordan River.

[7]But when he saw many of the Pharisees and Sadducees coming to where he was baptizing, he said to them: "You brood of vipers! Who warned you to flee from the coming wrath? [8]Produce fruit in keeping with repentance. [9]And do not think you can say to yourselves, 'We have Abraham as our father.' I tell you that out of these stones God can raise up children for Abraham. [10]The ax is already at the root of the trees, and every tree that does not produce good fruit will be cut down and thrown into the fire.

[11]"I baptize you with[b] water for repentance. But after me will come one who is more powerful than I, whose sandals I am not fit to carry. He will baptize you with the Holy Spirit and with fire. [12]His winnowing fork is in his hand, and he will clear his threshing floor, gathering his wheat into the barn and burning up the chaff with unquenchable fire."

[a]3 Isaiah 40:3   [b]11 Or *in*

NRSV

3 In those days John the Baptist appeared in the wilderness of Judea, proclaiming, [2]"Repent, for the kingdom of heaven has come near."[a] [3]This is the one of whom the prophet Isaiah spoke when he said,

"The voice of one crying out in the wilderness:
'Prepare the way of the Lord,
    make his paths straight.'"

[4]Now John wore clothing of camel's hair with a leather belt around his waist, and his food was locusts and wild honey. [5]Then the people of Jerusalem and all Judea were going out to him, and all the region along the Jordan, [6]and they were baptized by him in the river Jordan, confessing their sins.

[7]But when he saw many Pharisees and Sadducees coming for baptism, he said to them, "You brood of vipers! Who warned you to flee from the wrath to come? [8]Bear fruit worthy of repentance. [9]Do not presume to say to yourselves, 'We have Abraham as our ancestor'; for I tell you, God is able from these stones to raise up children to Abraham. [10]Even now the ax is lying at the root of the trees; every tree therefore that does not bear good fruit is cut down and thrown into the fire.

[11]"I baptize you with[b] water for repentance, but one who is more powerful than I is coming after me; I am not worthy to carry his sandals. He will baptize you with[b] the Holy Spirit and fire. [12]His winnowing fork is in his hand, and he will clear his threshing floor and will gather his wheat into the granary; but the chaff he will burn with unquenchable fire."

[a]Or *is at hand*   [b]Or *in*

COMMENTARY

Both Mark and Q began with the appearance and message of John the Baptist. Here Matthew begins to use these sources for the first time—in 3:1-6 rewriting Mark, in 3:7-12 rewriting Q with some overlap with Mark in v. 11. Prior to Mark and Q this material had circulated orally—3:1-6 in the form of a biographical legend about John, 3:7-12 as a brief collection of apocalyptic and prophetic sayings of John the Baptist.

John the Baptist was a significant figure in his

own right, a Jewish prophet with his own message and disciples, who ran afoul of Herod Antipas and was imprisoned and executed by him, as reported by Josephus.[86] The movement founded by John continued not only after the baptism of Jesus (Matt 9:14; 11:2-3), but also after the resurrection and beginning of the Christian community (Acts 19:1-7). Early Christianity experienced the Baptist's group as a competitor, and in various ways reinterpreted the traditions about John from the Christian perspective to incorporate them into the developing Christian tradition. Our earliest source, Q, had proportionally the most to say about John, and cast him in the most independent role—like Jesus, a prophetic spokesman for transcendent Wisdom (Matt 3:7-10/ Luke 3:7-9; Matt 3:11-12/ Luke 3:16-17; Matt 11:2-19/ Luke 7:18-35; 16:16, the Lukan form of 7:35 being closer to Q). The Gospel of Mark had already interpreted John as Elijah, who in Jewish tradition was expected to return as a harbinger of the eschatological advent of God (cf. Mal 3:1; 4:5-6; Mark 1:6; 9:11-13). Mark understood John exclusively as the forerunner of Jesus, having no independent message, and pictures him as a prefiguration of the Christian pattern of the proclaimer who is handed over to death, manifest in both Jesus and his disciples. Corresponding to Mark's view of the messianic secret, the Markan John the Baptist never recognizes or identifies Jesus as the Messiah. Except for the literary device of the secret messiahship, Matthew takes over the Markan pattern with which he had long been familiar. In doing so he both makes more explicit the Markan identification of John and Elijah (Matt 11:14; 17:13, both Matthean additions) and makes John and Jesus parallel and complementary figures (3:2 = 4:17; 3:5 = 4:23; 3:7 = 23:33; 4:12 = 21:15), although John is altogether subordinate to Jesus.

3:1-2. Matthew's lack of biographical interest is indicated by the vagueness of the chronological data. From the text, the reader gains no idea of how old Jesus was at the time of the settlement in Nazareth, nor of the age of John the Baptist at the time of his first appearance, nor of the age of Jesus when he first appears as an adult.

Unlike Mark and John, where the Baptist is

already on the narrative stage when the curtain opens, and in contrast to Luke, where elaborate preparation is made for his appearance in the lengthy chapters 1–2, John here appears abruptly in the Matthean story. His message that the kingdom of heaven has come near unites him with the preceding story, however, for chapters 1–2 have dealt with the incursion of God's kingdom into this world in the most unexpected manner.

3:3. The narrator identifies John for the reader by citing words from Scripture, differently from the Fourth Gospel, where John identifies himself by quoting this text (John 1:23). The Hebrew text reads:

A voice cries out:
"In the wilderness prepare the way of the LORD,
    make straight in the desert a highway for our God."
(Isa. 40:3 NRSV)

The parallelism clearly indicates that "in the wilderness" modifies "prepare the way of the LORD," with "LORD" meaning God, Yahweh. Isaiah 40:3 was already understood eschatologically in first-century Judaism, as illustrated by the Qumran community, which went into the wilderness to fulfill this scripture literally. The text of the LXX allows the voice of the prophet to be heard in the wilderness. Mark had already combined this text with Mal 3:1 and Exod 23:20 and applied it to the Baptist. The Isaiah segment follows the LXX exactly, except for the substitution of "his" for "our God," thus transferring Isaiah's prophecy of the advent of God to the Lord Jesus. Matthew omits the non-Isaiah part of the text, but otherwise follows Mark verbatim.

3:4-6. The description of John's clothing and food serves to separate him from elegant society and to identify him with the wilderness that was to be the scene of eschatological renewal. In Mark, too, it indicates that John is the expected Elijah (cf. 2 Kgs 1:8), an identification that Matthew will later make more explicit and place in the mouth of Jesus (11:14, added by Matthew to the Q context). "Locusts" are not carob pods (contra the popular tradition that has designated the species of tree that produces them as the "John the Baptist tree"), but actual locusts, described as ritually clean food in Lev 11:22 and eaten by the poorer people of the desert from ancient times until today.

---

86. Josephus *Antiquities of the Jews* XVII.5.2; for further, see the Commentary on 14:1-12.

The throngs come to be baptized, a distinctive practice that had given John his name. The verb for "baptize" (βαπτίζω *baptizo*) means to dip or to immerse, and John baptized these persons in the Jordan River. Various ritual immersions and washings in Judaism may have served as a model for John, as indicated by the pools/cisterns at Qumran and the *mikveh,* found in religious households as well as in public places, such as the Temple. Baptism for proselytes may have already been practiced.[87] But John did not simply take over a current practice. In contrast to the repeated washings at the Temple and Qumran, John's once-for-all baptism had eschatological implications, sealing the converts from the eschatological judgment to come (see vv. 7-12). Mark had related it to the forgiveness of sins (Mark 1:4), but Matthew omits that feature of John's baptism in order to attribute it exclusively to Jesus (26:28, where the same words occur) and to the church.

3:7. While Mark contains only John's preaching of the "mightier one" to come, Q reports John's scathing preaching of repentance. Matthew combines both. The Q introduction is better preserved in Luke 3:7, where John's preaching is addressed to the crowds who come to be baptized by him. Matthew changes the addressees of John's message to "Pharisees and Sadducees," and so can describe them only as coming "to where he was baptizing" (the NIV is here the more accurate translation), since in Matthew's view they represent the Jewish opposition who come to inspect John rather than to be baptized by him (cf. 21:23-27). Historically, in the Judaism of Jesus' time, the Pharisees and Sadducees were opposing religious parties, unlikely to work together.[88] Matthew is not reporting the historical situation of John's time, but wishes to describe the Jewish opposition as a united front, already manifesting itself against John as it would later against Jesus.

"Brood of vipers" in Q pictures the crowds as scurrying away from the coming eschatological judgment like snakes fleeing a forest fire. Since

Matthew understands the conflict initiated by the advent of Jesus in cosmic terms, for him the phrase (literally "sons of snakes") may suggest the dualistic opposition between the kingdom of God—appearing in Jesus and proclaimed by John—and the "sons of the evil one" represented by the Jewish leaders and those persuaded by them (13:38). "Vipers" is thus not merely an insulting term, but it pictures as well the predatory, poisonous false teachers who pervert the people.

3:8-10. The image of the ax at the root of the tree indicates the coming eschatological judgment that is already prepared, and the brief interval before it begins. Like other apocalyptic prophets, John sees the judgment as already on the horizon and the basis for his urgent call for repentance. An appeal to belonging to the elect group by virtue of descent from Abraham will not save one in the fiery judgment. Already Isa 51:1-2 had seen descent from Abraham and Sarah not as attainment but as the miraculous grace of God, who had produced a people from dead "rock" (cf. Gen 18:10-14). What God had done originally, God could do again. Matthew understands John's original preaching in a Christian sense: Inclusion in the holy people of God and acceptance at the last judgment is based not on descent from Abraham and belonging to empirical Israel, but on response to the call to decision, to baptism, and to the corresponding "fruits." John does not here specify what these fruits are, but Matthew will adopt this metaphor from Q as a fundamental representation of the life of discipleship to Jesus, which he will have Jesus elaborate at key junctures in the narrative (7:16-20; 12:33; cf. 13:8, 26; 21:18-19).

3:11-12. Matthew here combines Mark and Q with minimal changes. John contrasts his own mission and baptism with that of "the coming one." "The one who is to come" is an eschatological image, corresponding to the contrast between the present world and "the coming age" (העולם הבא *ha-'olam ha-ba'*; cf. Mark 10:30; Luke 18:30; Rev 1:4, 8; 4:8). While some Jewish apocalyptic views of the end had anticipated the advent of God as the judge, John seems to have looked forward to the imminent advent of another eschatological figure as God's representative. If one were not already convinced that John was the divinely appointed forerunner of the Messiah, one

87. If this ritual was already common in the first century, John's call for baptism would place his Jewish hearers in the same situation as Gentile outsiders, challenging them to start all over. See A. H. McNeile, *The Gospel According to St. Matthew: The Greek Text with Introduction, Notes, and Indices* (London: Macmillan, 1915; reprint 1961) 33-43; W. F. Flemington, "Baptism," *IDB* (Nashville: Abingdon, 1963) 1:348-53; M. H. Pope, "Proselyte," *IDB* 3:921-31.

88. See 16:1; 22:23-46; and Shaye J. D. Cohen, *From the Maccabees to the Mishnah* (Philadelphia: Westminster, 1987) 143-63.

would not read vv. 11-12 as referring to Jesus (see 11:2-3). While John baptized in water, a symbol of the eschatological judgment and purification, the one to come would baptize in fire—i.e., would accomplish the judgment itself, which would purify the righteous and burn up the unrighteous. While Mark has only the "Holy Spirit," Q had "fire," and may have read originally "wind and fire," corresponding to the metaphor of the threshing floor as the image of separation at the last judgment. Since the words for "wind" and "spirit" are identical in both Aramaic and Greek, "wind" could be understood by Mark in the positive sense as "[Holy] Spirit." John's original contrast of symbolic water baptism in the present and real fire baptism in the future—both of them

negative images of judgment—becomes in Mark the contrast between John's this-worldly baptism in water and the Messiah's eschatological baptism in the Holy Spirit, so that the contrast is not only between preliminary and final but between negative and positive as well. Matthew then combines Mark's "Holy Spirit" with Q's "fire," but it is not clear what he means by the Messiah's future baptism with the Holy Spirit, since he never refers to it again. Luke's understanding that this was fulfilled on Pentecost (Acts 1:5; 2:1-13) should not be read into Matthew. In all this, Matthew has interpreted John as a precursor of Jesus, a parallel figure who also already knows himself to be subordinate to the Messiah, unworthy even to carry his sandals.

REFLECTIONS

1. We know that Jesus did not in fact conform to John's expectations of what the "mightier one" would be (see 11:2-3). What did Matthew do with the picture of John that he received from his sacred documents? Matthew could have excluded John from his presentation, or completely transformed him so that John's picture of the coming one no longer clashed with messiahship as represented by Jesus (cf. the picture of John in the Fourth Gospel!). Alternately, he could have reinterpreted Jesus so that he fit more closely John's expectation of the violent eschatological judge. Yet Matthew's whole point is that christology must be reinterpreted in the light of Jesus' advent as the forgiving, accepting, non-retaliatory suffering-servant king whose strength is precisely in his meekness (12:14-21; 21:1-5). By incorporating John and his message within a Christian framework, Matthew was able to understand John's message from a Christian perspective and to preserve elements and emphases that Christians need to hear, even if that message is in tension with the main thrust of the Christian message. For example, John pictures eschatological judgment that will sort the Jewish people into "wheat" and "chaff." Matthew, however, applies this image to complacent Christians within the church, itself a mixed bag that is to be sorted out not by us but by the eschatological judge (see 13:30, 36-43).

2. John's rough contours, however, are not totally assimilated to Christianity. In Matthew, John remains a marginal figure, parallel to Jesus and subordinate to him, commended and respected, whom the reader must take seriously, yet who does not become a disciple; indeed, he has his own disciples, parallel to the group of Jesus' disciples. He is not quite "in," but neither is he "out," representing an ally in the cause of the kingdom of God who yet does not belong to the Christian community and cannot be incorporated within it. This is but one example of Matthew's openness to accepting others as God's servants and messengers even if he can find no legitimate place for them within his theological understanding of the church. The picture of John, who never became a disciple (read "Christian" from Matthew's post-Easter perspective), might be kept in mind when interpreting Matthew's more negative pronouncements against other Jews.

3. The abrupt appearance of John in Matthew's Gospel is a matter of theological design, not literary clumsiness. The action of God in history is often sudden, unexpected, and, to our eyes, even intrusive. The will of God cannot be equated with group progress, human growth, or social development, arising naturally out of the human possibility. God's will does not always work gently, climbing quietly like ivy up the lattice of history. Sometimes an Elijah appears, a nation repents, a Berlin Wall is dismantled, a Martin Luther King, Jr., strides across the landscape. God's will shatters the mold, violates the categories, breaks in on the world as a jarring surprise.

So the doors of Matthew's Gospel suddenly swing open, and there stands John in the wilderness of Judea, looking for all the world like Elijah of old. It's a shock to see him. Who could have guessed it? His surprising appearance is, itself, a claim that God's ways with the world are often strange, unforeseen, and unpredictable. Here at the beginning of Jesus' ministry, John the Baptist is a "call to worship" in the flesh—not a benign and cheery "Good morning," but a *real* call to worship that shakes the cobwebs off the pews: "Repent, for the kingdom of heaven has come near."

Matthew 3:13-17, The Baptism of Jesus

NIV

13Then Jesus came from Galilee to the Jordan to be baptized by John. 14But John tried to deter him, saying, "I need to be baptized by you, and do you come to me?"

15Jesus replied, "Let it be so now; it is proper for us to do this to fulfill all righteousness." Then John consented.

16As soon as Jesus was baptized, he went up out of the water. At that moment heaven was opened, and he saw the Spirit of God descending like a dove and lighting on him. 17And a voice from heaven said, "This is my Son, whom I love; with him I am well pleased."

NRSV

13Then Jesus came from Galilee to John at the Jordan, to be baptized by him. 14John would have prevented him, saying, "I need to be baptized by you, and do you come to me?" 15But Jesus answered him, "Let it be so now; for it is proper for us in this way to fulfill all righteousness." Then he consented. 16And when Jesus had been baptized, just as he came up from the water, suddenly the heavens were opened to him and he saw the Spirit of God descending like a dove and alighting on him. 17And a voice from heaven said, "This is my Son, the Beloved,[a] with whom I am well pleased."

[a] Or *my beloved Son*

COMMENTARY

The fact that Jesus was baptized by John is historical bedrock, having been questioned only by a few of the most skeptical historians. Jesus began his ministry by being baptized by John, and for an undetermined period was John's disciple ("after me" in 3:11 is not chronology but the phrase normally used for discipleship, as in 4:19). The story had already been interpreted in various ways when it came to Matthew. Mark had portrayed John's baptism as "for the forgiveness of sins," and had pictured Jesus being baptized by John without protest; John did not recognize Jesus as the Messiah. The question of Jesus' sinlessness

had not arisen for Mark (see Mark 10:18; cf. Matthew's rewriting in 19:17). Not only Matthew, but also his readers were thoroughly familiar with the Markan and Q forms of the story.

3:13. This background illuminates the meaning of the Matthean form of the story by throwing it into sharp profile. Matthew uses this scene to bring the adult Jesus on the narrative stage for the first time, to present him and his mission to the reader in terms of his own christology. The reader is already at the Jordan with John when Jesus arrives from Galilee. Matthew could have told the story otherwise, beginning with the reader and Jesus in Galilee, and having Jesus go to John (as in the *Gospel of the Nazarenes* 2). But Matthew incorporates Jesus into the story line in which John is already present rather than vice versa, preserving the history-of-salvation continuity from the OT through John to Jesus. Matthew adds an infinitive of purpose to Mark, indicating that Jesus had already decided in Nazareth to be baptized. This is a literary preemptive strike, the first hint that Jesus is in charge throughout this scene.

3:14-17. Although in Matthew's story there has been no previous contact between the two, John recognizes Jesus as his superior, and without making any christological confession tries to reverse the action that is about to take place (the verb is a conative imperfect, indicating attempted action). Jesus speaks for the first time in the Gospel, authoritatively taking charge of his own baptism in words that Matthew composes and adds to Mark. Both righteousness and fulfillment are key Matthean theological themes. *Righteousness* here means, as often elsewhere, doing the revealed will of God. Here, *fulfill* seems to mean simply "do, perform," and the meaning is that it is necessary for both John and Jesus to do God's will, which includes the baptism of Jesus. The plural *us* links John and Jesus together as partners in carrying out God's saving plan (11:2-19).

This scene is replete with eschatological overtones. The heavens are opened, a voice comes from heaven, the Spirit is given. The Judaism of Matthew's day tended to regard all of these elements as the revelatory gifts of God that had happened in biblical times and that no longer occurred, but would reappear in the last days. Matthew presents the appearance of the Messiah as the beginning of the eschatological events. The evocative symbol of the dove, which has never been neatly reduced to a single explanation, may connote (among other things) the eschatological event of the new creation, reminiscent of the dove-like movement of the Spirit over the chaotic waters of Genesis 1. Matthew thinks of the eschaton as the new creation (19:28) and has already used the word for "genesis" (γένεσις *genesis*; also meaning "genealogy," "birth," "story," "beginning") in his opening words (1:1, 18).

The heavenly voice speaks in the words of Scripture, a combination of Ps 2:7 and Isa 42:1.[89] The words are taken almost verbatim from Mark and represent a combination of christological themes that have become important to Matthew. Although Matthew has presented Jesus as the Son of God in the birth story (1:18-25; 2:15), he has withheld the direct announcement until this scene in which God confers the title. Matthew changes Mark's second-person address, "You are," to third person, "This is." Mark portrays the announcement as being made only to Jesus, and, in keeping with his perspective of the messianic secret, the other human characters in the story remain ignorant of Jesus' identity, which is disclosed to the reader. In Matthew the announcement is addressed to a wider circle—at least John, more likely the bystander public in general, since in chaps. 1–2 Jesus' identity is already a matter of family and public knowledge. Although John hears the heavenly voice, he does not become a disciple, but continues his own work with his own disciples.

---

89. The wording is identical to neither the MT nor the LXX of Isa 42:1, but reflects the version of Isaiah that Matthew uses or modifies in 12:18-21.

REFLECTIONS

There is no psychologizing of Jesus' "baptismal experience" in Matthew (or elsewhere in the Bible). Matthew does not speculate on what went on in the soul of Jesus. He does not encourage the reader to question whether Jesus already knew he was the Son of God, or had some unique relation to God, or whether his baptism was the occasion when his mission first became clear to him. This is the stuff of novels, not of Gospels. Nor is Matthew interested in metaphysical theories about what happened to the person of Christ at baptism. Matthew has made it clear that he excludes the view that, metaphysically speaking, Jesus became something at the baptism he had not been before (see 1:18-25).

From Matthew's perspective, the story of Jesus' baptism is christological narrative. The heavenly voice declares Jesus to be both Son of God and Suffering Servant; the two titles were already combined in the Markan source. Both titles are important to Matthew, but for him they are not unrelated, not two different special things about Jesus. Without minimizing the picture of Jesus as the Son, Matthew will emphasize the picture of Jesus as Servant, previously neglected in the tradition, as he already stresses it in this story. "My Son, the Beloved, with whom I am well pleased" (v. 17) reflects the first Servant Song of Isa 42:1. Matthew will later (12:18-21) cite the entire song (Isa 42:1-4), the longest scriptural quotation in his Gospel, as the concluding summary of Part One of his Gospel, representing Jesus' response to the conflict that his coming has initiated. The Servant picture fills in the content of the Son of God picture, affecting the way Jesus fulfills his mission. Precisely as the "mightier one" who will baptize with the Spirit, precisely as the Son of David and Son of God, he submits to baptism at the hands of one who is "lesser" (πραΰς *praus,* also translated "meek"; cf. 11:29; 21:5). Although he is the Son, he is baptized in obedience to the will of God. Precisely as the Son he is the obedient one. Already Jesus' obedience, which leads to his self-giving on the cross (27:43), and the prayer of 26:42 are anticipated. This obedience and this prayer bind together Jesus and his disciples (6:10; 16:24).

Thus Jesus' baptism has not only a christological message but an ecclesiological one as well, since Matthew considers Christ and the church an inseparable unity. It is not the case, however, that the baptism of Jesus is narrated as a model for Christian baptism, as though the meaning is "since Jesus was baptized, we should be too." It is, rather, the case that Jesus' baptism is painted with colors drawn from the palate of the Christian theology and practice of baptism. Just as disciples are to be baptized into the name of the Trinity (28:19), so also Father, Son, and Holy Spirit are all present in Jesus' baptism. Christian baptism is a matter of obedience and receiving the Spirit, and so was it for Jesus. As Christians are declared to be God's children in the act of baptism, Jesus was declared Son of God when he was baptized.

Matthew 4:1-11, The Temptation

NIV

4 Then Jesus was led by the Spirit into the desert to be tempted by the devil. [2]After fasting forty days and forty nights, he was hungry. [3]The tempter came to him and said, "If you are the Son of God, tell these stones to become bread."

[4]Jesus answered, "It is written: 'Man does not live on bread alone, but on every word that comes from the mouth of God.'[a]"

[5]Then the devil took him to the holy city and had him stand on the highest point of the temple. [6]"If you are the Son of God," he said, "throw yourself down. For it is written:

"'He will command his angels concerning you,
   and they will lift you up in their hands,
so that you will not strike your foot against a
   stone.'[b]"

[7]Jesus answered him, "It is also written: 'Do not put the Lord your God to the test.'[c]"

[a]4 Deut. 8:3   [b]6 Psalm 91:11,12   [c]7 Deut. 6:16

NRSV

4 Then Jesus was led up by the Spirit into the wilderness to be tempted by the devil. [2]He fasted forty days and forty nights, and afterwards he was famished. [3]The tempter came and said to him, "If you are the Son of God, command these stones to become loaves of bread." [4]But he answered, "It is written,

'One does not live by bread alone,
   but by every word that comes from the
   mouth of God.'"

[5]Then the devil took him to the holy city and placed him on the pinnacle of the temple, [6]saying to him, "If you are the Son of God, throw yourself down; for it is written,

'He will command his angels concerning you,'
   and 'On their hands they will bear you up,
   so that you will not dash your foot against
   a stone.'"

[7]Jesus said to him, "Again it is written, 'Do not put the Lord your God to the test.'"

NIV

⁸Again, the devil took him to a very high mountain and showed him all the kingdoms of the world and their splendor. ⁹"All this I will give you," he said, "if you will bow down and worship me."

¹⁰Jesus said to him, "Away from me, Satan! For it is written: 'Worship the Lord your God, and serve him only.'ᵃ"

¹¹Then the devil left him, and angels came and attended him.

ᵃ10 Deut. 6:13

NRSV

8Again, the devil took him to a very high mountain and showed him all the kingdoms of the world and their splendor; ⁹and he said to him, "All these I will give you, if you will fall down and worship me." ¹⁰Jesus said to him, "Away with you, Satan! for it is written,

'Worship the Lord your God,
     and serve only him.'"

¹¹Then the devil left him, and suddenly angels came and waited on him.

COMMENTARY

There was no Jewish tradition that the Messiah would be tempted by Satan. The story is an early Christian creation that appeared independently in Q and Mark. In Mark, the confrontation between Jesus and Satan is a test of strength, not a moral temptation, and no words are exchanged. The much more extensive Q story, followed by Matthew with only minor variations,[90] is a verbal battle between Jesus and Satan, in which the tempter tries to divert the obedient Son of God from his path. The Q version resembles haggadic tales of rabbis who battle each other with Scripture, and thus has something of the form of a controversy dialogue. The closest parallels are the debates between Jesus and the Jewish leaders (high priests, elders, Pharisees, Sadducees, scribes) in Matt 21:23-27; 22:15–23:36. It appears that a Christian scribe in the Q community composed the story on this model to portray Jesus' victory in his confrontation with Satan at the beginning of his ministry. Matthew creates a literary bracket by crafting this dispute with Satan so that it corresponds to the disputes with the Jewish leaders at the end of Jesus' ministry, thereby suggesting the underlying cosmic conflict that surfaces in the confrontation between Jesus and the Jewish leaders.

Matthew 4:1-11 does not begin afresh, but continues the narrative of the preceding scene

(see Overview for 3:1). This scene is connected with 3:1-17 by "Spirit," "wilderness," "Son of God," the motif of the voice of God (central to Deuteronomy, from which Jesus quotes), and, more subtly, by the resistance that both John and Satan offer to the obedient response of the Son to the Father's will.

Conflict with Satan is not limited to this pericope, but is the underlying aspect of the conflict between the kingdom of God and the kingdom of this world, which is the plot of the *whole* Gospel of Matthew. The friction between Jesus and the Jewish leaders throughout the Gospel, already anticipated in the conflict with Herod, the high priests, and the scribes (and even the hesitation of John to baptize Jesus) is actually a clash of kingdoms. Jesus is the representative of the kingdom of God; Satan also represents a kingdom (12:26). Thus elsewhere in the Gospel, "test" or "tempt" (πειράζω *peirazō*) is used only of the Jewish leaders (16:1; 19:3; 22:18, 35), and Jesus always resists them by quoting Scripture, as he does here. The conflict between Jesus and the Jewish leaders is a surface dimension of the underlying discord between the kingdom of God and the kingdom of Satan. This is what Matthew is *about.* God is the hidden actor, and Satan is the hidden opponent, *throughout* the Gospel; but God is always offstage, and Satan appears only here as a character in the story.[91] Satan is worked into

90. Luke 4:1-13 places the three temptations in a different order, ending with the Temple scene. Matthew is generally regarded as representing the Q order. Cf. John Kloppenborg, *Q Parallels: Synopsis, Critical Notes, & Concordance* (Sonoma, Calif.: Polebridge, 1988) 20.

91. The direct voice of God is heard twice within the narrative (3:17; 17:5), but God does not appear directly on the narrative stage as a character in the story.

the outline at strategic points, but the conflict between Jesus and Satan is not to be reduced to any one scene. In Matthew's theology, Satan, though defeated (12:28-29) continues to tempt Jesus during his ministry (16:23), at the crucifixion,[92] and into the time of the church (13:19, 39); Satan is finally abolished at the end time (25:41). The narrative of Jesus' ministry, which now begins, is told at two levels. It not only portrays the past life of Jesus, but also looks ahead to the post-Easter time, when the disciples must still confront demonic resistance to the gospel message (5:37; 6:13; 13:19, 39)—and not only from outsiders, but from other disciples as well (16:23).

4:1. Jesus came from Galilee for the purpose of being baptized (3:13), and now he is led by the Spirit to be tempted. All is part of the divine plan, and his submission to temptation is not an accident or a matter of being victimized by demonic power, but is part of his obedience to God.

Like his Jewish context and Q tradition, Matthew uses "devil," "Satan," "the evil one," and "Beelzebul" the "ruler of demons" as synonyms for the figure that had come to represent the personalized power of evil, also called "Beliar" and other names in early Judaism and the NT. In the Hebrew Bible, the satan (literally, "accuser") was a member of the heavenly court, the divine prosecuting attorney who implemented the will of God the heavenly Judge, by putting suspected offenders to the test (Job 1–2). With the development of apocalyptic thought between the testaments, Satan became a proper name for one sometimes thought to be a fallen angel who had rebelled against God, and who continued to resist God's will in the present age by attempting to lure human beings into sin.[93]

4:2. The period of forty days and forty nights is reminiscent of Moses (Exod 34:28; Deut 9:9; see Matt 5:1). The story also has overtones of the experience of Israel, the "son of God" (Exod 4:22-23; Deut 8:2-5), who passed through the waters into the wilderness, was tested—and failed, because of disobedience and worshiping other gods. Jesus, the true Son of God, who

recapitulates Israel's experience in coming out of Egypt (Matt 2:15), is tested in the wilderness and remains obedient to God, specifically refusing to worship another. The whole story can be seen as a typological haggadic story reflecting on Deut 8:2-3 (Jesus quotes exclusively from Deuteronomy). In contrast to Israel in the wilderness, whose faith wavered until it was restored by the miraculous manna, Jesus is hungry but remains faithful without a miracle.

Matthew pictures Jesus as voluntarily fasting, using the technical term for the cultic practice current in Matthew's church (6:16-18; 9:14-15, changing Mark). In Matthew, the temptation begins only after the forty-day period of fasting has ended, which has strengthened and prepared Jesus for the encounter with Satan, but has also left him hungry. Jesus' humanness is documented before the conflict begins.

4:3. "If" (εἰ *ei*) takes the statement at its face value, considering it a real case (as in 6:30, etc.); the word may also be translated "since." Thus the devil is not attempting to raise doubts in Jesus' mind, but is making an argument on a fact assumed to be true. The disputed issue is not whether Jesus is the Son of God, but what it means for Jesus to be the Son of God. It was a feature of some Jewish expectations of the Messiah that he would reproduce the miracle of the manna and that there would be a lavish supply of food in the messianic time. Jesus is challenged to show that he qualifies as Messiah by these criteria. Matthew has changed the singular "stone" and "bread" ("loaf") in Q to the plural "stones" and "loaves." Since one loaf would more than suffice for Jesus, the devil's argument is not only for Jesus to use his divine power for his own advantage, to alleviate his hunger (but denying his humanity and the trust in God Jesus teaches in 6:24-34), but also to use his divine power to provide food for all, meeting an obvious human need, corresponding to popular messianic expectations, and carrying enormous political power. In 21:18-22, Jesus does use his miraculous power to curse a fig tree that cannot provide him food when he is hungry, and he twice accomplishes a feeding miracle for the hungry multitudes (14:15-21; 15:32-38)—thus the problem of taking literally Jesus' power to provide food miraculously, whether he refuses to do so or not. (See Excursus

---

92. The phrase "Son of God" occurs in 4:6 in the devil's mouth and twice in the crucifixion scene: 27:40 in the mouth of the passers by, and 27:43 in the mouth of the high priests, scribes, and elders, both times added by Matthew (cf. 16:16, 23).

93. For a more extensive discussion, see T. H. Gaster, "Satan," in *IDB*, 4:224-28.

"Interpreting the Miracle Stories in Matthew," 241-51.)

4:4. Jesus responds only in the words of Scripture, each time from Deuteronomy (cf. 4:2). Jesus' words and deeds will later show the vital importance of providing food for hungry people (6:11; 14:13-21; 15:32-39; 25:31-46), but here he insists that a truly human life must be nourished by the Word of God. Although "Son of God" is an important christological title for Matthew, Jesus here insists on his own humanity by juxtaposing "human being" to the devil's "Son of God."[94]

4:5-7. The reference to the holy city is Matthew's addition. This somewhat rare phrase, like the expectation of manna in the first temptation, has eschatological overtones (Isa 48:2; 52:1; Dan 9:24; Matt 27:53; Rev 11:2; 21:2, 10). The identity of the pinnacle of the Temple is unclear, but it was not the roof or a spire. Although spectators are not mentioned, the temptation must be for Jesus to make some sensational demonstration that he is Son of God. The action is not obviously wrong or demonic (angels had protected Jesus in 2:1-23, and angels do come to serve him in 4:11), nor is the devil's quotation of Scripture for his purpose a case of obviously perverse exegesis.[95] Matthew is not merely reporting a once-upon-a-time encounter between Jesus and Satan, but is illustrating that even the well-intentioned theologies and interpretations of Scripture in his own community can become the vehicle of a demonic alternative to the path of obedient suffering that Jesus has chosen as the path of messiahship. The alternative between angelic help and obedience to God's will that leads to the cross is pointedly expressed in 26:36-53 (esp. v. 53). Again, Jesus resists the temptation with words from Scripture (Deut 6:16).

4:8-10. The "high mountain" is Matthew's addition, which he seems to have adopted from Mark 9:2 (cf. 5:1; 17:1 = Mark 9:2; 28:16). It strengthens the allusion to Moses. The offer of "all the kingdoms of the world" strikes the note of the struggle between the kingdom of God and the kingdom of Satan (12:26), which reverberates throughout the Gospel, and reveals the real conflict inherent in the temptation scene. The temptation is for Jesus to rule the kingdoms of the world—i.e., to assume the role presently played by the Roman emperor, and to do it by capitulating to the devil's kingship. The devil's command challenges Jesus to accept the status quo of the rebellious state of the world, to acknowledge that selfishness and practical atheism prevail, and to fit in with it. With Jesus' power, he could have it all. At the end of this section, Jesus takes up his task of proclaiming the advent of God's rule (4:17) and teaches his disciples to pray for it to occur in this world (6:10). Jesus will not deviate from worshiping the one true God, even for the noble-sounding purpose of taking over all the kingdoms of the world. At the conclusion of the story, on another mountain, Jesus announces that he has received all authority on earth, but it is from God—and after the cross (28:18).

For the third time Jesus resists the devil's proposal with the word of Scripture (Deut 6:13). For the first time, however, he adds his own words, "Away with you, Satan!" (v. 10). Only two Greek words comprise this text, expressing Jesus' authoritative command to which even Satan must now be subject.[96] Jesus and his disciples will continue to struggle against demonic powers throughout the Gospel, but it is a defeated enemy they face (see 12:26).

4:11. "Attended"/"waited on" here has the connotation of Jesus' being served food. By placing the kingdom of God first, even though it meant rejecting food and the help of angels, Jesus finally receives both, thus becoming an anticipatory example of his own teaching (6:33).

---

94. The NIV's "man" and the NRSV's "one" represent "human being" (ἄνθρωπος anthrōpos).

95. The devil's quoting of Psalm 91 does not exactly correspond to our biblical text, but it will not do to dismiss the devil's use of Scripture by saying he misquotes, since he is closer to the text than is Jesus' citation of Deuteronomy, or Matthew's typical formula quotations. Nor is the point that the devil misinterprets Scripture by ignoring the context, which Matthew himself frequently does. See Excursus "Matthew as Interpreter of Scripture," 151-54.

96. The NIV follows the MSS that read literally "Get behind me, Satan" (cf. C², D, L, and a number of later minuscules and versions), a reflection of Jesus' later words to Peter (16:23). Since in 16:23, unlike the present context, the phrase is a call to renewed discipleship, the NRSV reading not only has the better MSS attestation, but catches Matthew's theological point as well.

REFLECTIONS

1. Is Satan language passé? The interpreter's first question today may be whether there is still a place in our thinking for images of Satan, especially since such images can be abused by a literalism that uses "the devil made me do it" as an escape from personal responsibility and that brands its opponents as tools of the devil. Yet, language and imagery of the demonic played an important theological role for Matthew, and it can continue to do so for us. Such imagery provides a way of acknowledging the reality of an evil greater than our own individual inclinations to evil, a supra-personal power often called "systemic evil" today. Another valuable aspect of such language is that it can prevent us from regarding our human opponents as the ultimate enemy, allowing us to see both them and ourselves as being victimized by the power of evil.[97] From this perspective, Matthew's portrayal of the struggle between Jesus and the Jewish leaders as a cosmic conflict between God and Satan can be viewed as not only anti-Jewish but also as a theological move with some positive aspects.

2. How should Jesus' encounter with Satan be interpreted? The story of the temptation of Jesus has been interpreted in basically three ways.

The *biographical/psychological* interpretation understands the story as a reflection of Jesus' own inner turmoil after his baptism, as he attempted to sort out the meaning of his baptismal experience and his dawning messianic consciousness. Jesus is pictured as toying with various ways to exercise his messiahship. Such an approach does violence to the gospel genre, comprehending it as "report," and is uninterested in understanding the text in its concreteness.

The *ethical* interpretation seems more valid, since it makes contact with our own experience of being tempted. Jesus is presented as a model for resisting temptation (he quotes Scripture, refuses to use his power selfishly, prefers the Word of God to "material things," etc.). There may be some indirect value in this approach, but the interpreter should not move too quickly from this text to his or her own experience in quest of relevance. The text is not about the general activity of Satan in tempting people to do evil, for the temptations are not to lust and avarice, but to do things that were always considered good, supported by tradition and Scripture.

The third approach is *christological,* understanding this scene as an expression of one dimension of Matthew's christology. The issue is not the biographical/psychological one of how Jesus once thought of himself, but of how the Christians of Matthew's church (and ours) should think of Jesus as the Son of God. Matthew presents Jesus as the Son of God, who will work many miracles during his ministry, which is about to begin. Yet this opening scene presents us with a picture that not only rejects violence and miracles, but also considers them a demonic temptation. It is too easy to say, "He only rejected miracles performed in his own interest," for later in the story the Jesus who refuses to jump off the top of the Temple will show that he is the Son of God by walking on water (14:22-33); and he will match his refusal to turn stones into bread by turning five loaves into enough bread to feed thousands (14:13-21). Likewise, in 17:24-27, Jesus pays his taxes by means of a miraculous catch of a fish with a coin in its mouth.

A broad stream of New Testament christology pictured the earthly Jesus as weak and victimized, devoid of miraculous power, and saw God's saving action to be Jesus' obedience and identification with the victimized human situation. (See Excursus "Matthean Christology," 353-61.) In 4:1-11 Matthew presents Jesus from the christological perspective that pictures his earthly life as that of one who fully shares the weakness of our human situation (cf. Phil 2:5-11; Heb 2:5-18). The picture of Jesus as the obedient Son of God does not abolish or compromise the image of Jesus as truly human. The Christian community did not merely

---

97. See Paul S. Minear, *New Testament Apocalyptic* (Nashville: Abingdon, 1981) 108.

define Jesus in terms of his messiahship, but redefined the meaning of that messiahship in terms of the Jesus who went to the cross. Instead of the bread, circuses, and political power that "kingdom" had previously meant, represented in Jesus' and Matthew's day by the Roman Empire ("kingdom" and "empire" are from the same Greek word), in the Matthean Jesus we have an alternative vision of what the kingdom of God on earth might be. This is what was at stake in the temptation.

Thus we do not have in this pericope an example of a Jesus who "could have" worked miracles but chose not to do so as an ethical example for the rest of us. So understood, the text is of little help to us mortals who do not have the miraculous option. The same is true when the tempter reappears at the cross (27:40-44). To the extent that Jesus' temptation serves as a model for Christians, it might teach us that to be a "child of God" (a Matthean designation for Christians; see 5:9; cf. 28:10) means to have a trusting relationship to God that does not ask for miraculous exceptions to the limitations of an authentic human life.

Matthew 4:12-17, Beginning of Preaching Ministry

NIV

¹²When Jesus heard that John had been put in prison, he returned to Galilee. ¹³Leaving Nazareth, he went and lived in Capernaum, which was by the lake in the area of Zebulun and Naphtali— ¹⁴to fulfill what was said through the prophet Isaiah:

¹⁵"Land of Zebulun and land of Naphtali,
    the way to the sea, along the Jordan,
    Galilee of the Gentiles—
¹⁶the people living in darkness
    have seen a great light;
on those living in the land of the shadow of death
    a light has dawned."ᵃ

¹⁷From that time on Jesus began to preach, "Repent, for the kingdom of heaven is near."

ᵃ16 Isaiah 9:1, 2

NRSV

12Now when Jesusᵃ heard that John had been arrested, he withdrew to Galilee. ¹³He left Nazareth and made his home in Capernaum by the sea, in the territory of Zebulun and Naphtali, ¹⁴so that what had been spoken through the prophet Isaiah might be fulfilled:

¹⁵ "Land of Zebulun, land of Naphtali,
    on the road by the sea, across the Jordan,
        Galilee of the Gentiles—
¹⁶ the people who sat in darkness
    have seen a great light,
    and for those who sat in the region and
        shadow of death
    light has dawned."

¹⁷From that time Jesus began to proclaim, "Repent, for the kingdom of heaven has come near."ᵇ

ᵃGk he   ᵇOr is at hand

COMMENTARY

4:12. Matthew dates his story not in reference to the secular calendar but in relation to significant events in salvation history. Thus there is no indication of how much time has passed; it could be weeks, months, even years. Matthew follows Mark in beginning Jesus' ministry after John's arrest, in contrast to the Fourth Gospel, where Jesus and John the Baptist have overlapping ministries. The word translated "put in prison" (NIV; "arrested," NRSV) is the passive form of παραδίδωμι

(*paradidōmi*), which means "hand over," "betray," "deliver up." It is the same word used repeatedly both for Judas' act of betrayal and for God's act in delivering Jesus up for human sins. It reflects the picture of the Suffering Servant, whom "the Lord delivered up for our sins" (Isa 53:6 LXX, author's trans.). Elsewhere in Matthew, the passive is always used of God's act in delivering up Jesus. Its use here of John the Baptist, adapted from Mark 1:14, is another example of

Matthew's paralleling of John and Jesus, and another reminder that the story is still in the literary unit dealing with John the Baptist (see Introduction and above under 4:1-11).

The NRSV's "withdrew" catches the meaning of the Greek verb ἀναχωρέω (anachōreō), used ten times in Matthew and only twice elsewhere in the Gospels. Matthew uses it almost exclusively for Jesus' response to threats (see 12:15; 14:13). It is not out of cowardice, self-preservation, or strategy that he withdraws, but a representation of Jesus' alternate vision of kingship, which is non-violent and non-retaliatory; it also reflects the post-Easter experience of his disciples. Matthew develops the picture of Jesus as one who responds to aggression in a non-retaliatory withdrawal (5:38-42; 26:53-56) from its only use in Mark (3:7, also the response to the threat of 3:6), and makes it a *leitmotif* of his Gospel (2:14, 19-22; 4:12; 10:23; 12:14-21; 14:13; 15:21; cf. 2:12-13 for the magi as proleptic disciples).

4:13. Leaving Nazareth, where he had grown up, Jesus settles in Capernaum, the home of Peter and Andrew (8:5, 14), which will become his "own city" (9:1). Both towns are in Galilee, which had become Jesus' homeland in exile (2:19-21; 9:1; 13:54). Galilee plays something of a symbolic theological role, but it is not romanticized as though all Galileans are good and all Judeans are bad (11:20-24; 13:53-58). There was no "Galilean springtime" or idyllic Galilean period for Matthew. It is because of Galilee's association with Gentiles that Matthew emphasizes it as the arena of Jesus' ministry. Thus this pericope, which to superficial observation seems a minor biographical note, is not biographical at all, but is replete with Matthean theology—which he immediately moves to support from the Scripture.

4:14-16. This is Matthew's fifth formula quotation, which (like 2:6, 23) functions as a justification for the fact, unanticipated in messianic expectation, that Galilee was the principal locale of Jesus' ministry (see Excursus "Matthew as Interpreter of Scripture," 151-54). Isaiah 9:1-2 speaks of the grand reversal that will occur in the latter days, when the spiritual darkness of Galilee will be dispelled by the dawn of the new age when the ideal king appears. Matthew is drawn to the text not only by its messianic potential and Son of David connections (cf. Isa 9:3-7), but also

because it appropriately expresses the turn toward the Gentiles he saw being realized in the history of the church. Galilee, like much of Palestine, in Hellenistic times was a mixture of Jewish and Gentile cultures. Jews were perhaps a minority, but Matthew considers Galilee "Gentile" on the basis of this text, not on empirical demographics. Nazareth was in the territory of the Old Testament tribe of Zebulun; Capernaum was in Naphthali. Both were in Galilee, in the territory of Herod Antipas.

4:17. This statement marks a transitional point in the story line (see Overview). The summary of the message is an imperative, "repent," based on an indicative, "the kingdom of heaven has come near." Although Matthew places the imperative of human response in the emphatic first position, its basis is the logically prior indicative of God's act. "Kingdom of heaven" is the same as "kingdom of God" (see Excursus "Kingdom of Heaven in Matthew," 288-94). "Kingdom" refers to the active rule of God; "has come near" (NRSV) is better than "is near" (NIV) or "is at hand" (RSV) in that it describes an event, not a static condition. "Has come near" is a temporal statement, not a spatial one, referring to the eschatological kingdom that is already breaking in with the appearance of Jesus. Jesus announces that something has happened (the advent of the Messiah) and that this happening has brought near the final arrival of God's eschatological rule. This summary anticipates the announcement of the Christian message about Jesus, entrusted to the disciples in these very words (10:7); it also connects the church's and Jesus' message with that of John the Baptist (see on 3:2).

This eschatological reality is the basis for Jesus' call for repentance (as it was for John earlier and will be for the disciples later). "Repent" (μετανοέω metanoeō) in Matthew's Greek means literally "change one's mind," but it is loaded with the overtones of its Hebrew counterpart, "turn" "return" (שׁוּב šûb); it was not original with John or Jesus but was the standard prophetic and Jewish means of reconciliation with God. The word does not picture sorrow or remorse, but a change in the direction of one's life. "Get yourself a new orientation for the way you live, then act on it" catches both the Greek and Hebrew connotations. This new orientation is the response to the kingdom's having "come near."

REFLECTIONS

Matthew does not here call Jesus' message the *"gospel* of the kingdom," as in the Markan parallel 1:14. But in the bracketing summary references 4:23//9:35, Matthew does use this phrase, which is the identical description of the Christian message preached by the disciples after the resurrection (24:14; cf. 13:19). This means that Matthew affirms continuity between Jesus' message during his earthly ministry and the church's message about him. He avoids a problematic hermeneutical gap between Jesus as "proclaimer" of the kingdom and Jesus as the church's "proclaimed" Christ in two ways:

1. He makes the pre-Easter story of Jesus transparent to the post-Easter situation, retrojecting the concerns and responses of the post-Easter church into the narrative, so that the there-and-then story of Jesus and his disciples modulates into a here-and-now address to the church. This is done in the way the story is structured, not by first telling what happened back there and then making an application for today. Matthew retells the story of the saving act of God in Christ in such a way that the horizons between past event and present experience merge into one story. Teaching and preaching from Matthew can learn from the writer and utilize the same form.

2. Matthew makes the proclamation of the kingdom of God the common denominator between Jesus' preaching and that of the church—i.e., it is theocentric in both cases. As the church proclaims the act of God in Jesus, it also and thereby continues Jesus' own preaching of the kingdom of God. For Matthew the kingdom of God was not an ideal, a principle, or an abstraction, but was definitively revealed and embodied in the life and ministry of Jesus. This is why "kingship" language is so important throughout the Gospel of Matthew, from the opening scenes in which the newborn king is a threat to the kingdoms of this world (2:1-23), to the closing scenes, in which the "king of Israel" is the crucified one who gives himself for others (note the kingship language of 27:11-54) and then is vindicated and given "all authority" (28:16-20).

MATTHEW 4:18-22, THE CALL OF THE DISCIPLES

NIV	NRSV
[18]As Jesus was walking beside the Sea of Galilee, he saw two brothers, Simon called Peter and his brother Andrew. They were casting a net into the lake, for they were fishermen. [19]"Come, follow me," Jesus said, "and I will make you fishers of men." [20]At once they left their nets and followed him.	18As he walked by the Sea of Galilee, he saw two brothers, Simon, who is called Peter, and Andrew his brother, casting a net into the sea—for they were fishermen. [19]And he said to them, "Follow me, and I will make you fish for people." [20]Immediately they left their nets and followed him. [21]As he went from there, he saw two other brothers, James son of Zebedee and his brother John, in the boat with their father Zebedee, mending their nets, and he called them. [22]Immediately they left the boat and their father, and followed him.
[21]Going on from there, he saw two other brothers, James son of Zebedee and his brother John. They were in a boat with their father Zebedee, preparing their nets. Jesus called them, [22]and immediately they left the boat and their father and followed him.	

COMMENTARY

Despite its small size, this pericope represents a major subsection of Matthew's structure (cf. Introduction). The call of the first disciples is the beginning of the messianic community: the church. Jesus' baptism and temptation were not merely individualistic religious experiences of a "great man," but the recapitulation of the birth of Israel in the Red Sea and the wilderness testing; they lead to the formation of the new community, the Messiah's "people" (1:21). The story is not a straightforward report, but is transparent to the call of disciples in Matthew's church.

Matthew takes over the story from Mark 1:16-20 with only minimal (but significant) verbal changes, giving his own interpretation primarily by the literary structure into which he inserts the text rather than by substantial rewriting. In the oral tradition prior to Mark, the story had assumed the form of a pronouncement or *chreia* (cf. Introduction), with narrative biographical details held to a minimum and all emphasis placed on the sayings of Jesus. Roughly similar stories of teachers who called disciples who then leave everything to follow them are found in Hellenistic literature.[98] The story also is modeled on the call of Elisha by Elijah in 1 Kgs 19:19-21, and the call of prophets in general (cf. Amos 7:15). Just as Yahweh uprooted these prophets from their ordinary existence, so also Jesus represents the divine initiative in calling persons to discipleship.

4:18. Rabbis did not seek out students, but were sought out by applicants. Here, all the initiative is with Jesus, the primary actor. The narrator takes the reader with Jesus, walking beside the sea, until Simon and Andrew come on the narrative horizon. (The story could have been told with the narrator and reader already at the lakeside with the fishermen when Jesus appears. But that would not be the same.) Jesus comes to Simon and Andrew; they do not come to him. He sees them; they do not see him. He speaks; they do not.

4:19. Jesus' call is a command and a promise. Once again the imperative precedes the indicative, but is based on it (see Commentary on 4:17 above). "Follow me" is the command for them to become disciples. The meaning of the promise "I will make you fish for people" is not so clear. The fishing metaphor for the actions of deities has a long history in pagan and Jewish religion and tradition, and it must not be filled in by modern understandings of fishing.[99] The point will certainly be missed if it is thought that Jesus used the situation to construct an ad hoc metaphor. The image was used in a variety of ways in pagan and Jewish tradition, often of the deity's work in history in calling people to a new life, to participate in the god's own saving work. Here the picture seems to be that God's judging/saving mission to the world is represented by Jesus, who calls disciples to participate in the divine mission to humanity. The scene is thus utterly theological, not only picturing Jesus' pre-Easter call to certain Galileans, but also looking forward to the post-Easter situation in which the risen Christ calls disciples and sends them forth. Nothing in the text suggests that this is a special call to apostleship; rather, a theological perspective on the way every follower becomes a disciple is here presented. Thus this scene corresponds to 9:36–11:1, where it is properly completed (see Introduction).

4:20. Without a word, the fishermen leave their nets and follow Jesus. In contrast to the story in 1 Kgs 19:19-21, even parents are immediately abandoned (cf. 8:18-22; 10:21-22, 32-37; 19:16-30). In the Matthean story, these men have never seen Jesus before, have seen no miracles, heard no teachings. No explanation has been given them. They are not told why they should follow Jesus, what following him will mean, or where the path will lead them. We are met here with Jesus' first miracle, the miracle of his powerful word that creates following, that makes disciples. Jesus who calls takes the responsibility for making them fishers for people, just as he later declares that he will build his church (16:18). Thus far in Matthew, Jesus has spoken only brief staccato commands, each with authority (3:15; 4:1-11; 4:17). The meaning of the text will be missed by a biographical or psychological approach that

---

98. See Klaus Berger, M. Eugene Boring, Carsten Colpe, *Hellenistic Commentary to the New Testament* (Nashville: Abingdon, 1995).

99. See Wilhelm H. Wuellner, *The Meaning of "Fishers of Men"* (Philadelphia: Westminster, 1962).

speculates about previous contacts between Jesus and these fishermen, attempting to combine John 1:35-51 with this text or to somehow give a "rational" explanation for this miracle. The messianic community, the church, comes into being in response to Christ's own word.

The first disciple-to-be is Simon "Peter." The fact that he was first is important to Matthew (10:2; for discussion of Peter's name and role among the disciples, see Commentary on 16:16-18). He and his brother are fishermen. In first-century Galilee, this occupation could take one of three forms: (1) a tax collector with the fishing franchise, who sold fishing rights to local businessmen; (2) a person who owned or leased boats and employed day laborers; (3) or the seasonal day laborers themselves.[100] The first two types repre-sented upper and middle classes respectively, and would usually have been moderately well-educated, including having literacy in Greek. There are instances of Jewish scribes and rabbis who were in the fishing business, analogous to Paul the tent maker/leather worker. The third class were mostly poor and illiterate. Such information is helpful for the locating the social setting of the historical Jesus and his disciples, but is not so important for interpreting the text of the Gospel. The historical Simon Peter probably belonged to the middle class, but Matthew is so little inter-ested in biography that he does not fill in the picture enough for us to make that claim; Matthew even omits the Markan detail that Simon Peter and Andrew had hired servants (Mark 1:20).

100. See Wuellner, *"Fishers of Men,"* 26-64.

REFLECTIONS

How do people become disciples of Jesus Christ? As this story is retold in the Matthean community, this is the question Matthew is addressing, not the historical or biographical question of a past event. To be sure, the historical Jesus of Nazareth called actual people to be his disciples, but this story is focused to interpret the meaning of this fact to the readers' present. Thus interpretation must concentrate on interpreting the Matthean text, refusing to combine it with the other Gospels and with modern conceptions of either fishing or discipleship.

1. Modern readers are tempted to refashion the biblical pictures of discipleship into categories more comfortable with our own ideologies and idealisms. To become a disciple means to accept Jesus' principles for living, for example. There is an element of truth in such reinterpretations, but Matthew's understanding of discipleship cannot be reduced to this modern rationalism and idealism. In this text Jesus appears disruptively in our midst and calls us not to admire him or accept his principles, not even to accept him as our personal Savior, but to follow him. A reasonable response to his command "Follow me" would be "Where are you going?" The fishermen do not yet know the destination, which they must learn along the way (cf. 10:5-42; 16:13-28). Although Matthew does not use the vocabulary of "believe" and "faith" in this story, he here pictures the nature of faith that is at the heart of discipleship (cf. Heb 11:8). Where does such faith come from?

2. A panel discussion by a cross-section of Christians on the question "How did you become a believer?" would no doubt generate a variety of interesting and edifying stories. Some would be stories of dramatic suddenness, others of slow and painful groping and struggle; others would hardly relate to the question at all, but would never remember a time when they were "unbelievers." Perhaps Matthew too knows of these varied stories, but he dares to subsume them under a common denominator and to present them in this one picture: People become believers by the power of Jesus' word; they follow him because he has spoken to them, and his word generates faith. For Matthew, Jesus' call to discipleship was spoken not only to a few disciples in first-century Galilee but to the church throughout history (28:20). Jesus is the one who sows the word that produces good fruit (13:3, 18, 24, 37); he is the one who builds the church (16:18). In and through the words and deeds of preachers, missionaries, teachers, family, friends, and the nameless doers of Christian service, the voice of the Son of Man continues to speak and to generate faith. Whereas we may point to ourselves or to secondary causes as the source of faith, Matthew points to the One whose speaking makes us disciples.

3. The address "Follow me" is in the imperative, but the indicative of the divine initiative is fundamental. The fishermen are already at work, already doing something useful and important, thus they are not looking for a new life. Jesus' call does not fill an obvious vacuum or meet an obvious need in their lives, but, like the call of prophets in the Hebrew Bible, it is intrusive and disruptive, calling them away from work and family. The divine sovereignty is clothed in the call to human response: "I could not seek you, if you had not already found me."[101] "Discipleship is not an offer man makes to Christ. It is only the call which creates the situation."[102]

101. Augustine *Confessions* Book I.
102. Dietrich Bonhoeffer, *The Cost of Discipleship* (New York: Macmillan, 1959) 68.

MATTHEW 4:23–9:35, THE AUTHORITY OF THE MESSIAH

Matthew 4:23–7:29, The Sermon on the Mount

OVERVIEW

Matthew has given a summary of Jesus' message (4:17), but has not yet presented Jesus as teaching or as performing any miracle, except the call of the disciples. But with v. 17 he is preparing to give the first and major presentation of Jesus' teaching (the Sermon on the Mount, 5:3–7:29) and of Jesus' mighty works, including the calling and equipping of disciples (8:1–9:34). For Matthew, "words" precede "works," since he considers teaching to take precedence over and to validate miracles, not vice versa. "Miracles do not certify teaching; it is the other way round!"[103] This major unit is bracketed by verbally identical summary statements (4:23; 9:35). Thus 4:23–5:2 is no biographical summary, but Matthew's carefully prepared introduction to the centerpiece of his creative Part One (see Introduction).

The Sermon on the Mount is the first, the longest (uninterrupted), and the most carefully structured speech in Matthew's Gospel. Matthew and his church had long been thoroughly familiar with the Great Sermon in Q, which begins with beatitudes; continues with instruction on love, the "Golden Rule," attitudes toward others; and concludes with warnings about two kinds of ethical "fruit" and the story of the two builders.[104] Examination of the parallel material reveals that Matthew takes over all the material in the Q sermon, keeping all the intervening material in exactly the same order, except for his rearrangement of the sayings in Q's "On the Love of One's Enemies" (now preserved in Luke 6:27-36; see Fig. 4, Structure of the Sermon on the Mount). Matthew extracts 5:38-42 from its Q context and constructs a separate unit, reformulating these verses into two pairs of three antitheses (cf. Luke 6:27-30 and Fig. 4). He also relocates the Q text found in Luke 6:31 to make it the conclusion of the extensive didactic core of the sermon at 7:12,

103. Douglas R. A. Hare, *Matthew,* Interpretation (Louisville: Westminster/John Knox, 1993) 32.

104. Luke has essentially preserved the unexpanded Q form of the Sermon on the Mount in 6:20-49. The view of Hans Dieter Betz, *Essays on the Sermon on the Mount,* trans. L. L. Welborn (Philadelphia: Fortress, 1985), that the Sermon on the Mount is a pre-Matthean unit from a different setting, expressing a different theology from Matthew's has not been widely accepted (cf. Stanton, *Gospel for a New People,* 307-25).

at the same time adding his characteristic phrase "law and prophets" to make an inclusion with 5:17, the beginning of the main body of the sermon. Matthew thus preserves the basic three-part outline of the Q sermon, but by adding additional traditional material from elsewhere in Q, from M, from his own composition, and from occasional touches from Mark and by utilizing his favorite means of composing in triads using literary brackets, Matthew constructs a discourse with a new structure, corresponding more closely to his own theological interests.[105]

The following points are to be noted about this structure:

(1) The sermon is not a random collection of individual sayings, but a carefully composed discourse with a deliberate structure.

(2) Matthew 5:17, "the law or the prophets," corresponds to 7:12, "the law and the prophets," forming an inclusion that brackets the central core of the sermon.[106] The saying in 7:12 has been relocated, and the phrase "law and the prophets" has been added to create this inclusion. Thus we have good reason to see this as a basic element of the Matthean structure, separating the central instructional core from the introductory pronouncements and concluding warnings, demarcating the three major parts of the sermon.

(3) Matthew has elaborated the basic triadic structure already present in the Q sermon by composing many of the subunits in triads. This central core of the sermon corresponds to the pattern of a familiar rabbinic saying attributed to Simon the Just: "By three things the world is sustained: by the law, by the Temple service, and by deeds of loving kindness."[107] The Christian reformulation of these "Three Pillars of Judaism" in the sermon would have been recognized

by those who had this pattern in mind, since 5:17-48 deals with the Law, 6:1-18 is concerned with worship and religious practice, and 6:19–7:12 deals with trusting and serving God in social relationships and action.

(4) At the very center of the sermon is the Lord's Prayer, itself the triadic center in a structure composed of triads. Matthew thus gave the sermon a new center and point of orientation, since the Q sermon did not contain this section on prayer.

(5) The overall tripartite structure facilitates Matthew's explication of related theological themes. Part One begins with performative language in the indicative mode, characterizing the eschatological community and declaring the basis for its life to be in God's gracious act. Part Two, the didactic core of the sermon, is primarily in the imperative mode, giving instructions for the life of the eschatological community. In Part Three the imperative recedes, giving place to the future indicative warning of eschatological judgment.

(6) In all of this it is clear that the Sermon on the Mount is Matthew's composition.[108] Although some of the sayings are from the historical Jesus, the Sermon on the Mount is not a report of a speech actually given on a Galilean hillside. In the sixteenth century John Calvin had already taught that the sermon expresses the intention of the evangelist "of gathering into one single passage the chief headings of Christ's teaching, that had regard to the rule of godly and holy living"—i.e., it is the composition of the evangelist.[109]

---

105. Cf. Dale C. Allison, Jr., "The Structure of the Sermon on the Mount," *JBL* 106 (1987) 423-45.

106. The phrase is taken over by Matthew from Q 16:16 and made into a thematic label (see 5:17; 7:12; 22:40).

107. 'Abot 1:2. See W. E. Davies, *The Setting of the Sermon on the Mount* (Cambridge: Cambridge University Press, 1966) 307. It is likely that the destruction of Jerusalem, which brought the Temple service to an end, had made this saying a current topic of discussion in the Judaism with which

Matthew is in dialogue and confrontation. Graham Stanton, *Gospel for a New People* (Edinburgh: T. & T. Clark, 1992) 308, is critical of this possibility.

108. So say most scholars. Betz argues that the sermon was composed by a Jewish Christian in a pre-Matthean church and incorporated *en bloc* by Matthew. See Betz, *Essays on the Sermon on the Mount*.

109. John Calvin, *A Harmony of the Gospels Matthew, Mark, and Luke*, 3 vols. (Grand Rapids: Eerdmans, 1972) 1:168.

Figure 4: The Structure of the Sermon on the Mount

Introduction: Setting of the Sermon	4:23–5:2	Mark 1:39; 3:7-13
		Luke 6:12, 17-20*a*
I. Triadic Pronouncements That Constitute the Disciples as the Eschatological Community, 5:3-16		
A. The Beatitudes:		
Character and Destiny of the Disciples	5:3-12	Luke 6:20*b*-23
B. The Disciples as Salt	5:13	Luke 14:34-35
		Mark 9:49-50
C. The Disciples as Light and a City on a Hill	5:14-16	Luke 8:16; 11:33
		Mark 4:21
II. Tripartite Instructions on the Way of Life in the Eschatological Community, 5:17–7:12		
A. Part One: "The Law"	5:17-48	
1. The Law and the "Greater Righteousness"	5:17-20	Luke 16:16-17
2. Three Antitheses Modeling the Greater Righteousness, 5:21-32		
a. Anger	5:21-26	Luke 12:57-59
		Mark 11:25
b. Lust	5:27-30	Mark 9:43
c. Divorce	5:31-32	Luke 16:18
		Mark 10:3-4; 11:12
3. Three Antitheses for the Disciples' Application, 5:33-48		
a. Oaths	5:33-37	M
b. Retaliation	5:38-42	Luke 6:29-30
c. Love	5:43-48	Luke 6:27-28, 32-36
B. Part Two: "The Temple Service": Three Acts of Righteousness Before God, 6:1-18		
1. Giving to Charity	6:1-4	M
2. Prayer, 6:5-15		
a. Not like the hypocrites or the Gentiles	6:5-8	M
b. The Lord's Prayer	6:9-13	Luke 11:2-4
c. The condition of forgiveness	6:14-15	Mark 11:25(-26)
3. Fasting	6:16-18	M
C. Part Three: "Deeds of Loving Kindness": Additional Instruction in Authentic Righteousness, 6:19–7:12		
1. Serving God or Mammon	6:19-24	Luke 12:33-34
		11:34-36
		16:13
2. Anxiety	6:25-34	Luke 12:22-32
3. Judging	7:1-5	Luke 6:37-42
		Mark 4:24-25
4. Pearls Before Swine	7:6	M
5. Asking and Receiving	7:7-11	Luke 11:9-13
6. Concluding Summary: The Golden Rule	7:12	Luke 6:31
III. Three Eschatological Warnings, 7:13-27		
A. Two Ways	7:13-14	Luke 13:23-24
B. Two Harvests (False Prophets)	7:15-23	Luke 6:43-46;
		13:25-27
C. Two Builders	7:24-27	Luke 6:47-49
Conclusion of the Sermon	7:28-29	Mark 1:22

Matthew 4:23–5:2, Setting of the Sermon

NIV

[23]Jesus went throughout Galilee, teaching in their synagogues, preaching the good news of the kingdom, and healing every disease and sickness among the people. [24]News about him spread all over Syria, and people brought to him all who were ill with various diseases, those suffering severe pain, the demon-possessed, those having seizures, and the paralyzed, and he healed them. [25]Large crowds from Galilee, the Decapolis,[a] Jerusalem, Judea and the region across the Jordan followed him.

5 Now when he saw the crowds, he went up on a mountainside and sat down. His disciples came to him, [2]and he began to teach them, saying:

[a]25 That is, the Ten Cities

NRSV

23Jesus[a] went throughout Galilee, teaching in their synagogues and proclaiming the good news[b] of the kingdom and curing every disease and every sickness among the people. [24]So his fame spread throughout all Syria, and they brought to him all the sick, those who were afflicted with various diseases and pains, demoniacs, epileptics, and paralytics, and he cured them. [25]And great crowds followed him from Galilee, the Decapolis, Jerusalem, Judea, and from beyond the Jordan.

5 When Jesus[a] saw the crowds, he went up the mountain; and after he sat down, his disciples came to him. [2]Then he began to speak, and taught them, saying:

[a]Gk He   [b]Gk gospel

COMMENTARY

Matthew prepares to present the great central section on the words and deeds of the Messiah as the nuclear center of his creative Part One (see Overview and Introduction). While composed by Matthew for his own literary and theological purpose, the material is adapted and expanded from Mark (Matt 4:23 = Mark 1:39; Matt 4:24-25 = Mark 3:7-12; even the mountain of Matt 5:1 is from Mark 3:13). The reference to the disciples in 5:1 was probably already in Q (cf. Luke 6:20), but the concentric circle composition of Jesus/disciples/crowds is Matthew's own purposeful composition.

4:23-25. "Teaching" and "preaching" (NIV) or "proclaiming" (NRSV) are closely associated in Matthew (4:23; 9:35; 11:1). Preaching usually has "the good news of the kingdom of God" as its object. On the other hand, no content for teaching is given here or elsewhere in Matthew; the content of Jesus' teaching is not summarized in a phrase, but illustrated by Jesus' five great discourses, especially by the Sermon on the Mount. Prior to the resurrection, the disciples do not teach; Jesus is the only legitimate teacher (cf.

23:8). "Their" synagogues expresses the tension and alienation between the Matthean community and the synagogue, but does not solve the problem of the precise relationship between the two (see Introduction). Matthew replaces the Markan "Tyre and Sidon," with "Syria" (probably reflecting the home territory of the author and his church; see Introduction) and the Decapolis, a league of ten independent Greek-speaking cities mostly east of the Jordan with Gentile connotations.

The acts of healing are narrated not only to give the occasion for the gathering of the large and diverse crowd to hear the Sermon on the Mount, but also to place Jesus' instruction in the context of his own previous acts of announcing the kingdom and acting in mercy to illustrate its power and its nature. The people are healed without meeting any requirements or making any confession of faith. It is entirely the initiative and grace of the messianic representative of God's kingdom.

5:1-2. The Great Sermon in Luke occurs on the plain (Luke 6:17). Jesus' ascent of the mountain in Matthew is not to be explained biographically or psychologically, as though, having seen the crowds, he went up the mountain attempting to get away from them, but is part of Matthew's christological Moses typology. From the beginning, Matthew has related the story of Jesus in such a way as to evoke the figure of Moses as pictured in both the Scripture and Jewish tradition. In a dream, an angel announces Moses' birth and that he will work miracles and save his people.[110] Likewise, Jesus is conceived in a miraculous way (see 1:18-25); at his birth he is threatened by the wicked king; he is initially rejected by his own people; he comes out of Egypt; he passes through the water and is tested in the wilderness; he ascends the mountain and gives authoritative commands; he does ten great deeds of power in liberating the people of God (8:1–9:34; see further Moses parallels at 9:36; 17:1-9). The phrase "went up the mountain," common in the OT, is almost exclusively associated with Moses. Even the note that Jesus "sat down" while teaching may also reflect Moses on the mountain, since in some Jewish interpretations Deut 9:9 is understood to portray Moses as specifically sitting on Mount Sinai, and became a topic of rabbinic discussion.[111] Matthew understands that the advent of Jesus brought something qualitatively new (see 9:17), but it is important that Matthew does not specifically designate Jesus as a new Moses or his teaching as a new Torah, just as he refrains from calling the church a new Israel.[112] Nonetheless,

110. Pseudo Philo *Biblical Antiquities* 9.10.
111. W. D. Davies and Dale C. Allison, Jr., *A Critical and Exegetical Commentary on the Gospel According to Saint Matthew*, 2 vols., ICC (Edinburgh: T. & T. Clark, 1988–91) 1:424.
112. The structuralist analysis of Daniel Patte, *The Gospel According to Matthew: A Structural Commentary on Matthew's Faith* (Philadelphia: Fortress, 1987), 68, indicates that "new Moses" and "new Torah" may be the reader's view, which Matthew wants to affirm only partially and to transform. See also ibid., 41, and Dale C. Allison, Jr., *The New Moses: A Matthean Typology* (Minneapolis: Fortress, 1993).

Moses imagery looms in the background, and the sermon cannot be heard without reflection on how Jesus' authoritative teaching from the mount relates to the Torah given on Sinai—a live issue in the Matthean community. Although more than one Galilean hill has been identified by Christian tradition (and tourism) as the "mount of the beatitudes," the location of the Sermon on the Mount is not geographical but theological, the mountain of revelation that corresponds both to Mt. Sinai and the mountain of 28:16 (cf. also 15:29; 17:1; 24:3 for mountains as places of revelation).

As in 13:1 and 24:3, Jesus the teacher sits while teaching, the manner of the revered Jewish teacher (cf. Luke 6:17, where Jesus stands to give the Sermon on the Plain). Matthew pictures the sermon as being delivered primarily to the disciples, who are transparent to the post-Easter Christian community. By "disciples" Matthew cannot mean the Twelve, since only four have been called (4:18-22; cf. 9:9; 10:1-4). The disciples represent the church, not just the Twelve, and the time barrier between pre- and post-Easter already vanishes. In literary-critical terms, the real hearers of the sermon are the implied readers of Matthew's Gospel. The "report" of a sermon once delivered during Jesus' ministry becomes the present address of the Lord of the church, who continues to be present (1:23; 18:18-20; 28:20). At the end of the sermon, it is clear that the "crowds" who originally occasioned the sermon (representing potential disciples at this point in the narrative) have also "overheard" it (see 7:28-29).

Matthew 5:3-16, The Disciples as the Eschatological Community

MATTHEW 5:3-12, THE BEATITUDES

NIV	NRSV
3"Blessed are the poor in spirit, for theirs is the kingdom of heaven.	3"Blessed are the poor in spirit, for theirs is the kingdom of heaven.

NIV

[4] Blessed are those who mourn,
  for they will be comforted.
[5] Blessed are the meek,
  for they will inherit the earth.
[6] Blessed are those who hunger and thirst for
    righteousness,
  for they will be filled.
[7] Blessed are the merciful,
  for they will be shown mercy.
[8] Blessed are the pure in heart,
  for they will see God.
[9] Blessed are the peacemakers,
  for they will be called sons of God.
[10] Blessed are those who are persecuted because
    of righteousness,
  for theirs is the kingdom of heaven.

[11] "Blessed are you when people insult you, persecute you and falsely say all kinds of evil against you because of me. [12] Rejoice and be glad, because great is your reward in heaven, for in the same way they persecuted the prophets who were before you."

NRSV

[4] "Blessed are those who mourn, for they will be comforted.
[5] "Blessed are the meek, for they will inherit the earth.
[6] "Blessed are those who hunger and thirst for righteousness, for they will be filled.
[7] "Blessed are the merciful, for they will receive mercy.
[8] "Blessed are the pure in heart, for they will see God.
[9] "Blessed are the peacemakers, for they will be called children of God.
[10] "Blessed are those who are persecuted for righteousness' sake, for theirs is the kingdom of heaven.
[11] "Blessed are you when people revile you and persecute you and utter all kinds of evil against you falsely[a] on my account. [12] Rejoice and be glad, for your reward is great in heaven, for in the same way they persecuted the prophets who were before you."

[a] Other ancient authorities lack *falsely*

COMMENTARY

Most scholars agree that the core of the beatitudes goes back to the historical Jesus, who reversed the general value system by pronouncing blessing on the poor, the hungry, and those who weep (the Q form of 5:3-4, 6 = Luke 6:20*b*-21).[113] When the Q collection of Jesus' sayings was composed, these were combined with a fourth beatitude, 5:11-12/ Luke 6:22-23, which had been created in the church, probably by a Christian prophet, and had circulated independently. Most scholars attribute the eighth beatitude (Matt 5:10) to Matthew himself. Scholarship is divided on whether the remaining four beatitudes peculiar to Matthew and presumably not in Q (Matt 5:5, 7-9) represent Matthean composition or came to him in his expanded version of Q[Mt].

A *beatitude* (Latin) or *makarism* (Greek) is a

statement in the indicative mood beginning with a form of the adjective μακάριος (*makarios*), declaring certain people to be in a privileged, fortunate circumstance. The Greek adjective *makarios* means "fortunate," "happy," "in a privileged situation," "well-off."[114] In a religious context, *makarios* means "blessed" (by God), the LXX translation of the common *'ašrê* (אשרי) "blessed," "happy"). It connotes the German *Heil*, the Greek for "salvation" (σωτηρία *sōtēria*), the Hebrew for "peace," "well-being" (שלום *šālôm*) and the colloquial English "Okay."[115] Beatitudes normally occur in third-person forms, but are also found in the second-person direct address.

Neither Jesus nor Matthew invented the beatitude form, which occurs in the Old Testament and in both Jewish and pagan literature. Jesus and

---

113. For a detailed discussion of the methods and criteria for the following statements and results, plus additional bibliography, see M. Eugene Boring, "The Historical-Critical Method's 'Criteria of Authenticity': The Beatitudes in Q and Thomas as a Test Case," *Semeia* 44 (1988) 9-44.

114. *Makarios* (μακάριος) is to be distinguished from the other NT word translated "bless" (εὐλογέω *eulogeō*) and its derivatives, used primarily in the sense of praise, especially of God, as in Matt 21:9; 23:39.
115. This relation is indicated, e.g., by the NRSV's translation of 2 Kgs 5:21, "everything [is] all right" (שלום *šālôm*). Cf. 4:23-26.

early Christianity, including Matthew, reflect the use of beatitudes in the Jewish tradition, where they are found primarily in two settings: wisdom and prophecy. The setting gives the form a distinctive function and meaning: In the wisdom tradition, *makarisms* declare the blessing of those in fortunate circumstances, based on observation and experience (e.g., Sir 25:7-9), and declare their present reward and happiness. In the Prophets, makarisms declare the present/future blessedness of those who are presently in dire circumstances, but who will be vindicated at the eschatological coming of God's kingdom (Isa 30:18; 32:20; Dan 12:12). In the New Testament outside the Synoptics, most beatitudes are found in the prophetic book of Revelation (1:3; 14:13; 16:15; 19:9; 20:6; 22:7, 14).

The Matthean beatitudes were originally a wisdom form filled by early Christianity with prophetic eschatological content. Matthew's beatitudes are not practical advice for successful living, but prophetic declarations made on the conviction of the coming-and-already-present kingdom of God. This perspective calls for the following hermeneutical corollaries:

(1) The beatitudes declare an objective reality as the result of a divine act, not subjective feelings, and thus should be translated with the objective "blessed" instead of the subjective "happy." The opposite of "blessed" is not "unhappy," but "cursed" (cf. Matt 25:31-46; Luke 6:24-26).

(2) The indicative mood should be taken seriously, and not transformed into an imperative or exhortation. The beatitudes of the wisdom tradition are indicative in form but often imperative in function, a form of ethical exhortation toward the ideal expressed in the beatitude. For the prophets, the beatitudes were primarily a declaration of blessedness to those oriented to the future reality of God's kingdom, with a powerful but indirect ethical imperative in the form of a call to decision. They do not directly lay down demands for conversion, but declare the *notae ecclesiae,* the "marks of the church."

(3) There is, however, an ethical dimension to the beatitudes. The community that hears itself pronounced blessed by its Lord does not remain passive, but acts in accord with the coming kingdom. The life of those pronounced blessed is elaborated in Part II of the Sermon, the Instruction of 5:17–7:12.

(4) The beatitudes are written in unconditional performative language. They do not merely describe something that already is, but bring into being the reality they declare.[116] The form is not "if you will x, then y," or "whoever x, then y," but unconditionally declare that those who are x will be y. Like the patriarchal and priestly blessings, and like the prophetic word of the Scripture, the beatitude effects what it says, bringing into being what it states. As eschatological blessings, the beatitudes are not "entrance requirements" for outsiders, but a declaration about insiders. Nor do they form an introduction or prolegomenon to the heart of the sermon. They themselves constitute the foundation in the indicative mode for the commands in the imperative mode; they are gospel, not law, the kerygmatic basis of the didactic core of the sermon.

(5) Understood as a prophetic pronouncement, the truth claim of the beatitude is not independently true, but dependent on the speaker. In the prophetic tradition, the truth of the prophet's word depended on his or her being an authentic spokesperson for God, the active authority behind the pronouncement. The many allusions to Isa 61:1-11 in the beatitudes relate them to prophetic speech, and indirectly cast Jesus in the role of the "anointed one" of Isa 61:1. In the narrative context of the Sermon on the Mount, the speaker is more than a prophet, he is the Son of God and Lord of the church, already seen from the post-Easter perspective. The beatitudes, therefore, are not observations about reality that others of lesser insight had simply overlooked, such as the truths of mathematics or logic. They are true on the basis of the authority of the one who speaks. Thus for Matthew Jesus' beatitudes are related to the theme of the "authority" (ἐξουσία *exousia*) of Jesus (see 7:29; 8:9; 9:6; 21:23; 28:18). In the first words of the Sermon on the Mount, we do not meet general statements, the truth of which we can investigate on our own terms, with our own criteria, but a veiled, implicit christological claim that calls for taking a stand with regard to the speaker, not merely the content of his speech.

116. Examples of performative language are a baseball umpire's calling balls and strikes, a minister's pronouncing a couple husband and wife, a judge's pronouncing of sentence, and one person's saying "I apologize" or "I forgive you" to another. See J. L. Austin, *How to Do Things with Words* (Cambridge, Mass.: Harvard University Press, 1962).

(6) The beatitudes are not historical but eschatological. Since the blessedness of the subjects of typical beatitudes in Judaism and Hellenism was self-evident, it was not typical to have a justification for the pronouncement. The distinctive element in the synoptic beatitudes is that they are each grounded in a second clause beginning with "because" or "for" (ὅτι *hoti*), each of which points to the eschatological future coming of the kingdom of God (see Excursus "Kingdom of Heaven in Matthew," 288-94).[117] The first and last of the formally identical series 5:3-10 refer directly to the coming kingdom, and all the others express some eschatological aspect of it. The "comfort" of 5:4 refers to the eschatological salvation expected as the "consolation of Israel" (cf. Luke 2:25). "Inheriting the earth" of 5:5 is an eschatological image based on receiving the promised land in the Joshua story. "Being filled" (5:6) is an image of eschatological blessing that readily spoke and still speaks to a world where hunger is real. "Receiving mercy" (5:7), "seeing God" (5:8; cf. 1 Cor 13:12; Rev 22:4), and "being called [by God] 'Sons of God' " (5:9; cf. Hos 9:6) are not this-worldly practical realities, but elements of the eschatological hopes of Israel.

(7) The nine pronouncements are thus not statements about general human virtues—most appear exactly the opposite to common wisdom. Rather, they pronounce blessing on authentic disciples in the Christian community. All the beatitudes apply to one group of people, the real Christians of Matthew's community. They do not describe nine different kinds of good people who get to go to heaven, but are nine declarations about the blessedness, contrary to all appearances, of the eschatological community living in anticipation of God's reign. Like all else in Matthew, they are oriented to life together in the community of discipleship, not to individualistic ethics.

Matthew has previously pictured Jesus as announcing the nearness of the kingdom of God and calling disciples. In the beatitudes Matthew begins to fill in the content of both "kingdom" and "discipleship." Neither is what this-worldly wisdom anticipates.

5:3. The "poor" of Jesus' original pronouncement of blessing, preserved by Q and Luke, not only refers to literal poverty, but also connotes the lack of arrogance and sense of one's own need. Luke's beatitudes emphasize the literal, economic dimension. Matthew's addition of "in spirit" shifts the emphasis, but does not exclude literal poverty. (Cf. the similar addition of "for righteousness" to "hunger" in 5:6.) These changes ought not to be too quickly considered a "spiritualization" on Matthew's part, as though he were not interested in the literally poor (cf. 11:5; 25:31-46). From the time of the composition of the Psalms, "the poor" had been understood as a characterization of the true people of God, those who know their lives are not in their own control and that they are dependent on God. "Poor in spirit" makes this explicit. Persons who are pronounced blessed are not those who claim a robust ego and strong sense of self-worth, but those whose only identity and security is in God. Their identity is not in what they know, but in having a certain (poverty of) spirit. The exact phrase "poor in spirit" was not found in any extant Jewish literature until it emerged in the Dead Sea Scrolls of the Qumran community (1QM 14:7), which understood itself as the remnant, the true people of God over against the Jerusalem hierarchy. What is at stake in the phrase for both Qumran and Matthew is neither economics nor spirituality, but the identity of the people of God—a Matthean theme (1:21).

"Theirs is the kingdom." Thus far, Jesus has been presented as the king of the present and coming kingdom of God, the definitive one through whom God's rule is manifested. The kingdom has been presented as the summary and focus of Jesus' message, but no content has been given to the idea. In the Sermon on the Mount, Jesus will present the nature of the life of the kingdom he proclaims and represents. He has reversed the idea of human kingship, and those to whom his kingdom belongs correspond to this eschatological reversal. Just as the king is meek and poor in spirit (cf. on 5:5), so also are those to whom his kingdom belongs. Here and elsewhere, christology and discipleship are correlatives for Matthew.

5:4. It is not in their mourning as such that persons will receive the eschatological blessing. Matthew here taps into the deep biblical tradition

---

117. All of the beatitudes have the future tense in the second clause except 5:3 and its counterpart 5:10, which have the futuristic present (the future tense ["will be" (ἔσται *estai*)] in D is secondary).

that one of the characteristics of the true people of God is that they lament the present condition of God's people and God's program in the world (see Lamentations; the lament Psalms; etc.). In Isa 61:1-11, on which the beatitudes are based, the community laments the desolation of the holy city. This is the community that does not resign itself to the present condition of the world as final, but laments the fact that God's kingdom has not yet come and that God's will is not yet done (6:10). The grammatical form of the verb "shall be comforted" is the future passive. The passive voice was sometimes used by Jewish people to avoid saying God's name (divine passive). This text thus points to the eschatological future (as in vv. 6, 7, 9): "God will satisfy their yearnings by letting them see and participate in his eschatological celebration." On the tension between "mourning" here and its rejection as a characteristic of Jesus' followers in 9:15, see Reflections on 5:16.

5:5. Psalm 37:9, 11 is here reformulated as a beatitude and presented as a saying of Jesus. Since "meek," "gentle" (πραΰς *praus*) is a key Matthean word that characterizes the reversal of this-worldly ideas of kingship (11:29; 12:18-21; 21:5), Matthew may have formulated this saying himself. "Meekness" is here a synonym for "poor in spirit" (v. 3); it is not a matter of a particular attitude one is urged to adopt, but characterizes those who are aware of their identity as the oppressed people of God in the world, those who have renounced the violent methods of this-worldly power. "Inherit the land," originally referring to the promised land of Palestine, has here become an eschatological metaphor for participation in the renewed earth (19:28). Here is no strategy for worldly success; Matthew eliminates Mark's promise of rewarding the disciples with earthly goods (cf. Matt 19:29 with Mark 10:30).

5:6. All the references to "righteousness" or "justice" (δικαιοσύνη *dikaiosynē*) in the Sermon on the Mount have been added by Matthew. Thus Q's blessing on those who hunger becomes in Matthew a blessing on those who hunger and thirst "for righteousness" (see 5:3). Righteousness is a key Matthean concept, which retains both its primary meaning of actively doing the will of God (as in 6:1-18) and, like its Old Testament counterpart (צדקה *ṣĕdāqâ*), the rightwising eschatological activity

of God (6:33; cf. Isa 51:1, 5). Thus persons who hunger and thirst for righteousness are not those who merely long to be personally pious or idealistic dreamers or do-gooders, but, like those of 5:4, they are persons who long for the coming of God's kingdom and the vindication of right, which will come with it, and who on the basis of this hope actively do God's will now. This longing is no empty hope, but "shall be satisfied" (RSV), another divine passive—i.e., God will satisfy it.

5:7. Here Matthew uses the word for "mercy" (ἐλεήμων *eleēmōn*), which refers to concrete acts of mercy rather than merely a merciful attitude. As already illustrated by Joseph's actions in the opening scene of the Gospel, Matthew does not understand "justice" and "mercy" to be alternatives (1:19; see also 20:1-16, esp. v. 4). The key role mercy plays in Matthew's theology is illustrated by his twice adding "I desire mercy, not sacrifice" (Hos 6:6 NIV) to his sources at 9:13 and 12:7 (cf. the addition in 23:23 and the parable in 18:21-35, esp. v. 33). In none of the beatitudes is advice being offered for getting along in this world, where mercy is more likely to be regarded as a sign of weakness than to be rewarded in kind. Again the eschatological divine passive indicates that the merciful will receive mercy from God at the last judgment.

5:8. Psalm 24:3-4 has been cast in the form of a beatitude and presented as a saying of Jesus (cf. 5:5). "Purity of heart" is not merely the avoidance of "impure thoughts" (e.g., sexual fantasies), but refers to the single-minded devotion to God appropriate to a monotheistic faith. Having an "undivided heart" (Ps 86:11) is the corollary of monotheism, and requires that there be something big enough and good enough to merit one's whole devotion, rather than the functional polytheism of parceling oneself out to a number of loyalties. Faith in the *one* God requires that one be devoted to God with *all* one's heart (Deut 6:4-5; cf. Matt 22:37). This corresponds to the "single eye" of 6:22, the one pearl of 13:45-46, to Paul's "this one thing I do" (Phil 3:13 NRSV) and Luke's "one thing is needed" (Luke 10:42 NIV)—not one *more* thing. The opposite of purity of heart is a divided heart (Jas 4:8), attempting to serve two masters

(6:24), the "doubt" (διστάζω *distazō*; lit. "have two minds") of 14:33 and 28:17, and the conduct of the Pharisees (23:25).[118] "Seeing God" refers not to mystical vision in this world, but to the eschatological hope (1 Cor 13:12; Rev 22:4).

5:9. This beatitude was apparently added to the developing Q tradition in the particular form of Q that came to Matthew. The pre-70 Q community continued Jesus' own anti-militarist preaching. Their discipleship may be reflected in the tradition that the Jewish Christians of Palestine refused to fight in the 66–70 war against Rome. The Roman emperors called themselves "peacemakers" and "Sons of God." "Peacemakers" does not connote a passive attitude, but positive actions for reconciliation. Since military conflict was not directly part of Matthew's situation, he may have applied peacemaking to reconciliation of conflicting religious and cultural groups. Again, the eschatological divine passive points to God's claiming the peacemakers as "sons of God" in the last judgment, not to what people will say about those who work for peace in this world. To be declared "sons of God" is not a matter of individualistic identity but the eschatological fulfillment of Hos 1:10—i.e., to be accepted as belonging to the true people of God and entering into its inheritance—and has connotations of being welcomed among the "sons of God"—i.e., the angels.[119]

5:10. Verse 10 corresponds to 5:3, with which it forms a literary bracket. The group who will receive the eschatological blessing is not composed of the oppressed in general, but those persons unjustly persecuted because of their commitment to righteousness. The parallelism between "for righteousness' sake" (v. 10) and "for my sake" (v. 11) shows that righteousness is not an abstract concept for Matthew, but has a christological foundation and is one of several indications of the implicit christology of the Sermon on the Mount. Verse 10 was apparently composed by Matthew himself in order to conclude this series of beatitudes with a reference to righteousness, and to achieve nine beatitudes, corresponding to his pattern of composing in triads.

5:11-12. The transitional concluding beatitude of vv. 11-12 involves a shift in form. The beatitudes are indicative, but the body of the sermon 5:17–7:12 is basically instruction in the imperative mood. This transitional section shifts from third to second person, and includes the first imperative, "rejoice."[120] The joy to which the disciples are called is not in spite of persecution, but because of it. Rejoicing because of persecution is not the expression of a martyr complex, but the joyful acceptance of the badge of belonging to the eschatological community of faith, the people of God who are out of step with the value system of this age. Such people are like the prophets of Israel, who were also persecuted.[121] The introduction of the prophet imagery forms a transition to the next section, for prophets do not exist for themselves, but are entrusted with a mission to the world. The blessing pronounced on disciples in vv. 3-12 is for the purpose of their becoming the agents of blessing to others.

118. Augustine *Confessions* 2.1; Søren Kierkegaard, *Purity of Heart Is to Will One Thing* (New York: Harper and Bros., 1948). Compare Augustine's prayer, "While turned from Thee, the One Good, I lost myself among a multiplicity of things" and Kierkegaard's declaration that "purity of heart is to will one thing."

119. The NIV's preservation of "sons" for υἱοί (*huioi*), though not gender-inclusive as is the NRSV's "children," preserves the Jewish connotations of "son" (being an heir and belonging to the heavenly court) as well as the pagan overtones (contrast to the emperors' claim to be "sons of God" and "peacemakers").

120. Some scholars consider there to be only eight beatitudes and place vv. 11-12 with vv. 13-16 where the disciples are addressed directly. This has the advantage of clarifying what it means to be salt and light.

121. Matthew has added "who were before you" to Q's reference to prophets, suggesting that the Gospel's readers themselves belong to the prophetic tradition, and reflecting the presence of Christian prophets in the Matthean church (cf. 7:15-23; 10:41; 23:34).

REFLECTIONS

In the main, the beatitudes use two verbs: *are* and *will.* Each beatitude begins in the present tense—"blessed are . . ."—and moves to the future tense—"for they will. . . . " The present tense indicates that the beatitudes are expressions of what is already true about the Christian community. Of course, not every member of every congregation can claim to be meek, merciful, and pure in heart, but the beatitudes are addressed, not initially to individuals, but to the whole faith community. Among every authentic Christian congregation can be found persons of meekness, ministers of mercy, and workers for peace. Their presence and activity among us is a sign of God's blessing and a call to all of us to conform our common life more and more to these kingdom values.

The move to the future tense indicates that the life of the kingdom must wait for ultimate validation until God finishes the new creation. The future tense of the beatitudes resists all notions that Christianity is a "philosophy of life" designed to make people successful and calm today, in the present moment. Christianity is not a scheme to reduce stress, lose weight, advance in one's career, or preserve one from illness. Christian faith, instead, is a way of living based on the firm and sure hope that meekness is the way of God, that righteousness and peace will finally prevail, and that God's future will be a time of mercy and not cruelty. So, blessed are those who live this life now, even when such a life seems foolish, for they will, in the end, be vindicated by God.

MATTHEW 5:13, THE DISCIPLES AS SALT

NIV	NRSV
13"You are the salt of the earth. But if the salt loses its saltiness, how can it be made salty again? It is no longer good for anything, except to be thrown out and trampled by men.	13"You are the salt of the earth; but if salt has lost its taste, how can its saltiness be restored? It is no longer good for anything, but is thrown out and trampled under foot.

COMMENTARY

Although he uses material from Q, Matthew himself is responsible for the present form, location, and function of the salt and light sayings, which form a transition from the beatitudes to the instruction of 5:17–7:12. The life of discipleship is conceived throughout as life within the community of faith, a community charged with a mission to the world. The non-retaliatory essence of the new kingdom brought by Jesus is perfectly modeled; although out of step with the world and persecuted, like their master, Jesus' disciples live their lives for the sake of the world that persecutes them.

The saying is a metaphor with a brief rhetorical question, speaking of the disciples as salt. It is neither a parable, which requires narrative action, nor an allegory, in which each element can be univocally decoded into what it represents. The saying is evocative and has multiple layers of meaning, since salt had many connotations in Matthew's tradition and context—including sacrifice (Lev 2:13; Ezek 43:24), loyalty and covenant fidelity (Ezra 4:14; Num 18:19; eating together was called "sharing salt" and expressed a binding

relationship), purification (2 Kgs 2:19-22), seasoning (Job 6:6; Col 4:5), and preservative.[122]

The initial "you" is emphatic both by word choice (the pronoun ὑμεῖς [hymeis] is unnecessary in Greek; its presence indicates emphasis) and position, so that the sentence might be translated "It is you [and not the others—Pharisees? the Jewish people?] who are the salt of the earth." Yet there is no smugness, for the saying serves as a warning that if the disciples deny their mission, they (too) will be thrown out as useless. Salt loses its saltiness not by some impossible chemical miracle, but by becoming so impure, so mixed with other elements that it loses its function (see discussion of "purity of heart" above). The emphasis on "the earth" is Matthean. "Earth" is here the equivalent of "world" (cf. 5:14 par.). Matthew refers to "the world" nine times, never in a negative dualistic sense. The world does not belong to Satan. It is the creation of God (13:35; 24:21), the scene of the disciples' mission (5:14; 13:38; 26:13), where God's will shall finally be

122. Ignatius, *Letter to the Magnesians* 10. There may be a specific reference to salt's being used as a catalyst for fueling earthen ovens. When such salt lost its catalyzing potency, it was thrown out.

done (6:10). Salt does not exist for itself, nor do the disciples; their life is turned outward to the world. Here is no sectarian or provincial mentality—"the field is the world" (13:38).

MATTHEW 5:14-16, THE DISCIPLES AS LIGHT AND A CITY ON A HILL

NIV	NRSV
[14]"You are the light of the world. A city on a hill cannot be hidden. [15]Neither do people light a lamp and put it under a bowl. Instead they put it on its stand, and it gives light to everyone in the house. [16]In the same way, let your light shine before men, that they may see your good deeds and praise your Father in heaven."	14"You are the light of the world. A city built on a hill cannot be hid. [15]No one after lighting a lamp puts it under the bushel basket, but on the lampstand, and it gives light to all in the house. [16]In the same way, let your light shine before others, so that they may see your good works and give glory to your Father in heaven."

COMMENTARY

The disciples' mission in the world is further illustrated by the juxtaposition of two clashing metaphors. The light metaphor presents the disciples as illumination for the world. The primary function of light is not to be seen, but to let things be seen as they are. In a provocative contrast, the metaphor of the city on a hill presents the disciples as inevitably and unavoidably *being* seen (see Reflections below on the tension with 6:1-18).

The polemical overtone noted in 5:13 may be even stronger here, since "light" (to the nations) and "city on a hill" (to which the nations flow at the eschaton, Isa 2:2-5; 42:6; 49:6) were both used with reference to Israel's mission to the nations. Matthew believes that empirical Israel has failed to carry out this mission of the people of God and that the church of Jews and Gentiles is now charged with this task (28:18-20). Again, polemic against Jews is not the main thrust of the sayings, which function as a warning to disciples not to fail in their mission. The salt and light sayings picture mission as inherent to discipleship, as saltiness is essential to salt and shining is to light. For salt, being salty is not optional. With these three metaphors of salt, light, and city, the Matthean Jesus strikes the death blow to all religion that is purely personal and private. Just as the sermon is heard not only by the disciples but also by the "crowds" (7:28-29), so also the

church is not an esoteric community of initiates. The community that lives by the power of unostentatious prayer in the inner room (6:6) is not an introverted secret society shielding itself from the world, but is a city set on a hill whose authentic life cannot be concealed.

Matthew has rewritten the Q saying to emphasize the contrast between lighting a lamp and extinguishing it by placing it under a "bushel basket" (μόδιος *modios*; NIV "bowl"). The disciples are called to the active mission of "letting their light shine" to "all,"[123] but they do not generate the light any more than salt generates its own saltiness. The metaphors picture the church as having-been-lit, recipients of a light from which God is the source. They have been lit not for their own sakes, but for the sake of the world. Here, the community of disciples is light for the dark world, as is Jesus in 4:12-17 (cf. Isa 9:2). And as Jesus' deeds point not to his own glory but to the glory of God (9:8), so the purpose of the disciples' engaging in their acts of righteousness/justice before the world is not for their own sake but to glorify God. The disciples' mission is authorized and presupposed by Jesus' own mission and is the continuation of it (see 10:1).

The whole of Part I of the sermon is almost

123. Another indication of the universality of mission in the Gospel of Matthew (cf. 28:18-20).

exclusively in the indicative, but the following instruction is in the imperative. The conclusion of the "light" paragraph shifts from the indicative to the imperative, but is still based on it: "Be what you are."

REFLECTIONS

1. The "you are" of these sayings about salt and light is the Greek plural, addressed to the community of disciples. The disciples are what they are, not because of inherent potential that they are called upon to recognize and develop, but by Jesus' own word (see 4:18-22). These pronouncements are thus in continuity with the performative language of the beatitudes. The Matthean readers/disciples are not challenged to try harder to be salt and light, but are told that as followers of Jesus they are salt and light for the world. The text calls the reader not to more self-exertion, but to believe Jesus' word and to accept and live out the new reality it has already created in the call to discipleship.

2. Letting one's "light shine before others, so that they may see your good works" (v. 16) is in tension with 6:1-18 (cf. esp. 6:3 and 5:16) and other statements in Matthew. There are numerous such tensions in Matthew (e.g., 5:4 vs. 9:15; 5:9 vs. 10:34; 6:34 vs. 25:1-13; 8:12 vs. 13:38; 9:13 vs. 10:41; 16:6 vs. 23:3). Such tensions should not be pounced upon as examples of "contradictions in the Bible"; neither should they be too readily harmonized into a bland consistency, since they represent a potent dimension of scribal wisdom teaching (cf. e.g., Prov 26:4-5). This is the nature of proverbial wisdom in general: "look before you leap," but "he who hesitates is lost"; "fools rush in where angels fear to tread," but "damn the torpedoes—full speed ahead!" The charge of inconsistency may be an attack on one's integrity, but "consistency is the hobgoblin of small minds." Matthew composes as a Christian scribe, a tradent of proverbial Christian wisdom (cf. 13:52). The Gospel is not intended as *halakah,* a rule for life, but to stimulate imagination and personal responsibility. (See Commentary on becoming a "Jesus theologian" in struggling with the ethical directives of 5:21-48.) The jagged edges of Jesus' sayings should not be too quickly rounded off to make them consistent with other biblical teachings, or even with each other. Talk of the kingdom of God generates a certain wildness that is lost if it is domesticated. Again, Matthew can continue to be the church's teacher in this regard. He both preserves the radicality of Jesus' message and gives practical instruction on how to come to terms with it in the realities of everyday life. He does this not by writing an essay, but by modeling that life-style. This is one of the profundities of the next section of the Sermon on the Mount (5:17-48; see also Reflections on the sermon as a whole).

Matthew 5:17–7:12, Life in the Eschatological Community

MATTHEW 5:17-48, "THE LAW"

NIV	NRSV
17"Do not think that I have come to abolish the Law or the Prophets; I have not come to abolish them but to fulfill them. 18I tell you the truth, until heaven and earth disappear, not the smallest letter, not the least stroke of a pen, will	17"Do not think that I have come to abolish the law or the prophets; I have come not to abolish but to fulfill. 18For truly I tell you, until heaven and earth pass away, not one letter,[a] not
	ᵃGk *one iota*

NIV

by any means disappear from the Law until everything is accomplished. ¹⁹Anyone who breaks one of the least of these commandments and teaches others to do the same will be called least in the kingdom of heaven, but whoever practices and teaches these commands will be called great in the kingdom of heaven. ²⁰For I tell you that unless your righteousness surpasses that of the Pharisees and the teachers of the law, you will certainly not enter the kingdom of heaven.

²¹"You have heard that it was said to the people long ago, 'Do not murder,ᵃ and anyone who murders will be subject to judgment.' ²²But I tell you that anyone who is angry with his brotherᵇ will be subject to judgment. Again, anyone who says to his brother, 'Raca,'ᶜ is answerable to the Sanhedrin. But anyone who says, 'You fool!' will be in danger of the fire of hell.

²³"Therefore, if you are offering your gift at the altar and there remember that your brother has something against you, ²⁴leave your gift there in front of the altar. First go and be reconciled to your brother; then come and offer your gift.

²⁵"Settle matters quickly with your adversary who is taking you to court. Do it while you are still with him on the way, or he may hand you over to the judge, and the judge may hand you over to the officer, and you may be thrown into prison. ²⁶I tell you the truth, you will not get out until you have paid the last penny.ᵈ

²⁷"You have heard that it was said, 'Do not commit adultery.'ᵉ ²⁸But I tell you that anyone who looks at a woman lustfully has already committed adultery with her in his heart. ²⁹If your right eye causes you to sin, gouge it out and throw it away. It is better for you to lose one part of your body than for your whole body to be thrown into hell. ³⁰And if your right hand causes you to sin, cut it off and throw it away. It is better for you to lose one part of your body than for your whole body to go into hell.

³¹"It has been said, 'Anyone who divorces his wife must give her a certificate of divorce.'ᶠ ³²But I tell you that anyone who divorces his wife, except for marital unfaithfulness, causes her to

ᵃ21 Exodus 20:13   ᵇ22 Some manuscripts brother without cause
ᶜ22 An Aramaic term of contempt   ᵈ26 Greek kodrantes
ᵉ27 Exodus 20:14   ᶠ31 Deut. 24:1

NRSV

one stroke of a letter, will pass from the law until all is accomplished. ¹⁹Therefore, whoever breaksᵃ one of the least of these commandments, and teaches others to do the same, will be called least in the kingdom of heaven; but whoever does them and teaches them will be called great in the kingdom of heaven. ²⁰For I tell you, unless your righteousness exceeds that of the scribes and Pharisees, you will never enter the kingdom of heaven.

²¹"You have heard that it was said to those of ancient times, 'You shall not murder'; and 'whoever murders shall be liable to judgment.' ²²But I say to you that if you are angry with a brother or sister,ᵇ you will be liable to judgment; and if you insultᶜ a brother or sister,ᵈ you will be liable to the council; and if you say, 'You fool,' you will be liable to the hellᵉ of fire. ²³So when you are offering your gift at the altar, if you remember that your brother or sisterᶠ has something against you, ²⁴leave your gift there before the altar and go; first be reconciled to your brother or sister,ᶠ and then come and offer your gift. ²⁵Come to terms quickly with your accuser while you are on the way to courtᵍ with him, or your accuser may hand you over to the judge, and the judge to the guard, and you will be thrown into prison. ²⁶Truly I tell you, you will never get out until you have paid the last penny.

²⁷"You have heard that it was said, 'You shall not commit adultery.' ²⁸But I say to you that everyone who looks at a woman with lust has already committed adultery with her in his heart. ²⁹If your right eye causes you to sin, tear it out and throw it away; it is better for you to lose one of your members than for your whole body to be thrown into hell.ᵉ ³⁰And if your right hand causes you to sin, cut it off and throw it away; it is better for you to lose one of your members than for your whole body to go into hell.ᵉ

³¹"It was also said, 'Whoever divorces his wife, let him give her a certificate of divorce.' ³²But I say to you that anyone who divorces his wife, except on the ground of unchastity, causes her to commit adultery; and whoever marries a divorced woman commits adultery.

ᵃOr annuls   ᵇGk a brother; other ancient authorities add without cause   ᶜGk say Raca to (an obscure term of abuse)
ᵈGk a brother   ᵉGk Gehenna   ᶠGk your brother   ᵍGk lacks to court

NIV

become an adulteress, and anyone who marries the divorced woman commits adultery.

33"Again, you have heard that it was said to the people long ago, 'Do not break your oath, but keep the oaths you have made to the Lord.' 34But I tell you, Do not swear at all: either by heaven, for it is God's throne; 35or by the earth, for it is his footstool; or by Jerusalem, for it is the city of the Great King. 36And do not swear by your head, for you cannot make even one hair white or black. 37Simply let your 'Yes' be 'Yes,' and your 'No,' 'No'; anything beyond this comes from the evil one.

38"You have heard that it was said, 'Eye for eye, and tooth for tooth.'a 39But I tell you, Do not resist an evil person. If someone strikes you on the right cheek, turn to him the other also. 40And if someone wants to sue you and take your tunic, let him have your cloak as well. 41If someone forces you to go one mile, go with him two miles. 42Give to the one who asks you, and do not turn away from the one who wants to borrow from you.

43"You have heard that it was said, 'Love your neighborb and hate your enemy.' 44But I tell you: Love your enemiesc and pray for those who persecute you, 45that you may be sons of your Father in heaven. He causes his sun to rise on the evil and the good, and sends rain on the righteous and the unrighteous. 46If you love those who love you, what reward will you get? Are not even the tax collectors doing that? 47And if you greet only your brothers, what are you doing more than others? Do not even pagans do that? 48Be perfect, therefore, as your heavenly Father is perfect."

a38 Exodus 21:24; Lev. 24:20; Deut. 19:21   b43 Lev. 19:18
c44 Some late manuscripts enemies, bless those who curse you, do good to those who hate you

NRSV

33"Again, you have heard that it was said to those of ancient times, 'You shall not swear falsely, but carry out the vows you have made to the Lord.' 34But I say to you, Do not swear at all, either by heaven, for it is the throne of God, 35or by the earth, for it is his footstool, or by Jerusalem, for it is the city of the great King. 36And do not swear by your head, for you cannot make one hair white or black. 37Let your word be 'Yes, Yes' or 'No, No'; anything more than this comes from the evil one.a

38"You have heard that it was said, 'An eye for an eye and a tooth for a tooth.' 39But I say to you, Do not resist an evildoer. But if anyone strikes you on the right cheek, turn the other also; 40and if anyone wants to sue you and take your coat, give your cloak as well; 41and if anyone forces you to go one mile, go also the second mile. 42Give to everyone who begs from you, and do not refuse anyone who wants to borrow from you.

43"You have heard that it was said, 'You shall love your neighbor and hate your enemy.' 44But I say to you, Love your enemies and pray for those who persecute you, 45so that you may be children of your Father in heaven; for he makes his sun rise on the evil and on the good, and sends rain on the righteous and on the unrighteous. 46For if you love those who love you, what reward do you have? Do not even the tax collectors do the same? 47And if you greet only your brothers and sisters,b what more are you doing than others? Do not even the Gentiles do the same? 48Be perfect, therefore, as your heavenly Father is perfect."

a Or evil   b Gk your brothers

COMMENTARY

5:17-20, The Law and the "Greater Righteousness." Matthew has placed this section here as the preface to the antitheses that follow, the general principles to be explicated and illustrated in the six antitheses of 5:21-48. Matthew has expanded the core saying from Q on the permanent validity of Scripture now found in Luke 16:17 and rewritten the whole so as to form this programmatic statement that introduces the instructional core of the sermon, 5:17–7:12.

5:17. "The law or the prophets" forms a literary bracket with 7:12, setting off 5:17–7:12 as the instructional core of the sermon. "Law" here is the Torah or Pentateuch; "prophets" comprise both the Former Prophets (Joshua–Kings) and the Latter Prophets (Isaiah–Malachi). This was the central core of the Hebrew Bible (HB) of Matthew's day, the functional equivalent of "the Scripture."[124] The relevant point primarily concerns the law, but Matthew adds prophets because he regards the Scripture as a whole, including the Torah, as basically prophetic, looking forward to the eschatological time of fulfillment. (See Excursus "Matthew as Interpreter of Scripture" 151-54.)

The first saying is mostly Matthean redaction, although it may have a traditional nucleus. It is in the form of an "I have come" ($\mathring{\eta}\lambda\theta o\nu$ ēlthon) saying (see elsewhere in Matt 9:13 = Mark 2:17; 10:34-35; cf. Matt 20:28 = Mark 10:45; 8:29 = Mark 1:24). The closest formal parallel to 5:17 is 10:34, both peculiarly Matthean. The form can be used to express the post-Easter perspective that looks back on the meaning of the whole career of Jesus, presupposing Christian faith. Minimally, it expresses the authoritative prophetic consciousness of having been sent by God, and it is usually related to the eschatological kingdom and the reversal of expectations associated with it. In the Synoptics, which have no doctrine of Christ's preexistence, it does not mean "I have come from heaven. . . . "

"Do not suppose . . . " is only secondarily an apologetic statement directed to outsiders who accuse Christians of rejecting the Law. Matthew is addressed primarily to insiders who find themselves belonging to a community that in fact has made fundamental changes in its practice of the Torah. This community must both answer the charges of outsiders and clarify its own understanding of the relationship of Christian discipleship and Torah observance.

Jesus does not abolish the Law (cf. 19:16-19), but neither does he merely affirm the status quo. In Matthew's view, Jesus accomplishes an ultimately positive action with regard to the Law: He "fulfills" it. "Fulfill" is a key christological category in the Gospel of Matthew, which uses the category of "fulfillment" more than all the other Gospels together. Its meaning here has been variously understood. It does not mean merely "do,"

as though Jesus claims that he performs everything required by the Law, or "interpret," as though what he offers is only a new interpretation of the meaning of the Law, or "sum up," as though Jesus claims his teaching is only a summary of the Law (as Rom 8:4; 13:8-10; Gal 5:14; Matthew must not be explained in Pauline terms, and vice versa). In line with Matthew's general theology of fulfillment, the best approach to this difficult, but key, passage seems to be:

(1) The whole Scripture ("law and prophets") testifies to God's will and work in history. Matthew does not retreat from this affirmation. He does not play off the (abiding) "moral law" against the (temporary) "ceremonial law."

(2) God's work, testified to in the Scripture, is not yet complete. The Law and Prophets point beyond themselves to the definitive act of God in the eschatological, messianic future.

(3) The advent of the messianic king's proclaiming and representing the eschatological kingdom of God is the fulfillment of the Scripture—the Law and the Prophets. The Messiah has come. He embodies and teaches the definitive will of God. The Law and Prophets are to be obeyed not for what they are in themselves, but because they mediate the will of God. But in Matthew, Jesus declares that what he teaches is God's will and the criterion of eschatological judgment (7:24, 26; cf. 7:21), so there can be no conflict between Jesus and the Torah, which he fulfills. This is a tremendous, albeit implicit, christological claim.

(4) This messianic fulfillment does not nullify or make obsolete the Law and the Prophets, but confirms them. The incorporation of the Law in the more comprehensive history of salvation centered in the Christ-event is an affirmation of the Law, not its rejection.

(5) But this affirmation, by being fulfilled by Christ, does not always mean a mere repetition or continuation of the original Law. Fulfillment may mean transcendence as well (cf. 12:1-14). The Matthean Jesus elsewhere enunciates the critical principle that mercy, justice, love, and covenant loyalty are the weightier matters of the Law by which the rest must be judged (see 9:13; 12:7, both of which quote Hos 6:6; cf. Matt 23:23). Jesus' declaration that his own life and teaching are the definitive revelation of the will of God (cf. 11:25-27; 28:18-20) does indeed mean

124. For the combination "law and prophets," cf. 2 Kgs 17:13; Neh 9:26; Zech 7:12; Matt 5:17; 7:12; 22:40; John 1:45; Acts 13:15; 24:14; 28:23; Rom 3:21. The other books now in our OT canon, the Writings, were in the process of being officially canonized in Matthew's day. See Daniel J. Harrington, "Introduction to the Canon," *NIB* 1:7-21.

that neither the written Torah nor its interpretation in the oral tradition (see Commentary on chap. 15) is the final authority.

5:18. The affirmation of 5:17 is grounded in another declaration expressed in prophetic form; it probably originated not as a saying of the historical Jesus but as a pronouncement of an early Christian prophet. The freedom with which Jesus lived over against traditional understandings of Torah observance raised questions in the later church about the continuing validity of the Law, to which a variety of answers were given in early Christianity (see Acts 6–7; 10–11; 15:10-11; 21:20-24; Galatians; James). In some setting in which the early Palestinian church pondered whether the advent of the Messiah meant that the Law had been abolished, a Christian prophet speaking in Jesus' name responded with an absolute negative. The traditional "jot" and "tittle" (KJV), now translated into more contemporary form in both the NIV and the NRSV, represent the smallest letter of the Hebrew alphabet (׳ *yod*), and the minute strokes that distinguish one letter from another (e.g., ב and כ, *b* and *k*) or the ornamental strokes in Hebrew or accents in Greek that had no meaning at all. It is Matthew's way of affirming the continuing authority of Scripture in its totality as the revelation of God's will.[125]

"Truly I tell you" (NRSV) or "I tell you the truth" (NIV) is literally "Amen I say to you." "Amen" (ἀμήν *amēn*) is not from a Greek word, but is a transliteration of אמן (*'āmēn*), a responsive Hebrew affirmation to something said previously. The formula is characteristic of the Matthean Jesus, this being the first of thirty-two occurrences, but Matthew found it prefixed to sayings of Jesus in both Q and Mark. It is found twenty-five times in John as well (in doubled form, "amen, amen"). Beginning some of his pronouncements with "amen" was a unique aspect of Jesus' own authoritative speech. The form was adopted by Christian prophetic figures who continued to speak in Jesus' name in the later church, and then, in imitation of this, by non-prophetic types, such as Matthew. Thus "until heaven and earth pass away" is not a folk expression for "always," but

in apocalyptic fashion envisages a concrete event at the end of time, as does the identical expression in 24:35. The point is that, while the Law has continuing validity, it is not ultimate, in contrast to the word of Jesus, which is ultimately normative and will never pass away. The Law is affirmed, but relativized.[126]

5:19. Here the focus shifts from Christ to the disciples. The saying probably reflects a traditional saying circulating in Matthew's church, perhaps in Q^Mt. It is in the form of a "sentence of holy law" in which eschatological judgment is paralleled with present conduct. The form was characteristic of Christian prophets, another indication that 5:17-20 reflects debates in the post-Easter church on the role of the Law, to which Christian prophets gave revelatory responses, rather than being a transcription of the teaching of the historical Jesus. Such sayings spoken in the name of the risen Lord carried the Lord's authority. Matthew includes this saying as supporting his thesis that the Law has not been abolished for Christians, even though it is in tension with some of the ensuing examples of the "greater righteousness," which do in fact relax the OT Law (cf. Jesus' teaching on divorce, oaths, and retaliation).[127]

The saying has in view Hellenizing Christians who were understood to have abolished the Law or relaxed some of its demands. Paul and his followers were often so understood, although Paul too considered this a misunderstanding of his view (cf. Rom 3:21-31). The Matthean Jesus insists that even the "small" commands are important, as did the rabbis (see *'Abot* 2:1; 3:18; 4:21). Matthew insists on his point without excluding his opponents from the kingdom, but he considers them "least."

5:20. This saying is filled with Matthean vocabulary and appears to be entirely Matthew's own composition, created to link the programmatic statement about the "greater righteousness" to the six examples that follow. "Scribes and Pharisees" is a typically Matthean phrase, representing the Jewish religious leadership of his own day. Theirs was a high standard of piety and religious

---

125. The later Ebionites believed that not all of the Torah was from God, but contained passages of purely human origin. Matthew may be polemicizing against some who already solved the tensions between the Scripture and the new faith by abrogating part of the Torah. Matthew rejects this way out. His way is hermeneutical, not by excision.

126. For an alternative explanation, see John P. Meier, *Law and History in Matthew's Gospel: A Redactional Study of Matthew 5:17-48* (Rome: Biblical Institute Press, 1975). In Meier's understanding, the traditional saying declared that the authority of every word of the Law would last until the end of history. Matthew reinterpreted this to mean that this "end of history" is proleptically realized in the death and resurrection of Jesus.

127. "Relax" (RSV) better preserves the sense of λύω (*lyō*) in v. 19 in distinction to "abolish" (καταλύω *katalyō*) of v. 17.

practice, but Matthew considers them typically to be hypocrites (see on 23:1-33). Yet the standard of right living to which the sermon calls the disciples/readers is not merely to avoid hypocrisy. The following six antitheses (vv. 21-48) explicate what it means to exceed the righteousness of the scribes and Pharisees. (On entering the kingdom, see Excursus "Kingdom of Heaven in Matthew" 288-94.)

5:21-32, Three Antitheses[128] Modeling the Greater Righteousness. Matthew does not elaborate the meaning of this greater righteousness in an abstract essay, but explicates it by six concrete examples (better: "focal instances"[129]) that take up older materials and place them in a new interpretative structure.

Each of the six units begins with a juxtaposition of what *was* said (divine passive—i.e., by God through Moses) "to those of ancient times" (i.e., the Israelites at Sinai) and what *is now being said* by Jesus to his disciples. "You have heard" refers to hearing the Scripture read in the synagogue. The antitheses do not merely contrast Jesus' word with that of tradition or scribal interpretation, but with the Torah itself, which has been the subject since 5:17. Jesus' pronouncements do more than deepen or interpret the meaning of the written Law. The juxtaposition is not to be softened. Jesus does more than give a better interpretation of the old authority; he relocates authority from the written text of Scripture to himself—i.e., to God's presence in his life, teaching, death, and resurrection (see 1:23; 7:29; 18:18-20; 21:23-27; 28:18-20). Still, the point is that Jesus' teaching is not transgression of the Law, but its transcendence.

The Structure of the Whole, Arrangement of the Six. The antithetical form is not found in Scripture outside of Matthew 5. Elements of it are found in rabbinic literature, when a scribe or rabbi contrasts his own interpretation with others' by concluding "but I say to you." No rabbi or scribe ever contrasted his own pronouncements with what God had said in the Torah.

It has often been thought that this startling form must have originated with Jesus. It would correspond to the sovereign freedom with which he spoke and acted with reference to the Law and tradition, as expressed in numerous sayings and conflict stories (e.g., 12:1-8), and would express the implicit christology inherent in Jesus' acting and speaking with authority. If Jesus originated the form, however, it is very strange that it entirely dropped out of the tradition except for Matt 5:21-48. Since we know Matthew reformulated at least three sayings in his tradition to make them antitheses, and since there is no evidence for the earlier existence of the form, it is best to see Matthew as the originator of this form, which he imposed on the material as part of his careful structuring of the Sermon on the Mount.[130] The six antitheses are arranged in two triads, as indicated by the fresh beginning at 5:33 ("again" [πάλιν *palin*]), by the appearance of the full form only in 5:21 and 5:33, by the appearance of "that" (ὅτι *hoti*) and the "everyone who . . ." (πᾶς ὁ *pas ho*) form only in the first set, and by the fact that only the first set includes the "situational application" element (see below).

The Matthean Structure of Each Unit. The scribal interpreter Matthew, who "brings out of his treasure what is new and what is old" (13:52) elaborates each antithesis with other materials from his tradition to amplify the meaning or to interpret them to his situation. The threefold structure, seen most clearly in the first antithesis (5:21-26), is carried through in the first set of three, and then abandoned in the second triad— either because he had exhausted his materials for such elaboration or because the pattern had become clear and he leaves the hearers/readers to formulate their own applications.[131] The dynamic

128. The traditional term *antitheses* is retained, even though this label is contrary to the Matthean point that Jesus' teaching is not opposed to the Law and Prophets, but is their fulfillment, and that the righteousness of the disciples is not opposed to that of the scribes and Pharisees, but surpasses it. "Hypertheses" is more appropriate, so B. T. Viviano, "The Gospel According to Matthew," in *The New Jerome Biblical Commentary*, eds. Raymond E. Brown, Joseph A. Fitzmyer, Roland E. Murphy (Englewood Cliffs, N.J.: Prentice-Hall, 1990) 641.

129. Robert Tannehill, "The 'Focal Instance' as a Form of New Testament Speech: A Study of Matthew 5:39*b*-42," *JR* 50 (1970) 372-85.

130. Cf. M. Jack Suggs, "The Antitheses as Redactional Products," in Reginald H. Fuller, ed., *Essays on the Love Commandment* (Philadelphia: Fortress, 1978) 93-107.

131. H. D. Betz understands the Sermon on the Mount to belong to the literary genre of epitome, intended to present "the theology of Jesus in a systematic fashion." Although his understanding of the genre and tradition history of the sermon as a whole is difficult to accept, his succinct explanation does apply, especially to the antitheses. "The epitome is a composition carefully designed out of sayings of Jesus grouped according to thematic points of doctrine considered to be of primary importance. Correspondingly, its function is to provide the disciple of Jesus with the necessary tool for becoming a Jesus theologian. 'Hearing and doing the sayings of Jesus,' therefore, means enabling the disciple to theologize creatively along the lines of the theology of the master. To say it pointedly: The [Sermon on the Mount] is not law to be obeyed, but theology to be intellectually appropriated and internalized, in order then to be creatively developed and implemented in concrete situations in life." (Hans Dieter Betz, *Essays on the Sermon on the Mount,* trans. L. L. Welborn [Philadelphia: Fortress, 1985] 15.)

of this repeated structure is that it does not answer all ethical issues in advance, but asks the disciple to discern God's will in the light of Torah and Jesus' teaching and gives models for doing so. The threefold structure comprises reaffirmation of the Law, radicalization of the Law, and situational application of the radicalized Law:

Reaffirmation. Matthew reassures those who fear that Christians advocate the abolition of the Torah that this is a misunderstanding. Jesus' commands do not transgress the Law, but radicalize it—they go to the *radix,* the root of the command. The one who puts into practice what Jesus teaches in Matthew 5 will not violate any command of the Torah, which is not abolished but reaffirmed.

Radicalization. The fulfillment of the Law brought by the advent of the messianic king does not merely repeat the Law, but radicalizes it. The ultimate will of God was and is mediated by the Law, but sometimes in a manner conditioned by the "hardness of heart" of its recipients (cf. 19:3-9). The legal form fostered a casuistic approach, which Matthew opposes, since it does not go to the root of the matter (i.e., is not radical), but touches the surface, not the heart, of the ethical problem. (For Matthew's opposition to casuistry, see 23:16-21, the longest "woe" against the Pharisees, entirely "M" material.) Jesus' teaching deals with the inner springs of human conduct, which Law as such cannot regulate. Like the prophets of Israel, Matthew declares the unqualified will of God, which sometimes deepens or broadens the Law, expressing its ultimate intent, and sometimes qualifies or even negates its limitations, while affirming the ultimate will of God to which it pointed.

Situational "Between the Times" Application.[132] The call to live by the absolute will of God is not a counsel of despair. Prophets announce the absolute will of God and leave it to others to work out how this can be lived out in an imperfect world. Jesus spoke in this prophetic mode, and it had been continued by Christian prophets, including those in Matthew's tradition and church. But Matthew is a scribal teacher who is concerned not only to declare the absolute will of God as expressed in Jesus' radicalization of the

Torah, but also to provide counsel for day-by-day living for imperfect people who fall short of this call to live by the perfect will of God. Thus, without negating the call to perfection, Matthew selects other sayings of Jesus from his tradition that provide situational applications for disciples who both believe that the kingdom of God has come with the advent of Jesus and pray for its final coming (6:10). The new age has come in Jesus, but the old age continues and Christians live in the tension between the two. Disciples can take the antitheses seriously as models for their life in this world in the same way that they take the advent of the kingdom of God seriously as both present and yet to come. Most important, for Matthew, commitment to the messianic king means more than proper confession; it results in a changed life (repentance). But the messianic king, who makes these demands and who will use them as the criteria of the final judgment, which he will conduct, both lives them out himself during his earthly ministry and continues with the community in its struggle to discern and do God's will in ever-new situations (28:18-20). In the first set of three antitheses (5:21-32), the reality of Christian existence "between the times" of the Messiah's appearance and the eschatological coming of the kingdom is addressed by giving examples for the creative application of Jesus' teaching by his disciples. These examples are not casuistic new laws, but models for the disciples to adapt to their varied post-Easter situations. In the second set of antitheses (5:33-48), the concrete models are omitted, and the disciples are left to their own responsibility to be "Jesus theologians" (cf. note 131).

All six antitheses are expressions of the Great Commandment (22:34-40) and keep it from being trivialized or sentimentalized.

5:21-26, Love Shows No Hostility. *5:21, The Law Reaffirmed.* For the form, see above. All six of the antitheses deal with relations between human beings, not with religious rituals that express humanity's relation to God (see 6:1-18). The Matthean Jesus begins not with a peripheral matter of the Law, but with a verbatim quotation of the apodictic (unqualified, non-casuistic) command in the Decalogue against murder (Exod 20:13; Deut 5:18). The supplementary "whoever murders shall be liable to judgment" is not found

---

132. The shift from radicalizaton of the Law to situational application of the radicalized Law is signaled by the change from plural to singular forms.

verbatim in the Old Testament, but presents a paraphrasing summary of several legal texts in the Torah (Exod 21:12; Lev 24:17; Num 35:12; Deut 17:8-13). Matthew composes and includes it in order to introduce the word *judgment*, which plays a decisive role in Jesus' pronouncement.

5:22, The Law Radicalized. The command is not revoked, but is reaffirmed and then radicalized. Jesus pronounces that anger makes one subject to judgment, without distinguishing between "justified" and "unjustified" anger.[133] Likewise, the apparent distinctions between (1) anger that makes one accountable to a local court; (2) using an insulting term (such as *airhead* [ריקא *rêqā'*]), which makes one accountable to the Sanhedrin; and (3) calling someone a fool, which may be punished by hellfire, are only a parody of rabbinic casuistry, which Matthew lampoons and rejects (23:16-21). Matthew begins with what seems to be scribal wisdom and modulates the saying into a prophetic pronouncement of eschatological judgment. The fact that we do not have wooden legalistic casuistry here is clear both from the fact that the demand is difficult or impossible to carry out—becoming angry is not usually a matter under one's control—and from the absurdly disproportionate punishment, not to mention the fact that taken literally the Matthean Jesus violates his own injunction (23:17, 19). Verse 22 is not literally an escalating scale from local courts to the judgment bar of God, but a declaration of the absolute will of God, who wills not only that persons not kill each other, but also that there be no hostility between human beings. "This is not an injunction merely to avoid certain abusive expressions (that would be another form of legalism) but to submit our thoughts about other people, as well as the words they give rise to, to God's penetrating judgment."[134]

5:23-26, Situational Application. Despite their commitment to live by Jesus' command, the disciples find themselves involved in hostility. What then? Matthew selects two illustrations from his tradition of Jesus sayings (cf. Q =

Luke 12:57-59) that guide the disciples in applying Jesus' radical demand to their "between-the-times" situation of imperfect people living in an imperfect world. They are to consider reconciliation, overcoming alienation and hostility, to be even more important than worship at the altar (vv. 23-24); thus they are to work for reconciliation in the light of the eschatological judgment toward which they are journeying (vv. 25-26). Neither picture is to be taken legalistically as a literal case. The worshiper before the altar cannot literally leave the sacrificial liturgy half completed, find the offended or offending brother or sister (which may require a round trip of several days to Galilee and back), then return to the Temple and complete the liturgy. Corresponding to the antithesis of 5:22, this is not a realistic "case," but a non-literal, non-casuistic, parabolic pointer to the kind of greater righteousness appropriate to those who belong to the kingdom of God. Disciples are responsible for using this example creatively to apply Jesus' teaching in their own situations. As such it is a frontal attack on the legalistic system as an approach to the righteousness God demands. Likewise, the picture in vv. 25-26, originally perhaps a fragment of this-worldly wisdom, has in this context become a testimony to the urgency of reconciliation before arriving at the eschatological judgment of God.

5:27-30, Love Is Not Predatory. The formal structure devised by Matthew is also clearly seen in this pericope, which reaffirms the Law (5:27), radicalizes it (5:28), then provides two situational applications (vv. 29-30).

Reaffirmation. The Decalogue's absolute prohibition of "adultery" (μοιχεία *moicheia*; see Exod 20:14; Deut 5:18) refers specifically to a married woman's having sexual relations with a man other than her husband, and it is to be distinguished from "fornication" (πορνεία *porneia*; illicit sex in general). Adultery was considered a violation of the husband's exclusive right to his wife and the assurance that children born to her were his own. Both the woman and the man involved were considered guilty of adultery, whether or not the man was married.[135] Jesus' teaching does not

---

133. The mass of later MSS contain the scribal addition "without cause" (εἰκῇ *eikē*), which was printed in the Textus Receptus and hence became part of the KJV. There is no doubt that the reading adopted by the NIV and the NRSV, represented by B, ℵ, the Vulgate, and several of the early Church Fathers, best represents Matthew's original.

134. R. T. France, *Matthew*, Tyndale New Testament Commentaries (Grand Rapids: Eerdmans, 1987) 120.

135. So understood, adultery must involve a married woman. A married man who has extramarital relations with an unmarried woman was considered immoral, but not guilty of adultery, and likewise for the unmarried woman who has an affair with a married man.

abolish the Decalogue's command against adultery, but reaffirms it.

Radicalization. Jesus then radicalizes the intent of the Law with the pronouncement that every man who looks on the wife of another for the purpose of sexual desire is already an adulterer in his inmost being.[136] Although both men and women can be guilty of adultery, Jesus presupposes the patriarchal setting of both the original Decalogue and his own time by explicating his own command in terms of the man.[137] This is remarkable, since the woman was often considered the offending party (cf. John 7:53–8:1). Strictly interpreted, this text does not deal with natural sexual desire and its associated fantasy, but with the intentional lustful look at the wife of another. This observation, however, should not be used to domesticate Jesus' radical demand. As in 5:21-27, not only the physical deed, but the intention of the heart as well makes one guilty before the Law of God.

Situational Application. Once again the scribal Matthew does not leave the disciple who wants to live by the greater righteousness of the kingdom ethic standing helplessly before the radical, impossible-sounding demand. Without retreating from the command that expresses the absolute will of God, Matthew finds sayings of Jesus that, when brought to this context, show both that from time to time the disciple will in fact not measure up to this absolute standard and that such violations must be resisted by radical measures. The command to gouge out the eye and cut off the hand are found in another context in Mark 9:43, 47, which Matthew also uses in 18:8-9. This double usage may mean that Matthew found them in both of his major sources, but more likely that he simply used the Markan material twice, here as well as in its Markan context.[138] Thus we see the importance of Matthew's hermeneutical method of interpretation by context and interpretation by structure. Again, Matthew demonstrates that he does not interpret the Jesus tradition by citing it and then writing explanatory comments,

but by combining various sayings of Jesus from the tradition into a tensive structure that suggests and helps generate the disciples' own creative interpretation.

5:31-32, Love in Marriage. This antithesis is related to the preceding one in subject matter—namely, the continuing validity of the Torah's injunction against adultery. The issue is over what constitutes a violation of the seventh commandment. The teaching of the Matthean Jesus transcends the Jewish legal understanding that "adultery" (אָנַף *nāʾap*; μοιχεύω *moicheuō*) means extra-marital sexual relations between a married woman and a man, either married or not, which made both guilty of adultery. In the preceding pericope, the lustful look is already adultery. In this antithesis, divorce and remarriage, though socially acceptable and regulated by the Torah, are a violation of the seventh commandment—though there is a situational application, the so-called "exception clause."

The teaching of the Matthean Jesus in relation to the Law may be clarified by considering the following history of the hermeneutical tradition in which Matthew stands.

(1) There is no Torah command against divorce. The Law of Moses assumes the legitimacy of divorce; the issue is remarriage. Divorce had to be official and regulated by the community, thus offering some protection to the divorced woman by granting her legal status and permitting her to marry someone else. The decision to divorce was strictly the prerogative of the husband, who did not have to go to court, but could simply make the decision himself in the presence of certified witnesses.

(2) Deuteronomy 24:1-4 was the locus of the scribal discussion in Jesus' day and Matthew's, the issue between the rabbinic schools being how strictly the grounds for divorce ("something objectionable") should be defined. The strict school of Shammai interpreted this to mean sexual sins or perhaps gross impropriety, while the liberal school of Hillel argued that it could be anything that displeased the husband.[139] In either tradition, divorce was relatively easy to obtain and frequent in occurrence, encouraging a lax attitude toward marriage.

(3) Against both Law and tradition, the historical Jesus proclaimed the absolute prohibition of

---

136. The Greek construction πρὸς τὸ ἐπιθυμῆσαι (*pros to epithymēsai*) is a purpose infinitive best translated "for the purpose of."

137. The androcentric perspective is also retained in that adultery is not seen as an offense against the unfaithful man's wife, but against the husband of the unfaithful wife. Paul, too, continues to presuppose this perspective (see 1 Thess 4:6).

138. Here, Matthew rearranges the Markan order to place "eye" first, since the present text deals with the lustful *look.*

139. Burning his dinner (*m. Git.* 9:10) is often cited as the illustration.

divorce as the will of God. Mark 10:2-9 and 1 Cor 7:10-11 still reflect this oldest tradition, in which Jesus functions as a prophet who proclaims the unqualified will of God, without making any adjustments for the demands of practical necessities. Although one Old Testament text points in this direction (Mal 2:14-16), such an absolute prohibition of divorce is unprecedented in Judaism.[140]

(4) Matthew's primary sources, Mark and Q, both preserve Jesus' saying about divorce, but reintroduce the issue of remarriage, a practical necessity in the case of the divorced woman (Mark 10:11-12 added to Mark 10:2-9; Luke 16:18). In addition, Mark adjusts the saying to his Gentile context by adding the provision for a woman to divorce her husband (Mark 10:12). This provision was unknown in Jewish society except in exceptional cases, such as for royalty.

(5) Jesus' original proclamation, and the Markan and Q traditions that preserve it, indicates by its form that the man who divorced his wife is guilty of adultery. The pre-Matthean tradition had already reformulated this to fit the more traditional Jewish view that only the woman would be guilty of adultery (when she remarried), but preserves Jesus' charging the man with adultery by making him responsible for the woman's (subsequent) adultery (Matt 5:32).

(6) The whole stream of Christian interpretation has as its point of departure not the allowance of divorce, assumed by the Old Testament, but its absolute prohibition as initially proclaimed by Jesus. In this stream of tradition emanating from Jesus, marriage and the family are not a contractual arrangement regulated by law, but a part of the structure of creation itself, the good gift of God to humanity, and, therefore, not at human disposal. Matthew himself functions as a scribal interpreter of the whole tradition by including both the original demand of Jesus and both forms of its interpretation—the Jewish form here and the Gentile form in 19:3-12. He then adds the exception clause to both forms, allowing him to understand the teaching against divorce as another instance of his threefold pattern: Jesus (a) reaffirms the Law that had regulated the evil

of divorce by (b) radicalizing it, outlawing divorce entirely, then (c) built in a situational application for Jesus' radical demand by including one exception.

The exception clause has evoked much discussion; the following points may help to clarify Matthew's meaning. Despite the legal-sounding form, Jesus is not offering a new Law. Of the six antitheses, this one has been most often interpreted literally and legalistically, but such an interpretation misunderstands the nature of Jesus' teaching in the Sermon on the Mount and its relation to the Law (see above). Just as the preceding antitheses cannot be turned into law, so also is the case for those concerning divorce. Matthew does not offer a new casuistry but gives a model for creative affirmation and application of the radical demand of the will of God as proclaimed by Jesus. By including an exception clause, Matthew has in principle indicated that if there is one exception, there can be others. He does not attempt to prescribe what these might be but illustrates the fact that Jesus' teaching must be interpreted from case to case, without establishing a rigid law that makes an exception in only one case.

The exception clause itself can be understood in three ways, depending on whether *porneia* is taken to mean "fornication," "incest," or "adultery." (a) Although *porneia* can be distinguished from *moicheia* (as in 15:19), "fornication" is ruled out as the meaning here by the fact that a married woman is involved. (b) Likewise, *porneia* can mean "incest," as in 1 Cor 5:1. In the light of Acts 15:20, 29, several exegetes have argued that the term refers to what Jewish tradition considered incest on the basis of Leviticus 17–18—i.e., marriage within degrees of kinship prohibited by Jewish law but acceptable in the Gentile world. The exception would then in Matthew's situation refer to married Gentile couples admitted to the church but whose marriage was considered a violation of Jewish law. In this interpretation, such marriages could (or must?) be dissolved by divorce. Matthew is seen as a representative of conservative Jewish Christianity, approaching the matter legalistically and casuistically, intent on the legality of dissolving such marriages despite the prohibition of divorce (cf. Ezra 9–10). This is a very problematical interpretation in the light of

---

140. One Qumram text, 11QTemple 57:17-19, may provide evidence that divorce was forbidden by the Qumran sect, but the interpretation is disputed.

the preceding antitheses. (c) The most common interpretation—and the one supported here—is to understand *porneia* to mean adultery, since this is the most natural meaning of the word in the context, the issue uniting all of 5:27-32 being obedience to the command against adultery. An additional argument is that only if it is so understood does it fit the Matthean pattern we have delineated in all of the first set of antitheses.

5:33-48, Three Antitheses for the Disciples' Application. 5:33-37, Love Is Unconditionally Truthful. This antithesis is entirely M tradition and Matthean composition, with no parallels in the Gospel tradition. The similar saying in Jas 5:12, not dependent on Matthew, indicates that both Matthew and James derived the saying from an older tradition. Since there is no precedent in Judaism for the absolute prohibition of oaths, and since their complete rejection does not correspond to the practice of early Christianity, the core of the saying, which corresponds to his radical ethics, very probably goes back to Jesus.[141]

Matthew has formulated the material into an antithesis. It begins his second set of three, marked off from the first set by the introductory "again" (πάλιν *palin*), by the full introductory formula corresponding to 5:21, by changes in the formulation of Jesus' antithetical statement, and by the absence of the third element in the Matthean structure, the "situational application."

Matthew stands in the tradition of the HB and Judaism, sharing their horror of the misuse of language (see, e.g., 12:36-37, an M saying). Thus Judaism continued and elaborated the system of oaths and vows developed in the Old Testament to guarantee (some) words as especially true. The Mishnah has an entire tractate on oaths (*Shebuoth*) and another on vows (*Nedarim*). In both the Gentile and the Jewish worlds, an oath invoked the deity to guarantee the truth of what was said, or to punish the one taking the oath if what was affirmed was not true. Oaths involve communication between two parties, with the name of God (or a valid substitute) invoked as

guarantor. Vows were made directly to God. What was confirmed by an oath had to be true; what was vowed had to be done. This is somewhat analogous to the legal distinction made in United States courts between statements made under oath and other statements that are not. To testify falsely under oath is a crime. Other false statements may be considered morally wrong, but the oath system is considered necessary in order to guarantee the truth of at least some statements, and to tell when guilt has been incurred by falsehood and when not.

The Matthean Jesus formulates an antithesis that summarizes and paraphrases the Old Testament's teaching about oaths (Lev 19:12; Ps 50:14), then rules it out by his command that his followers take no oaths at all. Matthew 5:34*b*-36 is explicitly anti-casuistic (cf. 23:16-21), rejecting oaths that use substitutes for the name of God and those that avoid it altogether. Jesus abolished the distinction between words that must be true and those that must not, between words one is compelled to stand behind and those one must not, and calls for all speech to be truthful. As with divorce, Jesus' original prohibition was absolute, rejecting not only false or unnecessary oaths, but any effort to bolster our statement's claim to truth beyond the bare statement of it. It is a demand for the truthfulness of all our words.

Instructed by the models in the preceding antitheses, Jesus' disciples are called to make their own situational applications as they attempt to be guided by his call to speak the truth (see Commentary on 5:21-32). There may, indeed, be situations when utter candor violates the greatest command of love to God and neighbor, when a lie must to told in the service of love and truth, but Matthew refuses to give legalistic sanction or casuistic examples, casting the disciples on their own theological responsibility.

5:38-42, Love Does Not Retaliate. For the final two antitheses, Matthew returns to the pattern of the Great Sermon in Q, which had a section against retaliation framed by the twice-repeated command "love your enemies" (Luke 6:27-35). Matthew has broken up the material, rearranged it, and reformulated it into the antithesis form, retaining the love command as the goal and climax of the entire section.

The Old Testament does not command revenge,

---

141. In the Hellenistic world, the lax use of oaths was often criticized by both Gentiles and Jews, represented by Philo's complaint against "the evil habit of swearing incessantly and thoughtlessly about ordinary matters" (*On the Decalogue* 92, cf. 84-86; see also his *On the Special Laws*). Josephus's claim that the Essenes rejected oaths (*Jewish Wars* 2.135, 139, 142) seems to have been his misunderstanding now corrected by the Dead Sea Scrolls, which document at least an entrance oath to the community (CD 7.8; 9.9-12; 1QS 5.8; 6.27).

but had sought to curb the tendency to unlimited private revenge (see Gen 4:23-24) by incorporating the *jus talionis* into the institutionalized judicial system (Exod 21:24; Lev 24:20; Deut 19:21). Already prior to Jesus there was a stream of pagan, biblical, and Jewish tradition calling for restraint and opposing revenge.[142] Jesus radicalized this stream of Jewish tradition, which had already mitigated the retaliatory judicial approach. He not only affirmed the thrust of the Law in opposing unlimited revenge, but he called for his disciples to reject absolutely the principle of retaliatory violence as well. The command not to resist the "evil one" is unqualified. Retaliation and its associated violence represent the usurping counterkingdom of Satan, not the kingdom of God, represented by Jesus. "An evildoer" (ὁ πονηρός *ho ponēros*) can in this instance be understood individualistically as the evil individual who is the aggressor, abstractly as evil in general, or cosmically as the Evil One who is the adversary of the kingdom of God. These need not be considered mutually exclusive alternatives. The individual evil ones whom Jesus' disciples must not resist are manifestations of the cosmic kingdom of evil, which pervades the world, usurping God's rightful kingdom/rulership of the world. Thus this antithesis, like the others, is not a matter of commonsense wisdom, but is composed by Matthew in the perspective of the conflict of kingdoms, which pervades his Gospel (see 12:22-37; cf. Excursus "Kingdom of Heaven in Matthew," 288-94). That means that the enemy is seen not merely for what he or she is empirically, but is regarded in the light of the present-and-coming kingdom of God. This perspective takes evil seriously, but does not consider it ultimate. The eschatological kingdom of God, already breaking in with the advent of Jesus, embraces the enemy. Thus Jesus' command not to resist evil goes beyond passive resistance as a strategy. It is positive action in the interest of the aggressor, as the examples immediately show.

Superficially regarded, the five examples seem not to fit together. In the first three (being struck in the face, being sued in court, being requisitioned into short-term compulsory service for the occupying government), a person is victimized by powerful others, while in the last two the balance of power seems to have shifted, and one's help is sought by needy others (beggars, borrowers). From Matthew's perspective the common denominator for the five elements seems to be that they are all examples of aggression and pressure from other people who interfere with one's own selfish pursuits. What is called for is a response in terms of the good and needs of the other, not one's own rights.

In the first, a person has been struck in the face; Matthew adds "right" to Q's "cheek," indicating that it is a backhanded blow, more insult than physical injury. Instead of retaliating, the person is commanded to offer the other cheek.

In the example of verse 40, a court case is portrayed, in which a man is being sued and is literally losing his shirt (the χιτών *chiton* was a long nightshirt-like main garment). The victim is commanded not only to give it willingly, but also to give the cloak (ἱμάτιον *himation*), the toga-like outer garment that could not be legally taken away (Exod 22:25-26; Deut 24:12-13).[143] Since the willing victim ends up nude in the courtroom, here too Jesus' teaching is hardly intended literally. It is a matter of being secure enough in one's acceptance by God to enable one not to insist on one's rights, legal and otherwise, but empowering one to renounce them in the interest of others, a perspective on the life of discipleship also affirmed by Paul (1 Cor 6:1-11; 8:1–10:33; Rom 14:1–15:7).

The third example reflects the Roman practice taken over from the Persians, by which soldiers and government officials could compel citizens of the occupied country to give them directions or carry their equipment a prescribed distance (cf. 27:32, where Simon is compelled to carry Jesus' cross on the way to execution). Rather than resisting the evil government or plotting how to get even, the disciple is commanded to do more than the law requires.[144]

---

142. E.g., Prov 24:29; 1QS 10:18-19 "I will pay to no one the reward of evil; I will pursue the offender with goodness. For judgment of all the living is with God and it is He who will render to all their reward"; *b. Sabb.* 88b: "Our rabbis taught: Those who are insulted but do not insult, hear themselves reviled without answering, act through love and rejoice in suffering."

143. Luke 6:29 is the more original, where it is a matter of a mugging, and the order of the garments is reversed, since the robber begins with the outer and more valuable garments. Matthew's interest in judgment scenes and the influence of Isaiah 58 cause him to shift the setting.

144. Douglas R. A. Hare, *Matthew,* Interpretation (Louisville: Westminster/John Knox, 1993) 57, points out that "mile" (μίλιον *milion*) is the foreign, Roman measure of distance, never used elsewhere in the New Testament, where the local term στάδιον (*stadion*) is found. This sounds foreign to Jesus' and Matthew's audience, as "kilometer" still does in the United States, and is a reminder that the radical ethic of non-resistance applies even in the adverse political situation of an occupying power. "Freedom fighters in the audience must have regarded him as a traitor" (57).

5:43-48, Love Extends to the Enemy.

Matthew had already used some of the Q material for the preceding antithesis, but saved the love commandment for this climactic spot, forming his sixth and final antithesis. Leviticus 19:18 had commanded the love of neighbor, but the context made clear that "neighbor" includes only the fellow Israelite (19:17 "your kin"; both 19:16 and 19:18 place "your people" and "your neighbor" in synonymous parallelism.) There is no command to hate the enemy in the Old Testament, yet there are statements that God "hates all evildoers" (Ps 5:5; cf. 31:6) and statements that imply that others do, and should do, the same (Deut 23:3-7; 30:7; Pss 26:5; 139:21-22). The primary meaning is not aimed at personal vindictiveness or disdain, but at the religious rejection of those who do not belong to God's people and keep God's law. The group of insiders to be loved is constituted by the religious community; outsiders who are "hated" are those who do not belong.[145] This is made explicit in the Qumran community, who held it as a basic tenet of their faith that they were to "love all the children of light and hate all the children of darkness" (1QS 1:9-10; cf. 1:3-4). From a legal point of view, the question thus became how far the definition of *neighbor* must be extended (cf. Luke 10:25-29, 30-37). Judaism should not be caricatured as though it was always narrow and exclusive; there were elements and tendencies toward love for all peoples, including enemies.[146]

The Matthean Jesus makes love of God and neighbor the fundamental command on which all else depends (see 22:34-40 on the meaning of ἀγάπη *agapē*), and makes the command to love enemies specific and concrete. In its absoluteness and concreteness, it is without parallel in paganism or Judaism. The command should not be understood abstractly, "love all people, including even enemies." In Jesus' situation it referred particularly to the occupying Roman forces, and thus to national enemies as well as to competing religious groups and personal enemies. For Matthew

the focal instance was the concrete situation of the persecuted Matthean community. But such a concrete point of orientation then has the effect of making love universal.

Jesus bases the command not on a humanitarian ideal, a doctrine of human rights, or a strategy or utilitarian purpose (to win the enemy over) but (a) only on his authority to set his own command in juxtaposition to the Law (5:43), (b) on the nature of God who loves all impartially (5:45), and (c) on the promise of eschatological reward (5:46). The idea of reward is not mere selfishness, but a dimension of Jesus' fundamental proclamation of the present and coming kingdom as the basis for the radical life-style to which he calls his disciples. Thus "that you may be sons [υἱοί *huioi*] of your Father in heaven" also represents Matthew's inaugurated eschatology: Your conduct must be appropriate to your status as sons/children of God, which you already are (6:4, 6; cf. v. 18), and which will be revealed and acknowledged by God at the last judgment (cf. 5:9).

"Tax collectors" refers to the paid underlings of the Roman tax contractors. They were generally considered dishonest and were despised by the loyal Jewish population because of their unpatriotic job, and by the strictly religious because their work brought them into constant contact with Gentiles and thus rendered them ceremonially unclean. Although Jesus is presented as a friend of tax collectors and sinners (see 9:11; 11:19), and although Matthew's church includes Gentiles (28:18-20), he retains some of the vocabulary of the older Jewish-Christian tradition that disdained tax collectors and Gentiles—now understood not ethnically but as typical unbelievers.

What is the meaning of the troublesome *be perfect* in verse 48? In the Gospels, these words are used only by Matthew, who has changed Q's "merciful," preserved in the Lukan version in 6:36, just as he has inserted it into the Markan text in 19:21. It is thus not a problematic word he seeks to dilute, but a word he chose to sum up Jesus' demand in 5:21-48. Neither here nor in 19:21 does it express a two-level ethic, with "perfection" only for the elite, but is the command of Jesus to every disciple. While *perfect* should not be diluted for the comfort of the disciples, neither should it be understood in the Greek sense of absolute moral perfection, an impossible

---

145. *Hate* in biblical parlance does not necessarily imply personal hostility, but may mean "not choose; consider an outsider" (cf. Matt 6:24; Luke 14:26; Rom 9:13).

146. Cf., e.g., Prov 25:21; Jonah 4:10-11; *m. 'Abot* 1:12; 2:11; 4:3; for other examples see W. D. Davies and Dale C. Allison, Jr., *A Critical and Exegetical Commentary on the Gospel According to Saint Matthew*, 2 vols., ICC (Edinburgh: T. & T. Clark, 1988-91) 1:551-52.

ideal for human beings to attain. Contrary to the Greek abstract ideal of perfection, of being untarnished by concrete involvement in the material world, for Matthew it is precisely amid the relativities and ambiguities of concrete action in this world, which is God's creation despite its fallenness, that the disciple is called to be perfect. Nor does Matthew understand perfection in the Qumran legalistic sense of keeping all the laws of the community, an externally attainable goal that still leaves operating room for one's own selfish will. Matthew takes the word from his Bible (the LXX uses it often), particularly from texts such as Deut 18:13: "You shall be perfect before the Lord your God." The biblical word is תמים (tāmîm), which means "wholeness." To be perfect is to serve God wholeheartedly, to be single-minded in devotion to the one God, just as God is one, the ethical stance appropriate to a monotheistic faith (cf. Deut 6:4-6). It is the kind of living called for in all the antitheses, and it is their appropriate summary, corresponding to the "pure in heart" of 5:8.

REFLECTIONS

1. Modern Christians sometimes read New Testament commands that their church does not practice (foot washing, John 13:1-15; holy kisses, Rom 16:16; 1 Cor 16:20; fasting, Mark 2:20; exclusion of women from leadership, 1 Cor 14:33b-36; absolute prohibition of divorce Mark 10:2-12; etc.), and are perplexed by their own question (not merely the criticism of outsiders), "What does it mean that the Bible says 'do this' but our church, which claims to 'believe the Bible,' does not do it?" The prefatory declaration of 5:17 is a preemptive strike at what some Christian readers might think when they read 5:21-48, and as they reflect on the fact that their church simply no longer practices some of the clear commands of the Bible: circumcision, the food laws, animal sacrifice, (the Sabbath?). Jesus' clear "I have not come to abolish the Law" is directed both to those who *fear* that the new freedom of Christian faith has rejected the Bible and to those who (in their misunderstanding) *celebrate* that this is the case.

2. The reader of Matthew has also wondered, from the first scene on, how a righteous man such as Joseph could be commended for already having decided to act contrary to the Law (see 1:18-25). In 5:20 Matthew again introduces his focal "righteousness"/"justice" (δικαιοσύνη *dikaiosynē*). The Great Sermon in Q had been oriented to "love" (ἀγάπη *agapē*), also considered central by Matthew, but it contains no references to righteousness. Matthew has added five texts dealing with *dikaiosynē*, thereby shifting the orientation of the Sermon on the Mount to righteousness as doing the will of God (5:6, 10, 20; 6:1, 33). The disciples' righteousness is not adherence to an ideal standard, but is to be the righteousness of the eschatological community that lives in the conviction that the kingdom has already dawned in the advent of Jesus and lives with the prayer for and in the light of the coming kingdom of God. Their righteousness must, therefore, manifest that eschatological abundance characteristic of the messianic times. The demand does not remain general and abstract, but is immediately explicated and made concrete.

3. In 5:21-26, we can see the interplay between the vision of the kingdom of heaven and the practical ways that this kingdom is to be lived out in Christian community. The first half of the passage (5:21-22) says, in effect, that all anger and hostility are outside the bounds of God's kingdom. The second half of the passage (5:23-26) admits that Christians get angry and suffer through broken relationships, and tells us what to do when that reality occurs.

The difference between the two halves of the passage, between the vision and the practice, is not a matter of hypocrisy, but of promise and hope. A loving parent would say to a child, "I love and cherish you. Every good gift I know how to give is yours. I promise that nothing will ever change my devotion to you. Now, go into the rough and tumble of the world and live out this blessing." Just so, Jesus announces the good gift of God, a world where anger has no place, where destructive human relationships cannot endure, and then says, "Now, go into the rough and tumble of the world and live out what is already true about you."

4. In the area of sexual ethics, above all others, we hear "No one has any right to say anything to me about *this.* It is entirely my own personal business" (sometimes with the codicil "so long as it is not hurting anyone else"). The Sermon on the Mount proceeds from other presuppositions: (a) Our sexuality, like all else, is a gift of God, not our private possession to dispose of as we will. (b) Right and wrong are not a matter of individual decision, but of the revealed will of God. (c) My sex life does involve others, and may hurt them even if I am unaware of it. (d) There are orders or structures of human life established by God into which my individual life should fit, including sexual and family structures. (This is what the church has attempted to say in defining marriage as a sacrament.) (e) Even so, matters of right and wrong cannot be handled prescriptively, legalistically, casuistically, but go to the roots of human life in the heart and intentions.

5. The distinctive element in Jesus' ethic and the Sermon on the Mount has sometimes been described as Jesus' relocation of ethics "in the heart," using the external practices of "Jewish legalism" as the foil. This is historically incorrect and a slander on Judaism. There are Old Testament, Jewish, and pagan parallels to the "inwardness" of the Christian ethic—e.g., "I have made a covenant with my eyes;/ how then could I look upon a virgin?" (Job 31:1 NRSV). Eliezer ben Hyrcanus, a rabbi contemporary with Matthew, wrote: "The one who hates his neighbor, behold, belongs to those who shed blood."[147] Other parallels include: "A man who counts out money for a woman from his hand into hers or from her hand into his, in order that he might look at her will not be free from the judgment of Gehenna, even if he is [in other respects] like our master Moses";[148] "What is a crime for a person to do, is a crime for a person to think";[149] "As it is a sin to betray one's country, to use violence to one's parents, to rob a temple, where the offense lies in the result of the act, so the passions of fear, grief, and lust are sins, even when no extraneous result ensues."[150]

Many of the precepts of the Sermon on the Mount have parallels in the teaching of rabbinic Judaism as well.[151] The fundamentally distinctive element in the Sermon on the Mount is not items of content, but its christological and eschatological perspective on life in the light of the dawning kingdom of God.

6. These commands of Jesus must be taken with the utmost seriousness, but any attempt to take them literally as casuistic laws leads to absurdity. Obeyed, literally, 5:40 results in public nudity and arrest. The literal practice of these injunctions would result in anarchy and the multiplication of all the evil held in check by the legal system, a system that in our fallen world operates by violence or the threat of violence. Literal obedience can also result in suffering and oppression for those one is charged to love and protect. The sayings picture two-party transactions and challenge disciples to be willing to give up their own rights and even suffer violence at the hands of others rather than retaliating. Cases are not covered in which this line of non-action results in the injury or death of others. This alone shows that

---

147. *Derek Erez* 10 in Hermann L. Strack and Paul Billerbeck, *Kommentar zum Neuen Testament aus Talmud und Midrasch* (Munich: Beck, 1922–61) 1:282.
148. Baraita *Erubin* 18b; English translation p. 125.
149. Aristotle *Magna Moralia.*
150. Cicero *De Finibus Bon. et Mal.* 3.9.92.
151. For additional parallels, see Klaus Berger, M. Eugene Boring, and Carsten Colpe, *Hellenistic Commentary to the New Testament* (Nashville: Abingdon, 1995); and Morton Smith, *Tannaitic Parallels to the Gospels,* JBLMS 6 (Philadelphia: Society of Biblical Literature, 1951). See also the critique by Jacob Neusner, *Are There Really Tannaitic Parallels to the Gospels? A Refutation of Morton Smith* (Atlanta: Scholars Press, 1993).

the whole instruction is not casuistic. The sayings do not call for obedience to an abstract law to which the concrete good of others can be sacrificed. When it is a matter of protecting the weak and oppressed and setting aside the structures of injustice, disciples of Christ must, in fact, be ready to resist evil. But it is a different matter when disciples are called to set aside their own rights for the good of others. Yet not all of these objections and qualifications, which have been made many times, are to be understood as a rejection or domestication of these radical commands, or as a means of getting around them. Such considerations do not mean that these commands must be diluted or rejected, but that attempts at legalistic literal obedience are misunderstandings—as though they were new laws to be obeyed literally.

7. Although not given on an institutional level (Jesus does not legislate for worldly courts) but for the private lives of disciples, these commands still have implications for the involvement of these private lives in the public and political decisions for which Christians are responsible. These sayings indicate that Jesus himself must have resisted the militaristic tendencies of those who opposed Rome and who finally plunged the nation into a catastrophic war (66–70 CE). In preserving these sayings and making them the climax of his anthitheses, Matthew takes his stand with those who had resisted the catastrophic attempt at a "military solution," which he and his church had lived through.

8. None of this is a matter of strategy. To turn the other cheek is not to shame the opponent or win him or her over, to cause the enemy to repent. Going the extra mile is not a matter of prudence calculated to keep a low profile when you do not have power and need to "get along."[152] These sayings express the inherent rule of the kingdom of God, are God's ultimate way of dealing with humanity exhibited in the life and death of Jesus, who went to the cross. All such hermeneutical considerations are not a matter of watering them down, finding a meaning that does seem reasonable and with which we can live. They are not to be made "reasonable," for they violate the "common sense" of this world and point to another reality. They ask us whether we are oriented to the God who has redefined power and kingship in the life, ministry, death, and resurrection of Jesus of Nazareth.

152. See Luise Schottroff, "Non-Violence and the Love of One's Enemies," in *Essays on the Love Commandment,* ed. Reginald Fuller (Philadelphia: Fortress, 1978) 9-40.

MATTHEW 6:1-18, THE TEMPLE SERVICE

NIV

6 "Be careful not to do your 'acts of righteousness' before men, to be seen by them. If you do, you will have no reward from your Father in heaven.

[2]"So when you give to the needy, do not announce it with trumpets, as the hypocrites do in the synagogues and on the streets, to be honored by men. I tell you the truth, they have received their reward in full. [3]But when you give to the needy, do not let your left hand know what your right hand is doing, [4]so that your giving may be in secret. Then your Father, who sees what is done in secret, will reward you."

NRSV

6 "Beware of practicing your piety before others in order to be seen by them; for then you have no reward from your Father in heaven.

2"So whenever you give alms, do not sound a trumpet before you, as the hypocrites do in the synagogues and in the streets, so that they may be praised by others. Truly I tell you, they have received their reward. [3]But when you give alms, do not let your left hand know what your right hand is doing, [4]so that your alms may be done in secret; and your Father who sees in secret will reward you.[a]"

[a]Other ancient authorities add *openly*

NIV

5"And when you pray, do not be like the hypocrites, for they love to pray standing in the synagogues and on the street corners to be seen by men. I tell you the truth, they have received their reward in full. 6But when you pray, go into your room, close the door and pray to your Father, who is unseen. Then your Father, who sees what is done in secret, will reward you. 7And when you pray, do not keep on babbling like pagans, for they think they will be heard because of their many words. 8Do not be like them, for your Father knows what you need before you ask him.

9"This, then, is how you should pray:
" 'Our Father in heaven,
hallowed be your name,
10your kingdom come,
your will be done
on earth as it is in heaven.
11Give us today our daily bread.
12Forgive us our debts,
as we also have forgiven our debtors.
13And lead us not into temptation,
but deliver us from the evil one.*a*'

14For if you forgive men when they sin against you, your heavenly Father will also forgive you. 15But if you do not forgive men their sins, your Father will not forgive your sins.

16"When you fast, do not look somber as the hypocrites do, for they disfigure their faces to show men they are fasting. I tell you the truth, they have received their reward in full. 17But when you fast, put oil on your head and wash your face, 18so that it will not be obvious to men that you are fasting, but only to your Father, who is unseen; and your Father, who sees what is done in secret, will reward you."

a13 Or from evil; some late manuscripts one, / for yours is the kingdom and the power and the glory forever. Amen.

NRSV

5"And whenever you pray, do not be like the hypocrites; for they love to stand and pray in the synagogues and at the street corners, so that they may be seen by others. Truly I tell you, they have received their reward. 6But whenever you pray, go into your room and shut the door and pray to your Father who is in secret; and your Father who sees in secret will reward you.*a*

7"When you are praying, do not heap up empty phrases as the Gentiles do; for they think that they will be heard because of their many words. 8Do not be like them, for your Father knows what you need before you ask him.

9"Pray then in this way:
Our Father in heaven,
hallowed be your name.
10 Your kingdom come.
Your will be done,
on earth as it is in heaven.
11 Give us this day our daily bread.*b*
12 And forgive us our debts,
as we also have forgiven our debtors.
13 And do not bring us to the time of trial,*c*
but rescue us from the evil one.*d*

14For if you forgive others their trespasses, your heavenly Father will also forgive you; 15but if you do not forgive others, neither will your Father forgive your trespasses.

16"And whenever you fast, do not look dismal, like the hypocrites, for they disfigure their faces so as to show others that they are fasting. Truly I tell you, they have received their reward. 17But when you fast, put oil on your head and wash your face, 18so that your fasting may be seen not by others but by your Father who is in secret; and your Father who sees in secret will reward you.*a*"

aOther ancient authorities add openly bOr our bread for tomorrow cOr us into temptation   dOr from evil. Other ancient authorities add, in some form, For the kingdom and the power and the glory are yours forever. Amen.

COMMENTARY

With this unit we move to the second major section, the Instruction (cf. above on structure of the Sermon on the Mount). The tradition in this section is derived from M, with insertions of material also found in Q (6:9-13) and Mark (6:14-15). This section has no points of contact with

Q's Great Sermon, which Matthew has abandoned and will not resume until 7:1 (Luke 6:37).

If 6:7-15 is extracted, the remainder comprises three units composed almost exactly parallel to one another, with each having a negative and a positive section:

I. "When you . . . "(pl.)..........2a	5a	16a	
"do not . . ." do what the			
"hypocrites" do (pl.)..........2b-c	5b-c	16b-c	
"so that they may be			
praised/seen by human			
beings" 2d	5d	16d	
"Amen I say to you (pl.),			
they have received their			
reward" 2e	5e	16e	
II. Positive command to disciples			
(sg.) 3	6a-b	17	
"so that" + infinitive (sg.) .4a	6c	18a	
"And the Father who sees			
in secret will reward			
you" (sg.)...........................4b	6d	18b	

Verbs addressing the disciples are plural in the first, negative part and singular in the second, positive part.[153] This symmetrical structure is interrupted by the insertion of the unit on prayer (6:7-15), which itself is composed of three units to correspond to the triadic structure into which it is inserted. Since Matthew must be responsible for the insertion, the three units must have belonged to Matthean tradition. They were formulated in pre-Matthean Jewish Christianity, possibly including some authentic words of the historical Jesus, and had become sacred tradition in Matthew's church and influenced his own theology and vocabulary. Matthew has incorporated them almost intact, adding only 6:1 as a heading for the whole section.

6:1-4, Giving to Charity. 6:1.
This is the thematic heading that embraces the religious practices of almsgiving, prayer, and fasting, taken over by the church from Judaism under the common designation δικαιοσύνη (*dikaiosynē*; translated "righteousness/justice" in the preceding passage, but in this text often translated "piety"). There is no command to observe these religious practices; it is assumed that Jesus' disciples will continue to make these fundamental elements of Jewish practice part of their own lives.

By means of this heading, Matthew links this section thematically to the preceding one (cf. the similar thematic head in 5:20 for the following six examples of the "greater righteousness"). This also shows that he makes no distinction between devotion to God, expressed in acts of worship (6:1-18), and acts of personal integrity, justice, and love directed to human beings (5:20-48), *all* of which are called *dikaiosynē*.

In all three examples, this heading makes clear that the point of contrast between "the hypocrites'" behavior and that required of the disciples is not the contrast between public and private worship (Matthew affirms both),[154] nor the contrast between external and interior behavior (again, Matthew affirms both), but the contrast of motivations: the affirmation and applause of human beings, or the "reward" of being accepted by God.[155]

The word for "hypocrites" is a neutral term in Greek, literally meaning "stage actors," and is here applied metaphorically to those who perform their religious acts with an eye on the human grandstand. It should not be generalized to mean "the Jews," nor should this passage be used to contrast Jewish worship with Christian. Similar biting critiques of ostentatious acts of piety performed for human approval are found in contemporary Jewish writings along with similar praise for those who avoid such ostentation and seek only God's approval—e.g., "He who gives alms in secret is greater than Moses our teacher" (*B. Bat.* 6b).

6:2-3. The contrast is described in striking metaphors, neither of which is literal. Contrary to a popular explanation, there is no evidence that in the synagogue worship trumpets were sounded to call attention to the presentation of large gifts, but the meaning of this provocative metaphorical caricature is transparent. Nor is it literally possible for one hand to be unaware of what the other is doing. The emphasis is on doing one's religious duty to God—here, helping the poor—in such a manner that only God sees.

---

153. The verbs in 6:2 are singular, while the corresponding 5a and 16a are plurals. This minor formal disruption in the first unit was apparently caused by Matthew's adding the heading 6:1 with the plural.

154. Contrast *Gospel of Thomas* 14, which makes Jesus the opponent of all religious acts in the interest of the individual "spirit": "Jesus said to them, 'If you fast, you will bring sin upon yourselves, and if you pray, you will be condemned, and if you give to charity, you will harm your spirits.'"

155. The NRSV, seeking to make the language inclusive (contrast NIV's "men"), translates "others," which is open to the misunderstanding that the contrast is between "self" and "others." But the contrast is between conduct directed toward God and toward human applause.

The tension between this repeated note of privacy and even secrecy in doing good works, and the command to do them "before others" in 5:16, is somewhat relieved by the difference in motivation in each case. Yet the tension remains. Despite the differing motivations, in 5:16 people see the good works, and they should; in 6:3-4 the good works are not to be seen, regardless of motive. The tension is partly the result of Matthew's incorporating two different traditions, but is primarily due to the mode in which scribal wisdom functions (cf. Reflections on 5:16).

6:4. "Openly," found in the KJV, was added by some scribes in later manuscripts, and was read by some of the early versions and the Church Fathers, but is not found in ℵ, B, D, f^1, f^{13}, and is certainly not original. The promised reward is eschatological. God will reward with acceptance into the kingdom of God and the granting of eternal life. This-worldly reward for discipleship is not in Matthew's perspective.

6:5-15, Prayer. The tradition that came to Matthew had a unit on prayer in precisely the same form as the units on almsgiving and fasting. Matthew expands the central unit on prayer (6:5-6)—which he may have editorially relocated to make it the central unit—by adding the contrast between "Gentile" prayer and the authentic prayer of his disciples (vv. 7-8), the Lord's Prayer (vv. 9-13), and the condition of forgiveness (vv. 14-15), thus making the section on prayer the structural and theological center of the Sermon on the Mount, with the Lord's Prayer the core of this center (cf. "Structure" above).

6:5-6. This passage parallels vv. 1-4 and 16-18 and, by means of another provocative metaphorical picture, rejects ostentatious praying aimed at applause from a human audience and commands that prayer be directed to God alone. This shows that for Matthew prayer was not understood psychologically, for its effect on the one praying and those who hear it, but like all worship is God-centered and understood as an objectively real event in which God hears the worshiper.

Through the centuries Christian interpreters have sometimes taken the ostentatious and insincere practices here described to be typical of Jewish prayer in general. This is a grave and slanderous mistake. Jewish literature likewise contains similar criticisms of pretentious and hypo-

critical praying.[156] The hypocrites called attention to themselves as religious people by praying ostentatiously in the synagogue or on the street corners. Public prayer in the synagogue was normal; the synagogue was the house of prayer. Praying on street corners was not normal, nor was it necessary. As in the preceding unit against ostentatious giving of alms, it is not the act itself that is condemned, but the motive in performing for the applause of a human audience. Jesus does not here legislate against public community prayer, in which he expects the church to engage (18:19-20), otherwise he would have called for the abolition of the whole institution of Temple and synagogue. Rather, he commands that prayer be made to God alone. This is the meaning of going to the inner room or shed (KJV, "closet" [ταμεῖον *tameion*]), away from public view, to address only God in prayer. Prayer does not require a holy place, but is sanctified when addressed to God in a storeroom. As elsewhere in this section, the direction is not intended literally—one can also ostentatiously call attention to going to the inner room to pray.

6:7-8. In this addition to the tradition (see above), authentic prayer is contrasted not only with hypocrites in the synagogue but with perverse Gentile practice.[157] The "many words" of pagan prayer refers not merely to their length. The Greek word βατταλογέω (*battalogeō*) is obscure, absent from the LXX and used only here in the New Testament.[158] It may refer to the invocation of many gods; to the ritual repetition of prayer formulas; to empty, insincere talk; or to glossolalia. All such speaking supposes that one must impress or gain the attention of the deity or use the correct formula in order to ensure the effectiveness of the prayer, and thus understands prayer to be a manipulative function for the self-interest of the one praying. In contrast, Matthew

---

156. Cf. the discussion in E. P. Sanders, *Paul and Palestinian Judaism* (Philadelphia: Fortress, 1977) 107-10. Among his examples: The size of the offering does not matter; all are called "an odor of sweet savor," which teaches us "that it is all one whether a man offers much or little, if only he directs his mind toward Heaven [God]" (*Menaḥ* 13:11). Likewise, the scholar who studies much is not superior to his fellow, the common manual laborer, provided the latter "directs his heart to Heaven" (*Ber.* 17a). In much the same way it is said that the one who prays must "direct his heart" to heaven (*Ber.* 3.4).

157. There are good examples of noble, non-manipulative Gentile prayers, which Matthew does not here take into account. Cf., for example, the prayer of Cleanthes, part of which is quoted approvingly in Acts 17:28.

158. It is found in one manuscript, D, of Luke 11:2.

pictures Christians praying as an expression of trust in a God who knows our needs before we ask. Asking, then, is not a matter of informing or manipulating the deity, but of aligning ourselves in trust and acknowledging our need.

6:9-13, The Lord's Prayer. Over against such prayer, Matthew presents the Lord's Prayer as a pattern for the disciples. It has been relocated by Matthew to become the very center of the Sermon on the Mount, structurally and theologically (cf. Outline).

The Lord's Prayer was apparently a constituent part of Q (cf. Luke 11:2-4) and had been a part of the Matthean community's tradition and liturgy from its earliest days. The prayer consists of an address and two sets of three petitions. The first set of petitions has a certain rhythm and even rhyme, since they all begin with a third person imperative (-θήτω -thētō) and end with "your(s)" (σου sou). Each member of the second set contains a form of the word for "we" (ἡμεῖς hēmeis), known as the three "we petitions." Despite its context indicating private prayer, the pronouns that refer to human beings are in the plural throughout, indicating communal, corporate prayer. The prayer has formal similarities with other Jewish prayers current in the first century, especially the Kaddish and the Eighteen Benedictions, but the present form is due to Matthew and his community.

We can trace the history of the tradition of the prayer from the time of Jesus through Matthew to our own time:

(1) Jewish prayers of the first century addressed God as "Our Father," prayed for the hallowing of God's name and the coming of God's kingdom, and had other points of contact with the Lord's Prayer.

(2) Reflecting his own Jewish faith and background, Jesus taught his disciples a model prayer, originally in Aramaic, the common language of the people, not the Hebrew of official synagogue liturgy. This fact is indicated both by the use of אבא ('ābbā'), which apparently stood behind the original "Father" (πάτερ pater; see Commentary on 6:9), and by the use of "debts" (חבה ḥôbâ) instead of "sins," which was possible only in Aramaic. Jesus' original prayer was both in continuity with Jewish prayers and was distinguished from them—e.g., by its brevity and distinctive use

of *abba*. There is no (explicit) christology, nor anything un-Jewish about the prayer, which can serve as an ecumenical prayer shared by both Jews and Christians.

(3) This prayer was translated into Greek and preserved in Q. The short Q form reconstructed from the common elements in Matthew and Luke is very close to the original prayer of Jesus.

(4) Luke slightly adapted this prayer from his Q source for his Gentile church and incorporated it in his Gospel in 11:2-4.

(5) The Matthean church, founded by messengers of the Q community, had received the prayer as part of Q from its very beginning. In the course of a generation of use in the liturgy, it was slightly expanded and nuanced to correspond to the Jewish Christianity of Matthew's church.[159]

(6) The author of the Gospel of Matthew was deeply influenced by this prayer and its dominant themes (God as Father, the coming kingdom of God, doing the will of God, the need for receiving divine forgiveness and practicing human forgiveness), and incorporated it as the generative nucleus of the Sermon on the Mount, which he constructed from traditional sayings of Jesus.

(7) The Matthean form of the Lord's Prayer became dominant in the history of the church. In the Vulgate and the liturgy of the Roman Catholic mass, it formed the focus of the worship and prayer life of the church for more than a thousand years.

(8) When the Bible was translated into English, the forms of the Lord's Prayer in the dominant translations shaped the liturgy of the church and private devotion. The original Anglican Prayer Book adopted the translation of the Wycliffe (c. 1380), Tyndale (1526), and Coverdale (1535) Bibles: "Forgive us our trespasses, as we forgive those who trespass against us." This form became common in English-speaking countries in both Roman Catholic and Protestant settings, despite the presence of the alternate translation "Forgive us our debts as we forgive our debtors" in the KJV, which replaced the earlier translations as the primary translation of American Protestantism.

(9) As the English language evolves, minor changes are made in modern translations in order

---

159. The fact that the early church slightly elaborated and expanded the prayer is clear from comparing the Matthean version with the Lukan one (Luke 11:2-4), and from the expanded doxology in many MSS. Most scholars, however, consider the Q version to be substantially identical to Jesus' original prayer.

to continue to express the original meaning of the prayer in contemporary English. Since there is no uniform pattern of adopting contemporary English translations into the church's liturgy and private devotions, many people continue to pray using the version they have become accustomed to (e.g., "trespasses" vs. "debts") with the result that the wording of older English translations lives on in the life of the church.

6:9. Jesus' original invocation was to "Father" (as in Luke 11:2). "In heaven" represents the Matthean church's accommodation to the liturgical usage. In the first century both Jews and Greeks commonly addressed God as "Father." The common synagogue invocation was "our Father, our King" (אבנו מלכנו *'ābēnû malkēnû*). Jesus reflects this Jewish practice, with his own distinctive adaptation. It was characteristic of Jesus to pray to God simply as *abba,* which stands behind the simple Greek *pater* and is occasionally left untranslated (Mark 14:36; Rom 8:15; Gal 4:6). *Abba* is not only a child's term of endearment, like *Papa, Mama,* and *Dada,* but was also used by adult children in addressing their fathers.[160] It connotes the intimate personal relation of Jesus to God. For Jesus and Matthew, *Father* was not a general term for the deity, but was first of all Jesus' word for his own relation to God. He then included his disciples, and then human beings as such in this relationship. As children of the one God, they are "brothers and sisters" not only of one another but also of Jesus, sharing his personal relationship with God. *Father,* for Jesus, means the one who loves, forgives, and knows how to give good gifts to his children (7:11; Luke 15:11-32). This word for God and its associated imagery are very important to Matthew, as it is for the other Evangelists, especially the author of the Fourth Gospel. Father language dominates not only this section (6:1, 4, 6, 8, 9, 14, 15, 18), but is also found often elsewhere in the Sermon on

the Mount (5:16, 45, 48; 6:26, 32; 7:11, 21) and in the remainder of the Gospel. Matthew and the Matthean Jesus can also use other images for God, including feminine images, but the centrality of the father image in Matthew's theology and its basis in the teaching of Jesus should not be obscured.[161]

6:9b-10, Three "Thou" Petitions. Like all authentic worship, the Lord's Prayer is God-centered. It begins not with human needs and desires, but with the honor of God as God. The first three petitions are not for three separate items, but for the eschatological event in which God's name will be hallowed, God's kingdom will come, and the will of God will be done.[162] Thus all three are aspects of the central focus of Jesus' proclamation, the coming of the kingdom of God. (See Excursus "Kingdom of Heaven in Matthew," 288-94.) Each petition is primarily eschatological, with an impact on the present that calls for corresponding action. Even the address "Father" is eschatological, since the declaration of the disciples' "sonship" is a matter of future revelation at the last judgment, although already experienced in the present (cf. 5:9 and the similar theology of Rom 8:18-21).

"Hallowed be your name." A name in the biblical world was not a mere label, but represented the reality and presence of the person. *Hallow* means to honor as holy. The initial petition is that God will be honored as God, the Holy One. It is not a pious wish, but a prayer for a specific eschatological act of God (cf. Ezek 36:23-33). The prayer is intimate and direct, but not chummy. It preserves the awesome holiness of God and prays for it to be acknowledged by all.

"Your kingdom come." The eschatological nature of the whole prayer is focused in this one petition, which sums it up. Yet, as in each of the petitions, there is also a present dimension. For Jesus and his disciples, the kingdom was not only a future reality at the end of the world, but a present experience. (See Excursus "Kingdom of Heaven in Matthew," 288-94.) The prayer acknowledges that God is God and that God is finally responsible for bringing in God's rule, but

---

160. The view that Jesus' use of *abba* was absolutely unique, that it would have been scandalous to other Jews, and that it expressed his own christological consciousness as the unique Son of God, which he then conferred on his disciples, was advocated especially by Joachim Jeremias in numerous works, e.g., *The Prayers of Jesus,* SBT, 2nd Series 6 (Naperville, Ill.: Alec R. Allenson, 1967). This is now often considered too extreme a statement. Cf., e.g., Mary Rose D'Angelo, *"Abba* and 'Father': Imperial Theology and the Jesus Traditions," *JBL* 111 (1992) 611-30. If Jesus' usage was not absolutely unique or able to carry all the christological weight claimed by Jeremias, it was distinctive enough to make a profound impression on the early church, which preserved his practice even in Greek (Mark 14:36; Gal 4:6; Rom 8:15).

161. See Jouette Bassler, "God in the NT," *ABD* 2:1049-1055.

162. Cf. the eschatological beatitudes, which are not nine different statements, but nine statements of one theme. The Lord's Prayer is not a miscellaneous list of unrelated petitions, but two sets of three petitions all praying for the realization of God's kingdom.

one cannot pray this prayer without committing one's own will and action to fulfilling the will of God in the present and praying that other people will submit themselves to God's rule in the here and now (cf. 6:10*b* and 26:41). For Christians, submitting oneself to God's rule includes becoming disciples of Jesus the Christ.

"Your will be done." Rather than mythological pictures attempting to portray the meaning of "kingdom of God," the prayer expresses the content of the expression as doing God's will. Just as God's will is already done in heaven, so also at the consummation all creation will actualize the will of God. The kingdom image is (re-)uniting, bringing the rebellious earth back under the rightful sovereignty of the Creator. Thus heaven/earth corresponds to the already/not-yet nature of the kingdom. The statement "thy will be done," from the liturgy of the Matthean church, became very important to Matthew, who made it a theme of his Gospel. Jesus prays this prayer in Gethsemane (26:42, also peculiar to Matthew).

6:11-13, Three "We" Petitions. "Bread." The seemingly simple and natural prayer for daily bread has been interpreted in a wide variety of ways.

(1) Since the prayer as a whole is eschatological, and since in a hungry world bread is a widespread symbol of eschatological blessedness (cf. 22:16; Luke 14:15), the prayer is for the eschatological bread of the final coming of the kingdom of God. It was thought that the heavenly manna would reappear in the eschatological times, with bread from heaven for all (cf. John 6:22-58). This eschatological interpretation was widespread in the early church, both East and West. So understood, the prayer is for the eschatological blessing of the messianic banquet, when all God's people will sit down together, with enough food for all.

(2) Bread has been understood for normal this-worldly needs, for survival. For the poor people among whom Jesus lived and worked, it would be difficult to exclude this natural meaning. The prayer represents Jesus' own solidarity with the poor and his concern that they have the minimal means of survival. Praying this prayer, the church unites with the hungry and poor of the world, and hence the prayer constitutes a readiness of

those who have bread to share with those who have not.

(3) Since this prayer early became an element in the church's eucharistic liturgy, "bread" was often understood to refer to the sacramental bread. This could hardly have been part of Jesus' original meaning, and there is no indication that Matthew understands this petition eucharistically. The best interpretation combines (1) and (2): The prayer longs for the coming of God's kingdom, when there will be bread for all, and prays specifically for present physical needs.

"Daily" is the traditional translation of the unusual word ἐπιούσιος (*epiousios*), whose meaning is unknown since it occurs nowhere else in Greek literature independent of this text.[163] Based on etymology and its translation in ancient versions, it can mean "necessary," "continual," "for today," or "for tomorrow." The best linguistic evidence points toward "for tomorrow," which was also the Aramaic text of the *Gospel of the Nazarenes*. But asking today for tomorrow's bread seems to conflict with 6:31, 34. Yet what is forbidden there is not prayer for tomorrow's needs, but anxiety about them. The day laborer who lived from one day to the next could pray today for bread for tomorrow (especially as the evening prayer!) without being guilty of greed or wanting to store up reserves.

"Debts." We might first note that Jesus, like John the Baptist, Paul, and biblical theology in general, makes the assumption of universal sinfulness. Jesus assumes, and does not argue, that every person who comes before the Holy One in prayer comes as a guilty one who needs God's forgiveness. Sin is here thought of as a debt owed to God—a debt one cannot repay (cf. 18:21-35). Without presumption, but in confidence, the disciple is taught to ask for God's forgiveness. Like the rest of the prayer, the petition is primarily eschatological ("Grant me forgiveness in the last judgment"), but is also a prayer for present needs ("Grant me forgiveness here and now").

The binding of human forgiveness to God's, already present in Jesus' prayer and Q, expresses Matthew's dialectical understanding of forgiveness. God's forgiveness is unconditional, precedes human forgiveness of other human beings, and is

---

163. The one occurrence in a 5th-century papyrus (now lost) is fragmentary and without enough context to make the meaning clear.

its ground and cause. Yet prayer for God's forgiveness is unthinkable for one who is intentionally an unforgiving person (cf. 18:21-35). Here and elsewhere in the prayer, divine action and human action are not alternatives. When placed in a linear chronological framework, God's forgiveness corresponds to the already/not-yet of Matthean eschatology. We *already* have the unmerited, unconditional forgiveness of God. Whoever receives it is placed in a new relationship that calls for and makes possible forgiveness of others. But we do *not yet* have this forgiveness as a possession that cannot be lost in the final judgment. This dialectic goes back to Jesus and is preserved in the Q version of the prayer that came to Matthew. In his Jesus tradition, Matthew magnified this element of the danger of presuming on God's grace and, therefore, being an unforgiving person oneself, emphasizing it at the conclusion of the prayer in 6:14-15 and especially in 18:21-35.

"Lead us not into temptation; deliver us from the evil one." From the earliest times the church has been bothered by the apparent threat that God could lead Jesus' disciples into temptation, and had to be supplicated not do so. Beginning with the Old Latin, various translations have attempted to avoid that problem.[164] In accord with the orientation of the prayer as a whole, it is best to interpret the petition as originally having primarily an eschatological reference. In apocalyptic thought, just before the final victory of God and the coming of the kingdom, the power of evil is intensified, and the people of God endure tribulation and persecution. The disciple is instructed to pray that God, who always leads the people, will not bring them into this time of testing, when the pressure might be so great as to overcome faith itself (see 26:42, where the identical phrase occurs). Thus "evil one" is the proper translation of the final word of the prayer (as in NIV and NRSV), not "evil" in the abstract (KJV, RSV). Although originally primarily eschatological, the petition for deliverance from the final testing and the evil one also has a present dimension. The "ordinary" testings and temptations are seen not as petty peccadilloes, but as manifestations of the

ultimate power of evil. The disciple is instructed not to take them lightly, but to see them as a threat to faith and to pray for God's deliverance from them.

The manuscript tradition contains ten different endings to the Lord's Prayer, testifying to its frequent use and adoption in the life of the church. The oldest and best MSS do not contain the final doxology.[165] The mass of later MSS include some form of "for yours is the kingdom and the power and the glory forever, amen," derived from 1 Chr 29:11-13. Early English translations (such as the KJV) were unaware of the oldest Greek texts, which had not yet been rediscovered, with the result that the common English form of the Lord's Prayer used in public worship quite appropriately includes the doxology. There can be no doubt, however, that it is a later addition made long after Matthew's time.

6:14-15. On the connection between human and divine forgiveness, see Commentary on "Debts" in 6:11-13. These two verses have parallels in Mark 11:25-26, which may be a scribal gloss in Mark. If so, then vv. 14-15 are not derived from Mark and moved to this location, but are entirely M material, from Matthew's special tradition or, more likely, Matthean redaction. In this case, Matthew has composed a pair of paraenetic "sentences of holy law" in the style of the Christian prophets active in his community, to drive home the point that those who pray for God's forgiveness must themselves forgive.

6:16-18, Fasting. This is the third unit in the traditional "cultic catechism," taken over by Matthew, to which he returns after his insertion on prayer. Fasting means the voluntary abstention from food for a prescribed period as a sign of religious devotion. It was often accompanied by wearing sackcloth, placing ashes on the head, and abstaining from washing the body. The OT prescribed only one public fast, on the Day of Atonement (Leviticus 16). Later Jewish tradition developed two others, Rosh Ha-Shanah (New Year's Day) and the Ninth of Ab (lamentation for the destruction of Jerusalem by Nebuchadnezzar in 586 BCE and by Titus in 70 CE), but it is not known whether these were already official in Matthew's time. There were, however, voluntary fasts in which observant Jews could participate as

---

164. Some pre-Vulgate MSS read "ne patiaris nos induce in temptationem" ("Do not permit us to be led into temptation"), a reading followed by Tertullian and Cyprian. There can be no doubt that this is a scribal effort to "correct" Matthew's theology rather than the original reading of Matthew.

165. Including the majuscules אּ, B, D, 0170, the minuscules of f^1, f^{13}, and some ancient versions and quotations in the Fathers.

a sign of repentance, mourning, or devotion to prayer. Mondays and Thursdays were designated as appropriate days for such fasting.[166] It is such individual, voluntary fasts that are in view here, and it is assumed that the disciples participate in them (see further on 9:14-15).

As in the preceding instructions about almsgiving and prayer, the issue is whether such voluntary acts of piety are done with the goal of impressing a human audience, or as an act of devotion to God.[167] Thus the disciples are com-

manded not to call attention to themselves (by wearing sackcloth, placing ashes on their heads, or not washing or combing their hair), which makes it obvious they are fasting, but to perform their normal daily washing and anointing—so that only God will be aware of their devotion. Although this is not, as in the other examples, a metaphorical hyperbolic command, but is meant quite literally, it is still not merely a legal prescription, but an example of that devotion directed to God alone, which the disciple must apply creatively—for, again, it is possible to obey this literally and still find ways to be admired for one's strict religious devotion.

166. See *Did.* 8:1.
167. An ironic wordplay in the Greek is lost in translation—literally, "They make their faces *disappear* so that they may *appear* to other people to fast." Perhaps the following catches something of it: "They disfigure their faces because they figure on being seen by others."

REFLECTIONS[168]

1. Prayer is theology; theology is prayer. Karl Barth rightly affirmed, "The first and basic act of theological work is prayer."[169] Prayer is a theological act, the fundamental theological act. What one prays for simultaneously shapes and expresses one's theology. The use of the Lord's Prayer in Matthew's church has affected his theology (see above). Matthew's decision to place the Lord's Prayer at the center of the instruction of the Sermon on the Mount dissolves the line between worship and theology. Prayer is theology.

It is less often seen that theology is prayer. Thus Barth's dictum above is misunderstood if one takes it as piously recommending that one have a moment's prayer before beginning theological work. Barth's point (I think Matthew would agree) is that theological work itself, struggling to discern the contemporary meaning of God's revelatory self-disclosure, even when theological work struggles to affirm that there has been a divine relelvatory act or that the God purported to have acted in Christ is truly real—such theological struggle is itself prayer, wrestling with the angel until the blessing comes, even if one goes limping away (Genesis 32). The scribal Matthew comes from the same rabbinic milieu that generated the dictum: "An hour of study is in the eyes of the Holy One, blessed be He, as an hour of prayer."

2. You can tell what persons believe not so much by what they say in church, but by the assumptions on which they habitually act. The Lord's Prayer is an expression of faith, not only in what it says, but in what it assumes. There is an anthropological assumption, that the disciples of Jesus (and human beings as such) are true to themselves when they pray—and that they will pray. The text is not a command to pray or a scolding for not praying; it assumes that people do pray. The assumption is that human beings are not self-sufficient, but creatures of the creator God, pictured as their divine Father. It is not a sign of weakness to pray, but a sign of genuine humanity. Prayer is not merely for emergencies, but is thankful praise that acknowledges our true dependence on God.

3. Many thoughtful people have pondered what we are really doing when we pray. If there is a God at all, doesn't this God already know everything that we could possibly say in prayer?

168. The reader will note that here and elsewhere, much of the hermeneutical reflection is already built into the exegesis; the Reflections are not independent of the exegesis. In this section, for instance, hermeneutical and homiletical reflections on the individual petitions of the Lord's Prayer are integrated into the exegetical work, with the Reflection proper stepping back and taking a larger look at the implications of the text as a whole.
169. Karl Barth, *Evangelical Theology: An Introduction* (New York: Holt, Rinehart, and Winston, 1963) 160.

Does prayer really change anything? Is it even possible to truly worship a deity who can be swayed by our prayers? If there is a God at all, could this God be good if waiting to grant help or healing until we ask in the proper way? How could prayer be significant, if on many issues there are sincere people praying for opposite results? (One thinks not only of superficial illustrations from sports—though there is much praying during athletic contests, and much thanking God for victory afterward—but also of deep political struggles and wars.)

There is some help in realizing that prayer is a particular kind of language. Not all language is of the same kind.[170] The vocabulary of prayer is not the same as that for the application for a grant or a job. Since Matthew immediately prefaces the Lord's Prayer with his teaching that prayer language is not informational (6:8), he is quite aware that the language of prayer is in a different linguistic category from other types of language, even of other varieties of religious language. Prayer is the language of confession. By "confessional language" I do not mean merely admitting that we have done wrong, but confession in the sense of expressing faith, the language that gives expression to our deepest convictions. This kind of language is not merely expressive, a venting of emotions, but represents a reality of human life, even though it is a different kind of language from that used to express other realities. It is non-inferential—i.e., it cannot be made the basis for a series of logical inferences. It says what it says, not what it infers. It is the insider language of the community of faith, which makes no sense to the spectator perspective of the outsider. The believer asks for bread neither to inform the deity of a need nor to persuade a reluctant deity to supply it, but to confess our own need before God and to declare dependence upon God. And so it is with the prayer for forgiveness for sins, and for the coming of the kingdom. Once we realize something of the nature of the language of prayer, we are freed from the constrictions and hesitations we may have about praying—Do I really need to tell God that? Is my prayer going to change God's mind? Do I even want to pray to a God so subject to the power of suggestion? We can then confess our own need and lift up our intercessions and petitions to God without reservation. The Lord's Prayer offers a model for doing so. Matthew's text presents the opportunity for deepening our understanding of the nature of the language of prayer.

4. Jesus himself gave a model prayer to his disciples something like our earliest New Testament version (see above). One can reflect on, and preach from, the prayer as a prayer of Jesus, since there is a sense in which this prayer transcends all its NT literary contexts and brings us within sound of the very voice of Jesus.[171] Yet this is different from preaching from the Bible, for the Lord's Prayer in the New Testament is an integral part of the writing and theology of two (different) evangelists. From this point of view, it should make a difference whether one is preaching from the Matthean or Lukan text of the Lord's Prayer, and that not only regarding the slightly different wording. In each Gospel, the prayer is an expression of the theology of the Gospel in which it is embedded. "Your kingdom come," for instance, is verbally identical in the two versions. Yet two different sermons, lessons, or reflections should result from giving the context in each case its due. One must ask in each case, What does Matthew or Luke mean by the "kingdom of God"? This is a different question from asking what Jesus meant by it—and more readily answerable. We have the Gospels of Matthew and Luke on which to base our meaning, but we do not have the context in Jesus' ministry from which we can fill in the meaning of "kingdom of God" for him. Exegesis of Matthew (or Luke) will prevent us from filling in Jesus' meaning with the content of our own theology, tradition, or prejudice. Even so common a text as the Lord's Prayer is not only a call to prayer, but a call to study as well, and these may often be the same.

170. Cf. Reflections on Matthew 2:13-23, "The Other Babies of Bethlehem."

171. This was the point frequently developed by Joachim Jeremias, who believed that hearing the "very voice" of Jesus (distinguished from his "very words") could renew the church. Among his several publications on this topic, see *The Prayers of Jesus; The Lord's Prayer*, trans. John Reumann, Facet Books Biblical Series, 8 (Philadelphia: Fortress, 1964).

MATTHEW 6:19–7:12, MORE INSTRUCTION IN AUTHENTIC RIGHTEOUSNESS

NIV

[19]"Do not store up for yourselves treasures on earth, where moth and rust destroy, and where thieves break in and steal. [20]But store up for yourselves treasures in heaven, where moth and rust do not destroy, and where thieves do not break in and steal. [21]For where your treasure is, there your heart will be also.

[22]"The eye is the lamp of the body. If your eyes are good, your whole body will be full of light. [23]But if your eyes are bad, your whole body will be full of darkness. If then the light within you is darkness, how great is that darkness!

[24]"No one can serve two masters. Either he will hate the one and love the other, or he will be devoted to the one and despise the other. You cannot serve both God and Money.

[25]"Therefore I tell you, do not worry about your life, what you will eat or drink; or about your body, what you will wear. Is not life more important than food, and the body more important than clothes? [26]Look at the birds of the air; they do not sow or reap or store away in barns, and yet your heavenly Father feeds them. Are you not much more valuable than they? [27]Who of you by worrying can add a single hour to his life[a]?

[28]"And why do you worry about clothes? See how the lilies of the field grow. They do not labor or spin. [29]Yet I tell you that not even Solomon in all his splendor was dressed like one of these. [30]If that is how God clothes the grass of the field, which is here today and tomorrow is thrown into the fire, will he not much more clothe you, O you of little faith? [31]So do not worry, saying, 'What shall we eat?' or 'What shall we drink?' or 'What shall we wear?' [32]For the pagans run after all these things, and your heavenly Father knows that you need them. [33]But seek first his kingdom and his righteousness, and all these things will be given to you as well. [34]Therefore do not worry about tomorrow, for tomorrow will worry about itself. Each day has enough trouble of its own.

[a]27 Or *single cubit to his height*

NRSV

19"Do not store up for yourselves treasures on earth, where moth and rust[a] consume and where thieves break in and steal; 20but store up for yourselves treasures in heaven, where neither moth nor rust[a] consumes and where thieves do not break in and steal. 21For where your treasure is, there your heart will be also.

22"The eye is the lamp of the body. So, if your eye is healthy, your whole body will be full of light; 23but if your eye is unhealthy, your whole body will be full of darkness. If then the light in you is darkness, how great is the darkness!

24"No one can serve two masters; for a slave will either hate the one and love the other, or be devoted to the one and despise the other. You cannot serve God and wealth.[b]

25"Therefore I tell you, do not worry about your life, what you will eat or what you will drink,[c] or about your body, what you will wear. Is not life more than food, and the body more than clothing? 26Look at the birds of the air; they neither sow nor reap nor gather into barns, and yet your heavenly Father feeds them. Are you not of more value than they? 27And can any of you by worrying add a single hour to your span of life?[d] 28And why do you worry about clothing? Consider the lilies of the field, how they grow; they neither toil nor spin, 29yet I tell you, even Solomon in all his glory was not clothed like one of these. 30But if God so clothes the grass of the field, which is alive today and tomorrow is thrown into the oven, will he not much more clothe you—you of little faith? 31Therefore do not worry, saying, 'What will we eat?' or 'What will we drink?' or 'What will we wear?' 32For it is the Gentiles who strive for all these things; and indeed your heavenly Father knows that you need all these things. 33But strive first for the kingdom of God[e] and his[f] righteousness, and all these things will be given to you as well.

34"So do not worry about tomorrow, for to-

[a]Gk *eating*   [b]Gk *mammon*   [c]Other ancient authorities lack *or what you will drink*   [d]Or *add one cubit to your height*
[e]Other ancient authorities lack *of God*   [f]Or *its*

NIV

7 "Do not judge, or you too will be judged. ²For in the same way you judge others, you will be judged, and with the measure you use, it will be measured to you.

³"Why do you look at the speck of sawdust in your brother's eye and pay no attention to the plank in your own eye? ⁴How can you say to your brother, 'Let me take the speck out of your eye,' when all the time there is a plank in your own eye? ⁵You hypocrite, first take the plank out of your own eye, and then you will see clearly to remove the speck from your brother's eye.

⁶"Do not give dogs what is sacred; do not throw your pearls to pigs. If you do, they may trample them under their feet, and then turn and tear you to pieces.

⁷"Ask and it will be given to you; seek and you will find; knock and the door will be opened to you. ⁸For everyone who asks receives; he who seeks finds; and to him who knocks, the door will be opened.

⁹"Which of you, if his son asks for bread, will give him a stone? ¹⁰Or if he asks for a fish, will give him a snake? ¹¹If you, then, though you are evil, know how to give good gifts to your children, how much more will your Father in heaven give good gifts to those who ask him! ¹²So in everything, do to others what you would have them do to you, for this sums up the Law and the Prophets."

NRSV

morrow will bring worries of its own. Today's trouble is enough for today.

7 "Do not judge, so that you may not be judged. ²For with the judgment you make you will be judged, and the measure you give will be the measure you get. ³Why do you see the speck in your neighbor's*a* eye, but do not notice the log in your own eye? ⁴Or how can you say to your neighbor,*b* 'Let me take the speck out of your eye,' while the log is in your own eye? ⁵You hypocrite, first take the log out of your own eye, and then you will see clearly to take the speck out of your neighbor's*a* eye.

6"Do not give what is holy to dogs; and do not throw your pearls before swine, or they will trample them under foot and turn and maul you.

7"Ask, and it will be given you; search, and you will find; knock, and the door will be opened for you. ⁸For everyone who asks receives, and everyone who searches finds, and for everyone who knocks, the door will be opened. ⁹Is there anyone among you who, if your child asks for bread, will give a stone? ¹⁰Or if the child asks for a fish, will give a snake? ¹¹If you then, who are evil, know how to give good gifts to your children, how much more will your Father in heaven give good things to those who ask him!

12"In everything do to others as you would have them do to you; for this is the law and the prophets."

a Gk brother's   *b* Gk brother

COMMENTARY

This section corresponds to the third of the Three Pillars of Judaism, "Deeds of loving kindness." It begins with trusting and serving God with one's material possessions (6:19-34) and builds toward the "Golden Rule" (7:12). Much of the material in 6:19–7:12 resembles proverbial wisdom, and may have originally had this setting. In contrast to Parts One and Two, but like other wisdom material, this section is not tightly structured. Matthew's contextualization and relating

these instructions to Jesus' prophetic proclamation of the kingdom of God transforms it from prudent advice into expressions of the radical demands of discipleship.

6:19-24, Serving God or Mammon. A dualistic either/or pervades this unit:[172]

172. This is in continuity with the previous section, with its threefold contrast between piety done for observation by other human beings and piety to be seen by God alone.

treasures on earth/	treasures in heaven
the present/	the eschatological future
temporary goods that may be lost/	permanent goods that endure
clear eye and life in the light/	bad eye, confused life in the dark
serving things/	serving God

A comparison with the Lukan forms of this text shows that this antithetical form was not in the Q material, but has been imposed on it by Matthew, corresponding to the antitheses of Part One (5:21-48). What seems to begin as prudent advice on long-term investments turns out to be a radical challenge calling for the reorientation of one's whole life. The identification and location of one's "treasure" turns out to be a matter of one's total self (this is the meaning of "heart" in v. 21). How one handles property turns out to be not peripheral, but a matter of saving or losing one's whole being.

6:19-21. "Treasure in heaven" was a common Jewish image for eschatological reward. Matthew does not spell out how the disciples are to store up treasures in heaven. Here, too, he leaves room for the disciple's creative response in his or her particular situation.

"Rust" is the traditional translation of βρῶσις (*brōsis*, literally "eating"). Since there is a specific word for "rust" (ἰός *ios*, Jas 5:3), the word used here may refer to a kind of insect or worm that eats clothing, parallel to "moth."

6:22-23. In contrast to the modern understanding, which regards the eye as a window that lets light into the body, the common understanding in the ancient world was that the eye was like a lamp (Prov 15:30; 2 Sam 12:11; Dan 10:6; Tob 10:15), an instrument that projects the inner light onto objects so they may be seen.[173] In either case, however, if the eye is unsound, confusion and darkness reign within the person. Similar sayings are found in both paganism and Judaism. Of itself, the statement may have many meanings. By bringing it into this context, Matthew relates the saying to the issue of the disciples' attitude toward money and property, declaring that if the eye is not clear on this matter, the whole of one's life is perverted.

6:24. This statement assumes the existence of slavery, which is made specific in Q (still preserved in Luke 16:13). By omitting the word *slave*, Matthew applies it directly to the disciples. *Love* and *hate* do not refer to emotions, but represent the biblical idiom for "choose"/"not choose" (see 5:43). The point is that undivided service can be given to one master only; if there is more than one, every choice means a favoring of one and rejection of the other, hence a split in the disciple's loyalty. Like the beatitudes (esp. 5:8) and v. 24 below, this statement is a call for the unity of the person (cf. the vacillation expressed in "doubt" [διστάζω *distazō*] in 14:31; 28:17). Again, we see Matthew's radical dualistic understanding of discipleship that allows no middle ground (cf. 12:30).

Mammon is simply the Aramaic word for "property," including, but not limited to, money, and in itself has no sinister connotations.[174] It is a surprising turn to find Jesus placing worldly goods on a par with God as an object of service, an idolatrous rival to the one God. The presupposition behind all such statements is an affront to the common cultural understanding of the meaning of human life, both then and now. The concluding v. 24 only brings out the presupposition of the passage as a whole: that human life is not self-sufficient; that we find the meaning of our lives outside ourselves; that human life inescapably "serves" something that gives it meaning. The choice is not whether we shall serve, but what or whom we shall serve. This presupposition about who we are confronts our self-understanding with a radical challenge.

Matthew 6:25-34, Anxiety. The prohibition "do not be anxious" (RSV) signals the beginning of the second unit in this section (cf. 6:19) and is repeated throughout as its dominating theme (vv. 25, 27, 28, 31, 34 [twice]). Yet there is a connection with v. 24, which shows that the section is not directed to rich people only, those inclined to the arrogance that comes with wealth. Poor people can idolize what they do not have.

Again, the material seems to have come originally from the wisdom tradition, based on an appeal to common sense and the observation of

173. See Dale C. Allison, Jr., "The Eye Is the Lamp of the Body" (Matt 6:22-23 = Luke 11:34-36), *NTS* 33 (1987) 61-83.

174. The Aramaic Targum of Deut 6:5 uses it for the Hebrew word translated "might," "strength"; mammon could be a means of *loving* God with one's *substance*.

nature rather than to prophetic revelation, contrasting the life of trust in the one God with that of "Gentiles" (ἔθνη *ethnē*), outsiders to the elect people of God (see 5:47). Yet the present Matthean context binds this way of life to the kingdom of God proclaimed by Jesus (6:33).

6:26-29. The challenge to trust in God's providence does not exclude working and having property. The words are directed to people involved with sowing, reaping, storing in barns, toiling, and spinning, but who are called to see that their life is not based on these things. Such people are not called to become birds or lilies, but to consider God's providence for all creation, including birds, lilies, and human beings.

6:33. The Greek MSS, versions, and quotations in the Church Fathers have five different readings for "kingdom of God" and "his [i.e., the Father's] kingdom." While the meaning is approximately the same, the variations in the MSS betray an awkwardness in the text occasioned by Matthew's redactional addition of "and his righteousness" (or "and its righteousness"). It is clear that Matthew wants to relate his key word (δικαιοσύνη *dikaiosynē,* "righteousness"/"justice") both to the idea of the coming eschatological kingdom and to the idea of trust in the Father's providential care. While the word has the overtones of God's eschatological act of vindication at the end of history, its primary meaning here is not God's act, but the disciples' act in doing the will of God (cf. Excursus "Kingdom of Heaven in Matthew," 288-94, and the comments on 6:10). The command to seek first the kingdom is not intended chronologically, as though the disciples are free to pursue material goods after seeking the kingdom, but means that they are to seek God's kingdom above all else. The disciple can have only one priority: God's kingdom or will.

6:34. The conclusion, absent from Q, may either come from tradition or be Matthew's own composition. As an isolated saying, it can be understood in a pessimistic or cynical manner. In the present context, it is not intended to discourage planning for the future (25:1-13) but to be reassuring: Address each day's problems as they come, confident that your life is in the hands of a loving Father, who holds the whole world in his hands and will bring it to a worthy conclusion.

7:1-5, Judging. The instruction on human relationships continues, shifting from relation to things to relationships among people, particularly fellow members of the Christian community. The pericope has two elements: Jesus' absolute prohibition of judging (vv. 1[-2]), formulated in the plural, and qualifications that presuppose that judgments are actually made, formulated in the singular, which urge caution and a loving, nonjudgmental attitude (vv. [2-]3-5). The structure and function are thus reminiscent of the antitheses' radicalizing demand of Jesus, supplemented by situational qualifications (see 5:21-48). The absoluteness of the prohibition (v. 1) probably goes back to Jesus himself, while the supplementary qualifications (vv. 2-5) represent post-Easter church interpretation, either by placing original sayings from Jesus in this context or by secondary expansion. The wisdom material in the second part is interpreted by being placed within the eschatological prophetic demand of the first part, so that it is no longer prudent advice, but instruction on how the disciples must live in the light of the dawning kingdom of God. The word for "brother" (ἀδελφός *adelphos*), repeated three times and framing vv. 3-5, indicates that the primary scope of the saying concerns relationships within the Christian community, represented by the disciples.[175] Since the sermon is directed to the disciples but "overheard" by the crowds, however, the attitude here inculcated is not limited to community relationships but directed outward to all people.

7:1. Although Jewish tradition contains exhortations to moderation, toleration, and mercy, the absolute prohibition of judgment is without parallel. The Greek κρίνω (*krinō*) translates "judge"; in both Greek and English it is a general term with a broad spectrum of meanings, ranging from aesthetic judgments to proceedings in a court of law. In this verse it may mean either "be critical of" or "condemn." Jesus' original prohibition was absolute. It presumed the light of the dawning kingdom of God and the near advent of the last judgment. Here, as elsewhere, Jesus' teaching is not a strategy for success in this-worldly relationships, but a call to live in the light of the dawning kingdom of God.

---

175. The meaning of the word translated "brother" (*adelphos*), often generically rendered "brother or sister," is here obscured by the NRSV's "neighbor."

7:2-5. Here begins a series of qualifications that retain Jesus' original thrust, but adapt it to conditions in a continuing world. Verse 2 presupposes that judgments will in fact be made (discrimination, not necessarily condemnation). The concern is how they are made, for at the last judgment God will measure us by the same standard we have used for others. Thus those who show mercy will receive mercy (5:7; cf. 18:21-35). The grotesque imagery of the judgmental person, who is eager to remove a speck from the eye of a fellow member of the community, while having a log dangling from his or her own eye, emphasizes how hesitant disciples must be to identify and remove the faults of others. Yet the concluding v. 5 shows that Matthew does assume that occasions occur within the community when ethical discernment and community discipline are called for (cf. 7:15-20; 18:15-20), but they must be made by those aware of their own failures and of God's forgiveness.

7:6, Pearls Before Swine. This enigmatic saying is sometimes seen as a continuation of the preceding qualifications of Jesus' absolute demand against judging, in the sense that disciples must at least decide ("judge") who are "dogs" and "swine." The saying does not belong with vv. 2-5, however, since it introduces a new subject: holiness. Verses 2-5 deal with the sin of an erring member of the community, to which v. 5 is the proper conclusion. Verse 6 then introduces a new topic with the same formula used in 6:19, 25; 7:1.

Although there are analogous sayings in pagan literature, this saying is without parallel in the New Testament. "What is holy" is not an ethical term but is a biblical expression designating meat offered in sacrifice on the altar (Exod 29:37; Lev 2:3). For the Old Testament and Judaism, "swine" were the epitome of ritual impurity. "Dogs" are not pets, but semi-wild, dangerous stray animals, like the wolves of 7:15. The saying is constructed chiastically—the dogs tear to pieces, and the pigs trample the pearls in the mire. Thus the general proverbial meaning is clear enough: the truism that holy things should not be profaned. But the particular meaning remains unclear, opening the way for a variety of allegorical interpretations in the history of the church ("dogs" and "swine" refer to Gentiles or to heretics or to apostates). It

is not the case that "dogs" was a typical Jewish designation for Gentiles.[176] Already in the *Didache,* only slightly later than Matthew, the saying was understood to mean that the unbaptized should not be admitted to the eucharist (*Did.* 9:5). But the saying is a vivid metaphor, not an allegory to be decoded. It is thus easier to comment on what the saying does not mean than to explicate its meaning. In this case, we should simply acknowledge that the saying is provocatively obscure, both in its original context (if it goes back to Jesus) and in its Matthean setting.

7:7-11, Asking and Receiving. Matthew has made the Lord's Prayer the center of the sermon as a whole, and as he rounds off the Instruction on how the disciples are to live, he includes encouragement to pray. Matthew's emphasis on "works" is not to be understood from the Pauline perspective as an expression of human pride over against dependence on God, but as inextricably bound to the life of prayer and a joyful confession of confident childlike dependence.

The unit has two parts: vv. 7-8, containing three imperatives based on three unconditional promises, and vv. 9-11, which give further reason for confident prayer based on the analogy and contrast between human and divine fatherhood. Verses 7-8 may originally have been "beggars' wisdom," encouraging persistence—if you keep on asking, seeking, and knocking on doors, finally someone will help. Jesus or the early Palestinian church has transferred the picture to the relation between disciples and God and given it a transcendent meaning. The point is no longer human persistence, but divine goodness.

7:7-8. "Seeking" is often used in the Old Testament and Jewish tradition for prayer, with God's will as the object (e.g., Deut 4:29; Ps 105:4; Isa 65:1; cf. Jer 29:12-13). It is especially characteristic of the wisdom tradition (Prov 1:28; 6:12; 8:17; Eccl 7:23-25). "Knocking" (on the "doors of mercy") was a Jewish expression for prayer. Thus "ask," "seek," and "knock" are not three different actions—there are no stages of spiritual experience here—but three Jewish expressions for prayer. Yet the explication of "ask" by "seek" and "knock" gives a character to prayer that makes it more than a shopping list directed to a heavenly

---

176. See Israel Abrahams, *Studies in Pharisaism and the Gospels* (Cambridge: Cambridge University Press, 1917) 2:195.

dispensary. Prayer is a quest and an expectation. The divine passives "it will be given to you" and "it will be opened to you" point to God as the actor, while "will find" retains the human subject—again, divine action and human responsibility are not alternatives. The encouragement to bring human needs to God in prayer is not to inform or to persuade, but is an expression of the disciples' relation to God as dependent children who ultimately are not in control of their own lives.

Although directed to disciples, the universal "everyone" springs from the framework. The uncommitted "crowds" and the wider public as potential pray-ers emerge into the purview of the sermon again.

7:9-11. Bread and fish were the staples of the Galilean diet. Good human fathers are responsive and caring, and would never respond to their child's request for bread by mockingly substituting a stone for the needed bread or a snake for the expected fish. This would be a cruel joke, since there is a striking resemblance between the flat cakes of bread and Palestinian stones (cf. 4:3), and between eel-like fish and snakes.

"You then, who are evil . . . " (v. 11) is a Greek participle (literally, "You then, being evil") that presupposes universal sinfulness, including the fathers just mentioned and the disciples to whom the saying is directed. It is also striking that Jesus seems not to include himself among sinners, analogous to the way he speaks of "my Father" and "your Father." Neither here nor elsewhere in the Gospels does Jesus betray any sense of his own guilt or sin, but seems to look at the sinfulness of the human situation from a perspective that transcends it. There is no full-scale doctrine of the sinlessness of Christ here, yet the elements are present in Matthew for its later development (cf. 3:13-15 to Mark 1:4, 9; cf. 19:16-17 to Mark 10:17-18). Nor is there an explicit doctrine of original sin here, but universal sinfulness is all the more striking because it is simply assumed and mentioned as self-evident. It is a gross misunderstanding to juxtapose Jesus' "positive" view of humanity to Paul's "negative" view; Jesus, Paul, and Matthew have essentially the same view of human nature, as does the New Testament as a whole.[177]

---

177. See Rudolf Bultmann, "Jesus and Paul," in *Existence and Faith: Shorter Writings of Rudolf Bultmann,* ed. Schubert Ogden (New York: Meridian Books, 1960) 183-201.

7:12, The Golden Rule. This terse conclusion of the instruction is not a part of the preceding paragraph, to which it is unrelated, but a separate unit, making two pairs of three units in this section. The Golden Rule (as it has been popularly known since the eighteenth century) is a part of the Great Sermon in Q (cf. Luke 6:31), where it is integrated into the command to love one's enemies. Matthew has relocated the saying to make it the climax and conclusion of the Instruction, at the same time making redactional modifications that are minor in extent but major in significance.

(1) Matthew adds the introductory particle "so" (οὖν *oun,* left untranslated in NRSV). It does not here represent a logical inference from v. 11 or vv. 7-11, with which it does not connect, but is a summarizing particle referring to all that has gone before (as in Rom 12:1; Gal 5:1, where it has the same function), thus pulling together and declaring the result of the whole section (5:17–7:11). It could well be translated "So, then."

(2) Matthew adds the clause "for this is the law and the prophets." This forms an inclusion with the similar phrase in 5:17, thus bracketing 5:17–7:12 as the instructional body of the sermon. The clause further identifies the Golden Rule with the Great Commandment of love to God and neighbor, which Matthew identifies as the summary of the Law (22:40) and the hermeneutical key to its interpretation. In Matthew's understanding, the content of the Golden Rule is filled in by the Great Commandment, both of which are equated with the Law and the Prophets.

(3) Matthew adds *everything* as the opening word, making the Golden Rule an expression of the radical ethic of 5:21-47, especially of the Matthean perfectionism of 5:48.

There are numerous parallels to the Golden Rule prior to and alongside its canonical form. These are often stated in the negative form, such as "what you hate, do not do to anyone" (Tob 4:15 NRSV). The most well-known instance of such parallels is found in the story about Rabbi Shammai and Rabbi Hillel:

A certain heathen came before Shammai and said to him, "Make me a proselyte, on condition that you teach me the whole Torah while I stand on one foot." Thereupon he repulsed him with the builder's cubit which was in his hand. When he went before Hillel, he [Hillel] said to him, "What is hateful to you, do not do to your neighbor: that is the whole Torah, while the rest is commentary thereon; go and learn it." (*b. Ŝabb.* 31a)

This text also illustrates the fact that the connection between the Golden Rule as the summary of the Law was already present in the rabbinic tradition. It is not the case, however, that Jesus transformed the Jewish negative formulation into a positive Christian one, since the positive formulation was also current in contemporary Jewish and pagan tradition.[178] The negative form is also quoted in Christian sources, including *Did.* 1:2, shortly after Matthew, and in some MSS of Acts 15:20, 28, showing that early Christianity saw nothing particularly striking in the negative/positive variation.

178. See *Ep. Arist.* 207; *Testament of Naphtalai* 1; *2 Enoch* 61:1; Dio Cassius 52:34, 39; Isocrates *To Nicocles* [Cypr] 49; *Sentences of Sextus* 89.

REFLECTIONS

1. In the context of the ministry of Jesus, the message of 6:19-34 may well have been directed to his immediate disciples who had left homes and families to become, like Jesus, traveling teachers. In Matthew's Gospel, these words address not only the original disciples but also the post-Easter situation of Matthew's own church, where most had not taken this radical step of voluntary poverty. Through the centuries, the church has struggled to come to terms with these words without simply diluting them to later tastes. Like much else in the sermon, they should not be taken literally and legalistically. Yet they represent a radical call to decide to move away from cultural values into a life of trust and obedience.

The words are not given as advice to the general public on how to live, but are directed to disciples who are confronted with the demands of the sermon and may be wavering in their faith. For the first time, Matthew uses the words *little faith* (ὀλιγόπιστοι *oligopistoi*), found in his source (Q, Matt 6:30 = Luke 12:28), and he adopts it as a favorite expression for the disciples (8:26; 14:31; 16:8; 17:20). It affirms that they have faith, but that their faith is hesitant and needs reassurance. They are told not to be anxious, that the one who calls them to this radical style of life is also the creator who lovingly provides for the whole creation and who will finally bring the whole creation into his kingdom. The Preacher on the Mount is not an unrealistic exponent of romanticism, but one who knows that the sparrow will fall to the ground (10:29) and that trusting in God's providential care is not a strategy by which disciples can have it easy (5:10-12; 10:16-23).

2. Matthew 7:1-5 does not call for the obliteration of moral distinctions. The Matthean Jesus does not make each person a law to himself or herself, nor does he encourage the attitude that no one should be concerned to identify the moral failures of other members of the community and help them to overcome them. Even the act of forgiveness presupposes that one recognizes that another has done wrong; forgiveness entails a kind of judgment. Community discipline, involving judgment and forgiveness, may be an expression of the deepest love, while not judging the other by simply leaving her or him alone may be an easy way out that betrays authentic Christian love. Yet judging as condemnation is forbidden throughout.

3. In Matthew, prayer is not an abstract theological problem; it is a dynamic part of a relationship with God. We should not think of 7:7-11 as a formula for effective prayer. ("If you ask, seek, and knock, God will answer.") Instead, we should picture prayer within the context of the love between a parent and a child. In this setting, eager—even urgent and demanding—requests are met with gracious and wise gifts.

4. The Golden Rule is a formal principle that can function in several different ways, depending on the content with which it is filled. Not only could masochistic perversity use the principle to justify cruelty, but also the relatively common attitude of just wanting to be left alone, to "live and let live," not being bothered by others' attempts to "help," might use this formal principle as the justification for minding one's own business and failing to minister to the needs of others. There is thus nothing distinctively Christian about the Golden Rule in and of itself, nor is it a complete guide to Christian ethics. The distinctive Christian meaning is given by its identification with the Torah of Israel and the Great Commandment of love (see above), and by its placement in the overall flow of Matthew as a summary of the teaching of Jesus, who does not commend it as self-evident, but commands it as the crucified and risen Lord who speaks on his own authority (28:18-20). So regarded in its canonical context, the Golden Rule is not an egocentric rule of thumb for getting what one wants. Neither is the Golden Rule a matter of self-evident natural law, common ground between Jesus and the advocates of a commonsense ethic of enlightened self-interest. The focus is on doing for others, not on what one gets in return; "as you would have them do to you" (v. 12) is a guide for discerning what is right, calling the disciple to creative judgment. Not only is the Golden Rule at the farthest pole from a retaliatory *modus operandi* ("do unto others as they do unto you"), but also it is not even reciprocal, but initiatory (cf. 5:46-47). "As you would have them do to you" is the anticipatory mental act of discerning the loving thing to do that does not wait to respond to the action of another.

In this final saying of the Instruction, the disciples' action is related to human beings in general, "others" (οἱ ἄνθρωποι *hoi anthrōpoi*). Although spoken in the first place to disciples, and often focusing on inter-community relations, this summarizing statement is cast in a universal horizon that springs across all boundaries and relates to the greater righteousness to which disciples are called, not just to fellow members of the community, but to human relationships as such (5:20; 5:21–7:11; cf. 25:31-46).

Matthew 7:13-27, Three Eschatological Warnings

MATTHEW 7:13-14, TWO WAYS

NIV	NRSV
[13]"Enter through the narrow gate. For wide is the gate and broad is the road that leads to destruction, and many enter through it. [14]But small is the gate and narrow the road that leads to life, and only a few find it."	13"Enter through the narrow gate; for the gate is wide and the road is easy[a] that leads to destruction, and there are many who take it. [14]For the gate is narrow and the road is hard that leads to life, and there are few who find it."
	[a]Other ancient authorities read *for the road is wide and easy*

COMMENTARY

Matthew rewrites and amplifies the conclusion of the Great Sermon in Q to obtain another of his favorite triadic constructions.

The original saying presented two *gates* (Luke uses "doors"; which was original is not clear). Matthew (or perhaps his tradition) adds the motif of the two *ways* ("roads"), a common motif in both pagan and Jewish tradition.[179] The combination is somewhat awkward, causing confusion in the MSS as scribes attempted to make the imagery more consistent (the second "gate" in v. 13 is missing from many good MSS and, as the more difficult reading, is probably original; both the NRSV and the NIV follow the other MS tradition). It is thus not clear whether "gate" and "way" are two metaphors pointing to the same reality, or whether the "way" is thought of as leading up to the city "gate" or perhaps beginning with it. In either case, the narrow gate leads directly to salvation (for "life" as a metaphor for the kingdom of God and salvation, see 18:8; 19:16-17, 23-30; 25:46) and the wide gate to damnation. The "way" ("road"), in either case, is an ethicizing of

179. Cf., e.g., Deut 11:26; 30:15; esp. Jer 21:8 [Matthew is particularly interested in Jeremiah]; Ps 1:6; Sir 2:12; *Testament of Asher* 1:3-5; *2 Enoch* 30:15; 1QS 3:20. For pagan tradition see Hesiod *Works and Days* 286-92; Prodicus, cited in F. W. Beare, *The Gospel According to Matthew* (New York: Harper & Row, 1981) 194. In Jewish literature, the evil way is never pictured as easy, but sometimes the opposite (Ps 1:1; Prov 13:15; 15:19). Here, the Matthean Jesus is closer to the Gentile parallels.

the tradition. In Matthew's theology, the Christian life is thought of not in static terms, as a condition or once-for-all decision, but as the path or road of righteous living between the initial call of the disciple and the final goal of salvation. Thus he repeatedly emphasizes that many are called but few are chosen (9:13; 20:16; 22:14). The "many" here are then not outsiders, unbelievers, or Jewish opponents, but insiders, Christians who begin to follow but have "fallen by the wayside."

The "many" and "few" are not informational, but hortatory. They function not to give a doctrinal statement on how many will be saved, but to exhort and admonish lagging disciples of the urgency of decision, which must be made anew every day (12:30). Elsewhere, Matthew uses other imagery in which "many" are saved (8:11; 20:28). The initial warning sets the tone for the concluding section of the sermon, presenting Matthew's characteristic dualism of decision. There are two and only two doors, ways, kinds of fruit, final destinies.

MATTHEW 7:15-23, TWO HARVESTS (FALSE PROPHETS)

NIV

15 "Watch out for false prophets. They come to you in sheep's clothing, but inwardly they are ferocious wolves. 16By their fruit you will recognize them. Do people pick grapes from thornbushes, or figs from thistles? 17Likewise every good tree bears good fruit, but a bad tree bears bad fruit. 18A good tree cannot bear bad fruit, and a bad tree cannot bear good fruit. 19Every tree that does not bear good fruit is cut down and thrown into the fire. 20Thus, by their fruit you will recognize them.

21 "Not everyone who says to me, 'Lord, Lord,' will enter the kingdom of heaven, but only he who does the will of my Father who is in heaven. 22Many will say to me on that day, 'Lord, Lord, did we not prophesy in your name, and in your name drive out demons and perform many miracles?' 23Then I will tell them plainly, 'I never knew you. Away from me, you evildoers!' "

NRSV

15 "Beware of false prophets, who come to you in sheep's clothing but inwardly are ravenous wolves. 16You will know them by their fruits. Are grapes gathered from thorns, or figs from thistles? 17In the same way, every good tree bears good fruit, but the bad tree bears bad fruit. 18A good tree cannot bear bad fruit, nor can a bad tree bear good fruit. 19Every tree that does not bear good fruit is cut down and thrown into the fire. 20Thus you will know them by their fruits.

21 "Not everyone who says to me, 'Lord, Lord,' will enter the kingdom of heaven, but only the one who does the will of my Father in heaven. 22On that day many will say to me, 'Lord, Lord, did we not prophesy in your name, and cast out demons in your name, and do many deeds of power in your name?' 23Then I will declare to them, 'I never knew you; go away from me, you evildoers.' "

COMMENTARY

Just prior to the conclusion, the Great Sermon in Q has a brief section declaring that a person's words and deeds reveal the true self, just as the fruits of a tree reveal what kind of tree it is (cf. Luke 6:43-45). This Q theme (which also is expressed in Matt 3:7-10 = Luke 3:7*b*-9) had become very important to Matthew, and he uses it not only here and in 3:8, but also includes it in a fuller form in the key scene he composed as the climax of Part One (12:22-37). Here Matthew takes up this theme and restyles it into a direct warning to the disciples. The theme is important to him because (a) it fits his emphasis on deeds (rather than hearing/saying); (b) but the correct deeds alone are not adequate—they must represent the inward nature of the person doing them, otherwise they are hypocritical (6:1-18; 23:25-28); and (c) because it can be used as an image for both present identification of authentic discipleship ("know them by their fruits") and the future eschatological judgment when the good harvest will be gathered in and bad trees will be burned (chaps. 18–19).

Verse 15 is the heading for the whole unit, announcing false prophecy as the subject, to which v. 22 returns, bracketing the whole section together around the theme of charismatic activity. The sermon here clearly becomes transparent to the post-Easter situation of Matthew's church, which has charismatics among its leadership and membership. These are Christians who by the power of the Spirit speak the direct word of the exalted Lord (prophecy) and perform miracles (healings, exorcisms).

"False prophets" is not a code name for Pharisees, Zealots, or other opponents of the Matthean community, but refers to Christian prophets whom Matthew sees as dangerously misleading the church. These are would-be leaders within the community who appear innocent ("wolves in sheep's clothing" [see v. 15]) and who say "Lord, Lord" (v. 22) to Jesus. Matthew affirms charismatic speech and miraculous deeds as the gifts of the exalted Lord to his church (10:41; 23:34). It

is not prophecy as such that is suspect, but false prophets. What is Matthew's objection? They do not produce Christian "fruit," a common Matthean metaphor for true conversion, resulting in the kind of righteousness called for in the Sermon on the Mount (cf. 3:8-10; 12:33; 13:8, 26; 21:34, 41, 43). They do not do "the will of my [Jesus'] Father in heaven" (v. 21), but practice "lawlessness" (ἀνομία *anomia,* 7:23; paraphrased as "evildoers" by the NRSV and the NIV). Jesus quotes Ps 6:9 as his eschatological verdict. As in 13:41, 23:28, 24:12, this is Matthew's general word for unrighteousness, and it need not refer to some party or group advocating the abolition of the Mosaic law or to a Gnostic or Spirit-enthusiast group's rejection of all external norms. For Matthew, lawlessness is a rejection or perversion of righteous living as expressed in the Law and the teaching of Jesus, and summed up in the love commandment (see 7:12; 22:40). Matthew thus connects the lawlessness of false prophets and the relaxing of Christian love (24:12). The point is that neither correct confession of Christian christological titles ("Lord, Lord") nor the ability to perform spectacular miracles (which Matthew does not deny) will count in the final judgment, but whether one has done the will of God. This could be taken as works-righteousness, except for the fact that the warning is directed to disciples who confess their need of grace and forgiveness and pray for God's will to be done.

The Sermon on the Mount is not christological teaching about Jesus, but about the way of life to which the disciples are called. Yet, the implicit christology of the passage should not be missed. Already in the beatitudes and the antitheses, Jesus has assumed an authority that belongs only to God or God's unique representative. Here he pictures himself as acting in God's place as the Last Judge who decides the ultimate destiny of those who call him "Lord." One cannot flee from Paul to Jesus, nor from christology to the Sermon on the Mount. (See Reflections.)

MATTHEW 7:24-27, TWO BUILDERS

NIV	NRSV
24"Therefore everyone who hears these words of mine and puts them into practice is like a wise man who built his house on the rock. 25The rain came down, the streams rose, and the winds blew and beat against that house; yet it did not fall, because it had its foundation on the rock. 26But everyone who hears these words of mine and does not put them into practice is like a foolish man who built his house on sand. 27The rain came down, the streams rose, and the winds blew and beat against that house, and it fell with a great crash."	24"Everyone then who hears these words of mine and acts on them will be like a wise man who built his house on rock. 25The rain fell, the floods came, and the winds blew and beat on that house, but it did not fall, because it had been founded on rock. 26And everyone who hears these words of mine and does not act on them will be like a foolish man who built his house on sand. 27The rain fell, and the floods came, and the winds blew and beat against that house, and it fell—and great was its fall!"

COMMENTARY

The conclusion of the Great Sermon in Q is the double parable of the two builders (cf. Luke 6:47-49). Matthew has preserved the original form more closely, although also making redactional additions. The Matthean form is a splendid example of unadorned art, exquisitely symmetrical, the second half repeating the first almost verbatim. The power of the imagery is enhanced by the economy of words, the repeated short, unelaborated sentences having a staccato effect of hammer blows. The small changes in the second half of the parable bring into sharp profile the dualism of decision that has characterized the monitory conclusion since the "two ways" of 7:13:

wise/foolish[180]

rock/sand

doing/not doing

not fall/fall

Luke 6:47-49 has adapted the parable to the building practices of a Hellenistic city, but Matthew's version reflects the more original Palestinian situation where a house built during the dry season, when not a drop of rain falls in Palestine, seems secure until the fall storms come. Then the rain, wind, and floods that gush down the dry wadis overwhelm the house built on sand, while the house built on the rock stands secure. Although both builders seem to be getting along well in the present, only the one who has built with the coming storm in mind is secure. The difference between the "wise" (φρόνιμος *phronimos*) and the "foolish" (μωρός *mōros*) builders is not a matter of intellect, but one of insight into the eschatological situation—i.e., whether they are willing to hear in Jesus' words the revelation of God's will, and to act on them. Interpreters should not decode the parable as though it were pure allegory; one should not ask what the rock, house, rain, wind, and flood "stand for." Rather, a provocative picture is called to mind, showing the crucial difference between doing and not doing the will of God. The sermon knows of grace, but for it the grace of God is known only in that community committed to doing God's will revealed in Jesus. There can be no calculating "cheap grace" that keeps one from taking the Sermon on the Mount seriously as the revealed will of God to be lived.[181]

There are similar stories in rabbinic tradition, which contrast simply knowing the Torah or wisdom with both knowing and doing. Once again we see the implicit christology of the

---

180. This pair of terms is added by Matthew; cf. the similar pairing in 25:1-13.

181. See Dietrich Bonhoeffer, *The Cost of Discipleship*, rev. ed., trans. R. H. Fuller (New York: Macmillan, 1959). Cf. Ulrich Luz, *Matthew 1–7: A Commentary*, EKKNT (Minneapolis: Augsburg, 1989) 454.

Sermon on the Mount: No titles are here applied to Jesus, but Jesus places his own person and teaching as the revelation of God's will in place of the Torah.

Matthew 7:28-29, Conclusion of the Sermon

NIV	NRSV
[28]When Jesus had finished saying these things, the crowds were amazed at his teaching, [29]because he taught as one who had authority, and not as their teachers of the law.	28Now when Jesus had finished saying these things, the crowds were astounded at his teaching, 29for he taught them as one having authority, and not as their scribes.

COMMENTARY

Here is the first of Matthew's five concluding/transitional formulae that mark out the five key discourses (11:1; 13:53; 19:1; 26:1; cf. Introduction). With his statement about Jesus' authority and the response to his teaching, Matthew here briefly rejoins the Markan story line, which he had abandoned in order to insert the Sermon on the Mount (cf. Mark 1:22, 27). Matthew omits Mark's description of Jesus' teaching as "new" (cf. 5:17-20), but by adding "their" to "scribes" (cf. 4:23; 9:35; 10:17; Introduction) distances Jesus from the Jewish leaders.

REFLECTIONS

The following reflections are informed by the Sermon on the Mount as a complete unit.

1. At the conclusion of the sermon the crowds reappear (see 5:1-2). The crowds are not opponents, but neither are they disciples. They represent the uncommitted potential disciples to whom Jesus appeals throughout the Gospel. Jesus' teaching is not esoteric instruction for the initiated only. Although directed to disciples, it is "public" address that the uncommitted, potential disciples, represented by "the crowd," can also overhear and act upon. Matthew here presents a model for the church's missionary address to the world: The community of discipleship speaks its own language, makes its own confession, addresses its ethical demands to those who are committed to Jesus as the Christ and exalted Lord. Yet the church knows that it is not an esoteric group, but that it has responsibility to the world (28:18-20), so that even its "internal" talk is carried on with an awareness that the world is listening in. For Matthew, the line between church and world is not so sharp. This line not only runs through the community, to be made clear only at the eschaton (13:24-50), but through each person within the community as well. In addressing the difficult ethical issues of our own time, a church that takes Matthew's model seriously will neither attempt to legislate public morality for people of all religions and none, nor will it withdraw into a sectarian community concerned only about the ethical life of its own members. The text encourages the church to work out its own ethic based on the presuppositions of its own faith, but to do so with an eye on the crowds that share its ethical concerns, even if they do not share its faith or consider it irrelevant. Such ethical concern and action is a mode of evangelism, a mode that can be taken seriously by the contemporary world.

2. The crowds are not merely impressed; they are amazed. The NIV's "amazed" (ἐκπλήσσομαι *ekplēssomai*) is a strong word, almost "they were in shock." They were "astounded" (NRSV) at Jesus' authority. "Authority" (ἐξουσία *exousia*) is a key word in Matthew (cf. 8:9; 9:6, 8; 10:1; 21:23-27; 28:18). Etymologically, it connotes "out of one's own being" and represents both the form and content of Jesus' teaching. In contrast to the scribes, Jesus' teaching was not an exposition of an external authority, written Torah or oral tradition. He placed himself over both tradition and Scripture as a direct spokesman for God. With his "I say unto you," his authority transcends even that of the prophet's "Thus says the Lord." Matthew advocates a relocation of authority by virtue of the Christ-event. Jesus' teaching with authority is not merely a matter of speaking with volume and confidence, not a matter of tone of voice, but of how God's authority is mediated to us. The older configuration of book/tradition/persons who interpret them is replaced by one person. To be sure, the word of this person is now mediated to later generations by books/tradition/persons who interpret him. But the risen Christ continues in the process himself; the personal dimension is never reduced to book plus tradition. This corresponds to the combination of Jesus' teaching, all authority, and personal presence in the climactic conclusion at 28:16-20.

3. For the first time since 5:2, the voice of the narrator reappears (7:28). For three chapters, the hearer/reader has heard only one voice, that of Jesus, without interruption, question, dialogue, or comment by the narrator. At the conclusion of the sermon, there is no vocal response; the disciples are silent. The response of the crowds is reported, but not their words. All attention focuses on the word of Jesus. The hearers/readers almost forget that they are hearing a "sermon" in a story, for the authoritative instruction has become transparent to their own situation, functioning as address rather than report. This literary technique allows the hearers/readers to be directly addressed, as the disciples in the narrative become transparent to the readers' own post-Easter situation. This is one of the ways in which the continuing presence of Christ (18:20; 28:20) was experienced by the Matthean community and continues to be experienced by later readers.

4. Most of the church's struggle with the Sermon on the Mount has been oriented to the question How can anyone actually live this way? A more fundamental issue, and one more engaged with the contemporary perspective on ethics and the Bible, is the question Why would anyone even want to try to live this way in the first place? Superficial answers are available: The Sermon on the Mount is just common sense, or it helps one be happy and successful, or it is the way to gain heaven and avoid hell. Such answers are not only unhelpful, but also they are not Matthean. Matthew relates the sermon inseparably to the Preacher, and relates ethics inseparably to christology. To be sure, there is no explicit christology in the Sermon on the Mount. The subject matter of the sermon is not the person of Christ but the kind of life Christ's disciples are called to live. But the demands of the sermon are incomprehensible apart from the implicit christology found there (see 5:1-12, 17-20, 21-48; 7:21-27). One cannot avoid christology and appeal only to the teaching or great principles of Jesus, for these are inseparable from the claims of his person. But for Matthew the converse is also true: "Correct" christological understanding can never be a substitute for the kind of ethical living to which Jesus calls his disciples. Christology and ethics, like christology and discipleship, are inseparable for Matthew.

5. The traditional title for this passage has been the "Sermon on the Mount" since Augustine so labeled it in the fifth century, but the content represents Jesus' teaching more than his preaching, his *didache* rather than his *kerygma*. Matthew does not call it a sermon, but Jesus' "teaching" (5:2; 7:28-29). The core of the Matthean proclamation, shared by John the Baptist and Jesus' disciples, is the coming of the kingdom of God and the human response of repentance (3:1; 4:17, 23; 9:35; 10:7; 24:14; 26:13). Yet neither of these themes is found in the Sermon on the Mount. It is not directed to the general public, but presupposes the community of disciples who have already responded in faith to Jesus' preaching, who pray to God as Father and relate to each other as brothers and sisters. Unless this kerygmatic foundation is presupposed, one should be cautious in referring to it as a summary of Jesus' message.

6. Matthew's christological convictions are not communicated in essay form, but are inseparable from the narrative he has composed. The sermon is to be interpreted as part of the Matthean narrative, a speech made by the main character within the story Matthew has carefully constructed. The statements of the Sermon on the Mount are not general moral principles or advice of a religious genius or guru that can stand on their own. Both their meaning and their validity are derived from the story of what God has done in Jesus. Without the narrative context of the priority of grace, the sermon can be misunderstood synergistically as the ultimate legalism. Although it has many imperatives, the sermon is not a list of things we should do. As elsewhere in Matthew, the imperative of human response presupposes the indicative of God's action.

7. It has not been easy for a church that takes this text seriously to come to terms with it. Throughout the centuries, the main contours of the church's struggle to understand and obey its teaching may be classified under the headings of those to whom the church understood these instructions to be addressed and when these instructions were thought to apply. If it seems impossible that the sermon is intended to apply to everyone at all times, can its intention be better understood by limiting the persons or times to which it applies? This line of approach has resulted in the following categories of interpretation:

The Sermon Applies to Everyone, or to All Christians, and to All Times. (a) The literature of early Christianity assumes that the precepts of the sermon applied to all Christians, and that they were simply to be done with common sense being the guide.[182] Even after the "problem" with such precepts as literally turning the other cheek and giving away one's property became sharper, there have been individuals such as Leo Tolstoy and groups such as the Anabaptists who believed the sermon was simply to be literally practiced—which often meant a withdrawal from ordinary society.[183]

(b) A second way of applying the sermon to everyone relies on non-literal idealistic interpretation. Jesus and Matthew are thought of as wholesome idealists who gave us goals that, even if we cannot literally reach them, provide us with direction for our ethical striving. The older Protestant liberalism tended in this direction, reducing the sermon to principles and attitudes that should influence our practice. The center of the sermon became 6:1-18 as the key to the rest, and the purported legalism and externalism of "the Jews" became the foil for the "inner" ethic of Jesus.[184]

(c) Another approach, developed in the Lutheran tradition, applies the sermon to everyone in all times, but understands its function to be negative. In this tradition the sermon is understood to function as Law. Just as the Law was given to make us aware of our own inability to fulfill it and our need of God's grace, so also the sermon was given as a *praeparatio evangelica* intended to reveal to us our own impotence and drive us to despair, to compel us to stop exerting ourselves in establishing our own righteousness. This very Pauline understanding can lead either to a perverted view of cheap grace, or to a christological interpretation in which Jesus is the one who, as the Second Adam, fulfills the Law.[185]

The Sermon Applies Only to Certain People. A second major approach comes to terms with the perceived difficulty of the sermon's demands by arguing that it was not intended to

---

182. Cf. the sturdy no-nonsense comment of the *Didache,* "If you can bear the whole yoke of the Lord, you will be perfect, but if you cannot, do what you can" (*Did.* 6.1).

183. Hans Windisch, *The Meaning of the Sermon on the Mount* (Philadelphia: Westminster, 1951), argued that this was its meaning for Matthew, who was a legalist and perfectionist and who gives not a hint of human inability to fulfill the law, or of pride in self-achievement.

184. See Adolf Harnack, *What Is Christianity?* (New York: Harper and Bros., 1957).

185. See Eduard Thurneysen, *The Sermon on the Mount* (Richmond: John Knox, 1964).

apply to everyone, as all the above approaches assume, but only to certain people. During the Middle Ages the view, typified by Thomas Aquinas, was developed that the precepts of the Christian faith apply to all Christians, but that the "counsels of perfection" are only for priests, monks, and nuns. This seems to have some support from Matthew's own editing of Mark, where he adds to the Decalogue, required of all, the counsel "but if you would be perfect" (Matt. 19:21; cf. Mark 10:19). This need not be thought of as a compromise, but can represent the view that, if it is unrealistic to ask the majority to live strictly by the Sermon on the Mount, at least some should do so, not as a matter of self-righteousness or being better than others, but as a testimony to and embodiment of the will of God for all.

The Sermon Applies Only to Certain Times. A third major approach comes to terms with the sermon by arguing that it applies only at a certain time—i.e., that it is qualified eschatologically. There are three varieties of this view.

(a) The kind of dispensationalism popularized especially in America by C. I. Scofield's *Scofield Reference Bible* argues that the Sermon on the Mount was not intended for Jesus' hearers or for our own time, but is the kingdom ethic that will be practiced during the millennial kingdom, after the second coming of Christ.

(b) The rediscovery of eschatology in the teaching of Jesus was extremely important, for it had been discounted by Protestant liberalism.[186] While "kingdom of God" had been a matter of "the heart" in liberalism, Johannes Weiss and Albert Schweitzer showed that in the synoptic Gospels, it has an eschatological meaning, and argued that Jesus expected the apocalyptic end of the world to come very soon and that his teaching was intended to be practiced literally, since it applied only to the brief period before the end (the "interim ethic").

(c) Schweitzer's view is not advocated by any New Testament scholar now, but his rediscovery of the eschatological aspect of gospel ethics became the foundation for developing a view that has been influential. In this view, eschatology allowed Jesus (and Matthew) to perceive and announce the unconditional will of God, valid for all times, not just as an emergency matter for the interim. The Matthean Jesus is understood as one who sees the world and life in the light of the dawning kingdom of God (future/present), and who can thus reveal the life God requires in this light, without qualifications. This approach takes the historical situation and historical-conditionedness of the sermon seriously, without making it a relic separate from our own time and our own decisions.[187]

186. See Albert Schweitzer, *The Quest of the Historical Jesus* (New York: Macmillan, 1968).
187. See Günther Bornkamm, *Jesus of Nazareth* (New York: Harper and Bros., 1960). For further discussion of the Sermon on the Mount, see the Bibliography.

Matthew 8:1–9:34, Miracles and Discipleship

OVERVIEW

Matthew has previously given a summary statement of Jesus' healing and exorcisms (4:23-24), but here are the first miracle stories in the Gospel. Matthew has gathered them from his sources and arranged them to communicate his theological message. The miracle stories in 8:1–9:34 should not be interpreted in isolation, but each should be interpreted in the context of the section as a whole, since it has been constructed by Matthew as a single integrated unit presenting Jesus as "Messiah in deed" (cf. 11:2), corresponding to 5:1–7:29 as "Messiah in word" (cf. 7:28 and Introduction). The picture of Jesus speaking and acting with "authority" (ἐξουσία *exousia*) binds together the two sub-sections (implicit throughout (cf. 7:29; 8:9; 9:6-8).

From his sources (Mark and Q), Matthew has chosen stories of Jesus' "works" that picture God's

Figure 5: The Structure of Matthew 8:1–9:34

I. Christ Acts in Power for the Marginal and Excluded   8:1-17
    A. For a leprous person   8:1-4 = Mark 1:40-45
    B. For a Roman officer's paralyzed servant/slave   8:5-13 = Q; Luke 7:1-10
    C. For a sick woman and many others   8:14-15 = Mark 1:29-31
II. Christ's Mighty Acts Generate a Community of Disciples   8:18–9:17
    A. Christ calls into the storm, of which he is master   8:18-27 = Q; Luke 9:57-60; Mark 4:35-41
    B. Christ calls into new horizons, where he is master   8:28-34 = Mark 5:1-20
    C. Christ's call generates opposition, of which he is master   9:1-17 = Mark 2:1-22
III. Christ's Power Evokes Faith and Unbelief   9:18-34
    A. Faith in Jesus, who overcomes sickness,
      isolation, and death   9:18-26 = Mark 5:21-43
    B. Sight to the blind and the question of faith   9:27-31 = Mark 10:46-52)
    C. Faith and unbelief: healing a speechless, demonized man   9:32-34 = Q; Luke 11:14-15

saving power present in Jesus to deliver people victimized by circumstances and powers from which they cannot save themselves: leprosy, paralysis, sickness, earthquake and storm, demon possession, sin, speech and hearing disability, blindness, and death. Each story is a gospel in miniature that points to the meaning of the Christ-event as a whole. Several cases present people marginalized by Jewish society: the leprous man, the Gentile, the demonized person, the women, especially the woman with the hemorrhage (Matthew, like the other Gospels, presents no stories of Jesus healing a priest, a Pharisee, a scribe, an elder, or a Sadducee). Matthew has also made his selection correspond to the Scripture's description of eschatological salvation (Isa 35:5-6), which he will later quote, pointing back to this section (11:4-5).

Once again, Matthew's outline is triadic, with three sets of three miracle stories. Since one story has another inserted into it (9:18-26), there are actually ten miracles, another reflection of the Moses typology that shimmers through Matthew's compositional strategy. Just as Moses worked ten acts of power in delivering the people of God, so does Jesus as well. But Jesus' mighty deeds are all acts of mercy and deliverance—even for a Roman—rather than a judgment on the oppressor. As Matthew has transformed the violent, conquering "Son of David" into the healing King who does not retaliate but withdraws (see 12:9-21), he has replaced the violent acts of deliverance with acts of compassion.

The section is not composed exclusively of miracle stories, but includes elements that illustrate the meaning of discipleship, faith, and the conflict initiated by the incursion of the kingdom of God (8:18-22; 9:9-17). The discipleship material is not extraneous, but is integrated into the literary structure, which underscores the Matthean conviction that christology and discipleship (ecclesiology) are inseparably related. These considerations suggest the outline in Figure 5 as Matthew's own structure for this section.

The structure in Figure 5 has been carefully arranged to facilitate a certain movement to the story (to be experienced in the flow of the narrative, not seen as a static outline as presented above for analysis). The units are arranged to lead to a particular climactic scene. Matthew wanted to conclude with the divided response to the exorcism of 9:32-34 in order to present the Pharisee's charge of collusion with Satan as the last item in this series.

By 9:34, the reader is at a far different point in understanding the story of Jesus than at 8:1. For the first time in the Gospel, conflict emerges between Jesus and other people (at 9:2 the scribes protest Jesus' pronouncement of forgiveness). Previously, only the devil had opposed Jesus (4:1-11), the conflict between God's kingdom and Satan's having been prefigured in 1:18–2:23. Now, in response to Jesus' words and deeds of authority, a split occurs in Israel, and the community of Jesus' disciples is formed. The Pharisees join the conflict in 9:11, on the same issue: Jesus' acceptance of sinners. The conflict is not because of Jesus' offense against the Torah, which he explicitly keeps (8:4), but because he acts in the place of God to forgive sins and accept sinners (cf. 1:21-23). The conflict escalates so that finally the

Pharisees accuse him of acting by the power of Satan. Throughout all of 8:1–9:34 no one denies that the miracles really happened. One may respond to the Christ who works miracles either in faith or unfaith, all the while accepting the miracles. (See Excursus "Interpreting the Miracle Stories in Matthew," 241-51.)

Matthew 8:1-17, Christ Acts in Power for the Marginal and Excluded

MATTHEW 8:1-4, CHRIST HEALS A LEPROUS PERSON

NIV	NRSV
8 When he came down from the mountainside, large crowds followed him. ²A man with leprosy*a* came and knelt before him and said, "Lord, if you are willing, you can make me clean." ³Jesus reached out his hand and touched the man. "I am willing," he said. "Be clean!" Immediately he was cured*b* of his leprosy. ⁴Then Jesus said to him, "See that you don't tell anyone. But go, show yourself to the priest and offer the gift Moses commanded, as a testimony to them."	**8** When Jesus*a* had come down from the mountain, great crowds followed him; ²and there was a leper*b* who came to him and knelt before him, saying, "Lord, if you choose, you can make me clean." ³He stretched out his hand and touched him, saying, "I do choose. Be made clean!" Immediately his leprosy*b* was cleansed. ⁴Then Jesus said to him, "See that you say nothing to anyone; but go, show yourself to the priest, and offer the gift that Moses commanded, as a testimony to them."
a2 The Greek word was used for various diseases affecting the skin—not necessarily leprosy. *b3* Greek *made clean*	*a* Gk *he* *b* The terms *leper* and *leprosy* can refer to several diseases

COMMENTARY

A person afflicted with "leprosy" takes the initiative to come to Jesus. The biblical term for "leprosy" is not identical with Hansen's disease, leprosy as we know it in the modern sense, but covers a variety of skin diseases, several of them non-fatal. It is clear, however, that Matthew thinks of the plight of the afflicted man in terms of Leviticus 13–14, where leprosy is physically and socially a living death ("The person who has the leprous disease . . . shall wear torn clothes . . . and he shall cover his upper lip and cry out, 'Unclean, unclean.' . . . He shall live alone" [Lev 13:45-46 NRSV]).[188] The rabbis devoted an

extensive tractate in the Mishnah to it, *Nega'im,* and compared its healing to resurrection from the dead. Matthew has rearranged the sequence of his source to begin with this story, which symbolizes the human situation and the saving work of God in Christ, who restores people to life and community, and also to emphasize Jesus' respect for the Torah. Thus the man "worships" Jesus (προσκυνέω *proskyneō,* same word used in 2:2, 8; 4:10; etc.) and addresses him not as a magician or miracle-working holy man, but with the Christian title "Lord," used only by believers in Matthew. (See Excursus "Matthean Christology," 353-61.) He does not cry the required warning "unclean," but asks for help as in petitioning a

188. The difference between "clean" and "unclean" is a matter of ritual contamination, not of degrees of sanitation. What is "unclean" is not dirty, but is potentially dangerous, somewhat like the modern concept of being contaminated by radiation.

deity (cf. 7:7). Nor does he ask Jesus to heal him "if you can," but confesses faith appropriate to the post-Easter exalted Lord and makes everything depend on Jesus' sovereign will. Jesus' response corresponds to this. He does not invoke God's power or name, does not say "God wills" but "I will," speaking with the sovereign authority of one who is God with us (1:21).

A leprous person who had been cured could not reenter society until officially pronounced clean by a priest. The Torah prescribes a lengthy ritual to accomplish this cleansing (Leviticus 14). Jesus is portrayed as commanding strict adherence to the Law (e.g., 5:17-20). In Matthew's source, "say nothing to anyone" (v. 4) was part of the Markan "messianic secret"; here, it only means "Don't dawdle; go directly to the priest," underscoring Jesus' concern to keep the Law. The man, typifying the response appropriate to a disciple, does so. (Matthew omits Mark 1:45!) The man's act is "a testimony to them," both that he is certified as free from leprosy and that Jesus is Torah-observant; it also testifies to the reader that Jesus accomplishes the works of the Messiah (11:5). In this pericope Jesus both upholds the Law (as in 5:17) and transcends it, technically violating it (in touching the leper, 8:3; cf. Lev 5:3; 14–15). The pericope thus has the same dialectical attitude toward the Law as do the antitheses (see 5:21-48).

MATTHEW 8:5-13, CHRIST HEALS A ROMAN OFFICER'S SON/SERVANT[189]

189. Matthew's ambiguous παῖς (*pais*) can mean either "son" or "servant." Luke understands it unambiguously as "servant" (Luke 7:2), while the related story in John 4:53-54 speaks of the nobleman's "son" (John 4:47). Matthean usage suggests "son" as the meaning here (cf. 2:16; 17:14-21); "slave" in v. 9 translates a different word. The parallel to the Canaanite woman's daughter (15:22) also argues for "son" as the meaning here.

NIV

5When Jesus had entered Capernaum, a centurion came to him, asking for help. 6"Lord," he said, "my servant lies at home paralyzed and in terrible suffering."

7Jesus said to him, "I will go and heal him."

8The centurion replied, "Lord, I do not deserve to have you come under my roof. But just say the word, and my servant will be healed. 9For I myself am a man under authority, with soldiers under me. I tell this one, 'Go,' and he goes; and that one, 'Come,' and he comes. I say to my servant, 'Do this,' and he does it."

10When Jesus heard this, he was astonished and said to those following him, "I tell you the truth, I have not found anyone in Israel with such great faith. 11I say to you that many will come from the east and the west, and will take their places at the feast with Abraham, Isaac and Jacob in the kingdom of heaven. 12But the subjects of the kingdom will be thrown outside, into the darkness, where there will be weeping and gnashing of teeth."

13Then Jesus said to the centurion, "Go! It will be done just as you believed it would." And his servant was healed at that very hour.

NRSV

5When he entered Capernaum, a centurion came to him, appealing to him 6and saying, "Lord, my servant is lying at home paralyzed, in terrible distress." 7And he said to him, "I will come and cure him." 8The centurion answered, "Lord, I am not worthy to have you come under my roof; but only speak the word, and my servant will be healed. 9For I also am a man under authority, with soldiers under me; and I say to one, 'Go,' and he goes, and to another, 'Come,' and he comes, and to my slave, 'Do this,' and the slave does it." 10When Jesus heard him, he was amazed and said to those who followed him, "Truly I tell you, in no one[a] in Israel have I found such faith. 11I tell you, many will come from east and west and will eat with Abraham and Isaac and Jacob in the kingdom of heaven, 12while the heirs of the kingdom will be thrown into the outer darkness, where there will be weeping and gnashing of teeth." 13And to the centurion Jesus said, "Go; let it be done for you according to your faith." And the servant was healed in that hour.

[a] Other ancient authorities read *Truly I tell you, not even*

COMMENTARY

Matthew composes this scene by combining two sections of Q (Luke 7:1-10; 13:28-29). Matthew's combination and compression of the narrative focus attention on the sayings of both the centurion and Jesus.

8:5-6. In the Matthean story line, Jesus reenters Capernaum, his "own city" (cf. 9:1) for the first time since it was symbolically designated his residence in "Galilee of the Gentiles" (4:13-16). A Gentile military officer approaches Jesus, addressing him as "Lord" (as in 8:2). This is more direct than in the Lukan version, where the centurion never appears personally. He makes no request, but only states his need: At home is his paralyzed servant (or son) in great pain.

8:7-9. Punctuation marks do not appear in ancient MSS. Whether Jesus' response is to be understood as a statement (as in the NRSV and the NIV) or as a question is, like all such decisions, necessarily editorial and interpretative. The fact that Matthew intends Jesus' response to be understood as a question expressing hesitation ("I should come and heal him?") is probably indicated by the sentence structure (initial "I" [ἐγώ *egō*]) and by the parallel to the similar story in 15:21-28, where Jesus' initial response to a Gentile is negative. Matthew portrays Jesus as the Jewish Messiah, sent to the lost sheep of the house of Israel (10:5-6; 15:24), who is loyal to the Torah, as the preceding story and sermon emphasize, and is never pictured as entering a Gentile house (cf. Acts 10:28). Like the woman of 15:21-28, the centurion is not put off by Jesus' question, but considers it a test of faith—which he passes with flying colors. He explains that it is not necessary for Jesus actually to enter the house, but only to speak, and the child will be healed. "For I also" (καὶ γὰρ ἐγώ *kai gar egō*) at the beginning of v. 9 should be translated "If even I," so that the argument is not based on the similarity of his role to Jesus (which the initial address "Lord" repudiates), but means "If even I, who am under the authority of my superior officers,[190] can give commands and expect them to be carried

out, you, who are subject to no higher authority [cf. 28:17] need only say the word and the deed is done."

8:10. On "truly" (ἀμήν *amēn*), see 5:18. The note of disappointment that such faith has not been found in Israel comes as a surprise to the contemporary reader, since there have not yet been any negative experiences with the people of Israel in the Matthean story (except in the anticipatory birth story). The statement, like the following threat against the "heirs of the kingdom of heaven" seems to presuppose something not thus far present in the narrative. This is one of many indications (e.g., 10:38) that the Gospel was written for a particular readership already thoroughly familiar with Mark, Q, and their own past experience, all of which offered ample illustrations of lack of faith in Israel, and shows that the text should be interpreted historically (see Introduction).

8:11-12. Matthew emphasizes this perspective on the story by bringing vv. 11-12 into this context. The common interpretation is that "many from east and west" refers to believing Gentiles, like the centurion. Isaiah 2 pictures these believing Gentiles as making the eschatological pilgrimage to worship Israel's God, joining with the patriarchs of Israel in the eschatological banquet, while unbelieving Israel suffers the pain of final condemnation. This is the meaning of the terribly vivid imagery of "outer darkness" with "weeping and gnashing of teeth." Matthew combines two traditional images of Jewish eschatology and uses them against unbelieving Jews. This is not, however, necessarily a negation of the promises to Israel, for all Jews are not excluded. "Those from east and west" do not replace faithful Israelites, as the preceding story and Matthew in general make clear. Matthew does not expect the three patriarchs to be the only Jews at the eschatological party (cf. 19:28; 21:43; 23:39).

8:13. The brief conclusion declares that the miracle happened immediately, at a distance. As throughout the Gospel, however, the emphasis is not on the miracle as such, but on the faith of Gentiles, for whom "unbeliever" had been a common synonym. As elsewhere in Matthew, the man does not claim to have faith; it is Jesus who (twice) testifies to the man's faith (8:10, 13).

---

190. A centurion was in charge of 100 men, fitting into the military chain of command at approximately a sergeant's or lieutenant's level.

REFLECTIONS

If we were to first define *faith* so that we know clearly what it is, and then go looking for people (like ourselves) who have it, would we pass by this Roman officer? Even for us, he is an unlikely candidate for faith, and even more so for the other characters in Matthew's story. He is doubly the outsider, the first Gentile to appear in Matthew's story (after the magi of the birth narrative), and he is an army officer, part of the oppressive establishment.

One who is looking for evidence of faith in this man may first be struck by what is not said: There is nothing at all about his creed. So far as the story is concerned, we do not even know whether he was a theist, not to speak of monotheism.[191] Yet Matthew speaks of him as a model of faith. What does Matthew want to say to us in this story about the contours of real faith? The man feels compassion for someone else who depends on him. Matthew does not novelistically speculate on the details of the boy's illness or his relationship to the centurion. The story focuses on the centurion's concern for him, a concern that impels him to make a potentially humiliating request. He is not embarrassed to seek out an itinerant Jewish preacher and healer, confess his unworthiness to receive a personal visit, and ask him only to speak the authoritative word of healing for the child. There is a notable lack of swagger in all this. He understands the sickness to be a matter of authority and that Jesus' authority overrules the power that holds his son/servant in suffering and paralysis. This is what Matthew here identifies as authentic faith (cf. Reflections on 17:20, "faith that moves mountains").

Some of the categories are problematic for us (e.g., the view of the nature of authority presupposed). Yet there are ways in which we, too, may see the ills of life as a matter of authority, of who is finally in charge, and come to share the Gentile's faith, which trusts in an authoritative healing word that, once spoken, must have the last word. So understood, we may be saved from the simplistic reduction of this and similar stories to the formula "If I pray for healing and nothing happens, I don't have enough faith; if healing does come, it is because I have faith." Both self-centered guilt and self-centered pride can be dissolved by the faith that, in Jesus, the word of God is spoken, which finally transcends all boundaries and heals all wounds.

191. The form of this story in Luke 7:1-10 has additions that show that early Christian storytellers were also nervous about such issues, and that they made the centurion into a supporter of Judaism who had built a synagogue and was commended by Jewish elders as "worthy." None of this is in Matthew. Such comparisons remind us that in each case we are to interpret the text before us, not to make harmonizing reconstructions of "what really happened."

MATTHEW 8:14-17, CHRIST HEALS A SICK WOMAN AND OTHERS

NIV

14When Jesus came into Peter's house, he saw Peter's mother-in-law lying in bed with a fever. 15He touched her hand and the fever left her, and she got up and began to wait on him.

16When evening came, many who were demon-possessed were brought to him, and he drove out the spirits with a word and healed all the sick. 17This was to fulfill what was spoken through the prophet Isaiah:

"He took up our infirmities
and carried our diseases."[a]

a17 Isaiah 53:4

NRSV

14When Jesus entered Peter's house, he saw his mother-in-law lying in bed with a fever; 15he touched her hand, and the fever left her, and she got up and began to serve him. 16That evening they brought to him many who were possessed with demons; and he cast out the spirits with a word, and cured all who were sick. 17This was to fulfill what had been spoken through the prophet Isaiah, "He took our infirmities and bore our diseases."

COMMENTARY

The source of the story in this passage is Mark 1:29-34. However, Matthew, greatly abbreviating it to focus all attention on Jesus, inserts this scene into the story line at a different point in the narrative. The day is not a sabbath (cf. Mark 1:21-34). As in the case of the call to discipleship, all initiative is with Jesus, who is the subject of all the initiating verbs: He descends from the mountain, comes into Capernaum, enters the house, sees the sick mother-in-law of Peter, and touches and heals her. This emphasizes the sovereign power of Jesus, and is in contrast to Mark, where disciples are with Jesus and others tell him of the woman's need. This is a discipleship story, as is the following one in 8:18-22. Not only is the woman delivered from fever, but also she is restored immediately to complete health and vitality, demonstrated by the fact that "she got up and began to serve him" (v. 15; in Mark, "them").

Archaeologists have excavated a building in Capernaum that was originally constructed as a house in the first century BCE, then apparently was used as a meeting place for Christians in the late first century CE. Fourth- and fifth-century church buildings incorporated it, apparently venerating it as Peter's house, and may have been historically correct.[192]

192. See J. F. Strange and H. Shanks, "Has the House Where Jesus Stayed in Capernaum Been Found?" *BAR* 8 (1982) 26-37.

The first triad of miracle stories is brought to a close by the summary of v. 16. Although he has not yet told an exorcism story (8:28-34 is the first), by introducing exorcisms into the summaries (as in 4:24) Matthew keeps alive the picture that Jesus' ministry is a conflict of kingdoms—the kingdom of God vs. the kingdom of Satan—as he builds toward the key scene of 12:22-37 (see Introduction).

The quotation in 8:17 is from Isa 53:4, representing a translation of the Hebrew text independent of and different from the LXX. Although the figure of the suffering servant in the Servant Songs of Isaiah 42–53 has influenced Matthean christology, this is the only explicit citation of Isaiah 53 in Matthew or any of the canonical Gospels. Like the other formula quotations, it does not interpret the text in its historical context, so it would be a mistake to bring in the whole figure of the suffering servant. The one sentence Matthew cites should be understood in its Matthean context to mean that Jesus has removed our infirmities and sicknesses—i.e., that he has taken them away, not that he took them upon himself and suffered them in his own body. The vicarious suffering of the servant in Isaiah 53 has become the powerful Lord who conquers and removes our suffering, precisely as in the preceding three stories, and as in the Targum of Isaiah 53.

Matthew 8:18–9:17, Christ's Mighty Acts Generate a Community of Disciples

MATTHEW 8:18-27, CHRIST CALMS THE STORM

NIV

[18]When Jesus saw the crowd around him, he gave orders to cross to the other side of the lake. [19]Then a teacher of the law came to him and said, "Teacher, I will follow you wherever you go."

[20]Jesus replied, "Foxes have holes and birds of the air have nests, but the Son of Man has no place to lay his head."

NRSV

18Now when Jesus saw great crowds around him, he gave orders to go over to the other side. [19]A scribe then approached and said, "Teacher, I will follow you wherever you go." [20]And Jesus said to him, "Foxes have holes, and birds of the air have nests; but the Son of Man has nowhere to lay his head." [21]Another of his disciples said to

NIV

²¹Another disciple said to him, "Lord, first let me go and bury my father."

²²But Jesus told him, "Follow me, and let the dead bury their own dead."

²³Then he got into the boat and his disciples followed him. ²⁴Without warning, a furious storm came up on the lake, so that the waves swept over the boat. But Jesus was sleeping. ²⁵The disciples went and woke him, saying, "Lord, save us! We're going to drown!"

²⁶He replied, "You of little faith, why are you so afraid?" Then he got up and rebuked the winds and the waves, and it was completely calm.

²⁷The men were amazed and asked, "What kind of man is this? Even the winds and the waves obey him!"

NRSV

him, "Lord, first let me go and bury my father." ²²But Jesus said to him, "Follow me, and let the dead bury their own dead."

²³And when he got into the boat, his disciples followed him. ²⁴A windstorm arose on the sea, so great that the boat was being swamped by the waves; but he was asleep. ²⁵And they went and woke him up, saying, "Lord, save us! We are perishing!" ²⁶And he said to them, "Why are you afraid, you of little faith?" Then he got up and rebuked the winds and the sea; and there was a dead calm. ²⁷They were amazed, saying, "What sort of man is this, that even the winds and the sea obey him?"

COMMENTARY

Here begins a new triad of miracle stories. In the preceding triad (8:1-17) all attention focuses on the authority of Jesus (the disciples are not mentioned in any of the three; cf. Mark 1:29); the next triad (8:18–9:17) emphasizes discipleship. In contrast to the paragraphing of most translations and synopses, 8:18-27 is one story that begins with Jesus' command to go to "the other side," and is not concluded until the "other side" is reached in 8:28. This story in which Jesus commands his followers to cross the sea to new (Gentile) horizons, encountering a terrifying storm en route, reflects the experience of Matthew's church in entering into new horizons of the Gentile mission and presents differing responses to Jesus' command (cf. 28:18-20).

Matthew identifies the would-be disciple in v. 19 as a scribe ("a certain one" in Q; Luke 9:57). Although there are Christian scribes (13:52; 23:34), this scribe is marked as an outsider both by his addressing Jesus as "teacher" (which no real disciple ever does; cf. 12:38, and the "Lord" of 8:21) and by his presupposition that one can apply to Jesus as a rabbi who accepts students, the normal pattern in the Jewish setting. However, one does not petition to become a disciple;

the initiative is always with Jesus (see 4:18-22; 9:9).

Matthew 8:20 (and not some speculative theory about the scribe's motivations or sincerity) explains Jesus' brusque response. Since "Son of Man" can mean simply "human being," the saying taken by itself could be a proverbial reflection on the place provided by nature for birds and animals, while human beings alone are outsiders in this natural environment. This is not the meaning here, however, where "Son of Man" has christological content (see Excursus "Matthean Christology," 353-61). For Matthew and his readers, the paradoxical irony of Jesus' response is that while creatures of the field and sky have homes, the Son of Man, who is Lord of creation and Judge of the earth, is a wanderer without a place in this world to lay his head (even the "pillow" of Mark 4:38 is omitted in Matt 8:24). The applicant is not specifically rejected, but his understanding of discipleship is challenged; Jesus does not receive applicants, but takes the divine initiative in calling persons to a life in which all the world's priorities are reversed.

This theme continues in 8:21-22, which Matthew has slightly rewritten. If Luke 9:59 represents Q, Matthew has eliminated Jesus' "unsuccessful" call to a prospective disciple and has transformed the person who asks permission to bury his father into one who is already a disciple.[193] At one stroke, Matthew thus emphasizes that Jesus' call is "effective" and that the response to that call is not once-for-all, but must be made again and again.

Many attempts have been made to make both the request and Jesus' response more palatable. On the one hand, for example, the disciple's request has been explained as his asking to remain at home an indefinite time—until his father dies and is buried, until the estate is settled—and he then will be "free" to follow Jesus. On the other hand, Jesus' harsh response has been allegorized to mean "let the spiritually dead bury the physically dead," or some such meaning with which we can more easily come to terms conceptually and ethically. Both avenues are false escape hatches from a hard saying. The man's father has just died. According to tradition burial must take place the same day; this is a sacred obligation, especially to one's parents (cf. Gen 50:5; Tob 1:17-18; 6:14-15). One can hardly imagine a more legitimate, reasonable request—and that is the point. Absolutely nothing may take priority over Jesus' call to discipleship (cf. the "first" of 8:21; 6:33; and the story of Elijah's call of Elisha, 1 Kgs 19:19-21, intentionally evoked by this story). This is also the point of Jesus' saying in v. 22, which must be allowed to remain the scandalous, shocking statement it is, without being allegorized or otherwise made conceptually manageable.

Matthew rewrites Mark to emphasize that the disciples follow Jesus into the boat (8:23; cf. Mark 4:36). Recent redaction criticism has underscored

and elaborated the suggestion of patristic exegesis, which understood the boat to be a Matthean symbol of the church.[194] This story thus is for Matthew not primarily a "nature miracle," but represents the experience of the Christians of Matthew's church, who were called to new horizons of discipleship, but encountered terrifying storms along the way. The storm does not represent the "storms of life" on an individual level, but the stormy experience of those who follow Jesus into the Christian community. Matthew thus rewrites the disciples' exclamation, which smacks of outsider impiety (Mark 4:38, "Teacher, do you not care that we are perishing?" [NRSV]) into a liturgical-sounding cry for help ("Lord, save us!"[195]) to the Lord of the church, who is still present with it (1:23; 28:20). Corresponding to this, the storm (NRSV "windstorm"; NIV "furious storm") is initially described as an "earthquake" ($\sigma\epsilon\iota\sigma\mu\acute{o}\varsigma$ *seismos,* v. 24), inappropriate to the account as a there-and-then story of the pre-Easter Jesus, but evoking the experience of the post-Easter church, which experienced earthquakes as part of the eschatological terrors it must endure (cf. 24:7; Rev 6:12; 8:5; 11:13, 19; 16:18). Likewise, Matthew's added description of the disciples, "you of little faith" (v. 26), connotes not the condition of outsiders, but the situation of believers in the church whose faith falters at critical moments; it also evokes Jesus' call for trusting faith (6:25-34; cf. 6:30, 14:31; 16:8; 17:20). Thus the story, though not an allegory, is a symbolical narrative that makes contact with the personal experience of the Matthean Christians, who were indeed "in the same boat" as the disciples in the story.

193. Ἔτερος *heteros* may mean "another" or "a different one." The word is retained from Q, where it simply means "another." By adding "of the disciples," Matthew indicates that it refers to a person belonging to a different category—namely, a disciple. The scribe in the preceding story is not a disciple; this person is. Contrast Daniel Patte, *The Gospel According to Matthew: A Structural Commentary on Matthew's Faith* (Philadelphia: Fortress, 1987) 120, who argues that both were disciples.

194. Cf. especially the classic essay by Günther Bornkamm, "The Stilling of the Storm in Matthew," in *Tradition and Interpretation in Matthew,* eds. Günther Bornkamm, Gerhard Barth, Heinz Joachim Held (Philadelphia: Westminster, 1963) 52-57.

195. Matthew has only unbelievers address Jesus as "teacher," only disciples address him as "Lord."

REFLECTIONS

Jesus has a mission in the world. It involves crossing traditional boundaries. It will go on, for he goes before his disciples, calling them to follow, and some always will. Just as Jesus commanded the disciples to depart to the far shore, so he also makes clear to us that the call to discipleship is not the adding on of another worthy cause to our list of obligations, but the shocking transformation of all our previous understandings of discipleship. It may well be that we must endure a stormy passage, and the "other side" we cross to may be unfamiliar territory. We are not told how either the scribe or the disciple responded to Jesus' declarations; we are left to ponder our own understandings of what it means to be a follower of Jesus. Each of us must decide whether to be a part of Jesus' continuing mission in the world, or to remain safely on the familiar shore.

MATTHEW 8:28-34, CHRIST CALLS INTO NEW HORIZONS

NIV

28When he arrived at the other side in the region of the Gadarenes,[a] two demon-possessed men coming from the tombs met him. They were so violent that no one could pass that way. 29"What do you want with us, Son of God?" they shouted. "Have you come here to torture us before the appointed time?"

30Some distance from them a large herd of pigs was feeding. 31The demons begged Jesus, "If you drive us out, send us into the herd of pigs."

32He said to them, "Go!" So they came out and went into the pigs, and the whole herd rushed down the steep bank into the lake and died in the water. 33Those tending the pigs ran off, went into the town and reported all this, including what had happened to the demon-possessed men. 34Then the whole town went out to meet Jesus. And when they saw him, they pleaded with him to leave their region.

a28 Some manuscripts *Gergesenes*; others *Gerasenes*

NRSV

28When he came to the other side, to the country of the Gadarenes,[a] two demoniacs coming out of the tombs met him. They were so fierce that no one could pass that way. 29Suddenly they shouted, "What have you to do with us, Son of God? Have you come here to torment us before the time?" 30Now a large herd of swine was feeding at some distance from them. 31The demons begged him, "If you cast us out, send us into the herd of swine." 32And he said to them, "Go!" So they came out and entered the swine; and suddenly, the whole herd rushed down the steep bank into the sea and perished in the water. 33The swineherds ran off, and on going into the town, they told the whole story about what had happened to the demoniacs. 34Then the whole town came out to meet Jesus; and when they saw him, they begged him to leave their neighborhood.

aOther ancient authorities read *Gergesenes*; others, *Gerasenes*

COMMENTARY

The "other side" reached through stormy experiences and in obedience to Jesus' command (8:28) is Gentile territory, made clear not only by the geography but by the presence of the large herd of swine (8:30). There is great confusion in the textual tradition of the place name, with Gadara, Gerasa, and Gergesa being attested in some MSS of each of the Synoptics, plus other variations. The solution adopted by most text critics, reflected in most critical editions of the Greek New Testament and modern translations, is that Mark 5:1 and Luke 8:26 originally read "Gerasa," while Matthew originally read "Gadara." Mark's Gerasa (modern Jerash) was a Hellenistic city thirty-three miles from the Sea of Galilee. Matthew, better acquainted with Syrian and Galilean geography, seems to have recognized this as problematical and changed the location of the story to Gadara, a Hellenistic city six miles from the lake, with territory that may have extended to the shore. If one understands the story to be a realistic description of an actual event, this still poses a problem in view of the extremely rugged terrain and the trips from the shore to the city implied in 8:33-34. Thus Gergesa, assumed to be located directly on the shore of the sea, entered the textual tradition somewhat late as an effort to make the story more realistic (first attested in Origen, third century). It is not clear that Gergesa actually existed (although a site purported to be Gergesa is shown to tourists today).

On disembarking, Jesus is met by two demoniac men; the disciples are not mentioned in this story. Mark 5:1-20 has only one demoniac, but Matthew characteristically doubles some figures from his sources (Cf. the two blind men of 9:27-31 to the one in Mark 10:46-52; the doubling of the story itself in 20:29-34, where two blind men replace the one in Mark 10:46-52; and 21:1-7, where one donkey in Mark 11:1-7 is replaced by two; cf. also the reduction of Mark's witnesses to two, 26:60 vs. Mark 10:56-57.)

For Matthew, the exorcism story is not an isolated incident, not merely the sensational account of Jesus' power to help an individual or two, but represents the cosmic conflict between the kingdom of God and the kingdom of Satan. Matthew thus omits many of the novelistic details of the much fuller Markan account (5:1-20; twenty verses are compressed to seven), in order to concentrate all the attention on Jesus.

Like the devil in 4:3, 6, the demons recognize Jesus as Son of God, which no human being has yet done in Matthew. Their challenge, "What have you to do with us?" (v. 29) is not a question for information, but a formula of repudiation—literally, "What to you and to us?" meaning "What do we have in common? We belong to two different worlds" (cf. 2 Sam 16:10; 19:22; Mark 1:24; John 2:4; *Acts of Thomas* 45). In contrast to the Markan account, the demons do not tell Jesus what to do, and he does not enter into conversation with them. They only ask in consternation whether he has come to torment them before the allotted time, and ask to enter the swine. Matthew shares the apocalyptic concept that demonic powers, which seem to rule the world now, will be punished at the advent of the eschatological kingdom of God.[196] With Jesus' arrival, the eschatological judgment of evil powers is already underway (cf. 12:28, and the place of forgiveness of sins in the next pericope). In contrast to the Markan account, there is no bargaining, no granting of a concession, no struggle, no manipulation, no exorcistical formula or procedure, but only one word spoken by Jesus: "Go!" (v. 32).

---

196. See *1 Enoch* 15–16; *As. Mos.* 10:1ff; *Jub.* 10:8-9; *T. Levi* 18:12; cf. Matt 25:41; 1 Cor 6:3.

REFLECTIONS

The emphasis in this passage falls on the authority of Jesus. In contrast to Mark, Matthew does not heavily emphasize the healing of demon-possessed persons (we do not even get to see them restored; Matthew does not mention them again). Instead, Matthew wants the reader to see Jesus as powerful and authoritative. Jesus commands the chaos with a single word.

This passage, then, functions as a promise that no form of evil disorder—political, clerical, familial, psychological, physical—can endure forever. The healing, calming, restoring word of the gospel will ultimately subdue the forces of chaos, frenzy, illness, and death.

MATTHEW 9:1-17, CHRIST'S CALL GENERATES OPPOSITION

9 Jesus stepped into a boat, crossed over and came to his own town. [2]Some men brought to him a paralytic, lying on a mat. When Jesus saw their faith, he said to the paralytic, "Take heart, son; your sins are forgiven."

[3]At this, some of the teachers of the law said to themselves, "This fellow is blaspheming!"

9 [1]And after getting into a boat he crossed the sea and came to his own town.

2And just then some people were carrying a paralyzed man lying on a bed. When Jesus saw their faith, he said to the paralytic, "Take heart, son; your sins are forgiven." [3]Then some of the scribes said to themselves, "This man is blasphem-

NIV

⁴Knowing their thoughts, Jesus said, "Why do you entertain evil thoughts in your hearts? ⁵Which is easier: to say, 'Your sins are forgiven,' or to say, 'Get up and walk'? ⁶But so that you may know that the Son of Man has authority on earth to forgive sins. . . ." Then he said to the paralytic, "Get up, take your mat and go home." ⁷And the man got up and went home. ⁸When the crowd saw this, they were filled with awe; and they praised God, who had given such authority to men.

⁹As Jesus went on from there, he saw a man named Matthew sitting at the tax collector's booth. "Follow me," he told him, and Matthew got up and followed him.

¹⁰While Jesus was having dinner at Matthew's house, many tax collectors and "sinners" came and ate with him and his disciples. ¹¹When the Pharisees saw this, they asked his disciples, "Why does your teacher eat with tax collectors and 'sinners'?"

¹²On hearing this, Jesus said, "It is not the healthy who need a doctor, but the sick. ¹³But go and learn what this means: 'I desire mercy, not sacrifice.'^a For I have not come to call the righteous, but sinners."

¹⁴Then John's disciples came and asked him, "How is it that we and the Pharisees fast, but your disciples do not fast?"

¹⁵Jesus answered, "How can the guests of the bridegroom mourn while he is with them? The time will come when the bridegroom will be taken from them; then they will fast.

¹⁶"No one sews a patch of unshrunk cloth on an old garment, for the patch will pull away from the garment, making the tear worse. ¹⁷Neither do men pour new wine into old wineskins. If they do, the skins will burst, the wine will run out and the wineskins will be ruined. No, they pour new wine into new wineskins, and both are preserved."

^a13 Hosea 6:6

NRSV

ing." ⁴But Jesus, perceiving their thoughts, said, "Why do you think evil in your hearts? ⁵For which is easier, to say, 'Your sins are forgiven,' or to say, 'Stand up and walk'? ⁶But so that you may know that the Son of Man has authority on earth to forgive sins"—he then said to the paralytic— "Stand up, take your bed and go to your home." ⁷And he stood up and went to his home. ⁸When the crowds saw it, they were filled with awe, and they glorified God, who had given such authority to human beings.

9As Jesus was walking along, he saw a man called Matthew sitting at the tax booth; and he said to him, "Follow me." And he got up and followed him.

10And as he sat at dinner^a in the house, many tax collectors and sinners came and were sitting^b with him and his disciples. ¹¹When the Pharisees saw this, they said to his disciples, "Why does your teacher eat with tax collectors and sinners?" ¹²But when he heard this, he said, "Those who are well have no need of a physician, but those who are sick. ¹³Go and learn what this means, 'I desire mercy, not sacrifice.' For I have come to call not the righteous but sinners."

14Then the disciples of John came to him, saying, "Why do we and the Pharisees fast often,^c but your disciples do not fast?" ¹⁵And Jesus said to them, "The wedding guests cannot mourn as long as the bridegroom is with them, can they? The days will come when the bridegroom is taken away from them, and then they will fast. ¹⁶No one sews a piece of unshrunk cloth on an old cloak, for the patch pulls away from the cloak, and a worse tear is made. ¹⁷Neither is new wine put into old wineskins; otherwise, the skins burst, and the wine is spilled, and the skins are destroyed; but new wine is put into fresh wineskins, and so both are preserved."

^aGk reclined   ^bGk were reclining   ^cOther ancient authorities lack often

COMMENTARY

Matthew 9:1-17 is a single unit. Matthew's call to discipleship and the resulting dialogue and dispute at the following dinner party are all integrated into one story, forming the second half of the literary bracket begun at 8:18. The broader context makes the general meaning clear: Jesus' authoritative word and deed generate conflict and the beginning of a new community.

9:1. Jesus' "own town" is Capernaum, on the western side of the lake, no longer in Gentile territory (but cf. 4:13-16). In the scene that follows, Jesus forgives the sins of a paralyzed man who is brought to him by others. Like the other miracle stories, this is a typical, paradigmatic scene, transparent to the situation of Matthew's readers, picturing the response of God-in-Christ to human need. The story is not to be allegorized (i.e., to say that "paralysis" = "sin," etc.), but functions symbolically to express the meaning of the Christ-event as a whole. Otherwise, one must assume that the paralytic man was a notorious sinner, or one must answer such questions as why Jesus did not forgive the sins of other people, including those who demonstrated their faith by bringing the invalid to Jesus.

9:2. Matthew omits the colorful details of Mark 2:2-4; his whole attention focuses on Jesus and his authoritative word. Thus when he says that Jesus "sees their faith," he presupposes the details of Mark, familiar not only to Matthew but to his readers as well. Surprisingly Jesus does not first respond to the person's "obvious" need, and heals him later only to demonstrate his authority to forgive sins. It is difficult to accept this story as an objective report of an actual historical event, but is understandable as expressing Matthew's theology that Jesus represents God's Savior from sins. (Cf. Matthew's emphasis in 1:21; 6:12, 14-15; 26:28 and Commentary on these vv.) Jesus assumes the man's need of forgiveness not because the man is a notorious sinner, but because he represents the universal human need for God's forgiveness (cf. 6:12).

9:3. Jesus' pronouncement of forgiveness is considered blasphemy by the scribes. In Jesus' and Matthew's day, "blasphemy" (βλασφημία blasphēmia) was a general term, referring to anything considered derogatory to the dignity of God.

Jesus is charged with blasphemy because he acts in God's place (1:23). Apart from the anticipatory and paradigmatic birth story, this is the first appearance of opposition to Jesus in the Gospel. Matthew has stripped the previous stories of the conflict elements they had in Mark (over the sabbath, etc.), so that *blasphemy* might appear here in the context of Jesus' claim to forgive sins as the initial point of conflict. It will intensify into the scribes' charge of Jesus' collusion with Satan (9:34; 12:24), and then will reappear at Jesus' trial (26:65) as the capital charge against him.

The scribes are the first of three groups who oppose Jesus in this section (9:11, Pharisees; 9:14, disciples of John the Baptist). Matthew has revised Mark to get another triad and to represent the broad spectrum of Jewish groups in budding opposition to Jesus. By omitting Mark 2:7, Matthew leaves the scribes' charge without grounds. It is simply presupposed that they are evil, that they cannot do good because their hearts are evil (cf. 12:34-35; 15:19). In Matthew, the leaders who oppose Jesus are flat characters, incorrigible, and thus cannot be included in the group that praises God in v. 8 (thus Matthew substitutes "crowds" for Mark's "all").

9:4-5. Like God, Jesus "sees" their thoughts, for the scribes have not spoken aloud—only Jesus speaks in this scene. The logic of "which is easier" should not be pressed. The point is that the one who heals by the power of God (which can be seen and verified) can forgive by the power of God (even though it cannot be seen and verified). Jesus implicitly claims to act as the Son of Man (see Excursus "Matthean Christology," 353-61). As in the preceding story, the eschatological victory of God over the demonic forces is already present in Jesus' ministry, so here the eschatological pronouncement of acceptance or rejection by the Son of Man at the last judgment (10:32-33; 25:31-46) is already present in Jesus' ministry. Although the Gospel of Matthew has a strong futuristic eschatology, it also has a realized dimension: The coming kingdom of God is already present in Jesus (12:28).

9:6-8. Matthew regards the miracle as having actually happened, and as a demonstration of Jesus' authority. But he does not focus on the healing as such, omitting the details that Mark includes in his Gospel. For Matthew, the point of the story is Jesus' authority to forgive sins. Thus the closing chorus from the crowds does not praise God for the miracle (as in Mark), but for the authority to forgive sins, attributed not only to Jesus, but to "human beings." Here Matthew is thinking of the church, in which Jesus' authority to forgive sins continues (16:19; 18:15-20).

9:9-11. The theme of God's acceptance of sinners continues in the account of the call of Matthew and the disputes at the dinner party at his house. The pattern of the previous story is replicated here: forgiveness/objection/Jesus' concluding pronouncement. Jesus' authoritative word, which calms the storm (8:26) and pronounces forgiveness (9:2), also compels human response. As in 4:18-22, on which the story is modeled, Jesus' powerful word creates discipleship. The story should not be psychologized; nor should the reader speculate about previous contact between Jesus and Matthew, on the basis of which he was "ready" to follow. The point is that Jesus' call is effective. People do not volunteer to be disciples (see 8:18-20). Jesus rejects persons who suppose they can become disciples on their own initiative; likewise, here he calls the rejected. (On tax collectors, see 5:46.)

Levi, the tax collector of Mark 2:14, becomes Matthew in this story, thus identifying him with the Matthew of Mark 3:18, for the first time defining that Matthew as a tax collector. Yet there is no evidence for the tradition that Levi and Matthew were two names for the same person. In fact, it was rare for Jews to have two different Jewish names (see 10:1-5). The author may have chosen the name "Matthew" because of some association of the apostle Matthew with Q or traditional M materials, but there is no evidence for this either. The idea that the author is here using his own name to claim apostolic authorship is practically inconceivable, as well, since it would require that the author use Mark as a source to narrate his own call, and that he do it cryptically.

The coming of the kingdom of God was sometimes pictured as a great feast (e.g., 8:11), thus the dinner party over which Jesus presides has the overtones of the eschatological fellowship of the messianic banquet. With whom one chose to eat was a matter taken seriously in first-century Judaism (see Acts 10:1–11:3). As the previous objection had been from the scribes, Matthew changes Mark to identify the objectors here as Pharisees. Since the protest is made to the disciples and not directly to Jesus, the scene likely reflects not only the practice of the historical Jesus in extending table fellowship to those considered outcasts, but also the continuing acceptance of "sinners" into the fellowship of the church (cf. Commentary on 9:8).

9:12-13. Jesus' response is a common proverb in Hellenistic (but not strictly Jewish) literature. Matthew adds the quotation from Hos 6:6 (as he does in 12:7). In the light of 5:17-20, it cannot mean for Matthew the repudiation of the whole sacrificial system prescribed by the Law (nor did it mean this in Hosea). Since he writes after the destruction of the Temple, literal sacrifice is a moot issue in any case.[197] The point is that the mercy of God, extended to humanity in Christ, takes precedence over all else, so that everything in the Law must be understood in this light.

9:14-17. Despite the continuity between Jesus and John the Baptist, which Matthew emphasizes (see 3:2; 11:11-15), here John's disciples appear as a separate group (cf. Mark 2:18) in some tension with Jesus and his disciples. Here they raise the issue of fasting. Jesus has already been portrayed as affirming both the Torah, which commands one day of fasting per year (5:17-20; cf. Lev 16:1-34), and the later custom of more frequent fasting, for which he even gives rules (6:16-18). Jesus' response is threefold:

9:15. Jesus' first response is that wedding guests do not fast during the wedding. In other words, the presence of Jesus is the time of eschatological celebration, the presence of the kingdom of God (12:28), here pictured as the messianic wedding banquet.[198] Matthew's major

---

197. Rabbis, especially Johanan ben Zakkai, had found Hos 6:6 to be a useful text after the destruction of the Temple in 70 CE, so Matthew's attention to this text is in step with contemporary Judaism. In Matthew's source, the text had appeared as the quotation of a Jewish scribe to Jesus. The scribe was then commended by Jesus (Mark 12:32-33). Matthew, wanting to say nothing good about "their" scribes, incorporates the text here (and in 12:7) as a saying of Jesus.

198. From Isa 25:6-10 onward, the time of eschatological fulfillment was sometimes pictured as a great banquet (see *2 Bar* 29:3-8; *1 Enoch* 62:14; 1QSa 2.17-22; Matt 8:11-12; Luke 14:15; 22:28-30; Rev 19:9), sometimes presided over by the Messiah, or a great wedding celebration. The image of Yahweh as bridegroom and Israel as bride was prevalent in the Old Testament and Jewish tradition (e.g., Hosea 1–3) and continued in the Christian community, with the Christ representing the bridegroom and the church as the bride (2 Cor 11:2; Eph 5:25-32; John 3:29; Rev 19:7; 21:2, 9, 17). Here the images are combined, and the eschatological banquet is portrayed as a wedding banquet.

point is that the presence of the messianic King takes precedence over all else. Although he repeats Mark's words about fasting after the bridegroom is gone, appropriate to Mark's view of the absence of the Messiah during the time of the church (Mark 2:19-20; 14:25; 16:6), this is in tension with Matthew's own theology of the continuing presence of Christ with the church (1:23; 28:20).

9:16-17. The second and third responses are that one neither sews a patch of new cloth on an old garment, nor puts new wine in old wineskins. Whereas the first response is clearly connected to the challenge from John's disciples, the relevance of the second and third responses to the issue of fasting is not so easy to see. "In themselves, they are matter-of-fact observations about the danger of mixing the old and the new; they do not even hint whether they give superiority to the old or to the new. . . . Luke actually seems to take them as giving preference to the old."[199] Whatever the original point in the teaching of Jesus or the pre-Matthean church, Matthew slightly rewrites the saying about wineskins, which in Mark 2:22 had already expressed concern not only for the new wine but also for the old skins, to allow the ambiguous statement to be an affirmation of both old and new. By adding "so both are preserved," Matthew thus intends both the old wineskins and the new wine, not, as Mark could be understood, both new wine and new skins.

199. F. W. Beare, *The Gospel According to Matthew* (New York: Harper & Row, 1981) 231.

REFLECTIONS

The mixing of old and new is risky business. In the presence of old and new, the safe option is to reject one or the other. Thus both the superficial traditionalist rule of thumb, "always stay with the old," and the superficial iconoclastic rule of thumb, "always go for the new," are uncomplicated, unambiguous, and timidly safe. In every situation one always knows in advance what to do, knows who one's allies and enemies are.

The sayings about sewing a new patch on an old garment and putting new wine in old wineskins have often been interpreted to mean that Judaism was the old garment/wineskins and that Christianity is the new patch or new wine, the lesson being that the two should not be mixed. The interpretation goes: The old garment of Judaism could not contain the new patch of Christianity; the old Jewish wineskins could not contain the new Christian wine. This traditional Christian interpretation is not only a bit too self-serving, but also hardly fits the context, which affirms that while Jesus' disciples did not fast with either the Pharisees or the disciples of John the Baptist during the earthly life of Jesus, during the time of the church they would fast. Fasting is not something "new" brought by Jesus, but belongs to the "old," a command of the OT and a custom of the Jewish tradition.

To be sure, Matthew sees Jesus as having brought something eschatologically new, not merely a remodeling or patching up of the old. But Jesus brings the eschatologically new in such a way that it does not do away with the old, but fulfills and preserves it (see 5:17-20; 13:52; 26:28-29). Throughout his Gospel, Matthew affirms both old and new, refusing to join the superficial versions of either the conservative or the liberal movements in his church. Thus Matthew's Gospel can be read as quite conservative or very liberal, as "Jewish" or "Gentile," as traditional or avant garde, for it has elements of all of these (see Introduction). In this way he is a true representative of Jesus, "the man who fits no formula."[200] If both old and new are to be preserved, how does one know when to keep the old and when to choose the radically new? There is no neat answer in advance, no safe rule of thumb, no party handle one may always pull. Matthew walks the dangerous line between old and new, affirming them both, sometimes being considered the enemy by both conservative and liberal, never smugly sure that he has chosen the right way, but knowing this is the life to which Jesus calls us and that we are not alone in it.

200. See Eduard Schweizer, *Jesus* (Atlanta: John Knox, 1979).

Matthew 9:18-34, Christ's Power Evokes Faith and Unbelief

MATTHEW 9:18-26, CHRIST OVERCOMES SICKNESS AND DEATH

NIV

18While he was saying this, a ruler came and knelt before him and said, "My daughter has just died. But come and put your hand on her, and she will live." 19Jesus got up and went with him, and so did his disciples.

20Just then a woman who had been subject to bleeding for twelve years came up behind him and touched the edge of his cloak. 21She said to herself, "If I only touch his cloak, I will be healed."

22Jesus turned and saw her. "Take heart, daughter," he said, "your faith has healed you." And the woman was healed from that moment.

23When Jesus entered the ruler's house and saw the flute players and the noisy crowd, 24he said, "Go away. The girl is not dead but asleep." But they laughed at him. 25After the crowd had been put outside, he went in and took the girl by the hand, and she got up. 26News of this spread through all that region.

NRSV

18While he was saying these things to them, suddenly a leader of the synagogue*a* came in and knelt before him, saying, "My daughter has just died; but come and lay your hand on her, and she will live." 19And Jesus got up and followed him, with his disciples. 20Then suddenly a woman who had been suffering from hemorrhages for twelve years came up behind him and touched the fringe of his cloak, 21for she said to herself, "If I only touch his cloak, I will be made well." 22Jesus turned, and seeing her he said, "Take heart, daughter; your faith has made you well." And instantly the woman was made well. 23When Jesus came to the leader's house and saw the flute players and the crowd making a commotion, 24he said, "Go away; for the girl is not dead but sleeping." And they laughed at him. 25But when the crowd had been put outside, he went in and took her by the hand, and the girl got up. 26And the report of this spread throughout that district.

a Gk lacks *of the synagogue*

COMMENTARY

This story presupposes the reader's familiarity with the Markan version (5:21-43), which had been repeatedly read in the Matthean community for some time (cf. Introduction). Matthew places the story in a different sequence, with Jesus still reclining at the meal at the tax collector's house. (The fact that he was reclining may be assumed from "got up" in v. 19; cf. Mark 5:21, where Jesus has just stepped off the boat from the Gerasene territory.) As in Mark, the story is an intercalation, because of the insertion of the story of the woman's healing into the story of raising the ruler's daughter from the dead. But since in Matthew the child is already dead when the ruler arrives to make his request of Jesus, this arrangement has now lost its Markan effect of delay

and suspense. Matthew utilizes it for his own purpose, however.

Matthew transforms the Markan "leader of the synagogue" (Mark 5:22) into a civil administrator and omits his name, Jairus.[201] This facilitates reader identification with the father, since Matthew's community is alienated from the synagogue, and Matthew never has Jesus work a miracle for any Jewish leader. It also alleviates the question that would have been important for a synagogue official—namely, whether Jesus has been made (ritually) unclean by the touch of the sick woman. Like the Gentile magi (2:11), the Gentile woman (15:25), and the outcast leper (8:2), the ruler prostrates himself before Jesus

201. The NIV represents the Greek text; by adding "of the synagogue," the NRSV reverses Matthew's editorial work and so changes the meaning.

with his entreaty. This reflects the perspective of the later Christian community toward the exalted Lord, as does Jesus' response in accepting such worship. The post-Easter perspective is also seen in the fact that the child is already dead and the supplicant already confesses resurrection faith (cf. Mark 5:23). Thereby Matthean readers not only look back on the resurrection of Jesus, who conquered death, but also on the story in Mark.

En route, Jesus is touched by a woman who has suffered a menstrual hemorrhage for twelve years. As in the case of the leper (8:1-4), the woman's affliction is not only physical but also social, for according to Torah, everything she touches is ritually unclean. See Leviticus 15, which has elaborate precautions and rules for decontamination for both men and women who have abnormal bodily discharges. For "unclean" see footnote 187.

The woman has already made a decision to touch Jesus, believing the touch alone will heal her. This could be understood as magic thinking as well as selfishness, for by touching Jesus she runs the risk of transmitting her ritual uncleanness to him (cf. Lev 15:25-30). The fact that she comes up behind Jesus is a relic of the Markan story that has no point here, since Matthew has omitted the crowds and the disciples in order to concentrate all attention on Jesus. She touches Jesus' garment, and for the first time in the story Jesus speaks. He has read her internal monologue (so only in Matthew; in Mark she speaks aloud) and declares that her action is an expression of faith (not magic or superstition), which has saving power. Only then, on the basis of Jesus' word, does Matthew indicate that the woman is healed. This avoids the possible misunderstanding of the Markan story in which the woman is healed by the touch, without Jesus' intent. Here, as elsewhere, Matthew's retelling emphasizes Jesus' authority and the faith of the supplicant.

Jesus also dominates the scene at the ruler's house. The entourage, including the ruler himself, is no longer mentioned. The funeral is already in progress (the father being absent!), with the customary hired flute players and wailers. Jesus dismisses them with the word that the child is not dead but is only sleeping. The crowd takes Jesus' statement literally and laughs him to scorn. Some nineteenth-century rationalistic interpreters of Jesus' miracles likewise misunderstood Jesus' statement as literally true and explained the miracle as Jesus' saving the young woman from premature burial.[202] By having the crowd get a good laugh from this, Matthew indicates that their literal understanding of Jesus' words is false; the child is certainly dead. The use of "sleep" for "death" here is not a hiding of the reality of death, nor is it a general statement about the nature of death as "only" sleep, but a christological statement about the power of Jesus. From the post-resurrection perspective of the church's faith expressed in this story, Jesus is pictured as the one for whom death is already vanquished, and he raises the young woman from the "sleep" of death as he will raise all at the eschaton.[203] The story throughout is Matthew's confessional statement of faith in the power of the resurrected Jesus, of which the ruler and the woman are both examples. Matthew characteristically eliminates the "messianic secret" motif in the Markan conclusion (Mark 5:43), which was difficult to imagine in any case.

202. See, e.g., H. E. G. Paulus, reported in Schweizer, *Quest of the Historical Jesus*, 53.

203. Daniel Patte, *The Gospel According to Matthew: A Structural Commentary on Matthew's Faith* (Philadelphia: Fortress, 1987) 137, gives a structuralist argument that the meaning is "not that death is nothing else than sleep, but that death is transformed into sleep."

MATTHEW 9:27-31, CHRIST GIVES SIGHT TO THE BLIND

[27]As Jesus went on from there, two blind men followed him, calling out, "Have mercy on us, Son of David!"

[28]When he had gone indoors, the blind men

27As Jesus went on from there, two blind men followed him, crying loudly, "Have mercy on us, Son of David!" [28]When he entered the house, the blind men came to him; and Jesus said to them, "Do you believe that I am able to do this?" They

NIV

came to him, and he asked them, "Do you believe that I am able to do this?"

"Yes, Lord," they replied.

[29]Then he touched their eyes and said, "According to your faith will it be done to you"; [30]and their sight was restored. Jesus warned them sternly, "See that no one knows about this." [31]But they went out and spread the news about him all over that region.

NRSV

said to him, "Yes, Lord." [29]Then he touched their eyes and said, "According to your faith let it be done to you." [30]And their eyes were opened. Then Jesus sternly ordered them, "See that no one knows of this." [31]But they went away and spread the news about him throughout that district.

COMMENTARY

This story is a doublet twice over, since it represents Matthew's rewriting of the story in Mark 10:46-52 (also retained in Matt 20:29-34), and since in both cases the one blind man of Mark has become two in Matthew. Matthew pieces the story together with details from his sources and elements from his own stories he has used elsewhere. Three reasons for this are discernible from Matthew's overall plan: (1) The story fills out Matthew's triadic compositional pattern. (2) Matthew regards Jesus' deeds in 8:1–9:34 as the fulfillment of the picture of eschatological salvation in Isa 35:5, to which he will refer in 11:5. He thus needs a story of the healing of blind persons prior to 11:5. (3) In this section he is developing the tension between faith and unbelief; thus he has rewritten this Markan story to serve that purpose.

9:27-28. "Have mercy on us, Son of David!" is almost a prayer in Matthew, to whom the royal motif is important throughout (cf. 15:22; 20:30-31).[204] The fact that the men followed Jesus connotes more than "walking behind" him; *follow* is Matthew's word for "discipleship," and is added here to his Markan source (Bartimaeus does not follow Jesus until the end of the story in Mark 10:52). As in 9:18-26, when the Matthean story begins the central characters are already at the point to which they are brought at the end of the Markan story. The idea that this is a story about discipleship is also indicated by their addressing Jesus as "Son of David" and "Lord" (cf. Excursus

"Matthean Christology," 353-61) and by their faith. To readers in the Matthean church, the story does not picture conversion, but is for insiders. Blindness does not afflict only outsiders, for the church is a *corpus mixtum* in which spiritual blindness is present and is always a threat, but can be healed when "blind" Christians turn in faith to the risen Lord (13:10-17; 16:5-12, 15-24).

9:29-31. This may well explain the problematic ending to the story. After healing them, Jesus commands the blind men, strange and even unkind in itself, not to tell anyone about what he has done. Yet they disobey his command. Biographical or psychological explanations for the command should be avoided. This is not a strategic move on the part of the historical Jesus to avoid unwanted publicity; surely one with miraculous power to heal the blind could handle public relations matters. This element in the story functions at the level of Matthean theology, not literal history. Matthew wants to illustrate a theological point—namely, obedience to Jesus' commands (cf. 7:24-27; 28:18-20). Matthew looks through his sources to find an instance where Jesus' command is disobeyed. The Markan motif of the messianic secret, otherwise avoided by Matthew, provides such material. Matthew had omitted these words in their original setting (Mark 1:43, 45; cf. Mark 5:19-20), but now finds a use for them, re-incorporating them as an illustration of those who call Jesus "Lord" but do not do what he says. The essence of discipleship is not miraculous wonders, but obedience to Jesus' word (7:21-23).

204. See John R. Donahue, *The Gospel in Parable: Metaphor, Narrative, and Theology in the Synoptic Gospels* (Philadelphia: Fortress, 1988) 117.

MATTHEW 9:32-34, CHRIST HEALS A SPEECHLESS, DEMONIZED MAN

NIV

32While they were going out, a man who was demon-possessed and could not talk was brought to Jesus. 33And when the demon was driven out, the man who had been mute spoke. The crowd was amazed and said, "Nothing like this has ever been seen in Israel."

34But the Pharisees said, "It is by the prince of demons that he drives out demons."

NRSV

32After they had gone away, a demoniac who was mute was brought to him. 33And when the demon had been cast out, the one who had been mute spoke; and the crowds were amazed and said, "Never has anything like this been seen in Israel." 34But the Pharisees said, "By the ruler of the demons he casts out the demons."[a]

[a]Other ancient authorities lack this verse

COMMENTARY

Like each of the miracle stories, this one should not be interpreted as an isolated story of Jesus' amazing deeds, but only as part of the whole story told by Matthew. It fits into this overall structure as a meaningful conclusion to 8:1–9:34, forming the third story in the third triad in this section. The story is a doublet of 12:22-24, both being derived from the Q story preserved in Luke 11:14-15. There are four reasons for Matthew's duplicating the story, and for locating it here: (1) He needed a third story for his third triad. (2) Looking ahead to 11:5, he needed a story of the healing of a speech- or hearing-impaired person to complete the "works of the Messiah," fulfilling the picture of eschatological salvation in Isa 35:5-6.[205] (3) Although he has already pictured Jesus as master of the demonic powers in 8:28-34, Matthew concludes this section with a story that illustrates the opposition between the kingdom of God, represented by Jesus, and the satanic kingdom. (4) Matthew concludes this section of miracle stories with a scene that emphasizes the response of Israel, especially the unbelieving response of the leaders, to Jesus' mighty deeds. He thus rewrites and uses again the Q story of Luke 11:14-15, which had become central to the structure of his narrative (cf. Introduction and Commentary on 12:22-37).

The miracle itself is told briefly and without color, with all the emphasis on the response of the people. The contrasting responses of the people, already present in the Q story (cf. Luke 11:14-15), are sharpened by Matthew for his own purposes. On the one hand, the crowds, representing the neutral masses but potential believers, are amazed at Jesus' deeds. While admiration and amazement are not faith, the positive response of the crowds becomes the foil for the perversely negative response of the Pharisees, whom Matthew adds to this story. Throughout, Matthew's concern has not been the factual issue of whether the miracles actually happened, which no one in the story doubts, but their meaning. When the Pharisees "explain" Jesus' exorcisms by linking him with the power of Satan, they bring to a head the opposition that has been growing since 9:3, and anticipate the ultimately libelous charge that will be directed against Jesus in the key scene in 12:22-37, toward which Matthew is building and which will reemerge as the capital charge against Jesus in the trial scene (26:65).[206]

This concluding story brings to an appropriate climax the response of faith and unbelief portrayed in the final triad of miracle stories in this

205. Κωφός (kōphos, here translated "mute") means either "deaf" or "mute," or both deaf and mute. The same word is translated "deaf" in 11:5, as in Mark 7:32, 37; 9:25.

206. On "prince of demons = Beelzebul" see the discussion on 12:24. Verse 34 is missing in D, three old Latin MSS, the Sinaitic Syriac, the Diatessaron, and in the quotations in Juvencus and Hilary, all belonging to the Western text type. Its presence in all other MSS, including the oldest and best, and its literary and theological function (e.g., it is needed to prepare for 11:5) argue convincingly for its presence in Matthew's original text.

section. The series declines from the response of authentic faith (vv. 18-26), to faith that becomes disobedient (vv. 27-31), to conclude with the wonder of the crowds, which is still potential faith and could become authentic faith were it not for the perverse unbelief of the religious leaders (vv. 32-34).

Matthew 9:35, Transitional Summary: Preaching and Healing, Crowds and Compassion

NIV	NRSV
35Jesus went through all the towns and villages, teaching in their synagogues, preaching the good news of the kingdom and healing every disease and sickness.	35Then Jesus went about all the cities and villages, teaching in their synagogues, and proclaiming the good news of the kingdom, and curing every disease and every sickness.

COMMENTARY

Instead of responding to the charge of blasphemy, Jesus resumes his ministry of preaching, teaching, and healing.

Matthew 9:35 is a transitional summary, both concluding the unit 4:23–9:35 and setting the stage for the following section in which Jesus charges the disciples. On the one hand, it forms a literary bracket with 4:23, which it reproduces almost verbatim, making 4:23–9:35 the central section, which we might label "The Words and Deeds of the Messiah" (see Introduction). On the other hand, 9:35 prepares for the mission charge to the disciples. Matthew emphasizes the continuity between the mission of Jesus and the mission of the disciples (see Reflections on 11:1).

❖   ❖   ❖   ❖

EXCURSUS: INTERPRETING THE MIRACLE STORIES IN MATTHEW

MIRACLE STORIES IN MATTHEW

Matthew includes more miracle stories than any other Gospel. In addition to its twenty specific miracle stories, other miracles are mentioned often in summaries (4:23-24; 8:16-17; *9:35; 10:1;* 12:15; *14:14;* 14:35; 15:29-31; [cf. 13:58]; 19:2, *21:14;* italicized texts reflect Matthean additions of miraculous healings to Markan narratives and summary statements) and in sayings of Jesus (his own: 12:28; 16:9; his and the disciples': 11:5, 21-24; the disciples alone: 10:8).

Q had few narratives of any sort, with only two miracle stories, both of which Matthew takes over, using one twice (Q 11:14-15 = Matt 9:32-34 and 12:22-24).

The Markan miracle stories are Matthew's basic source, just as overall the Gospel of Mark has been the most influential source in Matthew's conception of his Gospel. Matthew has all the Markan miracles stories except three: Mark 1:21-28; 7:31-37; 8:22-26. Since Matthew

Figure 6: Miracle Stories in the Gospels

A. Miracles Performed Directly on Persons

1. Exorcisms
#1 Healing the Demoniac in the Synagogue in Capernaum
————————   Mark 1:21-28   Luke 4:31-34   ————————

#2 The Gadarene Demoniac(s)
Matt 8:28-34   Mark 5:1-20   Luke 8:26-39   ————————

#3 The Syrophoenician (Canaanite) Woman
Matt 15:21-28   Mark 7:24-30   ————————   ————————

2. Exorcisms/Healings
#4 The Speechless Demoniac
Matt 9:32-34   ————————   Luke 11:14-15   ————————

#5 On Collusion with Satan
Matt 12:22-30   (cf. Mark 3:22-27)   Luke 11:14-15   ————————

#6 Jesus Heals a Boy Possessed by a Spirit
Matt 17:14-21   Mark 9:14-29   Luke 9:37-43*a*   ————————

3. Healings
#7 Jesus Heals a Deaf Man (and Many Others)
————————   Mark 7:31-37   ————————   ————————

#8 A Blind Man Is Healed at Bethsaida
————————   Mark 8:22-26   ————————   ————————

#9 Cleansing of the Leper
Matt 8:1-4   Mark 1:40-45   Luke 5:12-16   ————————

#10 The Centurion of Capernaum
Matt 8:5-13   ————————   Luke 7:1-10   John 4:46*b*-54

#11 The Healing of Peter's Mother-in-law
Matt 8:14-15   Mark 1:29-31   Luke 4:38-39   ————————

#12 The Healing of the Paralytic
Matt 9:1-8   Mark 2:1-12   Luke 5:17-26   ————————

#13 (Jairus's Daughter and) the Woman with a Hemorrhage
Matt 9:18-26   Mark 5:21-43   Luke 8:40-56   ————————

#14 Two Blind Men
Matt 9:27-31   (cf. Mark 10:46-52) (cf. Luke 18:35-43) ————————

#15 Healing the Withered Hand
Matt 12:9-14   Mark 3:1-6   Luke 6:6-11   ————————

#16 The Healing of the Blind Man/Men
Matt 20:29-34   Mark 10:46-52   Luke 18:35-43   ————————

#17 The Healing of the Crippled Woman on the Sabbath
————————   ————————   Luke 13:10-17   ————————

#18 The Healing of the Man with Dropsy			
———	———	Luke 14:1-6	———
#19 The Cleansing of the Ten Lepers[207]			
———	———	Luke 17:11-19	———
#20 The Healing at the Pool			
———	———	———	John 5:2-47
#21 Jesus Heals the Man Born Blind			
———	———	———	John 9:1-41

4. Raising the Dead
#22 Jairus's Daughter (and the Woman with a Hemorrhage)

Matt 9:18-26	Mark 5:21-43	Luke 8:40-56	———
#23 The Widow's Son at Nain			
———	———	Luke 7:11-17	———
#24 The Raising of Lazarus			
———	———	———	John 11:1-44

B. Miracles Performed on Nature

5. Sea Miracles
#25 Stilling the Storm

Matt 8:23-27	Mark 4:35-41	Luke 8:22-25	———

#26 Walking on the Water

Matt 14:22-33	Mark 6:45-52	———	John 6:16-21

6. Miraculous Provision
#27 Five Thousand Are Fed

Matt 14:13-21	Mark 6:32-34	Luke 9:10b-17	John 6:1-15

#28 Four Thousand Are Fed

Matt 15:32-39	Mark 8:1-10	———	———

#29 Payment of the Temple Tax

Matt 17:24-27	———	———	———

#30 The Miraculous Catch of Fish

(cf. Matt 4:18-22)	(cf. Mark 1:16-20)	Luke 5:1-11	———

#31 The Marriage at Cana

———	———	———	John 2:1-11

7. Curse Miracles
#32 The Cursing of the Fig Tree; the Fig Tree Is Withered

Matt 21:18-19	Mark 11:12-14	———	———
Matt 21:20-22	Mark 11:20-26	———	———

207. One might add as #19a the Lukan note added to the Markan story of Jesus' arrest, that Jesus healed the ear of the high priest's servant (Luke 22:51b). This account is unique. Form critically, it is not a miracle story, but since it refers to a specific person, it does not belong to the category of general summaries of Jesus' miracles, such as Matt 21:14; it is the only reference in any Gospel to a healing miracle of Jesus in the passion story.

The above can be represented in tabular form:

	Matthew	Mark	Luke	John
Exorcisms	2	3	2	0
Exorcisms/Healings	3	1	2	0
Healings	8	8	10	3
Raising the Dead	1	1	2	1
Sea Miracles	2	2	1	1
Provision Miracles	3	2	2	2
Curse Miracles	1	1	0	0
Totals	20	18	19	7 = total 64 for Gospels

A total of thirty-two different miracle stories (not counting summaries) occur a total of sixty-four times in the four Gospels. It is clear that in the Gospels miracles cannot be regarded as incidental and relegated to the margin, for they are woven into the texture of the Gospel fabric. Whoever will interpret the Gospels has no option but to come to terms with miracles.

It is to be noted that, with the exception of the cursing of the fig tree (Matt 21:18-19 //Mark 11:12-14), all the miracles in the Gospels are performed for the benefit of human beings. Even the "nature miracles" are performed to help people in distress. Although some sayings speak metaphorically of "nature miracles" and do not address human needs (Mark 11:23//Matt 21:21; Luke 17:6//Matt 17:20; cf. 1 Cor 13:2), there are no such stories in the Gospels. Unlike writings of the Hellenistic world generally, including the apocryphal gospels and even the book of Acts, the canonical Gospels contain no stories in which miraculous power is used punitively against human beings (cf. Acts 5:1-11; 13:9-12). In the Gospels, the genre of miracle stories, already present in the Hellenistic world, has been transformed by the character of Jesus, who embodies and makes present the love of God (Matt 1:23).

tends to subsume exorcisms under healings (see below), he has an aversion to pure exorcisms. (He does include two others: 8:28-34 = Mark 5:1-20 [severely abbreviated], and 15:21-28 = Mark 7:24-30, involving Gentiles. Both express themes of his own theology apart from exorcism as such, as noted.) In Mark 7:31-37; 8:22-26, Jesus resembles the Hellenistic miracle worker who uses "magical" means and is not entirely Lord of the situation. This may be the reason why Matthew avoided them.

Matthew's own tradition is sparing in miracle stories. From M he has only the peculiar 17:24-27, where the point is not the miracle itself.

Matthew tends to subsume exorcisms under healings. He once retains Mark's distinction between exorcisms and healings in a summary statement (8:16-17 = Mark 1:32-34), but never adds exorcisms to a summary or story in his sources. In 12:15 he omits the Markan reference to "unclean spirits" (3:12), apparently including them in his "healed all," as in 4:24 as well. While the kingdom of God present in Jesus' works effects the expulsion of Satan from his domain (see Commentary on 12:22-37), this is typically portrayed as healing rather than exorcism. Matthew transforms even the picture of the "Son of David" as an exorcist, present in first-century Judaism, into the *healing* Son of David, who is meek and retiring (12:15-21; 21:1-9) and who inaugurates God's kingdom in the healing power of love and mercy (cf. Matt 12:22-23; 21:14-15).[208]

208. See Dennis C. Duling, "The Therapeutic Son of David: An Element in Matthew's Christological Apologetic," *NTS* 24 (1978) 392-410.

Matthew tends to abbreviate the narrative element in the miracle tradition he inherits (cf., e.g., Mark 5:1-43 and Matt 8:28-34; 9:18-26) and to emphasize the sayings and conversations included within them, with the result that formally the Matthean miracle stories are closer to apophthegms, conflict stories, and didactive narratives than they are to the miracle story form preserved in Mark.[209]

Matthew emphasizes the relationship between faith and miracle (cf. 8:10, 13; 9:2, 22, 28-29; 15:28; 21:21-22), but not as proof of Jesus' supernatural power in order to generate faith. Sometimes the faith of others, instead of the one healed, elicits the healing, suggesting that faith is not understood as the psychological precondition of receiving healing, nor the meritorious "work" that receives the miracle as reward. Faith is, rather, the act of prayer that receives the act of God as its response.

NON-MIRACULOUS TRADITIONS ABOUT JESUS

Jesus is also pictured in non-miraculous ways in the NT. The epistles, following Paul, portray the act of God in Jesus in the incarnation, crucifixion, and resurrection, never referring to any miracle story and never giving any indication that the earthly life of Jesus was full of divine, miraculous power. The Gospels also contain traditions in which the life of Jesus is pictured as being devoid of miraculous power.

Matthew 4:1-11[210]	(Mark 1:12-13)	Luke 4:1-13
Matthew 12:38-42	Mark 8:11-12	Luke 11:29-32
Matthew 16:1-4	(Mark 8:11-12)	Luke 12:54-56
Matthew 26–27	Mark 14–15	(Luke 22–23)

This juxtaposition of traditions that portray the truly human Jesus, who is subject to the limitations of finitude, with traditions such as the miracle stories, which represent Jesus as being filled with the power of God, is central to the literary genre of the Gospel.[211]

MIRACLE STORIES AS INDEPENDENT UNITS

The miracles stories were first told not as constituent elements of a "life of Jesus," but each as a complete story, summing up some aspect of the meaning of the Christ-event for Christian faith. Each one shows some aspect of human need, symbolizing human separation from God, authentic life, and the need for salvation (from hunger, sickness, meaningless-ness, subjection to demonic powers and the accidents of nature, sin, death). Each one pictures the act of God in Christ to deliver human beings from this threat to authentic life. Each one looks back on the life, death, and resurrection of Jesus and sums up the meaning of the whole Christ-event in one brief narrative. When the stories were incorpo-rated into the Gospel narratives, they did not lose their christological character as witnesses to the saving act of God in Christ, although each evangelist interpreted them within the framework of his own theology. Contemporary teaching and preaching from the miracle stories can let this message of salvation mediated by them be heard again, irrespective of how they are understood as literal history (see below).

209. See Hans Joachim Held, "Matthew as Interpreter of the Miracle Stories," in Bornkamm, Barth, Held, *Tradition and Interpretation,* 211-46.
210. The temptation story is not only non-miraculous, but also has a certain anti-miraculous polemic. See Commentary.
211. See Introduction and M. Eugene Boring, *Truly Human/Truly Divine: Christological Language and the Gospel Form* (St. Louis: Christian Board of Publication, 1984).

NEW TESTAMENT MIRACLE STORIES IN RELATION
TO OTHER MIRACLE STORIES IN THE GRECO-ROMAN WORLD

In the Greco-Roman world, miracle stories were told of others besides Jesus. Thus interpretation of NT miracle stories is illuminated by attending to both similarities and differences to other such stories.

According to the New Testament, Miracles Are Performed:

1. By God directly (Matt 27:51-53; Acts 2:1-4; 2:17).
2. By God, through an angel (Matt 1:18-25; 2:1-12; Acts 12:6-11; 12:20-23).
3. By Jesus (see above lists and charts). In the NT, miracle stories about Jesus are virtually peculiar to the Gospels. Acts and the epistles affirm the reality of miracles, but do not report miracles of Jesus.
4. By apostles (Matt 10:1, 8, 20//Mark 6:7, 13; 13:11//Luke 9:1-2; 12:12 [exorcisms, healings, raising the dead]; Acts 3:1-10; 5:1-11; 5:12-16; 9:32-25, 36-43; Rom 15:19; 2 Cor 12:12).
5. By good disciples, missionaries, ordinary Christians (Acts 6:8; 8:6, 13; 14:3; 8-12; 15:12; 16:16-18; 19:11; 1 Cor 12:10, 29; Gal 3:5; Heb 2:4).
6. By bad, false, and unbelieving disciples (Matt 7:22 [exorcisms, prophecy, "deeds of power" (δύναμεις *dynameis*]; Matt 24:24//Mark 13:22, false Christs and false prophets ["great signs and wonders" σημεία καὶ τέρατα *sēmeia kai terata*]).
7. By non-disciples: Jews and pagans (Matt 12:27//Luke 11:19 [= Q]), Pharisees (exorcisms, Acts 19:13-16; 2 Thess 2:9; Rev 13:13-14; 16:14; 19:20).

In the NT world, miracles were part of the given furniture of the world. Miracles belong to the realm of the possible. The fact that they happen is an accepted part of the worldview of most people. However, their *meaning* is disputed. The distinctive thing about Jesus is not that he works miracles and others do not. It is specifically not the case that Jesus is pictured as working miracles and others are pictured as not being able to work miracles, but that both Jesus and others are pictured in both miraculous and non-miraculous ways.

Miracles and Miracle Stories in First-Century Judaism

The word *nature* does not occur in the HB, which has no concept of "nature" in the sense of a self-contained and consistent system. The same is true for first-century Jewish thinking, except to the extent that it has been influenced by Hellenistic thought. In OT-Jewish thought, the world is not a closed system of "nature" that God must interrupt in a supernatural way in order to act. The world functions as it ordinarily does because God wills it so; God can occasionally will it otherwise. This extraordinary activity of God, who is always active in the "natural" order of things, is a "sign," a "wonder," or a "miracle," not a violation of "natural law."

Miracle stories are not evenly distributed in the HB. Some narratives have a high concentration of miracle stories: e.g., the Moses story and the Elijah-Elisha cycle. Some have only God performing miracles, but no human miracle workers: e.g., stories about Joshua and Daniel. Others have minimal or no miracles: the Samson-Saul-David stories. There are no exorcisms in the OT (the concept of Satan as a demonic figure developed late). Some narratives have two versions, miraculous and non-miraculous (1 Maccabees; 2 Maccabees).

Some streams of first-century Jewish thought supposed that these extraordinary acts of God or the Spirit were limited to the biblical period and would reappear at the eschaton. But stories of miraculous deeds were current among the rabbis and other Jews as well.[212] Rabbi Gamaliel calms a storm (*b. Baba Mezia* 59b), as does a Jewish boy (*b. Ber.* 9:1). Walking on the water has parallels in Jewish stories (cf. Bultmann, *History of the Synoptic Tradition*, 237). There are rabbis who heal and cast out demons (*b. Ber.* 34*b*), the most famous one being the first-century Rabbi Hanina ben Dosa, who healed the son of the famous Rabbi Gamaliel from a distance and who could tell if his prayer was effective by whether he could pray fluently or not. Bread is miraculously provided for the wife of Rabbi Hanina ben Dosa (*b. Ta῾ anit 24 b-25 a*).

The "point" of such stories is usually not the miracle itself, but a saying. Sometimes, the point of a miracle story is that disputed interpretations of Torah are not settled by miracles: "R. Eliezer used every argument to substantiate his opinion, but they [the other rabbis] would not accept them. He said, 'If the law is as I have argued, may this carob tree argue for me.' The carob tree uprooted itself and moved a hundred cubits from its place. Some say it moved four hundred cubits. They said 'From a tree no proof can be brought.' Then he said, 'May the canal prove it.' The water of the canal flowed backwards. They said, 'From a canal no proof may be brought.' Then he said, 'May the walls of this House of Study prove it.' Then the walls of the house bent inwards, as if they were about to fall. R. Joshua rebuked the walls, and said to him, 'If the learned dispute about the law, what has that to do with you?' So, to honor R. Joshua, the walls did not fall down, but to honor R. Eliezer, they did not become straight again. Then R. Eliezer said, 'If I am right, may the heavens prove it.' Then a heavenly voice said, 'What have you against R. Eliezer? The law is always with him.' Then R. Joshua got up and said, 'It is not in heaven (Deut 30:12).' What did he mean by this? R. Jeremiah said, 'The Torah was given to us at Sinai. We do not attend to the heavenly voice. For it was already written in the Torah at Mt. Sinai that, 'By the majority you are to decide (Exod 23:2).' 'R. Nathan met Elijah and asked him what God did in that hour. Elijah replied, 'He laughed and said, 'My children have defeated me.' "[213]

Pagan Miracle Stories in the Hellenistic World[214]

The Hellenistic world was filled with stories of miracles by gods, demi-gods, and specially endowed human beings. A brief listing of samples might include the following.

1. Many inscriptions on tablets from Epidauros, the "Lourdes of the Hellenistic world," give praise to the god Asclepius for miraculous healings (mostly from the 4th cent. BCE).

2. Pythagoras manifested a miraculous knowledge of the number of fish in a great catch, keeping the fish alive while they were being counted. Pythagoras (c. 6th cent. BCE) conversed with animals, who did as he commanded; he crossed the sea miraculously; he calmed strong winds, raging rivers, and seas; and he stopped plagues.

3. Vespasian (c. 69 CE) healed the blind with his saliva and healed a withered hand with pressure from his foot.

4. Lucian of Samosata's detailed (and skeptical) description of a Syrian exorcist, from *The Lover of Lies* 16. (2nd cent. CE).

---

212. For a selection of such, see David R. Cartlidge and David L. Dungan, *Documents for the Study of the Gospels* (Philadelphia: Fortress, 1980) 158-62 and Klaus Berger, M. Eugene Boring, Carsten Colpe, *Hellenistic Commentary to the New Testament* (Nashville: Abingdon, 1995) on Matt 8:1–9:34.

213. *b. Baba Mezia* 59b.

214. A good selection is offered by David R. Cartlidge and David L. Dungan, *Documents for the Study of the Gospels* (Philadelphia: Fortress, 1980) 151-66. See also Gerd Theissen, *The Miracle Stories of the Early Christian Tradition* (Philadelphia: Fortress, 1983); Howard Clark Kee, *Miracle in the Early Christian World: A Study in Sociohistorical Method* (New Haven: Yale University Press, 1983); Berger, Boring, Colpe, *Hellenistic Commentary to the New Testament* at relevant passages for Hellenistic parallels.

5. Pausanius's *Description of Greece* 6.16.1-2 (2nd cent. CE) describes the wine miracle in the temple of Dionysus at Elis.

6. Philostratus's (3rd cent. CE) *Life of Apollonius* contains many miracles, exorcisms, and healings but is written to "tone down" the even more sensational earlier stories and to present Apollonius (1st cent. CE) as a more philosophical sage.

A SPECTRUM OF HERMENEUTICAL APPROACHES

Miracle Stories as Literal Reports of Historical Events

Some interpretations have considered it theologically important to interpret the NT miracle stories as accurate reporting of historical events that literally happened. There are two variations of this view:

1. Miracles happened then and happen now

In this view the factuality of biblical miracles is the foundation for believing that such miracles continue to happen. Contemporary claims to miraculous acts are in continuity with the biblical story. "If God did it then, God can do it now" is the motto.

2. Miracles happened then, but not now

This view regards the biblical era as a special revelatory period in which God worked miracles through chosen messengers, and especially through Jesus, in order to provide miraculous proof of the truth of the revelation. Once the revelation had been given and recorded in Scripture, they had served their special purpose and hence ceased. Later claims to miraculous powers are not in continuity with the Bible and are usually to be considered false. This option was already available in first-century Judaism, some streams of which saw the miraculous activity of God and the Spirit limited to the biblical past (Ezra being the last chosen messenger), but expected to return in the eschatological age.

Rationalistic Explanations

Real events happened and were misunderstood as miracles, but can be explained naturally. Exorcisms and healings are examples of psychosomatic cures and the powerful, calming presence of Jesus and his word. Raisings of the dead were cases of (almost) premature burial. Feeding the 5,000 was a lesson in sharing. Walking on water was an optical illusion, mass hysteria, planned deception (a raft), or a misunderstanding of an earlier story occasioned by the ambiguity of the preposition translated "on" (ἐπί *epi* can also mean "at the edge of," i.e. in the surf).

Mythological Explanations

The miracle stories of the Gospels are neither rationalistic explanations of "what really happened" nor reports of the supernatural interventions of a transcendent deity. The most influential exponent of this view is still David Friedrich Strauss,[215] who understood miracle stories as imaginative forms that expressed the faith of early Christians. "Myth" in this sense is not a negative term, but a vehicle for the higher truth about Jesus. The significance of Jesus is not reduced to a timeless "concept," but is mediated by pictures of Jesus as the fulfiller of biblical and Jewish hopes for the Messiah, using biblical imagery. In this view, there may be

---

215. David Friedrich Strauss, *The Life of Jesus Critically Examined,* Lives of Jesus series (Philadelphia: Fortress, 1973).

a kernel of fact in several of the stories, but whether they report actual events is not only doubtful, but also beside the point.

MIRACLE STORIES AS PRIMARILY KERYGMATIC AND DIDACTIC NARRATIVES

There is a significant difference between Gospel stories about Jesus and similar stories about Hercules, Asclepius, and Apollonius. In the NT, the miracle stories point beyond themselves to *express* a christology; they are not primarily evidence to *prove* that Jesus is the Christ or evidence *for* faith. Since for first-century readers miracle stories were a part of the given furniture of the world, they do not possess probative value. They are vehicles for proclaiming a faith, not evidence on which faith is based. The Gospel of Matthew is not directed to outsiders to convert them by reciting miracle stories, but to insiders to express and clarify faith.

The Faith of Those Healed Is Not the Primary Meaning

While Matthew transforms several miracle stories in such a way that they illustrate the meaning of faith, even in Matthew the faith of those healed is not the primary meaning. Miracles do not typically happen as the reward for people's faith. The Gospels do not teach "If you believe well enough, you will have miracles too; if you don't have miracles, it is because you do not have enough faith." On the one hand, this can be a works righteousness; on the other, it can be used to induce guilt.

Miracles as an Eschatological Category

The "prophet like Moses" of Deut 18:15-18 was expected to renew the Mosaic miracles eschatologically. Isaiah 35:5-6 was understood to describe the eschatological season of miracles. Apocalyptic expectation pictured the coming of the kingdom of God as the expulsion of Satan (e.g., *As. Mos.* 10:1ff.). Miracle stories make the presence and power of the kingdom visible. They portray Jesus in such a way that messianic power is visibly present in him. They are stories of the coming of the kingdom and the messianic age, not stories of Jesus as a man with great power. They are thus, like all talk of the kingdom of God and the coming of the Messiah, theocentric rather than Jesucentric.

The expectation was that the eschatological age would be a manifestation of the kingly power of God. Jesus' deeds of love and liberation—and the saving action of God in Jesus' life, death, and resurrection, taken as a whole—were of such a character that they were seen by eyes of Christian faith as the fulfillment of these eschatological expectations. The early Christians did not invent miracle stories about Jesus from whole cloth, but as the appropriate form for conveying their faith that the eschatological age had been inaugurated by the way Jesus had actually lived and by God's vindication of him by the resurrection. This was also the point of Strauss's "mythical" interpretation, discussed above.

Miracle Stories as Incidental Elements

Miracle stories may serve as incidental elements in other didactic and conflict stories, as in the key scene Matthew 12:22-37.

HERMENEUTICAL SUGGESTIONS

The following principles result from bringing to bear the above information and insights on the interpretation of Gospel texts containing miracle stories.

(1) Distinguish the meaning and validity of the story from its strict factuality. The meaning and validity of the story may be appropriated both by those who affirm factuality and by those who question it. On the one hand, if one accepts the miracle story as reporting a factual event, one does not necessarily believe the gospel and have Christian faith; one does not necessarily even "believe the Bible." On this hermeneutical approach, one may believe in miracles but may not identify the acceptance of miracles with Christian faith. People in the stories believed in the facticity of the miracle but did not become disciples. Likewise, today some acknowledge that Jesus was a healer/exorcist but are not Christians.

On the other hand, if one does not accept the facticity of the miracle, or has questions about its facticity, this does not necessarily mean that one disbelieves the gospel and does not have Christian faith. The goal of the miracle story is not to convince the reader of the factuality of miracles (i.e., to change the reader's worldview), but to allow the miracle story to be a vehicle of the Christian gospel.

(2) Evaluate the story mode of presentation as positively as the Bible does. Do not look pejoratively at "stories," as though the choice were "they really happened" or "they are just stories." Most stories have non-factual elements.

(3) Attend to the linguistic category or categories (kind of language) to which miracle stories belong. All valid language does not belong to the same linguistic category and does not function in the same way.[216] The language of miracle most often fits the category of confessional language, which is non-objectifying and non-referential, akin to the language of prayer.

(4) Respect the differences between modern categories of thought and those of the first century. The concept of "natural law" that is "violated" by a miracle is a modern way of thinking and should not be imposed on the biblical materials. Specifically, the alternative "either natural or from God" is false from the biblical point of view.

(5) Avoid framing the issue in such a way that believing the gospel is equated with accepting a particular worldview or cosmology. The Gospels were written in an age when belief in miracles was already a part of the given worldview, irrespective of one's faith. Modern Christians live in a time when the world is perceived differently, again irrespective of one's faith. One's worldview is a given and cannot be changed at will. Just as we cannot decide to believe $2+2 = 5$ or that heaven is "up" by an act of faith or an act of the will, so we cannot decide by faith for or against a Newtonian or post-Newtonian view of the way the universe works. Miracle stories are to be interpreted in such a way that the original message of salvation expressed in the first-century worldview is translated into the modern worldview, being faithful to both the original message of salvation and the modern perception of the world.

(6) Guard against any view that restricts God's presence, power, and activity to the *extra*ordinary. An apologetic "God of the gaps" that locates the act of God only in what is not otherwise explainable reduces the sphere of God's activity to that of our ignorance. This can continually diminish the arena in which the presence of God is

---

216. See Frederick Ferre, *Language, Logic, and God* (New York: Collins, 1961); Ian T. Ramsey, *Religious Language: An Empirical Placing of Theological Phrases* (New York: Macmillan, 1957); John Macquarrie, *God-talk: An Examination of the Language and Logic of Theology* (London: SCM, 1967); Boring, *Truly Human/Truly Divine,* chap. 4, "The Gospel as Language," 91-114. See also "confessional language" in Reflections at Matthew 2:13-23, "The Other Babies of Bethlehem."

perceived, as well as discourage the expansion of one's knowledge by an appeal to faith.

(7) Avoid confusing hermeneutical differences with degrees of faith or unbelief. Do not equate faith with believing in miracles and lack of belief in miracles with lack of faith in general. Do not accuse others (or yourself) of a lack of faith as the reason for not believing in the factuality of miracle stories. The question of faith/non-faith must be posed in terms of *what* message the miracle story wants to communicate. Do not permit the offense of the miracle story to replace the offense of the gospel.

(8) Respect the ethical issues inherent in affirmations of God's working by means of miracles. The issue is not whether God can do such things, but whether God literally works in the way pictured by the language of miracle stories, and whether God *should* work this way—i.e., whether it accords with God's righteousness to work this way. Healings and resurrections, if understood as objectifying reports, raise the ethical question of why only a few are healed when one has the power to heal and raise all. If attention is focused on the miracle itself, it then becomes a problem, not merely of physics but of ethics as well, an obstacle to hearing what else the pericope wants to say. If the story of God's intervention to save the baby Jesus in Matt 2:13-18 is objectified as literal history, one must deal with the other babies of Bethlehem who were needlessly killed (see Commentary and Reflections on Matthew 2). Miracle stories should not be interpreted in a way that casts God in a questionable ethical role.

❖   ❖   ❖   ❖

MATTHEW 9:36–10:42, THE DISCIPLES AUTHORIZED AND SENT

OVERVIEW

This is the second of the five great discourses in Matthew's narrative (see Introduction). Like the other speeches, this is Matthew's composition from traditional materials. Both Mark (6:7-11) and Q (Luke 10:2-12) contain a missionary charge to the disciples. When each of his sources contains similar discourse material, Matthew's compositional policy is to combine them into one extensive speech, in contrast to Luke, who typically preserves each speech in a separate context (see 23:1–25:46). Matthew brings forward the Markan speech in the outline and amplifies it with material from the Q speech, as well as making exten-

sive additions from elsewhere in Mark, Q, and his own M traditions.

Just as Jesus has now been presented as the Messiah in word (chaps. 5–7) and deed (chaps. 8–9), so also now his authority and power, including the authority to forgive sins (9:8), are continued in the mission of the disciples. The commissioning of the disciples thus corresponds in Matthew's structure to their call in 4:18-22 (cf. Introduction). The discourse is prefaced by two scenes portraying the need of Israel and the divine compassion in sending apostles and disciples to minister to that need.

Matthew 9:36-38, Needy Crowds and Divine Compassion

NIV	NRSV
[36]When he saw the crowds, he had compassion on them, because they were harassed and helpless, like sheep without a shepherd. [37]Then he said to his disciples, "The harvest is plentiful but the workers are few. [38]Ask the Lord of the harvest, therefore, to send out workers into his harvest field."	[36]When he saw the crowds, he had compassion for them, because they were harassed and helpless, like sheep without a shepherd. [37]Then he said to his disciples, "The harvest is plentiful, but the laborers are few; [38]therefore ask the Lord of the harvest to send out laborers into his harvest."

COMMENTARY

9:36. "When he saw the crowds," plus a finite verb with Jesus as the subject is exactly the same construction as 5:1, is found only these two times in Matthew, and makes another bracket that encloses chapters 5–7 and 8–9 as "the words and deeds of the Messiah" (cf. Introduction). "Sheep without a shepherd" is an LXX phrase (Num 27:17; 1 Kgs 22:17; 2 Chr 18:16; cf. Jer 23:1-6; Ezek 34:8; Zech 10:12) taken from a different context in Mark 6:34.[217] Matthew relocates the phrase here to describe the plight of "the crowds," the uncommitted masses of Israel who are potential disciples but are in danger of being misled by their leaders. Matthew considers Jesus to be their true shepherd (cf. 2:6; 26:31), who has compassion on the harassed and helpless flock. Jesus has compassion for Israel, not animosity, understanding that it is his vocation to be sent to them (10:5; 15:24). Since in Num 27:17 the phrase "sheep without a shepherd" is used in the context of Moses' preparation for death and concern for a legitimate successor, its use here represents another aspect of Matthew's Moses' typology (see Commentary on 5:1). Just as Num 27:17 is concerned with the transfer of authority from Moses to Joshua ('Iησοῦς *Iēsous,* "a man in whom is

the Spirit"), so also here Jesus confers authority on the disciples (10:1, 7-8).

9:37-38. For Matthew, the shepherd image is already understood eschatologically,[218] but the eschatological perspective that dominates the following discourse is made more explicit when the metaphor shifts from shepherding to harvesting. The harvest is a frequent symbol for eschatological judgment (Isa 18:4; 27:12; Jer 51:53; Hos 6:11; Joel 3:13), used elsewhere by Matthew (3:12; 13:30, 39) and other writers in early Judaism and the New Testament (4 Ezra 4:26-37; 9:17; 2 Bar 70:1-2; Mark 4:26-29; 13:27; Rev 14:14-20). The disciples' mission is seen as an eschatological event. As such, it is God's act, though involving human workers rather than the angels as God's agents. Thus the disciples are instructed to pray for the Lord of the harvest (God) to send out laborers into the harvest. The response to this prayer is the mission of the disciples/ apostles, who in this context are represented as an expression of the divine compassion for the needy people of God, pictured in v. 36, and as participants in the Messiah's eschatological work of judging the people of God (cf. 4:18-22). The disciples' mission is not voluntary activity initiated by them; rather, they are chosen, authorized, and sent by God through Christ (10:10).

217. Jeremiah 23:5 and Ezek 34:23 picture the good shepherd to come as (son of) David. The Matthean theme of Jesus as true Son of David emerges here. See Excursus "Matthean Christology," 353-61, and 1:2-25.

218. See Matt 25:31-32, where the Son of Man as eschatological judge is portrayed as a shepherd who separates sheep from goats. The common denominator is the concept of kingship, for *shepherd* was not a "soft" word in the ancient Near East, but was often used as a metaphor for the absolute authority of kings (e.g., 1 Kgs 22:17; Isa 44:28; Jer 2:8; 3:15; 10:21; Ezekiel 34).

Matthew 10:1-5a, Disciples and Apostles

NIV

10 He called his twelve disciples to him and gave them authority to drive out evil[a] spirits and to heal every disease and sickness.

2These are the names of the twelve apostles: first, Simon (who is called Peter) and his brother Andrew; James son of Zebedee, and his brother John; 3Philip and Bartholomew; Thomas and Matthew the tax collector; James son of Alphaeus, and Thaddaeus; 4Simon the Zealot and Judas Iscariot, who betrayed him.

5These twelve Jesus sent out with the following instructions:

a1 Greek *unclean*

NRSV

10 Then Jesus[a] summoned his twelve disciples and gave them authority over unclean spirits, to cast them out, and to cure every disease and every sickness. 2These are the names of the twelve apostles: first, Simon, also known as Peter, and his brother Andrew; James son of Zebedee, and his brother John; 3Philip and Bartholomew; Thomas and Matthew the tax collector; James son of Alphaeus, and Thaddaeus;[b] 4Simon the Cananaean, and Judas Iscariot, the one who betrayed him.

5These twelve Jesus sent out with the following instructions:

aGk *he*   bOther ancient authorities read *Lebbaeus*, or *Lebbaeus called Thaddaeus*

COMMENTARY

Matthew has narrated only two call stories, in which only five disciples have been called (4:18-22; 9:9). Thus it comes as something of a surprise to the reader to learn that there are twelve disciples. Matthew's readers, however, knew Mark 3:13-14's narration of the selection of the Twelve, which is here presupposed.

Matthew generally speaks of the "twelve disciples" (10:1; 11:1; 20:17) or simply "the Twelve" (10:5; 26:14, 20, 47). Only here does he call them "apostles" (ἀπόστολοι *apostoloi*), a term that seems not to have been important to him. Our earliest tradition speaks of "the Twelve" and "all the apostles" as two distinct, overlapping groups (1 Cor 15:5-7). Luke's influence has led the church to think of the group as "the" twelve apostles. Historically, the apostles were a larger group of those to whom the risen Lord appeared and commissioned as his authorized representatives, as indicated by lists of those called apostles in Fig. 7.

The later need to identify the apostles with the Twelve, and thus establish a list of only twelve apostles (as already in Luke–Acts) has led to the traditional attribution of two or more names to

the same person (e.g., identifying Mark's Levi with Matthew's Matthew, and John's Nathanael with the Synoptics' Bartholomew). There is no historical evidence for such identifications, which is in any case unlikely, since evidence is lacking for the practice of giving two Hebrew names to Jewish males. The symbolism of the number twelve was important for Matthew and for early Christianity, as it had apparently been to Jesus, for it pictured the eschatological reconstitution of Israel as the people of God (cf. 19:28). The symbolism of the number twelve was more important than the persons who constitute the group.[219]

Except for Simon Peter, we know practically nothing about the other members of the lists.[220] "Simon the Cananaean" distinguishes this Simon from Simon Peter, and identifies him as a

219. This was also the case for the twelve tribes of Israel. The fact that there were twelve is symbolically important, despite the considerable variation among the OT lists of the tribes. According to C. U. Wolf ("Tribe," *IDB* 4:699-700) the OT lists more than twenty variant lists. The same is true of the "seven hills" of Rome and the "ten cities" of the Decapolis; the number remains constant, but the content of the lists changes.

220. A good summary of what little can be known about the apostles, from history and legend, is found in Hans Conzelmann, *History of Primitive Christianity* (Nashville: Abingdon, 1973), 148-55.

253

Figure 7: Apostles Identified in Matthew, Mark, Luke/Acts, John, and Paul

Matthew 10	Mark 3	Luke 6/Acts 1	John	Paul
1. Simon Peter	1. Simon Peter	1. Simon Peter	1. Simon Peter	1. Simon Peter
2. Andrew	4. Andrew	2. Andrew	2. Andrew	19. James brother
3. James	2. James	3. James	[3-4. "the sons of	of Jesus
4. John	3. John	4. John	Zebedee," 21:2]	(Gal 1:19)
5. Philip	5. Philip	5. Philip	5. Philip	[20. Andronicus
6. Bartholomew	6. Bartholomew	6. Bartholomew		(Rom 16:7)]
7. Thomas	8. Matthew	8. Matthew		[21. Junia(s)*
8. Matthew	7. Thomas	7. Thomas	7. Thomas	(Rom 16:7)]
9. James son of	9. James son of	9. James son of		[22. Paul
Alphaeus	Alphaeus	Alphaeus		(1 Cor 9:1, etc.)]
10. Thaddaeus	10. Thaddaeus			
11. Simon the	11. Simon the	11. Simon the		1 Cor 15:6 indicates
Cananaean	Cananaean	Zealot		that Paul knew of
12. Judas Iscariot	12. Judas Iscariot	12. Judas Iscariot	12. Judas Iscariot	more than 12 apostles.
(13. *Lebbaeus* for	(14. Levi son of	15. Judas son of	17. Nathanael	
Thaddaeus in	Alphaeus,	James	18. The Beloved	*Depending on
some MSS)	2:14)	(16. Matthias,	Disciple	accentuation, this name
		Acts 1)		can be read as either
				masculine (so RSV and
				NIV) or feminine
				(so KJV and NRSV).

Zealot.[221] Matthew explicitly lists Peter first (see 16:17-18) and Judas as last. Judas is identified as the one who "betrayed" Jesus (παραδούς *paradous*, aorist participle). This first explicit reference to the passion story is retrospective, one of the many instances indicating that the implied reader already knows the Jesus story and views it from a post-Easter perspective, of which this is a new interpretation (cf. 10:38).

By the insertion of "and" (καί *kai*) at strategic points, Matthew has consciously arranged the list into six pairs of two, perhaps a reminiscence of the sending "two by two" of Mark 6:7, which Matthew has omitted, or the "pairs" of leading rabbis prominent in the formulation of Jewish tradition (cf. *m. 'Abot* 2:8). This may suggest the missionary function of the disciples as well as the "two or three" of Matt 18:20 who are authorized to make decisions in Jesus' name, and Matthew's preference for "two's" (see 8:28-34; 9:27-31).

Matthew regards Jesus' mission as continuing in the work of the disciples, who are given the authority to speak and act in Jesus' name (10:1; cf. 10:19-20, 40)—i.e., to continue doing the same deeds of power Jesus himself has just done in 8:1–9:35 (however, authority to teach was not given to them until after the resurrection, 28:20). They preach the same message (4:17; 10:7) and receive the same response (9:34; 10:25). Thus the disciples are transparent to the post-Easter experience and mission of the church, and the mission discourse is to be heard as both Jesus' there-and-then address to his disciples in the pre-Easter setting of the story (for which 10:5*b*-6 may be representative) and as the address of the contemporary Christ who is still present with his church in its eschatological mission between the resurrection and the parousia (cf., e.g., 10:17-22, 32-33, which clearly depicts a post-Easter situation). Like the Gospel as a whole, this speech frustrates efforts to make neat distinctions between the past of Jesus' historical ministry and the present of Jesus' continuing ministry and presence in the work of his disciples.

221. The word *Zealot* derives from קנא (*qnʾ*, "jealous," "full of zeal") and is unrelated to the ethnic term *Canaanite* (cf. Luke 6:15; Acts 1:13). *Zealot* was not a technical term for a member of the revolutionary party in Jesus' day, as it became later at the time of the 66–70 war, to which Matthew looks back, but was applied to those "zealous for the Law" (cf. Acts 22:3-5; Gal 1:14; Phil 3:6).

Matthew 10:5b-42, The Missionary Discourse

OVERVIEW

The following outline corresponds to the units Matthew has adopted from his sources and reflects his tendency toward a chiastic structure. The first and last units are conflations of Mark and Q, with the central units alternating Mark and Q. The first, second, and last units conclude with "amen" (ἀμήν *amēn*) sayings. At the center of the discourse is the exhortation to fearless confession, taken from another context in Q, surrounded on either side by ominous predictions of the cost of discipleship. The whole discourse is bracketed by affirmations of the presence of Christ and his authority as continued in the disciples' mission.

A Sharing the Authority of Christ and
   His Reception, 10:5b-15
   (Mark 6:7-11/Q 10:2-12)
   B The Fate of the Disciples, 10:16-23
      (Mark 13:9-13)
      C Call to Courageous Confession,
         10:24-33
         (Q 6:40; 12:2-9)
   B' The Cost of Discipleship, 10:34-39
      (Q 12:51-53; 14:25-27; 17:33)
A' Sharing the Presence of Christ and
   His Reception, 10:40-42
   (Mark 9:37, 41/Q 10:16)

Matthew 10:5b-15, Sharing the Authority of Christ

NIV	NRSV
"Do not go among the Gentiles or enter any town of the Samaritans. ⁶Go rather to the lost sheep of Israel. ⁷As you go, preach this message: 'The kingdom of heaven is near.' ⁸Heal the sick, raise the dead, cleanse those who have leprosy,ᵃ drive out demons. Freely you have received, freely give. ⁹Do not take along any gold or silver or copper in your belts; ¹⁰take no bag for the journey, or extra tunic, or sandals or a staff; for the worker is worth his keep.	"Go nowhere among the Gentiles, and enter no town of the Samaritans, ⁶but go rather to the lost sheep of the house of Israel. ⁷As you go, proclaim the good news, 'The kingdom of heaven has come near.'ᵃ ⁸Cure the sick, raise the dead, cleanse the lepers,ᵇ cast out demons. You received without payment; give without payment. ⁹Take no gold, or silver, or copper in your belts, ¹⁰no bag for your journey, or two tunics, or sandals, or a staff; for laborers deserve their food. ¹¹Whatever town or village you enter, find out who in it is worthy, and stay there until you leave. ¹²As you enter the house, greet it. ¹³If the house is worthy, let your peace come upon it; but if it is not worthy, let your peace return to you. ¹⁴If anyone will not welcome you or listen to your words, shake off the dust from your feet as you leave that house or town. ¹⁵Truly I tell you, it will be more tolerable for the land of Sodom and Gomorrah on the day of judgment than for that town.
¹¹"Whatever town or village you enter, search for some worthy person there and stay at his house until you leave. ¹²As you enter the home, give it your greeting. ¹³If the home is deserving, let your peace rest on it; if it is not, let your peace return to you. ¹⁴If anyone will not welcome you or listen to your words, shake the dust off your feet when you leave that home or town. ¹⁵I tell you the truth, it will be more bearable for Sodom and Gomorrah on the day of judgment than for that town.	
ᵃ8 The Greek word was used for various diseases affecting the skin—not necessarily leprosy.	ᵃOr *is at hand* ᵇThe terms *leper* and *leprosy* can refer to several diseases

COMMENTARY

As the disciples function with the authority of Christ (10:1), the discourse begins by charging them to go to the same lost sheep of Israel as has Jesus (10:5b-6) to proclaim the same message (4:17; 10:7); to perform the same healings, exorcisms, and even raisings of the dead (8:1–9:35; 10:8); to live the same wandering, dependent life of poverty (8:20; 10:10); and to anticipate the same mixed reception (7:28-29; 8:16; 9:8 vs. 8:34; 9:34; 10:11-15). The list reflects the works of Christ in chapters 8–9, as it prepares for 11:4-6.

10:5b-8. The disciples are sent to Israel, all Israel, and only to Israel.[222] Historically the disciples were reluctant to go to the Gentiles even after Easter, so that it took a considerable time for the church under the guidance of the Spirit to develop a Gentile mission and become an integrated church (Acts 1–15; Galatians 1–2). Therefore 10:5b can hardly be historical, for Jesus would not have forbidden his disciples to initiate a Gentile mission to which they were in no way inclined anyway. Because historically the mission of the earthly Jesus was limited to Israel, this saying reflects the struggles within the early church to develop a Gentile mission, opposed by some in the name of Jesus. (This is the only reference to Samaritans or Samaria in Matthew; the inclusiveness of the Lukan perspective should not be read into Matthew.)

The sending of the disciples exclusively to Israel corresponds to the mission of the historical Jesus (cf. Rom 15:8) and is important in Matthew's theological story (15:24).[223] After Easter, the Great Commission ends this restriction by extending the mission to all nations (28:18-20). Since Jesus' previous prohibition of having contact with Gentiles and Samaritans was no longer valid for Matthew's own post-Easter situation, he could have omitted it, or declared that it was abolished. Instead, he preserves it, because it is valid for the time of Jesus. In Matthew's view the mission to Israel was not abolished by the later command

that lasts "until the end of the age," as though the church no longer carried on a mission to the land and people of Israel. The previous mission was taken up into the ultimate missionary mandate of the risen Lord, and is thus not abolished but "fulfilled"—although specific commands and limitations connected with it were rescinded. This is analogous to the relation between the commands of Torah and the commands of the risen Jesus, represented by the Sermon on the Mount (5:17-20).[224]

10:9-10. The original radicality of Jesus' own wandering life and of the Q missioners who probably founded Matthew's church (see Introduction) is retained in Matthew. Mark had already modified the strictness of the command, permitting each disciple to take a staff and sandals (Mark 6:8-11). Luke considers the prohibition of material goods a temporary command belonging only to the special period of Jesus' earthly ministry (Luke 22:35-36). Matthew preserves the original strictness as a witness to the radical call to discipleship once practiced by Jesus and the earliest disciples, and perhaps still practiced by the wandering charismatic missionaries sent out by the church in Matthew's day. Since any member of the community might be called upon to become such a missionary (if Acts 13:1-3 is representative), such commands are not dead relics of the past or an impossible ideal in Matthew's own situation. Nor are the prohibitions of money, knapsack, sandals, and staff a matter or strategy ("travel light") or an indication of ascetic tendencies. For both Jesus and his disciples, proceeding on a mission without even the basic equipment for sustenance and self-defense was a prophetic sign, an acting out of the presence of the kingdom similar to the symbolic actions performed by the biblical prophets (Isa 20:2, 4; Jer 13:1-11; 19:1-13; 27:1–28:14; Ezekiel 4; 5; 12; Hosea 1; 3).

At one point Matthew increases the strictness

---

222. The genitive expression does not designate only a part of Israel, but is an epexegetical or appositive genitive that identifies "lost sheep" with Israel as such.

223. Matthew omits or revises Markan stories that might portray a pre-Easter Gentile mission as being already underway (e.g., Mark 5:19-20; cf. Matt 8:34).

224. Contra Ulrich Luz, *Das Evangelium nach Matthäus* (Mt 8–17), Evangelisch-Katholischer Kommentar zum Neuen Testament I/2 (Benziger: Neukirchener Verlag, 1990) 2:92. For a thorough discussion of options in considering the historical origin of the saying, and the spectrum of opinions regarding Matthew's meaning in including this saying in obvious tension with 28:18-20, see Schuyler Brown, "The Two-fold Representation of the Mission in Matthew's Gospel," *Studia Theologica* 31 (1977) 21-32.

of the traditional predictions, changing Q's "the laborer deserves to be paid" to "laborers deserve their food" (cf. Luke 10:7). As Matthew opposes the developing rabbinic titles and status (cf. 23:5-12), so he also opposes missionaries who accept money for their work; they must be content with only the food necessary for survival. This may represent his polemic against an emerging tendency toward a paid class of clergy, and corresponds to the initial prohibition of traveling with money (v. 9; cf. 1 Cor 9:3-12).

10:11-15. These instructions incorporate practical wisdom for the early traveling missionaries who depended on the hospitality of fellow Christians. They are also an indirect prophetic warning to settled Christians to receive the wandering missionaries of the Matthean community. Hospitality, already a sacred obligation in the ancient Mediterranean world and emphasized in biblical stories (Gen 18:1-8; 19:1-11; 24:14-61; Judg 19:10-25; cf. Heb 13:2), is here placed in an eschatological framework, concluding the section

with a solemn prophetic ("amen" ἀμήν *amēn;* cf. Commentary on 5:18) pronouncement of eschatological judgment. *Didache* 11–13 illustrates both the importance of hospitality and the dangers of its abuse in the early Christian community. Sodom appears again as an analogous negative example in 11:23-24.

It was customary for the Palestinian Jew returning to the sacred land to shake off the dust of pagan countries before entering the holy land. In vv. 13-14, as in 3:7-10 and 10:16, Israel assumes the place traditionally occupied by pagan countries. These words need to be understood in the eschatological framework of the whole discourse, which commissions Jesus' disciples as though they were prophets not only announcing the last judgment but also anticipating it in their pronouncements and symbolic actions. Otherwise, there can be a danger of self-righteousness and lovelessness in the efforts of Jesus' disciples to live by these words.

Matthew 10:16-23, The Fate of the Disciples

NIV

[16]I am sending you out like sheep among wolves. Therefore be as shrewd as snakes and as innocent as doves.

[17]"Be on your guard against men; they will hand you over to the local councils and flog you in their synagogues. [18]On my account you will be brought before governors and kings as witnesses to them and to the Gentiles. [19]But when they arrest you, do not worry about what to say or how to say it. At that time you will be given what to say, [20]for it will not be you speaking, but the Spirit of your Father speaking through you.

[21]"Brother will betray brother to death, and a father his child; children will rebel against their parents and have them put to death. [22]All men will hate you because of me, but he who stands firm to the end will be saved. [23]When you are persecuted in one place, flee to another. I tell you the truth, you will not finish going through the cities of Israel before the Son of Man comes.

NRSV

16"See, I am sending you out like sheep into the midst of wolves; so be wise as serpents and innocent as doves. [17]Beware of them, for they will hand you over to councils and flog you in their synagogues; [18]and you will be dragged before governors and kings because of me, as a testimony to them and the Gentiles. [19]When they hand you over, do not worry about how you are to speak or what you are to say; for what you are to say will be given to you at that time; [20]for it is not you who speak, but the Spirit of your Father speaking through you. [21]Brother will betray brother to death, and a father his child, and children will rise against parents and have them put to death; [22]and you will be hated by all because of my name. But the one who endures to the end will be saved. [23]When they persecute you in one town, flee to the next; for truly I tell you, you will not have gone through all the towns of Israel before the Son of Man comes.

COMMENTARY

This section begins with a "heading" adapted from Q (Matt 10:16 = Q 10:3), continues with sayings taken almost verbatim from Mark (Matt 10:17-22 = Mark 13:9-13), and concludes with an *amen* (cf. 5:18) saying peculiar to Matthew (see v. 23). The beginning and end of this section correspond to the previous unit, beginning with an allusion to the people of God as "sheep" (10:5, 16) and concluding with a prophetic eschatological *amen* saying (10:13, 23).

10:16. As already in Q, the Christian missionaries are here seen as sheep—in solidarity with the "lost sheep" of Israel. But the leadership of empirical Israel, the unbelieving Jewish leaders perceived as persecutors of the Christian community, are pictured as dangerous wolves—a striking reversal of the Jewish tradition that compared the situation of Israel among the Gentiles to that of sheep among wolves (*1 Enoch* 89:55; 4 Ezra 5:18). In v. 16*b*, Matthew refashions a proverbial saying (cf. Rom 16:19; *Midr. Cant* 2:4). For him, the point is the disciples' discernment and single-mindedness (NIV and NRSV: "innocent"[225]).

The mission instructions in Mark 6:7-13 give no hint that the missioners will be persecuted and rejected. To let this represent the post-Easter missionary experience of the church, Matthew imports a section of the apocalyptic discourse in Mark 13 (Matt 10:17-25 = Mark 13:9-13). It is profoundly important for Matthew's interpretation to note that the remainder of this section is taken from the eschatological discourse in Mark 13, where Jesus is pictured as looking beyond the resurrection to the time of the church and the eschatological events. By bringing these words into the mission discourse that occurs earlier in the story line and applying it to the mission of the pre-Easter disciples, Matthew does three things:

(1) He breaks down the temporal distinctions between the there-and-then story of the pre-Easter Jesus and the here-and-now mission of his post-Easter readership.

(2) He underscores the fact that the mission of the church to the nations is not a mundane historical project initiated and carried on by persons who want to impose their religious views on others, but is a part of God's eschatological plan to bring all nations into the kingdom of God (Isa 2:4-2). Thus the troubles and persecutions the church must endure are part of the eschatological woes that will precede the coming of God's kingdom, here pictured as the advent of the Son of Man (10:23). The church will not be surprised at the fiery trials it must endure, for suffering is not incidental to mission; mission brings tribulation (cf. 1 Pet 4:12).

(3) Matthew casts the whole mission in the perspective of his motif of the conflict of kingdoms (cf. "before governors and kings," vv. 19-20), already introduced by the message that "the kingdom of God has come near" in 10:7.[226]

10:17. The floggings referred to here are not random mob violence, but official punishments for those considered guilty of blasphemy or gross violation of the Torah (cf. Deut 25:1-3, later elaborated in the Mishnah into punishments for heretics, blasphemers, and recalcitrant disturbers of the peace). Matthew's church apparently still had some relation to the synagogue, which subjected Jewish Christian missionaries to its discipline (as was Paul, cf. 2 Cor 11:24-25). Yet the synagogue, the ancestral home of Matthew's own faith and community, is now "their" synagogue.[227]

The fate of the disciples corresponds to that of their Master. The key expression is "handed over" (παραδίδωμι *paradidōmi*), which has important theological connotations. In the LXX of Isa 53:6, God "hands over" the Servant for our sins. This text may ultimately be in the background of the early Christian usage of this word for the passion of Jesus: God is the actor who delivers Jesus up to death for the salvation of others, a vicarious suffering for others, to which Jesus willingly submits. For Matthew as for Mark, John the Baptist stands in this tradition (Mark 1:14, reflected in Matt 4:12). The Matthean Jesus repeatedly and

---

225. The word means "unmixed"; cf. 5:8.

226. Cf. the juxtaposition of the newborn "king of the Jews" and "Herod the king" in the opening scenes of chaps. 1–2.

227. "Matthew's careful distinction between ἐκκλησία (*ekklēsia*, "church") and συναγωγή (*synagōgē* "synagogue") is striking. In six passages (4:23; 9:35; 10:17; 12:9; 13:54; 23:34) the evangelist has either modified an earlier tradition or has used his own words to emphasize the distance between the *ekklēsia* founded by Jesus and the *synagōgē* which is seen as the self-identification of the parent group" (Graham Stanton, "Matthew in Sociological Perspective," in *Gospel for a New People* [Edinburgh: T. & T. Clark, 1992] 97).

ambiguously uses the word in reference to his own passion (17:22; 20:18-19; 26:2) in such a way that it is unclear whether the action is divine ("delivered up for our salvation") or human ("betray," "hand over"). The disciples are also in this tradition, and they also will be "delivered up"/"handed over." Like Jesus, they will suffer for the sake of the divine mission in the world.

10:18. Prior to Easter, Jesus' disciples did not carry on a mission to Gentiles, did not suffer for the sake of Jesus' name, did not stand before governors and kings. The discourse here modulates even more clearly into the post-Easter address of Jesus to Christian disciples in Matthew's time. The unsuccessful mission to Israel already lay in the past for Matthew's church, which now carries on a mission to all nations (28:18-20). Matthew is concerned to emphasize that this turn to the Gentiles is not in order to find an easier task where people are more receptive. Not only were the early missionaries brought before "councils" (local Jewish courts; the same word is used for Gentile judiciaries), but Gentiles too will persecute faithful Christians, even bringing them before governors and kings.

10:19-20. A word of encouragement is pronounced for Christians who find themselves on trial. They will not need to depend on their own resources, but will be inspired by the Holy Spirit ("the Spirit of your Father," a uniquely Matthean expression) to speak words of witness. The Holy Spirit is an eschatological gift (see 3:11). "Do not be anxious" reminds the reader of 6:25, where the same words are used. There, the basis for encouragement is the Creator who cares for the creation. Here, eschatology forms the basis for encouragement. In Matthew's view, these are two aspects of the same God. Reminiscent of the Johannine concept of the Spirit as Paraclete, a word with forensic overtones, the Spirit aids Christian disciples in court. The courtroom is not merely a threat, it is an opportunity for mission ("as a testimony to them," v. 18*b*). This is the only reference in Matthew to disciples having the Holy Spirit (but cf. 3:11; 28:19). Rather than conceiving of the divine presence and help as the Holy Spirit's being given to the disciples between Easter and the parousia (as do Luke and John), Matthew thinks of the continuing presence of

Jesus (see Reflections on 1:23, "Jesus as the Continuing Presence of God").

10:21-22. In some streams of Jewish tradition, Mic 7:6 had already been interpreted to refer to the eschatological terrors (*1 Enoch* 100:2). Apocalyptic thought understood that immediately prior to the end and as a sign of its nearness, the natural structures of the world would break down, and even the most deeply rooted family loyalties would dissolve under the pressure of the approaching end. Matthew reflects the divisions that occurred in families as a result of Christian commitment and follows Mark in interpreting these as eschatological ordeals inherent in the church's mission. The promise to those who endure to the end is also thoroughly apocalyptic, referring not to the end of one's life or to the end of the temporary, this-worldly persecution, but to the ultimate end, the parousia (v. 23). In this discourse, the disciples of Matthew's church hear their Lord charging them with a mission that extends from the time of the earthly Jesus to the "end of the age" (28:20), a mission that after Easter expands from an exclusive concentration on Israel to include all nations.

10:23. The original form of this saying, found only here, may have been spoken by the historical Jesus, who expected the eschaton to come before the disciples returned from their mission.[228] Much more likely, it was originally an oracle of an early Christian prophet giving instructions for the conduct of Christian missionaries under duress.[229] The affirmation of the nearness of the end (which turned out to be a chronological mistake; see Reflections on 25:46) was thus for Matthew and his apocalyptic community not a conceptual problem to be solved or avoided, but a means of encouragement to mission. Since Matthew and his readers knew that the Son of Man did not come during the time of the historical Jesus, these instructions could be heard in his church as applicable to the continuing mission to Israel as part of the church's mission to all nations (28:18-20).

---

228. This was the cornerstone of Albert Schweitzer's reconstruction of Jesus' self-understanding in *The Quest of the Historical Jesus* (New York: Macmillan, 1968 [original German, 1906]).

229. See M. Eugene Boring, *The Continuing Voice of Jesus: Christian Prophecy and the Gospel Tradition* (Louisville: Westminster/John Knox, 1991) 250-51.

Matthew 10:24-33, The Call to Courageous Confession

NIV

NIV

²⁴"A student is not above his teacher, nor a servant above his master. ²⁵It is enough for the student to be like his teacher, and the servant like his master. If the head of the house has been called Beelzebub,ᵃ how much more the members of his household!

²⁶"So do not be afraid of them. There is nothing concealed that will not be disclosed, or hidden that will not be made known. ²⁷What I tell you in the dark, speak in the daylight; what is whispered in your ear, proclaim from the roofs. ²⁸Do not be afraid of those who kill the body but cannot kill the soul. Rather, be afraid of the One who can destroy both soul and body in hell. ²⁹Are not two sparrows sold for a pennyᵇ? Yet not one of them will fall to the ground apart from the will of your Father. ³⁰And even the very hairs of your head are all numbered. ³¹So don't be afraid; you are worth more than many sparrows.

³²"Whoever acknowledges me before men, I will also acknowledge him before my Father in heaven. ³³But whoever disowns me before men, I will disown him before my Father in heaven."

ᵃ 25 Greek *Beezeboul* or *Beelzeboul*   ᵇ 29 Greek *an assarion*

NRSV

²⁴"A disciple is not above the teacher, nor a slave above the master; ²⁵it is enough for the disciple to be like the teacher, and the slave like the master. If they have called the master of the house Beelzebul, how much more will they malign those of his household!

²⁶"So have no fear of them; for nothing is covered up that will not be uncovered, and nothing secret that will not become known. ²⁷What I say to you in the dark, tell in the light; and what you hear whispered, proclaim from the housetops. ²⁸Do not fear those who kill the body but cannot kill the soul; rather fear him who can destroy both soul and body in hell.ᵃ ²⁹Are not two sparrows sold for a penny? Yet not one of them will fall to the ground apart from your Father. ³⁰And even the hairs of your head are all counted. ³¹So do not be afraid; you are of more value than many sparrows.

³²"Everyone therefore who acknowledges me before others, I also will acknowledge before my Father in heaven; ³³but whoever denies me before others, I also will deny before my Father in heaven."

ᵃ Gk *Gehenna*

COMMENTARY

10:24-25. These two transitional verses are the axis on which the whole speech turns (see outline above). Just as the word *disciple(s)* occurs at the beginning and conclusion of the discourse (10:1, 42; 11:1), so also it appears precisely halfway through (v. 24), forming the thematic center as it introduces a new section. The fact that disciples are or become like their teacher is a bit of proverbial wisdom (cf. Q = Luke 6:40), here placed in the eschatological context of the whole speech and transformed into a foundational principle of Christian discipleship. Only Jesus can be understood as the teacher (cf. 23:8), so the saying is no longer general but refers concretely to the Christian's relation to Christ. "Servant" and "Lord" likewise portray the relation of the Chris-

tian to Jesus (this terminology was unproblematic to Jesus; see 11:29). Matthew underscores the parallel between Jesus and the disciples to whom he entrusts his mission. As he has been persecuted, likewise will they be. Just as he did not retaliate, but withdrew (see 12:14-21; cf. 5:38-41), so also the disciple is not to respond to hostility in kind or with prayers for vengeance, but is to withdraw and continue the mission elsewhere, in the glad confidence that the parousia of the Son of Man will bring the divine kingdom to full reality. Throughout, the discourse has emphasized the parallels between the disciples' lives and that of Jesus (see Commentary on 10:5b-15), including sharing the same fate of rejection and persecution. This is summed up and dramatically focused in the charge of working by the power of Beelzebul, directed first to Jesus and then to his disciples (see 9:34 and the key section 12:22-37).

10:26-33. The speech is directed to disciple-missioners who experience such rejection and persecution, and who may be afraid to speak out boldly for their new faith. Thus this section continues with a twice-repeated command not to be afraid (vv. 26, 31), concluding with a promise and a threat about publicly confessing (or acknowledging) Jesus (vv. 32-33). These sayings are not concerned with the initial confession of faith in conversion; all is addressed to disciples who already profess Christian faith, but are fearful of bearing public witness to it in the church's mission. The disciples' message is in continuity with

that of Jesus (and John) in proclaiming the kingdom of God (3:2; 4:17; 10:7). But the disciples not only preach what Jesus preached; they also proclaim Jesus ("confess me"). Jesus is pictured here (as also in the Sermon on the Mount, 7:21-23) as claiming to be the eschatological attorney before God the judge; the criterion of judgment will be the disciples' present confession of Jesus—or lack of it. As throughout, the post-Easter missionary situation of the church is presupposed.[230]

230. Matthew characteristically substitutes "I" for "Son of Man" in his source (cf. the Q form in Luke 12:8). Cf. the opposite exchange in Matthew 16:13, which has "Son of Man" for the "I" of Mark 8:27. The historical Jesus may have distinguished himself from the coming Son of Man, as still reflected in Luke 12:8 and Mark 8:38 (an independent tradition), but from Matthew's post-Easter perspective, Jesus is the Son of Man to come. (See Excursus "Matthean Christology," 353-61.)

Matthew 10:34-39, The Cost of Discipleship

NIV	NRSV
³⁴"Do not suppose that I have come to bring peace to the earth. I did not come to bring peace, but a sword. ³⁵For I have come to turn	³⁴"Do not think that I have come to bring peace to the earth; I have not come to bring peace, but a sword.

"'a man against his father,
    a daughter against her mother,
a daughter-in-law against her mother-in-law—
³⁶   a man's enemies will be the members of his
        own household.'ᵃ
	³⁵ For I have come to set a man against his father,
	    and a daughter against her mother,
	    and a daughter-in-law against her mother-in-law;
	³⁶ and one's foes will be members of one's own
	        household.

³⁷"Anyone who loves his father or mother more than me is not worthy of me; anyone who loves his son or daughter more than me is not worthy of me; ³⁸and anyone who does not take his cross and follow me is not worthy of me. ³⁹Whoever finds his life will lose it, and whoever loses his life for my sake will find it."	³⁷Whoever loves father or mother more than me is not worthy of me; and whoever loves son or daughter more than me is not worthy of me; ³⁸and whoever does not take up the cross and follow me is not worthy of me. ³⁹Those who find their life will lose it, and those who lose their life for my sake will find it."
ᵃ36 Micah 7:6	

COMMENTARY

10:34-36. Matthew has used material from three different passages in Q to compose this unit (cf. Luke 12:51-53; 14:25-27; 17:33), which in his chiastic structure corresponds to the dissension within families, characteristic of the eschatological tribulation (10:21-22). The "sword" here is not a political symbol, but an eschatological one (cf. Rev

6:4). The "I have come" form reflects the post-Easter perspective that looks back on the "coming" of Jesus as a whole and is present in all streams of the tradition (e.g., 5:17 = M; 9:13 = Mark 2:17; 10:34-35 = Q). The text reflects a real situation in Matthew's church, where people sometimes had to choose between their family and their faith. In some apocalyptic views, the breakdown of family structures is part of the terrors preceding the eschaton. Matthew finds this a meaningful framework within which to interpret the experience of his own church. Micah 7:6 had already been interpreted in Judaism as the prelude to the messianic times,[231] and had been adopted by the Q followers of Jesus as an affirmation that these times were already beginning. Matthew rewrites the Q allusion to correspond more closely to Mic 7:6 and to his previous allusion in 10:26b. Matthew also introduces the family theme here because the Beelzebul controversy in Mark 3, which he already has in view, is surrounded by material illustrating Jesus' "true family." Already the "members of the household" (οἰκιακός *oikiakos*) of v. 25 had alluded to the community of disciples as Christ's true family over against the charge of possession by Beelzebul and the disruptions of the ties of natural kinship (see 12:22-37). Thus Matthew's substitution of "Father" for Q's "God" (v. 29) is not only his typical Jewish reverence for God's name, but also his affirmation of the Christian community as the family of God where ties are closer and more demanding than natural family ties (cf. 10:32-33).

10:37-39. Although no christological titles are used, the reader should not miss the claim that loyalty to Jesus has priority over even the closest human relationships and life itself, a claim that represents an implied christology. Discipleship is

represented not as adding on another worthy cause to one's list of obligations, but a giving of self that is the ultimate self-fulfillment. Jesus here claims for himself what only a deity can appropriately claim.

The reader will be surprised by the abruptness of the reference to the cross, for which there is no explicit preparation in the preceding narrative. From reading chapters 1–9, the uninitiated reader would anticipate that the mission of the disciples would meet with spectacular success. But the discourse that begins with Jesus conferring his authority and power on the disciples concludes with the necessity of sharing Jesus' cross as well. In the narrative, the disciples' suffering is elaborated before that of Jesus. The decision of his opponents to kill Jesus is not narrated until 12:14. The disciples are not said to be surprised, however, nor were the original readers, who were already familiar with the story of Jesus, as it was handed on in Christian tradition and especially from their reading of the Gospel of Mark, which is here presupposed. Matthew and his Christian readers look back not only on the cross of Jesus, but on the martyrdoms of Christians that had already taken place.[232] Like the reference to Judas in 10:4, the reference to the cross illustrates the retrospective post-Easter perspective of the whole narrative.

231. *M. Sota* 9:15.

232. Cf. also 23:34. There is no evidence for the crucifixion of Christians by Jews in Palestine. By Matthew's time, however, it was well known that Christians—including Simon Peter, who was so important to Matthean Christianity—had been crucified in Rome under Nero.

Matthew 10:40-42, Sharing the Presence of Christ

NIV	NRSV
[40]"He who receives you receives me, and he who receives me receives the one who sent me. [41]Anyone who receives a prophet because he is a prophet will receive a prophet's reward, and anyone who receives a righteous man because he is a righteous man will receive a righteous man's reward. [42]And if anyone gives even a cup of cold water to one of these little ones because he is my disciple, I tell you the truth, he will certainly not lose his reward."	40"Whoever welcomes you welcomes me, and whoever welcomes me welcomes the one who sent me. [41]Whoever welcomes a prophet in the name of a prophet will receive a prophet's reward; and whoever welcomes a righteous person in the name of a righteous person will receive the reward of the righteous; [42]and whoever gives even a cup of cold water to one of these little ones in the name of a disciple—truly I tell you, none of these will lose their reward."

COMMENTARY

The conclusion of the speech returns to the opening affirmations that authorize and empower the disciples as representatives of Christ. Here is added the fact that Christ represents God—another implicit christological claim. The concluding lines also make clear that the perspective has shifted from the Twelve who were sent from Galilee to later disciples, both those who are sent and those who receive, both the "wandering missionaries" and the "settled Christians" of Matthew's church. This emphasizes again that the discourse as a whole deals with the nature of discipleship for all disciples, settled and itinerant, pre- and post-Easter, rather than only particular rules for traveling missionaries.

Since the sayings are Matthean revisions of older materials from Mark, Q, and Matthew's own tradition, there is some ambiguity as to who is referred to by "prophets," "righteous," and "little ones." Matthew's church included Christian prophets as a distinct class, whose ministry Matthew affirms as legitimate spokespersons for the risen Lord (here and 23:34), but whom he also regards with some hesitation (7:21-23). "Little ones" does not refer literally to children, but is Matthew's term for "ordinary" Christians, equivalent here to disciples (cf. 18:1-14).[233] The "righteous" seems here to represent a distinct group (perhaps traveling missionaries who are not prophets?), but elsewhere Matthew seems to have rewritten his tradition in order to get prophets and righteous as a pair representing the church as a whole (13:17; 23:29). "In the name of" is a Semitic expression meaning "because one is." "Settled" disciples who receive and support "itinerant" disciples engaged in the church's mission share in their work and receive the same reward.

---

233. In Zech 13:7 and 2 Bar 48:19, "little ones" is used as a synonym for the people of God. Matthew's egalitarian spirit may have chosen it in contrast to "rabbi," which means literally "my great one."

REFLECTIONS

1. To many modern Christians, this speech seems strange, even fanatical. Yet in every generation some disciples of Jesus have been in situations in which this "missionary discourse" of 10:5-42 speaks directly the word of the risen Lord. It is only for First World, "mainline" Christianity that this chapter as such may seem to represent another world, with its talk of witness, persecution, poverty, and martyrdom. To the extent that it seems alien, it is a call to reexamine our own version of Christianity and ask whether we have remade the Christian faith to our own tastes, and whether it is possible to so change faith and have it remain *Christian* faith.

From another perspective, this chapter need not be alien at all. It reveals in concentrated form what the Christian life essentially is: confession of (God's act in) Jesus, living toward the eschaton with a concern for mission in this world, letting go of both material possessions and fear of what others might think about us or do to us, placing of loyalty to the God revealed in Christ above all other loyalties, even the deepest ones of home and family, a life of non-resistance to violence, trust in God and God's future. The call to this life of mission is not directed to the Twelve only. For Matthew, all disciples are apostles; all participate in the apostolic mission.

How can disciples of Jesus find the courage to live such a life? In vv. 26-31, the Matthean Jesus gives three reasons, all adapted from Q (Luke 12:2-7), why the disciple, contrary to all appearances and common sense, need not be afraid:

(a) The eschatological judgment soon to come will make everything public, so attempting to keep one's faith private is ultimately futile (vv. 26-27). What was originally gnomic wisdom ("It's no use trying to keep things secret; everything becomes public sooner or later") had already been given an eschatological interpretation in Q (Luke 12:2), to mean that the final judgment will reveal all secrets. Matthew reformulates this threat into an imperative (10:27).

In the Matthean context, "what is heard in the darkness" refers to the nighttime meetings of the Matthean community, among whom Jesus' sayings were passed on and the Christian faith was sometimes expressed as charismatic revelations of the risen Lord.[234] The Christian message is to be publicly proclaimed and lived out by the disciples, not kept to themselves as private religion.

(b) The coming judgment of God, which can "destroy the soul," is more to be feared than the present judgments of human courts, which can harm only the body (10:28). The martyr tradition of Judaism (e.g., 2 Maccabees; 4 Maccabees) had already combined Jewish faith in the resurrection with the Hellenistic idea of the body and soul as two "parts" of the existing human being. As a teacher in a martyr church, Matthew stands partially in that tradition (cf. the parallel in Luke 12:4, which is more "Jewish" in thinking of human existence as a unity). Although Matthew here uses dualistic terminology to express human existence, he does not affirm the immortality of the soul. Matthew is not attempting to teach anthropological or eschatological doctrine. His point, made within the conceptual assumptions of his particular stream of Hellenistic Judaism, is parenetic, not doctrinal; there is a realm of human existence that the opponents cannot touch, but God can. Thus the fear of God (i.e., awe, due respect) and the ultimate judgment overcomes fear of what human courts can do and sets the disciple free to be a courageous witness. Encouragement lies in the awareness that it is ultimately God with whom we have to deal, not a theory about our own souls.

(c) God is the faithful creator who, however it may appear, cares for each creature (10:29-31). Sparrows were sold in the marketplace, sometimes in bundles of ten, and poor people bought them. Although sparrows are hunted and killed, this does not happen apart from the sovereign knowledge, power, and love of God the faithful creator. No theoretical explanation is given, but as in 6:25-34, trust in the one creator of all is called for. God as creator and God as eschatological redeemer are united as the basis for these words of encouragement. In Matthew's theology, creation and eschatology are not alternatives, but complementary perspectives on the one God who embraces the whole world.

2. These rigorous rules, more austere than those for the familiar traveling Cynic preacher, helped the Syrian churches to distinguish authentic missioners from entrepreneurs (cf. *Didache* 11–13). The church today is in dire need of such help, when the media make it possible for large sums of money to be made by enterprising preachers. Such commercialized evangelism has been a significant factor in discouraging some Christians from pursuing evangelism and mission at all. A church that heeds the Gospel of Matthew cannot abandon the evangelistic enterprise nor be suspicious of all evangelists. What is needed is discernment. From the earliest days, the church has been aware of the need for a critical sorting out of true ministers and prophets from those who are false, even if sincere (1 Cor 12:1-3; Phil 3:2-16; Eph 4:4-16; 1 Thess 5:12-13, 20-21; 1 John 4:1-3; *Didache* 11–13). The critical faculty that helps the church discern true from false ministers is itself a gift of the Spirit (1 Cor 12:10), which Matthew understands as the continuing presence of Christ in the church (Matt 1:23; 28:16-20).

234. "Whisper in the ear" reflects the language for the reception of oracles (cf. Job 4:12).

MATTHEW 11:1-19, THE MINISTRY OF JESUS IN RELATION TO JOHN THE BAPTIST

OVERVIEW

The overarching concern of this passage is christological: the identity and role of Jesus in saving history. The christological question is here posed in terms of the relation of Jesus to the identity and role of John the Baptist. So regarded, the unit has three subsections dealing with (1) the identity of Jesus, (2) the identity of John, and (3) the lack of discernment of "this generation," all of which is prefaced by the transitional conclusion to the preceding discourse.

A new unit begins after the concluding transitional summary of 11:1. The unit extends to 11:19, where the "deeds" (ἔργα *erga*) of v. 2 are repeated, forming a literary bracket. This is not apparent in the NRSV, which paraphrases "deeds" as "what the Messiah was doing." The intervention by the narrator in v. 20 then begins a new unit. Matthew has gathered all the remaining Q material about John the Baptist to form a literary unit corresponding to 3:1–4:17 (cf. Introduction).[235]

235. Matthew 11:2-19 corresponds to Luke 7:18-35, plus the additional Q reference in Luke 16:16. Matthew preserves the remaining references to John in Mark in their Markan context: Mark 6:14-25 = Matt 14:2-10; Mark 8:28 = Matt 16:14; Mark 11:30-32 = Matt 21:25-32.

Matthew 11:1, Transitional Conclusion: Jesus Departs

NIV

11 After Jesus had finished instructing his twelve disciples, he went on from there to teach and preach in the towns of Galilee.[a]

[a]1 Greek *in their towns*

NRSV

11 Now when Jesus had finished instructing his twelve disciples, he went on from there to teach and proclaim his message in their cities.

COMMENTARY

Surprisingly, and in contrast to his Markan source (Mark 6:12-13, 30 are omitted; cf. Luke 9:6, 10), after picturing the disciples as hearing the Mission Discourse, Matthew does not relate their departure, and no mission is recounted as part of the pre-Easter story. Thereby Jesus' address to the reader is more direct. The time of the Jewish mission continues and is contemporaneous with the reader.[236] Jesus' words about mission are more important than a narration of a past mission

236. On the mission to Israel as included in "all the nations/Gentiles" (πάντα τὰ ἔθνη *panta ta ethnē*), see Commentary on Matt 28:16-20.

of the Twelve. In the narrative the words are left hanging in the air, still addressing the post-Easter reader, and Jesus continues his preaching mission. Rather than connoting distance, as with "their" synagogues and "their" scribes, Jesus' preaching in "their" cities—the cities in which the disciples themselves preach—is another testimony that the risen Christ accompanies his church in its mission through history and is present and active in its preaching (cf. 1:23; 10:40; 13:37; 16:18; 18:20; 28:20).

Matthew 11:2-6, "Who Is Jesus?"

<table>
<tr><td>NIV</td><td>NRSV</td></tr>
</table>

NIV

2When John heard in prison what Christ was doing, he sent his disciples ³to ask him, "Are you the one who was to come, or should we expect someone else?"

⁴Jesus replied, "Go back and report to John what you hear and see: ⁵The blind receive sight, the lame walk, those who have leprosy*ᵃ* are cured, the deaf hear, the dead are raised, and the good news is preached to the poor. ⁶Blessed is the man who does not fall away on account of me."

ᵃ5 The Greek word was used for various diseases affecting the skin—not necessarily leprosy.

NRSV

2When John heard in prison what the Messiah*ᵃ* was doing, he sent word by his*ᵇ* disciples ³and said to him, "Are you the one who is to come, or are we to wait for another?" ⁴Jesus answered them, "Go and tell John what you hear and see: ⁵the blind receive their sight, the lame walk, the lepers*ᶜ* are cleansed, the deaf hear, the dead are raised, and the poor have good news brought to them. ⁶And blessed is anyone who takes no offense at me."

*ᵃ*Or *the Christ*   *ᵇ*Other ancient authorities read *two of his*
*ᶜ*The terms *leper* and *leprosy* can refer to several diseases

COMMENTARY

Matthew adapts the material from Q (Luke 7:18-23). Since Q begins with John's preaching (now found in Matt 3:7-12/ Luke 3:7-9, 16-17) but contains no reference to John's previous recognition of Jesus as the "coming one" or to John's arrest and imprisonment, in Q the story presents a positive view of John. In the course of his continuing ministry, John is beginning to wonder whether the "mighty one" whose near advent he had announced is in fact Jesus. In the Matthean story line, however, John has already recognized the messianic status of Jesus (3:14-15, a Matthean addition to his sources), and has been imprisoned (4:12, for which 14:1-12 is a flashback), so that the story in its present context represents the beginning of doubt rather than the dawn of faith.

From his prison cell, John hears of the deeds of Jesus and his disciples, designated in Matthew's terminology as "the works of the Christ." The phrase refers not only to Jesus' deeds in the collection of miracle stories in chapters 8–9, but to the similar works done by Jesus' disciples in chapter 10.[237] The fact that the question is not posed until after chapter 10, in which Jesus'

works had modulated into the disciples' works, illustrates once again the unity of christology and ecclesiology in Matthew's thought. The "coming one" (ὁ ἐρχόμενος *ho erchomenos*) is a generic term for the expected eschatological savior figure, widely used in early Christianity (cf. John's preaching in Matt 3:11; Matt 21:9 = Mark 11:9; Matt 23:39 = Q 13:39; John 6:35; Acts 19:4; Heb 10:37; Rev 1:8; 4:8). Since the "deeds of the Christ" of chapters 8–10 are acts of compassion rather than the fiery judgment of the "coming one" announced in 3:11-12, John backs off from his previous confidence and asks whether Jesus is indeed the expected one, or whether we should wait for another.[238]

Jesus' response is indirect, in terms of his works rather than christological confessions or titles. The words and deeds of Jesus and his disciples represent the works of the messianic age promised in Isa 35:5-6; 42:18. "What you hear and see" corresponds to Matthew 5–7 and 8–10, the "words and works of the Messiah," framed by

237. The literal translation, preserved in KJV and GNB, makes the literary bracket with 11:19 clear, where the same word appears. Both the NIV and the NRSV obscure the connotations of this Matthean term. Just as chapters 5–7 conclude with "his words," which impressed the crowds with their authority (7:28-29), so also "the deeds of the Messiah" summarizes chapters 8–10.

238. Different words are used by Matthew (ἕτερος *heteros*) and Luke (ἄλλος *allos*) for "another." Although these words can be used as synonyms (as in 2 Cor 11:4), Matthew's usage (but not Luke's) can also mean "one different in kind" and not merely another one of the same kind. Since Matthew uses the same word in 11:16, again in contrast to Luke, the nuance may be important here. So understood, John's question is not merely an inquiry as to whether Jesus is the one expected, but also "Should we wait for a different *kind* of Messiah?"

4:23 and 9:35. The literary bracket is made the more explicit in that the concluding reference to preaching the gospel to the poor corresponds to the beginning of the Sermon on Mount (11:5*b*/5:3). The key theme of "take offense," "fall away" (σκανδαλίζειν *skandalizein*; lit. "stumble over")

is here introduced. In the story line, it refers to Jesus' failure to conform to popular messianic expectations. The readers know it includes the scandal of a crucified Messiah and hear themselves included in the blessing.

Matthew 11:7-15, "Who Is John?"

NIV

⁷As John's disciples were leaving, Jesus began to speak to the crowd about John: "What did you go out into the desert to see? A reed swayed by the wind? ⁸If not, what did you go out to see? A man dressed in fine clothes? No, those who wear fine clothes are in kings' palaces. ⁹Then what did you go out to see? A prophet? Yes, I tell you, and more than a prophet. ¹⁰This is the one about whom it is written:

" 'I will send my messenger ahead of you,
    who will prepare your way before you.'ᵃ

¹¹I tell you the truth: Among those born of women there has not risen anyone greater than John the Baptist; yet he who is least in the kingdom of heaven is greater than he. ¹²From the days of John the Baptist until now, the kingdom of heaven has been forcefully advancing, and forceful men lay hold of it. ¹³For all the Prophets and the Law prophesied until John. ¹⁴And if you are willing to accept it, he is the Elijah who was to come. ¹⁵He who has ears, let him hear."

ᵃ10 Mal. 3:1

NRSV

7As they went away, Jesus began to speak to the crowds about John: "What did you go out into the wilderness to look at? A reed shaken by the wind? ⁸What then did you go out to see? Someoneᵃ dressed in soft robes? Look, those who wear soft robes are in royal palaces. ⁹What then did you go out to see? A prophet?ᵇ Yes, I tell you, and more than a prophet. ¹⁰This is the one about whom it is written,

'See, I am sending my messenger ahead of you,
    who will prepare your way before you.'

¹¹Truly I tell you, among those born of women no one has arisen greater than John the Baptist; yet the least in the kingdom of heaven is greater than he. ¹²From the days of John the Baptist until now the kingdom of heaven has suffered violence,ᶜ and the violent take it by force. ¹³For all the prophets and the law prophesied until John came; ¹⁴and if you are willing to accept it, he is Elijah who is to come. ¹⁵Let anyone with earsᵈ listen!"

ᵃOr *Why then did you go out? To see someone*
ᵇOther ancient authorities read *Why then did you go out? To see a prophet?*   ᶜOr *has been coming violently*
ᵈOther ancient authorities add *to hear*

COMMENTARY

11:7-10. The wilderness along the Jordan did contain reeds blowing in the wind and palaces inhabited by people dressed in royal robes—Herod's fortress palaces of Herodium, Machaerus, and Masada. Some Herodian coins bear the symbol of a reed from the Jordan valley. Since John, like Jesus, represents an alternative kingdom, the Matthean motif of the conflict of kingdoms may shimmer in the background. So understood, Jesus'

rhetorical question might mean "Reeds and royal robes are there, but that is not the reason you went into the wilderness. You went to see a *prophet.*" Or the thrust of Jesus' rhetoric might be simply a contrast to John: He was no weather vane who took his direction from changing political currents, but stood against the stream; he was dressed not in the finery of court lackeys, but, like Elijah, wore the rough garb of the wilderness prophet. In either case, Jesus' point is to affirm that John was a prophet (14:5; 21:26). Indeed, John is more than a prophet, in that he not only spoke of the eschatological events to come, but also played a role in these events; thus he was the object of prophecy (11:10). Matthew 11:10 follows the combination of Exod 23:20 and Mal 3:1, which had already appeared in Q (cf. Luke 7:27) and in Mark 1:2. God's promises to send the "angel of the LORD" in Exod 23:20 and the "messenger" in Mal 3:1 (Elijah; see Mal 4:5-6) are here interpreted as fulfilled by the coming of John the Baptist (11:14; 17:10-13). (But only "if you are willing to accept it." At the crucifixion, people still indulge in idle speculation about Elijah at the expense of the suffering of Jesus; cf. 27:46-49.)

11:11. John's borderline role in Matthew's theological scheme retains some ambiguity. On the one hand, John is paired with Jesus in having the same message of the kingdom (3:2 = 4:17), but on the other hand Matthew retains the traditional Q saying (cf. Luke 7:28) that distinguishes John from the least in the kingdom. It is not clear whether the "least in the kingdom" refers to Jesus or, more likely, to the disciples—i.e., Christian believers from Matthew's perspective. What is clear is that John plays a decisive role in the history of salvation, forming a dividing line. He is the last and greatest of the prophets of the old eon. What matters, however, is not personal greatness, but whether one belongs to the new era of God's reign, inaugurated by Jesus. In terms of salvation history, John is a borderline figure for Matthew. The prepositions used for "until" ($\H{\epsilon}\omega\varsigma$ *heōs* in Matthew; $\mu\epsilon\chi\rho\iota$ *mechri* in Luke) can be used either inclusively or exclusively. John has his own disciples and is never pictured as becoming a believer. Thus he represents a borderline in another aspect as well, standing between the disciples on the one hand and the

opponents on the other (cf. structure in the Introduction)

11:12-15. This passage must be important for Matthew, since he has moved it from a different context in Q (cf. Luke 16:16). It is, however, one of the most difficult and most disputed texts in Matthew.[239] The saying was already variously interpreted in early Christianity, as indicated by the different form and meaning in Luke 16:16. The chief issues are whether $\beta\iota\acute{\alpha}\zeta\epsilon\tau\alpha\iota$ (*biazetai*) is to be taken as middle voice (so NIV) or as a passive (so NRSV) and the related question of whether the $\beta\iota\alpha\sigma\tau\alpha\acute{\iota}$ (*biastai*) are "forceful" believers in the positive sense (so NIV) or "violent" opponents to the kingdom (so NRSV). It is, perhaps, best to regard this as another expression of the Matthean conviction that the non-violent eschatological kingdom represented by the advent of Jesus the meek king (21:1-9; cf. 12:22-37 and the Matthean addition in 21:5) has met violent opposition from representatives of the opposing kingdom. The advent of God's kingdom as represented by John and Jesus provokes violent opposition. Matthew's concluding point is clear: John is the eschatological Elijah, who stands at the turning of the ages. But like perceiving the advent of the kingdom in the parables, recognizing the prophets of the kingdom requires discernment: "Let anyone with ears [to hear] listen."[240]

---

239. W. D. Davies and Dale C. Allison, Jr., *A Critical and Exegetical Commentary on the Gospel According to Saint Matthew*, 2 vols., ICC (Edinburgh: T. & T. Clark, 1988–91) 2:254-55, list seven varieties of modern interpretations of this passage. See also P. S. Cameron, *Violence and the Kingdom: The Interpretation of Matthew 11:12*, ANTJ 5 (1984); David Catchpole, "On Doing Violence to the Kingdom," *IBS* 3 (1981) 77-92.

240. The original text of Matthew is probably represented by the NRSV's marginal reading, which includes "to hear" (as in $\aleph$, C, L, W, Z, Δ, Θ, f^1, f^{13} and most other MSS, but missing from a few MSS, including the important B), understood as "able to hear the real meaning"; cf. Commentary on 13:16. Matthew adopts the Markan phrase from Mark 4:9, 23; 8:18, itself a reflection of Deut 29:4 and Isa 42:20.

Matthew 11:16-19, The Call for Discernment and Response of "This Generation"

NIV

16"To what can I compare this generation? They are like children sitting in the marketplaces and calling out to others:

17" 'We played the flute for you,
and you did not dance;
we sang a dirge,
and you did not mourn.'

18For John came neither eating nor drinking, and they say, 'He has a demon.' 19The Son of Man came eating and drinking, and they say, 'Here is a glutton and a drunkard, a friend of tax collectors and "sinners." ' But wisdom is proved right by her actions."

NRSV

16"But to what will I compare this generation? It is like children sitting in the marketplaces and calling to one another,

17 'We played the flute for you, and you did
not dance;
we wailed, and you did not mourn.'

18For John came neither eating nor drinking, and they say, 'He has a demon'; 19the Son of Man came eating and drinking, and they say, 'Look, a glutton and a drunkard, a friend of tax collectors and sinners!' Yet wisdom is vindicated by her deeds."[a]

aOther ancient authorities read *children*

COMMENTARY

The preceding two sections have made clear the identity of Jesus and John. Jesus is the expected "coming one," and John is the final messenger promised by God to prepare the way. But "this generation"[241] lacks discernment (cf. 16:1-4), and recognizes neither John nor Jesus. In Jesus' analogy of children playing in the marketplace, one group wants to play a happy game (e.g., weddings), but the other group will not play. So the first group tries to get them to play funerals, but they reject that too. In Matthew's chiastic structure, the latter option corresponds to the gaunt and ascetic figure of John, whose message of coming judgment was too threatening, and whose life-style too unworldly for the sophisticates of "this generation." But when Jesus came in meekness, announcing the peaceable kingdom of unconditional love and forgiveness and celebrating the goodness of life with all, he was rejected as not "spiritual" enough. "This generation's" description of Jesus as a glutton and a drunkard is

reminiscent of Deut 21:20, suggesting more than merely an insult: Jesus is a rebellious Israelite worthy of stoning, one who should be executed in order to purge evil from the midst of the covenant community.

The Q community had originally understood both John and Jesus, as well as the members of their own prophetic community, as "children" of transcendent Wisdom, who vindicated the heavenly Wisdom by faithfully living out their prophetic mission and message (as in Luke 7:20). Matthew alters Q's "children" to "deeds," identifying Jesus with transcendent Wisdom, and not merely as one of a series of Wisdom's messengers.[242] As noted, the repetition of "deeds" here forms a literary inclusio with v. 2. This motif of Jesus identified as Wisdom continues into the next section (cf. esp. vv. 25-30).

241. The expression is Q's favorite description of the unbelieving last generation, found also in Mark.

242. See M. Jack Suggs, *Wisdom, Christology, and Law in Matthew's Gospel* (Cambridge, Mass.: Harvard University Press, 1970); F. W. Burnett, *The Testament of Jesus-Sophia: A Redactional-Critical Study of the Eschatological Discourse in Matthew* (Washington, D.C.: University Press of America, 1981). For a critique, see Marshal D. Johnson, "Reflections on a Wisdom Approach to Matthew's Christology," *CBQ* 36 (1974) 44-64.

REFLECTIONS

1. Matthew 11:1-19 presents another opportunity to reflect on the issue of the meaning of biblical interpretation. Is the John pictured here a historical figure or a character in Matthew's story world? This question presents a false alternative. There was certainly a historical John the Baptist; he is no more a fictional character than is Jesus. Yet taken as "pure" historical report, this story presents grave difficulties. Why, if as an inspired prophet John knew by divine revelation that Jesus was the Messiah (3:13-17), did John continue to have his own disciples who had their own rituals (9:14)? What did being a disciple of John mean? In addition, the interpreter must inquire how John could have communicated with his disciples from Herod's prison in the desert fortress-palace at Machaerus (the historical site of John's imprisonment), and imagine some way that this was historically possible. Further, the interpreter must psychologize John's experience, speculating on what had happened to him since the charismatic experience of seeing heaven opened and hearing the heavenly voice at Jesus' baptism. While this can make entertaining sermons, it has little to do with the text of the Bible and the Word of God that comes through it.

Alternatively, one could posit that the story presented here actually took place before John's arrest (despite 11:2), and so represents the dawn of faith rather than its decline and is not to be combined with the stories of Jesus' baptism and John's imprisonment. All such "historical" approaches require one to look outside the story world of the text for speculative answers.

The clue to Matthew's meaning lies elsewhere. Within the theological story world constructed by Matthew, John is a true prophet with a legitimate divine message, proclaiming the same message Jesus will proclaim, recognizing Jesus as the Messiah when he comes for baptism. John is imprisoned because his prophetic preaching offends the authorities, and later dies a martyr's death. Nonetheless, John wavers in his faith. For Matthew, this is the nature of discipleship and faith, which must be constantly renewed. John becomes an object lesson to Christian believers, who must not regard salvation as a static possession, but must take heed lest they also fall away (again, cf. Matthew's similar treatment of Peter in 14:28-31; 16:16-18, 23; 26:69-75). Even "spiritual experiences" do not guarantee acceptance on the Last Day (7:21-23). Such reflections, here applied to a relatively mild historical issue, apply to every pericope in Matthew.

2. Jesus is indeed the "coming one," but he has reversed the valences of the expectation. As the promised coming one, he is at the same time the stumbling block. He transforms the expectation in the act of fulfilling it. To say that *Jesus* is the Christ[243] is not only to say something about Jesus, but to transform the meaning of *Christ* as well. Faith does not grow from our testing Jesus against our criteria to see if he measures up; Jesus is not the best example of values we already have, validated on some other basis. One must overcome a certain "stumbling block" (σκάνδαλον *skandalon,* or "scandal," 11:6; cf. 13:21, 41; 15:12; 24:10; 26:31-33; 1 Cor 1:23; Gal 5:11) in order to come to faith and continue as a disciple.

3. The question is not merely whether Jesus was a great man or even a divine individual. Confession of Jesus as the Christ includes a confession about the messianic community: the church. The issue of Jesus' identity is not raised until John hears of the "works of the Christ," which in Matthew includes the disciples' mission, extending Jesus' authority and deeds as reported in chapter 10.

Likewise, the question of Jesus' identity cannot be dealt with apart from the question of Jesus' place in the saving history. As the Christ, Jesus is not merely a great individual, but the

---

243. It would be better to say that the Christ is Jesus. In all such christological statements, *Christ* is the subject and *Jesus* is the predicate. The function of such confessional statements is not to answer the question of the identity of Jesus, but to declare that the Christ has come.

fulfillment of the promises and presence of God in Israel, the one who stands at the turn of the ages. Thus the question of Jesus' identity cannot be dealt with apart from its context. This context includes the whole of Israel's history, including John the Baptist, the prophets, and the Jewish people.

4. To some extent John's question (11:3) may already be ours. John may speak for those who were once sure of their faith but now are not so sure, or for those who are impressed by Jesus' accomplishments but wonder whether there is some clue in them to the ultimate meaning of things, or for those who are beginning to doubt whether the way of gentleness and non-retaliation can ever really work in a world where a few have most of the power. Matthew does not consider the asking of such questions to close the door to faith. The pressure of events and the ways of the world force such questions on honest minds: Is there really a God who knows and cares? Does this God have a plan for the world? For me? If so, is Jesus the definitive revelation of that God, or should we look elsewhere for answers to ultimate questions? Those who seriously ask such questions may be closer to the kingdom than those who say that, of course, God exists and, of course, Jesus is God's Son.

On the other hand, John's question may not be ours, so that if we ask ultimate questions at all they may not take this form, and Matthew may intend to teach us how to ask such questions. His mode of asking, seeking, and knocking (7:7) excludes any individualistic me-and-Jesus approach and reshapes the christological question to include Israel and history. To ask whether Jesus is the one who is to come—i.e., the one in whom God is definitively revealed and acts for the world's salvation—is to ask what it is all about. Matthew's whole Gospel is the answer to John's question. The gospel message includes a cross for Jesus and imprisonment and death for John. But those who affirm that God is present with his people in the events to which the gospel bears witness know that they need not, and must not, look elsewhere for another, even if from time to time they continue to wonder whether he is the one. (Cf. Reflections on 21:23-27.)

MATTHEW 11:20–12:14, CONFLICT WITH THE KINGDOM OF THIS AGE

OVERVIEW

This section begins with "then he began" (τότε ἤρξατο *tote ērxato*) and an infinitive, signaling a turning point in the narrative much as the similar expression in 4:17 and 16:21. All three units of this section immediately deal with repentance, the radical reorientation of life to which Jesus calls. From Jesus' initial pronouncement of "woe" to the concluding resolution of the Pharisees to kill Jesus, this section describes growing conflict. Thus it corresponds to 2:1-23, the initial conflict in Matthew's chiastic structure of Part One (see Introduction). To discern Matthew's structure, the interpreter must disregard both the artificial division between chapters 11 and 12 and the para-graph divisions of the text found in synopses (which are arranged to facilitate source analysis rather than being oriented to the structure of each Gospel).

After the redactional v. 20, the whole section is composed of sayings material, first of oracles and other dominical sayings taken from Q, then of two conflict pronouncement stories taken from Mark.[244] Jesus first pronounces two woe oracles against Galilean cities (11:20-24). The central sec-

---

244. For the characteristics of pronouncement stories (or apophthegms [Bultmann]) see Introduction. Matthew's addition of sayings material to both stories has further subordinated the narrative element to the words of Jesus.

tion begins with a prayer of Jesus, to which are joined two other sayings of similar tone and meaning (11:25-30). The final section is composed of two conflict scenes concerning the Sabbath, each concluding with an authoritative pronouncement (12:1-14). The whole section is dominated by the word of the sovereign Jesus, who already speaks as the judge of the Last Day. This section, like the Sermon on the Mount, thus has a tripartite structure with Jesus' prayer at the center: (1) two woes against Galilean cities, 11:20-24; (2) Jesus' prayer, declaration, and invitation, 11:25-30; (3) two pronouncements from the Lord of the Sabbath, 12:1-14.

Matthew 11:20-24, Two Woes Against Galilean Cities

NIV	NRSV
²⁰Then Jesus began to denounce the cities in which most of his miracles had been performed, because they did not repent. ²¹"Woe to you, Korazin! Woe to you, Bethsaida! If the miracles that were performed in you had been performed in Tyre and Sidon, they would have repented long ago in sackcloth and ashes. ²²But I tell you, it will be more bearable for Tyre and Sidon on the day of judgment than for you. ²³And you, Capernaum, will you be lifted up to the skies? No, you will go down to the depths.ᵃ If the miracles that were performed in you had been performed in Sodom, it would have remained to this day. ²⁴But I tell you that it will be more bearable for Sodom on the day of judgment than for you."	²⁰Then he began to reproach the cities in which most of his deeds of power had been done, because they did not repent. ²¹"Woe to you, Chorazin! Woe to you, Bethsaida! For if the deeds of power done in you had been done in Tyre and Sidon, they would have repented long ago in sackcloth and ashes. ²²But I tell you, on the day of judgment it will be more tolerable for Tyre and Sidon than for you. ²³And you, Capernaum, will you be exalted to heaven? No, you will be brought down to Hades. For if the deeds of power done in you had been done in Sodom, it would have remained until this day. ²⁴But I tell you that on the day of judgment it will be more tolerable for the land of Sodom than for you."
ᵃ23 Greek *Hades*	

COMMENTARY

Matthew has brought this Q unit to this context to introduce his new section (cf. Luke 10:12-15). Jesus' first words introduce a new note, since nothing in the preceding narrative has prepared the reader for Jesus' pronouncement of woe. Like much else in the Gospel, the sayings are heard by the Matthean readers from the perspective of their own time, looking back on the ministry of Jesus as a whole. These two pronouncements may thus reflect not only Galilee's rejection of Jesus "in the days of his flesh," but also the unsuccessful mission conducted by the missionaries of the Q community and by Matthew's own church. The words may thus be partly or wholly from early Christian prophets rather than the historical Jesus.[245]

The woes are similar in form to the "woes against foreign nations" that are a common element of the prophetic books of the Hebrew Bible (e.g., Amos 1:3–2:3; Isaiah 13–23; Jeremiah 46–51; Ezekiel 25–32; Obadiah). But the Matthean oracles announce a great reversal: The Gentile cities of Tyre, Sidon, and Sodom, which had become biblical symbols of utter evil, will fare better in the judgment than will the Jewish cities of Chorazin and Bethsaida. Even Jesus' "own town" Capernaum (cf. 4:12-13; 9:1) is accused of "exalting itself to heaven," as did ancient Babylon and its king (Isa 14:13). Since previous references to Capernaum do not suggest wholesale rejection of Jesus, and Chorazin and Bethsaida are mentioned only here in Matthew, these oracles either indicate how spotty our knowledge of the ministry

245. See M. Eugene Boring, *The Continuing Voice of Jesus: Christian Prophecy and the Gospel Tradition* (Louisville: Westminster/John Knox, 1991) 174-76, 209.

of Jesus is or reflect the post-Easter missionary experience of the church; more likely, they suggest both.

The problem is not that the inhabitants were skeptical of miracles as such. Indeed, they believed that the miracles happened, but Jesus' call for repentance (4:17)—reorientation of life to accord with his announcement of the kingdom of God—had gone unheeded even by those who believed that Jesus and his disciples actually worked miracles. Like the OT prophetic pronouncements of doom, these proleptic pronouncements of eschatological judgment function not as the announcement of an unalterable fate, but as a call to repentance. (Cf. the Jonah story, shortly to be reflected in 12:38-41.)

REFLECTIONS

Capernaum, Jesus' adopted "own city" for his ministry, is found here in strange company, with strange language used about it. The great evil cities of history, those that had been denounced by the prophets for their wickedness and had received the fiery judgment of God for their sins, are here placed in the same category as little Capernaum, not known for bright lights and notorious sins. Nor had it ever consciously placed itself in the category of mighty Babylon, "exalting itself to heaven," asserting itself in the place of God, making an idol of itself. All it had done was to continue business as usual, while the signs of God's redeeming presence occurred in its midst without fanfare. That is all.

Matthew 11:25-30, Jesus' Prayer, Declaration, and Invitation

NIV

²⁵At that time Jesus said, "I praise you, Father, Lord of heaven and earth, because you have hidden these things from the wise and learned, and revealed them to little children. ²⁶Yes, Father, for this was your good pleasure.

²⁷"All things have been committed to me by my Father. No one knows the Son except the Father, and no one knows the Father except the Son and those to whom the Son chooses to reveal him.

²⁸"Come to me, all you who are weary and burdened, and I will give you rest. ²⁹Take my yoke upon you and learn from me, for I am gentle and humble in heart, and you will find rest for your souls. ³⁰For my yoke is easy and my burden is light."

NRSV

25At that time Jesus said, "I thank[a] you, Father, Lord of heaven and earth, because you have hidden these things from the wise and the intelligent and have revealed them to infants; ²⁶yes, Father, for such was your gracious will.[b] ²⁷All things have been handed over to me by my Father; and no one knows the Son except the Father, and no one knows the Father except the Son and anyone to whom the Son chooses to reveal him.

28"Come to me, all you that are weary and are carrying heavy burdens, and I will give you rest. ²⁹Take my yoke upon you, and learn from me; for I am gentle and humble in heart, and you will find rest for your souls. ³⁰For my yoke is easy, and my burden is light."

a Or praise   b Or for so it was well-pleasing in your sight

COMMENTARY

The tripartite structure of this unit is a result of Matthean composition. The first two elements (vv. 25-27) are from a different context in Q (Luke 10:21-22; Luke has made them a response to the jubilant return of the "seventy" from a successful preaching mission, which is absent from Matthew). Matthew has relocated them here and made them an integral part of this speech unit. The third element (vv. 28-30) is peculiar to Matthew, who either used his own traditions or composed it himself.

The audience is still "the crowds" of v. 7 (the disciples disappear at v. 1 and do not reappear until 12:1). Even the prayer of vv. 25-26 is overheard by the crowds and the reader, and the concluding invitation is to all. These striking sayings are thus not an isolated passage, but are firmly rooted in their context. Verse 25 is closely related to the preceding by the introductory "at that time" and the untranslated ἀποκριθείς *apokritheis* ("responded"; "answered" in KJV). By placing these sayings here, Matthew indicates that the negative woes and descriptions of the preceding paragraph are not the final and universal word. Jesus' message is rejected, but it finds acceptance as well—among the "babies," the unpretentious "little people" (cf. 18:6-14). If even John, who baptized him, had begun to question and the Galilean cities that knew him best had rejected his message, still some persons would have responded to Jesus on the basis of the gracious revelatory act of God (cf. 16:17).

This passage is unique in the synoptic tradition. It was once often considered to be similar to the declarations of Hellenistic savior figures, more akin to Johannine christological conceptions than to the Jesus of the Synoptics (cf. John 3:35; 5:19-20; 7:29; 10:14-15; 13:3; 17:2, 25).[246] The immediate background, however, seems to be the wisdom tradition of the OT and early Judaism. Beginning with a saying of the historical Jesus (11:25-26), the prophetic Q community expanded the saying by picturing Jesus as the messenger of transcendent Lady Wisdom (Sophia). Just as only God knows Wisdom (Job 28:12-27; Sir 1:6-9; Bar 3:32), so also only the Father knows the Son. Just as only Wisdom knows God (Wis 8:4; 9:1-18), so also only the Son knows the Father. Just as Wisdom makes known the divine mysteries (Wis 9:1-18; 10:10), so also Jesus is the revealer of God's hidden truths. As the personified divine Wisdom calls people to take up her yoke and find

246. Karl von Hase's label has become traditional: "a thunderbolt from the Johannine sky" (*Die Geschichte Jesu* [Leipzig 1876²], 422).

rest (Sir 51:23-30; cf. Prov 1:20-23; 8:1-36; Sir 24:19-22; *Odes of Solomon* 33:6-13), so Jesus extends the same invitation. For Matthew, Jesus is not merely the messenger of Wisdom, but is identified with the heavenly Wisdom of God; he speaks not only for Wisdom, but as the divine Wisdom (see Commentary on 11:20). Since Jesus' words are reminiscent of Exod 33:12-13, probably Matthew understood them also in terms of the Moses typology he develops elsewhere (see comments on 5:1).

11:25-26, Jesus' Prayer. Despite the rejection condemned in vv. 20-24, some persons accept Jesus' mission and message, and for this he gives thanks. In the context given them by Matthew, these words are not a thanksgiving for a successful mission (cf. Luke 10:21), but are a prayerful reflection on the "failure" of the Galilean mission. These words thus function parabolically and, as in vv. 20-24, portray another reversal: Those who accept are not the "wise and intelligent" ("learned," NIV), but the "infants" (NRSV). Since Matthew elsewhere regards wisdom and understanding as positive attributes of the disciples themselves, these words are not a tirade glorifying ignorance (7:24-27; 13:51; 23:34; 25:1-13; cf. the concluding command "learn," v. 29). As elsewhere (e.g., 16:17), Matthew affirms that those who recognize Jesus as the divine messenger do so not on the basis of superior religious status or individual intelligence or shrewdness, but by revelation, as the gift of the God to those who are open and unpretentious. The "little children" (NIV), persons without time, ability, or interest in religious learning and who have no religious basis for claiming the knowledge of God, are the ones to whom the divine revelation is given as sheer grace (cf. 18:1-14). In Matthew's own situation, the contrast is between the leadership of the Jewish synagogues, both scribal and Pharisaic, who have rejected Matthew's community and its message and the "little people" without religious status who comprise Matthew's Christian community.

11:27, Jesus' Christological Declaration. This contrast continues in v. 27, which pictures Jesus as having knowledge delivered to him directly from the Father, in contrast to the scribes and rabbis, whose tradition is on the human level alone (cf. 7:28-29; 15:1-20). Jesus is not pictured as a religious genius who has discovered the divine mystery, but as the beloved Son who is on intimate terms with the Father. It is the divine initiative of the Father who, in a statement anticipating 28:18, has given "all things" to the Son. This text has been understood since the second century in Johannine terms to affirm the pre-existence of the Son, and it played a role in the trinitarian controversies of the fourth century. For Matthew, however, who has no doctrine of pre-existence, the words do not describe a pre-historical heavenly transaction among the members of the Trinity, but, as in 28:18, express Matthew's retrospective faith in God's act in the Christ-event taken as a whole, seen from the post-Easter perspective. The statement claims exclusive mutual knowledge between the Father and the Son.

11:28-30, Jesus' Invitation. Speaking as the embodiment of the divine Wisdom, Jesus' invitation extends to all who are burdened. In his polemical situation, Matthew had in mind particularly the burden of religious obligation imposed by the scribes and Pharisees, which he understood as a barrier to communion with God (cf. 23:4). The saying has had a long life in the history of the church as a more general invitation to all those who are put off by the pretensions of human religion.

In the OT and Jewish tradition, "yoke" was a common metaphor for servitude, and hence obedience. In contrast to the rabbinic custom of speaking of the "yoke of the Torah" or the "yoke of the Kingdom," Jesus speaks of "my yoke," thereby claiming to be the expression of God's will. Like "rest," the "easy" yoke of Jesus is not an invitation to a life of ease, but of deliverance from the artificial burdens of human religion, which Matthew sees as a barrier to the true fellowship of the kingdom of God (23:4). "Learn" is an important Matthean aspect of discipleship (cf. 9:13; 28:19), added by him here to the traditional saying. Verse 29b disturbs the parallelism and contains key Matthean vocabulary ("meek" [πραΰς *praus*]) and is thus probably Matthew's own addition to the traditional saying.

Like the divine Wisdom (Sir 51:23-30), and like God in addressing Moses (Exod 33:14), Jesus offers "rest," which is not mere ease (cf. 10:17-39), but is a synonym for salvation, associated with the kingdom of God and eternal life (as in Heb 3:11, 18; 4:1, 3, 5, 10-11; Rev 14:13). The institution of the sabbath also had these overtones. Perhaps Jesus is here pictured as the true giver of sabbath rest and all that implies, setting the stage for his next pronouncements, set in the context of sabbath controversies.

REFLECTIONS

The perceptive reader is stunned by this section of Matthew, in which all those who should recognize the definitive revelation of God taking place in their midst instead fail to "get it." John the Baptist, who had baptized Jesus, knew his own unworthiness, and had heard the heavenly voice (11:2-14) did not get it. Those who had their own games to play and found that neither John nor Jesus met the predetermined criteria of their own values (11:16-19) did not get it. Chorazin, Bethsaida, and Capernaum, in whose presence Jesus had lived out the mighty acts of the dawning kingdom of God (11:20-24) did not get it. The scholars and the wise, who could explain much but missed the revelation in their midst (11:25a) did not get it. Those who did get it were the "babies," the unpretentious "little ones" who made no claims but could be given the gift of revelation, which comes from God alone (11:25b-27).

Is this an invitation to pride, to suppose that if we claim to get it, we belong to the chosen few? Or is it an invitation to resignation and despair, since God's revelation is God's own choice, and there is nothing we can do about it?

Who gets it? The passage closes with an invitation from the one who is himself meek and lowly in heart, an invitation to all who know themselves to be burdened and in need of salvation, an invitation to learn and become Jesus' disciples. Those who hear the invitation will know that they have the response-ability to answer the call, and when they do, they will understand that they must praise God, who has given them this gift of revelation.

Matthew 12:1-14, Lord of the Sabbath

NIV

12 At that time Jesus went through the grain-fields on the Sabbath. His disciples were hungry and began to pick some heads of grain and eat them. ²When the Pharisees saw this, they said to him, "Look! Your disciples are doing what is unlawful on the Sabbath."

³He answered, "Haven't you read what David did when he and his companions were hungry? ⁴He entered the house of God, and he and his companions ate the consecrated bread—which was not lawful for them to do, but only for the priests. ⁵Or haven't you read in the Law that on the Sabbath the priests in the temple desecrate the day and yet are innocent? ⁶I tell you that one*ᵃ* greater than the temple is here. ⁷If you had known what these words mean, 'I desire mercy, not sacrifice,'*ᵇ* you would not have condemned the innocent. ⁸For the Son of Man is Lord of the Sabbath."

⁹Going on from that place, he went into their synagogue, ¹⁰and a man with a shriveled hand was there. Looking for a reason to accuse Jesus, they asked him, "Is it lawful to heal on the Sabbath?"

¹¹He said to them, "If any of you has a sheep and it falls into a pit on the Sabbath, will you not take hold of it and lift it out? ¹²How much more valuable is a man than a sheep! Therefore it is lawful to do good on the Sabbath."

¹³Then he said to the man, "Stretch out your hand." So he stretched it out and it was completely restored, just as sound as the other. ¹⁴But the Pharisees went out and plotted how they might kill Jesus.

ᵃ6 Or something; also in verses 41 and 42   ᵇ7 Hosea 6:6

NRSV

12 At that time Jesus went through the grain-fields on the sabbath; his disciples were hungry, and they began to pluck heads of grain and to eat. ²When the Pharisees saw it, they said to him, "Look, your disciples are doing what is not lawful to do on the sabbath." ³He said to them, "Have you not read what David did when he and his companions were hungry? ⁴He entered the house of God and ate the bread of the Presence, which it was not lawful for him or his companions to eat, but only for the priests. ⁵Or have you not read in the law that on the sabbath the priests in the temple break the sabbath and yet are guiltless? ⁶I tell you, something greater than the temple is here. ⁷But if you had known what this means, 'I desire mercy and not sacrifice,' you would not have condemned the guiltless. ⁸For the Son of Man is lord of the sabbath."

⁹He left that place and entered their synagogue; ¹⁰a man was there with a withered hand, and they asked him, "Is it lawful to cure on the sabbath?" so that they might accuse him. ¹¹He said to them, "Suppose one of you has only one sheep and it falls into a pit on the sabbath; will you not lay hold of it and lift it out? ¹²How much more valuable is a human being than a sheep! So it is lawful to do good on the sabbath." ¹³Then he said to the man, "Stretch out your hand." He stretched it out, and it was restored, as sound as the other. ¹⁴But the Pharisees went out and conspired against him, how to destroy him.

COMMENTARY

The chapter division is unfortunate, since 12:1 does not begin a new section. The opening words (ἐν ἐκείνῳ τῷ καιρῷ *en ekeinō tō kairō*) bind this unit to the preceding text. The theme of conflict, which dominates 11:20–12:14, continues in this section, as well as the themes of rest/sabbath, the contrast of the "wise and understanding" versus the little people, the "easy yoke" ("mercy," v. 7), and the christological theme (the Son to whom the Father has given "all things" [11:27] is the Son of Man, who is Lord of the sabbath [12:8]). Nor does the composition shift from sayings to narrative, since the following two conflict stories are primarily sayings.

The two scenes of 12:1-14 are not two separate stories as they are in the Markan source (Mark 2:23–3:6), and as they are divided in most translations and synopses. Like the two-scene story of calling the disciples in 4:18-22, these two scenes form one unit.[247]

Matthew here refers to the sabbath for the first time, gathering all of his sabbath material into this one story.[248] Several layers of Jewish/Christian conflict are expressed in the present form of the story, from Jesus' original teaching and practice, through the use of this story in early Christian conflicts with Judaism, expressed in the pre-Markan oral tradition, in the Gospel of Mark, and finally in Matthew. We are concerned here with the meaning of the Matthean text in its final form (cf. Introduction).

It is misleading, superficial, and simplistic to attempt to understand the text in terms of a conflict between Jewish legalism and Jesus' or the church's freedom from the Law. To understand this text, one must first gain some sense of the meaning of the sabbath in first-century Jewish life.[249] The sabbath not only was commanded by God as part of the Decalogue, the fundamental covenant Law (Exod 20:8-11; Deut 5:12-15, in both cases expressed as the most elaborate of the Ten Commandments), but also was observed and blessed by God at the beginning of creation (Gen 2:2-3). The sabbath had served for centuries as the distinctive mark of the people of God that separated them from Gentiles and presented a constant testimony to their faith in the one God. Sabbath keeping was not superficial or casual; in

times of duress, faithful Israelites would die rather than break God's law by profaning the sabbath. To observant Jews, the sabbath was a joy, not a burden. The sabbath was a festive day of rest from labor, a day of eating and drinking on which it was forbidden to fast. From the beginning (Deut 5:14-15) an element of social justice had been expressed in the law, for servants and slaves received a much-needed rest of which they could not be deprived, and the poor and hungry joined in the eating and drinking.

Since the sabbath was central in Jewish life, its proper observance was important. In view of the ambiguity of the Scripture itself as to what constituted work, a body of tradition, having the force of religious law, had developed to guide the proper celebration of the sabbath (see comments on 15:1-20).[250] Humane considerations were paramount. Jewish tradition had already decided that "commandments that affect relations between human beings" take precedence over "commandments between God and human beings."[251] Thus to set aside strict observance of the sabbath for human need was in Judaism not understood as setting aside superficial ritual in favor of human good, for ritual laws were considered important, a way of honoring God. Nonetheless, God wills that human good take precedence over laws that concern God's honor, so setting aside the strict observance of the sabbath for human good was a way of honoring God. This point was already made in Judaism; its exact application was disputed, however.[252] Some rabbis taught that an animal that fell into a pit on the sabbath could be helped out; others (including the Essenes) specifically rejected this.[253] Some Jews considered healing on the sabbath to be permitted; others only if life was endangered. The latter qualification was often understood very broadly; hunger might be considered life threatening.

In the light of such considerations, the two scenes in 12:1-14, as rewritten by Matthew, should be seen as picturing Jesus' participation in

---

247. The second scene in 12:9 begins with "having gone on from there" (μεταβὰς ἐκεῖθεν *metabas ekeithen*), corresponding to the NRSV's "as he went from there" (προβὰς ἐκεῖθεν *probas ekeithen*) of 4:21, the second scene in the unified pericope of 4:18-22. Both scenes (vv. 1-8 and 9-14) occur on the same day, the sabbath, and are bound together by the issue of what is lawful to do on the sabbath, using the same technical terminology (ἔξεστιν *existin*; 12:2, 10, the latter being added by Matthew to unify them on this point). They are further bound together by the appearance of Pharisees at the beginning (v. 2) and end (v. 14). Thus in this instance Matthew's typical addition "their" synagogue (v. 9) refers specifically to the Pharisees, as well as to the general alienation Matthew and his community felt from the Jewish synagogue.

248. Surprisingly, there is no reference to the sabbath in the Sermon on the Mount, to the conflicts occasioned by Jesus' miracles in 8:1–9:34, or to the mission discourse of chapter 10. Matthew has eliminated previous references to the sabbath in his sources to obtain this effect.

249. Cf. Tractate *Sabbat* in Herbert Danby, ed., *The Mishnah* (Oxford: Oxford University Press, 1933) 100-20; Eduard Lohse, Σάββατον, *TDNT* 8:1-35; G. F. Moore, *Judaism in the First Three Centuries of the Christian Era* (Cambridge, Mass.: Harvard University Press, 1927) 2:21-39.

250. *M. Sabb.* 7:2 lists the thirty-nine main classes of work, which include reaping but not healing.

251. Cf. *M. Yoma* 8:9.

252. C. G. Montefiore, *Rabbinic Literature and Gospel Teachings* (New York: Macmillan, 1930), 242, considers Matt 12:7 "sound rabbinic doctrine; not very unusual." Cited by Ulrich Luz, *Das Evangelium nach Matthäus (Mt 8–17)*, Evangelisch-Katholischer Kommentar zum Neuen Testament I/2 (Benziger: Neukirchener Verlag, 1990) 2:234, who considers this an exaggeration of a valid point.

253. Cf. CD 11:13-14: "If an animal falls into a well or a ditch, it may not be lifted out on the Sabbath."

this Jewish debate as to the proper observance of the sabbath, not as a Christian rejection of "Jewish legalism." Matthew has taken care to rewrite the stories to emphasize that his position is not a rejection of the Law or the sabbath as such. He does not dismiss the issue, but enters into a debate still going on in Judaism. It is clear that Matthew does not pit the ceremonial law against the moral law (see 5:17-48) and that there is no polemic against the sabbath or the Law as such, nor is the sabbath denigrated as mere ceremony or ritual. It is not clear whether Matthew's community as a whole still continued to observe the sabbath (see 24:20).[254] But the way Matthew handles Mark's and Q's sabbath pericopes indicates that the way the sabbath is observed is still an important issue in Matthew's community.

12:1. Matthew's specific notation that the disciples "were hungry" is to be taken seriously as a Matthean motif (cf. 4:2; 21:18; 25:35-44; Jesus himself is hungry in Matthew only in 4:2 and 21:18). The picture is not of well-fed disciples enjoying a snack, but of those who have "left all" (4:20, 22; 19:27) to follow Jesus and are genuinely poor and hungry. The Law provided that such people could pluck grain in fields that did not belong to them (Deut 23:23-25); the issue was whether it could be done on the sabbath. The Pharisees here are concerned for God's honor in correctly observing the sabbath (not mere personal legal piety); their problem, from the point of view of this story, is that they neglect the real will of God expressed in the sabbath commandment, which is mercy, especially toward the poor and the hungry.

12:2. Matthew has omitted the question Why? from Mark. As a result, the Pharisees no longer ask a question, but make a charge, corresponding to the theme of conflict, which dominates the section 11:20–12:14.

12:3-4. The David story of 1 Sam 21:1-6 did not take place on the sabbath, but was so understood in rabbinic exegesis, as inferred from Lev 24:8. Matthew understands it in this rabbinic perspective. Jesus, like David, understood sabbath laws in the context of their real intent, God's

mercy for the poor and hungry. Jesus is Son of David but is also greater than David (cf. 1:2-25; 22:41-46); if David, on the basis of human need, could legitimately overrule standard ritual laws (including, in rabbinic understanding, the sabbath) and even violate the normal sanctity of the house of God, how much more can Jesus do so![255] All such arguments are intended to clarify and strengthen the faith of insiders, not to convince outsiders. The issue is christological, presupposing a view of Jesus' person and office shared by the Christian community, but not by others. Jesus as authoritative Son of David and Son of Man is the fulcrum of the argument, not commonsense humanitarianism versus Jewish legalism.

12:5-7. In rabbinic debate, a point of law (Halakah) could not be established on the basis of a story (Haggadah), but required a clear statement of principle from the Torah. Matthew, conditioned by this rabbinic context, adds an example from Num 28:9-10 (cf. the similar argument in John 7:22). Since the priests sacrifice according to the Law on the sabbath, sacrifice is greater than the sabbath. But mercy is greater than sacrifice, as the divine declaration makes clear (Hos 6:6 again; cf. Commentary on 9:13), so mercy is greater than the sabbath.

The declaration that "something" greater than the Temple is here is Matthew's adoption of a Q formula (cf. 12:41-42) and does not refer solely to the person of Jesus himself (the Greek word is neuter!). In Q, it may have referred to the kingdom of God, proclaimed and represented by Jesus. Here, in more open-ended terms, it refers provocatively to the *mercy* at the heart of God's sabbath commandment (cf. 23:23, with reference to tithing), as explicated in the following. It is to be explicitly noted that Jesus does not claim something "greater than the Torah" is present. There is no polemic against the Torah as such in this pericope.

This is the second time that Matthew has added a reference to Hos 6:6 to a Markan context (see 9:13). In the previous conflict with the Pharisees, Jesus had commanded them to "learn" what this means. The reader is aware of Jesus' invitation that to "learn" from him is the "easy yoke," which

---

254. A few years after Matthew wrote his Gospel, in the same locality, Ignatius argued for Sunday as the Christian holy day and against continued observance of the sabbath, which indicates that some Christians in his area were inclined to continue sabbath observance.

255. The common rabbinic hermeneutical principle of "light and heavy" (*qal vahomer*, an *a fortiori* argument) is here applied. Note that Mark's mistaken reference to Abiathar is omitted (Matt 12:4 vs. Mark 2:6).

contrasts with the burdensome interpretations of the Pharisees (11:29). The Pharisees have not accepted the call; they have not learned.

12:8. Jesus not only is the greater Son of David, but already exercises the authority of the eschatological judge, the Son of Man (see Commentary on 9:6 and Excursus "Matthean Christology," 353-61).

12:9-14. The story continues in a different setting. Except for the summary statements of 4:23 and 9:35, this is the first occasion for Jesus to be in a synagogue in Matthew (elsewhere only in 13:54). In Matthew, the synagogue is always an alien place of confrontation (cf. Luke 4:16; 6:6; 13:10). "Their" is added to Mark's synagogue, and Jesus is deliberately provoked by a test question rather than by merely being watched, as in Mark. The scene has the same structure and point as the preceding one. The Pharisees' "question" is hostile, posed not for information or discussion of a disputed legal point, but in order to accuse him—κατηγορέω (katēgoreō) is a technical legal term involving a court process. Sabbath violation does not, however, carry the death penalty, and it plays no role in the account of Jesus' trial in 26:57-75.[256]

Matthew again takes pains to recast the scene from Mark 3:1-6 into a dispute about proper observance of the sabbath, not about the legitimacy of the sabbath or the Torah as such.[257] He omits the Markan note of anger and introduces here a saying reflected in other contexts in Q (cf. Luke 13:15; 14:5), in which Jesus is represented as the advocate of the more liberal Jewish interpretation, presumably the one practiced by the peasant farmers of Galilee, and that can be assumed as common practice, whatever the leading Pharisaic opinion. The conclusion is in the form of a rabbinic ruling (v. 12b). Nonetheless, the Pharisees reveal their true nature by resolving to kill Jesus. Taken at the level of historical reporting, this might seem an overreaction to the modern reader. At the level of Matthew's story, it expresses the conflict of kingdoms, which is its main theme (cf. Commentary on 12:22-37; Excursus "Kingdom of Heaven in Matthew," 288-94). The reader, but not the characters in the story, knows that this plot will succeed, so that as this conflictive section comes to its climax, the shadow of the cross falls across it.

---

256. On the other hand "blasphemy" (βλασφημεῖ blasphēmeî), which emerged as the first point of conflict in 9:3, does play a role in the passion story.

257. Form critically, the story is not a miracle story, even though it contains a miracle. It is an expanded pronouncement story, the additions making it even more a conflict story in which sayings predominate than it was in Mark.

REFLECTIONS

1. In the history of Christian interpretation, this text has received a forced relevance by applying it to the question of what can be done on Sunday. Working on Sunday did not become an issue until after Constantine's time (4th cent. CE), when biblical sabbath legislation was applied to the Christian celebration of Sunday, not without hermeneutical violence. The Christian institution of the Lord's Day (Sunday), celebrating the resurrection of Jesus and traditionally concentrating on worship as the gathered Christian community, is a different kind of institution from the Jewish sabbath (Saturday), which is devoted to rest from labor and festive eating and drinking. The common ground between this sabbath text and Christian practice is not the issue of what is legal to do on the day of rest. Instead, we ponder where in our own situation is mercy more than sacrifice. Where is God's Law to be applied, not negated, in such a way that love is at its center?

2. It would be a mistake to understand this section as an affirmation of commonsense humanitarianism against petty legalism. Matthew does not understand the Torah in general or sabbath rules in particular to be a matter of pettiness (5:17-21). The "mercy not sacrifice" text from Hos 6:6 is not an abolition or negation of the sacrificial system or other ritualized practices of worship, but a Semitic way of expressing priority: mercy over sacrifice. (Matthew 5:23-24 specifically assumes the validity of the sacrificial system.) Throughout this section, sabbath rules are adjudicated not by common sense, but by the authority of the Son of Man (12:8), to whom the Father has given all authority (11:27; cf. 9:6, 28:18b). Precisely as in the Sermon on the Mount, the Torah is affirmed, but it is transcended by the authority of the one who speaks. Yet the crucial element for contemporary interpretation is the note sounded throughout Matthew: The one who speaks with transcendent authority is himself the representative of God's mercy for the hungering—and that is even greater than the Temple.

MATTHEW 12:15-21, THE SERVANT KING

NIV

¹⁵Aware of this, Jesus withdrew from that place. Many followed him, and he healed all their sick, ¹⁶warning them not to tell who he was. ¹⁷This was to fulfill what was spoken through the prophet Isaiah:

¹⁸"Here is my servant whom I have chosen,
the one I love, in whom I delight;
I will put my Spirit on him,
and he will proclaim justice to the nations.
¹⁹He will not quarrel or cry out;
no one will hear his voice in the streets.
²⁰A bruised reed he will not break,
and a smoldering wick he will not snuff out,
till he leads justice to victory.
²¹   In his name the nations will put their hope."^a

^a21 Isaiah 42:1-4

NRSV

15When Jesus became aware of this, he departed. Many crowds^a followed him, and he cured all of them, ¹⁶and he ordered them not to make him known. ¹⁷This was to fulfill what had been spoken through the prophet Isaiah:
¹⁸ "Here is my servant, whom I have chosen,
my beloved, with whom my soul is well pleased.
I will put my Spirit upon him,
and he will proclaim justice to the Gentiles.
¹⁹ He will not wrangle or cry aloud,
nor will anyone hear his voice in the streets.
²⁰ He will not break a bruised reed
or quench a smoldering wick
until he brings justice to victory.
²¹   And in his name the Gentiles will hope."

^aOther ancient authorities lack crowds

COMMENTARY

12:15. The conflict that first emerged in the ministry of Jesus in 9:1-8 came to its climax in 12:14 with the resolution of the Pharisees to put him to death. Jesus' response to this threat was to "withdraw" (ἀναχωρέω anachōreō). The withdrawal is not to passivity, but to the work of healing—still on the sabbath. Instead of retaliating, Jesus heals. Matthew makes this pattern a programmatic christological paradigm in which anachōreō becomes a key theological term.[258]

Jesus' "withdrawal" in the face of threat is not a matter of cowardice or strategy, but represents the divine response to human violence that will ultimately lead to the cross, in which human violence is met with divine self-giving. God willingly is edged out of the world and onto the cross.[259] Here

example of Jesus and good disciples; 2:14, 22, the baby Jesus proleptically models this; 4:12, Jesus' response to the arrest of John the Baptist; 14:13, Jesus' response to the murder of John the Baptist; 15:21, Jesus' response to the "scandalized" Pharisees, who have already decided to kill him). Thus eight of the ten instances of anachōreō in Matthew represent this christological pattern, the only exceptions being 9:24 and 27:5. The fact that the word is not simply a synonym for other, more common words for "go away" (ἀπέρχομαι aperchomai; ἐξέρχομαι exerchomai) is clear from Matthew's adding it to 15:21, which already had a Markan word for "go away" (cf. Mark 7:24).

258. This word was found once in Matthew's sources (Mark 3:7) where, in response to the death plot, Jesus does not retaliate but withdraws and heals. Matthew takes over this Markan scene as the climax of his creative Part One (12:15/ Mark 3:7; cf. Introduction), omitting Mark's disciples in order to focus on Jesus' act alone. Of the fourteen occurrences of ἀναχωρέω in the NT, ten are in Matthew, mostly with reference to Jesus, in a specifically theological sense (2:12-13, the magi follow the

259. See Dietrich Bonhoeffer, Letters and Papers from Prison (New York: Macmillan, 1953) 219.

we have not the renunciation of divine sovereignty, but its redefinition. It is the Christian redefinition of the Christ figure in terms of Jesus as the one who suffers at the hands of his enemies rather than making them suffer, the non-retaliatory mercy both taught (5:38-48) and practiced (26:50-54) by the sovereign Son of Man, who makes known his divine power in suffering love (16:21-23; 17:22-23; 20:17-19; 26:2).

12:16-17. In Mark, the command to silence is addressed to the demons who identify Jesus, corresponding to Mark's theory of the secret messiahship. Matthew does not share this perspective (cf. Excursus "Matthean Christology," 353-61). In Matthew, the command not to make him known is directed to those persons he has healed, and it is understood by Matthew as a dimension of his picture of Jesus as the meek servant of the Lord. Like the Servant of Isaiah, Jesus works quietly, avoiding publicity and acclaim, as expressed in the concluding formula quotation.

12:18-21. This Scripture quotation, the longest in Matthew, comes at a significant juncture in the structure of the Gospel, as the conclusion of Part One (cf. Introduction). Although directly related to its context, it contains much more than the context calls for and serves as a summary of the Matthean picture of the ministry of Jesus as a whole. Like the other formula quotations, it has its own textual form, closer to the MT than to the LXX, and it is particularly adapted to represent Matthean theology.[260] The following points are significant:

(1) The direct point of contact with the context is the retiring nature of the Servant, who does not wrangle or seek publicity, but quietly accepts those persons rejected by others. A bruised reed is "good for nothing"; it is "trash." A smoking wick must be thrown out or trimmed. But the Son/Servant rejects neither the one nor the other, just as Jesus calls as disciples those considered unacceptable by the religious authorities (11:25-30).

(2) The quotation is from Isa 42:1-4 (and 9), portraying the Servant of the Lord. This text was already considered messianic. The Targum reads:

"Behold my servant the Messiah." Since "my servant David" is a common biblical phrase, the term also has Davidic overtones. Matthew interprets Jesus in Davidic terms, but understands the powerful Son of God/Son of David to be identical to the meek (11:29; 21:5) Servant of the Lord who heals and suffers on behalf of others.

(3) It is God who speaks in this quotation from Isaiah, describing the Servant. This is similar to the heavenly voice at Jesus' baptism, which also uses Servant vocabulary in the context of the Spirit's being given to Jesus (3:16/12:18); the divine declarations that Jesus' Son/Servant ministry is filled with the Spirit forms a literary bracket around the entire ministry of Jesus (3:16-17/12:18; cf. 17:5, adapted from Mark to make it fit the Isaiah vocabulary more closely).

(4) Just as the quotation points back to the beginning of Jesus' ministry, so also it points forward to the conclusion, the last words of Part One striking exactly the same note as the conclusion of Part Two and the Gospel as a whole: the extension of the gospel to all nations.

(5) The announcement of judgment/justice to the Gentiles/nations anticipates not only the end of the Gospel, but also the beginning of Part Two, in which the rejection of Jesus and his message by the leaders of Israel becomes clear and "final." Until this point in the Gospel, Jesus and his disciples have preached exclusively to Israel. The offer has been refused by the Jewish leadership. A new community will be formed, comprising all nations. The double reference to nations/Gentiles (vv. 18, 21) anticipates and emphasizes this. The Servant will announce justice to the Gentiles as his disciples carry on the Christian mission after his death, a mission in which Jesus remains present and active in the work of his disciples (28:18-20; cf. 25:31-46).

(6) The Servant, although meek and quiet, is ultimately victorious. The conflict that will result in Jesus' death is anticipated. The Matthean reader who will follow Jesus into the conflicts and passion story of Part Two must see all that transpires in the light of this declaration. Jesus is not victim, but victor. His cause can do no less than triumph. But the way of universal victory is the way of the cross.

---

260. On Matthew's use of the OT, particularly the formula quotations, see Excursus "Matthew as Interpreter of Scripture," 151-54.

REFLECTIONS

A major theme of the Gospel of Matthew emerges again in this section. On the one hand, throughout 11:20–12:14, Jesus is pictured as the authoritative sovereign who represents the kingdom of God. He has authority to pronounce judgment (11:20-24); he is exclusively the one who knows and is known by the Father, who has given "all things" into his hand (11:27); he is the one who gives the ultimate "rest," salvation in the kingdom of God (11:28-30). He exercises the authority of the eschatological Son of Man and represents something greater than the Temple and is, therefore, Lord of the Sabbath (12:6, 8). Yet his self-description is that of the "meek" one (11:29), who declares that mercy, not ritual, is what God wants from us (12:7) and whose whole life is represented by acts of loving response to human need (12:1-8, 12-13). Jesus, who as the meek one represents the sovereign power of God, is at the heart of Matthew's message and summarizes his view of the Christian faith (see Commentary on 2:23; 21:4-5). Such titles as "Christ" and "Son of David" are redefined in terms of who Jesus actually is. Thus this section serves as the appropriate conclusion to Matthew's creative Part One, offering the final and climactic picture of the meek King, and serving as the transition to the key scene that has influenced the structure of 1:2–12:21 and for Matthew's theology as a whole.

MATTHEW 12:22–28:20

THE CONFLICT OF KINGDOMS DEVELOPED AND RESOLVED

OVERVIEW

I n Part One of his story, Matthew narrates the incursion of the kingdom of God into the world in the person of Jesus Christ, who redefines the meaning of kingship as suffering love and who provokes the opposition of the kingdom of Satan, represented by "this generation" and its leadership, the scribes and Pharisees, who finally resolve to kill Jesus. In Part Two, which begins at this point, the conflict develops, the disciples of Jesus become a separate community, and the opposition succeeds in killing Jesus. But this represents not the triumph of Satan's kingdom, but its defeat. (On the structure of Part Two, see the Introduction.)

MATTHEW 12:22-50, CONFLICT, DECISION, AND GATHERING THE TRUE COMMUNITY

This section has three units. In the first two, Jesus disputes with the Pharisees, competing with them for the loyalty of the crowds, who are present throughout and overhear his solemn pronouncements of judgment (12:23; cf. v. 46). In the third unit the new community of Jesus' disciples emerges after his rejection by "this generation."

Matthew 12:22-37, The Conflict of Kingdoms and the Necessity of Decision

NIV	NRSV
²²Then they brought him a demon-possessed man who was blind and mute, and Jesus healed him, so that he could both talk and see. ²³All the people were astonished and said, "Could this be the Son of David?"	22Then they brought to him a demoniac who was blind and mute; and he cured him, so that the one who had been mute could speak and see. ²³All the crowds were amazed and said, "Can this be the Son of David?" ²⁴But when the Pharisees
²⁴But when the Pharisees heard this, they said, "It is only by Beelzebub,^{a} the prince of demons, that this fellow drives out demons."	heard it, they said, "It is only by Beelzebul, the ruler of the demons, that this fellow casts out the demons." ²⁵He knew what they were thinking and said to them, "Every kingdom divided against itself is laid waste, and no city or house divided
²⁵Jesus knew their thoughts and said to them, "Every kingdom divided against itself will be ruined, and every city or household divided against	against itself will stand. ²⁶If Satan casts out Satan, he is divided against himself; how then will his kingdom stand? ²⁷If I cast out demons by Beelzebul,
a24 Greek Beezeboul or Beelzeboul; also in verse 27	

NIV

itself will not stand. ²⁶If Satan drives out Satan, he is divided against himself. How then can his kingdom stand? ²⁷And if I drive out demons by Beelzebub, by whom do your people drive them out? So then, they will be your judges. ²⁸But if I drive out demons by the Spirit of God, then the kingdom of God has come upon you.

²⁹"Or again, how can anyone enter a strong man's house and carry off his possessions unless he first ties up the strong man? Then he can rob his house.

³⁰"He who is not with me is against me, and he who does not gather with me scatters. ³¹And so I tell you, every sin and blasphemy will be forgiven men, but the blasphemy against the Spirit will not be forgiven. ³²Anyone who speaks a word against the Son of Man will be forgiven, but anyone who speaks against the Holy Spirit will not be forgiven, either in this age or in the age to come.

³³"Make a tree good and its fruit will be good, or make a tree bad and its fruit will be bad, for a tree is recognized by its fruit. ³⁴You brood of vipers, how can you who are evil say anything good? For out of the overflow of the heart the mouth speaks. ³⁵The good man brings good things out of the good stored up in him, and the evil man brings evil things out of the evil stored up in him. ³⁶But I tell you that men will have to give account on the day of judgment for every careless word they have spoken. ³⁷For by your words you will be acquitted, and by your words you will be condemned."

NRSV

by whom do your own exorcists^a cast them out? Therefore they will be your judges. ²⁸But if it is by the Spirit of God that I cast out demons, then the kingdom of God has come to you. ²⁹Or how can one enter a strong man's house and plunder his property, without first tying up the strong man? Then indeed the house can be plundered. ³⁰Whoever is not with me is against me, and whoever does not gather with me scatters. ³¹Therefore I tell you, people will be forgiven for every sin and blasphemy, but blasphemy against the Spirit will not be forgiven. ³²Whoever speaks a word against the Son of Man will be forgiven, but whoever speaks against the Holy Spirit will not be forgiven, either in this age or in the age to come.

³³"Either make the tree good, and its fruit good; or make the tree bad, and its fruit bad; for the tree is known by its fruit. ³⁴You brood of vipers! How can you speak good things, when you are evil? For out of the abundance of the heart the mouth speaks. ³⁵The good person brings good things out of a good treasure, and the evil person brings evil things out of an evil treasure. ³⁶I tell you, on the day of judgment you will have to give an account for every careless word you utter; ³⁷for by your words you will be justified, and by your words you will be condemned."

^aGk *sons*

COMMENTARY

This paragraph, usually designated the "Beelzebul Controversy," plays a key role in Matthew's thought. Matthew chose this pivotal point in the Markan narrative as the goal of his extensive and creative Part One; after this, he never varies from the Markan order of pericopes. The interpreter may recognize several reasons why Matthew considered this a crucially important scene. It was one of the few stories that occurred in both documents of his sacred tradition (Mark 3:20-29; Q = Luke 11:14-23). As it is rewritten by him,

several important elements of Matthew's theology converge in this one paragraph: the kingdom of God (12:28) over against the kingdom of Satan (12:26); the power of the Spirit in Jesus' work (12:28, 31-32); Jesus as Son of David (12:23); forgiveness of sins (12:31-32). Further, the charge of collusion with Beelzebul is particularly significant to Matthew, as a charge leveled at both Jesus and his disciples (9:34; 10:25; 12:24). Matthew's community, like the early Q community from which Matthew's community descends, apparently has been grievously offended by having heard this charge directed against them, which made a deep impression on them and on Matthew. The dualistic theme of the conflict of kingdoms was already in Q (Matt 12:26/ Luke 11:18; cf. Mark 3:26, which lacks the concept of Satan's kingdom).

Two kingdoms stand over against each other in this scene. Jesus represents the kingdom of God (12:28; cf. Excursus "Kingdom of Heaven in Matthew," 288-94). But in Matthew, Satan also has a kingdom, the alternative to God's kingdom revealed in Jesus (12:26). In this pericope, the Pharisees who oppose Jesus are portrayed as representatives of Satan's kingdom. These two kingdoms vie for the loyalty of "the crowds," who are present at both the beginning (12:23) and the end (12:46) of Jesus' pronouncements.

12:22. Matthew has used this scene from Q before (see Commentary on 9:32-34). The healing of a demon-possessed man who was blind and unable to speak was a great act of mercy, signaling the way the messianic King uses his divine power (cf. 11:1-6). Yet nothing is made of the miracle per se. Form critically, the pericope is not a miracle story, but a disputation, in which all attention focuses on the words of Jesus. As in the preceding sections (11:1–12:21), the minimal narrative serves as a framework for the authoritative pronouncements of Jesus.

12:23. Until the final scene in which they appear, the "crowds" in Matthew are potential disciples, neither aligned with the opposition nor committed to following Jesus (cf. 27:20-26). The last response of the crowds, in the earlier version of this same story, was wondering admiration (9:33). Here they go a step further in the direction of discipleship, entertaining the possibility that Jesus might indeed be the hoped-for Son of David, despite the fact that his merciful deeds do not correspond to the popular image of what the Son of David will be.[261]

12:24. Matthew changes the "scribes who had come down from Jerusalem" of Mark 3:22 to "Pharisees"—i.e., those who have already decided to put Jesus to death (12:14). The Pharisees, rivals for the loyalty of the "crowds," respond not to

Jesus but to the crowds' growing appreciation of him.[262] As before, they do not deny Jesus' miraculous healing and exorcism, but attempt to discredit him in the eyes of the crowds. In Matthew's perspective, their utter perversity is expressed by the fact that they attribute Jesus' mighty deeds of mercy to the power of Beelzebul, the prince of demons.[263] As Matthew pictures them, not only do they reject for themselves the kingdom of God, represented by Jesus, but their greater evil is that they attempt to block those who are entering the kingdom as well (23:13).

12:25-37. Review of this text in a synopsis of the Gospels makes clear that Jesus' response is a Matthean composition from materials in Mark and Q:

25b-26a	=	Mark 3:23b-26a (+ elements from Q; cf. Luke 11:17b)
26b-28	=	Q (cf. Luke 11:18b-20)
29	=	Mark 3:27
30	=	Q (cf. Luke 11:23)
31	=	Mark 3:28-29
32	=	Q (cf. Luke 12:10)
33-35	=	Q (cf. Luke 6:43-45)
36-37	=	M, or Matthew's own composition

Most of the sayings circulated as individual units and had their own meanings in their various pre-Matthean contexts. When placed together by Matthew, there is some tension between them, if they are understood in terms of their earlier meanings. Verse 28 functions on a different presupposition than v. 27, so they could hardly originally have been parts of the same speech. It

---

261. Questions introduced with μήτι (*mē ti*) usually anticipate a negative answer. Here, the question stops short of affirmation, but considers the possibility: "This one couldn't be the Son of David after all, could he?" On the "healing Son of David," see Commentary on 21:14-15.

262. Cf. 27:18, where jealousy for the loyalty of the crowds plays a role in the Jewish leaders' opposition to Jesus. Matthew's own situation, in which synagogue leadership and Christian missionaries competed for the loyalty of the Jewish laity, is here reflected.

263. Practically all Greek mss read Βεελζεβούλ (*Beelzeboul*), although both ℵ and B read Βεεζεβουλ (*Beezeboul*). Both are different from the traditional "Beelzebub" of the NIV, following the KJV, which had followed the Vulgate. No Greek ms reads "Beelzebub." This name was related to the Hebrew epithet given to the god of the Philistines in 2 Kgs 1:2, Baal-zebub, "god of flies." The etymology and the meaning of both Beelzebub and Beelzebul are disputed (cf. *IDB* 1:332, 374), yet "Beelzebul" may well have been used as the name of a pagan household god, "Lord of the House" ("Heavenly Temple"). Even if by Matthew's time the etymology had been forgotten, the name was then adapted in Judaism as a pejorative name for the chief demon, equivalent to Satan and Belial. There may be a play on words in the Pharisees' charge: Jesus, who claims to be Lord of the (Jerusalem) Temple (cf. 12:6), actually operates by the power of the pagan god/demon named "Lord of the Temple." The word play in 10:25 on "master of the house" (οἰκοδεσπότης *oikodespotēs*) suggests that Matthew knew this etymology.

is not the ability to perform exorcisms as such that distinguishes Jesus from the Pharisees, but the presence of the Spirit as the sign of the kingdom. Nor is the "knowing their thoughts" taken from Q necessary in the Matthean story line, where the Pharisees' charge is public. It is retained to show Jesus' sovereign power. Such considerations are important in order to understand the nature of the stratified texts we are interpreting, but we are primarily interested in the meaning at the level of the Matthean narrative (cf. Introduction). The Matthean Jesus refutes the Pharisees' charge with three pronouncements:

12:25-26. Satan does not work against himself. If so, even this shows that Satan's kingdom is at an end.

12:27. There were many Jewish exorcists.[264] Jesus here takes their existence as an ad hominem argument: If the Pharisees acknowledge exorcisms among their own group, how can they criticize Jesus?

12:28-29. The argument, which has previously appealed to common sense and experience, here shifts into a different, christological mode, which presupposes faith in Jesus as the one in whom the Spirit works. Matthew changed Q's "by the finger of God" (Luke 11:20; cf. Exod 8:19) to "Spirit" to correspond to Isa 42:1 (just quoted in 12:18) and to the declaration in 12:32. The presence of the Spirit in Jesus' ministry signals the arrival of the eschatological age. Verse 29 also appeals to traditional imagery: The eschatological victory of God will result in the binding of Satan (cf. Rev 20:2-3; *1 Enoch* 10:4-5; *Jub.* 48:15, 18; *T. Lev.* 18:12). Jesus proclaims that this is already happening; his messianic deeds, including exorcisms, represent the binding of Satan and the plundering of his "house."

12:30. Jesus' ministry is one of "gathering." This may connote imagery of the ingathering of the harvest and the lost sheep of the house of Israel (9:36-38, also with the "crowds" in view), or the regathering of the scattered people of Israel. All are eschatological pictures. With the advent of the Messiah, the eschatological king, there can be no neutrality. One can only "gather" with Jesus or oppose his eschatological ministry by "scattering." In the Matthean context, this pronounce-

ment is not an abstract statement but functions as a call to the crowds to become disciples.[265]

12:31-32. These sayings are not a separate statement on "the unpardonable sin," but in their Matthean context they are a constituent element of Jesus' response to the Pharisees' charge that he performs exorcisms and healings by the power of Beelzebul. In this case, the meaning of the text can be illuminated by a consideration of its trajectory from Jesus' original pronouncement through its various NT forms. The following sketch is, in the nature of the case, hypothetical but has substantial support.[266]

(1) Jesus' original saying was an absolute and universal pronouncement of divine forgiveness, "All things shall be forgiven to human beings, whatever they have blasphemed." "Human beings" was expressed in Aramaic by the generic בר נשא (*bar naša*), literally "son of man."

(2) This radical pronouncement was considered too revolutionary in early Christianity, so it was modified in a variety of ways:

(a) Some early Christians adapted a familiar Jewish pattern to describe a category of "unforgivable sins," expressed in a particular form ("All sins shall be forgiven/this sin shall not be forgiven"). In some situation in which the church's work in the power of the Spirit had been reviled, an early Christian prophet reformulated the radical word of Jesus as a pronouncement of judgment against those who had rejected the offer of salvation presented in the church's proclamation. Christian prophets speaking in Jesus' name anticipated and made present the verdict of the Judge at the last day. As in all prophecy, such pronouncements actually functioned as calls to repentance. This sin is called "unforgivable" because the Christian prophet speaks as the representative of the eschatological Judge; there can be no appeal from the proleptic verdict of the last judgment. After Jesus' original pronouncement, this is the earliest form of the saying as an "unpardonable sin" saying. This line of tradition is preserved in

---

264. Cf. Tob 8:1-5; Acts 19:13-16; Josephus *Antiquities of the Jews* 8.2.5; Justin *Dialogues* 85; Irenaeus *Against Heresies* 2.6.2.

265. So understood, this "exclusive" form is not in conflict with the "inclusive" form of Mark 9:40. The former is a warning against fence-straddling and a call to commitment; in its context, the latter is a call to an ecumenical perspective on the work of Christ.

266. For a more complete treatment and bibliography, see M. Eugene Boring, "The Unforgivable Sin Logion Mark 3:28-29/Matt 12:31-32/Luke 12:10: Formal Analysis and History of the Tradition," *NovT* 17 (1976) 258-79; *The Continuing Voice of Jesus: Christian Prophecy and the Gospel Tradition* (Louisville: Westminster/John Knox, 1991) 219-21.

Mark 3:28-29 and taken over by Matthew in 12:31.

(b) A second line of tradition further interpreted the saying by understanding "son of man" in the sense of a christological title, Son of Man. Whereas the original saying had distinguished the unforgivable sin against the Holy Spirit from all other sins, which are forgivable, this reinterpreted form distinguished speaking against Jesus, the Son of Man, which is forgivable, from speaking against the Holy Spirit, which is not.[267] This form of the saying came into the Q community. The meaning of this form has often been understood in terms of the difference between the earthly life of Jesus and the post-Easter time of the church: Those who misunderstood and reviled Jesus during his earthly life can be forgiven, but those who reject the work of the Holy Spirit in the time after Easter cannot. This is unlikely, however, since for Q the phrase "Son of Man," even when the reference was to the earthly Jesus, always had the connotation of the exalted apocalyptic Son of Man, not the lowly historical figure. A more satisfactory view is to understand the saying, in its Q setting, as declaring that even those who had in the past reviled the exalted Son of Man—i.e., had resisted the Q-community's christological claims about Jesus, could be forgiven, but those who continued to reject the final offer of forgiveness made by its eschatological prophet-missionaries in the power of the Spirit had rejected their final chance. Matthew adopts this Q form of the saying in 12:32, adding it to the Markan form he has preserved in 12:31.[268]

(c) The history of the saying's interpretation in early Christianity may help the contemporary reader understand the various forms of the saying in the NT. But exegesis is concerned with the meaning of the present form of the text in Matthew, which has incorporated both the Markan (Matt 12:31 = Mark 3:28-29) and the Q (Matt 12:32 = Luke 12:10) forms of the saying into his composition. In Matthew's context, the sayings are not speculative statements about which sin(s) may be unpardonable, but a pronouncement of judgment against the Pharisees. In Matthew, the Pharisees represent the kingdom of Satan, those who have already decided to kill Jesus (12:14), who block others from entering the kingdom of God (23:13), who are not planted by God but represent Satan's work (15:13-14) and are destined for condemnation at the final judgment. As elsewhere in Matthew, such pronouncements against the Pharisees at the narrative level function as warnings to church members and especially to church leaders. Their function is not to provide a doctrinal category of "unforgivable sins" about which Christians should be anxious.

12:33-35. The unit does not conclude until v. 37, with "then" (τότε *tote*) beginning afresh in v. 38. These are not general observations on "evaluating people by what they do," but a continuation of Jesus' polemical response to the Pharisees. Matthew has already used this Q material in the Sermon on the Mount (cf. 7:16-20). The general point of the metaphor that one's words and deeds represent one's inner reality, one's true self, is here refocused to make a double point. As applied to Jesus himself, it means that the Pharisees should have recognized God's work (not Satan's!) in Jesus' words and deeds (v. 33). The good fruit of healing the blind and mute demonized man could not have been produced by a bad tree. As applied to the Pharisees, it means that their evil speech (in attributing his works to Beelzebul) betrays who they really are, evil to the core. Their speaking against Jesus is not merely a superficial mistake of judgment, but shows, in Matthew's dualistic perspective, that the Pharisees belong to the kingdom of evil. It should not be forgotten that in the Matthean context these words are addressed to those who have already decided to kill Jesus (12:14) and who are perverting the way of those who might be coming to faith in him (12:23-24).

12:36-37. These sharp pronouncements, peculiar to Matthew and from his own tradition or created by him, reflect not only the Semitic and biblical perspectives on the importance of what one says (cf. on 5:33-37), but have a particular meaning in this context, which has to do with confession or denial of Christ. Matthew considers this act of verbal profession of one's faith to be very important (10:18-20, 26-27, 32-33). In the context of the synagogue, Matthean Christians

---

267. In 11:19 the opponents speak against the "Son of Man."

268. The two forms of the saying had come to have two different meanings and do not combine well into one coherent saying. They have different contrasts: v. 31 (= Mark 3:28-29): all sins that are forgivable/one sin is not forgivable; v. 32 (= Q) forgivable sin against the Son of Man/unforgivable sin against the Holy Spirit.

had been tempted to keep quiet about their faith in Jesus as the Christ, or even to join in saying scandalous things about Jesus. Like other parts of the NT (e.g., John 12:42-43; Rom 10:9-10), Matthew's Gospel makes one's verbal professions a matter of ultimate concern, for which one will be accountable at the last judgment.

REFLECTIONS

1. Discipleship to Jesus means mission to others. The call to follow Jesus is a call to participate in his mission of "gathering," a call that leaves no room for any middle ground. Matthew pictures the decision as being made in the context of a conflict of kingdoms, in which there can be no neutrality. In this situation, not to decide for is not to be *un*committed, but to be committed *against*.

In today's world, this means that those who take Matthew seriously cannot regard Jesus as merely a "personal savior" and the church as a religious support group for personal needs. Matthew's perspective lets us see our world as involved in a conflict of claims to sovereignty, a conflict in which we cannot be spectators, but must take sides. In this conflict, the church is a missionary community standing against the idolization of cultural values rather than putting a divine stamp of approval on them. To belong to the church as envisioned by Matthew is to be involved in its mission and participate in the struggle.

2. Matthew 12:31-32 has caused much anxiety in the history of the church. It has often been combined with other NT statements, such as Heb 6:4-8 and 1 John 5:16-17, to form a doctrine of "the unforgivable sin," despite the questions it raises about whether any creature can in fact ever get beyond the reach of God's mercy. It has been applied both to outsiders who never make the Christian confession and to insiders who make it and then fall away by becoming heretics or apostates. It is ironic that the great sinners of history have been unconcerned about their own guilt, while the most sensitive souls in the church have worried about it, sometimes to the point of despair. A good exegetical and historical rule of thumb might be that whoever is worried about having committed "the unpardonable sin" has not done so! Exegesis of the text challenges any approach that presupposes that there is an act that one may commit, even inadvertently, or a state into which one may "fall" or decide to enter, that takes him or her beyond the reach of God's grace. Yet the text is surrounded by challenges to discipleship and mission that prohibit its being understood as an offer of "cheap grace."

❖ ❖ ❖ ❖

EXCURSUS: KINGDOM OF HEAVEN IN MATTHEW

The language of "kings" and "kingdoms" is often thought to be passé, belonging to the social and thought world of another time and another place, at best quaint, at worst preserving and encouraging the kind of oppressive structures that responsible modern Christians need to reject. This may be a premature judgment. Before one can decide whether to reject, reaffirm, or reinterpret the Bible's kingdom language, one must first attempt to hear it in its own terms. This cannot be done in general, but only in terms of concrete texts. How should we understand Matthew's expression of faith through the language of the kingdom of heaven/God? I will summarize the important points for understanding Matthew's meaning and use of this language in the following five theses:

MATTHEW ADOPTS AND ADAPTS AN OLD AND WIDESPREAD TRADITION OF KINGDOM LANGUAGE

Matthew did not invent this manner of religious expression. His kingdom language comes from a rich background of religious usage in the ancient Near East, the OT, early Judaism, the preaching and teaching of Jesus, and early Christianity (cf. Bibliography). The kingdom of heaven/God had already formed a central element in both his major sources, Mark and Q, as it had in the teaching and preaching of Jesus.

The people for whom Matthew wrote used kingdom language as integral to their everyday secular world and had long been accustomed to its use in a meaningful religious sense. They did not need to have the meaning of words explained. In the opening paragraphs of his Gospel, Matthew presents the reader with a genealogy, tracing Jesus' ancestry through the kings of Israel and Judah. In it he includes the announcement of the birth of the "king of the Jews," King Herod's responsive effort to destroy Jesus, and John's announcement that the kingdom of heaven is "at hand" (1:2–3:2), none of which needed explaining for his first readers. The modern reader, on the other hand, does not live in a world where kings and kingdoms are an operative principle and must exercise historical study and imagination in order to understand what is being expressed in Matthew's affirmations of the kingdom of heaven/God.

THE KINGDOM OF HEAVEN IS CENTRAL TO MATTHEW'S THEOLOGICAL MESSAGE

The single most encompassing image within which Matthew's theological affirmations take place is that of the "kingdom of heaven." It unites the message of John (3:2), Jesus (4:17), and the disciples, pre- and post-Easter (10:7). The message the church continues to preach is the "good news of the kingdom" (24:14). Matthew uses kingdom language more than does any other NT author. While the cognate verb translated "rule" (βασιλεύω *basileuō*) is found only once (2:22, of Archelaus), "kingdom" and "king" are found a total of seventy-seven times. Of these, at least seventy-one are used in a theological sense, and the others have theological connotations; Matthew never uses the king/kingship vocabulary in a purely secular sense without theological overtones.[269]

"The Kingdom of Heaven" (32x) and "the Kingdom of God" (5x)

These two phrases mean exactly the same thing for Matthew, being used interchangeably in 19:23-24. In this phrase, "heaven" does not refer to the place of God's dwelling but is a reverential circumlocution used in Jewish circles to avoid pronouncing the sacred name of God. Since "kingdom" is a verbal noun whose primary connotation is not territory but ruling power, "reign" or "rule" often being the best translation, both "kingdom of heaven" and "kingdom of God" mean primarily "God's reign," "the sovereign power of God functioning as king."

---

269. The six cases not explicitly theological are: in 4:8, the devil's showing Jesus all the kingdoms of the world is itself a dimension of the devil's kingdom opposing the kingdom of God; in 10:18, disciples will be dragged before earthly kings because of the disciples' preaching of the kingdom of God; in 12:25, Jesus uses a "divided kingdom" as a negative example of the kingdom of God; in 24:27 (2 times) Jesus uses conflicts among earthly kingdoms as a negative example of eschatological "signs"; in 17:25, earthly kings are contrasted with the way things work in the kingdom of God.

God as King (6x)

God is indirectly called "king" once (5:35), and is represented as a king in two parables (18:23; 22:2, 7, 11, 13).

"The Kingdom of . . . Father" (3x)

Since "Father" is the Matthean Jesus' favorite expression for "God" (see 6:9), the kingdom of heaven/God can be called "the kingdom of their [the disciples'] Father" (13:43) or "the kingdom of my [Jesus'] Father" (26:29). Disciples who pray "Our Father" pray for the coming of "your kingdom" (6:9-10).

"The Kingdom" (8x)

When used as a genitive expression qualifying another noun ("good news," "word," "heirs," "children"), the kingdom of heaven/God is abbreviated simply to "the kingdom."

"The Kingdom of [Jesus or] the Son of Man" (3x); Jesus as King (8x)

Matthew twice refers to the Son of Man's having a kingdom (13:41; 16:28). Since Matthew identifies the Son of Man as Jesus, the one reference to Jesus' own kingdom (20:21) and the eight references to Jesus as "king" may be included here.[270]

Matthew knows of only one divine kingdom. Just as "kingdom of God," "kingdom of heaven," and "kingdom of [my/their] Father" all refer to the same dynamic reality, not to three separate kingdoms, so also the kingdom of the Son of Man is simply another name for the kingdom of heaven/God/the Father. The natural objection is that since "God," "heaven," and "Father" are all different ways of talking about the same figure (God), but Son of Man/Jesus is a separate figure, the kingdom of the Son of Man must refer to a separate or preliminary kingdom (as in some interpretations of 1 Cor 15:23-28). There are two reasons why this understanding of Matthew's kingdom language should be avoided, logical-sounding though it is: (1) It makes Matthew's message of the kingdom too much a concept, a schematic system, and misses the symbolic function of "kingdom of heaven/God" (see below). (2) In Matthew's christology Jesus is uniquely related to God as God's representative, so that talking about Jesus is a way of talking about God (see Excursus "Matthean Christology," 353-61). This implies that Matthew's affirmation of the kingdom of God is related to his picture of Jesus as king.

David as King

Since "Son of David" is an important christological category for Matthew, the singular opening reference to "King David" (1:6) is not an incidental reference to be categorized with other "secular" kingdoms, but a preliminary pattern of the rule of God in this world (see Excursus "Matthean Christology," 353-61).

The Opposing Kingdom

The devil, too, has a "kingdom," which has usurped and continues to oppose the true reign of God over the creation (12:26; cf. 4:8). The other kingdoms of this world (represented by the Jewish leaders and by the two king Herods) are pictured by Matthew as agents of this

---

270. Those references are "King of the Jews" (2:2; 27:11, 29, 37) and "King of Israel" (27:42), all but the first ironic; 21:5, at the triumphal entry into Jerusalem; 25:34, 40, Jesus represented as the eschatological king in the apocalyptic drama. In addition, the references to Jesus as "Son of David" belong in this category (see Excursus "Matthean Christology," 353-61).

kingdom. Herod the Great tried to destroy the Messiah; Herod Antipas killed John the Baptist (see Commentary on 2:1-23; 14:1-14). The conflict of these two kingdoms forms the plot of Matthew's narrative and the essence of his theology.

THE SYMBOL OF THE KINGDOM EVOKES A MYTH

Matthew's language of the kingdom functions as a symbol that evokes a myth: The sacred story of the creator God's saving act. By "myth" I mean the presupposed overarching framework of one's thought, within which one thinks about other things. "Myth" in biblical theology does not connote fiction or fairy tale, but is one's assumed way of thinking about what is most real, "the way things are." In Matthew's Jewish tradition, the symbol "kingdom of heaven/God" had become a shorthand means of evoking the story of the world, the "meaning of life," in four acts:

(1) God as creator and sovereign over all. Matthew presupposes the fundamental Jewish faith in one God, the creator, who has no superiors and no peers. Nothing exists that is not part of God's creation and for which God does not have the ultimate responsibility. The alternative is atheism or polytheism. "Kingdom of heaven/God" expresses this eternal sovereignty of the one God over the whole creation. Matthew's dualistic perspective on the world is penultimate; all that he says is predicated on the ultimate monotheistic faith of his Jewish tradition.

(2) The rulership of the world has been usurped by anti-God forces. The present condition of the world does not correspond to the will of the sovereign Creator. Real evil exists in the world. Something happened to subject the world to forces that usurp the kingly authority of the Creator, so that the world presently exists in a state of rebellion against its true sovereign. While Matthew assumes the reality of sin, he, like the Bible in general, does not elaborate this part of the myth. The Bible in general is very reticent to "explain" how the good creation of the one sovereign God came to its present fallen state. Genesis 3 is the Hebrew Bible's late and modest story of the origin of evil. Later apocalyptic speculations developed elaborate mythological descriptions of the fall/rebellion of angels and the like, but mainstream biblical theology, while accepting the fall as a given, conducted its thought world under the hard dome of heaven and in the givenness of the fallen historical world without curiosity as to what went on in the other world and before history. Gnosticism and certain kinds of apocalyptic mythology were regarded by canonical authors as pandering to unwholesome human appetites for matters reserved for God. Matthew resonates with the revelatory common sense of Deut 29:29; 30:11-14. Although God remains as King, we find ourselves in a rebellious world that gives its allegiance to other sovereignties. Indeed, we find ourselves to be sinners, which means not merely failing to live up to ideals, but rebelling against the sovereign God.

(3) God has "given" kingship to the chosen people, who accept the "yoke of the kingdom." The will of the sovereign God has not remained hidden. At Sinai, God gave the Torah to Israel, who accepted it, thereby voluntarily taking up the yoke of the kingdom of heaven/God. By Matthew's time, the symbol "kingdom of heaven/God" connoted not only God's eternal sovereignty, but also the particular community within this world that had subjected itself to God's revealed will. The faithful Jew who daily recites the Shema (Deut 6:4-9) reenacts the original acceptance of the Torah at Sinai, renewing and making personal the commitment as a member of the covenant people of Israel. It is in this sense that the kingdom had been "given" to Israel (Matt 21:43). While the world in general continues in its rebellious state against its sovereign Creator, there is a community to which God's will has been entrusted by revelation, and that has entered into a covenant to do God's revealed

will. The kingdom of heaven/God is not only an eternal ideal, but is present in this world as people do God's will as well.

(4) The consummation of God's kingdom is still future. Since God is the sovereign Creator whose will is mostly violated by the creatures, it is not a sufficient expression of God's kingdom that a small community imperfectly witnesses to the will of God and imperfectly lives by that revealed will. The myth evoked by the symbol "kingdom of heaven/God" has a significant future aspect without which it is not complete, a "not yet" that completes the "already" of the eternal sovereignty and the imperfect covenant community. Thus Jews of Matthew's day not only praised God the eternal king, and took upon themselves the yoke of the kingdom, but they also prayed for the final coming of God's kingdom in a way that would be manifest to all, would establish God's *de facto* sovereignty in fact over a creation over which God was already king *de jure.*

Matthew's own theology is constructed within the framework of this pre-Christian Jewish myth, which interprets it from the Christian perspective that modifies it at three significant points: (1) The rebellion of the creation, Act II of the mythical drama, is made more dualistic and concrete. A later form of the Jewish myth is elaborated, in which Satan is the ruler of the rebellious forces of creation, constituting his own "kingdom" as the presumed real rulership of this world. The fact that Satan headed up a rebellious kingdom opposing God's kingdom was already posited in Q (Matt 12:26/Luke 11:18) and became a key element in Matthew's perspective. (2) The advent of the Messiah has already begun to bring an end to the rebellious kingdom of Satan and to reestablish the reign of God in this world (12:26-28). Since the advent of the Messiah, taking up the "yoke of the kingdom" in the present now means committing oneself to live by the Torah as fulfilled by Jesus (5:17-48; 28:18-20), so that the community to which the kingdom is "given" is the messianic community of Jews and Gentiles, the church (cf. 21:43). (3) The consummation of the kingdom for which the community prays (6:10) is now the return of Jesus as Son of Man who as the messianic King will establish God's sovereignty over the whole creation. The nature of this final sovereignty, although still using the violent imagery of kings who reconquer rebellious territory, has been radically redefined by Jesus the meek king. (See Commentary on 11:28-30 and Excursus "Matthean Christology," 353-61.)

All this means that the "kingdom of heaven" is not a static concept, but a symbol of a dynamic process that moves through history from creation to eschaton. In this mythical sacred story of the saving acts of God, the kingly image is a unifying image, as the sovereign Creator restores a fragmented and rebellious universe to the unity corresponding to the one God, and brings back usurped territory under his gracious sovereignty.

MATTHEW UNDERSTANDS HIS OWN SITUATION IN TERMS OF THIS MYTH, AS A "CONFLICT OF KINGDOMS"

Matthew lived in a situation of extreme conflict (see Introduction). His theological interpretation of his situation identifies the Jewish opponents of his Christian community with the anti-kingdom of God forces. The Jewish leaders were not merely bad people; they were agents of the cosmic power of evil. Their opposition to Jesus and the church was not merely a matter of religious polemics and differences of interpretation, but represented the conflict between God the true king and the false and doomed kingdom of Satan (2:1-23; 12:22-37; 13:24-43; 23:1-39). While there are grave dangers in such a theological stance, such as understanding the characters in the story as agents of Satan in a way that legitimizes the demonizing of our own theological opponents, there is also positive theological potential: Our opponents are not themselves the ultimate enemy, but, like ourselves, are victimized by the powers of evil, which threaten to overwhelm us all, but which are ultimately doomed (the powers of evil, not necessarily our opponents!).

MATTHEW'S UNDERSTANDING OF THE KINGDOM OF HEAVEN HAS IMPORTANT HERMENEUTICAL CONSEQUENCES

Traditional Understandings of the Kingdom

(1) Some traditional understandings of the kingdom do not do justice to it. The kingdom of heaven cannot simply be identified with the church, just as it could not be identified with Israel. God "gives" the kingdom to the community of faith and obedience; God's kingdom can be manifest in and through it, but cannot be contained by or identified with it. The sovereignty of God resists such institutionalization, not to say imprisonment, in either a community or a theology.

(2) The kingdom of heaven cannot be identified with social programs. While the kingdom may be present and active in liberation movements outside the church, they must not be identified with God's kingdom. The legacy of the understanding of the kingdom of God popularized by Protestant liberalism of the early twentieth century is still present in talk of "spreading," "building," and "establishing" God's kingdom, all of which is alien to biblical theology in general and Matthew in particular.

(3) The kingdom of heaven/God is not a subjective experience of the "heart." In the Bible, the kingdom is the sovereign activity of God in the world and history, and it is never located in the heart.[271]

The Kingdom Is Dynamic, Not Static

"Kingdom" in the phrase "kingdom of heaven" is a noun of action, like the word *love* in the phrase "love of God." Just as God's love means God's acting in love for others, so also God's kingdom means God's active sovereignty over creation. God's kingdom does not exist as an abstraction in and of itself, but is God's act.

As God's saving action, the kingdom of heaven/God cannot be located temporally, but is a process that moves through history from creation to eschaton. To ask when the kingdom comes and whether it is present or future is to miss the dynamism of the symbol itself. The kingdom has eternal, past, present, and future aspects. It is Matthew's most encompassing image.

The Dynamism of the Kingdom Is Related to a Variety of Actions

In the preaching of John and Jesus, the kingdom itself "comes near" (3:2; 4:17) and "has come" in the exorcisms of Jesus (12:28) and "suffers violence" since the time of John (11:12). However, disciples are to pray that it will "come" in the future (6:10), and some of them will see it coming at the advent of the Son of Man (16:28).

People are threatened with not being able to "enter" it (5:20; 7:21; 18:3; 19:23-24; all future, all negative), but (the "wrong"!) people are "going into" it (21:31; in the present?). Some people not only are not going in themselves, but they lock others out of it as well (23:13, apparently in the present). On the other hand, Peter is given the keys to the kingdom (16:19; but see exegesis; this does not picture him as the gatekeeper at the pearly gates).

---

271. The modern tendency to locate the kingdom in the hearts of individuals is often related to the mistranslation of Luke 17:21, "the kingdom of God is within you," but the pronoun is plural and the preposition means "in your midst."

People can "inherit" it (25:34, future), be "heirs" of it (8:12) or "children" of it (i.e., "belong" to it, 13:38). It can "belong to" them (19:14) and be "theirs" (5:3, 10) as well.

In the eschatological future, people will eat and drink in the kingdom of heaven/God with the patriarchs of Israel (8:11) and with Jesus (26:29).

Since the kingdom of heaven/God is not an abstract concept or a territory, it may be spoken of in a number of ways that are too different to bring within one conceptual system.

The Dynamism of the Kingdom Is Communicated in Parables and Narratives

Neither the Matthean Jesus nor the narrator ever tells the reader what the kingdom is. This is due not only to the fact that readers were already familiar with the language of the kingdom (see above), but also because the language of the kingdom, as a species of God-talk, is talk of the transcendent, beyond our conception. Thus the Matthean Jesus repeatedly tells the reader what the kingdom is "like" (13:24, 31, 33, 44-45, 47, 52; 18:23; 20:1; 22:2).

Jesus' kingdom language uses the indirect parabolic (story) means of communication. Although Matthew sometimes misses the parabolic character of Jesus' message (see Overview at 13:1), nevertheless he presents his own message of the saving act of God in Jesus, the advent of the messianic king of the kingdom of heaven/God, not as an essay or explanation, but as a narrative.

The Dynamism of the Kingdom Is Related to Life, Not Abstract

Matthew is not interested in the "kingdom of heaven/God" as an abstract doctrine, but as the presupposition for ethics. The coming of God's kingdom means that God's will is done throughout the universe (6:10, where "your will be done on earth as it is in heaven" is Matthew's exegetical addition; cf. 26:42). A controversial and crucial text (21:43) added by Matthew relates the gift of the kingdom to bringing forth appropriate "fruits," a key ethical term for Matthew (3:8-10; 7:16-20; 12:33; 13:23; 21:19). Matthew associates God's kingdom and justice/righteousness very closely (5:10, 20; 6:33; 13:43).[272]

272. For further discussion of the kingdom of God, see the bibliography in the Introduction.

❖   ❖   ❖   ❖

Matthew 12:38-45, The Decisive Issue: The Resurrection of Jesus

NIV	NRSV
[38]Then some of the Pharisees and teachers of the law said to him, "Teacher, we want to see a miraculous sign from you." [39]He answered, "A wicked and adulterous generation asks for a miraculous sign! But none will be given it except the sign of the prophet Jonah. [40]For as Jonah was three days and three nights in the belly of a huge fish, so the Son of Man will be three days and three nights in the heart of the	[38]Then some of the scribes and Pharisees said to him, "Teacher, we wish to see a sign from you." [39]But he answered them, "An evil and adulterous generation asks for a sign, but no sign will be given to it except the sign of the prophet Jonah. [40]For just as Jonah was three days and three nights in the belly of the sea monster, so for three days and three nights the Son of Man will be in the heart of the earth. [41]The people of Nineveh

NIV

earth. [41]The men of Nineveh will stand up at the judgment with this generation and condemn it; for they repented at the preaching of Jonah, and now one[a] greater than Jonah is here. [42]The Queen of the South will rise at the judgment with this generation and condemn it; for she came from the ends of the earth to listen to Solomon's wisdom, and now one greater than Solomon is here.

[43]"When an evil[b] spirit comes out of a man, it goes through arid places seeking rest and does not find it. [44]Then it says, 'I will return to the house I left.' When it arrives, it finds the house unoccupied, swept clean and put in order. [45]Then it goes and takes with it seven other spirits more wicked than itself, and they go in and live there. And the final condition of that man is worse than the first. That is how it will be with this wicked generation."

a41 Or *something*, also in verse 42   b43 Greek *unclean*

NRSV

will rise up at the judgment with this generation and condemn it, because they repented at the proclamation of Jonah, and see, something greater than Jonah is here! [42]The queen of the South will rise up at the judgment with this generation and condemn it, because she came from the ends of the earth to listen to the wisdom of Solomon, and see, something greater than Solomon is here!

[43]"When the unclean spirit has gone out of a person, it wanders through waterless regions looking for a resting place, but it finds none. [44]Then it says, 'I will return to my house from which I came.' When it comes, it finds it empty, swept, and put in order. [45]Then it goes and brings along seven other spirits more evil than itself, and they enter and live there; and the last state of that person is worse than the first. So will it be also with this evil generation."

COMMENTARY

Matthew 12:38-45 is one literary unit framed by the reference to this "evil generation" (12:39/12:45). The three originally separate sayings (vv. 38-40; 41-42; 43-45) are taken by Matthew from their Mark and Q contexts, integrated into one unified speech, and placed in this context.

12:38-40. This unit is the continuation of the preceding one, interrupted only by the question of the scribes and Pharisees. In Matthew, their question—rather, their imperious demand—is specifically related to this context. Their response to Jesus' series of judgment pronouncements is to demand a sign. In Matthew, the address "Teacher" is the badge of the unbeliever; no disciple so addresses Jesus ("Lord" is the disciples' address). Jesus does on occasion respond to a challenge from unbelievers by working a miracle (see 9:6), but the story here moves on a different plane. By "sign" they mean not "miracle," (contra the NIV translation, Matthew never uses "sign" in this sense), but some unambiguous proof of his identity. The doublet in 16:1 adds "from heaven,"

apparently understood by Matthew to indicate some sort of cosmic sign, making his divine authority absolutely clear, in distinction from his exorcisms and miracles, which were capable of other interpretations, as 12:22-37 had just illustrated. Perhaps Matthew sees this as another facet of his Moses typology (cf. Exod 4:1-9, where Moses confronts an unbelieving Israel [not Egyptians]). In this context, the demand does not indicate openness awaiting convincing evidence, but hardness of heart. Matthew's addition of "adulterous" (as in 16:4) does not necessarily mean that his generation was characterized by unfaithfulness to marriage vows, but is metaphorical for Israel's relation to God (e.g., Hos 3:1; cf. Jer 3:9; 9:1; Ezek 16:30-52, esp. v. 38).

This incident appears in both of Matthew's sources. Mark 8:11-12 originally belonged to the stream of pre-Markan Christian tradition that saw the pre-Easter life of Jesus as unmessianic, with faith arising only on the basis of the cross and resurrection. In this tradition, Jesus declares absolutely that no sign will be given.[273] The Q tradition, preserved in Luke 11:29-30, makes the one exception: The sign of Jonah will be given to "this generation." It is unclear whether this refers to Jonah's preaching or the sign that Jonah himself was. Matthew uses both the Mark and the Q versions of this tradition (cf. Matt 16:1-4; Mark 8:11-13; Luke 11:29-30), but he makes the interpretation specific: The sign—the only sign—is the resurrection of Jesus, who will be in the earth three days, just as Jonah was in the great fish three days.

12:41-42. Jesus' promise of resurrection is not lost on the Pharisees, who remember it after the crucifixion and entombment (27:62-66). There they join the high priests in rejecting the ultimate sign of God's act in Jesus, providing an alternate rationalistic explanation, which shows that even the one sign given is ambiguous; there are no risk-free "signs." Their rejection of the message of the resurrected Christ, not their misunderstanding of the historical Jesus, seals their rejection. The gospel message then goes to the Gentiles/all nations (28:18-20). In vv. 41-42, Jesus proclaims that the Gentiles will rise up (be resurrected) in the last judgment and will condemn the unbelieving Jewish leaders—signalling the passion/resurrection and the Gentile mission, which, of course, Matthew and his readers look back on. Once again there is a shocking reversal of expectations. In a traditional picture of the last judgment, righteous Israel will condemn sinful Gentiles. Here the roles are reversed, as repentant Gentiles condemn unbelieving Jews. "Condemn" is meant seriously;

273. Mark had already combined this tradition with the miracle story tradition, which pictured the life of Jesus as full of divine power.

the righteous are pictured not merely as appearing as witnesses, but as judges, participating with the Son of Man in judgment (cf. Dan 7:22 LXX; Wis 3:8; Matt 19:28; 1 Cor 6:3; Rev 3:21; *Jub.* 24:29; *1 Enoch* 95:3; 96:1). As in 12:6, where Jesus represents "something greater than the temple," so here he represents something greater than Jonah and Solomon. The "queen of the south" refers to the Queen of Sheba's visit to Solomon (1 Kgs 10:1-13).

12:43-45. Whether taken in isolation as a saying of the historical Jesus or as a post-Easter creation of the early church, the original meaning of this saying is unclear. In a culture where sickness and demon possession were related, it represented a bit of folk wisdom based on the observation that cures/exorcisms often are not permanent, and that a relapse can be worse than the previous condition of sickness/possession. If the saying is from Jesus, he may have used it as a warning to those who wanted some of the benefits of his ministry but remained empty of commitment to the kingdom he proclaimed and lived. In their Matthean context, these words are an extension of Jesus' response to the Pharisees' demand for a sign, which was itself a continuation of the Beelzebul controversy. Despite Matthew's rewriting and insertion of additional material, he has preserved the connection present in Q, in which the saying about the return of the evil spirit was a response to the Pharisees' charge of collusion with Beelzebul. For the Matthean Jesus, the fragment of folk wisdom becomes an analogy of the experience of "this generation"—their last state is worse than the first. Their encounter with Christ, filled with saving potential, has turned out for them to be for the worse (cf. John 9:35-41).

REFLECTIONS

Matthew's declaration that the resurrection is the only sign given Jesus' generation is extremely important for the interpretation of the Matthean narrative as a whole, since it clearly indicates that every scene in the Gospel is narrated from the post-resurrection point of view of Easter faith. Each story and saying mediates the meaning of God's act in raising up the crucified one to be Lord of all. In Matthew's view, the characters *in* the story could not really understand what was going on merely by seeing and hearing the deeds and words of the earthly Jesus, for his true identity and God's saving act in his life and message became apparent only at the resurrection; only the *readers of* the story, from their post-Easter vantage point, could be confronted by the full message of the Gospel as a whole, the church's message about God's act in Jesus. Characters in the story who come to faith are transparent symbols of post-Easter believers. This further means that the pronouncements of judgment on the characters in the story are in fact directed to unbelievers of Matthew's own generation, including the Christian readers of his Gospel.

The wrenching reversal of expectations in this picture cannot be grasped by Christian readers who smugly identify with the Gentile judges in the last judgment in condemning unbelieving Jews. Resurrection itself, as God's grand reversal of all human values and expectations, cannot be possessed by the church as an unambiguous sign to be used against unbelievers, including unbelieving Jews, but remains the mysterious, unpredictable sign of God's overruling grace. Thus the picture might recover its original function for contemporary Christian readers if it were reinterpreted to portray Jews in the role of Ninevites, who will rise up in the judgment and condemn Christians who have for so many centuries kept the Jonah-sign of the resurrection as their own possession.[273]

273. See Luz, *Matthäus,* 2:285.

Matthew 12:46-50, The New Community of Disciples

NIV	NRSV
[46]While Jesus was still talking to the crowd, his mother and brothers stood outside, wanting to speak to him. [47]Someone told him, "Your mother and brothers are standing outside, wanting to speak to you."[a] [48]He replied to him, "Who is my mother, and who are my brothers?" [49]Pointing to his disciples, he said, "Here are my mother and my brothers. [50]For whoever does the will of my Father in heaven is my brother and sister and mother." a47 Some manuscripts do not have verse 47.	[46]While he was still speaking to the crowds, his mother and his brothers were standing outside, wanting to speak to him. [47]Someone told him, "Look, your mother and your brothers are standing outside, wanting to speak to you."[a] [48]But to the one who had told him this, Jesus[b] replied, "Who is my mother, and who are my brothers?" [49]And pointing to his disciples, he said, "Here are my mother and my brothers! [50]For whoever does the will of my Father in heaven is my brother and sister and mother." a Other ancient authorities lack verse 47 b Gk *he*

COMMENTARY

Despite the negative picture painted in the preceding denunciations of "this generation" that has rejected Jesus and his message, there are those who respond (cf. 11:25-27). Matthew reinterprets the scene in Mark 3:31-35 to portray the new community of disciples that emerges despite the failure of the mission to Israel. He rewrites Mark where the "crowd" (ὄχλος *ochlos*) is the "true family" to make it clear that they are potential disciples, but the true family is constituted by his "disciples" (μαθηταί *mathētai*).

The scene has no biographical interests. Jesus' mother reappears for the first time since the narrative of Jesus' birth, but no connection is made with the birth story. Jesus' brothers and sisters appear for the only time in the Gospel—but they are referred to by the villagers of Nazareth in 13:55-56. None of them plays any further role in the Gospel (unless the "other Mary" of 27:56, 61; 28:1 is the mother of Jesus). Matthew's only interest is in using Jesus' family as symbols for the Christian community, which here replaces his natural family.[275]

The crowds, as potential disciples, have been present throughout the disputation, overhearing Jesus' pronouncements against the Pharisees and "this generation." Matthew retains the Markan picture of Jesus' family standing "outside," which connotes religious distance, although

275. Thus speculation on the absence of Joseph from this scene misses Matthew's point. Historically, it is probably correct that Joseph had died, since he is never referred to after the birth story in any of the Gospels. But Matthew cannot use "father" as a symbol for members of the Christian community, since only God is Father (23:9).

he eliminated the Markan setting in a house when he omitted the embarrassing statement that Jesus' family thought him to be deranged (Mark 3:20-21), and the presence of the crowds indicates that Jesus was outside. Matthew's point is that those who have accepted Jesus' message, and thereby have been called to place the kingdom of God above even family loyalties, as he himself had done (8:21-22; 10:21-39; 19:29), have found a new family in the community of *disciples*—a term that Matthew specifically adds to his Markan source. Jesus "stretches out his hand" over them (also added to Mark), a gesture that, when used

of Jesus, signals his compassionate and direct response to those in need (8:3), his mighty act of deliverance to disciples in distress (14:31). The concluding pronouncement is doubly definitive: (1) Disciples are those persons who do the will of God. The essence of discipleship is not mere profession, right doctrine, or even charismatic phenomena, but doing the will of God (7:21-23). (2) Disciples are not only brothers and sisters of one another in the family of God, but also they are Jesus' "brothers and sisters," a relationship that is particularly important to Matthew as a designation of the members of the Christian community (cf. 23:8 [obscured there by the NRSV]; 25:40; 28:10).

REFLECTIONS

The exegetical discussion above raises the question of whether Matthew also reverses this equation: Those who do the will of God are Jesus' "brothers and sisters," even if they are not overtly disciples (see Commentary on 25:31-46). In any case, doing God's will, not formal identity with the community, is of fundamental importance. On the other hand, this passage also indicates that discipleship to Jesus cannot be an individualistic matter. To be a disciple is to belong to the wider family of the community of faith.

MATTHEW 13:1-52, SPEAKING IN PARABLES

OVERVIEW

What Is a Parable? Although Jesus has often used metaphorical speech before, (e.g., 5:13-16; 7:6, 24-27), here the reader encounters for the first time sayings that Matthew calls "parables."[276] The Greek word παραβολή (*parabolē*) itself means simply "something cast beside" something else to explain or clarify it—i.e., "comparison," "analogy." However, the synoptic Gospels[277] reflect the LXX, which employs the word to translate the wide range of meanings of משל (*māšāl*): "figure," "proverb," "aphorism," "riddle," "lesson," "allegory," or almost any kind of indirect or metaphorical speech. However, the meaning and function

of parables in the proclamation of Jesus and in the Gospel narratives cannot be settled on the basis of etymology and the use of the word elsewhere, but must be learned from the way parables actually function in the Gospels.

For centuries, the Gospel parables were understood to be primarily allegories—encoded teaching that could be decoded into edifying lessons for Christian life. Thus the three measures of flour into which the yeast was placed (13:33) could represent "Greeks, Jews, and Samaritans" (Theodore of Mopsuestia) or more individualistically "heart, soul, and spirit" (Augustine). Such an interpretation offers fertile ground for the preacher's imagination, but has little to do with the text of the Bible. The first major turning point in modern parable study was made by Adolf Jülicher's 1888 work, which made a sharp distinction between parable and allegory. An allegory has many points; a parable but one, which Jülicher

276. The opening description in 13:3 and the concluding transitional comment at 13:53 indicate that Matthew considers everything in between to be "parables," including v. 52. This is the first of three blocks of parables in Matthew, the others being 21:28–22:14 and 24:42–25:30. The first two involve public presentations, but only disciples are given the key to understanding. The third is given only to disciples (transparent for "readers"). All are expansions and elaborations from a Markan base.

277. The word occurs 48 times in the Synoptics (17 in Matthew; 13 in Mark; 18 in Luke) and not at all in the Fourth Gospel. Elsewhere in the NT, it appears only in Heb 9:9, 11:19.

understood to be a general point of moral or religious instruction. C. H. Dodd and Joachim Jeremias followed in this train, emphasizing that "the point" of each parable is eschatological, not a general moralism. For Dodd, each parable in its original setting in the message of Jesus communicated something about Jesus' realized eschatology—i.e., the presence of the kingdom; Jeremias modified this to "eschatology in the process of realization," understanding the kingdom in Jesus' message to be both "already" and "not yet."[278] Dodd's classic definition has served as the point of departure for much contemporary study of the parables: "At its simplest the parable is a metaphor or simile drawn from nature or common life, arresting the hearer by its vividness or strangeness, and leaving the mind in sufficient doubt about its precise application to tease it into active thought."[279] The parables have been studied with great intensity in recent years. While there are still disputed points, the following conclusions and perspectives on interpreting Gospel parables would find widespread support:

(1) Jülicher did a great service in demolishing the dominant allegorical interpretation, but made the distinction too neatly and firmly between parable and allegory, just as his distinctions among parable, similitude, and example story were too rigid.

(2) Parables are a means of disclosing new truth that cannot be reduced to non-parabolic, discursive language. Parables are not simply illustrations of truths that can be stated in other ways. Not only does a parable not have a number of points (as allegorical interpretation held), but also it has no "point" at all that can be stated in non-parabolic language. A parable is like a musical composition, a painting, or a poem in that it is not an illustration of a prosaic point, but is itself an inseparable unity of form and meaning. To reduce a parable to a "point" is to dismiss it as parable and domesticate its message to more comfortable and manageable categories.

(3) Parables generate new meaning in new situations. Thus parables are polyvalent. While a parable cannot "mean" simply anything (it is not a Rorschach blot), it has no one meaning that can be ferreted out by objective methods. It takes on mean-

ing as it forces the hearer/reader to participate in the construction of meaning. This process can subvert the meaning world of the hearer, opening up a new vision of reality. Parables thus often function by beginning in the familiar world of the hearer, but then present a different vision of the world, challenging the everyday expectations of the hearer.

(4) The parables are "secular." Although they are bearers of a religious vision, their content is not drawn from the religious life, but from the everyday world.

(5) Parables are more than generalizing metaphors. They are brief narratives, including one-liners, that presuppose a narrative.

Parables in the Ministry of the Historical Jesus. There can be no doubt that the picture of the synoptic Gospels is historically correct: Jesus characteristically taught in parables. They are a part of the original bedrock of the tradition. The newness of Jesus' message called for a new form of communication. While some Hellenistic teachers had used parable-like forms, there is nothing like them in either the HB or the LXX. While a certain kind of parable became common in later rabbinic teaching, as documented in the Mishnah and the Talmud, and while there existed in Jesus' day a traditional treasury of stock metaphorical ideas and characters (sowing, a king, etc.), Jesus' method of communicating in parables was not the typical practice of contemporary rabbis but a new and unsettling departure in religious communication. For instance, later rabbinic parables were concerned with exegesis of the Torah, a feature strikingly absent from the parables of Jesus in the Gospels, including Matthew, despite its portrayal of Jesus as an interpreter of the Torah (5:17-48).

In the preaching of Jesus, parables were not vivid decorations of a moralistic point but were disturbing stories that threatened the hearer's secure mythological world—the world of assumptions by which we habitually live, the unnoticed framework of our thinking within which we interpret other data. For example, capitalism, communism, the scientific worldview, competition, self-reliance, and individualism can all assume this unconscious mythological role. So long as this mythological framework remains intact, we can integrate Jesus' other teaching within our own framework of assumptions, domesticating his teaching and even making it into illustrations of our own values. Parables surreptitiously attack this

---

278. Adolf Jülicher, *Die Gleichnisreden Jesu,* 2 vols. (Tübingen: J. C. B. Mohr [Paul Siebeck] 1910; 1st ed. 1888); C. H. Dodd, *The Parables of the Kingdom* (New York: Charles Scribner's Sons, 1961); Joachim Jeremias, *The Parables of Jesus* (New York: Charles Scribner's Sons, 1972).
279. Dodd, *Parables,* 5.

framework of our thought world itself. This is why they were so disturbing then and remain so now, and why we are so eager to understand them as illustrations of points we are comfortable with already, rather than letting them be the disruptive vehicles of a new vision of how things are, a vision that challenges our secure world.

Parables in the Life of the Church. As the parables were handed on and around in the church's teaching and preaching, they were interpreted and modified to address new situations. These post-Easter additions and modifications can often be easily detected (see, e. g., 13:18-23, 36-43), but they are not merely to be stripped away to get back to the original parable. They illuminate the ways Jesus' potent message was heard and interpreted as the early Christians struggled to apply it to their own situations after Easter.

Parables in the Gospel of Matthew. Matthew took over the parables from his sources and tradition, including the reinterpretations they had already received in the life of the church, and made them an integral part of the story of Jesus. The reader of Matthew's Gospel may still be struck by the original explosive power of the parable as it projects itself through its later contexts. In this commentary, however, our primary concern is to discern the meaning of the text as presented to us in the Gospel of Matthew.

Matthew has located the "parable discourse" in the midst of the conflict section in which Jesus is being rejected by the leaders of Israel, the new community is being formed, and the inclination of the people as a whole hangs in the balance. The messianic words (chaps. 5–7), deeds (chaps. 8–9), and mission (chap. 10) had generated increasing conflict and rejection (chaps. 11-12). The section is preceded by the rejection of Jesus by the Pharisees and by his own family, culminating in the announcement of a new community of those who do God's will and are thus Jesus' "family" (12:22-50). Immediately following the parables discourse, Jesus is rejected with hostility in his own home town (13:53-58). Matthew created this structure, having already used the intervening Markan stories in his earlier section of miracle stories (Matt 4:23–5:53; 8:23-34; 9:18-26); as a result, Jesus' parables in 13:36-52 are his commentary on the meaning of his rejection by Israel and the founding of the new community. When Jesus gets into the boat (13:2),

the Matthean reader will remember the scene in 8:18-27, where, in the presence of the crowds Jesus called his disciples to follow him into the storm-tossed boat and undertake the perilous journey to the "other side" (Gentile territory), a reflection of the transitional experience of the Matthean church (see Commentary on 8:18-27).[280] The crowds did not follow, but the disciples did. This separation of the community of Jesus' disciples from the crowds is the specifically Matthean context and purpose of the parable collection. In its present context, the parables speak directly to the experience and history of Christians in the Matthean church, although this makes difficulties at the narrative level of Matthew's pre-Easter story.[281]

While "kingdom of God" was a central theme in Q, "kingdom" was not associated with parables. The word *parable* is not found in Q. The "parables of the kingdom" appear first in Mark 4, where they are understood in terms of Mark's "messianic secret." Matthew takes over the Markan connection between parables and kingdom of God and makes it into a major element in his portrayal of Jesus' message. In 13:1-52, Matthew constructs one of his five major discourses around this theme. All of the parables in Matthew 13 have an explicit reference to the kingdom of God/heaven; all but the first do this in their opening line—13:19 adds a kingdom reference to the interpretation of the parable of the sower, showing that for Matthew this too is a kingdom parable. Since judgment is at the heart of Matthew's view of the kingdom, this means that for Matthew "parables of the kingdom" means parables of the coming judgment. For Matthew, to know God's plan for history culminating in the judgment of the Son of Man is to know the mysteries of the kingdom of God.

Mark had arranged the parable discourse into the triadic pattern:

280. The setting in the boat in 13:2 seems to serve only this symbolic function, since it plays no further role (in contrast to Mark 4:33-36). It seems to be forgotten in 13:10 when the disciples "come to him," with vv. 10-17 addressed only to them; the next set of three parables (vv. 24-33) are addressed to the crowds again (cf. v. 34), with the final set of parables and interpretations addressed exclusively to the disciples back in the house (13:36-52).

281. There is no reason at the narrative level for the crowds to be spoken of so negatively in vv. 10-17 (cf. v. 34), but the Matthean readers understand this negative portrayal on the basis of the outcome of the story (here anticipated), in which the crowds play their own role in the rejection and crucifixion of Jesus, as well as from the experience of the post-Easter community in which the masses of Israel had remained indifferent or hostile.

A. parable
B. purpose: to conceal from outsiders
C. interpretation for insiders.

On the basis of the pattern already present in Mark, Matthew expands the discourse with ma-

terial from Q, M, and his own composition, structuring the additional components into two sets of three. The result is a threefold triadic structure: (see Fig. 8 below).

Figure 8: The Structure of Matthew 13:1-52

I. The Markan Parable Structure Adapted and Interpreted, 13:1-23
  A. A Parable
     Parable #1: "The Sower," 13:1-9
  B. Why Parables? 13:10-17
  C. The Parable of the Sower Interpreted, 13:18-23

II. Three Additional Parables in the Markan Pattern, 13:24-43
  A. Three Parables (introduced by "another parable" [ἄλλην παραβολήν *allēn parabolēn*])
     Parable #2: "The Weeds," 13:24-30
     Parable #3: "The Mustard Seed," 13:31-32
     Parable #4: "The Yeast," 13:33
  B. Why Speak in Parables? 13:34-35
  C. The Parable of the Weeds Interpreted, 13:36-43

III. Three Additional Parables in (a Variation of) the Markan Pattern, 13:44-52
  A. Three Parables (introduced by "the kingdom of heaven is like . . ."
     [ἡ βασιλεία τῶν οὐρανῶν ὁμοία ἐστίν *hē basileia tōn ouranōn homoia estivn*])
     Parable #5: "The Hidden Treasure," 13:44
     Parable #6: "The Pearl," 13:45-46
     Parable #7: "The Net," 13:47-48
  B. (C.) Parable of the Net Explained, 13:49-50[282]
  C. (B.) Understanding Parables:
     Concluding Parable #8 on Parables, 13:51-52

282. In the third triad, Matthew has switched the final two elements to round off the discourse with the disciples' understanding and a concluding parable about parables.

Matthew 13:1-23, The Markan Parable Structure Adapted and Interpreted

NIV

13 That same day Jesus went out of the house and sat by the lake. [2]Such large crowds gathered around him that he got into a boat and sat in it, while all the people stood on the shore. [3]Then he told them many things in parables, saying: "A farmer went out to sow his seed. [4]As he was scattering the seed, some fell along the path, and the birds came and ate it up. [5]Some fell on rocky places, where it did not have much soil. It sprang up quickly, because the soil was shallow. [6]But when the sun came up, the plants were

NRSV

13 That same day Jesus went out of the house and sat beside the sea. [2]Such great crowds gathered around him that he got into a boat and sat there, while the whole crowd stood on the beach. [3]And he told them many things in parables, saying: "Listen! A sower went out to sow. [4]And as he sowed, some seeds fell on the path, and the birds came and ate them up. [5]Other seeds fell on rocky ground, where they did not have much soil, and they sprang up quickly, since they had no depth of soil. [6]But when the sun rose, they were

NIV

scorched, and they withered because they had no root. [7]Other seed fell among thorns, which grew up and choked the plants. [8]Still other seed fell on good soil, where it produced a crop--a hundred, sixty or thirty times what was sown. [9]He who has ears, let him hear."

[10]The disciples came to him and asked, "Why do you speak to the people in parables?"

[11]He replied, "The knowledge of the secrets of the kingdom of heaven has been given to you, but not to them. [12]Whoever has will be given more, and he will have an abundance. Whoever does not have, even what he has will be taken from him. [13]This is why I speak to them in parables:

"Though seeing, they do not see;
    though hearing, they do not hear or understand.

[14]In them is fulfilled the prophecy of Isaiah:

" 'You will be ever hearing but never understanding;
    you will be ever seeing but never perceiving.
[15]For this people's heart has become calloused;
    they hardly hear with their ears,
    and they have closed their eyes.
Otherwise they might see with their eyes,
    hear with their ears,
    understand with their hearts
and turn, and I would heal them.'[a]

[16]But blessed are your eyes because they see, and your ears because they hear. [17]For I tell you the truth, many prophets and righteous men longed to see what you see but did not see it, and to hear what you hear but did not hear it.

[18]"Listen then to what the parable of the sower means: [19]When anyone hears the message about the kingdom and does not understand it, the evil one comes and snatches away what was sown in his heart. This is the seed sown along the path. [20]The one who received the seed that fell on rocky places is the man who hears the word and at once receives it with joy. [21]But since he has no root, he lasts only a short time. When trouble or persecution comes because of the word, he quickly falls away. [22]The one who received the seed that fell among the thorns is the man who hears the word, but the

[a]15 Isaiah 6:9,10

NRSV

scorched; and since they had no root, they withered away. [7]Other seeds fell among thorns, and the thorns grew up and choked them. [8]Other seeds fell on good soil and brought forth grain, some a hundredfold, some sixty, some thirty. [9]Let anyone with ears[a] listen!"

10Then the disciples came and asked him, "Why do you speak to them in parables?" [11]He answered, "To you it has been given to know the secrets[b] of the kingdom of heaven, but to them it has not been given. [12]For to those who have, more will be given, and they will have an abundance; but from those who have nothing, even what they have will be taken away. [13]The reason I speak to them in parables is that 'seeing they do not perceive, and hearing they do not listen, nor do they understand.' [14]With them indeed is fulfilled the prophecy of Isaiah that says:

'You will indeed listen, but never understand,
    and you will indeed look, but never perceive.
[15] For this people's heart has grown dull,
    and their ears are hard of hearing,
    and they have shut their eyes;
        so that they might not look with their eyes,
    and listen with their ears,
    and understand with their heart and turn—
        and I would heal them.'

[16]But blessed are your eyes, for they see, and your ears, for they hear. [17]Truly I tell you, many prophets and righteous people longed to see what you see, but did not see it, and to hear what you hear, but did not hear it.

18"Hear then the parable of the sower. [19]When anyone hears the word of the kingdom and does not understand it, the evil one comes and snatches away what is sown in the heart; this is what was sown on the path. [20]As for what was sown on rocky ground, this is the one who hears the word and immediately receives it with joy; [21]yet such a person has no root, but endures only for a while, and when trouble or persecution arises on account of the word, that person immediately falls away.[c] [22]As for what was sown among thorns, this is the one who hears the word, but the cares of the world and the lure of wealth choke the word, and it yields nothing. [23]But as for what was sown on good soil, this is the one

[a]Other ancient authorities add to hear   [b]Or mysteries   [c]Gk stumbles

NIV	NRSV
worries of this life and the deceitfulness of wealth choke it, making it unfruitful. ²³But the one who received the seed that fell on good soil is the man who hears the word and understands it. He produces a crop, yielding a hundred, sixty or thirty times what was sown."	who hears the word and understands it, who indeed bears fruit and yields, in one case a hundredfold, in another sixty, and in another thirty."

COMMENTARY

13:1-9, The Sower. Matthew 13:1 shows that Matthew thought of Jesus and "the crowds" as being in the house, despite his omission of Mark 3:20-21, which locates them there. The awkwardness of imagining the crowds in the house shows the symbolic dimension of the narrative. "That same day" clearly links chap. 13 with the preceding section.

It is difficult for later readers to hear the parable independently of the allegorical interpretation of 13:18-23, with which it came to be associated even prior to Mark. The later allegorical interpretation emphasized the four kinds of soil, with the implicit homiletical question "What kind of soil am I?" The original parable of Jesus focused on the surprisingly abundant harvest despite initial threats.[283] Neither this nor any of the seed parables is about the natural, slow, evolutionary progress of the kingdom of God, but portrays the mysterious, concealed working of God, who miraculously brings the harvest.

In first-century Palestine, fields could be sown in the fall or spring. Sometimes the field was first prepared by plowing, and sometimes the seed was sown first and then plowed in. The parable is not interested in agricultural details, hence there is no reference to the usual concerns of farmers, such as the vicissitudes of weather. All attention focuses on the fate of the seed in the various kinds of soil. "Sowing" was a stock metaphor for teaching or preaching, as was "harvest" for the eschatological ingathering and judgment.

The primary issue in interpreting the parable is whether the harvest in the final scene is intended to be realistic. There is some evidence that a

harvest of four- to tenfold was considered normal, with a harvest of fifteen times what was sown being exceptionally good.[284] On this understanding, Jesus' original parable, which is realistic until the final scene, portrays a fantastically surprising harvest. Recently, some scholars have been more persuaded by the evidence that seems to indicate that a harvest of one hundredfold was not considered exceptional, in which case the thrust of the parable remains in the everyday world throughout, picturing the kingdom as present in the ordinary rather than in apocalyptic pictures of the end.[285] Efforts to make the picture of the harvest realistic cite literary data from Greece, Italy, Africa, and Babylon, but convincing evidence that such a harvest in Palestine would be considered normal is still lacking.[286] The parable may be intentionally borderline or ambiguous on this point, being surprisingly extraordinary in comparison to everyday expectations, but still falling far short of the fantastic pictures of eschatological plenty prevalent in apocalypses. The decisive point for interpreting the original parable of Jesus may be the allusion to Gen 26:12. If that is true, then the only place where Galilean farmers would have heard of reaping a one hundredfold harvest was in the "unrealistic" world of the Bible. On this basis, Jesus' story begins in the ordinary world and concludes in the biblical world of hope and promise.

Although the parable originally focused more on the different kinds of soil and the final harvest, the Matthean interpretation at 13:18 changes Mark

---

283. This contrasts with the pessimistic picture of some apocalyptic thought, which used the picture of sowing and harvest to illustrate how few persons one must expect to be saved at the eschatological harvest (4 Ezra 8:41).

284. Ulrich Luz, *Das Evangelium nach Matthäus (Mt 8–17)*, Evangelisch-Katholischer Kommentar zum Neuen Testament I/2 (Benziger: Neukirchener Verlag, 1990) 2:307, cites A. ben David, *Talmudische Ökonomie* (New York: Olms, 1974) 1:104-5.

285. See Bernard Brandon Scott, *Hear Then the Parable* (Minneapolis: Fortress, 1989) 358.

286. A. H. McNeile, *The Gospel According to St. Matthew: The Greek Text with Introduction, Notes, and Indices* (London: Macmillan, 1915; reprint 1961) 188; Robert K. McIver, "One Hundred-fold Yield—Miraculous or Mundane? Matthew 13:8, 23; Mark 4:8, 20; Luke 8:8," *NTS* 40 (October 1994) 606-8.

to give the parable an informal title, "the sower," by which it has been known in practically all later interpretation. The sower himself plays a minor role in the story, disappearing after the opening line, but Matthew understands the parable christologically, identifying the sower with Christ.[287] For Matthew, Jesus accompanies his church through history (28:18), is himself the one who is present and active in the sowing of the word (13:37), identifies himself with his missionaries (10:40), himself builds the church (16:18) and is active in its discipline (18:18-20), and will finally be the judge who separates faithful from unfaithful disciples (13:41-43). Matthew sees all the parables in this chapter in the perspective of the sorting and evaluating event of the eschatological judgment. The christological focus has implications for discipleship. For him, the emphasis is on the responsibility of the individual believer to produce "fruit" (righteous deeds). Thus he changes Mark's collective singular "seed" to "seeds," thinking of categories of individuals' response to the word, and reverses Mark's climactic progression 30/60/100, corresponding to his judgment stories that begin with commending the most fruitful and proceed to pronouncements of judgment on the less fruitful (cf. 25:14-30). In Matthew's interpretation, a mind-blowing picture of an unexpected harvest corresponding to the biblical world has become a parable of judgment, even prior to the interpretation.

13:10-17, Why Speak in Parables? The setting in the boat seems to be forgotten. Verses 10-23 are directed only to the disciples, but the "them" of v. 24 must mean the crowds (cf. v. 34).

Matthew's source had pictured Jesus as using parables in order to prevent "outsiders" from understanding (Mark 4:10-12), a part of Mark's "messianic secret." Matthew does not share Mark's understanding of the secret messiahship and its corollary, the misunderstanding of the disciples.[288] Here we see him struggling to reinterpret a Markan hard saying within the framework of his own understanding of Jesus' ministry.

His considerable redactional expansion and modification of this passage begins with a clarifying of the question. Whereas in Mark a larger circle had asked about the meaning of the parables, now it is those who understand (the disciples alone) who ask specifically the reason for Jesus' speaking to "them" (the others) in parables. As they had asked specifically "Why?" Jesus responds with a specific "because."[289] The question receives a fivefold response, representing Matthean theology and moderating the difficult statements in Mark 4:10-12.

13:11. Understanding is not a human accomplishment, but a gift of God. This is a Matthean theme elsewhere (11:25-30; 16:17). For Matthew, "understanding" is not merely conceptual, but is understood biblically to include subjection to God's sovereignty. This is his understanding of Isa 6:9-10 (cf. Ps 119:34).

Matthew's source had used the singular "mystery," which tended to connote the secrets of the Hellenistic mystery cults and their exclusive insider/outsider mentality (Mark 4:11). Matthew changes to the plural "mysteries," more attuned to the OT understanding of the hidden plans of God for history and the ultimate establishment of the kingdom of God.[290]

13:12. Parabolic communication rewards good students and penalizes bad ones. Jesus speaks in parables because he is a good communicator who wishes to challenge those who want to understand; those who fail to understand show that they are poor students—i.e., wrong-headed, not merely intellectually dull. The reader of Mark 4:10-12 could well ask what kind of teacher generates only misunderstanding, and intends to do so. Matthew has corrected this in line with his view of Jesus as a good teacher, a dimension of his christology.[291] Matthew's view of parables is akin to that of Jesus ben Sirach, who saw them as a teacher's method of distinguishing perceptive students from indolent ones. This was standard scribal pedagogical strategy (cf. Sir 3:29; 21:11-15; 38:31-39:3). To express this understanding, Mat-

---

287. Matthew makes this explicit in 13:37, but his editorial modifications indicate that he understood the sower in each of the three seed parables christologically. Thus both Jesus and the sower "go out" (13:1, 3), Matthew adding the reference to Jesus in 13:1, even though he had dropped Mark's earlier reference to Jesus' being in a house (Mark 3:20; cf. Matt 12:46).

288. Matthew omits, modifies, or offers a supplemental correction for every passage in Mark that pictures the disciples as misunderstanding or failing to understand. Cf. Gerhard Barth, "Matthew's Understanding of the Law," in *Tradition and Interpretation in Matthew,* eds. Günther Bornkamm, Gerhard Barth, Heinz Joachim Held (Philadelphia: Westminster, 1963) 105-12.

289. Contrary to his usual style, Matthew adds the causal ὅτι *hoti* to preface v. 11, just as he had modified the vague "were asking" in Mark to "Why?" (Διὰ τί [*dia ti*] corresponds to ὅτι [*hoti*]; both are Matthean additions.)

290. Cf. the plural רזין (*rāzîn*) in Dan 2:28-29, 47; Raymond E. Brown, *The Semitic Background for the Term "Mystery" in the New Testament* (Philadelphia: Fortress, 1968).

291. It is to be noticed, however, that Matthew never refers to Jesus' parabolic communication to the crowds as "teaching," twice omitting Mark's terminology (Mark 14:2 = Matt 13:3).

thew moves Mark 4:25 to Matt 13:12, its new context provides an entirely new perspective. Only those who have committed themselves to follow Jesus as his disciples are given the mysteries of the kingdom. They have Jesus as their teacher (23:10) and can appropriate the meaning of the parables. For those who do not become disciples, the parables are not explained, and they function not as teaching but as judgment.

13:13. Matthew changes Mark's "in order that" (ἵνα *hina*) to "because" (ὅτι *hoti*), and omits the damning "so that they might not turn again and be forgiven." The result is that the crowds are described as failing to understand because they are already imperceptive, rather than as in Mark, where their lack of understanding is the intentional result of Jesus' teaching in parables.

13:14-15. The allusion to Isa 6:9-10, already present in the preceding passage, is now made specific, as Matthew adds the full quotation. Jesus, by speaking in parables, fulfills the Scripture. Some exegetes take these two verses as a later interpolation (with no MS evidence), but its appropriateness here is better explained as an aspect of Matthew's nervousness in dealing with Mark 4:10-12.

13:16-17. Matthew brings this reassuring word from another context in Q (cf. Luke 10:23-24), which affirms that the disciples not only see and hear the deeper meaning of what is happening before them, but also that what they experience is what prophets and righteous persons have longed to see and hear, the eschatological events of the time of fulfillment!

13:18-23, The Parable of the Sower Interpreted. The interpretation of the parable, here understood as an allegory, is given only to the disciples, who "came to him" with their question in v. 10.[292] Parables are not antithetical to allegory, and they are susceptible of allegorical interpretation. Jesus' original parable was not an allegory, even though the line between parable and allegory is not as firm as once thought. The interpretation is generally understood to be from the church (and rightfully

so[293]), but it has its own validity as one reading of the meaning of the polyvalent parable. In its present form, the interpretation represents the meaning generated by the parable in a later typical church situation, as Christian interpreters reflected on the meaning of the Christ-event and the church's experience in bearing witness to the gospel.

Matthew essentially adopts the interpretation of the parable of the sower as transmitted in Mark 4:13-20, with certain changes characteristic of Matthean theology. He designates the parable as that of "the sower," giving it a christological focus it had not had previously (cf. even more specifically 13:37). Matthew also slightly rewrites Mark 4:14 to avoid the direct clash between seed as word in v. 14 and seed as hearers in vv. 16, 18, 20—an attempt that does not quite succeed, since in 13:19*b* "what is sown in the heart" must be the word, but in vv. 20 and following "what was sown" is "the one who hears." Further, Matthew specifies that the word sown is the "word of the kingdom" (cf. Excursus "Kingdom of Heaven in Matthew," 288-94). The Matthean emphasis on the disciple as one who understands (see above) appears when he specifies that the problem with the first category of seed/soil is the lack of understanding, which forms a bracket with the Matthean addition to the final category, specifying that the good seed/soil "understands" (cf. also on 13:13, 15, 51). Further, Matthew has changed Mark's collective nouns to singulars, emphasizing individual responsibility. The closing summary portraying the good seed/soil adds distinctive Matthean themes to achieve the combination of hearing plus doing, understanding, and bearing fruit.

---

292. The same is true, of course, of the two other interpretations (of the parables of the weeds in vv. 37-43 and of the net in vv. 49-50). Even though Matthew does not share the Markan form of the messianic secret, he still has Jesus speak (not "teach," in Matthew) in such a way that the crowds cannot understand the real meaning of the parables, which are interpreted only to disciples. The scene of Matthew 13 is, therefore, not a realistic report but makes the theological point: only insiders understand. But all are invited to become insiders. This is valid for Matthew's post-Easter meaning, which means that Matthew 13 does not realistically report a pre-Easter teaching strategy of the historical Jesus, but represents Matthean theology to the reader.

293. For detailed reasons, see, e.g., J. Jeremias, *The Parables of Jesus* (New York: Charles Scribner's Sons, 1972) 77-79. Some main reasons: (1) The interpretation (mis-)construes the parable as an allegory. (2) A parable that must be explained is not from a master teacher. (3) The interpretation is not self-consistent (in Mark 4:16, 18, 20 seed = hearers; but in 4:14 seed = word); Matthew has noticed this and slightly adjusted it. (4) In the interpretation, much more attention is given to the losses than is the case in the parable, where the focus is on the surprising harvest. (5) The interpretation reflects the situation of the post-Easter church, not that of the pre-Easter Jesus (v. 17). (6) The vocabulary is that of the church, not of Jesus (e.g., absolute use of "the word"; several words that occur nowhere else in the teaching of Jesus, but occur regularly in early Christian paraenesis [instruction in Christian living], e.g., "sow" [σπείρω *speirō*] for "preach"; "deception" [ἀπάτη *apatē*]; "wealth" [πλοῦτος *ploutos*]; "unfruitful" [ἄκαρπος *akarpos*]; "bear fruit" [καρποφορέω *karpophoreō*] in a metaphorical sense). (7) The parable is eschatological; the interpretation is psychological and paraenetic. (8) The parable can be readily translated into Aramaic; the interpretation cannot, but seems to have been composed in Greek. (9) In the parable, the sower is active, and the seed produces the mysterious result; in the interpretation, the emphasis is on the soils. (10) In some streams of early Christianity, the parable circulated without the interpretation. Justin and the Pseudo-Clementine homilies used it without the allegorical interpretation, and the *Gospel of Thomas* has the parable in essentially the same form as Mark, but has no allegorical interpretation.

REFLECTIONS

The Matthean reading of Jesus' parable presents to the contemporary reader the following affirmations:

1. The victory of the kingdom of God is sure. The message of the parable is not an exhortation to work hard to bring in the harvest. As silent, mysterious, and unavailable to superficial observation as the germination of a seed in good soil, the kingdom for which the disciples pray (6:10) will certainly come. The seed has been sown by the Son of Man, who accompanies his church throughout history. The harvest is God's doing, and God is faithful.

2. But the line between sowing the word and reaping the kingdom harvest is not straight and unproblematical. The word encounters many difficulties between its original sowing and its eventual (but sure) harvest. Believers should not be surprised or discouraged that this is the case.

3. Although the responses and actions of believers do not effect the final coming of the kingdom, the choices they make are ultimately important, for they determine which side they are on at the final harvest. Believers may not blithely assume that they are the "good soil."

4. This picture of temporary and provisional pessimism, but ultimate optimism, also serves a theological purpose, similar to that of Romans 9–11. The parable and its interpretation served to interpret to Matthew's readers their own history in which the Messiah had been mostly rejected by his own people, yet the purpose of God (the "mysteries of the kingdom") remains sure and will be fulfilled.

These are not mere descriptions of what the text once meant to Matthew's church. When one gets within hearing distance of the text in its original setting, its message for today often becomes transparent.

Matthew 13:24-43, Three Additional Parables in the Markan Pattern

NIV	NRSV
²⁴Jesus told them another parable: "The kingdom of heaven is like a man who sowed good seed in his field. ²⁵But while everyone was sleeping, his enemy came and sowed weeds among the wheat, and went away. ²⁶When the wheat sprouted and formed heads, then the weeds also appeared.	24He put before them another parable: "The kingdom of heaven may be compared to someone who sowed good seed in his field; ²⁵but while everybody was asleep, an enemy came and sowed weeds among the wheat, and then went away. ²⁶So when the plants came up and bore grain, then the weeds appeared as well. ²⁷And the slaves
²⁷"The owner's servants came to him and said, 'Sir, didn't you sow good seed in your field? Where then did the weeds come from?'	of the householder came and said to him, 'Master, did you not sow good seed in your field? Where, then, did these weeds come from?' ²⁸He an-
²⁸"'An enemy did this,' he replied.	swered, 'An enemy has done this.' The slaves said
"The servants asked him, 'Do you want us to go and pull them up?'	to him, 'Then do you want us to go and gather them?' ²⁹But he replied, 'No; for in gathering the
²⁹"'No,' he answered, 'because while you are pulling the weeds, you may root up the wheat	weeds you would uproot the wheat along with them. ³⁰Let both of them grow together until the

NIV

with them. [30]Let both grow together until the harvest. At that time I will tell the harvesters: First collect the weeds and tie them in bundles to be burned; then gather the wheat and bring it into my barn.'"

[31]He told them another parable: "The kingdom of heaven is like a mustard seed, which a man took and planted in his field. [32]Though it is the smallest of all your seeds, yet when it grows, it is the largest of garden plants and becomes a tree, so that the birds of the air come and perch in its branches."

[33]He told them still another parable: "The kingdom of heaven is like yeast that a woman took and mixed into a large amount[a] of flour until it worked all through the dough."

[34]Jesus spoke all these things to the crowd in parables; he did not say anything to them without using a parable. [35]So was fulfilled what was spoken through the prophet:

"I will open my mouth in parables,
   I will utter things hidden since the creation
      of the world."[b]

[36]Then he left the crowd and went into the house. His disciples came to him and said, "Explain to us the parable of the weeds in the field."

[37]He answered, "The one who sowed the good seed is the Son of Man. [38]The field is the world, and the good seed stands for the sons of the kingdom. The weeds are the sons of the evil one, [39]and the enemy who sows them is the devil. The harvest is the end of the age, and the harvesters are angels.

[40]"As the weeds are pulled up and burned in the fire, so it will be at the end of the age. [41]The Son of Man will send out his angels, and they will weed out of his kingdom everything that causes sin and all who do evil. [42]They will throw them into the fiery furnace, where there will be weeping and gnashing of teeth. [43]Then the righteous will shine like the sun in the kingdom of their Father. He who has ears, let him hear."

[a]33 Greek three satas (probably about 1/2 bushel or 22 liters)
[b]35 Psalm 78:2

NRSV

harvest; and at harvest time I will tell the reapers, Collect the weeds first and bind them in bundles to be burned, but gather the wheat into my barn.'"

31He put before them another parable: "The kingdom of heaven is like a mustard seed that someone took and sowed in his field; 32it is the smallest of all the seeds, but when it has grown it is the greatest of shrubs and becomes a tree, so that the birds of the air come and make nests in its branches."

33He told them another parable: "The kingdom of heaven is like yeast that a woman took and mixed in with[a] three measures of flour until all of it was leavened."

34Jesus told the crowds all these things in parables; without a parable he told them nothing. [35]This was to fulfill what had been spoken through the prophet:[b]

"I will open my mouth to speak in parables;
   I will proclaim what has been hidden from
      the foundation of the world."[c]

36Then he left the crowds and went into the house. And his disciples approached him, saying, "Explain to us the parable of the weeds of the field." 37He answered, "The one who sows the good seed is the Son of Man; 38the field is the world, and the good seed are the children of the kingdom; the weeds are the children of the evil one, 39and the enemy who sowed them is the devil; the harvest is the end of the age, and the reapers are angels. 40Just as the weeds are collected and burned up with fire, so will it be at the end of the age. 41The Son of Man will send his angels, and they will collect out of his kingdom all causes of sin and all evildoers, 42and they will throw them into the furnace of fire, where there will be weeping and gnashing of teeth. 43Then the righteous will shine like the sun in the kingdom of their Father. Let anyone with ears[d] listen!"

[a]Gk hid in   [b]Other ancient authorities read the prophet Isaiah
[c]Other ancient authorities lack of the world
[d]Other ancient authorities add to hear

COMMENTARY

13:24-30, The Weeds. With 13:24 a new subsection of Matthew's composition begins (see above), composed by him from materials in Mark, Q, and the traditions unique to him. The phrase "for the kingdom of heaven may be compared to ... " occurs here for the first time in Matthew (cf. 13:31, 33, 44-45, 47; 18:23; 22:2). The Greek text represents an original Aramaic ל (*lĕ*), which means "it is the case with" the kingdom as with the following story as a whole, not restricting the comparison to one point. As a genuine metaphor, the parable *as a whole* is brought into relation to the real subject matter to which it points. Here, the kingdom is not like a man, but is described by the entire parable of the weeds.

As in the preceding subsection, it is difficult for readers to read the parable itself without the allegorical interpretation that follows in vv. 37-43. The most important issue then becomes whether the parable ever existed without the allegorical interpretation, or whether the parable was conceived as an allegory from the beginning, with the interpretation in view. The three views on this issue are (1) the parable goes back to Jesus, at least in its original structure, in which case it was a declaration against the building of boundaries and efforts to have a "pure" community, which is God's business and will be settled at the eschatological judgment. In this case, the parable was directed against tendencies in Israel and/or the pre-Easter Jesus movement toward becoming the same kind of exclusive, "pure" community attempted by Pharisees and Essenes. On this view, the allegorizing interpretation would have been composed by the church to apply this message to the growing problem of ecclesiastical discipline. (2) The parable was an allegory from the beginning, composed along with its interpretation by Matthew or Matthean Christians on the basis of Mark 4:26-29, which it replaces. (3) A mediating view regards the parable as having been composed by an early Christian teacher prior to Matthew, with the interpretation added by Matthew.[294]

There is, in fact, considerable evidence for the view that both the parable and its interpretation were composed, or at least heavily rewritten, by Matthew on the basis of Mark 4. The unrealistic aspects of the story[295] could be explained on the first possibility as the mind-teasing strangeness often found in Jesus' stories, on the second and third as a story composed from the beginning to fit the projected allegorical interpretation. In any case, the Matthean understanding of the story is presented in the following interpretation.

The precise botanical identification of "weeds" or "tares" (ζιζάνια *zizania*) is unclear, but obviously refers to a wheat-like weed (darnel, [as REB] "cheat") common throughout the Near East. Matthew makes nothing of the note that the weeds were sown "while everybody was asleep." Elsewhere in the NT, including the Gospel of Matthew, "sleep" is a metaphor for spiritual sloth or neglect (Mark 13:36; 1 Thess 5:6-8; cf. 1 Pet 5:8), but here it is more likely a reflection of the positive use of "sleep" in Mark 4:27, and it means simply "at night."

The distinctive element in this parable is that it involves two sowings. In the parable of the sower, the seed *per se* is a symbol of the (good and potent) word of God, which generates believers, and the issue is "What kind of soil are you?" (Despite the garbled interpretation that confuses seed and soil.) But in the parable of the weeds, there are two sowings, and the question is "Are you the good seed sown by the exalted Son of Man, or the evil seed sown by Satan?" Matthew's two-kingdoms view comes to expression again here (cf. Commentary on 13:36-43 and Reflections on 13:51-52).

13:31-32, The Mustard Seed. The parable

---

294. So F. W. Beare, *The Gospel According to Matthew* (New York: Harper & Row, 1981) 302-13. In favor of this view is the parable's emphasis on patience and waiting for the harvest—indeed its main point—yet entirely neglected in the interpretation.

295. (1) The setting is a large plantation operated by slave labor. Yet the owner himself sows the seed, and "reapers" do the harvesting. The slaves only ask questions. (2) Such weeds do not need to be sown, but appear on their own amid wheat. (According to R. T. France, *Matthew: Evangelist and Teacher* (Grand Rapids: Zondervan, 1989) 225, there were Roman laws against sowing darnel in a neighbor's field.) (3) Intentionally sowing weeds would require painstaking gathering of weed-seed, itself a strange process. An "enemy" who wanted to harm a neighbor's field could find easier ways. (4) The slaves register surprise that there are weeds among the wheat, although this is the natural expectation. (5) The slaves' questions are pointless; of course, the farmer sowed good seed, and, of course, they should be weeded out. (6) The master's response is extraordinary, however. Instead of weeding them out, they are to wait until the harvest. (7) The work of separating weeds from wheat at the harvest is not assigned to the slaves, but to a different group. (8) The order of burning weeds and gathering wheat at the harvest is a reversal of the normal order. Cf. Luz, *Matthäus*, 2:324.

came to Matthew in both its Markan (4:30-32) and its Q (cf. Luke 13:18-19) forms. The Q form was a genuine narrative parable of a one-time strange event; in Mark, it has become a general analogy. There is also a slightly different form of the parable in *Gospel of Thomas* 20. Matthew follows the Q form more closely. To understand this parable, one must first recognize that a mustard plant is an annual herb, whose proverbially small seeds (cf. 17:20) can indeed produce a plant normally from two to six feet in height (in extraordinary cases, nine to ten feet), but does not produce a *tree* of any kind.[296] The "tree" motif comes not from observation of mustard seeds and plants, but reflects the symbol of the imperial tree found in representations of empires, including apocalyptic imagery of the coming kingdom of God (cf. Ps 104:12; Dan 4:9, 18; Ezek 17:23; 31:6).

In the original parable of Jesus, the surprising, imagination-stretching, and presupposition-questioning tension resulted from the juxtaposition of the imperial tree image with the lowly mustard seed and plant. The view currently popular in some circles of NT scholarship that Jesus here lampoons apocalyptic views of the kingdom by comparing it to the mustard plant rather than to the apocalyptic tree is misplaced. The tree imagery is not dismissed or satirized. It remains, despite its inappropriateness as the final result of a mustard seed. The challenging feature is that the future tree-like glory is in continuity with the present smallness and ordinariness of the mustard plant. The presence of the hoped-for kingdom in Jesus, his works and disciples, is no more obvious than a garden herb—but the kingdom will come in God's power and glory nevertheless. A king who operates in meekness (11:25-30) and rides a donkey instead of a war horse (21:1-9) can be represented by a kingdom symbolized by a garden herb rather than a great tree. For Matthew's readers, the imagery was no longer surprising, for, like the modern reader, they had long since been accustomed to it from Mark's Gospel, their sacred tradition. For them (and us) the parable functions

not to upset our imagery of what the kingdom is as such, but as an encouraging/threatening image contrasting the present lowliness of the kingdom with its final greatness.

13:33, The Yeast. This parable is a narrative about the act of a specific woman, not a general analogy of the relation between yeast and the kingdom. The original parable of Jesus had three surprising features: (1) the positive use of yeast, which is almost always a symbol for corruption in Jewish tradition, including elsewhere in Matthew (cf. Exod 12:15-20; 23:18; 34:25; Lev 2:11; 6:10; Matt 16:6; 1 Cor 5:6-8; Gal 5:9). Like the mustard plant, it is a shocking juxtaposition with the hope for the kingdom of God (see Reflections below).

(2) The quantity of flour that was leavened is surprising as well, "three measures," being about ten gallons, making enough bread to feed 100-150 people. Like the ending of the parable of the sower, this parable is a picture of surprising extravagance. Just as there is a reminiscence of Gen 26:12 in 13:8 above, there may be here a reminiscence of Gen 18:6, where Sarai prepared "three measures" of flour (as well as a whole calf!) as a banquet for the heavenly visitors. The ending of the story pictures the celebratory banquet extravagance of the fantasy/biblical world. The focus of the parable is thus not on the natural process of development as Christianity spreads through the world, as the older Protestant liberalism interpreted both this and the other seed parables, but on the surprising, miraculous extravagance of the coming kingdom.

(3) The verb used for placing the yeast in the flour is unexpected: "hid" (so correctly KJV and RSV, unfortunately obscured by both NIV and NRSV, losing the connection with 13:35). One anticipates "placed" or "kneaded." But there is no action of the woman in bringing about the final extravagant supply of bread. The kingdom is at present hidden and silent, working by unexpected or even scandalous means, although the future will reveal its reality. This latter aspect of the parable is important to Matthew. In the context of the Matthean story, the parable seems to mean that the reality of the kingdom is hidden now to the religious leaders and general public, but it will be revealed later (but disciples already recognize it). The anointed king in the coming kingdom of

296. The Q form preserves the earlier designation of the mustard plant as a "tree," which the Markan form has adjusted to the more accurate "shrub," while preserving the original thrust that it is the "greatest" of these, with "large branches," and that birds "make nests in its shade." Even this is not botanically accurate, of course, but the parable communicates theology, not botany.

God is present with his community (1:23; 28:20 etc.), but this is a hidden presence, not a public spectacle. The advent of the coming king/judge will reveal it to all.

13:34-35, Why Speak in Parables? These words, which were the conclusion to the Markan parable discourse (Mark 4:33-34), are in Matthew a transition to the next subsection with a different audience, as in vv. 10-17. Similarly, Matthew introduces Ps 78:2 as the eighth of his formula quotations (see Excursus "Matthew as Interpreter of Scripture," 151-54). Matthew does not attend to the context and original meaning of Psalm 78, which deals not with the hiddenness of the revelation, but with its openness. In the rest of the Gospel, Jesus does not adhere to the principle enunciated in v. 34. Matthew is attracted to the saying by the word *parable* and is concerned to show that not only that the birth, ministry, and death of the Messiah were matters of prophecy and fulfillment, but also that he taught in parables.

The hidden/revealed schema corresponds to Deut 29:29 and Sir 3:22 (cf. comment on "mysteries" at 13:11 above). Matthew understands the OT as a whole and in all its parts to be prophecy, hence he can cite a psalm as "what had been spoken through the prophet."[297]

13:36-43, The Parable of the Weeds Interpreted. Since the language, style, and theology of this interpretation are thoroughly Matthean, most scholars regard it as his own composition, even if (an earlier form of) the parable of the weeds may derive from Jesus himself. The interpretation understands the parable to be a thoroughly allegorical portrayal of the eschatological judgment, a virtual little apocalypse, but not in a speculative sense—it urges a certain kind of conduct on the believer in the present.

13:36. The transition from the address to the crowds to the disciples is theologically significant in that the principal difference between "world" and "church" is that disciples are taken by Jesus into the house where he explains everything to them. Inasmuch as the reader is given the opportunity to accompany them into the house and

"overhear" Jesus' explanation, readers are implicitly understood to be within the in-group of disciples. Both the disciples in the story and the readers (are given the opportunity to) understand the mysteries of the kingdom of God, the ultimate meaning of the world and its destiny, which affects all, but is "known" only by those who receive Jesus as their teacher. In the Matthean perspective, this does not refer to a description of a once-upon-a-time event in the life of the historical Jesus, but portrays the situation of the church as the community who are privileged to be accompanied by the exalted Lord throughout their historical sojourn toward the coming of the kingdom at the last day.

The allegorized interpretation is selective. Some elements remain uninterpreted—e.g., sleeping, the initial servants and their question, and the fate of the good seed. All attention is focused on the coming judgment, as is also indicated by the "title" given the parable in the disciples' question (v. 36): "the weeds" (cf. the "title" given 13:3-9 in v. 18, "the sower"). Since the interpretation stands in a key position in the structure, the interpretation points to the Matthean understanding of the other parables as well, all of which he understands to be parables of the kingdom—i.e., parables of the coming judgment.

13:37. The Son of Man, who is the sower, is not only the historical Jesus, but is as well the exalted one who accompanies his church through history and the one who will judge both world and church at the end. The "seed" are sons/children/members of the kingdom—i.e., Christian believers—not "the word," as in Mark 4:14 and partially reflected in Matt 13:18-23.

The key to Matthew's understanding of this parable is the *second* sowing, done by "the enemy," the devil. Christians are the result of the "sowing" of the Son of Man. Unbelievers and opponents are the result of the activity of Satan. Matthew's dualistic perspective appears here once again, as in the conflict of kingdoms, which pervades his presentation (13:38 "sons of the kingdom"/"sons of the evil one"; cf. 15:15, and discussion at 12:22-37). Thus it is important that the field is the world, not merely the church (v. 38). The traditional interpretation urging Christians not to pronounce judgment on fellow members of the community is not incorrect, but it is

---

297. Matthew may have attributed this saying specifically to the prophet Isaiah, since this reading is supported by good MSS (א, Θ, f^1, f^{13}, and several of the Church Fathers), since it is the more difficult reading that is more likely to have been "corrected" by scribes than to have been introduced by them, and since Matthew makes a similar mistake later (see Commentary on 27:9).

too narrow. It is not only insiders that Christians are to refrain from judging. The admonition to forego efforts to root out the "weeds" corresponds to 15:12-14 with regard to the Pharisees; they are not "planted" by the Father, who will deal with them in due time. Jesus' disciples are not to try to uproot them, but to leave them be. Both the parable and the interpretation indicate that separation of authentic members of the covenant community from false members or disciples is God's business and must await the eschatological judgment. A tension between these texts and 18:15-20 may reflect a debate within Matthew's church.

Matthew affirms both the church discipline of chap. 18 and the perspective of tolerance and patience represented by chap. 13, without clarifying how this is to be worked out in practice.

13:42. "Weeping and gnashing of teeth" is a Matthean stereotyped formula adopted from Q (cf. Matt 8:12b = Luke 13:28) and added as a conclusion to five parables (13:42, 50; 22:13; 24:51; 25:30), highlighting Matthew's emphasis on the parables as pictures of eschatological judgment, focusing especially on the fate of the condemned. This is not glee over the fate of outsiders, but a warning to insiders.

REFLECTIONS

1. The parable of the weeds has many facets, but we can surely see, shimmering behind it, the experience of Matthew's church—and ours, too. It chronically comes as a shock to find that the world, that the family into which we were born, that even the church is not an entirely trustworthy place. The world has places of wonder, but alleys of cruelty, too. Families cause deep pain as well as great joy. The church can be inspiringly courageous one moment and petty and faithless the next. Good mixes in with the bad. "Where did these weeds come from?" is a perennial human cry.

When the master in the parable forbids the servants to go and weed out the field, this is not to be interpreted as a call to passivity in the face of evil. It is not a divine command to ignore injustice in the world, violence in society, or wrong in the church. It is, rather, a realistic reminder that the servants do not finally have the ability to get rid of all the weeds and that sometimes attempts to pluck up weeds cause more harm than good. This is the way it is.

Are we lost forever, then, in a hopelessly compromised world? No, the parable contains the promise that, in the wisdom of God, the weeds will ultimately be destroyed. Evil is temporary; only the good endures. The parable leads finally, then, to a place of joy and hope. We live in an imperfect world, and no human effort can eradicate that fact. But that was never our job anyway. We are given the task of living as faithfully and as obediently as possible, confident that the harvest is sure.

2. In both the parable of the mustard seed and the parable of the yeast, we find not the natural and the expected, but the supernatural and the surprising. The big tree growing from the tiny mustard seed is like those comic post cards illustrations of a farmer with a gargantuan tomato strapped to the back of a flatbed truck. That one, lone woman working with that massive amount of flour has either lost her mind or is working for the kingdom bakery. A modern analogy to these parables would be "The kingdom of heaven is like a preacher who preached every Sunday to a congregation of twenty-five people in a city of two million residents. The preacher kept on preaching until the whole city believed the gospel."

3. Jesus' original parables undermined preconceived ideas of how God must work to bring in the kingdom. So far as one can observe, its present form is like a garden herb; the future tree in which birds can nest is surrealistically unnatural. The parables are not about the "natural" progress of the kingdom from present smallness to future glory. The garden mustard plant and contaminating, corrupting, unclean yeast as symbols for the kingdom of God are as shocking as God's anointed king for the coming kingdom being represented by the humble crucified one. Matthew, though he reinterpreted the parables for his own situation, understood the parabolic representation of the kingdom and continued it. Contemporary readers who tend to respond a bit too smugly to ancient Jews' rejection of the Christ—because Jesus did not conform to their (biblical and traditional!) images of what the Christ was supposed to be—may learn from the parables not to have fixed images of what the kingdom of God must be. The presence of God's kingdom in our own world may scandalize our own (biblical and traditional!) ideas of where and how God's kingdom is supposed to be present.

4. The church through the centuries has tended to read itself rather triumphalistically into the parables, picturing itself as the small seed that grows to become a great tree, the yeast that will finally pervade the whole lump, the field that, despite containing both good and bad, will someday be purified to contain only the good. But the parables are about the kingdom, not the church, which somewhat self-righteously betrays its own self-understanding when it identifies itself with the "good" elements of the parables misunderstood as allegories. The parables speak of the final victory of the kingdom despite all appearances, and they challenge the church to respond to their message rather than find in them its guarantee of its own success.

Matthew 13:44-52, Three Additional Parables in a Variation of the Markan Pattern

NIV

44"The kingdom of heaven is like treasure hidden in a field. When a man found it, he hid it again, and then in his joy went and sold all he had and bought that field.

45"Again, the kingdom of heaven is like a merchant looking for fine pearls. 46When he found one of great value, he went away and sold everything he had and bought it.

47"Once again, the kingdom of heaven is like a net that was let down into the lake and caught all kinds of fish. 48When it was full, the fishermen pulled it up on the shore. Then they sat down and collected the good fish in baskets, but threw the bad away. 49This is how it will be at the end of the age. The angels will come and separate the wicked from the righteous 50and throw them into the fiery furnace, where there will be weeping and gnashing of teeth.

51"Have you understood all these things?" Jesus asked.

"Yes," they replied.

52He said to them, "Therefore every teacher of the law who has been instructed about the kingdom of heaven is like the owner of a house who brings out of his storeroom new treasures as well as old."

NRSV

44"The kingdom of heaven is like treasure hidden in a field, which someone found and hid; then in his joy he goes and sells all that he has and buys that field.

45"Again, the kingdom of heaven is like a merchant in search of fine pearls; 46on finding one pearl of great value, he went and sold all that he had and bought it.

47"Again, the kingdom of heaven is like a net that was thrown into the sea and caught fish of every kind; 48when it was full, they drew it ashore, sat down, and put the good into baskets but threw out the bad. 49So it will be at the end of the age. The angels will come out and separate the evil from the righteous 50and throw them into the furnace of fire, where there will be weeping and gnashing of teeth.

51"Have you understood all this?" They answered, "Yes." 52And he said to them, "Therefore every scribe who has been trained for the kingdom of heaven is like the master of a household who brings out of his treasure what is new and what is old."

COMMENTARY

The concluding triad varies from the pattern Matthew has been following by reversing elements B and C, in order to conclude with summary words about understanding parables rather than the interpretation of one particular parable. But the fact that vv. 44-52 were conceived as a unit is clear from the identical introductions to the three parables of this section, setting them apart from the preceding, and from the recurrence of the word *treasure* from the opening verse (v. 44) in the concluding verse (v. 52), forming a neat literary bracket for the subsection.

The parable of the net (vv. 47-48) and its interpretation has its counterpart in the preceding subsection's parable of the weeds and its interpretation. The primary hermeneutical problem for this section is constituted by the twin parables of the treasure and the pearl, which are without interpretation and seem out of place in this context. It is also unclear whether the parables belong together and are to be understood in parallel (as is the case in the Matthean context), or whether they were originally separate and not to be interpreted in the light of each other (as in the *Gospel of Thomas*). They do not occur elsewhere in the canonical Gospels.

13:44-46, Hidden Treasure and the Pearl. Matthew apparently intends the parable of the treasure to be interpreted together with the parable of the pearl, which immediately follows. The two parables do have common features: (1) In each case only a brief vignette of a crucial situation is given, without enough details to evaluate them as realistic stories. The interpreter should, therefore, be wary of filling in the gaps from pious imagination, but concentrate on what the parable does, in fact, portray. (2) The primary common feature is surely central to the meaning of each: The protagonist goes and sells everything for the sake of the one thing. This is the action of both the plowman and the merchant. This movement of the story as a whole is to be compared with the kingdom of God (cf. discussion of ל [lĕ] above), for the kingdom is "like" neither the "treasure" of v. 44 nor the "merchant" of v. 45, but in each case somehow like the story as a whole. In each case, the protagonist acts with the

single-minded response of the "pure in heart" (see Commentary on 5:8; cf. the *"one"* pearl). From the story in Mark 10:17-31, Matthew and his community had long known of the kingdom's demand of "all," and of one who had failed (cf. esp. Mark 10:21, where selling everything and giving it to the poor is connected with true "treasure"). These parables are Matthew's preemptive strikes at that issue of discipleship to be presented later.

The two parables are also different: (1) The plowman is doing his regular work, not looking for or expecting anything special, when he comes upon the treasure quite by accident. The merchant is actively seeking, knows what he is looking for, and still finds something beyond all his expectations. The kingdom can become real in either way (cf. 9:2, 22). (2) The great joy of the plowman is emphasized, but is altogether absent from the merchant. This does not mean that the merchant's selling everything in order to obtain the pearl was joyless, but it does mean that (subjective) joy is not the main point of either parable. (3) What the merchant did, although it may not have measured up to everyone's understanding of common sense, was unquestionably legal. The same cannot be said of the plowman, whose action may have been questionable, both legally and morally (we are not given enough details to know for sure). The disposition of buried treasure found on someone else's property was widely discussed in Roman legal discourse. Some of Matthew's readers may have expected a law-abiding plowman to have reported his find to the owner of the field rather than cashing in on it himself. Sensitive contemporary readers may wonder about the ethics of cheating the owner of the field out of his treasure, even if it was perfectly legal. The story does not legitimize the man's actions. Jesus was certainly able to use questionable actions of characters in his parables to picture the urgency of acting to gain the kingdom while the opportunity is there (cf. Matt 12:29's use of breaking-and-entering imagery, and more subtly, Luke 16:1-13).

In the story of the pearl, there is no moral or legal question at all, but still a surprising and provocative action. In the first-century Mediterranean world, the pearl was often a symbol of the highest good (as diamonds sometimes are in modern Western culture). Thus salvation is pictured in the Gnostic "Hymn of the Pearl" as the finding and safe return of a pearl lost in an alien land. Crossan has captured the movement of both the parable of the treasure and the parable of the pearl as advent/reversal/action, expressed in the parallel sets of verbs in vv. 44 and 45-46: finds/sells/buys.[298] The advent of the kingdom, sought for or not, brings about a reversal of values, leading to the crucial action that obtains the new. This action, puzzling and out of step with those who live by the old values, is central in each of these parables.

13:47-48, The Net. The net pictured here is a large dragnet, usually about six feet deep and up to several hundred feet wide, positioned in the lake by boats and requiring several men to operate (hence the plurals of v. 48). The picture is realistic, portraying an ordinary event with no surprising twists: The net brings in "every kind" of both good and bad fish, which are then sorted, the good being kept and the bad thrown out. Whatever the original meaning of the parable, Matthew's own ecclesiastical application already appears in the telling of the parable itself. The bad fish are called "rotten" ($\sigma\alpha\pi\rho\acute{\alpha}$ sapra), inappropriate to fish that have just been caught, but used four times previously in Matthew's description of bad "fruit" (works) presented by Christians, where it is appropriate (7:17-18; 12:33 twice; the word was taken over from Q [cf. Luke 6:43] and made into a Matthean theme). The fishers "sit" for the sorting, as will the Son of Man at the end (19:28; 25:31).

13:49-50, The Parable of the Net Explained. This interpretation is very like that of the parable of the weeds, vv. 36-43 (49a-50 is verbatim agreement with 40b, 42; 49b is very like 41). Like the preceding interpretation, it concentrates entirely on the fate of the wicked, whose destiny is to be cast into the furnace of fire, with weeping and gnashing of teeth—all typical Matthean language for eschatological judgment, but not appropriate to fish, which are buried or thrown back into the water, not burned. The

interpretation, allegorical as it is, does not represent the net to be the church, the fishers to be evangelists, etc. Matthew seems intentionally to forego the obvious opportunity to relate the parable to the story of the call of the fishers in 4:18-22. The parable is not a picture of evangelism, "fishing for people," but a parable of final sorting and separation.

13:51-52, Understanding Parables. The opening description in 13:3 and the concluding transitional comment at 13:53 indicate that Matthew considers everything in between to be parables, including v. 52. Thus, although commentators have liked to find exactly seven parables in the chapter, Matthew apparently considered the concluding picture of the scribe to be a parable as well, a parabolic concluding picture on the use of parables (cf. Fig. 8, p. 301).

The picture comes as an elaboration of the disciples' affirmative response to Jesus' question. They claim to understand. These words added to Mark are to make clear that, for Matthew, understanding is not an optional element of discipleship (see Commentary on 13:10-17).

Matthew understood that parables were constructed from a "treasure" ($\theta\eta\sigma\alpha\nu\rho\acute{o}\varsigma$ thēsauros) of conventional metaphors, in which, for example, "king" or "father" customarily point to God, "harvest" or "accounting" to eschatological judgment, and such.[299] Both Jesus and Christian scribal teachers did this. The uniqueness of Jesus or Matthew does not consist in the invention of radically new images, but in the surprising use to which they put the repertoire of familiar images. Vocabulary and style, as well as theology, indicate that Matthew himself has composed this concluding parable, with the (Jewish) scribe who has been trained (literally "discipled") for the kingdom of heaven being a cameo self-portrait (on Christian scribes, see 8:19-22; 23:34). Matthew affirms both the old and the new (see 9:17). Like a skilled scribe, he brings out of his storehouse the treasures of his Jewish past (Scripture, stock of traditional imagery, perspectives, and concerns), as well as older Christian tradition (Mark; Q). But he does not merely repeat the past. Alongside the

---

298. John Dominic Crossan, *In Parables: The Challenge of the Historical Jesus* (New York: Harper & Row, 1973) 26-36.

299. But not fishing and fishnets. "Leaven" is positively against the common stock of metaphors (see above). The use of transparent stock metaphors is different from allegorization, in which the code is more arbitrary.

old he introduces the new, presenting the old in a new light, reclaiming it for the new situation in which he finds himself, seeing all things in the light of the Christ-event and the coming of the kingdom. Even the unexpected order of "new and old" may be important: It is the new that provides the key to the appropriation of the old, not vice versa.

REFLECTIONS

1. With the parable of the net and its interpretation, the theme returns to the coming judgment, which dominates the chapter. It also forms a literary bracket with the opening of the chapter, where Jesus "sits" in the boat while the crowd stands on the shore (13:2). The judgment to come is already prefigured in the sorting, sifting scene of chap. 13, which is already separating humanity into disciples who understand, follow, and bring forth fruit, not only from scribes and Pharisees who actively oppose them (12:22-45) and from family and hometown folk who reject them (12:46-50; 13:53-58, framing the parable section), but also from "neutral" crowds who only hear without acting (13:2; cf. 7:24-27). The eschatological sorting described in the parables is happening as Jesus speaks and as people respond, or fail to do so. Thus the church is not identified with the net, or the fishers, just as it is not identified with the field or the yeast or any other item in the preceding parables. The church is to see itself reflected not in the elements in the parables, but in the scene of this chapter as a whole: those disciples who respond to the word of Jesus and become the new community, the family of God (12:49).

2. What is the meaning of the "predestination" language of the parables? To be sure, the explicit language of predestination is not used in Matthew (as it is by other NT authors; e.g., Acts 4:28; Rom 8:28-30; Eph 1:4-5; 1 Pet 1:2; Rev 13:8), yet his dualistic language makes clear that those who respond to the word of the parable of the sower do so because they are already of a certain nature, just as those who refuse to respond reveal their nature by their rejection. Even more clearly, the parable of the weeds pictures those who follow Jesus as the work of God, and those who reject him as the work of the devil. Three things need to be understood about such language: (1) It is indispensable to the biblical mode of God-talk. The sample references above, which could be multiplied many times, show that the language and conceptuality of predestination are not marginal elements of the NT's understanding of God, or limited to one author, but are near the mainstream of NT theology. To neglect it is to neglect something central. (2) The language of predestination wants to say something about *God,* not postulate a theory about two or more classes of human beings. It is strictly theological, not anthropological or soteriological. The affirmation: God is sovereign. Predestination language does not intend to make affirmations about human responsibility or the lack of it, but to point to God as Creator and Redeemer. Especially in an author such as Matthew, who emphasizes human responsibility, predestination language cannot be used to avoid our own responsibility for our actions. (3) Predestination language is the insider language of confession and praise, not the objectifying language that gives ontological status to some abstract system. It expresses the insider's praise rather than making objective claims about outsiders. It is the believers' mode of refusing to take credit for their own salvation, but to glorify God. Perhaps, then, a fourth note should be added: such God-talk is best done by telling stories, rather than (as here) making discursive, propositional statements. Preaching and teaching might learn from this, and let the story have its own effect rather than being crammed into the logical constraints of objectifying "explaining" language. As Hamlet said of the play, "Now let it work."

3. Matthew makes it clear that the parables can be understood only by disciples who are given the key by Jesus. Yet this is not merely the conceptual answer to a puzzle; understanding requires faith and obedience. The hope expressed in the parables of the kingdom is the against-all-expectations hope of the outcast and the oppressed. Matthew's community understood parables because they spoke to their situation in which hope could be only a gift of God. Contemporary, prosperous culture-Christianity can understand them only in solidarity with those who know the meaning of hope, because they recognize the limitations of their own power. To paraphrase Ulrich Luz: "In the pleasant lounge, the hope of the kingdom cannot be understood. On the sofa, the parables of the kingdom cannot be understood. Through exegesis alone, the parables of the kingdom cannot be understood."[300]

300. Paraphrase of Luz, *Matthäus*, 2:378-80.

Matthew 13:53–17:27, The Formation of the New Community Amid Continuing Conflict

OVERVIEW

Following the parables discourse, a new narrative section begins, extending to the next major discourse, 18:1-35 (see Introduction).[301] Apart from 16:21, there are no clear structural divisions in this section; Matthew simply follows the Markan order, with every pericope in this section based on Mark except the concluding 17:24-27. This does not mean, however, that the arrangement of individual events is merely arbitrary, for there was already a narrative logic present in

Mark, which Matthew adopts as his own. The story is carried forward by this particular order. Discipleship deepens, as does opposition. The crowds remain challenged by Jesus, but they neither reject him nor become disciples. The confrontation with Israel continues until 16:12. The dialogue between Jesus and the disciples/Peter at 16:13-20 forms a hinge, with the narrator's announcement (16:21) the most significant turning point in this section. From 16:21 onward, Jesus turns his attention to instructing the disciples in his destiny and what it means for the new community being formed.

301. The word translated "stumble," "take offense" (σκανδαλίζω *skandalizo*) is a key word/theme in both the opening scene (13:57) and Jesus' closing word (17:27) of this unit—another Matthean literary bracket.

Matthew 13:53–16:12, The Opposition of the Old Community

Matthew 13:53-58, Jesus Is Rejected at Nazareth

NIV	NRSV
[53]When Jesus had finished these parables, he moved on from there. [54]Coming to his hometown, he began teaching the people in their synagogue, and they were amazed. "Where did this man get this wisdom and these miraculous powers?" they asked. [55]"Isn't this the carpenter's son? Isn't his mother's name Mary, and aren't his brothers James, Joseph, Simon and Judas? [56]Aren't all his	[53]When Jesus had finished these parables, he left that place. 54He came to his hometown and began to teach the people[a] in their synagogue, so that they were astounded and said, "Where did this man get this wisdom and these deeds of power? [55]Is not this the carpenter's son? Is not his mother *a* Gk *them*

NIV

sisters with us? Where then did this man get all these things?" ⁵⁷And they took offense at him.

But Jesus said to them, "Only in his hometown and in his own house is a prophet without honor."

⁵⁸And he did not do many miracles there because of their lack of faith.

NRSV

called Mary? And are not his brothers James and Joseph and Simon and Judas? ⁵⁶And are not all his sisters with us? Where then did this man get all this?" ⁵⁷And they took offense at him. But Jesus said to them, "Prophets are not without honor except in their own country and in their own house." ⁵⁸And he did not do many deeds of power there, because of their unbelief.

COMMENTARY

In 13:53, Jesus resumes teaching.[302] The "hardening" of the misunderstanding crowds of the previous chapter does not deter Jesus from continuing his ministry to the Jewish public. He does not abandon them, but continues to teach and heal. This is another indication that the parable discourse reflects the experience of the Matthean church, rather than the plotted narrative at the level of the story. The disciples, apparently present, play no role in this scene and are not mentioned again until 14:15.

Matthew continues to follow the Markan order. Since he has previously used the Markan miracle stories of 4:35–5:43, he omits them here. This allows 13:53-58 to form a bracket with 12:46-50, Jesus' rejection by family and by hometown, bracketing the previous parabolic judgment discourse. Matthew follows closely the wording of this story taken from Mark 6:1-6, but makes the family connections more prominent, corresponding to 12:46-50. He also does this by tightening its structure to make it more clearly chiastic and to make the central part triadic. "Hometown" (v. 54) and "own country" (v. 57) are identical words in Greek. The concluding question of v. 56b is identical with the opening question of v. 54b. The result is a neat triadic chiasm:

A "hometown" (πατρίς *patris*) v. 54a

    B "Where did this man get . . ?"

        (πόθεν τούτῳ *pothen toutō*) v. 54b

        "Is not . . ?" (οὐχ *ouch*) v. 55a

        C "Is not . . ?" (οὐχ *ouch*) v. 55b

        "Are not . . ?" (οὐχι *ouchi*) v. 56

    B′ "Where did this man get . . ?"

        (πόθεν τούτῳ *pothen toutō*) v. 56b

A′ "own country" (πατρίς *patris*) v. 57

The identity of Jesus' family is central to Matthew's understanding of the new community being formed. The hometown folk misunderstand that. Their "taking offense" at him translates σκανδαλίζω (*skandalizō*), which in Matthew represents a fundamental theological and religious misstep, referring to something much deeper than irritation or personal pique.[303]

13:54. Both Mark and Matthew leave Jesus' hometown unnamed. Yet the familiar references to Jesus' family indicate that it is Nazareth, where Jesus grew up (2:22-23; cf. 21:11; 26:71), rather than Capernaum, the adopted center of his ministry (4:12-16; cf. 9:1).

The question about the origin of Jesus' authority is rhetorical, not informational, both anticipating 21:23-27 and looking back on 12:22-37. The question has to do with Jesus' authoritative teaching ("wisdom") and his mighty works, corresponding to the "words and deeds of the Messiah" of Matthew 5–7 and 8–9 respectively (see Introduction and Commentary on 4:23–5:2). The synagogue folk do not doubt that Jesus speaks and acts with authority; the issue is the source of this authority, precisely as in the case with the Pharisees of 12:22-37. The hometown here sides with the opposition; Jesus' family is constituted on another basis than physical relationship.

13:55-56. Matthew probably changes Mark's "carpenter" to "carpenter's son" since it is important to picture Jesus as Son of David, incorporated into the Davidic line as the legal son of Joseph

---

302. The parables discourse was not "teaching" in Matthew's view; see Commentary on 13:12.

303. The verb σκανδαλίζω occurs in 5:29-30; 11:6; 13:21; 15:12; 17:27; 18:6-9; 24:10; 26:31, 33; the related noun σκάνδαλον (*skandalon*) in 13:41; 16:23; 18:7 occurs eight times in Mark and once in Q. Matthew adopted it and used it more than all the other Gospels together (sixteen of twenty-eight occurrences in the Gospels are in Matthew).

(cf. 1:2-25) and to avoid Mark's "carpenter" and "son of Mary," both of which may have been offensive (cf. John 8:41). There is no suggestion in the text of Matthew that Jesus' brothers and sisters are anything but the children of Mary and Joseph, a view still advocated by Tertullian in the late second century with no suggestion that it was unorthodox. The later dogma of Mary's perpetual virginity generated other explanations. The notion that they are stepsiblings, Joseph's children from a previous marriage, was already advocated in the late second or early third century by the *Protevangelium of James* and later became the dominant view in the Greek Orthodox Church, advocated also by some Roman Catholics, such as the fourth-century Epiphanius. Jerome in the fifth century was the first to argue that they were cousins of Jesus, children of neither Mary nor Joseph, which became the dominant view in the later Roman Catholic Church. Matthew is untroubled by any of these later dogmatic problems.

13:57. Although "prophet" is not a major christological category for Matthew, the Matthean Jesus does identify himself with the true prophets of Israel (cf. 17:5; 21:11, 26, 46; 23:37).

13:58. Just as Matthew had rewritten Mark 4:12 in 13:10-17 above, making the unbelief the cause of his action rather than its result, so also here Matthew rewrites Mark to avoid the suggestion that Jesus' failure to work miracles in Nazareth was his own inability. (See Excursus "Interpreting the Miracle Stories in Matthew," 241-51.) When Matthew adds the charge of "unbelief" (ἀπιστία *apistia*) to the Markan story, it carries a depth of meaning that transcends the level of the story. It is not merely that the hometown folk doubted Jesus' ability to do miracles; unbelief places them in the category of those who have rejected the kingdom represented by Jesus. Since there are only two sides in this cosmic struggle (12:30), they have joined the opposition.

After being rejected in "their" synagogue (cf. on 4:23) at Nazareth, Jesus never returns to Nazareth, nor does he ever again enter a synagogue.

Matthew 14:1-12, The Death of John the Baptist

NIV

14 At that time Herod the tetrarch heard the reports about Jesus, ²and he said to his attendants, "This is John the Baptist; he has risen from the dead! That is why miraculous powers are at work in him."

³Now Herod had arrested John and bound him and put him in prison because of Herodias, his brother Philip's wife, ⁴for John had been saying to him: "It is not lawful for you to have her." ⁵Herod wanted to kill John, but he was afraid of the people, because they considered him a prophet.

⁶On Herod's birthday the daughter of Herodias danced for them and pleased Herod so much ⁷that he promised with an oath to give her whatever she asked. ⁸Prompted by her mother, she said, "Give me here on a platter the head of John the Baptist." ⁹The king was distressed, but because of his oaths and his dinner guests, he ordered that her request be granted ¹⁰and had John beheaded in the prison. ¹¹His head was brought in on a

NRSV

14 At that time Herod the ruler[a] heard reports about Jesus; ²and he said to his servants, "This is John the Baptist; he has been raised from the dead, and for this reason these powers are at work in him." ³For Herod had arrested John, bound him, and put him in prison on account of Herodias, his brother Philip's wife,[b] ⁴because John had been telling him, "It is not lawful for you to have her." ⁵Though Herod[c] wanted to put him to death, he feared the crowd, because they regarded him as a prophet. ⁶But when Herod's birthday came, the daughter of Herodias danced before the company, and she pleased Herod ⁷so much that he promised on oath to grant her whatever she might ask. ⁸Prompted by her mother, she said, "Give me the head of John the Baptist here on a platter." ⁹The king was grieved, yet out of regard for his oaths and for the guests, he commanded it to be given; ¹⁰he sent and had John beheaded

[a] Gk *tetrarch*   [b] Other ancient authorities read *his brother's wife*
[c] Gk *he*

NIV	NRSV
platter and given to the girl, who carried it to her mother. [12]John's disciples came and took his body and buried it. Then they went and told Jesus.	in the prison. [11]The head was brought on a platter and given to the girl, who brought it to her mother. [12]His disciples came and took the body and buried it; then they went and told Jesus.

COMMENTARY

Matthew here takes over the bizarre story of Mark 6:14-29 (see Commentary there), the only story in either Gospel not directly concerned with Jesus. His interest is entirely concentrated on using the story as a parallel and prefiguration of the Jesus story,[304] especially of the conflict that leads to Jesus' death, in order to make this story into a paradigm of the conflict of kingdoms, represented by the incursion of the kingdom of God into this world in the advent of Jesus (see Reflections below). Matthew streamlines the Markan story, reducing it from 302 to 172 words, eliminating everything that does not serve his purpose and modifying it to emphasize the conflict-of-kingdoms theme.

Just as both John and Jesus preach the kingdom of God (3:2; 4:17), so also both are explicitly identified as prophets (21:11, 26). In the preceding narrative, Matthew has not only followed both Q and Mark in picturing John in Elijah-like terms (see Commentary on 3:4) but also has gone beyond them in specifically identifying John as Elijah (see 11:14; cf. 17:10-12). This story too evokes the image of Elijah, since Herod/Herodias/John are parallel to Ahab/Jezebel/Elijah in 1 Kings 17–19. Despite Matthew's drastic condensation of the story, he adds words to Mark that specifically identify John as a prophet, in words that anticipate a similar identification of Jesus (14:5b; cf. 21:11, 46).

In Mark, the story is a "flashback" that fills the narrative space between the sending of the Twelve in 6:13 and their return in 6:30. Since Matthew had moved that section of Mark forward to 10:1-42, and never narrates the departure or return of the Twelve on their mission, the story of John's death now falls directly after the rejec-

tion at Nazareth, with only a new vague transitional phrase, "at that time" (cf. 3:1; 11:25; 12:1). While Herod's comment is no longer appropriate, as it was in its Markan context,[305] this altering of the chronology has the effect of placing Matthew's specific identification of John as a prophet immediately after Jesus' implicit self-designation as a prophet in 13:57. Matthew has adopted the deuteronomistic view of Israel's prophets, already incorporated in Q, that Israel always rejects the true prophet, whose destiny it is to suffer (5:12; 23:37).

14:1. Herod Antipas, the son of Herod the Great of the birth story 2:1-23, was the Roman puppet ruler of Galilee and Perea (cf. Luke 3:1). Despite Mark 6:14, Herod Antipas never had the title "king," which Matthew changes to the correct "tetrarch." Herod's almost casual identification of Jesus as John resurrected shows how widespread the idea of resurrection had become. It also illustrates that the Christian idea of the resurrection of Jesus is more than a mere resuscitation or return from the dead (see 28:1-20), for although Herod believes that Jesus is someone returned from the grave, in Matthew's view he by no means has Christian faith in the resurrection!

14:3. The Herodian family tree is large and complex, since Herod the Great had ten wives, with many sons and grandsons named Herod (see Fig. 9). Herod Antipas had married Herodias, the divorced wife of his brother (this is the meaning of "have" in 4b). According to Josephus, the two

---

304. Like Jesus, John preaches the kingdom of God, is regarded as a prophet, is "delivered up" (παραδίδωμι *paradidōmi*), is executed at the will of the Jewish authorities, and is placed in a tomb by his disciple(s). Herod's "Jesus is John" (14:2) both suggests and reinforces this parallel.

305. In Mark 6, Herod hears of the success of Jesus' mission and thinks he must be John the Baptist restored to life. In Matthew, there is nothing in the preceding pericope of the rejection at Nazareth to evoke this response from Herod. This is one of numerous passages in Matthew that presuppose Mark, and is additional evidence that Matthew used Mark as a source, and (consciously or unconsciously) assumed familiarity with it on the part of his intended readers.

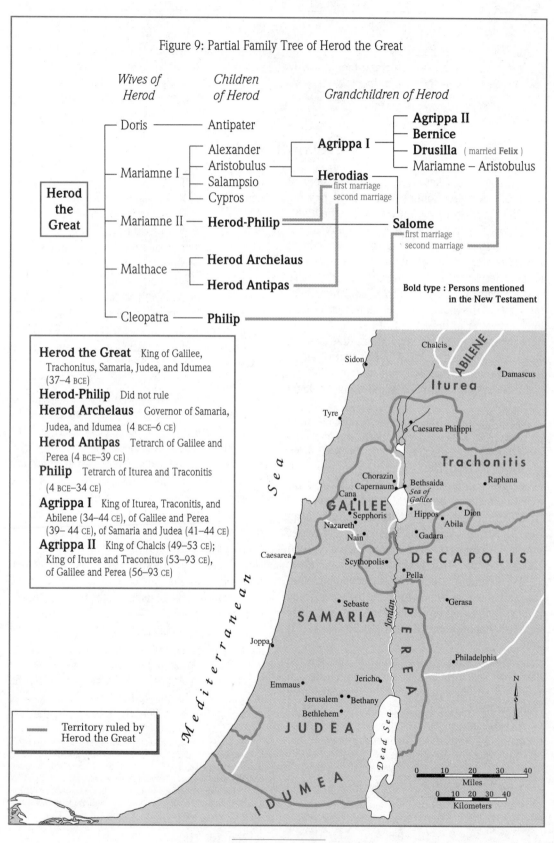

Figure 9: Partial Family Tree of Herod the Great

Wives of Herod — *Children of Herod* — *Grandchildren of Herod*

Doris —— Antipater

Mariamne I
- Alexander
- Aristobulus —— Agrippa I
  - Agrippa II
  - Bernice
  - Drusilla (married Felix)
  - Mariamne – Aristobulus
- Herodias
- Salampsio
- Cypros

first marriage
second marriage

Mariamne II —— Herod-Philip —————— Salome

first marriage
second marriage

Malthace
- Herod Archelaus
- Herod Antipas

Cleopatra —— Philip

Bold type : Persons mentioned in the New Testament

Herod the Great   King of Galilee, Trachonitus, Samaria, Judea, and Idumea (37–4 BCE)

Herod-Philip   Did not rule

Herod Archelaus   Governor of Samaria, Judea, and Idumea (4 BCE–6 CE)

Herod Antipas   Tetrarch of Galilee and Perea (4 BCE–39 CE)

Philip   Tetrarch of Iturea and Traconitis (4 BCE–34 CE)

Agrippa I   King of Iturea, Traconitis, and Abilene (34–44 CE), of Galilee and Perea (39– 44 CE), of Samaria and Judea (41–44 CE)

Agrippa II   King of Chalcis (49–53 CE); King of Iturea and Traconitus (53–93 CE), of Galilee and Perea (56–93 CE)

Territory ruled by Herod the Great

husbands were half-brothers. Josephus also reports the place of John's imprisonment as Machaerus, one of Herod's fortress palaces east of the Jordan, similar to the better-known Masada.[306] Matthew is not specific, but seems to locate the birthday party and execution of John in its more natural location in Galilee, for Galilean locations bracket this story in 13:58 and 14:13, with no suggestion of a change of location.

14:4. Royal honor and the legality of the royal marriage are both attacked by John. John's protest was not against the immorality of the Herodian court in general, but had to do with the Torah; he proclaimed the marriage of Herod and Herodias to be unlawful. In another parallel with Jesus, John too did not come to destroy the Law but as its advocate (cf. 5:17-20). The violation of Torah was not divorce and remarriage as such, which was provided for by the Law, but the violation of the purity code forbidding the marriage of close relatives (Lev 18:16; 20:21).[307] Also, the tetrarch's new marriage was a politically sensitive issue, since he had divorced the daughter of the Nabatean king in order to marry Herodias, a move that eventually became a factor in the hostilities that led to war between the two countries. At another level, the reader knows that Herod and Herodias live in violation of Jesus' teaching against divorce and oaths (5:31-37).

14:5. Over against John (and Jesus) as representatives of the kingdom of God, Matthew's understanding of Herod as representative of the anti-kingdom is also seen in his rewriting of Mark to make Herod the direct opponent of John. Mark 6:17-28 pictures Herod as an admirer and defender of John. In Mark, Herod is manipulated into executing him by the evil cunning of Herodias, responsible not only for his death but for his original arrest as well. Here, Herod himself arrests John and wants to kill him, his murderous intent restrained only by popular opinion of John as a prophet—precisely parallel to the conflict that will lead to Jesus' death (cf. 21:45-46). Thus in Matthew there is no basis for "was grieved" (περίλυπος *perilypos*), another instance of Matthew presupposing Mark.

14:6. The daughter of Herodias is not named in the Bible.[308] Nor does the Bible give her age (κοράσιον [*korasion*] refers to a girl at any age prior to marriage, as in 9:24-25) or represent her dance as lewd. This silence has given legend and art much room to develop the picture of Herodias as the conniving female and Salome as the lascivious dancer, a tradition that says more about the readers of the Gospels than the message of either Mark or Matthew.[309]

---

306. Josephus *Antiquities of the Jews* 18:136. For more details about the Herod dynasty, see Stewart Perowne, *The Later Herods: The Political Background of the New Testament* (Nashville: Abingdon, 1958). See also "Herod (Family)," *IDB* (Nashville: Abingdon, 1962) 2:585-94; "Herodian Dynasty," *ABD* (Garden City, N.Y.: Doubleday, 1992) 3:173-74.

307. According to Josephus, Herodias was not only the wife of Herod's brother, but also the niece of both of them.

308. The name "Salome" comes from Josephus *Antiquities of the Jews*, 18.5.4.

309. See Janice Capel Anderson, "Feminist Criticism: The Dancing Daughter," in Janice Capel Anderson and Stephen D. Moore, eds., *Mark and Method: New Approaches in Biblical Studies* (Minneapolis: Fortress, 1992) 103-34; provides much additional bibliographical information.

REFLECTIONS

1. Our lives are not lived in power vacuums or fire-free zones, but within an arena of clashing force fields. Matthew's story throughout brings the reader within the conflict of kingdoms, initiated by the advent of Jesus (see Overview of Part One, on 2:1-23, on 12:22-37, and Excursus "Kingdom of Heaven in Matthew," 288-94). In 14:9, Matthew preserves Mark's title "king," which he knows is historically incorrect (cf. 14:1) in order to express his view of the conflict of kingdoms inherent in this story. Matthew wants to picture Herod not merely as an evil or weak individual, but, along with other Jewish leaders, as a this-worldly representative of the kingdom of Satan, opposing the kingdom of God. Although John, Herod, and Herodias are historical figures, and the death of John, like the death of Jesus, occurred in history and not merely in a story, it is theology, not history, that dominates the narrative. This also means that the theological picture fails to do historical justice to the empirical Jewish leaders, who play a symbolic role in Matthew's theological story. The story should not be used to fuel the fires of anti-Semitism or anti-Judaism, or even to disparage the purported evil of first-century Jewish leaders. It calls on the reader to discern the demonic anti-kingdom-of-God powers that pervade our own time, and to take a stand with John and Jesus—though the story also makes clear who has the power in this-worldly confrontations, and serves as a call to faithful witness (see Jesus' mission charge to his disciples in 10:5-42, esp. 16-18, 24-33).

The story does not operate moralistically against oaths, divorce, partying, and dancing, but, like the conflict between Herod and Jesus in 2:1-23, portrays the fundamental struggle initiated by the kingdom of God and the fate of those who are committed to it. Who wins in this conflict? John appears to be just another example of those who take their stand on behalf of the revealed will of God against the powers that be. His fate is more absurd than most, expending his one and only life as the result of a birthday party dance. Matthew does not reassure the reader that John will somehow be vindicated or rewarded. The last picture we have of him is of his headless corpse being interred by his disciples. Yet the story intentionally evokes the story of Jesus, for whom "he was buried" is followed by "on the third day God raised him from the dead." Like everything else in the Gospel of Matthew, the story of John should not be proclaimed in isolation, but only as an element of the larger story of which it is a part. Each story calls the reader to faith in the crucified and risen one, and in the process redefines what it means to "win."

2. Matthew's rearrangement of the Markan narrative has enabled him to place this story just after the scenes in which Jesus has redefined the meaning of family relationships (see 13:53-58). Matthew values the sacredness of family relationships and uses language from the world of the family to express his deepest religious affirmations (brother and sister; father and mother). Yet the Herod story shows the problem with false and overvalued family relationships and the pressure of social relationships in general to line up with the wrong kingdom. It is Herod who, in defense of family honor and under the pressure of the presence of his guests at the party, kills the prophet of God. Matthew values family, colleagues, and friends, but does not sentimentalize, idealize, or absolutize relationships that can become an idolatrous alternative to commitment to the one God.[310]

310. See Patte, *Matthew,* 208.

Matthew 14:13-21, Healing and Feeding the Crowds

NIV	NRSV
[13]When Jesus heard what had happened, he withdrew by boat privately to a solitary place. Hearing of this, the crowds followed him on foot from the towns. [14]When Jesus landed and saw a large crowd, he had compassion on them and healed their sick. [15]As evening approached, the disciples came to him and said, "This is a remote place, and it's already getting late. Send the crowds away, so they can go to the villages and buy themselves some food."	13Now when Jesus heard this, he withdrew from there in a boat to a deserted place by himself. But when the crowds heard it, they followed him on foot from the towns. [14]When he went ashore, he saw a great crowd; and he had compassion for them and cured their sick. [15]When it was evening, the disciples came to him and said, "This is a deserted place, and the hour is now late; send the crowds away so that they may go into the villages and buy food for themselves." [16]Jesus said to them, "They need not go away;

NIV

¹⁶Jesus replied, "They do not need to go away. You give them something to eat."

¹⁷"We have here only five loaves of bread and two fish," they answered.

¹⁸"Bring them here to me," he said. ¹⁹And he directed the people to sit down on the grass. Taking the five loaves and the two fish and looking up to heaven, he gave thanks and broke the loaves. Then he gave them to the disciples, and the disciples gave them to the people. ²⁰They all ate and were satisfied, and the disciples picked up twelve basketfuls of broken pieces that were left over. ²¹The number of those who ate was about five thousand men, besides women and children.

NRSV

you give them something to eat." ¹⁷They replied, "We have nothing here but five loaves and two fish." ¹⁸And he said, "Bring them here to me." ¹⁹Then he ordered the crowds to sit down on the grass. Taking the five loaves and the two fish, he looked up to heaven, and blessed and broke the loaves, and gave them to the disciples, and the disciples gave them to the crowds. ²⁰And all ate and were filled; and they took up what was left over of the broken pieces, twelve baskets full. ²¹And those who ate were about five thousand men, besides women and children.

COMMENTARY

The contrast between the two kingdoms continues, as the banquet over which "King" Herod presides is implicitly contrasted with the meal provided by King Jesus. Matthew continues to follow the Markan order, directly connecting it to the preceding story, ignoring the Markan structure in which the story of John's death is a flashback. Matthew has little interest in such "realistic" chronology—in this very context, for instance, he has evening come twice on the same day (14:15, 23), and has Jesus depart in a boat, although the last mentioned location was the synagogue in landlocked Nazareth (13:54). Matthew has manipulated the chronological connections so that Jesus' withdrawal (ἀναχωρέω anachōreō) comes as direct response to the announcement of John's death. The geography here is not entirely clear; Matthew apparently wants the reader to understand that Jesus withdraws to the other side of the lake, where Herod Antipas has no authority. Once again, the sovereign representative of the kingdom of God, when faced with the hostile power of the kingdom of this world, does not respond with violence, but demonstrates the nature of his kingship by withdrawing.[311]

The mini-drama has three scenes: (1) setting the stage by Jesus' withdrawal to the other side of the lake (14:13-14; Matthew has no interest in the exact location), where he meets the crowds and heals their sick;[312] (2) the dialogue with the disciples (14:15-17); (3) the miracle itself (14:18-21). The central and longest part is the dialogue with the disciples. The story does not have the typical elements of a miracle story, lacking among other items the concluding response of the crowd.

In its journey through the pre-Gospel tradition and in its Markan form, this potent story has been reinterpreted in many ways (there are six versions of it in the NT) to express many dimensions of christological faith, incorporating numerous features from the Bible, Jewish tradition, and Christian experience:

❖ the wilderness setting for the people of God, en route from captivity to the promised land (Exod 13:18; "wilderness" occurs 92 times in Exodus–Deuteronomy)

❖ recalcitrant Israelites/disciples, who doubt that food can be provided in the wilderness (Exod 16:2-3 = Mark 6:35-38)

311. In Mark 6:30, Jesus' departure ("go away" [ἀπέρχομαι aperchomai], not "withdraw" [ἀναχωρέω anachōreō]) also is a response to an announcement from disciples, using the same word ("told" [ἀπήγγειλαν apēggeilan]), but there the announcement that incites Jesus' action is from his own returning disciples, a scene for which Matthew has made no place. On the key place ἀναχωρέω has in the Matthean story, see Commentary on 4:12 and 12:15.

312. Mark's "teaching" is replaced with "healing." With vv. 34-36, a bracket is formed, marking off 14:14-36 as a healing interlude within this conflict section. Conflicts resume at 15:1. Likewise, Matthew replaces Mark's "many" with his characteristic "crowds" to maintain continuity with the preceding. Despite their description in chap. 13, the crowds are still considered potential disciples.

❖ God leads the people, who are like sheep without a shepherd (Num 27:17 = Mark 6:34)

❖ the people are arranged in military companies (Exod 13:18 = Mark 6:40)

❖ God as shepherd triggers Psalm 23 and its "green grass" (Ps 23:2 = Mark 6:39 [an allusion to Scripture, not a historical botanical note])

❖ the giving of the manna (Exodus 16; Numbers 11; developed especially in the Johannine version of the story [John 6:1-58])

❖ Elisha's miraculous provision of food (2 Kgs 4:42-44). The miracle followed the death of Elijah (John, in the Gospel story). Elisha overcame protests and had a quantity left over—all of which are paralleled in the Gospel story.

❖ Jesus, accused of being a glutton (11:19), provided table fellowship to all, including "publicans and sinners."

❖ Jesus' eucharistic last meal with his disciples (Mark 14:17-25 = Matt 26:20-29), in which he assumes the role of head of the new family he is creating, providing food and pronouncing the table blessing (particularly appropriate in Matthew, where this story follows closely on 13:53-58)

❖ the messianic banquet as part of the eschatological imagery, which will include not only bread but also fish or sea creatures (cf. 2 Bar 29:3-8; 4 Ezra 6:52; cf. Ps 74:14; Isa 27:1).

Matthew does not develop all the overtones of this resonant story. He compresses the Markan version, making it one-third shorter, omitting and rewriting the elements that reflect badly on the disciples, omitting the features that picture the community as the wandering people of God in the wilderness, and concentrating especially on the eucharistic features, which he emphasizes.[313] The following parallels may be readily observed in the English translation, even more apparent in Greek:

14:15 "when it was evening"[314]	26:20 "when it was evening"
14:19 "sit down"	26:20 "took his place" (same Greek word, ἀνάκειμαι *anakeimai*)[316]
14:19 "Taking the five loaves"	26:26 "took a loaf of bread"
14:19 "and blessed"	26:26 "and after blessing it"[317]
14:19 "broke the loaves, and gave them to the disciples"[315]	26:26 "broke it, gave it to the disciples"
14:20 "ate"	26:26 "eat"
14:20 "all"	26:27 "all"

14:13. They are now on the east shore of the sea, Gentile territory, but the crowds are from the western, Jewish side. Does Matthew want the crowds (potential disciples) to see that following Jesus means eating among Gentiles? Or does Matthew note and use his geographical settings so subtly (cf. 15:29-39)?

14:15-17. The disciples are concerned for the crowds, who are not pictured as hungry and destitute, unable to purchase food, but as being so enthralled by Jesus' healing activity (Matthew has replaced Mark's "teaching" with "healing," v. 14) that they are reluctant to leave. Jesus encourages the continuing presence of the crowds, uncommitted as they are. His charge to the disciples, "you give them something to eat," is no longer met by the sarcastic response of Mark 6:37, but only by their volunteering the information of their inadequate resources.[318] Not misunderstanding, but lack of faith is the characteristic trait of Matthean disciples (although "little faith" [ὀλιγόπιστος *oligopistos*] does not explicitly occur until v. 31). The rewriting also avoids Jesus' having to ask an informational question, which Matthew is more hesitant to do than is his Markan source.

14:18-21. The sovereign Lord Jesus has known all along what he would do (cf. 16*b*). He

---

313. Matthew is not interested in preserving the wilderness motif in this story, and thus describes the location only as a "deserted place" (ἔρημος τόπος *erēmos topos*), not the "wilderness" (ἐρημία *erēmia*) as in 15:33. He likewise eliminates the Markan allusion to the military companies of the Israelites in the wilderness ("by fifties and by hundreds") and the "sheep without a shepherd" allusion to Num 27:17, which he had already used in 9:36. The eucharistic focus is emphasized by omitting all reference to the fish after 14:19*a*.

314. Matthew here modifies the Markan phrase to enhance the correspondence between the two scenes.

315. Matthew omits Mark's reference to the fish, not particularly appropriate to the eucharistic imagery. The retrospective discussion in 16:5-12 considers only the loaves, and not the fish.

316. The word ἀνάκειμαι connotes not merely sitting on the grass as at a picnic, but "reclining" in the Greco-Roman fashion, as at a formal banquet, another echo of the messianic banquet (see Commentary on 26:20).

317. Matthew here follows Mark in using the same Greek word for "blessing" in each case (εὐλογέω *eulogeō*), different from the Luke/Paul εὐχαριστέω (*eucharisteō*), which Matthew does use in the feeding of the 4,000 (15:36), again following Mark.

318. Here as elsewhere Matthew spares the disciples. See, e.g., Matthew's omission of a similar sarcastic comment from Mark 5:31 = Matt 9:21.

commands both the disciples and the crowds. In words and actions anticipating the eucharistic scene, Jesus breaks the bread (the fish are lost sight of after 19a), and the disciples distribute it to the crowd, satisfying their hunger. The abundance of leftover fragments is not a moralizing lesson in conservation, but a documentation of the greatness of the miracle. It is a counterpicture of the Mosaic manna, which could not be preserved (Exod 16:4-5, 13-21), and portrays the messianic times, when hunger will be replaced by extravagance.[319] Likewise, Matthew's addition of "besides women and children" (as in 15:38) is neither an inadvertent, condescending sexist comment nor an effort to be inclusive. Matthew exploits the ambiguity of the Markan word ἄνδρες (*andres*), which can be understood in an inclusive sense of "people" or in the limited sense of "males." Mark obviously intended it in the broader sense, but Matthew takes it in the limited sense, in order to expand the numbers of people present and thus the greatness of the miracle (cf. v. 35), and to evoke the image of the people of God in the wilderness, between Egypt and the promised land, sustained by manna, who are described in similar terms (Exod 12:37).

319. Cf. 2 Bar 29:3-8.

REFLECTIONS

On the issues involved in interpreting Gospel miracle stories in general, see Excursus "Interpreting the Miracle Stories in Matthew," 241-51.

This story was regarded as especially important in early Christianity, the only one recorded in all four Gospels (Matt 14:13-21; Mark 6:32-44; Luke 9:10b-17; John 6:1-15), with the variant "Feeding of the Four Thousand" in Mark 8:1-10 and Matt 15:32-39, making a total of six versions of the story. As in all Gospel stories (cf. Introduction), many layers of meaning shimmer through the present text, focusing on the levels of the historical Jesus, the tradition of the church, and the text of the Gospels.

The story certainly has a historical core in the sense that there was a historical Jesus who was a compassionate person who responded to people in need. The whole event of Jesus' life, death, and resurrection was pictured by Christian faith as God's response to humanity's deepest needs, here portrayed as hungering multitudes. Scholars are divided on whether there is a historical core to this particular story, however. The basic positions are:

(1) A miraculous event of feeding hungry people actually happened in the life of Jesus. This view is advocated not only by conservative and fundamentalist students who attempt to take everything in the Bible as literal history, but also by such scholars as Rudolf Otto, who regarded Jesus as a charismatic figure from whose presence sick people went away healed and hungry people went away filled.[320]

(2) The sacramental explanation of Albert Schweitzer, who argued that Jesus conducted a symbolic meal for multitudes of his followers in the desert in which bits of bread were distributed as a "veiled eschatological sacrament" proleptically celebrating the messianic banquet, and that the account of this event was later elaborated into a miracle story.[321]

(3) The rationalistic explanation of H. E. G. Paulus, who argued that "what really happened" was a lesson in unselfishness, as Jesus and his disciples shared the little food they had, which then shamed others into sharing their food, so that there was enough for all.[322] Ernst Renan's romantic *Life of Jesus* presented a similar non-miraculous explanation in which Jesus led his followers into the desert for a period during which time they lived frugally on skimpy rations, the account of which was later developed into a miracle story.[323]

320. Rudolf Otto, *Kingdom of God and Son of Man*, rev. ed. (London: Lutterworth, 1943), 333-76.
321. Albert Schweitzer, *The Quest of the Historical Jesus* (New York: Macmillan, 1968) 379.
322. H. E. G. Paulus, *Das Leben Jesu* (1828), cited in Schweitzer, *Quest of the Historical Jesus*, 52.
323. Ernst Renan, *The Life of Jesus* (Garden City: Doubleday, n.d.; original French edition 1863) 160.

(4) The story is not based on any particular event in the life of Jesus, but is a symbolic representation of the meaning of the Christ-event as a whole, with overtones of the eucharist and the eschatological pictures of fellowship and plenty for all. Many contemporary Gospel scholars subscribe to this view, which understands the story as a theological expression of the gospel rather than a report. "Symbol" does not mean "allegory," however. The story as a whole portrays God's act in Christ in meeting human need, but the five loaves do not represent the five books of Torah; the two fish do not represent the two covenants. Nor is the symbolic meaning of the story an alternative to its concrete picture of Jesus and his disciples meeting real human need. Just as the disciples' commission of chap. 10 follows the portrayal of Jesus' messianic power in chaps. 5–9, so also here Jesus' miraculous power involves his disciples.

However the story is interpreted, Jesus' charge to his disciples stands: "You give them something to eat."[324] The source of the feeding is God, but the resources are human. The work of the disciples, the "bread" of human effort, is honored, used, and magnified by Jesus.

324. See Leander E. Keck, "Limited Resources; Unlimited Possibilities," in *The Bible in the Pulpit: The Renewal of Biblical Preaching* (Nashville: Abingdon, 1978) 160-68.

Matthew 14:22-36, Walking on the Water and Healing the Sick

NIV

[22]Immediately Jesus made the disciples get into the boat and go on ahead of him to the other side, while he dismissed the crowd. [23]After he had dismissed them, he went up on a mountainside by himself to pray. When evening came, he was there alone, [24]but the boat was already a considerable distance[a] from land, buffeted by the waves because the wind was against it.

[25]During the fourth watch of the night Jesus went out to them, walking on the lake. [26]When the disciples saw him walking on the lake, they were terrified. "It's a ghost," they said, and cried out in fear.

[27]But Jesus immediately said to them: "Take courage! It is I. Don't be afraid."

[28]"Lord, if it's you," Peter replied, "tell me to come to you on the water."

[29]"Come," he said.

Then Peter got down out of the boat, walked on the water and came toward Jesus. [30]But when he saw the wind, he was afraid and, beginning to sink, cried out, "Lord, save me!"

[31]Immediately Jesus reached out his hand and caught him. "You of little faith," he said, "why did you doubt?"

[32]And when they climbed into the boat, the

[a]24 Greek *many stadia*

NRSV

[22]Immediately he made the disciples get into the boat and go on ahead to the other side, while he dismissed the crowds. [23]And after he had dismissed the crowds, he went up the mountain by himself to pray. When evening came, he was there alone, [24]but by this time the boat, battered by the waves, was far from the land,[a] for the wind was against them. [25]And early in the morning he came walking toward them on the sea. [26]But when the disciples saw him walking on the sea, they were terrified, saying, "It is a ghost!" And they cried out in fear. [27]But immediately Jesus spoke to them and said, "Take heart, it is I; do not be afraid."

[28]Peter answered him, "Lord, if it is you, command me to come to you on the water." [29]He said, "Come." So Peter got out of the boat, started walking on the water, and came toward Jesus. [30]But when he noticed the strong wind,[b] he became frightened, and beginning to sink, he cried out, "Lord, save me!" [31]Jesus immediately reached out his hand and caught him, saying to him, "You of little faith, why did you doubt?" [32]When they got into the boat, the wind ceased. [33]And those in the boat worshiped him, saying, "Truly you are the Son of God."

[a]Other ancient authorities read *was out on the sea*
[b]Other ancient authorities read *the wind*

NIV

wind died down. ³³Then those who were in the boat worshiped him, saying, "Truly you are the Son of God."

³⁴When they had crossed over, they landed at Gennesaret. ³⁵And when the men of that place recognized Jesus, they sent word to all the surrounding country. People brought all their sick to him ³⁶and begged him to let the sick just touch the edge of his cloak, and all who touched him were healed.

NRSV

34When they had crossed over, they came to land at Gennesaret. ³⁵After the people of that place recognized him, they sent word throughout the region and brought all who were sick to him, ³⁶and begged him that they might touch even the fringe of his cloak; and all who touched it were healed.

COMMENTARY

14:22-24. Mark's confusing geography is clarified by Matthew. The feeding of the five thousand took place on the east bank of the Sea of Galilee, and the disciples go by boat to the west bank, where they land.

For the first time in Matthew, the disciples are sent forth without Jesus—the Jesus who represents "God with us" (see Commentary on 1:23).[325] In the previous boat and storm scene, of which this is reminiscent, Jesus commands them to depart, but precedes them into the boat and they follow him (8:18, 23). They are in the storm-tossed boat, symbolic of the church's stormy missionary journey through history, but in that story he is with them on the sea, in the boat (see 8:23-27). In the present story they are sent forth alone, and Jesus, who represents the presence of God, is not with them. At the level of Matthean understanding, this may be the meaning of Jesus' "compelling" them to depart ("constrained," KJV; "insisted," J. B. Phillips). Matthew's rewriting of Mark emphasizes the separation between Jesus and the disciples; Jesus was "alone by himself" (κατ᾽ ἰδίαν *kat' idian* is added to Mark's μόνος *monos*), and the disciples are "far from the land" (literally "many stadia," replacing Mark's "in the midst of the sea"). Strangely enough, this is the first time in the Gospel that Jesus

is pictured as praying. He who will shortly act and speak in the person of God is first portrayed as praying in dependence on God. Although the phrase in v. 22 is reminiscent of 5:1, this is not the mountain of teaching, but the mountain of communion with God, as in 17:1-8. The boat/church symbolism of 8:23-27 is strengthened by representing the boat as "being tortured" (βασανίζω *basanizō*) by the waves (not the disciples laboring at rowing, as in Mark). This description is as strange as the "earthquake" in the sea of 8:24. In both cases, Matthew allows his symbolism to shape his description, for in both cases he is thinking of the suffering the church will experience during its mission on which it is sent forth "alone" (i.e., "without" the Jesus who promised to always be with them, 28:20).

The picture is not limited to its ecclesial and missionary symbolism, however. The sea itself in biblical thought connotes the forces of chaos, held at bay in the creative act of God, but always threatening (Gen 1:1-10; 7:11; Pss 18:15-16; 69:1-3; 107:23-32; 144:5-8). To the biblical mind, being on the sea is itself a threat, representing all the anxieties and dark powers that threaten the goodness of the created order. To be at sea evokes images of death, the active power that threatens the goodness of life. The sea is here a barrier that separates the disciples from Jesus, who represents the presence of God. In the midst of the chaos of the world, they are left alone in the boat/church, with only their fragile craft preserving them from its threat, buffeted by the stormy

325. The missionary discourse of 10:5-42 concludes without the disciples ever leaving; it is, in fact, Jesus who departs in 11:1.

The peculiar scene of v. 22, in which Jesus "compels" (ἀναγκάζω *anakazo*, an unusually strong word) the disciples to depart alone, so that he could "dismiss" the crowds (why do they need dismissing?), thus receives an explanation: The scene is contrived to set up the situation of the disciples being "alone" in the boat "without" Jesus, so the theological point can be made.

winds of conflict and persecution, mentioned three times (vv. 24, 30, 32).

14:25-27. It is impossible for Jesus, who mediates the presence of God, to be with them on this journey to the "other side," as he had promised (28:20). Yet he comes, in the latest and darkest part of the night, walking on the sea (the NIV retains Matthew's precise time as the fourth watch, 3:00 to 6:00 A.M.). Whereas the modern mind thinks of defying the law of gravity, the biblical mind thinks of the one who overcomes the power of chaos ("walking on" = conquest; "sea" = anti-creation chaos monster). From the *Epic of Gilgamesh* onward, it was a commonplace of ancient thought that no human being could perform this feat, reserved for deity.[326] In biblical thought, only God walks on the sea (Job 9:8; 38:16; Ps 77:19; Isa 43:16; 51:9-10; Hab 3:5; Sirach 24:5-6, of Divine Wisdom). Precisely in the midst of this symmetrically constructed story, Jesus does what only God can do, and speaks with the voice of God, "I am." There is no predicate nominative. The formula is first one of simple identification, "It is I [not a ghost as you fear]." But the phrase also evokes the self-identification of God, Yahweh (יהוה YHWH) the one who says absolutely "I am" (see Exod 3:13-15). This does not mean that Matthew here claims that Jesus is Yahweh (he had just pictured him as praying to God), but that the divine presence and assurance is mediated by Jesus, as promised in 1:23. The Matthean rewriting emphasizes the presence of Christ in and with the community in its mission.

14:28-31. These verses, probably composed by Matthew himself, are added to the Markan story (cf. Mark 6:50-51). With this Matthean addition, the ecclesial aspect of the story is underscored, since it is no longer a story about what

Jesus alone can do. The Christ who speaks with authority (chaps. 5–7), acts with authority (chaps. 8–9), and then confers this same authority on his disciples (chap. 10) here shares his power and authority with his disciples. The figure of Peter should not here (or elsewhere in Matthew) be psychologized as impetuous, but later failing. We do not have a psychological profile, but a character in a story representing all the disciples, portraying the theological meaning of discipleship as such. Peter addresses Jesus as a believer would, "Lord" (non-believers in Matthew use other titles). He has the right christological title and shows great personal faith, but he leaves the boat and the community. Then he sees the violence of the storm and begins to sink. For Matthew, Peter's problem was not only that he took his eyes off Jesus, but that he wanted proof of the presence of Christ, and so left the boat in the first place.[327] He cries out with the community prayer adopted from the psalms and common in Christian worship, "Lord, save me" (cf. 8:25). Jesus stretches out his hand, and Peter is saved.[328] The gentle rebuke identifies Peter as the typical disciple in Matthew; "little faith" is the dialectical mixture of courage and anxiety, of hearing the word of the Lord and looking at the terror of the storm, of trust and doubt, which is always an ingredient to Christian existence, even after the resurrection.[329] This last point is underscored by the peculiar word used here for "doubt" (διστάζω *distazō*), which connotes vacillation, not skepticism. It is used elsewhere in the NT only in Matt 28:17 of the disciples in the presence of the risen Lord (cf. Jas 1:6-8).

14:32-33. Matthew drastically rewrites the Markan ending of the story. Instead of utter astonishment, lack of understanding, and hardened hearts, we have falling down and worshiping Jesus, confessing that he is the Son of God. The conclusion is difficult to imagine in a small boat on the lake in Galilee, but reflects the response of a grateful church that experiences the impossible presence of Christ with it in its mission—as promised.

---

326. See *Gilgamesh* 10:71-77 (Shamash the sun god); Homer *Odyssey* 5.54 (Hermes, messenger of the gods); Virgil *Aeneid* 1.147 (Neptune, the sea god); Apollodorus *Bibliotheca* 1.4 (Orion, son of Poseidon the sea god); Dio Chrysostom 3.30 ("divine men" in general); Porphyry *Life of Pythagoreus* 19.91 (Pythagoreus). The motif is especially common in Indian literature, with the Buddhist text *Jataka* 190 telling of a disciple of Buddha who is able to walk on the water while meditating on the Buddha, but who begins to sink when his concentration falters. See W. D. Davies and Dale C. Allison, Jr., *A Critical and Exegetical Commentary on the Gospel According to Saint Matthew*, 2 vols. (Edinburgh: T. & T. Clark, 1988–1991) 2:500; Ulrich Luz, *Das Evangelium nach Matthäus (Mt 8–17)*, Evangelisch-Katholischer Kommentar zum Neuen Testament I/2 (Benziger: Neukirchener Verlag, 1990) 2:407-8; Klaus Berger, M. Eugene Boring, and Carsten Colpe, *Hellenistic Commentary on the New Testament* (Nashville: Abingdon, 1995).

327. To be sure, Jesus grants permission in the one word "come" (v. 29), as previously to the demons in 8:31-32. See Reflections below.

328. See Pss 18:17-18; 69:1-2, 14-15; 144:7-8. Midrashic reflection on these texts provides Matthew material for the amplification of his narrative.

329. See Luz, *Matthäus*, 2:410. For ὀλιγόπιστοι *oligopistoi* in 6:30; 16:8; and especially 8:26, as well as the cognate ὀλιγοπιστία *oligopistia* in 17:20.

The worshipful Christian confession with which the scene concludes illustrates the post-Easter perspective from which this and all the miracle stories are told. The story as a whole is reminiscent of the explicitly post-Easter John 21:1-14, especially the connection of feeding and the sea story, the initial lack of recognition preceding Jesus' self-identification, and Peter's getting out of the boat to come to Jesus. The only other occurrence of the disciples' worshiping Jesus, along with the only other use of διστάζω (distazō) is in the encounter with the resurrected Jesus in Matt 28:17. The revelatory "I am" suggests the post-Easter experiences of the disciples. Although in a pre-Easter narrative framework, this Gospel story resonates with the voice and deeds of the risen Lord.

14:34-36. With 14:14, added by Matthew, this scene forms a bracket that includes the feeding story and the miraculous coming of Jesus to his distressed disciples, a subunit that begins and ends with Jesus healing the multitudes. Prior to this unit, Jesus was engaged in conflict with outsiders, which immediately resumes in 15:1. Although the story of the advent of the kingdom of God inevitably generates conflict, Matthew here inserts an interlude portraying the healing presence of Christ.

REFLECTIONS

The distinctively Matthean meaning of this scene is set in sharp profile by the Matthean addition of vv. 28-31, usually called "Peter's walking on the water." This title misses the point of Matthew's message. Peter is the first disciple, and the typical one (see 16:13-19). However, Matthew will shortly make it clear that even Peter can become the agent and voice of Satan (16:23). This potentially demonic aspect of discipleship is already present in this story.

1. Peter's response ("if it is you") to Jesus' reassuring "I am" of the divine presence is similar to Satan's first words to Jesus (4:3). Peter hears Jesus' claim, just as the contemporary reader of the Gospel hears the Matthean claim that Jesus is the one who makes God present to us (1:23; 28:20). In a chaotic world where such a claim often appears false, hollow, or meaningless, many would like some experiential, spectacular reassurance that it is really so. Peter knows that Jesus had been left back on the beach, just as the modern reader knows that Jesus has been left back there in history. In both cases, it is clearly impossible that he could come to us. So when he appears, walking on the sea, it should be good news, if it could possibly be true. We can resonate with Peter, the typical disciple, when he proposes a test. It doesn't sound like the voice of Satan, especially since Peter is willing to risk death himself to prove the presence of the divine reality (4:5-7)! Just as Jesus had responded to the demons with a one-word granting of permission (8:32), so also with one word he allows Peter to leave the boat. But the initiative was with Peter, and it was an initiative grounded in a lack of faith and putting God to the test.

So the typical "lesson" derived from this text often borders on the demonic misunderstanding of the nature of faith, which Matthew wants to warn us against. The message is not "If he had had enough faith, he could have walked on the water," just as the message to us is not "If we had enough faith, we could overcome all our problems in spectacular ways." This interpretation is wrong in that it identifies faith with spectacular exceptions to the warp and woof of our ordinary days, days that are all subject to the laws of physics and biology. This is wrong because when our fantasies of overcoming this web are shattered by the realities of accident, disease, aging, and circumstance and we begin to sink, this view encourages us to feel guilty because of our "lack of faith."

2. What if the message of this text were "If he had had enough faith, he would have believed the word of Jesus that came to him *in the boat* as mediating the presence and reality of God"? Faith is not being able to walk on the water—only God can do that—but daring to believe, in the face of all the evidence, that God is with us in the boat, made real in the community of faith as it makes its way through the storm, battered by the waves.

3. We have had occasion to notice repeatedly that Matthew's way of telling the Jesus story is dualistic (see 3:7; 6:19-24; 10:26-31; 12:26, 33-35; 13:25, 37). The framework of the whole narrative is the conflict between the kingdom of God and the kingdom of Satan, and these are the only choices; everyone supports one or the other, is for or against Jesus and the kingdom of God he represents (12:30). The Jews and Pharisees of the story are not historical Jews and Pharisees, but represent the kingdom of Satan. The disciples belong to God's kingdom. The story is told with stark contrasts. Yet this dualism is not ontological or absolute. The crowds, though misunderstanding and hardened, are still potential disciples to whom Jesus continues to minister despite the dualistic framework of the story. And texts such as this one show that disciples are potential agents of the demonic. Matthew is not spinning out an ontological theory, but is addressing disciples, warning them not to give up on the recalcitrant crowds who may after all become disciples, and not to be too secure about their status as disciples, for even in their efforts to show their faith they may become agents of the demonic.[330]

330. For a different and less-hopeful reading of Matthew that takes his dualism as more determinative, see Fred W. Burnett, "Exposing the Anti-Jewish Ideology of Matthew's Implied Author," *Semeia* 59 (1992) 155-92.

Matthew 15:1-20, Defilement—Traditional and Real

NIV

15 Then some Pharisees and teachers of the law came to Jesus from Jerusalem and asked, [2]"Why do your disciples break the tradition of the elders? They don't wash their hands before they eat!"

[3]Jesus replied, "And why do you break the command of God for the sake of your tradition? [4]For God said, 'Honor your father and mother'[a] and 'Anyone who curses his father or mother must be put to death.'[b] [5]But you say that if a man says to his father or mother, 'Whatever help you might otherwise have received from me is a gift devoted to God,' [6]he is not to 'honor his father[c]' with it. Thus you nullify the word of God for the sake of your tradition. [7]You hypocrites! Isaiah was right when he prophesied about you:

[8]"'These people honor me with their lips,
　　but their hearts are far from me.
[9]They worship me in vain;
　　their teachings are but rules taught by men.'[d]"

[10]Jesus called the crowd to him and said, "Listen and understand. [11]What goes into a man's mouth does not make him 'unclean,' but what comes

a4 Exodus 20:12; Deut. 5:16　　b4 Exodus 21:17; Lev. 20:9
c6 Some manuscripts *father or his mother*　　d9 Isaiah 29:13

NRSV

15 Then Pharisees and scribes came to Jesus from Jerusalem and said, [2]"Why do your disciples break the tradition of the elders? For they do not wash their hands before they eat." [3]He answered them, "And why do you break the commandment of God for the sake of your tradition? [4]For God said,[a] 'Honor your father and your mother,' and, 'Whoever speaks evil of father or mother must surely die.' [5]But you say that whoever tells father or mother, 'Whatever support you might have had from me is given to God,'[b] then that person need not honor the father.[c] [6]So, for the sake of your tradition, you make void the word[d] of God. [7]You hypocrites! Isaiah prophesied rightly about you when he said:

[8] 'This people honors me with their lips,
　　but their hearts are far from me;
[9] in vain do they worship me,
　　teaching human precepts as doctrines.'"

[10]Then he called the crowd to him and said to them, "Listen and understand: [11]it is not what goes into the mouth that defiles a person, but it is what comes out of the mouth that defiles."

aOther ancient authorities read *commanded, saying*
bOr *is an offering*　　cOther ancient authorities add *or the mother*
dOther ancient authorities read *law*; others, *commandment*

NIV

out of his mouth, that is what makes him 'unclean.'"

¹²Then the disciples came to him and asked, "Do you know that the Pharisees were offended when they heard this?"

¹³He replied, "Every plant that my heavenly Father has not planted will be pulled up by the roots. ¹⁴Leave them; they are blind guides.[a] If a blind man leads a blind man, both will fall into a pit."

¹⁵Peter said, "Explain the parable to us."

¹⁶"Are you still so dull?" Jesus asked them. ¹⁷"Don't you see that whatever enters the mouth goes into the stomach and then out of the body? ¹⁸But the things that come out of the mouth come from the heart, and these make a man 'unclean.' ¹⁹For out of the heart come evil thoughts, murder, adultery, sexual immorality, theft, false testimony, slander. ²⁰These are what make a man 'unclean'; but eating with unwashed hands does not make him 'unclean.'"

[a]14 Some manuscripts guides of the blind

NRSV

¹²Then the disciples approached and said to him, "Do you know that the Pharisees took offense when they heard what you said?" ¹³He answered, "Every plant that my heavenly Father has not planted will be uprooted. ¹⁴Let them alone; they are blind guides of the blind.[a] And if one blind person guides another, both will fall into a pit." ¹⁵But Peter said to him, "Explain this parable to us." ¹⁶Then he said, "Are you also still without understanding? ¹⁷Do you not see that whatever goes into the mouth enters the stomach, and goes out into the sewer? ¹⁸But what comes out of the mouth proceeds from the heart, and this is what defiles. ¹⁹For out of the heart come evil intentions, murder, adultery, fornication, theft, false witness, slander. ²⁰These are what defile a person, but to eat with unwashed hands does not defile."

[a]Other ancient authorities lack of the blind

COMMENTARY

This subunit begins with the arrival of Pharisees and scribes from Jerusalem and extends to the withdrawal of Jesus in 15:21.[331] It is framed by the question of v. 1, to which Jesus returns only in the closing line of v. 20. Thus, although there are two changes of audience dividing the scene into three parts (vv. 1-9 to the Pharisees and scribes; vv. 10-11 to the crowds; vv. 12-20 to the disciples), all of vv. 1-20 is one unit pursuing a single theme. At the two extremes stand the Pharisees and scribes (opponents) and the disciples; the crowds stand in the middle and could go either way (wooed by the Pharisees but also addressed by Jesus as potential disciples). Formally, the unit 15:1-20 is an extended conflict story. After the healing/feeding interlude of 14:13-36, the conflict that dominates the section 13:53–17:27 resumes.

15:1-9, Scene 1—Pharisees and Scribes. Although historically unrealistic, identifying the

331. On Jesus' withdrawal, see 4:12; 12:15.

Pharisees and scribes as being from Jerusalem anticipates the passion story, where the conflict will conclude with the death of Jesus, just as it echoes 2:3, an anticipation of the passion. The question is not occasioned by a particular act, as in Mark 7:1-5, but assumes the absence of the hand-washing ritual as typical Christian practice. Here as elsewhere, the scene is not mere historical report (although it has elements that go back to the life of Jesus), but reflects the conflicts in Matthew's time between Jewish Christians in his church and the emerging Jewish leadership (see Introduction).

15:2. The hand washing at issue was not a matter of hygiene, but of ritual purity. The purity issue itself is not easy for modern Western readers to grasp, but it should not be trivialized as superficial legalism or regarded as primitive superstition. What is "clean" and "unclean" is a matter of maintaining the holiness to which the people of God are called, and it corresponds to God's own holiness. The OT itself takes the matter of holiness, cleanness/uncleanness very seriously and deals with it at length.[332]

Hand washing before meals, however, was not a part of the biblical regulations concerning ritual cleanliness. The only such regulations for laypersons in the Bible are found in Lev 15:11, where ritual impurity contracted by a bodily discharge is not transmitted if the ritually unclean person's hands are rinsed in water. In Exod 30:17-21, priests are instructed to wash their hands and feet as part of the ritual purification for ministering in the tabernacle (cf. Lev 22:4-7). Apparently the Pharisees, a lay movement alienated from the Temple priestly establishment, adapted this priestly practice for themselves as an expression of their conviction that all Israel was a "kingdom of priests" (Exod 19:6) and attempted to implement it as a standard practice in the reconstitution of Judaism after the destruction of the Temple in 70 CE.

The practice in question here is, therefore, neither an item of the biblical purity code (such as the sabbath and the kosher kitchen) nor of general practice in Judaism,[333] but a matter of specifically Pharisaic tradition. In the view of the Pharisees, however, this "tradition of the elders" was ancient, going back to the Sinai revelation, parallel to the written code given there and just as authoritative ('Abot 1:1). By no means did all Jews of Jesus' day share this view of the authority of the oral tradition. Even in Matthew's time, the Pharisees' view, though now dominant, was still competing with other groups as to the identity of the true Israel after the debacle of the 66–70 war and the destruction of the Temple. The Matthean church, though alienated from the synagogue and its leadership, participates in this inner-Jewish struggle. The issue that comes to expression in the Matthean text is, therefore, not "Judaism vs. Christianity" or "Tradition vs. Scripture," but part of an inner-Jewish debate in a particular situation. *"Your* tradition" (15:3) has therefore a very particular meaning: Jesus is responding to a Pharisaic charge and refers specifically to Pharisaic tradition.[334]

The issue is still alive in Matthew's context, where the Pharisees' successors attempt to enforce their understanding of tradition on Jewish-Christian communities still within their sphere of influence. In some, perhaps marginal way no longer clear to us (cf. Introduction), this includes Matthew's church, which is still affected by these debates. The Jesus who within the story speaks to the Pharisees also speaks to Matthew's readers about an issue still of vital importance for understanding what it means to belong to the holy people of God.

15:3-6. The foundation on which Matthew's response is based is not entirely clear. Two streams of Christian tradition have flowed into Matthew's own community: the earlier Q (and some M) traditions that represent a Christianity still loyal to the Torah, and the later Markan traditions representing Law-free Gentile Christianity (see Introduction). Historically, it is not clear how these had been combined in Matthew's community. In any case, Matthew's perspective must be constructed from the Gospel as a whole, not merely from this passage.

The question, which seems on the surface to be legitimate, does not receive a response until v. 20*b,* and then not to the Pharisees who ask it, but to the disciples in private.[335] This is another indication that the genre we are dealing with is not a verbatim report of an event in the life of Jesus, but a Christian interpretation of an issue in the life of the church. Instead of responding to the question, Jesus offers a counterattack, for at the level of the story the Pharisees are not asking a real question, since they have already decided to kill Jesus (12:14). Matthew tightens the entire interchange he finds in Mark, making the parallels and antitheses more striking and more damning; over against the commandment of God, the Pharisees place their own tradition; over against what "God said" (Mark: "Moses said") they place what they themselves say. In v. 6, Matthew actually has the Pharisees promulgating a commandment opposing God's command.

Verses 4-6 picture the Pharisees as interpreting the Torah in such a way as to provide an escape hatch for their members who had aging parents they did not wish to support. They could declare

332. See L. E. Toombs, "Clean and Unclean," *IDB* 1:641-48; James Muilenburg, "Holiness," *IDB* 2:616-25; Rudolf Otto, *The Idea of the Holy* (London: Oxford University Press, 1931); L. William Countryman, *Dirt, Greed, and Sex* (Philadelphia: Fortress, 1988).

333. Note that Matthew specifically omits Mark's generalizing comment about "all the Jews" (7:3), which in any case is historically incorrect. Pharisaic practice prevailed in later Judaism, however. Today, for example, the Passover seder includes the *rachaz,* the ritual of hand washing, with the following prayer: "Praised be thou, O Lord, king of the universe, who hast sanctified us with thy commandments and enjoined upon us the Mitzvah of washing the hands."

334. Here, the Matthean Jesus opposes Pharisaic perspectives. Elsewhere in Matthew, he sometimes supports them (e.g., 22:22-33). Pharisaism itself was not a monolith, but had internal disputes. Thus the Matthean Jesus is pictured as participating in the internal debates of Judaism.

335. Cf. the question from the Baptist's disciples in 9:14, introduced with the same "Why do?" (διὰ τί *dia tĭ*) which receives a reasoned response.

(some of) their property to be dedicated to the Temple, and thus not available to provide for their own parents in their time of need. It is implied that this is a perverse legal fiction designed to avoid keeping one of the most sacred commandments of the Decalogue. There is no documentation for such a practice outside the NT. Historically it is unclear whether in the first century items dedicated to the Temple by a vow could continue to be used by the one who had made the vow. The Mishnah (the later written codification of the rabbis' oral tradition) in fact has provisions for release from vows in cases of need, but we do not know what rules may have been in force in the first century. What we have here is Christian polemics, seen from outside the Jewish tradition. In all such situations, each side looks for data in its opponent's tradition and practice that can be interpreted adversely against the other side. Jews, for example, looking at Christian materials, could charge Christians with violating this same commandment of the Decalogue because they instructed their members to leave father and mother (10:34-37). Insiders on both sides of the conflict understand their own traditions differently from the ways polemical outsiders view them.

15:7-9. Once again Matthew concludes a subsection with a quote from Isaiah, portraying his opponents in a negative light (cf. 13:14-15). Matthew understands Isaiah's charge (Isa 29:13) against false worship of his own day (8th cent. BCE) as a "prophecy" of Matthew's own opponents (cf. Excursus "Matthew as Interpreter of Scripture," 151-54). The point is dependent on the LXX, which is quite different from the MT. The quotation (already in Mark, reflecting pre-Markan tradition), seems to broaden the scope of the polemic. What had previously been a conflict with the Pharisees is now a charge against "this people" as a whole, once again reflecting not the particulars of this context but anticipating the passion story, when the crowds finally join the leadership in rejecting Jesus.

15:10-11, Scene 2—The Crowds. Jesus has not given up on the crowds. They are not already condemned; despite the anticipatory 13:10-17, the option to understand and respond to Jesus' message is still there. The theme now shifts explicitly to the issue of what defiles (makes one ritually unclean, separating one from the holy community and the holiness of God). This was presumably the issue in the question about hand washing. In contrast to Mark 7:19c, which he omits, for Matthew, Jesus' blanket declaration that people are not made unclean by what enters their mouth but by what comes out of it is not a comprehensive pronouncement nullifying the laws of the Torah regarding ritual defilement, such as the food laws.[336] It is, rather, a thoroughly biblical and Jewish mode of declaring the relative importance of the inner commitments of the heart, as they come to expression in the way one speaks and acts, over against the ritual commandments, which are still not abolished. This is the way Matthew understands Hosea 6:6, quoted twice by him (9:13; 12:7), which makes mercy more important than sacrifice, without abolishing the latter—and corresponds to the original meaning of Hosea.

15:12-20, Scene 3—The Disciples. The scene changes again, and the disciples become the only addressees. Into the Markan story Matthew inserts vv. 12-14, mostly composed by him (with a Q point of contact; cf. Luke 6:39). Instead of its typical meaning in Matthew as "caused to stumble"/"sin," σκανδαλίζω (*skandalizō*) here means "were irritated, angered," though the typical meaning cannot be excluded even here as an overtone; their hypocritical encounter with Jesus only deepens the sin of those who have already hardened their hearts and decided against him. The Pharisees are pictured dualistically not as God's planting but the devil's, in terms reminiscent of 13:25, 39, and the same command is given as there: "leave them alone" (ἄφετε *aphete*), 13:30/15:14) for the eschatological judgment of God (but see 17:24-27 and Reflections on 14:28-32). The rhetorical question Jesus asks in Q, "Can the blind lead the blind?" (cf. Luke 6:39) is rewritten by Matthew as a declaration about the Pharisees. Again, this reflects the conflicts between Matthew's church and the Pharisaic leadership in the 70–90 period. It is a theological construal of the conflict from the perspective of the persecuted, not descriptive history (cf. Reflections). Since this is directed exclusively to the disciples, it functions more as warning to insiders

336. On Matthew's understanding of Jesus and the Torah, see 5:17-20 and 15:15-18.

against overrating ritual correctness than as polemic against outsiders.

15:15-18. Peter's question joins directly to v. 11, not to the preceding insertion of vv. 12-14. Jesus' declaration in v. 11 is understood to be a παραβολή (*parabolē*), a provocative wisdom saying whose meaning is not readily apparent. Matthew typically alters Mark's view that the disciples misunderstood, here by changing Mark's "so," "thus" (οὕτως *houtōs*) to the rare word for "still," "yet" (ἀκμήν *akmēn*), signaling that the disciples' misunderstanding is only temporary (cf. 16:11-12).[337] The fact that Matthew (unlike the Gentile Christian author of Mark) does not understand Jesus to be abrogating all the food laws of the Torah itself, but only rejecting the oral tradition of the Pharisees, is seen in his omitting Mark 7:19*c* ("Thus he declared all foods clean").[338]

15:19-20a. What defiles is what proceeds from the heart through the mouth. Matthew here adapts the "vice catalogue" from Mark, which belongs to a category of early Christian moral instruction adopted from Hellenistic Judaism, with many NT examples (e.g., Rom 1:29-31; 1 Cor 6:9-10; 2 Cor 12:20; Gal 5:19-20; Eph 5:3-5; Col 3:5, 8; 1 Tim 1:9-10; 2 Tim 2:3-5; Titus 3:3; 1 Pet 4:3; Rev 9:20-21; 21:8). Matthew concentrates particularly on sins of the heart/mouth— i.e., the linguistic sins that betray the orientation of the heart (cf. 12:34-37), and on the sins of the second table of the Decalogue, arranging them in the order found in Exodus 20 and adding "false witness" to Mark's list, which he has otherwise reduced from thirteen items to seven.

15:20b. The concluding pronouncement, which sounds very much like a rabbinic legal decision on a disputed item of Halakha, returns to the initial question of 15:2, not only rounding off the unit with a neat literary bracket, but also relating the whole discussion strictly to the Pharisaic oral tradition without offering any challenge to the prescriptions of biblical Torah.

---

337. Matthew omits or modifies all of the passages in which the Markan disciples misunderstand; cf. H. J. Held, "Matthew's Understanding of the Law," in *Tradition and Interpretation in Matthew,* eds. Günther Bornkamm, Gerhard Barth, Heinz Joachim Held (Philadelphia: Westminster, 1963) 105-12.

338. Similarly, Matthew 10:9-13 does not include Luke 10:8, instructing the missioners to "eat whatever is set before you," which may have been in Q.

REFLECTIONS

What we hear in this passage is one side of a conflict between church and synagogue in a particular situation at the end of the first century CE. Allowing for this and interpreting it in its historical context, what may we learn of the meaning of the Christian faith?

1. Preaching and teaching from this passage should avoid simplistic caricatures of the historical Pharisees, or portraying our theological opponents in the colors of the Pharisees in the text (*"We* adhere to the Word of God, while *they* are misled by human tradition"). Every religious community, including the NT Christian community, needs tradition as the vehicle for mediating and interpreting the Word of God (cf. 1 Cor 11:2; 2 Thess 2:15; 3:6). No one has, or can have, the pure "word of God" uncontaminated by human ideas or tradition. One meaning of the incarnation is that God affirms the relativity and fragmentariness of human ideas as the vehicle for God's own Word. The treasure is always in clay pots, and both are real—real treasure, real clay (2 Cor 4:7).

2. At the same time, this insight of biblical theology should not lead us to relativize everything as "only" human tradition. In and through human tradition, Jesus and the early church heard the Word of God in a fresh and definitive way. The church of every generation needs to continue to listen for that, not as an alternative to human tradition, but as the Word of the Lord that comes in and through it, transcending it.

3. At the level of the Matthean text, this pericope is a testimony to the dualistic *conflict of kingdoms.* Matthew sees the choice between the message from and about Jesus and the teaching expressed in Pharisaic traditions as an either/or choice between the kingdom of God and the demonic kingdom of Satan. There are only two choices (Matt 12:30). The Pharisees in the story represent the opposing kingdom of Satan. This can be a valid theological construct; in the welter of traditions and interpretations, especially our own, disciples of Christ are called to listen for the Word of God. But we must be wary of confusing theological constructs—Matthew's or our own—with historical reality and labeling Matthew's opponents or our own as "plantings of the devil." (For Matthew's own relativizing of this stark dualism, see 17:24-27 and Reflections on 14:28-32.)

4. The passage might give us a new insight into the meaning of holiness and the concern for purity, without trivializing it or considering it primitive. Empathizing with the concern of Matthew's community for ritual purity and guarding against ritual contamination, which can be seen as somewhat analogous to our own concern for protection from invisible viruses and radiation, may give us new insights into the meaning of the holiness of God and of the holy community, the people of God.

5. This concern for holiness is redirected by the Matthean Jesus toward a concern for the intent of the heart and what comes from it through the mouth. Our concerns are clearly not the same as those that separated the Pharisees and the Matthean church; ritual hand washing matters little to Christians one way or the other. But the text may have a meaning potential that bursts the bounds of the ancient situation. Without rejecting external concerns (Matthew does not), the passage might reorient contemporary readers to the danger of defilement of the heart and word. In the light of Jesus' example and teaching, Christians of every generation need to see themselves as belonging to a community called to holiness, and to ask what in our own time violates this holiness and nullifies the church's witness. There will be debate on this issue just as there was in Matthew's situation, but it is an issue worth debating, and inherent in the vocation to be God's people in a secular and pluralistic world—which as such is still God's world.

Matthew 15:21-28, The Syrophoenician (Canaanite) Woman

<table>
<tr><td>NIV</td><td>NRSV</td></tr>
<tr><td>

²¹Leaving that place, Jesus withdrew to the region of Tyre and Sidon. ²²A Canaanite woman from that vicinity came to him, crying out, "Lord, Son of David, have mercy on me! My daughter is suffering terribly from demon-possession."

²³Jesus did not answer a word. So his disciples came to him and urged him, "Send her away, for she keeps crying out after us."

²⁴He answered, "I was sent only to the lost sheep of Israel."

²⁵The woman came and knelt before him. "Lord, help me!" she said.

²⁶He replied, "It is not right to take the children's bread and toss it to their dogs."

²⁷"Yes, Lord," she said, "but even the dogs eat the crumbs that fall from their masters' table."

²⁸Then Jesus answered, "Woman, you have great faith! Your request is granted." And her daughter was healed from that very hour.

</td><td>

21Jesus left that place and went away to the district of Tyre and Sidon. ²²Just then a Canaanite woman from that region came out and started shouting, "Have mercy on me, Lord, Son of David; my daughter is tormented by a demon." ²³But he did not answer her at all. And his disciples came and urged him, saying, "Send her away, for she keeps shouting after us." ²⁴He answered, "I was sent only to the lost sheep of the house of Israel." ²⁵But she came and knelt before him, saying, "Lord, help me." ²⁶He answered, "It is not fair to take the children's food and throw it to the dogs." ²⁷She said, "Yes, Lord, yet even the dogs eat the crumbs that fall from their masters' table." ²⁸Then Jesus answered her, "Woman, great is your faith! Let it be done for you as you wish." And her daughter was healed instantly.

</td></tr>
</table>

COMMENTARY

Although this story concludes with a miracle, form critically it is more like a pronouncement story or controversy dialogue, with the series of interchanges between Jesus, the disciples, and the woman comprising the longest and central element in the unit. However, as Sharon Ringe points out, "the exchange between Jesus and the woman reverses the pattern usually found in such stories. Usually a situation or event provokes a hostile question from some onlooker to Jesus, to which Jesus responds with a correcting or reproving question and then drives home his point by a concluding statement which the opponent would be hard put to deny. In this story, however, it is Jesus who provides the hostile saying and the woman whose retort trips him up and corrects him."[339] It is questionable that Matthew would agree that the woman "trips up" and "corrects" Jesus, whose gift of healing is not exacted from him but is granted by his sovereign grace.[340] Yet Ringe's form-critical point is important, for the story does describe a reversal brought about by the woman's persistent faith.

15:21. Again Jesus' response to the threatening Pharisees of the previous story is to "withdraw" (ἀναχωρέω *anachōreō*),[341] this time into Gentile territory, which is emphasized both by the biblical phrase "Tyre and Sidon" (Mark had only "Tyre") and by designating the woman a "Canaanite" (Mark had "Syrophoenician"). The scene draws from biblical imagery to portray a dramatic contrast between the Jewish Messiah sent only to Israel on the one hand, and their archetypal enemies, subject to demons, on the other. Jesus does not enter a house (as he had in Mark 7:24, which adds that he did not want to be recognized, but Matthew is typically uninterested in Mark's messianic secret) to conform to Matthew's rule that Jesus never enters a Gentile house, and to avoid Mark's suggestion that Jesus' attempt at secrecy was unsuccessful.

15:22-25. Nonetheless, the woman addresses Jesus with the (later) Christian language of faith and worship: "Have mercy on me, Lord, Son of David"—all Christian confessions reflecting the liturgy of the church, adapted from the prayer language of the Psalter.[342] Jesus ignores her, and the disciples are likewise unsympathetic. Jesus responds to their request to send her away, somewhat incongruously, by repeating his restriction of 10:6 that his mission is only to the lost (i.e., leaderless) sheep of the house of Israel. The woman is undeterred, and in the kneeling posture of Christian worship continues to address her psalm-like petition to Jesus as "Lord."

15:26. For the first time Jesus addresses her directly. The crudeness of the analogy that compares Jews to children (of the "house of Israel" of v. 24) and Gentiles to dogs cannot be obviated by pointing to the use of the diminutive (κυνάριον *kynarion,* not κύων *kyōn,* as in 7:6), as though Jesus were only speaking affectionately of "puppies."[343] The word does, however, designate household animals as opposed to the semi-wild, stray dogs of Jewish culture. The metaphor presupposes a Gentile setting, since Jews did not typically have dogs as household pets. Nor in Matthew is the point simply a matter of chronology, Jews first, Gentiles later (as in Acts 3:26; 13:46; Rom 1:16; 2:9), since he has eliminated Mark 7:27*a,* "Let the children first be fed."

15:27. Seemingly unresentful of the analogy, the woman persists, and within the framework of Jesus' statement continues to plead her case—not that the "dogs" can eat later, but that they receive "crumbs" even as the "children" are being fed. Continuing to address Jesus as "Lord," she struggles with his reluctance to help just as the petitioners in the Psalms struggle with the One they addressed as LORD.

---

339. Sharon Ringe, "A Gentile Woman's Story," in Letty M. Russell, ed., *Feminist Interpretation of the Bible* (Philadelphia: Westminster Press, 1985) 67-68.
340. The woman addresses him three times as "Lord," used in Matthew only by believers.
341. On the theological significance of ἀναχωρέω in Matthew, see 4:12 and 12:15.

342. On the "healing Son of David," see 21:14-15.
343. There is no diminutive in Jesus' Aramaic. We are dealing with a character in the Greek text of Matthew, which is not an observer's report. Nor can one novelistically presuppose "a half-humorous tenderness of manner" in the tone of Jesus' voice, as does A. H. McNeile, *The Gospel According to Saint Matthew: The Greek Text with Introduction, Notes, and Indices* (London: Macmillan, 1915; reprint 1961) 231. Cf. R. T. France, *Matthew,* Tyndale New Testament Commentaries (Grand Rapids: Eerdmans, 1987) 247, who escapes from the difficulty by speaking of "Jesus' teasing challenge," and "jocular manner," and the "twinkle in his eye" as he spoke thus to her "to see how she would react"—none of which is in the text of Matthew.

15:28. Such persistent struggle in prayer Jesus designates as great faith (in contrast to 14:31), and immediately heals the woman's daughter. The exorcism is called a healing and is reported in words practically identical to the concluding words of the story of the centurion's son/servant (8:5-13), with which it has several points in common.[344]

344. (1) Both healings are for Gentiles. (2) Both are from a distance. (3) Both have an extensive dialogue prior to the healing in which Jesus' reluctance is overcome (taking 8:7 as a question). (4) Both petitioners are said to have great faith. (5) The concluding words are practically the same.

REFLECTIONS

Taken as a realistic report, the story raises difficult and inappropriate questions. Why is Jesus so harsh and offensive to this person? Does she finally best him in an argument and get him to do something he did not want to do? How did a Gentile come to have faith in Jesus as "Son of David"? What would it mean for someone to have (Christian!) faith in this setting? What happened to the woman? Is she now a disciple? Does she participate in a Christian community? Does she now keep the Law, as well as Jesus' teachings, as Matthean disciples are instructed to do? Does Jesus here already rescind his declaration of 10:6, so that the mission to the Gentiles is already opened by this act?

Such questions only demonstrate that the genre of the story is misconstrued when taken as a "report," from which the observer may make historical inferences. Rather, the woman emerges from the story and disappears again into it, to embody and communicate three Matthean points concerning the meaning of God's saving history and the meaning of human faith.[345]

1. God has a plan for salvation history in which salvation is offered first to the Jews (during Jesus' ministry, 10:6; 15:24) then broadened to include all nations after Easter (28:16-20). This story is a preliminary sign of what is to be. Like the kingdom of God, which is to come in its fullness only in the future, it already erupts into the present. Believing readers can see in this story the fact that salvation history as a theology, as an indispensable human effort to express the purpose of God, is still not absolute. God is not enslaved by any theology, even one announced by God's Son (see 24:22). Theology, valuable and necessary as it is, need not stand in the way of divine compassion or human faith. This text springs the boundaries of theology, without breaking it or abandoning it.

2. Worshipful struggle with the God represented by such a theology (cf. Genesis 32), rather than absolutizing it, rejecting it, or resigning in the face of it, is not unbelief, but here pronounced to be great faith. The contrast between her "great faith" and Peter's "little faith" only a few verses earlier can hardly be accidental (14:31; see Commentary and Reflections there). Had the woman said something like "If you are the Son of David, command my daughter to be healed," she would be in the same category as Peter, even if she had dared to proceed homeward on the assumption that the exorcism had taken place. Matthew has much to teach us on the nature of faith. We tend to assume we know what faith is, our main problem being that we do not have enough of it. Matthew's stories address our false assumptions about the meaning of faith itself.

3. It should not be lost that the example of such victorious faith is a Gentile woman, doubly an outsider. But the text should not thereby be embellished and placed in the service of an ideology, as though the Canaanite is an aggressive single parent who here defies cultural taboos and acts to free Jesus from his sexism and racism by catching him in a bad mood or with his compassion down, besting him in an argument and herself becoming the vehicle of

345. This is not to say that the story can be reduced to doctrinal points. Like Jesus' potent parables, such stories are themselves the indispensable vehicle of the truth to which they point, and their meaning is never exhausted by being focused in such summarizing statements.

his liberation and the deliverance of her daughter.[346] Rather, the story serves to challenge the sexism and racism of readers, ancient and modern, who tend not only to consider those of different gender and ethnicity as "the other," somehow more distant from God and the divine order and plan than our own group. Readers, ancient and modern, tend to identify with Jesus and his affirmation of God's order and plan. The story invites readers to place themselves in the role of the other, to struggle not only with God but also with our own perceptions of the other, and pronounces such enduring struggle to be great faith.

346. As in Sharon Ringe's interpretation; while several of her assertions are valid in their own right, the issue is whether they represent the meaning of this text.

Matthew 15:29-39, Healing and Feeding the Crowds

NIV

29Jesus left there and went along the Sea of Galilee. Then he went up on a mountainside and sat down. 30Great crowds came to him, bringing the lame, the blind, the crippled, the mute and many others, and laid them at his feet; and he healed them. 31The people were amazed when they saw the mute speaking, the crippled made well, the lame walking and the blind seeing. And they praised the God of Israel.

32Jesus called his disciples to him and said, "I have compassion for these people; they have already been with me three days and have nothing to eat. I do not want to send them away hungry, or they may collapse on the way."

33His disciples answered, "Where could we get enough bread in this remote place to feed such a crowd?"

34"How many loaves do you have?" Jesus asked.

"Seven," they replied, "and a few small fish."

35He told the crowd to sit down on the ground. 36Then he took the seven loaves and the fish, and when he had given thanks, he broke them and gave them to the disciples, and they in turn to the people. 37They all ate and were satisfied. Afterward the disciples picked up seven basketfuls of broken pieces that were left over. 38The number of those who ate was four thousand, besides women and children. 39After Jesus had sent the crowd away, he got into the boat and went to the vicinity of Magadan.

NRSV

29After Jesus had left that place, he passed along the Sea of Galilee, and he went up the mountain, where he sat down. 30Great crowds came to him, bringing with them the lame, the maimed, the blind, the mute, and many others. They put them at his feet, and he cured them, 31so that the crowd was amazed when they saw the mute speaking, the maimed whole, the lame walking, and the blind seeing. And they praised the God of Israel.

32Then Jesus called his disciples to him and said, "I have compassion for the crowd, because they have been with me now for three days and have nothing to eat; and I do not want to send them away hungry, for they might faint on the way." 33The disciples said to him, "Where are we to get enough bread in the desert to feed so great a crowd?" 34Jesus asked them, "How many loaves have you?" They said, "Seven, and a few small fish." 35Then ordering the crowd to sit down on the ground, 36he took the seven loaves and the fish; and after giving thanks he broke them and gave them to the disciples, and the disciples gave them to the crowds. 37And all of them ate and were filled; and they took up the broken pieces left over, seven baskets full. 38Those who had eaten were four thousand men, besides women and children. 39After sending away the crowds, he got into the boat and went to the region of Magadan.[a]

aOther ancient authorities read Magdala or Magdalan

COMMENTARY

These verses form a single unit, although vv. 29-31 are often printed as a separate pericope in synopses for convenience in noting parallels. Matthew has, in fact, composed them as his substitute for Mark 7:31-37.[347] Reminiscences of the Markan source remain, but in Matthew there is no break between v. 31 and v. 32, the whole unit being bracketed by geographical references (Sea of Galilee, v. 29; Magadan, v. 39). The unit now has a Matthean triadic structure, corresponding exactly to the earlier feeding story: (1) introductory setting of the stage in which the compassionate Jesus heals the multitudes; (2) the dialogue between Jesus and the disciples, which forms the central and longest element; (3) the miracle itself and transitional conclusion.

15:29-31. Matthew has abbreviated the strange itinerary of Mark 7:31, which seems to leave Jesus in Gentile territory, and has relocated the scene on a mountain near the Sea of Galilee. Since the location of Magadan, to which they depart (v. 39), is unknown, it is not clear whether Matthew pictures this scene on the east side of the lake (as clearly in Mark) or on the west side, an ambiguity not clarified by 16:5 and 13. Here, such geographical concerns seem unimportant to Matthew. Even if he intends to portray the scene on the east bank, there is no indication that this is a Gentile setting and that the crowds are Gentiles. Rather than geographical precision, the theological overtones of the mountain on which Matthew relocates the scene are of importance, reminiscent of 5:1 and 14:23 and anticipatory of 17:1. The traditional motifs related to Mount Zion may also be operative here, for "in Jewish expectation Zion is the eschatological gathering site of scattered Israel, a place of healing, and the place of the messianic feast."[348] Matthew maintains and strengthens the eucharistic overtones of the traditional story. The healings remind the reader of

the scene in 4:23, as well as the fulfillment of the messianic times promised in Isa 35:5-6 and reflected already in Matt 4:23; 9:35; 11:5. Thus, as the conflict gathers and deepens, this summary scene, which contains nothing new, recalls for the last time the ministry of the Messiah to his people Israel.

15:32-39. For interpretation of the details, see Commentary on the almost identical 14:13-21. The principal exegetical puzzle is why the doublet exists in the tradition in the first place—two feeding stories with essentially the same structure and meaning, differing only in minor details. Mark, Matthew's source, may have intended the first feeding for the Jews and the second for the Gentiles (5 and 12 supposedly being symbolism pointing to Jewish people, while 4 and 7 presumably point to "Gentiles"— details that should not be allegorized). This may be suggested by Mark 7:27, "let the children be fed *first*," in response to the Gentile woman's request, and the location of this pericope between the two feedings. But this cannot be the meaning in Matthew, who omits both Mark's "first" and Mark's clearly Gentile location in the Decapolis, as well as the Markan note that some had come from a great distance (Mark 8:3). Matthew's picture is thoroughly Jewish—the "God of Israel" who is praised in Matthew's conclusion is not a Gentile acclamation but the language of Israel's own liturgy (cf. Pss 40:14; 71:18; 105:48; Luke 1:68). In addition to preserving it simply because it was in Mark, Matthew seems to welcome another picture useful for this section that portrays Jesus acting compassionately for Israel while in conflict with the Jewish leadership. In Matthew's retelling, the two feedings have been assimilated to each other, so that he emphasizes the similarities between the two feedings rather than (as in the history of exegesis) their differences. The Messiah of Israel typically, almost stereotypically, heals and feeds. On the other hand, the disciples' lack of understanding is a relic of Markan theological perspective, not integral to Matthew's own view of the disciples.

The location of Magadan is unknown (see above), and has given rise to a number of variations in the MS tradition: Magdala, Magalan,

---

347. Matthew omits this Markan story not only in order to achieve a structural parallel between the two feeding stories, but also because it contains a number of elements objectionable to him: healing techniques that smack of magic (strange words, touching, use of saliva); Jesus sighs and groans like a pagan magician; Mark's secrecy motif; disobedience of Jesus' specific command.

348. W. D. Davies and Dale C. Allison, Jr., *A Critical and Exegetical Commentary on the Gospel According to Saint Matthew,* 2 vols. (Edinburg: T. & T. Clark, 1988–91) 2:566, who give copious references.

Magedan.[349] Matthew seems to picture Jesus sailing alone, omitting the disciples of Mark 8:10, who first rejoin the Matthean story at 16:5 (cf. Matthew's addition to Mark 8:14 there).

349. Cf. the situation with Gadara/Gerasa/Gergesa in 8:28.

Matthew 16:1-12, The Pharisees and Sadducees Seek a Sign

NIV

16 The Pharisees and Sadducees came to Jesus and tested him by asking him to show them a sign from heaven.

[2]He replied,[a] "When evening comes, you say, 'It will be fair weather, for the sky is red,' [3]and in the morning, 'Today it will be stormy, for the sky is red and overcast.' You know how to interpret the appearance of the sky, but you cannot interpret the signs of the times. [4]A wicked and adulterous generation looks for a miraculous sign, but none will be given it except the sign of Jonah." Jesus then left them and went away.

[5]When they went across the lake, the disciples forgot to take bread. [6]"Be careful," Jesus said to them. "Be on your guard against the yeast of the Pharisees and Sadducees."

[7]They discussed this among themselves and said, "It is because we didn't bring any bread."

[8]Aware of their discussion, Jesus asked, "You of little faith, why are you talking among yourselves about having no bread? [9]Do you still not understand? Don't you remember the five loaves for the five thousand, and how many basketfuls you gathered? [10]Or the seven loaves for the four thousand, and how many basketfuls you gathered? [11]How is it you don't understand that I was not talking to you about bread? But be on your guard against the yeast of the Pharisees and Sadducees." [12]Then they understood that he was not telling them to guard against the yeast used in bread, but against the teaching of the Pharisees and Sadducees.

a2 Some early manuscripts do not have the rest of verse 2 and all of verse 3.

NRSV

16 The Pharisees and Sadducees came, and to test Jesus[a] they asked him to show them a sign from heaven. [2]He answered them, "When it is evening, you say, 'It will be fair weather, for the sky is red.' [3]And in the morning, 'It will be stormy today, for the sky is red and threatening.' You know how to interpret the appearance of the sky, but you cannot interpret the signs of the times.[b] [4]An evil and adulterous generation asks for a sign, but no sign will be given to it except the sign of Jonah." Then he left them and went away.

[5]When the disciples reached the other side, they had forgotten to bring any bread. [6]Jesus said to them, "Watch out, and beware of the yeast of the Pharisees and Sadducees." [7]They said to one another, "It is because we have brought no bread." [8]And becoming aware of it, Jesus said, "You of little faith, why are you talking about having no bread? [9]Do you still not perceive? Do you not remember the five loaves for the five thousand, and how many baskets you gathered? [10]Or the seven loaves for the four thousand, and how many baskets you gathered? [11]How could you fail to perceive that I was not speaking about bread? Beware of the yeast of the Pharisees and Sadducees!" [12]Then they understood that he had not told them to beware of the yeast of bread, but of the teaching of the Pharisees and Sadducees.

a Gk him   b Other ancient authorities lack 2When it is . . . of the times

COMMENTARY

Matthew 16:1-4 is a doublet of 12:38-40 (see comments there). Despite the change of scene at 16:5, the section 16:1-12 is all one unit, framed by the unusual pairing of Pharisees and Sadducees at beginning and end (vv. 1, 12). Contrary to his usual practice, Matthew has not combined the Q and Markan accounts, but has used the Q version at 12:38-40 and the Markan version here (somewhat assimilated to the earlier version). Usually, when Matthew has excerpted a Markan unit to use in his creative Part One (see Introduction), he omits it when he comes to it in the Markan order. By repeating it here, he provides a frame for the whole unit 16:1-12, which is now thematically related both to the preceding unit and to what follows.

16:1. The combination of Pharisees and Sadducees is striking, occurring four times in this passage and nowhere else in the NT except in another Matthean passage (3:7). There as here, it is a Matthean editorial construction, replacing "crowds" in 3:7 and "Pharisees and Herodians" in the Markan parallel to this passage. Matthew wants to introduce the Sadducees here because of their role in the passion story. The historical Pharisees and Sadducees were mutually antagonistic groups, hardly likely to be speaking with one voice as here, just as it is historically unlikely that the aristocratic Jerusalem party would be found on the shore of the Sea of Galilee debating an itinerant preacher (3:7 is the only other NT reference to Sadducees outside Judea). The combination of Pharisees and Sadducees does not necessarily mean, however, that the author is a Gentile ignorant of historical reality.[350] It more likely points to Matthew's community, which, alienated from the synagogue leadership, now sees Judaism from the alienated ex-insider's perspective in which he and his group are outsiders to their own community.

The Pharisees and Sadducees "test" Jesus. This is the first use of "tempt" (πειράζω peirazō) since the temptation story of 4:1-11, used elsewhere only in 19:3 and 22:18, 35, each time of the Pharisees. Matthew sees continuity between the devil's opposition to Jesus and that of the Jewish leadership. The conflict of kingdoms, which is Matthew's major theme, reemerges. (See Excursus "Kingdom of Heaven in Matthew," 288-94.) This theme extends into vv. 5-12 and is another

reason for repeating 16:1-4 as its introduction. All of 16:1-12 thus leads into the key scenes of Peter's confession and Jesus' instruction to follow in 16:13-28, where the conflict between setting one's mind on "divine things" versus "human things" comes to sharpest focus. On the demand for a "sign from heaven" itself and Jesus' response, see 12:38.

16:2-4. The first part of Jesus' response is textually very uncertain, being absent from ℵ, B, X, f^{13} and most of the Syriac and Coptic tradition. Thus the REB omits it from the text, the NAB includes it within brackets, and both the NIV and the NRSV include it, but with a note as to its doubtful attestation. Whether original or secondary, it makes an important connection with the context, since "heaven" in 16:1 and "sky" in vv. 2-3 are from the same word in Greek (οὐρανός ouranos); there are no unambiguous signs, but even heavenly/sky signs must be interpreted. The Jewish leaders know how to interpret the sky, but not the only sign that will be given them, the death and resurrection of Jesus (cf. 12:38 and the Reflections following 12:45). This has to do with interpreting the "times" (καιροί kairoi), another key Matthean word (see 26:18). This lack of ability to interpret the sign constituted by Jesus is not a matter of intellectual acumen, but has to do with hardness of heart and lack of faith, as the following verses make clear. At the conclusion of this interchange, Jesus leaves the Pharisees and Sadducees. This is not the withdrawal from confrontation expressing the Matthean Jesus' non-retaliatory, non-violent response to hostility, signaled by his typical "he withdrew" (ἀναχωρέω anachōreō; see 4:12; 12:15), but Jesus' breaking off communication with the Jewish leadership (thus "abandon," "leave behind" [καταλείπω kataleipō], elsewhere in Matthew only 4:13; 19:5; 21:17). He will not see them again until the final confrontation, which begins in Judea (19:3; 22:23).

16:5-12. The disciples rejoin Jesus, who was apparently alone in the confrontation of vv. 1-4. Matthew has rewritten, streamlined, and relocated this Markan scene, which in Mark occurs in the boat during the crossing, so that it represents the interweaving of the two themes from the preceding two scenes: the feeding scene of 15:32-38, at which the disciples were last present, and the confrontation between Jesus and the

---

350. Contra John P. Meier, *The Vision of Matthew: Christ, Church, and Morality in the First Gospel* (New York: Paulist, 1979) 20-21; with more restraint, *Matthew,* New Testament Message series (Collegeville, Minn.: Liturgical Press, 1980) 178.

Pharisees and Sadducees of 16:1-4, with the disciples absent.

As Jesus has broken off communication with the Jewish leaders in the preceding scene, here he experiences a temporary breakdown of communication with his own disciples. The disciples are concerned with bread (v. 5). Jesus is concerned with warning the disciples against the teaching of the Pharisees and Sadducees (v. 6).[351] The common denominator is "yeast," which the disciples understand in terms of their own interest in literal bread (v. 8). With divine insight (cf. 12:25; 26:9-10) Jesus is aware of their misunderstanding, which is not merely at the intellectual level, but is a matter of "little faith" (ὀλιγόπιστοι *oligopistoi*). Jesus shifts from his own concern with the yeast/teaching of the Pharisees and Sadducees to deal with their concern. He had already taught them to trust in God for provisions (6:25-34, where the source of Matthew's favorite term ὀλιγόπιστοι was provided by Q), but they are letting concern for physical security take priority over spiritual realities. The next section toward

which this scene is building will designate this as setting their minds on human things rather than divine things (16:23). It is thus qualitatively different from the not-yet understanding that characterizes them in v. 9, which will be immediately remedied (v. 12). By worrying about literal bread, they are threatening to abandon Jesus' teaching in the Sermon on the Mount and join ranks with the Pharisees, who are on the side of the opposing kingdom and are united with Satan in "testing" Jesus—precisely as Peter is about to be accused of doing in the next section (16:23 again!). Jesus calls them to remember the extravagant divine provision manifest in the feedings of the five thousand and the four thousand, and then returns to his own agenda, which their *oligopistoi* had caused them to misunderstand: the teaching of the Pharisees and Sadducees. They get the point. Again in contrast to Mark (7:21), the disciples' misunderstanding is only a temporary aberration. In Matthew, the whole unit has been a teaching session, and a successful one, conducted by the master teacher and resulting in understanding disciples.

351. This section is in tension with 23:2-3, where the problem with the Pharisees is not their teaching as such, but their hypocrisy. Here, the "yeast" to be avoided is their teaching itself. Superficial harmonization should be avoided.

Matthew 16:13-28, The Disciples' Confession and the New Community

OVERVIEW

Matthew places this scene as the crucial midpoint of this extended section, portraying the formation of the church in response to Israel's rejection (see Overview at 13:53). In this scene, Peter declares the confession fundamental to the church's faith; Jesus pronounces Peter to be the foundation on which he will build his new community, and states the cost and meaning of adhering to this confession. Precisely in this ecclesiological section (13:53–18:35) Peter assumes a more prominent role, Petrine material being added to the Markan narrative at 14:28-31; 15:15; 16:17-19; 17:24-27; 18:21.

The unit extends from v. 13 through v. 28, being framed by references to the Son of Man in the beginning and ending verses, both added by Matthew. This single dialogue and teaching session occurs in one location in the district of Caesarea Philippi, with a change of scene beginning the unit (16:13) and closing it (17:1). Thus 16:13-28 is one unit with three sub-units, vv. 13-20, vv. 21-23, vv. 24-28. In this whole section Matthew has no other source than Mark and (for 16:17-20) traditions of his own community. He follows Mark closely, making his modifications and additions stand out dramatically.

Matthew 16:13-20, Jesus as Son of God; Peter as Rock

NIV

¹³When Jesus came to the region of Caesarea Philippi, he asked his disciples, "Who do people say the Son of Man is?"

¹⁴They replied, "Some say John the Baptist; others say Elijah; and still others, Jeremiah or one of the prophets."

¹⁵"But what about you?" he asked. "Who do you say I am?"

¹⁶Simon Peter answered, "You are the Christ,ᵃ the Son of the living God."

¹⁷Jesus replied, "Blessed are you, Simon son of Jonah, for this was not revealed to you by man, but by my Father in heaven. ¹⁸And I tell you that you are Peter,ᵇ and on this rock I will build my church, and the gates of Hadesᶜ will not overcome it.ᵈ ¹⁹I will give you the keys of the kingdom of heaven; whatever you bind on earth will beᵉ bound in heaven, and whatever you loose on earth will beᵉ loosed in heaven." ²⁰Then he warned his disciples not to tell anyone that he was the Christ.

ᵃ16 Or Messiah; also in verse 20   ᵇ18 Peter means rock.
ᶜ18 Or hell   ᵈ18 Or not prove stronger than it
ᵉ19 Or have been

NRSV

13Now when Jesus came into the district of Caesarea Philippi, he asked his disciples, "Who do people say that the Son of Man is?" ¹⁴And they said, "Some say John the Baptist, but others Elijah, and still others Jeremiah or one of the prophets." ¹⁵He said to them, "But who do you say that I am?" ¹⁶Simon Peter answered, "You are the Messiah,ᵃ the Son of the living God." ¹⁷And Jesus answered him, "Blessed are you, Simon son of Jonah! For flesh and blood has not revealed this to you, but my Father in heaven. ¹⁸And I tell you, you are Peter,ᵇ and on this rockᶜ I will build my church, and the gates of Hades will not prevail against it. ¹⁹I will give you the keys of the kingdom of heaven, and whatever you bind on earth will be bound in heaven, and whatever you loose on earth will be loosed in heaven." ²⁰Then he sternly ordered the disciples not to tell anyone that he wasᵈ the Messiah.ᵃ

ᵃOr the Christ   ᵇGk Petros   ᶜGk petra
ᵈOther ancient authorities add Jesus

COMMENTARY

This is the focal scene of the extended narrative unit 13:53–17:27. In the midst of what Matthew perceives as a blind and recalcitrant Israel, Jesus forms a new community of those who perceive and confess his true identity.

16:13. Caesarea Philippi, about twenty miles north of the Sea of Galilee, had earlier been the site of a Baal cultic center, then in Hellenistic times became known as Paneas because the god Pan had been worshiped in the famous grotto and spring there, but was renamed by Herod the Great after he built there a temple to Caesar Augustus. After Herod's death it was made part of the territory of his son Philip, who enlarged the town and renamed it after Tiberius Caesar and himself. During the war of 66–70, Caesarea was a recreation spot for the Roman general Vespasian, who began the siege of Jerusalem and then left his son

Titus in charge to complete it when he became emperor. After the fall of Jerusalem, Titus and his troops returned to Caesarea, where Josephus reports he had some of the Jewish captives thrown to wild animals.³⁵² Matthew's preservation of this location (dropped by Luke) may be only incidental, but since he did omit Mark's setting on the road, Matthew may have wished to emphasize that the significant scene took place in a setting with older nationalistic and religious associations, Jewish and pagan. He brings the scene of Jesus' confession as the Jewish Messiah into the shadow of a Caesar temple, where the Roman destroyers of Jerusalem had celebrated their victory, a revered site long associated with both pagan and Jewish revelatory events (cf. *1 Enoch* 12–16).

352. Josephus *The Jewish War* 3.9.7., 443-44; 7.2.1 23-24.

Jesus' question is for literary contrast with the disciples' response of faith, not because he needed to be informed of popular impressions of him. To enhance this contrast, Matthew does not mention "Son of David" previously expressed by the crowds (12:23) and by individuals (9:27; 15:22). Whereas Jesus' previous use of "Son of Man" (9:6; 11:19; 12:40; cf. 8:20) was not understood by opponents and crowds, Matthew has Jesus give his own self-identification as "Son of Man" in his question to the disciples (in contrast to his Markan source; cf. Mark 8:27). Jesus' true identity is not new to the disciples, who have heard Jesus refer to himself in christological terms before, have understood him, and have already worshiped him as Son of God (14:33). As a result, the scene here is not the christological breakthrough that it is in Mark, where no human being has correctly identified Jesus until Peter's confession of Mark 8:29. Rather, the emphasis is ecclesiological; this confession of faith in Jesus as the messianic representative of God's kingdom separates the new community he is forming from those who oppose and reject it.

16:14. The populace has high opinions of Jesus' identity. The common denominator of all those named is not only that they are prophets, but also that they all belong to the transcendent sphere. John and the other prophets are dead and must be thought of as resurrected in order to be identified with Jesus; Elijah was taken to heaven without dying. Jeremiah is added to the Markan list.[353] To identify Jesus as a prophet whom God had raised from the dead is a "high" christology—"just a prophet" could not be a Matthean phrase, for Jesus includes himself among the prophets (13:57). "Prophet," though not incorrect, is inadequate for Matthew's christological understanding (cf. 21:11, 46).

16:15-16. The pronoun "you" (ὑμεῖς *hymeis*) is emphatic: "But as for you, who do you say that I am?" (preserved better by the NIV). It is plural, addressed to all the disciples. Simon Peter answers on behalf of the group. In Mark, the disciples answer simply "the Christ," to which Matthew adds "the

Son of the living God" (cf. 26:63, where similar words recur in Jesus' own confession before the high priest, also concerned with building the new temple/community). "Son of God" is a matter of revelation, echoing the heavenly voice at Jesus' baptism (3:7), his own self-confession of 11:27 and the disciples' previous confession of 14:33, and will be confirmed by the heavenly voice of 17:14. (For the titles "Son of Man," "Christ," and "Son of God," see Excursus "Matthean Christology," 353-61.) In this context, the living God contrasts with the idolatrous associations of the locale.

16:17-19. Matthew's most important editorial change is the addition of these words to Jesus' response to Peter. Their origin continues to be disputed, but the majority of scholars would attribute them to pre-Matthean tradition or to Matthew himself, rather than tracing them back to the historical Jesus.[354] Whether the sayings were originally a unit or separate sayings, as well as the relation of 16:19 to 18:18, is disputed. The view presented here is that 18:18 was originally a Christian prophetic saying that circulated in the Matthean community as a saying of Jesus, from which 16:19 was derived.[355]

16:17. The plural address to all the disciples of v. 16 shifts to the singular. All the disciples have already received a similar pronouncement of blessing in 13:16-17, just as all have already confessed Jesus as Son of God in 14:33. Yet Jesus' singular blessing of Peter is significant, for in Matthew's Gospel Peter not only represents all the disciples as their spokesperson and, with all his strengths and weaknesses, stands for the typical Christian, but he also plays a unique and unrepeatable role in the founding of the new community (see Introduction). Peter is not blessed because of a personal attainment or insight he has

353. Matthew's interest in Jeremiah (mentioned by name in the NT only by Matthew: here, 2:17; 27:9) may be due to Jeremiah's association with the fall of Jerusalem, or his prophecy of the new covenant. Matthew himself may have felt a kinship with Jeremiah, who also was opposed by the religious establishment in his struggle with it for the loyalty of the people in a new situation after the destruction of Jerusalem.

354. Oscar Cullmann, *Peter: Disciple, Apostle, Martyr* (Philadelphia: Westminster, 1953), probably remains the most significant advocate of dominical origin, although he thought the original setting of the words was the last supper. The dominant scholarly view now regards the sayings, and perhaps the whole scene, as a retrojection of post-Easter confession into the narrative of Jesus' life. See Raymond E. Brown, Karl P. Donfried, and John Reumann, eds., *Peter in the New Testament* (Minneapolis: Augsburg, 1973); "Peter in the Gospel of Matthew," 75-107, esp. 86-89. Cf. Christoph Kähler, "Zur Form und Traditionsgeschichte von Matth. xvi. 17-19," *NTS* 23 (1976) 36-58, who argues that this was originally a post-Easter revelation to Peter, to whom Jesus first appeared (Luke 24:34; 1 Cor 15:5).

355. See M. Eugene Boring, *The Continuing Voice of Jesus: Christian Prophecy and the Gospel Tradition* (Louisville: Westminster/John Knox, 1991) 252-53.

achieved. Knowledge of Jesus' saving role comes by divine revelation—as gift, not attainment. In this, Peter is representative of Christian faith generally (cf. Matt 11:25-27; 1 Cor 12:3). The word for "revealed" (ἀποκαλύπτω apokalyptō; "apocalypse") connotes not some personal, individual spiritual experience, but the divine disclosure of the eschatological secret.[356]

There are three images of the role of Peter: v. 18, the rock on which the church is built by Jesus; v. 19*a*, the holder of the keys; and v. 19*b*, the one who binds and looses.

16:18, Peter as Rock. Peter is the foundation rock on which Jesus builds the new community. The name "Peter" means "stone" or "rock" (Aramaic כיפא, *Cepha;* Greek Πέτρος *Petros;* the English word *petrified* is a derivative). In Western countries, influenced by the Christian tradition, "Peter" is now a common name, but this simply reflects the influence the nickname Jesus gave his disciple Simon (Simeon) has had in Western culture. There are no documented instances of anyone's ever being named "rock" in Aramaic or Greek prior to Simon.[357] Thus English translations should render the word "stone" or "rock," not "Peter," which gives the false impression that the word represented a common name and causes the contemporary reader to miss the word play of the passage: "You are Rock, and on this rock I will build my church."[358] Peter is here pictured as the foundation of the church (see Reflections below).[359]

It is not clear whether Matthew understands that Peter is just now being given the name "Rock" by Jesus, or whether a previously given nickname is here being given a new significance. John 1:42 reflects a tradition in which Peter received his new name on his first encounter with Jesus, and in Matthew previously only the narrator has used "Peter" for Simon, which could be by anticipation. On the basis of Isa 51:1-2 (cf. Matt 3:9), some scholars have seen Peter as here paralleled to Abraham; just as Abram stood at the beginning of the people of God, had his name changed, and was called a rock, so also Peter stands at the beginning of the new people of God and receives the Abrahamic name "rock" to signify this. Since Matthew is particularly attracted to Isaiah to find illuminating parallels to Jesus and the church (cf. Excursus "Matthew as Interpreter of Scripture," 151-54), and since he regards Abraham as the beginning point of the story of the people of God (1:1-2; cf. 3:9), there may well be some truth in this. If so, this is only a connotation, and it goes too far to call Peter a "new Abraham."

Although Peter is the foundation, Jesus is the builder of the church. Thus Peter does not compete with Jesus.[360] Jesus himself is here portrayed as the one who constructs the new community, pictured as a building. This is part of Matthew's theology of the continuing active presence of Christ in the church (see Reflections on 1:23). The underlying image is that of the eschatological temple composed of the true people of God, common not only in early Christianity but also already at Qumran (cf. John 2:19-21; 1 Cor 3:16-17; 2 Cor 6:16; Eph 2:21; Rev 3:12; 4 QpPs37 3:13-16), and sometimes related to a foundation stone or one who is a *pillar* or *foundation* (cf. Gal 2:9 for "pillar" as a name for Peter, and Isa 28:14-22). In Jewish tradition, the Jerusalem Temple was built on a rock thought to be the center of the world, the present site of the Dome of the Rock). The word rendered "build" (οἰκοδομέω *oikodomeō*) is used here as in 26:21; 27:40.

356. Paul claimed to receive God's "revelation" of the "Son," not by "flesh and blood" (Gal 1:16). This language may be reflected here, showing that Peter, too, had a divine revelation. Conversely, Paul may be reflecting a claim made by or for Peter.

357. At least not in Greek. A fifth-century BCE Aramaic papyrus may have כיפא as a proper name. See Joseph Fitzmyer, "Aramaic Kepha and Peter's Name in the New Testament," in *To Advance the Gospel* (New York: Crossroad, 1981) 114-15. It is certain that "Cephas" was not used as a proper name among Palestinian Jews in the first century CE.

358. The words are identical to 16:16, "You are" (σὺ εἶ *su ei*). Peter and Jesus confess each other. Jesus responds to Peter's declaration about his unique role in the saving plan of God with a declaration about Peter's unique role.

359. This passage was not used for support of the papacy until the third century and later, and then was opposed by leading figures such as Origen and Augustine. In the seventeenth century, when this text was reinterpreted by Roman Catholic exegetes as referring to the founding of the papacy, this interpretation was opposed by Protestant exegetes, who denied that the passage referred to Peter as the foundation for the church at all. It has become traditional in Protestant polemics to point out the distinction between the masculine Πέτρος (*petros*) and the feminine πέτρα (*petra*) to support the view that the church is built on Peter's confession or his faith ("rock cliff" [πέτρα]), rather than on Peter himself ("stone" [Πέτρος]). This is a distinction in the Greek language, however, and the form כיפא (*Cephas*) shows that the name was originally given in Aramaic. In any case, if the conversation is historical, it

did not take place in Greek, but in Jesus' and Peter's native Aramaic, so to the extent that the conversation is thought of as historical, the Greek distinction is irrelevant. The distinction is made in this Greek text because as a man's name Πέτρος must be masculine rather than the feminine πέτρα.

360. First Cor 3:11, often cited to show that Peter could not be meant as the foundation on which the church is built, may be a Pauline reaction to this very idea promulgated by Petrine disciples in Corinth. On the other hand, Eph 2:20 and Rev 21:14 show that the founding generation of apostles played a unique role in the origin of the church and could be pictured as its foundation. In Matt 16:18 this apostolic role is focused uniquely on Peter.

"Church" (ἐκκλησία *ekklēsia*) is found only here and in 18:17 in the Gospels.[361] Etymologically, the word means "called out" and was used in Hellenistic Greek for the local political "assembly" (as in, e.g., Acts 19:32, 39-40). Neither etymology nor secular usage determines Matthew's meaning, however. He intends the renewed people of God, constituted by the disciples of Jesus, the heir and continuation of empirical Israel that has forfeited its standing and role (21:43). The *ekklēsia* represents the "congregation of Yahweh" (יהוה קהל *qāhāl yahweh*), the covenant people of God in the wilderness who received the Torah at Sinai, and is often so translated in the LXX. This does not mean that Matthew considered the church a replacement for Israel, but a special community of the new covenant within or alongside empirical Israel. Over against "their synagogues," Matthew has Jesus place "my church."[362]

Hades is the realm of the dead, not the place of punishment. The "gates of Hades" is a biblical expression (Isa 38:10) that can mean the same as the "gates of death" (Job 38:17; Pss 9:13; 107:18). In this case, the word translated "overcome" or "prevail over" means "be stronger than," and the meaning is that the realm of the dead, which no human being can conquer, is nevertheless not stronger than the church founded on the rock, and the church will always endure to the end of history, accompanied by its Lord (28:20).[363] Thus this text declares minimally that the church will never die. But "gates of Hades" may also refer to the portals of the underworld from which the powers of Satan emerge to attack the church, especially in the eschatological times (cf. the eschatological testing of Matt 6:13 and 26:41 and the dramatic imagery of Rev 9:1-11). Then the meaning would be that the church is under attack by the powers of evil, but will never be vanquished, because it is founded on the rock.[364] In neither case is the church pictured

triumphalistically, battering down the gates of Hades. Once again, the two kingdoms stand over against each other (see 12:22-37). The church does not escape from the power of Hades, but participates in the struggle between the two kingdoms with the sure promise that the opposing kingdom symbolized by the powers of death will never prevail.

16:19. For Matthew, each of these two kingdoms makes its influence felt by teaching. The "kingdom of heaven" is represented by authoritative teaching, the promulgation of authoritative Halakha that lets heaven's power rule in earthly things. The image of Peter with the keys is not that of the doorkeeper to heaven of popular piety and cartoons. As the next image makes clear, Peter's function is not to decide in the afterlife who is admitted and who is denied entrance to heaven; Peter's role as holder of the keys is fulfilled now, on earth, as chief teacher of the church. The similar imagery of Matt 23:13 and Luke 11:52 points to the teaching office, as does the introductory pericope Matt 16:1-12 and Matthew's concern for correct teaching in general. The keeper of the keys has authority within the house as administrator and teacher (cf. Isa 22:20-25, which may have influenced Matthew here). The language of binding and loosing is rabbinic terminology for authoritative teaching, for having the authority to interpret the Torah and apply it to particular cases, declaring what is permitted and what is not permitted. Jesus, who has taught with authority (7:29) and has given his authority to his disciples (10:1, 8), here gives the primary disciple the authority to teach in his name—to make authoritative decisions pertaining to Christian life as he applies the teaching of Jesus to concrete situations in the life of the church.[365] In 18:18, similar authority is given to the church as a whole, and the way the last three antitheses are presented in 5:33-48 (see discussion there) shows such application of Jesus' teaching is the task of the whole community of disciples, with Peter having a special responsibility as chief teacher as well as representative and model.

16:20. Matthew here returns to his Markan

---

361. The NRSV adds two more instances not in the Greek text by translating ἀδελφός (*adelphos*, "brother"/"sister") as "member of the church" in 18:15, 21.

362. It is hardly accidental that Matthew avoids "synagogue" (συναγωγή *synagōgē*) as a Christian designation here, although it was a common translation of קהל יהוה in the LXX and was used by other Christian writers for the church (Jas 2:2). Matthew opposes "church" and "synagogue," not "church" and "Israel."

363. So Ulrich Luz, *Das Evangelium nach Matthäus (Mt 8–17)*, Evangelisch-Katholischer Kommentar zum Neuen Testament I/2 (Benziger: Neukirchener Verlag, 1990) 2:464. Cf. Reflections on 1:23.

364. So Jeremias, "πύλη, πυλὼν," *TDNT* 6:924-28.

365. Within the narrative storyline, however, prior to Easter teaching is restricted to Jesus. The disciples never teach, and "teaching" is not included in the lists of 10:1 and 10:8. This authority first becomes effective after Easter, in the life of the church (28:16-20).

source and takes up these words, which were significant for Mark's theology of the messianic secret, but are somewhat vestigial in Matthew. These harsh-sounding words still have a theological meaning for Matthew, however. They are not to be understood in terms of the psychology or strategy of the historical Jesus, nor as an element of Mark's messianic secret, but as an affirmation of Matthean theology: the new community founded by Jesus has *insider* knowledge that distinguishes it from Israel, which has rejected Jesus as the Christ (13:10-17).

REFLECTIONS

1. For generations this passage has been a bone of contention between Protestants and Roman Catholics, with interpretations often falling along confessional lines. One of the achievements of contemporary ecumenical scholarship, however, is that both Protestant and Roman Catholic scholars generally agree that the original meaning of the text is that Jesus builds the church on Peter as the foundation (contrary to previous Protestant views) rather than on Peter's confession or Peter's faith, and that the position Peter held was unique and unrepeatable (contrary to previous Roman Catholic views). The text pictures Peter as playing a unique and unrepeatable role in the foundation of the church. Later theology—Roman Catholic, Eastern Orthodox, and Protestant—developed this meaning in its own ways, but there is now a general consensus as to the original meaning.[366]

For contemporary Christian life, this means that the text need not have the polemical edge it has developed in the older Roman Catholic/Protestant/Greek Orthodox debates, but can be heard again as the promise of Christ to build his church despite the forces of death arrayed against it. The church can take heart from this promise.

2. The Matthean pattern of revelation, blessing, name giving, and commissioning found here has already been applied to all the disciples in 5:3-16.[367] Christ as agent of God is the actor. Teaching and preaching from this text should point to the church not as a human achievement or fellowship of like-minded individuals who have formed a support group, but to God as the one who through Christ grants the revelation that generates faith, as the one who blesses those who receive the revelation, as the one who gives us a new name (identity, nature, not just label), and sends us to continue his work, including the authority to make decisions in his name.

---

366. Cf. the ecumenical statement edited by Raymond E. Brown, Karl P. Donfried, and John Reumann, *Peter in the New Testament* (Minneapolis: Augsburg, 1973).

367. Cf. M. Jack Suggs, "Expository Article: Matthew 16:13-20," *Int* 39 (1985) 291-95.

Matthew 16:21-23, Jesus as Suffering Son of Man; Peter as Stumbling Stone

21From that time on Jesus began to explain to his disciples that he must go to Jerusalem and suffer many things at the hands of the elders, chief priests and teachers of the law, and that he must be killed and on the third day be raised to life.

22Peter took him aside and began to rebuke him. "Never, Lord!" he said. "This shall never happen to you!"

21From that time on, Jesus began to show his disciples that he must go to Jerusalem and undergo great suffering at the hands of the elders and chief priests and scribes, and be killed, and on the third day be raised. 22And Peter took him aside and began to rebuke him, saying, "God forbid it, Lord! This must never happen to you."

NIV	NRSV
²³Jesus turned and said to Peter, "Get behind me, Satan! You are a stumbling block to me; you do not have in mind the things of God, but the things of men."	²³But he turned and said to Peter, "Get behind me, Satan! You are a stumbling block to me; for you are setting your mind not on divine things but on human things."

COMMENTARY

This is the first of the passion predictions, which form a constituent element of the narrative of each of the synoptic Gospels:

Matthew 16:21-23　Mark 8:31-33　Luke 9:22
Matthew 17:22-23　Mark 9:30-32　Luke 9:43b-45
Matthew 20:17-19　Mark 10:32-34　Luke 18:31-34
Matthew 26:2

Matthew and Luke incorporate the three Markan passion predictions, with Matthew adding an extra one at 26:2.[368] The most likely development of the tradition is as follows: (1) In view of the first-century Jewish understanding that rejection, suffering, and death belonged to the vocation of a true prophet, and in the light of what had happened to John the Baptist, the historical Jesus expected rejection, suffering, and death.[369] His imminent eschatological hope provided the theological framework for his conviction that God would vindicate him and his ministry in the near future, with the arrival of the eschatological kingdom. If he thought specifically of resurrection, as is likely, this will have been the general resurrection of God's people as part of the eschatological victory of God.

(2) After Easter, the earliest Christians developed the traditions of Jesus' sayings into more specific predictions, supplying details from their retrospective view (especially prominent in Mark 10:32-34) and from their reflection on the Scriptures. It is at this point that the precise dating of "after three days"/"on the third day" entered the tradition.[370] While Jesus will have expected a

speedy vindication after his death, his expectation will not have been so precise. Reflection on Hos 6:2, originally meant metaphorically of the "resurrection" of Israel, was reinterpreted as being fulfilled in the resurrection of Christ (cf. 1 Cor 15:4).

(3) Mark or the specifically pre-Markan tradition formulated and stylized these sayings, making them specifically Son of Man sayings with "hand over," "deliver up" (παραδίδωμι *paradidōmi*) as the primary verb. Mark made three such sayings structural markers in his narrative at 8:31; 9:31; 10:32-34.

(4) Matthew incorporates the three Markan passion predictions, although they no longer play the same structural role as in Mark, and slightly rewrites them to express his own theological message. We are here interested primarily in the Matthean level of meaning and will treat the three sayings together.

16:21. "From that time on" (ἀπὸ τότε *apo tote*) marks a turning point in the story, but is not a part of the fundamental structure of Matthew (cf. Outline; Introduction). Jesus here turns inward to instruct the disciples, a focus that continues through 20:34. From here to the end of chap. 18, there are no parables and no public instruction, and only one miracle-exorcism by Jesus (17:14-20). Matthew omits the crowds from the parallel narrative in Mark 8:34. The crowds disappear until 19:1 (except as part of the scenery in 17:14; they are not instructed). The opponents are absent until 19:3, where they appear only as props, the instruction being directed to the disciples.

Jesus' passion and the disciples' following are already presupposed and taught in Matthew (cf. 10:38), so this is not a dramatic new revelation (as in Mark), but now relates the confessional life of the disciples to the formation of the new

---

368. An additional fragmentary passion prediction, referring only to the approaching suffering of the Son of Man, is found in Mark 9:12 (Matt 17:12), omitted by Luke.

369. See 2 Chr 24:19-21; 36:15-16; Matt 23:29-37; Luke 13:31-34; Acts 7:52; Heb 11:32-38. Although the OT is silent about the destiny of Isaiah, the first-century CE or earlier *Martyrdom of Isaiah* pictures his violent martyrdom as something to be presupposed, since he was a faithful prophet.

370. Vincent Taylor, *The Gospel According to St. Mark* (New York: Macmillan, 1959) 378, assembles evidence showing that "in the LXX and in late Greek writers the two phrases were identical in meaning."

community. The instruction has specifically to do with the suffering of the Son of Man/Messiah, signaled by a new word for "instruction" (δεικνύω / δείκνυμι *deiknyō, deiknymi*), the same word used for revelatory instruction in Rev 1:1 (cf. ἀποκαλύπτω [*apokalyptō*] in 16:17). Matthew preserves Mark's "Son of Man" in all the other passion predictions, but omits it here because Jesus has already used it in 16:13 (on "Son of Man," see Excursus "Matthean Christology," 353-61).

Matthew does not elaborate a reason for Jesus' death, only that it is necessarily a part of God's divine plan (see 20:28). The suffering of the Son of Man is necessary ("must" NRSV; "destined" NIV), expressed by the apocalyptic δεῖ (*dei*; as in Rev 1:1, alluding to Dan 2:28 LXX). This does not mean "fate" in the Greek sense (ἀνάγκη *anagkē;* αἱμαρμένη *haimarmenē*), but in Matthew means God's will as revealed in Scripture. The verb used in 17:22; 20:18; and 26:2 (the other passion predictions) means both "hand over"/"betray" and "deliver up" (παραδίδωμι *paradidōmi*) by God, who delivers up the suffering servant in Isa 53:6.[371] The fact that God is the one who delivers up the Son of Man is clear in 17:22, where it is human beings to whom he is delivered (and not one group of people handing him over to another). Elsewhere, the word often expresses both meanings simultaneously, God being understood as the hidden actor at work in the actions of human beings. The word and its biblical background are thus carefully chosen to express the paradox of divine sovereignty and human responsibility at work in the suffering and death of Jesus.

By placing a single definite article at the beginning, Matthew joins "elders," "high priests," and "scribes" into one group, representing the united front of the Jewish leadership (cf. 16:1). Here, not the Jewish people as a whole, but their leadership, are held responsible for Jesus' coming death (cf. 27:24-26). The verbs for both "be killed" and "be raised" are in the passive voice, making clear that Jesus does not "rise" on his own, but that his resurrection is the act

of God.[372] Likewise, Mark's "after three days" is consistently changed to "on the third day," representing more adequately both the time between Friday and Sunday and the allusion to Hos 6:2.

16:22. Peter's response is to take hold of Jesus and rebuke him with prayer-like words, which Matthew has added to Mark.[373] Peter's objection can be understood as either a wrong idea of messiahship or personal love for Jesus, or both. Since Matthew has Jesus respond in terms of the meaning of discipleship, always for Matthew inseparable from one's understanding of messiahship, it is better to see Peter's response as theological rather than merely personal. This is all the more important since Peter continues in his representative role.

16:23. Jesus' counter response (Mark's "rebuke" is omitted) is to call Peter to renewed and deeper discipleship. "Get behind me" echoes the words of 4:19, the discipleship formula "behind me" (ὀπίσω μου *opisō mou*) being used in both cases. "Behind me" is not mere location, but the posture of the disciple. Jesus is going to the cross; the disciple is to follow. But there is also an echo of the address to Satan in 4:10, "go" (ὕπαγε *hypage*) being used in each place.

The testing that Jesus had met and overcome in his initial encounter with Satan was not once for all; it reappears in the sincere and prayerful remonstrance of the disciple. The temptation to accomplish his ministry in the way human criteria judge to be successful is, in fact, a demonic temptation (see Reflections on 14:22-33). Jesus' mission is to inaugurate an alternative kingdom, a radically different way of exercising rulership and authority. Here his opponent is none other than the rock on which he will build the new community. Peter the rock becomes Peter the

---

371. The NRSV of Isa 53:6 follows MT, "the Lord has laid on him the iniquity of us all." The LXX rendering stands behind Matthew's thought—and that of much early Christianity: "and the Lord delivered him up for our sins" (καὶ κύριος παρέδωκεν αὐτὸν ταῖς ἁμαρτίαις ἡμῶν *kai kyrios paredōken auton tais hamartiais hēmōn*).

372. Mark had used the ambiguous verb, which in the active and middle means "rise" (ἀνίστημι *anistēmi*). Matthew consistently changes it to ἐγείρω *egeirō* in the passive to express more clearly that just as Jesus does not "die" but is both killed by human beings and delivered over to death by God, so also he does not "rise" on his own but is raised by God. The fact that Matthew is sensitive to the distinction between these two verbs is clear from his rewriting of Mark 12:25-26, which had used them interchangeably, to eliminate this possibility (Matt 22:30-31).

373. "Take hold of" (REB) more adequately represents προσλαμβάνομαι (*proslambanomai*) than does "took him aside" of both the NIV and the NRSV (cf. NEB, "took him by the arm"). Peter's actual words (literally "[may God show] mercy to you Lord; this will not happen to you") can be understood as a conventional "God forbid" in the sense of "may it not happen," but can also represent a real prayer. In the light of the following reference to thinking God's thoughts or human thoughts, it is better to see it as an actual prayer; although Peter is oriented to a theology of "success" diametrically opposite to Jesus' theology of the cross, he supposes that he is representing God's will and expresses it in prayer.

stone of "stumbling" (the literal meaning of σκάν-δαλον [*skandalon*]; cf. Isa 8:11-15, esp. v. 14). There is also a "jarring juxtaposition"[374] by placing this immediately after the blessing pronounced on

Peter in 16:17-19. Despite his revelation from God (16:17), Peter continues to think as good human beings are accustomed to think: reasonably, egocentrically, and in terms of human friendship and "success."[375]

---

374. W. D. Davies and Dale C. Allison, Jr., *A Critical and Exegetical Commentary on the Gospel According to Saint Matthew*, 2 vols. (Edinburgh: T. & T. Clark, 1988–91) 2:665.

375. Cf. Luz, *Mattäus*, 2:489.

Matthew 16:24-28, The Cost and Promise of Discipleship

NIV	NRSV
[24]Then Jesus said to his disciples, "If anyone would come after me, he must deny himself and take up his cross and follow me. [25]For whoever wants to save his life[a] will lose it, but whoever loses his life for me will find it. [26]What good will it be for a man if he gains the whole world, yet forfeits his soul? Or what can a man give in exchange for his soul? [27]For the Son of Man is going to come in his Father's glory with his angels, and then he will reward each person according to what he has done. [28]I tell you the truth, some who are standing here will not taste death before they see the Son of Man coming in his kingdom."	[24]Then Jesus told his disciples, "If any want to become my followers, let them deny themselves and take up their cross and follow me. [25]For those who want to save their life will lose it, and those who lose their life for my sake will find it. [26]For what will it profit them if they gain the whole world but forfeit their life? Or what will they give in return for their life? [27]"For the Son of Man is to come with his angels in the glory of his Father, and then he will repay everyone for what has been done. [28]Truly I tell you, there are some standing here who will not taste death before they see the Son of Man coming in his kingdom."
[a]25 The Greek word means either *life* or *soul*; also in verse 26.	

COMMENTARY

These five sayings probably originally circulated independently, but had already been combined by the pre-Markan tradition or by Mark himself into a connected speech of Jesus. Matthew further integrates them into a unified response by making relatively minor changes—e.g., by omitting the new beginning at Mark 9:1 and thus joining that saying more closely to the preceding. Thus 16:24-28 becomes an integral part of the unified dialogue of 16:13-28 with a close-knit structure, integrating the motifs of christology and discipleship into a single, inseparable theme (cf. Outline).

16:24. Matthew omits the crowds introduced by Mark at this point, addressing the teaching exclusively to the disciples, in continuity with the preceding dialogue. Restricting the address to the disciples has the effect of focusing the instruction on the meaning of discipleship to those who are already within the community, those who have,

like Peter, made the Christian confession but are still "thinking according to human standards rather than the divine revelation" (cf. 23b). These words are not an invitation to discipleship for outsiders, but reflection on the meaning of discipleship for those who have already responded to the call of Christ. The NRSV's "If any want to become my followers" is thus misleading for Matthew's εἴ τις θέλει ὀπίσω μου ἐλθεῖν [*ei tis thelei opisō mou elthein*]. There is no word for "become" (cf. the NIV, which is better at this point). Θέλει (*thelei*) makes following a matter of the will, of decision, but not the initial decision. Jesus' announcement of the Son of Man's own way to the cross is also the way the disciple must follow; christology and discipleship are inseparable. Matthew's church was aware that some had actually been martyrs, including by crucifixion (Peter in Rome; see 23:34). In view of the shortness of the time before the parousia (v. 28), Matthew anticipates that the eschatological tribulation will intensify; so the call for disciples to take up their cross can be understood quite literally in his situation.[376]

16:25. This dramatic saying is not merely a general idealistic principle. Both the context and the qualifying phrase "for me"/"for my sake" make the giving of one's life a matter of commitment to the confession of Jesus as the Christ. Here as elsewhere, Matthew expresses his understanding of human existence somewhat Hellenistically. But ψυχή (*psychē*), often translated "soul," means "life," "life principle," and for Matthew is not an immortal "part" of human being, but is the true self, the living self. Those who seek to preserve their lives by living selfishly end up actually forfeiting themselves, for the decision about confessing or denying Christ must be seen in an eschatological perspective (vv. 27-28).

16:26. Again, in the context of Hellenistic "parallels," this could be seen as a general counsel of practical wisdom: What value are all the world's goods if one loses one's own life? People would trade all they have for their life, if that were the only option. Yet the saying must be seen in the light of its biblical background (Ps 49:7-9) and in the perspective of christological confession of the suffering and vindicated Son of Man, who is also the coming judge.

16:27. The Son of Man who has suffered has been vindicated by God and will be the eschatological judge. He will reward and punish "according to one's practice" (κατὰ τὴν πρᾶξιν *kata tēn praxin*), not on the basis of the confession one has made verbally, however orthodox. The fact that the Son of Man has God as his Father (cf. 25:31) means that "Son of Man" christology and "Son of God" christology should not be distinguished too sharply. Here as elsewhere, the way of the Son of Man through homelessness, suffering, and death to vindication by God fills in the content of the titles "Christ" and "Son of God." The entire christological dialogue is bracketed by Jesus' self-identification as Son of Man (16:13, 27-28). A similar identification takes place in the exchange between the high priest and Jesus in 26:63-64.

16:28. In order to conclude this dialogue with Jesus' self-declaration as Son of Man, Matthew reformulates the saying of Mark 9:1 into a Son of Man saying. This brings Jesus' preaching of the coming kingdom of God and his identity as Son of Man into very close relationship. The nearness of the coming kingdom/parousia of the Son of Man here functions as encouragement to follow the path of Jesus.

What "some standing here" are promised they will see before their death has been variously understood, some of the major options in church history being (1) the transfiguration, which immediately follows;[377] (2) the resurrection;[378] (3) Pentecost and the power of Christ at work in the church.[379] The most likely explanation, however, is that (4) Matthew refers to the parousia, which he expected to take place soon, when at least some of the first generation would still be alive. The chief problem with this apparently obvious meaning is, of course, that the parousia did not occur. This is, nonetheless, the most likely meaning. Allowing the early Christians to be chronologically incorrect in their eschatology does not nullify its theological validity, and it should be allowed to stand.[380]

376. Luke 9:23 already understands the Markan saying metaphorically of giving one's life for Christ by living it unselfishly. Matthew's interpretation includes this, but sees it as extending to actual martyrdom if need be.

377. Mark may have had this view, as did several of the early Church Fathers, including Augustine. This is not Matthew's view, however; he has rewritten the whole passage to include v. 28 with the preceding dialogue and separate it from the transfiguration.

378. Both Luther and Calvin so understood this text. This view must be at least partly correct, since Matt 28:16-20 has much Son of Man imagery, and Matthew certainly understood a major turning point in the history of salvation to occur at Jesus' resurrection, an anticipation of the eschatological event. Cf. Meier, *Vision,* 26-41 who argues too strongly for reducing Matthew's meaning to this view.

379. Gregory the Great and many later Roman Catholic exegetes so understood it, identifying the church with the kingdom too closely. Matthew's changing Mark's kingdom language to Son of Man language, relating it to the clear reference to eschatological judgment in v. 27, argues against it as Matthew's view, as does Matthew's lack of Luke's pattern of resurrection/ascension/Pentecost, having instead the continuing presence of Christ (see Commentary on 28:16-20).

380. See Reflections at 25:46 and M. Eugene Boring, *Revelation, Int.* (Louisville: Westminster/John Knox, 1989) 68-74.

REFLECTIONS

1. The function of this scene is to make an important theological claim about Jesus: His death occurred as a part of God's plan of salvation. "While the narrative function of the three passion announcements is to prepare the disciples, their theological purpose is to assure the readers, first that Jesus' violent death is not a meaningless accident of history but is part of God's plan, and, second, that Jesus was not a hapless victim but a knowing [and willing] partner in the divine strategy."[381]

2. The Christian life called for is not a reflection of, let alone the baptism and blessing of, the egocentric culture, but its polar opposite. Self-denial is not part of our culture's image of the "good life." But neither is the Matthean Jesus' call for denying oneself to be understood as asceticism or as self-hate. Just as Jesus' call to discipleship is not a joining in the cultural infatuation with self-esteem, neither is it the opposite. Nor is the self-denial to which Jesus calls the opposite of self-fulfillment. Just giving up things will not make one Christian; it will only make one empty. What is difficult for our culture to understand, indeed what it cannot understand on its own terms, is an orientation to one's life that is not focused on self at all, either as self-esteem or self-abasement, as self-fulfillment or self-emptying.

3. This call to discipleship is based on faith in Christ and confidence in the future victory of God; it is not a matter merely of high human ideals or noble principles. That is, the life called for here is not based on a reasoned conclusion about how things are, inferred from observation or general principles, but on faith that something has happened that makes everything different. To believe in Jesus as the Christ and to live accordingly means to reorient one's life toward the good news that God has acted decisively and ultimately in Jesus, not that Jesus has some good advice on how to live (by what criteria could such advice be judged to be good?). The call to discipleship here expressed is based on the past and future revelatory act of God. The call to discipleship of vv. 24-26 is inseparably related to the confession in v. 16 and to the expectation in vv. 27-28, all bound together with Jesus' self-proclamation as Son of Man in vv. 13 and 28. The christological confession of v. 16 is not abstract doctrine about the "person" of Jesus, but is realized only as it leads to the life called for in vv. 24-26.

4. This call to discipleship is a matter of confession, which means declaring one's faith in Jesus as the Christ, as God's definitive act of revelation and salvation. The word used to mean "confession" (μαρτύριον *martyrion*; Matt 8:4; 10:18; 24:14) also means "martyrdom," in the sense of witness. The giving of one's life is presented as an act of testimony to a truth bigger than oneself. Its result may be literal martyrdom, as had happened in Matthew's church and in every generation since, and continues today. But it may also mean the daily giving of oneself away in commitment to Christ (so Luke 9:23 explicitly). While many readers of this commentary will no longer live in a situation such as Matthew's in which the result of authentic Christian confession can be literal martyrdom, the call to give one's life as a testimony to the truth of the gospel is no less real. Orientation toward God, revealed in Christ as the Lord of one's life, rather than idolatrous self-orientation, is the decisive, crucial difference.

5. This call to discipleship is a matter of community. This is not an individualistic ethic of the solitary "I," but is the ethic of the community of disciples that confesses Jesus to be the Christ and lives toward the full coming of the kingdom of God for which it prays, accompanied by the presence of Christ during its time of mission.

6. The meaning of discipleship is learned along the way. The disciples in this story have been disciples for some time, called personally by Jesus (4:18-22; 9:9; 10:2-4), sent by him to preach and heal (10:5-8). They now learn the meaning and cost of discipleship, which cannot be explained in advance but must be learned en route. Many sensitive Christians may have wondered about the integrity of their own Christian life, since they "didn't know what they were doing" when they "joined the church." Neither did the Matthean disciples, who only

---

381. Douglas R. A. Hare, *Matthew*, Int. (Louisville: Westminster/John Knox, 1993) 232.

learn in 16:21-28 what following Christ means, and who will yet falter and fail before the story is over. There is encouragement here for Christians who are concerned about past lapses (with more sure to come) and who are sure they do not understand as much as they should about the Christian life, just as there is warning for Christians who are sure that they do understand and have no need to change their present conceptions of the way things are.

❖   ❖   ❖   ❖

EXCURSUS: MATTHEAN CHRISTOLOGY

Matthew does not develop christology as a separate doctrine. For Matthew, christology is an essential aspect of theology proper, the doctrine of God, and so cannot be abstracted and treated as a separate theme. Neither does christology deal with the person of Christ independently of discipleship and community. Just as christology and theology imply each other, so also do christology and ecclesiology.

THEOCENTRIC

Although Jesus appears in almost every scene of the Gospel of Matthew, the narrative is "about" Jesus only in the sense of Jesus as the Messiah, as the whole narrative and its title (1:1) make clear. The Messiah is the anointed one, the past participle implying the action of another.[382] Jesus is the Christ not by what he is in himself, but by the action of God, who made him to be the Christ. A gospel is a christological narrative (better: narrative christology) that by definition is theocentric. The active subject that constitutes Jesus to be the Christ is neither he himself, nor is it his disciples. Jesus is not chosen or elected to be the Christ by his admirers, as though he represented their ideals or the embodiment of their values. Contrary to all expectations, God anointed Jesus to be the Messiah.[383] Thus the affirmation that Jesus is the Messiah is an affirmation of the definitive act of God. Christology does not begin with the person of Jesus and inquire as to his identity and significance, but with the issue of whether God has acted to make him the Christ. What is at stake is not who Jesus is but who God is.[384] Christology is an aspect of the encompassing theocentric symbol "kingdom of heaven/God" (cf. Excursus "Kingdom of Heaven in Matthew," 288-94).

VARIETY OF PRE-MATTHEAN CHRISTOLOGICAL THOUGHT

Matthew has a number of different ways of expressing his fundamental conviction that God has definitively acted in Christ for the salvation of the world. There was considerable variety in Jewish messianic expectations. Not all Jews expected a messianic figure to play a role in the eschatological triumph of God. Where the messianic hope existed, it was manifested in a variety of forms. (Christians should thus avoid speaking of *the* Jewish hope for the Christ.) "Son of David," for instance, was not a universal or perhaps even general part of the messianic expectation. After the demise of the Davidic line and the ascendancy of the priestly Hasmoneans in the Maccabean period, the Davidic promises were reinterpreted in some circles to apply to priests, so that a levitical messiah could be expected alongside of, or as an alternative to, a Davidic messiah, as at Qumran. In early Judaism the

---

382. "Anointed one" (Χριστός *Christos*) belongs to that class of Greek adjectives that implies the action of another, such as "loved," "beloved" (ἀγαπητός *agapētos*) and "elected," "chosen" (ἐκλεκτός *eklektos*).

383. "Anointed" is the metaphorical shorthand term for "installed into office." Jesus receives no literal anointing in the narrative. See exegesis of 26:6-13; the woman who anointed him did so as anticipatory burial rites, not as a messianic anointing, for which a different word (χρίω *chriō*) is used, as well as a different substance (oil, not perfume).

384. See Schubert M. Ogden, *The Point of Christology* (San Francisco: Harper & Row, 1982).

Messiah was thought to have his ancestry in Judah (David), or Levi (Aaron), or Ephraim (Joseph), and sometimes these ideas "seem not to have been mutually exclusive."[385]

Likewise, early pre-Matthean Christianity had already developed a variety of ways of expressing the saving significance of (God's act in) Jesus.

The Christology of Q

The christological expressions used by the Q community seem to have developed over several decades. In the (relatively late?) form of Q used by Matthew, the sayings genre has the effect of picturing Jesus as primarily eschatological prophet and teacher of wisdom whose primary function is to speak the definitive word of God. Only a minimal range of christological titles is used:

- ❖ "The coming one" (ὁ ἐρχόμενος *ho erchomenos*) in Matt 3:11/Luke 3:16; Matt 11:3/Luke 7:19; Matt 23:39/Luke 13:35—all taken over by Matthew.
- ❖ "Son of God" (υἱὸς τοῦ θεοῦ *huios tou theou*) is found only in Matt 4:3, 6/Luke 4:3, 9, in the devil's challenge rejected by Jesus, and was apparently not a title for Jesus in the Q community. "Son" is claimed by Jesus in a unique sense in Matt 11:27/Luke 10:22.
- ❖ "Lord" (κύριος *kyrios*) is not used of Jesus christologically except in Matt 7:21-22/Luke 6:46, perhaps Matt 8:8/Luke 7:6; Matt 8:21/Luke 9:59.
- ❖ "Christ," "Son of David," "king," and "teacher" are not used of Jesus at all in Q.
- ❖ Jesus, along with John the Baptist, is represented as the definitive messenger of Wisdom in Matt 11:19*b*/Luke 7:35 and Matt 23:34-35 (cf. Luke 11:49-51).

The principal christological designation for Jesus in Q is "Son of Man," used eleven times. Three of these occurrences speak of Jesus, the Son of Man who is presently on earth, as homeless (Matt 8:20/Luke 9:58), as eating and drinking (and not ascetic; Matt 11:19/Luke 7:34), and as a sign to "this generation" by his preaching and presence (Matt 12:40/Luke 11:30).[386] The other eight Son of Man sayings in Q speak of Jesus as the exalted one who will come again as eschatological judge (Matt 5:11/Luke 6:22; Matt 10:32/Luke 12:8; Matt 12:32/Luke 12:10; Matt 19:28/Luke 22:28-30; Matt 24:27, 37, 39/Luke 17:24, 26, 30; Matt 24:44/Luke 12:40).

Although Q is aware of the crucifixion of Jesus (Matt 10:38/Luke 14:27), his suffering and death play no christological role, and there are no sayings about the suffering and dying of the Son of Man. The dominant image is that of Jesus as Son of Man who delivers the final message from God and who will return as eschatological judge. The criterion of judgment will be adherence to the message of Jesus by confessing him in word and deed. Matthew was deeply influenced by this christological imagery, which he and his community seem to have had as their dominant way of construing the significance of Jesus prior to the arrival of the Gospel of Mark in their community (see Introduction).

The Markan Revolution

While Q is a prophetic-sapiential anthology of sayings with only a smattering of narrative, Mark is primarily a narrative with only a minimum of sayings material. The Markan way of confessing faith in Jesus is thus radically different from that of Q, a revolutionary new narrative

---

385. Marshall D. Johnson, *The Purpose of the Biblical Genealogies,* SNTSMS (Cambridge: Cambridge University Press, 1969) 116.

386. Matthew has modified the more original form of Q found in Luke by interpreting it in terms of the resurrection. See Commentary on 12:40.

mode of christology that combined into one paradoxical narrative genre pictures of Jesus as the mighty Son of God with pictures of Jesus as humanly weak and victimized.[387] Matthew adopted the Markan narrative mode of christological confession as his own and made it basic to his presentation of Jesus. Mark's fundamental contribution to the development of Matthew's christology is the narrative mode of confession, but Mark also shifted the focus to christological titles that had previously played only a minimal role or none at all in Matthew's theology: Christ, Son of God, the suffering and dying Son of Man, teacher, prophet, king, Lord (only ambiguously in Mark), and Son of David (only negatively in Mark). See below for the Matthean adoption and reinterpretation of these titles.

M Emphases

From Matthew's special traditions he received an emphasis on Jesus as fulfiller of Scripture as well as stories of Jesus' birth and appearances after his resurrection, both of which were lacking in Mark.

NARRATIVE FORM AS A MEANS OF INCORPORATING A VARIETY OF CHRISTOLOGICAL EXPRESSIONS

The genius of narrative is that it can hold together contrary pictures that make problems for discursive logic; it can say different things without reducing them to a common denominator or arranging them into a systematic hierarchy of concepts, a theological mode that is difficult to achieve in abstract logic. Thus Matthew's christology is at the furthest pole from a list of titles or a philosophical discussion of christological topoi (e.g., person and work; nature and substance; divinity and humanity). While Matthew clearly believes that Jesus was uniquely the Son of God with a special divine mission, that he had died a truly human death and had been exalted to heavenly status, Matthew's christological thought is not oriented to the categories of divinity and humanity. Like most readers of the NT after him, Matthew accepts the Markan narrative resolution of this conceptual problem without reflecting on it himself. Thus "Son of God" is for him more a royal category related to kingship than a metaphysical one related to divinity, as illustrated by the way he develops the story of the miraculous birth. On the other hand, he simply assumes the true humanity of Jesus without reflecting on it as a disputed point, and he sees no problem in dropping the key Markan word for "human being" ($\check{\alpha}\nu\theta\rho\omega\pi\text{os}$ *anthrōpos*) in the climactic confession of the Roman soldier(s) at the crucifixion (cf. Mark 15:39 vs. Matt 27:54).

His christology works the way a narrative works, and is inseparable from experiencing the story itself. Thus literary criticism is an important avenue of christological insight, so that, for example, the first and last scenes are important as narratives, quite apart from titles and explicit christological reflection. The closing scene (28:16-20) to which the whole narrative builds portrays one who claims that all authority has been given to him but utilizes no titles. The opening scenes clearly affirm the virginal conception and birth of Jesus, yet Matthew does not relate them directly to his understanding of Jesus as Son of God. The story of the miraculous birth seems rather to be an element in his tradition that Matthew affirms but needs to explain in a way that allows the emphasis to fall on Son of David christology, which is important to Matthew (see below, and Commentary on 1:1-15).

Other distinctive Matthean christological emphases incorporated into his narrative are:

---

387. Cf. M. Eugene Boring, *Truly Human/Truly Divine: Christological Language and the Gospel Form* (St. Louis: Christian Board of Publication, 1984).

Jesus as Fulfillment of the Scripture

Matthew's narrative is not an independent story of Jesus but is the climax and fulfillment of the larger story, the biblical account of God and Israel, which points beyond itself to the ultimate fulfillment. Jesus is the fulfillment of this story, the definitive dénouement of the storyline, leading from creation through the fall, the call of Abraham and Sarah, the formation of Israel as the covenant people, the kingship under David, the decline and exile, the time of expectation. Matthew understands this story as a whole as prophecy, as promise that is fulfilled in Jesus (see Excursus "Matthew as Interpreter of Scripture," 151-54). The prophecy-and-fulfillment theme is so important throughout the narrative that it must be understood as a vehicle of Matthew's christology. Jesus is the fulfillment of the hopes and promises of all the Scripture, and he is portrayed in the colors drawn from the biblical palette, even when explicit christological claims are not present. The portrayal of Jesus evokes images of Moses, David, and the Suffering Servant of Isaiah 42–53.

Jesus Acts with Authority

The majestic apocalyptic vision of Daniel 7 has had a profound effect on Matthew, as may be seen especially in the closing scene of 28:16-20, although it is not explicitly cited and "Son of Man" terminology is not explicitly used. Rather, Jesus is presented as the one who has been given all authority. Again, the theocentric perspective is to be noted, as in "anointed"; in each case, the reader must ask "by whom?," transforming a surface-level picture of Jesus into a depth picture of the act of God. Jesus as the one who acts with authority is a thematic thread throughout, which comes to its climax in this scene.

Jesus Is Identified with Wisdom

Although not a central element in Matthew's christology, the picture of Jesus as identified with personified Wisdom is an important aspect of his view, as is evident from his amplification of this motif as found in Q.[388] It does seem that Matthew identifies Jesus with Wisdom, but still without a doctrine of preexistence.

Secrecy and Transparency in Mark and in Matthew

Mark had developed the incipient elements already in the pre-Gospel tradition into a full-blown messianic secret, according to which no human being understood the secret of Jesus' identity during his earthly life. In Mark, the messianic secret was a sophisticated literary device to allow the stories of Jesus' divine power to be told so that the readers, from their post-Easter perspective, could perceive the act of God in Christ, but the characters in the story remained blind to Jesus' identity until after the story was over, in order to preserve the necessity of the cross/resurrection for authentic Christian faith. "The secrecy theory is the hermeneutical presupposition of the genre Gospel."[389] Matthew did not need the messianic secret in this sense. He accepts Mark's narrative with its double picture of Jesus, but understands the narrative to work at two levels, both portraying the pre-Easter story and being transparent to the post-Easter situation. Thus the disciples in the story already are addressed as though they

---

388. M. Jack Suggs, *Wisdom, Christology, and Law in Matthew's Gospel* (Cambridge, Mass.: Harvard University Press, 1970), does regard sapiential christology as central to Matthew, who (along with John) develops Q's picture of Jesus as messenger of Wisdom into Jesus as the "incarnation" of Wisdom. Compare the appreciative but critical review of Suggs's argument by Marshall Johnson, "Reflections on a Wisdom Approach to Matthew's Christology," *CBQ* 26 (1974) 44-64.

389. Hans Conzelmann, "Present and Future in the Synoptic Tradition," *JTC* V:43.

live in the time after Easter. Matthew's Jesus can, therefore, be much more open in his self-revelation than the Markan Jesus, and the Matthean disciples can perceive the revelation at the level of the pre-Easter story (cf., e.g., Matthew's rewriting of Mark 6:51 at Matt 14:33). The secrecy elements still preserved in Matthew are mostly vestigial remains of the Markan way of telling the story.

Tradition and Reinterpretation; Picture of Jesus

To say that the Christ is Jesus not only interprets the meaning of "Jesus," but reinterprets the meaning of "Christ" in light of who Jesus actually was. This dynamic, fundamental to all christology, attains a particular focus in Matthew's delineation. The Christ who was to establish justice and inaugurate the kingdom of God was traditionally a violent figure, overthrowing the power of evil with righteous force. David was the paradigm. As the narrative unfolds to portray Jesus as the authentic king, God's representative and agent in inaugurating the kingdom of God, the traditional valences are reversed and the image is radically reinterpreted. Jesus is the meek king who conquers by suffering, who lives out his own teaching of loving the enemy and turning the other cheek.

This main substance of the storyline of Matthew is a narrative function, not a titular claim or philosophical discussion of Jesus' nature or being. The main point is made in a story. This is a scandalous story, one that poses a stumbling block for ordinary common sense (cf. the christological use of σκανδαλίζω [skandalizō] and σκάνδαλον [skandalon] at 11:6; 13:21, 57; 15:12; 16:23; 26:31).

Thus while Matthew's christology cannot be reduced to discussion of the various titles, the way that Matthew works the titles into the narrative is significant, and we may conclude with a summary of his specific titular usage.[390]

TITLES FOR JESUS IN MATTHEW

"Christ"/"Messiah" (17x)

Although in Gentile Christianity the strange Jewish word translated "Christ" (Χριστός Christos) quickly became a proper name for Jesus (for which "Lord" was often the titular designation); yet Matthew still preserves the original sense designating an office (e.g., 11:2). "Christ" is the first title given to Jesus in the title of the book (1:1), and it recurs in key scenes (16:16; 26:63). Jesus' response to Peter's declaration includes "Son of God" in the more encompassing "Christ" (16:16, 20).

The word itself means "anointed," reflecting the ancient Israelite ritual of pouring oil on the head of those being inaugurated into the office of prophet (cf. 1 Kgs 19:16; Isa 61:1), priest (Exod 28:41; Ps 133:2), or king (1 Sam 16:1-13; Ps 89:19-20). Thus while the classic exposition is correct in referring to the threefold office of the Messiah (prophet, priest, king), in first-century Palestine, it was the royal connotation that was most prevalent. *Messiah* means "king," God's chosen agent for inaugurating the eschatological kingdom of God. "Christ," "Son of God," and "king" all evoke the mythical picture of the eschatological restoration of the creation to the sovereignty of the Creator.

"King [of the Jews/Israel]" (8x)

Jesus as king is an important christological theme for Matthew, who closely links his view of Jesus with his theology of the kingdom of God. (See Excursus "Kingdom of Heaven in Matthew," 288-94.)

---

390. See Leander E. Keck, "Toward the Renewal of New Testament Christology," *NTS* 32 (1986) 362-77.

"The Coming One" (7x)

Although this does not seem to have been a traditional designation for the Messiah in Judaism, Matthew had found the christological use of ὁ ἐρχόμενος (*ho erchomenos*) in Q. He adopted it and used the title exclusively for Jesus, three times associating it closely with the Son of Man.

"Lord" (34x)

This common Greek word (κύριος *kyrios*) could be used simply as a polite form of address to a superior (27:63, the Jewish leaders to Pilate) or of human masters without any connotation of divine status (6:24; 10:24; 18:25-34, all in the words of Jesus). In biblical usage in the Jewish context, however, it was also the translation of the divine name "Yahweh," and thus meant "Lord" in the divine sense. While Q had been very restrained in using *kyrios* of Jesus and Mark never unambiguously did so, Matthew applies this term to Jesus thirty-four times, both in his own compositions and in insertions into Q and Markan contexts. Some of these are to be read at two levels—the characters in the story who address Jesus as *kyrios* meant something like "Sir," but the reader knows that it is the exalted Lord of the church's faith that is being addressed.

"Son"

Matthew adopts the one instance in Q in which "Son" is used absolutely in a christological sense (Matt 11:27/Luke 10:22), as well as using the phrases "Son of God," (9 times), "my Son" (with God as the speaker, 3 times), and parabolically representing Jesus as God's Son (21:37; 22:25-31 [cf. v. 34]). Since "Son" in various combinations is such a key term in NT christology, and since the biblical usage of this word is so different from its meaning in contemporary English, a brief explanation is in order.

Matthew uses the Greek word for "son" (υἱός *huios*) eighty-nine times, very often in ways that do not correspond to English usage (and thus often not translated "son" in English). In the OT "son" has the following meanings.[391]

(1) *Biological son, male child* (e.g., Gen 21:2, Isaac as son of Abraham and Sarah). This "normal" usage is found in Matthew (e.g., 1:21; 10:37; 13:55; 17:15), but less often than special theological uses influenced by his Hebrew background.

(2) *Child,* male or female (e.g., Gen 3:16, "in pain you shall bring forth children" [lit. "sons"]). Thus a male child can be specifically designated "male *son,*" as in Jer 20:15. The LXX translated "son" (בֵּן *bēn*) as "child" (τέκνον *teknon*) 134 times. When speaking literally, Matthew uses "son or daughter" for this inclusive sense (10:37; 7:9?) rather than "son" (or perhaps 7:9?), but can use "sons" inclusively in a metaphorical sense for "children" of God (e.g., 5:9, 45; cf. "adoption," lit. "sonship," Rom 8:15; Gal 4:5, which obviously is inclusive of male and female). When so used, though including male and female children, "son" has a different set of connotations and is not simply a synonym of "child."

(3) *Descendant* (e.g., Josh 22:27, "our children [lit. "sons"] in the generations after us"). In Matt 1:20, Joseph is "Son of David" in this sense, differently than Jesus.

(4) "Son" can be used of offspring of *animals* (Matt 21:5 of the donkey's colt, but in a quotation from Zech 9:9), of *plants,* and even of *inanimate things* (e.g., Job 5:7, "sons of the flame" [sparks]). The latter usage is not paralleled in the NT.

(5) *Inhabitants of a country* (e.g., Gen 23:3, "Hittites" [lit., "sons of Heth"]) or *membership* in

---

391. Cf. the standard Hebrew lexica and *TDNT* 8:340-62.

a nation or family (e.g., Exod 1:7; 3:10, "Israelites" [lit. "sons of Israel"; KJV "children of Israel"]). Matthew uses this meaning in 17:25; 27:9; 8:12 may belong here as well.

(6) *Belonging to a category* (Gen 6:2; Job 1:6, the RSV's "son of God" means "belonging to the divine category," thus the NRSV's "heavenly beings"; Ps 8:4, the RSV's "son of man" means "belonging to the human category," thus the NRSV's "human beings"; 2 Kgs 10:30, "sons of the fourth generation" means "belonging to the fourth generation"). Matthew's use of "Son of God" for Jesus may belong here, as well as in other categories. Does 13:38 belong here?

(7) *Members of a guild, order, or class* (1 Kgs 20:35, "sons of the prophets" [RSV]; Matt 9:15, lit. "sons of the wedding chamber" [members of the wedding party]; Matt 12:27, "sons" of the Pharisees [so RSV]).

(8) Metaphorical *term of endearment* (e.g., 1 Sam 3:6, Eli to Samuel; Exod 4:22; Hos 11:1, where God calls Israel "my firstborn son"; cf. Matt 2:15).

(9) Indicating a *quality or characteristic* (e.g., 1 Sam 14:52, "son of valor"; 2 Sam 3:34, "sons of wickedness" [evil people]; Matt 23:15, "child of hell" [lit., "son of Gehenna"]). Mathew 23:31 uses it in an ironic double sense, "sons of those who murdered the prophets," meaning both that they are their descendants (which they acknowledge) and that they are the same kind of people (the NRSV's "descendants" obscures the ironic twist here).

(10) *Legitimate heir* (2 Chr 13:9-10, "sons of Aaron" [legitimate priests, heirs of the Aaronic priesthood, not mere biological descent]). "Son of David" and "Son of Abraham" in Matt 1:1 may reflect this connotation, among others.

(11) The *Israelite king* (2 Sam 7:14; Pss 2:7; 89:26-27). Of course, there is nothing biological or metaphysical in this understanding of "son," which is a matter of honor, position, and "adoption." In biblical Hebrew, the move from "king" (Messiah, anointed one) to "son of God" is slight.

It is thus evident that in a Hebrew-Jewish context influenced by biblical usage, the term *son* is used in a variety of ways in addition to signifying a biological relationship. Although the word can be used generically to include both males and females, it is not equivalent to "child," which has other connotations.

"Son of David" (10x)

This term is found only in the synoptic Gospels (but cf. Rom 1:3; 2 Tim 2:8; Rev 3:7; 5:5; 22:16). It does not occur as a title in the OT, but does in *Pss. Sol.* 17:21 as a synonym for the "king" God will raise up in the eschatological times. It is the most frequently used messianic title in the Talmud and Midrash—that is, it is "Pharisaic," the stream from which Matthew comes and with which he is in most intensive dialogue.

Mark uses it only three times (10:47-48; 12:35), each time as a misunderstanding of the nature of Jesus' discipleship. Luke retains the Markan references and adds only the one reference in the genealogy (Luke 3:31). The phrase does not occur in John at all.

For Matthew, however, "Son of David" is a major christological title, as in Judaism it is a synonym for "Messiah." He includes it in the title to the Gospel (1:1), begins his narrative with a genealogy and "birth story" devoted to presenting Jesus as the authentic "Son of David" (1:2-25), and uses it more than the rest of the NT as a whole.

"Son of God" (9x)

In a Gentile context, "Son of God" would normally denote a divine or semi-divine being having only one human parent or no human parents at all. The expression was also used outside of the Bible for outstanding individuals who seemed to be superhuman in their status or accomplishments, such as the Caesars. In the context of the OT and Judaism, "Son of God" had a variety of meanings, resulting from the wide range of meanings of the Hebrew word בֵּן *bēn* (see above). Thus while in a Jewish context "Son of God" could not mean literal biological generation in which God played the role of the father, as in paganism, the phrase did take on a wide spectrum of meanings and was used in the following ways:[392]

(1) of Israel (Exod 4:22; Hos. 11:1);

(2) of particularly righteous Israelites (Wis 2:12-20);

(3) of angels, divine beings (Gen 6:1-4; Deut 32:8; Job 1:6; 2:1; 38:7);

(4) of the Israelite or Jewish king (2 Sam 7:14; Ps 2:7);

(5) of the coming Messiah (cf. Ps 2:7 in rabbinic exegesis; 4 Ezra 7:28-29).

While Matthew, like other NT writers, can refer to Christians as "sons of God" (5:9, 45; cf. Luke 20:36; Rom 8:14, 19; Gal 4:6; Heb 12:7; Rev 12:7), he uses "Son of God" of Jesus in a unique christological sense. While he affirms the supernatural origin and status of Jesus, his "Son of God" does not connote primarily divinity, but royalty: Jesus as the divinely appointed king in God's kingdom (cf. meaning #4 above and Excursus "Kingdom of Heaven in Matthew," 288-94). Thus Matthew uses the title to explicate the meaning of Messiah/Christ (16:16, where "Son of the living God" is added to Mark's "Christ"). While there is no doubt that "Son of God" is an important title for Matthew, it is not *the* title to which others are subordinate, for Matthew does not think of the christological titles as arranged hierarchically.[393]

"Son of Man" (30x)

This is the most difficult and most disputed of the christological titles. The expression "Son of Man" (ὁ υἱὸς τοῦ ἀνθρώπου *ho huios tou anthrōpou*) sounds as strange in Greek as it does in English, since it is not a native Greek term but is the literal translation of the common Hebrew בֶּן אָדָם (*bēn 'ādām*) or Aramaic בַּר אֱנָשׁ (*bar enōsh*), both of which mean simply "human being," as in Ezekiel (93 times) where the phrase designates the prophet as a mere human being in contrast to God (cf. meanings 6-7 above under the Hebrew usage of "son").

The NT uses the phrase as a designation of Jesus in a particular christological sense. Some features of NT usage:

(1) The articular singular is used only of Jesus.

(2) Except for Acts 7:56, the phrase is found exclusively in the Gospels. (The only other NT references are Mark 3:28 and Eph 3:5, where the plural is used of human beings in general, the citation of Ps 8:7 in Heb 2:6, and Rev 1:13 and 14:14, where the word without the article is used to mean "like a human figure.")

(3) In the Gospels, the phrase is found exclusively in the sayings of Jesus, as his self-designation (in John 12:34 the crowds questioningly repeat Jesus' own usage). The narrator never refers to Jesus as "Son of Man," nor does any character in the narrative, although several of the other christological titles are so used.

(4) The thirteen Johannine instances form a special category, but the sixty-nine Synoptic instances fall rather neatly into three groupings: (1) those that speak of the presence of the Son of Man; (2) those that speak of his suffering, death, and resurrection; and (3) those that speak of his eschatological advent. These three categories remain distinct; no saying speaks of the present Son of Man who will suffer and die, or of the dying and rising Son of Man who will come again.

(5) Son of Man sayings are found in all strata of the Synoptic tradition (Mark, Q, M, L), "present"

---

392. The meaning of υἱός (*huios*) or בֵּן (*bēn*) is often obscured in the NRSV's efforts to avoid gender-specific language.

393. Contra Jack Dean Kingsbury, *Matthew: Structure, Christology, Kingdom* (Philadelphia: Fortress, 1975) 62, 82, and numerous later essays. Kingsbury sees "Son of God" as "the central christological category of Matthew's Gospel" under which all the other titles are "subsumed."

and "coming" sayings are found in all strata, but "suffering, dying, and rising" sayings are found only in Mark and in literature dependent on Mark.

Under the influence of Daniel 7, the figure of the Son of Man was understood in some circles of first-century Judaism to be the apocalyptic deliverer who will come as judge at the end of time. Matthew and his community had adopted the centrality of "Son of Man" as a key christological title from Q (see above).

"Teacher"/"Rabbi" (14x)

Matthew is curiously ambivalent about using the titles "Teacher," "Master," or "Rabbi" for Jesus. On the one hand, he forbids aspiring disciples to use these titles of themselves, reserving them exclusively for Jesus, and presents Jesus throughout as the divinely authorized teacher (5:2–7:29; 28:16-20). On the other hand, only those who are outsiders or who misunderstand address Jesus as "Teacher" or "Master" (including Judas, 26:25, 49), while true disciples never use this form of address.

"Prophet"

For Matthew, this traditional messianic designation is a valid, but inadequate, title for Jesus (cf. 21:11, 46). Even John was more than a prophet (11:9). Matthew makes no explicit use of the expectation of an eschatological "prophet like Moses" (Deut 18:15-18; cf. Luke 24:19; Acts 3:22; 7:37).

"Servant"

Matthew has no specific servant christology, but has been influenced by the picture of the Servant of the Lord as the meek one who accomplishes God's will by his own suffering. The longest quotation in Matthew is from the first Servant Song, and comes at a crucial juncture in the Matthean narrative (12:18-20 = Isa 42:1-4).

❖　　　❖　　　❖　　　❖

Matthew 17:1-27, God's Confession and the New Community

Matthew 17:1-13, God's Confession and Jesus' Response

NIV

17 After six days Jesus took with him Peter, James and John the brother of James, and led them up a high mountain by themselves. [2]There he was transfigured before them. His face shone like the sun, and his clothes became as white as the light. [3]Just then there appeared before them Moses and Elijah, talking with Jesus.

[4]Peter said to Jesus, "Lord, it is good for us to be here. If you wish, I will put up three shelters—one for you, one for Moses and one for Elijah."

[5]While he was still speaking, a bright cloud

NRSV

17 Six days later, Jesus took with him Peter and James and his brother John and led them up a high mountain, by themselves. [2]And he was transfigured before them, and his face shone like the sun, and his clothes became dazzling white. [3]Suddenly there appeared to them Moses and Elijah, talking with him. [4]Then Peter said to Jesus, "Lord, it is good for us to be here; if you wish, I[a] will make three dwellings[b] here, one for you, one for Moses, and one for Elijah."

[a]Other ancient authorities read *we*　　[b]Or *tents*

NIV

enveloped them, and a voice from the cloud said, "This is my Son, whom I love; with him I am well pleased. Listen to him!"

⁶When the disciples heard this, they fell face-down to the ground, terrified. ⁷But Jesus came and touched them. "Get up," he said. "Don't be afraid." ⁸When they looked up, they saw no one except Jesus.

⁹As they were coming down the mountain, Jesus instructed them, "Don't tell anyone what you have seen, until the Son of Man has been raised from the dead."

¹⁰The disciples asked him, "Why then do the teachers of the law say that Elijah must come first?"

¹¹Jesus replied, "To be sure, Elijah comes and will restore all things. ¹²But I tell you, Elijah has already come, and they did not recognize him, but have done to him everything they wished. In the same way the Son of Man is going to suffer at their hands." ¹³Then the disciples understood that he was talking to them about John the Baptist.

NRSV

⁵While he was still speaking, suddenly a bright cloud overshadowed them, and from the cloud a voice said, "This is my Son, the Beloved;ᵃ with him I am well pleased; listen to him!" ⁶When the disciples heard this, they fell to the ground and were overcome by fear. ⁷But Jesus came and touched them, saying, "Get up and do not be afraid." ⁸And when they looked up, they saw no one except Jesus himself alone.

9As they were coming down the mountain, Jesus ordered them, "Tell no one about the vision until after the Son of Man has been raised from the dead." ¹⁰And the disciples asked him, "Why, then, do the scribes say that Elijah must come first?" ¹¹He replied, "Elijah is indeed coming and will restore all things; ¹²but I tell you that Elijah has already come, and they did not recognize him, but they did to him whatever they pleased. So also the Son of Man is about to suffer at their hands." ¹³Then the disciples understood that he was speaking to them about John the Baptist.

ᵃOr my beloved Son

COMMENTARY

Since there is a change of location at v. 9 and an apparent change from "Peter, James, and John" to (all?) "the disciples" at v. 10, this section appears at first to be two pericopes (as in many Gospel synopses; the Revised Common Lectionary includes only 17:1-9 as the unit). The troublesome Mark 9:9-13 (Matt 17:9-13) is simply eliminated by Luke. Matthew, however, links vv. 1-13 together into one unit (v. 9 is attached to 1-8 by the reference to "the vision"; v. 10 is attached to v. 9 by the inferential connective "then" [οὖν oun], and the explicit reference to the suffering Son of Man in v. 12 links vv. 10-12 to v. 9, all of which are Matthean additions. The Elijah motif also binds vv. 10-13 to vv. 1-9). Further, by omitting the reference to the disciples' lack of understanding (Mark 9:10) and concluding with the explicit declaration that the disciples do understand (17:13), Matthew has made all of vv. 1-13 an instructional session for the disciples. Just as the preceding scene (16:13-28) juxtaposes the

divine transcendence of Peter's confession of Jesus as Son of God based on a revelation from heaven (16:17) with Jesus' own teaching about the suffering Son of Man, so also in this scene the confession of the heavenly voice is juxtaposed with Jesus' self-confession as suffering Son of Man. Therefore, it is important to keep vv. 9-13 with vv. 1-8, just as it is important not to separate 16:21-23 from 16:13-20. The unit does have a two-pronged emphasis, however: Jesus the Messiah and Son of God is portrayed in Mosaic colors (vv. 1-9), while John is understood in terms of Elijah (vv. 10-13). John/Elijah is, then, understood as the forerunner and paradigm of Jesus, but in terms of his faithful witness and death at the hands of Herod, not in terms of miraculous power that delivered him from death. As with John, so with Jesus.

17:1-9, Jesus as (Greater Than) Moses. There are many layers of meaning to this story (cf. Reflections below). Here we concentrate on the Matthean level.

17:1. Every word is from Mark 9:2 except "his brother," which is added by Matthew. The addition is not only for biographical information, but also to remind the reader that the community of disciples is a family of brothers and sisters (12:46-50; cf. 18:35; 19:29, 28:10, as well as 7:3-5; 18:15; 23:8; 25:40, where the NRSV obscures the connection by translating ἀδελφοί [*adelphoi* "brothers and sisters"] in a variety of ways: "neighbors," "members of the church," "students," "members of the family"). The Markan "inner circle" Peter/James/John appears here for the first time in Matthew (cf. also 26:37).[394] Since "Son of David" is an important christological title for Matthew, he may regard these three as analogous to King David's inner circle of three (2 Sam 23:8, 18-23). If so, it would be another example of the redefinition of kingship accomplished by Jesus, for David's three were renowned for violence, as was David himself, while the disciples are called to give their lives for others, as does the Son of David.

Such precise chronological data as "after six days" is unique prior to the passion story. In Mark, it may be related to the preceding "after three days." Matthew has eliminated this connection by changing the preceding expression but not this one, thereby making this into an additional element in his Moses typology (from Exod 24:16, see Reflections below). The unnamed mountain corresponds to 5:1 and 28:16. To attempt to identify it (as in pilgrimages and Christian tourism of the Holy Land) is to confuse theology with geography.

17:2. "Transfigured" is literally "metamorphosed" (μεταμορφόομαι *metamorphoomai,* "to undergo a metamorphosis"). In the disciples' "vision" (17:9), Jesus glows with a transcendent glory reserved for heavenly beings, an anticipatory revelation of Jesus as belonging to the divine world (cf. 13:43; 28:3 for Matthean connotations). In Jewish tradition, this radiance was attributed to Adam, Abraham, and many others.[395]

The divine passive implies that the visionary transformation represents the act of God, who makes the revelation to the disciples (cf. 16:17). Matthew specifically adds that Jesus' face shone, another explicit allusion to Moses (cf. Exod 34:29-35; 2 Cor 3:18; Rev 1:16).[396]

17:3. By portraying Moses, Elijah, and Jesus as talking together in a scene of transcendent glory, Matthew confirms his view that Jesus is in continuity with and the fulfillment of God's work as represented by the OT. However, the pairing of Moses and Elijah does not specifically symbolize for Matthew the Scripture as a whole, the written "Law and the Prophets," since nothing here relates Moses to the Torah, nor did Elijah, who is not for Matthew the typical prophet, write anything preserved as Scripture. Moses and Elijah are here paired because they were both prophets who were initially rejected by the people but vindicated by God, both were advocates of the covenant and the Torah, both worked miracles, and both were considered by first-century Judaism to be transcendent figures who did not die but were taken directly to heaven.[397] They thus represent the heavenly world of divine vindication, the world to which, from Matthew's post-Easter perspective, Jesus also belongs. The fact that they were "speaking with" Jesus is another echo of Exod 34:35.

17:4-8. As in the preceding scene (16:13-20), Peter responds to the revelation, but here his lack of understanding as portrayed in Mark is somewhat alleviated (Mark 9:6 is omitted: "For he did not know what to say . . . "), and he speaks as a believer (Matthew's "Lord" for Mark's "Rabbi"). Peter speaks more respectfully than in Mark ("if you wish" added to Mark), but still without complete insight, like the people in general, still placing Jesus in the category of the prophets (17:4 = 16:14). Peter's proposal to build three "tents" (σκηναί *skēnai;* also "tabernacles," "huts") has been variously understood; the same word is used for ordinary tents, for the tabernacle, and for the

394. The pattern comes from Mark, who also has it in Mark 5:37, omitted by Matthew. Compare Mark 13:3, modified by Matthew to include all the disciples. These omissions and modifications lessen the significance of the "inner circle" for Matthew, perhaps because it detracts from his increased emphasis on Peter.

395. Cf. documentation in W. D. Davies and Dale C. Allison, Jr., *A Critical and Exegetical Commentary on the Gospel According to Saint Matthew,* 2 vols. (Edinburgh: T. & T. Clark, 1988–91) 2:692.

396. The description of a shining face and clothing also recalls the apocalyptic tradition (cf. *1 Enoch* 14:20; *2 Enoch* 1:5; 19:1; 4 Ezra 9:27; Rev 1:6). Second Macc 2:8 (1st cent. BCE) has the Moses/mountain motif, with the promise of glory and cloud to reappear in the eschatological times.

397. In interpreting the figure of Moses in the NT, one must keep in mind how Moses was understood in first-century Judaism, not only in the OT. Philo (*Life of Moses* 1.70) says Moses' face shone like the sun. And the idea that Moses did not die (despite Deuteronomy 34) but was taken directly to heaven (like Enoch and Elijah) is affirmed by Josephus *Antiquities of the Jews* 4.323-26; *b. Sota* 13*b;* cf. Jude 9; Origen *De Principiis* 3.2.1.; Clement of Alexandria *Strōmata* 1:23; 6:5.

temporary huts built at the Festival of Booths. Since some Jewish traditions associated the future advent of the kingdom of God over all the nations with the Feast of Booths (cf. Zech 14:9, 16), some understanding of the kingdom may lurk in the background of this saying, but if so, this was missed by Matthew despite his concentration on the theme of the kingdom. Rather, for Matthew, σκηνή (skēnē) connotes the tabernacle and Temple where the Shekinah, the fiery cloud that symbolized the continuing presence of God among the people, dwelt over the ark of the covenant. Matthew presents a threefold response to Peter's proposal:

(1) The heavenly cloud of God's presence appears, as on the tabernacle of Moses' day and the later Temple. As of old, the heavenly voice comes from the cloud, and the God who had previously spoken on Mount Sinai only to Moses speaks directly to them. The heavenly voice speaks in exactly the same words as at the baptism (see 3:17), confirming the identity and mission of Jesus declared there, and confirming the confession Peter himself had made in the preceding scene (16:16).

(2) Although three transcendent figures are present, the heavenly voice charges the disciples to hear *Jesus.* As in the Shema (Deut 6:4), "hear" carries its OT connotation of "obey" and is the same command given with regard to the "prophet like Moses" whom God would send (Deut 18:15; cf. 13:57). The disciples fall on their faces in fearful response to the theophany, as in Exod 34:30; Dan 10:9; and Hab 3:2 LXX.

(3) Jesus comes to them (only here and 28:18 in Matthew, another parallel between this scene and the resurrection appearances) and touches them, and they see no one but "Jesus himself alone." To focus all attention on Jesus and to distinguish him from Moses and Elijah, who have now disappeared, Matthew has added "himself" (αὐτός *autos*) and subtly rewritten Mark so that the word *alone* might stand here as the emphatic closing word of the scene. The heavenly visitors depart, but Jesus stays—Jesus alone. Without heavenly companions, without heavenly glory, *he* is the "tabernacle" (*skēnē*), the reality of God's abiding presence with us (cf. 1:23; 28:20). The disciples descend from the mountain into the mundane world of suffering and mission, accompanied by Jesus, God with us.

17:9. "Coming down the mountain" corresponds to going up the mountain in 17:1 and rounds off vv. 1-9 as a complete scene. Jesus' calling the event a "vision" (only so in Matthew) does not for Matthew connote the modern contrast between subjective experience and objective reality, which reduces the event to the disciples' subjectivity, for he raises no questions about the reality of the event. Rather, the designation "vision" relates the event to the visionary apocalyptic tradition, as has 16:17 (cf. Dan 8:16-17; 10:9-12, 16-19). The mention of Easter as the terminus is not an expression of the messianic secret, as in Mark, but has the effect of relating the vision to the Easter experiences (28:3-7; 28:16, 18-19) and indicates that it can only be understood from the post-Easter perspective of the Matthean readers, who are called to identify themselves with the disciples in the story.

17:10-13, John as Elijah. Whereas in Mark the conversation is still with only the three disciples of the preceding scene (cf. Mark 9:11, 14), Matthew has the scene modulate imperceptibly into a dialogue with the disciples, although he also follows the Markan picture of disciples remaining with the crowd (cf. 17:14, 16). The connection with vv. 1-9 at first seems forced, despite Matthew's adding "why then" (τί οὖν *ti oun*) to the disciples' question to relate it to the preceding topic. But v. 10 is not merely responding to v. 9, but looks back at all of 16:13–17:9, portraying the advent of Jesus as the eschatological event, as the Messiah/Son of God who fulfills his ministry as the rejected and dying Son of Man, who will be vindicated by God at the resurrection (cf. Overview at 13:53; 16:13). The disciples, who know already of Jesus' identification of John as Elijah (11:10, 14), voice the objection of the scribal opponents of Matthew's church to the Christian claims: How can the Christ have come already, since the Scripture says that Elijah must come first (Mal 4:5-6)?[398]

17:11. The phrase "restoration of all things," associated with the expected advent of Elijah, points to the eschatological restoration of creation

---

398. As often elsewhere in Matthew, the dialogue presupposes the concerns of Matthew's situation rather than the particulars of the pre-Easter life of Jesus.

to its pre-fallen state, not only salvation for human beings but also redemption of the creation itself (cf. 19:28, "the renewal of all things"). Jesus' reply may be punctuated either as a statement or a challenging question.[399] If, as is most likely, it is a statement, the future tense "he will restore all things" is problematic, since John, understood as the fulfillment of this expectation, had not "restored all things," but the world continued in its fallen, unredeemed state.[400] There are four possible explanations for the future tense: (1) The future verb in Matthew may simply reflect the form of the scriptural quotation (Mal 4:5-6), in which case it should be enclosed in quotation marks. (2) The future tense may reflect the scribal expectation, not Jesus' own. (3) Or in the view of the Matthean Jesus, while Elijah/John the Baptist has already come, the "restoration of all things" still belongs to the eschatological future. (4) More likely, Matthew affirms that the expectation of the future "restoration of all things" has already begun in the advent of John the Baptist, just as the kingdom of God has already appeared in the ministry of Jesus, but visible only to eyes of faith and awaiting its consummation at the eschaton (see Excursus "Kingdom of Heaven in Matthew," 288-94). The kingdom expectation, the Elijah expectation, the Son of Man expec-

tation, the expectation of the Messiah—all are variations of the redemptive hope that God has not abandoned his creation but will act decisively at the eschaton to redeem it. Matthew embraces all of these under the already/not yet of inaugurated eschatology: The hoped-for eschatological reality is already present, but is not reduced to present experience, for the consummation is yet to come. Thus declaring that "Elijah has come and he is John the Baptist" has the same scandalous quality as declaring "The Messiah has come, and he is Jesus of Nazareth."

17:12-13. "Elijah has already come" is an important declaration for Matthew, for a false Elijah expectation was a barrier to accepting the crucified Jesus as Messiah, even at the cross (16:14; 27:45). Elijah/John is paralleled to Jesus. He was sent from God, preached the kingdom of God, was opposed and killed by the representatives of the kingdom of this world, who failed to recognize him as the eschatological figure he was; he was Elijah, the forerunner of the Messiah. Since Elijah had never died, there was a special affront in speaking of the dead John the Baptist as Elijah, a scandal analogous to speaking of a crucified Messiah. Matthew's addition of "in the same way" (οὕτως καί *houtōs kai*; the NIV is better here) increases the John/Jesus parallelism precisely at the point of the suffering and death each of them endured in carrying out his mission. As with John, so with Jesus. Just as "this generation" under the sway of the opposing kingdom had failed to recognize John, so also Jesus' disciples recognize and understand and form the nucleus of the new community in the process of formation. The subsequent exorcism also brings out the conflict-of-kingdoms motif.

---

399. Since ancient MSS lack all punctuation, whether a sentence is declarative or interrogative is often an editorial decision.

400. This was and is the Jewish objection not only to the Christian claim that John was the promised Elijah, but that Jesus is the fulfillment of the hope for the Messiah as well. Christians who do not feel the force of this objection have hardly reckoned with the meaning of their own confession.

Some Christian scribes did see the problem, and they altered the future tense to the present (one major Greek codex, D, plus the majority of the Old Latin MSS, and MSS of two versions of the Syriac). The textual tradition of Mark 9:12 is unclear, with readings of both present and future. In the readings adopted by Nestle[27] and UBS[4], the problem is accentuated in that Matthew has changed the verb to the future from Mark's present.

REFLECTIONS

1. Many explanations have been given for the origin of this story,[401] from objective reporting of an event that literally happened (Cranfield), through various explanations of a subjective vision (V. Taylor; A. H. McNeile) or dream (Neander) of the disciples or their misunderstanding of a natural event (Schleiermacher; Paulus), to a purely symbolic story (D. F. Strauss) created either from the biblical apocalyptic tradition (Kee) or from the background of Hellenistic epiphanies (Kümmel; Conzelmann). There is some evidence that the story was originally an appearance story of the resurrected Christ, placed in its pre-Easter framework by Mark or the

---

401. See especially the thorough discussion of the options in Davies and Allison, *Matthew,* 689-93.

pre-Markan tradition (Wellhausen; Bultmann; Theissen; C. H. Dodd's form-critical analysis shows how *different* this story is from the Easter appearance stories).[402] The task of Christian preaching and teaching, however, is not to assess the historical probability of each of these proposals of what lies behind the text, but to interpret the meaning of the scriptural text.

2. In this we join Matthew as fellow interpreter, for the story comes to Matthew from his sacred tradition, the Gospel of Mark. Matthew's subtle rewriting highlights the following meanings:

(a) The transfiguration story recalls the baptism of Jesus, and the voice from heaven designates him both (powerful) Son of God and (weak) suffering servant (see 3:17). This commission is reconfirmed as Jesus begins to instruct his disciples on the meaning and cost of discipleship. Thus it is important that the scene follows the first passion prediction, *confirming* from heaven what had been *questioned* by Peter, whose mind was "not on divine things, but on human things" (16:23). The weak, crucified one (2 Cor 13:4) is also the divine glorious one, and vice versa.

(b) The transfiguration story recalls and confirms Peter's confession (16:16). Although Peter was still thinking in human categories, despite the revelation he had received, he had understood the identity of Jesus, and this confession is confirmed by the heavenly voice.

(c) The transfiguration story connects the confession of Jesus as Son of God and Jesus' self-identification as the Son of Man who suffers, is killed, is vindicated by God, and will appear as judge at the parousia. The content of "Son of God," confessed by Peter (16:16) and the heavenly voice (17:5), is filled in by the portrayal of the Son of Man who obediently goes to the cross (as in 26:63-64).

(d) The transfiguration story anticipates the eschatological events of the resurrection and the parousia of Jesus, giving the reader through the eyes of the disciples a glimpse of the eschatological glory of Jesus before the descent into the mundane world, which will lead to the cross. This is the truth of the theory that the transfiguration is a misplaced resurrection story, showing that the whole Jesus story is told from the post-Easter perspective in which the glory of the exalted one of Christian faith is retrojected into the pre-Easter narrative.

3. Matthew's reinterpretation especially emphasizes the eschatological role of Jesus in relation to Moses.[403] A number of Mosaic traits were already in the pre-Markan form of the story (cf. Exod 24:1-18; 34:29-35; Deut 18:15-18): "six days"; "high mountain"; a bright cloud over the mountain; a select group of three (Aaron, Nadab, Abihu = Peter, James, John); a voice from the cloud; the response of fear; the command "hear him" (Deut 18:15). These motifs must have all been present at the formation of the story, for Mark is not particularly interested in the Moses typology, but in relating the story to Jesus' prediction of the passion just given, so these features of the story do not come from him. Matthew, however, focuses his attention on Jesus in the role of Moses and develops this typology by mentioning Moses first, by adding the description of Jesus' face shining like the sun (Exod 34:29-35), by describing the cloud as "bright," making the cloud more like the Shekinah that rested on the tabernacle and the Temple, by having Jesus echo Moses' words about this "perverse and crooked generation" (17:17 = Deut 32:5), and by adding "with whom I am well pleased" to the heavenly voice. This last modification has the effect not only of making words of the heavenly voice precisely identical to the heavenly declaration at the baptism, but also, since they are from the address to the Servant of the Lord in Isa 42:1, relate Jesus to Moses, the Servant par excellence.

402. C. H. Dodd, "The Appearances of the Risen Christ: An Essay in Form-Criticism of the Gospels," in *Studies in the Gospels,* R. H. Lightfoot Festschrift, D. E. Nineham, ed. (Oxford: Blackwell, 1955) 9-36.

403. But not quite a "new" Moses; see Commentary on 5:1.

4. Moses and Elijah appear on the mount with Jesus and the disciples, then disappear in the cloud of the divine presence, leaving Jesus alone. The eschatological role of Elijah has been filled by John—who was killed. The eschatological role of Moses is filled by Jesus—who is to fulfill his ministry as the suffering servant. The disciples see Jesus surrounded by heavenly beings and glowing with heavenly glory, but the prophetic roles of Elijah and Moses are fulfilled by John and Jesus as they suffer and die. This is not human wisdom; it takes a revelation to understand this (cf. Matt 16:17; 1 Cor 1:17-18; Rev 11:1-13).

Matthew 17:14-20, Discipleship and Faith That Moves Mountains

NIV

[14]When they came to the crowd, a man approached Jesus and knelt before him. [15]"Lord, have mercy on my son," he said. "He has seizures and is suffering greatly. He often falls into the fire or into the water. [16]I brought him to your disciples, but they could not heal him."

[17]"O unbelieving and perverse generation," Jesus replied, "how long shall I stay with you? How long shall I put up with you? Bring the boy here to me." [18]Jesus rebuked the demon, and it came out of the boy, and he was healed from that moment.

[19]Then the disciples came to Jesus in private and asked, "Why couldn't we drive it out?"

[20]He replied, "Because you have so little faith. I tell you the truth, if you have faith as small as a mustard seed, you can say to this mountain, 'Move from here to there' and it will move. Nothing will be impossible for you.[a]"

[a]20 Some manuscripts *you.* 21*But this kind does not go out except by prayer and fasting.*

NRSV

[14]When they came to the crowd, a man came to him, knelt before him, [15]and said, "Lord, have mercy on my son, for he is an epileptic and he suffers terribly; he often falls into the fire and often into the water. [16]And I brought him to your disciples, but they could not cure him." [17]Jesus answered, "You faithless and perverse generation, how much longer must I be with you? How much longer must I put up with you? Bring him here to me." [18]And Jesus rebuked the demon,[a] and it[b] came out of him, and the boy was cured instantly. [19]Then the disciples came to Jesus privately and said, "Why could we not cast it out?" [20]He said to them, "Because of your little faith. For truly I tell you, if you have faith the size of a[c] mustard seed, you will say to this mountain, 'Move from here to there,' and it will move; and nothing will be impossible for you."[d]

[a]Gk *it* or *him*   [b]Gk *the demon*   [c]Gk *faith as a grain of*
[d]Other ancient authorities add verse 21, *But this kind does not come out except by prayer and fasting*

COMMENTARY

The story is closely attached to the preceding, to which it forms something of a counterpoint. This is rightly captured by Raphael's painting in the Vatican Museum, contrasting the glory of the transfigured Christ on the mountain and the misery of the human condition below to which he returns to minister. His disciples, who have been commissioned with Jesus' power and authority, have been "left" in the mundane world below and are frustrated by their failure. But Jesus is "with" them nevertheless, and he has power to heal despite their failure (cf. on 14:22-33). The primary focus of this pericope is this relationship of the power of Christ and the disciples' ministry in the world "below."

Matthew has shortened this Markan story by half (cf. Mark 9:14-29) and reformulated it so that, in terms of form and function, it is no longer a miracle/exorcism story expressing christology, but a pronouncement story that builds to Jesus' final declaration on the power of faith in vv. 19-20.

17:14-15. The crowd appears for the first time since 15:39, added here by Matthew to provide a proper referent for Jesus' declaration against "this generation" in v. 17. A man from the crowd "approaches him" (προσέρχομαι *proserchomai*; often used by Matthew of the reverential approach to deity) and addresses him with the believer's title "Lord" ("teacher" in Mark, which in Matthew is used only by outsiders) and with the prayerful cry for help, often found in the psalms, "Lord, save" (κύριε ἐλέησον *kyrie eleēson*; "Lord, have mercy"; cf. 15:22; 20:30-31). The afflicted boy is described as an epileptic (lit., "moonstruck," from the belief that epilepsy was caused by the moon or moon goddess). The reader does not learn that the boy is possessed by a demon until the incidental comment in v. 18. As in Mark 5:1-17 (= Matt 8:28-34), Matthew has condensed a vivid exorcism story, stripping it of its colorful details and reducing it to its bare essentials. Matthew has no interest in the exorcism as such, but uses the healing story to set the stage for the saying on the power of faith.

17:16. Matthew here reverts to the Markan arrangement of the narrative, in which only Peter, James, and John had been on the mountain with Jesus, and the other disciples had been unsuccessfully attempting to heal the boy (cf. the Overview and Commentary on 17:10). Matthew adds that the disciples are "unable" and omits Mark's question of whether Jesus is able to heal him; Matthew presupposes that, of course, Jesus is able to do it! The focus of the story remains on the disciples and on their inability, despite Jesus' conferral of power and authority on them in 10:1, 8. Matthew's rewriting of Mark shifts the conversation with the father to a dialogue with the disciples. The father is now a model of Christian faith; thus he forms a foil for the disciples' "little faith."

17:17-18. Matthew has added "perverse" to his characteristic "generation" (cf. Deut 32:5), which has the effect of further distancing Jesus from "this generation" (cf. 12:41-42; 22:16; 23:36; 24:34). As the Christ, the Son of God, and the suffering, dying, rising, and coming Son of Man, he is now forming the new community over against the "perverse generation" of empirical Israel, which rejects him. The disciples have iden-

tified him and made the correct confession, but whether they will become the authentic community he seeks to build or will regress into "this generation" is the struggle portrayed in this scene. Jesus has performed exorcisms and healings and has given the disciples authority and power to continue his ministry. They cannot do it with their own power, but only because Jesus is "with them," a Matthean theme called up by Jesus' sigh, "How long am I with you?"[404] Jesus heals the boy, and then the reader learns for the first time that he was possessed by a demon—i.e., was afflicted by the kingdom of Satan. Jesus' healing/exorcism is another instance of the kingdom, represented by Jesus, triumphing over the kingdom of Satan (cf. 12:22-37). Jesus is the one who accompanies his church through history, who builds the church, and whose power continues in it. The disciples should have been able to heal and do this work in the power of Jesus, as both they and Jesus recognize, but they could not.

17:19-20. Why? This is the point to which Matthew has (re)built the entire story. Matthew suppresses the Markan ending, imports a floating saying from a different context in Q (cf. Luke 17:6), and rewrites it as the concluding pronouncement of this story. The saying's importance to Matthew is seen in his using it again in 21:21. Matthew introduces this pronouncement with his own addition: The disciples' failure is due to one thing, "little faith" (ὀλιγοπιστία *oligopistia*, only here in the NT, but cf. the adjective ὀλιγόπιστος [*oligopistos*] in 6:30; 8:36; 14:31; 16:8). On the origin of the term, see Commentary on 6:30. It refers not only to Christian faith in general, but also to that faith in Christ representatively confessed by Peter (16:16), which distinguishes the Matthean Christians from "this faithless generation" (17:17). The faith in which they come up short is the trust in God's power that facilitates the extraordinary feats of the Christian mission (cf. 1 Cor 13:2).

17:21. This verse is missing from the most ancient Greek MSS (B, ℵ*, Θ, and others) as

---

404. Matthew has changed the Markan preposition from πρός (*pros*) to μετά (*meta*) to correspond to 1:23 and 28:20 and evoke this theme. Matthew plays on the presence/absence theme. Those "left behind" in Jesus' "absence" should still be able to do the messianic deeds, but they fail because of their "little faith." They call Jesus "Lord" but do not believe adequately in his continuing power even when he is "absent" (cf. the centurion of 8:5-13).

well as from a good part of the early Latin, Syriac, and Coptic translations. It was added in later MSS on the basis of Mark 9:29, but was not a part of the original text of Matthew.

REFLECTIONS

The proverbial saying about moving mountains is more than a rhetorical flourish. Matthew introduces it with a solemn "amen" (ἀμήν *amēn*) saying (see Commentary on 5:18). Like the parables, the saying resists reduction to pedestrian logic. One should not infer from it the guilt-inducing conclusion that when hoped-for miracles fail the problem must be our lack of faith, and that if we had "enough" faith we would be able to avert all tragedies and heal all afflictions. Neither can we infer from it that faith is itself a power that accomplishes miracles, for God is the one who acts, not an attitude called "faith." Like the story in 8:5-13, this is not a saying about the power of faith but about the power of God, even if God language is not used in either place (cf. also on 21:18-22). "And 'faith' in Matthew is always not a quality of the one praying, but a relationship of practical trust with the one to whom prayer is offered (8:10; 9:2, 22, 29; 15:28; 17:22)."[405] We might be tempted to reason that, if the smallest faith (mustard seed! see 13:31-32) moves mountains and our achievements seem quite ordinary, our faith must be smaller than the smallest—good math, but pedestrian exegesis. Rather, this disruptive picture pushes at us the gnawing reminder that as disciples we are agents of the church in which Christ himself is "with us," which means God-with-us (1:23; 28:20), and that with God nothing is impossible (see 19:26), a guard against fitting God into our ideas of what is possible and coming to terms too quickly with "the way things are."

405. R. T. France, *Matthew,* Tyndale New Testament Commentaries (Grand Rapids: Eerdmans, 1987) 304.

Matthew 17:22-23, The Second Passion Prediction

NIV

²²When they came together in Galilee, he said to them, "The Son of Man is going to be betrayed into the hands of men. ²³They will kill him, and on the third day he will be raised to life." And the disciples were filled with grief.

NRSV

22As they were gathering[a] in Galilee, Jesus said to them, "The Son of Man is going to be betrayed into human hands, ²³and they will kill him, and on the third day he will be raised." And they were greatly distressed.

ªOther ancient authorities read *living*

COMMENTARY

Here as elsewhere, Matthew, having no use for the Markan form of the messianic secret, omits Mark's secret journey (Mark 9:30), replacing it with "gathering" in Galilee. "Gathering" (συστρε-φομένων *systrephomenōn*) is a rare word (only here in Matthew; elsewhere in the NT only Acts 28:3),[406] chosen to express this process of select-

406. Thus replaced in later MSS by the more common "living," "staying" (ἀναστρέφοντες *anastrephontes*).

ing and building the new community, which is the theme of 13:53–17:27. The reference to Galilee points back to 4:12, recalling that Galilee is the scene of Jesus' ministry, but also anticipates 19:1, reminding the reader that this section of the ministry is drawing to a close. In this concluding section of the Galilean ministry, Jesus gathers the new community out of "this faithless and perverse generation" (17:17; see Overview at 13:53 on the section 13:53–17:27).

The theme of Jesus' instruction for his new community during this period is his messianic identity as the suffering and vindicated Son of Man, and what this means for discipleship. Thus the repetition of the passion prediction here is not merely a new increment of biographical information, but a concluding characterization of this period of gathering the new community as a whole.

On the passion predictions themselves, see 16:21. The distinctive feature of 17:22-23 is the contrast between God, who delivers over the Son of Man, and the human hands into which he is delivered. Thus the point in this saying is not only the betrayal by Judas and the culpability of the Jewish leaders who will deliver Jesus over to the Gentiles for execution, but that the Son of Man, who will be vindicated by God and return as judge of all at the parousia, is delivered by God into the power of human beings (cf. Rom 8:32).[407] The representative of God's kingdom is "meek" (πραυς *praus*). Although judge and Lord of all, he submits himself to become the victim of human power.

The disciples' response is not failure to understand as in Mark (9:32 is omitted) but sorrow—because they do understand. They have made progress since their initial protests in 16:21. The transfiguration and the period of instruction have had some effect. Their sorrow corresponds to their response at the last supper (26:22), when they learn of their own involvement in Jesus' being handed over, and to Jesus' own sorrow in Gethsemane, prior to his prayer and resolution of his commitment to God (26:37-38). The disciples have a way to go, but they are becoming the church Christ has promised to build out of such as they (16:18-20).

407. Thus παραδίδωμι (*paradidōmi*) is here better translated as "hand over" (GNB, NAB, REB, JB), "deliver into [the hands of]" (RSV), or "give up" (NEB) than the "betray" of both the NIV and the NRSV, which obscures the Matthean point and returns to the KJV! See Commentary on 16:21.

Matthew 17:24-27, Payment of the Temple Tax

NIV	NRSV
²⁴After Jesus and his disciples arrived in Capernaum, the collectors of the two-drachma tax came to Peter and asked, "Doesn't your teacher pay the temple tax*?" ²⁵"Yes, he does," he replied. When Peter came into the house, Jesus was the first to speak. "What do you think, Simon?" he asked. "From whom do the kings of the earth collect duty and taxes—from their own sons or from others?" ²⁶"From others," Peter answered. "Then the sons are exempt," Jesus said to him. ²⁷"But so that we may not offend them, go to the lake and throw out your line. Take the first fish you catch; open its mouth and you will find a four-drachma coin. Take it and give it to them for my tax and yours."	24When they reached Capernaum, the collectors of the temple tax^a came to Peter and said, "Does your teacher not pay the temple tax?"^a ²⁵He said, "Yes, he does." And when he came home, Jesus spoke of it first, asking, "What do you think, Simon? From whom do kings of the earth take toll or tribute? From their children or from others?" ²⁶When Peter^b said, "From others," Jesus said to him, "Then the children are free. ²⁷However, so that we do not give offense to them, go to the sea and cast a hook; take the first fish that comes up; and when you open its mouth, you will find a coin;^c take that and give it to them for you and me."
*a24 Greek *the two drachmas*	^aGk *didrachma* ^bGk *he* ^cGk *stater;* the stater was worth two didrachmas

COMMENTARY

This pericope comes at the conclusion of the extended section in which Jesus gathers the new community after his rejection by the leaders of Israel (see Overview of 13:53–17:27). In this section, Peter has figured prominently, having become the spokesperson for the new community as well as the representative figure in developing new teachings for its life (see 16:17-19). As a transition to the discourse on how community members are to live in relationship to one another (namely, in caring consideration for the well-being of one's brothers and sisters within the community), this pericope manifests the same concern with regard to outsiders: living in freedom as children of God, but concerned not to place a stumbling block in the way of others.[408] This scene thus joins the preceding passion prediction in forming an appropriate conclusion to this major section. Just as the Son of Man gives his life for others (17:22-23; cf. 20:28), so also the community lives its life aware of its freedom, but is so concerned with the welfare of others that it is willing to sacrifice its freedom for their sake.

17:24. Just as 17:22 begins to conclude the Galilean section, so also 17:24 narrows the focus to Capernaum, forming a bracket with 4:12. While in pre-70 Judaism it was generally assumed that loyal Jews would pay the two-drachma temple tax, precisely who should pay, how often, and how the tax was related to Scripture were disputed issues. Originally derived from Neh 10:32-33, where leading elements of the Jewish population take upon themselves a yearly obligation of one-third shekel for support of the temple cultus, the Pharisees later considered every male Jew throughout the world to be liable for half a shekel, and related it to Exod 30:11-16. Strangely enough, Sadducees argued that the annual payment should be a voluntary gift rather than an imposed tax, from which priests were exempt. Josephus and Philo indicate that diaspora Jews also (voluntarily) contributed their offering to the Temple.[409] The Qumran community understood the requirement in terms of Exod 30:11-16 as a one-

time only contribution. Thus the question was a live issue in the spectrum of pre-70 Judaism concerning which Jesus might have been asked and to which he may have responded.

Outsiders approach Peter with a question about Jesus' (and the disciples') practice. A problem of Matthew's own time is dealt with by telling a story in which Jesus confirms the Christian answer. The fact that Jesus is not asked directly suggests that the question presupposes a post-Easter setting, where the disciples' practice is at issue, as does the fact that Peter responds for Jesus. As promised in 16:18-19, Peter speaks on Jesus' behalf, and Jesus confirms Peter's answer as his own. The form of the question expects an affirmative answer, "Your teacher pays the temple tax, doesn't he?"

17:25-26. Jesus miraculously knows what has preceded (as in 9:4; 12:25; 26:10, 25) and confirms Peter's response with a probing analogy. Just as earthly kings do not tax their own children, but others, so also the children of God (lit., "sons," as 5:9, 45—Matthew's term for Christian believers) are free from the temple tax. Thus Jewish Christians are in principle free from supporting the Temple. This declaration may have originally been part of Jesus' own polemic against imposing a tax on Israel for what should be offered as a voluntary gift. The saying may have been taken up in this sense in a pre-Matthean stream of Jewish Christianity. It is not anti-Temple as such, or anti-Torah, but may be directed against a Pharisaic interpretation.

17:27. In the post-Easter situation, the saying becomes the occasion for Christian teaching on the proper use of freedom. In Matthew's time, the Temple no longer existed, but the Roman government had imposed a tax of two drachmas on all Jews for support of the temple to Jupiter in Rome, corresponding to the previous temple tax.[410] Although there was no legal choice for Jewish Christians in Matthew's church, the issue of whether to pay such a tax may have been a matter of conscience. In this situation, Matthew could, to his own advantage, separate his community from any identification with Judaism. That he

---

408. The "give offense" of 17:27 is literally "cause to stumble." See Reflections on 11:19. The σκάνδαλον / σκανδαλίζω (*skandalon/skandalizō*) terminology is taken up again in 18:6-9.

409. Philo *Special Laws* 1:77; Josephus *Antiquities of the Jews* 18:312.

410. Josephus *The Jewish War* 7.218-29.

did not take this view indicates that his community is not yet totally separated from Judaism and that, hostile as he is to the Jewish leadership, Matthew has a conciliatory attitude to the Jewish community as a whole.[411] In this setting, Matthew offers this story as a Christian lesson on the proper use of freedom, analogous to Paul's instructions in 1 Corinthians 8–9 and Luke's picture of Paul in Acts 21:17-26. Christians are to go the second mile (5:41) in their efforts to avoid placing a stumbling block before outsiders (and insiders with "weak" consciences, as in Romans 14).

This pericope is a further rehabilitation of Peter after the negative scene of 16:21-23. Peter is once again the representative speaker for both Jesus (to the opponents) and the disciples (to Jesus and the reader). Instead of being himself a "stumbling block" (σκάνδαλον *skandalon*; 16:13), he is now charged with the pastoral concern not to exercise his own freedom in a way that places stumbling blocks in the way of others (17:27). The story thus prepares for chap. 18, where concerns internal to the community are paramount.

The story does not report Peter's performance of Jesus' instruction to catch a fish with the tax money in its mouth, but it assumes it was carried out. This folkloristic motif is not integral to the point of the story, which has to do with avoiding the misuse of one's own understanding of Christian freedom as a disciple, for the sake of others and the Christian mission to them. Taken literally, the story has problems not only of physics but also of ethics, and it conflicts with other pictures of Jesus, who does not use his miraculous power for his own benefit (4:3-11, which considers such temptations demonic; cf. 26:36-42, 51-54; Excursus: "Interpreting the Miracle Stories in Matthew," 245-51).

---

411. The attitude here should also be contrasted with 15:12-14, where Jesus intentionally "scandalizes" the Pharisees, who are beyond redemption. Here, there is care not to unduly scandalize (cause to stumble) the opposition. Thus Matthew's dualistic view of the opposition should not be absolutized.

MATTHEW 18:1-35, LIFE TOGETHER

OVERVIEW

This is the fourth of Matthew's major discourses that form part of the basic structure of his Gospel (see Introduction). Like the others, it is not an isolated discourse, but is transitional, being related by Matthew especially to the preceding narrative section for which it forms a summary. The sayings have a different context in Mark, and still another in Luke, showing that context (and meaning) are primarily at the Matthean level (see Introduction). From 13:53 to 17:27, Jesus has been gathering and instructing the new community from the midst of "this generation," which rejects him. This transitional nature is emphasized by 18:1: "in that same hour" joins the discourse to the preceding, as does the concern for "giving offense" (σκανδαλίζω *skandalizō*), placing a stumbling block in another's way of 17:27 and 18:6-9.

Matthew is here following the order of Q injunctions, long familiar to his community (cf. Luke 17:1-4; Introduction). The discourse is divided into two sections, each of which is concluded by a parable and a concluding statement beginning with "so," "thus" (οὕτως *houtōs*), a reference to the heavenly Father and the subject of the preceding section (v. 14, "little ones"; v. 35, "forgiving the brother or sister"). The key term "little ones" serves as the structuring factor, beginning and ending units at vv. 6, 10, and 14. Each of the two major sections has Matthew's characteristic three subsections, giving the following outline of the discourse:

What the discourse presupposes is as important as what it prescribes: The life of discipleship is not an individualistic relationship to Christ, but *life together.*[412] How are disciples to relate to each other within the Christian community?

412. See Dietrich Bonhoeffer, *Life Together* (London: SCM, 1954). For a thorough study of 17:22–18:35, see William G. Thompson, S.J. *Matthew's Advice to a Divided Community* (Rome: Biblical Institute, 1970).

Matthew 18:1-14, Consideration for the "Little People"

NIV

18 At that time the disciples came to Jesus and asked, "Who is the greatest in the kingdom of heaven?"

[2] He called a little child and had him stand among them. [3] And he said: "I tell you the truth, unless you change and become like little children, you will never enter the kingdom of heaven. [4] Therefore, whoever humbles himself like this child is the greatest in the kingdom of heaven.

[5] "And whoever welcomes a little child like this in my name welcomes me. [6] But if anyone causes one of these little ones who believe in me to sin, it would be better for him to have a large millstone hung around his neck and to be drowned in the depths of the sea.

[7] "Woe to the world because of the things that cause people to sin! Such things must come, but woe to the man through whom they come! [8] If your hand or your foot causes you to sin, cut it off and throw it away. It is better for you to enter life maimed or crippled than to have two hands or two feet and be thrown into eternal fire. [9] And if your eye causes you to sin, gouge it out and throw it away. It is better for you to enter life with one eye than to have two eyes and be thrown into the fire of hell.

[10] "See that you do not look down on one of these little ones. For I tell you that their angels in heaven always see the face of my Father in heaven.[a]

[12] "What do you think? If a man owns a hundred sheep, and one of them wanders away, will he not leave the ninety-nine on the hills and go to look for the one that wandered off? [13] And if he finds it, I tell you the truth, he is happier about that one sheep than about the ninety-nine that did not wander off. [14] In the same way your Father in heaven is not willing that any of these little ones should be lost."

a10 Some manuscripts heaven. 11 The Son of Man came to save what was lost.

NRSV

18 At that time the disciples came to Jesus and asked, "Who is the greatest in the kingdom of heaven?" [2] He called a child, whom he put among them, [3] and said, "Truly I tell you, unless you change and become like children, you will never enter the kingdom of heaven. [4] Whoever becomes humble like this child is the greatest in the kingdom of heaven. [5] Whoever welcomes one such child in my name welcomes me.

[6] "If any of you put a stumbling block before one of these little ones who believe in me, it would be better for you if a great millstone were fastened around your neck and you were drowned in the depth of the sea. [7] Woe to the world because of stumbling blocks! Occasions for stumbling are bound to come, but woe to the one by whom the stumbling block comes!

[8] "If your hand or your foot causes you to stumble, cut it off and throw it away; it is better for you to enter life maimed or lame than to have two hands or two feet and to be thrown into the eternal fire. [9] And if your eye causes you to stumble, tear it out and throw it away; it is better for you to enter life with one eye than to have two eyes and to be thrown into the hell[a] of fire.

[10] "Take care that you do not despise one of these little ones; for, I tell you, in heaven their angels continually see the face of my Father in heaven.[b] [12] What do you think? If a shepherd has a hundred sheep, and one of them has gone astray, does he not leave the ninety-nine on the mountains and go in search of the one that went astray? [13] And if he finds it, truly I tell you, he rejoices over it more than over the ninety-nine that never went astray. [14] So it is not the will of your[c] Father in heaven that one of these little ones should be lost."

a Gk Gehenna   b Other ancient authorities add verse 11, For the Son of Man came to save the lost   c Other ancient authorities read my

COMMENTARY

18:1-5, Big People and Little People.
18:1. Matthew binds this scene to the preceding one by having the disciples come "at that time"—while Jesus and Peter are talking in the house in Capernaum. Matthew has rewritten Mark 9:33-34 to reflect more positively on the disciples, making the Markan narrator's description into a direct question that will provide the occasion for a teaching scene, corresponding to the whole following discourse. Matthew's aversion to disciples' wanting to be "greatest" may be reinforced by his disputes with formative Judaism, in which the rabbinic title is becoming prominent ("rabbi" [ῥαββί *rabbi*; רבי *rabbî*] 'means literally "my great one"; see Commentary on 23:8-11).

There is no dispute about greatness, as in the Mark 9:33 source, but only a question from the disciples about the kingdom. By inserting "kingdom" (βασιλεία *basileia*) language into the opening question, Matthew sets the whole discourse into the framework of the conflict of kingdoms (see Overview to Part One; 12:32-37; Excursus "Kingdom of Heaven in Matthew," 288-94). The concluding parable about a king brings out this contrast (see 18:23).

18:2-3. Jesus' response is a symbolic prophetic act, the radicality of which may be lost on modern Westerners who no longer share the dominant ancient Near Eastern view of children. Even in first-century Judaism, children were often regarded as inferior, without status or rights, treated more as property than as persons, and were never held up as a model for anything.[413] Matthew rewrites Mark 9:35-36 by having Jesus make the child an object lesson of the saying Matthew has rewritten (or, more likely, has an older form of) from Mark 10:15. Introduced with the solemn prophetic "amen" (ἀμήν *amēn;* cf. 5:18), Jesus first addresses their presupposition. The disciples had supposed that they were "in" the kingdom, and only asked about their relative rank. Jesus' radical prophetic reply challenges their assumption: To get "in," one must be converted, which means to become like a little child. This is the Synoptics' functional equivalent of John 3:3, 5, with the same gift and demand; following Jesus

is not adding on one more worthy cause, but calls for starting all over. Through the centuries, Christian preaching has derived many meanings from "become like a little child" (humble, innocent, without lust, open and trusting, spontaneous, vulnerable and dependent, allowing oneself to be given a gift without a compulsion to "deserve" it, etc.).

18:4. While the expression can, indeed, have many of these connotations, Matthew makes clear his own meaning by reformulating a Q saying he has also used in 23:12 (cf. Luke 14:11; 18:14). To become like a little child is to humble oneself, giving up all pretensions of self-importance, independence, and self-reliance and turning in trust to the heavenly Father (6:8, 32). The story is not a call to imitate the (presumed) character traits of children, but to accept a radically different understanding of status. The first rule for life together in the new community formed by Jesus is to abandon the quest for status and accept one's place as already given in the family of God.

18:5. This pericope comes to a neat conclusion with the last words of v. 4, which form a redactional bracket with the disciples' question in v. 1. Yet v. 5 is neither an unrelated appendage nor merely suggested by the catchword *child.* Rather, v. 5 is a concrete illustration of the meaning of humility called for in v. 4. To receive a child is to genuinely humble oneself, for the vulnerable, dependent child can do nothing to further one's selfish ambitions, and receiving the child can have no ulterior motives, no hidden agendas. One who receives a child has been converted to the ethos of the kingdom represented by Jesus, and is no longer concerned about being "greatest." In receiving a child, one then finds that in the child, Christ himself is received (cf. on 1:23).

18:6-10, Against Disdaining Little People. The subject now shifts (but only slightly) from those who are immature in years—i.e., children—to members of the Christian community who are immature in faith.[414] They are still "little

---

413. See Sirach 30; *m. ʾAbot* 3.11; Oepke, *TDNT* 5:636-53.

414. "Those who believe in me" appears only here in the synoptic Gospels, which are centered on the kingdom of God, not on faith in the person of Jesus. The phrase makes the post-Easter perspective of the passage transparent. "Children" quickly became in early Christianity a non-condescending label for "ordinary" Christians (Heb 2:13-14; 1 John 2:13, 18, 28; 5:21).

ones" without influence in the community, so that, like the children in the preceding pericope, they cannot advance one's religious career toward becoming "greatest" in the kingdom. What should the "mature" Christian's attitude be toward those "babes in Christ" (cf. 1 Cor 3:1-3)?

18:6-7. So far from being dispensable, the "little people" in the Matthean community are to be shown the greatest consideration, and that without condescension. The phrase "little ones" becomes the structuring principle of the whole discourse.[415] One must live one's own life of discipleship in such a way that no stumbling block is placed in the way of the weaker members of the community. Here, the same perspective on the responsible exercise of Christian freedom, explicated with reference to the outsider, is applied not only to the insider, but also to the weakest of them. Jesus' picture is hyperbolic and, therefore, memorable. The "great millstone" is literally "donkey millstone," the upper millstone of a large mill, which is pulled by a donkey, rather than the small domestic mill. The expression is proverbial (cf. Rev 18:21), but the application of it to the fate of one who places a stumbling block in the path of another's life of discipleship is unique with Jesus. Matthew elaborates the picture by inserting his modification of a Q saying (cf. Luke 17:1-2) on the necessity of such stumbling blocks. Although there is no avoiding living in a world where such things happen, the more mature members cannot use this as an excuse for their own lack of care for the little people of the community. The general woe pronounced against a world that does not care for the little ones need not, and must not, apply to *you.*

18:8-9. Similar words were already used in 5:29-30 as a call for the most radical measures to be taken against lust in one's own life. Here, rather than disciplining the sex drive, they are applied to disciplining the drive to power. Just as there the most stringent measures are called for in order to prevent one's sex drive from dominating one's life and making one into a predator against others, so also here the will to power (wanting to be "great" in the community, me-first

ambition at the expense of others) threatens to dominate one's existence, becoming a threat not only to oneself but to the faith of others and the life of the community as well. Thus the lack of continuity between vv. 6-7 and vv. 8-9 is only apparent. Both express the radical steps necessary to guard the life of the community.

18:10. This verse goes with vv. 6-9, "little ones" forming a bracket with v. 6. (The NIV's "look down on" is better than the NRSV's "despise," which might be misunderstood as "dislike," "hate.") The "big people" in the community are not tempted to hate the "little people," but to disdain them, to regard them as insignificant (cf. Rom 14:1-15:13). Although church leaders might be tempted to disdain them, the most exalted of the angels have been assigned to look after the little ones. Matthew assumes that the Son of Man who accompanies his church through history has attendant angels who perform his ministry (13:39, 41; 16:27; 24:31; 25:31; 26:53). They not only attended the Messiah (4:6, 11), but also attend the messianic people (18:10). In Judaism, God assigned heavenly beings to be responsible for earthly *nations,* including an angel that looked after Israel as its intercessor in heaven and guide and protector on earth (Dan 10:13, 21; cf. Deut 32:8). This concept was taken over by some streams of early Christianity (cf. Acts 12:15; Heb 1:5-14; Rev 1:20). Matthew adapts this picture and applies it to the weakest members of the congregation: Heaven has assigned only the most exalted angels, those that behold God's face, as helpers to the weaker members of the community. The point is clear: Heaven does not give up on the marginal, the lapsed, or the strayed, and what heaven values so dearly cannot be disdained by the "big people" in the church on earth.

18:11. This verse is absent from the oldest and best MSS representing several textual families and geographical locations. There can be little doubt that the verse was later added to Matthew from Luke 19:10 in order to supply what seemed to be a missing connection to the following parable. As we shall see, the continuity is already present.

18:12-14, Concern for Straying Members. Rather than disdaining the "little people," the alternative attitude that the "big people" in the community may take toward the "others" is

---

415. Matthew found the phrase "little ones" in Mark 9:42 (it does not occur in Q; cf. Zech 13:7 MT) and made it into a key phrase in his Gospel (10:42; 18:6, 10, 14) to describe the "ordinary" members of the Christian community who were likely to be considered insignificant by the relatively more mature.

to value them and seek them out when they go astray. As vv. 6-10 are directed to how "mature" Christians are to live their own lives with the spiritual welfare of others in view, so the parable that concludes this section is directed to actively seeking those members of the community who have gotten off the track, despite the community's concern not to put obstructions in their way.

During Israel's nomadic past, the people had developed the image of their nation as the flock of God, the good shepherd (Pss 23:1; 68:7; 100:3; Isa 40:10; 49:9; Jer 23:3; 31:10; 50:19; Ezek 34:1-31; Mic 4:6-8; 7:14). The people of God were called to be holy (Lev 11:45; 19:2; 20:26; Num 15:40). The original parable in Jesus' own situation may well have been a response to his critics' accusation that his table fellowship with tax collectors and sinners violated the holiness of the people of God (cf. Matt 9:11-12, where Jesus responds to this objection with the metaphor of the physician). Even more basically, Jesus' original parable may have been a fundamental critique of all conventional ideas of God and God's rule.[416]

We have neither the exact form of Jesus' original parable nor its original context. Jesus' parables were open-ended and polyvalent, with hermeneutical potential inviting their adaptation to new situations (cf. Commentary on 13:1-52). There are three extant forms of the parable, *Gospel of Thomas* 107;[417] Matt 18:12-14; Luke 15:3-7; in each case the meaning is adapted to the context. In *Gospel of Thomas,* the largest sheep goes astray, the others are not left behind in the desert or mountains, the motif of joy is lacking, and the conclusion is a rationalization in which the shepherd addresses the once-straying sheep, "I care for you more than the ninety-nine." In Luke 15:3-7,

the audience is composed of hostile critics, and the subject is evangelism of the lost outsider. In Matthew, on the other hand, the audience is Jesus' disciples, and the subject is seeking the strayed insider—pastoral care rather than evangelism, sanctification rather than justification. The Matthean version shows the influence of Ezek 34:6-8. The note of joy is sounded in both canonical versions.

In 18:12, Matthew begins with a question, as in Luke, but it is a different question. The question is redactional: "How does it seem to you?" (τί ὑμῖν δοκεῖ *ti hymin dokei*) is found only in Matthew in the Synoptics (18:12; 21:28; 22:42; 26:66), in John 11:56, and nowhere else in the NT. Jesus' original parable had portrayed a very dubious and risky decision, to leave the ninety-nine sheep in the desert (Luke) or on the mountains (Matthew) while going in search of the one lost sheep.[418] Matthew obviates this difficulty by posing the question in such a way that it self-evidently expects an affirmative answer, as even the Greek grammar indicates (question introduced by οὐχί [*ouchi*]). As is the case with many modern readers of the Bible, Matthew and his community had become so acclimated to the traditional form of the parable (in Q) that they already anticipated the fact that, of course, the "good shepherd" would seek the straying sheep. In Matthew's context, this focuses all concern on the plight of the lost sheep, not because it is more valuable than the others, but because it has strayed and needs to be restored, which the others do not. This is the point Matthew intends for his readers, who are too inclined to disdain the "little people" of the community, who can't keep up.

---

416. See Bernard Brandon Scott, *Hear Then the Parable* (Minneapolis: Fortress, 1989) 412-17.

417. *Gospel of Thomas* 107: "The kingdom is like a shepherd who had a hundred sheep. One of them went astray; it was the largest. He left the ninety-nine (and) sought for the one until he found it. After he had exerted himself, he said to the sheep, 'I love you more than the ninety-nine.' "

418. Various rationalizing explanations have been offered to lessen the shock: The shepherd naturally left kinsmen in charge, or put the sheep in a cave during his absence. All of this is absent from the text, as is the gospel song's "safely in the fold." This is precisely what is not said. Note that the KJV and TLB both avoid the difficulty by mistranslating, having the shepherd go into the mountains in search of the lost sheep, rather than leaving the ninety-nine in the mountains. The RSV was the first English translation to preserve the shock by translating correctly.

REFLECTIONS

1. In Matthew, the identity of the shepherd is not disclosed. The reader will think not only of God, but also of Jesus, who in Matthew represents the continuing presence of God with the church during its mission (see 1:23; Jesus is the shepherd who seeks the lost in 9:36; 15:24; 26:31). Yet Jesus has conferred his authority and ministry on his disciples (see 10:1-5a).

The God who values the straying and lapsed and seeks them out is embodied in his Son, the Messiah, but the continuing ministry of the Son is embodied in his disciples, the church. In Matthew's view, the church's *pastoral* care for its marginal and straying "little people" represents the continuing shepherding presence of God, made real in Jesus, God-with-us. In the church today, ministries of Christian education, nurture, pastoral care, support groups, crisis counseling, soup kitchens, overnight shelters for the homeless, and programs of financial assistance to the needy are ways that the community of faith responds to the needs of "the least of these."

2. The figure of the shepherd evoked more than one image in first-century Judaism (and Christianity, in Matthew's setting), images that were not readily at home with each other. On the one hand, traditional imagery, deriving from Israel's nomadic period, pictured God as the good shepherd. But by the first century, Jews in Palestine had long since ceased to be nomadic, and shepherds were a despised class, marginalized and categorized with tax collectors as those beyond the pale of proper Judaism. This tension in Jewish exegesis was overcome with elaborate explanations of why it was appropriate for the Bible to use such imagery for God. Matthew offers no such explanations, so there is a doubled radicality in his presentation. Not only are the straying marginal "little people" of Matthew's church considered of ultimate value, but also the Shepherd who seeks them is pictured without apology in an image disdained by the culture. The one who follows Jesus in ministry to the "little people" assumes a role that, already in the Bible, is not high on the cultural scale of images. Once in Western culture the "parson" was *the* "person" in the community. That time has ceased to be, and pastoral care must have another motive than cultural approbation. Matthew was already speaking to this need.

Matthew 18:15-35, Discipline and Forgiveness

Matthew 18:15-20, Church Discipline and the Presence of Christ

NIV

¹⁵"If your brother sins against you,ᵃ go and show him his fault, just between the two of you. If he listens to you, you have won your brother over. ¹⁶But if he will not listen, take one or two others along, so that 'every matter may be established by the testimony of two or three witnesses.'ᵇ ¹⁷If he refuses to listen to them, tell it to the church; and if he refuses to listen even to the church, treat him as you would a pagan or a tax collector.

¹⁸"I tell you the truth, whatever you bind on earth will beᶜ bound in heaven, and whatever you loose on earth will beᶜ loosed in heaven.

¹⁹"Again, I tell you that if two of you on earth agree about anything you ask for, it will be done for you by my Father in heaven. ²⁰For where two or three come together in my name, there am I with them."

ᵃ15 Some manuscripts do not have *against you*.　ᵇ16 Deut. 19:15
ᶜ18 Or *have been*

NRSV

15"If another member of the churchᵃ sins against you,ᵇ go and point out the fault when the two of you are alone. If the member listens to you, you have regained that one. ¹⁶But if you are not listened to, take one or two others along with you, so that every word may be confirmed by the evidence of two or three witnesses. ¹⁷If the member refuses to listen to them, tell it to the church; and if the offenderᶜ refuses to listen even to the church, let such a one be to you as a Gentile and a tax collector. ¹⁸Truly I tell you, whatever you bind on earth will be bound in heaven, and whatever you loose on earth will be loosed in heaven. ¹⁹Again, truly I tell you, if two of you agree on earth about anything you ask, it will be done for you by my Father in heaven. ²⁰For where two or three are gathered in my name, I am there among them."

ᵃGk *If your brother*　ᵇOther ancient authorities lack *against you*
ᶜGk *the brother*

377

COMMENTARY

These are not general rules for personal relations, but, like the preceding, are church rules for Christian congregational life (see Reflections below). As vv. 6-14 are concerned with marginal church members who are in danger of stumbling in their Christian life or have already wandered from the flock, so vv. 15-20 are concerned with members who are guilty of serious sin and remain unrepentant and disruptive participants in the congregational life. Although Matthew is opposed to casuistry of the rabbinic sort (see 5:21-48; 23:16-22), he here presents casuistic instructions for congregational life. (Nine clauses begin with the casuistic ἐάν [*ean*] + aorist subjunctive.)

18:15. In the light of v. 17, ἀδελφός (*adelphos*) does, indeed, mean "member of the church," but so translating *adelphos* obscures both the family nature of the church in Matthew's conception (cf. 12:46-50) and the fact that the word for "church" (ἐκκλησία *ekklēsia*) occurs in the Gospels only in 16:17 and 17:18. (Elsewhere, including later in this context, the NRSV often translates *adelphos* properly as "brother or sister"; e.g., in Matt 5:22-24; 18:35.)

"Against you" is not present in B ‫א‬ 1 and a few other MSS, and it is missing from the patristic quotations. Good arguments can be made for both inclusion and omission. Without the words, the verse refers to sin in general, and an interested Christian's intervention (as in the parallel Luke 17:3, thus likely so in Q). Then the case would be similar to Gal 6:1. If "against you" is accepted as what Matthew wrote, then it is the offended party who goes to the guilty one over a matter of personal offense. Matthew gives no list of specific sins that qualify for such response, but the fact that trivial matters are not in view may be inferred from the seriousness of the penalty in v. 17 (cf. the list in 1 Cor 5:11). Although the sin is a matter of community concern, the private conversation between offended and offender is to avoid embarrassment. Commitment to the priority of life together in community does not mean lack of sensitivity to the feelings of other persons, but precisely the opposite: Only by such sensitivity and care can people live together in the new family of God gathered by Jesus.

18:16. The offended person or community is to take the initiative; in some cases, the offender may be unaware of the offense. If the one-to-one encounter leaves the offending party unrepentant, the offended member attempts to resolve the problem by taking one or two fellow members of the congregation as "witnesses" (cf. Deut 19:15)—i.e., to protect from misrepresentation both the alleged offender and the one who claims to have been offended.[419] Matthew here Christianizes a longtime Jewish tradition of such reconciliatory acts on behalf of the community (cf. Lev 19:17-18; Deut 19:15; 1 Cor 5:1-4;, 11-13; Gal 6:1; 2 Thess 3:14-15; *y. Yoma* 45c; *T. Gad.* 6.3-5; 1QS 5.24–6.1).

18:17. "Church" here refers to the local congregation, unlike 16:17, where it is the universal body of believers. The injunction shows that the Matthean Christian community has meetings separate from the synagogue and that it exercises its own disciplinary program, but without making clear whether (at least some) members of the Christian community also participate in the synagogue. Cases of recalcitrant members who resist all private efforts to bring them to repentance are brought before the congregation, and if these persons do not heed the congregation's entreaty, they are expelled (cf. 1 Cor 5:1-4, 11-13; 2 Thess 3:14-15).

The language used seems strangely harsh, since Jesus (and his community) is accused of befriending tax collectors and sinners, as well as Gentiles (9:11; 11:19). The practice of excommunication also seems strange, from the perspective expressed in 7:1-5 and 13:37-43. These tensions may be due to the incorporation of conflicting traditions in the history of the community's development, or to applying them to different cases. It is clear, however, that if Matthew's church does not already have a procedure for disciplining dangerously errant members, one is here provided, spoken in the name of Jesus. While this procedure involves the judgment of "the congregation," it is not clear whether this presupposes the presence of church

---

419. The "progression" goes from "one or two" in v. 16 to "two" in v. 19 to "two or three" in v. 20. The numbers are not intended with mathematical precision, but in each case mean simply "a few."

leaders, through whom the congregation acts, or whether the assembly functions as a committee of the whole (see Introduction). In any case, the Christian community as a whole is concerned with the ethics of its individual members, and it intervenes in the spirit of love and forgiveness to take pastoral action that is more than mere advice. The goal is not only to maintain the holiness of the insiders, but to bring straying members to an awareness of their sins, to repentance, and eventual restoration as well (cf. 18:15, "gain").

18:18-20. With a pair of solemn *amen* sayings (see on 5:18), the Matthean Jesus assures the church of the divine ratification of its decisions.[420] The authority given Peter to make legal decisions for the church as a whole (16:9) is here given the

congregation in matters of its own discipline. By placing v. 19 in this context, Matthew applies an originally independent saying, encouraging group prayer, to the matter of church discipline. Likewise, in v. 20, an originally independent saying assuring the church of the continuing presence of Christ during the time of its mission—a major theme of Matthean theology (cf. on 1:23; 28:20)—is here applied to the particular case of the church's making its disciplinary decisions. Just as contemporary Judaism handed on sayings to the effect that wherever two or three discuss words of Torah they are attended by the divine presence,[421] so also Matthew's church proclaims that when it gathers in Jesus' name, Christ himself is present. The church is Christocentric rather than Torah-centric.

---

420. The MS attestation for ἀμήν (*amēn*) in v. 19 is almost evenly split: missing from ℵ D L Γ *f*[1] and other ancient MSS, but present in B (Θ) 058, 078, *f*[13] and most other MSS and versions. Verse 19 may originally have been the oracle of a Christian prophet (cf. Boring, *Continuing Voice of Jesus,* 252-53).

421. *'Abot* 3:3, 9; *b. Ber.* 6a.

REFLECTIONS

1. The instructions in this passage concern a matter not only of personal relations but also of preserving and reconciling a straying member of the community, while preserving the community's integrity as the holy covenant people of God. Matthew's community orientation and our individualistic one come into sharp conflict. Matthew offers a solution to something we hardly perceive as a problem, since we are inclined to see our sin as a matter between ourselves and God, or, at most, between ourselves and the person who has wronged us. That it is a matter of the Christian congregation to which we belong, and may damage its life, comes as a surprise to both us and them, if they are as individualistic as we are. Whatever we think of the solution Matthew offers, we might first ponder the nature of the Christian life it presupposes. A doctrine of the church as the people of God is here presupposed. To be Christian is to be bound together in community; to pray is to say *"our* Father," even in the privacy of our own room (Matt 6:6, 9).

2. Likewise, the setting of these instructions is what makes them both necessary and possible. Serious and stringent though these procedures are, they are in the context not of self-righteous vindictiveness, but of radical caring for the marginal and straying, and of grace and forgiveness beyond all imagining.

3. "Here we see developing the earliest legal procedures for excommunication, procedures designed to protect both the individual and the community. The sinner is guarded against arbitrariness and hasty action brought by a single individual or even by two or three leaders. The leader is protected from his own prejudices and from hasty action. The congregation is guarded from violent disruption and from the slow erosion of unresolved antagonisms."[422]

---

422. Paul S. Minear, *Matthew: The Teacher's Gospel* (New York: Pilgrim, 1982), 102.

Matthew 18:21-22, "Forgiveness" Without Grace

NIV	NRSV
[21]Then Peter came to Jesus and asked, "Lord, how many times shall I forgive my brother when he sins against me? Up to seven times?" [22]Jesus answered, "I tell you, not seven times, but seventy-seven times.[a]"	21Then Peter came and said to him, "Lord, if another member of the church[a] sins against me, how often should I forgive? As many as seven times?" [22]Jesus said to him, "Not seven times, but, I tell you, seventy-seven[b] times."
[a]22 Or *seventy times seven*	[a]Gk *if my brother* [b]Or *seventy times seven*

COMMENTARY

After the insertions of vv. 15*b*-20, Matthew now returns to his Q source (cf. Luke 17:4), rewriting Jesus' declaration in Q as a question from Peter and response from Jesus, which gives these two verses the form of a pronouncement story (and thus not merely the introduction to the following parable; cf. the analogous reformulation of Mark 9:34 into a question in Matthew 18:1). Already in Lev 19:17 the command to reason with the recalcitrant neighbor (fellow member of the covenant community) is followed immediately by the command to love the neighbor as oneself. Thus immediately after the instructions in vv. 15-20, Matthew adds this pronouncement story, which serves to guard them from a rigid or vindictive application. Only a congregation that operates in this spirit may act according to vv. 15-20.

Peter's proposal to forgive seven times sounds extravagantly generous, especially since there is no mention of repentance by the offending party (cf. Luke 17:4). It reverses the sevenfold pronouncement of vengeance in Gen 4:15. Jesus' response is far beyond Peter's proposal, and not only in greatly extending the quantity. The Greek number ἑβδομηκοντάκις ἑπτά (*hebdomēkontakis hepta*) can be legitimately understood as "seventy seven times" (as in Gen 4:24, again a reversal of Lamech's pronouncement of vengeance) or "four hundred ninety times" (as in the ancient translations of the NT). The difference between Peter's proposal and Jesus' pronouncement is not a matter of math or linguistics, but of the nature of forgiveness. Whoever *counts* has not forgiven at all, but is only biding his or her time (1 Cor 13:5). The kind of forgiveness called for is beyond all calculation, as the following story communicates.

Matthew 18:23-35, Grace Beyond Imagining

NIV	NRSV
[23]"Therefore, the kingdom of heaven is like a king who wanted to settle accounts with his servants. [24]As he began the settlement, a man who owed him ten thousand talents[a] was brought to him. [25]Since he was not able to pay, the master ordered that he and his wife and his children and all that he had be sold to repay the debt. [26]"The servant fell on his knees before him. 'Be	23"For this reason the kingdom of heaven may be compared to a king who wished to settle accounts with his slaves. [24]When he began the reckoning, one who owed him ten thousand talents[a] was brought to him; [25]and, as he could not pay, his lord ordered him to be sold, together with his wife and children and all his possessions, and payment to be made. [26]So the slave fell on
[a]24 That is, millions of dollars	[a]A talent was worth more than fifteen years' wages of a laborer

NIV

patient with me,' he begged, 'and I will pay back everything.' ²⁷The servant's master took pity on him, canceled the debt and let him go.

²⁸"But when that servant went out, he found one of his fellow servants who owed him a hundred denarii.ᵃ He grabbed him and began to choke him. 'Pay back what you owe me!' he demanded.

²⁹"His fellow servant fell to his knees and begged him, 'Be patient with me, and I will pay you back.'

³⁰"But he refused. Instead, he went off and had the man thrown into prison until he could pay the debt. ³¹When the other servants saw what had happened, they were greatly distressed and went and told their master everything that had happened.

³²"Then the master called the servant in. 'You wicked servant,' he said, 'I canceled all that debt of yours because you begged me to. ³³Shouldn't you have had mercy on your fellow servant just as I had on you?' ³⁴In anger his master turned him over to the jailers to be tortured, until he should pay back all he owed.

³⁵"This is how my heavenly Father will treat each of you unless you forgive your brother from your heart."

ᵃ28 That is, a few dollars

NRSV

his knees before him, saying, 'Have patience with me, and I will pay you everything.' ²⁷And out of pity for him, the lord of that slave released him and forgave him the debt. ²⁸But that same slave, as he went out, came upon one of his fellow slaves who owed him a hundred denarii;ᵃ and seizing him by the throat, he said, 'Pay what you owe.' ²⁹Then his fellow slave fell down and pleaded with him, 'Have patience with me, and I will pay you.' ³⁰But he refused; then he went and threw him into prison until he would pay the debt. ³¹When his fellow slaves saw what had happened, they were greatly distressed, and they went and reported to their lord all that had taken place. ³²Then his lord summoned him and said to him, 'You wicked slave! I forgave you all that debt because you pleaded with me. ³³Should you not have had mercy on your fellow slave, as I had mercy on you?' ³⁴And in anger his lord handed him over to be tortured until he would pay his entire debt. ³⁵So my heavenly Father will also do to every one of you, if you do not forgive your brother or sisterᵇ from your heart."

ᵃ The denarius was the usual day's wage for a laborer
ᵇ Gk brother

COMMENTARY

As in interpreting all the parables, the reader must distinguish between the original potent stories told by Jesus as a means of proclaiming the kingdom of God, and Matthew's later interpretations, applying them to life in the church. Frequently, as here, the later interpretation already understands the parable as an allegory (see Commentary on 13:1). Matthew's additions (v. [34 and] 35) transform the parable into a vivid lesson on forgiveness. The parable has become an allegorized negative example story: Don't be like the unforgiving servant. The later Matthean interpretation is the primary goal of understanding, but the power of Jesus' original disorienting story still penetrates through the Matthean overlay.[423]

18:23. For both Jesus' original story and Matthew's secondary application, the kingdom of God is somehow like the following story. For Jesus, the story was about a Gentile king and his servant, only secondarily pointing to God.[424] For Matthew, his allegorizing additions make the story from the beginning transparent to the relation between God and Christians. For Jesus, the king is a Gentile tyrant; for Matthew, the king already represents

---

423. For a perceptive reading of the original parable as heard in the pre-Easter situation of Jesus, see especially Bernard Brandon Scott, *Hear Then the Parable* (Minneapolis: Fortress, 1989) 267-80.

424. Gentile features of the story: (1) The vast amount of money (derived from tax revenue and its management) and power involved; (2) the king is "worshiped" by the servant (v. 26), impossible for a Jew; (3) Jewish law prohibited the wife and family from being sold into slavery (*m. Sota* 3.8); (4) in Judaism a man could be imprisoned for debt, but not tortured (βασινισται *basinistai*; v. 34 is literally "torturers"). The fact that the story is about a king is lost sight of after the opening lines; the story continues as a story about a master and his slaves. Matthew may have inserted "king" to interpret the story in his conflict-of-kingdoms theme.

God, and "debt" represents sin (cf. 6:12-15). The story unfolds in three scenes:

18:24-27, King and Servant. The servant is not a household slave, but a subordinate official (the NIV is here better than the NRSV). The debt was incurred through mismanagement of the king's resources and/or contracting to raise taxes from subject nations, not by personal expenditures. Even so, the figure is not realistic. A talent is the largest monetary unit (20.4 kg of silver), equal to 6,000 drachmas, the wages of a manual laborer for fifteen years. "Ten thousand" (μυριάς myrias, "myriad") is the largest possible number. Thus the combination is the largest figure that can be given. The annual tax income for all of Herod the Great's territories was 900 talents per year. Ten thousand talents would exceed the taxes for all of Syria, Phoenicia, Judea, and Samaria. The amount is fantastic, beyond all calculation.[425]

The debt is unpayable. Casting the servant into prison will be punitive—it will pay him back for his utter mismanagement—but it is utterly beyond the realm of possibility that the servant can repay his debt, no matter how much time is given. Both the servant and the king know this, despite vv. 25-26. The servant's situation is hopeless. He asks for mercy, and contrary to all expectation, the king responds with compassion.

18:28-31, Servant and Servant(s). The debt of the fellow servant is microscopic compared to what the first servant had been forgiven (1/600,000, if one attempts to be literal, but the figures are intended to represent an infinite contrast). Yet it is not an insignificant amount, representing 100 days' wages for an ordinary laborer (cf. 20:2).[426] When the first servant violently insists on repayment, it is not a trifling sum. The outrageous contrast between the way the first servant is treated by the king and the way the servant treats his fellow servant is not just a contrast of amounts owed. In the first scene, there was no reasonable way to repay such a debt; one could only be condemned or receive mercy. The parallel and contrast between the two scenes is that one is "reasonable" (the second) and one is not (the first). To interpret the first in terms of the second is a mistake; the whole thrust of the parable is to bring the second scene into line with the first. However, this does not happen. The servant does not respond to his fellow servant as he has been treated by the king. This outrages the other servants. The reader shares this outrage and is sympathetic when the other servants report the fellow's conduct to the king.

18:32-35, King and Servant. Again, the unthinkable happens. The king takes back his forgiveness, and the servant is condemned to eternal torment.[427] Some scholars think Jesus' original parable ended with the question of 18:33 (cf. the ending of Jonah, 4:11), others that v. 34 was the original conclusion. In any case, Matthew has added v. 35 to make the point in the parable's present context unmistakably clear (cf. 6:14-15).

---

425. Efforts have been made to make the figure more "realistic." On the one hand, it is explained that "ten thousand talents" is Matthew's exaggeration of an original ten talents (so T. W. Manson, *The Sayings of Jesus, as Recorded in the Gospels According to St. Matthew and St. Luke,* [London: SCM, 1949] 213) or ten thousand denarii (so M. C. De Boer, "Ten Thousand Talents? Matthew's Interpretation and Redaction of the Parable of the Unforgiving Servant [Matt 18:23-35]," *CBQ* 50 [1988] 214-32). On the other hand, the ten thousand talents are explained as the tax revenue promised the king by an official who had bid on the taxes for a large area, and then asked for a postponement of the debt when the anticipated revenue failed to materialize due to famine, bad crops, etc., in his assigned region (so J. D. Derrett, *Law in the New Testament* [London: Darton, Longman & Todd, 1970] 32-47).

426. Thus the NIV note "a few dollars" is misleading.

427. Again, this is the Matthean allegorical understanding of the parable, corresponding to 25:26, 30, 46.

REFLECTIONS

Matthew has clearly allegorized the parable, so that king = God; debt = sin; first servant = the one who is forgiven an enormous debt of sin by God; second servant = one who has committed an "ordinary" sin against a fellow human being or fellow Christian. When the Christian does not forgive as he or she has been forgiven, God's own forgiveness is then invalidated. The parable thus becomes a vivid illustration of a point that Matthew states elsewhere (6:14-15). This "moral of the story" can be psychologized by arguing that one who does not forgive others has never really received God's forgiveness in the first place, so it is not really "taken back." This may be a counsel of desperation in trying to make unilinear, non-parabolic sense of a disorienting parable. In the Matthean story, the problem remains that the king ("God") went back on his forgiveness. It is better to let the story remain unallegorized, so that it is an earthly king who reneges on his original gracious forgiveness, and let it illustrate, in an analogous way, the awfulness of failing to forgive as God forgives. This means that parables are often best preached as parables, even when Matthew has allegorized them. Matthew's legitimate allegorizing points can still be made independently of the parable, on the basis of Matthew's theology taken from the Gospel as a whole.

MATTHEW 19:1–22:46, CONFLICT AND ULTIMATE POLARIZATION

OVERVIEW

Matthew here shifts from discourse to narrative, but the theme of the preceding section continues: the meaning of life together in the Christian community in contrast to the community and values he understands to be represented by his opponents. This narrative unit is divided into two major sections, *Instructing the Disciples En Route to the Passion* (19:1–20:34) and *Jerusalem: The Final Confrontation* (21:1–22:46), thus extending the narrative to the next major discourse (see Introduction). Throughout, Matthew follows the Markan narrative line exactly, inserting additional sayings of Jesus from Q and M without varying the Markan order.

At one level, the outline of Matthew is geographical (see Introduction). The movement of chaps. 1–2 is from Judea, Jesus' home, to "exile" in Galilee of the Gentiles. This is where he calls his disciples and conducts his ministry (3:1–18:35).[428] At 19:1 the movement toward the passion begins, and Jesus returns to Judea for the first time since 4:12 (19:1–28:15).[429] Then the story moves back to Galilee for the commissioning to all the world (28:16-20).

The first narrative subsection 19:1–20:34 contin-

ues the theme of the Christian community as the true family of God (see from 12:46-50 on). By expansions and artful modifications of his source, Matthew has adjusted the Markan narrative so that the whole transitional section between Galilee and Jerusalem (19:1–20:34) becomes instruction to the disciples on the radically different kind of life called for by life together in the Christian community. All the teaching of 19:1–20:34 is now given directly to the disciples, except 19:3-9, 16-22, which becomes instruction to disciples by the additions 19:10-12, 23-26. Even the objections to Jesus' teaching are not made by opponents or bystanders, but by the disciples themselves (19:10, 13, 25; 20:24). After 19:1 the crowds disappear, only to reappear again at 20:29, thus forming brackets around a section in which they play no active role. This section is integrated by common themes that recur throughout: (1) The ethical life called for is not a matter of individualistic righteousness, but is represented by life together in the Christian community. (2) The kingdom of God as the basis and point of orientation for the life of the new community occurs at a key point in every pericope (19:12, 14, 23-24; 20:1, 21; cf. also the occurrences of "Son of Man" [19:28; 20:18, 28] and "Son of David" [20:30-31], both of which evoke the kingdom image). (3) This is an eschatological orientation, characterized by the reversal of present expectations and the values of this age. (4) The eschaton is already present in Jesus, the Son of Man who suffers, dies, and is raised. (5) This vision of how things ultimately (eschatologically) *are* is not seen clearly even by the disciples, whose blindness needs to be healed.

428. Cf. 2:6, 19-23. For Matthew, the "land of Israel" seems to be Judea and Galilee. Samaria belongs to the nations (10:5), not included until the post-Easter Great Commission (28:16-20). Judea is the "chosen" land, with the "holy city," where the "king of the Jews" should have been received. But he *was* received in "Galilee of the Gentiles."

429. Contrast the Fourth Gospel, in which the primary locus of Jesus' ministry is Judea and Jerusalem, from where he makes repeated visits to Galilee. These two views cannot be harmonized historically. This is only one illustration of the fact that the Gospels were not composed with biographical interests in mind, but that each evangelist constructed the storyline to express the theological meaning of the life of Jesus.

Matthew here includes Perea in Judea (cf. 4:25). He thinks theologically, not in terms of the political realities of Jesus' day, in which Judea was joined with Galilee under Herod Antipas.

Matthew 19:1–20:34, Instructing the Disciples En Route to the Passion

OVERVIEW

Matthew 19:1-26 is quite literally devoted to the new understanding of family (cf. 12:46-50), dealing with the place of divorce, remarriage, celibacy, children, and young people in the new Christian community. Matthew then grounds the radical reversal of cultural understandings called for by inserting and modifying a Q pericope (19:27-30 = Luke 22:30) and by presenting a parable intended to deal with the resentment generated within the community by this grand and gracious reversal (20:1-16). Matthew understands the theme of both the eschatological vision and the parable to be "the last shall be first and the first last" (19:30; 20:16). The eschatological reversal is already lived out in the career of the Son of Man, whose suffering and death are vindicated by God (20:17-19), but whose way of life is still misunderstood by ambitious and jealous disciples (20:20-28). Thus those who now confess their faith in Jesus with proper messianic titles still need to have their blindness healed—which Jesus is able to do (20:29-34). "From Galilee to Jerusalem" has thus been made by Matthew into a coherent thematic unit, whose movement is not merely geographical but represents growth in the meaning of discipleship en route from Galilee to the passion in Jerusalem. (For Overview of Passion Week, see 21:1.)

Matthew 19:1-12, Divorce, Remarriage, and Celibacy

NIV

19 When Jesus had finished saying these things, he left Galilee and went into the region of Judea to the other side of the Jordan. [2]Large crowds followed him, and he healed them there.

[3]Some Pharisees came to him to test him. They asked, "Is it lawful for a man to divorce his wife for any and every reason?"

[4]"Haven't you read," he replied, "that at the beginning the Creator 'made them male and female,'[a] [5]and said, 'For this reason a man will leave his father and mother and be united to his wife, and the two will become one flesh'[b]? [6]So they are no longer two, but one. Therefore what God has joined together, let man not separate."

[7]"Why then," they asked, "did Moses command that a man give his wife a certificate of divorce and send her away?"

[8]Jesus replied, "Moses permitted you to divorce your wives because your hearts were hard. But it was not this way from the beginning. [9]I tell you that anyone who divorces his wife, except for

a4 Gen. 1:27   *b5* Gen. 2:24

NRSV

19 When Jesus had finished saying these things, he left Galilee and went to the region of Judea beyond the Jordan. [2]Large crowds followed him, and he cured them there.

[3]Some Pharisees came to him, and to test him they asked, "Is it lawful for a man to divorce his wife for any cause?" [4]He answered, "Have you not read that the one who made them at the beginning 'made them male and female,' [5]and said, 'For this reason a man shall leave his father and mother and be joined to his wife, and the two shall become one flesh'? [6]So they are no longer two, but one flesh. Therefore what God has joined together, let no one separate." [7]They said to him, "Why then did Moses command us to give a certificate of dismissal and to divorce her?" [8]He said to them, "It was because you were so hardhearted that Moses allowed you to divorce your wives, but from the beginning it was not so. [9]And I say to you, whoever divorces his wife, except for unchastity, and marries another commits adultery."[a]

*a*Other ancient authorities read *except on the ground of unchastity, causes her to commit adultery*; others add at the end of the verse *and he who marries a divorced woman commits adultery*

NIV

marital unfaithfulness, and marries another woman commits adultery."

[10]The disciples said to him, "If this is the situation between a husband and wife, it is better not to marry."

[11]Jesus replied, "Not everyone can accept this word, but only those to whom it has been given. [12]For some are eunuchs because they were born that way; others were made that way by men; and others have renounced marriage[a] because of the kingdom of heaven. The one who can accept this should accept it."

[a]12 Or have made themselves eunuchs

NRSV

[10]His disciples said to him, "If such is the case of a man with his wife, it is better not to marry." [11]But he said to them, "Not everyone can accept this teaching, but only those to whom it is given. [12]For there are eunuchs who have been so from birth, and there are eunuchs who have been made eunuchs by others, and there are eunuchs who have made themselves eunuchs for the sake of the kingdom of heaven. Let anyone accept this who can."

COMMENTARY

19:1-2. This is Matthew's standard concluding formula to the five major speeches (see Introduction and Commentary on 7:28), combined with the transitional statement in Mark 10:1. Judea was the place of Jesus' birth, from which he was exiled to "Galilee of the Gentiles" by the Jewish opposition representing the kingdom of this age (see 2:22-23). Jesus returned to Judea to be baptized by John and tempted by Satan, but in Matthew, Jesus has not been in Judea since his withdrawal at 4:12.[430] Matthew here rewrites Mark to bring out the Galilee/Judea contrast, by adding "left Galilee and," omitting Mark's "and" after "Judea," thus making the region "beyond the Jordan" (Perea) specifically part of Judea. For Matthew, Jesus is in Judea from 19:1 on. Matthew's dualism is also geographical; there is no transition. Historically, Jews from Galilee en route to Jerusalem typically made a detour across the Jordan in order to avoid going through Samaria. As in his Markan source, the Matthean Jesus takes this route, but Matthew makes no point of it (cf. 10:5).[431] Matthew changes Mark's picture of Jesus teaching the crowds (Mark 10:1) to healing them, for in this entire section the Matthean Jesus restricts his teaching exclusively to the dis-

430. On "withdraw" (ἀναχωρέω *anachōreō*), see Commentary on 4:12; 12:15.
431. In Luke and John, Jesus goes through, not around, Samaria (cf. Luke 9:52; 17:11; John 4:4-39).

ciples (cf. 14:14 = Mark 6:34; see Overview above).

19:3. The specific identification of Jesus' opponents as Pharisees may be a Matthean addition (as in 3:7; 12:24; 15:12), since they are absent from some MSS of Mark 10:1, and the Markan text is often assimilated to that of Matthew. In the Matthean storyline, the Pharisees' question has three levels: (1) Matthew alters Mark's question on the legality of divorce as such to the grounds for a legitimate divorce. At one level, this casts the debate as part of the continuing rabbinic argument between the conservative Shammaites and the more liberal Hillelites (see Commentary on 5:31-32). (2) The word for "test" (πειράζω *peirazō*) reminds the reader of the last time Jesus was in Judea, "tempted" by Satan (4:1-11; cf. 16:1-12). Immediately on his return, he is tested by the Pharisees, who in Matthew's dualistic theology represent the kingdom of Satan. The ensuing dialogue is thus for Matthew more than a rabbinic dispute about interpretation of Torah; it is an expression of the continuing conflict of kingdoms (see 12:22-37), which intensifies as Jesus leaves Galilee and enters Judea. (3) In the Matthean story, Jesus is paired with John the Baptist, who has already been executed for objecting to Herod Antipas's divorce and remarriage to a divorcee (cf. 3:2; 4:12; 14:1-5). The

Pharisees' question uses the same vocabulary as John the Baptist in 14:4 ("it is lawful" [ἔξεστιν *exestin*]). The question thus evokes the conflict between the representatives of God's kingdom (John and Jesus) and the hostile kingship of this age, and reminds the reader that Jesus' destiny will be like John's.

19:4-9. Matthew has rearranged Mark 10:3-12 so that Jesus' answer corresponds to the pattern of ethical reflection developed in the antitheses (see 5:21-48, esp. 5:31-32). Whereas in Mark Jesus speaks of divorce as a command and the Pharisees speak of it as a concession (Mark 10:3-4), in Matthew these terms are reversed (19:7-8). And whereas in Mark Jesus begins with the concession and proceeds to the original will of God in creation, the Matthean Jesus begins with the absolute will of God and proceeds to the situational application (cf. on 5:21-48). The union of husband and wife as "one flesh" (physical, personal, parental) is the creation of God and is not at the husband's disposal. (The "man" who "separates" is not a third party, but the husband of v. 3; Matthew has changed Mark to have the identical "man" [ἄνθρωπος *anthrōpos*] in each case.)

In all of this, while still reflecting the first-century patriarchal culture, Jesus has transcended its views of marriage and the family by making marriage an element of the will of God, expressed in creation rather than merely a culturally conditioned contract on the human level. In the biblical story of creation, the first human pair were intended solely for each other, marriage being a God-given human relationship. Jesus' pronouncement is important in that (1) it constitutes the first definitive (but tacit) pronouncement in Jewish tradition against polygamy (sanctioned in the OT); (2) it places more responsibility on the husband than previously, tending toward removing the double standard by declaring the husband's relationship with the second woman as adulterous; and (3) it protects women from the arbitrary power of the husband's right to divorce at will.[432]

Matthew omits Mark 10:12, reflecting the Gentile provision for a woman's initiating a divorce as not applicable from his Jewish perspective.[433] As in 5:32 (see for a full discussion), Matthew builds an exception clause into Jesus' absolute prohibition of divorce, thus in principle making the teaching of Jesus a situational application of the absolute "ideal" will of God, rather than a legalistic code.

19:10-12. This addition to Mark seems to be entirely Matthean composition, part of his effort to have Jesus speak to the new situation of the Matthean church, which not only still has strong Jewish roots and perspectives, but also includes Gentiles with a completely different background and viewpoint. Verse 10 seems at first to portray the Twelve in their worst light, as people who judged all of Jesus' teachings only in the light of their own self-interest.[434] But the comment composed by Matthew functions only to set up Jesus' counterresponse. Thus the disciples' response, inappropriate when heard as a historical report, voices the objection of new Gentile members in the Christian community to the seemingly rigid marital ethic advocated by the Matthean Christians and serves to introduce the question of whether Christians should get married at all.[435]

The referent of "this teaching" (v. 11) is not entirely clear. (1) Some refer it to Jesus' teaching on divorce and remarriage in general (vv. 3-9), and thus make it applicable to all Christians, to whom "is given" the mystery of the kingdom (as 13:11). The following verses, however, seem to restrict the teaching's application to a limited group within the community. (2) The context has thus caused other scholars to argue that "the teaching" that is not for all applies to those divorced women who are forbidden by vv. 4-9 to remarry, but are to continue in their unmarried state as a mark of their obedience to God. (3) The view of most scholars is that while the pagan practice of literal castration as a religious practice is rejected (cf. Lev 22:24; Deut 23:1), those who "make themselves eunuchs for the sake of the

432. See Phillip Sigal, *The Halakah of Jesus of Nazareth According to the Gospel of Matthew* (Washington, D.C.: University Press of America, 1986) 83-118; Douglas R. A. Hare, *Matthew,* Interpretation (Louisville: Westminster/John Knox, 1993) 221.

433. This saying in Mark had been added to the traditional saying of Jesus to adapt it to a Gentile setting, where this was a possibility.

434. So Paul S. Minear, *Matthew: The Teacher's Gospel* (New York: Pilgrim, 1982) 105.

435. See 1 Cor 7:1-40 for another discussion of the Christian marital ethic derived from its Jewish roots, but launched into a Gentile situation.

kingdom of heaven" are members of the community who choose to remain celibate in order to commit themselves fully to Christian work. While marriage and family life were valued by Jesus and the Matthean church as a gift from God and were the normal life of the disciple, exceptional people such as prophets and missionaries sometimes remained unmarried as a mark of their special calling. John the Baptist, Jesus, and Paul apparently belonged to this group.[436] Matthew allows for it within the life of the church, but as with Paul (1 Cor 7:7) it is for the minority who "can" (v. 12) do this because "it is given" to them by God (v. 11).

436. See Boring, *Continuing Voice*, 134-37.

Matthew 19:13-15, Children in the New Community

NIV	NRSV
[13]Then little children were brought to Jesus for him to place his hands on them and pray for them. But the disciples rebuked those who brought them. [14]Jesus said, "Let the little children come to me, and do not hinder them, for the kingdom of heaven belongs to such as these." [15]When he had placed his hands on them, he went on from there.	[13]Then little children were being brought to him in order that he might lay his hands on them and pray. The disciples spoke sternly to those who brought them; [14]but Jesus said, "Let the little children come to me, and do not stop them; for it is to such as these that the kingdom of heaven belongs." [15]And he laid his hands on them and went on his way.

COMMENTARY

Whereas previously Matthew had used children as symbols of the "little people" in the Christian community (see Commentary on 18:1-10), here he is concerned with the place of actual children in church life. In contrast to contemporary Jewish and pagan religious life, the Christian community encouraged participation by the whole family.[437] Matthew thus changes Mark's ambiguous "touch"

437. There were pagan religions exclusively for men or women, but families did not participate together. The practice of the first-century synagogue is unclear, but it did allow some participation by women. See Elisabeth Schüssler Fiorenza, *In Memory of Her: A Feminist Theological Reconstruction of Christian Origins* (New York: Crossroad, 1983) 109; Bernadette Brooten, *Women Leaders in the Ancient Synagogue* (Chico, Calif.: Scholars Press, 1982). Male children prior to age twelve did not participate in synagogue worship; girls and younger women not at all.

to "lay hands on and pray," the typical acts of blessing by a revered teacher. It is likely that the practice of the Matthean church is reflected here, in which children are welcomed into the community in an act of blessing. This additional break with cultural mores did not happen without objection, again voiced by the disciples (v. 13; cf. v. 10). Children are not merely tolerated, but are regarded as models of how the kingdom of God is received. The kingdom "belongs" not only to them, but also to "such as these"—to all who receive it without presumption and self-justification.

Matthew 19:16–20:16, Successful Young People and the New Community

NIV	NRSV
[16]Now a man came up to Jesus and asked, "Teacher, what good thing must I do to get eternal life?" [17]"Why do you ask me about what is good?"	[16]Then someone came to him and said, "Teacher, what good deed must I do to have eternal life?" [17]And he said to him, "Why do you ask me about what is good? There is only one

NIV

Jesus replied. "There is only One who is good. If you want to enter life, obey the commandments."

¹⁸"Which ones?" the man inquired.

Jesus replied, " 'Do not murder, do not commit adultery, do not steal, do not give false testimony, ¹⁹honor your father and mother,'ᵃ and 'love your neighbor as yourself.'ᵇ"

²⁰"All these I have kept," the young man said. "What do I still lack?"

²¹Jesus answered, "If you want to be perfect, go, sell your possessions and give to the poor, and you will have treasure in heaven. Then come, follow me."

²²When the young man heard this, he went away sad, because he had great wealth.

²³Then Jesus said to his disciples, "I tell you the truth, it is hard for a rich man to enter the kingdom of heaven. ²⁴Again I tell you, it is easier for a camel to go through the eye of a needle than for a rich man to enter the kingdom of God."

²⁵When the disciples heard this, they were greatly astonished and asked, "Who then can be saved?"

²⁶Jesus looked at them and said, "With man this is impossible, but with God all things are possible."

²⁷Peter answered him, "We have left everything to follow you! What then will there be for us?"

²⁸Jesus said to them, "I tell you the truth, at the renewal of all things, when the Son of Man sits on his glorious throne, you who have followed me will also sit on twelve thrones, judging the twelve tribes of Israel. ²⁹And everyone who has left houses or brothers or sisters or father or motherᶜ or children or fields for my sake will receive a hundred times as much and will inherit eternal life. ³⁰But many who are first will be last, and many who are last will be first.

20 "For the kingdom of heaven is like a landowner who went out early in the morning to hire men to work in his vineyard. ²He agreed to pay them a denarius for the day and sent them into his vineyard.

³"About the third hour he went out and saw others standing in the marketplace doing nothing. ⁴He told them, 'You also go and work in my

---

ᵃ*19* Exodus 20:12-16; Deut. 5:16-20   ᵇ*19* Lev. 19:18
ᶜ*29* Some manuscripts mother or wife

NRSV

who is good. If you wish to enter into life, keep the commandments." ¹⁸He said to him, "Which ones?" And Jesus said, "You shall not murder; You shall not commit adultery; You shall not steal; You shall not bear false witness; ¹⁹Honor your father and mother; also, You shall love your neighbor as yourself." ²⁰The young man said to him, "I have kept all these;ᵃ what do I still lack?" ²¹Jesus said to him, "If you wish to be perfect, go, sell your possessions, and give the moneyᵇ to the poor, and you will have treasure in heaven; then come, follow me." ²²When the young man heard this word, he went away grieving, for he had many possessions.

23Then Jesus said to his disciples, "Truly I tell you, it will be hard for a rich person to enter the kingdom of heaven. ²⁴Again I tell you, it is easier for a camel to go through the eye of a needle than for someone who is rich to enter the kingdom of God." ²⁵When the disciples heard this, they were greatly astounded and said, "Then who can be saved?" ²⁶But Jesus looked at them and said, "For mortals it is impossible, but for God all things are possible."

27Then Peter said in reply, "Look, we have left everything and followed you. What then will we have?" ²⁸Jesus said to them, "Truly I tell you, at the renewal of all things, when the Son of Man is seated on the throne of his glory, you who have followed me will also sit on twelve thrones, judging the twelve tribes of Israel. ²⁹And everyone who has left houses or brothers or sisters or father or mother or children or fields, for my name's sake, will receive a hundredfold,ᶜ and will inherit eternal life. ³⁰But many who are first will be last, and the last will be first.

20 "For the kingdom of heaven is like a landowner who went out early in the morning to hire laborers for his vineyard. ²After agreeing with the laborers for the usual daily wage,ᵈ he sent them into his vineyard. ³When he went out about nine o'clock, he saw others standing idle in the marketplace; ⁴and he said to them, 'You also go into the vineyard, and I will pay you whatever is right.' So they went. ⁵When he went out again about noon and about three o'clock, he

---

ᵃOther ancient authorities add *from my youth*
ᵇGk lacks *the money*   ᶜOther ancient authorities read *manifold*
ᵈGk *a denarius*

NIV

vineyard, and I will pay you whatever is right.' ⁵So they went.

"He went out again about the sixth hour and the ninth hour and did the same thing. ⁶About the eleventh hour he went out and found still others standing around. He asked them, 'Why have you been standing here all day long doing nothing?'

⁷"'Because no one has hired us,' they answered.

"He said to them, 'You also go and work in my vineyard.'

⁸"When evening came, the owner of the vineyard said to his foreman, 'Call the workers and pay them their wages, beginning with the last ones hired and going on to the first.'

⁹"The workers who were hired about the eleventh hour came and each received a denarius. ¹⁰So when those came who were hired first, they expected to receive more. But each one of them also received a denarius. ¹¹When they received it, they began to grumble against the landowner. ¹²'These men who were hired last worked only one hour,' they said, 'and you have made them equal to us who have borne the burden of the work and the heat of the day.'

¹³"But he answered one of them, 'Friend, I am not being unfair to you. Didn't you agree to work for a denarius? ¹⁴Take your pay and go. I want to give the man who was hired last the same as I gave you. ¹⁵Don't I have the right to do what I want with my own money? Or are you envious because I am generous?'

¹⁶"So the last will be first, and the first will be last."

NRSV

did the same. ⁶And about five o'clock he went out and found others standing around; and he said to them, 'Why are you standing here idle all day?' ⁷They said to him, 'Because no one has hired us.' He said to them, 'You also go into the vineyard.' ⁸When evening came, the owner of the vineyard said to his manager, 'Call the laborers and give them their pay, beginning with the last and then going to the first.' ⁹When those hired about five o'clock came, each of them received the usual daily wage.ᵃ ¹⁰Now when the first came, they thought they would receive more; but each of them also received the usual daily wage.ᵃ ¹¹And when they received it, they grumbled against the landowner, ¹²saying, 'These last worked only one hour, and you have made them equal to us who have borne the burden of the day and the scorching heat.' ¹³But he replied to one of them, 'Friend, I am doing you no wrong; did you not agree with me for the usual daily wage?ᵃ ¹⁴Take what belongs to you and go; I choose to give to this last the same as I give to you. ¹⁵Am I not allowed to do what I choose with what belongs to me? Or are you envious because I am generous?'ᵇ ¹⁶So the last will be first, and the first will be last."ᶜ

ᵃ Gk a denarius   ᵇ Gk is your eye evil because I am good?
ᶜ Other ancient authorities add for many are called but few are chosen

COMMENTARY

Matthew 19:16–20:16 is one scene, created by Matthew by taking the story of the rich man from Mark 10:17-31, adding the saying at 19:28 from Q and the parable 20:1-16 from M, resulting in the following extended dialogue:[438]

438. A comparison with Mark 10:17-31 shows that Matthew has rearranged the speaking parts to get this neat back-and-forth of rabbinic dialogue. Matthew has the young man ask, "Which ones?" (as in 22:36) rather than having Jesus volunteer the information. The young man asks, "What do I still lack?" instead of simply having Jesus tell him, and the disciples respond to Jesus rather than to each other (19:25 vs. Mark 10:26).

Young man:	"What good deed must I do to have eternal life?"	(v. 16)
Jesus:	" . . . keep the commandments."	(v. 17)
Young man:	"Which ones?"	(v. 18*a*)
Jesus:	"You shall not murder, . . . love your neighbor."	(vv. 18*b*-19)
Young man:	"I have kept all these; what do I still lack?"	(v. 20)
Jesus:	"Go . . . sell . . . give . . . follow me."	(v. 21)
Young man:	No verbal response; goes away grieving.	(v. 22)
Jesus (to disciples):	" . . . it will be hard for a rich person to enter the kingdom."	(vv. 23-24)
Disciples:	"Then who can be saved?"	(v. 25)
Jesus:	"Impossible for humans; possible for God."	(v. 26)
Peter:	"What then will we have?"	(v. 27)
Jesus:	" . . . at the renewal of all things . . . eternal life" Kingdom parable as conclusion	(vv. 28-30) (20:1-16)

19:16-22. The "rich young ruler" appears in no NT document, but is a conglomerate of the figures in Mark (rich), Matthew (who alone adds "young") and Luke (who alone adds "ruler"). Matthew alone gives us the picture of a youth, twice calling him a "young man" (νεανίσκος *neaniskos*).[439] The point is not to speculate on the "real" age of the person in the story, but to accept Matthew's picture of him as a youth. In the present context, he represents wealthy, successful young people whom Matthew's church would like to attract to (or retain in) the way of Christian discipleship, but who often were uninterested in the different value system by which the Christian community lived.

19:16. The young man inquires about "eternal life," a term that occurs in Matthew only three times: here; in 19:29, forming a bracket for this scene; and in 25:46. His addressing Jesus as "teacher," although adopted from Mark, signals that he is an outsider—in Matthew, real disciples address Jesus as "Lord." Matthew's editing of the inquiry in Mark 10:17 has the effect of pairing this scene with 22:34-40, which also has an outsider address Jesus as "teacher," and who receives "love your neighbor as yourself" as the culminating response.

19:17-19. Matthew rewrites Jesus' reply in Mark, "Why do you call me good? No one is good but God alone" (Mark 10:18 NRSV) to avoid any misunderstanding that Jesus was not good (cf. Matt 3:14-15). In Matthew, Jesus represents God's goodness in this world (1:23). In the following parable, understood by Matthew as an allegory in which the employer represents God and Jesus, the employer's climactic declaration is that he is "good" (ἀγαθός *agathos*; 20:15). Matthew also edits his source to make Jesus' initial response more clearly an affirmation of the Torah. Jesus replies with the standard Jewish answer, "Keep the commandments." When the young man asks "Which?" again as in 22:34-40, Jesus' reply has been edited by Matthew to make both the order and the vocabulary correspond to the Decalogue in Exod 20:13-16 and Deut 5:17-20 (as in Matt 5:21).[440] Matthew wishes to make it clear that Jesus is an advocate of the Law rather than its opponent (5:17-20).

19:20. The young man has always been a law-keeping Jew who goes beyond the prohibitions of the Decalogue and attempts to live by the command of love for the neighbor. Yet he senses something is missing and asks, "What do I still lack?" (differently from Mark, in which Jesus takes the initiative in telling the man of his deficiency).

19:21. "If you would be perfect" has been traditionally understood as the basis for the distinction between two degrees of discipleship, the "ordinary" Christians who keep the basic commandments and the "perfect," those who belong

439. In his Markan source, it appears that the man is of mature years, because he claims to have kept the commands *"since* my youth" (Mark 10:20), omitted by Matthew. A "youth" (νεανίσκος *neaniskos*) is a person in his or her twenties, according to Philo *On the Creation* 105, quoting Hippocrates; from twenty to forty according to Diogenes Laertius *Lives of Eminent Philosophers*, "Pythagoras" 8.10.

440. Although there are text problems in Mark, which has been assimilated to Matthew in the manuscript tradition, it is clear that Mark's original aorist subjunctive prohibitions are changed by Matthew to the MT and LXX styles of future indicative; Mark's non-Decalogue "do not defraud" is omitted; the order of the Markan original is adjusted to correspond to that in Exodus.

to religious orders and live according to the extra "evangelical counsels" of poverty, chastity, and obedience. This interpretation serves to relieve "ordinary" Christians of the radical demand to dispose of property for the sake of the poor. More recently, the call for "perfection" has been understood as making a distinction between the Jewish way of salvation and the Christian way of discipleship; keeping the Law is the sufficient way to eternal life for Jews, but radical obedience is required of those who wish to become Christian disciples.[441] Both of these interpretations run aground on the fact that the passage does not distinguish two groups. The same goal is envisioned throughout, called "eternal life" (v. 16), "enter into life" (v. 17), "being perfect" (v. 21), "entering the kingdom of God" (v. 23), and "being saved" (v. 25). Verse 24 makes clear that selling all and giving to the poor is the requirement not only for the "second stage" for a Jew who is already saved to become a Christian, or for an "ordinary" Christian to become a "perfect" one, but also the condition for entering the kingdom of God at all. Further, τέλειος (teleios) does not mean "perfect" in the sense of sinless, but "whole," "undivided," "mature" as in 5:48, where it is the divine requirement not for a special class, but for all who strive to be obedient to God.[442] (On explanations for the demand to sell all, see the Reflections below.) Jesus' final word to the young man is verbatim the same as his call to Matthew, the wealthy publican who became a disciple (9:9; cf. 4:19, 21-22).

19:22. "This word" is identical to the expression translated "this teaching" in 19:11, binding this scene into the same series as 19:3-15 (see Overview). The young man is called and would be welcomed into Matthew's church, but he refuses. His sorrow contrasts with the joy of the person in the parable, who sells all to obtain the treasure of God's kingdom (13:44).

19:23-26. Jesus lets him go. His next words are not to the young man, but to the disciples, for whom the whole scene has been played out. Matthew reformulates it as an ἀμήν (amēn) say-

ing (see on 5:18), solemnly pronouncing that not only is it hard for a rich person to enter the kingdom, but it is impossible.[443] The disciples get the point, though many interpreters have attempted to moderate it (see Reflections below for comforting "explanations" of the needle's eye). Their exclamation only serves to set up Jesus' pronouncement that everything is possible for God (not "with God" [NIV] in the sense of collaboration). The scene could end on this dramatic note, but Matthew extends the dialogue, giving the eschatological basis for the radical style of life here called for and a parabolic conclusion intended to avoid misunderstanding and provoke further thought (see Overview).

19:27-30. It is important to see this paragraph as a continuation of the preceding dialogue, for taken by itself Peter's question seems purely selfish, a *quid pro quo* understanding of discipleship. In the present structure devised by Matthew, Peter's question provides the occasion for Jesus to affirm the eschatological reward for those who have not depended on their own goodness, but who by following Jesus participate in the eschatological reversal of all things symbolized by the kingdom of God. Jesus immediately explicates this.

19:28. The saying was originally most likely the oracle of a Christian prophet spoken in Jesus' name, announcing the reversal of present relationships at the last judgment.[444] In some strands of Jewish apocalyptic thought, the regathering of the dispersed twelve tribes of Israel is one of the blessings of the last days (*Pss. Sol.* 17:28; the tenth petition of the Eighteen Benedictions). The missionaries of the Q community in the early days of the post-Easter Jesus movement had carried on a mission to Israel announcing the time of the eschatological blessing and reconstitution of Israel. Their mission had been rejected, however, so the oracle announces that Israel will indeed be regathered at the eschaton—for judgment. As in other apocalyptic pictures, the saints participate with God, or the Son of Man, in this judgment scene in which the tables are turned and those now rejected will act as judges (*1 Enoch* 45:3;

441. So Daniel J. Harrington, *The Gospel of Matthew* (Collegeville, Minn.: Liturgical Press, 1991) 281.

442. This is borne out by the frequent use of τέλειος in the NT to characterize authentic Christian life as such; it may be translated "adult," "mature," or "perfect" (1 Cor 14:20; Eph 4:13; Phil 3:15; Col 1:28; Heb 5:14; Jas 1:4; 3:2).

443. It is important to remember throughout this section that the references to "kingdom of heaven" do not refer merely to "going to heaven" when one dies, but are Matthew's equivalent of "kingdom of God." See Excursus "Kingdom of Heaven in Matthew,"288-94.

444. See M. Eugene Boring, *The Continuing Voice of Jesus: Christian Prophecy and the Gospel Tradition* (Louisville: Westminster/John Knox, 1991), 229-30.

61:8; 62:2; 69:27; 108:12; 1 Cor 6:2; cf. Rev 20:4, 11). Matthew introduces the oracle here to portray the grounding of the life of discipleship in the vision of the present-and-coming kingdom of God and the reversal of values it expresses.[445]

"The renewal of all things" translates παλιγ-γενεσία (*paliggenesia*), a rare word that literally means "rebirth," as it is used in Titus 3:5, its only other NT occurrence, with reference to conversion and baptism. The word was a technical term in several Hellenistic religious traditions; it was also used by the Stoics for the periodic rebirth of the world after the cosmic conflagration. Matthew uses it to express the apocalyptic hope of the eschatological renewal of the earth. It is one way of picturing the meaning of the final coming of the kingdom of God, which will not negate the meaning of history, but will redeem and fulfill it (cf. "new heaven and new earth [new creation]" in Isa 65:17; 66:22; Rom 8:18-25; 2 Cor 5:17; Rev 21:1). This text has sometimes been understood as giving the twelve apostles authority to rule the "new Israel," the church, through the centuries. This is a misinterpretation, for three reasons: (1) The picture is eschatological, not historical. The "renewal of all things" occurs at the parousia, when the Son of Man comes and sits on the throne of judgment, as in 25:31-32, the only other instance of the Son of Man's sitting on a throne. Thus Matthew omits Mark 10:30, "now in this time," to make the eschatological orientation clear. (2) "Rule" is not the exclusive translation of κρίνω (*krinō*) here or anyplace else in Matthew, but means "judge" as well; nor does it mean exclusively "condemn," for which Matthew regularly uses κατακρίνω (*katakrinō*; 12:41-42; 20:18; 27:3). The twelve share the role of the Christ/Son of Man as eschatological ruler and judge, separating and sorting out, accepting and rejecting. The "twelve tribes" are eschatologically restored, but not *as such* saved. Some people are accepted, and some are rejected. Thus the church is in continuity with Israel, an Israel that must be sifted and judged. (3) The concept of the church as the "new Israel" is foreign to Matthew, who always uses "Israel" in the empirical sense. Because even eschatologically restored Israel must

445. Luke placed his edited form of this Q saying at the last supper (Luke 22:28-30).

be judged and sorted out like the church, the church is not simply identified with Israel.

19:29. Matthew here rejoins his Markan source, but keeps the picture oriented to the ultimate future. The Markan form of the saying pictures the disciples' present experience as receiving many houses and families in the Christian community in exchange for leaving their literal family to become disciples. Matthew elsewhere affirms this view of the church as the family of God (12:46-50; 18:1-35), but here preserves the contrast between present appearances and eschatological reality. Eschatological reward is not only for the Twelve, but also for everyone who, unlike the wealthy young man of 19:16-23, has left all to become a disciple. For Matthew, the kind of life to which the disciples are called, and for which they are instructed in this section (19:1–20:28), makes sense only when grounded in the eschatological vision of the ultimate triumph of God's kingdom. Thus "eternal life" recurs in v. 29 as the concluding response to the question asked in 19:16. Neither is 19:30 a pious generalization, but for Matthew it has a specific reference: The Matthean community's Pharisaic opponents will be rejected in the final judgment, and the Christian disciples whom they presently reject and persecute will receive eschatological vindication.

20:1-16. For contextual meaning, see Overview of 19:16–20:16 and structure under 19:16-26. Originally an independent pre-Matthean unit in the oral tradition, this parable of the laborers in the vineyard was told by Jesus in a context or contexts now lost. The original meaning(s) and function(s) in the context(s) of Jesus own ministry must be distinguished from its meaning and function in the Matthean literary context (see Commentary on 13:1). To hear it as Jesus originally told it, the reader must refrain from allegorically making the landowner into God and the payment the last judgment, for such a reading has the effect of letting the reader identify in advance with God, whose judgment is always right. Without this allegorical approach, the hearer tends to identify with those first hired, and the story can have its parabolic effect. The original parable ended at v. 13 or 14a; vv. 14(*b*)-16 are Matthean additions to enhance his allegorical interpretation. Exegesis of Matthew is interested not only in hearing the original parable in Jesus' terms, but also in understanding the meaning of the text as we have it in Matthew, where it is closely related to the preceding context (cf. the issue of the "good" in 19:16; 20:16 [see the NRSV footnote] and the similar ending with the sayings in 19:30 and 20:16).

The parable begins in the familiar world in which day laborers are hired at sunup and are paid at the end of the day, in accordance with Torah regulation and Jewish practice (Lev 19:13; Deut 24:14-15). A denarius was a normal day's pay for manual laborers hired by the day (cf. Tob 5:15; *Ber. Rab.* 61), but was barely enough to maintain a family at the subsistence level. The first-century reader feels at home in the world created by the story.

The parable gradually fades into another dimension from that of the everyday world, as unusual features begin to accumulate for which no explanation is given. Instead of sending his manager, the wealthy landowner himself goes to the market to hire laborers (cf. v. 8). The landowner goes repeatedly, even at the "eleventh hour" (5:00 P.M.). No explanation is given as to why those "standing idle" had not been hired on earlier recruitment visits. The first group of workers is hired on the basis of an oral contract for the normal amount; the later groups are promised "whatever is right," thus raising, but not answering, the question of what is "right" (δίκαιος *dikaios*; cf. 1:19). Although the first group has a "contract" and the second can only trust in the master's sense of justice, in reality both groups depend on the trustworthiness of the landowner. In the closing scene in which all are paid the same, the middle groups are ignored in order to focus on "first" and "last" (cf. 19:30; 20:16, which bracket the parable).

The closing scene in which payment is made contains the deeply disturbing element that makes the story a parable rather than an illustration of a logical "point." At the landowner's (now called "Lord," 20:8) order, those last hired are paid first (cf. 19:30). They receive a full day's pay. Those hired first now expect that fairness demands that they will receive more (v. 10)—but they receive the agreed-upon amount. Matthean readers, too, who assume they are committed to justice—equal pay for equal work—share the consternation of

those who have worked all day, enduring its heat and fatigue. Other Matthean texts encourage readers who share Matthew's sense of justice and his work ethic (cf., e.g., 25:14-30, esp. v. 29) to expect that those who work more get more, as does the preceding context (cf. 19:27-30 to 16-26).

The connection with 19:16-30 must not be lost sight of. As in 18:12-14 and 18:23-35, Matthew brings a unit to conclusion by inserting a parable (cf. structure of 18:1-35). Here as elsewhere, this is not in order to end with a rhetorical flourish, but to allow the parabolic conclusion both to block off possible misunderstandings and to provoke to further reflection. Although Matthew is attracted to this parable because it can be used to illustrate his themes of the reversal of first and last and good versus bad (he modifies the original story in this direction[446]), the original disturbing element in the parable still penetrates Matthew's redaction. The parable is upsetting because it functions to challenge and reverse conventional values, including the sense of justice and fairness among Matthew's religious readership, and this is one reason why Matthew chooses to preserve it and insert it here.[447] Although Jesus probably originally directed this story to those who criticized him for accepting publicans and sinners, Matthew includes this story as the climax of an extended section devoted to instructing insiders, not apologetics for outsiders. Here as elsewhere, Matthew understands the parable allegorically, so that for him the landowner is the eschatological judge, God or Jesus, who is indeed "good,"[448] and the payment at the end of the day is the last judgment (as in the preceding context, 19:27-29). The "first" and "last" in Matthew's view both refer to insiders, to Christians who have worked long and faithfully, and latecomers who have not. Some members of Matthew's church might read "first" as the old-line Jewish Christians and "last" as Gentile Christians who are now received on an equal basis.

446. See Scott's reading, *Hear Then the Parable* (Minneapolis: Fortress, 1989) 284-86.

447. One may contrast a rabbinic parable often pointed to as a "parallel," in which a king paid a laborer who had worked only two hours as much as those who had worked all day. When the latter complained, he explained that the others had done as much in two hours as they had done all day (*y.t. Ber.* 2.5.c.) Whereas Jesus' parable challenges conventional ideas of justice and fairness, the rabbinic story reinforces them.

448. Thus the reason for dropping Jesus' denial that he is "good" (Mark 10:18) appears at the conclusion of the parable (the NRSV's "generous" is ἀγαθός [*agathos*], the same word as "good" in 19:17 and Mark 10:18).

The parable deals with resentment toward others who have actually received the grace one affirms in theory. A comparison of v. 10 and v. 12 is instructive. Those who had worked all day begin not by objecting to the grace others had received, but by expecting that they themselves will receive more (v. 10). When they receive the just fulfillment of their contract, they object not to what they have in fact received, but that others have been made "equal" to them. They have what they have by justice; others have been made equal by grace. It is this last resentment that they find unbearable. Their objection to the lord's gracious acceptance of others as their equals alienates them, so that they are addressed by the distancing "friend" (ἑταῖρε *hetaire*).[449] Strategically placed at the conclusion of the section 19:16–20:16, the parable invites reflection on the sovereignty of the good God, the One with whom there can be no bargaining because he is the creator and the sovereign (cf. Romans 9–11). Likewise, the parable, while affirming the sovereign grace of God, rejects *presuming* on grace. Grace is always amazing grace. Grace that can be calculated and "expected" (v. 10) is no longer grace (cf. 22:11-14).

449. Although often translated "friend," ἑταῖρε does not mean "friend" in the personal sense. It is more like "mister" when used pointedly without a name. It is found only in Matthew in the NT, used always by a superior to a subordinate who is in the wrong (cf. 22:12; 26:50).

REFLECTIONS

Every sectarian group moving into the mainstream faces the question, "What about our (potentially) successful young people?" a question pushed by the young people themselves. Matthew changed Mark to get this dimension.

1. The most difficult thing for modern Western Christians to understand about this whole section dealing with marriage, divorce, children, money, success, and ambition is not the individual teachings, but that such matters are more than individual concerns to be decided by each person. Matthew's perspective calls for Christians to understand themselves as belonging to a community, so that no decision is purely personal and individual. Matthew's perspective calls for Christians to understand their lives as being lived in the light of the present and coming kingdom of God, which represents a reversal of cultural values rather than their confirmation. Thus the individual teachings of Matthew's Gospel cannot be understood on a paragraph-by-paragraph basis, unless and until one is converted to the Gospel's ecclesial and eschatological perspective.

2. Throughout this extended section, the "kingdom of heaven" is the point of orientation that makes possible the kind of life here called for. This does not mean "going to heaven." "Kingdom of heaven" is Matthew's usual term for "kingdom of God." Here as elsewhere in Matthew, two kingdoms collide, and the readers must decide with which one they are aligned (see Excursus "Kingdom of Heaven in Matthew," 288-94, and 12:22-37).

3. Both the story of the young man and the parable of the employer picture the triumph of grace. The young man is a fine specimen who "has it all": youth, money, morality, a sense that there is still something more, an interest in eternal things. Matthew resists the temptation to make the disciples (and his own church) look the better by painting the man in dark colors. He was a good, sincere, wealthy young man, and every church would be glad to "get" him. What did he lack? He anticipated being given one more commandment, one final achievement, and then his quest would be fulfilled. Not just the young man, but also the reader is surprised when he is told that he lacks all, that his salvation is impossible. At one level, the story communicates that salvation is not any kind of achievement, that on human terms entering the kingdom is not merely hard, but impossible. It is only when this "no" to all human claims is heard that the "yes" of God can be heard: But for God all things are possible. Binding this pronouncement to the call to discipleship keeps it from being cheap grace.

The rich young man is a picture of the rejection of grace by one who prefers to justify himself. The good employer is a picture of the resentment of grace toward others by those who have worked long and hard themselves.

4. The story of the rich young man who made the great refusal (19:16-23) is a hard text. Through the centuries, the church has squirmed under its difficulty and has devised some ways of coming to terms with it that are too easy:

In an effort to relieve the difficulty, at 19:24 some manuscripts (59; lectionary 183; the Armenian translation, and a few others) substitute "rope" for "camel" (κάμιλος [*kamilos*] for κάμηλος [*kamēlos*], one Greek letter difference; pronounced the same in Byzantine Greek). But even if this change makes the image more consistent, the solution only seems to help; it is also impossible to get a rope through the eye of a needle.

This story generated a medieval legend according to which there was a tiny gate in the Jerusalem wall called the Needle's Eye. It was too small for loaded camels to pass through, unless they were unloaded of their burdens, got down on their knees, and tried really hard. While it makes a "good" (but unbiblical) sermon, it misses the point of the story, which is not that it is hard for a rich person to get into the kingdom, but that it is impossible. Jesus clearly reached for the most extreme illustration of impossibility, and the disciples got the point (v. 25). In any case, the gate never existed in the wall of Jerusalem, but only in interpretations of this passage.

A traditional explanation is that Jesus distinguished two grades of discipleship, one for "ordinary" Christians and one for an elite group of the "perfect." While it is impractical for ordinary folk to sell their possessions and give all to the poor, the religious elite who belong to religious orders can do so. Thus the tension is resolved. This explanation shatters on the exegesis given above, and is abandoned by most exegetes, Protestant and Roman Catholic alike.

Some interpreters have argued that the rich young man was a special greedy case; his wealth stood between him and discipleship. Realizing this, Jesus made this demand of him alone. Selling our possessions and giving the proceeds to the poor is not necessary for others who do not let our worldly goods interfere with our Christian calling. This interpretation is particularly insidious in that it casts the whole scene in an individualistic light, as though the transaction were only between the young man and God, with his possessions constituting a roadblock to personal piety. But three parties are involved, not just two. The poor are those persons who need what the young man has, and they continue to be deprived by his refusal to give it up. Even on the individualistic level of personal piety, Robert Gundry well states, the fact that "Jesus did not command all his followers to sell all their possessions gives comfort only to the kind of people to whom he *would* issue that command!"[450]

Other interpreters have contended that in the special situation facing Jesus in 30 CE, he called a few chosen disciples to abandon home and family and travel about with him during the days of his earthly ministry (cf. 10:5-13). It is to this special vocation that he called the young man. Christian discipleship as such is unrelated to this special vocation. According to this historicizing (and somewhat self-serving) interpretation, a few people personally called by Jesus in 30 C.E. needed to sell all, but later disciples do not.

This text has sometimes been held up as an example of the purported contrast between Jewish teaching that earthly wealth is the reward of righteousness (Deut 28:1-14) and the Christians thought that wealth does not necessarily correlate to justice. But the OT and Judaism also warn of the dangers of wealth (e.g. Prov 15:16; 30:8-9; Ezek 7:19; Sir 31:5-7), and the NT pictures wealthy Christians (sometimes with obvious satisfaction; cf. Luke 8:1-3; 16:14-15; Acts 17:4).

450. Robert H. Gundry, *Matthew: A Commentary on His Literary and Theological Art* (Grand Rapids: Eerdmans, 1982) 388.

To be sure, Matthew, too, knows that all Christians did not sell their property and give to the poor and that there were wealthy disciples who are commended (27:57; cf. Introduction). The interpreter should, therefore, be wary of soothing "explanations" that allow us to live comfortably with this text. This story, like Jesus' parables, resists reduction to a clear explanation that fits comfortably within our customary categories. Like the parables, it offers a provocative and disturbing picture of the meaning of discipleship, but does not tell us precisely what to do. The tension remains.

Matthew 20:17-19, Third Passion Prediction

NIV	NRSV
[17]Now as Jesus was going up to Jerusalem, he took the twelve disciples aside and said to them, [18]"We are going up to Jerusalem, and the Son of Man will be betrayed to the chief priests and the teachers of the law. They will condemn him to death [19]and will turn him over to the Gentiles to be mocked and flogged and crucified. On the third day he will be raised to life!"	17While Jesus was going up to Jerusalem, he took the twelve disciples aside by themselves, and said to them on the way, [18]"See, we are going up to Jerusalem, and the Son of Man will be handed over to the chief priests and scribes, and they will condemn him to death; [19]then they will hand him over to the Gentiles to be mocked and flogged and crucified; and on the third day he will be raised."

COMMENTARY

Jerusalem was *announced* as the scene of Jesus' death in 16:21; this final passion prediction is made as they are actually on the way. Although the geography changes as Jesus makes his fateful way toward Jerusalem (20:17, 29), the themes of the preceding instruction to the disciples continue. (For contextual meaning, see Overview above.)

Matthew slightly rewrites Mark to make Jesus alone the subject of the sentence, emphasizing his christological sovereignty as fully in charge rather than his status as unwilling passive victim. Although Matthew is quite aware that the execution of Jesus was carried out by Gentile hands, he alters Mark to emphasize the divine sovereignty and, on the human level, Jewish responsibility. As

in Mark, this is the most detailed of the passion predictions; Matthew is even more precise than Mark, for the first time specifying crucifixion as the method of execution (but "cross" has occurred in 10:38 and 16:24). Thus Matthew shows Jesus to be fully aware of what lies ahead.

Another function of this "third passion prediction" is to present Jesus, the Son of Man, the ultimate Judge of the last day, as himself the model and basis for the kind of life to which he calls, instructs, and prepares his disciples. As always in Matthew, the life to which the church is called is grounded in christology; ecclesiology and christology are inseparable.

Matthew 20:20-28, The Disciples' Misunderstanding

NIV

20Then the mother of Zebedee's sons came to Jesus with her sons and, kneeling down, asked a favor of him.

21"What is it you want?" he asked.

She said, "Grant that one of these two sons of mine may sit at your right and the other at your left in your kingdom."

22"You don't know what you are asking," Jesus said to them. "Can you drink the cup I am going to drink?"

"We can," they answered.

23Jesus said to them, "You will indeed drink from my cup, but to sit at my right or left is not for me to grant. These places belong to those for whom they have been prepared by my Father."

24When the ten heard about this, they were indignant with the two brothers. 25Jesus called them together and said, "You know that the rulers of the Gentiles lord it over them, and their high officials exercise authority over them. 26Not so with you. Instead, whoever wants to become great among you must be your servant, 27and whoever wants to be first must be your slave— 28just as the Son of Man did not come to be served, but to serve, and to give his life as a ransom for many."

NRSV

20Then the mother of the sons of Zebedee came to him with her sons, and kneeling before him, she asked a favor of him. 21And he said to her, "What do you want?" She said to him, "Declare that these two sons of mine will sit, one at your right hand and one at your left, in your kingdom." 22But Jesus answered, "You do not know what you are asking. Are you able to drink the cup that I am about to drink?"[a] They said to him, "We are able." 23He said to them, "You will indeed drink my cup, but to sit at my right hand and at my left, this is not mine to grant, but it is for those for whom it has been prepared by my Father."

24When the ten heard it, they were angry with the two brothers. 25But Jesus called them to him and said, "You know that the rulers of the Gentiles lord it over them, and their great ones are tyrants over them. 26It will not be so among you; but whoever wishes to be great among you must be your servant, 27and whoever wishes to be first among you must be your slave; 28just as the Son of Man came not to be served but to serve, and to give his life a ransom for many."

[a]Other ancient authorities add *or to be baptized with the baptism that I am baptized with?*

COMMENTARY

There is a marked progression in the three Son of Man sayings in this section (cf. Excursus "Matthean Christology," 353-61). First, the ultimate future: The Son of Man will sit on his glorious throne (19:28). This declaration of the eschatological victory of God's kingdom represented by Jesus undergirds all the instruction of 19:1–20:34. Second is the immediate future: the picture of the Son of Man's suffering and vindication (20:18-19). This is what the disciples have to look forward to in the short term. Third is the present: the picture of the Son of Man's self-giving service for others (20:28). This is the model for the disciples' own

life and ministry in the present—i.e., the model Matthew presents to his own post-Easter Christian readers. The progression is from glory through suffering/glory to self-giving.

Matthew 20:20-28 adapts the scene from Mark 10:35-45, retaining the Markan pattern of (1) announcement, (2) misunderstanding, and (3) further instruction. Although Matthew has mostly eliminated or revised the Markan motif of the disciples' misunderstanding, he here retains elements of it in order to reinforce the point just made. In Mark, Peter is the focal example of misunderstanding the nature of Jesus' messianic rulership, and here James and John, also among those initially called, represent the misunderstanding characteristic of all the disciples. From a literary point of view, the disciples continue in their "blindness," "setting [their] minds not on divine things but on human things" (see Commentary on 16:23). This allows Jesus to reassert himself as the suffering Son of Man as the model for life in the kingdom and to prepare for the next and concluding scene, in which blindness is cured.

20:20. In order to spare the disciples, whom Matthew usually represents as understanding, Matthew replaces the disciples' own request with one represented by their mother. The woman identified as the "mother of the sons of Zebedee" appears only in Matthew, reappearing among the witnesses of the crucifixion (27:56), where she replaces Salome of Mark 15:40.

20:21. "Kingdom" replaces Mark's "glory" to tie in with the kingdom theme, which has undergirded the call to a radically different life throughout this section. The "right hand and left hand" imagery likewise reflects the rule of the Son of Man from his throne of 19:28.

20:22. The address shifts to the plural "you," and Jesus addresses the disciples directly. Matthew omits the image of baptism from Mark, focusing entirely on the image of the cup, which has a rich tradition in the HB and Judaism as a symbol of suffering, testing, rejection, judgment, and violent death (Deut 32:1; Pss 11:6; 16:5; 75:9 (8); Isa 51:17; Jer 25:15-29; Lam 4:21; Ezek 23:31-34; Zech 12:2; *Martyrdom of Isaiah* 5:13; Palestinian Targum on Gen 40:23; cf. Rev 14:10; 16:19; 17:4; 18:6). Since in some texts the cup is identified as the cup of God's *wrath,* some interpreters have understood Jesus' cup to be his death, conceived as the substitutionary death for sinners, absorbing God's wrath in their place. That cannot be the meaning here, since the disciples drink the same cup (v. 23). *Martyrdom of Isaiah* 5:13 shows that the cup can mean a death appointed by God, willingly accepted by the one being killed. Matthew's later use of this image at the last supper (26:27) and Gethsemane (26:39, 42) and Jesus' promise that the disciples will drink the same cup link the tradition of Israel's suffering with that of Jesus and the church.

The disciples are overconfident of their own ability, as in 26:35—but cf. their flight in 26:56. As was the case when Jesus called them and saw not merely what they were but what they would become in his service (4:18-22), so here he looks beyond their failure, knowing them better than they know themselves. Some of the disciples did become courageous martyrs, including the James here addressed (cf. Acts 12:2).

20:23. Even martyrdom does not gain the disciples the special places in the kingdom they (think they) want (see Commentary on 20:1-16). Not even Jesus will dispense such special rewards or claim to know to whom they will go (cf. 24:36). He is oriented to another perspective on leadership, to which he reorients the disciples.

20:25-27. Luke, having omitted the incident, includes a form of these words as part of Jesus' instruction at the last supper (Luke 22:24-27). In v. 25, Matthew drops the Markan "to them," allowing the disciples to become transparent to the post-Easter church and Jesus to address the reader directly. Jesus' vision of the style of leadership as servanthood corresponds to his alternative vision of kingship (see on 12:22-37). Over against the exalted and powerful terms used for worldly rulership, Jesus substitutes διάκονος (*diakonos,* "deacon," lit., a table servant, waiter or waitress, also used as a technical term for Christian ministry) and δοῦλος (*doulos,* lit., "slave"). Rather than replacing the image of kingship (potentially oppressive and always so in human kingdoms), Matthew reinterprets it in terms of Jesus as the revelation of God. First/servant ties into and further interprets the theme of reversal of first/last, dominant throughout this section and ties this pericope more closely to its context.

20:28. Matthew changes Mark's simple conjunction "and" to "just as" (ὥσπερ *hōsper*) to make more clear that Jesus as Son of Man is being reasserted as a model for the disciples' own lives and ministry. Again, ecclesiology rests on christology.

REFLECTIONS

Matthew adopts Mark's picture of Jesus' life as a "ransom," but does not elaborate it into a doctrine of the atonement (as Mark does not). The fact that Jesus' death effects forgiveness of sins and entering into a new covenant life with God (26:28) is important to Matthew, but he is not concerned to speculate on *how* this is "explained." "Ransom" (λύτρον *lytron*) in the LXX had already lost its specific idea of release by paying off the captor and had come to mean simply "rescue," "deliver" as an act of God's power (e.g., Exod 6:6; Deut 7:8). As in 26:28, Jesus' death is related to "many." In the Semitic idiom lying back of Matthew's Greek, "many" was often used in the inclusive sense (in contrast to "the few," "only a part") rather than in the exclusive sense (in contrast to "all"). Compare 1 Cor 10:17, where "many" and "all" are synonymous, and 1 Tim 2:5-6, which correctly renders the Semitic idiom "the man Christ Jesus, who gave himself a ransom for all."

Matthew 20:29-34, Blindness Healed

²⁹As Jesus and his disciples were leaving Jericho, a large crowd followed him. ³⁰Two blind men were sitting by the roadside, and when they heard that Jesus was going by, they shouted, "Lord, Son of David, have mercy on us!"

³¹The crowd rebuked them and told them to be quiet, but they shouted all the louder, "Lord, Son of David, have mercy on us!"

³²Jesus stopped and called them. "What do you want me to do for you?" he asked.

³³"Lord," they answered, "we want our sight."

³⁴Jesus had compassion on them and touched their eyes. Immediately they received their sight and followed him.

29As they were leaving Jericho, a large crowd followed him. ³⁰There were two blind men sitting by the roadside. When they heard that Jesus was passing by, they shouted, "Lord,ᵃ have mercy on us, Son of David!" ³¹The crowd sternly ordered them to be quiet; but they shouted even more loudly, "Have mercy on us, Lord, Son of David!" ³²Jesus stood still and called them, saying, "What do you want me to do for you?" ³³They said to him, "Lord, let our eyes be opened." ³⁴Moved with compassion, Jesus touched their eyes. Immediately they regained their sight and followed him.

ᵃOther ancient authorities lack *Lord*

COMMENTARY

For contextual meaning, see the Overview above. This is a doublet of 9:27-31, but not merely a repetition. There, the focus was christological, on the works of the Messiah (see Overview of 8:1–9:35). Here, as the conclusion of the section instructing and nurturing the disciples, the focus is on the disciples, who, like the blind men, must have their blindness cured by Jesus before they can see the new way of life to which Christian discipleship calls them.

Matthew sets the scene as they leave Jericho (cf. Luke), connecting it to the next city, Jerusalem, where "Son of David" significantly reappears (21:9). This scene and the next are also bound together by the crowd, though here it plays only the negative straight-man role to set up Jesus' word/action (like the disciples of 19:13, where the same verb is used, ἐπιτιμάω [*epitimaō*]). Unlike its Markan source, the story as interpreted by Matthew is not a symbolic story of conversion. Three times the blind men call Jesus "Lord," the mark of believers. [451] Twice they address him as "Son of David," a positive and correct christological title in Matthew (cf. Excursus "Matthean Christology," 353-61; on "the healing Son of David," see 21:14-15). The Markan emphasis on their faith is omitted, as are his "colorful details," so that Matthew can concentrate all attention on Jesus' compassion (added by Matthew) and his word. It is not their faith that occasioned the healing, but Jesus' powerful word. In yet another way Matthew indicates that discipleship is a gracious gift, not an achievement (see on 16:17). Precisely as the conclusion and climax of this section (19:1–20:34), in which Jesus has struggled to get his disciples to see the nature of the life to which he

calls them, Matthew places a story showing that when they finally "see it" it is a matter of Christ's giving sight to the blind.

As in 9:27-31, Matthew doubles the number of blind men. Although doubling is a stylistic trait of Matthew, who throughout has added "two" or doubled or reduced the number of individuals in Mark in order to get "two" (cf. 4:18, 21; 8:28; 9:27; 18:15-16, 19-20; 20:21, 24, 30; and even 21:2, 7, where Mark's one donkey becomes two), here it may be theologically significant as well. Just as the two sons of Zebedee represent all the disciples in the preceding pericope, so also here two blind men become transparent to all disciples who need to have their blindness healed (cf. 13:10-17). Doubling the number of blind men makes them legitimate witnesses (Deut 19:15; cf. Matt 18:16; 26:60) and a symbol of the community.

451. No one ever unambiguously calls Jesus "Lord" in Mark, who preserves it as a post-resurrection title of the exalted Lord. Matthew has throughout allowed insightful insiders to address Jesus in this way, in distinction from "blind" outsiders. When "blind" men call Jesus "Lord," it is a sign that they already represent the insider group, although it violates the narrative logic.

Matthew 21:1–22:46, Jerusalem: The Final Confrontation

OVERVIEW

From Jesus' entry into Jerusalem through the last supper, arrest, trial, crucifixion, and resurrection Matthew follows the Markan order exactly, except for slightly rearranging the fig tree incident (21:18-22 = Mark 11:22-26). In Matthew the "triumphal" entry and "cleansing" of the Temple occur on the same day, Jesus' first day in Jerusalem; in Mark they are divided into two separate days. Matthew preserves all of Mark's materials except the parable of the widow's mite (Mark 12:41-44). This means that the differences from Mark are additions of traditional material from Q and M, plus Matthew's own editorial additions and modifications.

On the "Great Tuesday," Matthew follows Mark's pattern of dispute over authority, parable of judgment (to which he adds two additional

parables, one from Q and one of his own), then four more disputes in rapid succession, leading to the final judgment discourse (23:1–25:46). The Matthean chronology, and the Markan chronology from which it is adapted, may be represented as follows:[452]

452. In both Mark and Matthew, the first identifiable day of the week is Wednesday, the "two days before the Passover" of Mark 14:1 = Matt 26:1. This day is fixed as Wednesday by Mark 15:42, which locates the crucifixion on Friday, the Passover having begun Thursday evening. Matthew omits this Markan date at 27:57, but confirms that he dates the crucifixion on Friday at 27:62. Thus from Wednesday onward, the chronology is the same for Mark and Matthew. By counting backward from Wednesday in their respective narratives, we arrive at Monday for the triumphal entry in Matthew, which was a Sunday in Mark. Matthew has reduced two Markan days to one by his rewriting of Mark 11:1-16 in Matt 21:1-22. For both Mark and Matthew, the dating that is important is not the day of the week but the day of the month—i.e., the relation to Passover/Unleavened Bread.

Figure 10: The Chronology of Jesus' Final Days in Jerusalem

Matthew	Mark
Day 1 (Monday)	*Day 1 (Sunday)*
Enters Jerusalem (21:1-9)	Enters Jerusalem (11:1-10) Looks around (11:11*a*)
"Cleanses" Temple (21:10-16) Leaves city (21:17)	Leaves city (11:11*b*)
Day 2 (Tuesday)	*Day 2 (Monday)*
Curses fig tree (21:18-19*a*) Fig tree withers (21:19*b*-22)	Curses fig tree (11:12-14)
	"Cleanses" Temple (11:15-17) Conspiracy against Jesus (11:18) Leaves city (11:19) *Day 3 (Tuesday)* Discovers fig tree withered (11:20-26)

Question about authority (21:23-27 = Mark 11:27-33)[453]
Three parables (21:28-22:14 = Mark 12:1-12)
On paying taxes to the emperor (22:15-22 = Mark 12:13-17)
Question about the resurrection (22:23-33 = Mark 12:18-27)
The Great Commandment (22:34-40 = Mark 12:28-34)
Question about David's Son (22:41-46 = Mark 12:35-37*a*)
Judgment discourse (23:1-25:46 = Mark 12:37*b*-13:37)
Day 3 "two days before the Passover" (Wednesday) (Mark's Day 4)
    Jesus' death plotted (26:1-5 = Mark 14:1-2)
    Anointing in Bethany (26:6-13 = Mark 14: 3-9)
    Betrayal by Judas (26:14-16 = Mark 14:10-11)
Day 4 (Thursday) (Mark's Day 5)
    Preparation, last supper, arrest, trial before Sanhedrin, Peter's denial
        (26:17-75 = Mark 14:12-72)
Day 5 (Friday) (Mark's Day 6)
    Trial before Pilate, crucifixion, burial (27:1-61 = Mark 15:1-47)
Day 6 (Saturday) (Mark's Day 7)
    The guard at the tomb (27:62-66; this day is not plotted in Mark, but allowed for)
Day 7 (Sunday) (Mark's Day 8)
    Discovery of empty tomb, appearances, Great Commission (28:1-20 = Mark 16:1-8*a*)

453. From this point on, the events happen on the same day of the week in Matthew and Mark. This makes "Tuesday" a long day in both Mark and Matthew.

Matthew 21:1-11, The Spectacular Entry: Conspicuously Meek

NIV

21 As they approached Jerusalem and came to Bethphage on the Mount of Olives, Jesus sent two disciples, [2]saying to them, "Go to the village ahead of you, and at once you will find a donkey tied there, with her colt by her. Untie them and bring them to me. [3]If anyone says anything to you, tell him that the Lord needs them, and he will send them right away."

[4]This took place to fulfill what was spoken through the prophet:

[5]"Say to the Daughter of Zion,
    'See, your king comes to you,
  gentle and riding on a donkey,
    on a colt, the foal of a donkey.'"[a]

[6]The disciples went and did as Jesus had instructed them. [7]They brought the donkey and the colt, placed their cloaks on them, and Jesus sat on them. [8]A very large crowd spread their cloaks on the road, while others cut branches from the trees and spread them on the road. [9]The crowds that went ahead of him and those that followed shouted,

"Hosanna[b] to the Son of David!"

"Blessed is he who comes in the name of the Lord!"[c]

"Hosanna[b] in the highest!"

[10]When Jesus entered Jerusalem, the whole city was stirred and asked, "Who is this?"

[11]The crowds answered, "This is Jesus, the prophet from Nazareth in Galilee."

[a]5 Zech. 9:9   [b]9 A Hebrew expression meaning "Save!" which became an exclamation of praise; also in verse 15   [c]9 Psalm 118:26

NRSV

21 When they had come near Jerusalem and had reached Bethphage, at the Mount of Olives, Jesus sent two disciples, [2]saying to them, "Go into the village ahead of you, and immediately you will find a donkey tied, and a colt with her; untie them and bring them to me. [3]If anyone says anything to you, just say this, 'The Lord needs them.' And he will send them immediately.[a]" [4]This took place to fulfill what had been spoken through the prophet, saying,

[5] "Tell the daughter of Zion,
    Look, your king is coming to you,
      humble, and mounted on a donkey,
        and on a colt, the foal of a donkey."

[6]The disciples went and did as Jesus had directed them; [7]they brought the donkey and the colt, and put their cloaks on them, and he sat on them. [8]A very large crowd[b] spread their cloaks on the road, and others cut branches from the trees and spread them on the road. [9]The crowds that went ahead of him and that followed were shouting,

"Hosanna to the Son of David!
    Blessed is the one who comes in the name
        of the Lord!
Hosanna in the highest heaven!"

[10]When he entered Jerusalem, the whole city was in turmoil, asking, "Who is this?" [11]The crowds were saying, "This is the prophet Jesus from Nazareth in Galilee."

[a]Or 'The Lord needs them and will send them back immediately.'   [b]Or Most of the crowd

COMMENTARY

Day 1: Monday. In the Matthean storyline, this is Jesus' first appearance in Jerusalem,[454] the city that joined with wicked King Herod in being troubled at the birth of Jesus (2:3), but that is nevertheless the "holy city" (4:5; 27:53, even

after the crucifixion) and the "city of the great king" (5:35). However, the traditional label "triumphal entry" can be used for this pericope only in Matthew's reversed sense that pictures Jesus as representative of the alternative view of kingship he has advocated throughout (cf. on 12:22-37). Likewise, the traditional Palm Sunday hardly fits the Matthean version of this story, narrated in all four Gospels, since "palms"

454. Matthew follows the storyline of Mark. Cf. the Fourth Gospel, where Jesus is repeatedly in Jerusalem and has "cleansed" the Temple on his first visit (2:13-17). In Luke, Jesus is dedicated in the Jerusalem Temple (2:22-39), visits it as a boy (2:41-52), visits it as a boy (2:41-52), then is absent until his final appearance in 19:45.

are mentioned only in John and in Matthew's chronology the event happened on Monday (see the Overview for Matt 21:1–22:46).

Matthew follows his Markan source closely, making three significant changes. (1) In vv. 4-5, he inserts his ninth "formula quotation," the first since 13:35 (see Excursus "Matthew as Interpreter of Scripture," 151-54). The image of Zech 9:9 had already made an impact on the (pre-) Markan form of the story, and perhaps influenced even Jesus' own symbolic act, but it is important to Matthew to make the reference to Scripture explicit. The quotation is not tacked on, but is fundamental to Matthew's understanding of the whole event, causing him to rewrite v. 1 to emphasize the Mount of Olives, scene of the eschatological event in Zech 14:4, and vv. 2-3 to allow for two animals (cf. Mark). Zechariah's prophecy of the meek king who would ride not on a war horse but on a donkey was expressed in poetic parallelism, picturing the animal as "a donkey, a donkey's colt." Although Matthew certainly understood the principle of parallelism in Hebrew poetry, he sees Scripture with rabbinic and scribal eyes, in which every detail is important. To emphasize the fulfillment of Scripture, he has the disciples fetch two animals and has Jesus ride on both of them (v. 7).[455] Matthew omits Zechariah's characterization of the king as "righteous and saving" (LXX; MT, "triumphant and victorious") in order to place all the emphasis on Jesus as the "humble" or "gentle" (πραΰς *praus*) king who redefines the nature of kingship. Thus "kingdom" from Mark has disappeared, replaced by Zechariah's "king," corresponding to the crowd's acclamation "Son of David," also added by Matthew.

(2) In this scene, Matthew explicitly adds the crowds three times to the Markan narrative.[456] As potential disciples, the crowds are contrasted with the "whole city" allied with the high priests and scribes (21:10 anticipated by 2:3). (Since 16:21

and especially since 19:1, the disciples have been in the center stage in the extensive section directed to their instruction and nurture.) Since the crowds were sent away in 15:39, they have been mostly absent or passive. Now they reappear as supporters and potential disciples. These crowds pave Jesus' way into the city with shouts of acclamation and with their own cloaks and branches, reminiscent of the jubilant royal entrances and processions of Solomon (Son of David!) in 1 Kgs 1:32-37, Jehu in 2 Kgs 9:13, Simon Maccabeus in 1 Macc 13:51, and Judas Maccabeus in 2 Macc 10:7. In their acclamation of Jesus, the crowds use words from Ps 118:25-26, the last of the Hallel psalms sung at Passover. "Hosanna" (ὡσαννά *hōsanna,* הושיעה נא *hôšî'â nā*) was originally a prayer, "Save, I/we beseech you," but by the first century had become a contentless, festive shout, something like a religious "hurrah," with no more literal meaning than "Good-bye" (also originally a prayer, "God be with you"). Similarly, the original meaning of Ps 118:26 was "Blessed in the name of the LORD is the one who comes [to the temple to worship]" (cf. NRSV footnote). But since "the one who comes" had developed eschatological and messianic overtones, the blessing is here applied to Jesus as a royal acclamation (cf. 11:3, "the one who is to come"; 23:39).

(3) Matthew adds vv. 10-11, in which the crowds who have accompanied Jesus through the narrative now identify him to the city's inhabitants, who have no previous experience of him. The people of Jerusalem are shaken by Jesus' appearance ("shake" [σείω *seiō*], as 27:51; 28:4; cf. 8:24; 24:7; also 2:3, where all the city is "troubled"). They ask the crucial question, "Who is this?" analogous to Jesus' own question in 16:13-15. The crowds' identification of Jesus as "the prophet" is not incorrect. They have previously rightly acclaimed him Son of David, a title toward which Mark is cool, but which Matthew considers central to the proper understanding of Jesus (see 1:2-25 and 22:41-46). So, too, is Jesus indeed a prophet (cf. vv. 11, 26, 46; 13:57; 17:5; 23:37; see also 21:23-27) who fits into the succession of prophets (21:33-37), the fulfillment of the hope of the "prophet like Moses" of Deut 18:15-18. Matthew knows that the crowd will finally fail and will shout "Crucify him!" but here their problem is not that their christology is in-

---

455. The doubling of the animals also corresponds to Matthew's general tendency to double items in his tradition, noticed before (see 20:29-34). Matthew slightly adjusts the preposition used by Mark (ἐπι *epi* to ἐπάνω *epanō*), which may indicate that Matthew intends to picture Jesus as being seated "on" the cloaks (actually the nearest antecedent of "them"), not on both animals. Whether it is possible to picture Jesus as somehow riding two animals (i.e., sidesaddle, with the cloaks draped over both of them) is beside the point, which is not a matter of Jesus' equestrian skills, but Matthew's understanding of the fulfillment of Scripture, for which both animals were important.

456. Matthew has added them a total of seventeen times to his sources; they play a specific narrative role.

correct, but that they will not transform their words into deeds (cf. 7:22-23). The perceptive reader will already have noted the untrustworthy character of the Matthean crowds who rebuke the blind men who are accepted and healed by Jesus (20:31). As Jesus, whose kingship is marked by a cross rather than a throne, enters Jerusalem to these shouts of acclamation from those who will later reject him, the deep irony in this opening scene in Jerusalem sets the tone for the passion story as a whole.

REFLECTIONS

When the crowds cry "Hosanna to the Son of David!" and "This is the prophet," they use the right words, but they still miss the point. They have all of the notes and none of the music. They have the theology straight, but they will still end up rejecting Jesus and calling for his death (27:20-23). Matthew is striking a familiar note: Knowing the truth is not the same thing as doing the truth (7:21). What one social psychologist said of university students is also true of the kingdom: "It is possible to make an A+ in the course on ethics and still flunk life."

Matthew 21:12-17, Encounter/Disruption in the Temple

NIV

[12]Jesus entered the temple area and drove out all who were buying and selling there. He overturned the tables of the money changers and the benches of those selling doves. [13]"It is written," he said to them, "'My house will be called a house of prayer,'[a] but you are making it a 'den of robbers.'[b]"

[14]The blind and the lame came to him at the temple, and he healed them. [15]But when the chief priests and the teachers of the law saw the wonderful things he did and the children shouting in the temple area, "Hosanna to the Son of David," they were indignant.

[16]"Do you hear what these children are saying?" they asked him.

"Yes," replied Jesus, "have you never read,

"'From the lips of children and infants
you have ordained praise'[c]?"

[17]And he left them and went out of the city to Bethany, where he spent the night.

NRSV

12Then Jesus entered the temple[a] and drove out all who were selling and buying in the temple, and he overturned the tables of the money changers and the seats of those who sold doves. [13]He said to them, "It is written,

'My house shall be called a house of prayer';
but you are making it a den of robbers."

14The blind and the lame came to him in the temple, and he cured them. [15]But when the chief priests and the scribes saw the amazing things that he did, and heard[b] the children crying out in the temple, "Hosanna to the Son of David," they became angry [16]and said to him, "Do you hear what these are saying?" Jesus said to them, "Yes; have you never read,

'Out of the mouths of infants and nursing babies
you have prepared praise for yourself'?"

[17]He left them, went out of the city to Bethany, and spent the night there.

aOther ancient authorities add of God   bGk lacks heard

COMMENTARY

The "temple" (ἱερόν *hieron*) refers to the whole complex of buildings and courts that made up the Temple precinct (like the Vatican), in distinction from the Temple proper (ναός *naos*), the sanctuary with its holy place, which only the priests could enter, and the holy of holies, entered only by the high priest on the Day of Atonement. There were separate courts for Jewish men, Jewish women, and the general public, including Gentiles. As a Jewish layperson, Jesus could enter the court of Israel, but not the sanctuary proper. This encounter takes place in the large Court of the Gentiles, where animals were sold for sacrifice and money was exchanged into the Tyrian coinage acceptable for gifts to the Temple. Both practices were necessary and valuable, since sacrificial animals could not easily be brought from a distance; these animals would then have to be certified as acceptable by the Temple priests. Foreign currency, often displaying idolatrous symbols, was inappropriate for Temple use. Both selling animals and exchanging money were also subject to abuse, but there is no evidence of this in Matthew. (On "den of thieves," see below.)

The Temple complex was large and secured by the Jewish Temple police, augmented by Roman soldiers during festivals. It included among other things an enormous barn with stalls for thousands of sacrificial animals, accommodations for the people who handled the animals, and a slaughter house—Jesus, even with the aid of his small band of disciples (of whom nothing is said) could not have closed down, or even disrupted, the Temple business, although he may have performed some dramatic symbolic act like those of the Israelite prophets.[457] In any case, the Temple was long since gone by the time Matthew wrote his Gospel, and he is not concerned with accurate reporting, but with theological meaning. Both Matthew and his opponents acknowledged the destruction of the Temple, which neither party expected to be rebuilt. The issue that divided them is what would replace the Temple as the effective symbol of God's presence among the people, and what

would be the way forward for the people of God, given the destruction of the Temple.

Matthew does not have a systematic and consistent "doctrine" of the Temple, but he does manifest more interest in it than do either of his sources. This scene is the first appearance of the Temple in Mark. In Q, after the opening scene in which Jesus is tempted by Satan to leap from the Temple pinnacle (Matt 4:5/Luke 4:9), the Temple is mentioned again only once, the significant "your house is left to you [desolate]" (Q; Luke 13:35). Matthew, on the other hand, has previous statements peculiar to him that assume the validity of Temple worship (5:23; 12:5-6; 17:24),[458] and will have more later (23:16-20), just as he extends the present scene taken from Mark to include two more incidents (see below). Jesus' action could not be understood by Matthew as a protest against the Temple and the sacrificial system as such, both of which were thoroughly grounded in biblical precepts. Yet Matthew does not lament the destruction of the Temple, which was indeed prophesied by Jesus (24:1-2), its coming destruction already symbolically intimated by the tearing of the veil during the crucifixion (see Commentary on 27:51). Thus while Matthew's view of the Temple is more nuanced than either Q's or Mark's view, there is still judgment.[459] By adding here the two additional scenes in the Temple (vv. 14-16), Matthew has transformed it into a christological scene, in which Jesus himself replaces the Temple as the locus of God's presence among the people (cf 1:23).

Thus this scene should not be labeled "cleansing the Temple," which implies that it had been ritually defiled and needed ceremonial cleansing (as in 2 Chr 29:16; 1 Macc 4:36-43; 2 Macc 10:3-5) or, as in much traditional Christian exegesis, that "the Jews" had profaned the Temple by making it into a price-gouging business enterprise. Neither interpretation has any basis in fact; the latter is particularly susceptible to anti-Jewish

---

457. See Jer 19:10; cf. Georg Fohrer, *Die Symbolische Handlungen der Propheten*, ATANT 25 (Zurich: Zwingli Verlag, 1953).

458. While he preserves Q's reference to "your house," he does not repeat it elsewhere. While he has "their" synagogues and "their" scribes, he never has "their" Temple.

459. See Matt 21:43; 23:38; 24:2; cf. Donald Senior, *The Passion of Jesus in the Gospel of Matthew* (Wilmington, Del.: Michael Glazier, 1985) 143.

propagandistic use. "Cleanse" is never used by any NT writer with reference to Jesus' symbolic act in the Temple. Matthew has Jesus perform three acts there:

(1) Following Mark, Jesus "casts out" both buyers and sellers and turns over the tables of the money changers.[460] For Matthew, who writes years after the Temple's destruction, this represents a retrospective vindication of God's judgment on the Temple and the people as a whole (cf. Commentary on 22:7). Matthew retains the combination of Isa 56:7 and Jer 7:11, quoted by Jesus, but drops the phrase "for all nations" from "My house shall be called a house of prayer." This is at first surprising, since Matthew advocates the post-Easter Gentile mission of his own church (28:18-20), but is understandable on closer reflection. Matthew has no interest in criticizing Judaism for its purported lack of openness to Gentiles; he is, in fact, sarcastic and critical of the Pharisees' Gentile mission (23:15). The contrast in this text is not between Judaism's purported narrowness and the church's openness to Gentiles. By removing the reference to Gentiles, which was confusing for his theological stance in any case, he allows the contrast between "house of prayer" and "den of thieves" to be all the more stark. "Den of thieves" does not refer to dishonest trade in the Temple. In its original context, Jeremiah addressed the people of Judah who adhered to a false Zion theology that regarded the Temple as a guarantee of divine protection, and charged them with regarding the Temple as a robber's hideout to which they could retreat in safety after their acts of injustice (Jer 7:1-11). Jeremiah's charge was thus directed against those who came to worship in the Temple rather than those who sold animals and changed money there. In the light of its destruction, which he understands as God's judgment, Matthew sees the Temple in the same perspective.

(2) Just as Jesus *casts out* the insiders who see the Temple as a safe place of refuge instead of prayer, so also he *welcomes* those who have been neglected and excluded, the blind, the lame, and children (v. 14), thus extending the messianic works he had done in Galilee to Judea and Jerusalem (cf. Mic 4:6-7; Zeph 3:19; and Commentary

on 11:5).[461] Jesus does this as Son of David, and he is acclaimed as such by another marginalized group in Israel, the children (see 18:1-14). Previously, Matthew specifically connected Jesus as Son of David with his ministry of healing (9:27-31; 12:22-24; 15:21-28; 20:29-34). As David was a violent person, the expected "Son of David" as a messianic figure was supposed to bring in God's reign with great violence against Israel's enemies. Matthew affirms Jesus as the fulfiller of the hopes associated with the Son of David (see 1:1-17), but transforms the image in the light of who Jesus actually was.[462] Evidence that this is the focus of Matthew's interest is that the addition to Mark's story of "cleansing" the Temple is more extensive than the original story taken from Mark and that the high priests and scribes, who raise no objection to Jesus' casting out the money changers (which they do not seem even to have noticed), challenge the children's ascription of "Son of David" to Jesus (vv. 15-16). As in 11:25-30, those who should "get it" by virtue of their position fail to do so, while the "little ones" unexpectedly do perceive what is really happening in the advent and presence of Jesus.

(3) Jesus accepts the acclamation "Son of David," given him by the children. David's son Solomon built the first Temple, which was destroyed by the Babylonians, an event interpreted by Jeremiah and others as punishment for the sinful lives of the people who rejected God's covenant (Jer 7:1-11). Jesus as Son of David builds a church—community, not building—in which the reality of God's presence is made known (1:23). This is recognized by the "little people," represented here by the children (see 11:25-27; 18:1-14), but rejected by the chief priests and scribes, who appear in the narrative for the first time since 2:4-6, where they "knew the Scriptures," but did not act on them.[463] Again Jesus

---

460. Since buyers are also thrown out, the romantic interpretation that pictures Jesus as acting against the rich merchants who are guilty of cheating the poor worshipers has no basis in the text.

461. This represents a modification of the Markan scheme, in which Jesus' saving acts of power, and all of his healing miracles, are done before he reaches Jerusalem; cf. 26:53. For the reversal, cf. Daniel Patte, *The Gospel According to Matthew: A Structural Commentary on Matthew's Faith* (Philadelphia: Fortress, 1987) 290. It is a reversal in another sense as well. David had excluded the lame and the blind from God's house (2 Sam 5:8). The true Son of David welcomes and heals them.

462. This transformation may have been prepared for by the image of Solomon, the son of David, who became something of an exorcist in Jewish tradition (Josephus *Antiquities of the Jews* 8:45-49; 11QPsAp[a], b. Gitt. 68*a*). See Dennis C. Duling, "The Therapeutic Son of David: An Element in Matthew's Christological Apologetic," *NTS* 24 (1978) 392-410.

463. In two of the passion predictions, Jesus had prophesied that they would reject and kill him (16:21, 20:18), so the reader is prepared for their reappearance and reaction.

quotes the Scripture, justifying the event (Ps 8:2; the point is dependent on the LXX; cf. Excursus "Matthew as Interpreter of Scripture," 151-54). There is no dialogue, only pronouncement.

Jesus is not at home in Jerusalem, and he finds lodging outside the city like other pilgrims at the festival (21:17). This is the first reference to Bethany in Matthew; the only other reference is 26:2, where Jesus has a dinner party at the house of Simon the Leper (cf. Luke and John, in which Jesus has friends, Mary and Martha [and, in John, Lazarus], whom he visits from time to time prior

to his final visit to Jerusalem, and with whom he stays during the festival). For Mark's pedestrian "go out" (ἐξέρχομαι *exerchomai*), Matthew substitutes a stronger word, "left" (καταλείπω *kataleipō*), which may also mean "abandon." Although Jesus will return the next day and teach in the Temple and engage its leaders (21:23–23:39), in which he will pronounce that "your house is left to you desolate" (23:38), this exit already anticipates the final separation from the Temple and its leadership in 24:1.

Matthew 21:18-22, Withering the Fruitless Tree

NIV	NRSV
[18]Early in the morning, as he was on his way back to the city, he was hungry. [19]Seeing a fig tree by the road, he went up to it but found nothing on it except leaves. Then he said to it, "May you never bear fruit again!" Immediately the tree withered.	18In the morning, when he returned to the city, he was hungry. [19]And seeing a fig tree by the side of the road, he went to it and found nothing at all on it but leaves. Then he said to it, "May no fruit ever come from you again!" And the fig tree withered at once. [20]When the disciples saw it, they were amazed, saying, "How did the fig tree wither at once?" [21]Jesus answered them, "Truly I tell you, if you have faith and do not doubt, not only will you do what has been done to the fig tree, but even if you say to this mountain, 'Be lifted up and thrown into the sea,' it will be done. [22]Whatever you ask for in prayer with faith, you will receive."
[20]When the disciples saw this, they were amazed. "How did the fig tree wither so quickly?" they asked.	
[21]Jesus replied, "I tell you the truth, if you have faith and do not doubt, not only can you do what was done to the fig tree, but also you can say to this mountain, 'Go, throw yourself into the sea,' and it will be done. [22]If you believe, you will receive whatever you ask for in prayer."	

COMMENTARY

Day 2: Tuesday. The origin of this story has been variously assessed, some scholars thinking it grew out of the parable of Luke 13:6-9, others thinking the parable is based on the story. Matthew found the story in Mark, where the two acts of pronouncing judgment on the tree on one day and discovering it withered on the next day surrounded and interpreted Jesus' action in the Temple (Mark 11:12-26). With the relocation, the disruption of the Temple business on Jesus' first day in Jerusalem (cf. chronological note above), the Markan intercalation collapses and the fig tree withers immediately, before the eyes of the disciples. Matthew also elimi-

nates the troublesome Markan note "it was not the season for figs," but the difficulty of Jesus' using his miraculous power for destructive purposes remains.[464]

What is the meaning of this strange story, traditionally called "cursing the fig tree" (though neither the Matthean nor the Markan form of the story refers to a "curse")? Most interpreters have seen the

---

464. Here Jesus seems to reverse his refusal (4:2-4) to use his miraculous power in reference to his own hunger. This is the only such miracle in the Gospels, although Mark 5:1-20 is also a "negative" miracle: the destruction of the swine. The apocryphal gospels are less hesitant in portraying Jesus as using his divine power destructively. See Patte, *Matthew*, 292.

fig tree as symbolic of Israel, hence they regard the cursing as a symbol of God's judgment on fruitless Judaism or the Jewish leadership. Matthew seems to present the story as a symbolic act prefiguring the condemnation of those in the following parables who do not bring forth the authentic fruits of righteousness and justice.[465] The Markan intercalation seems to support this interpretation.

In Matthew, the fig tree story still stands between Jesus' two visits to the Temple and thus has some connection with the judgment on Temple Judaism. The primary meaning for Matthew seems to focus on two points important to Matthew elsewhere:

(1) Matthew uses "fruit(s)" as a metaphor for good works seventeen times, more than any other writer in the NT. He never uses the word literally, but only in this ethical sense. The Lord comes seeking fruit from the tree, and when he finds only leaves, he causes it to wither. This represents the judgment of God on those who have the external appearance of productivity, but no real fruits. Matthew makes this point often (e.g., 3:10; 7:16-20, which makes the specific connection with fig trees; 21:43, which makes the connection with unbelieving Jews). It is not only a contrast between "fruitless Judaism" and "fruitful Chris-

tianity," but is also directed as a warning to insiders in Matthew's own community.

(2) These "fruits" are not self-justifying "works"; they are the products of faith, not its antithesis. Thus Matthew immediately makes the application to the prayer of faith, introduced by a solemn *amēn* saying (ἀμήν "truly," see Commentary on 5:18). Those who have faith will not only be able to do what Jesus has done—i.e., pronounce the withering judgment of God on fruitless religion (in the *church,* not in another religious community)—but also will remove any obstacle and will receive whatever they ask in prayer, if they believe. References to faith bracket this pronouncement. The reference to prayer connects it to the preceding pronouncement about the Temple (21:13), which further justifies Matthew's omission of "for all nations [Gentiles]"; the contrast is not between Jews and Gentiles, but between a house of prayer that has become dysfunctional and authentic prayer of faith. (For discussion of "faith that moves mountains," see Commentary on 17:20.) Since Jesus points to the power of faith as the meaning of the incident, it is not some power possessed by himself alone, but he and the believers share the role of being vehicles of the divine power. Thus the narrative is not basically a christological story pointing to the uniqueness of Jesus.[466]

---

465. Scholars, such as John Meier, emphasize the contact with texts like 21:43, and see this as symbolic of God's replacement of Israel as the people of God with the new Christian community (John Meier, *Matthew,* New Testament Message 3 [Collegeville, Minn.: Liturgical Press, 1990] 237). Daniel Harrington is representative of scholars who see the leadership but not the Jewish people as a whole as rejected, basing his interpretation on the contacts with Jer 8:13 and Hos 9:10, 16 (Daniel J. Harrington, *The Gospel of Matthew* [Collegeville, Minn.: Liturgical Press, 1991] 297-98).

466. See Patte, *Matthew,* 292.

Matthew 21:23–22:46, The Issue of Authority

OVERVIEW

When Jesus enters the Temple in 21:23, he remains until 24:1, departing for the final time after pronouncing it desolate in 23:38. It is a dramatic, symbolic scene, as Jesus, the authorized teacher of God's will (7:28; 28:18-20), makes his final challenge to the Jewish leaders within the sacred Temple court.

In Matthew's Markan source, this is the first of five controversy stories, with a parable be-

tween the first and second, concluded by woes against the scribes. Thus the series is not a list of topics on which Jesus gives teaching, as though he were lecturing on "The Nature of Authority," "Church and State," or "Life After Death," but a series of confrontations in which Jesus' opponents attempt to trap him, but are bested by him in public debate. Matthew extends and intensifies this series of encounters. By adding "Pharisees" in strategic locations, he makes the whole series into a confrontation between Jesus and the Pharisees and implicates them in the death of Jesus.[467] The two kingdoms of 12:22-37 stand over against each other. By adding two additional parables and incorporating the woes into the full-blown speech (23:1–25:46), Matthew restructures the unit symmetrically and more tightly:

467. Compare the series in Mark 11:27; 12:1, 12-13, 28, 35, in which the Pharisees are only incidental, with Matthew's rewriting and additions in 21:23 (21:45); 22:1, 15, 34, 41, then "Pharisees" eight times in chap. 23.

Introduction: The issue posed:		
Jesus' authority challenged		21:23
A Jesus' question		21:24-27
B Three parables		
1. The Two Sons		21:28-32
2. The Lord's Vineyard		21:33-45
3. The Great Supper		22:1-14
B' Three controversy stories		
1. Taxes to the Emperor		22:15-22
2. The Resurrection		22:23-33
3. The Great Commandment		22:34-40
A' Jesus' question		22:41-46

MATTHEW 21:23-27, JESUS' AUTHORITY CHALLENGED

NIV

[23]Jesus entered the temple courts, and, while he was teaching, the chief priests and the elders of the people came to him. "By what authority are you doing these things?" they asked. "And who gave you this authority?"

[24]Jesus replied, "I will also ask you one question. If you answer me, I will tell you by what authority I am doing these things. [25]John's baptism—where did it come from? Was it from heaven, or from men?"

They discussed it among themselves and said, "If we say, 'From heaven,' he will ask, 'Then why didn't you believe him?' [26]But if we say, 'From men'—we are afraid of the people, for they all hold that John was a prophet."

[27]So they answered Jesus, "We don't know."

Then he said, "Neither will I tell you by what authority I am doing these things."

NRSV

23When he entered the temple, the chief priests and the elders of the people came to him as he was teaching, and said, "By what authority are you doing these things, and who gave you this authority?" [24]Jesus said to them, "I will also ask you one question; if you tell me the answer, then I will also tell you by what authority I do these things. [25]Did the baptism of John come from heaven, or was it of human origin?" And they argued with one another, "If we say, 'From heaven,' he will say to us, 'Why then did you not believe him?' [26]But if we say, 'Of human origin,' we are afraid of the crowd; for all regard John as a prophet." [27]So they answered Jesus, "We do not know." And he said to them, "Neither will I tell you by what authority I am doing these things."

COMMENTARY

21:23. As in Mark, Jesus here enters the Temple for the last time. He is challenged by the high priests and elders, who will plot his death (26:3) and will sit in judgment on him (26:47, 57; 27:1). Pharisees are also present.[468] We thus have another ironic scene, in which Jesus' future

468. Jesus has previously been challenged by the Pharisees, who appear in 21:45 as also present here (cf. 22:14-15). They will not participate directly in his trial, but in retrospect are mentioned as being implicated (27:62).

judges pronounce judgment upon themselves in the following dialogue. Their question of authority is not a matter of personal petulance, nor a response to his action in the Temple, which is never mentioned. From Matthew's post-Easter perspective, it concerns the dispute in Judaism concerning who are the authoritative teachers for the reconstitution of the people of God in the aftermath of the war and destruction of Jerusalem and the Temple (see Introduction). Thus "authority" has played a role in Matthew's previous presentation of Jesus: In contrast to the scribes, he is recognized by the crowds to teach with authority (7:29); he has authority to heal, even at a distance, as recognized by a Gentile (8:9); he has authority to forgive sins, and confers his authority on his disciples (9:8; 10:1). At the climax of the Gospel he declares that God has given him all authority, including specifically to teach (28:18-20). Matthew has added to this scene the note that Jesus was teaching, which focuses the discussion on Jesus' authority to teach (but he keeps Mark's indefinite "these things," which in Mark would include Jesus' disruption of the Temple business).

21:24-25a. Jesus' response is more than a clever strategic move. By mentioning John the Baptist, Jesus evokes the picture of the stream of prophets through Israel's history, the authentic bearers of God's Word, although rejected and killed by the people's leaders. Jesus identifies John (and himself) with this succession of prophets "from heaven" (i.e., sent by God) but rejected by "this generation" (11:16; 12:41-42; 23:36-37); but his opponents' teaching is "of human origin"—i.e., they do not teach with God-given authority (7:29) but advocate human tradition (15:1-20).

21:25b-26. In contrast to Jesus, the chief priests and elders do respond with strategy and expediency rather than with a concern for truth.

They think over their alternatives, but Jesus knows their thoughts.[469] Their alternatives are to acknowledge that John's mission (i.e., his preaching and command to baptize) was from God, or to claim that it was only of human origin—i.e., that he was a false prophet. In the first case, they then would have to explain why they had not accepted his message; in the second case, they would run afoul of the popular opinion of John: that he was a true prophet. It is important for Matthew to show not only that the leaders are influenced by the crowd's opinion, since they seek popularity and are jealous of Jesus (27:18), but also that the crowd, which has played a positive role throughout the narrative but has not yet definitively decided for or against Jesus (see 21:10-11), does indeed have influence and responsibility. The leaders decide that it is better is not to answer at all.

21:27. Their original question was not, of course, for information, but a strategy to trap Jesus. They have now fallen into the trap themselves. Their refusal to answer allows Jesus to respond in kind, and to make their duplicity clear to all.

469. Matthew again replaces Mark's "argued with one another" (πρὸς ἑαυτούς *pros heautous*) with "in themselves" (ἐν ἑαυτοῖς *en heautois*), indicating that Jesus knew their silent thoughts (cf. 9:3, where ἐν ἑαυτοῖς replaces Mark's "in their hearts"; 16:7, where ἐν ἑαυτοῖς replaces the same expression as here; and Mark 2:8, where the expression clearly refers to silent thought). But Matt 21:38, where Matthew makes a similar substitution as here, shows that the expression can also refer to audible conversation.

REFLECTIONS

1. "We don't know" can be a legitimate religious response. Believers, even teachers of theology, have no vocation or commission to know all the answers. Even disciples who have been given the mysteries of the kingdom (13:10-17) do not know the eschatological secrets (24:42, 50; 25:13) and should not claim to know more than they do (20:22). Even Paul, who was not hesitant to declare his own convictions, emphasized that, inspired apostle or not, he did not claim to know such religious fundamentals as "how to pray" (Rom 8:26) and the nature of visions he had experienced himself (2 Cor 12:2). This is not feigned modesty, but a confession of the fragmentary nature of human knowledge as such, for Paul and for every Christian (1 Cor 13:12). "We do not know" can be a very Christian confession of faith.

But not here. The ambiguity of religious phenomena and theological truth should not veil a refusal to decide. Here the religious authorities are confronted with the different ministries of John and Jesus. They had, in fact, rejected both as authentic messengers from God. Yet when the yes or no question is pushed, they take refuge in "we don't know." Honest searching and struggle for the truth must finally decide, take a stand, even if one in some abstract sense still doesn't "know." The Jesus who taught his disciples to ask, seek, knock (7:7-8) also promised to be with them in the struggle (1:23; 28:20).

Although Matthew does not so formulate it himself, he would agree that those who want to do God's will can and must "know" that the message of Christ comes from God (John 7:17).

2. This text puts John and Jesus in the same category. Those who reject John also reject Jesus. Their question about Jesus' authority is restated—not avoided—as the question of John's authority. Both are from God, yet they are very different. Their differences embrace not only their different religious "styles" (9:14-17; 11:16-19), but also that John wavered and wondered (11:3), while Jesus spoke with unrelenting authority (7:29). For Matthew, God is also met in Christian missionaries, the "little ones" of the community, and in real children (10:40-42; 18:1-5). Yet this broad spectrum of figures in whom one may encounter authentic mediators of the divine presence does not mean that Matthew affirms a relativism in which all claims to divine authority are equally true and equally false. He calls for discernment (cf. Reflections on 11:16-19).

MATTHEW 21:28-32, THE TWO SONS

NIV

28"What do you think? There was a man who had two sons. He went to the first and said, 'Son, go and work today in the vineyard.'

29"'I will not,' he answered, but later he changed his mind and went.

30"Then the father went to the other son and said the same thing. He answered, 'I will, sir,' but he did not go.

31"Which of the two did what his father wanted?"

"The first," they answered.

Jesus said to them, "I tell you the truth, the tax collectors and the prostitutes are entering the kingdom of God ahead of you. 32For John came to you to show you the way of righteousness, and you did not believe him, but the tax collectors and the prostitutes did. And even after you saw this, you did not repent and believe him."

NRSV

28"What do you think? A man had two sons; he went to the first and said, 'Son, go and work in the vineyard today.' 29He answered, 'I will not'; but later he changed his mind and went. 30The father[a] went to the second and said the same; and he answered, 'I go, sir'; but he did not go. 31Which of the two did the will of his father?" They said, "The first." Jesus said to them, "Truly I tell you, the tax collectors and the prostitutes are going into the kingdom of God ahead of you. 32For John came to you in the way of righteousness and you did not believe him, but the tax collectors and the prostitutes believed him; and even after you saw it, you did not change your minds and believe him."

[a] Gk *He*

COMMENTARY

The three parables that follow are all directly addressed to the chief priests and elders as a continuation of Jesus' response to their challenge (cf. 21:28, 33; 22:1; cf. Luke 14:15; 20:9).

On the form of this dialogue unit, see below on 21:33-45. This parable, unique to Matthew and saturated with Matthean vocabulary, style, and themes, seems to have been composed by Matthew himself as the preface for the traditional saying found in another form in Luke 7:29-30 and introduced by Matthew as a sol-

emn *amēn* (ἀμήν) saying in 31*b*-32 (cf. 5:18).[470]

470. So Robert H. Gundry, *Matthew: A Commentary on His Literary and Theological Art* (Grand Rapids: Eerdmans, 1982) 442-43. Contra Bernard Brandon Scott, *Hear Then the Parable* (Minneapolis: Fortress, 1989) 80-85, arguing that the original, pre-Matthean form of the parable must be represented by the textual tradition in those MSS in which the second son says yes, does nothing, and is still accounted the one who did the father's will, although neither Scott nor any critical edition of the Greek NT regards this as the Matthean form. On the three different forms of the text, see Bruce Metzger, *A Textual Commentary on the Greek New Testament* (New York: United Bible Societies, 1971), 55-56. A variation on the text adopted by the NRSV and the NIV, in which the order of the two sons is reversed, so that the correct response is "the second," is preferred by the NEB and the REB, but this modification, made to make the parable correspond allegorically to the Jew/Gentile order, does not alter the meaning of the text.
Matthew may have been aware of a traditional story of two sons, such as Luke 15:11-32.

In addition to illustrating the general Matthean theme that God requires deeds rather than empty words (7:21-23), the specific meaning in the context is that the Jewish leaders originally said yes to the prophetic message from God delivered by John. Matthew has not forgotten that he has pictured the residents of Jerusalem, including the Pharisees and Sadducees, going out to hear John preach (3:5-7a). But the Pharisees and Sadducees did not accept his message and repent. Those who had been saying no to God's will revealed in the Torah, the tax collectors and prostitutes, changed their mind and accepted his message.

When Jesus asks "What do you think?" (21:28)[471] he does not allow their previous strategic silence to stand. Since the question is about characters in a story, it is indirect, and they cannot avoid answering it. When they do, they who will sit in judgment on Jesus already condemn themselves. Their attempt to trap Jesus has resulted in self-condemnation.

471. This is a pure Mattheanism, used six times in Matthew, always as Jesus' question; elsewhere in NT it is found only in John 11:56.

MATTHEW 21:33-46, THE LORD'S VINEYARD GIVEN TO OTHERS

NIV

33"Listen to another parable: There was a landowner who planted a vineyard. He put a wall around it, dug a winepress in it and built a watchtower. Then he rented the vineyard to some farmers and went away on a journey. 34When the harvest time approached, he sent his servants to the tenants to collect his fruit.

35"The tenants seized his servants; they beat one, killed another, and stoned a third. 36Then he sent other servants to them, more than the first time, and the tenants treated them the same way. 37Last of all, he sent his son to them. 'They will respect my son,' he said.

38"But when the tenants saw the son, they said to each other, 'This is the heir. Come, let's kill him and take his inheritance.' 39So they took him and threw him out of the vineyard and killed him.

40"Therefore, when the owner of the vineyard comes, what will he do to those tenants?"

41"He will bring those wretches to a wretched end," they replied, "and he will rent the vineyard to other tenants, who will give him his share of the crop at harvest time."

42Jesus said to them, "Have you never read in the Scriptures:

"'The stone the builders rejected
　has become the capstone[a];
the Lord has done this,
　and it is marvelous in our eyes'[b]?

43"Therefore I tell you that the kingdom of God

a42 Or cornerstone　　b42 Psalm 118:22,23

NRSV

33"Listen to another parable. There was a landowner who planted a vineyard, put a fence around it, dug a wine press in it, and built a watchtower. Then he leased it to tenants and went to another country. 34When the harvest time had come, he sent his slaves to the tenants to collect his produce. 35But the tenants seized his slaves and beat one, killed another, and stoned another. 36Again he sent other slaves, more than the first; and they treated them in the same way. 37Finally he sent his son to them, saying, 'They will respect my son.' 38But when the tenants saw the son, they said to themselves, 'This is the heir; come, let us kill him and get his inheritance.' 39So they seized him, threw him out of the vineyard, and killed him. 40Now when the owner of the vineyard comes, what will he do to those tenants?" 41They said to him, "He will put those wretches to a miserable death, and lease the vineyard to other tenants who will give him the produce at the harvest time."

42Jesus said to them, "Have you never read in the scriptures:

'The stone that the builders rejected
　has become the cornerstone;[a]
this was the Lord's doing,
　and it is amazing in our eyes'?

43Therefore I tell you, the kingdom of God will be taken away from you and given to a people that produces the fruits of the kingdom.[b] 44The one who falls on this stone will be broken to

aOr keystone　　bGk the fruits of it

NIV

will be taken away from you and given to a people who will produce its fruit. [44]He who falls on this stone will be broken to pieces, but he on whom it falls will be crushed."[a]

[45]When the chief priests and the Pharisees heard Jesus' parables, they knew he was talking about them. [46]They looked for a way to arrest him, but they were afraid of the crowd because the people held that he was a prophet.

[a]44 Some manuscripts do not have verse 44.

NRSV

pieces; and it will crush anyone on whom it falls."[a]

[45]When the chief priests and the Pharisees heard his parables, they realized that he was speaking about them. [46]They wanted to arrest him, but they feared the crowds, because they regarded him as a prophet.

[a]Other ancient authorities lack verse 44

COMMENTARY

It is disputed whether there was an original non-allegorical parable going back to Jesus.[472] The Markan form of this story is already understood as an allegory of Israel's rejection of God's prophets and final rejection of God's Son, resulting in Israel's replacement by "others" (Mark 12:1-12). Matthew makes the parable the centerpiece of Jesus' threefold parabolic response to the chief priests and elders, sharpening and extending its allegorical features to express the meaning given in the Matthean context. Matthew also reformulates the parable to correspond to the preceding one:

21:28a . . . . . . Jesus' introductory
              word 21:33a
21:28b-30 . . . The parable 21:33b-39
21:31a . . . . . . Jesus' question 21:40
21:31b . . . . . . Their self-incriminating
              response 21:41
21:31c . . . . . . Jesus' concluding
              pronouncement
              of judgment . . . . . 21:42-43 [44]

The two parables are also joined by their common elements of vineyard and son, as well as by

the theme of doing God's will (rather than merely claiming to do so).

21:33. Matthew identifies Mark's "man" as a "landowner" (οἰκοδεσπότης *oikodespotēs*; as 13:52; 20:1), thus making him more transparent to the allegorical meaning Matthew intends: the Lord of the vineyard is God (v. 40). The fence, wine press, and watchtower are the standard equipment of a vineyard and are not allegorized. The vineyard evokes the image of Isa 5:1-7, as does the language already in Mark, which Matthew slightly revises to conform more closely to the LXX text of Isaiah (showing that Matthew is thinking of the vineyard as Israel, as in Isa 5:7; but Matthew's addition of v. 43 makes the vineyard the kingdom).[473]

21:34. Matthew adds "the season of fruits" (ὁ καιρὸς τῶν καρπῶν *ho kairos tōn karpōn*; both the NIV and the NRSV obscure Matthew's repeated reference to "fruits," twice here and added again in v. 41). For "fruits" as his key term for "good works," see Commentary on 21:18-22. Unlike Mark, where the owner wants only his contracted share, here he unrealistically wants all the fruit, as allegorical meaning prevails over historical realism: God's claim can only be total.

21:35-36. Mark's series of three individuals'

472. Several scholars so argue, but disagree as to its meaning: (1) Radical action, like that of the murderous tenants, is called for to gain the kingdom (John Dominic Crossan, *In Parables: The Challenge of the Historical Jesus* [New York: Harper & Row, 1973] 86-96); (2) the kingdom will be taken from Israel's false leadership and given to the repentant publicans and sinners (Joachim Jeremias, *The Parables of Jesus* [New York: Charles Scribner's Sons, 1972] 70-77); (3) God relentlessly and recklessly searches for rebellious humanity, the searching God longing for response (John R. Donahue, *The Gospel in Parable: Metaphor, Narrative, and Theology in the Synoptic Gospels* [Philadelphia: Fortress, 1988] 53-55). If the parable goes back to Jesus, Donahue's is the most convincing interpretation of its original meaning.

473. The key hermeneutical problem here is whether Matthew retains the Markan allegorical meaning, in which the vineyard refers to Israel and the bad tenants to the bad leaders. Does Matthew's v. 43 change this, taking the "kingdom" (βασιλεία *basileia*) from Israel and giving it to the church, or taking bad leaders away from Israel and giving them Christian leaders? Since it is the *basileia* that is taken from Israel, it must refer to the sovereign act of God in electing Israel as the covenant people of God. At the Matthean level, the meaning seems to be that God's sovereign act of election, constituting one people as the covenant people, is taken from empirical Israel and given to the church of Jews and Gentiles.

being treated progressively worse, followed by "many," becomes in Matthew two groups of slaves sent by the vineyard's owner. Since for Matthew the slaves are transparently the prophets sent by God to rebellious Israel, the two groups probably represent the biblical categories of former and latter prophets.[474]

21:37-39. After the abuse and murder of several of his slaves, the landowner decides to send his son. Since this story is difficult to imagine as a realistic portrayal, Matthew understands the sending of the son retrospectively as an allegory of the destiny of Jesus, who was sent by God as the climax of the series of rejected prophets. When the tenants decide to kill the son and claim the vineyard as their own, their action may perhaps be less incredible than it at first appears if one considers the laws of the time (possession being determined by occupancy) and the sympathy of the common people against absentee landlords. But here, too, allegorical meaning, not historical realism, is transparently the point. The tenants represent the leaders of rebellious Israel, who conspire to kill Jesus. In the allegorical parable, Matthew can be uninhibited by history and can make the Jewish leaders totally responsible—there is no third party to whom the son is turned over for execution. Matthew reverses the Markan sequence in which the son is first killed and then unceremoniously dumped outside the vineyard; in Matthew, he is first taken outside and then killed, corresponding to the actual passion story (27:32) and showing again that the parable is dominated by its allegorical interpretation.

21:40-41. The landowner has now become the "Lord" (οἰκοδεσπότης *oikodespotēs* of 21:33 has become the κύριος *kyrios* of 21:40; cf. the identical development in 20:1, 8). Matthew changes the Markan verb to have the Lord "come," as at the parousia (cf., e.g., 25:31). At this point Matthew restructures the Markan form to have Jesus pose a question (as in v. 28; cf. above chart) that will allow the Jewish leaders to pronounce their own condemnation (cf. 2 Sam 12:7; 14:12-13)—again as in the preceding pericope. They declare that God will destroy the

wicked tenants and give the vineyard to other tenants. Matthew understands this as the destruction of Jerusalem and the growth of the church of Jews and Gentiles in unbelieving Israel's place. He then adds words that return the pronouncement to his principal charge, that the "tenants" have not given to their Lord the "fruit" (works of justice) he requires.

21:42. Jesus' final pronouncement (cf. structure above) begins with a verbatim quotation taken from Mark, who has followed the LXX of Ps 118:22-23 (cf. the use of Ps 118:25-26 in Matt 21:9). "Have you never read?" is a Matthean favorite expression (12:3, 5; 19:4; 21:6; 22:31) adapted from Mark (cf. 2:25; 12:10, 26), increasing the self-condemnation of those who know the Scripture (cf. 2:4-5). The parable ended with the death of the son. Here, the divine vindication (resurrection) is provided by the post-Easter church.

21:43. This verse is added by Matthew, apparently composed by him, and represents the major hermeneutical issue of this passage (and perhaps of Matthew). See Reflections below.

21:44. This text, which does not occur in several important MSS (D, 33, it, sy[s]) and is omitted in Eusebius's quotations of this passage, was once thought to be a scribal gloss imported from Luke 20:18 (cf. RSV, NEB, still missing from REB; NAB brackets it as a later addition). More recent evaluation tends to consider it a part of the original text of Matthew. It corresponds to the stone imagery of v. 42 and is related to the image of the kingdom of God as a great stone, as in Dan 2:44. If the verse had been added secondarily, a more natural place would be following v. 42. If, however, it is original, its present location would show how important Matthew considered v. 43 to be, since he would have broken the connection between v. 42 and 44 by inserting it. If original, v. 44 functions to intensify the judgment expressed in the parable and in v. 43: the rock/kingdom/Son, who should be Savior and Lord, becomes a terrible threat to the one on whom it falls or who falls against it.

21:45-46. It now appears that the Pharisees have been included with the chief priests and elders all the while (cf. 21:15, 23; 22:14-15). They represent Matthew's post-Easter opponents. The strange alliance of Jewish leaders would carry out their previous desire to arrest Jesus immedi-

---

474. In the OT of Matthew's day the Prophets were divided into the Former Prophets (Joshua–Kings) and the Latter Prophets (Isaiah–Malachi). Prophets were known biblically as slaves/servants of God (Jer 25:4; Amos 3:7; Dan 9:6, 10; Rev 10:7; 11:18).

ately except for the crowds who (correctly) view Jesus as a prophet (cf. 21:11, 24-26), again showing the influence the crowds have on the course of events. This has the effect of increasing the guilt of the crowds when they finally side with their leaders in demanding the death of Jesus (27:24-26).

REFLECTIONS

Who is represented by the "you" from whom the kingdom is taken? Who is the "nation" to whom it is given? In the context, the addressees are clearly the chief priests and Pharisees (the latter here added by Matthew)—i.e., the Jewish leadership, not the people as a whole. Thus some scholars (e.g., Saldarini and Harrington) have contended that Matthew here and elsewhere claims only that God will replace the present false leadership with faithful leaders. This requires understanding "nation" (ἔθνος *ethnos,* which is also the word for "Gentile") in an unusual sense, a new group of leaders for Israel. The more natural way is to understand *ethnos* as "nation" or "people," so that (as in 1 Pet 2:9) those to whom the kingdom is given are the renewed people of God, the church of Jews and Gentiles, who are called by God in place of unfaithful Israel.[475] Many Christians throughout history have been too willing to understand the text this way, which has fueled the fires of anti-Judaism and anti-Semitism. Many Christians today are hesitant to understand the text in any way that encourages a false understanding of supersessionism, that God has rejected Israel and replaced it with the church (Jewish and Gentile) as the people of God. Neither past mistakes nor present Christian sensitivity to Jewish-Christian relations should inhibit our allowing Matthew to mean whatever he meant. If he believed God had now rejected the Jews as the elect people of God and replaced them with the church composed of people called from all nations, including Jews, historical honesty should accept this. Historical exegesis may document this as Matthew's view, even if his situational-conditioned perspective must not be allowed to dominate our own, which must be informed not only by this text but by other canonical perspectives as well, such as that of Paul, another Jew who had become a Christian and who saw a larger plan of God that embraced both Israel and church (Romans 9–11).

This text does not speak explicitly, however, of Israel's being rejected, but of the "kingdom of God" being taken from "you"; in Matthew's view, the saving activity of God continues in that community where taking up the "yoke of the kingdom" means adherence to the Torah as fulfilled in the teaching of Jesus (cf. 5:17-48; 28:20; Excursus "Kingdom of Heaven in Matthew," 288-94). Matthew, like the modern reader, here struggles with a difficult problem, one that he perhaps had as much difficulty in resolving with systematic clarity and consistency as does his modern reader. Even if the objective meaning remains not entirely clear, contemporary readers can still legitimately ask whether they have set up other phony sovereignties in place of the one God, and thus might be addressed in the "you" from whom the kingdom is taken.

475. So, e.g., John Meier, *Matthew,* New Testament Message 3 (Collegeville, Minn.: Liturgical Press, 1990) 244-45.

MATTHEW 22:1-14, THE GREAT SUPPER

NIV

22 Jesus spoke to them again in parables, saying: [2]"The kingdom of heaven is like a king who prepared a wedding banquet for his son. [3]He sent his servants to those who had been invited to the banquet to tell them to come, but they refused to come.

[4]"Then he sent some more servants and said, 'Tell those who have been invited that I have prepared my dinner: My oxen and fattened cattle have been butchered, and everything is ready. Come to the wedding banquet.'

[5]"But they paid no attention and went off—one to his field, another to his business. [6]The rest seized his servants, mistreated them and killed them. [7]The king was enraged. He sent his army and destroyed those murderers and burned their city.

[8]"Then he said to his servants, 'The wedding banquet is ready, but those I invited did not deserve to come. [9]Go to the street corners and invite to the banquet anyone you find.' [10]So the servants went out into the streets and gathered all the people they could find, both good and bad, and the wedding hall was filled with guests.

[11]"But when the king came in to see the guests, he noticed a man there who was not wearing wedding clothes. [12]'Friend,' he asked, 'how did you get in here without wedding clothes?' The man was speechless.

[13]"Then the king told the attendants, 'Tie him hand and foot, and throw him outside, into the darkness, where there will be weeping and gnashing of teeth.'

[14]"For many are invited, but few are chosen."

NRSV

22 Once more Jesus spoke to them in parables, saying: [2]"The kingdom of heaven may be compared to a king who gave a wedding banquet for his son. [3]He sent his slaves to call those who had been invited to the wedding banquet, but they would not come. [4]Again he sent other slaves, saying, 'Tell those who have been invited: Look, I have prepared my dinner, my oxen and my fat calves have been slaughtered, and everything is ready; come to the wedding banquet.' [5]But they made light of it and went away, one to his farm, another to his business, [6]while the rest seized his slaves, mistreated them, and killed them. [7]The king was enraged. He sent his troops, destroyed those murderers, and burned their city. [8]Then he said to his slaves, 'The wedding is ready, but those invited were not worthy. [9]Go therefore into the main streets, and invite everyone you find to the wedding banquet.' [10]Those slaves went out into the streets and gathered all whom they found, both good and bad; so the wedding hall was filled with guests.

[11]"But when the king came in to see the guests, he noticed a man there who was not wearing a wedding robe, [12]and he said to him, 'Friend, how did you get in here without a wedding robe?' And he was speechless. [13]Then the king said to the attendants, 'Bind him hand and foot, and throw him into the outer darkness, where there will be weeping and gnashing of teeth.' [14]For many are called, but few are chosen."

COMMENTARY

Jesus tells a striking and troubling story in which all the invited guests to a dinner party at the last minute refuse to come, so the host rounds up a mélange of street people, who find themselves guests at a party they had never dreamed of attending. The story circulated in a variety of forms in early Christianity (Q; Luke 14:15-24; and *Gospel of Thomas* 64 as well as here), in each case being interpreted and modified in accordance with the theology of the author concerned. Matthew has adapted the Q form, placing it in this context to serve as the final item in his triad of judgment parables (see Overview above). As in the preceding parables, Matthew builds his allegorical interpretation into the story, making the parable an allegory of salvation history from the initial sending of the prophets to Israel through the renewed invitation by Christian prophetic missionaries, concluding at the last judgment when the good and bad in the church are sorted out. The original dinner party has become the messianic banquet given by the king (God) for his Son (Jesus), who invites guests who agree to come (Israel) to the wedding celebration (salvation, the messianic banquet), but who then refuse the final invitations delivered by both the first group of slaves (the Hebrew prophets) and the second (the prophetic Christian missionaries).

By extending its allegorical features, assimilating it to the preceding two parables, and placing it last, Matthew makes this story the climax of the progression of this three-parable set: The first of the triad, the parable of the two sons (21:28-32), focuses on the (more than a) prophet John; the second, the parable of the lord's vineyard given to others (21:33-46), pictures the whole prophetic line climaxing in Jesus, the Son who is killed. This third parable is understood from Matthew's own post-Easter perspective, facing the parousia and final judgment. This final parable thus follows the Q perspective in picturing the history of salvation from the original calling of Israel to the last judgment, and places Jesus and the church in the succession of Israel's prophets, persecuted and rejected by Israel.

22:1. In Matthew the parable has the same addressees as the preceding one, and he now specifically includes the Pharisees. Matthew's insertion of "again" (πάλιν *palin,* or "once more") binds the parable to the preceding one as well, as do all the points noted below in which this parable is assimilated to the preceding ones. This means that the Matthean meaning cannot be derived from the parable alone, but only from the narrative structure of which it is now an integral part.

22:2. Matthew introduced the kingship motif into the preceding parable (21:43). To correspond to this, the "man" of Q who gave a dinner party now becomes a king who gives a wedding feast for his son. The father/son motif binds together all three parables of this unit. The kingdom of heaven is not like a king, but is compared to the whole situation described by the story (see 13:1).

22:3. The story presupposes the two-stage custom documented both in rabbinic literature and Hellenistic papyri[476] according to which an invitation sent well in advance of the banquet was acknowledged and accepted by those invited, who then received a courtesy reminder on the day of the banquet itself. In Matthew's allegorical understanding, the original invitation corresponds to the call of Israel, who accepted God's covenant. As in the preceding parable (but differently from the Lukan parallel, which is closer to Q), the slaves who are sent correspond to the prophets of Israel. In Matthew, no excuses are offered (again, cf. the Lukan version; in the *Gospel of Thomas,* the excuse motif is elaborated into four specific excuses). Those who had committed themselves to attend the banquet simply declare their unwillingness to come (NIV, "but they refused to come" [οὐκ ἤθελον ἐλθεῖν *ouk ēthelon elthein*]). Refusal of a king's invitation, especially in concert suggesting conspiracy, is equivalent to rebellion (2 Sam 10:4; Josephus *Antiquities of the Jews* 9.13.2).

22:4-6. The king is patient (again, cf. the preceding parable) and does not retaliate, but sends a second group of slaves. This element of the story is peculiar to Matthew, necessary to fit his allegorical understanding, for it corresponds to the prophetic Christian missionaries.[477] Not only do those invited continue to refuse, but they abuse and kill the messengers as well. This is one of numerous unrealistic elements in the story that points to its allegorical meaning: prophetic Christian missionaries are killed, just as were the faithful prophets of Israel (see on 23:34, 37).

22:7. This element in the story cannot be made realistic. While dinner waits, the king wages war, kills those who had dishonored and rebelled against him, and burns "their" city, presumably also his own. On the historical level, this is not only an overreaction, but also hardly possible. The vocabulary reflects Matthew's theology: "destroyed" (ἀπόλλυμι *apollymi*) is the same verb

476. See Hermann L. Strack and Paul Billerbeck, *Kommentar zum Neuen Testament aus Talmud und Midrasch* (Munich: Beck, 1922–61) 1:880; and Chan-Hie Kim, "The Papyrus Invitation," *JBL* 94 (1975) 391-402.

477. On prophets in the Matthean community, see 5:17; 7:15; 10:41; 23:34; 24:11, 24. The fact that some of these deal with the danger of false prophets only strengthens the case for prophetic leaders in Matthew's church; only a community that accepts the prophetic phenomenon as such need worry about distinguishing authentic from false prophets. Matthew mentions apostles only in 10:2, and there are no warnings against false apostles.

used in 21:41; "murderers" reflects the same view as 23:31, 35. Matthew is thinking in terms of his view of salvation history, not of an actual king who waged war while dinner waited. Most scholars see this as Matthew's retrospective view of the destruction of Jerusalem, understood as a judgment on rebellious Israel, who had rejected the Messiah, although some explain it in terms of Matthew's reflection on Isa 5:24-25.[478] The explanations are not mutually exclusive; if one sees influence of the Isaiah text, this is not evidence against Matthew's post-70 date and perspective.

22:8-10. The rebellious first group has been judged, but the festival house is still empty. A third group of slaves is sent, representing the prophetic Christian missionaries, with a new invitation corresponding even in vocabulary to the Great Commission of 28:18-20.[479] The invitation is no longer restricted to those who had accepted the previous invitation, but is extended to all. Those who are "gathered in"[480] are both bad and good, corresponding to Matthew's realistic picture of the empirical church in other parables peculiar to him (13:24-30; cf. the interpretation in vv. 36-43; 13:47-50), and setting the stage for the appended conclusion of this scene.

22:11-13. This is not a separate parable, but functions only as an expansion of 22:1-10. The whole expansion seems to be Matthew's own composition, permeated with his vocabulary and theology. No trace of it is found in the Lukan and *Gospel of Thomas* forms of the story, and it fits awkwardly after vv. 8-10: How could those unexpectedly herded into the wedding hall from the streets wear the expected clothing, which all but one of them seem to do? Again, realism is sacrificed to theological meaning. In early Christianity,

the new identity of conversion was often pictured as donning a new set of clothes; the language of changing clothes was utilized to express the giving up of the old way of life and putting on the new Christian identity (see Rom 13:12-14; Gal 3:27; Eph 6:11; Col 3:12; cf. Luke 15:22; Rev 3:4; 6:11; 19:8). At the allegorical level, the man was expected to have the deeds of an authentic Christian life, corresponding to the "fruits" in the imagery of the preceding parable.[481] When confronted with his lack, the man has no response, for he is without excuse (reflecting Matthew's knowledge of the excuses offered in the Q form of the preceding parable, which he has omitted?).

The judgment seems harsh, but Matthew is thinking not of an actual wedding party, but of the last judgment; "weeping and gnashing of teeth" corresponds to 8:12; 13:42, 50; 24:51; 25:30, an apocalyptic Q expression (cf. Luke 13:28) that became a favorite of Matthew's to picture the terror of condemnation at the last judgment.

22:14. Matthew does not use "call" (καλέω *kaleō*) in the sense of "effective call," as does Paul, but in the sense of initial invitation to become a disciple. Whether one is actually "chosen" (ἐκλεκτός *eklektos*, "elected," i.e., accepted in the last judgment) depends on manifesting authentic Christian faith in deeds of love and justice. For the first time Matthew explicitly appropriates the term rendered "elect," referring it not to a specific group (Jews, Christians), but to those who will finally be accepted in the last judgment (see also 24:22, 24, 31). The focus of an elect people of God has shifted from the OT understanding of the people of Israel as a whole to that of the righteous "remnant," a shift already made in some streams of Judaism.[482] The dispute between Matthew and the Pharisaic leaders of his own time concerned who constituted this elect remnant, the continuing people of God.

---

478. See, e.g., Gundry, *Matthew*, 436-37, who has additional arguments against using this passage as support for a post-70 CE dating; cf. Donahue, *Parable*, 94.

479. Just as "worker" (ἐργάτης *ergatēs*) in the parable of 20:1-2; 8 is transparent to the same term used for Christian workers—i.e., missionaries (cf. 9:37-38; 10:10; 2 Cor 11:13; Phil 3:2; 1 Tim 5:18; 2 Tim 2:15), even more so with "slave" (δοῦλος *doulos*; e.g., Acts 4:29; 16:17; Rom 1:1; Gal 1:10). A king's official representatives were also called "slaves" (δοῦλοι *douloi*). The parable in Matthew does not picture household slaves, but officials. Thus prophets as God's authorized messengers are called "slaves" in both the OT (Jer 25:4; Amos 3:7; Dan 9:6, 10) and in the NT (Rev 10:7; 11:18).

480. "They were gathering together" (συνήγαγον *synēgagon*) is a pun on "synagogue," often used negatively by Matthew, but here obviously meaning the church, the "true synagogue" over against "their synagogues."

481. There is no evidence for the custom that kings provided the wedding attire for guests, an idea apparently originated by Augustine by inference from this parable and representing an attempt to understand this text by importing Pauline theology into Matthew (cf. Rom 10:1-13; Phil 3:7-9).

482. See Wis 3:9, 4:15; *1 Enoch*; *Apocalypse of Abraham* 29; cf. *TDNT* 4:145-72.

REFLECTIONS

The theological point of 22:11-14 is that those who find themselves unexpectedly included may not presume on grace, but are warned of the dire consequences of accepting the invitation and doing nothing except showing up. By concluding in this manner, Matthew makes it clear that such pictures in which unfaithful Israel is condemned are not an encouragement to smugness on the part of his Christian readers. The "elect" are not the church as a replacement for Israel, but those finally accepted in the last judgment. The whole section, in fact, is directed to the Matthean reader. It is instruction and warning to insiders, not a description of the fate of outsiders, confessional language rather than objectifying report. At this point, Matthew does join his voice with his fellow Jewish convert, who laments the present rejection of Israel: "So if you think you are standing, watch out that you do not fall" (1 Cor 10:12 NRSV; cf. Romans 9–11).

MATTHEW 22:15-22, ON PAYING TAXES TO THE EMPEROR

NIV

¹⁵Then the Pharisees went out and laid plans to trap him in his words. ¹⁶They sent their disciples to him along with the Herodians. "Teacher," they said, "we know you are a man of integrity and that you teach the way of God in accordance with the truth. You aren't swayed by men, because you pay no attention to who they are. ¹⁷Tell us then, what is your opinion? Is it right to pay taxes to Caesar or not?"

¹⁸But Jesus, knowing their evil intent, said, "You hypocrites, why are you trying to trap me? ¹⁹Show me the coin used for paying the tax." They brought him a denarius, ²⁰and he asked them, "Whose portrait is this? And whose inscription?"

²¹"Caesar's," they replied.

Then he said to them, "Give to Caesar what is Caesar's, and to God what is God's."

²²When they heard this, they were amazed. So they left him and went away.

NRSV

15Then the Pharisees went and plotted to entrap him in what he said. ¹⁶So they sent their disciples to him, along with the Herodians, saying, "Teacher, we know that you are sincere, and teach the way of God in accordance with truth, and show deference to no one; for you do not regard people with partiality. ¹⁷Tell us, then, what you think. Is it lawful to pay taxes to the emperor, or not?" ¹⁸But Jesus, aware of their malice, said, "Why are you putting me to the test, you hypocrites? ¹⁹Show me the coin used for the tax." And they brought him a denarius. ²⁰Then he said to them, "Whose head is this, and whose title?" ²¹They answered, "The emperor's." Then he said to them, "Give therefore to the emperor the things that are the emperor's, and to God the things that are God's." ²²When they heard this, they were amazed; and they left him and went away.

COMMENTARY

After the extended parabolic response to the opponents' first ploy, Matthew resumes the Markan storyline. This pericope does not represent "the teaching of Jesus on the separation of church and state," but is part of the controversy series initiated by those Pharisees who have already decided to kill him (12:14; see Overview). This is all the more ironic in that in each of the three following controversies (taxes, resurrection, the Great Commandment), Jesus affirms the Pharisees' positions (see 23:1-3). Despite their flattering introductory words, they are not seeking instruction or dialogue, but are trying to entrap him. Jesus is master of the situation and refuses to be caught. This, and not abstract doctrine on church and state, is the thrust of the narrative.

22:15-18. In contrast to Mark, the Pharisees are not the agents of the chief priests, scribes, and elders (cf. Mark 11:27; 12:1, 12-13), but are themselves in charge and take the initiative. As in 12:14 and 27:1, they "take counsel"/"plot"/"lay plans." Representing the opponents of Matthew's own time, they are the counterparts of Jesus as teacher of the Matthean church in that they too have disciples and echo Jesus' words "What do you think?" (21:28/22:17). Although the Herodians play no role in Matthew's time, he retains them from Mark, for they represent the overt supporters of the Roman regime and would support paying the tax. The Pharisees, on the other hand, were popular with the people because they in principle resented and resisted the tax, but did not go as far as the radical nationalists who publicly resisted its payment.

The tax issue was not general and abstract, but referred to a particular tax, the "census" (κῆνσος *kēnsos*), the Roman head-tax instituted in 6 CE, when Judea became a Roman province. This census triggered the nationalism that finally became the Zealot movement, which fomented the disastrous war of 66–70. Matthew looks back on this whole movement and its tragic consequences, but knows it was a divisive issue earlier and still engenders deep feelings (see 17:24-27). The tax could be paid only in Roman coin, most of which contained an image and inscription considered blasphemous by many Jews: *Tiberius Caesar Divi Augusti Filius Augustus Pontifex Maximus* ("Tiberius Caesar, august son of the divine Augustus, high priest"). Thus they are asking a trick question, calculated either to alienate the nationalists (if Jesus replied in the affirmative) or to make him subject to arrest by the Romans (if he declared against paying the tax). This clarifies Jesus' initial response, that their addressing him as "teacher" and accolades about his teaching are an insincere "putting me to the test" (the same word is used in 4:3; 16:1; 19:3; Satan and the Pharisees play the same role). The narrator's comment to the reader in Mark becomes Jesus' direct address to the Pharisees in Matthew, "Hypocrites!" and will become the keynote of 23:1-36.

22:19-22. Jesus asks for the "legal tender" with which the tax is paid. He does not have it himself, but the Pharisees, in the sacred precincts of the Temple, produce the coin with its idolatrous image and inscription and acknowledge that they are Caesar's. When Jesus pronounces that what is already the emperor's should be given to him, while avoiding either a direct yes or no, he in fact gives an indirect yes. It is not against the Torah (this was the form of the question in v. 17, "Is it lawful?") to pay taxes to the emperor. The Pharisees acknowledge this by participating in the economic system made possible by Rome, even by having Roman coins in the Temple area. Although unconvinced, the Pharisees are silenced and depart from this round "in shock" (ἐθαύμασαν *ethaumasan*).

REFLECTIONS

1. In the same breath in which he declares that paying taxes to support secular and pagan governments is not against the will of God, Jesus goes beyond their original question, declaring that what is God's must be given to God. This is not an in-principle division of the world into two realms with two sovereigns. Matthew's dualistic perspective is only penultimate; ultimately he is a monotheist who resists this kind of dualism. The kingdom of God represented by Jesus embraces all of life. Indeed, Matthew could hardly advocate the separation of religion and politics. He pictures Jesus and the Christian community as belonging to the series of Israel's prophets, who never made a split between religion and the political aspects of life.

2. While Matthew is clear that loyalty to God is a different and higher category than loyalty to Caesar, this text is not instruction on how people who live in a complex world of competing loyalties may determine what belongs to Caesar and what belongs to God. It simply declares that the distinction between what belongs to Caesar (as some things do) and what belongs to

God (the ultimate loyalty) must be made, and he leaves it to readers in their own situations to be "Jesus theologians" who, in the light of his own life and teachings, actualize the distinction (cf. 5:21-48).

MATTHEW 22:23-33, QUESTION ABOUT THE RESURRECTION

NIV

²³That same day the Sadducees, who say there is no resurrection, came to him with a question. ²⁴"Teacher," they said, "Moses told us that if a man dies without having children, his brother must marry the widow and have children for him. ²⁵Now there were seven brothers among us. The first one married and died, and since he had no children, he left his wife to his brother. ²⁶The same thing happened to the second and third brother, right on down to the seventh. ²⁷Finally, the woman died. ²⁸Now then, at the resurrection, whose wife will she be of the seven, since all of them were married to her?"

²⁹Jesus replied, "You are in error because you do not know the Scriptures or the power of God. ³⁰At the resurrection people will neither marry nor be given in marriage; they will be like the angels in heaven. ³¹But about the resurrection of the dead—have you not read what God said to you, ³²'I am the God of Abraham, the God of Isaac, and the God of Jacob'ᵃ? He is not the God of the dead but of the living."

³³When the crowds heard this, they were astonished at his teaching.

ᵃ32 Exodus 3:6

NRSV

²³The same day some Sadducees came to him, saying there is no resurrection;ᵃ and they asked him a question, saying, ²⁴"Teacher, Moses said, 'If a man dies childless, his brother shall marry the widow, and raise up children for his brother.' ²⁵Now there were seven brothers among us; the first married, and died childless, leaving the widow to his brother. ²⁶The second did the same, so also the third, down to the seventh. ²⁷Last of all, the woman herself died. ²⁸In the resurrection, then, whose wife of the seven will she be? For all of them had married her."

²⁹Jesus answered them, "You are wrong, because you know neither the scriptures nor the power of God. ³⁰For in the resurrection they neither marry nor are given in marriage, but are like angelsᵇ in heaven. ³¹And as for the resurrection of the dead, have you not read what was said to you by God, ³²'I am the God of Abraham, the God of Isaac, and the God of Jacob'? He is God not of the dead, but of the living." ³³And when the crowd heard it, they were astounded at his teaching.

ᵃOther ancient authorities read who say that there is no resurrection   ᵇOther ancient authorities add of God

COMMENTARY

22:23. This episode taken from Mark does not present Jesus' teaching about life after death, but is part of the series of confrontations with his opponents. Matthew adds that it occurred "the same day," Tuesday (see Overview above).

This is the only appearance of the Sadducees in Matthew's Markan source. Luke follows him in this (though the Sadducees appear five times in Acts). They do not appear in John at all. Matthew, however, has added them redactionally at 3:7; 16:1, 6, 11-12 to show that with the

Pharisees they form a united front against Jesus. They had disappeared in the war of 66–70 and its aftermath and, unlike the Pharisees, no longer formed a significant factor in Matthew's own situation. Since no primary sources from the Sadducees survived, and all we know about them is derived from later descriptions from groups and individuals more or less hostile to them, our characterization must be somewhat tentative.[483]

483. Reconstructions are based on the NT (Synoptics and Acts); Josephus *Antiquities of the Jews* 18; and Rabbinic sources—all hostile witnesses.

Apparently they belonged largely to the wealthy, land-owning class, tended to resist change and defend the status quo, and were closely related to the Priestly group ("Sadducee" is apparently derived from the Priestly name "Zadok"). They regarded only the Pentateuch as canonical. The doctrine of the resurrection of the dead made its first unambiguous appearance in the latest book of the OT (Dan 12:2), which they did not regard as canonical. The Sadducees were suspicious of such progressive apocalyptic doctrines that were not taught in the Scriptures they regarded as canonical but accepted by the Pharisees on the basis of the developing oral tradition (cf. Acts 23:8).[484] Unlike the impression one might receive by imposing modern categories on the text, the Sadducees' denial of the resurrection of the dead was not an expression of "modernism" that had abandoned the traditional belief, but an aspect of their biblicism and their theological conservatism, which resisted the "modern" idea of resurrection, advocated by the Pharisees.

22:24. The law of levirite marriage (from Latin *levir,* "brother-in-law") derives from the Pentateuch (Deut 25:5-6) and was considered important in Jewish tradition (cf. Gen 38:1-8 and the story of Tamar; Ruth 1–4. Both Tamar and Ruth are listed in Jesus' genealogy). The rationale for the law was the continuation of the family line into the future. The Sadducees affirm the importance of the law because of its assumption that one's life continues after death only in the lives of one's descendants, not in a heavenly world following the resurrection. To die without offspring was thought to be an incomplete life.

22:25-28. They thus present a case calculated to affirm the Torah but to show the absurdity of the idea of the resurrection. Their example, while probably fictional in Mark, is presented by Matthew as a real case (he adds "with us" [παρ' ἡμῖν *par' hēmin*]). The fact that it is not an utterly ludicrous example is illustrated by the Tobit story, in which Sarah had survived seven husbands (Tob 3:8; 6:14). Their question "Whose wife will she be?"

in the resurrection is calculated to display the absurdity of trying to sort out the tangle if all the relationships of this world are restored in some future life. This biblical law, part of the sacred Torah, obviously presupposes that there will be no future life in which this would become a problem.

22:29-32. The Sadducees are misled (cf. 24:4-5, 11, 24) on two fundamental points, since they know neither the Scripture nor the power of God. Jesus corrects their misapprehensions in reverse order, making yet another neat chiastic structure:

A Erroneous understanding of Scripture
  B Erroneous understanding of the
    power of God
  B′ Correct understanding of the power
    of God in the resurrection
A′ Correct understanding of Scripture

The structure first makes clear that affirmation of the resurrection is a matter not of correct theory, but of faith in the power of God (cf. Rom 1:4; Phil 3:10, 21; Rev 20:6). The life of the age to come is not a bigger and better version of this life—although categories of this life are our only means of conceptualizing it and expressing it. Rather, faith is a matter of the power of God to deliver on his covenant promises. Faith in the resurrection is not a theory of human nature or of "what happens when we die," but is trust in the power of God, who will, through that power, at the eschaton work an unimaginable transformation. Eschatological existence is not pictured literally, either as an abrogation of the life of this world or as its mere extension, so that questions about the untangling of earthly relationships are not only beside the point but also a denial of the power of God. If there is a problem here, it is God's problem, not ours.

Neither do the Sadducees understand the Scripture. When Jesus charges them with not "knowing" the Scripture, he does not mean that they have never read Exod 3:6 before; of course, they have. What is at stake is the proper interpretation of Scripture, in this and the next two scenes. Both Jesus and his opponents acknowledge Scripture and its authority; the issue that separates Matthew and his opponents is how to interpret it and who is authorized to do so.

---

484. Once again, Jesus apparently agrees with the Pharisees' position, not only affirming the resurrection, but contending that it is taught in the Pentateuch. Later rabbis accused the Samaritans (who also accepted only the Pentateuch as canonical and denied the resurrection) as obliterating the passages that taught it (*Sanh.* 90[b]). Cf. W. C. Allen, *A Critical and Exegetical Commentary on the Gospel According to St. Matthew,* ICC (New York: Scribner's, 1910) 239, for additional examples.

Although it will not be convincing to the modern Western mind,[485] the general hermeneutical approach here illustrated is shared by Jesus, Matthew, and their opponents. In this hermeneutic, the details of Scripture become an illustration and expression of a view arrived at on other grounds. Yet, the interpretation of Exod 3:6 as supporting the resurrection offered in Matt 22:31-32 is not as arbitrary as first appears. In the revelation of God's name—God's very nature—at the burning bush, God defines himself as the one who has bound himself willingly in covenant with people of past generations. These people are now dead and buried, but not gone forever. God maintains them in close relation. The imagery here must not be forced; even though they are still in their graves, the fact that they are also somehow still living is more appropriate to the concept of immortality than to resurrection (see Reflections on 28:1-20). The conceptualizations of immortality and resurrection are here blended, since on any understanding, Abraham, Isaac, and Jacob are not "risen." Although the two pictures of "immortality"

and "resurrection" are merged, the issue is clear: God's faithfulness and power is their hope for life beyond the grave, not something about their own nature.

None of this is abstract, speculative thinking. The one who declares it is on the way to his own death, freely accepted, and goes his way in the confidence that God will act beyond his death to continue the relationship of Sonship and to vindicate the meaning of his life (11:25-27; 16:21; 17:22-23; 20:18-19).

22:33. Matthew reintroduces the crowds and their response, taken from Mark 11:18b (as he had transferred 11:18a to 21:15).[486] The reference to teaching, introduced here, forms a bracket with the Sadducees' opening address to Jesus as "teacher." They were hostile, but the crowds are still positive and impressed. Matthew will reintroduce the Pharisees at the beginning of the next scene (both the crowds and the Pharisees are absent in Mark's Gospel). This concluding note has the effect of bringing the Pharisees' hostility into sharper profile.

---

485. The meaning of Exod 3:6 in its historical context is that Yahweh is the God worshiped in the past by the patriarchs. A second difficulty for moderns is that the continuation of personal existence after death, here affirmed to be implied in Exod 3:6, is still not *resurrection.*

486. The Markan contrast between the responses of the chief priests and scribes over against the crowds to Jesus' Temple expulsion (11:18a) becomes in Matthew a contrast between the Pharisees and the crowds over Jesus' teaching.

MATTHEW 22:34-40, THE GREAT COMMANDMENT

NIV	NRSV
[34]Hearing that Jesus had silenced the Sadducees, the Pharisees got together. [35]One of them, an expert in the law, tested him with this question: [36]"Teacher, which is the greatest commandment in the Law?" [37]Jesus replied: " 'Love the Lord your God with all your heart and with all your soul and with all your mind.'[a] [38]This is the first and greatest commandment. [39]And the second is like it: 'Love your neighbor as yourself.'[b] [40]All the Law and the Prophets hang on these two commandments."	34When the Pharisees heard that he had silenced the Sadducees, they gathered together, [35]and one of them, a lawyer, asked him a question to test him. [36]"Teacher, which commandment in the law is the greatest?" [37]He said to him, " 'You shall love the Lord your God with all your heart, and with all your soul, and with all your mind.' [38]This is the greatest and first commandment. [39]And a second is like it: 'You shall love your neighbor as yourself.' [40]On these two commandments hang all the law and the prophets."
a37 Deut. 6:5 b39 Lev. 19:18	

COMMENTARY

Matthew has already presented Jesus as teaching the centrality of love in the life of the disciples, and he has shown that love for "neighbor" includes the "enemy" (5:21-48, esp. 23-48). Here, the double commandment of love becomes part of the controversy series extending from 21:23 through 22:46. In the corresponding section of Mark, a friendly scribe makes a sincere inquiry, Jesus replies, the scribe commends him for his answer, and Jesus responds positively, declaring that the scribe is not far from the kingdom of God (12:28-34). Matthew's rewriting changes the form and character of the pericope from a scholastic dialogue to a controversy story.[487] The group of Pharisees present since 21:23 (cf. 45) reappear, but do not engage Jesus directly. Their gathering together reproduces verbatim the language of Ps 2:2, where the leaders gather together against the Lord and his anointed.[488] A professional theologian from their ranks (the only occurrence of "lawyer" [νομικός *nomikos*] in Matthew)[489] becomes their spokesman. His question is no longer sincere or collegial, as in Mark, but is to "test" Jesus (πειράζω *peirazō,* as in 4:1, 3; 16:1; 19:3; 22:18; only the devil and the Pharisees are the subject of this verb in Matthew). The address, "teacher," is insincere and stands in contrast to the believers' address, "Lord." Jesus has just defended the Pharisees' point of view, as he does throughout this section (cf. 23:1-2!), yet their response is to test him as did Satan.[490] In Matthew's understanding, this is more than a religious debate; once again, the two kingdoms confront each other (see on 12:22-37).

The nature of the test is not clear. The clue may be given by Matthew's addition "in the Law." The rabbis had counted 613 commands (248 positive commands, corresponding to the number of parts of the body; 365 negative commands, corresponding to the days of the year). Although rabbinical teachers could also indulge in giving summaries of the Law, there was also the view that all commandments were equal, with any ranking of them being mere human presumption in evaluating the divine law, all of which was equally binding. The lawyer may be attempting to draw Jesus into this debate and get him to make some statement that could be interpreted as disparaging toward (some part of) the Law, such as declaring the "moral law" more important than the "ceremonial law." This is a charge to which the Markan version of this story is very amenable, since not only Jesus but also the scribe subscribes to it.

In Mark as in Deut 6:4-5, the command to love God is part of the Shema, which begins with the confession of the oneness of God, the closest thing to a universal creed in Judaism. Why Matthew drops this initial confession is unclear. Although there was a rabbinic tradition of "summaries of the Torah," the combination of the command to love God and love neighbor is distinctive of the synoptic Jesus.[491] Matthew has slightly revised it to correspond more closely to the LXX text, omitting Mark's fourth element ("strength") and changing Mark's preposition three times from ἐξ (*ex*) to ἐν (*en*), both translated "with." Matthew's most dramatic change is to replace the Markan conclusion's positive interchange between Jesus and the scribe with Jesus' pronouncement (v. 40) that the whole of the law and the prophets "hang" from these two commandments. In the context of the Matthean narrative theology as a whole, this is more than another summary of

---

487. See Victor Paul Furnish, *The Love Command in the New Testament* (Nashville: Abingdon, 1972) 30-31.

488. Matthew uses "gather" (συνάγω *synagō,* the verbal form of συναγωγή *synagōgē* ["synagogue"]) twenty-four times, more than all the other Gospels together. Sometimes the verb is used with an ominous tone, reflecting the conflicts of Matthew's church with the synagogue (cf. 2:4; 22:34, 41; [24:28?]; 26:3, 57; 27:17, 27, 62), just as the term *synagogue* itself often has forbidding overtones (6:2; 10:17; 23:34). At other times, Matthew uses the verb indirectly of the "gathering(s)" of Jesus' disciples (12:30; 13:47; 18:20; 22:10).

489. Since "lawyer" is often used by Luke for "scribes," including in this passage, the word may not be original in Matthew but a copyist's intrusion from Luke. A few MSS support this possibility (λ, ε, sy³, arm; Or^lat.)

490. Here, too, Jesus affirms the Pharisaic point of view. The love command was one of the three texts regularly included in the phylacteries (*tephillin*) they wore (Exod 13:1-16; Deut 6:4-9; 11:13-21). Also in 17:24 Jesus sides with the Pharisaic view.

491. It is not found in the rabbinic corpus or Qumran texts, but a similar combination is found in the *Testaments of the Twelve Patriarchs* (under Christian influence? cf. *Test. Iss.* 5:2; 7:6; *Test. Dan.* 5:3). The pattern, but not the words, seems to be reflected in Philo *On the Special Law Books* 2:63; *On Abraham* 208.

the law. Nor is it a statement explaining that all the other commands of the law can be exegetically derived from these two commands. Rather, Jesus declares the command to love God and neighbor (on their unity as one command, see below) to be the hermeneutical key for interpreting all the divine revelation—not only the Law, but the Prophets as well.[492]

492. On the Law and the Prophets as a Matthean theme, see Commentary on 5:17 and 7:12. Matthew began his narrative with a situation in which a righteous man allowed love to be the interpretive principle to guide him in living by a law that seemed contrary to the will of God in that situation (1:18-25).

REFLECTIONS

Although the Sermon on the Mount has already included an extensive section of Jesus' teaching to his disciples on love as fundamental to the life of discipleship (5:21-48), in this concluding encounter with his opponents Matthew gives Jesus another opportunity to summarize the core of his teaching (as 7:12). There, the teaching was to his disciples; here, it is to his opponents, in the controversy situation showing his orthodoxy as an advocate of the whole of the Law and the Prophets. Since Matthew here focuses on the polemical aspect of the scene, he does not develop the theological issues that interest the contemporary interpreter (cf. Luke, who relocates the passage, 10:25-28): (1) the meaning of "love," (2) the meaning of "neighbor," and (3) the meaning of Jesus' responding with two commands.

1. The word used here for "love" is ἀγαπάω (agapaō), the verbal form of ἀγάπη (agapē). The interpreter should first dispel the tradition that has become almost sacrosanct that there is some magic in the meaning of the Greek word agapē. There is certainly something special about the Christian understanding of love for God, neighbor, and world as expressed in the NT. But this is not bound up with the meaning of a particular Greek word. The author who composed in Greek was in approximately the same situation as the English interpreter in having several words for "love" that overlapped in meaning. In Greek as in English there was and is no single Greek word with an inherent meaning that refers exclusively to the kind of love with which God loves the world and with which Christians are commanded to love God, each other, and their neighbors. Let it clearly be said: agapē was not such a word. Neither Jesus nor Christians invented this word, found in the LXX in a variety of senses: for the love of God (Deut 6:5) and neighbor (Lev 19:18) as here, but also of adulterous lust (e.g., Jer 2:25, 33), and of the love of money (Eccl 5:9). It is used as a synonym for ἐπιθυμία (epithymia) in Wisdom of Solomon 6, and for φιλία (philia) in 7:14; 8:2. The NT takes over this variety of usage of agapē. It is used in 2 Pet 2:15 for Balaam's love for money. In Luke 6:32 it is used for sinners' love for each other. In John 3:19 it is used for the love of evil people for the darkness. In addition, both agapē (noun) and agapaō (verb) are used as synonyms for φιλέω (phileō) / φιλία (philia), as in the celebrated but misunderstood John 21:15-17. Likewise, phileō, supposed in the traditional interpretation to express mutual love as in friendship, inferior to the self-giving love of agapē, is in fact used both for the deepest self-sacrificing love of both human beings and God (Matt 10:37; John 5:20; 11:3, 36; 16:27; 20:2; 1 Cor 16:22; Titus 3:15; Rev 3:19). When Christians use the word love with reference to God, to the deepest human relationships, and of the stance they are called to exercise toward the world, the content of this word is not to be filled in from the supposed meaning of a special Greek word, but from the understanding of God's nature made known in Christ. It is from this revelatory perspective that we come to know love as unmotivated and unmanipulated, unconditional and unlimited.[493] Such love is not a matter of feeling, which cannot be commanded in any case, but of commitment and action. It is at the farthest pole from sentimentality and is related to the OT word for "covenant love" or "steadfast love" (חסד ḥesed).

493. See especially the influential analysis of Anders Nygren, *Agape and Eros,* trans. Philip S. Watson (New York: Harper & Row, 1969).

2. In the OT context, a neighbor was one's fellow Israelite. Matthew's understanding has already extended the love to which the disciple is called to embrace even the enemy (see on 5:43; 25:31-46). This is in contrast to the Johannine love commandment, understood to be "new" rather than the core of the biblical revelation, which is restricted to the Christian insider (John 13:34; 1 John 2:9-10; 3:15, exclusively of "the brother or sister").

3. It is striking that Jesus is asked for one command but responds with two. Matthew alone specifically adds that the second is "like" (ὅμοια *homoia*) the first. This does not mean merely that it is similar, but that it is of equal importance and inseparable from the first. The great command to love God has as its inseparable counterpart the command to love neighbor. One cannot first love God and then, as a second task, love one's neighbor. To love God is to love one's neighbor, and vice versa (25:31-46).

MATTHEW 22:41-46, THE QUESTION ABOUT DAVID'S SON

NIV	NRSV

⁴¹While the Pharisees were gathered together, Jesus asked them, ⁴²"What do you think about the Christ*a*? Whose son is he?"
 	
"The son of David," they replied.
 	
⁴³He said to them, "How is it then that David, speaking by the Spirit, calls him 'Lord'? For he says,
 	
⁴⁴"'The Lord said to my Lord:
    "Sit at my right hand
until I put your enemies
    under your feet."'*b*
 	
⁴⁵If then David calls him 'Lord,' how can he be his son?" ⁴⁶No one could say a word in reply, and from that day on no one dared to ask him any more questions.
 	
a42 Or *Messiah*   *b44* Psalm 110:1
	41Now while the Pharisees were gathered together, Jesus asked them this question: ⁴²"What do you think of the Messiah?*a* Whose son is he?" They said to him, "The son of David." ⁴³He said to them, "How is it then that David by the Spirit*b* calls him Lord, saying,
	
	⁴⁴ 'The Lord said to my Lord,
	    "Sit at my right hand,
	        until I put your enemies under your feet"'?
	⁴⁵If David thus calls him Lord, how can he be his son?" ⁴⁶No one was able to give him an answer, nor from that day did anyone dare to ask him any more questions.
	
	*a*Or *Christ* *b*Gk *in spirit*

COMMENTARY

In Mark this was a concluding rhetorical question, part of a monologue by Jesus challenging the identification of the Messiah and Son of David. Mark affirmed Jesus as Messiah, but challenged the explication of this title in terms of "Son of David," which for him was associated too much with violence, military conquest, and a this-worldly kingdom. Matthew is positive about "Son of David" as a christological title for Jesus (cf. Excursus "Matthean Christology," 353-61, and esp. 1:2-25). He rewrites this scene as a bracket to 21:1-9, in which Jesus is properly hailed as Son of David. He transforms it from a monologue into a controversy dialogue in which Jesus exposes the Pharisees as inadequate interpreters of Scripture.

22:41. Again the Pharisees are introduced by Matthew, replacing Mark's general audience. Once more they are pictured as "gathering," with the negative overtones of the synagogue (see above on 22:34). Jesus is no longer "teaching," as in Mark, but takes the initiative (Matthew has inserted teaching into 21:23).

22:42. After overcoming the series of challenges from the Pharisees and other leaders in 21:23–22:40, Jesus takes the initiative with a direct question, "What do you think of the Messiah? Whose son is he?" In a Semitic context, "son" connotes more than biology and physical lineage; it has to do with character, the category to which one belongs and whom one obeys (see Excursus "Matthean Christology," 353-61).

On the surface, the Pharisees' response that the Christ is the Son of David is correct. In contrast to Mark, Matthew not only agrees but emphasizes this identification (1:1-25). Of course, Matthew and his Pharisee opponents disagreed as to whether Jesus is the Messiah, but not on whether "Son of David" is a valid christological title. In this regard, the issue is the meaning of "Son of David."

22:43-46. This is the point of Jesus' question in the text of Matthew, in which the key word "how" (πῶς *pōs*) has been relocated. It is no longer, as in Mark, a rhetorical question as to whether the scribes are correct in calling the Messiah "Son of David," implying that they are wrong (*pōs* as in 7:4; 12:26, 29, 34; 23:33). Now the question Matthew wants to deal with is the exegetical question of how David, presumed to be the divinely inspired author of Psalm 110, can call the Messiah "Lord" and yet have a "son" who is the Messiah, which Matthew emphatically affirms to be the case. The Pharisees, claiming to be the teachers of God's people, cannot explain this biblical question, but the teacher of Matthew's church can explain it: (1) As the Christ, Jesus is both Lord and Son of David—but one must have faith in Jesus as the Christ before this makes sense. (2) The Son of David idea is transformed in the process of Christian appropriation as a christological title. If the Son of David is *Jesus,* it has a new content.

Early Christianity found much support for its christological view in this psalm, the most cited passage in the NT, being directly quoted or alluded to thirty-seven times. It is unclear whether it was already interpreted messianically in contemporary Judaism. In the original psalm, the first "Lord" refers to Yahweh, the second one to the anointed Israelite king: God installs the king, called "my Lord" by the psalmist, on the throne at God's "right hand"—i.e., in the palace complex south of the Temple complex (the Hebrew word for "right" and "south" is the same). As an "anointed one," the king is here understood messianically. Thus the question is how David, the presumed writer of the psalm, could by divine inspiration address the Messiah as his "Lord," if the Messiah is also his "son." The Pharisees accept all the premises of this argument (so troublesome to moderns), but cannot answer, thereby showing themselves to be inadequate interpreters of the Scripture.[494] The chief function of this passage is to present Jesus as victor in the hostile series of disputes; they have challenged him unsuccessfully four times, but are put to silence the first time he takes the initiative. It is important to Matthew to show Jesus' superiority in advance of the trial, for he immediately turns to address his disciples and the crowds, who are still potential disciples. After having bested his opponents, Jesus will not confront them again until the trial, when he will be almost completely silent (23:13-39 is not actually addressed to the Pharisees). Henceforth, Jesus addresses only crowds and disciples. Thus 22:46 decisively brings the disputation to an end. Matthew relocates and rewrites Mark 12:34*b* in order to do so. Thus the "then" (τότε *tote*) of 23:1 is disjunctive and may indicate a new day.[495]

494. These issues have apparently been the object of reflection in Matthew's church. Matthean scribes can answer how the Christ (Jesus) is both Son of God and Son of David (see Commentary on 1:1-25). In the process, they have also transformed the meaning of "Son of David" from the militaristic savior who conquers by violence into the meek king who heals. For the faith expressed in their christology, both "Lord" and "Son of David" are proper titles for the Christ, because Jesus as the Christ has transformed the content of both titles.

495. Since 26:1 seems to relate the speech of 23:1–25:46 to what follows, Matthew may intend to locate this speech on Wednesday. His own day-by-day chronology does not become explicit until 26:1. (See chronology on p. 401).

REFLECTIONS

This passage, which pictures Jesus in a theological debate with the religious leaders, quotes one of the favorite Scripture verses of the early church: Psalm 110:1. As noted in the Commentary, this verse is the most often cited passage in the NT, appearing in some form thirty-seven times. It was surely a frequent part of early Christian worship. What must the first readers of Matthew have thought to hear something cherished from their worship coming from the lips of Jesus in a theological argument? It would be like watching a political debate, only to hear one of the candidates suddenly say, "When I survey the wondrous cross, on which the Prince of Glory died, my richest gain I count but loss and pour contempt on all my pride"!

At the very least, the readers of Matthew know that language of their worship is connected to the language of their Lord. They also realize, perhaps, that their worship is a kind of theological debate with the culture. Any group who dares to sing "Praise God, from whom all blessings flow" is engaging in a strenuous argument with a culture that sings "Praise the celebrities and the powerful and the rich, from whom everything the rest of us is after flows."

MATTHEW 23:1–25:46, THE JUDGMENT DISCOURSE

OVERVIEW

Day 2: Tuesday, continued. Chapter 23 is often seen as a separate speech, the "Woes against the Pharisees," with 24:1–25:46 constituting a distinct "Eschatological Discourse." The following considerations, however, make it better to interpret 23:1–25:46 as constituting in Matthew's understanding a single, unified speech, Jesus' final discourse.

(1) Matthew 22:46 has decisively brought the preceding confrontation with Jesus' opponents to an end (see above), so that at 23:1 Jesus turns to address his followers, actual and potential. The "then" (τότε tote) of 23:1 is thus disjunctive, constituting a new beginning.

(2) Matthew's overall structure calls for five major speeches (see Introduction). Unless 23:1-39 is included with chaps. 24–25, it must be seen as a lengthy speech unit in a "narrative" section.

(3) By adding the speech against the Pharisees to the beginning and additional eschatological warnings to the end, Matthew builds the apocalyptic discourse of Mark 13 into a grand concluding discourse that corresponds in length to the opening discourse (5–7 = 23–25). It also now corresponds in other ways as well: Whereas the Sermon on the Mount begins with blessings, this speech begins with woes (5:1-12 = 23:13-33); both speeches involve a mountain on which Jesus sits to teach, with crowds and disciples as hearers (5:1; 7:29 = 23:1; 24:3); in the closing scene of

each speech, false disciples say "Lord, Lord" and are told "I never knew you" (7:21-27 = 25:11).

(4) There is no concluding formula after 23:39. The change of location at 24:1 is not a conclusion, but a transition like that of 13:36, in which there is a shift of audience from crowds to disciples. Verse 36 does not divide the parable discourse into two separate speeches, despite the change of location and audience, nor does the transition at 24:1-3a (cf. also 15:1-20). The concluding formula is first found in 26:1, which both binds 23–25 together as one discourse and relates it to the other four major discourses in Matthew's structure.

(5) Even though Matthew is here following the Markan order, he omits the Markan story of the widow's offering (Mark 12:41-44) in order to bring together the judgments against the Pharisees and the eschatological discourse into one great speech of warning and judgment, and to connect the prediction of the Temple's destruction with 23:38.

(6) The insertion of 23:37-39, composed of a judgment lament and an eschatological promise, unites the preceding judgments with the following eschatology.

(7) Thematic connections bind the section 23:1–25:46 into one discourse: (a) The overarching theme of 23:1–25:46 is judgment, the present and coming judgment of God exercised by the Son of Man. Just as judgment comes at the

conclusion of each of the five great speech complexes (7:24-27; 10:32-42 [39, saving/losing; 40-42, future reward]; 13:47-50; 18:23-35), so also Jesus' final speech is one great judgment speech, leading up to the scene of the last judgment in 25:31-46, unique to Matthew and giving the key to the Matthean speech. (b) Matthew's addition of "kingdom of God" terminology at 23:13; 24:14; 25:1, 34, 40—none of which is in his sources—thematically unites the discourse, particularly by framing it with 23:13 ("closing the kingdom") and 25:40 ("entrance into the kingdom"). (c) Chapter 23 already has several thoroughly eschatological notes. Eschatology does not first begin in chap. 24; in 23:12, the initial admonitions are given an eschatological grounding. The woes of vv. 13-36 are an eschatological form as well. Other eschatological notes are found in 23:13, 32, 34-39.

The presumed break at 24:1-3 actually unites what precedes with what follows: "These things" of 24:3 refers to the destruction of the Temple in 24:2. But the temple motif connects 23:38 and 24:1-2.

(8) Matthean editing and composition has united the speech even in details. By adding "hypocrites" to 24:51, Matthew has related it to 23:13-36, just as the addition of "Christ" to 24:5

contrasts to 23:10. The repeated "coming" of the judge-figure in 24:30, 42-45; 25:10, 19, 27 corresponds to 23:35-39; the deeds of mercy called for in 25:31-46 correspond to the "weightier matters of the law" neglected in 23:23, where Matthew has added "mercy" and "faith[fulness]" to Q; the "desolating sacrilege" of 24:15 corresponds to 23:38, where "desolate" is added by Matthew.[496]

Matthew's composition has the effect of incorporating Mark's "little apocalypse" into a much larger discourse concerned with judgment, all addressed to insiders and potential followers. Rather than being seen as two speeches, one of which condemns outsiders and the other imparting eschatological instruction, the whole discourse functions as warning to insiders to live an authentic life devoted to deeds of justice and mercy, in the light of the eschatological victory of God and coming judgment on present unfaithfulness.

Like the Sermon on the Mount, this great speech complex is a Matthean composition from various sources.

496. Reading ἔρημος *erēmos* with B, L, *ff²*, sy[s], sa, bo[pt].

Figure 11: The Structure of the Judgment Discourse		
I. Judgment on the Present:		
To Crowds and Disciples	**23:1-39**	
A. Warnings	23:1-12	= M + Mark 12:37-40
		+ Q 11:39-47
B. Woes	23:13-36	= M + Q 11:39-52
C. Lament	23:37-39	= Q 13:34-35
II. The Coming Judgment: To Disciples	**24:1–25:46**	
A. Jesus' Prediction, Disciples' Question	24:1-3	= Mark 13:1-4
B. The "Little Apocalypse"	24:4-31	= Mark 13:5-27
1. The Beginning of Labor Pangs		
(ἀρχὴ ὠδίνων *archē ōdinōn*)	24:4-8	= Mark 13:5-8
2. The Great Tribulation		
(θλῖψις μεγάλη *thlipsis megalē*)	24:9-28	= Mark 13:9, 13,
		14-23;[497] Q 17:23-24, 37
3. The Parousia of the Son of Man		
(ὁ υἱὸς τοῦ ἀνθρώπου ἐρχόμενος		
ho huios tou anthrōpou erchomenos)	24:29-31	= Mark 13:24-27
C. Parables and Warnings	24:32–25:46	
1. The Fig Tree	24:32-35	= Mark 13:28-32
2. The Days of Noah	24:36-42	= Q 17:26-35, Mark 13:35
3. The Thief	24:43-44	= Q 12:39-40
4. The Good and Wicked Servants	24:45-51	= Q 12:42-46
5. The Ten Bridesmaids	25:1-13	1-10 = M; 11-13 = Q 13:25-8,
		Mark 13:33
6. The Talents	25:14-30	= Q 19:12-27
7. The Last Judgment	25:31-46	= M

497. Mark 13:9-13 was incorporated in the mission discourse, Matt 10:17-22.

Matthew 23:1-39, Judgment on the Present: To Crowds and Disciples

Matthew 23:1-12, Warnings

NIV

23 Then Jesus said to the crowds and to his disciples: [2]"The teachers of the law and the Pharisees sit in Moses' seat. [3]So you must obey them and do everything they tell you. But do not do what they do, for they do not practice what they preach. [4]They tie up heavy loads and put them on men's shoulders, but they themselves are not willing to lift a finger to move them.

[5]"Everything they do is done for men to see: They make their phylacteries[a] wide and the tassels on their garments long; [6]they love the place of honor at banquets and the most important seats in the synagogues; [7]they love to be greeted in the marketplaces and to have men call them 'Rabbi.'

[8]"But you are not to be called 'Rabbi,' for you have only one Master and you are all brothers. [9]And do not call anyone on earth 'father,' for you have one Father, and he is in heaven. [10]Nor are you to be called 'teacher,' for you have one Teacher, the Christ.[b] [11]The greatest among you will be your servant. [12]For whoever exalts himself will be humbled, and whoever humbles himself will be exalted."

[a]5 That is, boxes containing Scripture verses, worn on forehead and arm   [b]10 Or *Messiah*

NRSV

23 Then Jesus said to the crowds and to his disciples, [2]"The scribes and the Pharisees sit on Moses' seat; [3]therefore, do whatever they teach you and follow it; but do not do as they do, for they do not practice what they teach. [4]They tie up heavy burdens, hard to bear,[a] and lay them on the shoulders of others; but they themselves are unwilling to lift a finger to move them. [5]They do all their deeds to be seen by others; for they make their phylacteries broad and their fringes long. [6]They love to have the place of honor at banquets and the best seats in the synagogues, [7]and to be greeted with respect in the marketplaces, and to have people call them rabbi. [8]But you are not to be called rabbi, for you have one teacher, and you are all students.[b] [9]And call no one your father on earth, for you have one Father—the one in heaven. [10]Nor are you to be called instructors, for you have one instructor, the Messiah.[c] [11]The greatest among you will be your servant. [12]All who exalt themselves will be humbled, and all who humble themselves will be exalted."

[a]Other ancient authorities lack *hard to bear*   [b]Gk *brothers*
[c]Or *the Christ*

COMMENTARY

23:1-3a. In Matthew's chronology it is still Tuesday, and Jesus is still in the Temple precincts, where he has been since 21:23. The audience is different, as Jesus now turns to his disciples and the crowds (cf. 5:1). The crowds represent potential disciples who are still positive toward Jesus (21:8-9, 11, 26, 46; 22:33). Both groups are transparent to Christians and sympathizers in Matthew's own day. "Scribes" and "Pharisees" are distinct, but overlapping, categories. Scribes were

a professional class with formal training, somewhat like lawyers in contemporary American society.[498] They were schooled in the tradition and its application to current issues. Pharisees were a group within Judaism defined by strictly religious rules, composed mostly of laypersons without formal theological training (see Introduction). Some

498. The NIV's consistent translation as "teachers of the law" is thus sometimes misleading, e.g., at 23:34. Teaching is not the primary function of scribes.

scribes were also Pharisees, but few Pharisees were scribes. Together, they represent the Jewish leadership of Matthew's time (but not necessarily that of Jesus). The conflicts between synagogue and church, reflected in 23:1-39, indicate the growing Jewish-Christian conflict of the latter part of the first century.

"Moses' seat" is a metaphorical expression representing the teaching and administrative authority of the synagogue leadership, scribes and Pharisees. Surprisingly, and in contrast both to what precedes (16:6, 12) and to what immediately follows (23:4, 16-22), Jesus condemns only the practice of the scribes and Pharisees, not their teaching (see Reflections below). Jesus has, in fact, just been defending the doctrinal perspective of the Pharisees (22:23-40). Historically, there was more in common between earliest Christianity and the emerging Pharisaic leadership of formative Judaism than Matthean polemics suggest. Such commonalities are represented in elements of the tradition, as here. Matthew probably intends by the present passage that the Pharisees and scribes are right in founding their way of life on exposition of the Torah, which his Christian community also affirms (5:17-48), without here taking into account their differing interpretations (see Commentary on 15:1-20)

23:3b-7. Matthew's critique is three-pronged: (1) *They say but do not do* (23:3a).[499] Here as elsewhere, Matthew juxtaposes mere talking with actual conduct (6:1-18; 7:21-23; 21:28-32). The scribes and Pharisees also opposed such hypocrisy and emphasized that practice must correspond to teaching.[500] Of course, there were Christians whose life was a contradiction of their teaching, and it is these to whom the word of the Matthean Jesus is actually directed.

(2) *They burden others while failing to act themselves* (23:4). The Pharisees encouraged the people as a whole to live out their vocation as a priestly nation (Exod 19:6), especially after the destruction of the Temple and the cessation of functions of the actual priests. In other words,

they applied the Priestly purity laws to the people as a whole. Matthew understood their efforts as replacing God's law with human tradition, an intolerable and misdirected burden for ordinary people (15:1-20). The alternative to the "burden" placed on people's shoulders by the Pharisees is Jesus' own "yoke" (11:28-30), which is "easy" not because it is less stringent (5:17-48), but because it was oriented in another direction.

(3) *They act for the wrong reason: to make an impression on others* (23:5-7). After the destruction of Jerusalem in 70 CE, the emerging rabbinic leadership emphasized external signs of piety, not because they were hypocrites interested in externals, but as distinctive markers of the holy people of God in a pluralistic society. They were concerned that Judaism not become homogenized into the surrounding world after the destruction of their national shrine. Matthew's church was tempted to conform to these practices and was under pressure from the leadership of the synagogues to do so. Thus Matthew's critique, although at the story level represented as Jesus' critique of the Pharisees of his own time, functions in Matthew's time as warnings to the leadership of his own church against these practices. "Phylacteries" is Matthew's term for the *tephillin,* small leather boxes containing portions of the Torah (Exod 13:1-16; Deut 6:4-9; 11:13-32) strapped to the forehead and arm during the recitation of prayers, in literal obedience to Deut 6:8. The "fringes" are those commanded as part of the dress of every Israelite, later understood as the tassels attached to the prayer shawl (Num 15:38-39; Deut 22:12). The "best seats" in the synagogue refer to the place of honor at the front, facing the congregation, occupied by teachers and respected leaders. "Rabbi" in Jesus' day had become a generic honorific title, but in the restructuring of Judaism after 70 CE there was a tendency to restrict it to the official teachers of formative Judaism.

23:8-10. The disciples have been indirectly the addressees throughout. With an eightfold use of "you," Matthew now turns to them directly. The leadership of Matthew's church was tempted to imitate the clericalism he saw developing in his Jewish opponents; Matthew himself opposed it. As is typical of emergent groups from traditional ones, there is a strong egalitarian feeling and distrust of "official" leadership. Although the word

---

499. This was stock-in-trade of polemic in the Hellenistic world, Jewish and Gentile, a charge made by every philosophical school against its opponents. To understand the polemical rhetoric of 23:1-39 in its ancient context, very helpful is Luke T. Johnson, "The New Testament's Anti-Jewish Slander" *JBL* 108/3 (1989) 419-41. After citing much evidence documenting the nature of intra-Jewish polemic, Johnson concludes: "By the measure of Hellenistic conventions, and certainly by the measure of contemporary Jewish polemic, the NT's slander against fellow Jews is relatively mild" (441).

500. *m. ʾAbot.* 3:9, 17; *ʾAbot R. Nat.* A:24; B:31.

translated "rabbi" (רבי *rabbi*) literally means "my great one," it had become a customary term that evoked no more awareness of its literal meaning than does "sir" in English ("Lord," derived from κύριος *kyrios*). Matthew, however, may have had in view also the literal meaning in contrast to the Christian community as "little ones" (cf. 18:1-10). Matthew has Jesus addressed as "rabbi" only by outsiders and by Judas (cf. 26:25, 49).[501] Here, Matthew seems to forbid its use for Christian leaders, but allows it, or even encourages it, for Jesus. The NIV's "brothers [and sisters]" is better for ἀδελφοί (*adelphoi*) than the NRSV's "students," the point being that members of the Christian community are members of the family of God (12:46-50), where distinctions emphasized by titles are inappropriate.

Precisely this line of thought is continued in the reference to "father," a biblical and traditional honorific title (e.g., for Elijah and Elisha, 2 Kgs 2:12; 13:14; for revered Jewish teachers in *m. 'Abot*) that was being appropriated by formative Judaism. Just as he restricts "rabbi" to Jesus, so also he restricts "Father" to God.[502] "Father" is

Matthew's favorite designation for deity, reflecting the distinctive practice of Jesus (cf. 6:9).

"Instructor" (NRSV) or "teacher" (NIV) translates καθηγητής (*kathēgētēs*), used only here in the NT. It apparently reflects another title in use among Matthew's Jewish opponents, perhaps מורה (*môreh*), used of the "Teacher of Righteousness" at Qumran. As in the case of "rabbi," the title is restricted to Jesus.

Matthew's church did have a class of leaders (see Introduction), but Matthew regarded them in a more charismatic and egalitarian perspective. There may already have been tendencies in Matthew's church toward the form of church polity ("monarchical episcopate") advocated by Ignatius of Antioch only a few years later.[503] To be sure, one who claims to be "just" a "little one" can exercise more false pride than a sincere rabbi teaching the Torah. Here as elsewhere, externals such as titles are only pointers to the inner attitude, which is the realm of Matthew's real concern.

23:11-12. Leadership in the Christian community is to be servant leadership. A "minister" is a "servant" (διάκονος *diakonos*, "deacon").

501. Matthew omits "rabbi" from Peter's address in Mark 11:21 = Matt 21:20.

502. The fact that this is not uniform NT teaching is seen, e.g., from Paul's references to himself as "father" of his converts (1 Cor 4:15; cf. Acts 7:1; 22:1; 1 Thess 2:11; Phlm 10; 1 John 2:13).

503. E.g., *Trallians II, 1-2;* III, 1.

REFLECTIONS

1. The modern reader may hear a text about "making phylacteries broad and fringes long" as evidence of the irrelevance of the Bible, since such petty sins seem far removed from the sinful realities we are called to confront. Or it may seem directed to persons long ago and far away, or at least only to ostentatious examples of religiosity in our own time. From either perspective, such a text seems to have little to do with us. A closer reading may reveal that something near the center of our own life and being is here addressed, something that seems so right and human. We all like to be acknowledged at social gatherings; we all like to be greeted in the marketplace. It is not a matter of being hypocritical, but of being human: We are social creatures, and we like to be known and liked; it strikes at our sense of self-worth to be ignored or subtly put down socially. All of us live under internally imposed constraints of peer pressure and the desire to be accepted by others, to be insiders, to belong. Today's readers might well be wary of reading this text as a way of smugly criticizing the presumed ostentation of first-century Jews—easy to caricature from a distance and with our ignorance of Judaism—and instead attempt to address the text to our own desire to fit in and be recognized and appreciated (promotions, advancements!). *Should* this even be attempted? It strikes at the modern cultural idol of self-esteem. *Can* this be done, or are we all sentenced to playing out our lives as responses to these pressures for place and recognition? Matthew proposes an alternative world, a world seen from the perspective of the kingdom of God, an alternative family where the approval of God removes the heavy yoke of self-justification. There is more here than cheap shots at religious phonies in their long robes.

2. An irony of Christian history is that there has often been little correlation between the use of titles and the attitude here called for. Those in the Christian tradition who, despite the warning of this passage, adopted such titles as "Father" for leaders have often been truly humble servants. Those who insisted on being only "ministers" have sometimes been arrogant and tyrannical. The conclusion of this section points to the eschatological judgment when authentic greatness and humility will be revealed and rewarded on quite a different basis than the adoption of titles.

Matthew 23:13-36, Woes

NIV

13"Woe to you, teachers of the law and Pharisees, you hypocrites! You shut the kingdom of heaven in men's faces. You yourselves do not enter, nor will you let those enter who are trying to.[a]

15"Woe to you, teachers of the law and Pharisees, you hypocrites! You travel over land and sea to win a single convert, and when he becomes one, you make him twice as much a son of hell as you are.

16"Woe to you, blind guides! You say, 'If anyone swears by the temple, it means nothing; but if anyone swears by the gold of the temple, he is bound by his oath.' 17You blind fools! Which is greater: the gold, or the temple that makes the gold sacred? 18You also say, 'If anyone swears by the altar, it means nothing; but if anyone swears by the gift on it, he is bound by his oath.' 19You blind men! Which is greater: the gift, or the altar that makes the gift sacred? 20Therefore, he who swears by the altar swears by it and by everything on it. 21And he who swears by the temple swears by it and by the one who dwells in it. 22And he who swears by heaven swears by God's throne and by the one who sits on it.

23"Woe to you, teachers of the law and Pharisees, you hypocrites! You give a tenth of your spices—mint, dill and cummin. But you have neglected the more important matters of the law—justice, mercy and faithfulness. You should have practiced the latter, without neglecting the former. 24You blind guides! You strain out a gnat but swallow a camel.

NRSV

13"But woe to you, scribes and Pharisees, hypocrites! For you lock people out of the kingdom of heaven. For you do not go in yourselves, and when others are going in, you stop them.[a] 15Woe to you, scribes and Pharisees, hypocrites! For you cross sea and land to make a single convert, and you make the new convert twice as much a child of hell[b] as yourselves.

16"Woe to you, blind guides, who say, 'Whoever swears by the sanctuary is bound by nothing, but whoever swears by the gold of the sanctuary is bound by the oath.' 17You blind fools! For which is greater, the gold or the sanctuary that has made the gold sacred? 18And you say, 'Whoever swears by the altar is bound by nothing, but whoever swears by the gift that is on the altar is bound by the oath.' 19How blind you are! For which is greater, the gift or the altar that makes the gift sacred? 20So whoever swears by the altar, swears by it and by everything on it; 21and whoever swears by the sanctuary, swears by it and by the one who dwells in it; 22and whoever swears by heaven, swears by the throne of God and by the one who is seated upon it.

23"Woe to you, scribes and Pharisees, hypocrites! For you tithe mint, dill, and cummin, and have neglected the weightier matters of the law: justice and mercy and faith. It is these you ought to have practiced without neglecting the others. 24You blind guides! You strain out a gnat but swallow a camel!

<hr>

a13 Some manuscripts to. 14Woe to you, teachers of the law and Pharisees, you hypocrites! You devour widows' houses and for a show make lengthy prayers. Therefore you will be punished more severely.

aOther authorities add here (or after verse 12) verse 14, Woe to you, scribes and Pharisees, hypocrites! For you devour widows' houses and for the sake of appearance you make long prayers; therefore you will receive the greater condemnation b Gk Gehenna

NIV

25"Woe to you, teachers of the law and Pharisees, you hypocrites! You clean the outside of the cup and dish, but inside they are full of greed and self-indulgence. 26Blind Pharisee! First clean the inside of the cup and dish, and then the outside also will be clean.

27"Woe to you, teachers of the law and Pharisees, you hypocrites! You are like whitewashed tombs, which look beautiful on the outside but on the inside are full of dead men's bones and everything unclean. 28In the same way, on the outside you appear to people as righteous but on the inside you are full of hypocrisy and wickedness.

29"Woe to you, teachers of the law and Pharisees, you hypocrites! You build tombs for the prophets and decorate the graves of the righteous. 30And you say, 'If we had lived in the days of our forefathers, we would not have taken part with them in shedding the blood of the prophets.' 31So you testify against yourselves that you are the descendants of those who murdered the prophets. 32Fill up, then, the measure of the sin of your forefathers!

33"You snakes! You brood of vipers! How will you escape being condemned to hell? 34Therefore I am sending you prophets and wise men and teachers. Some of them you will kill and crucify; others you will flog in your synagogues and pursue from town to town. 35And so upon you will come all the righteous blood that has been shed on earth, from the blood of righteous Abel to the blood of Zechariah son of Berekiah, whom you murdered between the temple and the altar. 36I tell you the truth, all this will come upon this generation."

NRSV

25"Woe to you, scribes and Pharisees, hypocrites! For you clean the outside of the cup and of the plate, but inside they are full of greed and self-indulgence. 26You blind Pharisee! First clean the inside of the cup,[a] so that the outside also may become clean.

27"Woe to you, scribes and Pharisees, hypocrites! For you are like whitewashed tombs, which on the outside look beautiful, but inside they are full of the bones of the dead and of all kinds of filth. 28So you also on the outside look righteous to others, but inside you are full of hypocrisy and lawlessness.

29"Woe to you, scribes and Pharisees, hypocrites! For you build the tombs of the prophets and decorate the graves of the righteous, 30and you say, 'If we had lived in the days of our ancestors, we would not have taken part with them in shedding the blood of the prophets.' 31Thus you testify against yourselves that you are descendants of those who murdered the prophets. 32Fill up, then, the measure of your ancestors. 33You snakes, you brood of vipers! How can you escape being sentenced to hell?[b] 34Therefore I send you prophets, sages, and scribes, some of whom you will kill and crucify, and some you will flog in your synagogues and pursue from town to town, 35so that upon you may come all the righteous blood shed on earth, from the blood of righteous Abel to the blood of Zechariah son of Barachiah, whom you murdered between the sanctuary and the altar. 36Truly I tell you, all this will come upon this generation."

[a]Other ancient authorities add *and of the plate*   [b]Gk Gehenna

COMMENTARY

Although the address shifts here to the second person, the narrative does not picture the Pharisees as physically present. The addressees are exclusively the crowds and disciples. As in 11:21-24, the woes are in the literary form of an apostrophe (words addressed to someone not actually present). At the Matthean level of the discourse, the woes represent the conflict between the rabbinic movement and Matthean Christians, not an outburst of the historical Jesus against the 30 CE Pharisees, and it is Matthean readers who are actually addressed.

The woe form is from OT prophets (Isa 45:9-10; Jer 13:27; 48:46; Ezek 16:23). It was probably one form of Jesus' own prophetic speech. After Easter, the woe form was adopted by Christian prophets (Rev 8:13; 9:12; 11:14; 12:12). Q contained a collection of seven woes spoken in Jesus' name, which already reflected conflicts between the followers of Jesus and the Jewish leaders (cf. Luke 11:39-52). Matthew adapts this Q-speech to address his own opponents, represented by the "scribes and Pharisees" of his own time.

Although here and elsewhere Matthew is against insincerity, that may not be the primary meaning of ὑπόκρισις (*hypokrisis*) here. As in Gal 2:11-14, inconsistency between one's faith and one's action, whether one is aware of it or not, is the essence. In the Deuteronomistic theology adopted by Matthew from Q, hypocrisy represents godlessness, not merely phoniness.[504] The polemic is against placing too much value on the way one appears to others, which can be a form of idolatry. So understood, hypocrisy is not merely a transgression, but represents a lack of trust in God, a turning away from God toward what others think as the point of orientation for one's life.

23:13, Woe 1: Closing the Kingdom. Matthew transforms the Q woe into a saying about the kingdom (cf. Luke 11:52), corresponding to his view throughout that in the conflict between the Jewish leadership and the Jesus movement, two kingdoms confront each other (see 12:22-37). Matthew also rearranges the Q order, placing this woe first to make the conflict of kingdoms programmatic for the whole series. The woes are not a petty outburst, but proleptic pronouncements of the eschatological judge (cf. 25:31-46). The Pharisees are condemned because they neither enter the kingdom nor let others enter, perhaps a reference to expulsions of Christians from the synagogue in the wake of the developments at Jamnia (cf. John 9:34-35; 16:2-4) and in contrast to Peter's role in 16:19.

23:15, Woe 2: The Mission of the Opposing Kingdom.[505] Matthew, whose own church carries on a Gentile mission (28:18-20), understands the Pharisees to be carrying on a rival mission to the Gentiles, but of course requiring

them to keep the Law as a condition of becoming Jewish proselytes. Missioners of Matthew's community may have encountered resistance not only from the Pharisees, but also from their Gentile converts who were now zealous for the Law and opposed what they perceived as the Matthean Christians' lax attitude to the Torah. These hostile encounters may help the modern reader understand (not to say excuse) the vitriolic description of both Pharisees and their converts as "children of hell" (lit., "sons of" in the Semitic sense of "belonging to the category of"). This is the counterpart of Matthew's descriptions of Christians as "sons of" the kingdom (cf. 8:12; 13:38) and continues the imagery of the first woe, in which the kingdom of God is opposed by the alternative kingdom of Satan. We are aware of a few celebrated cases in which the Pharisees persuaded prominent Gentiles to convert to Judaism, but the existence of a large-scale Pharisaic mission to the Gentiles is unsupported by historical evidence.

23:16-22, Woe 3: Against Casuistry. There may have been legitimate grounding for the Pharisees' rules interpreting the biblical legislation on oaths and vows (see 5:33-37). The distinction between gold and Temple, or between sacrifice and altar, may have had to do with what a creditor could attach—i.e., they were the Pharisees' efforts to put the Law effectively into practice and prevent people from making meaningless oaths. Matthew understands the whole approach as casuistic hair-splitting, a devilish effort to find loopholes in the Law. His understanding of the teaching of Jesus has rejected the casuistic approach in principle (see 5:17-48), and the making of oaths in particular. Here, in order to condemn casuistry, he seems to accept the legitimacy of oaths. On the tensions between this speech and the Sermon on the Mount, see Reflections below.

23:23-24, Woe 4: Against Majoring in Minors. The Torah had commanded that a tenth of the increase of livestock, of fruit trees, and of grain, oil, and wine be presented to God for support of the priesthood and Levites (Lev 27:30, 32; Deut 12:17). While some passages seem to limit the tithe on agricultural produce to grain, oil, and wine (Deut 12:17; 14:23; cf. Neh 13:5, 12), other texts appear to extend the tithe to include all agricultural produce (Lev 27:30; Deut 14:22; cf. 2 Chr 31:5). To be sure that they

---

504. See Hubert Frankemölle, *Jahwebund und Kirche Christi; Studien zur Form-und Traditionsgeschichte des Evangeliums nach Matthäus* (Münster: Aschendorff, 1974), 285-86.

505. The original text of Matthew does not include 23:14; it is a later interpolation in some MSS from Mark 12:40. It is missing from B, ℵ, D, L, Z, Θ, λ 33, 892* pc, lat, sy^s, sa, bo^{pt}; Or, and would disrupt the pattern by making eight woes.

complied with God's law, the Pharisees tithed even small garden vegetables used for seasoning. Matthew rewrites the Q statement so that three "weighty obligations" correspond to the three minor ones. Justice, mercy, and faithfulness is another "summary of the law" dealing with responsibilities to one's fellow human beings. "Faith" here means "faithfulness," carrying out one's obligations under the covenant. The grotesque "gnat"/"camel" (גמלא / קלמא, *qalmāʾ/gamlāʾ*, which Matthew has reproduced in Greek) may reflect word play in Aramaic on the smallest and largest living things in normal experience. Both were (ritually) unclean (Lev 11:4, 41-44). Straining gnats out of liquids to be consumed in drinking or cooking represents the Pharisees' legitimate concern to comply with the Law. Matthew, too, is concerned with the importance of the "least" commandments (5:18-20). Matthew's critique is that in being concerned to filter out minor violations, they let major ones plop in unnoticed.

23:25-26, Woe 5: Inner and Outer. Although the imagery is unclear, the point is not: a polemic against concern with external appearance rather than internal integrity (6:1-18). The historical Pharisees were also against such hypocrisy. Matthew uses his picture of the Pharisees as a warning to church members and leaders. As in 15:1-20, purity is first a matter of the heart, proceeding from within to affect external actions. Matthew shows little appreciation for the Pharisees' concern for ritual purity, biblically based though it was. Yet, v. 26 shows that he does not replace "externals" with "internals"; real integrity requires both.

23:27-28, Woe 6: Whitewashed Tombs. As a public service, tombs were whitewashed to make them more obvious, since contact with the dead and with graves, even if unintentional, transmitted ritual impurity (Num 19:11-22). This was especially important to pilgrims at Passover time, who would not be familiar with the local sites and who, if they inadvertently touched a grave, would be prohibited from participating in the festival for which they had come to Jerusalem. Matthew commandeers the image of such a tomb to express his picture of hypocrisy: ostentatious exterior, corrupt interior.

23:29-36, Woe 7: Killer of Prophets. The final woe extends the tomb image and modulates

into the concluding theme: Israel's rejection of the prophets God has sent, including John, Jesus, and the Christian prophets. The tradition had long since developed that the true prophets of the past had been persecuted and killed.[506] The Pharisees showed their repentance for the sins of their ancestors by building monuments to the biblical prophets and declared that if they had lived in the days of their "fathers" who killed the prophets, they would not have participated in their murder. By exploiting the double Semitic meaning of the "father"/"son" terminology, Matthew turns both their word and their practice against them. Speaking of past generations as their "fathers" means that they acknowledge that they are "sons" of those who killed the prophets. In the Semitic meaning of *son,* this means not biological relationship but belonging to the same category (cf. Amos 7:14). Just as the beatitudes climax by placing Jesus' disciples in the group of persecuted prophets (5:11-12), so also the woes here climax by placing their opponents in the category of those who killed the prophets.

23:32. This passage is an ironic "command" like that of the biblical prophets (Isa 8:9-10; Jer 7:21; Amos 4:4; Nah 3:14-15), written retrospectively in view of actual persecutions of Christians by Jewish leaders in the two generations following Jesus' death.

23:33. This verse joins Jesus' prophetic denunciation both with that of John the Baptist (3:7) and with the following eschatological declarations (24:4–25:46).

"Gehenna" is the Greek form of "Ge-Hinnom" (גיא הנם),[507] the "Valley of Hinnom," a ravine immediately south of Jerusalem. Because it was the site of idolatrous worship during the time of the Judean kingship (2 Kgs 23:10; 2 Chr 23:8; Jer 7:31), it became a garbage dump where perpetual fire burned. By the first century CE it was already used metaphorically as a picture of the fiery eschatological judgment of God.

23:34-36. The series of woes in Q concludes with an oracle in which the transcendent Wisdom of God speaks, picturing the series of Wisdom's messengers rejected through the generations and now climaxed by the present generation's rejec-

---

506. See Heb 11:32-38; Charles Cutler Torrey, ed., *The Lives of the Prophets,* vol. 1, JBL Monograph Series, (Philadelphia: Society of Biblical Literature and Exegesis, 1946).
507. T. H. Gaster, "Gehenna," *IDB* 2:361.

tion of John, Jesus, and the Christian prophets (cf. Luke 11:49-51), who were pictured in Q as messengers of transcendent Wisdom. Matthew, however, identifies Jesus with divine Wisdom, so that the oracle is placed in Jesus' own mouth.[508] The Jesus of the narrative is transparent to the exalted Lord, identified with transcendent Wisdom, who has sent prophets in the past and who sends Christian prophets, sages, and scribes (leaders in the Matthean Christian community; cf. Introduction) to the present generation. Matthew knows from experience that they have been rejected and that some have been killed, and he sees the guilt of all the ages summed up in the present "evil generation" (cf. 11:16; 12:39, 41-42, 45; 16:4; 17:17; on "crucify," see 10:38).[509] Matthew understands his community to belong to the righteous who have always been persecuted, from Abel, the first victim (Matthew adds "righteous" to Q; cf. Luke 11:50), to Zechariah, the last martyr in the OT.[510] "This generation" is a com-

mon expression in Matthew, taken over from Q (see 11:16; 12:41-42; 24:34). The pronouncement of judgment is made on the generation contemporary with John the Baptist and Jesus, not on the Jewish people as such. These words about "all the blood [guilt] coming on this generation" are the last words of Jesus heard by the crowd (cf. 23:1) before Jesus leaves with his disciples (24:1). It is thus a moment of decision for them as to whether they will choose to belong to the kingdom of God, announced and lived out by Jesus, or to the opposing kingdom represented by the prophet killers. The next appearance of the crowd is at Jesus' arrest (26:55); their next words are to accept responsibility for Jesus' death, using words that echo Jesus' proleptic pronouncement here (27:25). By placing these words here as Jesus' own prophecy, Matthew shows that the Jesus who goes to the cross is identified with the transcendent Lord who is not an unwilling victim but master of the situation.

508. See M. Jack Suggs, *Wisdom, Christology, and Law in Matthew's Gospel* (Cambridge, Mass.: Harvard University Press, 1970) 31-62, although it is un-Matthean to speak of an "incarnation" of Wisdom.

509. See Douglas R. A. Hare, *The Theme of Jewish Persecution of Christians in the Gospel According to St Matthew* (Cambridge: Cambridge University Press, 1967).

510. The Zechariah referred to is the son of Jehoida of 2 Chr 24:20-22. Second Chronicles is the last book of the OT, so the description has the

ring of "from Genesis to Revelation." Matthew has confused this Zechariah with the prophet of Zech 1:1 and has added "son of Berachiah" (cf. Luke 11:51). Origen later mistakenly identifies this Zechariah with the father of John the Baptist.

Matthew 23:37-39, Lament

NIV

37"O Jerusalem, Jerusalem, you who kill the prophets and stone those sent to you, how often I have longed to gather your children together, as a hen gathers her chicks under her wings, but you were not willing. 38Look, your house is left to you desolate. 39For I tell you, you will not see me again until you say, 'Blessed is he who comes in the name of the Lord.'[a]"

a39 Psalm 118:26

NRSV

37"Jerusalem, Jerusalem, the city that kills the prophets and stones those who are sent to it! How often have I desired to gather your children together as a hen gathers her brood under her wings, and you were not willing! 38See, your house is left to you, desolate.[a] 39For I tell you, you will not see me again until you say, 'Blessed is the one who comes in the name of the Lord.'"

a Other ancient authorities lack desolate

COMMENTARY

Matthew has relocated these words (cf. Luke 13:34-35, spoken earlier in the narrative, long before Jesus had ever entered Jerusalem) to make

them Jesus' last words in Jerusalem and its Temple before he leaves it for the final time (24:1), to reenter the city only for his arrest, trial, and crucifixion. They continue the preceding theme of killing the prophets, but the form is different: They are a lament. Whereas the preceding woes are ostensibly addressed to scribes and Pharisees but actually function as a prophetic challenge to the crowds and disciples (23:1; also to the reader) not to belong to "this evil generation," these concluding words are an invitation ostensibly addressed to Jerusalem, but they function as an invitation to the crowds and disciples (and to the reader). They continue to picture Jesus as being identified with transcendent Wisdom, grieved at the rejection of her messengers. Thus "how often" refers not to previous occasions on which Jesus has been in Jerusalem—in Matthew this is his first and only visit to Jerusalem—but to transcendent Wisdom's repeated appeals to Jerusalem/Israel throughout history.

23:38. "Your" house corresponds to "their" synagogues (23:34; cf. 4:23; 9:35; 10:17). Matthew adds "desolate," looking back on the destruction of the Temple in 70 CE and in anticipation of Jesus' words in 24:2, 15.[511] For Matthew and his community, these words and the following explicit prediction of the Temple's destruction functioned as an apologetic, explaining how the destruction of the Temple fit into the divine program as a punishment for the people's sins in rejecting the prophets, including Jesus and the Christian prophets of the final generation (cf. Jeremiah, explicitly cited and mentioned by Matthew alone in the Gospels [2:17; 16:14; 27:9]).

23:39. This acclamation from Ps 118:26 has already been shouted by these same crowds during Jesus' "triumphal entry" into Jerusalem (see Matt 21:9), so it cannot in Matthew refer to this occasion as it does in Luke, where it occurs much earlier (13:35). In Matthew it must refer to the parousia, as the immediate context indicates. The crowds representing Jerusalem/Israel who presently will choose Barabbas over Jesus and shout "Let him be crucified!" (27:22) will eventually shout "Blessed is the one who comes in the name of the Lord." Does this mean that "the ritual greeting it will give then will be forced from it, and will be a recognition of its defeat and rejection"?[512] Or is Matthew's meaning that Israel's present rejection of the Messiah is not final, so that before the parousia they, too, will have been converted and will finally welcome him as God's representative (as Paul expects, Romans 9–11)?[513] For Reflections on 23:1-39, see the conclusion of the entire speech, 25:46.

511. Although omitted in B, L, ff[2], sa, bo[pt], and, therefore, in some editions of the Greek New Testament and English translations.

512. John Meier, *Matthew,* New Testament Message 3 (Collegeville, Minn.: Liturgical Press, 1990) 275. See also Douglas R. A. Hare, *Matthew, Int.* (Louisville: Westminster/John Knox, 1993) 272: "It will not be with joy but with the gloom of the condemned who are compelled to honor their judge (cf. Phil 2:10-11)." So already Calvin: "He [Jesus] will not come to them [the Jews] until they cry out in fear—too late—at the sight of his majesty, 'truly he is the Son of God' " (cited in Graham Stanton, *Gospel for a New People* [Edinburgh: T. & T. Clark, 1992] 249).

513. See W. D. Davies and Dale C. Allison, Jr., *A Critical and Exegetical Commentary on the Gospel According to Saint Matthew,* 2 vols. (Edinburgh: T. & T. Clark, 1988–91); Robert H. Gundry, *Matthew: A Commentary on His Literary and Theological Art* (Grand Rapids: Eerdmans, 1982) 474; G. Stanton has recently argued for this interpretation on the basis of the sin/exile/return pattern adopted from Deuteronomy and found also in Justin Martyr and the *Testaments of the Twelve Patriarchs* (see Stanton, *Gospel for a New People,* 248-51). Against the view that Paul in Romans 9–11 teaches a dramatic, universal conversion of empirical Israel as part of the eschatological events, see N. T. Wright, *The Climax of the Covenant* (Minneapolis: Fortress, 1993) 231-57.

Matthew 24:1–25:46, The Coming Judgment: To Disciples

Matthew 24:1-3, Jesus' Prediction, Disciples' Question

NIV	NRSV
24 Jesus left the temple and was walking away when his disciples came up to him to call his attention to its buildings. ²"Do you see all these things?" he asked. "I tell you the truth, not one stone here will be left on another; every one will be thrown down."	**24** As Jesus came out of the temple and was going away, his disciples came to point out to him the buildings of the temple. ²Then he asked them, "You see all these, do you not? Truly I tell you, not one stone will be left here upon another; all will be thrown down."

NIV	NRSV
[3]As Jesus was sitting on the Mount of Olives, the disciples came to him privately. "Tell us," they said, "when will this happen, and what will be the sign of your coming and of the end of the age?"	3When he was sitting on the Mount of Olives, the disciples came to him privately, saying, "Tell us, when will this be, and what will be the sign of your coming and of the end of the age?"

COMMENTARY

24:1-2. Matthew rewrites Mark 13:1, in which Jesus' leaving the Temple is mentioned only incidentally and only one disciple points out the grandeur of the Temple buildings, thereby making the scene Jesus' deliberate exit, to which all the disciples respond. Jesus has been in the Temple court since 21:23. When he now leaves, it is a symbolic act like that of the prophets of Israel, dramatizing his pronouncement of 23:38. Just as the "glory of the Lord," the symbolic presence of God in the Jerusalem Temple, once definitively left the Temple prior to its destruction and "rested" on the Mount of Olives before going into Gentile territory (Ezek 10:18; 11:23), so also Jesus, who definitively represents God's presence (1:23), now ceremonially departs the Temple for the final time. Jesus' departure precipitates a decision on the part of the "crowds and disciples" who have been listening (23:1). Only the disciples follow Jesus out of the doomed Temple; the crowds will appear next at the scene of the arrest (26:47). The die is now cast.

Jesus does not deny the impressiveness of the Herodian Temple architecture, the remains of which can still be seen at the base of the Temple Mount, part of which forms the "wailing wall." Matthew increases the prophetic solemnity of Jesus' prediction of the coming destruction of the Temple by making it an *amēn* (see 5:18) pronouncement.

24:3. Jesus has now left both Temple and city. Again, Matthew changes Mark, in which only the original four disciples hear Jesus' final discourse, so that all the disciples continue to be hearers— none of the crowds, all of the disciples.[514] The

Markan separation of four disciples from the others becomes the Matthean separation of the disciples from the crowds. As in the first great discourse of the Gospel (5:1–7:29), Jesus is seated on a mountain (the teaching posture; see Commentary on 5:1), but this time it is the Mount of Olives, rich in eschatological connotations (Zech 14:4). Jesus and the disciples are not, as in Mark, looking back at the Temple, which has now been left definitively behind (12:6).

In Matthew's Gospel, the disciples' question is explicitly eschatological. They are pictured as already understanding his teaching about his parousia, even though elsewhere they have difficulty grasping the death-resurrection (16:21-22; 26:56–28:17).[515] Although their question distinguishes the destruction of the Temple (which already lies twenty years in the past for Matthew and his readers) and the parousia, it (mistakenly) relates them as belonging to the same category of events and to the same chronological framework (see Reflections at 25:31-46 on interpreting Matthew's mistaken chronology). The eschatological question is not rejected (as in Acts 1:6-8). In Matthew, the question about the sign is explicitly connected to the parousia; it will dominate the following discourse and be explicitly answered in the Matthean addition 24:30, where it recurs. The Greek text binds "parousia" and "end of the world" together with a single article, showing that they refer to the same event.[516]

Matthew's answer to the question of the time

---

514. The generalizing address to "all" at the conclusion of the Markan discourse (13:37) is built into the Matthean discourse from the beginning, another indication that Matthew presupposes Mark and begins where he leaves off (see 9:18-26 = Mark 5:21-43).

515. This is the result of Matthew's combining the Markan picture of the disciples' misunderstanding with his own view of insightful disciples, each of which plays a significant theological role in its respective Gospel.

516. The fact that the second article (before "end of the world") was added in some MSS (D, W, 0138, f[13], and most later MSS) shows that some scribes thought of Jesus' "coming" as his "coming" for judgment in historical events, such as the destruction of Jerusalem, in distinction from the later parousia. It is clear that this is not Matthew's meaning, his text being preserved in ℵ, B, X, Λ, Θ, f[1], 33, 565, 892, and other MSS.

of the parousia is twofold. He incorporates Mark's "little apocalypse" (see Mark 13) in 24:4-31 with slight alterations, and extends it with seven para-bolic admonitions, encouraging an active vigilance until the advent of Jesus as the heavenly Son of Man. (See Reflections at 25:31-46.)

Matthew 24:4-31, The "Little Apocalypse"

NIV

[4]Jesus answered: "Watch out that no one deceives you. [5]For many will come in my name, claiming, 'I am the Christ,[a]' and will deceive many. [6]You will hear of wars and rumors of wars, but see to it that you are not alarmed. Such things must happen, but the end is still to come. [7]Nation will rise against nation, and kingdom against kingdom. There will be famines and earthquakes in various places. [8]All these are the beginning of birth pains.

[9]"Then you will be handed over to be persecuted and put to death, and you will be hated by all nations because of me. [10]At that time many will turn away from the faith and will betray and hate each other, [11]and many false prophets will appear and deceive many people. [12]Because of the increase of wickedness, the love of most will grow cold, [13]but he who stands firm to the end will be saved. [14]And this gospel of the kingdom will be preached in the whole world as a testimony to all nations, and then the end will come.

[15]"So when you see standing in the holy place 'the abomination that causes desolation,'[b] spoken of through the prophet Daniel—let the reader understand— [16]then let those who are in Judea flee to the mountains. [17]Let no one on the roof of his house go down to take anything out of the house. [18]Let no one in the field go back to get his cloak. [19]How dreadful it will be in those days for pregnant women and nursing mothers! [20]Pray that your flight will not take place in winter or on the Sabbath. [21]For then there will be great distress, unequaled from the beginning of the world until now—and never to be equaled again. [22]If those days had not been cut short, no one would survive, but for the sake of the elect those days will be shortened. [23]At that time if anyone says to you, 'Look, here is the Christ!' or, 'There he is!' do not believe it. [24]For false Christs and false

[a]5 Or Messiah; also in verse 23   [b]15 Daniel 9:27; 11:31; 12:11

NRSV

[4]Jesus answered them, "Beware that no one leads you astray. [5]For many will come in my name, saying, 'I am the Messiah!'[a] and they will lead many astray. [6]And you will hear of wars and rumors of wars; see that you are not alarmed; for this must take place, but the end is not yet. [7]For nation will rise against nation, and kingdom against kingdom, and there will be famines[b] and earthquakes in various places: [8]all this is but the beginning of the birth pangs.

[9]"Then they will hand you over to be tortured and will put you to death, and you will be hated by all nations because of my name. [10]Then many will fall away,[c] and they will betray one another and hate one another. [11]And many false prophets will arise and lead many astray. [12]And because of the increase of lawlessness, the love of many will grow cold. [13]But the one who endures to the end will be saved. [14]And this good news[d] of the kingdom will be proclaimed throughout the world, as a testimony to all the nations; and then the end will come.

[15]"So when you see the desolating sacrilege standing in the holy place, as was spoken of by the prophet Daniel (let the reader understand), [16]then those in Judea must flee to the mountains; [17]the one on the housetop must not go down to take what is in the house; [18]the one in the field must not turn back to get a coat. [19]Woe to those who are pregnant and to those who are nursing infants in those days! [20]Pray that your flight may not be in winter or on a sabbath. [21]For at that time there will be great suffering, such as has not been from the beginning of the world until now, no, and never will be. [22]And if those days had not been cut short, no one would be saved; but for the sake of the elect those days will be cut short. [23]Then if anyone says to you, 'Look! Here is the Messiah!'[a] or 'There he is!'—do not believe it. [24]For false messiahs[e] and false prophets will

[a]Or the Christ   [b]Other ancient authorities add and pestilences
[c]Or stumble   [d]Or gospel   [e]Or christs

NIV

prophets will appear and perform great signs and miracles to deceive even the elect—if that were possible. [25]See, I have told you ahead of time.

[26]"So if anyone tells you, 'There he is, out in the desert,' do not go out; or, 'Here he is, in the inner rooms,' do not believe it. [27]For as lightning that comes from the east is visible even in the west, so will be the coming of the Son of Man. [28]Wherever there is a carcass, there the vultures will gather.

[29]"Immediately after the distress of those days

" 'the sun will be darkened,
    and the moon will not give its light;
the stars will fall from the sky,
    and the heavenly bodies will be shaken.'[a]

[30]"At that time the sign of the Son of Man will appear in the sky, and all the nations of the earth will mourn. They will see the Son of Man coming on the clouds of the sky, with power and great glory. [31]And he will send his angels with a loud trumpet call, and they will gather his elect from the four winds, from one end of the heavens to the other."

NRSV

appear and produce great signs and omens, to lead astray, if possible, even the elect. [25]Take note, I have told you beforehand. [26]So, if they say to you, 'Look! He is in the wilderness,' do not go out. If they say, 'Look! He is in the inner rooms,' do not believe it. [27]For as the lightning comes from the east and flashes as far as the west, so will be the coming of the Son of Man. [28]Wherever the corpse is, there the vultures will gather.

29"Immediately after the suffering of those days

    the sun will be darkened,
        and the moon will not give its light;
    the stars will fall from heaven,
        and the powers of heaven will be shaken.
[30]Then the sign of the Son of Man will appear in heaven, and then all the tribes of the earth will mourn, and they will see 'the Son of Man coming on the clouds of heaven' with power and great glory. [31]And he will send out his angels with a loud trumpet call, and they will gather his elect from the four winds, from one end of heaven to the other."

COMMENTARY

Each of Matthew's major sources contains an apocalyptic section that climaxes with the coming of the Son of Man (Mark 13:5-37; Q = Luke 17:22-37; 18:18). They use different imagery, however, and have a different perspective on the relation of "signs" to the parousia. The Markan apocalypse predicts dramatic signs that discerning believers can recognize and thus determine their relative location on the apocalyptic timetable. In contrast, the Q apocalypse pictures the parousia as occurring suddenly, without warning. Along with other materials, Matthew integrates these into one grand discourse.[517] Although he includes the Markan "little apocalypse" *en toto* and incorporates the Q apocalypse into it, theologically he subordinates Mark's "signs" perspective to Q's

"no signs" perspective, which he has adopted as his own.[518] Matthew is not interested in encouraging apocalyptic speculation about "signs," but in having his community ready to meet the returning Son of Man whenever it happens.

Mark's "little apocalypse" was structured in three temporal acts: (1) a beginning phase characterized by wars, famines, and earthquakes, which were not to be taken as signs of the end time, (2) a period of intense suffering for the faithful people of God, the "tribulation," which was to immediately precede (3) the coming of the Son of Man. Matthew not only retains this threefold structure, he tightens and clarifies it.

---

517. Cf. his similar compositional procedure in 9:36–10:42, the missionary discourse, where he combines the missionary speeches in Mark and Q into one discourse; Luke's procedure in both cases differs (Luke 17:22-35 = Q; Luke 21:8-33 = Mark).

518. Q may have been the primary document representing the sacred tradition of Matthew's church, with Mark being accepted by the community only later; see Introduction. So far as narrative structure as a whole is concerned, Mark is primary and Q is inserted into it. But theologically Matthew has often remained closer to his older source, as here.

24:4-8, The Beginning of Labor Pains.
Wars, famines, and earthquakes were the stock-in-trade of apocalyptic speculation (Dan 2:28-29; 11:44; 4 Ezra 9:3-4; 13:30-32; 2 Bar 27:6-7). Mark's little apocalypse had already warned that these tragedies of history were not the signs that the end was to occur immediately, but they did signal the onset of the final period of history. This is the meaning of "birth pangs," a metaphor traditional in apocalyptic thought: The world of politics and nature goes through a period of suffering before the Messiah comes. For Matthew, this is a description of the period of the war of 66–70 and the events that led up to it. By looking back on this period through the lens of "birth pangs," he historicizes the metaphor and separates the past from the future eschatological events. His only significant change from Mark is the adding of "the Christ," to v. 5 to make it explicit that the deceivers are would-be messiahs in contrast to 23:10. Matthew does not intend to portray people claiming to be (the returned) Jesus, but the Jewish religious-military leaders who fomented and led the disastrous war against the Romans in 66–73, some of whom claimed to be the messianic savior promised by God and were so regarded by others.[519]

24:9-28, The Great Tribulation. A traditional segment of the apocalyptic schema adopted by Mark was a period of intense suffering immediately before the end. Matthew makes the Markan periodization even more crisp.[520] He signals the new period with "then" (τότε *tote*) and by inserting in v. 9 the quasi-technical term translated "tribulation" (θλῖψις *thlipsis*; the same word as 24:29, "distress" [NIV]; "suffering" [NRSV], here translated "be persecuted"/"be tortured"). It is clear that this is the final period before "the end" (vv. 13-14). It is characterized by persecution of the elect people of God (24:21-22) not only by Jewish opponents, as previously, but also by "all the nations"

(24:9).[521] "Because of my name" shows that it is the Christian confession that provokes the persecution.

24:10-12. In this final period, troubles are no longer only from outsiders, but the church is plagued also by internal disputes, betrayals, and a cooling of original commitments. "Fall away"/"turn from the faith" translates σκαν-δαλίζω (*skandalizō*; cf. 13:57); here it also reflects Dan 11:41, as much else in this speech that evokes Daniel's apocalyptic imagery (24:6 = Dan 2:28-29, 45; 24:30 = Dan 7:13-14; 24:15 = Dan 11:31; 24:21 = Dan 12:1; 25:46 = Dan 12:2; on "false prophets" and "lawlessness," see 7:21-23). Matthew's only use of the noun "love" (ἀγάπη *agapē*) evokes the previous discussion of the Great Commandment (22:34-40) and the conclusion of this speech 25:31-46, where deeds of love are what finally count in the judgment.

24:13-14. During the final eschatological woes, the church does not turn in on itself in a mode of passive waiting. The tribulation period is also the time of the church's worldwide mission to all nations (πᾶσιν τοῖς ἔθνεσιν *pasin tois ethnesin*; the same phrase is used in 28:19). Matthew's alteration of Mark designates the church's message as specifically the "gospel of the kingdom," again emphasizing the alternate kingship represented by the message and life of Jesus and continued by his disciples (cf. Excursus "Kingdom of Heaven in Matthew," 288-94, and 12:22-37). The mission of the church is to last until "the end"; the disciples' responsibility is to endure (cf. 10:23).

24:15-22. A climactic event of the period of the final tribulation is the appearance of the "desolating sacrilege" in the holy place. This phrase originally referred to a desecration of the Temple in 167 BCE by Antiochus IV Epiphanes, which became an apocalyptic image reinterpreted many times (see Dan 9:27; 11:31; 12:11; Mark 13:14). Matthew found it in his Markan source, where it is apparently applied to the desecration of the Temple and destruction of Jerusalem in 70 CE. It is not clear whether Matthew looks back on this prediction as already fulfilled in the events of 70, thus historicizing this part of the discourse, or

---

519. See Josephus, *The Jewish War* 6.5.2.; 7.11.1; *Antiquities of the Jews* 17.10.5-8; 17.271-85, gives three examples of self-proclaimed (messianic) "kings" and concludes with "anyone might make himself king." Cf. Richard A. Horsley and John S. Hanson, *Bandits, Prophets, and Messiahs: Popular Movements in the Time of Jesus* (Minneapolis: Winston, 1985).

520. Yet Matthew's eschatological thought is not mechanically or rigidly periodized. He retains the impressionistic, allusive character of apocalyptic language, so that these events, though past, can also be used as evocative images of the troubles that will immediately precede the end.

521. Matthew borrowed Mark 13:9-13 for his mission speech in 10:17-22a. He here repeats its first and last lines, but whereas previously persecution was from Jewish councils and synagogues, now it is from all the nations, the very peoples to whom the church is directing its mission.

whether (more likely) he regards this as an ominous event still to come. In Matthew's time, there was no longer a Temple to be defiled, but "holy place" could be understood more generally (2 Macc 2:18 uses the term to describe the Holy Land). Matthew's changing of the word translated "standing" from Mark's ungrammatical, but more specific, masculine ἑστηκότα (*hestēkota*) to the more correct, but more vague, neuter ἑστός (*hestos*) seems to indicate that he does not have a specific person or event in mind, which is therefore still in Matthew's future.

Likewise, Matthew's addition of "on the Sabbath" to the instructions for flight (24:20) seems to indicate that he still regarded the "desecrating sacrilege" as something in his own future. The reference to the sabbath could mean that on this point Matthew's church is still Torah-observant and that Christians are given a dispensation to flee, even though it violates the sabbath travel restrictions. More likely, the meaning is that in a Jewish context flight by a whole community on the sabbath would be both difficult and conspicuous, thus both more dangerous than on other days and scandalous and antagonistic to their opponents.[522]

The directive in 24:17-19 to leave everything and flee is neither cowardice nor eschatological panic, but is related by Matthew to the character of discipleship and the nature of the Christian mission. The disciples left everything when they were called to become "fishers for people" (4:18-22) and when they were sent out on a mission (10:5-10; "flee" in 10:23; cf. 19:27). The community scattered and fleeing is the community in a missionary mode. The regathering of the community is God's responsibility and promise at the eschaton (24:31).

The instruction to pray in 24:20-22 directs the community's view to God, who transcends the apocalyptic schema here being used. God is not bound to the apocalyptic timetable (cf. 4 Ezra 4:33-37, written about the same time!), but can make adjustments for the sake of the elect. Although using traditional apocalyptic ideas, Matthew directs his readers to put their faith in God, not in apocalyptic schedules. "The elect" (vv. 22, 24, 31) are now the disciples of Jesus: the church of Jews and Gentiles (see Reflections on 21:43).

Whatever these specific instructions for flight

may have meant as part of the (pre-)Markan apocalypse, for Matthew they no longer apply directly to his own community, which does not live in Judea. He repeats them as part of his sacred tradition, but they now function to underscore his major point that neither the general persecutions endured by the church nor the climactic event of the "desecrating sacrilege" should be misunderstood to mean that somehow the parousia had already occurred. This misunderstanding may have been encouraged in the Matthean community by the presence of Christian prophets whose speaking in the first person in the name of Jesus was taken as a claim that Christ had already returned. Likewise, Matthew's own repeated emphasis on the continuing presence of Christ may have been taken to mean that the future eschatological events had already happened: in effect, "Do not look to the future for the 'second coming,' for Jesus is already among us." Matthew resists this implication of his own teaching and emphasizes not only that the parousia is still future, but also that it will be so obvious that there will be no question about it. The final appearance of the Messiah will not be a "hidden Messiah" who must be sought out, but will be universally observable and as unambiguous as lightning— lightning is no private event!

24:23-28. The material taken over from Mark (vv. 23-25 = Mark 13:21-23) already made this same point (cf. also Matt 24:4-5 = Mark 13:5-6). Matthew augments this with sayings taken from the Q apocalypse (cf. Luke 17:23-24) that express the same warning. This compositional procedure illustrates how important the point was to Matthew. Thus, although 24:28 has often been understood with reference to the Roman army's destruction of Jerusalem in 70,[523] in Matthew's context it probably refers to the future parousia and means simply: "When the Messiah returns, it will be as clear as vultures circling over a dead body."

24:29-31, The Coming of the Son of Man. Even the third act of the apocalyptic drama is more concerned with dispelling misunderstandings by affirming the unmistakable public nature of the parousia than describing what will happen at the return of Christ. There will be no mistake

---

522. So Graham Stanton, *Gospel for a New People* [Edinburgh: T. & T. Clark, 1992) 192-206.

523. This was facilitated by the fact that ἀετός (*aetos*) can mean not only "vulture" but also "eagle," pointing to the eagles on the Roman standards.

that the parousia has occurred, because it will be signaled not by historical, this-worldly signs that need interpretation, but by cosmic events signaling the return to primeval chaos: The sun and moon will be darkened, and stars (not merely meteorites) will fall (standard elements in the traditional apocalyptic scenario [cf. Isa 13:10; 34:4; Ezek 32:7-8; Joel 2:31; 3:15; *Assumption of Moses* 10:5; Rev 6:13; 8:12; 12:4]). Likewise, the Son of Man will appear not privately or ambiguously, but universally visible, on the clouds of heaven. The "sign of the Son of Man," inserted by Matthew here, is the Son of Man himself (epexegetical genitive, like the "sign of Jonah" in 12:39—the sign that was Jonah himself, not something else pointing to Jonah). Thus Matthew's point is that there will be no sign in the sense of preliminary warnings: The first clear sign will be the end itself with its cosmic disruption and the indisputable appearance of the Son of Man. In v. 30 the disciples' question in v. 3 receives its definitive Matthean answer: The sign of his appearing will be the Son of Man himself.

Matthew also adds "all the tribes of the earth will mourn" to underscore the universality and unambiguous nature of the parousia. Since the *fact* of this universal mourning is Matthew's point, its *nature* remains unclear. "Mourn" (κόψονται *kopsontai*) may connote either sorrow directed toward Jesus—i.e., repentance and devotion to him (as Luke 23:7; *Gos. Pet.* 8:28; cf. Rev 1:7)—or sorrow and despair, lamenting one's own loss (Matt 11:17). Does it here express universal repentance and conversion (including the repentance of Israel) occasioned by the eschatological events? Or will it then be too late for repentance, so that the unconverted multitudes can only bewail the return of the judge

who will condemn them? The declaration is a prophetic combination of Dan 7:13 and Zech 12:10, whose original contexts indicate the mourning of repentance with subsequent service to the Son of Man.[524] This may be Matthew's meaning, too, yet he leaves the issue provocatively open.[525]

Matthew has little speculative interest in what will happen at the parousia. His "description" functions to warn against indifference and to encourage active vigilance. There is only one image: the powerful figure of the Son of Man sending out his angels to gather the elect. This is not a portrayal of the "rapture," in which Jesus comes back to take his disciples out of the world for a period prior to the end. This idea is foreign to Matthew's eschatology.[526] Rather than providing a sequence of eschatological events involving two second comings, Matthew portrays one great final event, which he describes under more than one image. The basic idea of the whole discourse is "judgment" (κρίσις *krisis*; κρίνω *krino*), the final identification, sorting out, and separation of good and evil. Here, the judgment/separation is pictured as sending out angelic harvesters to gather the elect to the Son of Man. Other pictures of judgment and separation are found in the parenetic parables and warnings to follow, which are elaborated and concluded in the final scene of the last judgment. (See Reflections at 25:31-46.)

524. Since this combination is also found independently in Rev 1:7, it apparently represents a firm early Christian tradition derived from a Christian scribal-prophetic school.
525. This is related to the interpretation of 23:39; see Commentary there.
526. See Robert Jewett, *Jesus Against the Rapture: Seven Unexpected Prophecies* (Philadelphia: Westminster, 1979). The idea of "gathering" is one way to express the separation involved in judgment, as in both the Markan apocalypse adopted here (cf. Mark 13:27) and in the Q apocalypse adopted in vv. 37-40 below. Cf. 25:34.

Matthew 24:32–25:46, Parables and Warnings

OVERVIEW

The remainder of the judgment discourse is composed of seven parables and monitory pictures that call the Matthean community to a life of active expectation of the parousia of the Son of Man. The first three and the fifth sections function as warnings to be alert, while sections 4 and 6 explicate the meaning of "being alert"—not mere passive waiting

but responsible action that corresponds to the nature of the coming kingdom. The seventh and concluding scene portrays the criterion of the coming judgment, serving as an indirect admonition to practice the deeds of love and mercy that will count in the judgment and completing the picture of the coming of the Son of Man begun at 24:29-31.

MATTHEW 24:32-35, THE FIG TREE

NIV

32"Now learn this lesson from the fig tree: As soon as its twigs get tender and its leaves come out, you know that summer is near. 33Even so, when you see all these things, you know that it^a is near, right at the door. 34I tell you the truth, this generation^b will certainly not pass away until all these things have happened. 35Heaven and earth will pass away, but my words will never pass away."

^a33 Or he   ^b34 Or race

NRSV

32"From the fig tree learn its lesson: as soon as its branch becomes tender and puts forth its leaves, you know that summer is near. 33So also, when you see all these things, you know that he^a is near, at the very gates. 34Truly I tell you, this generation will not pass away until all these things have taken place. 35Heaven and earth will pass away, but my words will not pass away."

^aOr it

COMMENTARY

This instructive analogy (not parable in the sense of 13:1-52) has two halves, the pictorial half that illustrates a reality in the corresponding historical half. In the picture half, the fig tree is an illustration of the sure sign of the coming of summer. Unlike most trees in Israel, which are evergreen, fig trees lose their leaves in winter. But unlike most deciduous trees, they do not usually bud at the beginning of spring, but at the very end. Thus while most trees indicate only that spring has begun, the budding of the fig tree indicates that spring is almost over and summer is near. In the Markan apocalypse, the budding of the fig is a picture of the near approach of the eschaton, which could be discerned by the signs of the great tribulation and the desolating sacrilege. Given Matthew's emphasis that the parousia will come without signs (see above and in Reflections at 25:31-46), these same words in Matthew point to the certainty and nearness of the parousia, not to its calculability.

The fig tree and summer are elements of the pictorial side of the analogy, while "these things" and the end belong to the world of history and eschatology:

Picture:
fig tree produces leaves   ➡   summer is near
Reality:
"all these things" happen   ➡ Son of Man is near

As the above exegesis indicates, for Matthew "all these things" are the climax of the great tribulation and the cosmic events that are part of the parousia itself, not this-worldly historical events that can be used as a basis for calculation of the end.[527] By combining Mark and Q, Matthew has rejected the idea that even attentive observers can perceive the precise eschatological timetable. What is clear for Matthew is that the parousia will happen in his own time, among the generation that experienced the presence of Jesus personally (24:34; cf. 16:28), and its certainty, since it is founded on the word of Jesus, is more enduring than the earth itself (24:35; cf. Commentary on 5:18).

527. In this analogy, there is no correlation between the fig tree and Israel, as though the budding of the fig tree corresponds to the reestablishment of the state of Israel in 1948. This once-popular interpretation confused the two halves of the analogy.

MATTHEW 24:36-42, THE DAYS OF NOAH

NIV

36"No one knows about that day or hour, not even the angels in heaven, nor the Son,[a] but only the Father. 37As it was in the days of Noah, so it will be at the coming of the Son of Man. 38For in the days before the flood, people were eating and drinking, marrying and giving in marriage, up to the day Noah entered the ark; 39and they knew nothing about what would happen until the flood came and took them all away. That is how it will be at the coming of the Son of Man. 40Two men will be in the field; one will be taken and the other left. 41Two women will be grinding with a hand mill; one will be taken and the other left.

42"Therefore keep watch, because you do not know on what day your Lord will come."

a36 Some manuscripts do not have nor the Son.

NRSV

36"But about that day and hour no one knows, neither the angels of heaven, nor the Son,[a] but only the Father. 37For as the days of Noah were, so will be the coming of the Son of Man. 38For as in those days before the flood they were eating and drinking, marrying and giving in marriage, until the day Noah entered the ark, 39and they knew nothing until the flood came and swept them all away, so too will be the coming of the Son of Man. 40Then two will be in the field; one will be taken and one will be left. 41Two women will be grinding meal together; one will be taken and one will be left. 42Keep awake therefore, for you do not know on what day[b] your Lord is coming."

a Other ancient authorities lack nor the Son
b Other ancient authorities read at what hour

COMMENTARY

24:36. In Mark this saying forms the conclusion of the Apocalyptic Discourse. In Matthew's rewriting, however, it is joined with the following sayings taken from Q (Matt 24:37-51 = Luke 17:26-27; 12:39-46; 13:28)[528] to form the thematic heading for the extended series of warnings of 24:36–25:30. It would be difficult to make the declaration more emphatic; even the Son of Man does not know the time of his own parousia.[529]

24:37-39. The comparison with the days of Noah (Genesis 6–9) is not the wickedness of that generation, but that life was going on as usual, with no striking or mysterious signs of the approaching judgment. Matthew's eschatological teaching is not that discerning disciples who know

how to decode the prophetic scriptures will be able to recognize when the end is near, but that people did not know, a theme Matthew emphasizes repeatedly (24:36, 39, 42-44, 48, 50; 25:13), thus playing down the traditional saying taken over from Mark, "by this you will know" (24:33). What the disciples do know is that the end could come at any time; this knowledge should spur active engagement in their assigned mission.

24:40-41. Modern dispensationalism has understood those who are "taken" as those who are temporarily removed from the world at the rapture. Matthew has no rapture in his eschatological understanding (see footnote 525). Those who are "taken" refers to being gathered into the saved community at the eschaton, just as some were taken into the ark. To be a believer is to endure faithfully the tribulation, which is part of the church's mission, not to escape from it. The point is that in the present the two men in the field and the two women grinding at the mill appear alike, but the parousia will disclose that one is saved and one is lost. The eschatological judgment

528. The "but" (δέ de) in 25:36 is adversative; "as" (ὥσπερ hōsper) of 25:37 joins it to the preceding. See Walter Bauer, *A Greek-English Lexicon of the New Testament and Other Early Christian Literature,* rev. ed. (Chicago: University of Chicago Press, 1979) 899.

529. Nor should any emphasis be placed on "day and hour." It is a counsel of desperation (and strange christology) to suggest that the Son of Man knows the general time of the parousia (or even the minute!), but not the exact day. The whole point is to discourage such speculation. This text later became problematic for trinitarian christology, was used by the Arians, and hence "nor the Son" was dropped from some MSS. Since it is "more difficult reading," and since Matthew has added "alone" (μόνος monos) to "Father," it is clear that it was in Matthew's original text.

has a revelatory function: The crucified Jesus is already the Christ, and the persecuted church is already the elect people of God, but the reality is hidden except to eyes of faith. The eschaton will make the present hidden reality apparent to all: when the crucified one is revealed to all, the Son of Man and his persecuted community will be revealed as the elect people of God.

Corresponding to his conflict-of-kingdoms theology, the present spectrum of church and humanity with an apparent broad middle ground will at the eschaton be separated into two—and only two—groups. The remaining parables and admonitions all emphasize this in their various ways (wise/foolish; faithful/evil; good and faithful/evil). (See Reflections at 25:31-46.)

MATTHEW 24:43-44, THE THIEF

NIV	NRSV
43"But understand this: If the owner of the house had known at what time of night the thief was coming, he would have kept watch and would not have let his house be broken into. 44So you also must be ready, because the Son of Man will come at an hour when you do not expect him."	43"But understand this: if the owner of the house had known in what part of the night the thief was coming, he would have stayed awake and would not have let his house be broken into. 44Therefore you also must be ready, for the Son of Man is coming at an unexpected hour."

COMMENTARY

It is a bold metaphor to picture the return of Jesus as the breaking and entering of a thief, but one that became traditional in the prophetic stream of early Christianity (1 Thess 5:2; Rev 3:3; 16:15). The fact that Matthew's metaphors are not to be interpreted as one consistent allegorical portrayal is seen from the fact that previously not

knowing is the reason for vigilance, while in this parable the one who *does* know is vigilant. The variety of pictures communicates the one point: The time of the parousia cannot be calculated. Disciples are to be busy with the assigned mission, not with apocalyptic speculation. (See Reflections at 25:31-46.)

MATTHEW 24:45-51, THE GOOD AND WICKED SERVANTS

NIV	NRSV
45"Who then is the faithful and wise servant, whom the master has put in charge of the servants in his household to give them their food at the proper time? 46It will be good for that servant whose master finds him doing so when he returns. 47I tell you the truth, he will put him in charge of all his possessions. 48But suppose that servant is wicked and says to himself, 'My master is staying away a long time,' 49and he then begins to beat his fellow servants and to eat and drink with drunkards. 50The master of that servant will come on a day when he does not expect him and at an hour he is not aware of. 51He will cut him	45"Who then is the faithful and wise slave, whom his master has put in charge of his household, to give the other slaves[a] their allowance of food at the proper time? 46Blessed is that slave whom his master will find at work when he arrives. 47Truly I tell you, he will put that one in charge of all his possessions. 48But if that wicked slave says to himself, 'My master is delayed,' 49and he begins to beat his fellow slaves, and eats and drinks with drunkards, 50the master of that slave will come on a day when he does not expect him and at an hour that he does not know. 51He will
	[a] Gk to give them

447

NIV	NRSV
to pieces and assign him a place with the hypocrites, where there will be weeping and gnashing of teeth."	cut him in pieces[a] and put him with the hypocrites, where there will be weeping and gnashing of teeth."
	[a]Or cut him off

COMMENTARY

This theme continues with a picture of a faithful and wise servant who meets responsibilities assigned by the absent Lord, without trying to calculate the date of his return. As in the conclusion of the Sermon on the Mount, the "wise" (φρόνιμος phronimos) servant is the one who obeys, not the one who calculates. This parable does not indicate that Matthew is developing a doctrine of the "delay of the parousia"; talk of delay is found only in the mouths of irresponsible servants who think they can predict the time of the parousia (v. 48). There must have been such talk in Matthew's church in the latter part of the first century, but Matthew opposes it. Since Matthew tended to interpret parables allegorically, he

probably understood this parable to be directed especially to church leaders who, in the light of what they perceived as a delay of the parousia, abused their authority for their own self-aggrandizement. Contrary to their calculations, the Lord will return unexpectedly and submit them to a horrible punishment, literally "cutting in two," the dismemberment traditionally practiced by Persian tyrants. Matthew adds to the Q saying that they will be counted among the unbelievers (which Matthew changes to "hypocrites"), making contact with the woes of 23:13-36 and showing once again that, as here, they are directed as warnings to Christian leaders.

REFLECTIONS

1. This passage is about the coming of the kingdom in its fullness, the return of Jesus. We might find ourselves asking: What do we know and what do we not know? It is easy to say what we don't know. We don't know the time—the year, the month, the day, or the hour. People who pore over the books of Daniel and Revelation, attempting to crack their code, are fooling themselves. We are called to be agnostics about the time of Jesus' return. We simply do not know.

What we do know, however, is what we are supposed to be doing in the meantime. Because we don't know the day or the hour, we are always to be "ready"; in the context of the Gospel of Matthew, that means doing the deeds of mercy, forgiveness, and peace that characterize kingdom people. Throughout church history, there have always been groups that, convinced they knew when the world would end, would quit their jobs and wait with eager anticipation for Christ's appearance. In Matthew's understanding of the Christian faith, the second coming doesn't cause us to quit the job of being the church in the world; rather, it calls us to take it up with even more urgency.

2. Matthew seems to be especially concerned with the proper exercise of authority in the church. On the one hand, he has a high view of churchly authority; the disciples share in the messianic authority of Jesus (cf. 10:1-5a; 19:28). But just as the kingship as proclaimed and lived out by Jesus is radically different from secular kingship (cf. 20:20-28), so also authority is seen in an entirely different way. Following Matthew's allegorical lead, John Meier points out that in 24:45-51 such authority is (1) derivative, (2) temporary, (3) for the good of others, and (4) democratic—in this parable the one appointed over others is also a servant.[530]

530. John Meier, *Matthew,* New Testament Message 3 (Collegeville, Minn.: Liturgical Press, 1990) 293, on 24:45-51.

MATTHEW 25:1-13, THE BRIDESMAIDS

NIV

25 "At that time the kingdom of heaven will be like ten virgins who took their lamps and went out to meet the bridegroom. ²Five of them were foolish and five were wise. ³The foolish ones took their lamps but did not take any oil with them. ⁴The wise, however, took oil in jars along with their lamps. ⁵The bridegroom was a long time in coming, and they all became drowsy and fell asleep.

⁶"At midnight the cry rang out: 'Here's the bridegroom! Come out to meet him!'

⁷"Then all the virgins woke up and trimmed their lamps. ⁸The foolish ones said to the wise, 'Give us some of your oil; our lamps are going out.'

⁹" 'No,' they replied, 'there may not be enough for both us and you. Instead, go to those who sell oil and buy some for yourselves.'

¹⁰"But while they were on their way to buy the oil, the bridegroom arrived. The virgins who were ready went in with him to the wedding banquet. And the door was shut.

¹¹"Later the others also came. 'Sir! Sir!' they said. 'Open the door for us!'

¹²"But he replied, 'I tell you the truth, I don't know you.'

¹³"Therefore keep watch, because you do not know the day or the hour."

NRSV

25 "Then the kingdom of heaven will be like this. Ten bridesmaids[a] took their lamps and went to meet the bridegroom.[b] ²Five of them were foolish, and five were wise. ³When the foolish took their lamps, they took no oil with them; ⁴but the wise took flasks of oil with their lamps. ⁵As the bridegroom was delayed, all of them became drowsy and slept. ⁶But at midnight there was a shout, 'Look! Here is the bridegroom! Come out to meet him.' ⁷Then all those bridesmaids[a] got up and trimmed their lamps. ⁸The foolish said to the wise, 'Give us some of your oil, for our lamps are going out.' ⁹But the wise replied, 'No! there will not be enough for you and for us; you had better go to the dealers and buy some for yourselves.' ¹⁰And while they went to buy it, the bridegroom came, and those who were ready went with him into the wedding banquet; and the door was shut. ¹¹Later the other bridesmaids[a] came also, saying, 'Lord, lord, open to us.' ¹²But he replied, 'Truly I tell you, I do not know you.' ¹³Keep awake therefore, for you know neither the day nor the hour.[c]"

a Gk *virgins*   b Other ancient authorities add *and the bride*
c Other ancient authorities add *in which the Son of Man is coming*

COMMENTARY

The chapter division here is particularly disruptive, for this story continues the theme developed above. Like all else in 23:1–25:46, the story is an integral part of the judgment discourse (see Overview at 23:1). There are points of contact with Mark 13:35 and Q (Luke 13:25-28), but the story itself is unique to Matthew.

While some have argued that an original parable of Jesus is at the core (Jülicher, Dodd, Jeremias), others have seen it as a Matthean allegorical composition by the early church (Linnemann; Perkins) or of Matthew himself (Bultmann, Bornkamm, Scott). The key issue is whether the details are realistic (parable) or seem contrived to fit the theological meaning (allegory). Unfortunately, we do not know the marriage customs of first-century Palestine well enough to make definitive judgments on this basis, and the story itself is unclear on the procedures of the wedding celebration. Where is the bride, who is never mentioned?[531] There do seem to be tensions with the customs described by Matthew in other

---

531. Some MSS add "and the bride" at the end of v. 1, "a natural but thoughtless interpolation" (W. C. Allen, *A Crticial and Exegetical Commentary on the Gospel According to St. Matthew*, ICC [New York: Scribner's, 1910] 262).

allusions to weddings. In 22:1-2 there are no bridesmaids awaiting the bridegroom's arrival, but all come to the home of the bridegroom; in 9:15 members of the wedding party are mentioned, but not "virgins" (the literal meaning for the word translated "bridesmaids" by the NRSV throughout). Further, details within the present story seem inherently unrealistic, whatever the wedding customs were: (1) the arrival of the bridegroom at midnight seems strange, but corresponds to the image of the thief in 24:43. (2) The notion that at midnight shops would be open where the foolish bridesmaids could go to buy oil also seems unrealistic and contrived. When one considers that numerous themes are thoroughly Matthean (see below) and that several details are entirely transparent to the theological points Matthew obviously wants to make, it seems likely that the story is an allegory constructed by Matthew to further illustrate and emphasize the theme of being ready for the coming of the Lord, despite the apparent delay.

The bridegroom is Jesus at his eschatological advent. This is clear from Matthew's previous use of this imagery (9:15; 22:1-3), in Jesus' being addressed as "Lord" and in speaking in solemn ἀμήν (*amēn*) pronouncements (25:12; cf. 5:18).

The bridesmaids represent the church, the present *corpus mixtum* that will be sorted out at the parousia. They all have lamps and oil, and all sleep, but only some are really prepared for the eschaton when it comes. Although the image of Yahweh as bridegroom and Israel as bride was prevalent in the OT and Jewish tradition, and continued in the Christian community with the bridegroom representing Christ and the church as the bride (John 3:29; 2 Cor 11:2; Eph 5:25-32; Rev 19:7; 21:2, 9, 17), that imagery does not fit Matthew's purposes here, and the bride does not appear at all. To represent the church, Matthew needed a group in which the members looked the same to external appearances, but who would be separated at the parousia. The scene is analogous to 13:36-43, also a Matthean allegory in which the present mixture of authentic and pseudo-disciples will be sorted out only eschatologically. The "wise" and "foolish" terminology corresponds to 7:24-27, where two men build houses that superficially appear alike, but only one of which meets the eschatological test.

The bridegroom's delay does not indicate that Matthew expects a further long delay (see 24:48 and Reflections below). In his situation there has already been a delay. His story points out that both those who thought the parousia would never take place and those who counted on a long delay and thus "still had time" were tragically mistaken.

The bridegroom's arrival is the parousia, with the same phrase, "to meet" (εἰς ἀπάντησιν *eis apantēsin*), used here as in 1 Thess 4:17. Since Matthew designates the story as "like the kingdom of heaven," this shows that the kingdom has a future aspect, that the final coming of the kingdom for which the church prays (6:10) is identical with the parousia of the Son of Man. Both Son of Man and kingdom of God have present and future aspects.

The oil, or rather *having* oil, represents what will count at the parousia: deeds of love and mercy in obedience to the Great Commandment (25:31-46).[532] This makes contact with Jewish traditions that used oil as a symbol for good deeds (*Num. Rab.* 13:15-16), while in other symbolism oil represents the Torah (*Deut. Rab.* 7). The problem was not having "oil" and not that they went to sleep, since both the "wise" and the "foolish" bridesmaids fall asleep. Here, Matthew pictures preparation for the parousia as responsible deeds of discipleship, not constant "watching" for the end.

The futile attempt to buy oil after the arrival of the bridegroom, though historically unrealistic, shows the futility of trying to prepare when it is too late. As in other Matthean scenes, there are finally only two groups: those who are ready and those who are not. As in the Sermon on the Mount, Matthew is not averse to closing on a negative note, with those who say "Lord, Lord" being excluded if they do not have the corresponding deeds of discipleship (cf. 7:21-27). The Sermon on the Mount has much more in common with the "eschatological discourse" than is generally noticed by those who are fascinated only by the one or the other. Both are thoroughly christological; both are thoroughly eschatological; both are thoroughly committed to the conviction that having the right confession without the corresponding life is ultimately disastrous.

532. The symbolism functions as in the parable of the talents; see note 536 below.

The conclusion in 25:13 is taken from Mark 13:35, but it is given a new content and meaning. In Mark, as the conclusion of a different parable, the identical words are properly translated "keep awake" (γρηγορέω *grēgoreō*). But in the Matthean story, the maidens' problem is not that they fall asleep, which both good and bad do. "Keeping awake" (or "keep watch" [NIV] translations of *gregoreō*), in the sense of constantly being on the alert for signs of the coming of the Son of Man, is not Matthew's understanding of responsible discipleship. Matthew opposes the frantic quest for eschatological information, and he pictures faithful disciples as those who do their duty at appropriate times and are thus prepared for the parousia whenever it comes. Such disciples can lie down to sleep in this confidence, rather than being kept awake by panicky last-minute anxiety. Thus the Matthean meaning for *grēgoreō* is "be prepared," not "keep awake"/"watch," and it might better be so translated in this context.

REFLECTIONS

Right at the beginning of the parable of the ten bridesmaids, Jesus tells us that five of them were foolish, and five were wise. The reason why he tells us this from the outset is that we cannot tell this just by looking at them. All ten have come to the wedding; all ten have their lamps aglow with expectation; all ten, presumably, have on their bridesmaid gowns. We would never guess from appearances that half are wise and half foolish.

No, it is not the looks, the lamps, or the long dresses that sets the wise apart from the foolish—it's the readiness. Five of the bridesmaids are ready for the groom to be delayed, but the other five are not. The wise have enough oil for the wedding to start whenever the groom arrives; the foolish have only enough oil for their own timetable. Five are prepared and ready, even for a delay; five are not.

Readiness in Matthew is, of course, living the life of the kingdom, living the quality of life described in the Sermon on the Mount. Many can do this for a short while; but when the kingdom is delayed, the problems arise. Being a peacemaker for a day is not as demanding as being a peacemaker year after year when the hostility breaks out again and again, and the bridegroom is delayed. Being merciful for an evening can be pleasant; being merciful for a lifetime, when the groom is delayed, requires preparedness.

At the beginning of the life of faith, you cannot really tell the followers of Jesus apart. They all have lamps; they are all excited about the wedding; they all know how to sing, "Lord, lord." Deep into the night, when we spot some persons attempting in vain to fan a dying flame to life, we begin to distinguish wisdom from foolishness.

MATTHEW 25:14-30, THE TALENTS

NIV	NRSV
[14]"Again, it will be like a man going on a journey, who called his servants and entrusted his property to them. [15]To one he gave five talents[a] of money, to another two talents, and to another one talent, each according to his ability. Then he went on his journey. [16]The man who had received the five talents went at once and put his money to work and gained five more. [17]So also, the one	14"For it is as if a man, going on a journey, summoned his slaves and entrusted his property to them; [15]to one he gave five talents,[a] to another two, to another one, to each according to his ability. Then he went away. [16]The one who had received the five talents went off at once and traded with them, and made five more talents. [17]In the same way, the one who had the two
[a]*15 A talent was worth more than a thousand dollars.*	[a]A talent was worth more than fifteen years' wages of a laborer

NIV

with the two talents gained two more. ¹⁸But the man who had received the one talent went off, dug a hole in the ground and hid his master's money.

¹⁹"After a long time the master of those servants returned and settled accounts with them. ²⁰The man who had received the five talents brought the other five. 'Master,' he said, 'you entrusted me with five talents. See, I have gained five more.'

²¹"His master replied, 'Well done, good and faithful servant! You have been faithful with a few things; I will put you in charge of many things. Come and share your master's happiness!'

²²"The man with the two talents also came. 'Master,' he said, 'you entrusted me with two talents; see, I have gained two more.'

²³"His master replied, 'Well done, good and faithful servant! You have been faithful with a few things; I will put you in charge of many things. Come and share your master's happiness!'

²⁴"Then the man who had received the one talent came. 'Master,' he said, 'I knew that you are a hard man, harvesting where you have not sown and gathering where you have not scattered seed. ²⁵So I was afraid and went out and hid your talent in the ground. See, here is what belongs to you.'

²⁶"His master replied, 'You wicked, lazy servant! So you knew that I harvest where I have not sown and gather where I have not scattered seed? ²⁷Well then, you should have put my money on deposit with the bankers, so that when I returned I would have received it back with interest.

²⁸"'Take the talent from him and give it to the one who has the ten talents. ²⁹For everyone who has will be given more, and he will have an abundance. Whoever does not have, even what he has will be taken from him. ³⁰And throw that worthless servant outside, into the darkness, where there will be weeping and gnashing of teeth.' "

NRSV

talents made two more talents. ¹⁸But the one who had received the one talent went off and dug a hole in the ground and hid his master's money. ¹⁹After a long time the master of those slaves came and settled accounts with them. ²⁰Then the one who had received the five talents came forward, bringing five more talents, saying, 'Master, you handed over to me five talents; see, I have made five more talents.' ²¹His master said to him, 'Well done, good and trustworthy slave; you have been trustworthy in a few things, I will put you in charge of many things; enter into the joy of your master.' ²²And the one with the two talents also came forward, saying, 'Master, you handed over to me two talents; see, I have made two more talents.' ²³His master said to him, 'Well done, good and trustworthy slave; you have been trustworthy in a few things, I will put you in charge of many things; enter into the joy of your master.' ²⁴Then the one who had received the one talent also came forward, saying, 'Master, I knew that you were a harsh man, reaping where you did not sow, and gathering where you did not scatter seed; ²⁵so I was afraid, and I went and hid your talent in the ground. Here you have what is yours.' ²⁶But his master replied, 'You wicked and lazy slave! You knew, did you, that I reap where I did not sow, and gather where I did not scatter? ²⁷Then you ought to have invested my money with the bankers, and on my return I would have received what was my own with interest. ²⁸So take the talent from him, and give it to the one with the ten talents. ²⁹For to all those who have, more will be given, and they will have an abundance; but from those who have nothing, even what they have will be taken away. ³⁰As for this worthless slave, throw him into the outer darkness, where there will be weeping and gnashing of teeth.' "

COMMENTARY

A talent is a large sum of money, equal to the wages of a day laborer for fifteen years (see 18:23). Precisely as a result of the wide circulation of this story, "talent" came into the English language in the Middle Ages as a term for God-given abilities, "gifts and graces." The talents in this story refer to money (25:18); the differing abilities of the recipients are referred to in other terms (25:15).

The story has undergone several transformations in its trajectory from Jesus' original parable through Q (where it first becomes observable to us; cf. Luke 19:11-27) and the differing versions and interpretations that appear in Matthew, Luke, and the *Gospel of the Nazarenes.*[533]

In Jesus' original parable, a man entrusts each of three servants with a large amount of money.[534] Upon his return, the first two have worked with the capital and doubled it. Attention focuses on the third, who has acted with proper caution not to lose what was entrusted to him and is able to return it whole to the master.[535] When challenged as to why he has not increased the money entrusted to him, he responds with a characterization of the master as a harsh and unjust man who inspires only fear and caution. The hearers of the parable are doubly surprised and do not know what to think. On the one hand, the hearers have just seen proof of the master's generosity to the first two servants. On the other hand, the story has led them to be sympathetic to the action of the one-talent man in carefully hiding the money. To his (and the hearers') surprise, the one-talent man is condemned for fearful inactivity, and his money is given to the first servant, who already has ten talents.[536]

The hearers must decide which characterization of the master to accept. The parable has led them in both directions, and it creates a dilemma rather than resolving one.

Matthew reads the Q parable as an allegory of the parousia, rewriting it to serve that purpose, and he inserts it into this context (cf. its different location in Luke 19). Matthew uses the story to fill in the content of the nature of the Christian life as "waiting" for the parousia. The meaning of being "good and faithful" is not mere theological correctness, passive waiting, or strict obedience to clear instructions, but active responsibility that takes initiative and risk (see on 5:21-48). In the story, the master gives no instructions as to what is to be done with the money, so faithfulness is not merely obedience to directions. Each servant must decide how to use his time during the master's absence.[537]

A comparison with related Matthean parables is instructive. (1) In 18:23-35 also a servant is entrusted with the great wealth of another, and a reckoning is called for (the words *talents* and *accounting* are found only in these two parables in the NT). In 18:23-25, the servant is forgiven a fabulous debt incurred by his mismanagement of his master's money; here, a servant is condemned, although he had lost nothing of his master's money. (2) In 24:45-51, as here, a servant is judged to be evil and receives exactly the same terrible punishment; there it is a matter of actively and profligately abusing his authority, while here the "evil" servant is cautiously circumspect. Such contrasts in Matthew's pictures of the judgment and the ultimate judge serve to guard the reader from too readily objectifying the meanings presented allegorically and to frustrate our efforts to summarize the way God works into neat coherent systems. The pictures point beyond themselves and resist systematization, while still speaking of the reality of judgment and the necessity for decision and responsible action. (See Reflections at 25:31-46.)

---

533. The *Gospel of the Nazarenes* presents the latest form, in which one servant multiplies the capital, one hides it, and one squanders it with harlots and flute girls. The first is rewarded, the second rebuked, the third cast into prison (see Wilhelm Schneemelcher, *New Testament Apocrypha: I Gospels and Related Writings* [Louisville: Westminster/John Knox, 1990] 161). This version is more satisfying to our aesthetic and moral sense; therefore, it is furthest removed from the original story of Jesus, which was upsetting to our ideas of justice.

534. See Bernard Brandon Scott, *Hear Then the Parable* (Minneapolis: Fortress, 1989) 217-36, for a good reconstruction of the original structure and impact of Jesus' parable.

535. Scott gives good evidence that the original hearers would have considered burying the money a responsible act, in contrast to the third servant in the Lukan version, who irresponsibly keeps the money in a napkin and is thus merely lucky to still have it at the master's return.

536. For the first time at 25:28-29, the hearer realizes that the vast amount of money originally thought to be entrusted to the servants only to manage has been given to them as their own. Only the third servant continues to regard the money as his master's (v. 25). With the realization that emerges at v. 28, the whole parable must be understood in terms of grace and the response to it, rather than stewardship of property that remains another's.

537. The talent itself does not stand for anything; it is what one does with the entrusted talent that represents the responsible deeds of Christian discipleship, just as oil in the preceding parable does not stand for anything, but responsible discipleship is represented parabolically by the whole act of being prepared by having oil.

MATTHEW 25:31-46, THE LAST JUDGMENT

NIV	NRSV

NIV

31"When the Son of Man comes in his glory, and all the angels with him, he will sit on his throne in heavenly glory. 32All the nations will be gathered before him, and he will separate the people one from another as a shepherd separates the sheep from the goats. 33He will put the sheep on his right and the goats on his left.

34"Then the King will say to those on his right, 'Come, you who are blessed by my Father; take your inheritance, the kingdom prepared for you since the creation of the world. 35For I was hungry and you gave me something to eat, I was thirsty and you gave me something to drink, I was a stranger and you invited me in, 36I needed clothes and you clothed me, I was sick and you looked after me, I was in prison and you came to visit me.'

37"Then the righteous will answer him, 'Lord, when did we see you hungry and feed you, or thirsty and give you something to drink? 38When did we see you a stranger and invite you in, or needing clothes and clothe you? 39When did we see you sick or in prison and go to visit you?'

40"The King will reply, 'I tell you the truth, whatever you did for one of the least of these brothers of mine, you did for me.'

41"Then he will say to those on his left, 'Depart from me, you who are cursed, into the eternal fire prepared for the devil and his angels. 42For I was hungry and you gave me nothing to eat, I was thirsty and you gave me nothing to drink, 43I was a stranger and you did not invite me in, I needed clothes and you did not clothe me, I was sick and in prison and you did not look after me.'

44"They also will answer, 'Lord, when did we see you hungry or thirsty or a stranger or needing clothes or sick or in prison, and did not help you?'

45"He will reply, 'I tell you the truth, whatever you did not do for one of the least of these, you did not do for me.'

46"Then they will go away to eternal punishment, but the righteous to eternal life."

NRSV

31"When the Son of Man comes in his glory, and all the angels with him, then he will sit on the throne of his glory. 32All the nations will be gathered before him, and he will separate people one from another as a shepherd separates the sheep from the goats, 33and he will put the sheep at his right hand and the goats at the left. 34Then the king will say to those at his right hand, 'Come, you that are blessed by my Father, inherit the kingdom prepared for you from the foundation of the world; 35for I was hungry and you gave me food, I was thirsty and you gave me something to drink, I was a stranger and you welcomed me, 36I was naked and you gave me clothing, I was sick and you took care of me, I was in prison and you visited me.' 37Then the righteous will answer him, 'Lord, when was it that we saw you hungry and gave you food, or thirsty and gave you something to drink? 38And when was it that we saw you a stranger and welcomed you, or naked and gave you clothing? 39And when was it that we saw you sick or in prison and visited you?' 40And the king will answer them, 'Truly I tell you, just as you did it to one of the least of these who are members of my family,[a] you did it to me.' 41Then he will say to those at his left hand, 'You that are accursed, depart from me into the eternal fire prepared for the devil and his angels; 42for I was hungry and you gave me no food, I was thirsty and you gave me nothing to drink, 43I was a stranger and you did not welcome me, naked and you did not give me clothing, sick and in prison and you did not visit me.' 44Then they also will answer, 'Lord, when was it that we saw you hungry or thirsty or a stranger or naked or sick or in prison, and did not take care of you?' 45Then he will answer them, 'Truly I tell you, just as you did not do it to one of the least of these, you did not do it to me.' 46And these will go away into eternal punishment, but the righteous into eternal life."

[a] Gk these my brothers

COMMENTARY

These are the last words of Jesus' last discourse, a climactic point to which Matthew has carefully built. Following the long series of six parables and warnings about living responsibly so as to be ready for the coming of the Son of Man (24:32–25:30), Matthew reverts to the actual coming already pictured in 24:29-31. This scene is unique to Matthew. It is not a parable, but an apocalyptic drama. Parables begin with familiar, this-worldly scenes, which then modulate into a new dimension of meaning. This scene, in contrast, begins with an other-worldly depiction of the parousia— the coming of the Son of Man with his angels and the gathering of all nations before his throne—and modulates into affirmations of the ultimate importance of ordinary, this-worldly deeds. While the evocative imagery cannot be reduced to a list of topics, Matthew has composed and located it so that several Matthean themes converge in this final scene.

The Two Kingdoms. The Son of Man, who comes at the end, is identified as the king (25:34, 40) who sits on his glorious throne (25:31) and who admits the righteous to the final kingdom of God (25:34). This is the triumph of the kingdom represented throughout the Gospel by Jesus as the alternative to the this-worldly demonic kingdom represented by his opponents (see Excursus "Kingdom of Heaven in Matthew," 288-94, and especially comments to 12:22-37). This negative counterkingdom is also represented in the imagery of the last judgment; the counterpart of the kingdom prepared from the foundation of the world (25:34) is the eternal fire prepared for the devil and his angels. The two kingdoms that are confused and interwoven in the ambiguities of history now stand disclosed at the end of history. There are only these two kingdoms: The Son of Man with his angels, the blessed righteous, and the kingdom of God prepared from eternity stand on one side; the devil and his angels, the accursed, and the destiny prepared for the devil and his own stand on the other. The kingdom of God is disclosed as the only true kingdom; in this final scene, kingdom language is not used of Satan's realm (cf. 12:26). The eschaton reveals that the apparent dualism of the present struggle of the two kingdoms is only penultimate, and that ultimately only God is King.

Christological Basis. A number of christological titles important throughout Matthew converge in this scene. Jesus is pictured as the Son of Man (25:31) who has God for his Father (25:34; thus an implicit Son of God christology is present here also). He is called "king," which connotes Messiah and Son of David in Matthew (1:1–2:2; 21:4-9), and is also called "Lord" (25:37, 44). He is the messianic shepherd who cares for the sheep (2:6; 9:36; 18:12; 26:31) and the judge who makes the final separation between sheep and goats. Even as "the one who comes" (25:31), Jesus fills a christological role (11:3; 23:39), anticipated by various figures in the preceding parables who "come" for a judgment scene (24:30, 42-44, 46; 25:10, 19, 27).

Thus the scene is through and through christological. For Matthew, this christology, and not a general humanitarianism, validates the ethic of love and mercy that becomes the eschatological criterion of judgment. This text cannot be used legitimately for biblical "support" for a general humanitarian ethic without coming to terms with the christology and apocalypticism in which it is inextricably embedded.

The Primacy of Ethics. Like the NT in general, Matthew has been very restrained, despite his apocalyptic orientation, in picturing what actually transpires when the Son of Man comes. This is the only scene with any details picturing the last judgment in the NT. To the reader's surprise (ancient and modern), the criterion of judgment is not confession of faith in Christ. Nothing is said of grace, justification, or the forgiveness of sins. What counts is whether one has acted with loving care for needy people. Such deeds are not a matter of "extra credit," but constitute the decisive criterion of judgment presupposed in all of vv. 23-25, the "weightier matters of the Law" of 23:23.

The Ultimacy of the Love Command. Jesus has taught that self-giving care for others is the heart of the revealed will of God in the Torah and its hermeneutical key (5:17-48; 7:12; 22:34-40). The messianic king has lived out his teaching that his kingdom consists of service to others (20:28). The same word translated "minister" (διακονέω *diakoneō*) recurs here as the final summary of the deeds performed by the righteous and neglected by the condemned (25:44).

All of this is clearly the major thrust of this scene. The particular Matthean meaning, however, has been disputed from earliest times. The large number of interpretations can be reduced to two issues and their variations.[538] (1) Who are "all the nations" (πάντα τὰ ἔθνη *panta ta ethnē*) and (2) who are "the least of these who are my brothers and sisters?" (ἀδελφοί *adelphoi*). (1) The major issue with regard to the "nations" is whether they (a) represent all the peoples of the earth, so that this is a picture of universal judgment, or (b) only a smaller group (Gentiles, Christians). Since *ethnē* is neuter, the shift to the masculine pronoun for "them" (αὐτούς *autous*) in 25:32 shows that it is individual human beings, and not nations as corporate political structures, that stand before the judgment. (2) The major issue concerning the "least of these" is whether they are (a) the world's needy generally or (b) specifically Christians or Christian missionaries. It seems that all the evidence can best be accounted for as follows:

The fundamental thrust of this scene is that when people respond to human need, or fail to respond, they are in fact responding, or failing to respond, to Christ. Yet this turns out to be a surprise to both groups (25:37, 44). Those who provide food, drink, clothing, shelter for the needy and visit the sick and imprisoned respond entirely on the basis of the needs of "the least of these" and are surprised to learn at the judgment that there was a deeper dimension to their acts of human compassion. Thus the needy brother or sister is not restricted to Christians or missionaries, for *adelphoi* is dropped in 25:45 and is sometimes used elsewhere in Matthew of any person whose need calls for response (5:22-24, 47; 7:3-5). If a form of this story goes back to

Jesus, this was its original meaning; if composed by Matthew, this "universal" meaning is its primary level, which is not obliterated by other applications.

However, Matthew focuses this general point on the reception of Christian missionaries, so that one concrete instance of the criterion of judgment would be whether the Gentiles to whom Matthew's church is carrying on a mission have supported or hindered the missionaries. This, indeed, fits with Matthean statements elsewhere, where Christ is met in the "little ones" he sends out as missionaries, and those who give them even a drink of cold water are responding to Christ himself (10:40-42). In Matthew's social setting, this apocalyptic language addresses those who experience themselves as outsiders and rejected by the powerful of this world and encourages them with pictures of the grand reversal at the eschaton. Matthew focuses the general meaning to fit the situation of his community in particular.

Yet even strictly historical exegesis makes clear that this judgment discourse (23:1–25:46) is not intended to give instruction on abstract themes, but functions as address to the implied reader. Here as elsewhere in the five discourses, Jesus speaks past the characters in the story who become transparent to the Christians of Matthew's church. Like the preceding six sections, the scene encourages and warns the Christian reader that what will count in the judgment are deeds of love and mercy performed for the needy. Although the apocalyptic scene may picture "all the nations" and their treatment of Christian missionaries, the actual address is not to the nations, but to the Christians themselves. The scene does not picture Gentiles who are condemned for failing to minister to Christians or Christian missionaries (see on 7:12). For the implied reader, "the problem in view is not opposition to mission but rather the more general one of endurance to the end. . . . It is Christians who are enjoined to *humanitarian service*."[539]

---

538. Sherman W. Gray, *The Least of My Brothers: Matthew 25:31-46, A History of Interpretation,* SBLDS 114 (Atlanta: Scholars Press, 1989), distinguishes thirty-two different interpretations. For a full discussion advocating the "particularist" interpretation, see Stanton, *A Gospel for a New People,* 207-31.

539. Russell Pregeant, "The Matthean Undercurrent: Process Hermeneutic and the 'Parable of the Last Judgment,'" SBLSP (Missoula, Mont.: Scholars Press, 1975) 145.

REFLECTIONS

The following reflections are informed by the Judgment Discourse as a complete unit.

Like other speeches of Matthean composition, this discourse has internal tensions and tensions with other teachings of Jesus in Matthew. The parousia will both be preceded by clear signs (24:3, 5-33) and come without warning (24:37-44); oaths, including swearing "by heaven," are presumed to be legitimate, despite earlier teaching to the contrary (23:22 vs. 5:34); Jesus himself calls others "fools" (23:17), despite the strict prohibition of 5:22. The Pharisees' teaching (but not their deeds) is to be accepted (23:1-3), despite 16:11. Some of these tensions may be made more understandable (though not made consistent) by appreciating Matthew's task of incorporating traditions of various origins in his Gospel. He wanted to preserve both the Q apocalypse (Luke 17:20-36) and the Markan one (13:5-37), even though the former understood the parousia to come without signs and the latter gave explicit signs by which its nearness could be recognized. Each way of conceiving of the last days had value, and Matthew respected both of them as part of his sacred tradition, preserving both as witnesses to the meaning of Jesus' teaching, despite their inconsistencies. As a teacher of Christian scribal wisdom, Matthew had less respect for logical consistency and more appreciation for imaginative, provocative sayings than many of his modern interpreters. (See Reflections on 5:14-16.) Exegetical ingenuity should not be strained to make Matthew more consistent than he was interested in being, or in fact was.

1. Matthew 24 is not an "eschatological discourse" that presents Matthew's or Jesus' doctrine of the end, but is part of chaps. 23–25, whose aim is pastoral care and encouragement. A synopsis will show that by incorporating the "little apocalypse" of Mark 13 into this larger framework, Matthew (affirms but) reduces the significance of apocalyptic per se, subordinating it to other, more directly pastoral, forms of discourse. What Matthew presents, and what is to be preached from these texts, is judgment and warnings on Christian discipleship oriented toward the eschatological victory of the kingdom of God, represented in Christ.

2. This is accomplished by a variety of pictures that are not to be harmonized conceptually. No one picture can do justice to the transcendent reality to which it points. There are basically two types of pictures: (1) In the first of these, the risen Christ is present with his church throughout its historical pilgrimage and mission. Matthew affirms the transcendent lordship of the living Christ, whose words are not merely the remembered teachings of a dead rabbi. This is expressed in pictures of Christ's continuing presence with his church through the ages, a major theme of Matthean theology (see 1:23; 28:20). In such a picture, there is no need for, and no room for, an ascension in which Christ departs, a period of Christ's "absence," and then a "return" of Christ, for the risen Christ never departs (cf. the last words of the Gospel). (2) In a second type of picture, the transcendence of the living Christ is pictured in a different way that had already become traditional in early Christianity—that of the departure of Christ at the resurrection/ascension and his return at the parousia. In the first picture, Christ continues to be present; in the second, Christ is absent from this world during the period between ascension and parousia. Only this second picture can speak of a "return" of Christ; only the first can speak of Christ's "presence." Each has its valid theological point to make, but they cannot be conceptually resolved. Matthew inherited and adopted both pictures. He affirmed them both. The tensive relationship of these two fundamental pictures must not be reduced to neat, manageable concepts, such that, e.g., Christ is now present "spiritually" but will return "physically" at the parousia, an attempt at explanation that falsely objectifies the mystery of each reality, a reality that can be conceptualized and spoken of only pictorially.[540] Thus the plurality of inconsistent pictures is a theological advantage, pointing beyond each way of conceiving the transcendent lordship of Christ to the reality itself that cannot be univocally represented. Matthew takes each way of talking about Christ's transcendent lordship with utmost seriousness as representing the eschatological reality. Christ is already present/Christ will come again. The final scene pulls these two together, but not in a conceptually neat way; the Son of Man who comes in glory at the end (25:31) is already present, not only in the high moments of inner-church life, but especially as the one who is met in the encounter with the poor and needy (25:40, 45).

3. Did Matthew expect the parousia to occur soon? This question must not be answered on the basis of our centuries-later perspective. As encouragement to his persecuted community, Matthew repeats as his own conviction the message of the first Christian generation that the end would come in their own time (16:28; 24:34; cf. 1 Cor 15:51-52; 1 Thess 4:15; Rev 1:3). As the first century drew to a close, this did not mean for Matthew that he devised a historical view that allowed for an indefinite "delay of the parousia." In Matthew's view, by his time there had already been a delay, which meant that the time of the end was closer than ever. By twice repeating the statement that some of Jesus' contemporaries would still be alive when the parousia occurs (16:28; 24:34), even near the end of the first century, Matthew affirms that the end is even nearer than previously thought.

The repeated references to "delay" (e.g., 24:48; 25:5) represent the contrary view, apparently in the air in Matthew's church, but always expressed by unfaithful characters in the story, never by the narrator. Matthew's own concern is to oppose this view, since it breeds complacency (cf. 2 Pet 3:3-13). Rather, Matthew's point is that he and his community already live in the time of the final tribulation; the days have been shortened (24:22), so the end will come soon—and may come at any time.

Near expectation is not incompatible with his emphasis on discipline and structure in the community, as Qumran amply illustrates. Matthew's conviction about the nearness of the parousia is not a speculative interest in calculating the time of the end, but a pastoral concern: He wants Christians to be ready by using the intervening time responsibly (24:39, 42, 50; 25:13).

4. Matthew expected the near parousia, and it did not occur. Although the church through the centuries has devised numerous ways to rescue Matthew from this error and explain texts that seem to affirm it in ways more congenial to later perspectives,[541] it is more in accord with the nature of Scripture and the integrity to which the interpreter is called to allow Matthew to express his faith in his own apocalyptic terms, including its mistaken temporal elements. Matthew will not be forced to become a modern man, and the contemporary reader can still be grasped by the apocalyptic message in all its urgency and compelling power.

So understood, what might Matthew's apocalyptic scenes say to contemporary readers?

(A) Such apocalyptic pictures can be heard as an affirmation of Jesus' and Matthew's radical monotheism—living our own lives in faith in the one God whose kingdom (rulership) is

---

540. It may be helpful to remember, however, that in secular Greek the basic meaning of παρουσία (*parousia*) is "presence." Early Christianity, including Matthew, made it into a quasi-technical term for the eschatological appearance of Christ, the "second coming." Yet even when Matthew uses it in the sense of future eschatological appearance, it is still resonant with the overtones of the continuing presence of Christ so prominent in Matthew's theology.

541. The frequent use of "seem" in such discussions should alert the church to the danger of a docetic view of both Christ and Scripture.

presently often hidden, but ultimately prevails. Atheism and polytheism sometimes make more conceptual sense. Especially, those whose thinking has been shaped by the Bible are tempted toward a polytheistic dualism, making the devil or evil a second god. But apocalyptic is an expression of the Shema, Israel's monotheistic confession faith, and these apocalyptic pictures call us to covenant faithfulness to this one God.

(B) The eschatological age has begun. To confess that the Christ has come, and that he is Jesus of Nazareth, is to say that there will be no further, supplementary revelation until this same God who is definitively revealed in the meekness and suffering love of Jesus is revealed at the end as the One and only God. Matthew was not off center to link his apocalyptic pictures with his confession of Jesus as the Christ. Matthew's pictures of the threat of false messiahs as the end approaches should not be heard in our time as specific predictions of deceitful figures to arise, but such pictures need not be discarded as outmoded apocalyptic baggage either. They can still speak to our own time of the urgent danger of accepting other values as ultimate and other means of redeeming our lives and world than the way revealed in Jesus the Messiah.

MATTHEW 26:1–28:28, JESUS' PASSION AND RESURRECTION

OVERVIEW[542]

The story of Jesus' suffering and death has traditionally been called the "passion story," but the term does not occur in the Bible. One might assume from the English meaning of the word that this is because the story deals with intense feeling, but *passion* in this context is related to the word *passive*. The designation suggests that in this section of the story, Jesus is not active but passive; he does not act but is acted upon. He does not "die," but is killed, does not "rise" but is raised. In the suffering and death of the Son of Man, human beings are the actors on the surface of the narrative, and God is the hidden actor behind the scenes; in the resurrection, God alone is the actor.

Matthew closely follows the Markan story, as elsewhere omitting some of Mark's more colorful details, but including every narrative element except 14:51-52 and adding within the Markan narrative only the stories of the fate of Judas (27:3-10) and the guard at the tomb (27:62-66).[543]

The distinctive Matthean meaning is expressed by subtle modifications to the Markan story and by enhancing its literary structure. The theological focus of the Markan narrative is shifted in the following directions:

(1) Mark had restricted the pictures of Jesus as powerful Son of God almost exclusively to the first half of the Gospel, portraying the Jesus of the passion story as the victimized servant who passively endures suffering and death. Matthew extends the features of the powerful Son of God into the passion story itself, showing Jesus to be master of his own fate,[544] but still preserving the picture of Jesus as dying a truly human death.

(2) In Mark, the passion story for the first time reveals the true identity of Jesus (14:61-62; 15:39), which previously is concealed from other characters in the story (the "messianic secret"). Jesus' identity in Matthew has been public since the first chapter, so that the emphasis shifts from secrecy to the rejection of the Messiah by his own people.[545]

---

542. On Matthew 26–28 as a whole, see Donald Senior, *The Passion of Jesus in the Gospel of Matthew* (Wilmington, Del.: Michael Glazier, 1985); Raymond E. Brown, *The Death of the Messiah,* 2 vols. (New York: Doubleday, 1994).

543. Mark 14:1–16:8 contains 2,002 Greek words. If the 202 words of 27:3-10 and 27:62-66 are subtracted, the corresponding Matthean section 26:1–28:8 contains 2,173 words, more than half of which are verbally identical (or almost so) with Mark's text (1,034 identical; additional 197 variant forms of same words = 1231, 57 percent). Matthew does, of course, add additional material to the end of Mark (Matt 28:8b-20).

544. The Markan Jesus performs no healings or exorcisms in Jerusalem. Contrast Matthew's addition at 21:14-16.

545. Nils Dahl, "The Passion Narrative in Matthew," *Jesus in the Memory of the Early Church* (Minneapolis: Augsburg, 1976) 45-50, argues that this is a shift from christology to ecclesiology. Cf. Frank J. Matera, *Passion Narratives and Gospel Theologies* (New York: Paulist, 1986) 81.

(3) The picture of Jesus as "king of the Jews," already prominent in Mark, connects with Matthew's dualistic picture of the confrontation of kingdoms, which is thematic in the rest of the Gospel. (See 12:22-37 and Excursus "Kingdom of Heaven in Matthew," 288-94.)

(4) On the other hand, Jesus as the meek king who exercises his kingship by suffering evil rather than retaliation does not, as previously, withdraw from the confrontation as his means of expressing the nature of God's kingdom, but resolutely confronts the evil embodied in the Jewish and Roman leadership, as well as in the failure of his disciples.

(5) By prefacing the whole narrative with a birth story that corresponds in many ways to the passion story, Matthew has constructed a frame around the whole Gospel. This has the effect of placing the passion story in a new light as well. As the following examples demonstrate, Matthew has often adjusted the Markan passion story to make this hermeneutical function clearer:

2:3	all Jerusalem in uproar	21:10
2:13-15	exodus/Passover recapitulated	26:1, 17-29
2:4	opponents: chief priests/elders of the people (Pharisees and scribes in the meantime)	26:3-4
1:20; 2:12-13, 19, 22	revelation by dream (dreams absent in meantime)	27:19
1:20, 24; 2:13, 19	angelic appearances ("angel of the Lord" absent in meantime)	28:5
2:2, 8, 11	see and worship	28:17
2:3	troubled	28:17
1–2	kingship/authority, "king of the Jews"	28:18
1–2	Son of David/Son of Man imagery	28:18-20
1:2ff.; 2:1ff.	Gentiles	28:19
1:16-23	Father/Son/Holy Spirit	28:19
1:2-17	past historical connection/rest of history	28:20
1:23	the divine presence ("with" [μετά *meta*])	26:18, 20, 29, 38, 40; 28:20

In contrast to the smaller narrative and sayings units, which have been compiled by the evangelists to comprise the bulk of the Gospel narrative, the story of Jesus' passion and resurrection is the longest sustained narrative in the synoptic Gospels, and it must be read and understood as a unit. Changes of location divide the narrative into twenty-one separate scenes, with transitions that divide the story into coherent units, as represented by Figure 12 (cf. also Fig. 8, p. 401).

	Figure 12: The Structure of Matthew's Narrative of Jesus' Passion and Resurrection

Day 3—Wednesday

Scene 1   Matthew 26:1-2—Jesus announces his passion
         Mount of Olives
         Jesus and the disciples

Scene 2   Matthew 26:3-5—Leaders plot Jesus' death
         Palace of the high priest Caiaphas
         Chief priests and elders of the people

Scene 3   Matthew 26:6-13—An insightful woman anoints Jesus for burial
         Bethany, house of Simon the Leper
         Jesus, the disciples, unnamed woman

Scene 4   Matthew 26:14-16—Judas agrees to betray Jesus
         High priest's palace (?)
         Wednesday (?)
         Judas, chief priests

Day 4—Thursday

Scene 5   Matthew 26:17-19—Disciples prepare Passover
         Location?
         Jesus and disciples

Scene 6   Matthew 26:20-30*a*—Jesus predicts the betrayal and inaugurates the eucharist
         Jerusalem, house of "a certain man"
         Thursday evening
         Jesus and the disciples

Scene 7   Matthew 26:30*b*-35—Jesus predicts desertion and promises reunion
         The Mount of Olives
         Thursday evening
         Jesus and the eleven

Scene 8   Matthew 26:36-56—Jesus prays and is arrested
         Gethsemane
         Thursday evening
         Jesus and the eleven; Judas; large crowd from chief priests and
           elders of the people

Scene 9   Matthew 26:57–27:1—Jesus is condemned by the Jewish leaders
        and denied by Peter
         Caiaphas's house
         Late Thursday night and early Friday morning
         Officers, Jesus, Caiaphas, scribes and elders [Peter, guards], whole council,
           many false witnesses, two false witnesses [first servant girl, another servant
           girl, the bystanders]

Day 5—Friday

Scene 10   Matthew 27:2—Jesus is delivered over to Pilate
         Location?; Friday morning
         High priests and members of the council; Jesus; Pilate

Scene 11   Matthew 27:3-10—Judas fails to make restitution and commits suicide
         Temple (v. 5)

Friday morning (?)
Chief priests and elders; Judas

Scene 12 Matthew 27:11-25—Jesus is condemned; Jewish people accept responsibility
for Jesus' death
  Location?
  Friday morning
  Jesus, Pilate, chief priests and elders, the crowd ("the people as a whole"),
   [Barabbas, Pilate's wife]

Scene 13 Matthew 27:26-31*a*—The true king is mocked
  The Praetorium
  Friday morning
  Jesus, Roman soldiers

Scene 14 Matthew 27:31*b*-32—Simon is compelled to carry Jesus' cross
  En route to Golgotha
  Friday morning
  Soldiers, Jesus, Simon of Cyrene

Scene 15 Matthew 27:33-56—Jesus is crucified
  Golgotha
  Friday morning to 3:00 P.M.
  Jesus, soldiers, passers-by, chief priests and elders, criminals

Scene 16 Matthew 27:57-61—Jesus is buried
  From Golgotha to the tomb
  Friday evening
  Joseph, Pilate, Mary Magdalene, the "other Mary"

Day 6—Saturday

Scene 17 Matthew 27:62-66—Jesus' tomb is guarded and sealed
  Pilate's residence; Saturday (the sabbath)
  Chief priests, Pharisees, Pilate, soldiers

Day 7—Sunday

Scene 18 Matthew 28:1-7—The two Marys discover the empty tomb
  The tomb outside the city
  Early Sunday
  Mary Magdalene, the other Mary, the angel of the Lord, the guards

Scene 19 Matthew 28:8-10—The two Marys encounter the risen Jesus
  The road between the tomb and the city
  Early Sunday
  The two Marys and the risen Jesus

Scene 20 Matthew 28:11-15—The guards are bribed by the chief priests
  The city
  Sunday
  The chief priests, elders, and the guards

Scene 21 Matthew 28:16-20—The risen Lord gives the Great Commission
  A mountain in Galilee
  Indefinite time after Easter
  The Eleven and Jesus

Matthew 26:1-16, Plot and Extravagant Devotion

Matthew 26:1-2, Jesus Announces His Passion

NIV

26 When Jesus had finished saying all these things, he said to his disciples, ²"As you know, the Passover is two days away—and the Son of Man will be handed over to be crucified."

NRSV

26 When Jesus had finished saying all these things, he said to his disciples, ²"You know that after two days the Passover is coming, and the Son of Man will be handed over to be crucified."

COMMENTARY

Day 3 Begins: Wednesday. Here is the final appearance of the formula that has concluded each of the five major discourses of Jesus in the Gospel of Matthew (cf. 7:28; 11:1; 13:53; 19:1). "All" is added here to signal that Jesus' teaching ministry is now concluded (another reminiscence of Moses; cf. Deut 31:30; 32:44). There will be no discourses of Jesus in the passion story, where Jesus is almost completely silent (Isa 53:7; cf. Matt 12:15-21; cf. also the Fourth Gospel). As previously, the formula serves as a transition to the following narrative.

Matthew launches the passion story with an additional passion prediction, a declaration from Jesus himself, expanded and transposed from the narrator's comment in Mark 14:1. The declaration recalls to the reader's mind the other passion predictions (see 16:21), showing that Jesus himself inaugurates the events to follow, which he will not only endure, but of which he is also in some sense master. The announcement is not mere information, but a preemptive overruling of the plot of the chief priests and elders, who decide not to apprehend him during the Passover festival (vv. 4-5). When the course of events shows that Jesus is in fact put to death during the Passover festival, the reader will perceive from Jesus' announcement that the chief priests and elders, supposedly in charge of events, are incorrect and without real authority. "You know" is not a casual comment, but includes the disciples as understanding the meaning of the coming events in advance, another indication of Matthew's abandonment of the Markan view that the disciples' did not understand until after the

resurrection. Crucifixion is not specifically mentioned in the Markan passion predictions, but Matthew has made the disciples and the reader aware of the cross as Jesus' destiny since 10:38 (cf. 23:34), and he has added the word to 20:19 (= Mark 10:34).

Although previous chronological indicators have been vague or ambiguous, at this point Matthew joins the Markan chronology, and the story progresses with measured chronological precision.[546] The scene pictured in 26:2 takes place on Wednesday. At evening of the next day, Passover begins.[547] This is the first passion prediction to specify Passover, the Jewish festival of liberation and salvation that looked back to the deliverance under Moses and forward to the final deliverance by the Messiah.[548]

546. Matthew follows Mark in giving the day of the *month*, not the day of *week*. See notes on the Matthean chronology of Holy Week at 21:1 and 23:1.
547. Matthew omits Mark's incorrect identification of this as also the Festival of Unleavened Bread, which began the next day (cf. Lev 23:5-6; Num 28:16-17).
548. In interpreting the meaning of the Passover, the Targum Neofiti on Exod 12:42 gives a "Poem of the Four Nights of Salvation" from the "Book of Memorials." The *first* night was the night of chaos, overcome by God at the creation of the world. The *second* night was when God revealed to Abraham and Sarah that, despite their age, they would miraculously become the parents of a child who would be the beginning of the covenant people of Israel. The *third* night was the night of the original Passover and the deliverance from Egypt. The *fourth* night is "when the world reaches its end to be dissolved: the yokes of iron shall be broken and the generations of wickedness shall be blotted out; and Moses will go up from the desert (and the king Messiah from on high). One will lead at the head of the flock and his Word will lean between the two of them, and I (God) and they shall proceed together. *This is the night of the Passover* to the name of the Lord: it is a night reserved and set aside for the redemption of all the generations of Israel" (Cited from Xavier Leon-Dufour, *Sharing the Eucharistic Bread* [New York: Paulist, 1987] 191, adapted by him from M. McNamara and M. Maher in Diez Macho, ed., *Neophyti 1. Targum Palestinense ms de la Biblioteca Vaticana II. Exodo* [Madrid: Consejo Superior de Investigaciones Cientificas, 1970] 442.

It was a time of fervent religious expectation and excitement, a time in which masses of pilgrims filled Jerusalem with explosive potential. During the festival, the Roman governor regularly came to Jerusalem from his usual residence at Caesarea Maritima, with additional troops to quell any attempted uprising. It is a bizarre, ironic story that Matthew unfolds, the Jewish leaders plotting to execute their Messiah at the festival of national salvation (like executing Abraham Lincoln on the Fourth of July!). The Jewish festival of liberation and salvation provides the framework for portraying the saving work of Jesus,

whose name Matthew has explained in salvific terms (cf. 1:21) as the one designated "to save his people from their sins."[549]

After this transitional scene, Matthew has placed a unit of three scenes, in which the plotting of the chief priests and the betrayal of Judas surround the scene of Jesus' anointing.

549. Matthew is especially conscious of the meaning of Jesus' name and its relation to the passion story; thus he adds Jesus' name to his sources a total of eighty times, in the passion story using Jesus' name thirty-eight times to Mark's seventeen in approximately the same amount of narrative.

Matthew 26:3-5, Leaders Plot Jesus' Death

NIV	NRSV
[3]Then the chief priests and the elders of the people assembled in the palace of the high priest, whose name was Caiaphas, [4]and they plotted to arrest Jesus in some sly way and kill him. [5]"But not during the Feast," they said, "or there may be a riot among the people."	3Then the chief priests and the elders of the people gathered in the palace of the high priest, who was called Caiaphas, [4]and they conspired to arrest Jesus by stealth and kill him. [5]But they said, "Not during the festival, or there may be a riot among the people."

COMMENTARY

During Jesus' ministry, his opponents have regularly been the scribes and Pharisees who have previously plotted his death (12:14) and who reappear after the crucifixion (27:62). The "chief priests and elders of the people" introduced here are not really new, however, for already in the birth story they collaborated with King Herod in the attempt to destroy the Messiah (2:3-4), and the passion predictions name them as the ones who will finally engineer Jesus' death (16:21; 20:18). They first enter the story as opponents of Jesus after he arrives in Jerusalem (21:15). Caiaphas has not been mentioned previously in Matthew; he does not appear at all in Mark. The religious leaders are "gathered" (a form of συνάγω [synagō]) against Jesus.[550] Like the Pharisees earlier (12:14),

they do not consider an investigation or fair trial; they have already decided on his death. Matthew has so constructed the story that the reader already knows that the powerful word of Jesus and the purpose of God will overrule the plot of the Jewish leaders, and that Jesus will die on the day he has already designated by faithfully submitting to God's will rather than as a victim of their will. Although "kingdom" language is not used, in this paragraph the conflict of kingdoms, which has been the *leitmotif* of Matthew's narrative, comes to expression again. Jesus guides the passion rather than merely enduring it.

550. Matthew uses this word more than all the other Gospels together (24 times; Mark 5 times; Luke 6 times; John 7 times). Matthew often adds it to his sources to connote the hostile forces gathered against Jesus (27:27 is parallel to 26:57, 59; 27:17, 62). Cf. Ps 2:2, in which the nations, peoples, and rulers "synagogue" against the Lord's anointed. Such usage reflects the hostility between synagogue and church in Matthew's own community.

Matthew 26:6-13, An Insightful Woman Anoints Jesus for Burial

NIV

⁶While Jesus was in Bethany in the home of a man known as Simon the Leper, ⁷a woman came to him with an alabaster jar of very expensive perfume, which she poured on his head as he was reclining at the table.

⁸When the disciples saw this, they were indignant. "Why this waste?" they asked. ⁹"This perfume could have been sold at a high price and the money given to the poor."

¹⁰Aware of this, Jesus said to them, "Why are you bothering this woman? She has done a beautiful thing to me. ¹¹The poor you will always have with you, but you will not always have me. ¹²When she poured this perfume on my body, she did it to prepare me for burial. ¹³I tell you the truth, wherever this gospel is preached throughout the world, what she has done will also be told, in memory of her."

NRSV

6Now while Jesus was at Bethany in the house of Simon the leper,ᵃ ⁷a woman came to him with an alabaster jar of very costly ointment, and she poured it on his head as he sat at the table. ⁸But when the disciples saw it, they were angry and said, "Why this waste? ⁹For this ointment could have been sold for a large sum, and the money given to the poor." ¹⁰But Jesus, aware of this, said to them, "Why do you trouble the woman? She has performed a good service for me. ¹¹For you always have the poor with you, but you will not always have me. ¹²By pouring this ointment on my body she has prepared me for burial. ¹³Truly I tell you, wherever this good newsᵇ is proclaimed in the whole world, what she has done will be told in remembrance of her."

ᵃThe terms *leper* and *leprosy* can refer to several diseases
ᵇOr *gospel*

COMMENTARY

As elsewhere in the passion story, Matthew closely follows Mark. Two other versions of the story appear in Luke 7:36-50 and John 12:1-8.

Although there are variations in content, all forms of the story have the same form or structure:

	Mark 14:3-9/Matt 26:6-13	Luke 7:36-50	John 12:1-8
Setting	Bethany House of Simon the Leper Reclining at table	(Not said:) Nain in Galilee House of Simon the Pharisee Reclining at table	Bethany House of Mary, Martha Reclining at table
Time	2 days before Passover	weeks before Passover	6 days before Passover
Identity of woman	woman	woman of the city who was a sinner	Mary, sister of Martha and Lazarus
Material	alabaster jar, very expensive (Mark: pure nard)	alabaster jar	litra of pure nard (approx. 12 oz.)

Action	breaks container pours on head	stands behind him cries wets feet with tears wipes feet with hair kisses feet	
	anoints head with μύρον (myron)	anoints feet with μύρον	anoints feet with μύρον
Objector	Mark = some people Matthew = disciples	Pharisee	Judas Iscariot
Objection	Why this waste? Could have been sold and (Mark: more than 300 denarii) given to poor	If he were a prophet, he would have known what kind of woman this is. Who is this who forgives sins? (Mark 2:7)	Why not sell and give 300 denarii to poor
Jesus' Counter- objection	She did it for my burial Always have poor Don't always have me	Parable of two debtors 500 denarii mentioned "Your faith has saved you" (= Mark 5:24)	She did it for my burial Always have poor Don't always have me

Such comparisons illustrate the transformations that stories receive in the process of transmission and reinterpretation, and make clear that each evangelist has composed the narrative structure of his Gospel. Our interest is not in harmonizing the various accounts or reconstructing the actual event, but attending to the Matthean meaning.

Lepers were considered ritually unclean (see 8:1-4); it is not said that Simon had been cleansed/cured by Jesus. The location contrasts with the palace of the high priest in the preceding scene. The woman, who remains anonymous in Matthew, appears only here. Matthew does not identify her as host, guest, bystander, or intruder, but focuses on her action: She pours very expensive perfume on Jesus' head. The "perfume" (μύρον myron) is a different substance from the oil used for anointing for office. The technical word for anointing for office is not used (χρίω chriō, as Luke 4:18; Acts 4:27; 10:38; Heb 1:9). This is not a christological anointing, but an extravagant act of devotion in preparation for burial (v. 12). Hence in Matthew, the women do not come to the tomb to anoint the body (Matt 28:1 vs. Mark 16:1), for that has already been done.

In the Markan passion story, where the power of Jesus is minimized, "some" object to the woman's action and Jesus overhears their objection. Matthew omits the Markan "to one another" (πρὸς ἑαυτούς pros heautous) and adds "having known" (γνούς gnous) to indicate that Jesus knows what they are saying within themselves, as in 9:4; 12:25, thereby continuing to retain more of the picture of the powerful Jesus who is in control. Matthew identifies the "some" who object in Mark specifically as disciples. The objection seems legitimate and in step with Jesus' own emphasis on giving to the poor (5:42; 6:2-4; 19:16-22; 25:31-46). Thus Jesus' reply that the poor are always present is not opposed to social humanitarian efforts as part of responsible Christian discipleship. In addition to being an allusion to Deut 15:11, which immediately enjoins helping the poor, the saying contrasts this duty with extravagant devotion to the crucified Jesus, which has an even higher priority. This is the confessional language of worship and devotion, in which there can be no higher priority than loving devotion to the deity (cf. 2:11 and 22:34-40 on the Great Commandment and relation of love of God and love for neighbor). Thus, although there is no explicit God-language or christological title, in its Matthean context the story serves as a christological affirmation about Jesus, as did the woman's original act.[551]

This is the only anointing/preparation for burial Jesus receives in Matthew (cf. Mark 16:1; John 19:39-40). Only the woman perceives that the one worshiped as Lord is the one who is crucified. Her act is a model of extravagant love and insight when others have been unseeing. "You will not always have me" is a vestigial remnant of the Markan emphasis on the absence of Jesus during the time of the church (Mark 2:20; 14:7, 25; 16:7), but it is out of step with Matthew's own theology of the continuing presence of Jesus with the church (1:23; 28:20). The saying thus serves in its Matthean context to distinguish between the constant priority of helping the poor and the unique priority of worshipful devotion to Jesus as

Lord.[552] Jesus praises her for having done a "good work" (ἔργον καλόν *ergon kalon*), the same term used for the deeds of discipleship in 5:16.

On "truly" (ἀμήν *amēn,* v. 13) see 5:18. The gospel that is to be proclaimed throughout the world after Jesus' death (24:14) is the Christian message of salvation, not Jesus' message of the kingdom or the book Matthew composes. "In memory of her" probably meant in the original version of the story "so that God will remember and vindicate her," as in Acts 10:4. It is not to be associated with or seen as an alternative to the memorial language of the eucharist, which does not occur in Matthew (cf. 1 Cor 11:24 = Luke 22:19*b*).

551. Elsewhere, Matthew is not hesitant to picture the "historical" Jesus as already being worshiped as the exalted "Lord" (κύριος *kyrios*) of the church (e.g., 14:33).

552. Douglas R. A. Hare, *Matthew, Int.* (Louisville: Westminster/John Knox, 1993) 294, points out that rabbis debated the relative merits of helping the poor and burying the dead and considered the latter to be the higher priority because (1) it could be done only at a certain time, while the poor could always be helped, and (2) it was a personal service.

Matthew 26:14-16, Judas Agrees to Betray Jesus

NIV	NRSV
[14]Then one of the Twelve—the one called Judas Iscariot—went to the chief priests [15]and asked, "What are you willing to give me if I hand him over to you?" So they counted out for him thirty silver coins. [16]From then on Judas watched for an opportunity to hand him over.	14Then one of the twelve, who was called Judas Iscariot, went to the chief priests [15]and said, "What will you give me if I betray him to you?" They paid him thirty pieces of silver. [16]And from that moment he began to look for an opportunity to betray him.

COMMENTARY

In the only previous reference to Judas (10:4) the reader has already been informed that Judas betrayed Jesus. Judas here takes the initiative and goes to the chief priests, asking for money, in profound contrast to the woman who has just given a very expensive gift to Jesus. Matthew suggests greed as Judas's motive (developed in John 12:5-6, which makes Judas the sole objector in the anointing scene). In Mark 14:11, the money is only promised, with no indication that Judas ever receives it, but in Matthew he is paid on the spot. There is no psychologizing of Judas's motives by Matthew, but the contrast between

the kingdom of God inaugurated by Jesus and the opposing kingdom dominated by selfish interest in money is clear (cf. 6:24, 33.).

The reference to "thirty pieces of silver" has been added by Matthew from Zech 11:12-13, the obscure connection to the wages of the shepherd, who puts the money back into the treasury (see Excursus "Matthew as Interpreter of Scripture," 151-54). In both places, the sum is considered paltry, the price of an injured slave (Exod 21:32). The contrast with the preceding story is intentional. "Betray" (v. 16) is the same word as "hand over" (v. 2; both are forms of παραδίδωμι [*paradidōmi*;

see 16:21), and makes the bracketing function of Scenes 1 and 3 the more apparent. The "divine passive" form in v. 2 is juxtaposed to the active form in v. 15: Both human responsibility and divine

sovereignty are fully present (see v. 24). Correspondingly, the "opportunity" (εὐκαιρία *eukairia*) Judas seeks is taken up from Jesus' side in v. 18 ("time" [καιρός *kairos*]).

Matthew 26:17-30a, Passover/Last Supper

Matthew 26:17-19, Disciples Prepare Passover

NIV	NRSV
[17]On the first day of the Feast of Unleavened Bread, the disciples came to Jesus and asked, "Where do you want us to make preparations for you to eat the Passover?" [18]He replied, "Go into the city to a certain man and tell him, 'The Teacher says: My appointed time is near. I am going to celebrate the Passover with my disciples at your house.'" [19]So the disciples did as Jesus had directed them and prepared the Passover.	[17]On the first day of Unleavened Bread the disciples came to Jesus, saying, "Where do you want us to make the preparations for you to eat the Passover?" [18]He said, "Go into the city to a certain man, and say to him, 'The Teacher says, My time is near; I will keep the Passover at your house with my disciples.'" [19]So the disciples did as Jesus had directed them, and they prepared the Passover meal.

COMMENTARY

Day 4 Begins: Thursday. According to Exod 12:1-20, the Passover lambs were to be killed on the afternoon of the 14th of Nisan, and the festival itself began with the ritual meal on the evening that began the 15th of Nisan. The Festival of Unleavened Bread began on the 15th and continued for seven days, during which no leaven should be found in the house. By the first century, the two festivals had merged and their names were used interchangeably. In addition, the pious practice of removing leaven one day early, the 14th, had become common, so that Mark's description of the 14th as the first day of Unleavened Bread, although technically incorrect, was common and is followed by Matthew despite his more precise awareness of Jewish law and customs.[553]

Preparation for the Passover involved (1) locating an appropriate place within the city walls of Jerusalem, the only legitimate location for eating the Passover meal; (2) searching the room for leaven and removing any items that might contain yeast

(bread crumbs, etc.); (3) obtaining a lamb and having it ritually slaughtered by the priests in the Temple; (4) roasting the lamb and preparing it with the other necessary items for the meal in the place previously arranged. While it is important to Matthew for theological reasons that the last supper was a Passover, he narrates none of the details associated with the Passover meal and ritual, concentrating his interest on the meal of the new covenant to be celebrated. Matthew abbreviates the Markan account to concentrate on the authority of Jesus, who simply commands and the disciples obey; the disciples' question in Mark becomes Jesus' command in Matthew. All the disciples are sent (apparently including Judas), not only two, as in Mark. By omitting the "colorful details" of Mark 14:13 (man with water jar; upper room), Matthew directs the reader's mind to the main point: the commanding authority of Jesus, which extends also to those addressed by the disciples.[554]

---

553. Josephus blends Passover and Unleavened Bread in *Antiquities of the Jews* 17. 213; 18.29; 20.106-109 and specifically labels the 14th as the "day of unleavened bread" in *The Jewish War* 5.98. Later detailed directions for removing leaven on the 14th are given in *m. Pesah.* 1:1-5, but probably reflect some of the practice in the first century.

554. Matthew's understanding of Jesus' authority being extended to the disciples, as in 10:1-42, is better than the novelistic historicizing speculation about a "secret arrangement" Jesus had made with friends in Jerusalem. Likewise, attempting to harmonize John's dating of the last supper one day earlier by claiming Jesus operated by a different calendar or staged his own "Passover" prematurely (and without a lamb!) are counsels of desperation.

Jesus announces that his "hour" (καιρός *kairos*) has come (a Matthean addition).[555] The *kairos* of Jesus contrasts with the "opportunity" (εὐκαιρία *eukairia*) for which Judas is looking. Even the

---

555. Καιρός (*kairos*), the special fulfilled time, is here distinguished from χρόνος (*chronos*), ordinary clock time. Matthew elsewhere uses it of the final time of God's eschatological victory (8:29; cf. 13:30; 16:3; 21:34). It corresponds to the "hour" of God's decisive action in the Fourth Gospel. Likewise, "is near" (ἐγγύς *engys*) resonates with the overtones of God's approaching kingdom (cf. 3:2; 4:17; 10:7; 21:34; 24:32-33; 26:45-46).

disciples' question to Jesus contrasts with that of Judas to the chief priests: He asks, "What are you willing [θέλετε *thelete*] to give me [μοι *moi*]." The disciples ask, "Where do you want [θέλεις *theleis*] us to prepare for you [σοι *soi*] to eat the Passover?" In each case, the emphatic pronoun is added by Matthew. Judas is focused on himself, the disciples on Jesus. The disciples obey.

Matthew 26:20-30a, Jesus Predicts the Betrayal and Inaugurates the Eucharist

NIV

20When evening came, Jesus was reclining at the table with the Twelve. 21And while they were eating, he said, "I tell you the truth, one of you will betray me."

22They were very sad and began to say to him one after the other, "Surely not I, Lord?"

23Jesus replied, "The one who has dipped his hand into the bowl with me will betray me. 24The Son of Man will go just as it is written about him. But woe to that man who betrays the Son of Man! It would be better for him if he had not been born."

25Then Judas, the one who would betray him, said, "Surely not I, Rabbi?"

Jesus answered, "Yes, it is you."[a]

26While they were eating, Jesus took bread, gave thanks and broke it, and gave it to his disciples, saying, "Take and eat; this is my body."

27Then he took the cup, gave thanks and offered it to them, saying, "Drink from it, all of you. 28This is my blood of the[b] covenant, which is poured out for many for the forgiveness of sins. 29I tell you, I will not drink of this fruit of the vine from now on until that day when I drink it anew with you in my Father's kingdom."

30When they had sung a hymn, they went out to the Mount of Olives.

a25 Or "You yourself have said it"   b28 Some manuscripts *the new*

NRSV

20When it was evening, he took his place with the twelve;[a] 21and while they were eating, he said, "Truly I tell you, one of you will betray me." 22And they became greatly distressed and began to say to him one after another, "Surely not I, Lord?" 23He answered, "The one who has dipped his hand into the bowl with me will betray me. 24The Son of Man goes as it is written of him, but woe to that one by whom the Son of Man is betrayed! It would have been better for that one not to have been born." 25Judas, who betrayed him, said, "Surely not I, Rabbi?" He replied, "You have said so."

26While they were eating, Jesus took a loaf of bread, and after blessing it he broke it, gave it to the disciples, and said, "Take, eat; this is my body." 27Then he took a cup, and after giving thanks he gave it to them, saying, "Drink from it, all of you; 28for this is my blood of the[b] covenant, which is poured out for many for the forgiveness of sins. 29I tell you, I will never again drink of this fruit of the vine until that day when I drink it new with you in my Father's kingdom."

30When they had sung the hymn, they went out to the Mount of Olives.

aOther ancient authorities add *disciples*   bOther ancient authorities add *new*

COMMENTARY

The Jewish day was reckoned from sundown of one day to sundown of the next. The identical expression "when it was evening" (ὀψίας γενομένης *opsias genomenēs*) in 27:57 identifies the intervening events from Scene 6 through Scene 15 (the last supper, Gethsemane, arrest, trials before chief priests and Pilate, crucifixion, and burial) as all happening within one day, the 15th of Nisan, Passover, the first day of Unleavened Bread.

26:20. No "coming" of Jesus is announced; he simply "takes his place"[556] with the Twelve, who are already there. Although Luke and especially John have a more elaborate series of incidents at the last supper, Matthew follows Mark in confining the narrative to two conversations: the announcement of the betrayer (26:21-25) and the institution of the eucharist (26:26-29).

26:21-25. The reader knows already that Judas will betray Jesus, but the characters in the story do not know.[557] Jesus has repeatedly announced that he will be "delivered up" (παραδίδωμι *paradidōmi*), but this may refer either to God's delivering up Jesus for humanity's sins, or to someone's betraying Jesus to his opponents.[558] For the first time, Jesus indicates to the characters in the story that one of his own inner circle of twelve will be the betrayer. (On "truly" [ἀμήν *amēn*] here and in vv. 13 and 34, see 5:18.) Strangely enough, Matthew drops the Markan allusion to Ps 41:9 (cf. v. 23). Mark had the disciples respond in unison. Matthew has individual responses so Judas can be featured in the incident Matthew adds at the end.

26:22-23. The disciples' response is not soul-searching, but confident rejection of Jesus' statement, though still leaving the possibility open and seeking reassurance; the interogative particle μήτι (*mēti*) implies a negative response (so both the NIV and the NRSV, better than earlier translations). Jesus does not further identify the betrayer

(in contrast to John 13:26), but only indicates that it is one who eats with him, sharing the common bowl. For Matthew, the announcement serves primarily a christological function for the reader: Jesus knows his fate in advance. Thus such speculations as whether this was overheard by the other disciples, and if so why they did not protest, and how to harmonize this with John 13:21-30 are all beside the point.

26:24. The dialectic of divine sovereignty and human responsibility in the passion is here finely expressed. God is not taken by surprise in the betrayal that leads to crucifixion; it goes according to the divine plan expressed in Scripture. But this does not relieve the burden of human responsibility. Matthew (who here follows Mark almost verbatim) does not parcel out the responsibility for Jesus' death between God and humanity: God is fully sovereign; humanity is fully responsible. The sharpness of the statement's contrast between the "Son of Man" (ὁ υἱὸς τοῦ ἀνθρώπου *ho huios tou anthrōpou*) and "man" (ἄνθρωπος *anthrōpos*) is preserved in the NIV and the RSV, but is obscured by the NRSV's translation.

26:25. Matthew adds this statement to make it clear that Jesus knows the identity of the betrayer in advance (nothing in Mark suggests this was the case), and to bring the hypocrisy of Judas into bold relief. The present participle παραδιδούς (*paradidous*) might better be translated "who was in the process of betraying him." Judas responds as do the other disciples, except for the address. They address Jesus as "Lord," the typical insiders' term; Judas uses "Rabbi" (ῥαββι *rabbi*) the outsiders' term.[559] Jesus' response, literally "You said it" (σὺ εἶπας *su eipas*), is not ambiguous, but a clear affirmative as in 26:64 and the similar σὺ λέγεις (*su legeis*) of 27:11, but without the slangy overtones of this English expression.

26:26-29, The Institution of the Eucharist. Influenced by the liturgical practice of the various streams of early Christianity, a number of different forms of this story developed: (1) The

---

556. Ἀνάκειμαι (*anakeimai*) means literally "recline," but it came to mean simply "be present to eat," with no indication of sitting (normal Jewish custom) or reclining (Greek and Roman custom). At Passover, Jews reclined in the Greco-Roman manner to show they were *free*. The posture is important in the Johannine narrative, but not in Mark or Matthew.

557. Not only from Matt 10:4, but from the Gospel of Mark, presupposed as familiar in the Matthean community (cf. Introduction).

558. See Commentary on the passion predictions at 16:21.

559. Matthew has an aversion to the title "Rabbi," deriving from the debate with developing Judaism (cf. 23:8-12). When Jesus is addressed as "Rabbi" by disciples in Mark, Matthew typically omits it (Mark 11:21 = Matt 21:20) or changes the address to "Lord" (Mark 9:5 = Matt 17:4; Mark 10:51 = 20:33).

form in the earliest extant Christian text (not necessarily the earliest form of the story) is the Pauline form found in 1 Cor 11:23-25 and in the long text of Luke 22:19-20, distinguished by the command to repeat the rite and by the phrase "for my remembrance" (εἰς τὴν ἐμὴν ἀνάμνησιν *eis tēn emēn anamnēsin*); (2) the form in the short text of Luke 22:15-19, distinguished by the order cup/loaf; (3) the form in Mark 14:22-25, characterized by Jesus' pledge not to drink of the cup until he drinks it anew with his disciples in the kingdom of God.[560] All forms of the tradition have had a complex development, resulting not only in different texts but also in numerous manuscript variations.[561] All forms of the text have both earlier and later elements; the point of exegesis is not to reconstruct Jesus' actual words at the last supper, but to interpret the meaning of the particular canonical text in view.

The Markan text had expressed Mark's theology of the absence of Jesus between crucifixion and parousia (see Mark 2:20; 14:7, 25; 16:7).[562] Despite Matthew's own understanding of the presence of Jesus with his church during the time of mission between resurrection and parousia (see 1:23; 28:20), Matthew adopts the Markan form of the tradition, apparently the only form he knew. Matthew probably found his own understanding of the continuing presence of Christ in the words "This is my body." There is no indication, however, that Matthew adopts the Hellenistic-Pauline understanding of the church as the body of Christ (1 Corinthians 11–12). Matthew probably understands the words of institution in relation to their Aramaic background. Since Aramaic (unlike Hebrew and Greek) does not have a word for "body," Jesus' original word was probably גוף (*gûp*), meaning "body" in the sense

of "self," "ego." According to Eduard Schweizer, the sentence would then have originally meant "This is myself." This saying assures the church, then, that the risen Lord himself is present at the supper.[563]

Matthew follows Mark in using different verbs for the prayer over the bread ("pronounce a blessing" [εὐλογέω *eulogeō*]) and for the wine ("give thanks" [εὐχαριστέω *eucharisteō*]). Both are directed to God, not to the bread or wine, resembling the standard Jewish table blessings ("Blessed art thou, O Lord, king of the universe, who dost bring forth bread from the earth"; "Praised be thou, O Lord, king of the universe, Creator of the fruit of the vine."). The connotation of God as king and the repeated reference to the kingdom of God in v. 29 set this text in the context of Matthew's theme of the conflict of kingdoms (cf. 12:22-37; Excursus "Kingdom of Heaven in Matthew," 288-94). Matthew has already used "cup" as a symbol of Jesus' giving his life for others (20:22) and will do so again in Gethsemane (26:39). Matthew preserves the awkward reference to "cup" (rather than "wine," which would be parallel to "bread") in order to maintain the connotations of Passover, which had several references to "the cup."

Matthew's most distinctive changes to the Markan meaning are these: (1) The Markan narrator's words about the cup, "and they all drank of it," are made into a parallel command to the words over the bread, so that each action comprises a command of Jesus and the disciples' obedient response. (2) The command to "eat" is then added to the words over the bread, to enhance the parallelism to the newly formulated command to "drink." (3) The whole action is related to "the forgiveness of sins," the identical words dropped from Mark's description of John's baptism (Mark 1:4). Forgiveness is dissociated from John's baptism and related to Jesus' covenant-renewing death. The forgiveness of sins is Jesus' primary mission (1:21; cf. 9:1-7). Forgiveness is accomplished by Jesus' death, understood here in terms of the sacrifice that seals the bond between God and the covenant people (cf. Exod 24:8; Isa 53:12; but see Matt 9:2). In Exod 24:3-8, the covenant sacrifice is unrelated to for-

---

560. In addition, the Johannine tradition, which has no eucharistic sayings at the last supper, has incorporated eucharistic sayings in the extensive discourse on the bread of life, added to the story of the feeding of the five thousand (John 6:51-58).

561. On text-critical issues, see especially Metzger, *Textual Commentary*, 173-77, on the six forms of the Lukan text. On the eucharistic tradition in general, see Joachim Jeremias, *The Eucharistic Words of Jesus* (New York: Charles Scribner's Sons, 1966), which concentrates on reconstructing the original words of Jesus; and Xavier Leon-Dufour, *Sharing the Eucharistic Bread: The Witness of the New Testament* (New York: Paulist, 1987), more oriented to exegesis of the NT texts themselves.

562. On this motif in Mark, see Vernon K. Robbins, "Last Meal: Preparation, Betrayal, and Absence (Mark 14:12-25)," and John Dominic Crossan, "Empty Tomb and Absent Lord (Mark 16:1-8)," in Werner H. Kelber, ed., *The Passion in Mark: Studies on Mark 14–16* (Philadelphia: Fortress, 1976), 21-40, 135-52.

563. See Eduard Schweizer, *The Lord's Supper According to the New Testament* (Philadelphia: Fortress, 1967) 17.

giveness of sins, for which there were other sacrifices. But Jesus' death is pictured by Matthew as replacing the sacrificial blood of the old covenant law, so he adds "for forgiveness of sins." (4) In the phrase "for many," Matthew changes the Markan preposition from ὑπέρ (*hyper*) to περί (*peri*), both translated "for," but *peri* being more common in sacrificial contexts (cf. Isa 53:4, 10; Heb 5:1, 3; 1 Pet 3:18; 1 John 2:2). On the inclusive sense of "for many," see Commentary at 20:28. (5) Matthew adds "with you" in v. 29, corresponding to his emphasis throughout on the presence of Jesus with his disciples—though here it is the future fellowship of the kingdom of God. (6) Mark's "kingdom of God" becomes "my father's kingdom" (cf. 10:32-33//Luke 12:8-9; Matt 12:50//Mark 3:35 for other instances of Matthew's replacing "God" in his tradition with "my Father" in sayings of Jesus).

Matthew's reference to the "blood of the covenant" does not explicitly use the word *new,* but it is implicit in his interpreting Jesus' death in terms of (the eschatological renewal of) the God's covenant with Israel.[564] In all such contexts, "new" means eschatologically renewed, not "new and improved" in the cultural sense. (Cf. Paul's use of "new creation," 2 Cor 5:17; Gal 6:15; John's use of "new Jerusalem," Rev 22:1-2, 5; the Fourth Gospel's use of "new commandment,"

John 13:34, all of which connote ultimacy, not "more recent and therefore better.") Matthew affirms the eschatological newness brought through Jesus and its continuity with the "old," which is still valued (Matt 9:17; 13:52).

26:30a. Although Matthew has specifically identified this meal as a Passover (26:2, 17-19), he has narrated none of the Passover ritual during the meal itself. The drinking of wine is not specifically related to Passover, since it was included in many festive meals and Jesus and his disciples were known to drink wine together on many occasions (11:19). In contrast to the Passover, which emphasizes "why this night is different from all other nights" by serving unusual foods (unleavened bread, bitter herbs), the food and drink blessed by Jesus is ordinary food (unless the Passover framework means the bread must have been unleavened, but there is nothing in the pericope to suggest this). This transitional note thus gives the only point of contact with the usual Passover ritual, which included the singing of the "Hallel" series of psalms (113–118), 113–114 near the beginning and 115–118 near the conclusion.[565] This is the only reference to singing in the Gospels, and it is absent from the Lukan and Johannine accounts of the last supper. With the songs that conclude the Passover, the (redactional) frame around the last supper is complete.

---

564. The word rendered "new" (καινῆς *kainēs*) is found in some important MSS and text traditions (A, C, D, W, 074, *f*[1], *f*[13], 𝔐, latt, sy, sa, bo, Ir[lat]) but is missing from others (𝔓[37], ℵ, B, L Z, Θ, 33, pc, mae, bo[mss]). Similar textual phenomena are found in the MSS of Mark 14:24. The original text of both Mark and Matthew probably originally lacked "new" before "covenant," the MSS variants resulting from assimilation to Luke 22:20 and 1 Cor 11:25, where "new covenant" is the original reading.

565. This is the order in the later version of the Passover ritual, which rests on very old tradition, however. The fact that the Passover motifs occur only in the transitional beginning and ending of the pericope, with no reference to the Passover in the account itself, suggests that the dating represents the theologically motivated editorial work of the early church rather than remembered calendar dating; cf. the Johannine last supper, located on the night before the Passover meal (cf. John 18:28; 19:14, 36).

REFLECTIONS

As a symbolic action, the eucharist expresses meaning not reducible to words. Realities beyond verbal expression are acted out. Yet the act is rife with meaning and invites theological explication, although theological statements never exhaust the symbol's hermeneutical potential. Five dimensions of Christian faith are implicit in the eucharistic meal as such, but not all are actualized in each account.

1. The Passover context emphasized by Matthew already gives the eucharistic meal the character of a memorial celebration of the liberating act of God that created the covenant people. The meal thus points *backward* both to the death of Jesus for the forgiveness of sins, and to the life of Jesus in which he provided fellowship meals, both with his disciples and with outsiders and marginalized persons (cf. 9:10-13; 11:19; 26:6-13). Especially in the ancient Near East and in Jewish tradition, persons' eating together was a sacred bond of hospitality and sharing of life. The eucharistic meal pointed back to the life of Jesus when he made God's openness and acceptance real by eating with sinners. The meal had a gift character; it is provided by Jesus and given to all, including tax collectors and sinners. This dimension appears in the stories of the miraculous feedings, where the gift is amazingly unlimited as well as unmerited. The meal specifically recalls Jesus' last supper with his disciples on the night before his death, and the reality of his giving his body and blood (the expression simply means his life, in its concrete reality) for our salvation. So regarded, every eucharist is a memorial to something that actually happened in history. Although memorial terminology is not explicitly found in the Matthean form of the eucharistic narrative, Matthew's Gospel as a whole points to the significance of this history.

2. The meal points *forward* to its fulfillment in the kingdom of God. The primary meaning is eschatological, anticipating the joy of the messianic banquet, but also pointing forward from Jesus' time to the life of the church, which celebrates the messianic banquet and the kingdom of God by anticipation. So regarded, every eucharist is a promise of the final victory of God's kingdom. The conflict of kingdoms is a major theme of Matthew. The eucharist is a proleptic celebration of the victory, which is sure.

3. The meal points *inward* as a call to self-examination on the part of the participants. Although this element is not specifically found in Matthew (as it is in 1 Cor 11:28), by placing the story of the supper in the context of the announcement of betrayal and the disciples' response (26:21-25), Matthew too evokes the response of self-examination.

4. The meal points *upward*—i.e., to the heavenly realm where the risen and exalted Christ is enthroned. The symbols of the body and blood of Jesus now point beyond themselves to the transcendent realm (cf. Reflection 3 on interpreting the eschatological judgment discourse, after 25:31-46). Later Christian theology developed a variety of ways of explicating this dimension of eucharist faith; Matthew preserves only the enigmatic words "This is my body" and "This is my blood," without explaining how they are to be understood.

5. The meal points *outward* to the whole church and to the world. This is made explicit in the Pauline and long Lukan forms, where the command to repeat is given and the meal is explicitly described as a testimony to others (1 Cor 11:26). Matthew has this dimension of Christian faith elsewhere (e.g., 5:16; 10:32-33), and he specifically includes concern for others in the eucharistic overtones of the account of the feeding of the five thousand: "You [disciples] give them [the 'outsider' crowds] to eat" (14:16).

Matthew 26:30*b*-56, Abandonment, Betrayal, Arrest

Matthew 26:30*b*-35, Jesus Predicts Desertion and Promises Reunion

NIV	NRSV
[30]When they had sung a hymn, they went out to the Mount of Olives. [31]Then Jesus told them, "This very night you	[30]When they had sung the hymn, they went out to the Mount of Olives.

NIV

will all fall away on account of me, for it is written:

" 'I will strike the shepherd,
and the sheep of the flock will be scattered.'[a]

[32]But after I have risen, I will go ahead of you into Galilee."

[33]Peter replied, "Even if all fall away on account of you, I never will."

[34]"I tell you the truth," Jesus answered, "this very night, before the rooster crows, you will disown me three times."

[35]But Peter declared, "Even if I have to die with you, I will never disown you." And all the other disciples said the same.

NRSV

[31]Then Jesus said to them, "You will all become deserters because of me this night; for it is written,
'I will strike the shepherd,
and the sheep of the flock will be scattered.'
[32]But after I am raised up, I will go ahead of you to Galilee." [33]Peter said to him, "Though all become deserters because of you, I will never desert you." [34]Jesus said to him, "Truly I tell you, this very night, before the cock crows, you will deny me three times." [35]Peter said to him, "Even though I must die with you, I will not deny you." And so said all the disciples.

COMMENTARY

Matthew reproduces this Markan scene almost exactly. Instead of returning to the more comfortable surroundings of Bethany (21:17; 26:6-13), Jesus takes the disciples to the Mount of Olives, calling to mind the themes of the apocalyptic discourse (esp. 24:9-13). The triumphal Passover hymns are replaced by Jesus' somber prediction that all his disciples will stumble over him (σκανδαλίζω skandalizō, sometimes translated "be offended"; Matthew specifically adds "because of me" [ἐν ἐμοί en emoi]). Skandalizō is a significant word in Matthew. Jesus' representation of the kingdom of God is contrary to all expectations. John and his disciples are in danger of stumbling over it (11:6). Jesus' hometown folk stumble at him (13:57), as do the Pharisees (15:12). But believers who have accepted the Word of God superficially, without deep roots, can also stumble "when trouble or persecution arises on account of the word" (13:21). That is precisely what Jesus predicts will now happen to all the disciples—i.e, they will stumble at the prospect of a Christ who chooses to be crucified rather than to retaliate.

Matthew has portrayed Jesus as the messianic king who will shepherd the people of God (2:1-6), who has compassion on the people as sheep without a shepherd (9:36), and who understands his mission as regathering and reconstituting the lost sheep of the house of Israel into the eschatological community of the people of God (10:6; 15:24). Now the paradox of v. 24 is renewed (v. 31). Although human beings deny and betray, it is God who will strike the shepherd, and the sheep will be scattered (Matthew expresses his ecclesiological interest by adding "of the flock"). The thought that Jesus' fate is the fulfillment of Zech 13:7 shows that God is the ultimate actor in Jesus' being given up to death, overruling human actions.[566] Yet this is not the final word. Corresponding to the passion and vindication of the Son of Man, the community goes through its own scattering, but will be regathered by the risen Jesus, who like a shepherd "goes before" his flock and will rejoin them and reconstitute them in Galilee.

Just as Peter had originally responded to the prediction of Jesus' passion and resurrection with rejection and disbelief (16:21-23), so also here he directly contradicts Jesus' prediction of the disciples' immediate failure and subsequent redemption. Whereas Peter had previously been spokesperson for the disciples, here he distinguishes himself from them, claiming to be an

---

566. Mark had already changed Zechariah's imperative "Strike the shepherd" (LXX "shepherds") to the indicative "I [God] will strike. . . ." Matthew preserves this change, even though it agrees with neither the MT nor the LXX, to emphasize the divine sovereignty.

exception. In Jesus' last ἀμην (amēn) saying (cf. 5:18), he solemnly predicts that Peter will deny him three times (i.e., definitively) before the third watch of the night is signaled by the cock's crow (cf. Mark 13:35 for "cock crow" as the third watch, 12:00–3:00 A.M.).

Matthew 26:36-56, Jesus Prays and Is Arrested

NIV

36Then Jesus went with his disciples to a place called Gethsemane, and he said to them, "Sit here while I go over there and pray." 37He took Peter and the two sons of Zebedee along with him, and he began to be sorrowful and troubled. 38Then he said to them, "My soul is overwhelmed with sorrow to the point of death. Stay here and keep watch with me."

39Going a little farther, he fell with his face to the ground and prayed, "My Father, if it is possible, may this cup be taken from me. Yet not as I will, but as you will."

40Then he returned to his disciples and found them sleeping. "Could you men not keep watch with me for one hour?" he asked Peter. 41"Watch and pray so that you will not fall into temptation. The spirit is willing, but the body is weak."

42He went away a second time and prayed, "My Father, if it is not possible for this cup to be taken away unless I drink it, may your will be done."

43When he came back, he again found them sleeping, because their eyes were heavy. 44So he left them and went away once more and prayed the third time, saying the same thing.

45Then he returned to the disciples and said to them, "Are you still sleeping and resting? Look, the hour is near, and the Son of Man is betrayed into the hands of sinners. 46Rise, let us go! Here comes my betrayer!"

47While he was still speaking, Judas, one of the Twelve, arrived. With him was a large crowd armed with swords and clubs, sent from the chief priests and the elders of the people. 48Now the betrayer had arranged a signal with them: "The one I kiss is the man; arrest him." 49Going at once to Jesus, Judas said, "Greetings, Rabbi!" and kissed him.

50Jesus replied, "Friend, do what you came for."[a]

a50 Or "Friend, why have you come?"

NRSV

36Then Jesus went with them to a place called Gethsemane; and he said to his disciples, "Sit here while I go over there and pray." 37He took with him Peter and the two sons of Zebedee, and began to be grieved and agitated. 38Then he said to them, "I am deeply grieved, even to death; remain here, and stay awake with me." 39And going a little farther, he threw himself on the ground and prayed, "My Father, if it is possible, let this cup pass from me; yet not what I want but what you want." 40Then he came to the disciples and found them sleeping; and he said to Peter, "So, could you not stay awake with me one hour? 41Stay awake and pray that you may not come into the time of trial;[a] the spirit indeed is willing, but the flesh is weak." 42Again he went away for the second time and prayed, "My Father, if this cannot pass unless I drink it, your will be done." 43Again he came and found them sleeping, for their eyes were heavy. 44So leaving them again, he went away and prayed for the third time, saying the same words. 45Then he came to the disciples and said to them, "Are you still sleeping and taking your rest? See, the hour is at hand, and the Son of Man is betrayed into the hands of sinners. 46Get up, let us be going. See, my betrayer is at hand."

47While he was still speaking, Judas, one of the twelve, arrived; with him was a large crowd with swords and clubs, from the chief priests and the elders of the people. 48Now the betrayer had given them a sign, saying, "The one I will kiss is the man; arrest him." 49At once he came up to Jesus and said, "Greetings, Rabbi!" and kissed him. 50Jesus said to him, "Friend, do what you are here to do." Then they came and laid hands on Jesus and arrested him. 51Suddenly, one of those with Jesus put his hand on his sword, drew it, and struck the slave of the high priest, cutting off his ear. 52Then Jesus said to him, "Put your

aOr into temptation

NIV

Then the men stepped forward, seized Jesus and arrested him. ⁵¹With that, one of Jesus' companions reached for his sword, drew it out and struck the servant of the high priest, cutting off his ear.

⁵²"Put your sword back in its place," Jesus said to him, "for all who draw the sword will die by the sword. ⁵³Do you think I cannot call on my Father, and he will at once put at my disposal more than twelve legions of angels? ⁵⁴But how then would the Scriptures be fulfilled that say it must happen in this way?"

⁵⁵At that time Jesus said to the crowd, "Am I leading a rebellion, that you have come out with swords and clubs to capture me? Every day I sat in the temple courts teaching, and you did not arrest me. ⁵⁶But this has all taken place that the writings of the prophets might be fulfilled." Then all the disciples deserted him and fled.

NRSV

sword back into its place; for all who take the sword will perish by the sword. ⁵³Do you think that I cannot appeal to my Father, and he will at once send me more than twelve legions of angels? ⁵⁴But how then would the scriptures be fulfilled, which say it must happen in this way?" ⁵⁵At that hour Jesus said to the crowds, "Have you come out with swords and clubs to arrest me as though I were a bandit? Day after day I sat in the temple teaching, and you did not arrest me. ⁵⁶But all this has taken place, so that the scriptures of the prophets may be fulfilled." Then all the disciples deserted him and fled.

COMMENTARY

Matthew follows the Markan narrative closely, but with subtle alterations that shift the focus of the presentation from the failure of the disciples to the sovereignty of Jesus, who continues to be the teacher who embodies his teaching in his own life.

26:36. The command for the disciples to "sit here" while Jesus separates himself for worship and prayer is reminiscent of Gen 22:5, from the *Akedah,* the story of the binding of Isaac, which seems to have been understood in Judaism as a willing sacrifice for others. Matthew's changing the Markan word for "here" (from the common ὧδε *hōde* to the rare αὐτοῦ *autou,* used in the LXX of Gen 22:5) strengthens this connection.

26:37-38. The three disciples are the same small, privileged group who were allowed to see Jesus' glory at the transfiguration (17:1) and who claimed to be willing to drink the same cup as Jesus (20:22)—i.e., willing to die for him (26:33). Matthew softens Mark's picture of Jesus from "distressed" to "sorrowful," but does not eliminate the picture of a truly human anxiety in the face of death. He who makes the presence of God

real to others (1:23) longs for human companionship in his hour of need. "Stay awake" is not merely directed to the disciples' sleepiness, but echoes the apocalyptic warning of 24:42 (cf. 25:13) and points to the time of "testing" that draws near in the eschatological event of Jesus' death and resurrection, which approaches (cf. πειρασμός *peirasmos,* 26:41). Matthew adds references to Jesus' being "with" (μετά *meta*) his disciples and wanting them to be "with" him (26:18, 20, 29, 38, 40).

26:39-46. Jesus falls prostrate before God in prayer (lit., "on his face," as in Gen 17:3, 17; Num 14:5; 2 Sam 9:6; 1 Kgs 18:39; and as the disciples themselves had done in 17:3). Matthew rewrites Mark, who has three occasions on which Jesus finds the disciples sleeping, explicitly to delineate three periods of prayer, shifting the focus from the failure of the disciples to Jesus as himself a model of prayer. The contrast between the willing spirit but the weakness of the flesh in v. 41 is not a dualistic anthropology, but represents two aspects of the whole person that struggle with each other. Jesus himself is caught up in this struggle, and his prayer moves from praying for deliverance from death (as often in the Psalms; Ps 118:17-18 had just been sung) to trust and commitment to God's will, using the identical words he had taught his disciples in 6:10. Jesus' three prayers form a dramatic contrast to the three denials of Peter, who sleeps instead of praying. After the prayer, Jesus is resolute and sovereign, and he announces the arrival of the betrayer in words that also connote the advent of the kingdom.[567]

26:47-50. To the reader who does not already know the story, the arrival of Judas must be a surprise, for Matthew has not previously narrated his departure. So far as the reader has been able to tell, Judas has been present through all the last supper and Gethsemane scenes with the other disciples (cf. John 13:30). Judas is at the head of a large, armed crowd from the chief priests and elders of the people. No police are specifically mentioned, but Matthew must understand those who arrest Jesus to be the temple police (cf. 26:58; "guards" = temple police). Matthew's narrative does not involve the Roman soldiers until later (27:27; cf. the cohort [600 troops] present at the arrest in the Fourth Gospel, John 18:3, 12). Judas addresses Jesus with the customary greeting, "hello" (χαῖρε *chaire,* the same term as 27:29 when the soldiers mockingly salute him) and repeats the outsiders' term "Rabbi" rather than the disciples' term "Lord" (κύριος *kyrios*; note the contrast introduced by Matthew in vv. 22 and 25). Jesus responds with the distancing "friend" (ἑταῖρε *hetaire*), but in the sense of the politely cool generic form of address to someone whose name one does not know (cf. its use in 20:13 and 22:12, its only other NT occurrences). The remainder of Jesus' response is grammatically ambiguous and can be a question ("Why have you come?"), a statement ("This is why you have come [namely, to betray me with a kiss]"), or a command ("Do that for which you have come"). Since the words are added by Matthew, they most likely are an additional expression of Jesus' sovereignty and should be translated as a command. "Then" (τότε *tote,* a characteristic Matthean addition)—

i.e., only after Jesus has given the command—they arrest him, and the predicted "handing over" is accomplished.

26:51-54. Mark represents one of those standing by as having drawn a sword, apparently one of the armed group that had come to arrest Jesus, and in the chaotic mêlée having accidentally cut off the ear of a servant of the high priest. Matthew makes this one of the disciples (the Fourth Gospel will make it specifically Peter) and makes it the occasion of Jesus' continuing to teach. Even in Gethsemane, Jesus remains the teacher, making three points:

(1) The way of non-violence, non-retaliation, love of enemies, is to be pursued to the end. What Jesus has taught, he lives out, at the cost of his life (5:38-39, 43-48). Just as he practiced the prayer he taught his disciples, so also he practices non-retaliatory self-giving. Violence is self-destructive and futile, resulting only in a vicious spiral of violence. The sword is a symbol not only of mob violence or self-defense, but also of government itself (cf. Rom 13:4, which speaks, as Matthew does, of "authority" [ἐξουσία *exousia*] and "sword" [μάχαιρα *machaira*]). Jesus represents a redefinition of kingship; the way of God's kingdom is to absorb evil rather than inflict it, and bring the spiral finally to an end.

(2) Jesus is not arrested against his will. A legion is six thousand troops; twelve corresponds to Jesus and the remaining eleven disciples. He is confident of the Father's angelic protection, but will not ask for it (cf. 4:6-7, 11). In this statement, added to Mark, Jesus is less the truly human victim than in Mark. Matthew here extends the picture of the powerful Son of God further into the passion story than does Mark. Yet even here, the power is in God's hands, not in the hands of Jesus as a divine being, and his human trust in God is what is exhibited. (Again, cf. Matthew 4, where Jesus places himself on the "human" [ἄνθρωπος *anthrōpos*] side of the equation.)

(3) The Scriptures must be fulfilled. Matthew emphasizes this conviction (found in Mark 14:49) by including it twice (vv. 54 and 56). The Matthean Jesus does not mean that the prophecies are a pre-written script that Jesus must dutifully act out, but that the Scriptures represent the plan and will of God, to which Jesus willingly and trustingly submits (see Excursus "Matthew as In-

---

567. "The one handing me over" can be either God or Judas; "has come near" is the same word used of the coming kingdom, and it may refer either to God's act in delivering up Jesus or to the near approach of Judas the betrayer. Throughout, Matthew maintains the tension between divine sovereignty and human responsibility.

terpreter of Scripture," 151-54). Jesus' prophecy that *all* will abandon him (26:31), denied by the protestations of *all* (26:35), is fulfilled when *all* desert him (26:56). Except for Peter, we see none of them again until after the resurrection (28:16-17), again fulfilling Jesus' own prophecy (26:32). All of vv. 52-54 is Matthean composition, with v. 54 based on Mark 14:49*b*, which Matthew will use again at v. 56.

26:55. "Bandit" (NRSV) or "[one] leading a rebellion" (NIV) translates λῃστής (*lēstēs*), used by Josephus for the terrorists/freedom fighters who offered armed resistance to the Roman occupation (cf. Matt 27:38, 44). Matthew adds to Mark's description that he "sat" in the Temple (as in 5:1)—i.e., in the posture of an authoritative teacher.

The note that Jesus taught in the Temple "day after day" is taken over from Mark 14:49, even though it does not fit Matthew's chronology in which Jesus had taught in the Temple only on the "long Tuesday" (cf. 21:1). The Markan reference is also problematic, and probably indicates a pre-Markan source in which Jesus had taught in the Temple for an extended period, which is in fact historically more likely. Matthew and Mark value theological meaning higher than the accuracy of historical chronology, however, and the modern interpreter might take this clue from them. Both Matthew and Mark seem to preserve this note to emphasize the guilt of those who arrest Jesus by stealth and betrayal.

Matthew 26:57–27:1, Jewish Trial: Jesus' Confession and Peter's Denial

NIV

⁵⁷Those who had arrested Jesus took him to Caiaphas, the high priest, where the teachers of the law and the elders had assembled. ⁵⁸But Peter followed him at a distance, right up to the courtyard of the high priest. He entered and sat down with the guards to see the outcome.

⁵⁹The chief priests and the whole Sanhedrin were looking for false evidence against Jesus so that they could put him to death. ⁶⁰But they did not find any, though many false witnesses came forward.

Finally two came forward ⁶¹and declared, "This fellow said, 'I am able to destroy the temple of God and rebuild it in three days.'"

⁶²Then the high priest stood up and said to Jesus, "Are you not going to answer? What is this testimony that these men are bringing against you?" ⁶³But Jesus remained silent.

The high priest said to him, "I charge you under oath by the living God: Tell us if you are the Christ,ᵃ the Son of God."

⁶⁴"Yes, it is as you say," Jesus replied. "But I say to all of you: In the future you will see the Son of Man sitting at the right hand of the Mighty One and coming on the clouds of heaven."

ᵃ63 Or *Messiah*; also in verse 68

NRSV

⁵⁷Those who had arrested Jesus took him to Caiaphas the high priest, in whose house the scribes and the elders had gathered. ⁵⁸But Peter was following him at a distance, as far as the courtyard of the high priest; and going inside, he sat with the guards in order to see how this would end. ⁵⁹Now the chief priests and the whole council were looking for false testimony against Jesus so that they might put him to death, ⁶⁰but they found none, though many false witnesses came forward. At last two came forward ⁶¹and said, "This fellow said, 'I am able to destroy the temple of God and to build it in three days.'" ⁶²The high priest stood up and said, "Have you no answer? What is it that they testify against you?" ⁶³But Jesus was silent. Then the high priest said to him, "I put you under oath before the living God, tell us if you are the Messiah,ᵃ the Son of God." ⁶⁴Jesus said to him, "You have said so. But I tell you,

From now on you will see the Son of Man
  seated at the right hand of Power
  and coming on the clouds of heaven."

⁶⁵Then the high priest tore his clothes and said, "He has blasphemed! Why do we still need wit-

ᵃOr *Christ*

NIV

⁶⁵Then the high priest tore his clothes and said, "He has spoken blasphemy! Why do we need any more witnesses? Look, now you have heard the blasphemy. ⁶⁶What do you think?"

"He is worthy of death," they answered.

⁶⁷Then they spit in his face and struck him with their fists. Others slapped him ⁶⁸and said, "Prophesy to us, Christ. Who hit you?"

⁶⁹Now Peter was sitting out in the courtyard, and a servant girl came to him. "You also were with Jesus of Galilee," she said.

⁷⁰But he denied it before them all. "I don't know what you're talking about," he said.

⁷¹Then he went out to the gateway, where another girl saw him and said to the people there, "This fellow was with Jesus of Nazareth."

⁷²He denied it again, with an oath: "I don't know the man!"

⁷³After a little while, those standing there went up to Peter and said, "Surely you are one of them, for your accent gives you away."

⁷⁴Then he began to call down curses on himself and he swore to them, "I don't know the man!"

Immediately a rooster crowed. ⁷⁵Then Peter remembered the word Jesus had spoken: "Before the rooster crows, you will disown me three times." And he went outside and wept bitterly.

27 Early in the morning, all the chief priests and the elders of the people came to the decision to put Jesus to death.

NRSV

nesses? You have now heard his blasphemy. ⁶⁶What is your verdict?" They answered, "He deserves death." ⁶⁷Then they spat in his face and struck him; and some slapped him, ⁶⁸saying, "Prophesy to us, you Messiah!ᵃ Who is it that struck you?"

69Now Peter was sitting outside in the courtyard. A servant-girl came to him and said, "You also were with Jesus the Galilean." ⁷⁰But he denied it before all of them, saying, "I do not know what you are talking about." ⁷¹When he went out to the porch, another servant-girl saw him, and she said to the bystanders, "This man was with Jesus of Nazareth."ᵇ ⁷²Again he denied it with an oath, "I do not know the man." ⁷³After a little while the bystanders came up and said to Peter, "Certainly you are also one of them, for your accent betrays you." ⁷⁴Then he began to curse, and he swore an oath, "I do not know the man!" At that moment the cock crowed. ⁷⁵Then Peter remembered what Jesus had said: "Before the cock crows, you will deny me three times." And he went out and wept bitterly.

27 When morning came, all the chief priests and the elders of the people conferred together against Jesus in order to bring about his death.

ᵃOr Christ   ᵇGk the Nazorean

COMMENTARY

This entire scene takes place at one location: the house of Caiaphas the high priest. It is a complex scene with many characters and is composed so as to juxtapose Jesus' confession before the high priest with Peter's denial in the high priest's courtyard. The contrast is dramatically highlighted in that Jesus' confession uses the identical words of Peter's previous words of confession (16:16; 26:63-64; cf. 10:32-33)—the Peter who now denies (and curses) him.

26:57-58. Matthew's whole account adopts and intensifies Mark's view that the Jewish leaders were the major culprits in the arrest and

execution of Jesus, tending to minimize Roman involvement.[568] He has rewritten Mark in order to use a form of "gathered" (συνάγω *synagō*; cognate of the noun "synagogue"; cf. 26:3), which often had sinister connotations for him and his community. Matthew preserves Mark's technique of intercalation (narrative "sandwiches" in the form ABA'). The scene of Peter seated among the temple guards is introduced here, then the narrative camera

568. Our purpose in explicating the meaning of the Matthean text is not to reconstruct the actual history. From the historical point of view, the story lying behind the Johannine narrative is more plausible, in which the Romans are involved in Jesus' arrest from the first, there is only a Jewish hearing with the actual trial taking place before Pilate, and the Johannine chronology does not call for the arrest of Jesus and a meeting of the Sanhedrin on the actual holy day of the Passover.

switches to Jesus before the council, then back to Peter's denial in vv. 69-75. Thus the stories of Jesus' confession and Peter's denial are interwoven.

26:59-63a. Matthew adds "false" before "testimony" (cf. Mark 14:55) to emphasize the hypocrisy of the Jewish authorities who have already decided on Jesus' death (from 12:14 on!) and are only looking for a pretext. Their quest for false witnesses does not succeed. In Mark the chief priests look for authentic testimony and find false witnesses; in Matthew they look for false witnesses and end up with the truth. Matthew rewrites Mark to show that the testimony of the final two witnesses is, in fact, true.[569] For Matthew, Jesus is able to destroy the Temple, the δύναμαι (*dynamai*) of v. 61 corresponding to that of v. 53.[570] In each case, Jesus is able, by his divine power, to do something he does not, in fact, do. Like the suffering servant (Isa 53:7), Jesus is silent in the face of his accusers.

26:63b-64. Since Jesus does not deny the last charge, the high priest infers that Jesus does indeed claim to operate with power that belongs only to God, and that such a claim is blasphemous (cf. 9:2-3). Thus the discontinuity between vv. 59-62 and 63-65 is not as abrupt as it first appears. Using language reminiscent of Peter's confession in 16:16—i.e., the Christian confession of Matthew's church—he places Jesus under oath and charges him with claiming to be the Messiah, the Son of God. By answering clearly but indirectly, Jesus shows that he practices his own precepts (5:33-37; cf. 23:16-22) and avoids using the oath to confirm his word.[571] Jesus' response is nonetheless a clear affirmative (see 26:25). Meanwhile, Peter voluntarily denies with an oath (vv. 72, 74). Jesus affirms that he is the Christ, the Son of God, but shifts to the title he has used as a self-designation throughout: "Son of Man" (see Excursus "Matthean Christology," 353-61). The meaning of Mat-

thew's addition "from now on" is not clear. Does it refer to the heavenly reign of the Son of Man, which is to start immediately? If so, how can the high priest "see" this? Does it refer to the eschatological events that accompany the crucifixion and resurrection (27:51-53; 28:2-4)? Is it a proleptic pronouncement of the Son of Man who will judge them at the last day—but they are unaware of it? The "you" was the singular σύ (*su*) in "you have said so," but immediately becomes the plural "you" (ὑμεῖς *hymeis*) and may refer to the post-Easter present of the reader/believers, who from 28:16 on have seen Jesus as the exalted Son of Man who both continues to be present with his church during its mission and will come as eschatological judge.

26:65-66. Jesus' self-identification as Messiah, Son of God, and Son of Man is considered blasphemy, corresponding to the original objection against him for claiming to act in God's place by forgiving sins (see 9:3), and now becomes the grounds for the verdict. Jesus is found guilty of a capital offense. "Deserves death" echoes the judgment against Jeremiah, who also had spoken against the Temple (Jer 26:1-19; cf. Matthew's particular interest in Jeremiah at 2:17 and 16:14), and switches back to the original charge of destroying the Temple. Tearing the garments is not a spontaneous emotional response. Originally an expression of sorrow, along with disheveled hair, tearing the garments had become a ritual expression of indignation when one hears blasphemy. The garments of the high priest were sacred, a matter of Torah and tradition, such a sacred sign of authority that the Romans sometimes kept those garments in custody. Tearing them is explicitly forbidden (Lev 10:6; 21:10). Does Matthew picture the high priest as violating the Torah in the very act of condemning Jesus?

26:67-68. There is no change of scene (unlike 27:27-31), and Mark's "some" is omitted, with the result that the high priests and elders are portrayed as themselves spitting on Jesus and striking him—even worse than Pilate. Again, the scene evokes the picture of the Suffering Servant of Isaiah (cf. Isa 50:6). As Jesus had been an example of his own teaching on prayer and oaths, so he lives out his teaching of non-retaliation ("strike" [ῥαπίζω *rapizō*] is used only here and 5:39 in Matthew). The blindfold of Mark 14:65

---

569. Matthew omits Mark's "false," adds "two" in accord with Deut 17:6 and 19:15, and sets this sentence off from the preceding one with an adversative "now" (δέ *de*) instead of Mark's conjunctive "and" (καί *kai*) and by adding "at last" (ὕστερον *hysteron*).

570. Jesus has made no such claim in Matthew (cf. 24:2), so that the charge comes as a surprise to the reader. A saying of Jesus relating to the destruction of the Temple circulated in early Christianity and was understood in a variety of ways in and out of the Christian tradition (cf. 24:1-2; 27:40, 51; John 2:19; Acts 6:14; 1 Cor 3:16-17; 6:19; 2 Cor 6:19; Eph 2:21; 1 Pet 2:5-6).

571. Matthew changes Mark's "I am" (ἐγώ εἰμι *ego eimi*) to "you say [so]" (σὺ εἶπας *su eipas*) to achieve conformity with Jesus' own teaching.

has been omitted, so the action is no longer a cruel parody of "blind man's buff," but a mockery of Jesus' messianic claims. By saying "Prophesy, Christ," the Jewish leaders specifically reject him as Messiah (the Romans will reject only his supposed political claims). If he is the Christ, he should have the prophetic power to identify those who strike him (cf. Luke 7:39). The scene has several layers of irony, for in Matthew's view not only are the prophecies of the Scriptures being fulfilled, but also the Jesus they mockingly challenge to prophesy is being doubly proved to be a prophet, since his previous passion predictions are now being fulfilled and in the courtyard his prophecy about Simon Peter is in the course of fulfillment. Further, although they strike him (παίω *paiō*), Jesus has already prophesied that God will be the one to strike him (26:31, πατάσσω *patassō*, a synonym).

26:69-75. The scene concludes by switching back to Peter in "the courtyard" (αὐλή *aulē*), recalling the similar location of Judas's betrayal (26:3). Matthew replaces Mark's "below" with "outside" (ἔξω *exō*), recalling the position of Jesus' mother and brothers as outsiders (12:46-47), in contrast to his true family, those who do the will of God. The fire in Mark is missing (though preserved by Luke and John). The charge is being "with" Jesus, important in the Matthean narrative (cf. 26:18, 29, 36, 38, 40, and the theological explication at 1:23). Matthew varies the Markan sequence (two challenges by a servant girl and one by bystanders) so that the three challengers are a first servant girl, a second servant girl, and bystanders.[572] Just as Matthew has previously made one blind man, one demoniac, one mute person, and one donkey into two of each (8:28-34; 9:27-31; 9:32-33/12:22; 20:29-34; 21:1-9), so also here he makes one servant girl into two. And just as he has added two witnesses to the trial in which Jesus confesses the Christian truth, so also Matthew has two witnesses for Peter's denial of that truth.

There is no doubt that Peter denied that he was a disciple during Jesus' trial; it is a story unlikely to have been invented. The stories themselves, however, are the product of Christian theological imagination rather than accurate memory or investigative reporting. The theological importance is in the portrayal of Peter as a representative disciple: even the great Christian leader failed; even the failure repented and became a faithful disciple, entrusted with the Christian mission. The vocabulary echoes 10:32-33 and 5:16 (as its reversal). Whereas Jesus was strengthened for the coming test by praying three times in Gethsemane, and Peter had fallen asleep three times in Gethsemane, here he denies three times that he knows Jesus. Whereas Jesus had stood firm in his confession three times (false witnesses, true witnesses, Caiaphas), Peter denies in each of his three confrontations. Whereas Jesus had forthrightly made his confession under the probing of the high priest, Peter crumbles when confronted by the high priest's maid. Whereas Jesus had refused to confirm his word with an oath, Peter here volunteers one.[573] He adds to his oath a curse (against himself if he is lying, or against Jesus to show that he is not a disciple?). "Curse" (καταθεματίζω *katathematizō*), used only here in the NT, is usually transitive rather than reflexive, and suggests that Peter cursed Jesus (cf. 1 Cor 12:3, using a different word). Matthew has rewritten Mark's ambiguous closing line to make it clear that Peter repents and will be reinstated as a good disciple who carries on the church's mission in 28:16-20 (cf. the despair of Judas, 27:3-10).

27:1. In Matthew, the political element present in Mark recedes, and it is Jesus vs. the Jewish leaders throughout.[574] This scene concludes with the early morning (re-?)assembling of the council in order to (officially?) take action to condemn Jesus and deliver him to the Roman authorities (cf. 20:18; 27:3). There is no break in the Matthean story, which gives the impression that the trial and mocking lasted throughout the night. In Mark, Jesus had already been condemned during the late evening session (14:64), and the council reconvenes the following morning.

---

572. This also differs from John 18:12-27, where the challengers are "the woman who guarded the gate" (at the house of Annas, not Caiaphas), "they" (after the transfer to Caiaphas's house) and "one of the [male] slaves of the high priest." Luke 22:54-62 has a servant girl and two unnamed men, without designating which high priest's house is the location. Interpreters, such as Harold Lindsell, *The Battle for the Bible* (Grand Rapids: Zondervan, 1976) 174-76, who regard the truth of the Gospel as dependent on their accuracy in reporting facts, "harmonize" the accounts by claiming there were a total of six denials. This approach not only arrives at a conclusion not found in any of the Gospels, but misconstrues the nature of Gospel truth as well.

573. "Oath" (ὄρκος *horkos*) here does not mean that Peter reverted to profanity, but that, contrary to the teaching and example of Jesus, he attempted to confirm the truth of his statement with an oath (see 5:33-37).

574. Even "in the trial before Pilate it is not so much a question of the King of the Jews (27:11; cf. Mark) but rather of Ἰησοῦς ὁ λεγόμενος χριστός *Iēsous ho legomenos Christos* ['Jesus the one called "Messiah" ')] (27:17, 22)" (Nils Dahl, *Jesus in the Memory of the Early Church* [Minneapolis: Augsburg, 1976] 46).

Matthew 27:2-31a, Roman Trial: Jesus Condemned and Mocked

Matthew 27:2, Jesus Is Delivered Over to Pilate

NIV	NRSV
2They bound him, led him away and handed him over to Pilate, the governor.	2They bound him, led him away, and handed him over to Pilate the governor.

COMMENTARY

Day 5 Begins: Friday. This verse concludes the preceding scene and transfers the action to the next setting: Pilate's court. Pilate, prefect,[575] has played no prior role in the Matthean story (so also Mark and John; cf. Luke, who mentions Pilate prior to the passion story in 3:1; 13:1; 20:20). The historical situation is disputed with regard to the measure of local autonomy the Roman authorities permitted the Jewish leaders. They may have had some authority in cases involving religious matters, but Pilate as the Roman governor represented the real political power. On the basis of John 18:31, it has often been believed

that during the Roman governors' administration of Judea (6–40, 44–66 CE) the Jewish leaders did not have the power of capital punishment, but this has been disputed. The evidence for the Jewish right of capital punishment all seems to point to exceptions, however, and John 18:31 seems to represent the historical situation.[576] Whatever the historical reality may have been, in Matthew's portrayal the Jews have the authority to condemn Jesus, but Pilate must carry out the execution.

575. The NT throughout uses the generic term "governor" (ἡγεμών *hēgemōn*), but literature about the NT often uses the title "procurator" (from Josephus and Tacitus). We now know, on the basis of an inscription found at Caesarea Maratima in 1961, that Pilate had the title "prefect" and that the later title "procurator" was used anachronistically.

576. So the majority opinion, as represented, e.g., by W. F. Albright and C. S. Mann, *Matthew*, AB (Garden City, N.Y.: Doubleday, 1971) 334-36; Eduard Lohse, *Die Geschichte des Leidens und Sterbens Jesu Christi* (Gütersloh: G. Mohn, 1964) 78. For the argument that the Sanhedrin did have the power of capital punishment, see Hans Lietzmann, *Der Prozess Jesu* (Berlin: Berlin Academy of Sciences, 1931); followed by Paul Winter, *On the Trial of Jesus* (Berlin: De Gruyter, 1961).

Matthew 27:3-10, Judas Fails to Make Restitution and Commits Suicide

NIV	NRSV
3When Judas, who had betrayed him, saw that Jesus was condemned, he was seized with remorse and returned the thirty silver coins to the chief priests and the elders. 4"I have sinned," he said, "for I have betrayed innocent blood." "What is that to us?" they replied. "That's your responsibility." 5So Judas threw the money into the temple and left. Then he went away and hanged himself. 6The chief priests picked up the coins and said,	3When Judas, his betrayer, saw that Jesus*a* was condemned, he repented and brought back the thirty pieces of silver to the chief priests and the elders. 4He said, "I have sinned by betraying innocent*b* blood." But they said, "What is that to us? See to it yourself." 5Throwing down the pieces of silver in the temple, he departed; and he went and hanged himself. 6But the chief priests, taking *a* Gk *he* *b* Other ancient authorities read *righteous*

NIV

"It is against the law to put this into the treasury, since it is blood money." [7]So they decided to use the money to buy the potter's field as a burial place for foreigners. [8]That is why it has been called the Field of Blood to this day. [9]Then what was spoken by Jeremiah the prophet was fulfilled: "They took the thirty silver coins, the price set on him by the people of Israel, [10]and they used them to buy the potter's field, as the Lord commanded me."[a]

[a]10 See Zech. 11:12,13; Jer. 19:1-13; 32:6-9.

NRSV

the pieces of silver, said, "It is not lawful to put them into the treasury, since they are blood money." [7]After conferring together, they used them to buy the potter's field as a place to bury foreigners. [8]For this reason that field has been called the Field of Blood to this day. [9]Then was fulfilled what had been spoken through the prophet Jeremiah,[a] "And they took[b] the thirty pieces of silver, the price of the one on whom a price had been set,[c] on whom some of the people of Israel had set a price, [10]and they gave[d] them for the potter's field, as the Lord commanded me."

[a]Other ancient authorities read *Zechariah* or *Isaiah*
[b]Or *I took*   [c]Or *the price of the precious One*
[d]Other ancient authorities read *I gave*

COMMENTARY

Before continuing with the action, Matthew inserts a new scene into the Markan outline, one of only two such additions (see Overview above).[577] The scene fits poorly into Matthew's storyline, for it requires the chief priests to be in the Temple, while the context is the gathering of the chief priests and elders at the house of Caiaphas. Matthew thus has a reason for inserting this tragic interlude at this particular point: It separates the trial before the Sanhedrin even further from the trial before Pilate. Also, by interweaving the story of the trial before Pilate with that of Judas's death, Matthew casts each in a different light, just as was the case in the intertwining of the account of the trial before the Sanhedrin with that of Peter's denial and repentance.

Matthew's is the only Gospel to continue the story of Judas after the scene of Jesus' arrest in Gethsemane.[578] Having realized that he had made a great mistake, Judas seems to have done all the

right things: He is sorry; he returns the money; he acknowledges Jesus' innocence and his own guilt. Yet Matthew seems to hold him up as a model of failed discipleship, one who would have been better off if he had not been born (26:24). Why is his action unacceptable to Matthew, who pictures him as despairing and taking his own life? The answer is not to be found in the supposed distinction between the word used for Judas's repentance (μεταμέλομαι *metamelomai* ["regret," "repent," "change one's mind"]) and the more robust and biblical word usually used by Matthew for genuine repentance (μετανοέω *metanoeō*, "change one's mind," "feel remorse," "repent," "be converted," "reorient one's life"; cf. Matt 3:2; 4:17; 11:20-21; 12:41). *Metamelomai* is also used by Matthew positively (21:30-32). Although Matthew is obviously contrasting Peter in the previous scene and Judas in this one, the difference be-

577. A. H. McNeile, *The Gospel According to St. Matthew: The Greek Text with Introduction, Notes and Indices* (London: Macmillan, 1915; reprint 1961) 264, reads this scene as a continuation of the preceding one, with Judas appearing while the Sanhedrin is still in session, but v. 5 seems to place it in the Temple court at a later time. The ambiguity as to how the reader should visualize time and place for this scene illustrates the non-reportive nature of the material.

578. Acts 1:15-20 recounts Peter's speech in which a different story of the end of Judas is reported (not itself narrated). The Acts story is so different as to preclude harmonization with the Matthean story. The major differences: (1) Matthew: Judas throws the money into the Temple, which the priests use to buy a field; Acts: Judas buys a field with the money himself. (2) Matthew: It is a "field of blood" because of Jesus' blood; Acts: It is a "field of blood" because of Judas's blood. (3) Matthew: Judas takes

his own life by hanging himself; Acts: Judas dies accidentally, by falling. The two stories share common elements of tradition, however: Judas dies a violent death, and a "field of blood" is associated with his destiny. In addition, both stories are developed from scriptural motifs, Matthew's being developed from 2 Sam 17:1-23 as well as Jer 18:2-3, 19:4; 32:7-9; Zech 11:12-13, with Luke's being related to the cursing ordeal of Num 5:21-27.

A third story of Judas's death is told in Papias, Fragment 3: "Judas walked about in this world a sad [literally "big"] example of impiety; for his body having swollen to such an extent that he could not pass where a chariot could pass easily, he was crushed by the chariot, so that his bowels gushed out." This story was in turn grotesquely elaborated in later versions. For the original texts and commentaries, see Kirsopp Lake, "The Death of Judas," in K. Lake and R. J. Foakes-Jackson, eds. *Beginnings of Christianity,* 5 vols. (London: Macmillan, 1920-33; reprint Grand Rapids: Baker, 1979) 5:22-29.

tween them is more than terminological. (The word used for genuine repentance, *metanoeō,* is not used of Peter either.) From Matthew's point of view, what Judas lacks and what Peter has is that fundamental reorientation from the kingdom of this world, represented by thinking human things, to the kingdom represented by Jesus ("thinking divine things"; cf. 16:21-23).

The reader perceives the importance of this fundamental reorientation not from this pericope, but from its context in Matthew as a whole, oriented to the new kingdom represented by the meek Son of David (cf. 12:22-37). Thus Matthew has developed the story in terms of the biblical story of David, whose kingdom was threatened by an opposing kingdom and who had a friend who betrayed him and then hanged himself (2 Sam 17:1-23; the verb "hanged" [ἀπάγχομαι *apagchomai*] occurs only these two times in the Bible). This story is not merely about the tragic situation of Judas, nor does it speculate on his eternal destiny. For Matthew, the story becomes another expression of the conflict of kingdoms, an illustration of how terrible it is to cast one's lot with the wrong side (12:25-30). It also has echoes of the story of Esau, who sold his birthright and never found the way to true repentance (Gen 27:1-40; Heb 12:16). Unlike Peter, Judas does not return to the community of disciples, where forgiveness abounds (18:21-35), but dies in private despair.

The high priests are represented as flat characters, uniformly evil. Just as they had decided in advance to kill Jesus and sought *false* witnesses, making a sham of the "trial" before the Sanhedrin, so also they have only used Judas, and now that his purpose is served literally have no more use for him. The priests consider the money paid to Judas, now retrieved from the Temple, to be unclean, thus acknowledging their own guilt. Yet their religious scrupulosity prohibits their placing it in the Temple treasury. They officially decide (the same phrase as 27:1) to use the money to purchase the "potter's field," which became known as the "field of blood." In all of this, there is a mixture of historical tradition and the confusion between "potter" (יוֹצֵר *yôṣēr*) and "treasury" (אוֹצָר *'ôṣār*) in the MSS of Zech 11:12-13, along with the blending of Zechariah 11 and Jeremiah 18–19; 32:6-15. Thus the fulfillment quotation, mostly from Zechariah, is labeled as being from Jeremiah. (On Matthew's use of Scripture, see Excursus "Matthew as Interpreter of Scripture," 151-54.) Matthew is not concerned to resolve the mystery of why one of Jesus' own betrayed him, and then could not repent even though he was remorseful. Matthew's interest focuses on the religious leaders, who appear all the more callous and guilty by appearing in this scene.

Matthew 27:11-25, Jesus Is Condemned

NIV

[11]Meanwhile Jesus stood before the governor, and the governor asked him, "Are you the king of the Jews?"

"Yes, it is as you say," Jesus replied.

[12]When he was accused by the chief priests and the elders, he gave no answer. [13]Then Pilate asked him, "Don't you hear the testimony they are bringing against you?" [14]But Jesus made no reply, not even to a single charge—to the great amazement of the governor.

[15]Now it was the governor's custom at the Feast to release a prisoner chosen by the crowd. [16]At that time they had a notorious prisoner, called Barabbas. [17]So when the crowd had gathered,

NRSV

11Now Jesus stood before the governor; and the governor asked him, "Are you the King of the Jews?" Jesus said, "You say so." [12]But when he was accused by the chief priests and elders, he did not answer. [13]Then Pilate said to him, "Do you not hear how many accusations they make against you?" [14]But he gave him no answer, not even to a single charge, so that the governor was greatly amazed.

15Now at the festival the governor was accustomed to release a prisoner for the crowd, anyone whom they wanted. [16]At that time they had a notorious prisoner, called Jesus[a] Barabbas. [17]So

[a]Other ancient authorities lack *Jesus*

NIV

Pilate asked them, "Which one do you want me to release to you: Barabbas, or Jesus who is called Christ?" ¹⁸For he knew it was out of envy that they had handed Jesus over to him.

¹⁹While Pilate was sitting on the judge's seat, his wife sent him this message: "Don't have anything to do with that innocent man, for I have suffered a great deal today in a dream because of him."

²⁰But the chief priests and the elders persuaded the crowd to ask for Barabbas and to have Jesus executed.

²¹"Which of the two do you want me to release to you?" asked the governor.

"Barabbas," they answered.

²²"What shall I do, then, with Jesus who is called Christ?" Pilate asked.

They all answered, "Crucify him!"

²³"Why? What crime has he committed?" asked Pilate.

But they shouted all the louder, "Crucify him!"

²⁴When Pilate saw that he was getting nowhere, but that instead an uproar was starting, he took water and washed his hands in front of the crowd. "I am innocent of this man's blood," he said. "It is your responsibility!"

²⁵All the people answered, "Let his blood be on us and on our children!"

NRSV

after they had gathered, Pilate said to them, "Whom do you want me to release for you, Jesusᵃ Barabbas or Jesus who is called the Messiah?"ᵇ ¹⁸For he realized that it was out of jealousy that they had handed him over. ¹⁹While he was sitting on the judgment seat, his wife sent word to him, "Have nothing to do with that innocent man, for today I have suffered a great deal because of a dream about him." ²⁰Now the chief priests and the elders persuaded the crowds to ask for Barabbas and to have Jesus killed. ²¹The governor again said to them, "Which of the two do you want me to release for you?" And they said, "Barabbas." ²²Pilate said to them, "Then what should I do with Jesus who is called the Messiah?"ᵇ All of them said, "Let him be crucified!" ²³Then he asked, "Why, what evil has he done?" But they shouted all the more, "Let him be crucified!"

²⁴So when Pilate saw that he could do nothing, but rather that a riot was beginning, he took some water and washed his hands before the crowd, saying, "I am innocent of this man's blood;ᶜ see to it yourselves." ²⁵Then the people as a whole answered, "His blood be on us and on our children!"

ᵃOther ancient authorities lack *Jesus*   ᵇOr *the Christ*
ᶜOther ancient authorities read *this righteous blood*, or *this righteous man's blood*

COMMENTARY

In this scene Matthew follows Mark closely, making two additions (27:19, 24-25) and subtle modifications, all of which have the effect of making the decision of the Jewish crowds and the responsibility of the Jewish leaders all the clearer.⁵⁷⁹ Matthew's additions structure the scene into three episodes: (1) Jesus' confession and silence before the governor, vv. 11-14; (2) the people's choice of Barabbas and rejection of Jesus, vv. 15-23; (3) Pilate's proclamation of his innocence and the people's acceptance of responsibility for Jesus' death, vv. 24-25.

27:11-14. After his insertion of the story of Judas's death in 27:3-10, Matthew adds a transitional sentence to bring the storyline back to Jesus' trial. "Jesus stood before the governor" also has the effect of paralleling Jesus' fate and that of the disciples (10:17-18).

Pilate's question is clearly a political charge, treason or rebellion against Rome, and is clearly a capital offense.⁵⁸⁰ Jesus' response is a clear affirmative, as in 26:25, 64 (the NIV is the better translation here). As in 26:64, Jesus confesses his

579. The location of this scene is unclear in the Synoptics, which, following Mark, do not bring Jesus into the Praetorium ("governor's headquarters," NRSV) until Matthew 27:27 par. In contrast, John 18:28 has the whole Roman trial take place in the Praetorium, having a different chronology that incorporates the Synoptics' later Roman flogging and mocking scene into an earlier location in the Roman trial.

580. Presumably, the reader is to understand that the Jewish leaders have translated the religious term *messiah* as "king" for Pilate (in v. 22 Pilate keeps their term). *Messiah* itself was also a highly charged political term, the distinction between "religious" and "political" being alien to Jewish understanding.

own identity (though Matthew's readers understand the affirmation differently than does Pilate; cf. 2:1). These are Jesus' only words in the Roman trial; he will speak only once more before his death, the cry from the cross in 27:46.[581] Pilate is amazed, but the well-versed reader will think of Isa 52:14-15; 53:7.

27:15-23. Matthew adopts the Markan picture of the annual custom of releasing one prisoner at the festival. The practice is not documented outside the NT and is omitted by Luke, who is more sophisticated in Roman matters. It is historically unlikely that the authorities would release a popular political prisoner at a nationalistic festival when patriotic and religious emotions were highest. In the Gospels, the episode has the literary and theological effect of heightening the contrast between Jesus' true identity as the one who saves his people (1:21) and who is the true Son of the Father (11:27) and Barabbas, "son of his father" (Βαραββᾶς *Barabbas,* בּר־אבּא *Bar-abbā*). Matthew heightened this contrast if, as is probable, he added "Jesus" as Barabbas's given name.[582] The choice is between two men named "Jesus" ("God saves," see on 1:21): Jesus the criminal, son of (whoever was) his father, and Jesus the Messiah, who saves his people from their sins, the true Son of the Father (3:17; 11:25-27; 17:5).[583] Once again, two kingdoms stand over against each other. Kingship language is ironically used repeatedly of Jesus, the "Righteous One" (v. 19) who cannot be charged with evil (v. 23), while the Jewish leaders will persuade the people to choose a notorious criminal. Such is Matthew's understanding.

27:19. This addition seems to have been composed by Matthew, reflecting his favorite themes of Jesus as the righteous one (cf. 3:15; 21:32) and divine revelation by dreams ("by a dream" [κατ' ὄναρ *kat' onar*] is used in the NT

only here and in the Matthean birth story, 1:20; 2:12-13, 19, 22). These words may be taken as increasing Pilate's guilt—he now knows by divine revelation that Jesus is innocent, and he is commanded by God to have nothing to do with him. Matthew, however, probably understands the following episode of hand washing to represent Pilate's obedience to the divine message communicated by the dream, so that the words serve to release him from responsibility and heap guilt on the Jewish people.

27:20-23. The crowds have throughout been pictured by Matthew as an uncommitted group, potential disciples, sometimes quite friendly to Jesus (21:11, 46; cf. 26:5), but also courted by the Pharisaic opposition. Their first sign of opposition is their presence at Jesus' arrest (26:47). Here they make their final decision, corresponding to the rejection of the Christian message by the masses of Jewish people in Matthew's own experience. The ominous note of 27:1 finds its fulfillment. Pilate, desiring to release Jesus, miscalculates, counting on the crowd to overrule the intent of the Jewish leaders to kill Jesus. But now it is no longer the leaders alone who bear responsibility. Persuaded by their leaders, "all" cry out for Jesus' crucifixion. ("All" is added by Matthew in v. 22; cf. v. 25, "all the people," another Matthean addition.) When asked for reasons, they only turn up the volume. This is the last time we see the crowds in Matthew (cf. Luke 23:48; see also Reflections below on role of the crowds).

27:24-25. Here Matthew makes his second addition to enhance the contrast between Jewish guilt and Roman innocence. Writing from the post-Easter perspective of the (mostly) failed Christian mission to Jews and the success of the Gentile mission, he pictures Pilate as absolving himself of guilt and the Jewish people accepting the responsibility for Jesus' death.[584] (The "crowds" [ὄχλοι *ochloi*] become "the people as a whole" [πᾶς ὁ λαός *pas ho laos*] in v. 25.[585]) The scene is only in Matthew and

---

581. Contrast the Johannine Jesus, who is pictured as talkative and magisterial, in charge of his own trial and death, representing a different theology of Jesus' death: victor rather than victim.

582. The NRSV, but not the NIV, adopts the reading "Jesus Barabbas," found in Θ, *f*¹, 700*, sy*ˢ*. "Jesus" is missing from most ancient MSS, but Origen and about twenty medieval MSS contain a note that many ancient copies here read "Jesus Barabbas." It is more likely to have been omitted by pious scribes than added.

583. The Markan identification of Barabbas as a freedom fighter against the Romans, significant in the time of the Jewish war reflected in Mark (66–73 CE) is dropped by Matthew as no longer relevant to his 90 CE situation. For Matthew, Barabbas is simply a notorious criminal like the two "bandits" (λῃσταί *lēstai*) crucified with Jesus (cf. 27:38).

584. Pilate is not pictured as entirely innocent; he does finally deliver Jesus to be crucified (v. 26). But over against the Markan picture, one can see in Matthew the developing tendency to exonerate Pilate and condemn the Jews. In the *Acts of Pilate* and Tertullian *Apologeticum* 21.24, for example, Pilate is pictured as a secret disciple who acknowledges the divinity of Jesus. Later Christian tradition made him into a Christian martyr, then, along with his wife Procla or Procula, into a saint (as in the Ethiopic and Coptic churches).

585. The identical phrase πᾶς ὁ λαός is found listing the opponents of Jeremiah at Jer 26:8 (cf. Jer 26:15, where shedding the "innocent blood" of the prophet brings disaster upon the city). Here as elsewhere, Jeremiah texts have had a deep influence on Matthew's narrative.

was probably composed by Matthew himself. The symbolic act is not Roman, but has numerous biblical overtones (Deut 21:1-9; Pss 26:6-10; 73:13; Isa 1:15-16). Pilate's words to the Jews are identical to the Jewish leader's words to Judas: "You see to it."

The people respond with words accepting the guilt (for the biblical idiom (cf. Lev 20:9-16; Josh 2:19-20; 2 Sam 1:16; 14:9; Jer 26:15; 51:35). These words were destined to be tragically misinterpreted by Christians of later centuries who continued to blame the Jewish people as a whole for the death of Jesus. Matthew, however, looks back on the destruction of Jerusalem in 70 CE as divine punishment for rejection of the Messiah (cf. 22:7; 23:34-36, 39). The people in Matthew's story do not invoke guilt on all future generations, but on themselves and their children—i.e., the generation that experienced the devastation of Jerusalem and the destruction of the Temple. Matthew is engaged in the anti-Jewish polemic of

his time, and he offers his theological interpretation of a tragic event that had already happened as part of his polemic. He does not wish for revenge or pronounce a sentence on all Jews forever.

In the light of Matthew's overall dualistic theological perspective of the alternative kingdoms represented by Jesus and the rulers of this world (both Jewish and Gentile), one should see this scene as the confrontation of two kingdoms. These two kingdoms are not, however, Rome and the kingdom of God (cf. Revelation), but the options of royal power exerted through violence and the authority and power of God present in meekness, the latter represented by Jesus and the former by both the Jewish and the Gentile rulers. It is the Jewish crowds who stand before the decision here, and they opt for rule by violence. Jesus' kingship represents God's kingdom, but they reject it. This is immediately dramatized (vv. 27-31a).

Matthew 27:26-31a, The True King Is Mocked

NIV

26Then he released Barabbas to them. But he had Jesus flogged, and handed him over to be crucified.

27Then the governor's soldiers took Jesus into the Praetorium and gathered the whole company of soldiers around him. 28They stripped him and put a scarlet robe on him, 29and then twisted together a crown of thorns and set it on his head. They put a staff in his right hand and knelt in front of him and mocked him. "Hail, king of the Jews!" they said. 30They spit on him, and took the staff and struck him on the head again and again. 31After they had mocked him, they took off the robe and put his own clothes on him.

NRSV

26So he released Barabbas for them; and after flogging Jesus, he handed him over to be crucified.

27Then the soldiers of the governor took Jesus into the governor's headquarters,a and they gathered the whole cohort around him. 28They stripped him and put a scarlet robe on him, 29and after twisting some thorns into a crown, they put it on his head. They put a reed in his right hand and knelt before him and mocked him, saying, "Hail, King of the Jews!" 30They spat on him, and took the reed and struck him on the head. 31After mocking him, they stripped him of the robe and put his own clothes on him.

aGk the praetorium

COMMENTARY

27:26. Whereas the Jewish trial concluded with the mocking of Jesus as "Christ" by the Jewish leadership, the Roman trial concludes with the Gentiles mocking him as "king." Just as 26:68

corresponds to 26:63, so also 27:29 corresponds to 27:11. The mocking is preceded by the flogging, a terrible beating administered on the bare back with a leather whip, often studded with pieces of metal or bone to increase the torture (cf. Acts 16:22; 22:24-25). Its severity was sometimes fatal. In the Fourth Gospel, it was administered to Jesus early in the Roman trial as a part of Pilate's failed strategy to obtain sympathy for Jesus (John 19:1-6). Matthew follows Mark in placing it after the trial as a result of the guilty verdict and sentencing. Matthew, like the other Gospels, avoids graphic description (see Reflections below).

27:27-31a. In contrast to both the flogging and the crucifixion, the mocking scene is given in vivid detail (though still without the sensationalism of the martyr stories of 4 Maccabees). Thus the irony of the scene is what is important for Matthew. Jesus is indeed king, but kingship is here redefined. The mock coronation is a parody of Jesus' own (coming) pronouncement in 28:18*b*. The scene is set in the Praetorium for the first time, but Pilate is not present (cf. the earlier mocking by the Jews, in which the leaders participate, 26:67-68). The soldiers "assemble" (συνάγω *synagō*) against Jesus, changing Mark's neutral word to the verbal cognate of the word for "synagogue"; cf. 26:3). All the accoutrements and insignia of royalty are mockingly noted: Jesus is a clown-king, complete with "robe," "crown," "scepter," "kneeling," and "acclamation." The crown of thorns is not just for additional torture; the sharp points radiating outward represent the rays of divinity surrounding the ruler's head, used on coins to portray Hellenistic kings. Matthew makes the ironic scene complete by adding the reed/scepter to Mark and by changing the (imperial) purple robe for an ordinary red chlamus, the Roman soldier's cape instead of an emperor's robe. The latter is not only more historically realistic (where would soldiers get an emperor's robe?), but also heightens the irony, making the ordinary "robe" the same kind of parody as the thorns/crown and the stick/scepter. In contrast to the homage paid the true king of the Jews by the magi (2:11), Jesus is greeted by being spit upon and struck, and in contrast to the universal practice of kingship in this world, the true king receives violence rather than inflicting it (5:38-40; 26:52-54).

Matthew 27:31*b*-66, Jesus' Crucifixion and Burial

Matthew 27:31*b*-32, Simon Is Compelled to Carry Jesus' Cross

NIV	NRSV
Then they led him away to crucify him.	Then they led him away to crucify him.
[32]As they were going out, they met a man from Cyrene, named Simon, and they forced him to carry the cross.	32As they went out, they came upon a man from Cyrene named Simon; they compelled this man to carry his cross.

COMMENTARY

Matthew takes this scene from Mark 15:20*b*-21. It is capable of much dramatic elaboration (a tendency already present in Luke 23:26-32). Matthew has actually abbreviated it; here as elsewhere he is more interested in theological meaning than gruesome details. The vertical crucifixion stake was fixed in the ground at the place of execution; as further humiliation, the condemned prisoner was usually forced to carry the heavy crossbar himself. Matthew follows Mark in picturing Jesus as not carrying his own crossbar; a passerby named Simon was requisitioned by the Romans for the task (see Matt 5:41).[586] Simon is no longer "coming in from the

586. Matthew adopts the Markan picture, in which Jesus is passive and victimized at the crucifixion and another carries his cross, in accord with the declaration of 16:24 that discipleship is cross-bearing. Contrast John's picture of Jesus carrying his own cross (19:17), exemplifying John's interest in picturing Jesus as divinely powerful and in charge of his own death (John 10:17-18; 18:2-11). These pictures should not be combined or historically harmonized; each has its theological point to make.

country"[587] or identified as the father of Alexander and Rufus, apparently because they had been known in Mark's community but not in Matthew's. The fact that Simon is originally from Cyrene (modern Libya) anticipates the mission to the Gentiles. In the Matthean story, the only person present with Jesus at Golgotha whose

name we know is an outsider.[588] That a stranger named Simon is forced to carry Jesus' cross emphasizes the abandonment of Jesus' own disciples, especially the one named Simon (cf. 16:24; 26:33, 56, 69-75).

587. The Markan phrase connotes work in the fields, so Simon is thought of as a resident of Judea, not a visitor from Cyrene for the Passover. After the last supper scene, Matthew follows Mark in no longer attending to the chronology that would place the execution on Passover. Historically, it is as unlikely that an execution would be carried out on the Passover as is Simon's working in the fields on a holy day, on which work was strictly forbidden.

588. The Fourth Gospel's placing of the Beloved Disciple and the mother of Jesus (and one or two other women) at the cross is probably an idealized scene communicating Johannine theology, not historical fact. In any case, Matthew's narrative has it otherwise. Unlike the Fourth Gospel's use of the Beloved Disciple, Mark and Matthew make nothing of the presence of Simon as a source or guarantor of the tradition (cf. John 19:35; 21:24).

Matthew 27:33-56, Jesus Is Crucified

NIV

[33]They came to a place called Golgotha (which means The Place of the Skull). [34]There they offered Jesus wine to drink, mixed with gall; but after tasting it, he refused to drink it. [35]When they had crucified him, they divided up his clothes by casting lots.[a] [36]And sitting down, they kept watch over him there. [37]Above his head they placed the written charge against him: THIS IS JESUS, THE KING OF THE JEWS. [38]Two robbers were crucified with him, one on his right and one on his left. [39]Those who passed by hurled insults at him, shaking their heads [40]and saying, "You who are going to destroy the temple and build it in three days, save yourself! Come down from the cross, if you are the Son of God!" [41]In the same way the chief priests, the teachers of the law and the elders mocked him. [42]"He saved others," they said, "but he can't save himself! He's the King of Israel! Let him come down now from the cross, and we will believe in him. [43]He trusts in God. Let God rescue him now if he wants him, for he said, 'I am the Son of God.'" [44]In the same way the robbers who were crucified with him also heaped insults on him.

[45]From the sixth hour until the ninth hour darkness came over all the land. [46]About the ninth hour Jesus cried out in a loud voice, *"Eloi, Eloi,[b] lama sabachthani?"*—which means, "My God, my God, why have you forsaken me?"[c]

NRSV

[33]And when they came to a place called Golgotha (which means Place of a Skull), [34]they offered him wine to drink, mixed with gall; but when he tasted it, he would not drink it. [35]And when they had crucified him, they divided his clothes among themselves by casting lots;[a] [36]then they sat down there and kept watch over him. [37]Over his head they put the charge against him, which read, "This is Jesus, the King of the Jews."

[38]Then two bandits were crucified with him, one on his right and one on his left. [39]Those who passed by derided[b] him, shaking their heads [40]and saying, "You who would destroy the temple and build it in three days, save yourself! If you are the Son of God, come down from the cross." [41]In the same way the chief priests also, along with the scribes and elders, were mocking him, saying, [42]"He saved others; he cannot save himself.[c] He is the King of Israel; let him come down from the cross now, and we will believe in him. [43]He trusts in God; let God deliver him now, if he wants to; for he said, 'I am God's Son.'" [44]The bandits who were crucified with him also taunted him in the same way.

[45]From noon on, darkness came over the whole land[d] until three in the afternoon. [46]And about three o'clock Jesus cried with a loud voice, "Eli, Eli, lema sabachthani?" that is, "My God,

[a]35 A few late manuscripts *lots that the word spoken by the prophet might be fulfilled: "They divided my garments among themselves and cast lots for my clothing"* (Psalm 22:18) [b]46 Some manuscripts *Eli, Eli* [c]46 Psalm 22:1

[a]Other ancient authorities add *in order that what had been spoken through the prophet might be fulfilled, "They divided my clothes among themselves, and for my clothing they cast lots."* [b]Or *blasphemed* [c]Or *is he unable to save himself?* [d]Or *earth*

NIV

⁴⁷When some of those standing there heard this, they said, "He's calling Elijah."

⁴⁸Immediately one of them ran and got a sponge. He filled it with wine vinegar, put it on a stick, and offered it to Jesus to drink. ⁴⁹The rest said, "Now leave him alone. Let's see if Elijah comes to save him."

⁵⁰And when Jesus had cried out again in a loud voice, he gave up his spirit.

⁵¹At that moment the curtain of the temple was torn in two from top to bottom. The earth shook and the rocks split. ⁵²The tombs broke open and the bodies of many holy people who had died were raised to life. ⁵³They came out of the tombs, and after Jesus' resurrection they went into the holy city and appeared to many people.

⁵⁴When the centurion and those with him who were guarding Jesus saw the earthquake and all that had happened, they were terrified, and exclaimed, "Surely he was the Sonᵃ of God!"

⁵⁵Many women were there, watching from a distance. They had followed Jesus from Galilee to care for his needs. ⁵⁶Among them were Mary Magdalene, Mary the mother of James and Joses, and the mother of Zebedee's sons.

ᵃ54 Or a son

NRSV

my God, why have you forsaken me?" ⁴⁷When some of the bystanders heard it, they said, "This man is calling for Elijah." ⁴⁸At once one of them ran and got a sponge, filled it with sour wine, put it on a stick, and gave it to him to drink. ⁴⁹But the others said, "Wait, let us see whether Elijah will come to save him."ᵃ ⁵⁰Then Jesus cried again with a loud voice and breathed his last.ᵇ ⁵¹At that moment the curtain of the temple was torn in two, from top to bottom. The earth shook, and the rocks were split. ⁵²The tombs also were opened, and many bodies of the saints who had fallen asleep were raised. ⁵³After his resurrection they came out of the tombs and entered the holy city and appeared to many. ⁵⁴Now when the centurion and those with him, who were keeping watch over Jesus, saw the earthquake and what took place, they were terrified and said, "Truly this man was God's Son!"ᶜ

55Many women were also there, looking on from a distance; they had followed Jesus from Galilee and had provided for him. ⁵⁶Among them were Mary Magdalene, and Mary the mother of James and Joseph, and the mother of the sons of Zebedee.

ᵃOther ancient authorities add *And another took a spear and pierced his side, and out came water and blood*
ᵇOr *gave up his spirit*   ᶜOr *a son of God*

COMMENTARY

27:33. The actual location of the crucifixion scene is unknown. The traditional site at the Church of the Holy Sepulcher in the Old City was identified by Helena, mother of Constantine, in the fourth century, along with many other sites she specified during her pilgrimage to the Holy Land. "Gordan's Calvary," just outside the present city walls, was identified by a British general in the nineteenth century on the basis of the shape of the hill. But Golgotha (Latin *calvaria,* both words mean "skull") is never called a "hill" in the Bible. Its location on a hill is unlikely, since crucifixions were intended to have a public message and were located by the Romans on busy public thoroughfares. Matthew follows Mark in locating the site of execution outside the city walls, which itself may represent theology rather than history (Matt 21:39; cf. Lev 24:14; Num

15:35-36; John 19:20; Heb 13:12). Matthew omits Mark's specification of the beginning of the crucifixion at 9:00 A.M., with noon being his first noting of the time (contrast even further John 19:14, which has the proceedings before Pilate still in progress at noon).

27:34. Mark had pictured Jesus being offered myrrhed wine, itself a delicacy, but also used as a narcotic to ease the pain of the condemned (cf. Prov 31:6).[589] Matthew changes "myrrh" to "gall," corresponding to Ps 69:21.[590] Mark's helpful narcotic becomes in Matthew a cruel joke. In

589. Babylonian Talmud Sanhedrin 43a.

590. Continuing this tendency, the vast majority of MSS change Mark's "wine" (οἶνος *oinos*) to "vinegar" (ὄξος *oxos*) from Psalm 69, but Matthew originally wrote οἶνος, as in ℵ B D K L Θ, *f*¹, *f*¹³, 33 and the Latin, Syriac, and Coptic MSS traditions.

Mark, Jesus refuses the drink, no reason being given. Matthew has Jesus taste, fulfilling the Scripture, and then refuse. Since the narrative is not eyewitness reporting but theological interpretation of the evangelists, who present a variety of portrayals, meaning should be sought at the level of the theological intention of the evangelists. None of the evangelists wishes to portray a drugged or unconscious Jesus on the cross, but one who can speak.[591]

27:35. As with the flogging, the actual crucifixion is mentioned in one word, a Greek adverbial participle that becomes a subordinate clause in English, not even the main verb of the sentence (see Reflections below).[592] The main verb deals with dividing the garments of the condemned, expressed in words taken from Ps 22:19. In earliest Christianity, Psalm 22 became a key source of imagery for portraying the passion. In the psalm, a desperately sick person laments to God that relatives are already dividing up his or her belongings. Matthew follows the (pre-)Markan tradition that had already interpreted this as being fulfilled in the Roman custom of dividing the condemned man's clothes among the execution squad.

27:36. Matthew adds the detail that the soldiers sat down and watched Jesus. This is not only part of Matthew's apologetic to certify the actual death and burial of Jesus, but it also corresponds to the note of expectation he builds into other scenes by adding this same phrase (27:54, 61).[593]

27:37. The deep irony of the whole trial, mocking, and crucifixion scene is concentrated on the placard placed on the cross. It was intended as a coarse joke, but the reader knows it is profoundly true at a level the participants in the story cannot imagine. Matthew emphasizes this by adding "This is . . . " transforming the insult into a Christian confession that even the executioners will acknowledge before the scene is over (v. 54).

27:38. The two crucified with Jesus are described, as in Mark, as "bandits" (λῃσταί *lēstai*, which can refer to criminals, to robbers [as in Matt 21:13; Luke 10:30; John 10:1; 2 Cor 11:26] or to revolutionaries, terrorist/freedom fighters [as Josephus, *The Jewish War* 2.254]). Matthew had not described Barabbas in these terms (see 27:16, omitting the description in Mark 15:7). In Matthew, Jesus is not classed with revolutionaries, but with common criminals, thus increasing the humiliation (cf. Isa 53:3, 9, 12).

27:39-44. While Jesus is on the cross, he is derided by three groups. (1) The passersby "derided" him (the verb is βλασφημέω *blasphēmeō*, literally "blasphemed," the same as 26:65) with the charge of claiming to destroy and rebuild the temple (see on 26:61). The "wagging of their heads" is an act of derision taken from Ps 22:8 (cf. Ps 109:25; Lam 2:15). Their challenge for the one who saved others to save himself is not, as they think, the refutation of his claims, but ironically the very truth taught by Jesus (16:25). "If you are the Son of God" is added by Matthew, reflecting Wis 2:13, 18-20, itself an interpretation of Ps 22:9. Matthew adds "Son of God" because it is important to his christology (cf. his similar addition in 16:16; 26:63), and to make the challenge of the passersby correspond to 4:3, 6, where the devil issued a similar challenge using the identical words. There, too, Jesus placed himself in the category of humanity, as he does here by the most human act of all, dying a human death.[594] The jeer of the passersby is thus more than a cruel taunt; it represents an opposing theology rejected by the canonical Gospels.

(2) The whole Sanhedrin is pictured as present, as the chief priests, scribes, and elders join in the

---

591. Interpreters have often understood this historically and combined it with a theory of the atonement, such as expressed by McNeile, *Matthew:* "A voluntary death for others required full exercise of will and consciousness to the last" (418). There can be no doubt that Jesus suffered terrible physical abuse and pain. However, the connection between Jesus' experiencing pain and God's reconciling act in the crucifixion of Jesus should not be interpreted in a sadistic or masochistic manner, just as docetism should be avoided (see Reflections below).

592. Matthew's readers were familiar with the horrible details of execution by crucifixion. The contemporary reader may obtain a historical understanding of the practice of crucifixion in the Roman world from Martin Hengel, *Crucifixion in the Ancient World and the Folly of the Message of the Cross* (Philadelphia: Fortress, 1977); Joseph Fitzmyer, "Crucifixion in Ancient Palestine, Qumran Literature, and the New Testament," *CBQ* 40 (1978) 493-513; Pierson Parker, "Crucifixion," *IDB* 1:746-47; J. F. Strange, "Crucifixion, Method of," *IDBSup,* 199-200. Nails and blood are from John, not the Synoptics.

593. This is analogous to the later mention of the women as observing the crucifixion, death, and burial and coming to the tomb on Easter morning, providing continuity of documentation and avoiding in advance the charge that Jesus did not really die or that the wrong tomb was discovered empty.

594. On the basis of a docetic misunderstanding of the doctrine of the divinity of Christ, some early Christians were reluctant to portray the crucifixion as a genuine human death (cf. *Acts of John, Gospel of Basilides, Gospel of Peter,* and docetism in general). Matthew struggles with this also and enhances the Markan picture of Jesus as weak and victimized by adding touches of divine power to the passion story (e.g., 26:52-54), but ultimately resists the temptation to make Jesus' suffering and death a sham.

taunt, this time using the very words of Ps 22:9 and Wis 2:13-20, with "Son of God" added again to the Markan text.[595] They call Jesus specifically the "King of Israel" and "Son of God," and they challenge him to come down from the cross. So not only do two christologies stand over against each other here, but two understandings of kingship and the kingdom of God as well.

(3) The robbers join in the same derision; there is no repentant thief in Matthew. Jesus suffers among criminals, with no friend, relative, disciple, or convert present. The narrator lets the reader be present when all others have abandoned Jesus.

27:45. The noon to three P.M. period is taken from Mark, where it is part of a schematic division of the day into three-hour periods. Matthew does not adopt this schema, so this is his first reference to time. The word translated "land" (γῆ *gē*) can refer either to the "land" in the national sense (i.e., "Judea") or to the whole earth. Since Matthew has other cosmic signs accompany the crucifixion, he probably intends the darkness to be worldwide.[596] This is the first of the signs that the crucifixion/resurrection of Jesus is (a prolepsis of) the eschatological event, a prefiguration of the parousia (cf. Exod 10:22 [darkness over Egypt at the first Passover]; Amos 8:9; Matt 24:29). Matthew's text is closer to the LXX Exodus text than to his Markan source, one of many indications of the formative influence exercised by the Bible on the formation of the passion story.

27:46-49. Jesus' only articulate word from the cross is the first line of Psalm 22, a lament of a suffering righteous person who calls out for divine vindication, which the psalm itself goes on to promise and celebrate, the Gentiles themselves finally joining in the celebration. The Matthean reader, who knows the whole story, can rightfully think of Psalm 22 as an outline of the whole cross/resurrection salvation-event, which leads to the Gentile mission. But the Matthean Jesus should not be pictured as merely reciting the opening line for an outline of salvation

history.[597] The human Jesus is pictured as dying with a cry of anguish and abandonment on his lips, and yet not of despair. In the darkness and pain, he still addresses his lament to God, and as "my God." Matthew has slightly adjusted the language from Mark's Aramaic citation to reflect the text of the HB more exactly, Mark's "Eloi, Eloi" becoming "Eli, Eli" (אלי [*ēlê*], ἠλι [*ēli*], rhyming with the English word *daily*). This also facilitates the bystanders' (mis-)understanding that Jesus is calling for Elijah ('Ηλίας *Elias*), which sounds very similar in Greek (but not in Hebrew).[598]

Matthew has clarified the somewhat confusing scene of Mark 15:36. One of the bystanders wants to offer Jesus a drink of some of the cheap wine carried by soldiers ("vinegar") in order to prolong his life a little. But others, wanting to increase his distress and thus the chance that Elijah will come to save him, forbid it (or simply join in to say "wait"; there is a translation difficulty here). Matthew changes Mark's "take him down" to "save," another reflection of the vocabulary of Psalm 22. Their hesitation, whether motivated by speculation that Jesus may in fact be the kind of righteous person Elijah would come to save, or mere curiosity in seeing a miracle, is vain—the Matthean reader knows that Elijah has already come (cf. 11:14; 17:10-13). The addition to v. 49 mentioning the spear thrust and water and blood, although found in some ancient MSS (א, B, C, L, al), is not an original part of the Matthean text, but a later scribal incursion from John 19:34.

27:50. By adding the word for "again" to Mark and changing the verb to "cried" (often in Psalm 22 and other lament psalms for prayer to God), Matthew has transformed the final, inarticulate scream with which Jesus dies in Mark 15:37 into a continuation of his earlier lamentation of v. 46. Likewise, the change from "he expired" to "he yielded up his spirit" (so RSV; cf. NRSV textual note) reflects Matthew's view of a Jesus

595. Historically it is, of course, very unlikely that the ruling religious council of the land would *en masse* attend an execution, especially on the sacred Passover. Matthew, however, has forgotten that the chronological framework he presupposes now makes this the Passover, which plays no role after 26:2, 19.

596. Contrast Luke 23:44-45, which historicizes the event in terms of an eclipse—not possible at the Passover, the time of the full moon.

597. Douglas R. A. Hare, *Matthew, Int.,* (Louisville: Westminster/John Knox, 1993) 322, points out that "this evasion is precluded" by the considerations that (1) Luke couldn't hear it this way, and thus substituted another psalm he considered more appropriate (Luke 23:45 = Ps 31:6) and (2) that the bystanders in the Matthean story did not hear it as an affirmation of all of Psalm 22, but as a cry for help.

598. Thus here is another indication that the story was composed in Greek. While the crucifixion of Jesus was itself certainly an actual historical event, the narrative does not reflect an eyewitness report, but the theological composition of the Christian community, including the later Greek-speaking church.

who dies a truly human death, but still with the lordly dignity of one who is Son of God.

27:51-53. The eschatological signs that began with the darkness of v. 45 continue as Jesus dies. Matthew makes them into a connected series:

(1) The Temple curtain is split from top to bottom. Matthew has in mind the veil that separates the most holy place from the rest of the Temple (Exod 26:31-35; 40:21). Ripping this curtain effectively demolishes the Temple as the site of God's presence and is a prolepsis of the Temple's destruction. Matthew looks back on the destruction of Jerusalem and the Temple, which he saw as divine judgment on Israel for rejecting the Messiah (see 22:7). Jesus had predicted the destruction of the Temple as part of the eschatological events (24:1-2). With his death, the judgment and destruction begin, as do the eschatological events themselves.

(2) The preceding sign was already in Mark, but understood differently by him. The remaining ones are added by Matthew. The eschatological signs continue with an earthquake that splits the rocks (cf. 24:8; 28:2).

(3) The tombs of Israelite saints, surrounding the city and the Temple Mount, are opened as Jesus dies. The rock tombs anticipate the rock tomb in which Jesus will be buried (27:60), and join Christ and the saints in solidarity. These saints are Jewish people who are brought to life by Jesus' death—but not "this generation," which has rejected him.[599] Since Matthew wants to connect the raising of the Israelite saints with the death of Jesus, seen in eschatological terms, but also wants Jesus' own resurrection to be primary (as, e.g., 1 Cor 15:20), this results in the peculiar picture of the saints' being resurrected on Good Friday but remaining in their tombs (or in the open country) until after the Easter appearances of Jesus. That we have theology in narrative form, and not bare historical reporting, is clear. Although no theory of the atonement is elaborated, it is clear that for Matthew the death of Jesus is not a mere minus that will be negated by the resurrection. Already in the death of Jesus the eon-changing, dead-raising power of God breaks in.

27:54. Jesus' death and the eschatological

events it triggers have a profound effect not only on Jewish saints, but also on Gentiles. The Roman execution squad is converted by seeing these events (in Mark it is the centurion alone, on the basis of Jesus' death alone), and become a prefiguration of the Gentiles who will be converted and form a large element of Matthew's own church. They signify this by reciting in unison the Christian affirmation rejected by "this generation": "Truly, this one was the Son of God."[600]

27:55-56. Matthew follows Mark in picturing certain women as viewing the crucifixion from a distance, who will be able to validate the death and burial and who will serve as witnesses to his resurrection (28:1). Mary Magdalene is clearly identified; the identities of the others is not clear. "Mary the mother of James and Joseph" (in Mark, "Joses," a different person) may be the mother of Jesus (cf. 13:55), but if so this is a peculiar way to identify her. Mark's "Salome" has been replaced by the mother of James and John, who plays a role earlier in the Gospel (20:20), where she is also a Matthean addition to Mark. The description of her as "the mother of the sons of Zebedee" reminds the reader of the absence of Jesus' disciples and the presence of the women as their substitutes.[601] In Mark, the surprising appearance of women at this point in the story, and the surprising fact that they have been Jesus' disciples back in Galilee, plays a literary role.[602] Matthew takes them over from Mark, but they no longer are Jesus' followers in Galilee; they follow him *from* Galilee—i.e., they made the pilgrimage trip south with him and his followers. Although Matthew minimizes the role of these women as earlier followers/disciples/ministers with Jesus, they have a key role as witnesses to the crucifixion and resurrection, and they are still present after all the male disciples have fled (26:56).

---

599. Interpretation of Matthew's view of the fate of Jewish people as a whole should not forget that the first people affected by the eschatological event of Jesus' death were Jewish people who had made no Christian confession.

600. The word rendered "man" (ἄνθρωπος *anthrōpos*), present in Matthew's source (Mark 15:39), is not in Matthew's Greek text, but is added in the NRSV by the translators. Matthew misses the sharpness of Mark's christological affirmation, when the centurion declares that this *human being* was the Son of God, effectively anticipating the Chalcedonian christology (truly human/truly divine). Matthew's perspective is here more focused on ecclesiological insight than christology, concentrating on the renewed people of God, composed of Jews and Gentiles.

601. Matthew reserves the title "disciples" for certain male followers (cf. 28:7-8); thus he does not name the women disciples, in spite of their substituting for the "disciples," doing what the disciples should have done. See J. C. Anderson, "Matthew: Gender and Reading," *The Bible and Feminist Hermeneutics,* ed. Mary Ann Tolbert, *Semeia* 28 (Chico, Calif.: Scholars Press, 1983) 3-27, esp. 17-20.

602. See Mary Ann Tolbert, *Sowing the Gospel* (Minneapolis: Fortress, 1982) 288-99.

Matthew 27:57-61, Jesus Is Buried

NIV

[57]As evening approached, there came a rich man from Arimathea, named Joseph, who had himself become a disciple of Jesus. [58]Going to Pilate, he asked for Jesus' body, and Pilate ordered that it be given to him. [59]Joseph took the body, wrapped it in a clean linen cloth, [60]and placed it in his own new tomb that he had cut out of the rock. He rolled a big stone in front of the entrance to the tomb and went away. [61]Mary Magdalene and the other Mary were sitting there opposite the tomb.

NRSV

[57]When it was evening, there came a rich man from Arimathea, named Joseph, who was also a disciple of Jesus. [58]He went to Pilate and asked for the body of Jesus; then Pilate ordered it to be given to him. [59]So Joseph took the body and wrapped it in a clean linen cloth [60]and laid it in his own new tomb, which he had hewn in the rock. He then rolled a great stone to the door of the tomb and went away. [61]Mary Magdalene and the other Mary were there, sitting opposite the tomb.

COMMENTARY

One might wish the chapter division had been made here rather than at 28:1, since this scene and the next one are preludes to the resurrection rather than postludes to the crucifixion. The exact phrase of 26:20 is repeated, "when evening came" (ὀψίας δὲ γενομένης *opsias de genomenēs*), marking off the events from 26:20 through 27:56 as one portentously eventful twenty-four-hour period that is now over and a new day is beginning.[603] Jesus was not buried by relatives or the Twelve, but by Joseph of Arimathea, introduced into the story for the first time. Burial of the dead, especially those killed by oppressive governments hostile to the Jewish community, was an act of piety much revered in Judaism (cf. Tob 1:17-18; 2:4, 7; 12:12-13).

Joseph is a distinctive figure in the Matthean presentation: (1) In contrast to Mark, he is not a member of the Sanhedrin—i.e., he is unrelated to the events that led to the condemnation of Jesus. In Matthew, the Jewish leadership are flat characters, uniform in their opposition to Jesus. (2) In Mark, Joseph is "waiting for the kingdom of God," but in Matthew, Joseph is explicitly a disciple. Although Jesus is not buried by any of the Twelve, who have abandoned him, neither is he buried by a benevolent member of the opposition, but, in another parallel to John the Baptist,

he is buried by a disciple (cf. 14:12). (3) Only in Matthew is the tomb Joseph's own tomb, and only in Matthew had Joseph hewn it out of the rock himself. (4) Only in Matthew is Joseph wealthy (cf. Isa 53:9), which coheres with his owning an expensive tomb, but not with his hewing it out himself. These touches make the burial more personal and also serve an apologetic function: Jesus was not buried in an unmarked tomb that might be later mistaken.[604] In the Matthean story, both the Jewish leaders and Jesus' disciples know exactly which tomb he is buried in. Joseph's wealthy status also places him in solidarity with (some of) the members of the Matthean church, themselves more wealthy than average (see Introduction). Matthew drops the Markan note that Joseph purchased a linen shroud, perhaps remembering that in his chronology all this is transpiring on the Passover, but more likely because it is unnecessary if Joseph is

603. See Claus Westermann, *A Thousand Years and A Day: Our Time in the Old Testament* (Philadelphia: Muilenburg, 1962). The thousand years are the history of Israel, climaxed in the last day of Jesus' life.

604. The 1969 discovery of the remains of a crucified man in a family tomb near Jerusalem makes the burial story historically plausible, rather than supposing the Romans threw the body in an unmarked grave or left it on the cross to be eaten by vultures. See J. F. Strange, "Crucifixion, Method of," *IDBSup* 200-201.

An apologetic tendency was developing in the recounting of the passion story, warding off objections, anticipated or real. Mark's story had already emphasized the certification of Jesus' death (Mark 15:44-45), the objection to the resurrection being "He didn't really die." Matthew omits this note, replacing it with v. 36, which performs the same function, and adds the story of bribing the guards (the objection being "He did really die and was buried, but the disciples stole the body"). Both Mark and Matthew include the series of witnesses to guarantee continuity and preempt the objection that the wrong tomb was discovered empty.

wealthy; he already possesses it. Just as the tomb is "new," so also the linen is (ritually) "clean."

These distinctively Matthean touches add to the reflective, muted atmosphere that, in contrast to the previous scene, pervades the burial account. This is enhanced when, once again, the male disciple "leaves" and the women sit down to keep vigil over the tomb. This provides continuity of witnesses, although the "many" has now dwindled to the two Marys.[605] Their silent vigil before the tomb also communicates a note of expectancy (cf. the similar comment about the soldiers [27:36], whose "keeping watch" led to their seeing the eschatological events that generated their Christian confession [27:54]). None of those who have heard Jesus' promises of resurrection are present; even Joseph, having performed his last service for his teacher, "went away" and is never heard from again.[606] The Easter events will take place without him.

605. Again, it is not clear that Matthew wants the reader to identify the "other Mary" as the mother of Jesus.

606. Later legends made much of him. The Matthean story should not be historicized to ask what "really happened" to Joseph. As a "disciple," he is one who has (or should have) heard Jesus' passion and resurrection predictions (16:21; 17:22-23; 20:18-19), since even his enemies are aware of them (27:63).

REFLECTIONS

1. Preachers and teachers should be wary of simplistic reductions of the mystery of the passion and the atonement. Matthew does not present Jesus' death as something that must happen so that God could be forgiving, nor Jesus' wavering in Gethsemane as endangering God's ability to forgive. In Matthew's presentation of the passion of Jesus, God is present and active for the salvation of humanity. The human Jesus struggles with the fear of death and is not an actor reciting the lines of a pre-written drama.

2. The fact that Jesus' suffering is not mentioned should not be interpreted in stoic terms of his own courage in silently enduring pain, nor in docetic terms as though as a divine being he only appeared to suffer and die (though the silence about Jesus' suffering gave Docetism the opportunity, just as Matthew's anti-Judaism gave later anti-Semitism the opportunity). The Gospels avoid the gory details of the flogging and the crucifixion, not from prudishness or squeamishness, but because the story of Jesus' suffering and death functions not by its psychological effect on the reader but by its theological meaning.

3. Matthew, in accordance with all the other canonical Gospels, provides no speculation on the physical cause of Jesus' death. Various popular explanations have combined Mark's note that Jesus died sooner than most (Mark 15:44-45) and John's description of the blood and water that came from Jesus' side from the soldier's spear thrust (John 19:34) to mean that Jesus died from a "broken heart" or "the weight of the world's sins." Such speculations are alien to the meaning of the biblical text, which affirms that God acted for humanity in the death of Jesus, but presents no pseudo-medical or pseudo-theological theories as to how this was the case.[607] Matthew affirms the atoning death of Jesus (20:28; 26:28, 31; all from Mark), but elaborates no doctrine of the atonement; nor does he provide materials for one. The stark narrative of the crucifixion is interpreted without reference to atonement theory.

4. The story of Jesus' suffering and death is interpreted positively by Matthew. The earth trembles and the sky grows dark to show that what happens is not merely a human tragedy, but the eschatological act of God (see Commentary on 27:45-54). In contrast to Paul, Hebrews, and John, however, there is no emphasis on the saving efficacy of the act of crucifixion as such, or of Jesus' shedding his blood (in Matthew the crucifixion is bloodless). Matthew takes

607. A sophisticated version of this approach is found in William D. Edwards et al., "On the Physical Death of Jesus Christ," *Journal of the American Medical Association* (March 21, 1986) 1455-63. A good refutation of this approach is given by Dennis Smith, "An Autopsy of an Autopsy," *Westar* (April 1987) 3-6.

up and reaffirms the rare instances in which Mark had interpreted the death of Jesus as the saving act of God (see Commentary on Matt 20:28 = Mark 10:45; Matt 26;27-28 = Mark 14:23-25), but does not amplify this atonement theology by adding material from his own tradition or editorial composition. It is the main features of the theology of the Gospel as a whole that all come to expression in the passion story (see Overview at 26:1):[608]

(A)*Jesus Messiah Is the Son of God.* The crucifixion of the royal Son of God presents God as the one who suffers violence rather than perpetrate it on others, redefining the meaning of kingship (26:37, 67-68; 27:40-43).

(B)*The Rejection of Jesus Messiah.* The crucifixion not only says something about God, but it reveals humanity's rejection of God's ways as well, and that not by the thugs and hoodlums of this world, but officially, by the highest forms of religion and government (27:15-26). Not only humanity's worst, but also humanity's best is indicted by this story. As throughout the Gospel, those who are expected to respond reject the Messiah, and those without claims surprise us by accepting.

(C)*God's New Nation, the Church.* The Roman soldiers are only the symbolic representatives in the narrative for that larger community of Jews and Gentiles, women and men, who respond in faith and are formed by God into the continuing people of God (27:54-56).

(D)*Jesus the Model of Righteousness.* Just as in his life and teaching, so also in his death, Jesus models the meaning of being a righteous man, and the story that began in 1:19 comes full circle. (See Commentary on 26:36-56; 27:43.)

608. See also Frank J. Matera, "Matthew's Gospel Theology," in *Passion Narratives and Gospel Theologies* (New York: Paulist, 1986) 121-49.

Matthew 27:62-66, Jesus' Tomb Is Guarded and Sealed

NIV

[62]The next day, the one after Preparation Day, the chief priests and the Pharisees went to Pilate. [63]"Sir," they said, "we remember that while he was still alive that deceiver said, 'After three days I will rise again.' [64]So give the order for the tomb to be made secure until the third day. Otherwise, his disciples may come and steal the body and tell the people that he has been raised from the dead. This last deception will be worse than the first."

[65]"Take a guard," Pilate answered. "Go, make the tomb as secure as you know how." [66]So they went and made the tomb secure by putting a seal on the stone and posting the guard.

NRSV

[62]The next day, that is, after the day of Preparation, the chief priests and the Pharisees gathered before Pilate [63]and said, "Sir, we remember what that impostor said while he was still alive, 'After three days I will rise again.' [64]Therefore command the tomb to be made secure until the third day; otherwise his disciples may go and steal him away, and tell the people, 'He has been raised from the dead,' and the last deception would be worse than the first." [65]Pilate said to them, "You have a guard[a] of soldiers; go, make it as secure as you can."[b] [66]So they went with the guard and made the tomb secure by sealing the stone.

[a]Or *Take a guard*   [b]Gk *you know how*

COMMENTARY

Day 6 Begins: Saturday, 27:62. This story is of a piece with 28:11-15, for which it is a preemptive strike. Both are unique to Matthew, are written in Matthean style and vocabulary, and are probably composed by Matthew himself, perhaps with a traditional core. In Matthew's chronology, the day is not only during the Festival of Unleavened Bread, but also is an especially holy sabbath (awkwardly expressed, not to say concealed, by the roundabout "the day after the day of the Preparation"; cf. 28:1).[609] "Gathered" again translates συνήχθησαν (*synēchthēsan*) with the same connotations of the hostile synagogue of Matthew's own day as previously (see 26:3).

27:63. The Pharisees reappear for the first time since 23:29 (= 22:41). Matthew has followed Mark in absenting them from the passion story proper, but here reintroduces them in order to implicate them in the death of Jesus, and because they were present when Jesus indirectly predicted his resurrection (12:40).[610] The Jewish leaders address Pilate as κύριε (*kyrie*), which may mean only "Sir" when used as a form of polite address to human beings, but is used elsewhere in Matthew only of God, by the believers addressing Jesus as Lord, or by figures in Jesus' parables (the Jewish leaders always address Jesus as "Teacher" or some such title, never as "Lord").

They call Jesus an "impostor" (πλάνος *planos*); the later Christian teaching about him uses "deception" (πλάνη *planē*)—two forms of the same word later used by Judaism to characterize Jesus and his disciples (lit., "those who lead astray").

27:64-65. As in the Roman trial scene, of which this scene is reminiscent, Pilate has the authority, but is persuaded by the evil Jewish leadership to fulfill their wishes. The Jews appear more and more hardened and guilty, Pilate more and more manipulated and innocent. Matthew's "Christianizing" of Pilate may come nearer the surface, however, when Pilate grants them a contingent of Roman soldiers,[611] but with the sardonic comment "Make it as secure as you can." Sealing the tomb is probably derived from the similar scene in Dan 6:17, an association also made in later Christian art, following Matthew's lead. The setting of the guard and sealing of the tomb are only in Matthew, to answer in advance the charge apparently current in Matthew's Jewish environs that the disciples stole the body (cf. 28:11-15).[612] As the story moves toward Easter morning, two affirmations about the future are juxtaposed: Jesus' own prediction of the resurrection and the Jewish leaders' united front trying to guarantee that it could not happen. The two kingdoms that have stood over against each other throughout Matthew await the third and decisive day.

609. This has sometimes been understood as avoiding or repudiating the Jewish institution of sabbath observance (so McNeile, *Matthew*, 428), but this is unlikely (see 24:20). The oblique identification of the day seems to intentionally forego the chance to charge the Jewish leaders with violating the sabbath and reverse their charges against Jesus (12:1-14). Matthew seems more interested in minimizing historical difficulties such as presenting the chief priests as violating the sabbath. The apologetic tendency noted above comes to expression once again. In response to objections, real and anticipated, the kerygma becomes more and more historicized, changing to some extent its original character.

610. Jesus' explicit predictions of his death and resurrection (16:21; 17:22-23; 20:18-19) were made in private to his disciples. Yet Matthew may not be thinking so precisely of 12:40, heard by the Pharisees, but may be presupposing the post-Easter understanding that Jesus predicted his own resurrection as generally known.

611. Grammatically, ἔχετε (*echete*) can be indicative ("You have a [Jewish] guard") or imperative ("Take a [Roman] guard"), but the former option, adopted by the NRSV, makes it unnecessary that they ask Pilate in the first place and conflicts with "soldiers" in v. 12, as well as their responsibility to Pilate in v. 13. Here the second option, chosen by the NIV, is better.

612. The historical development was however: first, Christian proclamation of the resurrection; Jewish "explanation" of the empty tomb; then this story as the Christian counterresponse.

Matthew 28:1-20, Jesus' Resurrection

OVERVIEW

The proclamation of the resurrection in the canonical Gospels consists of the discovery of the empty tomb and appearances of the risen Jesus. Neither Matthew nor any of the other canonical Gospels narrate the resurrection event itself, which remains hidden in mystery.[613] For the dis-

been laid against the entrance to the sepulcher started of itself to roll and gave way to the side, and the sepulcher was opened, and both young men entered in. Now when those soldiers saw this, they awakened the centurion and the elders—for they also were there to assist at the watch. And whilst they were relating what they had seen, they saw again three men come out from the sepulcher, and two of them sustaining the other, and a cross following them, and the heads of the two reaching to heaven, but that of him who was led of them by the hand overpassing the heavens. And they heard a voice out of the heavens crying, 'Thou hast preached to them that sleep,' and from the cross there was heard the answer, 'Yea.' Those men therefore took counsel with one another to go and report this to Pilate" (from Ron Cameron, ed., *The Other Gospel: Non-canonical Gospel Texts* [Philadelphia: Westminster, 1982] 80-81).

613. In contrast, e.g., to the *Gospel of Peter* 35–42, "Now in the night in which the Lord's day dawned, when the soldiers, two by two in every watch, were keeping guard, there rang out a loud voice in heaven, they saw the heavens opened and two men coming down from there in great brightness and draw nigh to the sepulcher. That stone which had

covery of the empty tomb, Matthew has only his Markan source, which he follows to its end at Matthew 28:8*a* (= Mark 16:8*a*). Some earlier studies of the Gospels suggested that the "lost" ending of Mark was available to Matthew, who utilizes it as his own conclusion. This is unlikely, since (1) Mark almost certainly intended to end his narrative at 16:8*a,* and (2) the distinctive

Matthean style, vocabulary, and theology of 28:8*b*-20 indicate it is Matthew's own composition, while containing some peculiarly Matthean traditional elements peculiar to his tradition.

Matthew brings his Gospel to an end by adopting the closing scene from the Gospel of Mark and composing three additional scenes climaxing in the Great Commission.

Matthew 28:1-7, Two Marys Discover the Empty Tomb

NIV

28 After the Sabbath, at dawn on the first day of the week, Mary Magdalene and the other Mary went to look at the tomb.

²There was a violent earthquake, for an angel of the Lord came down from heaven and, going to the tomb, rolled back the stone and sat on it. ³His appearance was like lightning, and his clothes were white as snow. ⁴The guards were so afraid of him that they shook and became like dead men.

⁵The angel said to the women, "Do not be afraid, for I know that you are looking for Jesus, who was crucified. ⁶He is not here; he has risen, just as he said. Come and see the place where he lay. ⁷Then go quickly and tell his disciples: 'He has risen from the dead and is going ahead of you into Galilee. There you will see him.' Now I have told you."

NRSV

28 After the sabbath, as the first day of the week was dawning, Mary Magdalene and the other Mary went to see the tomb. ²And suddenly there was a great earthquake; for an angel of the Lord, descending from heaven, came and rolled back the stone and sat on it. ³His appearance was like lightning, and his clothing white as snow. ⁴For fear of him the guards shook and became like dead men. ⁵But the angel said to the women, "Do not be afraid; I know that you are looking for Jesus who was crucified. ⁶He is not here; for he has been raised, as he said. Come, see the place where he*ᵃ* lay. ⁷Then go quickly and tell his disciples, 'He has been raised from the dead,*ᵇ* and indeed he is going ahead of you to Galilee; there you will see him.' This is my message for you."

*ᵃ*Other ancient authorities read *the Lord* *ᵇ*Other ancient authorities lack *from the dead*

COMMENTARY

Day 7 Begins: Sunday, 28:1. Matthew's interpolated scene in setting the guard (27:62-65) had interrupted the continuity established by the women witnesses of the crucifixion (27:56) and the burial (27:61). Now, without accounting for their activity on the sabbath (cf. Luke 23:56), Matthew resumes the continuity, providing the necessary two witnesses (Deut 19:15; cf. Matt 18:16; 26:60). The initial phrase (ὀψὲ δὲ σαβ- βάτων *opse de sabbatōn*) could be translated "late on the sabbath"—i.e., Saturday evening⁶¹⁴—

but the following phrase makes it clear that early Sunday morning is meant. Matthew modifies Mark so that the women come only to "see the tomb"—i.e., continue their vigil—rather than to "anoint the body," since the guard posted in Matthew makes anointing impossible, and since the body was already anointed for burial in 26:12. Likewise, they do not wonder who will roll away the stone, since they are not intending to reopen the tomb and anoint the body, which in any case is made impossible in Matthew by the guard.

28:2-4. The eschatological drama of the crucifixion continues (cf. 27:51-53). There is another

614. So Robert H. Gundry, *Matthew: A Commentary on His Literary and Theological Art* (Grand Rapids: Eerdmans, 1982) 585.

earthquake, and the angel of the Lord descends (appearing for the first time since 2:19, and replacing the "young man" in Mark 16:5).[615] His appearance is described with phrases reflecting the descriptions of the divine beings in Dan 7:9 and 10:6, but less than the splendor of the transfigured Christ (Matt 17:2). In this case, the apocalyptic signs do not convert (cf. 27:51-54). In contrast to the soldiers at the crucifixion, the guards at the tomb are "shaken up" and become like "dead men" themselves.

28:5-7. The perfect participle used by the angel identifies the risen Jesus as "the crucified one" (τὸν ἐσταυρωμένον *ton estaurōmenon*). Since the Greek perfect tense indicates a completed act with ongoing consequences, Jesus' crucifixion was not a temporary episode in the career of the Son of God, a past event nullified, transcended, or exchanged at the resurrection for heavenly glory. Even as the risen one, he bears the mark of his self-giving on the cross as his permanent character and call to discipleship (16:24). The angel commands the women to carry the message to the disciples, making them not only the initial witnesses of the empty tomb, but the first bearers of the glad message that "he has been raised [by God] from the dead."[616] In the Markan plot, the women were overcome with fear and kept silent, and the story ends by leaving the task of proclaiming the Easter message the responsibility of the reader (Mark 16:8*a*). Matthew continues the story by adding joy to the note of fear, and the women become positive figures who obediently go to tell the disciples. Matthew adds "quickly" and that they "ran." Peter is singled out in the command of Mark 16:7, but, although prominent in Matthew's pre-Easter narrative (26 references), he is strikingly absent here. Jesus had told the disciples that he would meet them in Galilee (26:32), but the women had not heard this. Matthew thus adjusts the Markan "as he told you" to "I [the angel] have told you." Galilee is for Matthew not mere geography, but theology, "Galilee of the Gentiles" (cf. 4:12-17), the appropriate setting for the Great Commission to all nations (28:16-20). As in Mark, Matthew has no appearances of Jesus to the disciples in Jerusalem or Judea, and no room in the narrative for any such appearances (cf. Luke 24; John 20). The stories of appearances of the risen Jesus cannot be harmonized into one narrative; each story is a testimony to the church's resurrection faith, not part of a single historical report. (See Reflections at 28:16-20.)

615. Earthquake is an eschatological sign in Isa 29:6; Hab 3:6; Hag 2:6, 21; Zech 14:4-5; Matt 24:7; 27:54; Rev 6:12; 8:5; 11:13, 19; 16:28. Angels often appear in eschatological scenes, e.g., Zech 12:8 (specifically the "angel of the Lord"); 1 Thess 4:16; 2 Thess 1:7; Rev 7:1-2, 11; 8:2-4; 10:5, 7; 14:6, 19; 16:1–17:1; 18:1, 21; 19:9, 17; 20:1; 21:9–22:8. For angels in Matthew as apocalyptic imagery, see 13:39, 41, 49; 16:27; 24:31; 25:31.

616. Ἐγείρω *egeirō* in the aorist passive can be either transitive, "raise," "arouse" someone else (e.g., 8:25), or intransitive "rise," "rouse" oneself (e.g., 8:26). Ἠγέρθη *ēgerthē* here can be translated "he has risen" (NIV, RSV, JB) or "he has been raised" (NRSV, NEB, REB, GNB). In view of Matthew's changing the ambiguous ἀνίστημι (*anistēmi*) in the passion predictions (Matt 16:21; 17:23; 20:19; 26:32), "he has been raised" with God as the actor is the preferable translation, as in 27:52.

Matthew 28:8-10, Two Marys Encounter the Risen Jesus

NIV	NRSV
[8]So the women hurried away from the tomb, afraid yet filled with joy, and ran to tell his disciples. [9]Suddenly Jesus met them. "Greetings," he said. They came to him, clasped his feet and worshiped him. [10]Then Jesus said to them, "Do not be afraid. Go and tell my brothers to go to Galilee; there they will see me."	[8]So they left the tomb quickly with fear and great joy, and ran to tell his disciples. [9]Suddenly Jesus met them and said, "Greetings!" And they came to him, took hold of his feet, and worshiped him. [10]Then Jesus said to them, "Do not be afraid; go and tell my brothers to go to Galilee; there they will see me."

COMMENTARY

This scene was composed by Matthew (see Overview). In Matthew, the women are not only the first witnesses of the empty tomb, but they receive the first appearance of the risen Christ as well (cf. 1 Cor 15:5). Jesus "meets" them—i.e., joins and accompanies them (the word ὑπαντάω [hypantaō], its variant in some MSS, ἀπαντάω [apantaō], and their cognates all connote "go to meet and accompany back," as in 25:1, 6; [27:32 D]; Acts 28:15; 1 Thess 4:17). They are already en route on their mission when they are joined by the risen Christ, a paradigm of Matthew's understanding of the reassuring presence of the risen Christ in the missionary activity of the church (cf. 1:23; 10:40; 13:37; 14:22-33; 16:18; 17:17; 18:5, 20; 28:20). Matthew uses no christological titles in the resurrection story; the risen Lord is simply "Jesus," like "the crucified one" (v. 5), binding the exalted Lord of the church's faith and experience to the crucified man of Nazareth. The scene is almost a doublet of the encounter with the angel: Jesus too tells them not to fear—a standard element of angelophanies and theophanies—and he repeats the angel's commission to carry a message to the disciples. There is an added dimension, however: The disciples are now called "brothers" by Jesus himself. We have not seen the disciples since they all "deserted him and fled" (26:56), except for Peter, who denied him, and Judas, who betrayed him and then killed himself. The alienation has now been healed from the divine side; the disciples may know that they again/still belong to the family of believers (12:46-50, Jesus' true family identified with "his disciples"). The women become not only missionaries of the resurrection message, but also agents of reconciliation.

Matthew makes nothing of the nature of the resurrected body of Jesus, and he seems to take pains to make the scene as normal as possible. Jesus addresses them with the normal greeting (lit., "rejoice" [χαίρετε chairete]), but functioning as ordinary greeting language comparable to our "hello." Their reverent "approach" (προσέρχομαι proserchomai), taking hold of his feet, and "worshiping" him (προσκυνέω proskyneō) is Matthew's way of showing both the reality of the resurrection (Jesus is not a ghost or phantom) and the continuity between the pre- and post-Easter person of Jesus (they do the same things prior to Easter, also illustrating the retrojection of the Easter faith into scenes of the pre-Easter narrative). Matthew will shortly present a picture of the risen Christ as a spiritual presence through all the ages. He has more than one way of conceiving the reality of the resurrection, a testimony to his view that the reality of the thing itself is not to be confused with, or identified with, any one way of conceptualizing it. (See Reflections at 28:16-20.)

Matthew 28:11-15, The Guards Are Bribed

11While the women were on their way, some of the guards went into the city and reported to the chief priests everything that had happened. 12When the chief priests had met with the elders and devised a plan, they gave the soldiers a large sum of money, 13telling them, "You are to say, 'His disciples came during the night and stole him away while we were asleep.' 14If this report gets to the governor, we will satisfy him and keep you out of trouble." 15So the soldiers took the money and did as they were instructed. And this story has been widely circulated among the Jews to this very day.

11While they were going, some of the guard went into the city and told the chief priests everything that had happened. 12After the priests[a] had assembled with the elders, they devised a plan to give a large sum of money to the soldiers, 13telling them, "You must say, 'His disciples came by night and stole him away while we were asleep.' 14If this comes to the governor's ears, we will satisfy him and keep you out of trouble." 15So they took the money and did as they were directed. And this story is still told among the Jews to this day.

[a] Gk they

COMMENTARY

28:11. Rather than following the women on their mission, the narrative camera swings back to the guards. This scene is thus the completion of the story begun in 27:62-66, both scenes peculiarly Matthean insertions that interrupt the narrative flow. The scene with the guards forms a perverse parallel to that of the women, with corresponding sets of verbs (vv. 7-8/11, 13). Although the women have been commissioned to "go and tell" (ἀπαγγέλλω apangellō) the good news of the resurrection and reconciliation, the guards, who have seen the same things as the women, "went" and "told (apangellō) "everything that had happened." Observing the spectacular events themselves thus did not generate faith in the eschatological event of the resurrection, which is different from merely being convinced that Jesus' body came out of the tomb. (See Reflections at 28:16-20.)

28:12-15. Again the chief priests and elders (16:21; 21:23; 26:3, 47; 27:1, 3, 12, 20, 41; cf. 27:62, "chief priests and Pharisees") "held an official consultation" (συμβούλιον λαβόντες *symboulion labontes*, as 12:14; 22:15; 27:1, 7). On "gathered," see the note to 26:3. This is the height of irony, as they now become the perpetrators of the very story that setting the guard and sealing the tomb were designed to prevent, and the height of hypocrisy, which Matthew has opposed to discipleship throughout (6:2, 5, 16; 7:5; 15:7; 22:18; 23:13, 15, 23, 25, 27-29; 24:51). As in the case with Judas, money oils the wheels of hypocrisy—but here the sum is greater. It costs more to suppress the resurrection message than to engineer the crucifixion. The chief priests and elders were callous to Judas, but they seem to be more concerned with the welfare of the soldiers—actually

it is the spread of the false message to which they are committed. The soldiers end up as (false) "witnesses," accepting money to risk their lives for what they know to be a lie. The Gospel concludes with the polar opposites of the two kingdoms represented throughout the Gospel (cf. 12:22-30, esp. the "dualism of decision," represented by 12:30).

The use of "soldiers" (στρατιῶται *stratiōtai*) indicates that the guard was Roman soldiers rather than Temple police, as does their anxiety about Pilate's response (cf. Acts 12:18-19). The fact that Roman soldiers would report to the chief priests is one of the indications that the story is not literal history, but part of Matthew's theological understanding of the resurrection. The vocabulary of Matthew's comment that the soldiers did as they were "instructed" (διδάσκω *didaskō*) and that the "story" (λόγος *logos,* "message") has been circulated among "the Jews" reflects the controversies between the synagogue and the church of Matthew's own time. The Christian story of the resurrection was opposed by a counterstory circulated by the synagogue. The phrase "the Jews" has been used previously in Matthew only as part of the phrase "king of the Jews" (2:2; 27:11, 29, 37). The term is an outsider's wording, expressing some distance.[617] Its use here indicates that after the eschatological event of the crucifixion/resurrection, in Matthew's view the "people" of unbelieving Israel are now "the Jews," no longer as such the chosen people of God, but one of the nations of the world to whom the universal mission is directed.

---

617. Contrast the magis' and the Romans' term "Jews" with the chief priests' term "Israel" (2:1; 27:29, 37 vs. 27:42). Elsewhere, Matthew himself uses "Israel" in both positive (10:6, 23; 15:24, 31) and negative (8:10; 19:28; 27:9) connotations.

Matthew 28:16-20, The Great Commission

NIV	NRSV
¹⁶Then the eleven disciples went to Galilee, to the mountain where Jesus had told them to go. ¹⁷When they saw him, they worshiped him; but	16Now the eleven disciples went to Galilee, to the mountain to which Jesus had directed them. ¹⁷When they saw him, they worshiped him; but

NIV

some doubted. [18]Then Jesus came to them and said, "All authority in heaven and on earth has been given to me. [19]Therefore go and make disciples of all nations, baptizing them in[a] the name of the Father and of the Son and of the Holy Spirit, [20]and teaching them to obey everything I have commanded you. And surely I am with you always, to the very end of the age."

[a]19 Or *into*; see Acts 8:16; 19:5; Romans 6:3; 1 Cor. 1:13; 10:2 and Gal. 3:27.

NRSV

some doubted. [18]And Jesus came and said to them, "All authority in heaven and on earth has been given to me. [19]Go therefore and make disciples of all nations, baptizing them in the name of the Father and of the Son and of the Holy Spirit, [20]and teaching them to obey everything that I have commanded you. And remember, I am with you always, to the end of the age."[a]

[a]Other ancient authorities add *Amen*

COMMENTARY

28:16. This is the first scene in which the disciples have appeared since they fled during the arrest of Jesus (26:56).[618] Presumably, Matthew understands that they remained in Jerusalem until they received the announcement of the women (which is not narrated), on the basis of which they returned to the mountain Jesus had appointed for their post-resurrection rendezvous (cf. 26:32). The disciples thus have already come to faith in the risen Jesus and the reconciling message that they are again/still his brothers. The basis for this faith is not an appearance of Jesus to them, but the testimony of the women, which they have accepted. The Jerusalem appearances of Jesus to his disciples recounted in Luke 24:13-43 and John 20:19-29 cannot be accommodated within the Matthean storyline. The mountain corresponds to the mountain of 5:1 and 17:1 (cf. 14:23; 24:3); its meaning should be sought in Matthew's theology rather than in geography.[619]

28:17. Jesus appears to them, and they "see" him. Matthew does not describe the risen Jesus. As in 28:9-10, the event is narrated as though it were an ordinary, this-worldly event. Like the women in 28:9, their response is not amazement, fascination, or curiosity, but kneeling in worship.[620] There is also the element of hesitation and doubt.[621] The concluding clause of v. 17 may legitimately be translated "but some doubted," referring to others besides the eleven (NIV and NRSV; so also KJV, ASV, NEB), "but *some* of them doubted," implying that while some of the eleven worshiped, others of them doubted (GNB, REB),[622] or "but *they* doubted," referring to the same group that worshiped (NAB). The latter translation represents Matthew's own theological understanding of the meaning of discipleship, which is always a matter of "little faith," faith that by its nature is not the same as cocksureness, but incorporates doubts within itself in the act of worship. "Doubt" here is not theoretical skepticism, but the risky wavering of the one who must decide when more than one possibility seems reasonable and right. The word is διστάζω (*distazō*), elsewhere found in the NT only at 14:31, in a scene composed by Matthew, reminiscent of this one. Thus the same elements of worship, doubt, and little faith inhere in the church after Easter as before. Whatever the nature of the resurrection event, it did not generate perfect faith even in those who experienced it firsthand. It is

---

618. The mention of "eleven" recalls to the reader the absence and fate of Judas, who was never reconciled to Jesus, a preliminary contrast to those who are about to be reunited with their master. Matthew gives no indication that Judas is to be replaced (cf. Acts 1:12-26).

619. In each case, it is a matter of a particular mountain, Jesus who teaches with authority, and the disciples as standing between Jesus and the general uncommitted population. The mountain of 28:16 is analogous to that of 5:1, but not identical with it. The text does not indicate the disciples' return to the site of the Sermon on the Mount.

620. The only previous occasion on which the disciples "worshiped" Jesus is 14:33, which has characteristics of a resurrection story and illustrates the fluidity of the tradition, which did not firmly distinguish between pre-Easter and post-Easter stories, since the whole tradition was permeated with the faith in the risen Lord.

621. Form criticism may offer a helpful perspective here, since in the commissioning form that may be at the base of this narrative, the patriarch, prophet, or apostle being called and commissioned often responds to the numinous presence of the divine messenger with an objection, hesitancy, fear, or unbelief (cf., e.g., Exod 3:6*b*; Judg 6:13; Jer 1:6).

622. This understanding is defended on grammatical grounds by P. W. van der Horst, "Once More: The Translation of *hoi de* in Matthew 28:17," *JSNT* 27 (1986) 27-30.

not to angels or perfect believers, but to the worshiping/wavering community of disciples to whom the world mission is entrusted.

28:18-20. As in 17:7 at the transfiguration, Jesus comes to the disciples (typically they come to him in Matthew). The risen Jesus comes to his wavering church, as in 14:25. Jesus' only action is to speak. Matthew sacrifices all curiosity-titillating details to the word of Jesus, which continues to be spoken to the disciples after Easter.

Acts 1–15 narrates the gradual process in which the community of Jesus' disciples after Easter came to realize under the guidance of the Spirit that the risen Lord wills that the church be a universal, inclusive community of all nations. This process is here concentrated into one scene, composed by Matthew on the basis of traditions alive in his church.[623] The scene represents Matthew's theological interpretation of the mission of the church in obedience to the command of the risen Christ. There are traditional elements reflecting the Christian prophetic activity in Matthew's community, but the composition is Matthew's. If the scene were merely a report of a scene in which Jesus had literally commanded all the disciples to carry on a Gentile mission, it would be difficult to understand their struggles in Acts 1–15.

The basis for the words of commission is the claim of the risen Jesus that all authority has been given to him by God (cf. 11:27). The risen Jesus is pictured as Lord of heaven and earth—the cosmic ruler in God's stead (cf. Phil 2:5-11; Col 1:15-18; Heb 1:1-3), the king in the present-and-coming kingdom of God, the one who represents God's cosmic rule. The babe worshiped by Gentiles and mocked at his crucifixion as "king of the Jews" (2:1; 27:11, 29, 37) has assumed his throne and begun to reign. The lowly Son of Man has been enthroned as the exalted Son of Man (cf. Dan 7:13-14); his resurrection was not only his vindication but also his enthronement. As he is God's representative, there is no competition between God as king and the authority of Jesus, just as there is no idolatry inherent in the worship of

Jesus—who had declared that only God may be worshiped (4:9-10). Matthew has no explicit doctrine of the "deity of Christ," but presents the Jesus story in such a way that to encounter Jesus is to encounter the God who is defined in Jesus (cf. John 20:28).

The commission is to all the "nations" (ἔθνη ethnē, "Gentiles"). An important hermeneutical issue concerns the relationship to the Great Commission of 28:18-20 to the previous missionary command of 10:5-6. Is it understood as rescinded, here replaced with the mission to Gentiles, in which case the Gentile church now replaces Israel? Or is it the case that Israel, now having lost its status as the people of God, is included among the nations to which the church's mission is directed? In the former case, there is no longer a mission to Israel, and *ethnē* should be translated as "Gentiles." But if 10:5b-6 is understood as supplemented, in the sense of two concentric circles, the latter of which embraces the former (as argued above in Matthew 10), then "nations" or "peoples" is the translation, one of which is now Israel.[624]

The nations are to be "discipled" (Matthew has used *disciple* as a verb in 13:52 and 27:57; it is found elsewhere in the NT only in Acts 14:21). Previously, Matthew has adopted the Markan usage in which "disciples" are exclusively the inner group of twelve men who have left all to follow Jesus, although Matthew has told the story in such a way that they become transparent for Christians in the post-Easter church.[625] After the resurrection, the invitation to discipleship is open to all people of all nations. That is, people are not called to become individual believers but are to be enlisted as disciples within the Christian community, whose reception of the Christian message in faith must be actualized in their lives. The call to the fishers (4:18-22), the tax collector (9:9), and the rest of the Twelve (10:1-4) is now extended to all, as an extension of the call to

623. The vocabulary and style are thoroughly Matthean, but Matthew may have composed the final command of the risen Jesus on the basis of prophetic pronouncements in his community. See Benjamin J. Hubbard, *The Matthean Redaction of a Primitive Apostolic Commissioning: An Exegesis of Matthew 28:16-20,* SBLDS (Missoula, Mont.: Scholars Press, 1974); M. Eugene Boring, *The Continuing Voice of Jesus: Prophecy and the Gospel Tradition* (Louisville: Westminster/John Knox, 1991) 247-49.

624. For "Gentiles," see, e.g., Luz, *Matthäus,* 2:92; Douglas Hare and Dan Harrington, "Make Disciples of All the Gentiles (Matt 28:19)" *CBQ* 37 (1975) 359-69. For "nations," including Israel, see, e.g., John P. Meier, "Gentiles or Nations in Matt 28:19?" *CBQ* 39 (1977) 94-102. The fact that "all the nations" includes Israel is suggested from the use of the phrase in such passages as 2 Chr 6:33 and Zech 2:10-11, where all the nations of the world become the people of God. In Matt 24:9, "nations" must include Israel.

625. Matthew 8:21 shows that the Gospel is not absolutely rigid in this usage.

Abraham and in accord with the promise that all nations would finally be blessed through him (Gen 12:1-3).

Baptism is the act marking a transition from outside the Christian community to discipleship within it. Previously in Matthew, baptism has been associated only with John the Baptist; neither Jesus nor his disciples have carried on a baptismal ministry (cf. John 3:22; 4:1-2). It is not clear whether "in the name of" with the trinitarian formula refers to the authority by which baptism is carried out, to the liturgical formula pronounced over the baptized, or to fellowship with the divine reality into which the candidate is baptized (or elements of each of these meanings). In any case, there is a contrast to "baptism in Jesus' name" as represented in Acts (2:38; 8:16; 10:48; 19:5; cf. 1 Cor 6:11).

Like the rest of the NT, the Gospel of Matthew has no developed doctrine of the Trinity. Although he has pictured both the earthly Jesus and the risen Lord as acting in the place of God (e.g., 9:1-7; 25:31-46) and has "Father, Son, and Holy Spirit" appear in the same scene (e.g., 3:13-17), he attempts no speculative discursive explanation of how or whether the "Son" and the "Spirit" are "co-eternal with the Father." Yet Matthew, like other NT authors, has found that God-talk in the light of the Christ-event does modulate into a threefold pattern without denying the fundamental Jewish monotheistic affirmation (12:28; 22:43; cf., e.g., Rom 1:3-4; 8:3-4; 14:17-18; 15:30; 1 Cor 12:3-6; 2 Cor 13:13; Eph 3:14-19; 4:4-6; 1 Thess 1:2; Titus 3:4; Heb 2:3; 6:4; Luke 1:35;

2:25-28; John 3:34; 1 Pet 1:1-2; 1 John 4:2; 5:6-9 [NRSV and NIV, but not KJV]; Jude 20; Rev 1:4-5; 14:13). Matthew is in step with late first-century CE Syrian Christianity that is developing these rudiments into liturgical formulas (cf. *Did.* 7.1). The essential point is that the one encountered in Jesus as the Son of God and in the Spirit-led church as the people of God is not some subordinate deity, but the one true God.

Now the disciples are given authority not only to baptize, but also to teach. Although they have previously shared in Jesus' authority (cf. 10:1), prior to Easter the disciples had not been authorized to teach. After baptizing disciples, the continuing Christian community is to instruct them in all that Jesus has taught. "All" here reflects the "all" of 26:1, and it refers not only to the Sermon on the Mount but to all of Jesus' teaching contained in the Gospel as well, especially the five great discourses. Nothing is said of the Torah. Jesus' teaching that fulfills the Torah (cf. 5:17-20) is the sole content of the disciples' teaching, as it will be the sole criterion on the last day (7:24-27).

The Matthean Jesus does not ascend.[626] His last words are a promise of his continuing presence during the church's mission (cf. 1:23; 10:40; 13:37; 16:18; 17:17; 18:5, 20; 26:29).

---

626. Matthew also, of course, has pictures of the parousia in which Jesus, the exalted Son of Man, comes on the clouds of heaven. Since Matthew has pictures both of the continuing presence of Christ with the church and of the Christ who comes from heaven at the end of history, neither can be intended as a literal, objectified statement about the present location of the risen Lord. Each has its own distinct and important theological function, but they cannot be combined on the basis of literalism. (See Reflections at 25:46.)

REFLECTIONS

Matthew's specific hermeneutical approach to the resurrection should be interpreted in the context of the variety of theological perspectives on the resurrection found in the NT.[627] Important Matthean emphases are:

1. The resurrection is an eschatological event, the ultimately decisive event for human history, not merely something spectacular that happened to Jesus. Thus resurrection faith is

---

627. For the NT in general, see esp. Oscar Cullmann, *Immortality of the Soul: Or Resurrection of the Dead?* (London: Epworth, 1958); C. F. D. Moule, ed., *The Significance of the Message of the Resurrection for Faith in Jesus Christ,* SBT, 2nd series 8 (London: SCM, 1968); Xavier Leon-Dufour, *Resurrection and the Message of Easter* (New York: Holt, Rinehart and Winston, 1971); Ulrich Wilkens, *Resurrection: Biblical Testimony to the Resurrection; An Historical Examination and Explanation* (Atlanta: John Knox, 1978); Marinus de Jonge, *Christology in Context: The Earliest Christian Response to Jesus* (Philadelphia: Westminster, 1988) chap. 11.

For Matthew's interpretation of the resurrection, see Otto Michel, "The Conclusion of Matthew's Gospel," in Graham Stanton, ed., *Issues in Religion and Theology 3: The Interpretation of Matthew* (Philadelphia: Fortress, 1983); Jerome Neyrey, *The Resurrection Stories* (Wilmington: Michael Glazier, 1988) chap. 2; Raymond E. Brown, *A Risen Christ in Eastertime: Essays on the Gospel Narratives of the Resurrection* (Collegeville, Minn.: Liturgical Press, 1991) chap. 2.

not merely believing that a dead body came back to life, or that the tomb was empty on Easter morning. Those who believed that Jesus was John the Baptist risen from the dead did not have resurrection faith (14:1; 16:14). The soldiers and chief priests who knew the fact that Jesus had "come back to life" did not have Christian faith in the resurrection (28:11-15).

2. The resurrection itself is not to be described. Matthew does not narrate the resurrection, but the discovery of the empty tomb and the appearances. He renounces all speculative interest in attempting to describe the mystery, and has it happen offstage, a matter of testimony and proclamation, not of empirical observation (unlike the *Gospel of Peter*, in which the narrator and the reader get to be spectators).

3. Resurrection faith is not identical with affirming the historical factuality of any of the Gospels' resurrection stories. The story is the vehicle of the faith, but is not to be identified with it. The Easter stories are not to be harmonized, but each is to be interpreted as mediating some dimension of the Easter faith. Matthew makes this clear by telling the story more than one way, frustrating any attempt to identify message with form.[628] The message, however, cannot be abstracted from the NT forms. "Christ arose" is not a general declaration that may be separated from its concrete canonical expressions.

4. The resurrection is not merely the happy ending of an almost-tragic story of Jesus, a postscript at the end. The resurrection perspective permeates the story throughout, so that all of Matthew's story is testimony to the risen Lord of the church. The resurrection is thus to be preached from all twenty-eight chapters, not only from the last. It is a fundamental misunderstanding of the gospel genre to suppose that, even though one may have difficulty proclaiming Matthew's message of chapter 28, twenty-seven chapters remain. Without the resurrection, the whole story evaporates.

5. The resurrection is not Jesus' final accomplishment, in continuity with his other miracles, but is the act of God for Jesus who suffers the victimization of a truly human death and enters into the realm of death as powerless as any other human being. Resurrection is not an optional christological extra, but is a matter of theology strictly defined.

6. Resurrection faith does not arise on the basis of evidence, of which the chief priests and soldiers had plenty, but on the basis of the experienced presence of the risen Christ (28:8-10, 16-17), by testimony of those to whom he appeared (28:10, 16), and by his own continuing presence among his disciples (28:20).

7. Faith in the resurrection is a matter of worship, not of analysis and inference (28:16). Even so, it does not exclude doubt, but takes doubt into itself (cf. 28:17).

8. Resurrection faith is not to be identified with faith in an empty tomb. Matthew affirms both, but also knows that it is possible to believe in an empty tomb without resurrection faith (28:11-15). The whole NT affirms the resurrection, but stories of the empty tomb are only one way of expressing it, a way found only in the Gospels.

---

628. E.g., the resurrected body of Jesus is both graspable (28:8-10) and speaks (28:10, 18-20), but is also a spiritual presence that continues in the life of the church (28:20).

THE GOSPEL OF MARK

INTRODUCTION, COMMENTARY, AND REFLECTIONS
BY
PHEME PERKINS

THE GOSPEL OF
MARK

INTRODUCTION

AN ORIENTATION TO MARKAN STUDIES

B y the early twentieth century, most scholars accepted the hypothesis that Mark provided the basic narrative framework behind the Gospels of Matthew and Luke. These two Gospels, it was believed, had supplemented Mark with material derived from a collection of Jesus' sayings (designated Q, from the German *Quelle,* meaning "source") and with other traditional material unique to each evangelist. Although more complicated theories of the relationships among the Gospels are occasionally defended, this view still provides the clearest way of understanding the synoptic Gospels.[1] Initially, this insight, combined with the brevity and simple style of the Markan narrative, led commentators to assume that Mark's Gospel contains an early summary of what was known about Jesus.[2] This view seemed to agree with the ancient testimony in Eusebius's *History of the Church* that Mark's Gospel derives from Peter's remembrances, recorded by Mark, who had been with him in Rome.[3]

Form Criticism. The simple view of Mark as someone who collected earlier traditions about Jesus did not survive further critical analysis of the Gospel. Form criticism taught

1. For a detailed analysis of the argument for the two-source theory of gospel composition, see Joseph A. Fitzmyer, *The Gospel According to Luke I–IX,* AB 32 (Garden City, N.Y.: Doubleday, 1981) 63-97. For an analysis of the hypotheses concerning a possible pre-Markan passion narrative, see M. Soards, "The Question of a Premarkan Passion Narrative," in Raymond E. Brown, *The Death of the Messiah: From Gethsemane to the Grave. A Commentary on the Passion Narratives in the Four Gospels,* vol. 2 (Garden City, N.Y.: Doubleday, 1994) appendix IX.

2. See Vincent Taylor, *The Gospel According to St. Mark,* 2nd ed. (New York: St. Martin's, 1966).

3. Eusebius *History of the Church* 3.39.5.

scholars to analyze the individual units as examples of established patterns in the oral tradition. It also taught them that the use of particular types of material in the life of a community influences the form and content of what becomes traditional material. In some instances, Matthew and Luke may have taken a saying or parable of Jesus from a tradition that is less developed formally than the Markan version. The duplication of groups of miracle stories surrounding the feeding of the multitudes (Mark 6:30-44; 8:1-10) and the stilling of the storm (Mark 4:35-41; 6:45-52) suggests that Mark may have used two versions of the same cycle of miracles. Analyses of the types of miracle stories in antiquity raised questions concerning the function of such narratives. Stories of rescue at sea belong to the type of story in which the epiphany of a divine being delivers individuals from distress.[4] If the reason for reciting miracle stories in the early communities was to identify Jesus as a divine being, then stories about him could have been shaped to fit that type. No individual miracle story has an *a priori* claim to represent what happened in the life of Jesus. Form-critical analysis suggests that miracles, conflict stories, and even individual sayings had all been shaped by oral tradition before the evangelist composed his Gospel, which itself was composed with the listening audience in view.[5]

Determining which features of Mark's account represent theological concerns that are peculiar to the evangelist is more difficult than in the case of Matthew and Luke. With the latter, analysis of how each evangelist has treated Mark and the common material shared by them enables scholars to suggest literary and theological emphases unique to each evangelist. The storm at sea episode is one example. In Mark's version (4:35-41), the exchange between Jesus and his disciples is very harsh. They accuse Jesus of not caring if they perish. He replies that the disciples have no faith. In Matthew's version (8:23-27), the disciples' request is formulated as a petition in a rescue story that expects a divine being to act. Matthew's Jesus comments on the disciples' "little faith" prior to his calming the sea. One might conclude that the miracle then cured their deficiency in faith. Luke (8:22-25) keeps the comment on the disciples' faith after the miracle but moderates both the disciples' request and Jesus' comment on their faith. A survey of other passages involving the disciples would show that Matthew and Luke usually moderate the harsher elements in the Markan account.

Treatments of Mark as a simple report of what was remembered often assume that negative images of the disciples are evidence of early tradition. The modifications in Matthew and Luke could then be described as part of the process of turning Jesus' disciples into heroes. After all, the picture of Peter in Acts shows no lack of faith or unwillingness to confront suffering. So if Mark, as an earlier source, says the disciples had no faith, he must be reporting what they were actually like. However, more careful analysis of the type of material Mark is using has led scholars to reject that simple solution. Based on the

4. See Gerd Theissen, *The Miracle Stories of the Early Christian Tradition,* trans. F. McDonagh (Philadelphia: Fortress, 1983) 100-103.
5. See the extensive discussion of oral characteristics in Markan style by Christopher Bryan, *A Preface to Mark: Notes on the Gospel in Its Literary and Cultural Settings* (New York: Oxford, 1993) 67-151.

results of form criticism, many scholars now believe that the traditions from which Mark crafted his portrait of the disciples would not have carried such negative evaluations. For example, the usual point of a rescue miracle was to lead the audience to acknowledge the presence of the deity. A collection of miracles that leads to misunderstanding rather than confession does not make sense. Therefore, scholars began to suspect that Mark had created his picture of Jesus' disciples by altering the traditional conclusions of such stories. One controversial solution to the problem even suggests that Mark sought to counter the influence of a Christology of the "miracle-working Jesus" that had been associated with the Twelve,[6] a view that turns the ancient theory of Markan origins on its head. Not only was Mark not a follower of Peter, but also he thought that the Twelve had misunderstood the true significance of Jesus' life and death on the cross. Most interpreters, however, do not accept this understanding of Mark's depiction of the disciples. Mark's narrative highlights the dichotomy between the divine and the human. The disciples' failure highlights the fact that Jesus transcends the purely human.[7]

Since Mark's Gospel appears to have been the earliest written account, much of the discussion during the first half of the twentieth century centered on using Mark to draw up a picture of the historical Jesus. The fact that Jesus often commanded others to remain silent about his miraculous deeds (e.g., 1:34, 44) and told his disciples not to tell anyone that he was the Messiah (8:29) was thought to indicate a deliberate policy on Jesus' part. He did not wish to draw attention to himself as a populist, political leader. That apparently simple solution, however, does not account for the Gospel's persistent motif of Jesus' authority. Even though it is not an indication of perceptive understanding, astonishment and awe can be attached to Jesus' teaching (1:22, 27), exorcism (1:27), healing (2:12), nature miracles (4:41), public activity in general (6:2), and, finally, the angelic announcement of his resurrection (16:8). Markan summaries emphasize the size of the crowds pressing around Jesus (1:32-34, 45). Since the summaries are probably Mark's composition, he can hardly have intended to suppress the popularity of Jesus with the crowds.

Redaction Criticism. During the second half of the twentieth century, redaction criticism made scholars aware of the fact that the evangelist was more than a collector of traditional material. Mark writes from a consistent point of view. Keys to his intentions have been sought in the repetitions, summary passages, stories embedded within each other, and the narrative move from the miracle worker and authoritative teacher of the opening chapters to the crucified Son of God at the close. A common approach has been to discuss Markan redaction in terms of the christology of the Gospel. As soon as Jesus is acknowledged by the disciples as the Messiah, he begins to teach them the necessity of suffering (8:27-33). A select group sees Jesus transfigured and hears God declare him "Son," only to be warned not to tell anyone until after the death and resurrection of Jesus

6. See T. J. Weeden, *Mark: Traditions in Conflict* (Philadelphia: Fortress, 1971).
7. See Philip G. Davis, "Mark's Christological Paradox," *JSNT* 35 (1989) 3-18.

(9:2-13). These examples suggest that Mark wishes to qualify the theology of glory with the cross, because it is only in offering himself on the cross that Jesus is truly Son of God (15:39).

In recent decades, the same redaction-critical questions that were applied to Mark have been applied to the sayings source (Q) used by both Matthew and Luke. Scholars have isolated strata within Q that identify Jesus with divine Wisdom and as an eschatological prophet who anticipated the coming of God's kingdom. This latter stage is associated with the apocalyptic Son of Man. The Q collection appears to have taken its final, written shape by 60 CE, some years earlier than Mark. Comparisons between the two raise further questions about Markan redaction.[8] Q depicts Jesus as a prophetic figure, with controversy stories and miracles understood as evidence for his authority to speak as God's representative. Like John the Baptist, Jesus suffers the fate of prophets who offend the wealthy and powerful. Mark, on the other hand, has made the cross the key to Jesus' identity (although Jesus' prophetic role remains important). Q associates Jesus' disciples with his mission much more closely than Mark does. They take up the message and the fate of their master and participate in his apocalyptic glory. When the Son of Man judges the nations, he will be assisted by the Twelve (Luke 22:30//Matt 19:28). For Mark, the Twelve only accompany Jesus during his ministry. They are chosen to "be with him" (3:14) but fail to complete the journey because they flee when Jesus is arrested. Yet the judgment that their "flight" represents a complete failure from Mark's point of view must be nuanced. Jesus predicted their flight, which fulfills the prophetic word about the flock that is scattered when its shepherd is struck down (Mark 14:27-28, citing Zech 13:7).[9] Throughout the passion narrative, Jesus' prophecies are fulfilled.

Literary Criticism. Finally, as the analysis of sources, layers of tradition, and their editing becomes more complex and less likely to yield certain historical evidence, scholars have turned to other methods. Sparked by interest in literary criticism, especially questions of how a narrative shapes the responses of its readers, literary theories are invoked to describe the impact of Mark's narrative as a whole. Individual episodes cannot be treated apart from their place in the story. Mark teaches readers what to anticipate as the Gospel progresses. They share a perspective with the narrator that differs from that of any of the characters in the story. A number of puzzling features in the Gospel, especially the fact that it ends with the women fleeing the tomb and not telling anyone, can be resolved quite differently, depending on what assumptions an interpreter thinks Mark's reader will bring to the story from the earlier narrative. If they remember that Jesus' promise to see the disciples again forms the second half of the comment on their flight (Mark 14:28), then the readers know that they will be restored as a community. If they remember the prophecies

8. See Dieter Lührmann, "The Gospel of Mark and the Sayings Collection Q," *JBL* 108 (1989) 51-71; *Das Markusevangelium,* HNT (Tübingen: J.C.B. Mohr [Paul Siebeck], 1987).

9. See Raymond E. Brown, *The Death of the Messiah: From Gethsemane to the Grave. A Commentary on the Passion Narratives in the Four Gospels,* vol. 2 (Garden City, N.Y.: Doubleday, 1994) 128-30.

concerning the future of believers in Mark 13 or the comment that the sons of Zebedee will share Jesus' baptism of suffering (Mark 10:39), then readers know that the disciples did take up the cross. If readers bring forward the negative examples of the disciples' behavior from the earlier narrative, then the conclusion heightens Jesus' abandonment by all his followers.

Pastoral experience shows that the insights gained from methods of narrative analysis are often the most useful for preaching and Bible study. One must contend with the fact that most parishioners encounter the text only in isolated fragments, however. All of the synoptic Gospels sound the same; therefore, people find it difficult to attend to the larger structural features in each individual Gospel. One of the most endearing features of Mark's narrative on the pastoral level is the evident weaknesses of Jesus' disciples. They seem to become more bewildered and frightened as the story unfolds. For many laypersons that depiction lends a consoling air of reality to Mark's vision of Christian discipleship. No ordinary person can be like Jesus, but Mark's description of Peter sets a standard that is within reach.

Social-Scientific Criticism. Another recent development in New Testament scholarship, social-scientific criticism, looks to the social sciences for categories of analysis.[10] Models of peasant societies developed in the twentieth-century cultural anthropology are applied to the New Testament evidence. How do such societies view charismatic leaders? What is the mechanism by which persons gain and lose honor? How are social boundaries drawn and maintained? What cultural and social values are maintained by religious groups in the society? Such questions about the social, economic, and political contexts of early Christian texts tries to locate Christianity's impact on the larger social structures of its time. Sometimes concrete details in the stories provide clues about the circumstances in which a tradition originated. Gerd Theissen has observed that Mark 2:13-14 speaks of tax collectors in Capernaum. That fact requires a boundary in the vicinity. After 39 CE there would not have been such a toll station, because the territory that had belonged to Philip was united to eastern Galilee. Therefore, storytellers familiar with the situation must have framed such stories before 39 CE. This observation shows that some of Mark's traditions came from ancient Palestine and may have been collected in written form within a decade of Jesus' death.[11] However, the Palestinian origin of its traditions does not demonstrate that the Gospel was composed in Palestine.

MARK'S AUDIENCE

Redaction criticism has fostered a number of attempts to reconstruct the situation of the church for which Mark wrote.[12] The traditional view that Mark wrote down

10. See John H. Elliott, *What Is Social-Scientific Criticism?* (Minneapolis: Fortress, 1993); Gerd Theissen, *The Gospels in Context: Social and Political History in the Synoptic Tradition* (Minneapolis: Fortress, 1991); Bruce J. Malina and Richard L. Rohrbaugh, *A Social-Science Commentary on the Synoptic Gospels* (Philadelphia: Fortress, 1992).

11. Theissen, *Gospels in Context,* 119-20.

12. See Joel Marcus, "The Jewish War and the *Sitz im Leben* of Mark," *JBL* 111 (1992) 441-62; C. Clifton Black, "Was Mark a Roman Gospel?" *ExpTim* 105 (1993) 36-40; Theissen, *Gospels in Context,* 235-89.

remembrances of Peter in Rome either before Peter's death or shortly thereafter lead to a number of hypotheses. The emphasis on suffering was thought to depict the persecutions in Rome under Nero's rule. However, as we know from Paul's letters (e.g., 2 Cor 1:8-11; 1 Thess 2:14-16), Christians suffered persecution elsewhere in the empire. Other readers have noted the concern with false messianic prophecies and with the fate of the Temple in Mark 13. They also point out that the advice to flee (Mark 13:14-22) correlated with the promise that Jesus would go ahead of his disciples to Galilee (Mark 14:28; 16:7). Therefore, they suggest, Mark was written somewhere in Syro-palestine during the turmoil generated by the revolt against Rome. Because of their links to Judaism, Gentile Christians could not side with the other Gentiles in the region. Because they know that Jesus was Messiah and not any of the false prophets or leaders of the Jewish rebellion, Gentile Christians could not be associated with the Jewish resistance. The extent to which Mark 13 can be taken to refer to the community depends on whether the evangelist has employed earlier apocalyptic formulations.

Discussions of the social context that is presupposed by Mark now figure prominently on both sides of the debate. Demographic descriptions of the Roman house church congregations during the first two centuries provide a possible context for the Gospel.[13] The majority of Roman Christians were lower-class immigrants, both Jew and Gentile, organized in several quite diverse house church communities. Mark commonly portrays Jesus explaining his public teaching to the disciples inside a house (1:29-33; 2:1, 15; 3:19; 7:24). This detail may have reminded readers of their own instruction in household churches. Christianity had emerged among the Jewish population in Rome by 48 CE. A few Roman Christians enjoyed higher status than the artisans, laborers, and tradespersons of the majority. Paul's letter to Roman Christians seeks to inculcate toleration and solidarity between the various factions (Rom 11:13-36; 14:1–15:13). By the time Paul wrote Romans (c. 57 CE), Gentile Christians were in the majority and had to be warned against lording it over the Jewish Christians who had founded the churches in the city. If Paul's comments on respect for governing authorities (Rom 13:1-7) address the concrete danger of rebellion against market taxes imposed by Nero, then Mark's insistence that Christians avoid the political turmoil in Palestine may address the Roman situation as well.

A number of details in the Gospel show that the author was not familiar with places referred to in his tradition; geographical mistakes occur at several points (5:1; 6:53; 7:31; 10:1). We also find Matthew correcting Mark's citations of Scripture. For example, Mark attributes a combination of Isa 40:3 and Mal 3:1 to Isaiah (1:2-3), but Matthew cites only the Isaiah section (Matt 3:3). Mark must explain Jewish customs to his audience, and often does so with some uncertainty (7:3-4; cf. Lev 22:1-16; 7:11, 19*b*). He retains a number of Semitic words from his traditions but must explain them to readers (5:41; 7:34; 14:36; 15:22, 34, 42). Replacement of external purity rules by emphasizing moral virtues

13. On Roman Christianity see Peter Lampe, *Die stadrömischen Christen in den ersten beiden Jahrhunderten: Untersuchungen zur Sozialgeschichte* (Tübingen: J.C.B. Mohr [Paul Siebeck], 1987); J. S. Jeffers, *Conflict at Rome: Social Order and Hierarchy in Early Christianity* (Minneapolis: Fortress, 1991).

(7:14-23) may be typical of Hellenized Jews as well as Gentiles, but the assertion that "all foods are clean" (v. 19b), made by the narrator, would not be typical of that environment. Nor would challenges to sabbath observance (2:23-28) be characteristic of a Jewish community. Matthew modifies both stories so that the generalizing conclusions that Mark draws from them are no longer present. Jesus, who is greater than David, suspends sabbath obligation in the interests of the mercy God commanded in the prophet (Matt 12:1-8). Matthew omits Mark's parenthetical comment that Jesus declared all foods clean (Matt 15:15-20). Those exegetes who agree that Mark's audience was Gentile Christians, but hold that Mark himself was a Palestinian Jew,[14] seem to ignore both the internal evidence as well as the evidence from Matthean corrections that Mark is not personally familiar with Jewish practice.

By the mid-first century CE, Christians were distinguishable from Jews, so the Christians were singled out as scapegoats for the great fire during Nero's reign.[15] Mark refers to persecution as the cause for many to fall away (4:17) and for fraternal betrayal (13:9). These comments might easily refer to the type of betrayal experienced by the Roman Christians during this persecution, which would cost both Peter and Paul their lives.[16] In 2 Tim 4:9-16, Paul injects this note of betrayal into Paul's last days, when those who should have defended the apostle abandoned him instead. None of these correspondences demand a Roman locale for the audience projected by Mark's narrative. The traditional assumption that Mark was written at Rome was based on the tradition that linked Mark with Peter. Early Christian writings from Rome contain no evidence of familiarity with Mark. Therefore, the best one can say for the traditional view that Mark's intended audience was the Roman house churches c. 70 CE is that the Gospel can be understood as reflecting that experience. The understanding of discipleship it projects would incorporate the situations faced by Christians in Rome.[17]

Other exegetes remain unconvinced by the claim that early Palestinian Jesus tradition, preserved among Roman Christians, accounts for the Palestinian elements in the Gospel of Mark.[18] They locate Mark's church among the Gentile communities of the eastern provinces, possibly in Palestine or Syria. With the number of Hellenistic cities in that area, such a change in venue may not contribute much to understanding the social context of the Gospel itself. The Latinisms found in Mark (12:42; 15:16) may have been commonplace anywhere Roman soldiers were quartered.

Those who think that Mark was written from a Syro-palestinian perspective, point to chapter 13 as their major evidence. Its prophecies of false prophets, war, denial, and

14. Such as Dieter Lührmann, *Das Markusevangelium,* 6-7; Robert A. Guelich, *Mark 1–8:26,* WBC 34A (Dallas: Word, 1989) xxviii.

15. Tacitus *Annals* 15.44.

16. *1 Clem* 5.4-7; 6.1; Ign. *Rom.* 4.2-3.

17. See Black, "Was Mark a Roman Gospel?"

18. See, e.g., Howard Clark Kee, *Community of the New Age: Studies in Mark's Gospel* (Philadelphia: Westminster, 1977); Lührmann, "The Gospel of Mark and the Sayings Collection Q"; Marcus, "Jewish War"; Theissen, *Gospels in Context.*

betrayal (vv. 6-13) fit the turmoil associated with the civic strife that accompanied the Jewish war against Rome.[19] The focus on the Temple's destruction (13:1-2), as well as Jesus' condemnation of the Temple as a "house of brigands" (11:17), may allude to events at the end of that revolt. Zealot leaders had taken over the Temple as their headquarters (perhaps motivated by prophecies from Daniel[20]). Titus destroyed the Temple completely, leaving not one stone standing. The Jewish civil war created serious problems for Gentile Christians as well, who were easily caught up in the violence erupting between Gentiles and Jews in the Hellenistic cities of Palestine during the revolt. Josephus describes massacres by both Jews and Gentiles of each other.[21] Mark's emphasis on Jesus' positive stance toward Gentiles and its sharp attacks on Jewish leaders have been seen as responses to such violence.[22] Since Josephus describes the zealots who occupied the Temple as defiling it,[23] Mark's advice to flee when sacrilege occurs has been read as an allusion to that event (13:14). The Jewish leaders are seen as responsible for the destruction that has come upon the nation (Mark 12:9).

As in the case for a Roman provenance, the hypotheses of Palestinian origins provides a possible explanation for some of the details in the narrative. Josephus's own account of the Jewish war shows that it was possible for a Jew living in Rome to offer an account of those events some years after Mark's Gospel was written. Josephus's writing serves an apologetic function. Unlike the Zealots, whose excessive pride God punished by destroying the Temple, the Romans demonstrated reverence for Jerusalem as a holy place.[24] Mark need not have written his Gospel in immediate proximity to the events of the Jewish revolt to use them as evidence for the truth of Jesus' predictions concerning the Temple and the fate of Israel.

The difficulty in determining a concrete sociopolitical context for Mark's Gospel has been further complicated by the influence of narrative criticism. Literary critics have warned scholars against making quick judgments about the historical communities that lie behind a text. They point out that narratives can project an implied audience, which may be quite different from the actual readers. Unlike the apocalyptic visions of Daniel 7–12, Mark does not correlate prophecies, specific historical figures, and events. Therefore, Mark does not seem interested in providing an apocalyptic history to explain events in the recent past. Mark 13 remains subordinate to the larger framework of events that led to Jesus' death on the cross, since Mark has woven the

19. For sociological studies of the situation in Judea during this period, see Richard Fenn, *The Death of Herod: An Essay in the Sociology of Religion* (Cambridge: Cambridge University Press, 1992); Martin Goodman, *The Ruling Class of Judea: The Origins of the Jewish Revolt Against Rome A.D. 66–70* (Cambridge: Cambridge University Press, 1987); for a discussion of Judea in the context of Roman policy in the Near East see Fergus Millar, *The Roman Near East 31 B.C.–A.D. 337* (Cambridge, Mass.: Harvard University Press, 1993).

20. See Marcus, "Jewish War."

21. Josephus *The Jewish Wars* 2.18.1-2; secs. 457-61.

22. See Marcus, "Jewish War," 453. Theissen makes the more probable suggestion that Gentile Christians in these cities would have fallen victim to attack by both sides (*Gospels in Context*, 268-70).

23. Josephus *The Jewish Wars* 4.6.3; sec. 388.

24. See ibid., 5.362-74. See also Hans Conzelmann, *Gentiles, Jews, Christians: Polemics and Apologetics in the Greco-Roman Era*, trans. E. M. Boring (Minneapolis: Fortress, 1992) 203-11.

discussion of the Temple's fate into the narrative of Jesus' death. Both occur according to God's plan.[25]

AUTHORSHIP AND DATE OF COMPOSITION

Since Mark must have been written before Matthew and Luke, and since the turmoil in Judea, which led to the destruction of the Temple, appears to have been in progress or recently completed by the time the Gospel was written, most scholars agree that Mark wrote his Gospel probably around 70 CE. Those who hold out for the tradition of a Roman origin prior to Peter's martyrdom opt for the earlier end of the spectrum, c. 62–64 CE. The tradition that Mark's Gospel was associated with Peter first appeared in the second century. Eusebius cites a statement by Papias (c. 120/130 CE): "Mark, who became Peter's interpreter, accurately wrote, though not in order, as many of the things said and done by the Lord as he had remembered."[26] Eusebius goes on to explain that Mark collected anecdotes from Peter, but did not possess an ordered account from the apostle. The Papias tradition does not actually affirm that Mark was in Rome when he met Peter, although most later authors presumed that was the case. Since the Papias tradition refers only to anecdotes, the statement could merely be a defense of the apostolic origin of the Gospel. However, when its traditions are compared with the other Gospels and with evidence for pre-Gospel tradition in Q, one finds that the anecdotes cannot be a collection of stories from a single source. Mark, itself, contains variants of a single tradition. Some of Mark's material had already been collected into larger units, and other episodes appear to be preserved in a more primitive form in Q.

Therefore, those scholars who do not wish to dismiss the ancient testimony completely presume that Papias correctly identifies the author of the Gospel as a second-generation Christian named Mark. Since "Mark" was a common name, that clue does not provide much help in locating the Gospel or its author. The New Testament refers to a Jewish Christian named Mark who was initially associated with Paul (Acts 12:12; 13:5, 13; Col 4:10; Philemon 24). First Pet 5:13 refers to Mark as an associate of the imprisoned Peter. Since 1 Peter speaks of its city of origin as "Babylon," a well-established code for Rome (cf. Rev 17:5),[27] later Christians would conclude that Mark received his material from Peter at Rome. Whether or not these references to "Mark" refer to one and the same person cannot be determined. First Pet 5:12 claims that the letter was written down by another Pauline follower, Silvanus (2 Cor 1:19; 1 Thess 1:1). Therefore, it appears that the author of 1 Peter seeks to assimilate Peter's image to that of Paul by including two figures from the Pauline mission. The Mark referred to in 1 Pet 5:13 is probably the "John

25. See Robert A. Guelich, "Anti-Semitism and/or Anti-Judaism in Mark?" in *Anti-Semitism and Early Christianity,* ed. C. A. Evans and D. H. Hagner (Minneapolis: Fortress, 1993) 92-95.

26. Eusebius *Ecclesiastical History* 3.39.15.

27. On the connection between Peter and Rome in Eusebius, see Pheme Perkins, *Peter: Apostle for the Whole Church* (Columbia: University of South Carolina Press, 1994) 41-43; on the Papias tradition, see Charles M. Nielsen, "Papias: Polemicist Against Whom?" *TS* 35 (1974) 529-35.

Mark" associated with the Pauline mission, but that connection does not provide any significant information about the author of the Gospel of Mark.

Since the evidence clearly does not support one theory of authorship or social context over the other, the commentary that follows has not been written to defend a particular hypothesis about the author or the community for which the Gospel was composed. Awkward explanations of Jewish customs do suggest that the community consisted of Gentiles (cf. Mark 7:3-4; 14:12; 15:42). Mark has inherited multiple versions of some miracles. Other units of the narrative, such as the discourse on parables (Mark 4:1-34), the apocalyptic discourse (Mark 13), and the passion narrative, seem to embody several levels of tradition. Therefore, the Gospel reflects a more complex history than the ancient tradition might suggest. Mark was not composed to record historical remembrances about Jesus. Mark 1:1 refers to what follows as the "beginning of the gospel of Jesus Christ." In Paul's letters, "gospel" (εὐαγγέλιον *euangelion*) refers to the message of salvation that the apostle preached (Rom 1:1, 16; 10:16; 11:28; 1 Cor 4:15; Gal 1:6-9). Mark 1:14-15 retains that sense of *gospel* as "preached message." Therefore, the opening words of Mark suggest that what follows fulfills the function of earlier preaching.

LITERARY GENRE

By attaching the noun *gospel* to the beginning of a narrative, Mark signals a transition from the oral form of "preached message" to the designation of a written account of Jesus as a "gospel." As scholars have come to appreciate the marked contrast between speech and writing in the dynamics of cultural transmission, that shift in meaning has taken on new importance. The privileged authority for the tradition shifts away from lineal descendents, charismatic prophets, or wise elders charged with remembering and restating the tradition. In the moment of speaking and hearing, the audience encounters directly the founding authority of its faith. Interpretation and personal communication are embedded in the oral performance quite differently from the way they are in writing.[28] Papias's version of the origins of Mark's Gospel suggests an attempt to recapture a world that is passing by looking for a tradition that links writing with having heard the apostles; the materials in Mark's narrative exhibit numerous characteristics of oral transmission.[29] Yet, the Gospel ends on a note of silence (16:8), which sets the oral world at risk.[30]

By recognizing the tension between the oral and written in Markan tradition, we can appreciate the difficulties built into the question of genre. The usual question posed by Mark 1:1 is whether the evangelist has created a new written genre, "the gospel." Since a genre cannot emerge without antecedents, what comparative experiences with texts would readers or hearers bring to the gospel? Or has Mark merely adapted a familiar genre,

28. See the seminal study by Werner Kelber, *The Oral and the Written Gospel* (Philadelphia: Fortress, 1983) 90-139.

29. See ibid., 44-89; Christopher Bryan, *A Preface to Mark: Notes on the Gospel in Its Literary and Cultural Settings* (New York: Oxford, 1993) 67-84.

30. Kelber (*Oral and Written Gospel*, 128-29) insists that Mark deliberately destroys the hopes of the disciples to be representatives of the risen Lord.

such as a Hellenistic biography, to the traditional material available? A century of vigorous debate saw the question of the gospels as ancient biographies eclipsed by form criticism, only to return to the former way of thinking when it became clear that the evangelists did more than collect and edit earlier complexes of tradition. The intentionality evident in the construction of the narrative poses the question of what conception of genre guided the process.[31]

In 1901 Wilhelm Wrede's book *The Messianic Secret in the Gospels* was published, a book that has played a critical role in discussions of gospel genre.[32] Wrede emphasized the tension between the confession that Jesus is Messiah and Lord and the pre-resurrection life and deeds of Jesus. He proposed that Mark took the idea of a "messianic secret" from his sources to combine his christological confession with a non-christological version of Jesus' deeds. The disciples are depicted as unable to perceive the truth about Jesus until after the resurrection. By making this combination, Mark provides a christological context for the Gospel's readers. Therefore, the gospel genre has a confessional shape, which distinguishes it from the common Greco-Roman biographies.

Ancient biographies emphasize the unusual birth, the childhood exploits that prefigure the hero's later life, and the extraordinary nature of the characters. A life should end with triumph and honor. If the hero is condemned, like Socrates, then he should exhibit wisdom in fearless nobility and a wise saying. Biographies of Moses by Jewish writers like Philo and Josephus follow all the conventions of their time.[33] The Gospels, however, do not fit the model provided by such biographies. Some scholars have resolved the dilemma by arguing that Mark chooses to narrate history in an apocalyptic mode.[34] This hypothesis has its own difficulties, since Mark does not employ the symbolic or prophetic typologies to encode the account of Jesus' ministry and death into a cosmic vision of salvation.

The apocalyptic analogies do highlight an important element in the gospel genre: The truth about its hero cannot be divorced from a revelation of God's purposes. Without that post-resurrection perspective, the life of Jesus, unlike that of Moses, would not be sufficiently noteworthy to merit attention. Some scholars prefer to treat Mark as the foundation story for an early Christian community that had no interest in history or biography.[35] This view assumes that a non-messianic Jesus tradition can be reconstructed from Q, which reflects the original emphasis of Jesus' ministry. Consequently a narrative that depicted him as the suffering Son of Man could only be the product of extensive communal myth-making.

31. See Theissen, *Gospels in Context,* 235; David E. Aune, *The New Testament in Its Literary Environment* (Philadelphia: Westminster, 1987) 17-76; Adela Yarbro Collins, *The Beginning of the Gospel* (Minneapolis: Fortress, 1992) 1-38.

32. Wrede's book was translated as *The Messianic Secret* (Cambridge: Clarke, 1971).

33. See Louis H. Feldman, *Jew and Gentile in the Ancient World* (Princeton: Princeton University Press, 1993) 242-87; Aune, *The New Testament in Its Literary Environment,* 27-66; Bryan, *Preface to Mark,* 22-64.

34. So Collins, *Beginning of the Gospel,* 4-38.

35. See Burton L. Mack, *A Myth of Innocence* (Philadelphia: Fortress, 1988).

Part of the difficulty in assigning a particular literary genre to the Gospel lies in the nature of its sources. The fact that Mark's literary skills do not approach those of most ancient biographers may indicate that he was unaware of the rhetorical conventions associated with composing the life of a famous figure. Mark also appears to have been constrained by his sources. They were not christologically neutral but had been shaped by emerging Christian beliefs.[36] Despite the elements of eschatology and the peculiar death of its hero, which stretch the boudaries of what was commonly thought to be a biography or a "life," Greco-Roman readers would have to conclude that Mark is an exercise in biography. Recent stage productions demonstrate that Mark's oral character makes it possible to envisage the entire Gospel's being performed before an audience.[37]

Wrede correctly pointed out that the Gospel has a confessional agenda to establish the fact that Jesus is the Son of God. Some scholars add to this emphasis the necessity of explaining how the Son of God came to be crucified. The scandal of the cross must be absorbed into the larger explanation of God's saving purposes. Both of these concerns have been embedded in the structure of the narrative itself.

Scholars generally agree that the Gospel of Mark can be divided between the initial account of Jesus' divine authority in miracles and teaching and the preparation for the passion, which begins at 8:27. There is less agreement about smaller divisions within the two halves of the Gospel. The evangelist often initiates an episode, interrupts it to recount another event, and then returns to the first episode (e.g., 3:20-21, 31-35; 5:21-24a, 35-43; 11:12-14, 20-25; 14:1-2, 11-10). By interlocking individual stories, Mark encourages the reader to interpret one episode in the light of the other. At the same time, the interruptions reflect typical patterns of oral storytelling. Another pattern of organization that makes it easy for hearers to follow the progress of the story is by geography. The Prologue contains John the Baptist's witness to Jesus as the "Coming One" in the desert (1:1-8). Prior to the turn toward the passion, Jesus' ministry takes place in and around Galilee (1:9–8:21). Then Jesus begins a journey that moves toward Jerusalem while he instructs the disciples about the cross (8:22–10:52). His passion and death conclude a series of events that take place in and around Jerusalem (11:1–15:41). Finally, a series of events take place at the tomb, ending with the angel's announcement and the flight of the women (15:42–16:8).[38]

36. This notion is contrary to Wrede.
37. The videotape of the British actor Alec McCowan reciting the King James Version of Mark is distributed by the American Bible Society.
38. See Bryan, *Preface to Mark*, 82-84.

BIBLIOGRAPHY

Best, Ernest. *Mark: The Gospel as Story.* Edinburgh: T. & T. Clark, 1983. Informed by the best in Markan scholarship, a series of short chapters present the major issues in Markan theology.

Collins, Adela Yarbro. *The Beginning of the Gospel: Probings of Mark in Context.* Minneapolis: Fortress, 1992. Treats four controversial areas in Mark: the gospel genre, suffering and healing, apocalyptic, and the passion narrative and empty tomb.

Fowler, Robert M. *Let the Reader Understand: Reader-Response Criticism and the Gospel of Mark.* Minneapolis: Fortress, 1991. Application of modern literary theory to Mark, emphasizing the Gospel's rhetoric of indirection.

Guelich, Robert A. *Mark 1–8:26.* WBC 34A. Dallas: Word, 1989. A scholarly commentary on the Greek text, using form and redaction criticism to explain how the evangelist reshaped traditional material.

Gundry, Robert H. *Mark: A Commentary on His Apology for the Cross.* Grand Rapids: Eerdmans, 1993. Massive survey of scholarly research that rejects common views of Mark. Treats the Gospel as an apology for the scandal of the cross.

Hooker, Morna D. *The Gospel According to St. Mark.* London: A. & C. Black, 1991. Commentary for general readers and theological students, highlighting the Jewish background to Mark.

Kingsbury, Jack Dean. *The Christology of Mark's Gospel.* Philadelphia: Fortress, 1983. Treats the christology of the Gospel from the perspective of Mark's use of christological titles, particularly "Son of God."

Räisänen, Heikki. *The "Messianic Secret" in Mark.* Translated by C. Tuckett. Edinburgh: T. & T. Clark, 1990. A challenge to the view that the secret of Jesus' messianic identity is the key to Markan christology; argues for diverse uses of secrecy in the Gospel.

Taylor, Vincent. *The Gospel According to St. Mark.* 2nd ed. New York: St. Martin's, 1966. The first edition (1952) of this commentary on the Greek text established the tradition of form-critical analysis of Mark.

Tolbert, Mary Ann. *Sowing the Gospel: Mark's World in Literary-Historical Perspective.* Minneapolis: Fortress, 1989. Literary analysis of Mark finds the key to its narrative dynamic in the parable of the sower: responses to the word are dramatized in the Gospel.

OUTLINE OF MARK

I. Mark 1:1–8:26, Jesus Heals and Teaches with Power

A. 1:1-45, The Beginning of Jesus' Ministry
1:1, Introduction
1:2-8, John the Baptizer Appears
1:9-15, Jesus, the Son of God, Appears
1:16-20, Jesus Calls the First Disciples
1:21-28, Exorcism in the Synagogue
1:29-45, Healing Increases Jesus' Reputation

B. 2:1–3:35, Controversy at Capernaum
2:1-12, Healing the Paralytic
2:13-17, Jesus Calls Sinners
2:18-28, Jesus Defends His Disciples
3:1-6, Doing Good on the Sabbath
3:7-12, Crowds Flock to Jesus
3:13-19, Choosing the Twelve
3:20-30, Jesus Is Charged with Demonic Possession
3:31-35, Jesus' True Family

C. 4:1-34, Parables of the Kingdom
4:1-9, The Parable of the Sower

B. 11:1–13:37, Jesus' Ministry in Jerusalem
>   11:1-11, Entry into Jerusalem
>   11:12-14, Cursing a Fig Tree
>   11:15-19, Cleansing the Temple
>   11:20-25, Sayings on Prayer
>   11:27-33, Challenge to Jesus' Authority
>   12:1-12, Parable of the Vineyard Tenants
>   12:13-17, Paying Taxes to Caesar
>   12:18-27, Resurrection of the Dead
>   12:28-34, The Greatest Commandment
>   12:35-37, The Son of David Is Lord
>   12:38-40, Warning About the Scribes
>   12:41-44, The Widow's Offering
>   13:1-37, The Apocalyptic Discourse
>>   13:1-2, The Temple Will Be Destroyed
>>   13:3-13, Evil Times Are Not the End Time
>>   13:14-23, Flee the End-time Turmoil
>>   13:24-27, The Coming of the Son of Man
>>   13:28-31, Certainty of End-time Salvation
>>   13:32-37, Exhortation to Be Watchful

C. 14:1–15:47, The Passion and Death of Jesus
>   14:1-2, Decision to Arrest Jesus
>   14:3-9, Jesus Is Anointed
>   14:10-11, Judas Agrees to Betray Jesus
>   14:12-31, The Passover Meal
>   14:32-42, Prayer in Gethsemane
>   14:43-52, Jesus Is Arrested
>   14:53-65, Trial Before the Sanhedrin
>   14:66-72, Peter Denies Jesus
>   15:1-20, Jesus Before Pilate
>   15:21-41, Jesus Is Crucified
>   15:42-47, The Burial of Jesus

D. 16:1-20, Jesus Is Risen

MARK 1:1–8:26

JESUS HEALS AND TEACHES WITH POWER

MARK 1:1-45, THE BEGINNING OF JESUS' MINISTRY

OVERVIEW

The first chapter depicts the beginning of Jesus' ministry near the Sea of Galilee and in Capernaum. A number of motifs that will figure prominently in the narrative already appear: the boats on the sea (v. 20), the crowds pushing in on Jesus (vv. 32-33), the demons resisting a powerful exorcist (vv. 23-24, 34), Jesus' withdrawal into houses with his disciples (v. 29), and Jesus' retreat to deserted places to be alone (vv. 12, 35) before returning to the crowds. Mark links brief episodes and summaries of Jesus' activity with a chain of temporal markers (vv. 32, 35) and geographical indicators (vv. 14, 16, 21, 39). By the end of the chapter, crowds seek out Jesus even in the deserted places (v. 45). Those persons present in the synagogue where Jesus performs his first miracle recognize that his teaching will set him at odds with the scribes (v. 22).

References to "Spirit" in this first chapter prepare readers to view the ministry of Jesus as a contest between the Holy Spirit and evil spirits. The first voice in the desert, that of John the Baptist, announces that the one who is to come will baptize with the Holy Spirit (v. 8). The Spirit descends upon Jesus when he is baptized (v. 10) and drives Jesus into the wilderness to be tempted by Satan (v. 12). Jesus' first miracle involves driving an unclean spirit out of a man (vv. 23-27). The first evidence that the Holy Spirit is working through Jesus occurs in these episodes. Satan appears to be no match for Jesus in Mark's Gospel, since the evangelist never describes the two as being locked in serious combat.[39] Jesus' opponents

in this Gospel will turn out to be human beings. Scribes from Jerusalem accuse him of using demonic power (3:22-27). Peter's rejection of Jesus' passion prediction leads him to call Peter "Satan" for refusing to accept God's plan and thinking like ordinary humans (8:33). Satan is not the source of Peter's protest. The struggle lies in the distance between the human and the divine.[40]

The first chapter also demonstrates the gap between human understanding of who Jesus is and God's truth. From the human point of view, there are four groups who respond differently to Jesus: John the Baptist, Jesus' disciples, the crowds, and the religious authorities. Only the first three appear in this chapter, although the authorities are mentioned in the instructions to the leper (v. 44) and in the comparison drawn between Jesus' teaching and that of the scribes (v. 22), who will appear on the scene as Jesus' opponents in the series of controversy stories, beginning in chapter 2.[41] John the Baptist establishes Jesus' identity as the one who fulfills the prophetic promises concerning the agent of salvation. The disciples are ready to leave everything to follow Jesus (vv. 18, 20). At the same time, they do not understand the purpose of Jesus' activity (v. 38). The crowds acknowledge the extraordinary power behind Jesus' teaching and healing activity (vv. 27, 32-34, 45).

At the human level, only John the Baptist states who Jesus is. However, an unclean spirit recognizes Jesus as "the Holy One of God" (v. 24). This formula alerts readers that the power by

---

39. Philip G. Davis, "Mark's Christological Paradox," *JSNT* 35 (1989) 6-7, challenges the view that Mark presupposes an apocalyptic struggle between Jesus and Satan by noting how rarely Satan appears in the Gospel. Mark never has Jesus proclaim that Satan has been vanquished (cf. Matt 25:41; Luke 10:18; John 12:31 *b*).

40. See ibid., 7.

41. For a detailed study of Mark's treatment of the religious authorities, see Michael J. Cook, *Mark's Treatment of the Jewish Leaders,* NovTSup 51 (Leiden: E. J. Brill, 1978).

---

which Jesus heals and teaches is a function of his unique relationship with God. Direct statements about Jesus are also contained in the epithets "messiah" (i.e., Christ) and "Son of God" (v. 1). These two titles for Jesus will appear at climactic moments in the story—e.g., Peter's confession at Caesarea Philippi (8:29) and the centurion's announcement at the cross (15:39).[42] At Jesus' trial, the high priest asks the question about Jesus' identity that has been running through the entire narrative, "Are you the Messiah, the Son of the Blessed One?" (14:61 NRSV).

The term *messiah,* or *anointed,* did not have a fixed referent in the first century CE.[43] Use of the adjective *messianic* in modern scholarly literature to refer to persons who claimed to be the agents of God's end-time salvation confuses analysis of the term with discussions of function. Figures who claimed prophetic or royal status and gathered groups of followers are often referred to as "messianic."[44] Mark 13:22 warns of "false christs and false prophets" who will lead the people astray. In that context the term *christ* may refer to persons who claimed to be charismatic, political leaders in the Davidic tradition. If understood politically, the title "messiah" would be the basis for the execution of Jesus on the charge of claiming to be king of Israel. However, the expression may have been used more loosely to designate any number of persons who claimed to have been raised up by God to lead the people.[45]

For early Christians, the titles "messiah" and "Son of God" were closely associated, as they are in the opening of Mark's Gospel. The citation of a prophetic text immediately following Mark 1:1 points to a different dimension in the use of such titles: the claim that Jesus is the one predicted in Scripture. Evidence from the Qumran documents shows that collections of scriptural texts were

made to describe the prophet, king, or priest who would be the agent of God's salvation in the last days.[46] The Essenes expected different individuals to fulfill these roles. Members of their community were to hold fast to the precepts of the Law "until there shall come a prophet and the messiahs of Aaron and Israel."[47]

The expression "Son of God" had its origins in the Israelite royal cult, where it referred to the relationship between God and the Davidic king (2 Sam 7:14; Ps 2:7). Essene exegetes combined Psalm 2 and 2 Samuel 7 in an interpretation of the "scion of David," who would stand alongside the Interpreter of the Law to fulfill the prophecy of Amos 9:11 and save Israel.[48] The expression "Son of God"/"Son of the Most High" appears in another fragmentary Essene text that describes a victorious king.[49] The interpretation of this text is disputed, however. Although it may refer to a king who will bring the elect people of God to final victory over their enemies, Joseph Fitzmyer insists that the king referred to as "Son of God" is not the end-time ruler.[50] In any case, non-Christian evidence for use of the titles "Son of God" and "messiah" to designate particular figures is extremely rare. The Essene evidence shows that sectarian exegetical work appears to have been responsible for taking the language of being begotten by God to apply to the end-time Davidic messiah.[51] However, it does not provide an unambiguous example of the move from the begetting language of Pss 2:7 and 110:3 to calling this figure "Son of God."[52]

By the time Mark's Gospel was written, both "messiah" ("Christ") and "Son of God" were established designations for the Jesus in whom Christians found salvation. Outsiders had given Jesus' followers the name "Christian" (Χριστιανοί *christianoi;* see Acts 11:26). These expressions were not understood as variants of the claim to be a Davidic figure (cf. Mark 12:35-37). Romans 1:3-4, an early creedal formula, treats

42. On christological titles as the key to Mark's picture of Jesus, see J. D. Kingsbury, *The Christology of Mark's Gospel* (Philadelphia: Fortress, 1983).

43. See M. de Jonge, "The Use of the Word 'Anointed' in the Time of Jesus," *NovT* 8 (1966) 132-48; J. H. Charlesworth, *Messiah* (Minneapolis: Fortress, 1993).

44. See Richard A. Horsley, "Like One of the Prophets of Old: Two Types of Popular Prophets at the Time of Jesus," *CBQ* 47 (1985) 435-63; "Popular Messianic Movements Around the Time of Jesus," *CBQ* 46 (1984) 471-95. For precision in the use of terminology in analyzing the christological titles in the Gospels, see Joseph A. Fitzmyer, *The Gospel According to Luke I–IX,* AB 32 (Garden City, N.Y.: Doubleday, 1981).

45. See D. Hill, "Jesus and Josephus' 'Messianic Prophets,' " in *Text and Interpretation: Studies Presented to M. Black,* eds. E. Best and R. Wilson (Cambridge: Cambridge University Press, 1980) 143-54.

46. See 4Q 175.

47. 1QS 9,10-11.

48. 4Q 174 1,11-13.

49. 4Q 246.

50. Joseph A. Fitzmyer, "The Aramaic Language and the Study of the New Testament," *JBL* 99 (1980) 14-15.

51. 1QSa 2,11-12.

52. See the extensive discussion of these issues in Raymond E. Brown, *The Death of the Messiah: From Gethsemane to the Grave* (New York: Doubleday, 1994) 465-83.

Davidic descent as a fact about Jesus that is well known. However, the significant christological fact about Jesus is not his descent from David, but the fact that as of the resurrection Jesus had been established as Son of God with power.[53]

Although Jesus' teaching and deeds demonstrate his power, none of the human participants in the Markan story address Jesus as Son of God during his lifetime. Mark's Christian readers, however, knew that the one whom the disciples, crowds, and religious authorities do not recognize is in fact Son of God. They have the testimony

of God for that confession (1:11; 9:7). Since both the baptism and the transfiguration of Jesus involve elements of theophany, Mark's readers must have understood the title "Son of God" to imply that Jesus is not merely human.[54] This conviction establishes a tension between the reader's understanding and the life of Jesus presented in the Gospel. Neither Jesus' deeds nor his teaching are sufficient to demonstrate the truth of his identity to others, even those closest to him, while he is alive. Instead, a complete outsider, the centurion, recognizes Jesus as Son of God after his death on the cross (15:39).

53. See the discussion of this formula in Joseph A. Fitzmyer, *Romans,* AB 33 (New York: Doubleday, 1993) 229-30, 234-37.

54. Davis, "Mark's Christological Paradox," 12-15.

Mark 1:1, Introduction

NIV	NRSV
1 The beginning of the gospel about Jesus Christ, the Son of God.[a]	**1** The beginning of the good news[a] of Jesus Christ, the Son of God.[b]
[a]1 Some manuscripts do not have *the Son of God.*	[a]Or *gospel* [b]Other ancient authorities lack *the Son of God*

COMMENTARY

The first sentence appears to serve as a title for the whole work as well as the introduction to the first episode. However, scholars disagree over whether such a sentence could stand by itself as the title of a book.[55] Some interpreters prefer to treat this sentence as an introduction to the citation of Scripture that follows in vv. 2-3. Elsewhere Mark uses the word for "as" (καθώς *kathōs*) to attach a phrase to what comes before (4:33; 9:13; 11:6; 14:16, 21; 15:8). However, the citation does not clarify verse 1 but refers to John the Baptist. The opening word, "beginning" (Ἀρχή *Archē*), may refer either to a temporal beginning or to the opening of the narrative. Those who treat the term as a temporal marker assume that the opening sentence refers to the introductory episode. The term *gospel* (εὐαγγέλιον *euangelion*) reappears

in Mark 1:14-15. There, Jesus initiates his own preaching of the gospel message.[56] Its claim to refer to the whole narrative that follows lies in the connection between the titles used for Jesus and what follows. Peter's recognition that Jesus is "the Christ" constitutes the turning point in Mark (8:27-30).

The expression "Son of God," which follows "Jesus Christ" in some manuscripts, is textually insecure.[57] However, it represents the pivotal confession about Jesus in the Gospel (1:11; 9:7; 15:39). It may have been dropped in some manuscripts because it concludes a long line of abbreviations beginning with "gospel." By the time Mark was written, "Christ" was so commonly used as a designation for Jesus that without further specification the word did not imply a particular dignity. Therefore, a title that expresses

55. Matthew 1:1 is the closest parallel to Mark 1:1. See D. E. Smith, "Narrative Beginnings in Ancient Literature and Theory," *Semeia* 52 (1991) 1-9. Some examples of the ancient biographies begin in the midst of the action without a prologue. See Christopher Bryan, *A Preface to Mark: Notes on the Gospel in Its Literary and Cultural Settings* (New York: Oxford, 1993) 33-35.

56. Many interpreters treat these verses as the opening of the narrative proper rather than as the conclusion to the prologue. See Scaria Kuthirakkattel, *The Beginning of Jesus' Ministry According to Mark's Gospel (1,14-3,6): A Redaction-Critical Study,* AnBib 123 (Rome: Editrice Pontificio Istituto Biblico, 1990) 4-22.

57. The most recent Greek editions (Nestle-Aland[27]; UBS[4]) treat "Son of God" as possibly the original reading.

Jesus' unique dignity would be necessary to highlight the significance of the narrative to come. Thus the combination of "messiah" and "Son of God" (i.e., "Son of the Blessed One") appears in the high priest's question at Jesus' trial (14:61).

Although modern readers associate the word *gospel* (NRSV "good news") with written accounts of the life of Jesus, Mark probably uses the word in the sense of the Pauline epistles. There *gospel* refers to the oral preaching that Jesus is the source of salvation (cf. Rom 1:1, 9, 16; 2:16). Later, we learn that followers of Jesus must be ready to suffer for the sake of the gospel (Mark 8:35; 10:29; 13:10). This usage shows that the genitive "of Jesus Christ" indicates the one about whom the gospel speaks, not a record of Jesus' preaching. Romans 1:1 describes the apostle as set apart for the "gospel of God," and an elaborate creedal formula refers to the risen Lord as "Son of God" (Rom 1:3-4). The associations between the beginning of Mark and the Pauline use of "gospel" for the preached message about Jesus Christ captures the significance of oral testimony as the root of Christian faith.

Paul's letters show that the designation "Christ" (a Greek rendering of the Aramaic for "anointed") was commonly used with "Jesus" as a proper name (e.g., Rom 1:1). Thus many readers may not have recognized "Christ" as a title, implying that Jesus had a special dignity as God's anointed agent. The Gospel will use "Christ" as a messianic title. It forms the content of Peter's confession (8:29), where it represents an insight that distinguishes Jesus' disciples from the popular opinions about Jesus.

"Son of God" occupies a special place in Mark's presentation of Jesus. During the ministry of Jesus, God refers to Jesus as "beloved Son" (1:11; 9:7). Demons also acknowledge Jesus as the Son of God (3:11; 5:7), whose appearance marks the end of their hold on human beings. During the passion, Jesus accepts the title (14:62) and is acknowledged Son of God by the centurion who witnesses his death (15:39). Yet to an audience in that time, the expression "Son of God" would not suggest the incarnate divinity, which Christians came to associate with its use for Jesus. In Ps 2:7 (also 2 Sam 7:14; Ps 89:27) the expression belongs to royal terminology. The newly anointed king is declared God's adopted son. Early Christians fre-

quently used this psalm text as evidence for the exalted status of the risen Lord (cf. Heb 1:5; 5:5).

Although Mark does not quote Ps 2:7 directly, many exegetes think that he presumed his readers would fill out the expression "Son of God" with the allusions to this psalm. The descent of the Spirit and divine voice at Jesus' baptism suggest anointing and divine adoption. However, other royal imagery in which Jesus is described as son of David or king of Israel surfaces only in the context of Jesus' passion. Therefore, Mark does not assume that human beings confessed that Jesus was "Son of God" prior to the crucifixion. There it reflects a truth that is properly understood only when it is used of the crucified. Upon entering Jerusalem, Jesus heals a blind man who hails him as "Son of David" (10:47, 51). Jesus is executed on the false charge of claiming to be "king of Israel"—i.e., leader of an insurrectionist movement (15:6-32). The soldiers and crowds mock the lowly, crucified "king," who cannot save himself. Exegetes are divided over whether Mark intends the reader to attach a new meaning to such royal terminology or to reject it as inadequate to understanding Jesus. The Markan apocalypse warns readers against following false "christs" who will arise during a time of turmoil and war and claim to lead the people in Jesus' name (13:5, 21-22).[58] Mark's reluctance to use royal imagery for Jesus apart from the passion itself undercuts the plausibility of persons who might allege that they embody the messianic, royal authority of Jesus.

The use of the expression "Son of God" by demons suggests another context for understanding the expression. Greek-speaking readers unfamiliar with the Jewish context of "Son of God" might understand the expression in a more general sense to refer to an individual who possesses some form of divine power. Mythology contains stories of demigods and heroes, and popular tales of miracle workers and other extraordinary individuals assumed that such unusual traits bespeak a special relationship to the gods. No fixed set of traits is associated with such

---

58. Joel Marcus argues for the full reading of Old Testament allusions behind Mark's use of the title "Son of God." See Marcus, *The Way of the Lord: Christological Exegesis of the Old Testament in the Gospel of Mark* (Minneapolis: Fortress, 1992) 66-77. Jesus' royal authority guarantees his superiority to the human powers that dominate the earth as well as his mastery of the cosmic forces of chaos.

figures in antiquity. Mark may have known a tradition of exorcism stories in which Jesus was addressed as "Son of God." In that context, the expression merely indicates that Jesus possesses power superior to that of any of the demons. The fact that Mark composed the summary statement in 3:11 indicates that he was not uncomfortable with the inference that Jesus' miracles are a function of his status as Son of God. However, that understanding does not form the basis of the believer's confession that Jesus is Son of God. For the Gospel of Mark as a whole, emphasis on the miraculous power of Jesus is subordinated to the presentation of Jesus as the beloved Son of God who accomplishes God's will on the cross.[59]

59. Adela Yarbro Collins rightly insists that both the OT background and the imagery of Jesus as a powerful, divine figure play a part in Mark's picture of Jesus as a healer. See *The Beginning of the Gospel* (Minneapolis: Fortress, 1992) 52-61.

REFLECTIONS

Modern Christians find three surprises in the beginning of Mark's Gospel: its abruptness, the meaning of a gospel as proclamation, and the importance of the titles "messiah" and "Son of God." Our experience with the other Gospels, as well as the annual celebration of Christmas, leads us to expect either a birth story, as in Matthew and Luke, or a poetic meditation on Jesus' pre-existence with God, as in John. The danger of the infancy narratives lies in speculations about the childhood of Jesus and his family, which may take over from the real story of salvation. In early Christianity, a number of writings provided readers with that emphasis, and even in modern times writers claiming special psychic wisdom have produced works that claim to fill in details of the hidden life of Jesus. The abrupt beginning of Mark provides an opportunity to highlight a different feature of our Christmas celebration: the fulfillment of God's promises of salvation. Information about Jesus' childhood, or even speculation that he spent time with the Essenes or in some other part of the world, that one finds in these pseudo-gospels has no bearing on the plan of salvation. The public ministry, death on the cross, and resurrection of Jesus are the events in which God's love comes to humanity.

We can demonstrate the importance of the message about salvation by reminding people that the word *gospel* originally meant "proclamation" or "good news." Christianity did not begin with a new book. Its Scripture was that of the Jewish people. Christianity began with a "new message" about what the God known through that Scripture had done in Jesus Christ. The sayings of Jesus and stories about him had circulated by word of mouth for years before Mark was written. Unlike a technical manual, these stories do not depend on writing to be remembered. Compared to the difficulties of Sanskrit religious writings from India, for instance, the story about Jesus is amazingly simple. If one expects long ascetic training, complex rituals, and obscure writings for a religion to be profound, then the gospel form comes as a surprise. The good news itself is a simple message of salvation in Jesus, which people can take anywhere in the world.

The titles for Jesus are so familiar that it is difficult to hear "Christ" or even "Son of God" as though for the first time. How can modern men and women recapture the eager expectation that God will redeem humanity from the cosmic and human powers of suffering, evil, and injustice? All too often the modern versions of those false prophets who appropriate Christ's name and the human longings for an end time have led their followers to a sectarian isolation from the larger community. Christians should not be taken in by such latter-day prophets. Yet we have been warned that the title "God's anointed" belongs to Jesus alone. Others hear "Son of God" and immediately isolate Jesus from the real world of human experience. Mark's Jesus is not so isolated; he exhibits a range of human emotions. Although he possesses divine power, Jesus cannot overcome the hostility of his enemies or the fearful misunderstanding of his own disciples. We must learn to hear in "Son of God" praise for the faithful human suffering that Jesus exhibits.

Mark 1:2-8, John the Baptizer Appears

NIV

²It is written in Isaiah the prophet:
"I will send my messenger ahead of you,
    who will prepare your way"ᵃ--
³"a voice of one calling in the desert,
 'Prepare the way for the Lord,
    make straight paths for him.'"ᵇ
⁴And so John came, baptizing in the desert region and preaching a baptism of repentance for the forgiveness of sins. ⁵The whole Judean countryside and all the people of Jerusalem went out to him. Confessing their sins, they were baptized by him in the Jordan River. ⁶John wore clothing made of camel's hair, with a leather belt around his waist, and he ate locusts and wild honey. ⁷And this was his message: "After me will come one more powerful than I, the thongs of whose sandals I am not worthy to stoop down and untie. ⁸I baptize you withᶜ water, but he will baptize you with the Holy Spirit."

a2 Mal. 3:1   *b3* Isaiah 40:3   *c8* Or *in*

NRSV

2As it is written in the prophet Isaiah,ᵃ
"See, I am sending my messenger ahead of you,ᵇ
    who will prepare your way;
³ the voice of one crying out in the wilderness:
 'Prepare the way of the Lord,
    make his paths straight,'"
⁴John the baptizer appearedᶜ in the wilderness, proclaiming a baptism of repentance for the forgiveness of sins. ⁵And people from the whole Judean countryside and all the people of Jerusalem were going out to him, and were baptized by him in the river Jordan, confessing their sins. ⁶Now John was clothed with camel's hair, with a leather belt around his waist, and he ate locusts and wild honey. ⁷He proclaimed, "The one who is more powerful than I is coming after me; I am not worthy to stoop down and untie the thong of his sandals. ⁸I have baptized you withᵈ water; but he will baptize you withᵈ the Holy Spirit."

ᵃOther ancient authorities read *in the prophets*
ᵇGk *before your face*   ᶜOther ancient authorities read *John was baptizing*   ᵈOr *in*

COMMENTARY

Mark immediately connects the good news with the Old Testament prophecies of salvation. The position of the quotations suggests that they belong to the gospel concerning Jesus Christ. However, the one who will prepare the way in the wilderness is John the Baptist. The other Gospels do not refer to Isa 40:3 until after John has been introduced (Matt 3:1-3; Luke 3:2-4; John 1:19-23).

The citation attributed to Isaiah in vv. 2-3 combines the reference to a messenger who will prepare God's way from Mal 3:1 with Isaiah's description of the way in the wilderness (Isa 40:3); these two passages are linked by the phrase "prepare the way." The messenger figure com-

bines Mal 3:1 with the angel who guarded Israel in the wilderness (Exod 23:20). That prophecy appears in a different context in Q (Matt 10:11; Luke 7:27).[60] Including the angel of Exodus in the prophecy reminds readers of the importance of the wilderness in salvation history. Salvation traditionally comes from the wilderness. Moses, Elijah, and David all had to flee to the wilderness (Exod 2:15; 1 Sam 23:14; 1 Kgs 19:3-4). Likewise, Jesus will emerge from the wilderness to begin preaching the good news and will return

60. Bryan, *Preface to Mark,* 138; Marcus, *Way of the Lord,* 12-17, thinks that Mark was responsible for conflating the two independent Q sayings into a single prophecy.

there several times (Mark 1:35, 45; 6:31-32, 35; 8:4).[61]

The voice crying in the wilderness uses the words of the prophet to sound the beginning of the good news. The prophetic texts suggest that the one for whom the messenger prepares the way is God, whose royal power will liberate a captive people (cf. Isa 40:9-10). Both John (v. 4) the baptizer and Jesus (vv. 12-13, 35, 45) emerge from the wilderness to preach to the people. The *Community Rule* found at Qumran indicates the importance of this Isaiah tradition. Members of that Jewish sect looked upon their wilderness community as the place in which the righteous prepared the way of the Lord.[62] However, unlike the Essenes, Jesus is not merely founding a community whose faithful obedience to the Law would anticipate God's final coming in judgment, such as we find at Qumran. Instead, Jesus *is* the Lord.

Some exegetes treat 1:1-3 as the introduction to the whole Gospel. The command "prepare the way of the Lord" contains a double reference. On the one hand, it refers to the preparation that John the Baptist's preaching will make for the coming of Jesus. On the other, it reminds Christian readers to prepare for the return of the Lord in judgment. Thus when John the baptizer appears, his summons to a baptism of repentance is described as a preparation for the Lord. National repentance was commonly depicted as the prelude to the "day of the Lord"—that is, the day when God will judge the nation for its sins (cf. Joel 2:12-17). Historically, John the Baptist exemplifies a form of prophetic leadership among the people that galvanizes popular hopes for renewal and liberation. His execution by Herod Antipas indicates that such figures may be a serious threat to the established order.

Josephus has explained John's preaching in philosophical categories that were more comprehensible to a Hellenized audience. He exhorted the people to an inner moral reform that was symbolized in the external ritual of baptism.[63]

From Josephus's perspective, only the inner moral reform constitutes forgiveness. The soul cannot be cleansed by a washing of the body. Mark's report that John's baptism was a vehicle for forgiveness (v. 4) is probably closer to the view held by the common people. Several Jewish texts of the period associate washing in the flowing (i.e., living) waters of a river as part of the appeal to God for forgiveness.[64] The desire for repentance, forgiveness, and purification was motivated by John the Baptist's warning that the day of the Lord—the day of judgment—was drawing near.[65]

From the Christian perspective, John the Baptist did not awaken a repentance that heralded God's judgment. Rather, the repentance and anticipation evoked by John's preaching provided a receptive audience for Jesus' ministry. This evaluation of the Baptist contains a historical core. The eschatological context of John's preaching implies that baptism is not merely a purification ritual that can be repeated whenever individuals are defiled by sin or ritual impurity. Rather, the crowds who come to be "gathered together by baptism"[66] are the remnant, the redeemed who will experience God's coming as a day of salvation. Since Jesus announced that God's reign was at hand, some of those who had responded to the Baptist's call were certainly among Jesus' earliest followers (as the Fourth Gospel suggests, John 1:35-38).

John's imprisonment will mark the beginning of Jesus' mission in Galilee (Mark 1:14). John's execution by Herod Antipas (Mark 6:14-29) anticipates Jesus' own death. Since the Baptist's disciples retrieved his body for burial (6:29), Mark acknowledges that followers of the Baptist continued to exist as a recognizable group after Jesus began his ministry. Mark 11:27-33 returns to the link between the preaching of the Baptist and that of Jesus. Jesus demands that the religious leaders tell him the source of John's authority before he will defend his own activities. Trapped by their unwillingness to acknowledge John and their fear of the crowd's reaction if they deny that the Baptist was from God, the authorities cannot answer Jesus. Such fears reflect plausible political concerns in the first century. Josephus alleges that Herod executed John because Herod feared the popu-

---

61. Joel Marcus, *The Way of the Lord: Christological Exegesis of the Old Testament in the Gospel of Mark* (Minneapolis: Fortress, 1992) 23-26. The salvation that comes from the wilderness in this second exodus does not merely repeat the first, because there will no longer be room for human disobedience.

62. 1QS 8, 12-16.

63. Josephus *Antiquities of the Jews* 18.116-19. See also Robert L. Webb, *John the Baptizer and Prophet: A Socio-historical Study*, JSNTSup 62 (Sheffield: JSOT, 1991).

64. *T. Levi* 2.3B2-8; *Sib. Or.* 4.165-67; *Apoc. Mos.* 29.11-13.

65. Webb, *John the Baptizer*, 180-97.

66. See Josephus *Antiquities of the Jews* 18.117.

larity the baptizer enjoyed with the people. Such persuasive speech may lead to rebellion, so Herod Antipas decided to rid himself of the problem before any rebellion could occur.[67]

Neither Josephus nor the Fourth Gospel makes any comment about John's dress or diet. However, both are important elements in the wilderness symbolism that Mark introduces with the prophetic citation.[68] John's clothing recalls the prophet Elijah in 2 Kgs 1:8: "A hairy man, with a leather belt around his waist" (NRSV). Just as Mal 3:1 depicts Elijah as the forerunner of the Lord, so also Mark 9:13 makes explicit the identification of John with the prophet Elijah. John's diet of locusts and wild honey, as abstention from meat and wine, also marked him as a prophet (cf. Dan 1:8).

Although Mark and Josephus agree on the general outlines of the Baptist's ministry and his popularity with the people, Mark sees the Baptist as the forerunner of Jesus. Consequently, John's baptism cannot be an end in itself. The crowds who flock to John from Judea and Jerusalem were not necessarily expecting another to come after the Baptist. The double saying (vv. 7-8) points away from the theme of repentance to the coming of a "greater one" and a further cleansing. The concept of a cleansing by the Holy Spirit appears in the Qumran rule.[69] *The Testament of Levi* 18:6-8 associates the coming of the Spirit with the revelation of a true high priest in the line of Levi. Consequently, the claim to have received the Spirit may mark members of the elect prior to the messianic age as in the Qumran rule. Or the Spirit may be linked to the appearance of the final age of salvation, as in *The Testament of Levi.* Therefore, some interpreters have suggested that the saying about the stronger one may have referred either to God or to an indeterminate messianic figure before it was applied to Jesus. In the double-membered form of the saying, the superiority of the coming one is demonstrated both by the Baptist's unworthiness to undo his sandals and

by the fact that he brings the Spirit. An anthropomorphic use of the shoe as a sign of divine wrath appears in the psalms (Pss 60:8; 108:9). However, the saying more naturally suggests a human agent.[70] Both Q and Mark suggest that the Baptist announced the coming of God's judgment. On the level of human affairs, he may well have expected the coming of a human agent whose activity would inaugurate the end time.[71]

John's baptism was not a purification rite to be repeated. Nor did it establish a righteousness that could never be lost. Those who repented and received baptism from John would be the elect, who are prepared to receive the one to come. Since the comparison between John and the coming one presumes a qualitative difference between the two, "baptism with the Holy Spirit" suggests a permanent change in an individual's relationship with God that will come about only at the eschaton. Repentance and water baptism, as practiced by John the Baptist or in the purification rituals that marked persons who joined the Essene sect, may only designate a reorientation of a person's life. The Essenes entered a community that had already tested their determination to reform and walk obediently according to the Law. Members of the sect received the "Spirit of the true counsel of God."[72] John had not gathered the elect into a separate community but asked the nation as a whole to repent. Some interpreters conclude that forgiveness of sin is to be associated with baptism in the Spirit.[73] However, the prophetic promises of cleansing and receiving the Spirit at the end time are less concerned with past sin than with future holiness (cf. Ezek 36:25-27). The elect will never turn away from the Lord.

The description of John the Baptist in Q includes examples of oracles that warn of impending judgment (Matt 3:7-12; Luke 3:7-18). If Mark was familiar with that tradition about the Baptist's preaching, he refocused it. The Baptist's role is to introduce Jesus as the coming one, not to warn that divine judgment is near. Mark's version of the saying about baptism with the Spirit lacks the

---

67. Josephus *Antiquities of the Jews* 18.118-19. Herod Antipas may have had a particular reason to be concerned about his standing with the populace. Construction of the city Tiberias over an ancient cemetery was so contrary to custom that only the poor and foreigners could be induced to live there. See Richard Fenn, *The Death of Herod: An Essay in the Sociology of Religion* (Cambridge: Cambridge University Press, 1992) 41.

68. Cf. J. D. Kingsbury, *The Christology of Mark's Gospel* (Philadelphia: Fortress, 1983) 58-59; Christopher Bryan, *A Preface to Mark: Notes on the Gospel in Its Literary and Cultural Settings* (New York: Oxford, 1993) 139.

69. 1QS 4:20-21.

70. David R. Catchpole, *The Quest for Q* (Edinburgh: T. & T. Clark, 1993) 71-73. Catchpole argues that Mark has edited the earlier Q version of the saying.

71. Webb, *John the Baptizer,* 260-306.

72. 1QS 3.6-8; 11.14; CD 3.18; 4.6; 9.10; 1QH 4.37; 7.30; 11.10.

73. Robert A. Guelich, *Mark 1–8:26,* WBC 34A (Dallas: Word, 1989) 20, argues that the Qumran evidence links forgiveness and the presence of the Spirit in the community.

second term attached to the Q version, "with fire" (Matt 3:11; Luke 3:16). Fire is a common symbol of judgment in the Old Testament (Amos 7:4; Isa 31:9; Mal 3:2). The Qumran *Rule of the Community* describes an eschatological cleansing of the elect by fire and the Spirit in which all traces of evil are removed from the righteous. The Spirit is compared to purifying water.[74] For the elect, fire has a purifying function rather than a judgmental one. Some exegetes think that Q originally referred only to "baptism with fire" and that the version "with the Spirit and fire" represents a conflation of Mark and Q. However, both "Spirit" and "fire" designate the coming end time; "Spirit" points toward the salvation experienced by the elect, "fire" to divine judgment. Since John's baptism prepared the elect for the end time, reference to salvation would have been been appropriate to an early variant of the saying.[75]

Mark focuses attention on the prophetic saying with which the Gospel begins. John the Baptist appeared to prepare the way in the wilderness for Jesus. By highlighting the difference in dignity between Jesus and the Baptist, Mark points to Jesus' uniqueness. One who is unworthy to untie the sandals of another establishes a social distance greater than that between a master and a slave. Such an exaggerated claim of unworthiness played an important function in honor/shame cultures in indicating that the speaker will not threaten the honor of the superior party.[76] With the aid of the OT references to God's triumphant march through the wilderness to Zion, as well as the titles used for Jesus in v. 1, Mark's readers should identify Jesus' appearance with the approach of God.

74. 1QS 4.20-21.
75. The combination of Spirit/wind and fire at Pentecost (Acts 2:1-4) should not be read into the pre-Christian form of this saying.

76. See Bruce J. Malina and Richard L. Rohrbaugh, *A Social-Science Commentary on the Synoptic Gospels* (Philadelphia: Fortress, 1992) 175.

REFLECTIONS

1. Since preparing the way of the Lord forms the central focus of the Advent readings, this account of John the Baptist is often used on the Sunday before Christmas, because it asks us to consider what it means to prepare for the Lord's coming. The Isaiah passages, which feature prominently in the Advent season, bring words of hope to those discouraged by years of exile and the bleakness of the Jerusalem to which they returned. The ancient mythological imagery of God as the triumphant divine warrior bringing the exiles home through the wilderness served Isaiah as a word of hope.[77] The good news in Mark is that those hopes have finally been fulfilled.

2. However, the Lord does not come to a people who are unprepared. What is required of them? Repentance, forgiveness of sin, and baptism—themes that we associate with the liturgical season of Lent. In the ancient church, catechumens prepared for baptism and penitents for reconciliation with the community in the Lenten season. These traditions emphasize conversion and reform. Sometimes the call to reform our lives suggests that humans build the "way of the Lord" by their obedience to the ethical vision of Christianity. That perspective endangers the element of divine grace, which belongs to the gospel message. In the exodus, God, through an angel, led the people. In Isaiah, God is responsible for the return of the exiles through a wilderness that has been turned into a paradise. These images of hope, promise, and renewal remind us that human obedience, walking in the way of the Law, is a proper response to God's grace. We do not build the highway and then wait for God to come. God has already drawn near to us before we repent.

77. On the mythology behind the Isa 40:3 passage, see Marcus, *Way of the Lord,* 26-29.

Mark 1:9-15, Jesus, the Son of God, Appears

NIV

9At that time Jesus came from Nazareth in Galilee and was baptized by John in the Jordan. 10As Jesus was coming up out of the water, he saw heaven being torn open and the Spirit descending on him like a dove. 11And a voice came from heaven: "You are my Son, whom I love; with you I am well pleased."

12At once the Spirit sent him out into the desert, 13and he was in the desert forty days, being tempted by Satan. He was with the wild animals, and angels attended him.

14After John was put in prison, Jesus went into Galilee, proclaiming the good news of God. 15"The time has come," he said. "The kingdom of God is near. Repent and believe the good news!"

NRSV

9In those days Jesus came from Nazareth of Galilee and was baptized by John in the Jordan. 10And just as he was coming up out of the water, he saw the heavens torn apart and the Spirit descending like a dove on him. 11And a voice came from heaven, "You are my Son, the Beloved;[a] with you I am well pleased."

12And the Spirit immediately drove him out into the wilderness. 13He was in the wilderness forty days, tempted by Satan; and he was with the wild beasts; and the angels waited on him.

14Now after John was arrested, Jesus came to Galilee, proclaiming the good news[b] of God,[c] 15and saying, "The time is fulfilled, and the kingdom of God has come near;[d] repent, and believe in the good news."[e]

a Or my beloved Son   b Or gospel   c Other ancient authorities read of the kingdom   d Or is at hand   e Or gospel

COMMENTARY

1:9-11. Mark follows the prediction of the one to come with the baptism of Jesus. After John's words about the superior status of the one to come, Jesus' baptism would seem to be out of place. Since others who had come to be baptized confessed their sins (v. 5), the ancient tradition of the sinlessness of Jesus (2 Cor 5:21) makes this detail inappropriate in his case. The other evangelists either provide an explanation (Matt 3:13-15), sidestep the issue (Luke 3:21), or effectively deny that Jesus, the Son of God, was baptized (John 1:32-34). Since later writers find Jesus' baptism embarrassing, the comment that he was baptized by John the Baptist probably reflects historical tradition.[78]

The fact that Jesus was baptized by John only suggests that Jesus associated himself with the need to gather the elect and to prepare for the Lord's coming with a gesture of repentance. The revelation scene in which Jesus is declared Son of God (vv. 10-11) appears in this context in all of

the Gospels. The Fourth Gospel has the Baptist receive a revelation about Jesus' identity by witnessing the descent of the Spirit, like a dove, upon him (John 1:32).[79] Was the vision story added to the baptism by Christians in order to explain why Jesus was baptized? Some authors treat the vision as a "call" that represents Jesus becoming conscious of his own unique role. For Mark, this episode is central to the Gospel's christology.

Jesus' unique status as Son of God is confirmed by the descent of the Holy Spirit (v. 10). Readers might have expected the Baptist to identify Jesus as the coming one as he does in Matthew and John. Instead, Jesus is the only one who sees the heavens open and the Spirit descend, and only he hears the divine voice (vv. 10-11). Thus Mark's readers are shown the identity of Jesus, while that knowledge remains hidden from characters in the narrative.

The descent of the Spirit shows that Jesus is

78. See John P. Meier, *A Marginal Jew: Rethinking the Historical Jesus* (New York: Doubleday, 1991) 168-69.

79. On the various explanations for the use of a dove to represent the Spirit, see Stephen Gero, "The Spirit as a Dove at the Baptism of Jesus," *NovT* 18 (1977) 17-35.

the suffering servant of God who was to bring salvation to the nations (Isa 42:1). God's Word confirms Jesus' status as the unique source of salvation for humanity. The title "Son of God" derives from Ps 2:7, where it originally referred to the Davidic king, and Isa 44:2, where it designated the people Israel as a whole. God's gift of the Spirit to the one who would bring salvation also appears in Isa 63:11.[80]

Elements of apocalyptic symbolism—the open heavens (Isa 63:19), the descent of the Spirit, and the divine voice—also call attention to the fact that Jesus is the agent of God's salvation. Therefore, the episode is not intended to supply information about the state of Jesus' own self-understanding, as though the encounter with John triggered Jesus' recognition of his relationship to God. Rather, the episode continues the opening theme of prophetic fulfillment. In the New Testament, those with whom God is "well pleased" will play a role in the coming of salvation. Mark may have thought that Jesus was designated messiah when he received the Spirit at his baptism. However, the brevity of the narrative does not make that conclusion certain.[81] Although the Baptist's predictions were directed to the crowd, the vision of the Spirit and the Word of God are perceived by Jesus alone. Readers have a privileged position that is not shared by the characters in the narrative. This view enables the reader to recognize that Jesus is indeed the Lord whose coming was foretold by the prophet Isaiah.

The links between the episodes that introduce Jesus (vv. 9-15) and the Isaiah prophecy show that this section belongs to the introductory section of the narrative. The introduction concludes when Jesus, who had come from Galilee to John in the wilderness, returns to Galilee to begin preaching the gospel. Jesus, himself, alerts the audience that the "time" or "crucial moment" (καιρός *kairos*) has arrived (v. 15). Ancient biographical writings expected the hero to be prepared for his mission through some signs of divine favor. The theophany associated with Jesus' baptism meets that criterion.[82]

1:12-13. The Spirit immediately drives Jesus into the wilderness. This episode marks another

important feature of ancient narrative: testing the hero. However, the brevity of Mark's version surprises readers who are familiar with the dramatic exchange between Jesus and Satan, found in Q (Matt 4:1-11; Luke 4:1-13). The entire story is encapsulated in a single verse, which is divided into two parallel, double-membered clauses: (a) Jesus was in the desert forty days being tested by Satan; and (b) Jesus was with wild beasts, and angels ministered to him. Echoes of the testing of the Israelites in the wilderness may have shaped this temptation story; Mark's version states that Jesus was tested by Satan for forty days, just as God had tested Israel for forty years. From early Christian times onward, interpreters have also seen the picture of Christ in the wilderness with the animals as an antitype of Adam in the garden. Although wild animals suggest the dangers posed by the desert regions, the juxtaposition of this notice with the concluding reference to angels who ministered to Jesus makes the alternate reading possible. The enmity between humans and wild animals, which was a consequence of Adam's fall, does not apply to Jesus. Jewish legends also described angels coming to take the dead body of Adam into the heavens. The allusions to the Adam story as well as to Israel's wilderness experience show the reader that Jesus' relationship to God demonstrates what would have been the case for humanity if Adam had not sinned. A wilderness transformed into paradise formed part of the hope for salvation depicted in Isaiah (Isa 11:6-9; 32:14-20; 65:25). Unlike the Q version of the temptation, which emphasizes the conflict between Jesus and Satan, Mark's tradition uses the reference to the animals and ministering angels to highlight the specific characteristics of the new exodus.

Unlike the ancient Israelites, Jesus lacks all human company in the desert. Ordinarily, such isolation would be an indication of madness or demonic possession. However, the angels are a sign of Jesus' relationship to God: Although he lacks human company, the Son of God can rely on divine assistance.[83] The brevity of Mark's reference to Satan leads to different conclusions. Some scholars presume that Jesus is locked in conflict with Satan throughout the narrative. However, Satan rarely appears in the rest of the

80. See Marcus, *Way of the Lord,* 46-56.
81. See ibid., 73-75.
82. See Bryan, *A Preface to Mark,* 86-87.

83. See Malina and Rohrbaugh, *Social-Science Commentary,* 176.

Gospel as the agent of temptation. Jesus quickly proves able to expel any demon. Therefore, Mark probably intends readers to assume that Jesus had already broken Satan's power before his ministry began.[84]

1:14-15. Once Jesus has been introduced as the unique Son of God, the one who will embody the Spirit and even reverse the story of sinful humanity, his public ministry can begin. Mark notes that Jesus came to Galilee to preach after the arrest of John the Baptist (v. 14). His return to Galilee cannot have been an attempt to escape danger, since Herod Antipas, who executed John the Baptist (6:14-29), ruled Galilee and Perea. Some historians think that the public activity of the two overlaps, as the Fourth Gospel alleges (John 3:22-24). Mark's notice assumes that John's arrest triggers the ministry of Jesus. The Greek verb translated "arrest" (παραδίδωμι *paradidōmi*) is used later in Mark for the "handing over" of Jesus to the authorities (9:31; 10:33; 14:21, 41). Therefore, the end of the Baptist's ministry reminds the Christian of the fate awaiting Jesus. Since the two figures are not merely parallel, Jesus' death will have a significance quite different from that of the Baptist. Jesus' death will be the source of salvation for humanity.

The summary of Jesus' message in vv. 14*b*-15 combines John the Baptist's preaching of repentance with a phrase that would have been familiar to Mark's readers from early Christian preaching, "believe in the good news." John the Baptist had predicted the coming of one who would baptize with the Spirit. "The time is fulfilled" (v. 15*a*) indicates that Jesus' ministry will bring about the age of salvation anticipated by this prediction. Jesus announces that the "kingdom of God has come near." Some exegetes treat vv. 14-15 as the introduction to Jesus' ministry, not the conclusion of the Gospel's prologue.[85] The pericope looks in both directions: Jesus had to leave Galilee for the baptism and temptation in the wilderness of Judea (v. 9), and v. 14 explains Jesus' return. Readers are left with some uncertainty about the time that elapsed between the testing of Jesus in the wilderness and the arrest of John the Baptist. Mark may have linked John's arrest with the preaching of Jesus in this fashion as a further indication that Jesus is the one to "come after" the Baptist. Since Jesus is driven into the wilderness by the Spirit after his baptism and then begins preaching in Galilee, there is no suggestion that Jesus was a disciple of John. Mark does not explain why John was imprisoned, nor does he indicate who arrested John, until he recounts John's death (6:14-29). Some interpreters take the passive verb rendered "handed over" (παραδοθῆναι *paradothēnai*) as a divine passive, indicating that John's death was also part of God's plan. This interpretation is not confirmed by other claims about the death of John. However, the verb does appear as a divine passive in connection with the death of Jesus (9:31; 10:33; 14:21, 41). If his preaching led to the arrest of the Baptist, then Jesus' activity must involve similar dangers.

The content of Jesus' preaching in v. 14, "the gospel of God," echoes the opening of Mark, "the gospel of Jesus Christ, the Son of God." The summons to repent echoes the description of John's preaching a "baptism of repentance for the forgiveness of sins" (v. 4). As the earlier parallels between the Baptist and Jesus establish, Jesus' appearance is to mark the coming of salvation. Repentance has a different object: the gospel. Although John's preaching points to judgment, the time that Jesus announces refers to the approaching reign, or kingdom, of God.

The summons that concludes the summary of Jesus' ministry, "repent and believe in the gospel," seems to represent early Christian preaching. Repentance and belief are linked (Acts 11:17-18; 20:21; Heb 6:1). The parallelism with the earlier statement about the kingdom suggests that the gospel is linked to Jesus' preaching about the kingdom.

---

84. See Ernest Best, *The Temptation and Passion: The Markan Soteriology*, 2nd ed., SNTSMS 2 (Cambridge: Cambridge University Press, 1990) xviii-xx.

85. This interpretation is also reflected in the page layout of Nestle-Aland[27]. The United Bible Societies' edition inserts titles and parallels for each pericope; it identifies vv. 14-15 as the beginning of Jesus' Galilean ministry.

REFLECTIONS

1. The opening scenes in Mark raise the question of what it means to prepare for the coming of the Lord. Christians encounter this theme during the Advent season. The juxtaposition of Advent with Christmas tends to lead us to think of the preparations we make for a new baby: reorganizing the home and schedules, planning for the trip to the hospital, organizing baby showers, settling on a name, and even anticipating receiving the child into the church community. Unless there are medical difficulties or family problems, a joyful excitement surrounds the event.

If we use these experiences to understand what the gospel means by "preparing the way of the Lord," we miss the more stern notes evident in the summons to repentance, the testing of Jesus, and the arrest of John the Baptist. The Lord does not come to the people as a little baby. The Lord comes as judge and redeemer. In order to establish the peace and justice that the prophets anticipate, the Lord must confront human sinfulness. The prophet Hosea depicts God reducing the sinful nation to the wilderness again so that the people would learn that all prosperity comes from the Lord (Hos 2:1-15). When the Qumran community or John the Baptist withdraw into the wilderness to "prepare the way of the Lord," they testify against the corruption of the larger society. Only those who repent, who return to following the Lord, will experience the coming rule of God as a time of blessing and peace.

2. Unlike Matthew and Luke (Matt 4:1-11; Luke 4:1-13), Mark does not explain how Satan tested Jesus in the wilderness. The stories of Israel in the wilderness and of Adam and Eve in the garden provide examples of what it means to be tested and fail. One frequent element in these stories is the lack of confidence in the Word of the Lord. Even though they have been delivered from Pharaoh's army, the Israelites think that God might leave them to die in the wilderness (Exod 16:2-3). Even though they can see God's presence on Mt. Sinai in thunder, cloud, and trumpet blast (Exod 19:16-20; 24:15-18), the people think that Moses has perished and persuade Aaron to make them a calf idol (Exod 32:1-6). Jesus, on the other hand, remains faithful to God. In return, the wild animals are peaceful, and angels provide nurture for him.

To prepare for the Lord's coming, people must make a radical return to God. They must entrust themselves to God's Word and not go looking for their own insurance policy. Excessive anxiety about success and security often leads to compromises with our religious values and personal well-being. We allow activities associated with work or school to eat away at time for family, for worship, and for service to others in our community. The good news is that we can still experience the rule of God in our lives. It will not be a smooth road to fulfilling all our dreams, however; Jesus begins to preach in Galilee after the king has imprisoned John the Baptist. Turning to the Lord means turning away from all the voices calling us to walk some other path. The call of Jesus' first disciples, which follows this section, begins to spell out an important meaning of the way of discipleship.

❖   ❖   ❖   ❖

EXCURSUS: REIGN OF GOD IN MARK

The phrase "reign" or "kingdom" of God (ἡ βασιλεία τοῦ θεοῦ *hē basileia tou theou*) frequently designates the subject of Jesus' message in the synoptic Gospels.[86] Although more common in Matthew and Luke, this phrase occurs fourteen times in the Gospel of Mark. In the Old Testament, God's rule over Israel would usher in the age of justice and peace. Isaiah 52:7 heralds good news, peace, salvation, and the reign of God to the nation. Since God's rule would also be the day of vengeance against the wicked (cf. Isa 61:1-2), the summons to repent implies the need to prepare the nation for the coming of the rule of God. However, the Hebrew expression "kingdom of God," or its Greek equivalent, appears only twice in the Old Testament (1 Chr 28:5; Wis 10:10). In the apocalyptic tradition, God's rule always exists in heaven. When that rule finally holds sway on earth, the kingdoms of earthly rulers will be destroyed (Dan 2:44; Rev 11:15).

Consequently, statements about entering the kingdom suggest conditions that persons must fulfill in order to be counted among the elect who are part of the kingdom God establishes (cf. Mark 10:23-24; Rom 14:17-18). "Entering" sayings suggest a future dimension to the kingdom. Those who fulfill the stipulated conditions now will belong to the kingdom that is to come. In the beatitudes the kingdom can be said to belong to particular persons (Matt 5:3, 10; Luke 6:20); the same expression appears in Jesus' saying about the children (10:13-16).

Mark's description of Joseph of Arimathea as one who awaits the kingdom of God (15:43) suggests that the kingdom's presence is not the direct result of human activity; God must be responsible for its approach. The crowd's acclamation in Mark 11:10 refers to the "kingdom of our father David that is coming." Reference to a "secret" associated with the kingdom (Mark 4:11) suggests that believers have an understanding of the kingdom that differs from expectations held by the crowd. Some of Jesus' sayings suggest that the kingdom is not yet present but can be anticipated by his disciples (Mark 9:1; 14:25). The parables, which are introduced as examples of the kingdom of God (4:26, 30), suggest a hidden presence of the kingdom's beginning. Its arrival appears both inevitable and somewhat beyond human control.

The juxtaposition of the critical time being fulfilled and the kingdom drawing near in the introduction to Jesus' ministry (1:4-15) creates ambiguity over how the kingdom of God is related to the ministry of Jesus. On the one hand, Jesus' preaching and ministry seem intended to make the rule of God present to those who believe. On the other hand, the cosmic judgment which will make God's rule over the world visible to all nations remains in the future. One solution is to treat the fulfillment as a reference to the promises in the prophetic quotation of 1:2-3, while the incompleteness of the kingdom looks toward the future. Jesus' ministry has inaugurated the coming of the kingdom.[87]

86. See George R. Beasley-Murray, *Jesus and the Kingdom of God* (Grand Rapids: Eerdmans, 1986); Joel Marcus, "Entering into the Kingly Power of God," *JBL* 107 (1988) 663-75; J. C. O'Neill, "The Kingdom of God," *NovT* 35 (1993) 130-41; Roy A. Harrisville, "In Search of the Meaning of 'The Reign of God' " *Int* 47 (1993) 140-51.

87. Cf. Aloysius M. Ambrozic, *The Hidden Kingdom: A Redaction-Critical Study of the References to the Kingdom of God in Mark's Gospel,* CBQMS 2 (Washington, D.C.: Catholic Biblical Association, 1972) 19-25.

❖   ❖   ❖   ❖

Mark 1:16-20, Jesus Calls the First Disciples

NIV	NRSV
[16]As Jesus walked beside the Sea of Galilee, he saw Simon and his brother Andrew casting a net into the lake, for they were fishermen. [17]"Come, follow me," Jesus said, "and I will make you fishers of men." [18]At once they left their nets and followed him.	16As Jesus passed along the Sea of Galilee, he saw Simon and his brother Andrew casting a net into the sea—for they were fishermen. [17]And Jesus said to them, "Follow me and I will make you fish for people." [18]And immediately they left their nets and followed him. [19]As he went a little farther, he saw James son of Zebedee and his brother John, who were in their boat mending the nets. [20]Immediately he called them; and they
[19]When he had gone a little farther, he saw James son of Zebedee and his brother John in a boat, preparing their nets. [20]Without delay he	

NIV	NRSV
called them, and they left their father Zebedee in the boat with the hired men and followed him.	left their father Zebedee in the boat with the hired men, and followed him.

COMMENTARY

Jesus' first disciples are fishermen from Capernaum, a settlement that stretched along the lakefront; archaeologists have uncovered groups of small houses that were clustered around courtyards with adjoining houses that may have been occupied by related families. Jesus calls two pairs of brothers, Peter and Andrew, and James and John. Although nothing distinguishes either the town or its inhabitants, readers familiar with the Old Testament will recognize that this story depicts a divine calling, such as that of Elisha, the disciple and successor of the prophet Elijah, who called him away from plowing the fields (1 Kgs 19:19-21). The call story has three parts: (1) setting: fishermen by the sea (vv. 16, 19); (2) summons: come and follow (vv. 17, 20a); and (3) response: they left and followed (vv. 17, 21).

The fact that these men drop both occupation and family obligations to follow the one who summons them demonstrates that their call comes from God. The disciples are pictured as prosperous enough to own houses and employ hired hands to assist in the fishing enterprise. In a traditional society, such a break with family and occupation is extraordinary. Yet, Mark indicates that Peter and Andrew left immediately to follow Jesus. To the ancient reader, the summons to follow Jesus—i.e., to become a disciple—was an extraordinary disruption in a person's life (cf. Mark 10:28). It might even have seemed offensive. If the labor of the sons was critical to the fishing enterprise in which the two families were engaged, then such a departure might appear to put the welfare of the whole family at risk.[88]

In the summons to Peter and Andrew, Jesus provides a substitution for their old occupation, "I will make you fish for people" (v. 17). Christian readers recognize the expression as a reference to the later missionary activity of the disciples. Mark indicates that Jesus gives his disciples a share in his own mission (3:14-15; 6:7-12, 30). Their encounter with the risen Lord will be in Galilee (14:28; 16:7). Consequently, the "gospel of Jesus Christ," the message about the crucified and risen Lord, will begin to be preached in Galilee, just as Jesus began preaching the kingdom there.

Old Testament references to hooks and nets generally carry a negative overtone, one of ensnaring persons (e.g., Jer 16:16; Ezek 29:4-5; Amos 4:2; Hab 1:14-17). God sets traps for those who deserve judgment. The instances in which the disciples participate in Jesus' mission involve healing, preaching, and exorcism. They suggest that those who are "caught" by this new fishing activity are actually saved, not destroyed. Just as the preaching of Jesus shifts away from the tone of judgment associated with the Baptist to one of fulfillment, so also the metaphor of fishing for people is used in a context that suggests the positive function to be performed by preaching, bringing the good news to others.

88. On the economics of fishing in the first century CE, see Malina and Rohrbaugh, *Social-Science Commentary,* 180.

REFLECTIONS

1. Modern readers sometimes find this story disquieting. It suggests instances of young people who inexplicably renounce everything to join a cult or a Christian sect. The genre of a call story explains the abruptness and total commitment demonstrated by the disciples. The socioeconomic picture of prosperous fishermen indicates that they were not naive youth but established members of local society. Peter's family home in Capernaum becomes a center from which Jesus and his followers operate. The apostle was married, had his mother-in-law living in his household (Mark 1:29-31), and may have had children (as later tradition assumes).

This detail, along with the fact that pairs of brothers became followers of Jesus, suggests that we are dealing with a choice whose burdens are shared by the entire family. Although the disciples gave up their routine occupations to follow Jesus, they were not cut off from their families.

2. As established, relatively prosperous fishermen, the disciples probably had some education. The idea that they were impoverished, persons on the margins of society is unlikely. Of course, the wealthy, privileged aristocracy might consider Jesus and his followers "nobodies," but that judgment would have been applied to the majority of the population. This story reminds us that discipleship always has a cost. We must be willing to give up something in order to bring the good news to others.

Mark 1:21-28, Exorcism in the Synagogue

NIV

²¹They went to Capernaum, and when the Sabbath came, Jesus went into the synagogue and began to teach. ²²The people were amazed at his teaching, because he taught them as one who had authority, not as the teachers of the law. ²³Just then a man in their synagogue who was possessed by an evil[a] spirit cried out, ²⁴"What do you want with us, Jesus of Nazareth? Have you come to destroy us? I know who you are—the Holy One of God!"

²⁵"Be quiet!" said Jesus sternly. "Come out of him!" ²⁶The evil spirit shook the man violently and came out of him with a shriek.

²⁷The people were all so amazed that they asked each other, "What is this? A new teaching—and with authority! He even gives orders to evil spirits and they obey him." ²⁸News about him spread quickly over the whole region of Galilee.

[a]23 Greek *unclean*; also in verses 26 and 27

NRSV

21They went to Capernaum; and when the sabbath came, he entered the synagogue and taught. ²²They were astounded at his teaching, for he taught them as one having authority, and not as the scribes. ²³Just then there was in their synagogue a man with an unclean spirit, ²⁴and he cried out, "What have you to do with us, Jesus of Nazareth? Have you come to destroy us? I know who you are, the Holy One of God." ²⁵But Jesus rebuked him, saying, "Be silent, and come out of him!" ²⁶And the unclean spirit, convulsing him and crying with a loud voice, came out of him. ²⁷They were all amazed, and they kept on asking one another, "What is this? A new teaching—with authority! He[a] commands even the unclean spirits, and they obey him." ²⁸At once his fame began to spread throughout the surrounding region of Galilee. .

[a]Or *A new teaching! With authority he*

COMMENTARY

The opening scenes in Mark 1 place more emphasis on the power of Jesus' word than on explaining the content of the message summarized in vv. 14-15. Jesus enters the synagogue at Capernaum and astonishes the crowd with the authority of his teaching (vv. 21-22).[89] Teaching in the syna-

gogue brings Jesus into conflict with the scribes, who were experts in interpreting the Law (2:6). Mark consistently sets up Jewish religious leaders as opponents of Jesus. Scribes appear alongside most of the other groups mentioned in the Gospel. They are associated with local Pharisees in the Galilean ministry (2:16; 7:5) and work with Jerusalem officials during the passion narrative (14:1, 43, 53; 15:1, 31). As the story unfolds,

89. Archaeologists have uncovered and partially reconstructed the white limestone synagogue building that stood on this site (4th cent. CE?). A much simpler basalt structure with a cobbled floor stood in Jesus' day.

readers learn that the scribes and Pharisees are disturbed by the challenge that Jesus' teaching and activity pose to their traditions (2:16; 3:22; 7:5).[90]

Instead of continuing with an example of Jesus' teaching, Mark uses an exorcism story to demonstrate the authority of Jesus' word (v. 27). The crowd is overwhelmed with astonishment (6:2; 7:37; 10:26; 11:18). Exorcism stories generally include an encounter between the afflicted person and the exorcist (vv. 23-24), the action by the exorcist (v. 25), and the demon's departure (v. 26). Demons typically take over the personality of their victim in such stories and attempt to resist the exorcist's efforts to expel them. Mark concludes this episode by describing the crowd's response to Jesus' teaching and the spread of Jesus' reputation in the surrounding countryside (vv. 27-28). Mark includes three more exorcism stories (5:1-20; 7:24-30; 9:14-29). Summaries of Jesus' activity include exorcism as a prominent example of the activity that generated a following among the crowds (1:34, 39; 3:11-12, 15, 22-23; 6:13; 9:38). This tradition preserves an element in the historical ministry of Jesus.[91]

The conclusion of this story, "He commands even the unclean spirits, and they obey him," has been created by the evangelist to parallel the previous episodes. Jesus established his authority over Satan in the temptation story (vv. 12-13). Jesus' disciples then responded immediately to his word and followed him (vv. 16-20). Now readers learn that Jesus has such authority that even demons obey instantly. These demons in Mark's retelling prove to be more perceptive theologically than the human audience. They acknowledge Jesus' status as "Holy One of God" and the fact

that his coming marks the end of their own domination over human beings (v. 24). The end of demonic power is a sign that the present evil age is coming to an end (cf. *1 Enoch* 55:4). The crowd sees Jesus as a powerful miracle worker, but they do not recognize that he is Son of God.

Satan's power is being broken up because the Lord has come to redeem the people. Therefore, the exorcism indicates what it means for the kingdom of God to draw near. The kingdom cannot be separated from the person of Jesus, who embodies God's power. The unclean spirit is the antithesis of the Holy Spirit, whom Jesus possesses. When attempting to resist the exorcist, the demon speaks for the entire kingdom of evil spirits by using the plural, "Have you come to destroy us?" (v. 24).

The swift, violent reaction of the demons proves the truth that Jesus is the Holy One of God. The demons provide insight into Jesus' identity for readers of the Gospel but not for characters within the story. Demonic confessions are usually contrasted with the perplexed or awestruck questions about Jesus' identity that come from the crowd (1:27; 2:7; 4:41; 6:3).[92] The amazement over Jesus' powers does not mean that the people believe in him. The danger that may be posed by having a reputation as an exorcist is met by Jesus' command for the demon to be silent (1:25). Comparisons between Mark's stories and conventional exorcism accounts show that the evangelist is not interested in exorcism for its own sake. His narratives lack abjurations and formulae used against the demons by the exorcist. Nor does he have to make an incantation or appeal to God. Instead, the focus of the story remains the divine authority exercised by Jesus.[93]

---

90. See Elizabeth S. Malbon, "The Jewish Leaders in the Gospel of Mark: A Literary Study of Marcan Characterization," *JBL* 108 (1989) 259-81.

91. See the argument for historicity in Gregory E. Sterling, "Jesus as Exorcist: An Analysis of Matthew 17:14-20; Mark 9:14-29; Luke 9:37-43a," *CBQ* 55 (1993) 467-93.

92. See J. D. Kingsbury, *The Christology in Mark's Gospel* (Philadelphia: Fortress, 1983) 86-87.

93. See Robert H. Gundry, *Mark: A Commentary on His Apology for the Cross* (Grand Rapids: Eerdmans, 1993) 77-78.

Mark 1:29-45, Healing Increases Jesus' Reputation

NIV	NRSV
[29]As soon as they left the synagogue, they went with James and John to the home of Simon and Andrew. [30]Simon's mother-in-law was in bed with	29As soon as they[a] left the synagogue, they entered the house of Simon and Andrew, with
	[a]Other ancient authorities read *he*

NIV

a fever, and they told Jesus about her. ³¹So he went to her, took her hand and helped her up. The fever left her and she began to wait on them.

³²That evening after sunset the people brought to Jesus all the sick and demon-possessed. ³³The whole town gathered at the door, ³⁴and Jesus healed many who had various diseases. He also drove out many demons, but he would not let the demons speak because they knew who he was.

³⁵Very early in the morning, while it was still dark, Jesus got up, left the house and went off to a solitary place, where he prayed. ³⁶Simon and his companions went to look for him, ³⁷and when they found him, they exclaimed: "Everyone is looking for you!"

³⁸Jesus replied, "Let us go somewhere else--to the nearby villages--so I can preach there also. That is why I have come." ³⁹So he traveled throughout Galilee, preaching in their synagogues and driving out demons.

⁴⁰A man with leprosy[a] came to him and begged him on his knees, "If you are willing, you can make me clean."

⁴¹Filled with compassion, Jesus reached out his hand and touched the man. "I am willing," he said. "Be clean!" ⁴²Immediately the leprosy left him and he was cured.

⁴³Jesus sent him away at once with a strong warning: ⁴⁴"See that you don't tell this to anyone. But go, show yourself to the priest and offer the sacrifices that Moses commanded for your cleansing, as a testimony to them." ⁴⁵Instead he went out and began to talk freely, spreading the news. As a result, Jesus could no longer enter a town openly but stayed outside in lonely places. Yet the people still came to him from everywhere.

a40 The Greek word was used for various diseases affecting the skin—not necessarily leprosy.

NRSV

James and John. ³⁰Now Simon's mother-in-law was in bed with a fever, and they told him about her at once. ³¹He came and took her by the hand and lifted her up. Then the fever left her, and she began to serve them.

32That evening, at sundown, they brought to him all who were sick or possessed with demons. ³³And the whole city was gathered around the door. ³⁴And he cured many who were sick with various diseases, and cast out many demons; and he would not permit the demons to speak, because they knew him.

35In the morning, while it was still very dark, he got up and went out to a deserted place, and there he prayed. ³⁶And Simon and his companions hunted for him. ³⁷When they found him, they said to him, "Everyone is searching for you." ³⁸He answered, "Let us go on to the neighboring towns, so that I may proclaim the message there also; for that is what I came out to do." ³⁹And he went throughout Galilee, proclaiming the message in their synagogues and casting out demons.

40A leper[a] came to him begging him, and kneeling[b] he said to him, "If you choose, you can make me clean." ⁴¹Moved with pity,[c] Jesus[d] stretched out his hand and touched him, and said to him, "I do choose. Be made clean!" ⁴²Immediately the leprosy[a] left him, and he was made clean. ⁴³After sternly warning him he sent him away at once, ⁴⁴saying to him, "See that you say nothing to anyone; but go, show yourself to the priest, and offer for your cleansing what Moses commanded, as a testimony to them." ⁴⁵But he went out and began to proclaim it freely, and to spread the word, so that Jesus[d] could no longer go into a town openly, but stayed out in the country; and people came to him from every quarter.

a The terms leper and leprosy can refer to several diseases
b Other ancient authorities lack kneeling
c Other ancient authorities read anger   d Gk he

COMMENTARY

Preaching and healing continue to increase Jesus' reputation until he cannot be alone, even in the "deserted regions" (v. 45). This development may carry ominous connotations. The temptation story demonstrates that Jesus may go to the wil-

derness without being harmed. He withdraws to pray there before leaving Capernaum to engage in preaching throughout Galilee (v. 35). When the crowds pursue him even into such deserted places, their presence may carry hints of danger.

Mark's Gospel can be read against the turmoil of the years that led up to the Jewish revolt, when charismatic figures who gathered crowds in the deserted places usually sought to inaugurate rebellion. Mark is careful to show readers that Jesus did not lead a crowd out into such places. They would seek him on their own.

References to desert places around Capernaum in Galilee make no sense as literal geography. They do provide another parallel between the opening of Jesus' ministry and the preaching of John the Baptist. Just as crowds had gone out from Jerusalem and the Judean countryside to be baptized by John (v. 5), so also crowds from the Galilean towns came to Jesus to be healed.

1:29-34. Mark alternates between scenes in which Jesus is surrounded by a crowd and others in which he teaches his disciples alone inside a house (cf. 4:10, 34; 7:17). The first healing episode occurs inside Simon and Andrew's house (vv. 29-31).[94] The healing of Peter's mother-in-law compresses the typical features of a healing story: (a) description of the illness, (b) request for healing, (c) action by the healer, and (d) evidence that the ailing person has been restored to health. Jesus immediately cures the woman, who then gets up and welcomes the guests and prepares a meal for them.

Mark complements this healing with a summary reference to the response of the townspeople to Jesus' presence. They crowd the door of the house with all those who are ill or demon possessed. Readers would anticipate Jesus' ability to heal all (vv. 32-34). The concluding words, "he would not permit the demons to speak, because they knew him" (v. 34), belong to a famous puzzle in Markan interpretation: the function of commands to silence in the narrative.[95] Here, Mark's comment "because they knew him" reminds readers of the possessed man in the synagogue. The demon knew who Jesus was and what his mission would accomplish (v. 24).

Why would Jesus object to such testimony? Some interpreters have suggested that the solution lies in the link between "Son of God" and exorcist

94. Archaeologists have uncovered the remains of what may have been a house church from the late first century CE under the octagonal church of the fifth century CE. This building traditionally marks the house of Simon Peter.

95. See Heikki Räisänen, *The "Messianic Secret" in Mark* (Edinburgh: T. & T. Clark, 1990).

or miracle worker. Although Jesus has come to destroy Satan's power, he has not come to do so by exercising miraculous powers. Jesus must suffer and die. His enemies will taunt him with the fact that he is unable to save himself from crucifixion (15:31-32). According to this interpretation, commands to silence are part of Mark's christology. Jesus, the Son of Man, came to suffer and die, not to win the adulation of the crowds through working miracles. Other exegetes emphasize the fact that the demons are the source of testimony in this instance. The reference to silencing them may be merely a summary reference to the silencing that forms part of the exorcism rite. The demon attempts to use knowledge about the exorcist to ward off its own destruction (v. 24). However, we have seen that Mark has deliberately focused on the authority and identity of Jesus in retelling the exorcism stories. Therefore, it does not seem sufficient to attribute the silence command merely to the exorcism story genre.

Later in the Gospel, readers learn that scribes from Jerusalem refer to the exorcisms as evidence that Jesus is a magician, one who uses satanic power (3:22). Since accusations of practicing magic may lead to severe penalties, such as banishment or death, the charge posed a threat to Jesus' life. Consequently, the commands to silence are an indirect way of indicating that such charges are false.

1:35-39. The reader soon learns that the crowds at Capernaum create a problem for Jesus' ministry as well. He did not come to settle in the town as a local healer and holy man, but to preach throughout the region. Leaving Peter's house in the darkness well before dawn, Jesus returns to a deserted place to pray (v. 35). Because there are no deserts around Capernaum, translations often resort to speaking of "a lonely place" (RSV). Such adaptations mask the obvious parallel with the temptation story. During that episode, Jesus' special status as Son of God is underlined by the fact that angels minister to him. Mark does not need to specify what Jesus withdraws to pray about in such examples (also 6:46). They clearly indicate that Jesus comes to do God's will, not to seek his own advantage or popularity. After Simon and the other disciples pursue him to bring him back to the crowds at Capernaum, Jesus insists that he must go and repeat his preaching and healing in the rest of Galilee (vv. 36-39).

1:40-45. The final episode, the healing of a leper (vv. 40-45), brings such an increase in Jesus' reputation that he can no longer enter the towns but must remain in deserted areas. Mark presents this excessive popularity as the consequence of an act of disobedience. Instead of remaining silent and showing himself to the priest as ordered (v. 44), the leper goes and spreads the word of his healing (v. 45).

The encounter between Jesus and the leper contains several verbs that describe Jesus' emotional state. How they are translated plays an important role in the tone of the passage. The textual tradition indicates that uncertainty over the emotional tone of the passage also existed in antiquity. Most manuscripts describe Jesus' initial reaction to the leper's appeal (v. 41), rendered "filled with compassion" or "moved with pity" (σπλαγχνισθείς *splagchnistheis*), the verb used in other miracle accounts (Mark 6:34; 9:22). This reading is accepted by modern editors of the Greek text. Some manuscripts, however, read "becoming angry" (ὀργισθείς *orgistheis*; cf. Mark 9:19, 23). Luke 5:13 and Matt 8:3 resolve the problem by omitting the references to Jesus' reaction. Several modern commentators have argued for the reading *orgistheis* as the more difficult. It also matches the violent emotional reaction attributed to Jesus in verse 43.[96] However, accommodation to the latter may have led to the substitution of "anger" for "compassion" in verse 41. Reading *orgistheis* suggests that Jesus is moved with violent emotion in response to the leper's approach and request. Retaining *splagchnistheis* associates the strong emotions with the charge that Jesus gives the man after he has been healed.

The leper approaches Jesus as a suppliant (some manuscripts lack the verb for "kneeling" in v. 40). Instead of requesting healing, the man makes a statement about Jesus' ability to heal, "If you choose, you can make me clean" (v. 40). The ability to "make clean" if one chooses technically should apply only to God. Variants of the expression "If you choose, you can" appear in ancient

prayer formulae. They are an acknowledgment of the sovereign will of the gods. Magical formulae often take the opposite approach, in which the magician claims to possess power to compel the deity.[97] Jesus uses a similar "if you will" formula in Gethsemane (Mark 14:36). Therefore, the leper's approach indicates that he recognizes Jesus as one whose power conforms to the will of God. Indirectly, the passage begins to teach Mark's readers how they should pray.

The Hebrew term that we translate "leprosy" (צרעת *ṣāʿrat*) designates any of a number of scaly skin diseases. Persons afflicted with this disease may contaminate others with ritual impurity. Therefore, in Mark's day they were expected to act in a way that indicated their situation, such as dress in torn clothing and warn others not to come too close (Lev 13:45). Leviticus 13–14 provides the rules by which the priests were to determine which class of scale disease an individual had contracted, his or her level of impurity, whether the disease had been cured, and the rites for purification after recovery from the disease.[98] Some interpreters have preferred the rendering of the leper's plea as "pronounce me clean" rather than "make me clean" in order to avoid the theological difficulty of attributing God's power to Jesus. The rest of the story, however, acknowledges the existing legal tradition, which held that only a priest had authority to designate persons impure or pure. One Essene rule book insists that a priest must make the pronouncement even if he has to be instructed in the Law by a nonpriestly expert, "Even if he [the priest] be an imbecile, he alone shall quarantine him; for theirs is the judgment."[99] Rabbinic rulings contain a similar provision.[100] Therefore, there is no reason to interpret Jesus' action as usurping the determination to be made by priests.

Other interpreters who focus on the social boundaries and conventions evident in the story think that it represents a peasant culture's treat-

---

96. See Robert A. Guelich, *Mark 1–8:26,* WBC 34A (Dallas: Word, 1989) 72; Rudolph Pesch, *Das Markusevangelium I. Teil,* HTKNT II (Freiburg: Herder, 1977) 1:144; Joachim Gnilka, *Das Evangelium nach Markus. 1 Teilband Mk 1–8, 26,* EKKNT II (Zürich: Benziger, 1978) 1:92-93.

97. See Sharyn Echols Dowd, *Prayer, Power and the Problem of Suffering: Mark 11:22-25 in the Context of Markan Theology,* SBLDS 105 (Atlanta: Scholars Press, 1988) 136-44.

98. For an extensive discussion of this legislation, which includes legal material from Qumran as well as the rabbis, see Jacob Milgrom, *Leviticus 1–16,* AB 3 (New York: Doubleday, 1991) 768-889; Hannah K. Harrington, *The Impurity Systems of Qumran and the Rabbis,* SBLDS 143 (Atlanta: Scholars Press, 1993) 181-213.

99. CD 13.6-7.

100. *m. Neg.* 3:1.

ment of persons with such diseases. Although the law required such persons to keep their distance for a time after the priest had declared a person clean, the lepers in the New Testament remain in contact with the larger society (Matt 8:1; Mark 14:3).[101] Jesus' own behavior in reaching out to touch the man violates the restraints imposed on those concerned with ritual purity. This gesture may represent the power that Jesus possesses as the "Holy One of God." Human beings can be contaminated by such ritual impurities, but the one who possesses God's holiness cannot be made impure. God's presence creates holiness.

A violent emotional response is attributed to Jesus in v. 43. Since Jesus heals the man as easily as he did Peter's mother-in-law (vv. 41-42), the emotional notes in v. 43 seem more appropriate to an exorcism, with its conflict against the demonic, than to a healing miracle. The NIV and the NRSV fail to capture the tone of this verse. "Sent away" hardly captures the elements of force or violence of the Greek word, which may also be translated "drive away" or "cast out" (ἐκβάλλω ekballō); the harsher form was used to translate the verb in 1:12. Similarly, "sternly warned" hardly conveys the emotional agitation attached to the verb (ἐμβριμάομαι embrimaomai), which expresses anger or displeasure; it may refer to shaking the head or snorting. Why does Jesus become agitated and push the man away from his presence? The NIV and the NRSV renderings assume that the verb serves to underline the seriousness of Jesus' instruction to keep quiet and go to the priest.

Some interpreters think that Jesus' response indicates anger at the social conventions surrounding the treatment of persons with scale diseases. If the assumption that such diseases were signs of divine anger was widely shared, Jesus might have been troubled by the view that God was responsible for the man's condition. Others think this verse may have come from a variant of the episode in which a sufferer's condition was attributed to demonic influence. Leprosy was often attributed to a divine curse. Since Jesus' emotional response follows a healing, the possibility that his

reactions are dictated by the social codes surrounding the disease appears more probable. Ordinary tradespeople and laborers, like Jesus and his disciples, probably did not have the concern for ritual purity found among priests and scribes. Another possibility emerges if one considers what drove the man to approach Jesus. Had he already been refused a declaration of cleanness by the priests before coming to Jesus?

Jesus' orders to the man (v. 44) respect the conditions of the Law. Although Jesus has healed the man, he cannot rejoin the larger community without a priest's certification. When Jesus directs the man to say nothing but go and make the required offerings "as a testimony to them," "them" may refer to the priests, and not the people. Some commentators suggest that Jesus' anger is directed at that system and anticipates the explicit conflicts over the Law later in the narrative. The man's cure, once certified by these authorities, will demonstrate the false standards on which the system of religious classification has been built. It might be that readers assume that the man has no chance of being pronounced clean by the priests. Legislation from the Qumran community shows meticulous concern with the details of the week-long purification after apparent healing. The common people probably had little patience for such prescriptions.

If this is so, then the reader should greet the man's apparent disobedience with approval. Jesus had told him to remain silent and go through the legal procedures. Instead, the man rejects the demands of the Law in order to spread the message about Jesus. This behavior might have been interpreted in antiquity as due respect for one's benefactor. In the honor/shame code of ancient societies, it would be offensive not to spread the praises of one's benefactor. Turning from behavior that may be anticipated in Jesus' original audience to Mark's Gentile readers, one would expect even less concern for the peculiarities of the Law. On the one hand, Jesus demonstrates his respect for established tradition concerning purification of persons who have scale diseases. On the other hand, the man's response shows that nothing should keep people from telling others about what Jesus has done for them.

---

101. See Carl R. Kazmierski, "Evangelist and Leper: A Socio-cultural Study of Mark 1:40-45," *NTS* 38 (1992) 37-50.

REFLECTIONS

1. Although Christians today rarely attribute mental illnesses or epilepsy to demonic possession or other diseases to divine anger, they are aware of the spiritual dimensions of healing. Communal healing services supplement our ministry to shut-ins, to the sick, and to the dying. Most people have experienced both the joy of a better-than-expected recovery and the pain and anger of unexpected medical complications or even death. The cycle of self-accusation or anger at family members that often accompanies severe illness or death can be as devastating as the disease itself. Serious mental illness, even when controlled by medication, also strains the resources of family and friends. Sometimes we may think that it would be easier to attribute such afflictions to demons than to endure the dashed expectations accompanying each new type of therapy and the lurking fear of suicide.

2. How can we read these stories about Jesus, the exorcist and healer, without feeling cheated? God or Jesus has only to will it, and a person is healed. Does God will that person's suffering? If anything would make Jesus angry, it would surely be the charge that God wills the suffering and evil in our world. Even Jesus does not escape suffering and death—and he exercises God's healing power! There is a flaw in our common talk about health and sickness. The persistent emphasis on personal responsibility for keeping ourselves healthy has a backside: blaming those who become ill for their condition. Paradoxically, the person who is "possessed" cannot be blamed. He or she has been invaded by a stronger power, which only God can expel.

3. Another feature of illness that many of the healing stories in the Gospel of Mark illustrate is isolation. Peter's mother-in-law lies wracked with fever. She cannot fulfill the role of preparing and serving a meal to the guests, which would have fallen to her as the senior woman in the household. Jesus' healing restores her to her social position within the household. Many women today react negatively to the picture of a woman getting up after a severe illness to serve male guests. That sentiment hardly seems appropriate to the complex gender and social roles involved in the household. Certainly, Peter's wife or a female servant may have prepared food. The privilege of showing hospitality to important guests falls to Peter's mother-in-law as a matter of honor, not servitude. We even exhibit similar behavior. When special guests are expected for dinner, no one gets near the kitchen without clearance from the person who has the privilege of preparing the food.

Social isolation and reintegration are more evident in the case of the leper. He cannot resume normal associations with other people until a priest has inspected his condition and he has performed the required purification rites. Today, we react in a similar way to AIDS patients or even to persons with cancer. Many persons battling such illnesses report that their family and friends become timid about touching them. When they need most the human contact of a hug, a hand to hold, or a pat on the back, they find others drawing back. Dying persons suffer even more acute forms of isolation. When they begin to look too ill, even their closest friends stop visiting them. We may no longer confine persons with highly communicable diseases to isolation, but the subtle forms of social isolation we practice can be just as devastating. Jesus did not cut himself off from the leper. Instead, he healed the man by reaching out to touch him.

4. The stories also teach readers lessons about prayer. Jesus withdrew into the wilderness to pray to God before beginning his mission throughout the towns and villages of Galilee. The leper approaches Jesus in the proper stance to be used in making a request of God. Jesus is the source of the blessings that God wishes for human beings. Even when God does not appear to respond to prayer as we anticipate, we should remember the compassion that Jesus shows toward those who approach him for healing.

MARK 2:1–3:35, CONTROVERSY AT CAPERNAUM

OVERVIEW

Jesus' return to Capernaum, which is now described as his home (2:1, 3a, 19b), inaugurates a series of controversy stories, ending with a plot against Jesus' life (3:6). In these stories, Jesus demonstrates the superiority of his new teaching to that of the scribes and Pharisees. Increasing hostility develops throughout the controversies in Mark 2:1–3:6—scribes challenge Jesus' authority to forgive sin (2:6); they ask why he associates with tax collectors and sinners (2:16b); Jesus is asked why his disciples do not fast (2:18b); Pharisees ask why Jesus' disciples break the sabbath (2:24); they watch to trap Jesus healing on the sabbath (3:2). Finally, the Pharisees and Herodians plot to destroy Jesus (3:6).[102] At this point, readers know that what Jesus does on the sabbath is good, but it has led to determined enemies. The coming of God's reign in Jesus has brought healing and forgiveness for others, but for Jesus it will mean opposition and death.[103]

Jesus ultimately must withdraw from the synagogue at Capernaum to the sea (3:7). A summary of his activities reminds readers of what they have already learned about his ministry (3:7-12). He calls the rest of the group of twelve disciples who will have a special share in his ministry (3:13-19). Then disputes over the source of Jesus' power to exorcise separate him from his natural family and establish the disciples, those who do the will of God, as his true family (3:19b-35). Although Jesus had ordered the leper to fulfill the law of Moses (1:44), the controversy stories in 2:1–3:6 display opposition to the conventions of sabbath observance.

The reader begins to learn how Jesus' teaching with authority (1:27) differs from that of the scribes. The scribes cannot forgive sin. They have no power to heal the afflicted and no compassion for those who are suffering. The separation of Jesus from his natural family (3:20-21, 31-35) forms the nucleus of the second half of this section. Using Mark's technique of framing one episode with the two halves of another, one sees division in Jesus' family as the framework within which Jesus' enemies try to turn the crowd against Jesus as an agent who manipulates satanic powers. By the end of this section of the gospel, readers recognize the positive effect of his ministry insofar as it brings repentance and creates a new people devoted to doing the will of God. The account also displays the negative side of the same events: division and enmity.

This section introduces a new type of story: the controversy story. Wise men and rabbis were often the subjects of such tales. In Hellenistic biographical writing, the *chreia* was a brief episode that enshrined some facet of the hero's character or illustrated a point of his teaching. The controversy stories that figure so prominently in Mark open with a challenge that Jesus will be forced to meet. Such stories belong to oral traditions as well as to written ones. They enable an audience familiar with the techniques of oral memory to recall the points of teaching more easily than asking them to remember the list of sayings that represent the climax of such stories. It is also characteristic of the story to have some dramatic tension in the setup (e.g., the paralyzed man whose friends must let him down through the roof, 2:3-4).[104]

---

102. Mark has woven traditional stories together in the section by creating the sequence of hostile acts by the Pharisees: warning Jesus (2:24); watching him with the intent to gain evidence to accuse him (3:2, 4); their decision to destroy him (3:6). See Kuthirakkattel, *Beginning of Jesus' Ministry,* 176-239.

103. See Joanna Dewey, *Markan Public Debate: Literary Technique, Concentric Structure and Theology in Mark 1:1–3:6,* SBLDS 48 (Chico, Calif.: Scholars Press, 1981) 119; Christopher Bryan, *A Preface to Mark: Notes on the Gospel in Its Literary and Cultural Settings* (New York: Oxford, 1993) 89-91.

104. This is the oral way of teaching: not by discussion of principle but by vivid presentation of precept. See Bryan, *Preface to Mark,* 128.

Scholars dispute whether it is possible to reconstruct the traditional cycle of controversy stories that the evangelist has redacted in developing the material for this section. The controversies in this section must have originated in the ministry of Jesus. Jewish issues, such as sabbath observance, do not appear to be a pressing issue for Mark's Gentile audience. Fasting, on the other hand, has been resumed in the community (2:20). Thus these episodes portray Jesus as the one who sets the conditions of discipleship for his followers. He has determined that the most important characteristic of the disciple is devotion to God (3:31-35). Compassion overrides the external details of sabbath observance. The scribes and Pharisees, as well as the disciples of John the Baptist, appear unable to discern what the will of God really is. Just as the story of the former leper contains a veiled hint that Jesus exercises the healing power of God (1:40-41), so also the first controversy in this cycle turns on Jesus' claim to forgive sins, also a divine prerogative (2:5-6).

Most scholars agree that the controversy stories were inherited from the earliest Palestinian community. The standard opponents are scribes, persons versed in Scripture. Thus the debates take place as disputes between those learned in the Law. Outsiders are forcing Jesus to define the boundaries of the new community. Unlike the ancient philosophical texts that refer to details of the teaching of individual philosophers, Mark appears to use this material to create some distance between the Jewish community and Jesus and his followers.[105]

105. See Gerd Theissen, *The Gospels in Context: Social and Political History in the Synoptic Tradition* (Minneapolis: Fortress, 1991) 114-21.

Mark 2:1-12, Healing the Paralytic

NIV

2 A few days later, when Jesus again entered Capernaum, the people heard that he had come home. [2]So many gathered that there was no room left, not even outside the door, and he preached the word to them. [3]Some men came, bringing to him a paralytic, carried by four of them. [4]Since they could not get him to Jesus because of the crowd, they made an opening in the roof above Jesus and, after digging through it, lowered the mat the paralyzed man was lying on. [5]When Jesus saw their faith, he said to the paralytic, "Son, your sins are forgiven."

[6]Now some teachers of the law were sitting there, thinking to themselves, [7]"Why does this fellow talk like that? He's blaspheming! Who can forgive sins but God alone?"

[8]Immediately Jesus knew in his spirit that this was what they were thinking in their hearts, and he said to them, "Why are you thinking these things? [9]Which is easier: to say to the paralytic, 'Your sins are forgiven,' or to say, 'Get up, take your mat and walk'? [10]But that you may know that the Son of Man has authority on earth to forgive sins . . . ." He said to the paralytic, [11]"I tell you, get up, take your mat and go home." [12]He got up, took his mat and walked out in full

NRSV

2 When he returned to Capernaum after some days, it was reported that he was at home. [2]So many gathered around that there was no longer room for them, not even in front of the door; and he was speaking the word to them. [3]Then some people[a] came, bringing to him a paralyzed man, carried by four of them. [4]And when they could not bring him to Jesus because of the crowd, they removed the roof above him; and after having dug through it, they let down the mat on which the paralytic lay. [5]When Jesus saw their faith, he said to the paralytic, "Son, your sins are forgiven." [6]Now some of the scribes were sitting there, questioning in their hearts, [7]"Why does this fellow speak in this way? It is blasphemy! Who can forgive sins but God alone?" [8]At once Jesus perceived in his spirit that they were discussing these questions among themselves; and he said to them, "Why do you raise such questions in your hearts? [9]Which is easier, to say to the paralytic, 'Your sins are forgiven,' or to say, 'Stand up and take your mat and walk'? [10]But so that you may know that the Son of Man has authority on earth to forgive sins"—he said to the paralytic— [11]"I say to you, stand up, take your mat

[a] Gk *they*

NIV	NRSV
view of them all. This amazed everyone and they praised God, saying, "We have never seen anything like this!"	and go to your home." [12]And he stood up, and immediately took the mat and went out before all of them; so that they were all amazed and glorified God, saying, "We have never seen anything like this!"

COMMENTARY

This episode combines the formal characteristics of a healing miracle with those of a pronouncement story. The healing miracle describes the cure of a paralyzed man in response to the faith shown by his friends: (a) severity of the illness and his being carried on a pallet by four men (v. 3); (b) the request for healing, implied in the men's making a hole in the roof of the house to let him down before Jesus (v. 4); (c) action by the healer and word of forgiveness (v. 5) and command (v. 11); evidence of the cure in that the man rises and carries away his pallet, to the amazement of the crowd (v. 12). A controversy over Jesus' claim to forgive sin erupts in the middle of the healing miracle (vv. 5-10). The successful healing serves as the response that defeats the argument offered by the scribes.

The juxtaposition of a healing miracle with a debate over Jesus' authority to forgive sin raises a question about the pre-Markan history of the tradition. A variant story of Jesus' healing a paralytic in John 5:1-9 has the man healed by the command to carry his pallet off. Only after the man has been challenged by the Jewish authorities for violating the sabbath does Jesus find him in the Temple and warn him to sin no more (John 5:1-14). The Johannine example shows that it is possible to separate the debate over sin from the healing of a paralyzed person. However, if Mark 2:5*b*-10 were originally an independent tradition that has been woven into the miracle story, then the statement about forgiveness must have replaced some other word of reassurance.[106] The miracle ends with the common assertion that all were amazed and gave glory to God (v. 12). However, that conclusion hardly incorporates the

scribes, who are locked in controversy with Jesus over forgiveness.

Mark uses the immense popularity of Jesus with the crowds, established in the summary statements (1:27-28, 32-34, 45; 2:2) to create an obstacle for the men seeking a miracle.[107] They cannot get near Jesus, and their determination to do so exhibits the faith that moves Jesus to heal the man (v. 5*a*). In the healing of the leper, the form of the petitioner's request exhibits appropriate piety concerning God's power. This story adds a different dimension to the miracle stories: faith as a condition of healing. Faith may be understood merely as a variant of the earlier petition. In many ancient miracle accounts, the faith attributed to the petitioner means that the individual recognizes the deity's ability to grant the request.[108] The Markan stories have an additional dimension to this faith. Whenever faith appears in the healing miracles, the persons involved must overcome physical or social obstacles (5:21-24, 35-43; 10:46-52). Their faith is directed toward Jesus as the one who is able to exercise God's healing power. Lack of faith limits Jesus' ability to perform miracles in his native village of Nazareth (6:5-6*a*).

Jesus' statement that the man's sins are forgiven hardly follows from the request for healing, as we have seen. Some interpreters try to avoid the implication that Jesus usurped God's prerogative (Exod 34:6-7; Isa 43:25; 44:22) by suggesting that the statement was intended to reassure the man that God would forgive him (as in 3:28; 4:12). Or they point to Old Testament passages in which illness is associated with sin (2 Sam 12:13;

---

106. See the discussion of the formal elements in the story by Gerd Theissen, *The Miracle Stories of the Early Christian Tradition,* trans. Francis McDonagh (Philadelphia: Fortress, 1983) 164-66.

107. Use of a summary statement to exaggerate the popularity of a teacher with the crowd is typical of ancient biographical accounts. See Charles W. Hedrick, "The Role of Summary Statements in the Composition of the Gospel of Mark: A Dialogue with Karl Schmidt and Norman Perrin," *NovT* 26 (1984) 307-9.

108. See Theissen, *Miracle Stories,* 130-33.

Ps 103:3; Isa 6:7). Jesus' defense, however, does not respond to the charge of blasphemy with an appeal to Scripture. Nor does he respond directly to the charge that he claims God's authority. The Gospel's readers might also wonder why he does not refer to the forgiveness that was associated with John's baptism (1:4). God remains the agent of forgiveness in that context.

Jesus' words to the man may be understood as an expression of similar assurance about the forgiveness that comes from God. However, he responds first with a saying that depends on the assumption that it is more difficult to tell the man to walk than to say, "Your sins are forgiven" (v. 9). The logical juxtaposition is unclear. Both are statements about powers that belong to God. The latter would be more rapidly disconfirmed if the man were not cured.[109] By juxtaposing the issue of forgiveness and the command that Jesus will give the man, Mark makes it clear that the healing is a sign that the man has been forgiven.

The evangelist has expanded Jesus' words with a saying about the authority of the Son of Man (v. 10). The term translated "authority" ($\dot{\epsilon}\xi o \upsilon \sigma \acute{\iota} \alpha$ *exousia*) appears in earlier crowd reactions to Jesus' exorcisms (1:27). A similar Son of Man saying is attached to the assertion of freedom from sabbath restrictions in Mark 2:28. Both sayings use the title "Son of Man" to claim a present authority that sets Jesus and his followers over against Jewish authorities. The textual tradition is uncertain in locating the phrase "on earth." Some place it after "Son of Man," others at the end of the clause. The phrase seems intended to contrast God, who is in heaven, with the Son of Man. Since the Son of Man figure in Dan 7:14 is a human who ascends to the divine throne, the use of Son of Man here presumes a Christian identification of Jesus as Son of Man. The distinction between God and Jesus as Son of Man is maintained by the specification of the appropriate sphere in which the Son of Man exercises authority: on earth.

With the exception of Mark 2:28, all other references to the Son of Man appear after the passion prediction in 8:31. The authority of the Son of Man in that context is established only after the Son of Man is confessed as the one who

died on the cross and who will come to judge the world. The coming of the Son of Man in judgment will vindicate Jesus against those who maliciously accuse him of blasphemy at his trial (14:62-64). His death on the cross atones for the sins of humanity (10:45). Although Mark's readers were certainly familiar with the passion and future judge types of the Son of Man saying, nothing in the narrative prompts the reader to supply that use for the sayings in chapter 2. The judgment saying in Mark 8:38 correlates the attitude people take toward Jesus in this world with the attitude the heavenly Son of Man will take toward them in the judgment. In that context, people encounter Jesus on earth—that is, in this evil generation, and the Son of Man in heaven. Thus the present-authority form of the Son of Man saying found in these passages is quite unusual.[110] Mark has probably derived these two sayings from his tradition. The crowd recognizes that God is the final source of the miracle they witness (v. 12).

How the expression "Son of Man" came to be used to designate Jesus remains the subject of scholarly debate. The phrase is never used by others as a confessional statement about Jesus in the Gospel. Jesus uses the expression as a form of self-reference. As a colloquial Aramaic expression, "son of man" (אנשׁ בר *bar 'ĕnāš*) could be used as an indirect third person.[111] In that case, a saying about the authority of the Son of Man may have been used by Jesus to imply that "a person" or "humans" have such authority. When "Son of Man" is juxtaposed with Jesus, the evangelists intend the expression to refer to Jesus' special status. Passion predictions treat the suffering of the Son of Man as a paradox, challenging conventional views of power, authority, and honor (8:31-33). A final group of sayings describes the Son of Man as one who comes in glory with the angels of God to execute judgment (8:38). The apocalyptic picture of the Son of Man as judge can be linked with the vision of "one like a son of Man" in Dan 7:13-14 (other elements of Dan 7:13-14 are used in Mark 8:38; 13:26; 14:62). In that vision, the seer sees a heavenly figure with a human form ascending to God's throne and being endowed with an eternal rule over the

109. See Pesch, *Markusevangelium I,* 159f.

110. See Guelich, *Mark,* 89-93.

111. See Joseph A. Fitzmyer, *The Gospel According to St. Luke I–IX,* AB 28 (Garden City, N.Y.: Doubleday, 1981) 210-11.

nations. As the representative of the righteous persons who have suffered persecution, the Son of Man heralds the destruction of their persecutors (Dan 7:21-22, 27).[112] Echoes of the heavenly Son of Man, who represents the suffering righteous, provide the most plausible source for the use of the expression in reference to Jesus. Even so, "forgiveness of sins" represents an innovation in that tradition.

Mark's reader is familiar with Jesus' authority to heal. In its present form, this story portrays healing as evidence of Jesus' authority to forgive sin. In what some interpreters take as ironic reversal, Jesus argues that it is "easier" to pronounce forgiveness of sins than to heal a paralyzed

112. See John J. Collins, *Daniel* (Minneapolis: Fortress, 1993) 79-82, 304-22.

person. By applying the common rule of argument, if the greater case holds, so the lesser. Jesus insists that if he heals the man, then his enemies must recognize his authority to forgive sin. Jesus has already demonstrated something of divine omniscience by recognizing the sins of the man before him and the hostile thoughts of his opponents. The scribes' charge of blasphemy, made against Jesus, though without credible evidence, at his trial (14:64) could warrant the death penalty. Jesus takes the initiative in unmasking the inner thoughts of the scribes. His ability to know what is in the human heart is another attribute reserved only to God. Although Jesus' demonstration of divine authority does not convert his enemies, the crowd responds appropriately by glorifying God.

REFLECTIONS

1. Jesus began his ministry with an attack on the powers of demonic possession and illness (1:21-45). The approach of God's rule meant healing of severe physical afflictions, which separated persons from the larger human community. In this story, another barrier falls: that of sin. Resistance to Jesus' words and actions of forgiveness shows that the separation of the sinner from God is not the only barrier created by sin. Humans divide themselves into categories of "righteous" and "sinners," but Jesus rejects that division. The "righteous" think they know the conditions under which persons may expect to receive mercy from God. Those who experience God's mercy and compassion are already trying to shape their lives by God's law. Their desire for holiness is not wrong. The failure occurs when the scribes mistake Jesus' ministry to sinners as blasphemous disregard for God's holiness.

2. Jesus establishes a pattern of holiness that invites the outsider into fellowship. Forgiveness is essential to the new community around Jesus. The story of the paralytic also reminds us that forgiveness is central to healing. Psychoanalysis has taught the twentieth century that deep-seated, irrational guilt and self-hatred can generate imprisoning physical symptoms. That story highlights another important feature of the social context of illness: The faith of the paralyzed man's four friends initiated the healing encounter with Jesus. For many people, the most difficult part of enduring a severe illness is helplessness, the need to rely on others for one's basic functions of daily life.

Mark 2:13-17, Jesus Calls Sinners

NIV	NRSV
[13]Once again Jesus went out beside the lake. A large crowd came to him, and he began to teach them. [14]As he walked along, he saw Levi son of Alphaeus sitting at the tax collector's booth. "Fol-	13Jesus[a] went out again beside the sea; the whole crowd gathered around him, and he taught them. [14]As he was walking along, he saw Levi [a] Gk *He*

NIV

low me," Jesus told him, and Levi got up and followed him.

[15]While Jesus was having dinner at Levi's house, many tax collectors and "sinners" were eating with him and his disciples, for there were many who followed him. [16]When the teachers of the law who were Pharisees saw him eating with the "sinners" and tax collectors, they asked his disciples: "Why does he eat with tax collectors and 'sinners'?"

[17]On hearing this, Jesus said to them, "It is not the healthy who need a doctor, but the sick. I have not come to call the righteous, but sinners."

NRSV

son of Alphaeus sitting at the tax booth, and he said to him, "Follow me." And he got up and followed him.

15And as he sat at dinner[a] in Levi's[b] house, many tax collectors and sinners were also sitting[c] with Jesus and his disciples—for there were many who followed him. [16]When the scribes of[d] the Pharisees saw that he was eating with sinners and tax collectors, they said to his disciples, "Why does he eat[e] with tax collectors and sinners?" [17]When Jesus heard this, he said to them, "Those who are well have no need of a physician, but those who are sick; I have come to call not the righteous but sinners."

[a]Gk reclined   [b]Gk his   [c]Gk reclining   [d]Other ancient authorities read and   [e]Other ancient authorities add and drink

COMMENTARY

Having established Jesus' authority to forgive sin, Mark now portrays Jesus reaching out to outcasts and sinners. Levi's occupation as "tax collector" was to collect customs due on the goods crossing the border. Since toll collectors determined what price persons bringing goods across the boundary must pay, a toll collector might enrich himself by demanding more than the required amount. As long as the toll collector was able to cover the tax revenue promised in his contract with the authorities, he could keep whatever was left for himself. Thus they were unpopular among the people, who suspected them of dishonesty. Those who managed to exploit the system to become wealthy employed slaves and other agents to do the actual collecting.[113] The story of Levi's call to discipleship repeats a number of features in the earlier story about the call of the fishermen. Like the fishermen, Levi is beside the sea, engaged in his usual occupation. At Jesus' word, Levi drops everything to follow him (v. 14).

Just as Jesus dined at Peter's house, so also now he goes to Levi's house and eats with toll collectors and sinners (vv. 15-17). The expression "sinner" reflects the social contempt in which tax collectors were held. In a loose way, even the

common people might be referred to as sinners by the Pharisees and Essenes, who sought to embody all the details of holiness and purity in their daily lives. Although there were no explicit prohibitions against persons like Jesus and his disciples eating with fellow Jews, even if they were engaged in a despised trade like toll collecting, Pharisees, who sought to maintain a higher standard of holiness than ordinary people, would probably not have done so. Meals played an important role in the religious and social life of ancient peoples, and, further, Jewish meals had to comply with kosher laws. Wealthy individuals might invite guests of different rank to dine with them. Guests who reclined in the inner dining room with the host might eat much better food and wine than other retainers who might be invited to the same gathering.[114] These small houses, grouped together around courtyards typical of ancient towns, made it easy for outsiders to look in and learn what the inhabitants were doing, and when the scribes of the Pharisaic sect discovered Jesus dining with "sinners," they voiced their objections to Jesus' disciples.

The first half of Jesus' response to their objection (v. 17a) cites a common proverb, "Those who

113. See Bruce J. Malina and Richard L. Rohrbaugh, *A Social-Science Commentary on the Synoptic Gospels* (Philadelphia: Fortress, 1992) 189-90.

114. See Ibid., 191-92.

are well have no need of a physician." The second half applies the proverb to Jesus' own ministry: He did not come for the righteous. In order to appreciate the challenge posed by this response, one must take "the righteous" as a reference to persons who are sincerely attempting to follow the way of life set forth in the Law (cf. Psalm 1). The label "sinners" designates persons who deliberately reject or flaunt the Law. The Old Testament frequently describes the "wicked" as persons who think that God's judgment does not apply to them. The presence of Gentiles, Greco-Roman culture, and foreign rulers posed additional problems of assimilation for righteous Jews. Although suspected injustice seems to be the major reason for classifying toll collectors as sinners, their ties to the ruling authorities may have added to the general suspicion about them. Such persons could hardly be expected to observe the ritual requirements surrounding food and meals.

Nor do the "wicked" have any concern for religious matters. They do not belong to the crowds that came to Jesus. Instead, Jesus seeks them out. This activity defines a new meaning for the "coming of the Lord." As we have seen, the common expectation was that the righteous who suffered oppression at the hands of the wicked would be delivered and their oppressors punished. Jesus redefined the coming of God's rule as the time of salvation, when people are freed from the power of Satan. They are healed, and their sins are forgiven. In this story, Jesus goes even further. He seeks out those whom society considers evil. He accepts their hospitality and with it the complex, reciprocal obligations that go with such a relationship. Scholars often describe Jesus as a person who sought to break down the barriers that existed in his time. Certainly, the offer of forgiveness and table fellowship to such persons here is just as radical as the healing and forgiveness of sin in the previous episode.

REFLECTIONS

1. The story of Levi's call shows that no occupation makes one less a disciple of Jesus. Businesspeople in the parish often make remarks that show they think their occupations make them "less holy" than others who are farmers, teachers, health-care workers, or involved in a profession concerned with assisting people in some direct way. Jesus looks beyond the social prejudices against toll collectors to call forth the disciple in Levi.

2. Meals play an important role in identifying the new community that is beginning to form around Jesus' preaching. The meals described so far in Mark follow a call to discipleship. Peter and Andrew became disciples. After Jesus healed Peter's mother-in-law, she was able to serve them a meal, and her participation suggests that Peter's whole family supported Jesus' mission. Now that Levi has been included in the circle of disciples, he invites his friends to a banquet, which Jesus attends.[115] These meal scenes contribute to a Christian understanding of the two meals that define their community: the Lord's Supper and the heavenly banquet that will be celebrated when the kingdom is fully realized (Mark 14:17-26).

We should take care to make our celebrations the occasion for healing, for reconciliation, for breaking down barriers that exclude others, and even for reaching out to invite others to discover God's presence in our midst. The task is not easily accomplished, as Paul's experience with the Corinthians demonstrates (1 Cor 11:17-34). The Corinthians permitted the Lord's Supper to become an opportunity for the wealthy members of the church to demonstrate their superiority over its poor members.

115. Readers may be intended to see that banquet as a celebration of Levi's call to discipleship. See Robert A. Guelich, *Mark 1–8:26*, WBC 34A (Dallas: Word, 1989) 101.

Mark 2:18-28, Jesus Defends His Disciples

¹⁸Now John's disciples and the Pharisees were fasting. Some people came and asked Jesus, "How is it that John's disciples and the disciples of the Pharisees are fasting, but yours are not?"

¹⁹Jesus answered, "How can the guests of the bridegroom fast while he is with them? They cannot, so long as they have him with them. ²⁰But the time will come when the bridegroom will be taken from them, and on that day they will fast.

²¹"No one sews a patch of unshrunk cloth on an old garment. If he does, the new piece will pull away from the old, making the tear worse. ²²And no one pours new wine into old wineskins. If he does, the wine will burst the skins, and both the wine and the wineskins will be ruined. No, he pours new wine into new wineskins."

²³One Sabbath Jesus was going through the grainfields, and as his disciples walked along, they began to pick some heads of grain. ²⁴The Pharisees said to him, "Look, why are they doing what is unlawful on the Sabbath?"

²⁵He answered, "Have you never read what David did when he and his companions were hungry and in need? ²⁶In the days of Abiathar the high priest, he entered the house of God and ate the consecrated bread, which is lawful only for priests to eat. And he also gave some to his companions."

²⁷Then he said to them, "The Sabbath was made for man, not man for the Sabbath. ²⁸So the Son of Man is Lord even of the Sabbath."

18Now John's disciples and the Pharisees were fasting; and people^a came and said to him, "Why do John's disciples and the disciples of the Pharisees fast, but your disciples do not fast?" ¹⁹Jesus said to them, "The wedding guests cannot fast while the bridegroom is with them, can they? As long as they have the bridegroom with them, they cannot fast. ²⁰The days will come when the bridegroom is taken away from them, and then they will fast on that day.

21"No one sews a piece of unshrunk cloth on an old cloak; otherwise, the patch pulls away from it, the new from the old, and a worse tear is made. ²²And no one puts new wine into old wineskins; otherwise, the wine will burst the skins, and the wine is lost, and so are the skins; but one puts new wine into fresh wineskins."^b

23One sabbath he was going through the grainfields; and as they made their way his disciples began to pluck heads of grain. ²⁴The Pharisees said to him, "Look, why are they doing what is not lawful on the sabbath?" ²⁵And he said to them, "Have you never read what David did when he and his companions were hungry and in need of food? ²⁶He entered the house of God, when Abiathar was high priest, and ate the bread of the Presence, which it is not lawful for any but the priests to eat, and he gave some to his companions." ²⁷Then he said to them, "The sabbath was made for humankind, and not humankind for the sabbath; ²⁸so the Son of Man is lord even of the sabbath."

^aGk *they* ^bOther ancient authorities lack *but one puts new wine into fresh wineskins*

COMMENTARY

The next two episodes begin with questions about the behavior of Jesus' disciples. They eat when others fast (2:18-22) and pluck grain to eat when others would observe the sabbath prohibition against the work of preparing food (2:23-28). Jesus defends their actions by insisting that the conventional rules do not apply. Both cases involve issues about which individual Jewish teachers might differ. Mark's presentation of the two traditional controversy stories suggests that while Christians have adopted the practice of fasting, they do not consider themselves bound to observe the Jewish sabbath regulations. (Matthew 6:16-18 distinguishes the Christian practice of fasting from that of the Jews.) Christians do not adopt visible signs of fasting, such as torn clothing, since God knows the piety of a person's heart.

The difference between fasting and sabbath observance would have been critical to Mark's audience of Gentile Christians. Others do not need to observe that persons are fasting. If non-Jews began to observe the well-known Jewish sabbath rules, then others would be affected by their change in behavior.[116] To Christians, who were already experiencing persecution, the conclusions drawn from these stories about Jesus and the sabbath had important implications. For Jesus' Jewish audience, the question was not whether to observe the sabbath but what constituted sabbath observance.

2:18-22. The pericope on fasting combines a pronouncement story that rejects fasting (vv. 18-19*a*), an affirmation that fasting will be appropriate after Jesus' death (vv. 19*b*-20), and two proverbs, which defend the need for new practices to apply to the time of Jesus (vv. 21-22). The coming kingdom has brought new experience of salvation in healing and forgiveness. The opening question, which raises the difference between Jesus' practice and that of John the Baptist (v. 18), reminds readers that Jesus is the one who comes after the Baptist to inaugurate the new age.

The Law requires fasting only on the Day of Atonement (Lev 16:1-34; 23:26-32; Num 29:7-11), although fasts might be declared in times of national emergency (Esth 4:16; Isa 58:3-6; Jer 3:6-9; Joel 1:14; 2:15; Jonah 3:5) or as a personal expression of supplication, mourning, or repentance (1 Sam 1:7-8; 2 Sam 3:35; 12:21; 1 Kgs 21:27; Neh 1:4; Dan 9:3). Fasting, prayer, and almsgiving were signs of a righteous person (cf. Tob 12:8-9). The Pharisees were said to fast twice a week (Luke 18:12; *Did.* 8.1). Therefore, outsiders expect Jesus' disciples to observe the pious custom of fasting as do the members of other Jewish sects devoted to holiness.

The people's question treats Jesus as a prophet or religious teacher on the same level as John the Baptist. But Mark's readers know that Jesus is more than that. He fulfills the hope for a time of salvation. The use of wedding and banquet imagery to symbolize the presence of salvation is familiar from the OT. Jesus' reply by counterexample fits a common form of oral debate, using analogies to demonstrate the absurdity of an opponent's proposal. No one thinks of fasting while a wedding feast is in progress (v. 19*a*). Since Mark understands the "bridegroom" to refer to Jesus, a somber note appears in the celebration, for Jesus will be taken away. In fact, readers soon learn that Jesus' enemies are plotting his death (3:6). After Jesus' death, his disciples will have opportunity to fast (v. 20). The expression "on that day" creates difficulty for those who assume that Mark intends the two days of fasting (Wednesday and Friday) later adopted by Christians (*Did.* 8:1). The expression may designate simply the mourning appropriate to the day of Jesus' death. Other exegetes point out that the Christian fast days were not tightly linked to the death of Jesus.[117]

The *Gospel of Thomas* (104) contains a variation of the challenge and response that generalized the question. Encouraged to fast by unnamed persons (perhaps the disciples), Jesus first rejects the proposal, because it appears to suggest that he is a sinner. Then he replies that they may fast when the bridegroom leaves. This version appears to be a later development, since it lacks the concrete connection with the ministries of Jesus and John the Baptist. The christology of Jesus as the one whose ministry inaugurates the new age of salvation has been replaced by one that emphasizes the sinlessness of Jesus as the divine revealer.

From a social perspective, the counterquestion about the bridegroom sets those who propose fasting in a negative light. Since fasting was a public gesture of penance or mourning, guests who fasted during a wedding would appear to disapprove of the marriage. Their behavior would be perceived as a serious insult to the host.[118]

Two further analogies shift the focus to the absurdity of trying to combine the new with the old. An attempt to patch a garment with unshrunk cloth or to put new wine in old skins results in even worse loss. The sayings about the patch and the wineskin are examples of proverbial wisdom.[119] The conclusion emphasizes the necessity

---

116. On sabbath observance as a well-known feature of Jewish behavior, see Louis Feldman, *Jew and Gentile in the Ancient World* (Princeton: Princeton University Press, 1993) 158-67.

117. So Joseph A. Fitzmyer, *The Gospel According to Luke I–IX*, AB 32 (Garden City, N.Y.: Doubleday, 1981) 599.

118. See Malina and Rohrbaugh, *Social-Science Commentary*, 194.

119. These proverbs appear in a different collection of proverbial sayings in *Gospel of Thomas* 47.

of what is new. The reader learns that Jesus cannot be comprehended by the inherited religious categories.

2:23-28. The dispute over sabbath observance takes the challenge to an area of Jewish law that was widely known among Gentiles. Since details of what is required to keep the sabbath were not specified in the Law, different teachers might disagree over whether the disciples are violating the Law. If picking off the heads of grain is considered reaping or harvesting, then the disciples violate the Law (Exod 34:21; *Jub.* 2:29-30; 50:6-13). Once again, others hold Jesus responsible for determining the behavior of his disciples. The response begins with a counterexample (vv. 25-26), followed by statements about the purpose of the sabbath (v. 27) and the authority of the Son of Man (v. 28).

The counterexample moves from a greater to a lesser case: David's violation of the sanctuary and priestly privilege to feed his men (1 Sam 21:1-6). This analogy suggests that the disciples were picking off the grain in order to eat it. The Markan version adds details to the story that make it a more appropriate analogy to Jesus and his disciples. David had his companions with him and sought to satisfy their hunger, so he went into the sanctuary and took the bread. If David could commit such a sacrilege on behalf of his followers, no one should accuse Jesus' disciples of being law breakers.[120]

The generalization that follows provides a principle, which covers both cases, illustrating the humanitarian intent of the Law. The argument was not foreign to Judaism. Individual and human emergencies could always take precedence over sabbath rules (e.g., 1 Macc 2:39-41; 2 Macc 5:19). Severe hunger might constitute such an emergency. Although such an explanation might be advanced for this story prior to its inclusion in the Gospel, its present context makes the emergency explanation implausible. The reader has heard of dining in Levi's house and of disciples who do not fast, so hunger is not a probable motive within that context. Therefore, the generalization (v. 27) appears to argue that any per-

ceived human need justifies suspension of sabbath rules.

Mark has already introduced the issue of Jesus' authority in connection with healing (2:10). The previous episode contrasts Jesus and his disciples with disciples of John the Baptist. This one sets Jesus as a teacher over against the Pharisees. Although explicit references to Jesus as "Son of David" do not appear until Jesus approaches Jerusalem for the passion (10:48), Mark's account of the OT episode focuses on David as the central actor. Indirectly, Jesus associates himself with David.[121] However, Jesus is greater than David (Mark 12:35-37). The generalizing conclusion indicates that Jesus has done more than resolve a particular problem of sabbath observance. The gnomic saying in v. 27 may have been added to the pericope during its oral transmission. It enunciates a general principle for evaluating sabbath rules, which is not inherently linked to either the grain plucking episode or the statement about the Son of Man, which follows.[122]

The original episode may have originated in the ministry of Jesus. The point of the gnomic saying in verse 27 is not that human beings can determine what they should do with regard to the sabbath. Rather, it states an authoritative interpretation of God's intention in giving the Law.[123] The final saying makes the christological implications of the story and its application evident. Scholars are divided over whether the Son of Man saying originated with Mark or had already been attached to the story. Although the Aramaic expression "son of man" can be used as a generic term, the view that v. 28 is merely a reformulation of v. 27 and asserts human sovereignty over the sabbath does not fit the christological interests of the Markan narrative.[124] This conclusion underlines the references to Jesus' authority that dominate the chapter. The authority to determine religious practice forms a piece with the authority

120. See Damià Roure, *Jesús y la Figura de David en Mc 2,23-26*, AnBib 124 (Rome: Pontificio Istituto Biblico, 1990) 13-32. Roure examines other examples in which David was credited with the ability to establish rulings on the Law.

121. See Paul Achtemeier, "He Taught Them Many Things": Reflections on Markan Christology," *CBQ* 42 (1980) 471. Mark follows his practice of transforming claims about Jesus into sayings about the Son of Man by adding verse 28. Roure argues that Chronicles treats David as a figure like Moses. Consequently, David can issue commandments concerning the Law. David was also understood to speak with prophetic authority (*Jesús y la Figura de David*, 39-50, 78-79. See also 11QPs³ 27,11).

122. See Joachim Gnilka, *Das Evangelium nach Markus. 1 Teilband Mk 1–8, 26*, EKKNT II (Zurich: Benziger, 1978) 1:119-21.

123. See Rudolph Pesch, *Das Markusevangelium I. Teil*, HTKNT II (Freiburg: Herder, 1977) 1:183-85.

124. See Guelich, *Mark*, 124-26.

to forgive sin on earth, since it determines the meaning of sin in the context of commandments about worship. Jesus' concern for sinners shows that he will not establish norms that isolate sinners from the righteous. The emphasis on the new in the pericope on fasting suggests that Jesus has authority to reject earlier tradition. Without the christological affirmation, developed in the dispute over forgiveness (vv. 5-10), that Jesus' authority cannot be distinguished from that of God, such an assertion would be blasphemous. The following story, which also takes place on the sabbath (3:1-5), illustrates that Jesus does not intend to abolish sabbath observance as such. Rather, he insists that the principle of doing good should govern behavior on the sabbath.

Some interpreters suggest that the overriding focus of these stories lies in the urgency of Jesus' mission to preach the kingdom. The disciples pluck grain to eat because they are on the way to preach the gospel. They cannot remain at home, where their food would have been prepared the previous day.[125] The fasting episode signifies that, because they are with Jesus, the disciples act as though the kingdom of God is present.[126]

125. Ibid., 127.
126. See Joanna Dewey, *Markan Public Debate: Literary Technique, Concentric Structure and Theology in Mark 1:1–3:6*, SBLDS 48 (Chico, Calif.: Scholars Press, 1981) 119.

REFLECTIONS

As was the case in the question of eating with sinners, the issues in these examples concern what was considered appropriate behavior for a religious teacher and his disciples. Even the sabbath violation suggested by the grain-picking episode can be disputed. Accustomed to pluralism and individualism in religion, most modern readers applaud Jesus' freedom of actions and presume that the opponents are narrow-minded bigots. Yet, Jesus sets aside neither fasting nor sabbath observance completely. Fasting, which is inappropriate when Jesus is present, will have its place after his death. Sabbath rules have a humanitarian purpose, which should be respected.

1. This passage raises different issues for Christian readers today than it would have in a society accustomed to regulating behavior according to religious traditions. Does freedom from stipulated fasts mean that Christians need never consider fasting and penance necessary to their relationship with God? Many people today are accustomed to donating the cost of one meal to groups that aid the hungry around the world. Fasting as an expression of charity and solidarity with human suffering should certainly be part of any Christian spirituality. Motivated by economic reasons, the secular legal protection conventionally accorded the Christian sabbath (Sunday "blue" laws) has been removed either partially or completely. Christians find themselves faced with difficult choices. Should they or their children participate in sports, activities, and jobs that routinely interfere with the weekly times for worship, religious instruction, or family activities? Do religious leaders have the responsibility to guarantee that our society put a priority on human spiritual needs over economic gain?

2. Mark's emphasis on Jesus' authority raises another issue for today's Christians. We are most comfortable with the universalizing interpretation of v. 27, which suggests that persons are free to establish their own approach to the sabbath. A more restrictive interpretation of the pericope sees Jesus as the one who is Lord of the sabbath. Thus Christians who acknowledge Jesus as Lord should keep the sabbath in the same spirit that Jesus exhibits in these stories. The parishioner who has only recently been released from the hospital should not feel compelled to attend church. But those who never consider corporate worship an important part of faith should reconsider whether Jesus is Lord for them.

Mark 3:1-6, Doing Good on the Sabbath

NIV

3 Another time he went into the synagogue, and a man with a shriveled hand was there. ²Some of them were looking for a reason to accuse Jesus, so they watched him closely to see if he would heal him on the Sabbath. ³Jesus said to the man with the shriveled hand, "Stand up in front of everyone."

⁴Then Jesus asked them, "Which is lawful on the Sabbath: to do good or to do evil, to save life or to kill?" But they remained silent.

⁵He looked around at them in anger and, deeply distressed at their stubborn hearts, said to the man, "Stretch out your hand." He stretched it out, and his hand was completely restored. ⁶Then the Pharisees went out and began to plot with the Herodians how they might kill Jesus.

NRSV

3 Again he entered the synagogue, and a man was there who had a withered hand. ²They watched him to see whether he would cure him on the sabbath, so that they might accuse him. ³And he said to the man who had the withered hand, "Come forward." ⁴Then he said to them, "Is it lawful to do good or to do harm on the sabbath, to save life or to kill?" But they were silent. ⁵He looked around at them with anger; he was grieved at their hardness of heart and said to the man, "Stretch out your hand." He stretched it out, and his hand was restored. ⁶The Pharisees went out and immediately conspired with the Herodians against him, how to destroy him.

COMMENTARY

Jesus returns to the synagogue at Capernaum, where another conflict over sabbath observance ensues. His first appearance in that synagogue (1:21-22) led the crowd to contrast the authority of his teaching with that of the scribes. Since Mark 2:28 has just affirmed Jesus' authority over the sabbath, the incident that follows demonstrates that authority. It also introduces a new level of hostility against Jesus. Unlike the previous episode, the miracle itself does not involve any violation of sabbath law; the man in this passage is healed as soon as he obeys Jesus' command to stretch out his hand. Nor is the principle expressed by Jesus' words to his adversaries problematic. When doing good is a matter of saving someone's life, no one would dispute the necessity of action. The apocryphal *Gospel of the Nazareans,* which recognizes the fact that the healing of a withered hand might not appear to be a life-and-death issue, portrays the man as a stone mason, who needs both hands in order to earn a living.[127] Modern exegetes often follow a similar

line and argue that the perceived offense lies in Jesus' performing a miracle without a compelling reason to act on the sabbath. That reading ignores the fact that Jesus does nothing to break the sabbath rest. His only offense lies in words. The question he poses to his opponents about whether it is "lawful to do good or to do harm on the sabbath, to save life or to kill," would not have been disputed by any rabbi. Doing good and saving life always take precedence over sabbath obligations. There is no evidence to support the assumption that Jews of Jesus' day were such rigid legalists that they had forgotten this principle.[128]

This objection makes it difficult to reconstruct a controversy from the life of Jesus in this particular episode. Structurally, the episode in 3:1-6 has been constructed to parallel the one with which this series opens, the healing of the paralytic (2:1-12). In both cases a healing serves to evoke controversy, the result of which is the determination of Jesus' opponents to seek his death. In the first case, he was accused of blas-

---

127. See frag. 10 in Wilhelm Schneemelcher, ed., *New Testament Apocrypha,* vol. 1: *Gospels and Related Writings,* trans. R. McL. Wilson, rev. ed. (Louisville: Westminster/John Knox Press, 1991) 160.

128. See Guelich, *Mark,* 134-36; cf. Gnilka, *Das Evagelium nach Markus,* 1:127.

phemy. Now they are determined to see him die.[129]

Mark sets the scene quite differently from the previous sabbath controversy. Some people in the synagogue are watching Jesus and hoping he will perform a healing that they can use to bring a charge against him. Mark's reader knows that Jesus is able to discern the unspoken malice in persons around him (2:8). Jesus forces the issue by calling the man out from the crowd and challenging his opponents to state the truth about the sabbath law. Silence in this instance is evidence of a plot. Jesus frames the question in a way that reveals the ulterior motives at work: "to do harm, to kill" (v. 4). Anyone who truly cares about the Law will agree with Jesus. The strong emotional reaction on Jesus' part—anger and sadness at the people's hard heartedness—highlights the extent to which Jesus' opponents have cut themselves off from any possibility of accepting Jesus' word. This reaction is more clearly motivated by the hostility being directed against Jesus in this episode than the earlier example of anger associated with the cleansing of the leper (1:43).

Some exegetes suggest that v. 6 was added to an earlier story by the evangelist. Initially, those who are seeking a reason to accuse Jesus are anonymous (v. 2). If Mark has formulated this episode as a conclusion to the series, then the reader would assume that "they" refers to the opponents of the earlier episode, the Pharisees, who are already determined to destroy Jesus. This note warns readers that Jesus' ministry will lead to death. Pharisees had no political authority during this period. Retained by others as advisors, the Pharisees were able to gain influence in powerful circles.[130] The Herodians were not a well-defined political party. Used as a general designation, the expression would appear to refer to those wealthy aristocrats who are friends and retainers of Herod Antipas. Although Hellenizing influences in court circles would make association with such persons, unusual for observant Pharisees, some members of the Pharisee party were from those circles. In Luke 13:31 Pharisees associated with Herod Antipas come to warn Jesus about the hostility of Herod.[131]

Mark's readers know that John the Baptist has already been imprisoned by Herod. The Pharisees in question are engaged in a political plot against Jesus, who exposed their malice when he challenged them to interpret the Law and then healed the man without breaking the Law. The episode demonstrates Jesus' superiority over his opposition. He recognizes their intentions. Although they only plot against Jesus on the sabbath, they are determined to "do evil or kill"—clear violations of the Law. The next cycle of controversies with religious authorities will make the implied accusation more explicit. The Pharisees and scribes have no concern for God's will. They substitute human traditions for the truth, which comes from God (7:8, 13).[132] Readers accustomed to the dynamics of shame and honor in ancient societies would recognize that public exposure humiliates the opposition. By consciously evoking a controversy with the religious authorities, Jesus has put himself at risk. Those whose honor has been challenged must seek to restore it. Thus Mark's readers might anticipate the Pharisees' response: eradicate the one who has caused their shame.[133]

---

129. See Guelich, *Mark,* 132-33.

130. See Anthony J. Saldarini, "The Social Class of the Pharisees in Mark," in *The Social World of Formative Christianity and Judaism: Essays in Tribute to Howard Clark Kee,* ed. J. Neusner et al. (Philadelphia: Fortress, 1988) 69-77.

131. Luke generally treats the Pharisees as greedy and hostile; hence, the tradition of friendly Pharisees is somewhat surprising. See Sean Freyne, *Galilee, Jesus and the Gospels: Literary Approaches and Historical Investigations* (Philadelphia: Fortress, 1988) 100-102.

132. See ibid., 45; Elizabeth S. Malbon, "The Jewish Leaders in the Gospel of Mark: A Literary Study of Marcan Characterization," *JBL* 108 (1989) 265-66.

133. See Malina and Rohrbaugh, *Social-Science Commentary,* 196.

REFLECTIONS

1. Christians have a special obligation to avoid anti-Semitic stereotyping of the Pharisees and other religious authorities as bound by intolerant legalism. Even some scholarly commentaries on the controversy stories rely on improper generalizations about Jewish legalism. The Pharisees, scribes, and other religious authorities performed a socially necessary function of interpreting the Law so that people could use it to shape their lives. Disputes over proper interpretation of the Law are as necessary a part of their social and religious landscape as are Supreme Court decisions in the United States.

2. These stories use religious and political authorities as foils to Jesus. Their resistance provides an occasion for Jesus to demonstrate his insight into human character and the superiority of his teaching. But they also raise a disturbing historical possibility. Jesus' mission involves shaking up the strongly held religious and social convictions of his time. Often Christians today think that Jesus disturbed his contemporaries because of their lack of humanitarian concern for others. After viewing a film on the death of Jesus, a group of eighth graders was asked to tell who they had identified with: the disciples, the Jews, or the Romans. "None of them," the youth insisted. "Because they all were jerks; just out for themselves. Jesus was the only good person in the film." Challenged to explain why people in the film wanted to kill a person who was so clearly non-violent and much weaker than his enemies, the youth were more perplexed. "God told Jesus that he had to die," several suggested. Then one of them noticed that Jesus always insisted on the truth in the movie. "Truth upsets people," he volunteered. This story can be read as an example of that way of understanding Jesus.

Mark 3:7-12, Crowds Flock to Jesus

NIV	NRSV
⁷Jesus withdrew with his disciples to the lake, and a large crowd from Galilee followed. ⁸When they heard all he was doing, many people came to him from Judea, Jerusalem, Idumea, and the regions across the Jordan and around Tyre and Sidon. ⁹Because of the crowd he told his disciples to have a small boat ready for him, to keep the people from crowding him. ¹⁰For he had healed many, so that those with diseases were pushing forward to touch him. ¹¹Whenever the evil*ᵃ* spirits saw him, they fell down before him and cried out, "You are the Son of God." ¹²But he gave them strict orders not to tell who he was.	⁷Jesus departed with his disciples to the sea, and a great multitude from Galilee followed him; ⁸hearing all that he was doing, they came to him in great numbers from Judea, Jerusalem, Idumea, beyond the Jordan, and the region around Tyre and Sidon. ⁹He told his disciples to have a boat ready for him because of the crowd, so that they would not crush him; ¹⁰for he had cured many, so that all who had diseases pressed upon him to touch him. ¹¹Whenever the unclean spirits saw him, they fell down before him and shouted, "You are the Son of God!" ¹²But he sternly ordered them not to make him known.
a11 Greek unclean; also in verse 30	

COMMENTARY

A summary account recapitulates motifs that have been repeated several times.[134] Jesus cannot appear in public without being pressed by great crowds of persons seeking to be healed. In oral composition, repetitions provide variations on previous versions. This passage expands the range of people who come to Jesus. His reputation has spread beyond the cities and towns of Galilee to include Judea, Jerusalem, Idumea, the Transjordan, and the coastal towns of Tyre and Sidon (vv. 7-8). Although Jesus has not preached in these areas, his reputation has spread to them already. Not all testimony to

134. Attempts to use these accounts to determine the structure of Mark's narrative require too many exceptions to be persuasive. See the discussion in Charles W. Hedrick, "The Role of Summary Statements in the Composition of the Gospel of Mark: A Dialogue with Karl Schmidt and Norman Perrin," *NovT* 26 (1984) 294-96. The summary statements are clear indicators of the oral style of Markan composition. See Christopher Bryan, *A Preface to Mark: Notes on the Gospel in Its Literary and Cultural Settings* (New York: Oxford, 1993) 131-32; Dewey, "Oral Methods of Structuring Narrative in Mark," *Int* 43 (1989) 36.

Jesus' identity is welcome, however. Once again, Mark tells the reader that Jesus silences the demons, who know that Jesus is Son of God (v. 12; cf. 1:24).

Several elements are involved in this silencing of the demons. The pre-Markan exorcism stories would have had the demons use the exorcist's name in an attempt to ward off his power. Silencing them belongs to the exorcism rite as such.[135] Mark has used the ritual silencing of demons to reject their testimony as evidence for Jesus' identity. Readers already know that Jesus is the Son of God, but the controversy stories show us that those opposed to Jesus have no interest in God's will. Instead, they accuse the one who possesses God's powers of blasphemy (2:7).

The crowds who press around Jesus for healing are not necessarily believers or disciples. The large crowds also explain the need for Jesus to select more disciples as apostles to participate in

his mission (vv. 13-14). The unusual word used to describe the crowd, "multitude" ($\pi\lambda\hat{\eta}\theta\circ\varsigma$ *plēthos*), combined with the expanded geographical notice, demonstrates that Jesus' influence extends further than that of John the Baptist.[136]

The necessity for Jesus to retreat to a boat indicates that the large crowds are physically endangering his life (v. 9). The suffering, which also belongs to Jesus' mission as Son of God, forms a sharp contradiction to the picture of Jesus as the one who has power over the demons and the other forces of the cosmos. Mark has reformulated the silencing command in v. 12 to suggest that Jesus had to exorcise demons in order to keep them from revealing that he is the Son of God.[137] Although their confession is not false, it is not appropriate without the cross.

135. See Gerd Theissen, *The Miracle Stories of the Early Christian Tradition,* trans. Francis McDonagh (Philadelphia: Fortress, 1983) 140-45.

136. See Robert H. Gundry, *Mark: A Commentary on His Apology for the Cross* (Grand Rapids: Eerdmans, 1993) 157.

137. See Robert A. Guelich, *Mark 1–8:26,* WBC 34A (Dallas: Word, 1989) 149.

Mark 3:13-19, Choosing the Twelve

NIV

13Jesus went up on a mountainside and called to him those he wanted, and they came to him. 14He appointed twelve—designating them apostles[a]—that they might be with him and that he might send them out to preach 15and to have authority to drive out demons. 16These are the twelve he appointed: Simon (to whom he gave the name Peter); 17James son of Zebedee and his brother John (to them he gave the name Boanerges, which means Sons of Thunder); 18Andrew, Philip, Bartholomew, Matthew, Thomas, James son of Alphaeus, Thaddaeus, Simon the Zealot 19and Judas Iscariot, who betrayed him.

a14 Some manuscripts do not have *designating them apostles.*

NRSV

13He went up the mountain and called to him those whom he wanted, and they came to him. 14And he appointed twelve, whom he also named apostles,[a] to be with him, and to be sent out to proclaim the message, 15and to have authority to cast out demons. 16So he appointed the twelve:[b] Simon (to whom he gave the name Peter); 17James son of Zebedee and John the brother of James (to whom he gave the name Boanerges, that is, Sons of Thunder); 18and Andrew, and Philip, and Bartholomew, and Matthew, and Thomas, and James son of Alphaeus, and Thaddaeus, and Simon the Cananaean, 19and Judas Iscariot, who betrayed him.

Then he went home;

a Other ancient authorities lack *whom he also named apostles*
b Other ancient authorities lack *So he appointed the twelve*

COMMENTARY

A sudden geographical transition from the sea to the mountain marks an important shift in the narrative. Mountains have a particular significance as places of prayer (6:46) and divine revelation

(9:2, 9). Jesus' selection of a special group of twelve from the larger group of disciples (vv. 13-15), along with the list of their names (vv. 16*b*-19), was an established tradition. Parallel references to the Twelve as apostles (vv. 14*b*, 16*a*) may have been formulated by the evangelist to tie together two independent pieces of tradition.[138] Traditionally, the number twelve makes this group representative of the tribes of Israel, and it indicates that Jesus has come to restore Israel. When the apostles are finally sent on a successful mission (6:7-13, 30-31), it becomes clear that their activity makes the kingdom present as effectively as does Jesus' ministry.[139]

For Mark, this group has been appointed to accompany Jesus and share his mission. Jesus not only commissions the Twelve to preach, but also confers on them authority over demons (vv. 14-15). This notice adds to the growing picture of Jesus' divinity. Some interpreters have suggested that "being with" Jesus and "being sent out" are contradictory. However, the Twelve have a special relationship with Jesus, which ensures that they are his representatives. Before they actually embark on that mission, the Twelve will receive special instruction from Jesus (cf. 4:10, 34).

The list of names probably came to Mark from tradition. He may have rearranged it to place the three examples of renaming first. The substitution of "Peter" (Πέτρος [*Petros*] from πέτρα *petra,* "rock"—derived from the Aramaic nickname "Cephas" or "rock") for "Simon," probably originated with Jesus. Paul's letters show that it was accepted as Simon's name by Jewish Christians in Jerusalem (Gal 1:18) and Corinth (1 Cor 1:12).[140] Since "rock" appears more appropriate to Peter's role in reestablishing the community of disciples after the resurrection (cf. Luke 24:34; 1 Cor 15:3-5), some exegetes have suggested that the change in name from "Simon" to "Peter" should be linked to Peter's vision of the risen Lord.[141]

The nickname given the sons of Zebedee, "sons of thunder" (Βοανηργές *Boanērges*), did not stick. The three disciples will later form an inner group who accompany Jesus apart from the rest (5:37; 9:2; 14:33). The list of the Twelve does not include "Levi, the son of Alphaeus" (Mark 2:14) but does identify a second James as "son of Alphaeus" (v. 18). The epithet may have moved from one individual to the other. Some interpreters suggest that Levi was not called to be one of the Twelve, but was one of the larger group of disciples who followed Jesus. A simpler explanation for the divergence in the two names would be to assume that both variants had become attached to traditional accounts of the calling of disciples prior to Mark's use of these stories.

The final notice has an ominous ring (v. 19). Judas Iscariot will betray Jesus. The plots being hatched by Jesus' enemies (v. 6) provide a narrative context for such betrayal. Its actual fulfillment does not occur until the conclusion of the Gospel (14:1-2, 10-11).

138. See Rudolph Pesch, *Das Markusevangelium I. Teil,* HTKNT II (Freiburg: Herder, 1977) 1:203.
139. See Gundry, *Mark,* 167-68.

140. Mark is careful to use Simon, Peter's given name, for the apostle prior to this incident and Peter after 3:16. See Mary Ann Tolbert, *Sowing the Gospel: Mark's World in Literary-Historical Perspective* (Minneapolis: Fortress, 1989) 145.
141. See Pesch, *Das Markusevangelius,*1:206. However, the tradition in John 1:42 also attributes the nickname to Jesus.

Mark 3:20-30, Jesus Is Charged with Demonic Possession

NIV	NRSV
[20]Then Jesus entered a house, and again a crowd gathered, so that he and his disciples were not even able to eat. [21]When his family heard about this, they went to take charge of him, for they said, "He is out of his mind." [22]And the teachers of the law who came down from Jerusalem said, "He is possessed by Beelzebub[a]! By the prince of demons he is driving out demons."	[20]and the crowd came together again, so that they could not even eat. [21]When his family heard it, they went out to restrain him, for people were saying, "He has gone out of his mind." [22]And the scribes who came down from Jerusalem said, "He has Beelzebul, and by the ruler of the demons he casts out demons." [23]And he called them to him, and spoke to them in parables, "How can Satan cast out Satan? [24]If a kingdom is divided against
a22 Greek Beezeboul or Beelzeboul	

NIV

²³So Jesus called them and spoke to them in parables: "How can Satan drive out Satan? ²⁴If a kingdom is divided against itself, that kingdom cannot stand. ²⁵If a house is divided against itself, that house cannot stand. ²⁶And if Satan opposes himself and is divided, he cannot stand; his end has come. ²⁷In fact, no one can enter a strong man's house and carry off his possessions unless he first ties up the strong man. Then he can rob his house. ²⁸I tell you the truth, all the sins and blasphemies of men will be forgiven them. ²⁹But whoever blasphemes against the Holy Spirit will never be forgiven; he is guilty of an eternal sin."

³⁰He said this because they were saying, "He has an evil spirit."

NRSV

itself, that kingdom cannot stand. ²⁵And if a house is divided against itself, that house will not be able to stand. ²⁶And if Satan has risen up against himself and is divided, he cannot stand, but his end has come. ²⁷But no one can enter a strong man's house and plunder his property without first tying up the strong man; then indeed the house can be plundered.

²⁸"Truly I tell you, people will be forgiven for their sins and whatever blasphemies they utter; ²⁹but whoever blasphemes against the Holy Spirit can never have forgiveness, but is guilty of an eternal sin"— ³⁰for they had said, "He has an unclean spirit."

COMMENTARY

As soon as Jesus returns home—i.e., to Capernaum—crowds gather around him. Just as the episode by the sea notes that the vast crowds endanger Jesus, so also in this case the crowd practically has Jesus and the disciples blockaded in the house (cf. 2:2). This time the evangelist tells us that Jesus and his apostles cannot even eat (v. 20).

This section contains two episodes, one embedded inside the other, a common technique of Markan composition. Jesus' relatives fear that he has lost his mind and come to get him (vv. 21, 31-35). Meanwhile, enemies among the Jerusalem scribes appear to accuse Jesus of being possessed (vv. 22-30).[142] They provide a formal, legal charge against Jesus: that he exercises satanic powers (vv. 21*b*-22). Since persons charged with doing magic could be either banished or executed, such suspicions could not be left unchecked.

3:21. Mark introduces the encounter between Jesus and the scribes with the note that Jesus' relatives intended to take him away by force (κρατῆσαι *kratēsai*; v. 21*a*). The encounter between Jesus and his family will resume after the charge of his using satanic powers has been an-

swered (vv. 31-35). In the second half of the episode, the question of Jesus' sanity is no longer mentioned. Once he has responded to the scribes, readers, at least, know that all of Jesus' activities are motivated by the Holy Spirit. Instead, his family are kept outside by the large crowd in and around the house. Jesus responds to the statement that they wish to see him by pointing to those around him. He insists that his true family are those who do the will of God (v. 35). Mark frequently alternates inside and outside, between those around Jesus and the crowds.[143] Opponents are always outside. Those who charge Jesus with being in league with Satan are outsiders, because they have rejected what comes from God. What about Jesus' family? Mark is responsible for bringing together vv. 21 and 31-35. The saying about their desire to see Jesus, stripped of the suspicion that he is possessed, does not place them in a negative light. Rather, it indicates the seriousness of Jesus' devotion to doing the will of God. With the addition of v. 21 and the insertion of the charge that he is in league with Satan, the tone of the incident becomes more negative. Jesus' relatives seem to harbor suspicions similar to those of the scribes.

3:22-27. Just as Jesus flushed out the scheming of those in the synagogue earlier, so also he

---

142. When two episodes are intertwined in Mark, they illuminate each other. In this case, Mark brings together two stories that involve reaction to Jesus' activity and the role of his disciples. See John Donahue, *Are You the Christ? The Trial Narrative in the Gospel of Mark,* SBLDS 10 (Missoula, Mont.: Scholars Press, 1973) 81.

143. See S. H. Smith, " 'Inside' and 'Outside' in Mark's Gospel," *ExpT* 102 (1991) 363-67.

now addresses the Jerusalem scribes. They do not confront Jesus directly. Instead, he calls them and speaks to them "in parables" (ἐν παραβολαῖς *en parabolais*; v. 23). The word for "parable" (παραβολή *parabolē*) refers to various forms of metaphoric speech, from riddles and proverbs to short narratives that illustrate a point of teaching.[144] In the next chapter, *parabolē* refers to the short narratives that illuminate the mystery of the kingdom of God. The examples given here are expanded proverbs. As a rhetorical device, proverbial sayings turn the tables against the opponent by showing that any intelligent person would recognize the absurdity of the opponent's view. Parables and proverbial sayings form a central element in the teaching of Jesus. Proverbs, riddles, and illustrative stories are fundamental to oral cultures. The memorable comparisons, stock characters, and contrasts fix the speaker's point in an audience's mind.[145] Since the proverbial retort does not convert the opposition to Jesus' point of view, some interpreters suggest that the element of judgment attached to the parables in Mark 4:10-12 belongs here as well.[146] Common wisdom condemns their malicious argument.

Jesus' opponents claimed that his power to cast out demons was a sign that Jesus had received his authority from the chief demonic power, Beelzebul. Readers familiar with the ancient magical texts might recognize that Jesus does not use the magical names and formulae associated with magicians. The demons had been using Jesus' name "Son of God" against him. Jesus repeatedly silences them with a word of command.[147] The argument given, however, does not employ this defense. Instead, v. 23 highlights the impossibility of what the scribes assume—that Satan could cast out himself. (Mark's readers know, of course, that the demons recognize that Jesus is the "Holy One of God," not one of them.) Proverbial sayings about divided kingdoms and households are also applied to the situation (vv. 24-25). Satan could not permit the rout of his forces to be carried out

by Jesus and expect to maintain his dominion over humans.

Instead, Jesus proposes a counterimage: robbing a strong man (v. 27). The only way to seize the goods of a powerful person is for someone stronger to tie him up. This example demonstrates the strength of the parable as metaphor. Jesus speaks indirectly about his own activity. He is no agent of Satan. His actions demonstrate that demonic powers are being broken up. Jesus is stronger than Satan and is able to bind Satan and raid his kingdom. Papyri of the time contain spells in which the exorcist uses the divine name to drive out demons.[148] Properly understood, Jesus' exorcisms are evidence that God's rule is becoming present in Jesus' ministry.

3:28-30. Mark concludes the episode with another saying of Jesus about the unforgivable sin. Variants of this saying occur in Q (Matt 12:31-32; Luke 12:10) and *The Gospel of Thomas* 104.[149] Mark uses these sayings to charge Jesus' opponents with being blasphemers themselves, since they are treating the Spirit of God as a satanic spirit (v. 30). Mark's conclusion to the episode in v. 30 makes it clear that the harsh judgment saying in v. 29, "whoever blasphemes against the Holy Spirit can never have forgiveness, but is guilty of an eternal sin," applies to the religious authorities who had come from Jerusalem to investigate Jesus. Most exegetes think that the saying about the "eternal sin" was formulated by a Christian prophet speaking in the name of Jesus. The Q form is a double-membered parallel saying, "If anyone speaks a word against the Son of Man, it can be forgiven him, but if he speaks against the Holy Spirit, it cannot be forgiven him."[150] Mark's formulation seems to have derived from a different tradition, which opened with the assertion that all sin could be forgiven human beings except that against the Holy Spirit.[151]

As an isolated saying from an early Christian prophet, this logion's significance cannot be precisely determined. Such a prophetic word must be directed to a concrete situation. Depending on the situation, the weight could fall on the fact

---

144. See Bernard Brandon Scott, *Hear Then the Parable: A Commentary on the Parables of Jesus* (Minneapolis: Fortress, 1989) 7-54. See also Robert C. Tannehill, "The Gospels and Narrative Literature," in this volume.

145. See Walter Ong, *Orality and Literacy* (New York: Methuen, 1982) 33-36.

146. See Joachim Gnilka, *Das Evangelium nach Markus. 1 Teilband Mk 1–8, 26*, EKKNT II (Zurich: Benziger, 1978) 1:149.

147. See Theissen, *Miracle Stories*, 141-42, 233.

148. See Gundry, *Mark*, 181.

149. See M. Eugene Boring, "The Unforgivable Sin Logion Mark III 28-29, Matt XII 31-32/Luke XII 10," *NovT* 18 (1977) 258-79.

150. Ibid., 267.

151. Ibid., 274-77.

that sins can be forgiven as long as people do not cut themselves off from the source of forgiveness, the Holy Spirit. Or it could fall on the second half of the logion, emphasizing that certain persons have cut themselves off from forgiveness. The latter might have originated as a prophetic word against those who were persecuting the community. Christians are exhorted to rely on the Holy Spirit when they are brought to trial for preaching the gospel (Mark 13:11).

Within the larger context of Mark's narrative, the two sayings sharpen the separation between those who accept Jesus' word and the opponents gathering against him. Jesus has demonstrated that God's forgiveness is offered to all humans (2:1-12). The crowd has recognized that a new power of God is at work and has praised God (2:12). Local scribes have accused Jesus of blasphemy (2:7); use of the term *blasphemy* (v. 29) reminds readers of that earlier accusation. When the Pharisees were looking to trap him, Jesus was angered by such hard heartedness (3:5). Now, he pronounces a word of judgment against such persons: They cannot be forgiven. The evangelist's comment in v. 30 shows that the judgment saying is directed against those who have charged Jesus with using Satan's power.

The opponents in all these stories are depicted as scribes and Pharisees—persons who claim to be concerned with observing God's Law. In this instance, the scribes are sent from Jerusalem. The presumption that Jerusalem authorities will investigate what occurs elsewhere also appears in accounts of the earliest church in Acts; Paul goes from Jerusalem to arrest Christians in Damascus (Acts 9:1-2), and apostles from Jerusalem regulate admission of new converts elsewhere (Acts 8:14-16; 15:14-30). Although there is no clear evidence that Jerusalem scribes regulated affairs in Galilean synagogues during Jesus' lifetime,[152] Mark has created a consistent picture of the malicious blindness of religious authorities. The Jerusalem scribes provide the link between local scribes and Pharisees and their charges against Jesus and the Jerusalem authorities. The latter will eventually bring about Jesus' death on charges of blasphemy (14:64).[153]

152. Sean Freyne (*Galilee, Jesus and the Gospels: Literary Approaches and Historical Investigations* [Philadelphia: Fortress, 1988] 210) is finally forced to conclude that Mark's tradition is correct. Scribal activity was centered in Jerusalem and spread from there to Galilean synagogues. But he admits that there is no early evidence for the social position of scribes in Galilee during this period. Synagogue evidence is also disappointingly rare.

153. See ibid., 47-52.

REFLECTIONS

1. Many readers find it difficult to imagine how Jesus' healings can lead to such hostile interpretations. Yet people today might be just as suspicious of someone with the dramatic mass appeal of Jesus. We might wonder whether the masses are being defrauded in some way. Ancient societies often used charges of magic to rein in persons whose extraordinary position, gifts, or behavior challenged the established order.[154] Many people prefer to maintain the traditional patterns in personal, family, or social life rather than make radical changes that might bring greater health or happiness to a troubled situation.

2. Here, Jesus takes an aggressive posture by exposing the malice and absurd premises of his accusers. The saying about the Holy Spirit reveals that more is at stake than Jesus' own personal feelings of honor or shame. What is at stake is the truth about the saving power of God at work in the ministry of Jesus. Since the saying is directed against those who are trying to destroy Jesus' authority with the crowds by typing him as satanic,[155] the "sin against the Holy Spirit" is not a special, reserved class of sin. The saying makes a statement about Jesus' enemies. Christians, who participate in the Holy Spirit from their baptism, should remember

154. The second-century Roman orator and novelist Apuleius left a record of his defense against the charge of practicing magic. Most of that defense avoids direct reference to the issue, although he does suggest that if his opponents really thought he had magic power, they would worry about the possibility that the angry magician would turn against them. See his *Apology,* chap. 26. See also Howard Clark Kee, *Medicine, Miracle and Magic in New Testament Times,* SNTSMS 55 (Cambridge: Cambridge University Press, 1986) 95-99.

155. On the prevalence of type casting and its relationship to social roles and authority in antiquity, see Bruce J. Malina and Richard L. Rohrbaugh, *A Social-Science Commentary on the Synoptic Gospels* (Philadelphia: Fortress, 1992) 200-201.

the words and examples of universal forgiveness. People who feel cut off from God or even imagine that they have committed this sin need a word of healing. Jesus came to bind Satan and set his victims free. The Holy One of God drives out spirits, which are set against God. Mark's narrative expresses the irony of the fact that some human beings are more closed to God's presence in Jesus than are the demons themselves.

Mark 3:31-35, Jesus' True Family

NIV	NRSV
31Then Jesus' mother and brothers arrived. Standing outside, they sent someone in to call him. 32A crowd was sitting around him, and they told him, "Your mother and brothers are outside looking for you."	31Then his mother and his brothers came; and standing outside, they sent to him and called him. 32A crowd was sitting around him; and they said to him, "Your mother and your brothers and sisters[a] are outside, asking for you." 33And he replied, "Who are my mother and my brothers?"
33"Who are my mother and my brothers?" he asked.	34And looking at those who sat around him, he said, "Here are my mother and my brothers!
34Then he looked at those seated in a circle around him and said, "Here are my mother and my brothers! 35Whoever does God's will is my brother and sister and mother."	35Whoever does the will of God is my brother and sister and mother."
	[a] Other ancient authorities lack *and sisters*

COMMENTARY

Mark now returns to the episode in which Jesus' relatives have come to take him away (v. 21). By introducing Jesus' family prior to the dispute over the agency behind Jesus' miracles, Mark creates the impression that the family's motives are hostile as well. Consequently, some interpreters have even suggested that the negative picture of Jesus' family is aimed at James, the brother of the Lord, the leader of the Jerusalem church (Acts 15:13; Gal 2:9). However, attempts to suggest a historical occasion for this narrative element seem inappropriate. Mark 6:1-6 treats persons from Nazareth who know Jesus with equal severity.[156] The issue is not opposition to Jerusalem but the danger of attachments to family, village, and traditional ties. Readers already know that Jesus' first disciples left family and occupation in order to follow him (1:16-20).[157]

Mark often has Jesus move from a public scene with opponents and crowds to an inside scene with his disciples and other followers. Consequently, the fact that his mother and brothers must call to Jesus from outside (v. 31) indicates that his family are not disciples. The narrative has already suggested that Jesus has moved away from his natural family by referring to Peter's house in Capernaum as the place to which Jesus comes home after preaching in surrounding regions (2:1). It is difficult to determine how much historical information lies behind these notices. They have an exemplary character for Markan Christians, who have detached themselves from their original families. Jesus defines *family* in terms of discipleship, "those who do the will of God" (v. 35).

Both the reference to Jesus' natural family and his redefinition of the family of disciples refer only to his mother and siblings, with no mention of Jesus' father. The description of Jesus' family in Mark 6:3 follows the same pattern. Jesus is described as "son of Mary"; several brothers are named and a general reference to sisters is included. The simplest explanation is that Mary's husband had died some time before. No reference

---

156. See Smith, " 'Inside' and 'Outside,' " 365.
157. Malina and Rohrbaugh, *Social-Science Commentary,* 202, suggest that the new Christian "fictive kin group" would have to supply the socioeconomic ties that its members lost as a result of their conversion.

to a father appears in connection with Peter and Andrew either. By contrast, James and John are working with their father when they answer Jesus' call and are identified as sons of Zebedee. Some interpreters find deep significance in the omission of a mention of a father. Only God is Father to the community of disciples. Jesus rejects the relationships of power and subordination that were invested in the father as the male head of an extended household that includes adult sons and their wives, just as he rejects the sociopolitical form of such relationships (Mark 10:41-45).

The interpreters who think that this pericope indicates hostility toward Jesus' family presume that tensions between Jewish and Gentile Christians were responsible for the judgment that Jesus' family were "outsiders" to his mission. One of the brothers, James, was a prominent leader in the Jerusalem community. He is linked by Paul to those Jewish Christians who expected Gentiles to be circumcised and adopt Jewish food restrictions (Gal 1:19; 2:1-12). And Paul alleges that people sent from James persuaded Peter, Barnabas, and other prominent members of the Antioch church to break off their accustomed table fellowship with Gentile believers (Gal 2:11-14). However, the tone of Mark's narrative does not suggest a violent break between Jesus and his family. Jesus shows those who refer to his family's presence that familial authority cannot be set above doing the will of God. As adult converts in a traditional society, most of Mark's audience had probably experienced such a crisis in their own families.

REFLECTIONS

1. The presence of women in Jesus' description of the new family of disciples distinguishes his followers from those who surrounded popular teachers of the Law or popular philosophical teachers. There, teacher-disciple relationships implied male teachers and followers. The household setting of the early community also facilitated participation by women. The realm of public testimony, preaching, and exorcising, remains the arena in which males engage in verbal combat with each other. This division between the public arena with its use of verbal combat as a means of gaining honor and the private household, which embraces women and children, is foreign to many modern readers. It is easier to look at the issues raised by this passage in terms of power and influence.

2. Neither Jesus nor any of his followers belongs among the powerful of their society. Jesus does not have the religious credentials of the scribes and Pharisees, especially those from Jerusalem. He certainly lacks any ties to the powerful aristocrats associated with the king, the so-called Herodians. Instead, Jesus draws on the proverbial wisdom and the religious instincts of very ordinary persons. By watching Jesus unmask the authorities and experts of their society, such persons learn their own value in the sight of God. They may have a better understanding of what it means to do the will of God than the experts from Jerusalem. In a society dominated by experts, people today constantly make decisions about how far they can trust the authorities. Sometimes wisdom lies in everyday common sense.

MARK 4:1-34, PARABLES OF THE KINGDOM

OVERVIEW

Jesus has just used parables, extended proverbial sayings, to defeat charges leveled against him (3:23-27). Although the parable illustrates the absurdity of the opposing view, it does not overcome the hard heartedness of those who are bringing accusations against Jesus. Only those who are already disciples of Jesus can appreciate the significance of his words. Mark now draws together several of Jesus' parables into an extended discourse.[158] These parables are more typical examples of the narrative parables of Jesus, in which brief stories drawn from common experiences take a drastic or surprising turn. The point of the parable lies in the reversal, the unusual or exaggerated image, or the new twist on an established theme in the story. As was true of the proverbial examples in the previous chapter, the narrative parables do not require elaborate allegorization to make their point. The unusual element in each parable challenges readers to imagine the new reality of the kingdom of God.

The ability to formulate striking images from everyday realities, such as we find in parables and proverbs, characterizes the teaching of Jesus.[159] The scale of the parables in Mark remains very much the world of Galilean villagers, among whom Jesus preached.

This section includes a statement about parables that seems to undermine their function as illustrations of Jesus' teaching grounded in everyday experience (4:10-12). Only the insiders get the point of the parables. This saying about the purpose of the parables may have been taken from tradition. It corresponds to another meaning of the Aramaic word for "parable" (משל *mās̆āl*), meaning a riddling or enigmatic saying. Any figurative or non-literal use of language depends on the ability of readers to recognize the fact that the image points to a reality that is not a literal statement of facts.[160] We have seen that the parables in the controversy stories perform a similar

function. The reader/disciple knows that Jesus' example proves his enemies wrong, but Jesus' opponents remain unconvinced. Thus it is not unreasonable to conclude that Jesus' parables always combine elements of clarity and hiddenness. Those disposed to respond positively to his message that the kingdom of God is near understand the parables as depictions of the new reality that Jesus makes possible. But those who are hostile to Jesus find the exaggeration or the unusual twists in the story either incomprehensible or offensive.

Mark sets this section of the Gospel alongside the Sea of Galilee. Earlier, Jesus escaped the press of the crowd by withdrawing in a boat (3:9). Now he goes out in the boat to teach the crowd on the shore (v. 1). Mark has composed the discourse on the parables from a diverse collection of material. The parables of the sower (Mark 4:2-9; Matt 13:3-9; Luke 8:4-8; *Gospel of Thomas* 9), the reason for speaking in parables (Mark 4:10-12; Matt 3:10-17; Luke 8:9-10), and the allegorical explanation of the parable of the sower (Mark 4:13-20; Matt 13:18-13; Luke 8:11-15) form the first half of the section. The second half begins with a series of proverbial sayings that appear in different versions in the other Gospels: the parables of the lamp (4:21), what is hidden will be manifested (4:22), "let those with ears to hear, hear" (4:23), "the measure you give, you will get" (4:24), and "to the one who has, more will be given (4:25). Although the sayings circulated individually outside this context, the Gospel writer has placed them in a setting in which parables are being told. Hearers must be careful to grasp the mystery of the kingdom being revealed through the parables. From this point on, Jesus will struggle to make his disciples understand his teaching. His efforts may even appear to be in vain when we come to the passion narrative. This emphasis is not so much a historical statement about the disciples in the past as it is a warning to Mark's persecuted and struggling community.[161] Finally, two short parables, the seed growing secretly (4:26-29) and the mustard seed (4:30-31; Matt 13:31-32; Luke 13:18-19; *Gospel of Thomas* 20), form the end of the discourse.

Mark's use of alterations between what occurs

---

158. See John R. Donahue, *The Gospel in Parable* (Philadelphia: Fortress, 1988) 28-62; Madeleine I. Boucher, *The Mysterious Parable: A Literary Study,* CBQMS 6 (Washington: Catholic Biblical Association, 1977) 17-63; Scott, *Hear Then the Parable,* 21-25. See also Tannehill, "The Gospels and Narrative Literature," in this volume.

159. The only other parables of Jesus preserved in Mark occur in 12:1-12, the wicked tenants; 13:28-29, the fig tree; and 13:34-37, the doorkeeper. All of Mark's parables reappear in other Gospels. Although Matt 13:34-30 replaces the parable of the seed growing secretly of Mark 4:26-29 with the image of wheat and tares, the saying part of the seed growing secretly is preserved in the conclusion of the *Gospel of Thomas* 21. The *Gospel of Thomas* 9 contains a version of the parable of the sower without the allegorical explanation found in the synoptic Gospels (Mark 4:13-8). Since the *Gospel of Thomas* version is more concise than the version in Mark, many scholars suggest that Mark expanded the traditional version of the parable that he received from his tradition. See John Dominic Crossan, *In Parables* (Philadelphia: Fortress, 1973) 42-43.

160. Scott, *Hear Then the Parable,* 10.

161. So Aloysius Ambrozic, *The Hidden Kingdom: A Redaction-Critical Study of the References to the Kingdom of God in Mark's Gospel,* CBQMS 2 (Washington, D.C.: Catholic Biblical Association, 1972) 89.

"outside" in the presence of the crowds and what occurs "inside" with his circle of disciples confuses the geographical sequence somewhat. Initially, Jesus is speaking from a boat to the crowds (vv. 1-2). He has somehow moved away when he explains the reason for using parables and interprets the parable of the sower. The question is put by "those who were around him along with the twelve" (v. 10). However, the proverbs and parables of the second half are apparently addressed to the people. The verses that conclude the section distinguish the "them" to whom Jesus addresses the parables from the disciples, to whom Jesus explains everything in private (vv. 33-34).

This distinction reinforces the earlier claim that the disciples had been given the secret of the kingdom, which was unintelligible to the crowds (4:12). Just as the disciples consistently fail to understand who Jesus is and the necessity of his suffering in the rest of the narrative, so also readers are forced to wonder whether the disciples truly are "insiders."[162]

162. See Smith, " 'Inside' and 'Outside,' " 366. Against proposals to identify the disciples with a group that holds an unacceptable view of Jesus as a powerful miracle worker or as a church leader, see Ernest Best, *Mark: The Gospel as Story* (Edinburgh: T. & T. Clark, 1983) 47-50. Flawed disciples might invite the community to identify with them or serve as a literary device to highlight the greatness of the teacher.

Mark 4:1-9, The Parable of the Sower

NIV

4 Again Jesus began to teach by the lake. The crowd that gathered around him was so large that he got into a boat and sat in it out on the lake, while all the people were along the shore at the water's edge. [2]He taught them many things by parables, and in his teaching said: [3]"Listen! A farmer went out to sow his seed. [4]As he was scattering the seed, some fell along the path, and the birds came and ate it up. [5]Some fell on rocky places, where it did not have much soil. It sprang up quickly, because the soil was shallow. [6]But when the sun came up, the plants were scorched, and they withered because they had no root. [7]Other seed fell among thorns, which grew up and choked the plants, so that they did not bear grain. [8]Still other seed fell on good soil. It came up, grew and produced a crop, multiplying thirty, sixty, or even a hundred times."

[9]Then Jesus said, "He who has ears to hear, let him hear."

NRSV

4 Again he began to teach beside the sea. Such a very large crowd gathered around him that he got into a boat on the sea and sat there, while the whole crowd was beside the sea on the land. [2]He began to teach them many things in parables, and in his teaching he said to them: [3]"Listen! A sower went out to sow. [4]And as he sowed, some seed fell on the path, and the birds came and ate it up. [5]Other seed fell on rocky ground, where it did not have much soil, and it sprang up quickly, since it had no depth of soil. [6]And when the sun rose, it was scorched; and since it had no root, it withered away. [7]Other seed fell among thorns, and the thorns grew up and choked it, and it yielded no grain. [8]Other seed fell into good soil and brought forth grain, growing up and increasing and yielding thirty and sixty and a hundredfold." [9]And he said, "Let anyone with ears to hear listen!"

COMMENTARY

The parable of the sower is one of Jesus' best-known parables. It begins and ends with the summons "Listen!" Those who prove themselves capable of apprehending the message of the parable will become followers of Jesus. In the early church, this parable encouraged believers who had already accepted the word to nourish its

growth in their lives, and it explained why some people failed to respond or to become mature Christians.[163] Although we refer to the parable by its main

163. Different interpretations of the parable meet these concerns in different ways. See C. H. Dodd, *The Parables of the Kingdom* (New York: Scribners, 1961) 145. On the early Christian vocabulary found in the allegorical interpretation of the parable, see Joachim Jeremias, *The Parables of Jesus* (New York: Scribners, 1972) 77-78.

character, the sower, the emphasis lies on the fate of the seed. Christian readers quickly identify the sower with Jesus and the seed with his preaching. The previous episode (vv. 31-35) distinguishes those who do the will of God as "brothers and sisters of Jesus" from those who fail to understand the true source of his power. Therefore, Mark's Gospel has prepared the reader for a parable in which Jesus distinguishes different responses to his mission.

The seed falls on three areas that keep it from bearing fruit: a path, rocky ground, and among thorns. Despite the loss of many seeds, some fall on good soil and yield a good harvest. The bad soils have been arranged in order from (a) soil that gives the seed no opportunity to sprout to (b) soil that does not allow deep roots to (c) soil that chokes the seed after it has grown, before it can yield fruit. The triadic description of the harvest—thirty, sixty, and a hundredfold—matches the triad of bad soils.

The agricultural practices presumed in the story have raised considerable dispute among exegetes. Some assume that Mark merely reported Palestinian peasant practices of scattering seed and then plowing it into the ground. More recent studies of agricultural sources have made that account appear implausible. Jewish sources from the time of Jesus credit Abraham with inventing a plow that enabled farmers to till the soil before sowing the seed. As a consequence, they were able to cover the seed before the birds could get to it.[164] Mark's audience either assumed that the sower had already prepared the ground, but had sowed in such a way that not all of the seed fell on good ground, or that the story took place before the invention of appropriate plowing techniques. Some interpreters suggest that the parable assumes a second planting when the ground was not as thoroughly prepared as it would be in the spring.

Another disputed item of agricultural information concerns the size of the harvest. The triad of thirty, sixty, a hundredfold belongs to a common technique in oral storytelling. Repetition in a sequence underlines the point being made. The other versions vary the order or refer only to the

hundredfold (Luke). Would Jesus' audience perceive this harvest as unusually large? Or merely a good year? Most scholars have presumed that the dynamics of loss and harvest in the parable imply a surprisingly abundant harvest. Its size is understood as an indication of the eschatological blessing of the kingdom of God.[165] Others have attempted to calculate normal yields based on the interest and taxes that peasants had to return for the seed they borrowed to plant.[166] The numbers associated with the yield refer to the fruit of the remaining seeds, not to the harvest as a whole in comparison with a normal harvest. Since the dynamics of the parable focus our attention on the failures attendant in the process of sowing, the ordinary harvest may be experienced as a miracle.[167]

As with the shorter proverbial sayings, the point of the parable depends on the context to which it is applied. The focus on the contrast between the dangers awaiting the seed sown by being scattered on the ground and the harvest may demonstrate that the word of God will produce a fruitful harvest even though many are unresponsive (cf. Mark 3:6, 20-35; Isa 55:10). The warning to "Listen!" which frames the story (vv. 3, 9) might be taken to focus attention on the bad soils. The readers have some responsibility to avoid being like that unfruitful ground. Interest in the types of unfruitful ground led to expansion of the description of the rocky ground in Mark's version of the parable. The statement of what happens to the seed there is twice as long as in the other examples. Two items contribute to the fate of the seed: It lacks enough soil to grow productive roots; as a consequence, it cannot survive the scorching sun. If the parable refers to the kingdom as unexpected blessing, then the emphasis on destroyed seed serves to highlight the blessing associated with God's kingdom.[168]

Some interpreters think that Mark begins with this parable in order to direct the reader's attention back to the fate of Jesus' preaching. Several verbs describe actions taken against the seed by

164. See Scott, *Hear Then the Parable,* 353; Pheme Perkins, *Jesus as Teacher* (Cambridge: Cambridge University Press, 1990) 39. The Abraham story, found in *Jub.* 11:10-24, treats the practice of scattering seed and then sowing as wasteful and archaic. By inventing the plow, Abraham provided his people with a better technology.

165. So Jeremias, *Parables,* 150.
166. See K. D. White, "The Parable of the Sower," *JTS* 13 (1964) 301-2.
167. See Scott, *Hear Then the Parable,* 361-62.
168. See John R. Donahue, *The Gospel in Parable* (Philadelphia: Fortress, 1988) 34. Donahue notes that the repeated comments about failed seed lull the reader into complacency, which is shattered when the harvest arrives.

outside forces: birds eat it (v. 4); sun scorches it (v. 6); and thorns choke it (v. 7). The charges against Jesus in the previous controversy stories show that the gospel faces violent opposition. Other interpreters think that the scorching sun was added to represent the persecution suffered by early Christian communities, since it disrupts the progression of root systems: no roots, shallow roots, and roots but no fruit. (See Reflections at Mark 4:13-20.)

Mark 4:10-12, The Secret of the Kingdom

NIV	NRSV

¹⁰When he was alone, the Twelve and the others around him asked him about the parables. ¹¹He told them, "The secret of the kingdom of God has been given to you. But to those on the outside everything is said in parables ¹²so that,
 	
  " 'they may be ever seeing but never perceiving,
      and ever hearing but never understanding;
  otherwise they might turn and be forgiven!'ᵃ"
 	
 ᵃ12 Isaiah 6:9,10
	10When he was alone, those who were around him along with the twelve asked him about the parables. ¹¹And he said to them, "To you has been given the secretᵃ of the kingdom of God, but for those outside, everything comes in parables; ¹²in order that
	 'they may indeed look, but not perceive,
	   and may indeed listen, but not understand;
	  so that they may not turn again and be
	          forgiven.' "
	
	 ᵃOr mystery

COMMENTARY

Mark disrupts the public discourse to introduce the element of private instruction for Jesus' followers.[169] The injunctions to "Listen!" warn readers that some persons are unable to grasp Jesus' message. The comments about those who are unable to hear exploit another usage of the term *parable*. Instead of using a proverb or an everyday situation to make its meaning clear, the parable is instead a "riddle." Only those hearers who grasp the solution to the riddle understand what is being referred to. The core saying for this scene (vv. 11-12) is probably a piece of independent tradition in which the Isaiah citation was used as a proof text.

"Those who were around him along with the twelve" (v. 10) suggests that the larger group of disciples from whom the Twelve were selected are included in this instruction. They have been identified as Jesus' new family (3:31-35). Consequently, they have already shown themselves responsive to the preaching of Jesus.[170] This formulation, however, makes ambiguous the referents of "[they] asked . . . " (v. 10), "he said to them" (v. 13), and "his disciples" (v. 34). Does "his disciples" include a group larger than the Twelve? Most interpreters assume that the Twelve pose the question in v. 10 and receive the private instructions in v. 34. The ambiguity makes it difficult to determine who understands the parable/riddle.[171] The ability to perceive the parable—i.e., to hear the preaching of Jesus and bear fruit—appears to distinguish followers in general from others in the crowd. The private instruction that Jesus gives the disciples (v. 34) suggests that the smaller group is intended. Since the disciples have been called to "fish for people" (1:17), they must understand what Jesus is preaching.

Verse 11 distinguishes insiders who know the secret of the kingdom from outsiders for whom everything Jesus teaches is a parable, a riddle. The term translated "secret" (μυστήριον *mystērion*) serves as the Greek rendering of the Aramaic term *rāz* (רז; cf. Dan 2:18-19). Apocalyptic texts refer to the

169. See Aloysius Ambrozic, *The Hidden Kingdom: A Redaction-Critical Study of the References to the Kingdom of God in Mark's Gospel*, CBQMS 2 (Washington, D.C.: Catholic Biblical Association, 1972) 46-54.

170. See Robert H. Gundry, *Mark: A Commentary on His Apology for the Cross* (Grand Rapids: Eerdmans, 1993) 196.

171. Cf. Guelich, *Mark*, 200-201.

secrets of God's plan for the end time. Only the elect, members of the sect instructed by their teachers, know the meaning of the symbolic visions in which the events of the end time are depicted.[172] Paul uses the term *mystērion* for the Christian economy of salvation (Rom 11:25; 1 Cor 2:7-8). The parable of the sower hardly qualifies as the type of discourse that would require such revelation. The sequence of soils does not correspond to an apocalyptic schema for the end time. The saying about those who have received the secret of the kingdom may have been associated with a collection of parables from which Mark has taken the material for this chapter. Verse 11 appears to promise that the reader is about to be told the "mystery" of the kingdom of God. Yet no such revelation occurs.[173]

Another possibility for understanding Mark's use of vv. 11-12 is to situate this motif within the larger discussion of the messianic secret in Mark.[174] The secret of the kingdom of God must be associated with the identity of Jesus as the bearer of salvation. The demons, who hail Jesus as "Holy One of God," are silenced because they know him (1:34). The disciples, who acknowledge him as Messiah and witness the transfiguration, will be silenced until after the passion (9:9). However, the overall tenor of 4:11 does not suggest secrecy in the sense of either silencing or failed comprehension. The saying is much closer to the apocalyptic idea of a "mystery" as knowledge available only to members of the sect. Although Jesus' preaching is identified with the sower, nothing in the parable discourse focuses the reader's attention on christology. Therefore, the parable theory probably does not belong to the christological use of "messianic secret."[175] The disciples continue to receive private teaching throughout the Gospel (4:34; 7:17; 9:2-9, 28-29, 30-31*a*; 10:10-12, 23; 12:43; 13:1-3). In each case this teaching either involves new sayings of Jesus or interprets teaching just given.

Verse 12 cites Isa 6:10 as though it provides the reason for Jesus' use of parable/riddles. The "hardening" saying need not suggest that parabolic speech is a deliberate attempt to exclude people from hearing the message. Jesus would not endorse the policy of cutting off access to forgiveness, since he came to offer forgiveness and to call sinners (1:15; 2:5, 10, 17). Isaiah 6:10 describes the hard heartedness of the nation, which makes them deaf to the prophets' words. Such hardening is viewed as an act of divine judgment. Jesus has encountered this attitude in those persons who seek to destroy him (3:6). The disciples will be charged with hard heartedness when they fail to have confidence in Jesus' power to rescue them (6:52). Mark may be thinking of a narrower group when he uses the citation from Isaiah— namely, the scribes and Pharisees, who are explicitly hostile to Jesus' deeds and his teaching.[176] However limited their comprehension, Jesus constantly shows himself willing to teach both the crowds and the disciples. Mark consistently composes didactic scenes (4:3-20; 7:14-23; 8:14-21; 10:1-12) in which a public event or teaching is followed by a change of place, a request for explanation, a retort by Jesus, and further explanation.[177]

The prophetic citation does not clarify the meaning of the expression "secret of the kingdom of God" (v. 11), as one might have expected. It may have been traditionally attached to a comment on Jesus' parables, since Mark inserts this saying between a request for an explanation of the sower and Jesus' actual interpretation. The interpretation begins with a rebuke (v. 13). The parable has a fairly clear meaning as a general comment on the fate of the word, which comes from God. Therefore, the interpretation given the parable does not appear to represent the "secret of the kingdom." However, the parable in its entirety might be understood to refer to the coming of the kingdom. The remaining parables in the chapter are introduced as stories about the kingdom (vv. 26, 30).

---

172. *1 Enoch* 51:3; 1QS 3:13–4:1.

173. See Robert M. Fowler, *Let the Reader Understand: Reader-Response Criticism and the Gospel of Mark* (Minneapolis: Fortress, 1991) 169; Bernard Brandon Scott, *Hear Then the Parable: A Commentary on the Parables of Jesus* (Minneapolis: Fortress, 1989) 24.

174. See Joachim Gnilka, *Das Evangelium nach Markus. 1 Teilband Mk 1–8, 26,* EKKNT II (Zurich: Benziger, 1978) 1:166-70.

175. See Heikki Räisänen, *The "Messianic Secret" in Mark* (Edinburgh: T. & T. Clark, 1990) 76-92.

176. So Ambrozic, *The Hidden Kingdom,* 56-57.

177. See Philip Sellew, "Composition of Didactic Scenes in Mark's Gospel," *JBL* 108 (1989) 613-34.

Mark 4:13-20, Interpretation of the Parable of the Sower

NIV

[13]Then Jesus said to them, "Don't you understand this parable? How then will you understand any parable? [14]The farmer sows the word. [15]Some people are like seed along the path, where the word is sown. As soon as they hear it, Satan comes and takes away the word that was sown in them. [16]Others, like seed sown on rocky places, hear the word and at once receive it with joy. [17]But since they have no root, they last only a short time. When trouble or persecution comes because of the word, they quickly fall away. [18]Still others, like seed sown among thorns, hear the word; [19]but the worries of this life, the deceitfulness of wealth and the desires for other things come in and choke the word, making it unfruitful. [20]Others, like seed sown on good soil, hear the word, accept it, and produce a crop—thirty, sixty or even a hundred times what was sown."

NRSV

[13]And he said to them, "Do you not understand this parable? Then how will you understand all the parables? [14]The sower sows the word. [15]These are the ones on the path where the word is sown: when they hear, Satan immediately comes and takes away the word that is sown in them. [16]And these are the ones sown on rocky ground: when they hear the word, they immediately receive it with joy. [17]But they have no root, and endure only for a while; then, when trouble or persecution arises on account of the word, immediately they fall away.[a] [18]And others are those sown among the thorns: these are the ones who hear the word, [19]but the cares of the world, and the lure of wealth, and the desire for other things come in and choke the word, and it yields nothing. [20]And these are the ones sown on the good soil: they hear the word and accept it and bear fruit, thirty and sixty and a hundredfold."

[a]Or *stumble*

COMMENTARY

Jesus begins the exposition of the parable of the sower with a word of reproach. Anyone who cannot understand this parable will not be able to comprehend the others (v. 13). This remark follows more naturally on the question in v. 10 than it does the saying about insiders' being given the secret of the kingdom. It also marks a shift in the narrative treatment of Jesus' disciples. From this point on, the disciples will often appear uncomprehending, weak in faith, and even hard hearted (4:40; 6:52; 8:33; 9:32).

The allegorical interpretation of the sower appears to be secondary to the parable itself. The *Gospel of Thomas* shows that the parable circulated without the allegorical interpretation of the soils, which reflects the experiences of the early Christian community. The identification of the seed with the word may have belonged to the initial reading of the parable. The extended types of soil can be lumped together as failures, contrasted with the good soil responsible for the

harvest. Since a bountiful harvest is assured, readers should not be no more concerned about rejection or failure than they would be over the seed lost during sowing (cf. 4 Ezra 8:31-44).

The verb *fell* (vv. 4, 5, 8) has been replaced with the verb *sown*. This explanation includes exhortation aimed at members of the community who might abandon the faith they have embraced. The first group never really receive the word because Satan snatches it away. The second, those who lack roots, cannot withstand persecution. The third, those strangled by thorns, lose their faith because concern for wealth and other cares of the world stifle belief. Nevertheless, the word still bears a rich harvest. These examples depict the missionary efforts of the early community: Not only do some reject the message outright, but also others seem to have accepted the message, only to abandon it. This typology of belief moderates the dualism of insiders and outsiders, reflected in the saying about receiving the secret of the kingdom. Rather than be discouraged by these inevitable failures, Mark's readers should be encouraged by the concluding promise of a rich harvest.

The opening rebuke, "Do you not understand this parable? Then how will you understand all the parables?" suggests that readers should learn from this example how to approach the parables that follow. The catalogue of reactions indicates that even persons who appear to accept Jesus' teaching cannot be trusted. Some will quickly lose their initial enthusiasm, whereas others will be unable to face the coming persecutions (13:9-13). The love of riches and worldly cares causes the rich man to reject Jesus' offer of discipleship (10:17-22). Since failure to receive the word is attributed to Satan, Mark later has Jesus call Peter "Satan" when he protests Jesus' word about future suffering (8:33). Although this comment suggests an element of divine election at work in determining who believes and who does not, most examples hint at personal responsibility for the fate of the word once a person has responded to it.

REFLECTIONS

1. The parable of the sower invites us to reflect on the complexities of faith. No matter how sophisticated our pastoral strategies or how extensive our religious education programs, we cannot take credit for the emergence or growth of faith. Genuine growth in faith can be measured only by the developments in a person's life. Does faith endure prosperity as well as hardship? Does it yield fruit? Or is it like the tool we go looking for in an emergency, hoping we remember how it works? The self-help culture that sells people guaranteed quick fixes for all the difficulties of life often creates the expectation that faith should be the same way—a comforting solution to the problems and pain of life. The interpretation given the parable of the sower reminds us that true discipleship does not provide such solutions. Some will meet with hostility from others because of their faith. Others will choose the ever-present concerns for comfort and security instead of sacrifice and discomfort. They may not even realize that their lives have been taken over by the demands of success. Religion becomes a holiday accessory.

2. Faced with disbelief among their own families and communities, many lifelong Christians become discouraged. Parents and grandparents ask themselves anxiously what they have done wrong in bringing up their children. Faced with the difficulties of maintaining a vibrant faith community in today's world, many begin to wonder whether the effort is worth it. This parable provides encouragement for those darker moments, too. The word of the gospel is not too weak for the job. Loss has been part of the process from the beginning. Despite the vigorous opposition to the word, it still yields a rich harvest. Despite the dramatic evidence of Jesus' relationship to the divine, even he was not able to elicit an enduring faith from all who heard his message.

3. We also learn an important lesson from the image of Jesus' parables as riddles that require that sudden ability to connect the images of the riddle with its referent, which it does not depict directly. At first a riddle puzzles us. Even if we cannot solve it, we cannot get it out of our mind, and when we have solved a riddle its clever metaphorical twist may continue to give us pleasure. There are some people who are simply no good at riddles. They never understand them or take pleasure in them—even when they are simple enough for a child to grasp. Sometimes faith is like that. Some people just do not find religious language and practice meaningful.

Mark 4:21-25, A Series of Proverbs

NIV

²¹He said to them, "Do you bring in a lamp to put it under a bowl or a bed? Instead, don't you put it on its stand? ²²For whatever is hidden is meant to be disclosed, and whatever is concealed is meant to be brought out into the open. ²³If anyone has ears to hear, let him hear."

²⁴"Consider carefully what you hear," he continued. "With the measure you use, it will be measured to you—and even more. ²⁵Whoever has will be given more; whoever does not have, even what he has will be taken from him."

NRSV

21He said to them, "Is a lamp brought in to be put under the bushel basket, or under the bed, and not on the lampstand? ²²For there is nothing hidden, except to be disclosed; nor is anything secret, except to come to light. ²³Let anyone with ears to hear listen!" ²⁴And he said to them, "Pay attention to what you hear; the measure you give will be the measure you get, and still more will be given you. ²⁵For to those who have, more will be given; and from those who have nothing, even what they have will be taken away."

COMMENTARY

Two groups of proverbs frame a double exhortation to take care how one hears the word (vv. 23, 24a). As general sayings, proverbs take their particular meaning from the context in which they are used. Since the sayings in this collection also appear separately in other Gospels, Mark may have been responsible for bringing them together in this particular grouping.[178] The interpretation of the parable of the sower introduces the issue of losing faith or bearing a fruitful harvest. Reference to persecution (v. 17) suggests the reason why some persons might prefer to conceal their faith. This collection of proverbial sayings makes testimony the necessary condition for growth in faith.

4:21-23. It would be easy for Christians to take the apparently deterministic distinction between insiders and outsiders as evidence that preaching to an uncomprehending or hostile world does no good. Let those who find themselves enthralled by religious language seek out the community and learn the secret of the kingdom. The first group of sayings rejects that view. Light is not hidden but exposed where all can see it (v. 21). Mark's formulation of the lamp proverb is unusual (cf. Luke 8:16; Matt 5:16//Luke 11:33; *Gospel of Thomas* 33). The other versions speak of people lighting a lamp and then placing

it somewhere. Mark speaks of a lamp "coming" or possibly "being brought" in order to put it under a bushel. The construction requires that "lamp" be a metaphor for a subject that may come. Mark's narrative context provides two possibilities for this subject: Jesus or the kingdom. Since the mystery of the kingdom has been revealed to Jesus' disciples in the parable (4:11), the kingdom appears to be the referent of the lamp saying.

The attached proverb, "there is nothing hidden, except to be disclosed" (v. 22), may have been used in isolation as a warning to those who think they can conceal evil. But such an application does not fit this context. Attached to the saying about the lamp, this proverb counters a possible misunderstanding of the fact that Jesus instructs his disciples apart from the crowds. This teaching is not hidden or esoteric. The Twelve were called to be with Jesus and to preach (3:14). Thus any private instruction he may give them will serve the later public proclamation of the gospel.[179]

The transition from what is small, insignificant, and hidden to what is visible to all reappears in the ensuing seed parables. Both a seed that grows of itself and one that is tiny, like the mustard

---

178. So Guelich, *Mark,* 226-27. For an argument in favor of a pre-Markan collection, see Ambrozic, *The Hidden Kingdom,* 103.

179. Gundry, *Mark,* 212, suggests that the saying originally understood the "hidden"/exposure contrast in an apocalyptic setting. The "hidden" things that are exposed at the judgment will bring God's sentence against those who thought their activities were not known by God.

seed, produce a sufficient harvest (vv. 26-29, 30-32). This movement from a precarious sowing to harvest provides an analogy for Jesus' proclamation of the kingdom of God.

4:24-25. The second set of proverbs picks up the issue of increasing faith, which depends on giving away what one has. If this injunction refers to the parable of the sower and its interpretation, then the proverb might be addressed to those who let other concerns swamp their faith. Originally, the sayings about appropriate measures probably referred to generosity. The saying, which contrasts rich and poor, seems to reflect an economic truism. Ancient societies were structured in a way that made this parable particularly apt. Legal proceedings were the vehicle for wealthy individuals to increase their holdings and their prestige. Those who think that they can preserve or even increase their faith in secrecy will find that they have nothing. The passive verbs suggest that God will increase the faith of those who give away what they have and will take away the faith of those who fail to do so.

Mark 4:26-34, Two Parables About Seeds

NIV	NRSV
26He also said, "This is what the kingdom of God is like. A man scatters seed on the ground. 27Night and day, whether he sleeps or gets up, the seed sprouts and grows, though he does not know how. 28All by itself the soil produces grain— first the stalk, then the head, then the full kernel in the head. 29As soon as the grain is ripe, he puts the sickle to it, because the harvest has come."	26He also said, "The kingdom of God is as if someone would scatter seed on the ground, 27and would sleep and rise night and day, and the seed would sprout and grow, he does not know how. 28The earth produces of itself, first the stalk, then the head, then the full grain in the head. 29But when the grain is ripe, at once he goes in with his sickle, because the harvest has come."
30Again he said, "What shall we say the kingdom of God is like, or what parable shall we use to describe it? 31It is like a mustard seed, which is the smallest seed you plant in the ground. 32Yet when planted, it grows and becomes the largest of all garden plants, with such big branches that the birds of the air can perch in its shade."	30He also said, "With what can we compare the kingdom of God, or what parable will we use for it? 31It is like a mustard seed, which, when sown upon the ground, is the smallest of all the seeds on earth; 32yet when it is sown it grows up and becomes the greatest of all shrubs, and puts forth large branches, so that the birds of the air can make nests in its shade."
33With many similar parables Jesus spoke the word to them, as much as they could understand. 34He did not say anything to them without using a parable. But when he was alone with his own disciples, he explained everything.	33With many such parables he spoke the word to them, as they were able to hear it; 34he did not speak to them except in parables, but he explained everything in private to his disciples.

COMMENTARY

4:26-29. Mark now includes two parables about seeds, commonly called the parable of the seed growing of itself (vv. 26-29) and the parable of the mustard seed (vv. 30-32), with a short conclusion on Jesus' use of parables (vv. 33-34). The introduction to the first parable links the parable of the sower to the promised secret of the kingdom (v. 26). As in the earlier parable, the sower is not involved with the subsequent growth of the seed. It grows and produces "of itself" (v. 28). As soon as ripe grain appears, the sower comes to harvest the crop; harvesting often appears as a symbol for the final judgment (see Joel 4:13). If the eschatological harvest is the focus of the parable, then the strangely passive sower might be seen as a reference to God. This reading makes the parable consistent with the previous warnings to see to it that faith increases.

An alternate reading treats the passivity of the sower as a comment on the certainty of growth. Earth's producing fruit "of itself" might be understood as a reference to fields that lie fallow in the sabbatical year. Even they produce fruit that can be harvested, much like seeds from annual plants, which reseed themselves and grow on their own. The introductory reference to sowing the seed, however, weakens the probability of a sabbath year explanation. The central inaction may still lie at the heart of the parable.

Apocalyptic visions of the coming rule of God envisage a cosmic scene of judgment in which the wicked are destroyed. This parable suggests that the kingdom can be present like the seed prior to the appearance of ripe fruit. Its emergence is unnoticed by many, but they will have no difficulty recognizing the ripe fruit.[180] Even though Jesus' ministry may not appear to be establishing the kingdom, it is certainly present. In this parable, the farmer's roles shift with the season. Although he is passive during the period in which the seed is maturing, he reacts swiftly when it is time for the harvest. Matthew substitutes the parable of the wheat and tares for this parable, thus sharpening the allusion to judgment, since the tares will eventually be gathered and burned (Matt 13:24-30, 36-43). Mark's audience might associate the harvest images in this parable with the apocalyptic prediction that on the day of judgment, God's angels will gather the elect from the ends of the earth (Mark 13:27).[181] Depending on the perspective from which the parable is viewed, the seed growing secretly may be a warning about the suddenness of the coming judgment. No one knows when the hour will come (Mark 13:20-23, 32). When it does arrive, the kingdom that has been hidden will be manifested to all.[182] Or it may be understood as a word of consolation for those who feel that God delays decisive action.[183] Human actions can neither hasten nor delay the coming of the kingdom, which has begun in Jesus' ministry.[184]

4:30-32. The second seed parable continues the imagery of small, apparently insignificant seeds being transformed into mature plants. Instead of speaking of harvest as the result of the process, this parable highlights the function of the full-grown plant. The mustard bush provides shelter for birds who nest on the ground in its shade. Other versions of the parable of the mustard bush indicate that the parable appeared in different contexts. A shorter version of the Markan type appears in *Gospel of Thomas* 20, in which seed from a wild mustard bush, the "smallest of all seeds," happens to fall on tilled ground and grows into a large bush. The formulation in Mark, in which the seed is sown on the ground, may have been created to provide an introduction parallel to the previous two seed parables. As with the earlier parable, Mark's version of this seed parable is more expansive in describing the subsequent development of the bush than is the *Gospel of Thomas* account. Mark speaks of large branches designed to enable the birds to nest in its shade; the *Gospel of Thomas* merely speaks of birds taking shelter in the plant. Echoes of the OT may be responsible for this formulation; the LXX of Ezek 17:23 has birds "under its shade" rather than "in the shade" of the tree.

Matthew 13:31-32 and Luke 13:18-19 represent another version of the parable (Q) in which a person sows the seed, which grows into a tree. The shade or shelter provided by the bush has been replaced by the branches as a place for the birds to make their nests. This variant highlights the OT use of great trees to depict the kingdoms of the world (Ezek 17:23; 31:6; Dan 4:12, 20-22).[185] The great tree in Dan 4:20-22 corresponds to a kingdom that rules all the peoples of the world. The image of a mighty cedar of Lebanon symbolizes Assyria (Ezek 31:2) and Judah (Ezek 17:3-4). Thus it must have seemed contradictory to use the image of a bush to represent the kingdom of God. Changing the image for the kingdom from a bush to a tree emphasizes that the kingdom of God is greater than all human kingdoms.

180. Cf. Scott, *Hear Then the Parable,* 364-71.

181. See Rudolph Pesch, *Das Markusevangelium I. Teil,* HTKNT II (Freiburg: Herder, 1977) 1:529.

182. C. H. Dodd, *The Parables of the Kingdom* (New York: Scribners, 1961) 141-44, suggested that Jesus understood his own ministry as inaugurating the end-time judgment. The challenges to hear the parables in this chapter may be understood as highlighting that reality for the audience.

183. The seer in 2 Esdras raises this question about Israel's experience persistently. See 2 Esdr 4:22-25.

184. See Joachim Jeremias, *The Parables of Jesus* (New York: Scribners, 1972) 151-53.

185. See Scott, *Hear Then the Parable,* 376-77.

In order to explain how the bush provides shelter for all the birds of the air, Mark observes that the full-grown bush has large branches. Even when fully grown, the kingdom of God does not appear unusually large if it is compared to great trees. Yet, as bushes go, the mustard bush is the greatest. Birds that nest on the ground are sheltered by its branches. Jesus may have told this parable to counter the impression that God's rule had to appear among the great and powerful. It may have been an expression of God's providence in creation (Ps 104:12; Matt 6:26-30).

Mark uses the parable to conclude the discourse on parables. The certainty with which small mustard seeds take over the tilled soil into which they fall contrasts with the precariousness of the seed scattered by the sower and the mysterious appearance of the harvest from the seed that grows of itself. The overtones of divine judgment attached to the harvest in the two earlier parables are also missing. Thus this parable suggests that the secret of the kingdom of God can be found by Jesus' disciples in their present experience. God has already provided protection for the faithful. The next episode, a rescue at sea, joins the christology of Mark with the certainty of God's protection for suffering disciples.[186] Jesus

makes God's salvation present just as his preaching announces the coming of God's rule.

4:33-34. The general summary combines the suggestion that parables are intended to aid understanding (v. 33) with the division between the crowd and the disciples (v. 34). Yet the disciples are unable to understand the parable of the sower without Jesus' explanation (vv. 10, 13). The need to explain the meaning to the disciples points to the inherent ambiguity of the parable genre. Mark's repeated demands to hear the parables link the diverse traditions together in this discourse (vv. 3, 9, 23, 24, 33) and point beyond the narrative time in which Jesus addressed those around him to the actual readers of the Gospel. The interpretation supplied for the parable of the sower reminds them that parables are a summons to hear the word of God and to follow Jesus. Those who hear and do not understand (v. 12) remain outside the circle of disciples. The explanation also insists that being a disciple has three steps: hearing, accepting the word, and bearing fruit.[187] By reminding readers of Jesus' explanation (v. 34), Mark does not intend to exclude them from understanding the parables. Rather, he invites them to construct their own understanding of discipleship.

186. Cf. John R. Donahue, *The Gospel in Parable* (Philadelphia: Fortress, 1988) 51.

187. See ibid., 49-50.

REFLECTIONS

1. The seed parables point to the certain harvest that stems from next-to-invisible beginnings. The lack of human agency during the growth process does not mean that disciples should sit back and wait for God to bring the harvest. The proverbial sayings on how faith increases warn against such a conclusion. Instead, the image of a certain harvest from invisible beginnings promises that even though our testimony to the gospel appears insignificant or even fruitless, Christians should not be discouraged or give up. Christians should beware of giving in to the mania for statistics as evidence of success, which dominates modern life. When the harvest is ripe, it will be time for the reaper.

2. The image of a mustard bush as the kingdom of God set over against the alternative vision of the nations as great trees points to another feature of God's rule. The kingdom does not replicate the kind of greatness that human nations attempt to build for themselves.

3. The passivity of human figures during the growth process challenges a common reading of these parables. They do not describe an evolutionary process by which Christians build the kingdom. The proverbial sayings warn Christians that faith cannot remain private. We must give away what we have received. This evangelical emphasis counters a common modern tendency to think of religion as a matter of private preference that is best worn lightly in the presence of others. These proverbs and parables suggest that God does not give the gift of faith (or secret of the kingdom) to individuals as their private possession. Rather, the gift provides light for others and shelter for the birds of the field.

MARK 4:35–6:6a, MIRACLES AROUND THE SEA OF GALILEE

OVERVIEW

Mark follows the parables with a series of miracle stories on and around the Sea of Galilee. These stories emphasize the extraordinary character of Jesus' powers as he subdues the raging sea (4:35-41), casts out a legion of demons (5:1-20), heals a woman who has been ill for twelve years (5:24b-34), and raises a young girl who has just died (5:21-24a, 35-43). The miracles in this section show that Jesus has power over nature, demons, and death.[188] Yet when Jesus comes to his hometown, the people's lack of faith makes it impossible for him to perform many miracles (6:4-6). Mark frames these dramatic miracles with references to the deficient faith of persons whom the reader might presume to be believers: the disciples (4:40) and people who had known Jesus all his life (6:6).

188. See Guelich, *Mark*, 263.

Mark 4:35-41, The Storm at Sea

<table>
<tr><td>NIV</td><td>NRSV</td></tr>
<tr><td>

³⁵That day when evening came, he said to his disciples, "Let us go over to the other side." ³⁶Leaving the crowd behind, they took him along, just as he was, in the boat. There were also other boats with him. ³⁷A furious squall came up, and the waves broke over the boat, so that it was nearly swamped. ³⁸Jesus was in the stern, sleeping on a cushion. The disciples woke him and said to him, "Teacher, don't you care if we drown?"

³⁹He got up, rebuked the wind and said to the waves, "Quiet! Be still!" Then the wind died down and it was completely calm.

⁴⁰He said to his disciples, "Why are you so afraid? Do you still have no faith?"

⁴¹They were terrified and asked each other, "Who is this? Even the wind and the waves obey him!"

</td><td>

35On that day, when evening had come, he said to them, "Let us go across to the other side." ³⁶And leaving the crowd behind, they took him with them in the boat, just as he was. Other boats were with him. ³⁷A great windstorm arose, and the waves beat into the boat, so that the boat was already being swamped. ³⁸But he was in the stern, asleep on the cushion; and they woke him up and said to him, "Teacher, do you not care that we are perishing?" ³⁹He woke up and rebuked the wind, and said to the sea, "Peace! Be still!" Then the wind ceased, and there was a dead calm. ⁴⁰He said to them, "Why are you afraid? Have you still no faith?" ⁴¹And they were filled with great awe and said to one another, "Who then is this, that even the wind and the sea obey him?"

</td></tr>
</table>

COMMENTARY

This story combines a nature miracle with the imagery of a divine epiphany.[189] Ancient Near Eastern mythology depicted the storm god triumphing over the raging waters of the monster of chaos (e.g., Baal vs. Yam; Marduk vs. Tiamat). Even Hebrew poetry sometimes describes God as the victor in combat with the forces of chaos (cf. Ps 107:23-25). (The description of Jesus asleep on a cushion in the stern of the boat may have reminded readers of the prophet Jonah [Jonah 1:5-6].) The mythological and poetic imagery of God triumphing over the raging waters makes clear the response to the final question, "Who then is this . . . ?" (v. 41). He is no mere human being. Jesus has God's power to still the storm. Once again, readers know that Jesus is Son of God (1:1, 11, 24). Yet the disciples seem unable to decipher the significance of Jesus' identity.

Several details in the narrative seem out of place. When Jesus calms the storm, he speaks to the wind as though to a demon (cf. 1:24), leading some interpreters to describe this story as an exorcism. Use of exorcism language provides a cosmological context for the story. Just as the sea monster in ancient mythology represents the powers of evil, so also the raging storm here reflects all the powers of chaos and evil. Jesus' exorcisms are evidence that he is the stronger one, able to break up Satan's kingdom (3:23-27). Mark refocuses this impressive demonstration of Jesus' divine power by underlining the disbelief that Jesus' disciples exhibit during the episode. Miracles like those Jesus performed early in his ministry could have been performed by other miracle workers, exorcists, or magicians. However, no one but Jesus could still the raging storm.

Readers are told that other boats had set out across the lake as well (v. 35). This detail may have come from Mark's source, since it plays no role in the story that follows.[190] Given the fact that at least four of the disciples were professional fishermen and must have experienced such storms before, their terror indicates the severity of the incident. The usual pattern for a sea rescue mir-

acle involved a plea to the deity for help, but Mark's version lacks such a formula. Matthew reformulates the disciples' words to Jesus to fit the anticipated pattern, "Lord, save us! We are perishing!" (Matt. 8:25 NRSV). In Mark, however, when the disciples awaken Jesus, they accuse him of being indifferent to their plight. The tone of this accusation also parallels the story of Jonah, where the captain charges the prophet with not caring about the fate of those on the ship (cf. Jonah 1:6). He then follows the normal pattern of a sea rescue miracle by asking Jonah to pray to his God. Mark permits the disciples' accusation to stand without any request.

The lack of a request to the deity raises the question of whether the disciples believe that Jesus can rescue them from the storm. The complete calm that follows Jesus' command to the sea and the wind leaves no doubt about his power to do so. Jesus then chides the disciples for their fear and lack of faith. Given the details that exhibit how severe the storm is, such fear is plausible. In order to transcend fear, the disciples must recognize that Jesus is not a human being with unusual abilities to preach, heal, and exorcise. They must acknowledge that Jesus is the Son of God.

This episode creates distance between Mark's readers and the disciples. It intensifies the doubts about the disciples, first voiced in response to the request for an interpretation of the parable of the sower (4:13). Despite their privileged position, the disciples are unable to grasp the significance of Jesus' words and deeds and do not understand who Jesus really is. Beginning with Jesus' move onto a boat to teach in 4:1, the sea provides the fixed geographical location for the narrative world in Mark's Gospel through 8:26.[191] It will disappear from the story following Peter's confession that Jesus is Messiah (8:27-30). After that confession, the question of Jesus' identity shifts to the cross.

---

189. See Gerd Theissen, *The Miracle Stories of the Early Christian Tradition,* trans. Francis McDonagh (Philadelphia: Fortress, 1983) 101-2.

190. Some exegetes think that its primary function was to provide other witnesses to the incident. Others suggest that the rest of the boats were lost during the storm. See ibid., 102.

191. See Norman R. Petersen, "The Composition of Mark 4:1–8:26," *HTR* 93 (1980) 194-97. This section of the Gospel can be divided into three units that have the same structure: (1) Jesus interacts with a crowd at the seaside (4:1-34; 6:30-44; 8:1-12); (2) an incident while on a boat challenges the disciples to recognize Jesus' identity (4:35-41; 6:45-52; 8:13-21); (3) Jesus heals (5:1-20; 6:53-56; 8:22-26). For a different reading of the three divisions in this section, see Elizabeth Struthers Malbon, "Echoes and Foreshadowings in Mark 4–8: Reading and Rereading," *JBL* 112 (1993) 213-22.

The disciples must learn the necessity of Jesus' suffering.

At the same time, Mark may have formulated the story with the suffering and uncertainty of his own church in mind. It should reassure them that Jesus has the power to save believers even in the worst circumstances.

REFLECTIONS

1. The question of Jesus' identity appears repeatedly in Mark. When the disciples suddenly show a lack of trust in God's power working through Jesus and even accuse Jesus of not caring, readers are challenged to examine their own faith. Merely repeating the confession that Jesus is Son of God means little if Jesus does not represent God for us. A suspicion that God does not really care what happens to us will corrode our religious life. The results of such sentiments in daily life are familiar. Human relationships die when we sense that others do not care what happens to us.

2. Doubts about God also emerge in times of crisis. Mark's readers were familiar with the destructive effects of persecution. The weaknesses exhibited by Jesus' disciples encourage later believers to persist despite doubts about God's saving presence. In the end, they will discover the one whom wind and sea obey.

3. When the disciples say to Jesus, "Teacher, do you not care that we are perishing?" their panic separates them from Jesus. How can he not care? He is in the boat with them! Jesus does not react to their panic. He speaks first to the raging elements, the wind and sea. Then he asks his stunned disciples about their faith. On the human level, we often act like the disciples. We expect others to share our panic or distress. If they seem detached from the situation, we accuse them of not caring about our suffering. Panic reactions can divide us from others who might help just as they can cause us to doubt God's love for us.

Mark 5:1-20, The Gerasene Demoniac

NIV

5 They went across the lake to the region of the Gerasenes.[a] [2]When Jesus got out of the boat, a man with an evil[b] spirit came from the tombs to meet him. [3]This man lived in the tombs, and no one could bind him any more, not even with a chain. [4]For he had often been chained hand and foot, but he tore the chains apart and broke the irons on his feet. No one was strong enough to subdue him. [5]Night and day among the tombs and in the hills he would cry out and cut himself with stones.

[6]When he saw Jesus from a distance, he ran and fell on his knees in front of him. [7]He shouted at the top of his voice, "What do you want with me, Jesus, Son of the Most High God? Swear to

[a]*1 Some manuscripts* Gadarenes; *other manuscripts* Gergesenes
[b]*2 Greek* unclean; *also in verses 8 and 13*

NRSV

5 They came to the other side of the sea, to the country of the Gerasenes.[a] [2]And when he had stepped out of the boat, immediately a man out of the tombs with an unclean spirit met him. [3]He lived among the tombs; and no one could restrain him any more, even with a chain; [4]for he had often been restrained with shackles and chains, but the chains he wrenched apart, and the shackles he broke in pieces; and no one had the strength to subdue him. [5]Night and day among the tombs and on the mountains he was always howling and bruising himself with stones. [6]When he saw Jesus from a distance, he ran and bowed down before him; [7]and he shouted at the top of his voice, "What have you to do with me, Jesus, Son of the Most High God? I adjure you by God, do not torment

[a]*Other ancient authorities read* Gergesenes; *others,* Gadarenes

God that you won't torture me!" [8]For Jesus had said to him, "Come out of this man, you evil spirit!"

[9]Then Jesus asked him, "What is your name?"

"My name is Legion," he replied, "for we are many." [10]And he begged Jesus again and again not to send them out of the area.

[11]A large herd of pigs was feeding on the nearby hillside. [12]The demons begged Jesus, "Send us among the pigs; allow us to go into them." [13]He gave them permission, and the evil spirits came out and went into the pigs. The herd, about two thousand in number, rushed down the steep bank into the lake and were drowned.

[14]Those tending the pigs ran off and reported this in the town and countryside, and the people went out to see what had happened. [15]When they came to Jesus, they saw the man who had been possessed by the legion of demons, sitting there, dressed and in his right mind; and they were afraid. [16]Those who had seen it told the people what had happened to the demon-possessed man— and told about the pigs as well. [17]Then the people began to plead with Jesus to leave their region.

[18]As Jesus was getting into the boat, the man who had been demon-possessed begged to go with him. [19]Jesus did not let him, but said, "Go home to your family and tell them how much the Lord has done for you, and how he has had mercy on you." [20]So the man went away and began to tell in the Decapolis[a] how much Jesus had done for him. And all the people were amazed.

[a]20 That is, the Ten Cities

me." [8]For he had said to him, "Come out of the man, you unclean spirit!" [9]Then Jesus[a] asked him, "What is your name?" He replied, "My name is Legion; for we are many." [10]He begged him earnestly not to send them out of the country. [11]Now there on the hillside a great herd of swine was feeding; [12]and the unclean spirits[c] begged him, "Send us into the swine; let us enter them." [13]So he gave them permission. And the unclean spirits came out and entered the swine; and the herd, numbering about two thousand, rushed down the steep bank into the sea, and were drowned in the sea.

[14]The swineherds ran off and told it in the city and in the country. Then people came to see what it was that had happened. [15]They came to Jesus and saw the demoniac sitting there, clothed and in his right mind, the very man who had had the legion; and they were afraid. [16]Those who had seen what had happened to the demoniac and to the swine reported it. [17]Then they began to beg Jesus[a] to leave their neighborhood. [18]As he was getting into the boat, the man who had been possessed by demons begged him that he might be with him. [19]But Jesus[b] refused, and said to him, "Go home to your friends, and tell them how much the Lord has done for you, and what mercy he has shown you." [20]And he went away and began to proclaim in the Decapolis how much Jesus had done for him; and everyone was amazed.

[a]Gk he   [b]Gk they   [c]Gk him

COMMENTARY

The city of Gerasa was one of the ten cities of the Decapolis, which lay across the Jordan in the territory ruled by Philip.[192] Geographically, Jesus has ventured well into Gentile territory. The description of the locale within the story, however, fits none of the traditional sites, since Gerasa lies thirty miles southeast of the sea. Jesus is breaking down barriers that separate Jews from Gentiles,

clean from unclean. The sea, which might have been a barrier between the two ways of life, will hereafter be crossed repeatedly.[193] The ominous signs of social and religious chaos attached to this story are as dramatic as the storm at sea that attended the crossing. The demoniac's condition forms the antitype to the civilized, Hellenistic city nearby. He lives like a wild animal among the dead, and repeatedly injures himself because not

192. See S. Applebaum and A. Segal, "Gerasa," *The New Encyclopedia of Archaeological Excavations in the Holy Land,* E. Stern, ed. (New York: Simon & Schuster, 1993) 2:470-79.

193. See Sean Freyne, *Galilee, Jesus and the Gospels: Literary Approaches and Historical Investigations* (Philadelphia: Fortress, 1988) 54-55.

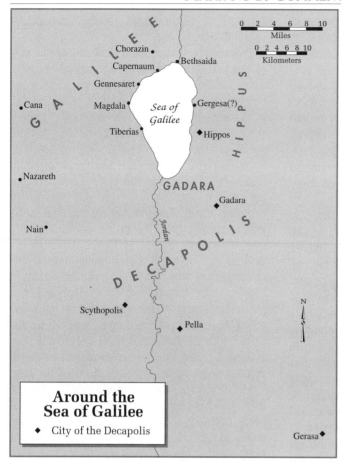

Around the Sea of Galilee

◆ City of the Decapolis

Jewish ritual practices separate the world into categories of clean and unclean. When heard within that context, the elements of impurity in this story are piled one upon another: unclean spirit, dwelling among tombs, and a large herd of swine. This description may also be a deliberate echo of Isa 65:4-5, where the nation that should seek God has lapsed into impure paganism and its citizenry dwell among tombs at night, eat swine's flesh, brew abominable things, and claim to be holy.[196] Mark's Gentile readers may not have sensed the anomaly of Jesus' venturing so dramatically into the chaos of ritual impurity as would Jewish readers, but the description of the possessed man raving among the tombs would evoke the horror of being outside the ordering power of civilization. The dramatic expressions of the man's completely asocial behavior, even to the point of howling like a wild animal rather than using language (v. 5), makes the point dramatically enough for any reader. The demons have stripped this man of every shred of humanity.

Unlike the demoniacs earlier in the story, this man has been driven from all human contact.[197] God created humankind in the divine image (Gen 1:26); this man, however, appears to have lost even the "image of God" that makes him human. Like the demons preceding in earlier stories, this man immediately recognizes that Jesus is the Holy One of God. Unlike the earlier stories, this recognition takes place at a distance. Although his rushing up to prostrate himself before Jesus suggests a gesture of worship appropriate to Jesus' identity (v. 6), the demoniac's words reflect a desire to drive Jesus away that is characteristic of the exorcism genre (v. 7).[198] This juxtaposition may

even the most primitive form of human restraint, chains, can contain him.[194]

Formally, the episode is much more expansive than a normal exorcism story. It ends with two reports about the episode: (1) swineherds rush to carry news to the city (v. 14), and (2) the cured demoniac begins spreading throughout the Decapolis the news about what Jesus has done (v. 20). In addition, the extended description of the man's condition (vv. 3-5) heightens anticipation over what will happen when he encounters Jesus. Finally, the description of the swine's being drowned, which fits the geographical assumptions of Mark's Gospel that the episode took place near the sea, was probably added to a description of a disturbance among the swine that demonstrated the demons' departure.[195]

---

194. Freyne (ibid., 55) suggests that the reference to binding in v. 3 looks back to Jesus' saying about binding the strong man in 3:27.

195. See Robert A. Guelich, *Mark 1–8:26,* WBC 34A (Dallas: Word, 1989) 273.

196. Cf. Rudolph Pesch, *Das Markusevangelium I. Teil,* HTKNT II (Freiburg: Herder, 1977) 1:286.

197. See Mark 1:21-28, where the demoniac is present in the synagogue; in the summary in 1:39, teaching in synagogues and casting out demons are coordinated.

198. See Robert H. Gundry, *Mark: A Commentary on His Apology for the Cross* (Grand Rapids: Eerdmans, 1993), 259.

have belonged to the tradition as Mark knew it, since he explains the demon's response by telling readers that Jesus had already told the demon to leave (v. 8).

Some interpreters have suggested that the demon's name, "Legion," contains a veiled reference to the devastation of people and property caused by the Roman occupation.[199] The Tenth Legion, which used the boar as a symbol on its standard, had been stationed there since 6 CE. The imperial powers that controlled the region perceived themselves to be the source of civilization and peace.[200] The local populace, faced with powers it could not resist, had a very different perception, regarding imperial power as oppressive. Jesus, whose cosmological power was demonstrated at the sea, shows that the presence of God's rule can also disrupt the structural violence done to persons in this setting.[201]

The verbal exchange between the demoniac and Jesus expands the concise pattern of earlier exorcism stories (see Mark 1:23-27). Readers know that Jesus silenced the demons because they were identifying him as Son of God (3:12). This identification was an attempt to ward off the power of the exorcist. Here, the demon engages in an even more elaborate exchange. He first approaches Jesus as suppliant, kneeling before him (v. 6). He then attempts to invoke God's name to drive Jesus away (v. 7). A second exchange between Jesus and the demon forces the demon to reveal his name (v. 9). This revelation provides a striking explanation for the terrible situation in which this man has found himself. At full strength, a legion consisted of 6,000 infantry, 120 cavalry, and associated auxiliaries. The term *legion* might also be used for a battalion of 2,048, which is closer to the number of pigs in the herd.[202] An astonishing visual image results: As soon as Jesus steps into this Gentile territory, a legion prostrates itself

before him. God's kingly power has subdued imperial domination.[203]

Presumably recognizing that he will not be able to ward off Jesus, Legion tries to strike a bargain. Instead of expelling the demons from the territory, permit them to enter the herd of swine grazing in the area (vv. 10-12). True to their character, the Legion destroy the swine by causing them to stampede into the sea and drown (v. 13). The symbolic power of Mark's geographical condensation comes into play at this point, since a violent sign of the demon's exit commonly appears in exorcism stories. The storm at sea has evoked the mythic cosmology of the divine warrior's victory over the chaos monster (4:35-41). Although the demons try to avoid being driven out of the country, they wind up in the sea (the waters of chaos), where they belong. To a Jewish audience the loss of such an enormous number of swine might have been a humorous reversal in the story.[204] Or, if the impurity of the setting was evoked by the swine, the drowned legion of demons suggests that Jesus has cleansed the area.

The story type requires some evidence that the individual has been cured. In this case, the swineherds, fleeing in terror from the epiphany of divine power in Jesus, bring people out from the city.[205] They see that the man who was once completely asocial is in his right mind and wearing clothes (v. 15). Like the demon, the citizens also want Jesus to leave the area (v. 17). Mark does not supply a reason for that request, although suspicion of Jesus' power over the demons (similar to the earlier charges that Jesus was in league with Satan [3:22]) could be presumed to be the reason. Concern over the economic loss of the herd of pigs would seem to be a less likely motive in a story that originated among Jews, who considered swine unclean.

Although the exorcism story proper ends with the evidence that the man has been healed, this episode has been expanded to provide Jesus with his first Gentile missionary (vv. 18-20). Although refusing the man's request to become one of the

199. Lührmann notes that this comparison aims at describing the destructive power of the demons. The demons are being compared to the Roman legions; the legions are not compared with demons. See Dieter Lührmann, *Das Markusevangelium,* HNT (Tubingen: J.C.B. Mohr [Paul Siebeck], 1987) 100.

200. See Klaus Wengst, *Pax Romana and the Peace of Jesus Christ* (Philadelphia: Fortress, 1987) 7-54.

201. See ibid., 66; Gerd Theissen, *The Gospels in Context: Social and Political History in the Synoptic Tradition* (Minneapolis: Fortress, 1991) 110.

202. See Gundry, *Mark,* 263.

203. Mark's narrative echoes assume that readers repeat their experience of hearing the gospel (cf. Malbon, "Echoes and Foreshadowings," 229-30). Therefore, this symbolic gesture echoes the dramatic recognition of Jesus as Son of God on the cross (15:39).

204. See Gundry, *Mark,* 262.

205. This assumes that "flight and fear" (vv. 14-15) were originally attached to the exorcism itself. The herdsmen were not merely running to tell what had happened to the pigs. See Guelich, *Mark,* 284.

disciples, Jesus does empower him to preach the good news and sends the man home to family and friends to tell them what God has done for him. If "Lord" refers to the God of Israel, the injunction evokes the story of Naaman the leper (2 Kgs 5:1-19). Mark concludes the episode by presenting the man as a missionary in the cities of the Decapolis. Although some exegetes have suggested that his departure to preach in the Decapolis represents an element of disobedience similar to the leper's in Mark 1:44-45, the command here does not silence the man. Even though Jesus departs from the territory, the good news begins to spread among the Gentiles. This mission prepares for the later journey that Jesus himself makes throughout the region of the Decapolis (Mark 7:31).

This story is a dramatic illustration of Jesus' earlier claim that his exorcisms represent the binding of Satan (3:27). Its allusions to the OT, to cosmological myths, to powerful experiences of impurity and chaos, and to the political powers of the time have stretched the story beyond the normal elements of an exorcism. Some interpreters have argued that all of Mark's exorcisms belong to the imaginative effort of creating Christianity's founding myth, and thus have no grounding in historical reality.[206] This story does present a clear example of the mythological dimensions of such traditions. However, the ubiquity and social functions of exorcism traditions in antiquity and in traditional, pre-modern cultures suggests that there is no reason to reject the tradition that Jesus was an exorcist. Demons were believed to harass persons from outside (e.g., the demon Asmodeus in Tob 3:7-15), or, in other cases, to take over an individual's personality. Cultural anthropologists have described the social functions of possession and exorcism in traditional societies. Social tensions can be enacted and resolved through exorcism rites.[207] Likewise, in many of the miracles and exorcisms of Jesus, healing involves breaking down traditional boundaries so that persons formally excluded from the community are included.[208] Tales of Jesus as an exorcist may have spread among non-Christians (cf. Mark 9:38-40) more readily than did Jesus' sayings.[209]

206. See Burton L. Mack, *A Myth of Innocence* (Philadelphia: Fortress, 1988) 215.

207. Cf. Adela Yarbro Collins, *The Beginning of the Gospel* (Minneapolis: Fortress, 1992) 46-56; Howard Clark Kee, *Medicine, Miracle and Magic in New Testament Times,* SNTSMS 55 (Cambridge: Cambridge University Press, 1986) 75-79.

208. See Kee, *Medicine, Miracle and Magic,* 79.

209. See Theissen, *Gospels in Context,* 110-12.

REFLECTIONS

1. The story of the man possessed by Legion pits Jesus against the breakdown of every civilizing and humanizing power. Some of the mentally ill homeless persons in large cities, especially those who exhibit violent behavior, evoke the same fear and repulsion in people today that the demoniac must have inspired in ancient Palestinians. Unlike the possessed man in Mark's story, most of the homeless and mentally ill persons in our cities continue to wear clothes, use language, and appear to be functioning members of human society in other interactions with people. Yet volunteers at homeless shelters or at homes for the mentally ill often struggle to overcome their fear and aversion of the persons they are trying to help. But if volunteers do overcome that fear and aversion, they are often surprised to discover human beings beneath the rags, smell, and foul language. They may also become sensitive to the ways in which other volunteers keep the clients at a distance.

2. When the man is healed, he progresses from the non-human life of a rabid animal to that of a person with a home and friends. But he does not return home to take up life as usual. Healing has given him a new mission: to let others know that God's healing power can overcome the worst evils in human experience. Healing has a mission. It involves transformation, not mere restoration to the status quo.

Mark 5:21-43, Two Healing Stories

NIV

21When Jesus had again crossed over by boat to the other side of the lake, a large crowd gathered around him while he was by the lake. 22Then one of the synagogue rulers, named Jairus, came there. Seeing Jesus, he fell at his feet 23and pleaded earnestly with him, "My little daughter is dying. Please come and put your hands on her so that she will be healed and live." 24So Jesus went with him.

A large crowd followed and pressed around him. 25And a woman was there who had been subject to bleeding for twelve years. 26She had suffered a great deal under the care of many doctors and had spent all she had, yet instead of getting better she grew worse. 27When she heard about Jesus, she came up behind him in the crowd and touched his cloak, 28because she thought, "If I just touch his clothes, I will be healed." 29Immediately her bleeding stopped and she felt in her body that she was freed from her suffering.

30At once Jesus realized that power had gone out from him. He turned around in the crowd and asked, "Who touched my clothes?"

31"You see the people crowding against you," his disciples answered, "and yet you can ask, 'Who touched me?'"

32But Jesus kept looking around to see who had done it. 33Then the woman, knowing what had happened to her, came and fell at his feet and, trembling with fear, told him the whole truth. 34He said to her, "Daughter, your faith has healed you. Go in peace and be freed from your suffering."

35While Jesus was still speaking, some men came from the house of Jairus, the synagogue ruler. "Your daughter is dead," they said. "Why bother the teacher any more?"

36Ignoring what they said, Jesus told the synagogue ruler, "Don't be afraid; just believe."

37He did not let anyone follow him except Peter, James and John the brother of James. 38When they came to the home of the synagogue ruler, Jesus saw a commotion, with people crying and wailing loudly. 39He went in and said to them,

NRSV

21When Jesus had crossed again in the boat[a] to the other side, a great crowd gathered around him; and he was by the sea. 22Then one of the leaders of the synagogue named Jairus came and, when he saw him, fell at his feet 23and begged him repeatedly, "My little daughter is at the point of death. Come and lay your hands on her, so that she may be made well, and live." 24So he went with him.

And a large crowd followed him and pressed in on him. 25Now there was a woman who had been suffering from hemorrhages for twelve years. 26She had endured much under many physicians, and had spent all that she had; and she was no better, but rather grew worse. 27She had heard about Jesus, and came up behind him in the crowd and touched his cloak, 28for she said, "If I but touch his clothes, I will be made well." 29Immediately her hemorrhage stopped; and she felt in her body that she was healed of her disease. 30Immediately aware that power had gone forth from him, Jesus turned about in the crowd and said, "Who touched my clothes?" 31And his disciples said to him, "You see the crowd pressing in on you; how can you say, 'Who touched me?'" 32He looked all around to see who had done it. 33But the woman, knowing what had happened to her, came in fear and trembling, fell down before him, and told him the whole truth. 34He said to her, "Daughter, your faith has made you well; go in peace, and be healed of your disease."

35While he was still speaking, some people came from the leader's house to say, "Your daughter is dead. Why trouble the teacher any further?" 36But overhearing[b] what they said, Jesus said to the leader of the synagogue, "Do not fear, only believe." 37He allowed no one to follow him except Peter, James, and John, the brother of James. 38When they came to the house of the leader of the synagogue, he saw a commotion, people weeping and wailing loudly. 39When he had entered, he said to them, "Why do you make

[a]Other ancient authorities lack *in the boat*   [b]Or *ignoring*; other ancient authorities read *hearing*

NIV	NRSV
"Why all this commotion and wailing? The child is not dead but asleep." [40]But they laughed at him. After he put them all out, he took the child's father and mother and the disciples who were with him, and went in where the child was. [41]He took her by the hand and said to her, *"Talitha koum!"* (which means, "Little girl, I say to you, get up!"). [42]Immediately the girl stood up and walked around (she was twelve years old). At this they were completely astonished. [43]He gave strict orders not to let anyone know about this, and told them to give her something to eat.	a commotion and weep? The child is not dead but sleeping." [40]And they laughed at him. Then he put them all outside, and took the child's father and mother and those who were with him, and went in where the child was. [41]He took her by the hand and said to her, "Talitha cum," which means, "Little girl, get up!" [42]And immediately the girl got up and began to walk about (she was twelve years of age). At this they were overcome with amazement. [43]He strictly ordered them that no one should know this, and told them to give her something to eat.

COMMENTARY

5:24b-34. Mark combines the story of a woman who has been hemorrhaging for twelve years with the cure of Jairus's daughter by having the former occur while Jesus is on the way to Jairus's house. In contrast to the esteemed synagogue official, the woman remains a nameless member of the crowd. The length of her affliction and the fact that she has been impoverished by spending all of her resources on doctors who have only made her condition worse underline the crisis of her situation (v. 26). Her flow of blood poses the danger of ritual impurity for anyone who comes into contact with her (Lev 15:19-33).[210] Therefore, she must have been subject to social isolation similar to that of the man with the scale disease (1:40-42).

The leper was healed as soon as Jesus touched him. In this story, the woman concludes on the basis of Jesus' reputation that merely touching his clothes will be sufficient to heal her (vv. 27-29). This gesture depicts Jesus as a thaumaturge (a performer of miracles). Magical power flows from the charismatic healer to his clothing and anything that touches it. (Acts 5:15 attributes healing power to even the shadows of Peter and John.[211]) Her instantaneous healing demonstrates that Jesus has such power, but the story does not end with that conclusion. The instant result separates

Jesus from other healers, especially the doctors on whom whom she has spent her resources, only to become worse (vv. 25-26). In addition, the woman's condition has made her "impure." Therefore, she must overcome social and ritual boundaries to approach and touch Jesus. Struggling through the crowd demonstrates her ability to overcome obstacles that would separate her from Jesus.[212]

In the controversy stories, Jesus shows himself aware of the inner thoughts and motives of his opponents. Here, he immediately recognizes the healing power that has passed from him to the woman (v. 30). By indicating that Jesus had this realization, Mark demonstrates that Jesus' clothes are not endowed with magical powers. The significance of the miracle requires a confrontation between Jesus and the woman. In that exchange, her faith will be identified as the real source of her healing (v. 34). Although the woman, acting merely on Jesus' reputation, was healed, Jesus' disciples continue to be ignorant of Jesus' real power. They provide the expected obstacle to public disclosure of the miracle by wondering at Jesus' claim that someone has touched him. In a crowd, many people would do so (v. 31).

The woman's fear at being discovered suggests the magical view of such healing powers. She might be accused of stealing what belongs to the

210. Cf. Marla J. Selvidge, *Woman, Cult and Miracle Recital: A Redaction-critical Investigation on Mark 5:24-34* (Lewisburg: Bucknell University Press, 1990).
211. See Pesch, *Das Markusevangelium,* 1:302.
212. See Gundry, *Mark,* 269.

healer without appropriate supplication (or payment)![213] Other interpreters suggest that her fear stems from the possible accusation of ritual contamination. Purification legislation from Qumran equates women with a flux of blood and males with a genital discharge. After the discharge stops, a seven-day purification period, followed by laundering clothing, is required before those who touch such a person are free from that contamination.[214] Readers know that Jesus was not concerned about the problems of ritual contamination, since he had touched the leper (1:41), and the woman is said to be familiar with Jesus' reputation. Therefore, ritual impurity does not appear to be the primary focus of Mark's narrative. Unlike the story of the leper's healing, Jesus does not instruct the woman to observe the required period of purification.

The exchange between Jesus and the woman removes any suggestion that Jesus' clothes were endowed with magical power, nor does Jesus condemn her for attempted "theft" of his power. Jesus does not possess a magic force that accounts for his ability to heal. Instead, healing reflects the presence of God's saving power (Deut 32:39; Isa 35:4-6; 53:4-5; Hos 11:3; Mal 4:1-3),[215] and Jesus' saving and healing presence demonstrates that the kingdom of God is near.[216] The woman's gesture of pushing through the crowd to touch Jesus' garment resembles the faith exhibited by those who brought the paralytic to Jesus (2:5a). Jesus points to the woman's faith as the real agent of healing and pronounces the cure permanent (v. 34).[217]

The fear the woman exhibits as she responds to Jesus' question stems from her knowledge of what has happened to her (v. 33). In other words, she recognizes the extraordinary divine power possessed by Jesus. Fear and trembling are common responses to the presence of the divine. The disciples were "filled with a great fear" after Jesus calmed the storm (4:41). In that situation, they were accused of having no faith (4:40). Likewise, the Gerasenes were so afraid of Jesus' powers that they asked him to leave their country (5:15-17). Jesus addresses the woman as "daughter," suggesting that she now has a personal relationship to Jesus as one of his family (3:35). (Some see his form of addressing her as an indication of the difference in social status between the two, although it appears to narrow the gap exhibited by the woman's falling at Jesus' feet.[218]) The term may have been introduced when this story was combined with the cure of Jairus's daughter (v. 35). It carries more personal overtones than would the term "woman," which had been used for her in the rest of the story.

5:21-24a, 35-43. Jairus stands at the opposite end of the socioeconomic scale from the unnamed woman. His status as a "ruler of the synagogue" marks him out as a wealthy and influential member of the community.[219] He would have been accustomed to having others beg him for favors. One might expect such a person to send an emissary to ask Jesus to come and heal the little girl.[220] The fact that the father comes and throws himself at Jesus' feet begging for help shows that he is as desperate as the hemorrhaging woman. He, too, knows Jesus' reputation as a healer and is certain that if Jesus lays his hands on the girl, she will recover (vv. 22-23). Mark's readers may be somewhat surprised to find the synagogue leader pleading for help, since Jesus' last healing in a synagogue led to a plot against him (3:1-6). However, they also know that Mark does not attribute that hostility to the local synagogue leaders but to scribes of the Pharisee party, Pharisees,

---

213. The need to pay physicians, which had exhausted the woman's resources (5:26), was apparently commonly noted in antiquity. Philo notes that the Essenes had a fund to pay for the medical care of all of their members. See Philo *Every Good Man Is Free* 87; cf. Kee, *Medicine, Miracle and Magic,* 25.

214. 4QThoharot A1.9 (=4Q274). Harrington, *Impurity Systems,* 85-87.

215. Kee, *Medicine, Miracle and Magic,* 12-17

216. Ibid., 73.

217. See Gerd Theissen, *The Miracle Stories of the Early Church Tradition,* trans. Francis McDonagh (Philadelphia: Fortress, 1983) 129-33. The contrast of faith in the power of a god to heal to skepticism appears in Greco-Roman miracle stories. Some tales show the god Asclepius healing a person who claimed to doubt the god's power. Faith, or its equivalent hope in the Epidaurus inscriptions, may be a characteristic of the suppliant, or it may emerge after the healing.

218. Bruce J. Malina and Richard L. Rohrbaugh, *A Social-Science Commentary on the Synoptic Gospels* (Philadelphia: Fortress, 1992) 209-10, suggest that by addressing the woman as a family member Jesus demonstrates that the social ostracism caused by her disease has been overcome.

219. Inscriptions suggest that the "ruler of the synagogue" (ἀρχισυνάγωγος *archisynagōgos*) was in charge of supervising the worship of the community. Such persons might also be "leaders" (ἄρχοντες *archontes*) of the Jewish community, a status indicated by use of the title ἄρχων *archōn*. See E. Schürer *A History of the Jewish People in the Time of Jesus Christ,* rev. ed. (Edinburgh: T. & T. Clark, 1986) 3:100-101.

220. The man uses a diminutive of "daughter" (θυγάτριον *thygatrion*). Other diminutives are used later in the story: "child" (παιδίον *paidion*; vv. 39, 40) and "little girl" (κοράσιον *korasion*; vv. 41, 42). Only the messengers who bring news of her death use the common form (θυγάτηρ *thygatēr*; v. 35). The diminutives contribute a sense of familial affection; so Gundry, *Mark,* 279.

and Herodians—that is, religious and political officials independent of the local community.[221]

By interrupting the journey to Jairus's house with the story of the hemorrhaging woman, Mark is able to show that Jesus can heal a chronic condition without even touching the person directly. Her story also highlights the importance of faith to the healing. Jesus is not a healer with magic powers to sell. The interruption also creates a time delay in the narrative, providing space for the girl to die, messengers to report to the father, and mourners to gather at the house (vv. 35, 38).

The messengers present an obstacle to the healing by advising the father to leave Jesus alone, since the girl has died. Jesus takes the initiative by telling Jairus to have faith (v. 36). The reference to faith picks up the conclusion to the healing of the woman. By interweaving the two stories, Mark has provided an opportunity for the father to witness that scene.

Associates and friends continue to provide an obstacle to the healing. When Jesus and those with him arrive at the house, the mourners laugh at his claim that the girl is not dead (vv. 38-40). However, their response assures readers that the girl is indeed dead. Funeral rites have already begun. Such discouraging mockery (v. 40) fits the commonplace element in Greco-Roman miracle traditions of the miracle's being the god's answer to those who doubt his powers. As in the lengthy account of the woman's illness, the mourners' skepticism shows the reader how extraordinary Jesus' powers really are. He will overcome death, not a mistaken diagnosis.

Unlike the earlier miracles, which were performed in public, Jesus limits the audience for this one. The three disciples who accompany him—Peter, James, and John—will serve as an inner group at the transfiguration (9:2) and in Gethsemane (14:33). This limitation of witnesses echoes two OT scenes: (1) Elijah's taking the widow's son apart to his own chamber when he restores the boy's life (1 Kgs 17:17-24) and (2) Elisha and his servant's going into the room alone to restore life to the Shunammite woman's son (2 Kgs 4:32-37). Although in the OT examples the mother is excluded, here Jesus includes the parents. Con-

trasted with the earlier pattern of a prophet's restoring life, Jesus does not engage in extended prayer and physical gestures toward the body before life is restored. Taking the girl's hand, Jesus immediately restores her to life, just as the woman had been immediately cured when she touched Jesus' garment.

Formally, this story has a two-part conclusion. The girl shows that she has been healed by getting up and walking. The astonished reaction of witnesses indicates that a miracle has taken place. Yet, Jesus apparently provides another proof of the cure when he commands them to feed the girl (v. 43).[222] The parallel versions adjust their accounts to the conventional form. Matthew 9:25 shortens the whole episode and omits the feeding. Luke 8:55 relocates the feeding prior to the concluding references to amazement and the command to silence. Since there are complex links between the sections of Mark 4:1–8:21, Mark may have shifted feeding to the end of the story. Two major feeding miracles appear in the account that follows (6:31-44; 8:13-21).[223]

Mark attaches a command to silence to the conclusion of this miracle (v. 43). A similar command to the leper had been immediately disregarded (1:44). On the other hand, the Gerasene demoniac had been told to return home and tell others what God had done for him (5:19). No reaction is described in this context. Given the narrative context, the command makes no sense. Jesus has expelled a crowd of mourners from the house. Friends and associates have been involved with the family from the beginning. Clearly, the girl's cure will not remain a secret. If the small group of witnesses remains silent about what happened in the room, then perhaps Jesus' explanation to the crowd, "not dead, but sleeping" (v. 39), might prevail. This development contradicts the usual response to skeptics in Greco-Roman healing stories. The accounts inscribed at shrines like Epidauros demonstrate to the unbelieving that the god (and his shrine) had healing powers. Some scholars think that collections of Jesus' miracles played a similar role. They served as demonstrations that God's divine power was in Jesus, the Son of God. The miracle itself provokes the ques-

221. See Elizabeth S. Malbon, "The Jewish Leaders in the Gospel of Mark: A Literary Study of Marcan Characterization," *JBL* 108 (1989) 264-67.

222. See Guelich, *Mark*, 293.
223. See Elizabeth Struthers Malbon, "Echoes and Foreshadowings in Mark 4–8: Reading and Rereading," *JBL* 112 (1993) 220-21.

tion of Jesus' identity and awe over the power he exercises.[224] Since Mark also emphasizes the necessity of Jesus' death on the cross, commands to remain silent caution readers against treating the miracles as evidence for the true identity of Jesus.

Jairus's request expresses confidence that if Jesus touched the girl she would "get well," a secular rendering of "be saved" (σωθῇ *sōthē*). The woman with hemorrhaging was assured that her faith had made her well ("saved her," 5:34). Use of the verb *save* in a context that anticipates a miracle (cf. 6:56) is a prominent feature in the crucifixion story: Jesus is challenged to "save" himself (15:30); scribes and Pharisees comment that although Jesus could save others, he cannot save himself (15:31); they challenge him to come down so that they can "see and believe" (15:32). Commands to silence concerning Jesus' power over death may anticipate Jesus' command to the same three disciples not to tell anyone about the transfiguration until after the resurrection (9:9).

Other exegetes think that the command belongs to the pre-Markan version of the story.[225]

The later episodes of the Syrophoenician woman's daughter (7:24-30) and the healing of a deaf man (7:31-36) will make it clear that Jesus cannot hide from the crowds (7:24). His commands to silence are routinely disobeyed and do not generate faith, only amazement at his powers (7:36-37). Two examples in which Jesus commands silence involve the use of Aramaic phrases as part of the healing (5:41; 7:34). This element, the use of "secret words," provides another traditional reason for a command to silence, along with removing the crowd from the room prior to the miracle.[226] For Mark, both the woman and Jairus came to Jesus with the faith appropriate to disciples. Without such faith, merely witnessing Jesus' powerful deeds will not convert the scornful crowd into believers. The next episode (6:1-6a) suggests that Jesus cannot work miracles among those who lack faith.[227]

---

224. See Theissen, *Miracle Stories*, 212-14.

225. See Gundry, *Mark*, 276. Gundry thinks that Mark would not have permitted the tension between this command and the Gerasene demoniac

to stand if the silence command had not been traditional. He argues that feeding the girl is a strategy designed to permit Jesus to leave the area before the crowd discovers the miracle he has performed.

226. See Theissen, *Miracle Stories*, 149-50; Rudolph Pesch, *Das Markusevangelium I. Teil*, HTKNT II (Freiburg: Herder, 1977) 1:311-12.

227. See Pesch, *Das Markusevangelium*, 1:314.

REFLECTIONS

1. The story of a nameless woman who has exhausted her resources seeking medical treatment for a chronic condition strikes a responsive chord with many older adults today. When they were younger, doctors seemed able to provide cures. Now these persons seem to have an ever-expanding list of medical complaints. As one man in his seventies put it, "After a certain age, you are never really well. Just less sick." The financial drain and emotional difficulty of dealing with the bureaucratic, impersonal, and compartmentalized medical establishment compound the difficulty.

2. While the woman is a hero of persistence and faith, Jesus and the disciples appear to represent negative experiences associated with visits to the doctor: impersonal and sometimes crowded waiting rooms; the sense that the doctor wants to get the patient out of the way, and the dismay when the patient does not respond to treatment as anticipated. Jesus at first appears to condemn the woman rather than celebrate her healing. The strong affirmation he gives to her faith at the end of the story alleviates the apparent harshness in the search for the woman. Jesus does not take the credit for making her well but points to her faith as the real source of healing.

3. Every parent with a seriously ill child can identify with Jairus. Parents find it more painful to entrust a young child to the hospital knowing that the youngster is about to undergo a risky or lengthy surgical procedure than to undergo similar treatment themselves. Parents and other family members feel the burden of reassuring the child that the doctors will make him or her all better, even when they know that the prognosis is not good. Stories like this one seem to promise too much. For every family whose child makes a complete recovery from major surgery or life-threatening illness, there is another family whose child dies. Where is faith and healing in that situation?

Faith and healing come after the fact, as families learn to remember with gratitude the child they have lost. The mourners who mock Jesus in the story may not have believed that the little girl had any future. Some interpreters have suggested that since the verb for "rise up" (ἐγείρω *egeirō*) used here is also used for the resurrection, this story contains a message about resurrection for Christian readers. Jesus cares for the girl just as much, whether she returns to earthly life or passes to life with God after death.

Those interpreters who think that the command to silence points toward the cross remind us that faith acknowledges that the crucified is Son of God. Christians do not base their faith in Christ on miracles.

Mark 6:1-6*a*, Disbelief in Nazareth

NIV

6 Jesus left there and went to his hometown, accompanied by his disciples. ²When the Sabbath came, he began to teach in the synagogue, and many who heard him were amazed.

"Where did this man get these things?" they asked. "What's this wisdom that has been given him, that he even does miracles! ³Isn't this the carpenter? Isn't this Mary's son and the brother of James, Joseph,*a* Judas and Simon? Aren't his sisters here with us?" And they took offense at him.

⁴Jesus said to them, "Only in his hometown, among his relatives and in his own house is a prophet without honor." ⁵He could not do any miracles there, except lay his hands on a few sick people and heal them. ⁶And he was amazed at their lack of faith.

*a*3 Greek *Joses*, a variant of *Joseph*

NRSV

6 He left that place and came to his hometown, and his disciples followed him. ²On the sabbath he began to teach in the synagogue, and many who heard him were astounded. They said, "Where did this man get all this? What is this wisdom that has been given to him? What deeds of power are being done by his hands! ³Is not this the carpenter, the son of Mary*a* and brother of James and Joses and Judas and Simon, and are not his sisters here with us?" And they took offense*b* at him. ⁴Then Jesus said to them, "Prophets are not without honor, except in their hometown, and among their own kin, and in their own house." ⁵And he could do no deed of power there, except that he laid his hands on a few sick people and cured them. ⁶And he was amazed at their unbelief.

*a*Other ancient authorities read *son of the carpenter and of Mary*
*b*Or *stumbled*

COMMENTARY

The three miracles in chapter 5 demonstrate the divine powers evident in Jesus' miracles. Jesus overcomes the life-destroying powers of demonic possession, chronic illness, and death. Jairus and the hemorrhaging woman sought Jesus' help because they had faith in what they had heard about him. Their faith forms a striking contrast to the reception Jesus receives in his hometown. His

ministry there begins as did his initial ministry in Capernaum. Jesus astonishes those gathered in the synagogue with his teaching and healing (vv. 1-2; Mark 1:21-28). Readers might expect an example of healing or exorcism to follow as in Capernaum, but it does not.

Jesus' natural family were excluded from the circle of believers in an earlier episode (3:21,

31-35). That episode establishes the contrast between the Twelve, whom Jesus chose to be with him (3:14); the natural family of Jesus (3:21, 31); and the wider circle of Jesus' followers, his new family, those who do the will of God (3:35). Jesus' return to Nazareth, with members of his new family (the disciples; v. 1) raises the question left open in the earlier episode: Will those with familial and social ties to Jesus believe?

Jesus' human origins form a road block to the belief that should follow from experiencing the extraordinary wisdom and healing power exercised by Jesus. Reading the episode against the backdrop of honor and shame in peasant villages provides some insight into the hostile reception.[228] Jesus has stepped out of the status and role in society that he had in the village of 1,600 to 2,000 people. Our only evidence in the New Testament for Jesus' occupation is the term commonly translated "carpenter" (τέκτων tektōn; 6:3). This word can be used to describe anyone who works in wood or other hard materials. In that day, people would not have built whole houses out of wood, so as a carpenter, Jesus would have been called upon to produce door frames and other wooden objects, and would not build complete dwellings.[229] Since Galilee was prosperous during this period, Jesus and his family were not impoverished tenant farmers or day laborers. But his status as a local craftsman would have been considerably lower than that of a member of the educated class, who could devote himself to learning the Law. Villagers commonly resent those who attempt to elevate their position above that to which they are entitled by birth. The attempt by Jesus' family to stop his wandering and public preaching in 3:21 implies that from the perspective of the village, Jesus was thought to be dishonoring his family.

Mark shows no knowledge of any tradition about Jesus' conception and birth. Designating Jesus as "son of Mary" rather than "son of Joseph" (v. 3) may have been intended as an insult by the crowd. The question "Where did this man get all

this [wisdom and power]?" (v. 2) may imply a hostile answer: Perhaps he is the offspring of someone other than his father.[230] As belief in the perpetual virginity of Mary emerged in later centuries, interpreters had to find other explanations for the siblings referred to in these passages (v. 3).[231] Mark 6:17 uses the term *brother* for the half-brothers, Herod and Philip, who were Herod's sons by different mothers. Therefore, it is not possible to tell whether the brothers and sisters of Jesus are biological children of Mary or her stepchildren. Mark is not interested in specifying the precise relationship between Jesus and his other siblings. The townspeople are scandalized by the human origins of Jesus, whom they know as a carpenter.

As Mark's readers would expect, Jesus responds to what people are thinking about him. The proverbial saying "Prophets are not without honor, except in their hometown" (v. 4) has been expanded with two clauses: "among their kin" and "in their own house." The original proverb spoke about the "homeland" (πατρίς patris). The qualifying clauses narrow the region down to the prophet's household and relatives. If this retort is understood as an insult, then Jesus has responded to his critics in kind.[232] Since the miracles in the previous chapter emphasize the importance of faith in those who approach Jesus for healing, the conclusion that Jesus is unable to work many miracles in Nazareth is hardly surprising. Mark moderates that conclusion somewhat by commenting that Jesus did heal some people (v. 5). The next sentence applies the verb rendered "to marvel," "to be amazed" (θαυμάζω thaumazō) to Jesus. The same verb designates the response of those in the Decapolis to the possessed man's story about Jesus' healing (5:20) and to Pilate's reaction to Jesus' refusal to answer (15:5) and his early demise (15:44). The term does not imply either faith or insight into Jesus' identity. In an ironic twist, Jesus is amazed at the lack of faith in his home village.

228. See Bruce J. Malina and Richard L. Rohrbaugh, *A Social-Science Commentary on the Synoptic Gospels* (Philadelphia: Fortress, 1992) 212-13.

229. See John P. Meier, *A Marginal Jew: Rethinking the Historical Jesus* (New York: Doubleday, 1991) 280-85. Meier finds no evidence to support the thesis proposed by other exegetes that Jesus was a master builder involved in constructing the new cities in Galilee, like Sepphoris and Caesarea. The Gospels never show Jesus having anything to do with the urban centers in Galilee.

230. See Malina and Rohrbaugh, *Social-Science Commentary,* 214. The use of such a social insult should not be taken as "historical information" any more than the tradition of trading insults about the opponent's mother among some teenagers today conveys facts about their respective mothers. The point of the insults is to cut the speaker down to size.

231. See Meier, *A Marginal Jew,* 318-32.

232. See Malina and Rohrbaugh, *Social-Science Commentary,* 212.

REFLECTIONS

1. The episode in Nazareth forms a somber counterpoint to the astounding success that has surrounded Jesus in other towns. Someone who can go into the chaos of the Gentile territory across the Sea of Galilee and emerge victorious cannot convert those in his own town! Since Paul assumed that Christians in Galatia were familiar with the fact that James, the brother of the Lord, was a prominent leader in the Jerusalem church (Gal 1:19; 2:9), Mark's readers probably knew that members of Jesus' family eventually came to believe in Jesus; 1 Cor 15:7 reports that the risen Lord appeared to James. Another brother in the list, Jude, was credited with composing a brief epistle.

Many people are surprised by this story. They think that the people who know Jesus best should have been the first to follow him. Yet they also know human experiences of rejection when attempts to reach out and help family members are rebuffed. People who are able to help others solve complicated personal problems are helpless when their own children are in trouble. When some eighth graders were asked why they thought Jesus was rejected, one boy commented, "Wasn't his father, Joseph, dead? Well, what was he doing running out on his mother? She might have starved." Mark's list suggests that Mary had plenty of people to care for her, but this point has merit. The oldest son was expected to take his father's place in the extended family. Jesus' behavior must have been a painful puzzle to his family.[233]

2. The comments attributed to the townspeople remind us of an important fact about Jesus: He was a real human being. He had spent much of his adult life at a trade, working with wood. Some scholars even surmise that he might have spent time working on building the magnificent Gentile cities, like Sepphoris, that were not far from his village. The knowledge that Jesus gains of rich persons and their servants while working at this trade reappears in his parables. Modern readers, who find the divine powers are exhibited in the miracles difficult to imagine, find this passage reassuring. Jesus did not overwhelm people as though he were a larger-than-life action hero. If you were to meet Jesus at Levi's dinner or on the job, Jesus would appear to be just another human being. Faith overcomes the scandal of the ordinary appearance of Jesus when it recognizes that God's healing power comes to humanity through him.

233. Luke explicitly incorporates this motif into the infancy narratives by having Simeon predict this situation to Mary (Luke 2:34-35).

MARK 6:6b–8:26, JESUS CONTINUES PREACHING IN GALILEE

OVERVIEW

Jesus now departs from Nazareth for another circuit of Galilean villages (6:6b). The disciples, who were selected during the first journey to be with Jesus and to participate in his ministry (3:14-15), begin to participate in preaching the gospel (6:7-13). John the Baptist, whose arrest signaled the beginning of Jesus' ministry, is executed (6:14-29). (Some interpreters prefer to begin the second major section of the narrative with John the Baptist's death, since the Gospel opens with the Baptist.[234]) Jesus rescues the disciples from another storm at sea (6:47-52). He then engages in controversies over observance of the Law (7:1-23)

234 Christopher Bryan, *A Preface to Mark: Notes on the Gospel in Its Literary and Cultural Settings* (New York: Oxford, 1993) 95. Bryan suggests that the sending out of the Twelve is a hinge to the next section.

and continues to attract crowds (6:53-56). The meals in other peoples' houses, found in the previous section of the Gospel, are replaced by two feeding miracles in which Jesus provides for large crowds (6:33-44; 8:1-9). Most of these episodes confirm the picture of Jesus that has been drawn during the first preaching journey. The feeding miracles introduce a new note of Jesus' compassion for the crowds (6:32; 8:2).

The miracle of healing the blind man in

Bethsaida concludes the series of events around the sea (8:22-26).[235] Since a matching cure occurs as Jesus enters Jerusalem (10:46-52) other interpreters prefer to see this episode as the beginning of the final segment in Jesus' Galilean ministry.[236]

---

235. See Norman R. Petersen, "The Composition of Mark 4:1–8:26," *HTR* 93 (1980) 198-99.
236. Cf. Elizabeth Struthers Malbon, "Echoes and Foreshadowings in Mark 4–8: Reading and Rereading," *JBL* 112 (1993) 225-26.

Mark 6:6b-13, Sending Out the Disciples

NIV	NRSV
Then Jesus went around teaching from village to village. [7]Calling the Twelve to him, he sent them out two by two and gave them authority over evil[a] spirits. [8]These were his instructions: "Take nothing for the journey except a staff—no bread, no bag, no money in your belts. [9]Wear sandals but not an extra tunic. [10]Whenever you enter a house, stay there until you leave that town. [11]And if any place will not welcome you or listen to you, shake the dust off your feet when you leave, as a testimony against them." [12]They went out and preached that people should repent. [13]They drove out many demons and anointed many sick people with oil and healed them.	Then he went about among the villages teaching. [7]He called the twelve and began to send them out two by two, and gave them authority over the unclean spirits. [8]He ordered them to take nothing for their journey except a staff; no bread, no bag, no money in their belts; [9]but to wear sandals and not to put on two tunics. [10]He said to them, "Wherever you enter a house, stay there until you leave the place. [11]If any place will not welcome you and they refuse to hear you, as you leave, shake off the dust that is on your feet as a testimony against them." [12]So they went out and proclaimed that all should repent. [13]They cast out many demons, and anointed with oil many who were sick and cured them.

[a]7 Greek *unclean*

COMMENTARY

Jesus has chosen the Twelve to participate in his ministry (3:14-15). He now sends them out with the authority to expel demons (vv. 7, 12-13) as well as to preach the news of the kingdom. Thus, unlike the individuals who responded to being healed by telling others about Jesus (1:45; 5:20), the Twelve participate directly in Jesus' own activity of bringing about the rule of God. Jesus gives them the power to undermine the power of evil during their mission. However, most of the attention Mark gives to the disciples focuses on their failure to understand who Jesus is.[237] This

section deliberately recalls the initial choice of the disciples. Jesus calls the disciples to him (3:13; 6:7), and he intends for them to preach and exorcise (3:14b-15; 6:7, 12). Since their mission is successful, this section demonstrates that the disciples were able to carry out the ministry for which Jesus had chosen them. At the same time, they do not possess independent authority. They are extensions of Jesus' own activity.[238]

The early Christian practice of anointing the

---

237. See Ernest Best, *Mark: The Gospel as Story* (Edinburgh: T. & T. Clark, 1983) 44-50.

238. Mark may be instructing missionaries of his own time in the meaning of their own authority as well. See ibid., 49. Generally, the disciples are typical followers of a powerful teacher rather than missionaries and leaders.

sick (cf. Jas 5:4) is attached to the mission of the disciples (v. 13). This correspondence encourages readers to see the origins of early Christian missionary activity in the authority and ministry of Jesus.[239] Missionary pairs appear to have been characteristic of early Christianity. Jesus initially called pairs of brothers (1:16-20). Acts refers to Peter and John (Acts 3:11; 8:9), to Barnabas and Paul (Acts 11:25-26), and to companions whom Peter takes with him to Cornelius (Acts 10:23). The dangers of travel in antiquity make such arrangements necessary.[240] Other interpreters have suggested that the use of pairs should be associated with the legal requirement for two witnesses to testify in a case (Num 35:30; Deut 19:15). A judicial note is introduced in the gesture of judgment against those who refuse to hear the messengers of the gospel (v. 11).[241]

A collection of rules to govern the conduct of traveling missionaries forms the central section of this pericope (vv. 8-11). The variants in Q (Matt 10:8-14; Luke 9:3-6; 10:2-12) contain even more radical conditions, emphasizing the urgency of eschatological judgment. The towns that reject the message can expect to experience God's wrath (Luke 10:11-12). Although Mark's "testimony against them" (v. 11) suggests condemnation in the judgment, there is no hint that this mission confronts people with the eschatological summons to repent.

The lists of provisions for the journey vary in all versions of the missionary command (Matt 10:9-10; Mark 6:8; Luke 9:3; 10:4). Such variations would be anticipated in rules passed on by oral tradition.[242] Mark permits staff and sandals, apparently an accommodation to early Christian missionary practice.[243] Q rejects these. The Q formulation echoes the views of ancient cynic philosophers who challenged the presumptions of culture by claiming that it created unnatural needs and passions, although the Cynics were noted for carrying a bag and a staff; the staff was sometimes used against the audience as well as against animals. Consequently, the details may have been intended to distinguish Jesus' disciples from such wandering preachers.[244] Mark's instructions permit disciples adequate clothing, but not a second tunic, which would have provided protection from the cold night air. Rather, they are to trust God to provide lodging each night. They are not permitted to carry money or extra provisions from one place to another. Thus it is clear that the disciples are not engaged in preaching and healing in order to make money, which may have subjected them to the charge of being religious charlatans or magicians. The disciples were to depend on local hospitality. Since they were required to remain in the first house that welcomed them (v. 10), they could not move to a household that offered more luxurious accommodations. Mark lacks telling the reason for such hospitality referred to in Q (Matt 10:10; Luke 10:7) and Paul (1 Cor 9:14, 17-18): "The worker is worthy of his pay."[245]

The final instruction provides a response for those who reject the disciples. Shaking dust off one's feet was a gesture of cursing a place. The elements of curse and divine condemnation are more evident in Q (Matt 10:14; Luke 10:10-12). On the day of judgment, the rejecting towns will be worse off than Sodom and Gomorrah. Shaking dust off the feet may reflect the shaking of one's clothing as a sign of renunciation (Neh 5:13; Acts 18:6). Clearing away even the dust under one's sandals suggests an even more thorough rejection than shaking out garments or washing one's hands (Matt 27:24). Mark may have moderated the severity of the judgment oracle in Q, since he does not anticipate Christian missionaries calling down curses on unreceptive towns. The tradition merely stands as a testimony before God that the

239. See Rudolph Pesch, *Das Markusevangelium I. Teil*, HTKNT II (Freiburg: Herder, 1977) 1:325-26. Pesch argues that the early Christian etiology for its missionary activities is preserved in a more primitive form in Q (Matt 9:37-38; 10:7-16; Luke 10:2-12). Mark's introduction of narrative elements into the collection of missionary sayings seems to be a secondary historicizing of the tradition. Cf. Dieter Lührmann, "The Gospel of Mark and the Sayings Collection Q," *JBL* 108 (1989) 62-63.

240. See Lionel Casson, *Travel in the Ancient World* (Baltimore: Johns Hopkins Press, 1994) 72-73.

241. So Joseph A. Fitzmyer, *The Gospel According to Luke X–XXIV*, AB 28A (New York: Doubleday, 1985) 847.

242. See the chart in W. D. Davies and Dale C. Allison, Jr., *A Critical and Exegetical Commentary on the Gospel According to Saint Matthew, VIII–XVIII*, 2 vols., ICC (Edinburgh: T. & T. Clark, 1988–91) 2:171.

243. So Davies and Allison, ibid., 172. They also note a possible OT allusion: Exodus 12:11 instructs the Israelites to eat the Passover with sandals on their feet and a staff in their hand.

244. Or Mark even used the lack of a staff as a sign of pacifism. See Ibid., 173. According to Josephus, the Essenes took nothing but weapons to protect themselves against robbers (*War* 2.125).

245. Matthew's version substitutes "food" or "nourishment" (τροφή *trophē*) for "wages" (μισθός *misthos*) in the Q saying, apparently to lessen the conflict with the prohibition against carrying money. See ibid., 174.

town has refused to hear God's word. Mark's judgment sayings correlate witness to or rejection of the Son of Man with a person's status in the judgment (Mark 8:38).

REFLECTIONS

1. The Twelve share in Jesus' authority and mission. They do not become independent of Jesus. Both the teaching and healing they perform are extensions of Jesus' own ministry. All ministry in the church recognizes an obligation to continue Jesus' work. It sometimes appears that the church has set its own institutional survival ahead of the gospel. Religious leaders sometimes appear to engage in ministry to fulfill a personal need for prestige, influence, or even material gain. These simple instructions, which reflect the practice of early Christian missionaries, call those engaged in ministry back to the fundamental basis of all preaching, healing, and teaching: the ministry and person of Jesus. Whatever material resources ministers possess should serve the needs of those to whom they bring the gospel.

2. The variations in the rules for missionaries show that the earliest Christians recognized the need to adapt to the circumstances in which they found themselves. The important point made by the early rules takes a very different form when we think about Christian missions today. The principle that the gospel comes to bring healing, peace, and good news to people means that missionaries must adapt to the culture of those they come to serve. They are not agents of colonialism or political expansion. Even so, Christian missionaries sometimes die as martyrs when local violence breaks out around them. Sometimes a situation may become too dangerous or difficult for the missionaries to remain. The gesture of shaking dust off one's shoes does not have to mean cursing those who will not listen. It acknowledges the mysterious elements in human freedom. Even the most sophisticated and culturally sensitive presentation of the gospel can be rejected. Christians are not to waste their resources in such situations. Others are waiting to hear the gospel.

Mark 6:14-29, The Death of John the Baptist

[14]King Herod heard about this, for Jesus' name had become well known. Some were saying,[a] "John the Baptist has been raised from the dead, and that is why miraculous powers are at work in him."

[15]Others said, "He is Elijah."

And still others claimed, "He is a prophet, like one of the prophets of long ago."

[16]But when Herod heard this, he said, "John, the man I beheaded, has been raised from the dead!"

[17]For Herod himself had given orders to have John arrested, and he had him bound and put in prison. He did this because of Herodias, his brother Philip's wife, whom he had married. [18]For John had been saying to Herod, "It is not lawful

[14]King Herod heard of it, for Jesus'[a] name had become known. Some were[b] saying, "John the baptizer has been raised from the dead; and for this reason these powers are at work in him." [15]But others said, "It is Elijah." And others said, "It is a prophet, like one of the prophets of old." [16]But when Herod heard of it, he said, "John, whom I beheaded, has been raised."

[17]For Herod himself had sent men who arrested John, bound him, and put him in prison on account of Herodias, his brother Philip's wife, because Herod[c] had married her. [18]For John had been telling Herod, "It is not lawful for you to have your brother's wife." [19]And Herodias had a grudge against him, and wanted to kill him. But she could not, [20]for Herod feared John, knowing

*a14 Some early manuscripts *He was saying*

*a*Gk *his*   *b*Other ancient authorities read *He was*   *c*Gk *he*

NIV

for you to have your brother's wife." [19]So Herodias nursed a grudge against John and wanted to kill him. But she was not able to, [20]because Herod feared John and protected him, knowing him to be a righteous and holy man. When Herod heard John, he was greatly puzzled[a]; yet he liked to listen to him.

[21]Finally the opportune time came. On his birthday Herod gave a banquet for his high officials and military commanders and the leading men of Galilee. [22]When the daughter of Herodias came in and danced, she pleased Herod and his dinner guests.

The king said to the girl, "Ask me for anything you want, and I'll give it to you." [23]And he promised her with an oath, "Whatever you ask I will give you, up to half my kingdom."

[24]She went out and said to her mother, "What shall I ask for?"

"The head of John the Baptist," she answered.

[25]At once the girl hurried in to the king with the request: "I want you to give me right now the head of John the Baptist on a platter."

[26]The king was greatly distressed, but because of his oaths and his dinner guests, he did not want to refuse her. [27]So he immediately sent an executioner with orders to bring John's head. The man went, beheaded John in the prison, [28]and brought back his head on a platter. He presented it to the girl, and she gave it to her mother. [29]On hearing of this, John's disciples came and took his body and laid it in a tomb.

[a]20 Some early manuscripts *he did many things*

NRSV

that he was a righteous and holy man, and he protected him. When he heard him, he was greatly perplexed;[a] and yet he liked to listen to him. [21]But an opportunity came when Herod on his birthday gave a banquet for his courtiers and officers and for the leaders of Galilee. [22]When his daughter Herodias[b] came in and danced, she pleased Herod and his guests; and the king said to the girl, "Ask me for whatever you wish, and I will give it." [23]And he solemnly swore to her, "Whatever you ask me, I will give you, even half of my kingdom." [24]She went out and said to her mother, "What should I ask for?" She replied, "The head of John the baptizer." [25]Immediately she rushed back to the king and requested, "I want you to give me at once the head of John the Baptist on a platter." [26]The king was deeply grieved; yet out of regard for his oaths and for the guests, he did not want to refuse her. [27]Immediately the king sent a soldier of the guard with orders to bring John's[c] head. He went and beheaded him in the prison, [28]brought his head on a platter, and gave it to the girl. Then the girl gave it to her mother. [29]When his disciples heard about it, they came and took his body, and laid it in a tomb.

[a]Other ancient authorities read *he did many things*
[b]Other ancient authorities read *the daughter of Herodias herself*
[c]Gk *his*

COMMENTARY

Earlier, Pharisees had enlisted the Herodians' help in plotting to destroy Jesus (Mark 3:6). Now Jesus' growing reputation brings his name to the attention of Herod himself (v. 14). Juxtaposing this notice with the mission of the disciples suggests that their mission in the villages of Galilee is responsible for the fact that Jesus' activity has come to the attention of the court.[246] According to the Jewish historian Josephus, John the Baptist's popularity with the crowds was the reason for his arrest.[247] Emergence of another popular prophet would cause similar concerns.[248] Mark lists three opinions about Jesus, said to be circulating in court circles (vv. 14-16). Some believed that Jesus was John the Baptist raised from the dead. Others believed that Jesus was Elijah. Since Malachi (3:1;

246. See Bryan, *Preface to Mark,* 95.

247. Josephus *Antiquities of the Jews* 18.5.2.

248. See Robert L. Webb, *John the Baptizer and Prophet: A Socio-historical Study,* JSNTSup 62 (Sheffield: JSOT, 1991), 333-48.

4:5-6) predicted that Elijah would appear before the day of judgment, Jesus' message of repentance in view of the approaching rule of God (1:15) could be taken as a message of impending judgment. The final opinion merely takes Jesus to be like one of the prophets of old. He is not identified with the Baptist or with the impending judgment. This threefold identification of Jesus with a series of prophetic figures reappears when Jesus asks his disciples to tell him who people think he is (8:28). By deciding the issue in favor of identifying Jesus with John the Baptist (v. 16), Herod shows that he recognizes that Jesus is the successor to John.[249]

Herod's profession provides Mark the narrative opportunity to tell the story of John the Baptist's martyrdom (vv. 17-29). Mark's account, which diverges from Josephus's version, appears to be a legendary development based on earlier stories of prophets and the wicked rulers. Herod Antipas had divorced his first wife in order to marry Herodias, who at the time was the wife of his brother, also called Herod.[250] The tradition that John the Baptist offended Herod by criticizing his marriage to Herodias may have originated in a sectarian legal context. Mark's source for the death of the Baptist probably circulated in a Jewish context that revered the Baptist.[251] Although condemnation of the marriage of Herod might seem less troubling than popularity with the crowds,

it had serious consequences. The legitimacy of Herodian rule was weak. A king whose marriage might offend God would have trouble holding the loyalty of the people.[252]

Mark's story makes it appear that the birthday party and the execution of the Baptist took place in Galilee. According to Josephus, Herod executed John the Baptist at his fortress Machaerus, on the eastern shore of the Dead Sea. The portrait of a drunken king trapped into fulfilling a rash vow by a malicious queen has no parallel in Josephus. Popular Old Testament stories may have provided the details that led to the development of this legend about John the Baptist. The story of Elijah's conflicts with Ahab and Jezebel reflect a clash between a prophet and a king regarding marriage (1 Kings 21). The motif of a rash vow leading to disaster when the person who makes the vow must kill an innocent person originates with the story of Jephthah's daughter (Judg 11:29-40). The popular tale of Esther depicts a banquet in which the heroine beguiles the king into pledging up to half his kingdom (Esth 1:1-22; 2:9; 5:3; cf. Herod's promises in v. 23). The heroine Judith, having seduced the king, beheads the drunken Holofernes (Jdt 13:1-10). She takes the head out of the tent in a pouch and later displays it to the assembled Israelites (Jdt 13:14-16). Mark's version of the death of John the Baptist fits the mold of such popular narratives. The story suggests deep-seated hatred of the Herodian court. Its wickedness compares with that of Ahab, who was dominated by the idolatrous Jezebel, and the courts of Israel's oppressors. As in the Ahab and Jezebel story, this tale shifts the blame away from the king onto the wicked queen.[253]

249. Although the formulation of Herod's remarks is that Jesus is John the Baptist "risen" (v. 16), it would be a mistake to think that Herod was expressing a belief in resurrection or some form of reincarnation. The belief in resurrection was peculiar to circles of the righteous, like the Pharisees. Traditional Jewish martyr traditions contain a scene in which the wicked person who condemns the righteous or the persecutor king is confronted with the exalted sufferer. It would be appropriate for Herod to sense that the "righteous one" whom he had executed has come back to haunt him. Mark will make further use of this martyr tradition in the passion material. See George W. E. Nickelsburg, "The Genre and Function of the Markan Passion Narrative," *HTR* 73 (1980) 153-84.

250. The full name of Herodias's first husband is unknown. Mark identifies him as Philip. Josephus identifies him as Herod, presumably as a family name. Herodias was Herod Antipas's niece. Marriage between an uncle and his niece was permitted by most interpretations of the Law, but is rejected in Essene law. What made her marriage to Antipas clearly objectionable was the violation of the Mosaic law prohibiting marriage to a brother's wife while the brother was still alive (Lev 18:16; 20:21).

251. So Rudolph Bultmann, *History of the Synoptic Tradition* (New York: Harper & Row, 1968) 301-2; Pesch, *Das Markusevangelium,* 1:339, suggests that the legendary details of the king's banquet were influenced by the popular Jewish stories in Esther.

252. See Robert A. Guelich, *Mark 1–8:26,* WBC 34A (Dallas: Word, 1989) 327; Webb, *John the Baptizer,* 375. Webb notes that other populist prophets were put down by the Romans when they gathered crowds in Roman controlled territory. The execution of John the Baptist has a private side, which suits the Markan suggestion that John was eliminated because he challenged Herod's marriage.

253. However, to the populace the king's behavior, a drunken party with courtiers at which a female relative seduces him with an erotic dance, is shockingly dishonorable. See Malina and Rohrbaugh, *Social-Science Commentary,* 216.

REFLECTIONS

1. By using the legend of the righteous person in a wicked court, Mark alerts his readers to the dangers awaiting Jesus. Herod recognizes that Jesus is in some sense the successor to John the Baptist. Yet repentance does not accompany his statement. The murderous scene may be repeated if Jesus runs afoul of the authorities. The literary genre of the tale provides the means to separate the king from responsibility for John the Baptist's death. Yet, as in the case of Pilate, such attempts to shift blame onto others are not entirely persuasive. Herod thinks more of the drunken oaths he has sworn and his honor before the assembled guests than he does of the prophet whom he was allegedly protecting. Willingness to sacrifice others to maintain honor, prestige, and power remains one of the great temptations of persons in positions of authority.

2. Although the world of Herod and his court is foreign to most readers, the destructive dynamics of sexual and power politics remains a very real feature of human life. Many women find themselves unable to implement new ideas unless a male coworker proposes them. Use of sexual attractiveness to gain access to power, a common element in all of these stories, poses another problem in the workplace. The legend of John the Baptist shows us that justice is the ultimate victim in such situations.

Mark 6:30-44, Feeding the Five Thousand

NIV

³⁰The apostles gathered around Jesus and reported to him all they had done and taught. ³¹Then, because so many people were coming and going that they did not even have a chance to eat, he said to them, "Come with me by yourselves to a quiet place and get some rest."

³²So they went away by themselves in a boat to a solitary place. ³³But many who saw them leaving recognized them and ran on foot from all the towns and got there ahead of them. ³⁴When Jesus landed and saw a large crowd, he had compassion on them, because they were like sheep without a shepherd. So he began teaching them many things.

³⁵By this time it was late in the day, so his disciples came to him. "This is a remote place," they said, "and it's already very late. ³⁶Send the people away so they can go to the surrounding countryside and villages and buy themselves something to eat."

³⁷But he answered, "You give them something to eat."

They said to him, "That would take eight

NRSV

30The apostles gathered around Jesus, and told him all that they had done and taught. ³¹He said to them, "Come away to a deserted place all by yourselves and rest a while." For many were coming and going, and they had no leisure even to eat. ³²And they went away in the boat to a deserted place by themselves. ³³Now many saw them going and recognized them, and they hurried there on foot from all the towns and arrived ahead of them. ³⁴As he went ashore, he saw a great crowd; and he had compassion for them, because they were like sheep without a shepherd; and he began to teach them many things. ³⁵When it grew late, his disciples came to him and said, "This is a deserted place, and the hour is now very late; ³⁶send them away so that they may go into the surrounding country and villages and buy something for themselves to eat." ³⁷But he answered them, "You give them something to eat." They said to him, "Are we to go and buy two hundred denarii*a* worth of bread, and give it to them to eat?" ³⁸And he said to them, "How many loaves have you? Go and see." When they had

a The denarius was the usual day's wage for a laborer

599

NIV

months of a man's wages[a]! Are we to go and spend that much on bread and give it to them to eat?"

[38]"How many loaves do you have?" he asked. "Go and see."

When they found out, they said, "Five—and two fish."

[39]Then Jesus directed them to have all the people sit down in groups on the green grass. [40]So they sat down in groups of hundreds and fifties. [41]Taking the five loaves and the two fish and looking up to heaven, he gave thanks and broke the loaves. Then he gave them to his disciples to set before the people. He also divided the two fish among them all. [42]They all ate and were satisfied, [43]and the disciples picked up twelve basketfuls of broken pieces of bread and fish. [44]The number of the men who had eaten was five thousand.

[a]37 Greek take two hundred denarii

NRSV

found out, they said, "Five, and two fish." [39]Then he ordered them to get all the people to sit down in groups on the green grass. [40]So they sat down in groups of hundreds and of fifties. [41]Taking the five loaves and the two fish, he looked up to heaven, and blessed and broke the loaves, and gave them to his disciples to set before the people; and he divided the two fish among them all. [42]And all ate and were filled; [43]and they took up twelve baskets full of broken pieces and of the fish. [44]Those who had eaten the loaves numbered five thousand men.

COMMENTARY

The story of John the Baptist's death provides a temporal break in the narrative for the disciples to accomplish their mission and return (v. 30). Their report to Jesus involves both what they did and what they taught. Mark refers to the disciples as "apostles" here for the only time, recalling the verb for "send" (ἀποστέλλω apostellō) from 6:7. The term apostle, a technical term for the early Christian missionaries, indicates that they are official agents (שׁלח šāliah). Returning to report to the one who sent them is a function of official emissaries. It shows readers that apostolic teaching is based on the teaching of Jesus.

A brief interlude separates the disciples' return and Jesus' next miracle. The term rendered "uninhabited place" (ἔρημος τόπος erēmos topos) appeared in the opening chapter, describing both where Jesus spent forty days in the desert before his ministry began (erēmos, 1:12-13) and the place to which he withdrew to pray after his first healing miracles (1:35). The suggestion that the disciples need to withdraw to rest from their mission recalls the latter incident. But by the end

of the first chapter the crowds have gone into the "deserted places" to find Jesus (1:45). A similar transition occurs in this section.[254] When the crowd sees the boat leaving the shore, they race to its destination ahead of Jesus and his disciples (v. 33). The Greek sentence is awkwardly overloaded. The term many is located after the two verbs saw and recognized, but prior to the conjunction and. The sentence could refer to an indefinite "they" who saw Jesus and the disciples leave, a smaller group who recognized those in the boat, and that group plus others who ran to the spot where the boat is going. The journey is evidently along the shore of the lake on the same side. The fact that people come from "all the cities" ahead of Jesus indicates his immense popularity in the region (cf. 1:45; 3:7-8).[255]

254. See Guelich, Mark, 338-39. The notice that the size of the crowd made it impossible for Jesus and his disciples to eat looks back to 3:20-21, 31-35.

255. See Robert H. Gundry, Mark: A Commentary on His Apology for the Cross (Grand Rapids: Eerdmans, 1993) 322-23. Gundry's use of the word magnetism to depict the populace's response to Jesus seems inappropriate, as it suggests an irrational attractive force rather than the power of Jesus' reputation. The response of the crowds everywhere else contrasts with the lack of faith in Jesus' home village (6:1-6a).

Seeing the crowd, Jesus has compassion on them because they are like sheep with no shepherd (v. 34).[256] The comparison evokes a well-established metaphor. Moses prays that the people will have a leader so that they will not find themselves "like sheep without a shepherd" (Num 27:17). The prophets condemned kings for failing to act as shepherds (1 Kgs 22:17). Ezekiel promises a new age in which God will shepherd the people (Ezek 34:5-6). Jesus responds to the plight of the people by teaching the crowd "many things" (v. 34). Thus he presents himself as their shepherd. Some interpreters include the "green grass" on which the crowd is told to recline (v. 39) in the shepherd image, claiming Jesus' actions reenact Ps 23:2.[257]

This claim is enhanced by the feeding miracle that follows. The disciples, concerned about the late hour and isolated place, propose sending the people away to buy food. When Jesus challenges the disciples to feed the people, they protest that it would cost two hundred days' wages (vv. 35-37), indicating the size of the crowd.[258] The suggestion that the disciples might buy food for the crowd is somewhat anomalous, since their missionary instructions prohibited them from carrying any money or provisions.

The precise details incorporated into the story

highlight the extraordinary character of the meal: The people are carefully arranged in groups; the five loaves and two fish are distributed; twelve baskets of scraps remain; five thousand men had eaten. As with previous events in Mark, the feeding of the five thousand draws on OT imagery. Moses arranged the people in groups under their leaders (Exod 18:25). A similar feeding miracle was associated with Elisha (2 Kgs 4:42-44), whose servant protested giving twenty barley loaves to the people.[259] Not only does the miracle evoke images of the people eating in the wilderness or of the prophet providing food, but it also points toward the future. The banquet in the messianic age would repeat the wilderness miracle (4 Ezra 6:52; 2 Bar 29:4).

Early Christians also saw this story as an anticipation of the eucharist. When he orders the people to recline on the grass (v. 39), Jesus takes the position of a host giving a banquet for his guests.[260] The gestures by which Jesus blesses the bread before giving it to the disciples to distribute (v. 41) recall the eucharistic blessing (Mark 14:22), even though the meal itself does not consist of bread and wine. The primary function of the feeding miracle in this section of the Gospel is to demonstrate that the people now have a true shepherd in Jesus. Although some of the people in the previous episode had thought Jesus was Elijah or one of the prophets of old, Jesus demonstrates that he is even greater than Elijah.[261]

256. The concern that Jesus exhibits for his weary disciples (v. 31) may be an anticipation of his concern for the crowd. Robert H. Gundry, *Mark: A Commentary of His Apology for the Cross* (Grand Rapids: Eerdmans, 1993) 322-23, contrasts the inability of the disciples to get anything to eat with the feeding of the crowd, which follows.

257. See Robert A. Guelich, *Mark 1–8:26*, WBC 34A (Dallas: Word, 1989) 341. However, there is no verbal link between the two passages.

258. Their protest underlines a common element in this type of miracle story. No one expects or requests a miracle of the holy man or prophet. See Gerd Theissen, *The Miracle Stories of the Early Church Tradition*, trans. Francis McDonah (Philadelphia: Fortress, 1983) 104-5. Gundry's suggestion that the statement demonstrates the disciples' willingness to do anything Jesus asks, even spend their money to feed the crowd, makes no sense in the ancient context (*Mark*, 324-25). On the value of the denarius, see Bruce J. Malina and Richard L. Rohrbaugh, *A Social-Science Commentary on the Synoptic Gospels* (Philadelphia: Fortress, 1992) 219.

259. Barley was the staple grain of poor people in antiquity. See Malina and Rohrbaugh, *Social-Science Commentary*, 217.

260. See Rudolph Pesch, *Das Markusevangelium I. Teil*, HTKNT II (Freiburg: Herder, 1977) 1:352-53.

261. The Johannine variant of this episode concludes with a lengthy discourse that emphasizes the exodus typology (John 6:1-14, 22-51). It makes explicit an association that may have been implicit in Mark: Jesus is also greater than Moses. He has gathered and fed the leaderless people in the wilderness.

REFLECTIONS

1. Mark reports that the crowds rush from around the Sea of Galilee to a deserted place when they discover where Jesus is going. They are so hungry to hear Jesus' words that they make no preparations for physical hunger, yet stay all day. Their action, as well as Jesus' compassion, points to Jesus as the promised shepherd. The miracle becomes a sign of God's salvation coming to the people. What motivates people to drop everything and seek Jesus today?

2. This passage begins with Jesus expressing compassion for the crowd. Teaching and feeding show that Jesus is the shepherd. The combination represents a variant of the teaching and healing that have been characteristic of all of Jesus' ministry. People today find it difficult to balance those two aspects of Christian responsibility. Some think that the social ministries of the church are all that is necessary to make Christ present in the world. Others think that the church should have nothing to do with feeding and healing except when it is necessary to help someone in the local community. The church's ministry, so the argument goes, is to preach the gospel and provide for public worship.

Both sides are wrong. There is no Christianity without proclaiming the gospel. Teaching and learning the Word of God are as essential to faith as are prayer and belonging to a Christian community. A community that has the same compassion for the suffering that Jesus exhibited cannot be content with only preaching the gospel to the already converted. Christians must also attempt to meet the pressing social and material needs of others, even if few of those who receive such services ever become members of the church.

Mark 6:45-56, Walking on Water

NIV

45Immediately Jesus made his disciples get into the boat and go on ahead of him to Bethsaida, while he dismissed the crowd. 46After leaving them, he went up on a mountainside to pray.

47When evening came, the boat was in the middle of the lake, and he was alone on land. 48He saw the disciples straining at the oars, because the wind was against them. About the fourth watch of the night he went out to them, walking on the lake. He was about to pass by them, 49but when they saw him walking on the lake, they thought he was a ghost. They cried out, 50because they all saw him and were terrified.

Immediately he spoke to them and said, "Take courage! It is I. Don't be afraid." 51Then he climbed into the boat with them, and the wind died down. They were completely amazed, 52for they had not understood about the loaves; their hearts were hardened.

53When they had crossed over, they landed at Gennesaret and anchored there. 54As soon as they got out of the boat, people recognized Jesus. 55They ran throughout that whole region and carried the sick on mats to wherever they heard he was. 56And wherever he went—into villages, towns or countryside—they placed the sick in the marketplaces. They begged him to let them touch even the edge of his cloak, and all who touched him were healed.

NRSV

45Immediately he made his disciples get into the boat and go on ahead to the other side, to Bethsaida, while he dismissed the crowd. 46After saying farewell to them, he went up on the mountain to pray.

47When evening came, the boat was out on the sea, and he was alone on the land. 48When he saw that they were straining at the oars against an adverse wind, he came towards them early in the morning, walking on the sea. He intended to pass them by. 49But when they saw him walking on the sea, they thought it was a ghost and cried out; 50for they all saw him and were terrified. But immediately he spoke to them and said, "Take heart, it is I; do not be afraid." 51Then he got into the boat with them and the wind ceased. And they were utterly astounded, 52for they did not understand about the loaves, but their hearts were hardened.

53When they had crossed over, they came to land at Gennesaret and moored the boat. 54When they got out of the boat, people at once recognized him, 55and rushed about that whole region and began to bring the sick on mats to wherever they heard he was. 56And wherever he went, into villages or cities or farms, they laid the sick in the marketplaces, and begged him that they might touch even the fringe of his cloak; and all who touched it were healed.

COMMENTARY

6:45-52. Jesus sends the disciples ahead so that he may pray alone (vv. 45-46). As we have seen in the introduction to the previous section, his withdrawal to a deserted place reminds readers of the opening scenes of Jesus' ministry (1:35). Twice Jesus separates himself from the crowds and even from his disciples in order to pray (1:35; 6:46). Both examples mark significant developments in Jesus' ministry. When the disciples come to get Jesus after the first instance, he leaves Capernaum to go through all the towns of Galilee. In this case, Jesus has symbolically established a new relationship with the people: He is the messianic shepherd of Israel. The eucharistic images that appear for the first time in the preceding episode point forward to the messianic banquet, which will be the culmination of the kingdom (Mark 14:25). But unlike Matthew and Luke, in Mark's Gospel Jesus does not begin to teach his disciples about prayer until he approaches Jerusalem for the passion (11:22-25).[262]

This separation also sets the stage for a second divine epiphany during a storm at sea. A number of references in the story make the divine character of Jesus walking on water evident. In the OT, God is described as the one who appears on the waters (Job 9:8; 38:16). The description of Jesus as intending to "pass them by" (v. 48) also evokes an image of God's presence (Exod 33:19, 22). Therefore, the reader is probably intended to hear the "I Am" with which Jesus identifies himself, "Take heart, it is I; do not be afraid" (v. 50), as the formula of divine self-revelation. The disciples' fear at the sudden appearance of Jesus belongs to the genre of an epiphany story.[263] Just as in the earlier sea miracle (Mark 4:39-40), so also here the raging storm stops immediately (v. 51). In the previous case, Jesus had rebuked the disciples for their lack of faith. Mark puts the conclusion to this story in the third person, but it is

even more devastating. The disciples are said to be "hard hearted." Mark's readers know that this term originally applied to hostile outsiders (3:5). Prior to the evangelist's comment on the reason for the disciples' amazement, the epiphany demonstrates that Jesus has God's power to rescue the faithful from the raging waters of the sea.[264]

The disciples, who have witnessed all of Jesus' miracles and have been part of his mission, suddenly appear no better than the worst unbelievers! They cannot understand who Jesus really is. Their fear and lack of understanding at this point in the narrative prepare the reader for the disciples' failure during the passion. The first sea miracle introduced doubts about how well the disciples understood Jesus in spite of their special instruction (4:10-12, 34; 4:39-41). Their response to these even more dramatic miracles challenges the normal tendency of the reader to identify positively with the disciples.[265]

6:53-56. The summary that concludes the chapter (vv. 53-56) avoids all ambiguities. Jesus continues to attract huge crowds because of his healing powers. Even the miracle of healing from touching Jesus' cloak is repeated. This summary may have been taken from a pre-Markan cycle of stories used in this section.[266] A similar series of events will be repeated in chapter 8, concluding with an exchange between Jesus and the disciples in a boat (8:13-21). Despite their inability to understand his answer, the disciples persist in asking the key question of who Jesus is.[267]

---

262. See Sharon Echols Dowd, *Prayer, Power and the Problem of Suffering: Mark 11:22-25 in the Context of Markan Theology*, SBLDS 105 (Atlanta: Scholars Press, 1988) 1-33.

263. See Theissen, *Miracle Stories*, 93-97.

264. Elaborate debates over whether the story was originally an epiphany that has been turned into a rescue miracle or vice versa ignore the combination of epiphany and salvation in appearances of Yahweh (e.g., Exod 33:2-9; 34:5-6). See Pesch, *Das Markusevangelium*, 1:358-60; Guelich, *Mark*, 346-47.

265. See Mary Ann Tolbert, *Sowing the Gospel: Mark's World in Literary-Historical Perspective* (Minneapolis: Fortress, 1989) 101-3. Tolbert, who uses the allegory of the parable of the sower as the hermeneutical key to the whole Gospel, suggests that the decay of relationships between Jesus and the disciples, which culminates with their flight (14:50), indicates that they are like the seed that lacks roots (4:6, 17). See ibid., 130.

266. See Paul J. Achtemeier, "Toward the Isolation of Pre-Markan Miracle Catenae," *JBL* 89 (1970) 265-91.

267. See Elizabeth Struthers Malbon, "Echoes and Foreshadowings in Mark 4–8: Reading and Rereading," *JBL* 112 (1993) 227.

REFLECTIONS

1. The two sea miracles might have been variants of a single epiphany tradition. By separating Jesus from the disciples, Mark makes the obstacle in the second case greater than in the first. Even so, the disciples' persistent failure to understand who Jesus is seems perplexing. If miracles alone create faith, the disciples have witnessed more than enough for their faith to be strong. Instead, the disciples are repeatedly shown how weak their faith really is.

A similar situation can occur to anyone. We discover that our grasp of something that we know well is not as secure as we thought. It may take a crisis to determine where our real priorities lie. We face the challenge of constantly overcoming our hard heartedness and disbelief. Our disbelief has less to do with the anticipation that God will do miracles than with the suspicion that perhaps life would be just the same even if we did not put out the effort to be active members of the Christian community.

2. The combination of danger and rescue in these miracles conveys another message for a suffering church: Jesus has not abandoned his followers. Jesus is there to help them through the difficulties of life. Such confidence does not need to be expressed in a dramatic miracle.

Mark 7:1-23, Controversy over Purification Rules

NIV

7 The Pharisees and some of the teachers of the law who had come from Jerusalem gathered around Jesus and ²saw some of his disciples eating food with hands that were "unclean," that is, unwashed. ³(The Pharisees and all the Jews do not eat unless they give their hands a ceremonial washing, holding to the tradition of the elders. ⁴When they come from the marketplace they do not eat unless they wash. And they observe many other traditions, such as the washing of cups, pitchers and kettles.[a])

⁵So the Pharisees and teachers of the law asked Jesus, "Why don't your disciples live according to the tradition of the elders instead of eating their food with 'unclean' hands?"

⁶He replied, "Isaiah was right when he prophesied about you hypocrites; as it is written:

" 'These people honor me with their lips,
    but their hearts are far from me.
⁷They worship me in vain;
    their teachings are but rules taught by men.'[b]

⁸You have let go of the commands of God and are holding on to the traditions of men."

[a]4 Some early manuscripts *pitchers, kettles and dining couches*
[b]6,7 Isaiah 29:13

NRSV

7 Now when the Pharisees and some of the scribes who had come from Jerusalem gathered around him, ²they noticed that some of his disciples were eating with defiled hands, that is, without washing them. ³(For the Pharisees, and all the Jews, do not eat unless they thoroughly wash their hands,[a] thus observing the tradition of the elders; ⁴and they do not eat anything from the market unless they wash it;[b] and there are also many other traditions that they observe, the washing of cups, pots, and bronze kettles.[c]) ⁵So the Pharisees and the scribes asked him, "Why do your disciples not live[d] according to the tradition of the elders, but eat with defiled hands?" ⁶He said to them, "Isaiah prophesied rightly about you hypocrites, as it is written,

'This people honors me with their lips,
    but their hearts are far from me;
⁷ in vain do they worship me,
    teaching human precepts as doctrines.'

⁸You abandon the commandment of God and hold to human tradition."

9Then he said to them, "You have a fine way of rejecting the commandment of God in order to

[a]Meaning of Gk uncertain   [b]Other ancient authorities read *and when they come from the marketplace, they do not eat unless they purify themselves*   [c]Other ancient authorities add *and beds*
[d]Gk *walk*

NIV

⁹And he said to them: "You have a fine way of setting aside the commands of God in order to observe[a] your own traditions! ¹⁰For Moses said, 'Honor your father and your mother,'[b] and, 'Anyone who curses his father or mother must be put to death.'[c] ¹¹But you say that if a man says to his father or mother: 'Whatever help you might otherwise have received from me is Corban' (that is, a gift devoted to God), ¹²then you no longer let him do anything for his father or mother. ¹³Thus you nullify the word of God by your tradition that you have handed down. And you do many things like that."

¹⁴Again Jesus called the crowd to him and said, "Listen to me, everyone, and understand this. ¹⁵Nothing outside a man can make him 'unclean' by going into him. Rather, it is what comes out of a man that makes him 'unclean.'[d]"

¹⁷After he had left the crowd and entered the house, his disciples asked him about this parable. ¹⁸"Are you so dull?" he asked. "Don't you see that nothing that enters a man from the outside can make him 'unclean'? ¹⁹For it doesn't go into his heart but into his stomach, and then out of his body." (In saying this, Jesus declared all foods "clean.")

²⁰He went on: "What comes out of a man is what makes him 'unclean.' ²¹For from within, out of men's hearts, come evil thoughts, sexual immorality, theft, murder, adultery, ²²greed, malice, deceit, lewdness, envy, slander, arrogance and folly. ²³All these evils come from inside and make a man 'unclean.'"

[a]9 Some manuscripts set up   [b]10 Exodus 20:12; Deut. 5:16
[c]10 Exodus 21:17; Lev. 20:9   [d]15 Some early manuscripts 'unclean.' [16]If anyone has ears to hear, let him hear.

NRSV

keep your tradition! ¹⁰For Moses said, 'Honor your father and your mother'; and, 'Whoever speaks evil of father or mother must surely die.' ¹¹But you say that if anyone tells father or mother, 'Whatever support you might have had from me is Corban' (that is, an offering to God[a])— ¹²then you no longer permit doing anything for a father or mother, ¹³thus making void the word of God through your tradition that you have handed on. And you do many things like this."

14Then he called the crowd again and said to them, "Listen to me, all of you, and understand: ¹⁵there is nothing outside a person that by going in can defile, but the things that come out are what defile."[b]

17When he had left the crowd and entered the house, his disciples asked him about the parable. ¹⁸He said to them, "Then do you also fail to understand? Do you not see that whatever goes into a person from outside cannot defile, ¹⁹since it enters, not the heart but the stomach, and goes out into the sewer?" (Thus he declared all foods clean.) ²⁰And he said, "It is what comes out of a person that defiles. ²¹For it is from within, from the human heart, that evil intentions come: fornication, theft, murder, ²²adultery, avarice, wickedness, deceit, licentiousness, envy, slander, pride, folly. ²³All these evil things come from within, and they defile a person."

[a]Gk lacks to God   [b]Other ancient authorities add verse 16, "Let anyone with ears to hear listen"

COMMENTARY

7:1-13. The feeding miracle began with Jesus' disciples "assembling" (συνάγονται *synagontai*) with Jesus and telling him what they had done and taught (6:30). Mark now uses the same verb to signal a challenge posed to Jesus' authority as a teacher who also teaches disciples (v. 1). This time Pharisees, who represent Jesus' local opposition (2:18, 24; 3:6), and scribes from Jerusalem (3:22)

assemble with Jesus to challenge the behavior of his disciples (cf. 2:18, 24). Controversy stories ordinarily begin with a question or challenge, and the retort follows quickly. But both the question over customs of purification (v. 5) and the reply are delayed in this episode (vv. 14-15). Instead, Jesus turns against his opponents by taking up the remark about the "tradition of the elders" that served as a warrant for their criticism (vv. 8-9). He challenges them by citing authorities that everyone in the debate would recognize as superior to ancestral traditions: the Law (v. 10; Exod 20:12; Deut 5:16) and the prophets (vv. 6-7; Isa 29:13 LXX).[268] This section of Mark develops the picture of Jesus as teacher on a new level. The challenge by opposing teachers enables the master to demonstrate the superiority of his system.[269]

Since Mark has just presented Jesus as the true shepherd of Israel, his conflict with the Pharisees and Jerusalem scribes over the traditions of the elders can be viewed as a rejection of the false teaching of those whom Jesus replaces. As in the earlier controversy about fasting (2:18), the initial question concerns matters that were typical of pious sects like the Pharisees. The implication of the question is that if Jesus does not teach his disciples such rules of piety, he cannot be a religious teacher. Dispute over such traditions divided sects within Judaism from one another. The arguments in this section may have been formulated when Jewish Christians had to defend their failure to observe such pious customs. Mark and his readers are uninterested in the details of Jewish legal debates. The explanation Mark provides for the reader (vv. 3-4) reflects an outsider's almost sarcastic view of Jewish customs.[270] Both Pharisaic and Essene legislation shows that these sects required their followers to eat food in a state of ritual purity.[271] The traditions about eating made distinctions between requirements for laity and priest. Exceptions dealt with situations in which individuals might have to eat without performing ritual washing.

The Pharisees and scribes from Jerusalem are familiar enemies of Jesus (3:6, 22). Their question seeks to embarrass Jesus in front of the crowds and thus undermine his authority as a teacher. Mark's stereotyped account of Jewish customs ensures that his readers have no sympathy with the issue being raised.[272] Jesus' response provides a threefold reason for rejecting the claim that interpretations of the Law, which are said to stem from the "elders," should govern a person's behavior. He first challenges the "elders" with a quotation from Isaiah (vv. 6-7; Isa 29:13) that castigates the people because they substitute human teaching for true devotion to God. The quotation introduces the distinction between outward piety and devotion to God in one's heart. What is "in the heart" forms the basis for the teaching that follows the exchange between Jesus and his enemies. There Jesus substitutes a new understanding of purity. The exchange is dominated by sarcasm. Each citation of scripture is introduced with the charge that the adversaries fulfill or set aside its words "excellently" (καλῶς *kalōs*; vv. 6, 9).[273] The word that they should keep, "honor father and mother," instead they set aside. The one they should avoid, "teaching human traditions with a heart far from God," they fulfill.

Jesus' second challenge refers to another custom, that of declaring goods "Corban" (κορβᾶν [Hebrew קרבן *qōrbān*])—that is, dedicating them to the Temple (vv. 9-13). Archaeologists have discovered an ossuary lid marked "Corban," which indicates that the practice was typical of Jesus' time.[274] Although the term could mean no more than an item offered to the Temple, it appears to have taken on the status of a vow attached to goods, which meant that they could not be used for any other purpose. Later rabbinic legislation discusses cases in which an individual can be released from such a vow. The need to obey the command to "honor father and mother" (to support aging parents) was explicitly decided in favor of the Mosaic commandment.[275] The existence of that dispute in later Judaism suggests that the issue raised by Jesus was probably a matter of contention in his time as well.

---

268. See Elizabeth S. Malbon, "The Jewish Leaders in the Gospel of Mark: A Literary Study of Marcan Characterization," *JBL* 108 (1989) 271-72.

269. So Vernon K. Robbins, *Jesus, the Teacher: A Socio-rhetorical Interpretation of Mark* (Philadelphia: Fortress, 1984) 127.

270. Rules concerning food preparation and consumption effectively separated Jews from their Gentile neighbors and hence contributed to the general reputation for "hatred of humanity" attached to the Jews. See Feldman, *Jew and Gentile*, 128-29.

271. See Hannah K. Harrington, *The Impurity Systems of Qumran and the Rabbis*, SBLDS 143 (Atlanta: Scholars Press, 1993) 267-81.

272. Malina and Rohrbaugh, *Social-Science Commentary*, 221, interpret this exchange as an example of the conflict between the "great tradition"—scribal traditions based on written texts and generally advocated by the urban elite—and the "little tradition"—peasant perceptions of religion. Peasants have often adapted "official" religious practice to the realities of their lives.

273. See Gundry, *Mark*, 350.

274. See Joseph A. Fitzmyer, *Essays on the Semitic Background of the New Testament*, SBLSBS 5 (Missoula, Mont.: Scholars Press, 1974) 93-100.

275. *m. Nedarim* 9.1.

The argument given in Mark takes the position that by claiming that a vow could not be retracted on any grounds, the elders were teaching people to disregard the commandment of God.[276]

Verse 13 generalizes from this specific case to the general practice of teaching such traditions. A progression of verbs indicates the disastrous effect of such teaching. The opponents are said to progressively "abandon the commandment of God" (v. 8), "reject the commandment" (v. 9), and finally "make void the word of God" (v. 13). This generalization removes the discussion from the question concerning particular traditions. It rejects all such interpretation as opposed to the word of God.

7:14-23. The initial retort was addressed to Jewish teachers. The resolution to the issue they had raised comes when Jesus resumes his role as authoritative teacher (cf. 1:27). Jesus summons the crowds to him *again*. Their response demonstrates that Jesus has retained the authority to teach, which his opponents sought to discredit.[277] The episode with the crowd and the disciples follows a pattern for didactic scenes already employed in the first example of Jesus' teaching, the parable of the sower: a public statement or event (vv. 14-15), followed by a shift in locale (v. 17a); a request for an explanation (v. 17b); a retort by Jesus, suggesting that the disciples should have understood (v. 18a); and a further explanation (vv. 18b-23).[278]

Jesus asserts that nothing one eats or drinks can defile a person (v. 15a). The connection between washing and "pure food" belongs to the original legal context, since both define what is required to eat in a state of purity.[279] Instead of concern with external categories,[280] Jesus insists that impurity comes from within. Hellenistic Jewish writers explained Jewish rules concerning

clean and unclean animals in moralizing terms. Animals that Jews are not permitted to eat exhibit undesirable moral traits.[281] The original challenge did not concern food that is either impure or non-kosher but ritual washing associated with meals. Jesus' reply, which refers to what is "taken into" and "comes out" of a person, shifts to rules that governed the behavior of all Jews. Readers have seen that Jesus was not concerned with being defiled by contact with persons like the leper (1:41) and the hemorrhaging woman (5:30-34). He could even command the leper to carry out the purification rites required by the Law (1:44). The conflict over whether Gentile converts must be required to observe kosher rules (cf. Acts 15:19-21) shows that this saying did not necessarily resolve that issue.

Mark's Gentile audience clearly did not observe any restrictions about foods. However, all of the controversies in which Jesus comes to the defense of his disciples (cf. 2:15-28) concern eating. Table fellowship between Jewish and Gentile Christians created considerable strain in the early community (Acts 11:1-9; 15:1-29; Gal 2:11-14).[282] The private explanation addressed to the disciples in the final section substitutes the order provided by inner purity for the discipline of kosher rules. By treating the pronouncement in v. 15 as a parable, Mark presents the disciples' request for further teaching negatively. They should have been able to understand this parable, just as they should have understood the parable of the sower (v. 18; cf. 4:13). The evangelist's comment in v. 19b, "thus he declared all foods clean," removes the ambiguity over what practical consequences this tradition is to have for his readers. Kosher food rules have been abrogated. Some interpreters find a contradiction between the second argument, in which Jesus castigates the Pharisees and scribes for using tradition to set aside the Word of God, and the example of Jesus' setting aside the distinction between clean and unclean animals, which is also part of God's Law. They suggest that this tension forces readers to recognize this as another example of the authority of the Son of Man over the Law (cf. 2:28). The general conclusion, all foods are clean, does not appear as a statement from Jesus. Rather, Mark presents it as the correct understanding of what Jesus meant. The interjected

276. See W. D. Davies and Dale C. Allison, Jr., *A Critical and Exegetical Commentary on the Gospel According to Saint Matthew*, 2 vols., ICC (Edinburgh: T. & T. Clark, 1988–91) 2:523-24; Gundry, *Mark*, 364, rightly rejects the suggestion that this stricter view originated in diaspora Judaism. The original conflict represents a Palestinian setting.

277. Mark assumes that the crowd listens to and accepts Jesus' teaching. So Malbon, "Jewish Leaders," 272.

278. Philip Sellew, "Composition of Didactic Scenes in Mark's Gospel," *JBL* 108 (1989) 620. Sellew suggests that the schema for presenting Jesus as a teacher was already available in Mark's environment. The sayings of Jesus may have been treated as mysterious revelation, which required explanation (623-24).

279. See Harrington, *Impurity Systems*, 273-75.

280. See the detailed map of the purity system in Malina and Rohrbaugh, *Social-Science Commentary*, 222-24.

281. *Letter of Aristeas* secs. 140-171.

282. See Tolbert, *Sowing*, 184-85.

remark suggests that this tradition may have originally been used in a more limited context. Sayings of the Lord do not appear in early Christian disputes over table fellowship. Some interpreters think that this explanatory comment (like 7:2-4) had already been incorporated into the story prior to Mark.[283]

The first half, "what goes in cannot defile," is justified by an anatomical observation. Food travels through the digestive tract into the latrine; it never comes near a person's heart (vv. 18-19). The second half, "what comes out defiles," uses a catalogue of vices to depict the inner corruption of the heart. The vices include actions proscribed in the Ten Commandments (theft, murder, adultery, avarice or envy, deceit). Consequently, Jesus continues to uphold the commandment of God, which his opponents undermine.[284]

Rejection of kosher rules and other purification rituals takes away the observable outward markers that separate Jews from their Gentile neighbors. A Jewish teacher might insist that the moral virtues in Jesus' list are just as important as kosher rules and that both are central to Jewish identity. External rules remind Jews that they are different from other nations. Mark's generalization makes a claim about the Christian community as a whole. External practices do not distinguish its members from their non-Christian neighbors. This claim has important implications for the next episode, in which Jesus enters Gentile territory and heals the child of a Gentile woman.[285]

283. See Guelich, *Mark*, 356.
284. See Gundry, *Mark*, 356.

285. See Pesch, *Das Markusevangelium,* 1:384; Guelich, *Mark*, 380.

REFLECTIONS

1. Most Christian readers today habitually think of purification rites and kosher food rules as evidence of an unenlightened Jewish legalism. This prejudiced view must be set aside in thinking about the issues raised by the debate in this portion of Mark. The Israelite community needed to remember that it was different from the nations in order to preserve its faith in God as the true creator, ruler, and judge of the world. Otherwise, the gods of the more powerful nations that conquered Israel would seem to be the appropriate objects of worship.

2. The tendency that Jesus criticizes in the Pharisees and scribes appears in most religious groups. People come to hold on to merely human traditions as if they were divinely revealed. At the same time, the very basic virtues of love, reconciliation, and the good news that God has come among us as savior get lost. Religious groups can very easily sacrifice faith to save the tradition, even when everyone knows that the tradition in question was established by human beings, not God.

3. Finally, the sayings on defilement challenge readers to think about the real challenge posed by the gospel. It would, in fact, be much easier to follow any number of ritual practices than to transform our hearts. The list includes both obvious external transgressions (murder, theft, adultery) and inner feelings that give rise to such transgressions (avarice, wickedness, licentiousness, envy, pride).

Mark 7:24-30, The Syrophoenician Woman

NIV	NRSV
²⁴Jesus left that place and went to the vicinity of Tyre.ª He entered a house and did not want anyone to know it; yet he could not keep his presence secret. ²⁵In fact, as soon as she heard about him, a woman whose little daughter was possessed by an evilᵇ spirit came and fell at his feet. ²⁶The woman was a Greek, born in Syrian Phoenicia. She begged Jesus to drive the demon out of her daughter.	24From there he set out and went away to the region of Tyre.ª He entered a house and did not want anyone to know he was there. Yet he could not escape notice, ²⁵but a woman whose little daughter had an unclean spirit immediately heard about him, and she came and bowed down at his feet. ²⁶Now the woman was a Gentile, of Syrophoenician origin. She begged him to cast the demon out of her daughter. ²⁷He said to her, "Let the children be fed first, for it is not fair to take the children's food and throw it to the dogs."
²⁷"First let the children eat all they want," he told her, "for it is not right to take the children's bread and toss it to their dogs."	
²⁸"Yes, Lord," she replied, "but even the dogs under the table eat the children's crumbs."	²⁸But she answered him, "Sir,ᵇ even the dogs under the table eat the children's crumbs." ²⁹Then he said to her, "For saying that, you may go—the demon has left your daughter." ³⁰So she went home, found the child lying on the bed, and the demon gone.
²⁹Then he told her, "For such a reply, you may go; the demon has left your daughter."	
³⁰She went home and found her child lying on the bed, and the demon gone.	
ª24 Many early manuscripts *Tyre and Sidon* ᵇ25 Greek *unclean*	ªOther ancient authorities add *and Sidon* ᵇOr *Lord*; other ancient authorities prefix *Yes*

COMMENTARY

The boundaries that have been set aside in Jesus' treatment of the purity rules are crossed in this episode. Jesus ventures into Gentile territory. While there, he heals a Gentile child after losing a verbal sparring match to her mother. Mark formulates the introduction to the story so that Jesus' reputation in the Gentile region is evident. He is no more able to remain alone by entering a house here than he was in Galilee.[286] The woman seeks him out immediately. Her understanding of Jesus' teaching puts the misunderstanding of his opponents, and even of his disciples, in a bad light. Where the reader might expect Jesus to praise the woman for her faith (as he does in Matt 15:28), he instead attributes the healing to her victory in argument (v. 29). Although the girl is possessed (v. 26), Jesus heals her from a distance; he does not have to confront the demon directly, as in the case of the Gerasene demoniac. Some interpreters suggest that Jesus healed Gentiles at a distance because the evangelists know that Jesus, himself, never preached in the Gentile cities of Galilee, such as Tiberias and Sepphoris. Or the motif may have been part of the original stories about healing Gentiles in order to demonstrate that Jesus did not violate purity rules.[287]

Jesus asserts his mission to the lost sheep of Israel before commenting on food thrown to dogs.[288] At the same time, the expression "let the children be fed first" accepts the possibility of a Gentile mission.[289] But the story poses a number of exegetical difficulties. The "bread" metaphor suggests teaching, yet the woman asks for healing. Perhaps more striking, however, is the way Jesus rebuffs the woman, suggesting that his ministry is to Israel (Matt 15:24-26 emphasizes this point),

286. Gundry, *Mark*, 376, emphasizes the fact that the house probably belonged to Jewish residents of the region and entering did not involve Jesus in violating ritual boundaries.

287. See Guelich, *Mark*, 382.

288. Matthew also drops Mark 7:27 a, the suggestion that Gentiles will have their turn later. See Gerd Theissen, *The Gospels in Context: Social and Political History in the Synoptic Tradition* (Minneapolis: Fortress, 1991) 61.

289. See Pesch, *Das Markusevangelium*, 1:386-88.

especially since Jesus has already exorcised one Gentile demoniac and even sent him to announce what the Lord had done for him (5:19). Mark's introduction to the story, however, tells readers that Jesus did not come to the Gentile territory to preach but to escape the crowds (v. 24). Thus the narrative exchange between Jesus and the woman shows Gentile readers why Jesus did not preach to them.

Theissen suggests a historical reason for the original reply that differed from Mark's concern for the Gentile mission. He notes that the universal consensus that this story advocates breaking down the barriers between Jews and Gentiles that consistently threatened that mission[290] does not explain why Jesus' reply was preserved in such a hostile form.[291] Therefore, Theissen looks for socioeconomic causes of hostility between the Jewish populace in the outlying regions around Tyre and Sidon and Gentiles dwelling in those cities. Upper Galilee exported produce through the coastal cities. The cities, in turn, depended on these regions for food. In periods of crisis or food shortage, the populace of the hinterlands may have resented producing goods for the wealthy cities. Jesus' saying "Let the children be fed first, for it is not fair to take the children's food and throw it to the dogs" (v. 27) can be read in the light of that situation. Those who produced the food, Jewish peasant farmers, see their work consumed by others.[292] The term translated "dog" (κυνάριον kynarion) is a diminutive form of the word. Some interpreters have sought out the references to small dogs as pets and companions in order to moderate the hostility apparent in Jesus' remarks.[293] Nevertheless, the term was usually an insult intended to degrade those of whom it was used (1 Sam 17:43; Prov 26:11; Eccl 9:4; Isa 56:10-11; Matt 7:6; Phil 3:2). There is no hint in this saying that pet dogs are intended. Rather, the saying has been formulated as a sharp rebuke.[294]

290. See Joachim Gnilka, *Das Evangelium nach Markus. 1 Teilband Mk 1–8, 26,* EKKNT II (Zurich: Benziger, 1978) 1:294-95.
291. See Theissen, *Gospels in Context,* 64.

292. Ibid., 72-77.
293. See Epictetus, *Dissertationes* 4.1.111; Tob 5:17.
294. See Theissen, *Gospels in Context,* 64-66.

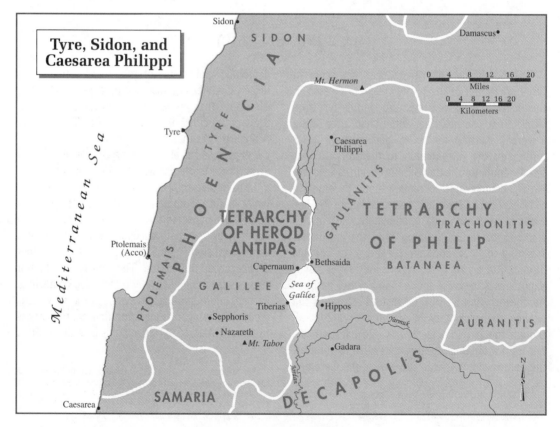

Tyre, Sidon, and Caesarea Philippi

The Syrophoenician woman's reply shows that she is able to engage the challenge posed by Jesus' saying better than his own disciples do. This form of oral combat requires an ability to respond with a saying of equal power. Her response uses the ambiguity surrounding the term *dog* to turn the demeaning metaphor to her advantage.[295] While it would be wrong to feed the dogs food that the children need, everyone knows that dogs are permitted to eat what the children drop under the table. This retort reverses the prejudices on both sides of the debate. Jewish peasants might consider themselves superior to the Gentiles of the city. Jesus, who usually overwhelms his opponents, allows the Gentile woman's reply to stand. Consequently, Theissen has suggested that this story should not be considered a miracle of healing at a distance. The miracle is the overcoming of prejudice and boundaries that separate persons.[296] Mark had Jesus enter Gentile territory to be alone, not to engage in a mission. The exchange with the woman points toward the future in which Gentiles will be included; their faith will bring them salvation. Jesus' initial response to the woman has been formulated to safeguard the priority of his mission to Israel.[297]

295. Bruce J. Malina and Richard L. Rohrbaugh, *A Social-Science Commentary on the Synoptic Gospels* (Philadelphia: Fortress, 1992) 225, who are usually sensitive to the riposte in the Gospels fail to comment on this example. They treat the episode as evidence of the woman's confidence in Jesus as the one who can broker God's power.

296. See Gerd Theissen, *The Gospels in Context: Social and Political History in the Synoptic Tradition* (Minneapolis: Fortress, 1991) 79-80.

297. See Robert A. Guelich, *Mark 1–8:26,* WBC 34A (Dallas: Word, 1989) 388-89.

REFLECTIONS

1. Many modern readers are offended by Jesus' initial conduct. He treats a non-Jewish woman with a severity that he has not shown to any of the others who have sought healing. At the same time, Jesus acknowledges that the woman's word has overthrown his own. She uses the same technique on Jesus that he has used on his opponents. Mark's readers know that the temporal sequence implied in "the children first" was a reality. Dogs under the table are within the household; they are not strangers to the family.

Today, the discomfort caused by this story challenges Christians to examine how they treat the "Gentiles," persons from another racial or ethnic background, in their midst. Do the poor or persons from minority groups find themselves unwelcome in our churches? Do they get what is left over after a denomination's main churches have been provided for?

2. This passage also reminds pastors, teachers, and others in positions of authority how to lose an argument. When Jesus recognizes that the woman's argument is stronger than his own, he grants her petition. Many of us do not have nearly so much graciousness. Even when we know that the other person is right, we may try to justify ourselves rather than agree and get on with the business at hand.

3. Those interpreters who suggest that Jesus' reply acknowledges the hardship of Jewish farmers who saw their labors used to feed the Gentile cities remind us of how real are the barriers that divide people. It was not easy for a Gentile woman to approach a Jewish teacher for help. Yet her love for her child had brought her across boundaries of gender, religion, and ethnic origins. The Jesus who healed her child would never turn away those who seek help. Christians continually work to make the church a place in which all people are welcome as brothers and sisters in God's family.

Mark 7:31-37, Healing a Deaf Man

NIV

³¹Then Jesus left the vicinity of Tyre and went through Sidon, down to the Sea of Galilee and into the region of the Decapolis.ᵃ ³²There some people brought to him a man who was deaf and could hardly talk, and they begged him to place his hand on the man.

³³After he took him aside, away from the crowd, Jesus put his fingers into the man's ears. Then he spit and touched the man's tongue. ³⁴He looked up to heaven and with a deep sigh said to him, *"Ephphatha!"* (which means, "Be opened!"). ³⁵At this, the man's ears were opened, his tongue was loosened and he began to speak plainly.

³⁶Jesus commanded them not to tell anyone. But the more he did so, the more they kept talking about it. ³⁷People were overwhelmed with amazement. "He has done everything well," they said. "He even makes the deaf hear and the mute speak."

ᵃ31 That is, the Ten Cities

NRSV

31Then he returned from the region of Tyre, and went by way of Sidon towards the Sea of Galilee, in the region of the Decapolis. ³²They brought to him a deaf man who had an impediment in his speech; and they begged him to lay his hand on him. ³³He took him aside in private, away from the crowd, and put his fingers into his ears, and he spat and touched his tongue. ³⁴Then looking up to heaven, he sighed and said to him, "Ephphatha," that is, "Be opened." ³⁵And immediately his ears were opened, his tongue was released, and he spoke plainly. ³⁶Then Jesusᵃ ordered them to tell no one; but the more he ordered them, the more zealously they proclaimed it. ³⁷They were astounded beyond measure, saying, "He has done everything well; he even makes the deaf to hear and the mute to speak."

ᵃ Gk *he*

COMMENTARY

The geographical route used to bring Jesus back to the Sea of Galilee from Tyre makes no sense on the map (v. 31). The geographical confusion makes it difficult to determine whether the deaf man of the story is a Gentile. The features of the story are already familiar from the other healing miracles. Although this episode is unique to Mark's Gospel, Matt 15:29-31 contains a summary of Jesus' activity along the Sea of Galilee that includes healing of those who are unable to speak. As in the story of the paralyzed man, friends bring the deaf man to Jesus and plead healing for him (v. 32; cf. 2:3-5a). This story also has several similarities to that of Jairus's daughter: Jesus goes away from the crowd to heal the person (v. 33; 5:40); Jesus gives the command in Aramaic (v. 34; 5:41); the person immediately demonstrates that she or he has been cured (v. 35; 5:42); and Jesus commands the individuals to remain silent about the miracle (v. 36; 5:43a). Mark does

not tell the reader what Jairus did, although the situation (where Jesus has interrupted a funeral) makes it impossible to keep the miracle unknown. In this case, we are told that the deaf man and his friends reject Jesus' repeated commands to remain silent (v. 36).

As in the earlier story of the disobedient leper (1:45), the publicity enhances Jesus' reputation. The crowd praises Jesus for bringing the salvation promised in the prophets (Isa 35:5-6). Disobedience seems even more necessary in this instance, since the only way for the deaf man to show that he is healed is to talk to others. The conclusion indicates an important element in the crowd's response: They recognize that Jesus is to be praised for these activities (v. 37). The response "he has done everything well" may be associated with the judgment on creation expressed in Gen 1:31 (LXX). Healings of blind, deaf, and disabled persons are all signs of the arrival of the messianic age (Isa 35:5-6).[298] This confessional response provides an initial key to the way in which Mark's readers are to understand Jesus' miracles, and it

anticipates the disciples' report of the crowd's opinions about Jesus (8:27-28), which initiates the revelation that Jesus is the Messiah (8:29).

298. See Joachim Gnilka, *Das Evangelium nach Markus. 1 Teilband Mk 1–8, 26,* EKKNT II (Zurich: Benziger, 1978) 1:298.

REFLECTIONS

1. This miracle follows a familiar format. However, the positive conclusion reminds readers of the significance of healing miracles. They are not some form of special magic or a promise that God will protect believers from illness. By linking the conclusion with God's creative power, Mark indicates the true source of all healing. God's power is at work, whether the healing takes place through our normal medical interventions or as an unexpected event.

2. Hearing and speech have a symbolic role to play in Mark's narrative. The Syrophoenician woman was so skilled in speech that Jesus healed her daughter. Jesus' disciples, on the other hand, have shown increasing difficulty in understanding what Jesus is telling them. They clearly need some form of healing that will enable them to truly hear—that is, to understand.

Understanding, on the other hand, can be expressed to others only if we speak. Young children learn how the world around them works, whether that is the physical world or the world of human interactions, by repeating everything they hear. Schoolteachers once required that pupils recite their lessons. Now that such training has become rare, college and graduate students often fail to understand what they read, and trying to explain it without using the words of the source material creates havoc. It is fair to say that unless people can tell others what they know, they do not really know it. Believers need to recognize the need to speak about their experience of salvation. They speak to others in testimony and to God in thanksgiving and praise.

Mark 8:1-10, Feeding the Four Thousand

NIV

8 During those days another large crowd gathered. Since they had nothing to eat, Jesus called his disciples to him and said, [2]"I have compassion for these people; they have already been with me three days and have nothing to eat. [3]If I send them home hungry, they will collapse on the way, because some of them have come a long distance."

[4]His disciples answered, "But where in this remote place can anyone get enough bread to feed them?"

[5]"How many loaves do you have?" Jesus asked.

"Seven," they replied.

[6]He told the crowd to sit down on the ground. When he had taken the seven loaves and given thanks, he broke them and gave them to his disciples to set before the people, and they did so. [7]They had a few small fish as well; he gave

NRSV

8 In those days when there was again a great crowd without anything to eat, he called his disciples and said to them, [2]"I have compassion for the crowd, because they have been with me now for three days and have nothing to eat. [3]If I send them away hungry to their homes, they will faint on the way—and some of them have come from a great distance." [4]His disciples replied, "How can one feed these people with bread here in the desert?" [5]He asked them, "How many loaves do you have?" They said, "Seven." [6]Then he ordered the crowd to sit down on the ground; and he took the seven loaves, and after giving thanks he broke them and gave them to his disciples to distribute; and they distributed them to the crowd. [7]They had also a few small fish; and after blessing them, he ordered that these too should be distributed. [8]They ate and were filled;

thanks for them also and told the disciples to distribute them. ⁸The people ate and were satisfied. Afterward the disciples picked up seven basketfuls of broken pieces that were left over. ⁹About four thousand men were present. And having sent them away, ¹⁰he got into the boat with his disciples and went to the region of Dalmanutha.

and they took up the broken pieces left over, seven baskets full. ⁹Now there were about four thousand people. And he sent them away. ¹⁰And immediately he got into the boat with his disciples and went to the district of Dalmanutha.ᵃ

ᵃOther ancient authorities read *Mageda* or *Magdala*

COMMENTARY

Parallels between Mark 6:31–7:37 and 8:1-21 (or 8:26) have led scholars to suggest that Mark is here incorporating a variant of the earlier material. However, there is considerable disagreement over how much of the sequence is pre-Markan and how much was composed by the evangelist himself.²⁹⁹ The major blocks of material in the sequence are (a) feeding miracle (6:31-44; 8:1-9 [10]); (b) exchange with Pharisees (7:1-13; 8:11-13); (c) healing that restores ability to perceive (7:31-37; 8:22-26); (d) boat scene/private instruction about Pharisees (6:45-52/7:17-23; 8:14-21).

Mark's development of this entire section, which ends with Jesus healing a blind man (8:22-26),³⁰⁰ leads readers to acknowledge the blindness of Jesus' own disciples.³⁰¹ The boat episode following the first feeding miracle introduces the possibility that the disciples' hearts are hardened (6:52). The first feeding story (Mark 6:35-44) was initiated by the disciples' concern for the crowd. In this variant, Jesus takes the initiative (cf. John 6:5). The length of time the crowd has been without food and the distance from any source of food (desert, no surrounding villages) have been highlighted. However, the parallels with the earlier story make the disciples' inability to understand what Jesus will do a clear failure in their faith.³⁰²

Mark inserts 8:1-10 into the narrative without providing a transition to explain how Jesus came to be instructing a large crowd for three days (v. 2). The evangelist has crafted the comment that Jesus summoned the disciples to him.³⁰³ Some interpreters think that the setting of the previous episode, possibly in Gentile territory, was intended as the setting of this story as well.³⁰⁴ In that case, Mark intends Gentile readers to think that this story represents them just as the earlier story referred to a Jewish audience. The story's proximity to the encounter with the Syrophoenician woman hints that the crumbs left by the children will be substantial.³⁰⁵

Jesus' exchange with the disciples is less elaborate than in the previous version of the story. However, it enables Mark to underline the great distance people must travel to hear Jesus. Their faith forms a sharp contrast to the opponents, who fail to recognize that Jesus is from God (8:11-12). The disciples' comment that it is impossible to feed so many people in a desert introduces the element of difficulty, which one expects in a miracle account. In this variant, seven loaves and a few small fish are blessed and distributed separately. Mark emphasizes the fact that the crowd eats and is satisfied (v. 8). The banquet indicates the abundance of the messianic age, for Jesus has not merely provided enough food for the crowd to get home.³⁰⁶

299. See Guelich, *Mark,* 401-3; Elizabeth Struthers Malbon, "Echoes and Foreshadowings in Mark 4–8: Reading and Reading," *JBL* 112 (1993) 214-28; Philip Sellew, "Composition of Didactic Scenes in Mark's Gospel," *JBL* 108 (1989) 617-27; Norman R. Petersen, "The Composition of Mark 4:1–8:26," *HTR* 93 (1980) 119-217.

300. Some interpreters prefer to treat the healing of the blind man (8:22-26) as the beginning of the next section, which will conclude with another healing of the blind (10:46-52). See Malbon, "Echoes and Foreshadowings," 214.

301. See Petersen, "Composition," 205-7.

302. See Robert M. Fowler, *Let the Reader Understand: Reader-Response Criticism and the Gospel of Mark* (Minneapolis: Fortress, 1991) 69-70.

303. "Call to him" (προσκαλέομαι *proskaleomai)* is typical of Markan editorial work. See Gnilka, *Das Evangelium nach Markus,* 1:301.

304. Four of the five miracle stories in Mark 6:45–8:10 take place in territory that is either clearly Gentile or on the borders. See Howard Clark Kee, *Community of the New Age* (Philadelphia: Westminster, 1977) 33.

305. See Rudolph Pesch, *Das Markusevangelium. I Teil,* HTKNT II (Freiburg: Herder, 1977)1:391.

306. See Robert H. Gundry, *Mark: A Commentary on His Apology for the Cross* (Grand Rapids: Eerdmans, 1993) 394.

REFLECTIONS

By incorporating another version of the feeding story, Mark highlights its significance. Readers are reminded of Jesus' compassion for the crowds. The geographical progression from crowds who gathered in the populated areas to those who followed Jesus out into the wilderness has been further intensified. This crowd followed him into the wilderness and remained there without food for three days.

A priest from Senegal once told the story of a trip back home from studying in America. Tribal people are used to going with very little food and then holding a large feast after a successful hunt. They had heard stories about the plentiful food in America, so they asked him if Americans ate a lot. Compared with the Senegalese banquet, Americans do not eat a lot, the priest assured them, but they eat all the time. They expect food to be provided the instant they notice that they are hungry. "Fast food" on demand is a hallmark of American culture.

African Christians relate better to this story than do North Americans. Africans know that people can undertake a journey of several days with very little food and water. Christians from the developed countries might ask themselves two questions: Is there something about Jesus that would justify going to a deserted place to hear him without any "fast food" for three days? Do we really need all of the resources that we consume for ourselves, or should compassion for others motivate us to share more of what we have?

Mark 8:11-13, Demand for a Sign

NIV	NRSV
[11]The Pharisees came and began to question Jesus. To test him, they asked him for a sign from heaven. [12]He sighed deeply and said, "Why does this generation ask for a miraculous sign? I tell you the truth, no sign will be given to it." [13]Then he left them, got back into the boat and crossed to the other side.	11The Pharisees came and began to argue with him, asking him for a sign from heaven, to test him. [12]And he sighed deeply in his spirit and said, "Why does this generation ask for a sign? Truly I tell you, no sign will be given to this generation." [13]And he left them, and getting into the boat again, he went across to the other side.

COMMENTARY

This brief notice seems to have been awkwardly inserted into the narrative sequence. After the feeding miracle the disciples and Jesus go off in a boat (v. 10), and they are in a boat when the next episode begins (v. 14). The boat framework, however, may have been developed by the evangelist in connection with the geographical framework in which the Sea of Galilee separates Jesus' mission into both Jewish and non-Jewish areas.[307] Jesus apparently disembarks at an unknown location and encounters the Pharisees. The Pharisees' demand for a sign is, in fact, part of a traditional

sequence that involved the feeding and a sea miracle. The Gospel of John contains an independent tradition in which the wilderness feeding miracle is followed by both a storm at sea and demands that Jesus perform a sign (John 6:1-21, 25-31). Whereas John interprets the feeding miracle as a "sign," which Jesus' opponents fail to recognize, Mark does not use the word *sign* to mean "miracles." An independent version of the demand for a sign occurs in Q (Matt 12:38-42; Luke 11:29-32); in that version, Jesus uses the examples of the Queen of Sheba and the Ninevites to castigate his genera-

307. See Gnilka, *Das Evangelium nach Markus,* 1:305.

tion for their blindness.[308] The Markan form of the demand may have been earlier than the expanded saying. The response to Jesus' preaching of the kingdom should be sufficient evidence for the source of his authority.[309]

The Pharisees ask for some form of divine authentication. Readers know that the heavenly sign was already provided at Jesus' baptism (1:9-11). They also know that the Pharisees have already challenged Jesus concerning his interpretations of the Law (2:18-28; 10:1-12)[310] and that nothing Jesus might say or do can persuade them that he is from God. Their traditions blind them to the word of God (6:13).

By presenting Jesus' refusal to perform a sign as his rejection of "this generation," Mark's account reflects the tradition of Israel in the wilder-

ness. Those who came out of Egypt and murmured against God were an evil generation (Deut 32:20; Ps 95:10-11).[311] Jesus could not work miracles in Nazareth because of its inhabitants' disbelief (6:6a), and neither can he give a sign to the unbelieving generation represented by the Pharisees. Jesus' strong emotional reaction to their demand ("sighed deeply" [ἀναστενάζω *anastenazō*]) reflects the permanence of the disbelief that confronts Jesus.[312] By shifting from the Pharisaic antagonists to "this generation" and using an elliptical oath formula, "if a sign be given to this generation . . . ,"[313] Jesus appears as a prophet announcing God's judgment against his generation.

---

308. See David R. Catchpole, *The Quest for Q* (Edinburgh: T. & T. Clark, 1993) 241-43.

309. Ibid., 247.

310. See Elizabeth S. Malbon, "The Jewish Leaders in the Gospel of Mark: A Literary Study of Marcan Characterization," *JBL* 108 (1989) 267.

311. See Gnilka, *Das Evangelium nach Markus,* 1:307.

312. See Sean Freyne, *Galilee, Jesus and the Gospels: Literary Approaches and Historical Investigations* (Philadelphia: Fortress, 1988) 48-49.

313. The formula would normally conclude with a curse upon the speaker. See Guelich, *Mark,* 415.

REFLECTIONS

This brief saying reminds readers of the paradox of faith. Unless people recognize that God is present, speaking, and acting in Jesus, no form of testimony will persuade them to follow him. This dilemma resembles the earlier discussion about catching on to the mystery of the rule of God in the parables. No amount of explanation or evidence can provide that initial evidence of faith. Although Jesus' refusal seems to be harsh, it acknowledges the reality of human freedom.

We may exhort, persuade, offer support, and more, but in the end faith remains a mysterious gift of responding to God's Word. Sometimes we need to walk away from hostile demands for proof of our faith in God. People who seek arguments with us out of a need to justify their own anger with God or the church are best left with a short refusal to such debate.

Mark 8:14-21, Against the Leaven of the Pharisees

NIV	NRSV
[14]The disciples had forgotten to bring bread, except for one loaf they had with them in the boat. [15]"Be careful," Jesus warned them. "Watch out for the yeast of the Pharisees and that of Herod." [16]They discussed this with one another and said, "It is because we have no bread." [17]Aware of their discussion, Jesus asked them: "Why are you talking about having no bread? Do you still not see or understand? Are your hearts	14Now the disciples[a] had forgotten to bring any bread; and they had only one loaf with them in the boat. [15]And he cautioned them, saying, "Watch out—beware of the yeast of the Pharisees and the yeast of Herod."[b] [16]They said to one another, "It is because we have no bread." [17]And becoming aware of it, Jesus said to them, "Why are you talking about having no bread? Do you still not perceive or understand? Are your hearts
	[a]Gk *they* [b]Other ancient authorities read *the Herodians*

NIV

hardened? ¹⁸Do you have eyes but fail to see, and ears but fail to hear? And don't you remember? ¹⁹When I broke the five loaves for the five thousand, how many basketfuls of pieces did you pick up?"

"Twelve," they replied.

²⁰"And when I broke the seven loaves for the four thousand, how many basketfuls of pieces did you pick up?"

They answered, "Seven."

²¹He said to them, "Do you still not understand?"

NRSV

hardened? ¹⁸Do you have eyes, and fail to see? Do you have ears, and fail to hear? And do you not remember? ¹⁹When I broke the five loaves for the five thousand, how many baskets full of broken pieces did you collect?" They said to him, "Twelve." ²⁰"And the seven for the four thousand, how many baskets full of broken pieces did you collect?" And they said to him, "Seven." ²¹Then he said to them, "Do you not yet understand?"

COMMENTARY

This exchange between Jesus and the disciples in a boat concludes the long sequence that began with Jesus teaching the crowds from a boat (4:1-8). Three sea incidents depict the decline in the disciples' ability to perceive who Jesus is. The first two were miracles demonstrating that Jesus possessed God's power to save.[314] References in this third episode to the earlier feeding stories make the disciples' understanding of Jesus' saying particularly obtuse. Although readers expect disbelief from the Pharisees, the lack of understanding demonstrated by Jesus' disciples in this episode makes it appear that they are also part of the unbelieving generation (v. 12), not recipients of a privileged insight (4:11).

Mark makes sure that the reader knows the disciples have one loaf of bread (v. 14), even though they act as though they have none (v. 16). Likewise, the feeding stories combine assertions by the disciples that they have no way to feed the crowd with the discovery of a number of loaves. The parable of the sower shows that the disciples had not originally understood Jesus' meaning (4:13). Now, Jesus asks them twice if they have "not yet" (οὔπω *oupō*) perceived or understood (8:17, 21).[315]

Jesus' saying (v. 15) could stand as an independent warning against the influence of the Pharisees (see Luke 12:1). Jesus has just rebuffed the Pharisees. The phrase "and of Herod" has no

immediate connection to Mark's narrative (an independent saying about Herod appears in Luke 13:32). Mark may intend for his readers to recall the opinions Herod expressed earlier about Jesus' identity (6:14-16). Some manuscripts recognize the difficulty and emend "Herod" to say "Herodians." The Pharisees and Herodians have been sworn enemies of Jesus from the beginning (3:6).

As a metaphor, leaven or yeast frequently carries negative overtones, since it was thought to work by creating decay in the dough. Passover observance required cleansing the home of all traces of leaven (1 Cor 5:6; Gal 5:9), and leaven could not be part of cereal offerings to the Lord (Lev 2:11).[316] Therefore, the metaphor itself was not problematic. The context does not specify the content to be attached to "leaven." Presumably, only the Pharisees' influence was at stake in the original saying.

Mark, however, uses the episode as a further comment on the disciples.[317] Their misunderstanding assumes that Jesus is rebuking them for not bringing food with them (v. 16). Yet, in fact, Jesus rebukes the disciples for their hard heartedness. His query "Do you have eyes, and fail to see?" (v. 17), which takes up the Isaiah citation that had been applied to outsiders (4:12), raises a serious question about Jesus' disciples. Could they fulfill the second half of that citation—that is,

314. See Elizabeth Struthers Malbon, "Echoes and Foreshadowings in Mark 4–8: Reading and Rereading," *JBL* 112 (1993) 241-45.

315. See Norman R. Petersen, "The Composition of Mark 4:1–8:26," *HTR* 93 (1980) 211.

316. See Bernard Brandon Scott, *Hear Then the Parable: A Commentary on the Parables of Jesus* (Minneapolis: Fortress, 1989) 324-35.

317. Sellew, "Didactic Scenes," 617-19, thinks that Mark has composed the whole episode around the leaven saying.

could they fail to repent and thus not be forgiven? After the second rescue at sea, the narrator charges the disciples with lack of understanding and hard heartedness (6:52). Because they have failed to understand the truth about Jesus, manifested in the feeding miracle, they are terrified during the storm at sea. However, the didactic scenes involving the disciples in the following chapters (9:14-29; 10:1-12) will lack such sharp rebukes. Although they will continue to misunderstand Jesus, the disciples are learning the truth about who he is. As we move into the second half of the Gospel, Jesus will begin to make even more extensive demands on those who would be his disciples.[318]

Jesus expands upon his earlier comment by interrogating the disciples about the results of each of the feeding miracles (vv. 19-21). This dramatic episode provides a solemn context for the initial word of warning. Perhaps the disciples have been corrupted by the leaven of Jesus' opponents. They are able to state the number (and type) of baskets filled at each of the feedings, yet that knowledge has not generated faith in Jesus' ability to provide for his followers. This doubt echoes their reactions to the earlier rescue miracles. They continue to be astounded by Jesus' power, and yet forget who is with them. Although the repeated question about their understanding might suggest despair, the "not yet" (*oupō*), contrasted with Jesus' emotional response to the Pharisees, may be intended to suggest that they will eventually understand.[319]

318. See ibid., 628-29.

319. See Guelich, *Mark*, 425-26.

REFLECTIONS

1. The shocking picture of the disciples painted by this episode has generated elaborate explanations. Some make the disciples representative of opinions or groups that Mark opposed in the early church. Other interpreters have suggested that the disciples' plight demonstrates the impossibility of understanding Jesus apart from the cross and resurrection. Jesus' opponents have provided readers with examples of very differing interpretations of the same events. The crowds treat Jesus' healings and exorcisms as evidence of his authority. He is the shepherd whom the sheep need. His family thinks that Jesus may have gone insane. His opponents feel that he uses satanic powers. Jesus cannot be a religious teacher, since he shows disregard for training his disciples in piety and careful interpretation of the Law. Christians often assume that the disciples could not have been affected by such contrary views, since they had been with Jesus and even shared in his ministry. Yet, Christians also know the passion story: One disciple betrays Jesus, another denies him, and the rest flee.

2. If readers identify with the disciples, then the disciples' weaknesses may provide some encouragement. Misunderstanding, fear, and even flight do not separate believers from the Lord as long as they are willing to continue following him. This episode also highlights the warning Jesus makes to the disciples: "Watch out—beware of the yeast of the Pharisees and the yeast of Herod." Today, many sources of leaven tempt us to become deaf to the gospel. Advertising media, public opinion, and popular ideologies all contain messages that undermine the gospel.

Mark 8:22-26, Healing a Blind Man at Bethsaida

NIV	NRSV
[22] They came to Bethsaida, and some people brought a blind man and begged Jesus to touch him. [23] He took the blind man by the hand and led him outside the village. When he had spit on	22 They came to Bethsaida. Some people[a] brought a blind man to him and begged him to touch him. [23] He took the blind man by the hand and led him
	[a] Gk *They*

NIV

the man's eyes and put his hands on him, Jesus asked, "Do you see anything?"

²⁴He looked up and said, "I see people; they look like trees walking around."

²⁵Once more Jesus put his hands on the man's eyes. Then his eyes were opened, his sight was restored, and he saw everything clearly. ²⁶Jesus sent him home, saying, "Don't go into the village.ᵃ"

ᵃ26 Some manuscripts *Don't go and tell anyone in the village*

NRSV

out of the village; and when he had put saliva on his eyes and laid his hands on him, he asked him, "Can you see anything?" ²⁴And the manᵃ looked up and said, "I can see people, but they look like trees, walking." ²⁵Then Jesusᵃ laid his hands on his eyes again; and he looked intently and his sight was restored, and he saw everything clearly. ²⁶Then he sent him away to his home, saying, "Do not even go into the village."ᵇ

ᵃGk *he* ᵇOther ancient authorities add *or tell anyone in the village*

COMMENTARY

This healing story is at the center of three miracles that deal with the senses: the deaf man (7:31-37), the blind man at Bethsaida (8:22-26), and the blind Bartimaeus outside of Jericho (10:46-52). These healings indicate that Jesus has fulfilled the prophecy of Isa 35:5-6.[320] The questions with which Jesus challenged his disciples in the previous episode (v. 18) provide a symbolic dimension to the healing of eyes that fail to see and ears that fail to hear. Can Jesus heal those who are deaf and blind to the rule of God as he has done for those physically afflicted? The rescue at sea—which follows on the heels of the disciples' inability to understand the miracle of the loaves—occurred during a crossing to Bethsaida (6:45). Since that is the only other appearance of the name in Mark's Gospel, this healing episode may be intended as a hint to the reader that the disciples will also be healed.[321]

This episode is similar to the healing of the deaf man. Jesus takes the man aside and touches the afflicted eyes with saliva. He also sends the man home with a command to avoid going into the village, apparently a variation on the command to tell no one. As in the story of Jairus's daughter (5:43), readers are not told whether the man obeys

the command. This miracle has an unusual structure in that the first attempt at healing provides only partial vision.[322] The original story may have used the double healing gesture to prove that Jesus was able to restore sight to a person who had been completely blind, not someone whose blindness is due to disease or eye irritation.

Mark's use of this story as a commentary on Jesus' relationship with the disciples leads many interpreters to suggest that the double healing reflects the process that will be necessary to overcome their blindness. Malbon points to the double confession of faith required of Peter in the next episode. Although Peter correctly identifies Jesus as "Messiah" (v. 29), he is still unable to perceive Jesus as the suffering Son of Man (v. 33). Peter continues to be half-blind.[323] Because this is the first time Jesus cures a blind person, the episode points forward to what will come; both giving sight and the slowness and difficulty of the process forecast the next section of the narrative.[324]

322. See Theissen, *Miracle Stories,* 63; Ralph Jackson, *Doctors and Diseases in the Roman Empire* (Norman: University of Oklahoma Press, 1988) 82-83. Eye diseases were among the most common medical ailments in the Greco-Roman world, and human saliva was commonly used as a remedy. See Pliny *Natural History* 28.7; Theissen, *Miracle Stories,* 63. Medical historians suggest that much of the adult population of the ancient Near East suffered from myopia.

323. See Malbon, "Echoes and Foreshadowings," 225.

324. See Christopher Bryan, *A Preface to Mark: Notes on the Gospel in Its Literary and Cultural Setting* (New York: Oxford, 1993) 99.

320. Some interpreters treat the two healings of blind men as a framework for the instructions on discipleship in 8:31–10:45. Others argue that this episode forms the conclusion to this section of the Gospel. So Malbon, "Echoes and Foreshadowings," 225, and Petersen, "Composition," 216.

321. The evangelist has probably introduced the name of the town from the earlier episode. See Gnilka, *Das Evangelium nach Markus,* 1:313.

REFLECTIONS

Today many blind people are able to function independently and engage in many of the same activities as sighted people. Ancient societies lacked the services and education that make this quality of life possible. Blind persons had to be led everywhere by others. This man is led to Jesus by friends and then led apart by Jesus. Once cured, he can depart for home on his own. Readers certainly expect an instant cure, so the intermediate stage comes as something of a surprise. Certainly the man was better off with partial vision than with none. Did he show a tinge of disappointment when he first looked out?

Readers sometimes feel that such a two-stage healing honors Jesus less than those that occur immediately. Others observe that this process provides a better model for physical and spiritual healing than do instant cures. Sometimes people treat the first stage as though it were the final one and walk away. When patients begin to feel better, they begin to skip prescribed treatments. Without a firm commitment to "seeing clearly," people may mistake impaired health for true spiritual health.

MARK 8:27–16:20

THE SON OF MAN MUST SUFFER

MARK 8:27–10:52, PREPARING THE DISCIPLES FOR SUFFERING

OVERVIEW

The hints about Jesus' identity that have been built up in the first half of the Gospel culminate in Peter's confession that Jesus is Messiah (8:27-30) and God's testimony to the Son (9:2-8). Peter's confession distinguishes what the disciples know about Jesus from the common views about him (v. 28; cf. 6:14-15).[325] The transfiguration supplies the divine testimony demanded by the Pharisees (8:11). The divine revelation that Jesus is Son of God, associated by the reader with Jesus' baptism (1:10-11), is repeated in the presence of the inner circle of disciples, Peter, James, and John (5:37). Both episodes conclude with a warning not to tell anyone (8:30; 9:9). These injunctions are linked to the predictions of Jesus' passion, which follow: The Son of Man did not come merely to exercise authority on earth, but also to suffer (8:31-32; 9:12-13, 30-32; 10:32-34). The first half of the Gospel has hinted at the coming death of Jesus (1:14; 3:6; 6:14-29), although the christological emphases in that section of the narrative fell on the power and authority of Jesus. However, discordant elements were introduced in the hostility of the Pharisees and scribes, the misunderstanding of the disciples, and the limits on Jesus' healing power in the face of unbelief (6:6). In the first section of the narrative, Jesus apparently does not wish to be known as a miracle worker, but his commands to remain silent were regularly disobeyed (1:44-45; 5:19-20; 7:36-

37).[326] The portrayal of the disciples, however, raises questions about the suitability of a faith based on witnessing miracles. Although Peter and the others appear to have reached the correct insight that Jesus is Messiah, that confession will be misunderstood if suffering is not the central truth about Jesus' identity. The second half of the Gospel, therefore, completes the initial confession that Jesus is Messiah and Son of God (1:1; 8:29; 9:7) with the threefold repetition of the passion predictions (8:31-32a; 9:30-31; 10:32-34).[327]

Since the disciples participate in the ministry of Jesus, they must also learn to share the suffering of the Son of Man. Each of the passion predictions is followed by an expression of disbelief, misunderstanding, or fear and then instruction on the necessity of suffering (8:34-38; 9:33-37; 10:35-45). Their journey has turned toward Jerusalem (10:32); Jesus uses the opportunity to instruct his disciples. The description of the journey ends with the healing of blind Bartimaeus outside of Jericho as Jesus and the disciples approach Jerusalem for the passion (10:46-52). That episode will introduce another partial recognition of Jesus' messianic status, "Son of David."[328]

---

325. Although Matt 16:17 suggests that Peter has received special insight from God to make this confession, Mark simply has Peter respond to a question that was put to all the disciples. There is no indication that his reply sets him above the others.

326. See Robert Tannehill, "The Gospel of Mark as a Narrative Christology," *Semeia* 16 (1979) 66-71.

327. See Rudolph Pesch, *Das Markusevangelium I. Teil,* HTKNT II (Freiburg: Herder, 1977) 2:1-6. Pesch suggests that material from a pre-Markan passion narrative begins in 8:27. Against the possibility of a connected pre-Markan narrative of the passion, see M. Soards, "The Question of a Premarcan Passion Narrative," in R. Brown, *The Death of the Messiah* (New York: Doubleday, 1994) 1492-1524.

328. See J. D. Kingsbury, *The Christology of Mark's Gospel* (Philadelphia: Fortress, 1983) 90-91.

Mark 8:27-30, Jesus Is the Messiah

NIV	NRSV
27Jesus and his disciples went on to the villages around Caesarea Philippi. On the way he asked them, "Who do people say I am?" 28They replied, "Some say John the Baptist; others say Elijah; and still others, one of the prophets." 29"But what about you?" he asked. "Who do you say I am?" Peter answered, "You are the Christ.*a*" 30Jesus warned them not to tell anyone about him.	27Jesus went on with his disciples to the villages of Caesarea Philippi; and on the way he asked his disciples, "Who do people say that I am?" 28And they answered him, "John the Baptist; and others, Elijah; and still others, one of the prophets." 29He asked them, "But who do you say that I am?" Peter answered him, "You are the Messiah."*a* 30And he sternly ordered them not to tell anyone about him.

a29 Or Messiah. "The Christ" (Greek) and "the Messiah" (Hebrew) both mean "the Anointed One."

aOr the Christ

COMMENTARY

Mark 6:14-16 described the opinions about Jesus held by those associated with Herod, people who had only heard of Jesus by reputation. Herod himself adopted the incorrect opinion that the reader knows is closest to the truth: Jesus is John the Baptist returned. Now Jesus asks the disciples about the common opinion of who he is. They repeat the views already listed in the previous episode: John the Baptist, Elijah, one of the prophets (vv. 27-28). Jesus then puts the same question to the disciples. Peter replies, "the Messiah" (v. 29). This confession is the first correct human statement about Jesus' identity in the Gospel. The shouted confessions of demons that Jesus had to silence are now replaced by human witness.[329]

The setting for the episode is awkward, "into the villages of Philip's Caesarea." One would expect "region" of Caesarea Philippi (5:1, 17; 7:24, 31; 8:10). "Villages" may reflect the previous episode, which was set in a village (vv. 22-26). Although the region was twenty-five miles north of the Sea of Galilee,[330] Mark shows no interest in the Gentile character of the region.

Caesarea Philippi was built by Herod Philip as the capital of his tetrarchy. Perhaps, its distance—two days' journey—and northern location served to isolate Jesus and his disciples from the crowds that attended his every move earlier in the ministry.

The term *Messiah,* or *Christ,* was used as a christological confession of Jesus' identity by Mark's community. It even appears in the opening verse (1:1). Scholars have no evidence that "the anointed" designated a specific figure, since persons could be hailed as being anointed in a variety of contexts. Anointing represents God's affirmation that the prophet, priest, or king is the divinely chosen leader of the people. Jewish texts of the period describe a king who is to be the agent of God's restoration of the people in the end time.[331] The epithet may have been used to describe the historical Jesus as an agent of God's saving power without implying that he alone filled that role. Mark reflects early Christian confessions that treat "Messiah" as an indication of the unique role played by Jesus in salvation history.[332]

The silence command that concludes this episode applies explicitly to the confession that Jesus

329. See Mary Ann Tolbert, *Sowing the Gospel: Mark's World in Literary-Historical Perspective* (Minneapolis: Fortress, 1989) 200-201.

330. See Robert H. Gundry, *Mark: A Commentary on His Apology for the Cross* (Grand Rapids: Eerdmans, 1993) 427; Pesch, *Das Markusevangelium,* 2:30.

331. *Pss. Sol.* 17:32; *1 Enoch* 48:10; 52:4; 4 Ezra 12:32; *1QS* 9:11.
332. Joseph A. Fitzmyer, *The Gospel According to Luke I–IX,* AB 28 (Garden City, N.Y.: Doubleday, 1981) 197-99.

is Messiah. Some exegetes assume that the point of the command when it relates to a christological title is to acknowledge the gap between the pre-Easter Jesus and the risen Lord. The crucified and risen Jesus is the only one who can be designated Lord. Thus the ministry of Jesus was non-messianic. Whatever the historical merits of such a view, Mark clearly presents Jesus' ministry as a manifestation of God's power and rule throughout the narrative.

Readers might expect a word of praise for the confession, since it demonstrates that the disciples are superior to the crowds in their understanding of who Jesus is. Instead, the command to tell no one is introduced with the verb for "rebuke" (ἐπιτιμάω epitimaō), the same verb Mark uses to describe Jesus' response when the demons

acknowledge him as Son of God (3:12). Thus the rebuke does not impugn the correctness of the title being used.[333] The problem with the confession is the inappropriateness of the time (prior to the passion), the context (exorcism and healing miracles), or the witnesses (spoken by demons). Since the episodes surrounding the two affirmations of Jesus' identity in this section demonstrate that the disciples do not understand that suffering lies at the heart of Jesus' mission, they are no more able to use the titles "Messiah" and "Son of God" correctly than the demons are. Jesus will accept both titles publicly during his interrogation by the Sanhedrin (Mark 14:62).

333. See Kingsbury, *Christology*, 93-96.

REFLECTIONS

Most Christians today find christological titles like "Messiah" and "Son of God" so shopworn that they are devoid of meaning. The difficulty is not that they might convey inappropriate expectations about the ministry of Jesus but that they do not convey any expectations at all. Mark's concern for the context in which such expressions are used provides some assistance in this dilemma. We should think of "Messiah," "Son of God," "Son of Man," and the other, lesser christological titles as code words for stories of how salvation comes to be present in human life through Jesus.

In order to make the titles meaningful, we need to remember the central elements in the story. An age that allows media advertising campaigns to "anoint" its leaders needs to be reminded that God chooses unlikely persons to convey salvation. Human beings cannot manipulate the truth to create their own savior figures. Mark's messianic secret warns us against those who appear bent on "selling themselves" as servants of God. Both "Son of God" and "Son of Man" link Jesus with the heavenly world. Although the designation "Son of God" may have been used of a human figure, Mark presents it as God's word about Jesus. The demons use it because of the healing power that is effective in Jesus. But "Son of Man" is associated with exaltation, vindication, and judgment.

Although many Christians practice meditative prayer and find it meaningful, we must not be lulled into a belief that meditation is a means unto itself. As Christians, we believe that God is not just a feeling of power, bliss or harmony but that God became present to and among human beings in Jesus, Son of God. As exalted Son of Man, the one who was manifested in Jesus is the norm by which we judge or evaluate all things. The titles that some think are just empty words remind us of the special ways we know God.

Mark 8:31-33, First Passion Prediction

NIV	NRSV
[31]He then began to teach them that the Son of Man must suffer many things and be rejected by	31Then he began to teach them that the Son of Man must undergo great suffering, and be

NIV

the elders, chief priests and teachers of the law, and that he must be killed and after three days rise again. [32]He spoke plainly about this, and Peter took him aside and began to rebuke him.

[33]But when Jesus turned and looked at his disciples, he rebuked Peter. "Get behind me, Satan!" he said. "You do not have in mind the things of God, but the things of men."

NRSV

rejected by the elders, the chief priests, and the scribes, and be killed, and after three days rise again. [32]He said all this quite openly. And Peter took him aside and began to rebuke him. [33]But turning and looking at his disciples, he rebuked Peter and said, "Get behind me, Satan! For you are setting your mind not on divine things but on human things."

COMMENTARY

A saying about the suffering Son of Man sparks a new exchange between Jesus and Peter. As does the previous exchange (vv. 27-30), this episode concludes with a rebuke (v. 33). The parallelism between the rebuke in v. 30, "not to tell anyone" and v. 33, "Get behind me, Satan! For you are setting your mind not on divine things but on human things," suggests that the second rebuke explains the first. When Peter hears Jesus explain that the Son of Man must suffer, Peter has the audacity to take Jesus aside and rebuke Jesus! Since the verb for "rebuke" (ἐπιτιμάω *epitimaō*) has been used to refer to silencing demons, Peter appears to have fallen into the same trap as Jesus' relatives. He thinks that Jesus is insane and needs to be exorcised. Even without the sharp language, anyone growing up in a traditional society would be horrified to observe a disciple taking this tone with his teacher.[334] Jesus' swift reaction, even calling Peter "Satan," is appropriate after such an affront.[335]

Clearly, Peter attaches significance to the title "Messiah" that excludes suffering. The passion prediction uses the title "Son of Man" for Jesus rather than "Messiah" or "Son of God." Readers have seen Jesus use this expression in controversies with his opponents. It encodes the claim to exercise God's authority to forgive sin (2:10) and to determine suitable behavior on the sabbath (2:28).[336] The OT image of a heavenly "son of man" (Dan 7:13-14), ascending to the divine throne provided a framework for understanding

the resurrection of Jesus and the expectation that Jesus would return as judge. The passion predictions form a third type of Son of Man saying. Since the other images clustered around the Son of Man expression suggest divine authority that can be exercised by Jesus either in the present or in his future coming as judge, the sudden reference to suffering does seem out of place. Jesus claims authority similar to God's in his teaching; he claims to be able to forgive sin and to be the one who will come in judgment. Jesus' teaching and forgiveness now will be upheld in heaven. Thus the expression "Son of Man" highlights elements of conflict and vindication in Mark's Gospel.[337]

More sophisticated readers might know that the figure in Daniel is identified with the righteous of Israel who suffer. That identification appears to be more one of metaphor than the anticipation that the heavenly defender of the righteous will somehow actually share their fate.[338] To those who are being persecuted for remaining loyal to their Jewish faith, it promises that God has not abandoned them to the evils of the oppressor. They will be vindicated. If Jesus had said no more than that he would suffer like other prophets and righteous persons before him and that like them he would be vindicated by God, the cross would not be central to the gospel. Peter's objections would reflect the fear of suffering that will lead him to deny Jesus (14:66-72).

The passion predictions about the suffering Son of Man suggest something more than what is found in the traditional metaphor. The Son of

---

334. See Tolbert, *Sowing*, 202.
335. Malina and Rohrbaugh (*Social-Science Commentary*, 232) suggest that this scene is similar to the temptation scene, which opens the Gospel. Peter's rebuke is a test of Jesus' loyalty to God.
336. See Kingsbury, *Christology*, 96-97.

337. Ibid., 170-71.
338. Particularly because the primary associations made with the "son of man" figure suggest an angelic protector of the people rather than a human being as the referent of the symbol. See John J. Collins, *Daniel* (Minneapolis: Fortress, 1993) 304-10.

Man does not identify with the righteous from the distance of heaven but actually experiences their plight. The imperative "must" (δεῖ *dei*; "it is necessary") conveys the idea of a divinely established plan. The necessity involved is not a cruel, blind fate. Nor is it the necessity of corrupt and imperfect human institutions, though they serve as its vehicle. The authority and vindication associated with the expression "Son of Man" are retained because Jesus suffers out of obedience to God.[339] This necessity is grounded in God and cannot be evaded (9:12; 14:21, 49). The contrast between setting one's mind on divine things or on merely human ones will be demonstrated in the teaching on discipleship, which follows.

The prediction establishes a pattern that will play an increasingly important part in the concluding chapters of Mark: Jesus' ability to predict what will happen to himself and to his disciples (cf. 10:39). Knowledge of the circumstances of one's own death was a sign of wisdom or a gift of extraordinary persons in the Greco-Roman world.[340] Given the fate of John the Baptist and the unrelenting hostility of religious leaders in Jerusalem during Jesus' last days, the historical probability that he spoke of his own death and sought to understand it within the context of the coming of God's kingdom is very high.[341] Jesus

also must have expressed the conviction that God would vindicate him. The Gethsemane tradition (Mark 14:32-42) and the tradition of Jesus' prayer in Heb 5:7-10 show that Peter's protest may express a struggle that Jesus himself underwent in confronting his fate. Therefore, Jesus' rebuke should not be taken as evidence of hostility toward Peter. The difference between Peter's attempt to ward off Jesus' prediction of the passion and Jesus' prayer in Gethsemane lies in the fact that the one praying is willing to accept what God chooses.[342] Peter treats Jesus' prophecy as the words of one possessed who must be exorcised.

Although one can assign a high degree of historical plausibility to Jesus' recognition that God's plan might include his own death, the passion predictions as we have them in the Gospels are hardly original.[343] They have been formulated in the light of the passion narrative, which will follow. The editorial comment that Jesus told them this "boldly" or "directly" (v. 32*a*) removes any suspicion that Jesus' death took him by surprise. Despite their hostile intent, Jesus' enemies have not triumphed in gaining his death. Ironically, they become part of God's plan even in their hostility.[344]

---

339. See Kingsbury, *Christology*, 174.
340. See Philo *Moses* 2.51 secs. 290-91; Suetonius *Domitian* 15.3. See also Gundry, *Mark*, 428.
341. See Raymond E. Brown, *The Death of the Messiah: From Gethsemane to the Grave. A Commentary on the Passion Narratives in the Four Gospels*, vol. 2 (Garden City, N.Y.: Doubleday, 1994) 234.

342. On Gethsemane, see ibid., 166.
343. Gundry (*Mark*, 429) adopts the view that the expression "suffer many things" (8:31) derives from an Aramaic substratum that might go back to Jesus. He also detects an allusion to Ps 118:22 in "be rejected."
344. See Tannehill, "Narrative Christology," 78-80.

REFLECTIONS

1. This episode does not explain how or why the death of Jesus lies at the heart of God's plan of salvation. It merely insists that it does. The shock of this insight has been prepared by the previous depiction of Jesus in the Gospel. Readers know that Jesus can control even the cosmic forces. How can he permit the enemies who wish to destroy him to succeed, as they had in destroying John the Baptist? Paul was right to insist that the gospel of the cross makes a mockery of all our human conceptions of success (1 Cor 1:18-25).

2. Confronted with the necessity of suffering, most people react exactly like Peter. The necessity of suffering is not simply a pious desire to imitate Jesus; much of what is truly worthwhile can be accomplished only by those who are willing to trust Jesus' word that suffering belongs to God's plan. In a "pain-killer" culture, a balanced understanding of suffering is difficult to achieve. Jesus sets out the challenge for us to think as God does, not as human beings normally do. Jesus' healing miracles and his compassion for the crowds at the feeding miracles make it clear that God does not delight in human suffering. The disciples were sent out to heal as well as to preach the gospel. Yet danger lies in concluding that suffering and self-sacrifice are always undesirable. Despite everything the Bible tells us about the suffering of truly righteous people, Christians frequently think that if we pray enough God will remove all trials from our lives. A family with a drug-addicted teenager might be pressured to "pray harder and the kid will come around," rather than for the strength to care for their child and to find the right treatment and support. Parents whose asthmatic child has life-threatening allergies are convinced that if they pray before the child eats certain foods the child won't have an allergic reaction. One emergency trip to the hospital has not convinced them that perhaps God is trying to tell them something else. Somehow these devout Christians have grasped the Jesus of the miracles but have ignored the word of the cross. Prayer is important in healing, but prayer is an opening up of ourselves to what God wills, not an exercise in forcing God to do our will.

Mark 8:34–9:1, Taking Up the Cross

NIV

³⁴Then he called the crowd to him along with his disciples and said: "If anyone would come after me, he must deny himself and take up his cross and follow me. ³⁵For whoever wants to save his life[a] will lose it, but whoever loses his life for me and for the gospel will save it. ³⁶What good is it for a man to gain the whole world, yet forfeit his soul? ³⁷Or what can a man give in exchange for his soul? ³⁸If anyone is ashamed of me and my words in this adulterous and sinful generation, the Son of Man will be ashamed of him when he comes in his Father's glory with the holy angels."

9 And he said to them, "I tell you the truth, some who are standing here will not taste death before they see the kingdom of God come with power."

a35 The Greek word means either *life* or *soul*; also in verse 36.

NRSV

34He called the crowd with his disciples, and said to them, "If any want to become my followers, let them deny themselves and take up their cross and follow me. ³⁵For those who want to save their life will lose it, and those who lose their life for my sake, and for the sake of the gospel,[a] will save it. ³⁶For what will it profit them to gain the whole world and forfeit their life? ³⁷Indeed, what can they give in return for their life? ³⁸Those who are ashamed of me and of my words[b] in this adulterous and sinful generation, of them the Son of Man will also be ashamed when he comes in the glory of his Father with the holy angels."

9 ¹And he said to them, "Truly I tell you, there are some standing here who will not taste death until they see that the kingdom of God has come with[c] power."

aOther ancient authorities read *lose their life for the sake of the gospel*   bOther ancient authorities read *and of mine*   cOr *in*

COMMENTARY

8:34-38. Jesus summons the crowd before giving instruction about discipleship and suffering (v. 34*a*). This act represents a striking reversal of the usual pattern in which Jesus withdraws from the crowd to instruct his disciples. By including the crowd, Mark brings the audience into the picture.[345] These sayings, which begin "If any

345. See Christopher Bryan, *A Preface to Mark: Notes on the Gospel in Its Literary and Cultural Setting* (New York: Oxford, 1993) 100.

want to become my followers," refer to an ongoing reality of Christian life. Discipleship sayings circulated in a number of variants: A disciple must take up the cross (v. 34*b*; Matt 10:38; Luke 14:27; *Gospel of Thomas* 55*b*); must be willing to lose his or her life (v. 35; Matt 10:39; Luke 17:33; John 12:25); and must not deny Jesus when challenged by others (v. 38; Matt 10:33;

Luke 12:9).[346] Mark 8:34-38 (Matt 16:24-27; Luke 9:23-27) connects these independent sayings with the argument that nothing is gained by rejecting Jesus and saving one's life, since those who turn away from discipleship will be condemned. The Son of Man, who calls them to follow his suffering, is the exalted One who will testify about his followers before God (v. 38).

The primary cause of the persecution and possible death envisaged in the sayings about taking up one's cross and losing one's life is testimony to the truth of the gospel (v. 35). This possibility anticipates the sacrifice disciples will make as they spread the gospel—even members of their own families will hand Christians over for punishment (Mark 13:9-13). Mark has clearly formulated this version of the discipleship sayings with an eye toward the concrete sufferings endured by Christians in his time.[347] Mark also recognizes that denying oneself is not limited to situations in which witnessing to the gospel brings physical danger. The interpretation of the parable of the sower reminds readers that others lose their faith because concern for wealth and other earthly things take over (4:19).

The picture of a condemned criminal carrying the cross bar to the place of execution (v. 34) forms a shocking requirement for discipleship. Human standards cannot explain the necessity of such a commitment to the will of God. Mark emphasizes the necessity of this commitment by concluding the series of discipleship sayings with a judgment saying, "Whoever is ashamed of me and of my words in this adulterous and sinful generation, of them the Son of Man will also be ashamed when he comes in his glory" (v. 38). This saying exploits the image of the Son of Man as the one who will execute God's judgment over humanity. Fidelity to Jesus brings persecution, because the disciples live in an age that is contrary to God. Jesus had passed a prophetic judgment against his generation when he refused the demand for a sign (8:12). The adjectives *evil* and *adulterous* echo the words of the OT prophets (Isa 1:4, 21; Jer 3:3). Some interpreters treat the distinction between Jesus, "ashamed of me," and the "Son of Man" in this version of the saying as evidence that Jesus did not identify himself with the heavenly figure of Dan 7:13-14. Use of Son of Man sayings to establish Jesus' authority and the identification of Jesus as exalted judge in the pre-markan tradition, however, indicates that Mark expects readers to recognize that Jesus is referring to his own return. The expression "in the glory of his Father" links the Son of Man christology with the identification of Jesus as Son of God, which will be expressed in the transfiguration (9:2-8).[348]

The image of the Son of Man holds out both promise and warning. Those who confess Jesus to be Messiah and Son of God must be faithful disciples. They cannot expect the gospel to match the desires and demands of the larger society. Later in the narrative, readers learn that the sons of Zebedee are to be martyred (10:38-39) and that Christians will have to stand trial because they preach the gospel (13:9). Those who remain faithful can be confident that they will be among the elect at the judgment. The Jesus whom they follow is exalted with God. But those who are "ashamed of Jesus"— that is, who accept the judgment of a "wicked and adulterous age," will discover that their savior treats them in the same way.[349]

9:1. The reference to the Son of Man's coming in glory (8:38) provides Mark an opportunity to attach another saying of Jesus about the end time. Attention turns from the glorious coming of the Son of Man back to the kingdom of God, which was the subject of Jesus' preaching.[350] If the two forms of "coming"—the Son of Man in judgment and the kingdom coming in power—are variants of the same event, then the promise that some of those who hear Jesus will not die until they see the rule of God was not fulfilled in the apocalyptic sense that the combination suggests. Daniel 7:13-14 pictures a son of man being invested with God's eternal rule. Daniel 7:27 affirms that the persecuted righteous share in that eternal dominion. If the saying about the coming of the kingdom was associated with the coming of the Son of Man, then it might be intended to make a similar promise to the persecuted disciples. The judgment that condemns their enemies also vindicates those who have suffered for the sake of the gospel. Since Mark links the suffering and resurrection of Jesus

---

346. See Pesch, *Das Markusevangelium,* 2:58-65.
347. See Bryan, *Preface to Mark,* 100-101.

348. See Joachim Gnilka, *Das Evangelium nach Markus. 1 Teilband Mk 1–8, 26,* EKKNT II (Zurich: Benziger, 1978) 2:26-27.
349. See Kingsbury, *Christology,* 176.
350. Gnilka, *Das Evangelium nach Markus,* 2:27.

with the expectation of the parousia, the period in which the disciples preach the gospel lies between the two events.[351]

Isolated from its Markan context, the saying simply promises that the reign of God is not delayed (13:30; 1 Cor 15:51-52; 1 Thess 4:13-18).[352] Jesus' ministry began with the announcement that the kingdom was near (1:15), and this saying reiterates that promise. Some interpreters have suggested that the "mystery of the kingdom" (4:11) lies in the discovery that God's power is present, even though Jesus' followers must follow him in suffering.[353]

Mark formulates the saying with the verb in the past tense, "has come with power." This formulation suggests that the reader will discover that the promise has been fulfilled. Many interpreters point to the transfiguration narrative as the logical referent for the saying. When Peter, James, and John see Jesus transformed, they will recognize that dominion has been conferred upon him.[354] Others look beyond the transfiguration to the passion, especially the climax when the Temple veil is torn and the centurion acknowledges that Jesus is the Son of God (15:38-39). The coming of the kingdom upsets normal human views of power. The series of sayings in 8:34–9:1 has shifted from the cross of Jesus to discipleship that can sustain its own suffering by anticipating the coming of the kingdom in power. The journey to the cross has just begun.[355]

351. Ibid., 28.
352. Dieter Lührmann, *Das Markusevangelium*, HNT (Tübingen: J.C.B. Mohr [Paul Siebeck], 1987) 153.
353. Bryan, *Preface to Mark*, 101.

354. Joel Marcus, *The Mystery of the Kingdom of God*, SBLDS 90 (Atlanta: Scholars Press, 1986) 52. Marcus emphasizes the connection between the reference to the kingdom of God in v. 1 and the royal connotations of the title "Son of God" in v. 7. See also E. Nardoni, "A Redaction-Critical Interpretation of Mark 9:1," CBQ 365-84.
355. Dorothy A. Lee-Pollard, "Powerlessness as Power: A Key Emphasis in the Gospel of Mark," SJT 40 (1987) 178-79.

REFLECTIONS

1. The disciples have participated in Jesus' ministry of preaching and healing (6:7-13, 30). Now they discover that they must also participate in the ministry of suffering. Anyone who attempts to call the world to account before the gospel must be ready to sacrifice self-interest. The gospel was not formulated for the convenience of those who would preach it to others. The instructions for missionaries, which required radical dependence upon those to whom they ministered (6:8-10), provided concrete examples of "denying self." Christians do not have to invent some fancy form of persecution complex in order to practice this saying. There are many ways in which the gospel calls us to deny self in order to be more like Christ.

2. The church continues to be a martyr throughout the world. In our day those Christians who work to bring justice and peace to suffering peoples around the world are often victims of the violence they are trying to end. Sometimes death squads single out religious leaders and missionaries for particularly brutal execution in the hope of frightening the people. Even Christians who are not called upon to be martyrs have a responsibility to pressure their governments to oppose the deaths of these modern martyrs. When a very prominent religious leader is assassinated, the world reacts. Many other Christian martyrs are known in church circles but ignored by the larger society. Christians must be concerned about every innocent victim. The least believer is just as important as a prominent church figure.

3. In addition to solidarity with the martyr church, Christians should consider whether there are situations in which public pressure may lead them to deny their faith. We may feel that pressure at any age. Many adults know that Christian faith is not always welcome in the workplace, so they learn to cloak their Christian identity when morally questionable practices seem to be the order of the day. Children and youth can feel the pinch, too. Coaches sometimes threaten to throw kids off teams if they insist on attending church rather than practice on Sunday morning (even Easter Sunday!). Compared to the dangers faced by a martyr church, our discomfort with religion in the public forum may seem trivial. But fidelity to Christ in such situations is not unimportant. As Fred Craddock pointed out in an address to pastors, the reality for most Christians in this country is seldom a life-and-death matter.

> We think giving our all to the Lord is like taking a $1,000 bill and laying it on the table—"Here's my life, Lord. I'm giving it all."
>
> But the reality for most of us is that he sends us to the bank and has us cash in the $1,000 for quarters. We go through life putting out 25¢ here and 50¢ there....
>
> Usually giving our life to Christ isn't glorious. It's done in all those little acts of love, 25¢ at a time.[356]

356. Fred Craddock, cited in *Leadership* (Fall 1984) 47.

Mark 9:2-13, The Transfiguration of Jesus

NIV

²After six days Jesus took Peter, James and John with him and led them up a high mountain, where they were all alone. There he was transfigured before them. ³His clothes became dazzling white, whiter than anyone in the world could bleach them. ⁴And there appeared before them Elijah and Moses, who were talking with Jesus.

⁵Peter said to Jesus, "Rabbi, it is good for us to be here. Let us put up three shelters—one for you, one for Moses and one for Elijah." ⁶(He did not know what to say, they were so frightened.)

⁷Then a cloud appeared and enveloped them, and a voice came from the cloud: "This is my Son, whom I love. Listen to him!"

⁸Suddenly, when they looked around, they no longer saw anyone with them except Jesus.

⁹As they were coming down the mountain, Jesus gave them orders not to tell anyone what they had seen until the Son of Man had risen from the dead. ¹⁰They kept the matter to themselves, discussing what "rising from the dead" meant.

¹¹And they asked him, "Why do the teachers of the law say that Elijah must come first?"

¹²Jesus replied, "To be sure, Elijah does come first, and restores all things. Why then is it written that the Son of Man must suffer much and be rejected? ¹³But I tell you, Elijah has come, and they have done to him everything they wished, just as it is written about him."

NRSV

2Six days later, Jesus took with him Peter and James and John, and led them up a high mountain apart, by themselves. And he was transfigured before them, ³and his clothes became dazzling white, such as no one[a] on earth could bleach them. ⁴And there appeared to them Elijah with Moses, who were talking with Jesus. ⁵Then Peter said to Jesus, "Rabbi, it is good for us to be here; let us make three dwellings,[b] one for you, one for Moses, and one for Elijah." ⁶He did not know what to say, for they were terrified. ⁷Then a cloud overshadowed them, and from the cloud there came a voice, "This is my Son, the Beloved;[c] listen to him!" ⁸Suddenly when they looked around, they saw no one with them any more, but only Jesus.

⁹As they were coming down the mountain, he ordered them to tell no one about what they had seen, until after the Son of Man had risen from the dead. ¹⁰So they kept the matter to themselves, questioning what this rising from the dead could mean. ¹¹Then they asked him, "Why do the scribes say that Elijah must come first?" ¹²He said to them, "Elijah is indeed coming first to restore all things. How then is it written about the Son of Man, that he is to go through many sufferings and be treated with contempt? ¹³But I tell you that Elijah has come, and they did to him whatever they pleased, as it is written about him."

a Gk *no fuller*   *b* Or *tents*   *c* Or *my beloved Son*

COMMENTARY

9:2-10. The transfiguration episode is said to follow the Caesarea Philippi instruction "after six days." A similar expression ("after two days") links the passion account to the apocalyptic discourse. The christological emphases of the previous episode are repeated in the transfiguration story.[357] Jesus' status as Messiah is confirmed by the divine testimony that he is God's beloved Son (8:29; 9:7; 14:61); the predicted glory of the coming Son of Man (8:38) is anticipated by the shining white garments of Jesus (9:3).[358] Finally, the disciples were instructed to tell no one that Jesus was Messiah (8:30), and now those who witness the transfiguration are to tell no one until the Son of Man has risen (9:9).

The three disciples who are singled out for this manifestation of Jesus' identity as Son of God are the ones who witnessed the healing of Jairus's daughter (5:37). They will also witness the agony in Gethsemane (14:33).[359] Although the healing and the transfiguration suggest a special manifestation of Jesus' divine power and glory, this group of disciples does not demonstrate exceptional insight or fidelity. Peter has already been castigated for rejecting the necessity of suffering (8:33). James and John will soon show themselves preoccupied with greatness rather than service (10:35-37). All three will fail to watch with Jesus during the agony in the garden (14:33-41). These failures become all the more striking because the divine voice has instructed them to listen to the Son (9:7), an allusion to Deut 18:15. Jesus is the promised Mosaic prophet.[360]

Although some exegetes think that the transfiguration story originated as a resurrection appearance of Jesus and was relocated,[361] there is no evidence that Mark considers this episode out of place. Form critically, the transfiguration lacks the commissioning elements that are associated with resurrection stories.[362] The literary genre is that of an epiphany, a sudden manifestation of the divine. The human recipients of such a revelation are typically thrown into a state of fear or confusion. Mark 9:6, however, transforms the original motif of fear to an explanation of Peter's suggestion that they build booths on the mountain. For Mark, the primary point of this motif is to demonstrate Peter's lack of understanding.[363] The exchange between Jesus and the disciples that follows the vision itself (vv. 9-13) reverts to the themes of passion and resurrection (8:31). Jesus' clear supremacy over two of the three figures whom Jews considered alive in the presence of God—Moses and Elijah (Enoch being the third)—should have permitted the disciples to understand what resurrection meant.[364]

Details in the episode evoke several Old Testament stories, even though no particular passage is quoted directly.[365] The dazzling white clothing signals heavenly rather than earthly beings (Dan 7:9; 12:3). The mountain, cloud, and divine voice all remind readers of God's appearance in Exod 24:15-18. Jewish tradition held that Moses, whose burial place is unknown (Deut 34:5-8), and Elijah, who was taken up in a chariot (2 Kgs 2:1-11), did not die but were living in heaven. Peter's immediate response to the vision, "let us make three dwellings" (v. 5) seems somewhat con-

---

357. Cf. Morna D. Hooker, " 'What Doest Thou Here, Elijah?' A Look at Mark's Account of the Transfiguration," in *The Glory of Christ in the New Testament: In Memory of George Bradford Caird,* L. D. Hurst and N. T. Wright, eds. (Oxford: Clarendon Press, 1987) 59-60.

358. Shining garments typically indicate angelic figures (2 Bar 51, 5; *1 Enoch* 38:4; 50:1; 104:2; *T. Levi* 8:2). On the transfiguration as an anticipation of Jesus' parousia as Son of Man, see Howard Clark Kee, *Community of the New Age* (Philadelphia: Westminster, 1977) 132-35. The transfiguration was already understood as evidence for the parousia in 2 Pet 1:16-18. Second Peter does not mention the other figures; it depicts the incident as an "enthronement": God confers glory and power on Jesus by naming him "beloved Son." See Jerome Neyrey, *2 Peter, Jude,* AB 37C (Garden City, N.Y.: Doubleday, 1993) 172-74.

359. The parallels between the Gethsemane scene and the transfiguration are particularly close. The group of disciples goes from witnessing Jesus' power (in healing Jairus's daughter) to God's word about the Son to his anguish. Brown suggests that witness, not revelation, links the episodes. Jesus' closest disciples were unable to understand either the glory or the suffering of the Son of God. See Brown, *Death of the Messiah,* 151-52.

360. See Pesch, *Das Markusevangelium,* 2:76.

361. See James M. Robinson, "Jesus: From Easter to Valentinus (or to the Apostles' Creed)," *JBL* 101 (1982) 5-37.

362. See W. D. Davies and Dale C. Allison, Jr., *A Critical and Exegetical Commentary on the Gospel According to Saint Matthew,* 2 vols., ICC (Edinburgh: T. & T. Clark, 1988–91) 2: 690-93. They suggest that an unusual event in the life of Jesus led to comparison between Jesus and Moses on Sinai. The divine voice from heaven was incorporated from the baptismal epiphany scene.

363. See Pesch, *Das Markusevangelium,* 2:76.

364. See James M. Tabor, "Returning to Divinity: Josephus' Portrayal of the Disappearances of Enoch, Elijah and Moses," *JBL* 108 (1989) 259-81. Tolbert, *Sowing,* 206-7, describes the dialogue during the descent as lampooning the ignorant disciples.

365. See Marcus, *Way of the Lord,* 80-93.

fused.[366] Since Moses and Elijah dwell with God in heaven, erection of dwellings on the mountain does not make sense. Some interpreters think that this detail refers to the booths used at the Feast of Tabernacles (Lev 23:43). Mark may have thought of Peter's suggestion as an attempt to replicate the Mosaic tent of meeting (Exod 33:7-11).

Mark's readers recognize the content of the divine voice from the revelation to Jesus at his baptism. Now God commands the disciples to obey the word of the Son. This revelation makes it clear that Jesus is greater than Moses and Elijah,[367] yet he will enter his glory through suffering and death. The conversation during their descent brings the story back to the necessity of suffering.[368] This version of the command to remain silent (v. 9) differs from the others in limiting the period of silence to the time before the resurrection. The disciples are unable to understand what Jesus is referring to, even though the earlier passion prediction included a reference to resurrection (8:31). Mark's readers may have seen the transfiguration as evidence for the heavenly exaltation of Jesus. It demonstrates that the kingdom that Jesus is preaching has been implemented. Despite the turmoil of the world, experienced by the Markan Christians, they can recognize that Jesus is superior to their persecutors and is already controlling the world.[369]

9:11-13. The question put to Jesus about the coming of Elijah returns to the theme of judgment. Elijah, it was said, would precede the Lord's coming in judgment (Mal 3:23-24). Daniel 12:2-3 indicates that resurrection is linked to the end-time judgment.

The disciples, however, ascribe this view to the teaching of the scribes rather than to Scripture. Presuming that resurrection evokes the imagery of judgment, the question about Elijah's coming first might include resurrection as part of the judgment events. Apocalyptic literature frequently includes visions and dialogues with the angel who reveals the events of the end time. Thus the disciples may put their question presuming that Moses and Elijah had revealed such details to Jesus. Earlier discussions of Jesus' identity had the crowds identifying him with Elijah (Mark 6:15; 8:28). Since the disciples recognized that Jesus was greater than Elijah, the query about his coming seems odd in the larger narrative sequence.

Jesus replies by suggesting that John the Baptist was Elijah. John's death indicates the fate awaiting the Son of Man (vv. 12-13). "As it is written" (v. 13) implies that the death of the Baptist also fulfills a divine plan that was predicted in the prophets. Malachi 3:22-23 (LXX) describes Elijah as the one who comes before the day of judgment. Although there is no specific text behind the comment that the Son of Man must suffer and be rejected (v. 12c), this formulation represents a common early Christian understanding of the death of Jesus as the fulfillment of the prophetic testimony, with the further conclusion that similar prophecies were made about Elijah (v. 13c). Marcus proposes that we understand vv. 11-13 as an example of reconciling apparent contradictions in Scripture. Malachi 3:22-23 suggests that Elijah will lead the people to reconciliation, an expectation that contradicts the testimony that the Messiah must suffer. The harmonization explains that Elijah "came first" and suffered as well.[370] This dual example reminds Mark's community that they are participants in the suffering of these figures. God has not abandoned them but permits Christians a chance to be part of the sufferings that herald the coming of God's rule.

366. See Tolbert, *Sowing,* 207. Hooker's suggestion, "Mark's Account," 65-66, that Peter's proposal is an expression of hospitality for unexpected visitors does not do justice to the fact that it occurs during an epiphany. The "divine visitors" are not hidden from the view of the participants.

367. See Morna D. Hooker, " 'What Doest Thou Here, Elijah?' A Look at Mark's Account of the Transfiguration," in *The Glory of Christ in the New Testament: In Memory of George Bradford Caird,* L. D. Hurst and N. T. Wright, eds. (Oxford: Clarendon Press, 1987) 68-69.

368. Mark consistently links glory and suffering (8:38; 10:37; 13:26). See ibid., 70.

369. See Joel Marcus, *The Way of the Lord: Christological Exegesis of the Old Testament in the Gospel of Mark* (Minneapolis: Fortress, 1992) 92-93.

370. Ibid., 94-107. The Son of Man has been assimilated to the tradition of the suffering servant.

REFLECTIONS

Despite providing the most dramatic evidence of Jesus' relationship to God of any epiphany scene in the Gospel, the transfiguration cannot override the necessity of Jesus' suffering and death. It does sharpen the paradox of the cross. Although God spared Moses and Elijah from the normal processes of death, not only does God's own beloved Son die, but also his death is at the hands of his enemies. Even the affirmations of exaltation and entry into the glory of his Father (8:38) cannot nullify the scandal of the cross. God's command to heed the word of Jesus gives his teaching the authority of divine revelation.

Christians frequently think of the divinity of Jesus in terms of heavenly glory or the triumph of the parousia without recognizing the real presence of God on the cross. We tend to think that Jesus is most clearly Son of God in glory, not in suffering. This passage challenges us to revise our understanding of how God's presence comes to the world. The command to silence reminds Christians that glory and suffering cannot be separated. Appearances of glory do not provide evidence for God's truth. Sometimes people expect historians to describe Jesus as such an overpowering personality that others will be compelled to believe. Or they are scandalized by books that treat Jesus as someone whom the educated elite of his time would hardly have noticed. Mark warns that faith grasps hold of a different reality. Dramatic miracles and heavenly visions do not create faith. Christians know that the crucified Jesus is now risen and is exalted with God. Jesus Christ is present to believers without signs and wonders.

Although Mark never lets us forget the reality of the cross, the transfiguration also reminds us of the heavenly basis for our faith in Jesus. At Jesus' baptism (Mark 1:9-11) God declared, "You are my Son, the Beloved." The transfiguration confirms that testimony just as Jesus begins to instruct his disciples about the cross. The presence of Moses and Elijah reminds us that the death and resurrection of Jesus are the goal of the story of God's salvation in the Law and the Prophets. The God who delivered Moses and Elijah will certainly be with Jesus and his disciples. The living presence of Moses and Elijah also reminds us that Jesus is not merely a great figure from the past. The Jesus of Christian faith lives as God in a way that transcends the life of the saints in heaven. As Paul says in Romans, "Neither death, nor life . . . nor anything else in all creation, will be able to separate us from the love of God in Christ Jesus our Lord" (Rom 8:38-39 NRSV).

Mark 9:14-29, Healing a Possessed Boy

NIV

[14]When they came to the other disciples, they saw a large crowd around them and the teachers of the law arguing with them. [15]As soon as all the people saw Jesus, they were overwhelmed with wonder and ran to greet him.

[16]"What are you arguing with them about?" he asked.

[17]A man in the crowd answered, "Teacher, I brought you my son, who is possessed by a spirit that has robbed him of speech. [18]Whenever it seizes him, it throws him to the ground. He foams at the mouth, gnashes his teeth and becomes rigid. I asked your disciples to drive out the spirit, but they could not."

[19]"O unbelieving generation," Jesus replied, "how long shall I stay with you? How long shall I put up with you? Bring the boy to me."

[20]So they brought him. When the spirit saw Jesus, it immediately threw the boy into a con-

NRSV

14When they came to the disciples, they saw a great crowd around them, and some scribes arguing with them. [15]When the whole crowd saw him, they were immediately overcome with awe, and they ran forward to greet him. [16]He asked them, "What are you arguing about with them?" [17]Someone from the crowd answered him, "Teacher, I brought you my son; he has a spirit that makes him unable to speak; [18]and whenever it seizes him, it dashes him down; and he foams and grinds his teeth and becomes rigid; and I asked your disciples to cast it out, but they could not do so." [19]He answered them, "You faithless generation, how much longer must I be among you? How much longer must I put up with you? Bring him to me." [20]And they brought the boy[a] to him. When the spirit saw him, immediately it convulsed the boy,[a] and he fell on the ground and

[a] Gk him

vulsion. He fell to the ground and rolled around, foaming at the mouth.

²¹Jesus asked the boy's father, "How long has he been like this?"

"From childhood," he answered. ²²"It has often thrown him into fire or water to kill him. But if you can do anything, take pity on us and help us."

²³" 'If you can'?" said Jesus. "Everything is possible for him who believes."

²⁴Immediately the boy's father exclaimed, "I do believe; help me overcome my unbelief!"

²⁵When Jesus saw that a crowd was running to the scene, he rebuked the evil[a] spirit. "You deaf and mute spirit," he said, "I command you, come out of him and never enter him again."

²⁶The spirit shrieked, convulsed him violently and came out. The boy looked so much like a corpse that many said, "He's dead." ²⁷But Jesus took him by the hand and lifted him to his feet, and he stood up.

²⁸After Jesus had gone indoors, his disciples asked him privately, "Why couldn't we drive it out?"

²⁹He replied, "This kind can come out only by prayer.[b]"

[a]25 Greek *unclean*   [b]29 Some manuscripts *prayer and fasting*

rolled about, foaming at the mouth. ²¹Jesus[a] asked the father, "How long has this been happening to him?" And he said, "From childhood. ²²It has often cast him into the fire and into the water, to destroy him; but if you are able to do anything, have pity on us and help us." ²³Jesus said to him, "If you are able!—All things can be done for the one who believes." ²⁴Immediately the father of the child cried out,[b] "I believe; help my unbelief!" ²⁵When Jesus saw that a crowd came running together, he rebuked the unclean spirit, saying to it, "You spirit that keeps this boy from speaking and hearing, I command you, come out of him, and never enter him again!" ²⁶After crying out and convulsing him terribly, it came out, and the boy was like a corpse, so that most of them said, "He is dead." ²⁷But Jesus took him by the hand and lifted him up, and he was able to stand. ²⁸When he had entered the house, his disciples asked him privately, "Why could we not cast it out?" ²⁹He said to them, "This kind can come out only through prayer."[c]

[a]Gk *He*   [b]Other ancient authorities add *with tears*   [c]Other ancient authorities add *and fasting*

COMMENTARY

Mark's introduction to this exorcism story presents the other disciples as being engaged in activities typical of Jesus' ministry: They have gathered a crowd, are debating with the scribes, and have attempted to exorcise a possessed boy (vv. 14, 18b). Upon first seeing Jesus, the crowd is "overcome with awe" (v. 15a). The narrator does not give the reason for their awe. Perhaps the referent is a lingering remnant of the transfiguring glory, which causes his garments to glisten, as did Moses' face when he encountered the glory of God (Exod 34:29). The episode as a whole follows the pattern of other didactic scenes. After the public event, Jesus instructs the disciples privately (vv. 28-29). Attentive readers will notice that a change has occurred in this scene. Jesus answers the disciples' question directly, without first commenting on their lack of understanding.[371]

The issue turns to whether Jesus can heal the severely afflicted boy (vv. 17-27). The story itself is the only exorcism in the second half of Mark's Gospel. Apparently, this story was very popular in early Christianity, since Matthew and Luke appear to have employed a different version of the story from the oral tradition. The simple contest between Jesus and the violent world of the demon, typical of the longer exorcism stories, has been modified to include the father's report about Jesus' disciples, who are unable to cure his son. Mark has rewritten the introduction (vv. 14-16), re-

371. See Philip Sellew, "Composition of Didactic Scenes in Mark's Gospel," *JBL* 108 (1989) 631-32. Despite their failures, Jesus is preparing this group of disciples to carry on his teaching.

touched the traditional story (vv. 17-25), and reshaped the conclusion (vv. 26-27) to lead into the traditional material (vv. 28*b*-29). Mark is also responsible for highlighting the activities and the failure of the disciples.[372] Another exorcism report will be used after the next passion prediction to show that the disciples still do not understand the truth about Jesus' mission (vv. 38-41).

Although more dramatically narrated than any of the exorcisms in the narrative so far, this episode repeats a pattern that is familiar to Mark's readers. The exchange between Jesus and the boy's father is punctuated with outbursts of anger, which heighten the characteristic violence of the exorcism scene. As with the Gerasene demoniac, this demon throws the boy into fits that endanger his life (5:5; 9:22). The conversation with the father is much longer than a normal exorcism, providing information that the narrator introduced in the case of the Gerasene demoniac. The father explains the boy's condition twice, and in between the demon throws the boy into a fit as soon as he is brought into Jesus' presence. Since the demon renders the boy unable to speak, it cannot cry out Jesus' name as other demons have done. The demon's violent exit leaves the boy apparently dead. Jesus raises the boy up, perhaps an indirect allusion to the resurrection.

The outbursts punctuating this story alert the reader that it carries an additional message. The father reports that Jesus' disciples have failed to drive out the demon (v. 18). Although one might have expected a comment on the disciples, whose failure led the father to seek Jesus' assistance, Jesus responds with an angry denunciation of his generation as "faithless" (v. 19; cf. Deut 32:5, 20). Jesus has previously condemned his generation as wicked and adulterous (8:38), and his own healing activity was restricted when those from his hometown did not believe in him (6:5-6). Possibly the general disbelief among the crowd, evident in the dispute taking place at the foot of the mountain, rather than the actual request should be taken as the cause of the first outburst.[373] The crowd's argument with the disciples

must have suggested that Jesus' abilities would be just as limited as those of his disciples.

When the father asks Jesus to take pity on him and cast out the demon if he is able to, Jesus becomes angry again (v. 23). He insists that "all things are possible for the believer" (v. 23). (The NRSV translation, "All things can be done for the one who believes," limits the agent of such benefits to Jesus or God.) This exchange specifies the cause of Jesus' anger: It is the disbelief that has been exhibited in the situation. The father responds by confirming his participation in the "unbelieving generation" and by asking Jesus to heal his unbelief. Readers are familiar with characters who expressed absolute faith in Jesus' power to heal: Jairus ("lay your hands on her, so that she may be made well" [5:23]) and the hemorrhaging woman ("If I but touch his clothes, I will be made well" [5:28]). The successful exorcism suggests that the father's faith has been strengthened. Although the father responds to Jesus' outburst (v. 23) by including himself among the unbelieving generation (v. 24),[374] he also insists that he believes. The disciples' failure and the dispute that had arisen among the crowd are the cause of his uncertainty.

Mark has expanded a traditional exorcism account to highlight the obstacle to faith in Jesus posed by the crowd. Jesus does not perform this miracle in order to impress the crowd, although their arrival precipitates his action. Like the healing of the blind man (8:22-26), this cure takes place in two stages. As in the earlier case of Jairus's daughter, Jesus takes him by the hand and raises him up (v. 27; 5:41-42). But the crowd's tendency to disbelief remains. After the demon's violent exit, they think that the boy has died (v. 26). This marks a shift: The second half of the Gospel focuses on faith in the suffering Son of God, not the powerful miracle worker.

The unanswered question in the passage concerns the disciples' inability to heal the boy. When Jesus sent them out to preach, they were able to exorcise demons (6:13). Mark characteristically follows the public episode with a private exchange "in a house" between Jesus and the disciples,[375] where the disciples seek an explanation for their failure (vv. 28-29). Jesus' reply, "This kind can come out only through prayer," points to an

---

372. See Gregory E. Sterling, "Jesus as Exorcist: An Analysis of Matthew 17:14-20; Mark 9:14-29; Luke 9:37-43a," *CBQ* 55 (1993) 471-85.

373. See Robert H. Gundry, *Mark: A Commentary on His Apology for the Cross* (Grand Rapids: Eerdmans, 1993) 489.

374. See ibid., 489.

375. See Sellew, "Didactic Scenes," 631.

alarming gap in the disciples' relationship to God. Can it be that they know nothing about prayer? Jewish miracle traditions commonly insist that God works in response to prayer. Prayer indicates that the individuals involved have faith in God's power to bring about the requested outcome.[376] The fact that Jesus can exorcise such a difficult demon with the same direct command that he uses on other demons provides another indication of his unique relationship to God.

At this point in the Gospel, Jesus has always withdrawn by himself to pray (1:35; 6:46). The disciples have received no teaching about prayer or even witnessed Jesus himself praying. Their earlier mission succeeded because they had been sent out by Jesus to share his ministry. This episode shows a group of the disciples attempting what they have not been sent to do. Their failure demonstrates that they lack the faith and understanding required to undertake such activity on their own. When an outsider is able to use Jesus' name to exorcise demons (9:38-39), the disciples attempt to prevent him from doing so.

376. See Sharyn Echols Dowd, *Prayer, Power and the Problem of Suffering: Mark 11:22-25 in the Context of Markan Theology,* SBLDS 105 (Atlanta: Scholars Press, 1988) 102-14.

REFLECTIONS

The somewhat humorous picture of the disciples attempting to copy Jesus and failing has a sobering side. Jesus' response to the father shows that the basic trust in God's healing power was lacking. Many Christians pray in a way like the father speaking to Jesus, leaving God an option not to act. As one woman put it, "God probably has more significant things to deal with, so I always say 'It'll be all right.'" Others are nervous about the saying "all things are possible to the believer." What about the unanswered prayers of people who are suffering? Of course, we know that a prayer is unanswered only if we have dictated the answer in advance. We are like children who have a definite idea of what presents they are going to get for Christmas. They cannot appreciate the other presents until the desired item has made its appearance.

Faith is not dictating the response to God. Peter's earlier attempt to talk Jesus out of suffering falls into the category of dictating divine action. Faith means learning to think as God does, not according to human standards.

Mark 9:30-32, Second Passion Prediction

30They left that place and passed through Galilee. Jesus did not want anyone to know where they were, 31because he was teaching his disciples. He said to them, "The Son of Man is going to be betrayed into the hands of men. They will kill him, and after three days he will rise." 32But they did not understand what he meant and were afraid to ask him about it.

30They went on from there and passed through Galilee. He did not want anyone to know it; 31for he was teaching his disciples, saying to them, "The Son of Man is to be betrayed into human hands, and they will kill him, and three days after being killed, he will rise again." 32But they did not understand what he was saying and were afraid to ask him.

COMMENTARY

Despite the extraordinary power exhibited in the exorcisms, Jesus still must suffer. The return through Galilee from Caesarea Philippi to Jerusalem is not the occasion for a new mission but for instruction of the disciples,[377] wherein Jesus predicts the passion and resurrection for the second

377. See Joachim Gnilka, *Das Evangelium nach Markus. 1 Teilband Mk 1–8, 26,* EKKNT II (Zurich: Benziger, 1978) 2:53.

time. Each of the three passion predictions in this section of the Gospel is followed by instructions on discipleship and incidents that show that the disciples have not understood Jesus' teaching, just as Peter, James, and John did not understand what resurrection meant earlier (9:10). This passion prediction alters several elements from the previous version. Instead of being rejected by the religious leaders, Jesus is to be handed over to "human hands." The verb has shifted from the passive "be killed" (8:31) to the active "they will kill him" (9:31). The variant may refer to the Roman trial and execution of Jesus.[378] When Jesus announces that the hour has come, he refers to being handed over to "sinners" (14:41).

The initial notice of the disciples' response shows a deepening separation from Jesus. Earlier, Peter had protested the first passion prediction (8:31-33), and the group, who failed to understand the meaning of resurrection, discussed it and asked Jesus whether Elijah would indeed have to come first (9:10-11). Now they are afraid to ask Jesus about the word they do not understand (v. 32). Fear plays a prominent role in the passion narrative. Fear and silence conclude the whole Gospel when the women flee from the tomb (16:8).

---

378. Rudolph Pesch, *Das Markusevangelium I. Teil,* HTKNT II (Freiburg: Herder, 1977) 2:99, who treats the passion predictions as part of a pre-Markan passion narrative, assumes that "human hands" refers to the Jewish people as a whole.

Mark 9:33-37, Dispute over Greatness

NIV

[33]They came to Capernaum. When he was in the house, he asked them, "What were you arguing about on the road?" [34]But they kept quiet because on the way they had argued about who was the greatest.

[35]Sitting down, Jesus called the Twelve and said, "If anyone wants to be first, he must be the very last, and the servant of all."

[36]He took a little child and had him stand among them. Taking him in his arms, he said to them, [37]"Whoever welcomes one of these little children in my name welcomes me; and whoever welcomes me does not welcome me but the one who sent me."

NRSV

[33]Then they came to Capernaum; and when he was in the house he asked them, "What were you arguing about on the way?" [34]But they were silent, for on the way they had argued with one another who was the greatest. [35]He sat down, called the twelve, and said to them, "Whoever wants to be first must be last of all and servant of all." [36]Then he took a little child and put it among them; and taking it in his arms, he said to them, [37]"Whoever welcomes one such child in my name welcomes me, and whoever welcomes me welcomes not me but the one who sent me."

COMMENTARY

After the disciples' failure to exorcise the demon and the subsequent revelation that they do not know how to pray, this episode shows their incredible lack of perception. Jesus and the disciples have returned to a house in Capernaum (v. 33), perhaps the house of Simon Peter and Andrew (1:29). Jesus apparently returned there after his first preaching journey around Galilee (2:1).

Unlike earlier scenes, when the disciples solicited instruction from Jesus, Jesus now asks the disciples what they have been discussing on the journey (v. 33). Their silence shows that they recognize that a dispute over greatness is not appropriate.

Jesus responds to their behavior with two independent sayings (vv. 35-36), showing that he knows what they had been discussing. Sitting before speaking (v. 35) puts Jesus in the formal position of a teacher. Those to whom he addresses these words are identified as "the Twelve." What follows is presented as an authoritative word about rank among Jesus' followers (cf. 10:43-44).[379] The first saying requires a reversal of status and values in the kingdom (v. 35; cf. 10:31). The second example is even more surprising for a religious teacher and his male disciples. Jesus takes a child from the household into his arms[380] and tells the disciples that those who receive a child receive Jesus, and those who receive Jesus receive God (v. 37). The shocking element in this episode cannot be appreciated by modern readers. Our social conventions have exalted childhood as a privileged time of innocence, this romantic view is usually imported into these passages. However, the child in antiquity was a non-person (cf. Gal 4:1-2).[381] Children should have been with the women, not hanging around the teacher and his students (cf. 10:13-16). To say that those who receive Jesus receive God does not constitute a problem. A person's emissary was commonly understood to be like the one who sent him.[382] But to insist that receiving a child might have some value for male disciples is almost inconceivable. Roman authors convey little information about children prior to adolescence, when they enter into adulthood. There appears to have been little interest in children as such, even among medical writers. Childless Romans who needed heirs commonly adopted adults rather than children.[383] When Jesus pointed to his new family as those who do the will of God (3:35), he spoke of mother, brothers, and sisters, not children.

This example treats the child, who was socially invisible, as the stand-in for Jesus. It suggests that the greatness or desire to be "first" being disputed among the disciples involved which one would be Jesus' representative. Even the failed exorcism and their fear at Jesus' repeated passion prediction did not undermine their confidence that they could follow Jesus. The opening words, "first must be last of all and servant of all" (v. 35), hint that the death Jesus predicted was a sign of his own self-offering on behalf of all. Since the child in question may have been a household slave, there is no likeness between such a figure and Jesus or God.

Jesus demands that the child be received "in my name." In the next episode, a non-disciple will use Jesus' name to cast out demons (vv. 28, 39, 41), something the disciples have been unable to do.[384] Now they are challenged to do something else "in Jesus' name": to receive someone as inconsequential as a child. They cannot be concerned about their status as adult male followers of a famous teacher; association with Jesus should enhance their status. Some interpreters suggest that v. 36 was formulated along the lines of Mark 10:16. The original saying in v. 37 was equivalent to Matt 10:40b, which refers to the reception of Jesus' disciples when they were engaged in missionary activity.[385] In Mark's version, the lesson about hospitality to the lowly is directed toward the disciples.

---

379. See ibid., 2:104; similarly 4:1; 13:3.
380. The ancient household consisted of an expanded family. Mark 1:29 includes Andrew as part of the household. Children of household slaves might also be present. There is no evidence in this passage for the suggestion that this child was Peter's.
381. See Bruce J. Malina and Richard L. Rohrbaugh, *A Social-Science Commentary on the Synoptic Gospels* (Philadelphia: Fortress, 1992) 238.
382. *m. Berakot* 5:5.

383. See Suzanne Dixon, *The Roman Family* (Baltimore: Johns Hopkins, 1992) 98-113.
384. See Pesch, *Das Markusevangelium,* 2:105.
385. See Gnilka, *Das Evangelium nach Markus,* 2:55.

REFLECTIONS

1. Greatness in the kingdom overturns the usual perceptions of greatness and honor. The challenge to learn to think as God does runs counter to well-established behavior patterns. We often pay service to the view that the "first shall be last," so long as we are not challenged to put that view to the test of accepting someone whom we consider a real "outsider." Karl Barth describes the radical acceptance of others as the basis of Christian ethics: "To think of *every human being,* even the oddest, most villainous or miserable as one to whom Jesus Christ is Brother and God is Father; and we have to deal with him on this assumption."[386] One of

---

386 Karl Barth, *The Humanity of God* (Atlanta: John Knox, 1976), 53.

the most difficult tasks for volunteers at soup kitchens, homeless shelters, and other service organizations is to learn to treat with dignity the people whom they are helping.

2. Our social conventions about children are so radically different from those of antiquity that we do not react with the surprise that people would have in ancient times at the special attention given to a child. Although we may be annoyed when children become disruptive in public places, we assume that even young children have individuality and dignity. Some interpreters have suggested that these stories in which Jesus uses children as examples made it possible for children to be accepted in the early Christian communities (cf. 1 Tim 4:12).

Social commentators have begun to wonder whether North Americans have lost their desire to make the well-being of children a central concern. Certainly, too many children in our society are discounted, either by individuals who should be their caregivers or by policies that do not help provide caregivers with the resources they need to nurture children. We would do well to recall Jesus' suggestion that the way we treat the youngest and least is a good measure of our discipleship.

Mark 9:38-41, An Outsider Uses Jesus' Name

NIV

38"Teacher," said John, "we saw a man driving out demons in your name and we told him to stop, because he was not one of us."

39"Do not stop him," Jesus said. "No one who does a miracle in my name can in the next moment say anything bad about me, 40for whoever is not against us is for us. 41I tell you the truth, anyone who gives you a cup of water in my name because you belong to Christ will certainly not lose his reward."

NRSV

38John said to him, "Teacher, we saw someone[a] casting out demons in your name, and we tried to stop him, because he was not following us." 39But Jesus said, "Do not stop him; for no one who does a deed of power in my name will be able soon afterward to speak evil of me. 40Whoever is not against us is for us. 41For truly I tell you, whoever gives you a cup of water to drink because you bear the name of Christ will by no means lose the reward."

[a]Other ancient authorities add *who does not follow us*

COMMENTARY

The disciples are certainly not ready to accept a child as though she or he were Jesus. John comes hoping to be praised for attempting to stop an unnamed outsider from using Jesus' name to exorcise. The issue of unauthorized prophets appears in the Old Testament as well (Num 11:26-30). Use of the "name of Jesus" played an important role in the early church (Acts 3:6, 16; 4:7, 10, 30; Jas 5:14).[387] Jesus takes the view that anyone who is able to exorcise in his name should be free to do so. Unlike the scribes, who accused Jesus of being possessed (3:22), this exorcist will not speak badly of Jesus. Verse 40 introduces a proverb to demonstrate the truth of the situation, "Whoever is not against us is for us."

Mark has added an independent saying that promises that those who have provided for Jesus' disciples will be rewarded (v. 41). References to the "name of Christ" provide the verbal link that binds the saying to the previous episode. The story has an ironic tone in the context of the larger narrative; the disciples attempt to prevent another from doing what they had just failed to do (9:18).

387. See Pesch, *Das Markusevangelium*, 2:108-9.

REFLECTIONS

1. The "foreign exorcist" raises a problem for today's churches. In an age of fiscal and personnel constraints, we need to learn cooperation. There is no reason for churches in the same locale to duplicate each other's services to the larger community. However, we quickly become possessive. Each group wants to keep its own territory. Even though ecumenism has taught us to respect other churches, real cooperation is more difficult. We tend to add shared efforts on top of our regular worship or social outreach and then wonder why people loose their drive for shared ministry.

2. The final saying (v. 41) reminds the disciples of the conditions of their mission. They are to depend on those among whom they work. Therefore, they must trust others to provide the basic necessities of life. Such outsiders will also receive a reward. Unlike the scribes and Pharisees, Jesus seeks to draw the boundaries between those who are "with Jesus" to include as many people as possible. He came for sinners, not for the righteous. The disciples fall into the trap that snares many religious groups: They wanted to restrict salvation to their group alone.

Mark 9:42-50, Sayings on Scandal

NIV

42"And if anyone causes one of these little ones who believe in me to sin, it would be better for him to be thrown into the sea with a large millstone tied around his neck. 43If your hand causes you to sin, cut it off. It is better for you to enter life maimed than with two hands to go into hell, where the fire never goes out.[a] 45And if your foot causes you to sin, cut it off. It is better for you to enter life crippled than to have two feet and be thrown into hell.[b] 47And if your eye causes you to sin, pluck it out. It is better for you to enter the kingdom of God with one eye than to have two eyes and be thrown into hell, 48where

" 'their worm does not die,
and the fire is not quenched.'[c]

49Everyone will be salted with fire.
50"Salt is good, but if it loses its saltiness, how can you make it salty again? Have salt in yourselves, and be at peace with each other."

NRSV

42"If any of you put a stumbling block before one of these little ones who believe in me,[a] it would be better for you if a great millstone were hung around your neck and you were thrown into the sea. 43If your hand causes you to stumble, cut it off; it is better for you to enter life maimed than to have two hands and to go to hell,[b] to the unquenchable fire.[c] 45And if your foot causes you to stumble, cut it off; it is better for you to enter life lame than to have two feet and to be thrown into hell.[b,c] 47And if your eye causes you to stumble, tear it out; it is better for you to enter the kingdom of God with one eye than to have two eyes and to be thrown into hell,[b] 48where their worm never dies, and the fire is never quenched.

49"For everyone will be salted with fire.[d] 50Salt is good; but if salt has lost its saltiness, how can you season it?[e] Have salt in yourselves, and be at peace with one another."

[a]Other ancient authorities lack *in me* [b]Gk *Gehenna*
[c]Verses 44 and 46 (which are identical with verse 48) are lacking in the best ancient authorities [d]Other ancient authorities either add or substitute *and every sacrifice will be salted with salt*
[e]Or *how can you restore its saltiness?*

[a]43 Some manuscripts *out,* 44*where / " 'their worm does not die, / and the fire is not quenched.'* [b]45 Some manuscripts *hell,* 46*where / " 'their worm does not die, / and the fire is not quenched.'* [c]48 Isaiah 66:24

COMMENTARY

This section contains a series of sayings against those who cause others to sin. It has been attached to this context by association with the concluding sayings of the previous two sections. The "little ones who believe in me" points backward to the "little children" received in Jesus' name (v. 37) and to those given a cup of water because they bear the name of Christ (v. 41). In that setting, this collection begins with a judgment oracle against anyone who causes a disciple to sin (v. 42). A shift to the second person warns Jesus' followers that they would be better off losing a body part than committing a sin that would exclude them from the kingdom. An obscure proverb about fire and salt concludes the series (vv. 49-50). The shift to second-person exhortation in this section reflects use of these sayings in early Christian exhortation, as does the expression "it would be better if . . . " (καλόν ἐστίν *kalon estin*; cf. 14:21).[388]

9:42. The opening saying is clear. It utters a sharp denunciation of those whose hostility leads one of Jesus' disciples to sin. To "scandalize" or "cause to stumble" (σκανδαλίζω *skandalizō*) indicates a loss of faith (4:17; 14:27, 29). The designation "little ones" is used of Christians in general (cf. Matt 18:10, 14; 25:40, 45). The evils of the end time make "scandal" a clear danger for the faithful (13:5-6, 21-22). Such hostile outsiders are the opposite of those who provide hospitality or assistance to Jesus' disciples. Both types were included in the earlier instruction prior to the disciples' preaching mission in Galilee (6:10-11).

9:43-47. The sayings about maiming oneself rather than falling into sin seem extraordinarily harsh. Many of Jesus' sayings and parables employ such striking metaphors to drive home their point. These sayings follow a reference to persons who might actually lead Christians to abandon their faith. The interpretation of the parable of the sower contains examples of loss of faith that were familiar to Mark's audience: hardship or persecution on account of the Word, worldly concerns, delight in riches, and desire for other things (4:17-19). Jesus is not making a rule that directs Christians to amputate parts of their body. The list of parts—hand, foot, and eye—reflects the most

common injuries to a rural population of agricultural laborers and craftsmen. Also, ancient audiences were familiar with such stories as that of Oedipus, who gouges out his eyes rather than look upon the children he produces with his own mother.[389] Yet Jesus' example is less radical than the Oedipus story, since Jesus' story assumes that only a single eye is lost. The idea that it is better to sacrifice a body part than to allow a person to fall into vice had become proverbial by Jesus' time: "Cast away every part of the body which leads you to intemperance; for it is better to live temperately without it, than to live whole."[390] The metaphor shows the audience how serious the question of sin is. Disciples would rather undergo amputation than turn away from Jesus.

9:48-49. The reference to fire (v. 48) provides the catchword to attach sayings about salt and fire. "Fire and worms" were common descriptions of the punishment awaiting the wicked (Sir 7:17; Jdt 16:21). The expression "for everyone will be salted with fire" may have been proverbial. Hence the "everyone" need not imply that Mark is referring to universal judgment rather than to the disciples.[391] Some commentators have pointed to the use of fire and salt in preserving food as the root metaphor.[392] The saying would be appropriate to situations in which persons are being tested or tried in some way. No one can escape, but such trials are the necessary salt that preserves integrity or faith. They need not destroy it. The psalms speak of God refining (i.e., testing with fire) persons to demonstrate their integrity (cf. Pss 17:3*b*; 26:2). The process of refining also implies purifying the people (Dan 11:35; 12:10). Since v. 49 is unique to Mark's Gospel, it suggests that the evangelist had the sufferings of his own community in view (13:9-13). Mark 13:13*a* warns, "You will be hated by all because of my name."

---

388. See Pesch, *Das Markusevangelium,* 2:113.

389. Hans Dieter Betz, *Galatians* (Philadelphia: Fortress, 1979) 226-28, notes that this motif had been turned into proverbial examples of self-sacrificial friendship (so used in Gal 4:15).

390. Sextus *Sentences* 13. For further examples, see W. D. Davies and Dale C. Allison, Jr., *A Critical and Exegetical Commentary on the Gospel According to Saint Matthew,* 2 vols., ICC (Edinburgh: T. & T. Clark, 1988–91) 2:765-67.

391. See Gundry, *Mark,* 527, who argues for a reference to universal judgment.

392. See Pesch, *Das Markusevangelium,* 2:116-17.

9:50. The second proverbial saying about salt refers to the worthlessness of salt that has lost its ability to season and preserve (v. 50a). The saying appears in Q as well (Matt 5:13; Luke 14:34-35), which concludes with the observation that such salt will be thrown out. The apparent absurdity of salt's becoming unsalty may have been part of the original saying. Although salt does not lose its chemical properties, it could be contaminated and so lose its value. The exhortation to apply the saying "have salt and be at peace" (v. 50b) is unclear. Pure salt was a valuable commodity. It is required as part of the sacrificial offering (Exod 43:24; Lev 2:13[393]).

Eating salt with someone is a sign of friendship and loyalty (Ezra 4:14).[394] The expression "salt of the covenant" appears in the OT (see Lev 2:13).[395] Mark may understand the sayings as a general exhortation to hospitality and covenant loyalty. In that case, Mark directs these comments at the disputes that had broken out among the disciples. The divisions created by persecution in his own time may also have been in view.

393. See also *Jub.* 21:1; *11Q Temple* 20.

394. See also Philo *On Dreams* 2.210.
395. See W. D. Davies and Dale C. Allison, Jr., *A Critical and Exegetical Commentary on the Gospel According to Saint Matthew*, 2 vols., ICC (Edinburgh: T. & T. Clark, 1988–91) 1:472-73.

REFLECTIONS

1. This collection of sayings is very difficult for Christians to hear. The amputation metaphors, with their references to the fires of hell, are inevitably perceived in legalistic terms as words of damnation, not grace. Yet we should be able to recognize the metaphoric use of language in these sayings, which were part of familiar proverbs in Jesus day. His audience would have had no difficulty recognizing the fact that Jesus was speaking metaphorically and was not literally suggesting that we remove an offending body part.

These sayings challenge us to examine the quality of our discipleship. Is following Christ at the core of our being, something too precious to be surrendered lightly? Or is our Christianity merely a matter of taste and convenience, something we shelve at the slightest difficulty or inconvenience? Belief that is easily set aside cannot be the faith that Jesus calls for among his disciples.

2. The final saying, suggesting hospitality and communal solidarity, reminds Christians that they have obligations to one another as well. We should not wait for a time of personal crisis to look for support from others. Neither should we assume that the way we live our lives is merely a private matter. Everyone around us is either better off or worse off than we are, depending on the kind of "salt" found among Christians and their communities.

Mark 10:1-12, The Permanence of Marriage

NIV	NRSV
10 Jesus then left that place and went into the region of Judea and across the Jordan. Again crowds of people came to him, and as was his custom, he taught them.	**10** He left that place and went to the region of Judea and[a] beyond the Jordan. And crowds again gathered around him; and, as was his custom, he again taught them.
²Some Pharisees came and tested him by asking, "Is it lawful for a man to divorce his wife?"	²Some Pharisees came, and to test him they asked, "Is it lawful for a man to divorce his wife?"
³"What did Moses command you?" he replied.	³He answered them, "What did Moses command
⁴They said, "Moses permitted a man to write a certificate of divorce and send her away."	
	[a]Other ancient authorities lack *and*

NIV

5"It was because your hearts were hard that Moses wrote you this law," Jesus replied. 6"But at the beginning of creation God 'made them male and female.'*a* 7"For this reason a man will leave his father and mother and be united to his wife,*b* 8and the two will become one flesh.'*c* So they are no longer two, but one. 9Therefore what God has joined together, let man not separate."

10When they were in the house again, the disciples asked Jesus about this. 11He answered, "Anyone who divorces his wife and marries another woman commits adultery against her. 12And if she divorces her husband and marries another man, she commits adultery."

a6 Gen. 1:27   *b7* Some early manuscripts do not have *and be united to his wife*.   *c8* Gen. 2:24

NRSV

you?" 4They said, "Moses allowed a man to write a certificate of dismissal and to divorce her." 5But Jesus said to them, "Because of your hardness of heart he wrote this commandment for you. 6But from the beginning of creation, 'God made them male and female.' 7"For this reason a man shall leave his father and mother and be joined to his wife,*a* 8and the two shall become one flesh.' So they are no longer two, but one flesh. 9Therefore what God has joined together, let no one separate."

10Then in the house the disciples asked him again about this matter. 11He said to them, "Whoever divorces his wife and marries another commits adultery against her; 12and if she divorces her husband and marries another, she commits adultery."

a Other ancient authorities lack *and be joined to his wife*

COMMENTARY

Jesus now leaves Capernaum in Galilee to go to Jerusalem through the Transjordan region, where he continues to instruct the crowds (v. 1). The present tense of the verb translated "travel together" (συμπορεύομαι *symporeuomai*) indicates that the crowds habitually followed Jesus. Earlier, Mark included people from this region among the multitudes drawn to Jesus in Galilee (3:7-8).[396] The ensuing scene combines traditional material with the standard pattern of a didactic scene in which a public episode (vv. 2-9; Matt 19:3-9) is followed by private instruction of the disciples inside a house (vv. 10-12; Matt 5:31-32; Luke 16:18).

Mark's readers know that the Pharisees are intent on destroying Jesus. The primary challenge posed by Pharisees and scribes has been to Jesus' treatment of traditional teaching (2:1–3:6; 7:1-23). Readers know that Jesus will challenge such traditions by appealing to Scripture (7:9-13).[397] Mark presents the Pharisees' question about whether a man is permitted to divorce his wife as their attempt to test or entrap Jesus (v. 2*a*). Given the Law's stipulations for granting the woman a divorce decree (Deut 24:1), the question "Is it lawful for a husband to divorce his wife?" (v. 2*b*) seems inappropriate. When Jesus demands that they tell him what the Law says, the Pharisees demonstrate that they are familiar with that law (v. 4). Therefore, their question cannot have been posed out of any desire for knowledge about Mosaic teaching. The other examples of "tests" put to Jesus—the demand for a sign (8:11) and the question of whether disciples should pay taxes (12:15)—were more clearly challenges to his authority. Jesus' counterquestion, an element in stories of verbal combat, turns the tables on his opponents by demonstrating that they are only interested in preserving the Law as they understand it, not in doing God's will.[398]

Essene interpretations of the Law argue for the permanence of marriage. Polemic against the polygamy or divorce and remarriage of the kings of Israel was generalized to apply to members of the

396. See Philip Sellew, "Composition of Didactic Scenes in Mark's Gospel," *JBL* 108 (1989) 625.

397. See Elizabeth S. Malbon, "The Jewish Leaders in the Gospel of Mark: A Literary Study of Marcan Characterization," *JBL* 108 (1989) 271. Matthew 19:3 makes the question conform to Jewish disputes over divorce by having the Pharisees ask whether a divorce can be obtained "for any reason." See Joachim Gnilka, *Das Evangelium nach Markus. 1 Teilband Mk 1-8, 26,* EKKNT II (Zurich: Benziger, 1978) 2:70.

398. See Rudolph Pesch, *Das Markusevangelium I. Teil,* HTKNT II (Freiburg: Herder, 1977) 2:123.

sect as well.[399] The Essene argument against divorce appealed to Gen 1:27; 7:9; and Deut 17:17. The political implications, hence the danger to which the Pharisees hoped to expose Jesus, become clearer when one recognizes that the Essene legislation was formulated on the basis of rulings about what it was permissible for a king to do. He was not permitted to have more than one wife. Nor could he divorce his wife to marry another. Viewed in the light of marriages and divorces among members of the Herodian family, as well as the political manipulation of political marriages in Rome,[400] the Pharisees' question is much more dangerous. Readers of the Gospel did not need to be familiar with the Herodian family history. Mark's version of John the Baptist's execution has made it clear that the royal court was sensitive to prophetic criticism of the fact that Herod Antipas had divorced his wife in order to marry his brother's former wife (6:17-19). The connection between the execution of John the Baptist and this question put to Jesus would be even stronger if the geographical notice in v. 1 refers to Herod Antipas's other territory, Perea. Despite Mark's assumption that the Baptist was held in Galilee, John was probably arrested while preaching on the east bank of the Jordan in Perea and was confined and executed in the fortress Machaerus, east of the Dead Sea.[401] Mark quotes John the Baptist as saying to the king, "It is not lawful for you to have your brother's wife" (6:18), thus making it clear that the Baptist had made a statement about the Law in this particular case. Although Mark was probably unfamiliar with laws against divorce among the Essenes, he knew that royal marriages and divorces are politically dangerous. Behind the apparently stupid question posed by the Pharisees

lurks the execution of John the Baptist, so Jesus answers their question at his own peril.[402]

Instead of commenting on the Law by debating the circumstances under which a husband might be permitted to divorce his wife, Jesus asks about what God intended in the creation. Essene law also appealed to Genesis to argue against divorce. Jesus does not deny that Moses established a procedure by which a husband might divorce his wife, but he insists that its existence resulted from the hard heartedness of humanity (v. 5). Mark's readers know that the kingdom of God inaugurated by Jesus' ministry does not belong to the hard-hearted, faithless generation with which Jesus constantly has to contend (9:19).[403]

Readers also know that Jesus opposed substituting human traditions for the commandment of God (7:9-13). The conclusion Jesus draws from the Genesis passage is consistent with the picture of Jesus and the Law already presented in the Gospel.[404] God intended men and women to be permanently joined in marriage, so no human tradition can claim the authority to override that fact (v. 9). Jesus exploits the metaphoric possibilities of Gen 2:24, "they become one flesh," to exhibit the absurdity of thinking that divorce "law," whatever conditions it sets down, represents God's will. Divorce would be like trying to divide one person into two.[405]

The initial story does not culminate in any form of legal ruling. Instead, it castigates the Pharisees for co-operating with the hard heartedness of an evil generation by substituting human traditions for God's intention. Jesus also avoids taking sides on the hidden question about Herod Antipas's marriage to his sister-in-law. Instead, Jesus sticks with what concerns disciples: God's intention in creating human beings. The close

399. See 11QTemple 57:17-19; also CD 4:21–5:2. See also Joseph A. Fitzmyer, "The Matthean Divorce Texts and Some New Palestinian Evidence," *TS* 37 (1976) 197-226; Raymond F. Collins, *Divorce in the New Testament* (Collegeville: Liturgical Press, 1992) 80-85.

400. Since some of Herod's sons and grandsons were reared in imperial Roman circles and depended on imperial whim for succession, the standards of Roman justice determined what happened within the ruling families of Judea. See Richard Fenn, *The Death of Herod: An Essay in the Sociology of Religion* (Cambridge: Cambridge University Press, 1992) 117-29.

401. On Herod Antipas's marriage and the execution of the Baptist, see E. Schürer, *A History of the Jewish People in the Time of Jesus Christ,* rev. ed. (Edinburgh: T. & T. Clark, 1986) 1:344-45. Herodias took the more unusual step of divorcing her first husband, son of Herod the Great and Mariamne. The sectarian legislation may reflect a desire to strengthen the authority of male heads of household. See Martin Goodman, *The Ruling Class of Judea* (Cambridge: Cambridge University Press, 1987) 70.

402. The earlier alliance between the Pharisees and Herodians in seeking to destroy Jesus (3:6) also contributes to the associations between this scene and the death of the Baptist.

403. See Dan O. Via, *The Ethics of Mark's Gospel: In the Middle of Time* (Philadelphia: Fortress, 1985) 77.

404. The determination to seek God's will for humanity in creation, not in the conditions of a world marked by sin, appears to have been central to the teaching of Jesus. See Pheme Perkins, *Jesus as Teacher* (Cambridge: Cambridge University Press, 1990) 51-54.

405. The manuscript traditions differ over whether the citation from Gen 2:24 in v. 7 includes the full text, "and cling to his wife," or an elliptical, "leave father and mother, and the two shall become one flesh." Both modern editions of the Greek text now opt for the longer reading, although the shorter one appears in reliable MSS. See Collins, *Divorce,* 67-68.

association between this incident and the tradition concerning Herod's marriage and the death of John the Baptist makes it unlikely that the episode was created by Mark to illustrate the general teaching about divorce in v. 11.[406]

Mark typically has Jesus provide further instruction for the disciples apart from the crowd. The disciples continue to press the point. A different saying of Jesus forms the basis of this reply (vv. 11-12; cf. Matt 5:31-33; Luke 16:18;

1 Cor 7:10). Unlike the initial dispute, which was framed according to Jewish Law, where only the husband could dissolve the marriage, this formulation assumes the usual Greco-Roman practice in which either party could do so. That twist also fits the story of Herod Antipas's second marriage, since his sister-in-law had to divorce her husband in order to marry him. In any case, divorce did not require elaborate legal procedures. All an individual needed to do was declare that she or he no longer wished the marriage to continue. The original marriage contract usually contained stipulations about prop-

___

406. See Collins, *Divorce*, 74-79. Collins treats the whole section, including v. 11, as a conflict story created by the evangelist.

Jesus' Journey to Jerusalem

→ Jesus' journey

erty disposal and other matters that would apply in the case of divorce.[407]

If one assumes that the bond between husband and wife is permanent, then the party who repudiates a spouse to marry another is committing adultery. Indirectly, this general comment describes a well-known and widespread practice of members of the royal court.[408] As one of the Ten Commandments, the prohibition of adultery does not belong to those legal stipulations that might be described as human tradition. Earlier in Mark, Jesus used the commandment to honor father and mother against the tradition of Corban (cf. 7:9-13). The Pharisees' question here (v. 2) assumes the Jewish tradition, in which only a husband could divorce his wife. But Mark 10:11-12 reflects common Hellenistic practice. The variant in Luke 16:18, which is formulated as a description of the husband's behavior, probably comes closer to an actual saying of Jesus.[409] Attempts to reconcile Mark 10:12 with Jewish practice are evident in some textual variants that refer to the wife as "leaving her husband and marrying another"—that is, she is assumed to be committing bigamy. Given both the ease of divorce and the evidence that Jewish women also divorced their husbands, the variant probably reflects a scribe's attempt to fix Mark's text so that it matches the initial question, not an earlier, more Jewish, reading.[410]

Although the statement makes Jesus' understanding of marriage clear, it does not provide the basis for creating a new legal code concerning divorce and remarriage. The formulation presumes that the party responsible has followed the customary legal forms and might consider his or her actions "blameless," as Herod Antipas attempted to do.[411] In this case, as in most of the political examples from aristocratic circles, the divorce is sought for the purpose of marrying another.[412] Mark 10:11-12 does not stipulate what the injured party should do once his or her spouse has remarried. Jewish Law prohibited remarriage between two divorced persons if the wife had been married to and divorced from another man in the interim. Paul concluded that it would be in the spirit of Jesus' word on marriage for a Christian whose non-Christian spouse had divorced him or her to remarry (1 Cor 7:15). In principle, Paul thought that Christians should not seek divorce. By remaining unmarried after their divorce, a Christian couple leave open the possibility of their reconciliation (1 Cor 7:10-11). The several NT variations on Jesus' teaching about divorce suggest that the subject was of considerable importance to early Christians. At the same time, Jesus refused the grounds for the original question asked by the Pharisees. He could not be accused of breaking the Law, because his views coincided with those of teachers who were stricter in their interpretation. On the other hand, he has sided with John the Baptist's dangerous view of the marriage between Antipas and Herodias; that case and others like it are equivalent to adultery. Jesus wishes to insist that God's intentions for human beings, set forth in the Decalogue, take priority over other provisions of the Mosaic Law.[413] Jesus does not intend to create new legislation.

407. See Naphtali Lewis, *Life in Egypt Under Roman Rule* (Oxford: Oxford University Press, 1983) 56-57. Divorce could be by consent or unilateral repudiation (as in the cases described in Mark), well into the Justinian period. Christians eventually created a more complex set of marriage and divorce laws than had been typical in antiquity. See also Suzanne Dixon, The *Roman Family* (Baltimore: Johns Hopkins, 1992) 77-83.

408. First Cor 7:10-11 follows Mark 10:11-12 in assuming that either the husband or the wife might repudiate a spouse to marry someone else. The variant in Matt 5:31-32 and Luke 16:18 follows the Jewish tradition, in which only the male can divorce his wife. (In fact, Jewish women could and did divorce their husbands, so the formulation of the Law should not be taken as evidence for social practice.) For divorces by Jewish women, see Bernadette Brooten, "Koonten Frauen im alten Judentum die Scheidung betreiben?" *EvT* 42 (1982) 65-80; an example of such a divorce decree from 13 BCE can be found in Ross S. Kraemer, *Maenads, Martyrs, Matrons, Monastics* (Philadelphia: Fortress, 1988) 88.

409. So Gnilka, *Das Evangelium nach Markus*, 2:75; Joseph A. Fitzmyer, *The Gospel According to Luke X–XXIV*, AB 28A (Garden City, N.Y.: Doubleday, 1985) 1120-21.

410. See Gnilka, *Das Evangelium nach Markus*, 2:75; Collins, *Divorce*, 69.

411. The main social constraint preventing someone from repudiating a spouse to marry another, especially in the case of women rejected by their husbands, was the woman's male kin. Since Herod Antipas's first wife, the daughter of the Nabatean king Aretas IV, managed to escape Herod and return to her father, Herod had to face hostility and eventual defeat by Aretas (36 CE).

412. While on a visit with his brother-in-law, Antipas had persuaded Herodias to seek a divorce to marry him. In some Roman cases, a woman's father might order her to divorce her husband and marry another man to seal a political alliance. The Antipas-Herodias union makes the comment about committing adultery against the repudiated spouse clearer. The desire to possess another's spouse existed prior to any actions, legal or illegal, of the parties in question.

413. See Collins, *Divorce*, 100.

REFLECTIONS

1. Christians have not been as adept as was their founder at avoiding the divorce business. Some have created an elaborate legal system for determining when a marriage may be declared void. Others are experimenting with ritualizing divorce. One cannot come away from this Markan story without the sense that Jesus would have declared both approaches attempts to put human traditions in place of God's intention for humanity. A failed marriage represents a human tragedy for everyone involved. The pastoral responsibility of the church is to participate in healing, not in exacerbating or legitimating the tragedy of human hard heartedness. By the time most couples resort to divorce, the rift between them is too great for reconciliation. At the same time, we are increasingly aware of the emotional toll paid by children of divorced parents. Churches have been working hard to counsel couples contemplating marriage to work at gaining basic respect for each other and the ability to negotiate differences before they get married. Other programs aim to help couples and families strengthen their commitments to each other or to help single parents rear their children. None of these programs can help those who fall into the category of the "hard hearted," those persons who lack compassion and refuse to make a change of heart. Jesus was looking at the selfish individualism of the Herodian court when he made his comments in answer to the Pharisees' question. He was not telling a battered woman that she and her children must risk physical and psychological torment every day just to avoid divorce.

2. By treating marriage as grounded in God's creative love, Jesus removes it from the realm of law. The first-century audience was familiar with marriage as a contract. As with any contract, it could be nullified. Indeed, marriage contracts often anticipate that happening. Sometimes people enter into marriage assuming that it will not last. Jesus was not the only one to challenge the casual attitude of his day, but, unlike the Essenes, he did not think new laws would create the spirit in which disciples would live out his teaching. Sometimes people think that Jesus is merely the product of a stricter society. In fact, the legal protections around marriage were much more individual in his day than in ours. The questions he poses about a hard-hearted or utilitarian view of marriage are still crucial for our reflection, not because we want tough laws against divorce, but because we seek to make Christian families what God intended them to be.

Mark 10:13-16, Jesus Receives Children

NIV

13People were bringing little children to Jesus to have him touch them, but the disciples rebuked them. 14When Jesus saw this, he was indignant. He said to them, "Let the little children come to me, and do not hinder them, for the kingdom of God belongs to such as these. 15I tell you the truth, anyone who will not receive the kingdom of God like a little child will never enter it." 16And he took the children in his arms, put his hands on them and blessed them.

NRSV

13People were bringing little children to him in order that he might touch them; and the disciples spoke sternly to them. 14But when Jesus saw this, he was indignant and said to them, "Let the little children come to me; do not stop them; for it is to such as these that the kingdom of God belongs. 15Truly I tell you, whoever does not receive the kingdom of God as a little child will never enter it." 16And he took them up in his arms, laid his hands on them, and blessed them.

COMMENTARY

Jesus made an example of a little child to overturn the disciples' arguments about which of them was the greatest in Mark 9:33-37. That episode was followed by the disciples' trying to prohibit an outsider from using Jesus' name (9:38-39). This episode begins with the disciples' attempting to enforce the standard social mores. Children should not be allowed to disturb the teacher and his students (10:13). Once again, this behavior shows that the disciples do not understand the point of Jesus' ministry, which is inclusive, not exclusive. Including the children also made it possible for the women who had the responsibility of caring for them to hear Jesus' teaching.[414] After affirming that the reign of God belongs to children, Jesus challenges his disciples again: "Whoever does not receive the kingdom of God as a little child will never enter it" (v. 15). Children were not considered persons in their own right. They had no status or power. Yet Jesus insists that God's rule exists for the lowly (v. 14*d*).

Verse 15 turns toward the disciples. Once again, Jesus is warning the disciples that they must give up the normal human calculations of greatness if they are to participate in the rule of God. Jesus' saying that one who does not "receive the kingdom of God like a child shall not enter it"

(v. 15) is puzzling. Modern ideas about the innocence of children cannot be carried back to the first century.[415] In the philosophical context of the teacher and student, "babes" are those who are still without any real understanding of serious teaching (see 1 Cor 3:1-4). Therefore, it is not likely that the image referred to the disciples as recipients of Jesus' teaching.[416] The child in antiquity was radically dependent upon the *pater familias.* The father decided whether the child would even be accepted into the family. Children belonged to their father and remained subject to his authority even as adults. The saying "to receive the kingdom like a child," which most scholars treat as originally independent of the scene about accepting children, must, therefore, refer to the radical dependence of the child on the father for any status, inheritance, or, in families where children might be abandoned, for life itself. It warns the disciples that they are radically dependent upon God's grace—they cannot set the conditions for entering the kingdom.[417]

---

414. Bruce J. Malina and Richard L. Rohrbaugh, *A Social-Science Commentary on the Synoptic Gospels* (Philadelphia: Fortress, 1992) 243, suggest a model from peasant society to explain this scene: The women brought their children so that Jesus could touch them and protect them from evil.

415. See Robert H. Gundry, *Mark: A Commentary on His Apology for the Cross* (Grand Rapids: Eerdmans, 1993) 548.

416. See Aloysius Ambrozic, *The Hidden Kingdom: A Redaction-Critical Study of the References to the Kingdom of God in Mark's Gospel,* CBZMS (Washington, D.C.: Catholic Biblical Association, 1972) 151-52.

417. See Pesch, *Das Markusevangelium,* 2:133-34; Marcus, "Entering," 672-74.

REFLECTIONS

Modern readers find it difficult to avoid romanticizing the ideal of the child. They typically look at some characteristic of children, like innocence or dependence or acceptance, as the meaning of "become like a child." However, ancient societies lacked such romantic notions of childhood. Jesus directs his comments to adult male disciples who are shoving away the "non-persons." In the early church, the Lukan variant of this passage, which substitutes "babies" for "little children" (Luke 18:15-17), was used to support the practice of receiving children into the community through baptism.

Today, Jesus would not use comparison with a child to score the point about who belongs to the kingdom of God. Disciples must be challenged to identify with a group of non-persons. In U.S. society, homeless "street people" are often regarded as non-persons. In many parts of the world, particularly in under-developed nations, indigenous peoples might provide a more telling example.

Mark 10:17-22, The Rich Man

<table>
<tr><td>NIV</td><td>NRSV</td></tr>
<tr><td>

¹⁷As Jesus started on his way, a man ran up to him and fell on his knees before him. "Good teacher," he asked, "what must I do to inherit eternal life?"

¹⁸"Why do you call me good?" Jesus answered. "No one is good—except God alone. ¹⁹You know the commandments: 'Do not murder, do not commit adultery, do not steal, do not give false testimony, do not defraud, honor your father and mother.'ᵃ"

²⁰"Teacher," he declared, "all these I have kept since I was a boy."

²¹Jesus looked at him and loved him. "One thing you lack," he said. "Go, sell everything you have and give to the poor, and you will have treasure in heaven. Then come, follow me."

²²At this the man's face fell. He went away sad, because he had great wealth.

a19 Exodus 20:12-16; Deut. 5:16-20

</td><td>

17As he was setting out on a journey, a man ran up and knelt before him, and asked him, "Good Teacher, what must I do to inherit eternal life?" ¹⁸Jesus said to him, "Why do you call me good? No one is good but God alone. ¹⁹You know the commandments: 'You shall not murder; You shall not commit adultery; You shall not steal; You shall not bear false witness; You shall not defraud; Honor your father and mother.'" ²⁰He said to him, "Teacher, I have kept all these since my youth." ²¹Jesus, looking at him, loved him and said, "You lack one thing; go, sell what you own, and give the moneyᵃ to the poor, and you will have treasure in heaven; then come, follow me." ²²When he heard this, he was shocked and went away grieving, for he had many possessions.

a Gk lacks *the money*

</td></tr>
</table>

COMMENTARY

The story of the rich man who turns down the invitation to discipleship illustrates the fact that desire for wealth can stifle the seed sown by the Word (4:19). The rich man addresses Jesus as "Good Teacher" when asking what is required to inherit eternal life (v. 17). Jesus immediately switches the focus from himself to God: "No one is good but God alone" (v. 18). Jesus is not imposing his word on that of God.[418] Jesus does not replace God in any way, but represents the coming of God's rule. God's order for human life has already been revealed in the commandments. Reference to God as the only one who is good recalls the opening of the Decalogue (Deut 5:6). The Decalogue, which has figured in two earlier controversy stories (7:9-13; 10:11-12), serves as a summary of the Law. Another acclamation of the sovereignty of God introduces a formulation of the command

to love God (Deut 6:4-5).[419] The rich man states that he has followed all of the commandments from the time he was a young man (v. 20). Jesus' response, "looking at him, loved him" (v. 21), gives the reader no reason to doubt the truth of the man's claim. Readers understand that Jesus knows the unspoken thoughts of those around him.

Jesus then extends to the man the call to join his circle of disciples. To do so, he must first divest himself of his property; the disciple-missionary possesses only the basic items of clothing (6:9).[420] A disciple cannot be a rich person with all the accompanying complex socioeconomic ties and relationships. This invitation also illustrates the earlier saying about becoming like a child insofar

---

418. John R. Donahue, "A Neglected Factor in the Theology of Mark," *JBL* 101 (1982) 563-94, emphasizes the importance of single-minded devotion to God in Mark's Gospel. The concern for Markan christology sometimes obscures the emphasis that Mark places on God's action and God's will.

419. The double love command appears as the summary of the Law in the episode of the scribe who is "not far from the kingdom" (12:28-34), which concludes Jesus' public controversies. See Pesch, *Das Markusevangelium,* 2:139-40.

420. On the dual portrayal of wealth and the ambiguities of attitudes toward it in the Gospels, see Perkins, *Jesus as Teacher,* 90-92; Joseph A. Fitzmyer, *The Gospel According to Luke X-IX,* AB 28 (Garden City, N.Y.: Doubleday, 1981) 247-51. Much of the negativity toward "the rich" in the Bible must be evaluated in the context of a limited-goods society, in which one person's wealth means poverty for others. See Malina and Rohrbaugh, *A Social-Science Commentary,* 244.

as it requires setting aside all the elements that confer status and power over others. Even the man's exemplary piety might have been rewarded with approval by others who witnessed it (cf. Matt 6:1-18).[421] Despite the rich man's sincere devotion to the Word of God, he cannot bring himself to accept the call. The sadness with

421. Christopher Byran, *A Preface to Mark: Notes on the Gospel in Its Literary and Cultural Setting* (New York: Oxford, 1993) 102, sees a pattern of reversal throughout this section: the strong yield to the weak, the privileged convey privilege to the lowly, and the wealthy are asked to forgo the fruits of their wealth.

which he departs distinguishes him from the enemies of Jesus, who are hostile when they leave, and suggests that he had hoped for some association with Jesus. Yet he cannot let go of the socioeconomic prestige of being a "rich man" in order to be a disciple. Ironically, the arguments about greatness among the disciples suggest that they might prefer a form of discipleship that would permit them to have some form of prestige or influence as well.

REFLECTIONS

1. Readers respond to this story differently, depending on their socioeconomic status. For some, the story is discouraging. If someone who had been committed to living justly and had experienced Jesus' love walks away sad, who can follow Jesus? For others, the story is encouraging. It explains the difficulty they have in dealing with wealthy people regarding some issues of Christian social teaching. Even well-meaning wealthy persons may balk at taking stands on behalf of the poor or oppressed if it costs them power or prestige.

2. It is easy to suppose that the story of the rich man illustrates an actual event in the life of Jesus. It calls to mind the commitment of unusual persons like St. Francis of Assisi, who stripped himself of every stitch of the rich clothing his cloth merchant father had given him, or Mother Teresa, who gave up a "comfortable life" in a religious order to help those abandoned to die on the streets of Calcutta. Such saints are not "loners." Others join their vision and enrich the world. Like Jesus and his disciples, those who give up everything enter into a special relationship with the rest of the community: They depend on the hospitality described in Jesus' instructions to his disciples (6:7-13).

3. If we are not called to such radical sacrifice, we are constantly reminded of the generous hospitality practiced in the early Christian communities. All Christians should think seriously about their stewardship of money and material possessions. Resisting the pressures of a consumer culture, which generates perpetual needs for more and newer possessions, is difficult for many Christians today. Our excess consumption may deprive others of resources they need just to survive. It is a hidden form of structural greed that wastes the world's resources and creates suffering for others we may never meet.

Mark 10:23-31, Wealth and Discipleship

NIV	NRSV
[23]Jesus looked around and said to his disciples, "How hard it is for the rich to enter the kingdom of God!" [24]The disciples were amazed at his words. But Jesus said again, "Children, how hard it is[a] to	23Then Jesus looked around and said to his disciples, "How hard it will be for those who have wealth to enter the kingdom of God!" [24]And the disciples were perplexed at these words. But Jesus said to them again, "Children, how hard it is[a] to
[a]24 Some manuscripts *is for those who trust in riches*	[a]Other ancient authorities add *for those who trust in riches*

NIV

enter the kingdom of God! ^{25}It is easier for a camel to go through the eye of a needle than for a rich man to enter the kingdom of God."

^{26}The disciples were even more amazed, and said to each other, "Who then can be saved?"

^{27}Jesus looked at them and said, "With man this is impossible, but not with God; all things are possible with God."

^{28}Peter said to him, "We have left everything to follow you!"

^{29}"I tell you the truth," Jesus replied, "no one who has left home or brothers or sisters or mother or father or children or fields for me and the gospel ^{30}will fail to receive a hundred times as much in this present age (homes, brothers, sisters, mothers, children and fields—and with them, persecutions) and in the age to come, eternal life. ^{31}But many who are first will be last, and the last first."

NRSV

enter the kingdom of God! ^{25}It is easier for a camel to go through the eye of a needle than for someone who is rich to enter the kingdom of God."

^{26}They were greatly astounded and said to one another,^{a} "Then who can be saved?" ^{27}Jesus looked at them and said, "For mortals it is impossible, but not for God; for God all things are possible."

^{28}Peter began to say to him, "Look, we have left everything and followed you." ^{29}Jesus said, "Truly I tell you, there is no one who has left house or brothers or sisters or mother or father or children or fields, for my sake and for the sake of the good news,^{b} ^{30}who will not receive a hundredfold now in this age—houses, brothers and sisters, mothers and children, and fields with persecutions—and in the age to come eternal life. ^{31}But many who are first will be last, and the last will be first."

^{a}Other ancient authorities read *to him*   b Or *gospel*

COMMENTARY

The story shifts from the public encounter to Jesus' instructions to the disciples. These sayings highlight the conflict between wealth and discipleship. The ancient patronage system in which the wealthy were celebrated as communal benefactors made it appear that the local aristocracy was endowed with wealth and power by God, the divine king and patron. The wealthy provided funds to support synagogues and Temple sacrifices, thus exhibiting their special relationship to the divine. The OT prophets constantly challenged the assumption that God cared about such lavish worship in the absence of justice and concern for the poor and weak (cf. Isa 1:12-23). Nevertheless, people naturally assumed that the wealthy elite were closer to God and more likely to be saved than were the common people. Jesus' lament that it is very difficult for persons with such attitudes to experience God's saving power ("enter the kingdom") is an explosive shock (vv. 23-24a).[422]

The proverbial comment about a camel's passing through the eye of a needle (v. 25) provides

the metaphorical intensification of the point typical of the sayings of Jesus.[423] Although the disciples have left home and occupations to follow Jesus (1:18, 20), they are astonished by this example. "Then who can be saved?" they ask Jesus (v. 26).[424] Jesus' reply invokes a theological maxim that will reappear in the discussion of prayer (11:22-24): "For God all things are possible" (v. 27). Jesus also repeats this affirmation during his own prayer in Gethsemane (14:36). This axiom was well known in antiquity, in which stock examples of impossible things could be used to contrast the fixed world of nature and human experience with the divine; prophetic oracles, such as Jer 13:23 and Isa 49:15, use this rhetorical device. Humanly speaking, the situation in question is impossible, but God's power is not limited by

422. See Malina and Rohrbaugh, *Social-Science Commentary,* 244.

423. See Perkins, *Jesus as Teacher,* 42-46.
424. This reply demonstrates that the explanation that the "eye of a needle" refers to a narrow gate in the wall around Jerusalem—i.e., something that a real camel could get through but with difficulty—are completely off the mark. The saying means what it says: real camels and real needles. The metaphor of the camel was traditional, but the particular formulation of this saying may have been attached to the warning in v. 24b from the beginning. See Pesch, *Das Markusevangelium,* 2:141.

such constraints.[425] Jesus' miracles demonstrate that he possesses the power of God to do things that are otherwise impossible. The exchange between Jesus and the father of the possessed boy in Mark 9:22-24 insisted upon faith in Jesus' power to perform such a miracle. In this passage, the disciples' incredulous "If the rich can't be saved, no one can" is turned around. God can save even the rich—that is, get the camel through the needle's eye. Therefore, God can save anyone.

Despite their astonishment at what Jesus has said, the disciples, as described by Peter, have left everything to follow Jesus (v. 28). Jesus replies as though the statement was a question about the reward that will come from such renunciation (vv. 29-30). The saying reassures the disciples that what they have renounced will be replaced by the new Christian family in both the present life and the eternal life to come.[426] Jesus himself depicts those who "do the will of God" as his mother, brothers, and sisters (3:35). His home village of Nazareth has been replaced by Capernaum and his family house by that of Peter. Disciples were sent out to preach with the instruction to accept the hospitality of the first house to take them in (6:10). Those who give disciples even a glass of water will be rewarded (9:41). Therefore, the promise that what has

been renounced will be replaced a hundred-fold in this life does not imply a return to one's previous socioeconomic situation.

Renunciation takes primary place for Jesus and Mark's Gospel. The rewards in this life involve both the benefits of inclusion in the new family gathered around Jesus and the hardship of persecutions. Mark unexpectedly inserts persecutions into the list of "goods" that are repaid a hundredfold (v. 30). Persecutions were to be expected as long as Christians are witnessing to the gospel in the world. Mark does not trivialize the pain or danger of persecution. It costs people their faith (4:17). If God had not shortened the time of the persecutions, no one would survive (13:20). Mark's church has been marked by the persecution and turmoil of the 60s CE, when Nero martyred Christians in Rome, including Peter and Paul. Those in Palestine were caught between Jews and their pagan neighbors when Jews initiated a revolt against Rome. Jesus has already warned that following him requires disciples to take up their cross (8:34-35). Jesus is leading his disciples toward Jerusalem and his own death.

The series concludes with an independent reversal saying, which already appeared in the dispute over greatness (9:35). Both in the present and in the future, earthly measures of power and status do not apply in the kingdom of God. Every example in the chapter has involved some reversal of the normal human understanding of greatness. Jesus is about to remind the disciples of the one reversal for which they are still unprepared: his own death.

425. See the discussion and examples of this form in Sharyn Echols Dowd, *Prayer, Power and the Problem of Suffering: Mark 11:22-25 in the Context of Markan Theology,* SBLDS 105 (Atlanta: Scholars Press, 1988) 70-78.
426. See Bruce J. Malina and Richard L. Rohrbaugh, *A Social-Science Commentary on the Synoptic Gospels* (Philadelphia: Fortress, 1992) 244.

REFLECTIONS

1. This collection of sayings provides an important example of how the apparent impossibility of renouncing all things to follow Jesus can be both possible and even rewarding. The key lies in Christianity as a new community, the "family" gathered around Jesus. Christians should also recognize that their faithfulness to the gospel is God's gift. The same God has called together the community and even those non-believing benefactors who provide crucial assistance.

2. Those who find it difficult to enter such a community may resist renouncing power and prestige and the ability to dictate the behavior of others as much as wealth. Interviews with millionaire philanthropists in the United States have revealed that power and influence, the ability to get things done, is generally mentioned as the greatest advantage of wealth. The church as a family of disciples cannot permit those standards of influence to distinguish one person from another.

3. Today's culture is so saturated with the demand for pleasure and instant gratification that Jesus' words about suffering often strike people as sour grapes. It is significant that Mark has inserted the word *persecutions* into the list of goods that Christians will receive from God. Perhaps one of the best proofs that Christianity is not a projection of unrealistic psychological wishes is the realism with which it speaks about the world and the life of those who bear witness to the gospel. Christians do not hide from evil or suffering. They overcome those realities through loving service.

Mark 10:32-34, Final Passion Prediction

NIV	NRSV
32They were on their way up to Jerusalem, with Jesus leading the way, and the disciples were astonished, while those who followed were afraid. Again he took the Twelve aside and told them what was going to happen to him. 33"We are going up to Jerusalem," he said, "and the Son of Man will be betrayed to the chief priests and teachers of the law. They will condemn him to death and will hand him over to the Gentiles, 34who will mock him and spit on him, flog him and kill him. Three days later he will rise."	32They were on the road, going up to Jerusalem, and Jesus was walking ahead of them; they were amazed, and those who followed were afraid. He took the twelve aside again and began to tell them what was to happen to him, 33saying, "See, we are going up to Jerusalem, and the Son of Man will be handed over to the chief priests and the scribes, and they will condemn him to death; then they will hand him over to the Gentiles; 34they will mock him, and spit upon him, and flog him, and kill him; and after three days he will rise again."

COMMENTARY

The picture of Jesus and his frightened disciples walking toward Jerusalem (v. 32) brings readers back to the reality of the passion. Mark's introduction is a heavy-handed combination of several short phrases, but it effectively demonstrates the separation between Jesus and his followers. He once again tries to prepare the Twelve for the events to come. The passion prediction gives readers a detailed summary of the episodes to come: delivered to chief priests and scribes (cf. 14:53), who condemn him to death (14:64) and deliver him to the Gentiles (15:1); they mock (15:16-20), spit upon (15:19), scourge (15:15), and finally kill him (15:20-39); but after three days he will rise (16:1-8).

Mark 10:35-45, James and John Request Positions of Honor

NIV	NRSV
35Then James and John, the sons of Zebedee, came to him. "Teacher," they said, "we want you to do for us whatever we ask." 36"What do you want me to do for you?" he asked. 37They replied, "Let one of us sit at your right and the other at your left in your glory." 38"You don't know what you are asking," Jesus said. "Can you drink the cup I drink or be baptized with the baptism I am baptized with?"	35James and John, the sons of Zebedee, came forward to him and said to him, "Teacher, we want you to do for us whatever we ask of you." 36And he said to them, "What is it you want me to do for you?" 37And they said to him, "Grant us to sit, one at your right hand and one at your left, in your glory." 38But Jesus said to them, "You do not know what you are asking. Are you able to drink the cup that I drink, or be baptized with

39"We can," they answered.

Jesus said to them, "You will drink the cup I drink and be baptized with the baptism I am baptized with, 40but to sit at my right or left is not for me to grant. These places belong to those for whom they have been prepared."

41When the ten heard about this, they became indignant with James and John. 42Jesus called them together and said, "You know that those who are regarded as rulers of the Gentiles lord it over them, and their high officials exercise authority over them. 43Not so with you. Instead, whoever wants to become great among you must be your servant, 44and whoever wants to be first must be slave of all. 45For even the Son of Man did not come to be served, but to serve, and to give his life as a ransom for many."

the baptism that I am baptized with?" 39They replied, "We are able." Then Jesus said to them, "The cup that I drink you will drink; and with the baptism with which I am baptized, you will be baptized; 40but to sit at my right hand or at my left is not mine to grant, but it is for those for whom it has been prepared."

41When the ten heard this, they began to be angry with James and John. 42So Jesus called them and said to them, "You know that among the Gentiles those whom they recognize as their rulers lord it over them, and their great ones are tyrants over them. 43But it is not so among you; but whoever wishes to become great among you must be your servant, 44and whoever wishes to be first among you must be slave of all. 45For the Son of Man came not to be served but to serve, and to give his life a ransom for many."

COMMENTARY

Despite the previous discussions of discipleship as taking up the cross and of the lowly as heirs of the kingdom, James and John ask for the chief positions of honor when Jesus enters his glory (vv. 35-37). Since exaltation and glory come only after the suffering of the passion, Jesus asks the brothers if they are able to participate in his suffering (v. 38; the present tense of the verbs used, "drink" [πίνω *pinō*] and "baptized" [βαπτίζω *baptizō*], indicate that Jesus has already begun to experience the suffering of his passion).

Two metaphors are used to describe such participation: drinking the cup that Jesus will drink and being baptized with his baptism. The "cup" (ποτήριον *potērion*) plays a prominent role in the passion. The cup of wine represents the blood Jesus will shed to establish the new covenant (14:24). Jesus' prayer to be spared the cup if it is God's will makes the cup stand for all the suffering of the passion (14:36). In the OT, the word for "cup" is used metaphorically to refer to divine wrath or punishment (Pss 75:9; Isa 51:17; Jer 25:15-16; Ezek 23:33). Thus Jesus might be said to drink the "cup" as the sacrificial victim whose death atones for the sinfulness that merited God's wrath (Rom 3:24-26; 2 Cor 5:21; Gal 3:13). But that view

does not explain how the disciples can drink the cup. They are being asked if they can accept the same kind of suffering that Jesus now faces.[427] The use of "baptism" in parallel with "cup" indicates that it is also a metaphor for suffering. Old Testament references to waters overwhelming the sufferer in lament psalms may have provided the origin for this metaphor (Pss 42:8; 69:3).[428]

Since the disciples have just been described as a fearful band following Jesus to Jerusalem, the confident assertion that they can share Jesus' suffering must strike the reader as naive. However, Jesus predicts that they will share his suffering (v. 39), and, indeed, Acts 12:2 informs us that James was martyred in Jerusalem by Herod Agrippa (c. 44 CE; Gal 2:9 suggests that John survived his brother). Mark's readers know that Jesus' prophetic word was fulfilled.[429] Nevertheless, Jesus does not determine the positions people have in the kingdom (v. 40). Once again, Mark calls readers back to the fact that God stands behind Jesus' ministry. God is the one

---

427. See Raymond E. Brown, *The Death of the Messiah: From Gethsemane to the Grave. A Commentary on the Passion Narratives in the Four Gospels*, vol. 2 (Garden City, N.Y.: Doubleday, 1994) 169-70.
428. See Rudolph Pesch, *Das Markusevangelium I. Teil*, HTKNT II (Freiburg: Herder, 1977) 2:158.
429. See ibid., 2:159.

who determines who will share Jesus' glory. This qualification over what Jesus controls reappears in the apocalyptic discourse. Only God knows the time of the end (13:32).

Jesus' prophecy concerning the martyrdom of James and John reminds the reader that the failures of the disciples during Jesus' lifetime are not the final word about their faithfulness as followers of Jesus. Although they will run away during the passion, these same disciples will later share the suffering of Jesus.

Since greatness was a topic of contention among them, the other disciples become angry with James and John. A series of sayings about authority and discipleship makes the rejection of power and status in the new community clear (vv. 42-44). Only those willing to be slaves in the service of others have any claim to greatness (vv. 43-44).[430] This insistence on service distinguishes Jesus' understanding of the new order from many apocalyptic visions. Frequently, apocalyptic visions of liberation picture the afflicted and suffering righteous triumphing over their former masters and persecutors. For example, Dan 7:27 pictures dominion as passing to the persecuted, who will enjoy everlasting rule over the nations.

The reply to James and John highlights the exemplary character of the death of Jesus. The final saying points once again to the Son of Man as the one who has come to serve—not the glory the disciples had in mind. It also states the reason for Jesus' death: "a ransom for many" (v. 45). This formulation distinguishes Jesus' death from those of martyr disciples, like James and John. The disciple shares Jesus' suffering but does not offer his or her own life as a sacrifice for the sins of others.[431]

The Pauline epistles show that sacrificial understandings of Jesus' death were well-established in early Christianity (Rom 3:24-26; Gal 2:20). The image of a "ransom" appears in Paul's "bought with a price" (1 Cor 6:20; 7:23). Mark 10:45 only uses the image of ransoming "many"; it does not specify the relationship between Jesus' death and the forgiveness of sin. Therefore, this passage does not draw its imagery directly from the suffering servant of Isa 53:10-12, whose death is an offering for the "sins of many." Mark's readers may have presumed that this picture of Jesus' death as atonement for sin was behind the expression. Other interpreters insist that a ransom liberates persons from slavery.

This final section parallels the opening exhortation to bear one's cross in imitation of the Son of Man, who came to serve (8:34-38). The self-denial associated with the cross does not always mean martyrdom, even in Mark. Another form of self-denial has been emphasized throughout these chapters: denying the human demand for honor, power, and status. The repeated struggles for honor among the disciples show what a difficult task that reversal of values is.[432] The image of ransom as liberation from slavery opens up an additional dimension of Jesus' self-sacrifice. It is the true meaning of the victory over evil, which has been enacted in Jesus' healings and exorcisms.[433]

---

430. See Ernest Best, *Mark: The Gospel as Story* (Edinburgh: T. & T. Clark, 1983) 89-90.

431. See Best, ibid., 89. Mark makes it clear that the only reason why disciples can share Jesus' suffering at all is because Jesus has given his life for them.

432. See Malina and Rohrbaugh, *Social-Science Commentary*, 245-46.

433. See Adela Yarbro Collins, *The Beginning of the Gospel* (Minneapolis: Fortress, 1992) 68-71.

REFLECTIONS

1. Jesus' disciples continue to resist his teaching about the passion and about suffering service. This episode suggests why this teaching is so difficult: It requires surrendering ingrained ideas of honor and dishonor, power and weakness. Although readers may think the disciples foolish to demand positions of honor with Jesus, a serious attempt to put the ethic of self-denying service into practice quickly shows how much we demand honor from others. We all know how quickly jealousy breaks out when a small group seems to have acquired a privilege that others could not share or did not know about.

2. We often undercut the exemplary side of the death of Jesus by overemphasizing its unique place in salvation history as an offering on behalf of sinful humanity. This passage insists upon the death of Jesus as a pattern in which his followers participate. Since the first meaning of participating in the death of Jesus is the renunciation of ordinary greatness to be a slave in service of others, all Christians have an obligation to service (except the weakest and oppressed who have nothing to give up). This image does not legitimate inaction in the face of the suffering of those who are victims of the powerful. (See also Reflections on Mark 15:1-20.)

Mark 10:46-52, Healing Blind Bartimaeus

NIV

46Then they came to Jericho. As Jesus and his disciples, together with a large crowd, were leaving the city, a blind man, Bartimaeus (that is, the Son of Timaeus), was sitting by the roadside begging. 47When he heard that it was Jesus of Nazareth, he began to shout, "Jesus, Son of David, have mercy on me!"

48Many rebuked him and told him to be quiet, but he shouted all the more, "Son of David, have mercy on me!"

49Jesus stopped and said, "Call him."

So they called to the blind man, "Cheer up! On your feet! He's calling you." 50Throwing his cloak aside, he jumped to his feet and came to Jesus.

51"What do you want me to do for you?" Jesus asked him.

The blind man said, "Rabbi, I want to see."

52"Go," said Jesus, "your faith has healed you." Immediately he received his sight and followed Jesus along the road.

NRSV

46They came to Jericho. As he and his disciples and a large crowd were leaving Jericho, Bartimaeus son of Timaeus, a blind beggar, was sitting by the roadside. 47When he heard that it was Jesus of Nazareth, he began to shout out and say, "Jesus, Son of David, have mercy on me!" 48Many sternly ordered him to be quiet, but he cried out even more loudly, "Son of David, have mercy on me!" 49Jesus stood still and said, "Call him here." And they called the blind man, saying to him, "Take heart; get up, he is calling you." 50So throwing off his cloak, he sprang up and came to Jesus. 51Then Jesus said to him, "What do you want me to do for you?" The blind man said to him, "My teacher,[a] let me see again." 52Jesus said to him, "Go; your faith has made you well." Immediately he regained his sight and followed him on the way.

[a] Aramaic *Rabbouni*

COMMENTARY

A final healing miracle concludes the ministry of Jesus outside Jerusalem. The crowd's attempts to silence the beggar's cries for help provide the obstacle that his faith must overcome. By continuing to resist the crowd's attempts to silence his cries for help, Bartimaeus exhibits great faith in Jesus.[434] Unlike the earlier two-step cure of a blind man (8:22-26), Jesus does not use saliva or touch this man. Instead, he sends Bartimaeus on his way with the assurance that his faith has healed him (v. 52a; cf. 5:34). Unlike the earlier incident, this cure does not seek to have the man avoid pub-

licity (cf. 8:26). Now that Jesus has entered his passion, the commands to be silent about his identity cease.[435]

In appealing for help, Bartimaeus addresses Jesus as "Son of David" (vv. 47-48). Mark has not used images of Jesus as the anointed king in the line of David prior to this point. Now that Jesus is approaching Jerusalem, the imagery of Zion's king coming to the sanctuary can be invoked to describe his arrival (Ps 118:26; Zech 9:6). Barti-

434. See J. D. Kingsbury, *The Christology of Mark's Gospel* (Philadelphia: Fortress, 1983) 103.

435. Christopher Bryan, *A Preface to Mark: Notes on the Gospel in Its Literary and Cultural Setting* (New York: Oxford, 1993) 104, sees this episode as a transition between the journey section and the events in Jerusalem. Jesus' messianic titles are associated with his crucifixion.

maeus's acclamation precedes the entry into Jerusalem. Once healed, Bartimaeus joins the crowd that accompanies Jesus into the city. Therefore, his initial acclamation sets the tone for the entry when the crowd hails the coming of the "kingdom of our ancestor David" (11:10).

Attempts to connect the title "Son of David" with healing activity in Second Temple Judaism have not offered a convincing explanation of the use of the title in this episode.[436] (The expression "scion of David" for a messianic figure appears at Qumran.[437]) Therefore, the title has been introduced into the healing miracle to anticipate the Davidic motifs in the passion narrative. Readers soon learn that the Messiah, Son of David, is actually "Lord," not son as a descendent on the same level as his famous ancestor (12:35-37).[438]

The Bartimaeus episode may have a symbolic function in the narrative as well. Many interpreters have noted that he spontaneously leaps up and abandons his cloak when told that Jesus has called him. Although told, "Go, your faith has healed you," Bartimaeus begins to follow Jesus along the road. Such behavior reverses the image of the rich man who would not follow Jesus (v. 22), and Bartimaeus's spontaneous enthusiasm provides a counterpoint to the fear, silence, and hesitation with which the Twelve are following Jesus up to Jerusalem (v. 32). Although the notice that Bartimaeus "follows" Jesus probably does not imply that he joins the larger circle of disciples,[439] the story does demonstrate the power that Jesus has to awaken faith in others.

436. See Dennis C. Duling, "Solomon, Exorcism and the Son of David," *HTR* (1975) 235-52; Vernon K. Robbins, "The Healing of Blind Bartimaeus (10:46-52) in the Marcan Theology," *JBL* 92 (1973) 224-43.
437. See 4QFlor 1:11; 4QPBless 1:3-4. See also Fitzmyer, *Luke X–XXIV*, 1216.
438. See Kingsbury, *Christology*, 106-17.

439. See the extensive discussion of the attempts to treat the verb for "follow" as an indicator of discipleship in Robert H. Gundry, *Mark: A Commentary on His Apology for the Cross* (Grand Rapids: Eerdmans, 1993) 599-603.

REFLECTIONS

Some interpreters think that Mark has placed the healing of a blind man as the final event in Jesus' ministry outside Jerusalem to show that the disciples would eventually be healed of their spiritual blindness. However, the actual details of the miracle play a minor role in the episode. Bartimaeus exhibits the type of faith that forms the basis for healing. He also cries out the truth that Jesus is the merciful Son of David, and the crowd cannot silence him. Such faith points to the success of Jesus' ministry, despite the voices of opposition and the misunderstanding of those closest to Jesus. Christians through the centuries have repeated a variant of Bartimaeus's cry for mercy. The prayer "Jesus, have mercy" was repeated continuously to remind the faithful that God's mercy is always present.

MARK 11:1–13:37, JESUS' MINISTRY IN JERUSALEM

OVERVIEW

The Bartimaeus episode has shown that Jesus' reputation as a healer was well known in the vicinity of Jerusalem. In fact, scribes and Pharisees from Jerusalem had challenged Jesus' authority in Galilee as both healer and teacher (3:22; 7:1). However, Jesus' ministry in Jerusalem will consist only of teaching, which will lead to his popularity with the crowds and to the determination of the chief priests and scribes to have him executed (11:18).

The Temple forms the symbolic center of these chapters.[440] The entry into the city ends at the Temple, where (11:11) on the following day, Jesus

440. See Donald Juel, *Messiah and Temple: The Trial of Jesus in the Gospel of Mark* (Missoula, Mont.: Scholars Press, 1977).

cleanses the Temple (11:15). When Jesus walks into the Temple area, the chief priests, scribes, and elders challenge his authority (11:27), initiating a series of controversy stories in which Jesus silences successive opponents: chief priests, scribes, and elders (11:27, 32; 12:12); Pharisees and Herodians (12:13, 17); Sadducees (12:18); and a scribe (12:28, 34). Jesus then answers the challenge to his authority (12:35-37), instructs his disciples to watch out for the scribes (12:38-40), and, sitting opposite the Temple treasury, uses a widow's offering as an example to once again challenge the economic arrangements attached to the Temple (12:41-44). Upon leaving the Temple, Jesus predicts its destruction (13:1-2) and, seated opposite the Temple on the Mount of Olives, delivers a series of oracles on the future, regarding the disciples and the end time (13:3), the latter to be signaled by the erection of a desolating sacrilege in the Temple (13:14). Finally, the death and resurrection of Jesus will mean the end of the Temple cultus.[441]

This focus on the Temple makes it clear that the struggle between Jesus and his opponents concerns religious issues—specifically, who speaks God's word to the people. Jesus did not enter Jerusalem as Son of David or anointed king in order to liberate the people from foreign domination. The Temple and its custodians have lost the authority to mediate God's presence to the people. They are responsible for the fact that Israel will no longer have the messianic destiny of being the place of prayer for all nations. A new temple will emerge in the community that Jesus brings into being.[442]

441. See Ernest Best, *The Temptation and Passion: The Markan Soteriology,* 2nd ed., SNTSMS 2 (Cambridge: Cambridge University Press, 1990) lii.
442. See ibid., xxxvii.

Mark 11:1-11, Entry into Jerusalem

NIV

11 As they approached Jerusalem and came to Bethphage and Bethany at the Mount of Olives, Jesus sent two of his disciples, [2]saying to them, "Go to the village ahead of you, and just as you enter it, you will find a colt tied there, which no one has ever ridden. Untie it and bring it here. [3]If anyone asks you, 'Why are you doing this?' tell him, 'The Lord needs it and will send it back here shortly.'"

[4]They went and found a colt outside in the street, tied at a doorway. As they untied it, [5]some people standing there asked, "What are you doing, untying that colt?" [6]They answered as Jesus had told them to, and the people let them go. [7]When they brought the colt to Jesus and threw their cloaks over it, he sat on it. [8]Many people spread their cloaks on the road, while others spread branches they had cut in the fields. [9]Those who went ahead and those who followed shouted,

"Hosanna![a]"

"Blessed is he who comes in the name of the Lord!"[b]

[10]"Blessed is the coming kingdom of our father David!"

"Hosanna in the highest!"

[a]9 A Hebrew expression meaning "Save!" which became an exclamation of praise; also in verse 10   [b]9 Psalm 118:25,26

NRSV

11 When they were approaching Jerusalem, at Bethphage and Bethany, near the Mount of Olives, he sent two of his disciples [2]and said to them, "Go into the village ahead of you, and immediately as you enter it, you will find tied there a colt that has never been ridden; untie it and bring it. [3]If anyone says to you, 'Why are you doing this?' just say this, 'The Lord needs it and will send it back here immediately.'" [4]They went away and found a colt tied near a door, outside in the street. As they were untying it, [5]some of the bystanders said to them, "What are you doing, untying the colt?" [6]They told them what Jesus had said; and they allowed them to take it. [7]Then they brought the colt to Jesus and threw their cloaks on it; and he sat on it. [8]Many people spread their cloaks on the road, and others spread leafy branches that they had cut in the fields. [9]Then those who went ahead and those who followed were shouting,

"Hosanna!
Blessed is the one who comes in the name of the Lord!
[10] Blessed is the coming kingdom of our ancestor David!
Hosanna in the highest heaven!"

NIV	NRSV
[11]Jesus entered Jerusalem and went to the temple. He looked around at everything, but since it was already late, he went out to Bethany with the Twelve.	11Then he entered Jerusalem and went into the temple; and when he had looked around at everything, as it was already late, he went out to Bethany with the twelve.

COMMENTARY

Three episodes comprise Jesus' entry into Jerusalem: obtaining the colt on which Jesus rides (vv. 1-6), approaching the city with the acclamation of the crowd (vv. 7-10), and Jesus' visit to the Temple (v. 11). Throughout the passion narrative, Jesus demonstrates his knowledge of impending events.[443] The finding of the colt incorporates a common folklore technique in which signs identify the desired person or object. These signs may include details of an encounter with strangers in the process. Roman soldiers routinely requisitioned animal and human labor from the populace. Jesus' promise to return the animal promptly distinguishes him from the ruling forces.

Matthew's version of this episode includes a citation of Zech 9:9, in which Jerusalem is called to rejoice because its victorious king comes "humble, and mounted on a donkey,/ and on a colt, the foal of a donkey" (Matt 21:5). The notice that the animal is unbroken (Mark 11:2) may have been taken from the Zechariah tradition, but Mark does not refer to the passage explicitly. The use of Zech 9:9 as a proof text in Matt 21:5 provides a more explicitly messianic interpretation for the account of Jesus' entry into the city. The tradition reflected in Mark suggests that Jesus came into Jerusalem with a crowd of jubilant pilgrims. At the historical level, the crowd's gesture does not imply that Jesus was treated as a messianic figure.[444]

Verbal associations between vv. 3 and 7 are strengthened by the reference to sitting on the colt as well as to bringing it to Jesus. Without the OT citation as evidence for the significance of the colt (as in Matt 21:5; John 12:15), finding the colt appears to have been independent of the entry

in vv. 8-10.[445] The references to outer garments link vv. 7 and 8. The disciples who brought the young donkey put their garments on the colt. Then people in the crowd ("many") lay their garments on the road; the road in question leads from the Mount of Olives (v. 1a) to the Temple (v. 11a). Spreading cloaks out before a king to walk on recalls the account of Jehu's accession to the throne in 2 Kgs 9:13.[446] When Jesus begins the journey along the road toward Jerusalem, he goes ahead of the disciples, who follow afraid (10:32). Now that he has arrived in the vicinity of the city, the road is covered with garments and branches and the throng is both "going ahead" and "following" him (v. 9).

Although Christians have become accustomed to remembering this event by processing and waving palm branches in the annual celebration of Palm Sunday, Mark does not describe the branches as palms. The tradition of waving palms, found in John 12:13, probably arose from the use of such branches to celebrate the Feast of Tabernacles (Lev 23:39-43)—a feast that plays an important role in the symbolism of the Fourth Gospel. Palm branches were also used to celebrate Hanukkah (2 Macc 10:7). According to Mark's account, the crowd cuts leafy branches growing in the fields and uses them along with their garments to cover the road along which Jesus rides.

The crowd's acclamation combines two pilgrimage psalms (118:26a; 148:1). Psalm 118 was a part of the liturgy of the Jewish celebration of the Passover seder, where reciting the Hallel (Psalms 115–118) follows the drinking of the third cup of wine (m. Pesah. 10:1-7). The structural counterpart occurs in Mark 14:26 as Jesus and the

---

443. See Gundry, *Mark*, 624.

444. See Joseph A. Fitzmyer, *The Gospel According to Luke X–XXIV*, AB 28A (Garden City, N.Y.: Doubleday, 1985) 1244-45. Hence speculation about why the political authorities did not take action against the crowd's demonstration is irrelevant. See Gundry, *Mark*, 632-64.

445. The two may have been combined in the tradition prior to Mark, so Joachim Gnilka, *Das Evangelium nach Markus. 1 Teilband Mk 1-8, 26*, EKKNT II (Zurich: Benziger, 1978) 2:114.

446. See Rudolph Pesch, *Das Markusevangelium I. Teil*, HTKNT II (Freiburg: Herder, 1977) 2:182.

disciples sing the final hymns before leaving the upper room after Last Supper to go from Jerusalem to the Mount of Olives. However, the Passover rituals of the first century CE are not necessarily reflected in the rabbinic sources, which are almost two centuries later. Mark's audience may have thought only of hymns familiar to them, not the Hallel psalms.[447] The line that parallels the clause of Ps 118:26 acknowledges Jesus' arrival as a sign that the "kingdom of David" is coming. Placed parallel to the psalm citation, this expression reminds the reader of the announcement that inaugurated Jesus' ministry in Galilee: "The kingdom of God has come near" (1:15).

Some interpreters have suggested that Mark's narrative poses a dilemma. Why do authorities not intervene when the crowd expects Jesus to inaugurate the kingdom of David? This question assumes that the crowd has identified Jesus as the one about to establish that kingdom by claiming the authority of David for himself. Mark, however, has avoided any suggestion of a triumphal entry by confining the demonstration to the road leading up to the city. On the other hand, Mark's first-century readers were certainly familiar with certain triumphal entries crucial to the fate of Jerusalem. Those familiar with the events of the Jewish revolt might think of the coup when the people welcomed Simon bar Giora, who then drove Eleazer and his faction from the Temple.[448] Those who lived in Rome might have witnessed the triumphal procession of the Emperor Vespasian in celebrating the defeat of the Jews.[449]

Mark links the enthusiastic demonstration on the road with Jerusalem and the Temple (v. 11). Even in the last days of the Jewish revolt against Rome, the rebels thought that God might deliver them from defeat on the site of the ruined Temple. Their leader, Simon bar Giora, who presented himself in royal attire as though he were the anointed of the Lord, suddenly appeared and was captured on the spot, presumably hoping for a divine intervention.[450] Mark's readers know that the Temple cannot be a source of divine power. Jesus "entered Jerusalem and went into the temple; and . . . looked around at everything." The only purpose of this visit is to see the precincts, not to occupy the area, as in the case of the rebels during the Jewish revolt, nor even to excite the crowds in the city (cf. Matt 21:10-11).[451]

Mark confines Jesus' activity in Jerusalem to either the Temple area (cf. 14:36) or, in the case of the apocalyptic discourse, to the Mount of Olives facing the Temple (13:1-3). Further, Jesus' only activity is teaching. Here he will challenge the religious authorities responsible for his death. From a narrative point of view, Mark may intend readers to recognize that Jesus has taken over the area that his opponents claimed for their own.[452] At night he leaves the Temple area with the Twelve for Bethany, a village just east of Jerusalem on the slope of the Mount of Olives (where he had borrowed the donkey; 11:1), where Jesus and the Twelve find a hospitable reception (cf. 6:10; 14:3). Mark's narrative fits the historical description of first-century Jerusalem, to which huge crowds thronged for Passover; Josephus speaks of almost three million pilgrims.[453] To meet the needs of such numbers, the slaughter of lambs in the Temple began at noon on the day before the feast. Even if Josephus's numbers are exaggerated, such crowds would require visitors to find places to stay outside the city.

447. See Brown, *The Death of the Messiah*, 124-25.
448. See Josephus *The Jewish War* 4.19.11-12; secs. 574-78; Joel Marcus, "The Jewish War and the *Sitz im Leben* of Mark," *JBL* III (1992) 459.
449. See Bryan, *Preface to Mark*, 105n. 6.
450. See Marcus, "Jewish War," 458.
451. See Gnilka, *Das Evangelium nach Markus*, 2:119.
452. See Sean Freyne, *Galilee, Jesus and the Gospels: Literary Approaches and Historical Investigations* (Philadelphia: Fortress, 1988) 59-60.
453. Josephus *The Jewish War* 2.14.3; sec. 280. See also Brown, *The Death of the Messiah*, 372, 1354.

REFLECTIONS

1. The excitement shown by the crowd demonstrates the hope for salvation, which focuses on Jesus. Pilgrims journeying to Jerusalem for the Passover feast would be particularly conscious of God as the one who liberates the people. The hopes for a renewal of society when God's anointed king enters Zion and establishes true peace and justice shaped much of the prophecy and poetry of post-exilic Judaism. Christians read many of these prophecies during the seasons of Advent and Lent. The language that expresses the desire for a society of peace and justice may be strange to modern sensibilities. Yet, whenever a new government administration takes office or a new religious leader is installed, people speak of their hopes for an order that will be different from the past.

2. Major religious holidays bring out both the hopes and the tensions within families. Some people dread family holiday celebrations because the expectations that are raised cannot help leading to disappointment. Conscious of his impending death on the cross, Jesus knows that crowds are not reliable. The joyful expectations for God's salvation that attend his approach to the city will leave him abandoned on the cross. This story reminds us that faith is not built on such cycles of hope and disappointment. Jesus knows the patient suffering and apparent lack of success required for the coming of God's rule. The power of God, which the crowd hopes to witness, will be demonstrated, but it will occur only on the cross.

3. Anthropologists have studied the phenomenon of pilgrimage in religious traditions around the world. The pilgrimage provides a special time of separation from a person's usual social world and relationships. The great feasts of Israel, like Passover, were occasions of pilgrimage to Jerusalem for all but the residents of the city, providing a visible sign of the unity of the people as they gathered at the Temple. Those who, as a result of the diaspora, resided long distances from Jerusalem might make the journey only once in a lifetime. Today, both Christians and Jews often celebrate the annual feasts without including the time of preparation provided by the pilgrimage. The Christian liturgical cycle provides penitential seasons of Advent and Lent as a time of preparation for the annual celebrations of the central mysteries of the faith. Do we take the time to prepare for Christmas and Easter spiritually by changing our routine, standing back from the busyness of the holiday season? In our consumer-driven society, we need encouragement not to treat Advent as an early Christmas celebration, with so much activity that everyone is exhausted on the day itself. Likewise, Lent should be a time for a communal journey in which adults share their faith and prepare for the three days that celebrate the Easter mysteries: Maundy Thursday, Good Friday, and Easter Sunday.

Mark 11:12-14, Cursing a Fig Tree

NIV

12The next day as they were leaving Bethany, Jesus was hungry. 13Seeing in the distance a fig tree in leaf, he went to find out if it had any fruit. When he reached it, he found nothing but leaves, because it was not the season for figs. 14Then he said to the tree, "May no one ever eat fruit from you again." And his disciples heard him say it.

NRSV

12On the following day, when they came from Bethany, he was hungry. 13Seeing in the distance a fig tree in leaf, he went to see whether perhaps he would find anything on it. When he came to it, he found nothing but leaves, for it was not the season for figs. 14He said to it, "May no one ever eat fruit from you again." And his disciples heard it.

COMMENTARY

This is the only miracle in the passion narrative. Its apparently destructive character does not fit the pattern of Jesus' other miracles. Readers know that Jesus provided food for thousands in the wilderness, so his annoyance over finding no figs when he is hungry hardly seems in character, especially given the fact that the only edible vegetation that might have been found on a fig tree so early in the season would have been buds from which the fruit would develop.454 However, since the second half of the fig tree story (vv.

454. See Gundry, *Mark,* 636.

20-21) follows Jesus' prophetic action in the Temple (vv. 15-19), Mark invites readers to give the episode a symbolic significance by associating the fate of the fig tree with that of the Temple, which has lost its place as a "house of prayer for all nations" (v. 17).[455] As a prophetic word about the situation of his people, the example of the fig tree echoes the judgment oracle in Jer 8:13. Although this fig tree, since it has green leaves, does not appear

like the tree in Jer 8:13, its leaves will be withered when Jesus and the disciples return the next day (v. 20). Even the root will be dried up, fulfilling Jesus' curse that no one would ever eat from that tree again.

Mark 11:14 concludes with the notice that Jesus' disciples hear what he is saying. That note is picked up on the next day when Peter observes the tree and comments on its condition (v. 21). This incident provides a dramatic illustration of the power of Jesus' word.[456]

455. Use of the fig tree episode to frame the Temple episode is unique to Mark's Gospel. In Matthew, it follows the cleansing of the Temple (Matt 21:18-22). Luke omits the episode but includes an independent parable about the man who comes looking for figs on an unfruitful tree (Luke 13:6-9).

456. See W. R. Telford, *The Barren Temple and the Withered Tree,* JSNTSup 1 (Sheffield: JSOT, 1980) 56.

Mark 11:15-19, Cleansing the Temple

NIV

15On reaching Jerusalem, Jesus entered the temple area and began driving out those who were buying and selling there. He overturned the tables of the money changers and the benches of those selling doves, 16and would not allow anyone to carry merchandise through the temple courts. 17And as he taught them, he said, "Is it not written:

"'My house will be called
   a house of prayer for all nations'[a]?

But you have made it 'a den of robbers.'[b]"

18The chief priests and the teachers of the law heard this and began looking for a way to kill him, for they feared him, because the whole crowd was amazed at his teaching.

19When evening came, they[c] went out of the city.

a17 Isaiah 56:7   b17 Jer. 7:11   c19 Some early manuscripts he

NRSV

15Then they came to Jerusalem. And he entered the temple and began to drive out those who were selling and those who were buying in the temple, and he overturned the tables of the money changers and the seats of those who sold doves; 16and he would not allow anyone to carry anything through the temple. 17He was teaching and saying, "Is it not written,

'My house shall be called a house of prayer
   for all the nations'?
   But you have made it a den of robbers."

18And when the chief priests and the scribes heard it, they kept looking for a way to kill him; for they were afraid of him, because the whole crowd was spellbound by his teaching. 19And when evening came, Jesus and his disciples[a] went out of the city.

a Gk *they:* other ancient authorities read *he*

COMMENTARY

The historical significance of a denunciation of Temple money changers and pigeon sellers has been hotly debated.[457] Such an act would have affected only a small area in the huge Temple compound. The center of the episode,

457. See Craig A. Evans, "Jesus' Action in the Temple: Cleansing or Portent of Destruction?" *CBQ* 51 (1989) 237-70; David Seeley, "Jesus' Temple Act," *CBQ* 55 (1993) 263-83.

however, lies not in Jesus' actions but in the prophetic saying, a combination of Isa 56:7, that the Temple is a "house of prayer for all peoples" and Jer 7:11, "den of robbers" (both NRSV).

This episode is commonly referred to as the "Cleansing of the Temple," even though it does not involve ritual purification of a sanctuary that has been defiled, which requires actions

Plan of the Temple Mount

1. Antonia Fortress
2. Pool of Israel
3. Solomon's Portico
4. Beautiful Gate
5. Court of Women
6. Nicanor's Gate
7. Court of Israel
8. Altar
9. Laver
10. Court of the Priests
(surrounding the Temple building)
11. Sanctuary
12. Holy of Holies
13. Court of the Gentiles
14. Royal Portico
15. Royal Bridge

All Reconstructions by Dr. Leen Ritmeyer

The Temple Facade

Figure 13: The Temple Mount of Herod the Great

by priests.[458] The Feast of Hanukkah celebrates the cleansing of the Temple after its defilement by pagan cult objects under Antiochus IV (see 1 Macc 4:50-51; 2 Macc 2:12).[459] No reader in Mark's day would suppose that Jesus' actions of themselves could restore purity to the sacred space.[460] On the other hand, Mark's readers know that the Temple area was taken over by zealot revolutionaries and then destroyed by the Romans (13:1-2). The word translated "robber" (ληστής lēstēs) in 11:17b is not the term usually used for a thief but refers to a "brigand."[461]

Jesus' actions involved commercial traffic that provided coinage and some animals for offering in the Temple, both necessary for the normal activities at the Temple (v. 15). Coins that bore the images of pagan deities—often combined with that of the emperor—were in violation of the commandment against making graven images (Exod 20:4). So worshipers had to exchange them for coins minted at Tyre in order to place an offering in the Temple treasury. Vendors provided sacrificial animals for pilgrims, doves being the traditional offering of the poor people.[462] Mark adds a further note that Jesus was prohibiting anyone from carrying vessels (NRSV, "anything") through the Temple (v. 16). The referent is unclear, but "vessel" may refer to ritual vessels, or it may mean ordinary vessels that were connected with money changing and trafficking in small animals. In either case, the comment suggests that Jesus has authority over the activity in the Temple area. While overturning the tables might be a symbolic act of protest, the ability to stipulate what may be carried through a section of the Temple requires that others recognize Jesus' power to determine subsequent activity there.[463] Jesus' authority in the Temple parallels the earlier assertion of his authority over the Sabbath (2:28). Coins will play a role in two further episodes: the question about taxes for Caesar (12:15-17) and the widow's mite (12:41-44).

Mark presents the hybrid prophetic text as the content of Jesus' teaching. Some interpreters take the expression "bandit" from the Jer 7:11 citation as a reference to the zealot leaders who had occupied the Temple area during the revolt against Rome, especially since Mark's apocalyptic discourse warns Christians against following false prophets and messiahs. The events of their own time are not evidence that the end time has come (Mark 13:4-8). However, a political interpretation for the term translated "robbers" (lēstēs) is not required by the narrative, since that word also appears in the Greek translation of Jer 7:11. Those in charge of the Temple, the chief priests and scribes, perceive this teaching as an attack on them (11:18), although their response is delayed until the next day (11:27-33). In the interim, the ultimate failure of the Temple is depicted symbolically; however, the disciples (and the reader) will learn that the "house of prayer" is not the only place where prayers can be heard by God (11:24-25).[464] The question of what is truly God's will becomes the focus of the final controversies in Jerusalem (12:13-34).[465]

Jesus and his disciples leave the city to return to the village where they are staying in the evening. When they return to the city in the morning (vv. 20-21), the fig tree, which had green leaves the day before, has withered to its roots. By framing the episode in the Temple with the cursing of the fig tree, Mark suggests that the Temple will suffer a similar fate. It no longer fulfills the purpose for which God intended it. Some interpreters have suggested that the juxtaposition of the withered tree and the Temple depicts another Old Testament prophecy in reverse: Ezekiel 47:12 predicts that in the messianic age waters from the

---

458. See E. P. Sanders, *Jesus and Judaism* (Philadelphia: Fortress, 1985) 61-76. Sanders concludes that Jesus' action of overturning tables and speaking a prophetic word was symbolic of the destruction of the Temple. Evans's defense of the traditional cleansing title rightly insists that the critique of the Temple and its cult in the first century assumes some form of restored worship and hence purification (Evans, "Jesus' Action," 252-64). However, his claim that Mark 11:17 unambiguously refers to the episode as a "cleansing" (237) is not that clear. Mark's comments in this passage may be directed against the zealots of his own time, whose revolt had led to the destruction of the Temple.

459. See also Josephus *Antiquities* 12.7.7.

460. Robert H. Gundry, *Mark: A Commentary on His Apology for the Cross* (Grand Rapids: Eerdmans, 1993) 641-42, suggests that we speak of "cleansing" in a non-ritualistic sense. Jesus did intend to remove from the Temple area persons and activities that he considered inappropriate.

461. Josephus used the term for the zealot revolutionaries. See Joel Marcus, "The Jewish War and the *Sitz im Leben* of Mark," *JBL* 111 (1992) 449-56.

462. See Gundry, *Mark,* 642.

463. See Seeley, "Temple Act," 271-81, concludes that there are so many implausible details in this account that it could not possibly be historical.

464. On the Markan community as the new "house of prayer," see Sharyn Echols Dowd, *Prayer, Power and the Problem of Suffering: Mark 11:22-25 in the Context of the Markan Theology,* SBLDS 105 (Atlanta: Scholars Press, 1988) 52-54.

465. Donahue, "Neglected Factor," 371, emphasizes the fact that the christological affirmations recede at this point.

renewed Temple will flow in such abundance that the trees on both sides of the bank will never wither and will bear fresh fruit every month, and their leaves will have medicinal properties.

REFLECTIONS

Jesus' action in the Temple has inspired numerous political interpretations in our time. Some allege that it legitimates Christian attempts to unseat corrupt regimes, especially those whose power is supported by religious leaders who ignore the abuses of human rights by the wealthy, powerful majority. Others have used this passage in debates with Christians who oppose war, claiming that Jesus' behavior in the Temple shows that he accepted a legitimate role for violence. Both views go too far. Although Mark set the stage for Jesus to arrive in the Temple as God's anointed king, in this passage he did not use the imagery of the king entering his sanctuary. Instead, Mark turned to the prophets. God's house of prayer for all nations has been corrupted by mercenary concerns.

Christians often face a similar dilemma without realizing it. With buildings and programs to support, they may fall into the trap of marketing religion. Sometimes when marketing means keeping the big donors happy, the gospel suffers. Controversial issues, such as attempts to bring into a church community persons who are different racially, socially, or economically, are often avoided for fear that donations may suffer. Similar fears may appear when churches engage in programs to aid others outside the local community or suggest that certain governmental policies are morally questionable.

Even without engaging in controversial issues, Christians may find it difficult to avoid the marketing orientation of a successful church. How fast is it growing? How many people attend services regularly? What's the average weekly collection? Just as he did on questions about the sabbath and divorce, so also here Jesus calls us back to the only question that counts: What did God intend? A house of prayer for all peoples.

Mark 11:20-25, Sayings on Prayer

NIV	NRSV
[20]In the morning, as they went along, they saw the fig tree withered from the roots. [21]Peter remembered and said to Jesus, "Rabbi, look! The fig tree you cursed has withered!" [22]"Have[a] faith in God," Jesus answered. [23]"I tell you the truth, if anyone says to this mountain, 'Go, throw yourself into the sea,' and does not doubt in his heart but believes that what he says will happen, it will be done for him. [24]Therefore I tell you, whatever you ask for in prayer, believe that you have received it, and it will be yours. [25]And when you stand praying, if you hold anything against anyone, forgive him, so that your Father in heaven may forgive you your sins.[b]"	[20]In the morning as they passed by, they saw the fig tree withered away to its roots. [21]Then Peter remembered and said to him, "Rabbi, look! The fig tree that you cursed has withered." [22]Jesus answered them, "Have[a] faith in God. [23]Truly I tell you, if you say to this mountain, 'Be taken up and thrown into the sea,' and if you do not doubt in your heart, but believe that what you say will come to pass, it will be done for you. [24]So I tell you, whatever you ask for in prayer, believe that you have received[b] it, and it will be yours. [25]"Whenever you stand praying, forgive, if you have anything against anyone; so that your Father in heaven may also forgive you your trespasses."[c]
a22 Some early manuscripts If you have b25 Some manuscripts sins. 26But if you do not forgive, neither will your Father who is in heaven forgive your sins.	*aOther ancient authorities read "If you have bOther ancient authorities read are receiving cOther ancient authorities add verse 26, "But if you do not forgive, neither will your Father in heaven forgive your trespasses."*

COMMENTARY

The Temple was to have been a "house of prayer for all peoples" (v. 17*a*; Isa 56:7). However, Isaiah's prophecies of Gentiles coming to the renewed Jerusalem will not be fulfilled directly,[466] because the Temple has ceased to be the true "house of God." At Jesus' death, the Temple veil will be torn (15:38).[467] The sayings that follow the symbolic withering of the fig tree demonstrate to Mark's readers that believers will nevertheless be able to approach God without the Temple and its sacrificial cult. The association of faith, prayer, and miracles (vv. 22-23) is hinted at earlier in the Gospel. Bartimaeus is healed by his faith (10:52). The disciples are not able to cast out a demon because that type requires prayer (9:29).[468] The possessed boy's father draws a sharp rebuke from Jesus when the father expresses doubt over whether Jesus can cure his son: "All things can be done for the one who believes" (9:23). Peter's amazement over the withered fig tree provides the opening for a series of sayings on prayer.

The first saying in this collection uses a dramatic metaphor to drive home the point that the prayer of those who have unwavering faith is always answered. Such a person could even cause a mountain to cast itself into the sea! Sayings about mountains being moved belong to the category of "impossible things." Some ancient authors argue that only the gods can do such feats, others that not even the gods can do what is impossible.[469] The earlier episode with the possessed boy has established Jesus as one who exercises God's power to do impossible things.

Discussions of unanswered prayer in antiquity often asked whether the gods had failed to respond because they were unable to or because they were unwilling to grant a request. Mark claims that God is both able and willing to respond.

The question about the power of prayer also sets the stage for Jesus' prayer during the passion. Jesus accepts the necessity of the passion; he does not die because God is unwilling or unable to save the Son.[470]

The second saying (v. 24) repeats the assertion that believers can be confident that their prayer will be answered if they believe that they have received what they ask, and it applies the general principle stated in v. 23 to the prayer of the community.[471] Other versions of this saying show that early Christians felt the need to introduce qualifications: Prayer must be in the name of Jesus (John 14:13-14; 15:16*b*; 16:23); the request must reflect that Jesus' word abides in the person praying (John 15:7); God will grant the requests of Christians united in prayer (Matt 18:19; *Gospel of Thomas* 41); prayer must come from an undivided heart (Jas 1:8), but one that is righteous like Elijah (Jas 5:17-18); Christians will not ask for things that merely respond to individual desires (Jas 4:3). In addition, figures like Abraham and Moses are often described as having had the privilege of speaking boldly to God,[472] so that God responds directly to their requests. This particular saying (v. 24) generalizes that special confidence, and it applies to all believers.

The final saying (v. 25) introduces a theme more familiar from its Matthean variant in the Sermon on the Mount (Matt 6:11, 14-15). The forgiveness that the Son of Man exercises on earth (2:10) is available to all who are willing to forgive others. Jesus agrees with his critics that "God alone forgives sin" (2:7). Those who learn to forgive others can be certain that God has forgiven them. Forgiveness was understood to be a condition for God's response to prayer.[473] Luke 17:3-6 links the requirement that Christians forgive those who have sinned against them to the saying about faith that can move mountains. James treats unsuccessful prayer (Jas 4:3) in a series of sayings

---

466. See *Pss. Sol.* 17:32-33.

467. See Elizabeth S. Malbon, *Narrative Space and Mythic Meaning in Mark* (San Francisco: Harper & Row, 1986) 120-26.

468. Mary Ann Tolbert, *Sowing the Gospel: Mark's World in Literary-Historical Perspective* (Minneapolis: Fortress, 1989) 194-96, sees this episode as confirmation of the failure of Jesus' disciples. The withered tree recalls the plants without roots (4:6).

469. Dowd, *Prayer,* 70-92, rightly insists that there is no compelling evidence to interpret the saying about "moving a mountain" as an eschatological reference to uprooting the Temple mount or to the splitting of the Mount of Olives at the Messiah's appearance (Zech 14:4). Mark 11:23-25 refers to what human beings with faith can do. It does not suggest that faith causes the messianic woes (Ibid., 73-74).

470. See ibid., 96-121.

471. Mark has formulated the two sayings to be linguistically parallel. Dowd, *Prayer,* 63-64, suggests that the emphasis on divine agency in these sayings ensures that "moving mountains" or doing other miracles that result from prayer will not be understood as examples of magical powers.

472. See Harold W. Attridge, " 'Heard Because of His Reverence' (Heb 5:7)," *JBL* 98 (1979) 90-93.

473. See Dowd, *Prayer,* 65.

about the passions. Refraining from speaking evil of others or judging them belongs to the Christian discipline of the passions (Jas 4:11-12); John 15:16-17 links the prayer saying and the love command. Divine forgiveness is associated with the coming of the kingdom in Mark (1:4, 15) and in the Lord's Prayer (Matt 6:11; Luke 11:4). The community that expects God to be attentive to its prayer must be a place in which the kingdom is experienced in mutual love and forgiveness.[474]

Jesus also instructs the disciples to regard God as their Father, a notion that does not appear in the earlier list of relationships shared by disciples, who are Jesus' family. Older scholarship treated Jesus' habit of referring to God as "father" as a linguistic innovation on Jesus' part. Some theologians even claimed that the use of the Aramaic term *Abba* (אבא), described as the name young children used for their father, provided a window into the unique consciousness of Jesus' experience as Son of God. More recent evidence from the Qumran scrolls requires that this view be modified.[475] The word *abba* is, instead, a vocative, nominative form.[476] Joseph, praying for rescue, addresses God as "my father."[477] Other prayers that address God as "Father" contain a similar emphasis on God as the one who rescues the afflicted, especially those oppressed by Gentiles (3 Macc 6:3-4, 7-8; Sir 23:1; *Joseph and Aseneth* 12.8–15:1). Appeals for mercy and forgiveness are also associated with use of "Father" for God. Since God is the king whose providence governs all things, God can again rescue Israel from oppression (3 Macc 6:3-4, 7-8). Thus the tradition of suffering, righteous persons who depend on God's power to rescue them underlies prayer to God as "Father." So although the Aramaic term *abba* is unusual as an individual address to God, it is not the Aramaic form used by young children, and it does not provide a direct window into Jesus' experience as Son of God. On the other hand, Christians' preference for the term in personal prayer probably goes back to Jesus, himself. His use of the term made such an impression on his followers that it became a defining characteristic of Christian prayer.[478]

---

474. Joachim Gnilka, *Das Evangelium nach Markus 1. Teilband Mk 1–8, 26,* EKKNT II (Zurich: Benziger, 1978) 2:135, suggests that the forgiveness saying also prohibits the use of prayer to bring evil on another, a misunderstanding that might result from the cursed fig tree.

475. See Mary Rose D'Angelo, "Theology in Mark and Q: *Abba* and 'Father' in Context," *HTR* 85 (1992) 149-74.

476. See the discussion in Raymond E. Brown, *The Death of the Messiah: From Gethsemane to the Grave. A Commentary on the Passion Narratives in the Four Gospels,* vol. 2 (Garden City, N.Y.: Doubleday, 1994) 172-75.

477. 4Q372 1.16-20.

478. Paul assumes that Gentile Christians were taught to address God as "Father" at the time they were baptized (cf. Rom 8:15; Gal 4:6).

REFLECTIONS

1. Many Christians find the sayings on confidence in prayer difficult to apply to their own experience. Jesus can make such statements because of his special relationship to God, but surely no ordinary believer can have such certainty! Frequently, Christians mistake the metaphorical illustration of a mountain throwing itself into the sea as though it conferred on humans the ability to completely rearrange the material world. Others make the mistake of thinking that prayer is like a young child begging its parents for something. The image of God as Father does not apply to humans who are insistent toddlers. The Jewish examples all refer to adults turning to God in situations of real need. Human power and ingenuity alone cannot get one through such situations. As Christians, we can pray with confidence because we know that our prayer is part of the prayer Jesus offers to God. The Epistle to the Hebrews speaks of Jesus as the compassionate high priest to whom we turn (Heb 4:14-16). Paul points to the role of the Spirit in bringing what is in the depths of our hearts to God (Rom 8:26-27).

2. Another sign of dissatisfaction with prayer is the number of Christians who jump from one how-to-pray method to the next. One day a person may be enthusiastic about a particular workshop, book, or prayer group as though that person had never prayed before. Three or four weeks later that same person is discontented. "The parish needs to do something about prayer," he or she says. Jesus does not propose an elaborate method for prayer. The only requirement is simple: Pray confidently, because God does hear and can help. Pray forgiving others, and God will forgive your sins. Complicated methods of prayer and meditation are no substitute for daily prayer. Making time for God every day builds a foundation of faith, hope, and love that we may not be aware of. We need to step aside from the rush of our daily routine to find God's presence. Mark has shown us that Jesus withdrew from the crowds and even the disciples to pray. We need to do the same.

3. This teaching on forgiveness is particularly important as we turn to the controversies between Jesus and his opponents. Jesus does not hate those who put him to death. The Dalai Lama gave a striking example of compassion. Asked by an interviewer if he hated the Chinese who were torturing his people and destroying Tibetan culture, he replied, "Hardly at all. No." He went on to explain that he felt compassion for their fear, hatred, and anger. They are the victim of their own violence. In a radio interview, author André Dubus described the importance of prayer in learning forgiveness. It took him several years of praying for the driver who hit him and left him paralyzed before he could actually feel forgiveness. His experience provides a wonderful example for Christians. We do not have to feel love and compassion toward those for whom we pray. It may take time, but persistant prayer for those who have injured us will replace bitterness of spirit with compassion.

Mark 11:27-33, Challenge to Jesus' Authority

NIV

²⁷They arrived again in Jerusalem, and while Jesus was walking in the temple courts, the chief priests, the teachers of the law and the elders came to him. ²⁸"By what authority are you doing these things?" they asked. "And who gave you authority to do this?"

²⁹Jesus replied, "I will ask you one question. Answer me, and I will tell you by what authority I am doing these things. ³⁰John's baptism—was it from heaven, or from men? Tell me!"

³¹They discussed it among themselves and said, "If we say, 'From heaven,' he will ask, 'Then why didn't you believe him?' ³²But if we say, 'From men' ...." (They feared the people, for everyone held that John really was a prophet.)

³³So they answered Jesus, "We don't know."

Jesus said, "Neither will I tell you by what authority I am doing these things."

NRSV

27Again they came to Jerusalem. As he was walking in the temple, the chief priests, the scribes, and the elders came to him ²⁸and said, "By what authority are you doing these things? Who gave you this authority to do them?" ²⁹Jesus said to them, "I will ask you one question; answer me, and I will tell you by what authority I do these things. ³⁰Did the baptism of John come from heaven, or was it of human origin? Answer me." ³¹They argued with one another, "If we say, 'From heaven,' he will say, 'Why then did you not believe him?' ³²But shall we say, 'Of human origin'?"—they were afraid of the crowd, for all regarded John as truly a prophet. ³³So they answered Jesus, "We do not know." And Jesus said to them, "Neither will I tell you by what authority I am doing these things."

COMMENTARY

On the next day, the conflict initiated by Jesus' prophetic action in the Temple (v. 18) is resumed when the religious authorities demand that Jesus explain what right he has to act as he does. The issue of Jesus' "authority" forms a counterpart to the first statement about Jesus in the Gospel: "He taught them as one having authority, and not as the scribes" (1:22).[479] Com-

479. Mark consistently uses controversy stories to illustrate Jesus' authority over against opponents who insist that they are the leaders of Israel. This dynamic separates Jesus from the Cynics, who treated society at large as their opposition. See Gerd Theissen, *The Gospels in Context: Social and Political History in the Synoptic Tradition* (Minneapolis: Fortress, 1991) 114-16.

bined with the parable of the wicked vineyard workers (12:1-12), this section sharpens the contrast between Jesus, who has the authority to determine activity in the Temple and to teach, and the official leaders of Judaism, whose authority God is taking away.[480] Jesus' response to their challenge plays on the fear of the crowd's reaction, which concerns the religious authorities (v. 18). He promises to answer if they will tell him whether John the Baptist's baptism was of divine origin or merely a human matter. Fear of exposure dictates both possibilities that the scribes and Pharisees contemplate. They know that if John is "from God" they are guilty of not obeying the voice of God's prophet. If they deny the divine origin of John the Baptist's mission, they fear what the crowd might do. Trapped by their own fears of either public

embarrassment or public anger, the authorities state that they cannot answer. Since Josephus says that Herod imprisoned and executed the Baptist out of concern over the influence he held over the crowds, the motive attributed to the religious leaders may be considered plausible.[481] When the leaders are afraid to answer, Jesus refuses to answer their question concerning his authority. The choice between "from God" or "human arrangement" is easily made by readers who are familiar with the Gospel. Both the Baptist and Jesus derive their power from God. Unlike their leaders, the people respond to the authority of those who have been sent by God.[482]

480. See Rainer Kampling, *Israel unter dem Anspruch des Messias,* SBB 25 (Stuttgart: Katholisches Bibelwerk, 1992) 153-56.

481. The link between Jesus and John the Baptist in this episode suggests that it may have been associated with early christological debates. See Kampling, *Israel,* 156-60.

482. Kampling, *Israel,* 155, emphasizes the importance of seeing this episode as a paradigm for the conflict between Jesus and the authorities. Mark has been careful to separate their hostility from the response of the people, who are not opposed to Jesus.

REFLECTIONS

1. The clever strategy Jesus uses to avoid answering the authorities' question shows that his opponents should know the answer already. Like John the Baptist, Jesus' authority is from heaven. Further, the religious authorities can recognize a prophetic voice behind John's words. They also know that they have a responsibility to heed the word of God. Jesus is able to deflect their hostile question because the authorities are not acting sincerely. Any time people attempt to evade what they know is their responsibility, they run the risk of putting themselves in a similar bind.

2. One of the ongoing tensions of Christian life revolves around the authority of witness to the gospel that offends persons in power. Mark's Jesus has not come to provoke the violent overthrow of religious or civic leaders. His popularity with the crowds makes it clear that, if he had chosen to do so, Jesus could have acted like the prophets and populist leaders who sprang up during the period of revolt against Rome. But the alternative to revolution was not lack of controversy. Jesus was able to speak out against evils in his time with a prophetic voice that the leaders could not ignore. They rightly understood that Jesus challenged their authority to speak in God's name.

Mark 12:1-12, Parable of the Vineyard Tenants

NIV	NRSV
12 He then began to speak to them in parables: "A man planted a vineyard. He put a wall around it, dug a pit for the winepress and built a watchtower. Then he rented the vineyard	**12** Then he began to speak to them in parables. "A man planted a vineyard, put a fence around it, dug a pit for the wine press, and built a watchtower; then he leased it to tenants

NIV

to some farmers and went away on a journey. ²At harvest time he sent a servant to the tenants to collect from them some of the fruit of the vineyard. ³But they seized him, beat him and sent him away empty-handed. ⁴Then he sent another servant to them; they struck this man on the head and treated him shamefully. ⁵He sent still another, and that one they killed. He sent many others; some of them they beat, others they killed.

⁶"He had one left to send, a son, whom he loved. He sent him last of all, saying, 'They will respect my son.'

⁷"But the tenants said to one another, 'This is the heir. Come, let's kill him, and the inheritance will be ours.' ⁸So they took him and killed him, and threw him out of the vineyard.

⁹"What then will the owner of the vineyard do? He will come and kill those tenants and give the vineyard to others. ¹⁰Haven't you read this scripture:

" 'The stone the builders rejected
has become the capstone[a];
¹¹the Lord has done this,
and it is marvelous in our eyes'[b]?"

¹²Then they looked for a way to arrest him because they knew he had spoken the parable against them. But they were afraid of the crowd; so they left him and went away.

a10 Or cornerstone   b11 Psalm 118:22,23

NRSV

and went to another country. ²When the season came, he sent a slave to the tenants to collect from them his share of the produce of the vineyard. ³But they seized him, and beat him, and sent him away empty-handed. ⁴And again he sent another slave to them; this one they beat over the head and insulted. ⁵Then he sent another, and that one they killed. And so it was with many others; some they beat, and others they killed. ⁶He had still one other, a beloved son. Finally he sent him to them, saying, 'They will respect my son.' ⁷But those tenants said to one another, 'This is the heir; come, let us kill him, and the inheritance will be ours.' ⁸So they seized him, killed him, and threw him out of the vineyard. ⁹What then will the owner of the vineyard do? He will come and destroy the tenants and give the vineyard to others. ¹⁰Have you not read this scripture:

'The stone that the builders rejected
has become the cornerstone;[a]
¹¹ this was the Lord's doing,
and it is amazing in our eyes'?"

12When they realized that he had told this parable against them, they wanted to arrest him, but they feared the crowd. So they left him and went away.

a Or keystone

COMMENTARY

Although the chief priests, scribes, and elders (11:27) were silenced by Jesus' challenge to indicate the source of John the Baptist's authority, they do not leave the area until they have heard this parable, which Jesus addresses to the crowd (v. 12), who had presumably witnessed the earlier exchange. An oral culture requires witnesses to the challenge and counterchallenge by contending authorities.[483] The passion predictions have indicated that chief priests, scribes, and elders would

be responsible for the death of Jesus (8:31; 10:32), but they will not do so without involving others (9:31). The conflicts that persist throughout the chapter are carried on by surrogates for this group (cf. 12:13).[484]

Although the introduction refers to parables, the condemnation of the religious authorities consists of a single parable (vv. 1-9) and a citation of Ps 118:22-23 (vv. 10-11a). The authorities, who have indirectly admitted that they should have listened to the Baptist (11:31), recognize that the parable contains an indictment against them (v.

483. Bruce J. Malina and Richard L. Rohrbaugh, *A Social-Science Commentary on the Synoptic Gospels* (Philadelphia: Fortress, 1992) 254-55, highlight the insulting character of Jesus' initial response. The parable of the vineyard tenants intensifies the dishonor directed at his opponents in the eyes of the audience.

484. See Elizabeth S. Malbon, "The Jewish Leaders in the Gospel of Mark: A Literary Study of Marcan Characterization," *JBL* 108 (1989) 269.

12). This insight only hardens their determination to destroy Jesus, thus carrying out the actions portrayed in the parable.[485] The dynamics of this episode illustrate Mark's earlier comment on the function of parables (4:10-12). Those who possess the secret of God's rule—that Jesus is the Son of God—can understand the parable. Others will neither see nor hear, and so they will not repent. The authorities are hardened in their determination by this exchange with Jesus. They know what the point of the story is, but they are unable to repent. The people, on the other hand, are sheep without shepherds (6:34).[486]

The initial comparison of a man to his vineyard evokes the Old Testament image of Israel as God's vineyard. The people turn away from the Lord despite the care God lavishes upon the nation (Isa 5:1-7). Some scholars assume that the original version of this story lacked the Isaiah allusion as well as the concluding saying about the rejected cornerstone (vv. 9-11). Comparison of the four surviving variants of the story (Matt 21:33-41; Mark 12:1-9a; Luke 20:9-16a; *Gospel of Thomas* 65) suggests a simpler sequence of events in which an absentee owner sends two servants to collect the produce, each of whom is beaten and returns empty handed. Then the owner sends his only son to deal with the ruthless tenants.[487] Scholars also disagree over whether the death of the son forms part of the initial story. Some scholars insist that the parallels between the son and Jesus led early Christian narrators to transform a hostile rejection into death. The adaptation of the story to the salvation history of the gospel continues in Mark's version. Prior to the death of the son, numerous servants are sent. Some are killed, and one is wounded in the head (vv. 3-5). This extended series may highlight the certainty of divine judgment to come, or it may be a way of underlining the long-suffering patience of God, who has persistently sought to call the people to repentance (Jer 3:11-14; Ezek 16:59-63; Hos 2:2, 14-20).[488]

The details of the interaction between the vineyard owner and his tenants reflect common stipulations in leases of the period. The owner was responsible for suitable preparation of the vineyard.

The tenants were to give to the owner or an agent the stipulated amounts of grapes or wine at the time of the harvest in lieu of rent. Even the violence in the parable echoes conflicts that can be documented in legal material. Some cases describe violence against widows or physically impaired heirs by others who wished to seize their property. Villagers could take over land from an absentee landlord, if the villagers felt the landlord was too weak to enforce the claims. Thus the only shocking thing about this parable is the escalating nature of the tenants' violence, which culminates in murder.

The concluding question, which turns the audience's attention to the fact that the owner will seek revenge for the death of his son, returns to the Isaiah imagery. There God sees bloodshed in the land instead of justice. This injustice has been used by the wealthy to increase their holdings. God responds by taking away the fruitfulness of the land (5:7-10). However, it is possible to see the original parable as ending with a question about what the owner will do. If the owner has only one or two servants and a single son, he would not necessarily be able to exact physical vengeance on the tenants.[489] Since the Law permits the son to act on behalf of his father, the legal definition of *agency* implies that dishonor and insult to the son would be equivalent to dishonoring the one who sends him. The expectation attributed to the tenants that they would inherit if the son died also fit socioeconomic conditions of the time. If the father had died and the only son had come to inspect or claim his inheritance, then his death would leave the vineyard ownerless.[490]

The parable of the vineyard tenants takes the prophetic imagery and the analogies to daily life as its basis. The conquest of Palestine by successive powers in the Hellenistic and Greco-Roman periods had shattered normal patterns of property being held and inherited by an established aristocracy and landed peasantry. Although most readers today easily recognize the pathos of the owner's story, Jesus' audience may have exhibited a broader range of emotion.[491] The landless peasant

---

485. See Kampling, *Israel,* 160-65.
486. Ibid., 179.
487. See Bernard Brandon Scott, *Hear Then the Parable: A Commentary on the Parables of Jesus* (Minneapolis: Fortress, 1989) 246-48.
488. See John R. Donahue, *The Gospel in Parable* (Philadelphia: Fortress, 1988) 55.

489. The designation, "beloved" (v. 6) emphasizes the allegorical possibilities of the parable. The whole orientation of the story suggests that this is the man's only son. So Joseph A. Fitzmyer, *The Gospel According to Luke X–XXIV,* AB 28A (Garden City, N.Y.: Doubleday, 1985) 1284.
490. See Gundry, *Mark,* 661-62.
491. Luke's audience expresses dismay at the destruction that will come upon the tenants when the owner responds to what they have done (Luke 20:16). Their response shows that it was possible for ancient readers to identify with the tenants.

day laborers might have dreamed of a day when they would gain their own land. Some emigrated to the Hellenistic cities. Others formed the nucleus of the bands of robber-revolutionaries during the period of revolt against Rome.[492]

As if to clarify the ambiguous emotions evoked by the root story, Mark's narrative intensifies both the patience of the owner and the wickedness of the tenants. The owner sends an excessive number of servants to collect from the tenants. These servants meet with increasing levels of violence. The servant wounded in the head (v. 4) reminds readers of the fate suffered by John the Baptist. After the tenants' vicious determination has been demonstrated, the owner's decision to send his only son seems foolhardy. Nevertheless, the owner gives the tenants one last chance to comply with the original conditions of their contract. Additional details enable the audience to identify the man's son as Jesus (cf. "beloved son," Mark 1:11; 9:7).

The central episode cannot be treated as an allegory based on Isa 5:1-7 with no grounding in the experience of its audience. The correlation with socioeconomic problems of the period demonstrate that the parable presents a striking image of what the present evil age is like. The familiar image of Israel as God's vineyard makes it possible for the audience to link the application of this shocking story to the confrontation between Jesus and his opponents. Mark's version focuses on the horror of rejecting Jesus, the Son of God. This event becomes the culmination of a long history of similar incidents. Just as a human owner has the option of replacing the original tenants, so also God finds a new covenant community—that is, the community of disciples, which Jesus calls into being.[493]

The link between the parable and a community founded on Christ is expressed by a saying about the cornerstone from Ps 118:23. It points to Jesus as the cornerstone of the new people of God, which is now compared to a building (cf. 1 Cor 3:9-15) rather than a vine. Unlike the image in Isa 5:1-7, God's judgment does not lead to the destruction of the vineyard, since the failure to provide fruit in Jesus' parable was due to the actions of the

tenants, not to the lack of a harvest. Some commentators detect an optimism in the saying about the stone that appears to clash with the tone of judgment in the parable. God has made the "rejected one" the cornerstone.[494] The surprise of finding a "rejected stone" at the most prominent position in a building also conveys a note of local color: The magnificent Temple complex begun by Herod the Great was still under construction at the time Jesus was speaking. Later, Jesus responds to his disciples' statement about the magnificent stones of the Temple by predicting its complete destruction: "Not one stone will be left here upon another" (13:1-2). Throughout the Gospel, readers have seen Jesus and his disciples in borrowed spaces: in other peoples' homes; in wilderness areas; in boats; in Gentile territory. Eventually, even Jesus' tomb is borrowed. Jesus is the cornerstone of a community that will not be identified with the architectural grandeur of the Temple.[495]

Mark's treatment of the parable opens up a new understanding of its significance for Christians in his day. The inner Jewish conflict between religious authorities and charismatic figures like John the Baptist and Jesus anticipates the conflict between two religious communities, each with a claim to be God's vineyard. Throwing out the tenants no longer means replacing the old leaders; now it means reestablishing the entire community. The death and resurrection of Jesus stand behind the image of the rejected stone that becomes the corner. The verb rendered "reject" (ἀποδοκιμάζω *apodokimazō*) appears only in 12:10 and in the first passion prediction of 8:31. The community that will come into existence represents the reversal of expectations in another way. Psalm 118:10-12 depicts God as the triumphant holy warrior who defeats the nations Gog and Magog in order to establish his people Israel. The renewal of Israel is to be the light that summons the Gentiles to worship at the Temple (Isa 2:2-4). Mark begins a challenge to that eschatological vision that will be carried through the apocalyptic discourse in chap. 13. God's triumph will mean the end of the

492. See Martin Goodman, *The Ruling Class of Judea: The Origins of the Jewish Revolt Against Rome A.D. 66–70* (Cambridge: Cambridge University Press, 1987) 62-63.

493. This interpretation of the salvation history in the parable suggests that the failures of the disciples during the passion should not be taken as an indication of the forfeiture of their position as the foundation of the new Israel.

494. See Joel Marcus, *The Way of the Lord: Christological Exegesis of the Old Testament in the Gospel of Mark* (Minneapolis: Fortress, 1992) 111.

495. Elizabeth S. Malbon, *Narrative Space and Mythic Meaning in Mark* (San Francisco: Harper & Row, 1986) 137-40, suggests that the anti-architectural sentiments in Mark work against concluding that Mark understands the cornerstone as the foundation of the community as a Temple.

Temple, as the withered fig tree suggests, and will incorporate the nations into the community founded on the rejected one, the Son of God, whom the vineyard workers murdered.[496]

496. See Marcus, *Way of the Lord,* 114-19.

REFLECTIONS

1. Many interpreters think that this entire parable was expanded by Mark into an allegory against Israel. The original parable of Jesus was not against Israel. It combined the prophetic voice of Isaiah with the realism of everyday life to describe the evil age in which people find themselves. A modernday parable would probably turn to violence on inner-city streets or in public schools to make its point. By drawing our attention to the larger pattern of social violence, the parable explains how it is that allegedly religious people came to oppose Jesus, even though he was the Son of God. People become blinded by their own desires, concepts of what constitutes the future, and attachment to particular authorities.

2. Christians today must be careful not to let the conflict between the Christian and Jewish communities, evident in Mark's version of the parable, become the dominant element in its interpretation. Jesus had compassion on his people because they were like sheep without a shepherd (6:34). His rejection of the particular religious leaders of his day does not imply rejection of the people as a whole. The controversy stories consistently show why Jesus challenges the religious leaders: They are not concerned about God's Word at all but only about their own prestige and traditions.

Mark 12:13-17, Paying Taxes to Caesar

<table>
<tr><td>NIV</td><td>NRSV</td></tr>
<tr><td>

[13]Later they sent some of the Pharisees and Herodians to Jesus to catch him in his words. [14]They came to him and said, "Teacher, we know you are a man of integrity. You aren't swayed by men, because you pay no attention to who they are; but you teach the way of God in accordance with the truth. Is it right to pay taxes to Caesar or not? [15]Should we pay or shouldn't we?"

But Jesus knew their hypocrisy. "Why are you trying to trap me?" he asked. "Bring me a denarius and let me look at it." [16]They brought the coin, and he asked them, "Whose portrait is this? And whose inscription?"

"Caesar's," they replied.

[17]Then Jesus said to them, "Give to Caesar what is Caesar's and to God what is God's."

And they were amazed at him.

</td><td>

13Then they sent to him some Pharisees and some Herodians to trap him in what he said. [14]And they came and said to him, "Teacher, we know that you are sincere, and show deference to no one; for you do not regard people with partiality, but teach the way of God in accordance with truth. Is it lawful to pay taxes to the emperor, or not? [15]Should we pay them, or should we not?" But knowing their hypocrisy, he said to them, "Why are you putting me to the test? Bring me a denarius and let me see it." [16]And they brought one. Then he said to them, "Whose head is this, and whose title?" They answered, "The emperor's." [17]Jesus said to them, "Give to the emperor the things that are the emperor's, and to God the things that are God's." And they were utterly amazed at him.

</td></tr>
</table>

COMMENTARY

Although the chief priests, scribes, and elders have left, they send Pharisees and Herodians, already enemies of Jesus (3:6), to trap him (v. 13; cf. 10:2). Mark 12:13-37 contains a series of four questions: Is it lawful to pay taxes? If a woman has been married to seven brothers successively, which one's wife will she be in the resurrection? What is the greatest commandment? If David calls the messiah "Lord" how can he be David's son? Interrogating a teacher with a series of questions formed a staple element in Rabbinic rhetoric.[497]

The opening statement demands a ruling on how to obey the Law. The ironic flattery of their initial greeting (v. 14) implies that Jesus is being asked for this ruling because his impartiality mirrors that of God.[498] Although they think that they can trap Jesus into either making himself unpopular with the crowd by supporting Roman rule as legitimate or politically suspect to the authorities by rejecting the payment of tribute, Jesus eludes the trap by continuing to insist that people focus on what really belongs to God. The initial flattery also adds a more subtle threat to the first question. The statement "You are sincere, and show deference to no one; for you do not regard people with partiality, but teach the way of God in accordance with truth" (v. 14), which readers recognize as a true description of Jesus' teaching, underlines the fact that Jesus rejects all standards except those that come from God. Jesus' opponents hope to force him to demonstrate that he has no regard for the power represented by Caesar.

The episode repeats the pattern of the earlier challenge posed by the Pharisees who sought to trap Jesus with their question about divorce. The question attempts to put Jesus in the position of ruling on the Law by creating a situation in which he will deny the Law. The technique requires that the teacher formulate a counterquestion that illustrates the malicious character of his opponents. Ordinarily, a ruling on the Law would also require citation of scriptural authority. Therefore, some interpreters propose to reconstruct that reference on the basis of Gen 1:26 and Exod 13:9. Human

beings bear the image of God and of the Law written on the hand, eyes, and mouth. Thus the denarius may belong to Caesar, but the human being belongs to God.[499]

Jesus finds a way to show his audience that the Pharisees and Herodians are hypocrites and that the dilemma they pose does not pit loyalty to God against loyalty to Caesar. Instead, as he had done in the question about divorce (10:2-9), Jesus turns from the sociopolitical issue to the theological issue. What does God require of human beings? Jesus' earlier statement that the Temple was to be the house of prayer for all peoples suggests that God's rule does not require that God's people be defined by a theocracy embodied in a particular nation.[500]

The key to the dynamic retort in the pericope lies in the challenge for Jesus' opponents to produce a coin (12:15b-16).[501] The pagan religious imagery used on coins violated Jewish rules against making images and idolatry. The inscriptions on Roman coins also proclaimed the emperor divine, clearly offensive to Palestinian Jews. Thus the presence of the money changers in the temple precincts permitted Jews to exchange such coins for those acceptable for making an offering in the Temple. In addition, one solution to the inevitable necessity of using such coins in everyday dealings was not to look at them. Jesus, however, demands that his opponents, who were able to produce a coin easily, take a look at it. That demand must have caught his audience off guard.[502]

Archaeologists can describe precisely the sort of coin in question. Mark 12:14b says that the tax the Pharisees were asking about was the "poll tax" (κῆνσος kēnsos), levied by the Romans on every adult listed in the census. It could be paid only in a silver denarius from the imperial mint—one side of the coin was inscribed with the emperor's wreathed head; the other had a female figure,

---

497. See David T. Owen-Ball, "Rabbinic Rhetoric and the Tribute Passage (Mt. 22:15-22; Mk. 12:13-17; Lk. 20:20-26)," *NovT* 35 (1993) 2-4.

498. See John R. Donahue, "The Neglected Factor in the Theology of Mark," *JBL* 101 (1982) 574.

499. See Owen-Ball, "Tribute Passage," 6-12.

500. See Donahue, "Neglected Factor," 574; Rudolph Pesch, *Das Markusevangelium I. Teil,* HTKNT II (Freiburg: Heider, 1977) 2:228.

501. See Paul Corby Finney, "The Rabbi and the Coin Portrait (Mark 12:15b, 16): Rigorism Manqué," *JBL* 112 (1993) 631.

502. See ibid., 632-37. The history of the period shows that Jews were willing to protest violations of the prohibition against images quite vigorously. They even risked death in opposing Pilate's attempt to bring Roman standards into Jerusalem, so the question about images was not unimportant.

probably the embodiment of peace, wearing a crown and holding a scepter in one hand and an olive or palm branch in the other.[503] Archaeological findings show that these coins were not in everyday use, even in the Gentile cities in Galilee; the coinage in everyday use by Jews living under Herod Antipas was free of images. Since neither Jesus nor his followers are likely to have encountered such a coin, it must have been produced by one of Jesus' opponents, more likely the pro-Roman Herodians of Antipas's court than the Pharisees.[504] As soon as Jesus' opponents identify the image and inscription as Caesar's, Jesus has the

503. See ibid., 633.
504. See ibid., 640-43.

solution: The coin must belong to Caesar, so it should be returned to him.

For Jesus and his disciples, concern over the images on coins was a non-issue. By redefining the significance of the coin away from being a sign of tribute paid to an occupying power and making it merely another's property, Jesus defuses the political tension inherent in the question. He does not let his opponents escape without reminding them of what really counts: returning to God the things that belong to God. Mark's reader should supply an understanding of the "things of God" in terms of Jesus' instructions about discipleship. A subsequent exchange with one of the scribes defines what belongs to God in terms of the double command to love God and neighbor (12:28-34).

REFLECTIONS

1. The conclusion to the story about paying tribute forms a parallel to the emphasis on giving the fruit of the vineyard to its owner. Jesus is always able to escape the dilemmas and traps set by his opponents, because he has a clear idea of what God's truth really is. The Pharisees and Herodians were right in describing Jesus as they did (v. 14). He does care only for what God intends. In order to see what the things of God are, people must step out of the categories in which human traditions have framed an issue. The question is not which of two opposing sides is right but which one represents God's viewpoint?

2. This story has long been pondered in Christian theological reflection on the problem of Christian citizenship. It was most commonly used to show that Christians could be both loyal citizens and committed believers. It has also been used to justify the separation of church and state. The church does not have to rule in the political order.[505] However, Jesus does not set the "things of Caesar" and the "things of God" on the same level. God always has priority.[506] The question of how Christians should relate to the demands of the state would be different if there was a conflict between what faithfulness to God requires and what the state demands. The tribute coin is "indifferent" in Jesus' view. But when the emperor demanded that Christians show their respect by actually participating in a cultic sacrifice, the situation changed (cf. Revelation 13). Then Christians accepted martyrdom rather than violate the worship that belonged to God alone.

3. Most Christians today are not placed in such life-and-death situations as those that early Christians faced. However, some Christians may run into similar dilemmas at work or in the military. They may be ordered to falsify a report, pass a defective product, or put up with some other form of wrongdoing. In some cases, the presence of other persons who are equally concerned changes the dynamics of the situation. Sometimes it is possible to use personal contacts with others in an organization to intervene. In other cases, people have suffered retaliation or lost their jobs altogether for "blowing the whistle." In such cases, the whole community has an obligation to support the person who is suffering because he or she put the "things of God" first.

505. See J. S. Kennard, *Render to God: A Study of the Tribute Passage* (New York: Oxford University Press, 1950); Charles H. Giblin, "The 'Things of God' in the Question Concerning Tribute to Caesar (Lk 20:25; Mk 12:17; Mt 22:21)," *CBQ* 33 (1971) 510-27.
506. See Joseph A. Fitzmyer, *The Gospel According to Luke X–XXIV,* AB 28A (Garden City, N.Y.: Doubleday, 1985) 1292.

Mark 12:18-27, Resurrection of the Dead

NIV

¹⁸Then the Sadducees, who say there is no resurrection, came to him with a question. ¹⁹"Teacher," they said, "Moses wrote for us that if a man's brother dies and leaves a wife but no children, the man must marry the widow and have children for his brother. ²⁰Now there were seven brothers. The first one married and died without leaving any children. ²¹The second one married the widow, but he also died, leaving no child. It was the same with the third. ²²In fact, none of the seven left any children. Last of all, the woman died too. ²³At the resurrection[a] whose wife will she be, since the seven were married to her?"

²⁴Jesus replied, "Are you not in error because you do not know the Scriptures or the power of God? ²⁵When the dead rise, they will neither marry nor be given in marriage; they will be like the angels in heaven. ²⁶Now about the dead rising—have you not read in the book of Moses, in the account of the bush, how God said to him, 'I am the God of Abraham, the God of Isaac, and the God of Jacob'[b]? ²⁷He is not the God of the dead, but of the living. You are badly mistaken!"

a23 Some manuscripts resurrection, when men rise from the dead,
b26 Exodus 3:6

NRSV

18Some Sadducees, who say there is no resurrection, came to him and asked him a question, saying, ¹⁹"Teacher, Moses wrote for us that if a man's brother dies, leaving a wife but no child, the man[a] shall marry the widow and raise up children for his brother. ²⁰There were seven brothers; the first married and, when he died, left no children; ²¹and the second married the widow[b] and died, leaving no children; and the third likewise; ²²none of the seven left children. Last of all the woman herself died. ²³In the resurrection[c] whose wife will she be? For the seven had married her."

24Jesus said to them, "Is not this the reason you are wrong, that you know neither the scriptures nor the power of God? ²⁵For when they rise from the dead, they neither marry nor are given in marriage, but are like angels in heaven. ²⁶And as for the dead being raised, have you not read in the book of Moses, in the story about the bush, how God said to him, 'I am the God of Abraham, the God of Isaac, and the God of Jacob'? ²⁷He is God not of the dead, but of the living; you are quite wrong."

aGk his brother   bGk her   cOther ancient authorities add when they rise

COMMENTARY

The belief that (i.e., only the righteous) humans would return to life when God's judgment establishes true justice developed during the two centuries prior to the birth of Jesus. This response to the persecution of Jews who remained faithful to the Law explains how these persons' faithfulness is rewarded, even though they appear to have died in vain. Daniel 12:2-3 promises a special, angelic immortality to those who teach holiness in an evil age. But since this belief does not have extensive support in the Scriptures, many Jews did not accept it.[507] The Sadducees, especially, were known to think that belief in resurrection was an unjustified innovation (Acts 23:8).[508] After the resurrection of Jesus, early Christians were firmly committed to proclaiming resurrection (cf. 1 Cor 15:3b-5). The story in its present form serves to vindicate Christian preaching by responding to two distinct objections: the use of the custom of levirate marriage (Gen 38:8; Deut 25:5) to demonstrate the absurdity of the belief (vv. 19-25); and the claim that resurrection of the dead is among the "impossible things" that not even God can do (vv. 26-27).

The controversy story contains two replies to

507. See George E. Nickelsburg, Resurrection, Immortality and Eternal Life in Intertestamental Judaism, HTS 26 (Cambridge, Mass.: Harvard University Press, 1972).

508. See Josephus The Jewish War 2.8.14; sec. 165.

the absurd case posed by the Sadducees. The first corrects a false understanding of what belief in the resurrection implies, but it does not provide a specific interpretation of Scripture (vv. 24-25). The second uses Scripture to establish the credibility of belief in the resurrection. Only the first speaks directly to the case of levirate marriage. Although the custom also appears in Ruth 4:1-12, the evidence that it was actually observed in first-century Palestine is weak. Consequently, the audience may have recognized the case as being "trumped up," a rhetorical challenge to defeat a popular teacher.[509] Jesus' reply rejects the idea that such human institutions continue in the life to come. He points to the tradition in Daniel and elsewhere that the resurrected are like angels. They are no longer constrained by the limits or relationships of earthly bodies (Dan 12:2-3).[510]

The second argument (vv. 26-27) is based on God's self-revelation to Moses in Exod 3:6-16. Since God claims to be God of the patriarchs, they must still be living. Use of Exod 3:6-16 to demonstrate the truth of life after death appears to have originated independently of the apocalyptic tradition about resurrection, referred to in the first argument. There, transformation into the likeness of angels is associated with the end time. This argument is directed toward the possibility of immortality in general, not to resurrection as God's eschatological promise.[511] The OT frequently points out that God cannot be God of what is dead. God is asked to rescue the sufferer because there can be no praise of God in Sheol (Pss 6:6; 88:4-6; Qoh 9:4-10; Isa 38:18-19). Wisdom of Solomon 2:1-11 indicates that this tradition had been combined with philosophical skepticism by the first century. The wicked conclude that if there is no return from Hades, and if the body and spirit merely dissolve into the elements, then they should live this life for themselves; Wis 5:1-16 reverses that argument by showing that the righteous have a glorious eternal life in God's presence. Only the wicked vanish without a trace (Wis 5:14). Use of Exod 3:6-16 as evidence that God grants eternal life to the righteous probably originated in a similar context. Contrary to the skeptics, who think that there is no life beyond the grave, Scripture proves that God has the power to restore life to the righteous.

The cumulative result of the two-pronged argument is summed up in a very short statement, "You are very much mistaken" (v. 27b). The Sadducees, who thought they would bring a materialist argument against belief in the resurrection, turn out to be as mistaken about God's life-giving power as are the materialist skeptics, who believe in nothing. Throughout the debate, Jesus emphasizes the fact that those who do not believe in the resurrection are denying the reality of God's power to give life. Just as the parable about the vineyard tenants prepares readers to understand the death of Jesus, so also this debate prepares them for the resurrection.

509. Fitzmyer, *Luke X–XXIV*, 1304, points to Josephus (*Antiquities of the Jews* 4.8.23; secs. 254-56) as possible evidence for the existence of the practice, but he agrees that the audience may have seen the question as a bogus challenge.

510. See Pesch, *Das Markusevangelium*, 2:233. See also *1 Enoch* 15:6-7; 104:4; *2 Baruch* 51:10b.

511. See Donahue, "Neglected Factor," 579-80.

REFLECTIONS

1. Many Christians today are just as confused as the Sadducees over the question of resurrection. The mental images we form at funerals of the deceased joining his or her family and loved ones feel suspect. A six-year-old surprised his mother by asserting, "Mom, I just can't wait to die." After attending several funerals, the boy had developed the idea that he could go into a box and join the grandfather whom he had hardly known. Since we have no other images available but those formed on the basis of existence in this world, we are bound to use such language to describe the resurrection. Yet when we do so, we run the risk of setting up absurdities.

2. Once again, Jesus does an end-run around the problem by highlighting the basic principles involved in the whole discussion. The point is not what kind of biological or psychological dynamics are involved—we don't know. We do know that resurrected persons belong to that other dimension of reality that we call heaven. Such "bodies" and relationships have different properties from those we experience here on earth. The basic principle about God is even more fundamental: God seeks to be God of living persons, not of dead ones. The power of God works to create and sustain life at all times.

3. The skeptical challenge to belief in life after death, presented in Wisdom of Solomon 2 shows the importance of such beliefs for the way people live in this life. Paul makes a similar comment to the Corinthians (1 Cor 15:32-33). If the dead are not raised, then people may as well devote this life to getting as much pleasure as they can. There is no reason to sacrifice our individual desires for the welfare of others, and certainly no reason for all the suffering the apostle went through so that the Corinthians could know Christ. The Greek philosopher Plato recognized that justice and truth require some form of immortality. As Paul told the Corinthians, Christians have a firmer foundation for their devotion to God's will in this life: the resurrection of Jesus Christ.

Mark 12:28-34, The Greatest Commandment

NIV

28One of the teachers of the law came and heard them debating. Noticing that Jesus had given them a good answer, he asked him, "Of all the commandments, which is the most important?"

29"The most important one," answered Jesus, "is this: 'Hear, O Israel, the Lord our God, the Lord is one.ᵃ 30Love the Lord your God with all your heart and with all your soul and with all your mind and with all your strength.'ᵇ 31The second is this: 'Love your neighbor as yourself.'ᶜ There is no commandment greater than these."

32"Well said, teacher," the man replied. "You are right in saying that God is one and there is no other but him. 33To love him with all your heart, with all your understanding and with all your strength, and to love your neighbor as yourself is more important than all burnt offerings and sacrifices."

34When Jesus saw that he had answered wisely, he said to him, "You are not far from the kingdom of God." And from then on no one dared ask him any more questions.

ᵃ29 Or the Lord our God is one Lord   ᵇ30 Deut. 6:4,5   ᶜ31 Lev. 19:18

NRSV

28One of the scribes came near and heard them disputing with one another, and seeing that he answered them well, he asked him, "Which commandment is the first of all?" 29Jesus answered, "The first is, 'Hear, O Israel: the Lord our God, the Lord is one; 30you shall love the Lord your God with all your heart, and with all your soul, and with all your mind, and with all your strength.' 31The second is this, 'You shall love your neighbor as yourself.' There is no other commandment greater than these." 32Then the scribe said to him, "You are right, Teacher; you have truly said that 'he is one, and besides him there is no other'; 33and 'to love him with all the heart, and with all the understanding, and with all the strength,' and 'to love one's neighbor as oneself,'—this is much more important than all whole burnt offerings and sacrifices." 34When Jesus saw that he answered wisely, he said to him, "You are not far from the kingdom of God." After that no one dared to ask him any question.

COMMENTARY

After the hostility and blindness of various religious authorities, this story comes as a surprise.

A scribe who overhears the disputes and recognizes that Jesus' answers are good asks about the commandments. He is an exception to the hostile questioner, since he proves able to acknowledge and repeat the truth in what Jesus says.[512] Jesus' reply is consistent with the emphasis on God that runs throughout this section. The confession "God is one" (the Shema; Deut 6:5-6), introduces the summary of the Law in the double command to love God and neighbor (vv. 29-31).[513] The summary of the Law as love of God (Deut 6:6) and love of neighbor (Lev 19:18) appears in Hellenistic Jewish texts.[514] When the scribe repeats this summary with approval, he observes that love of God and love of neighbor are more important than all burnt offerings and sacrifices (v. 33). The scribe's repetition demonstrates that he accepts Jesus' teaching and draws the proper conclusion from it. Jesus concludes the encounter by declaring the scribe "not far from the kingdom of God" (v. 34).[515]

Like the previous episode, this exchange involves two parts. The question about what is the greatest commandment is answered in vv. 29-31.[516] The expanded discourse with the scribe (vv. 32-34) appears to have been added to the tradition. Why demonstrate that the scribe has understood Jesus' teaching correctly? Despite the negative view of the scribes, which runs throughout Mark's account (cf. 12:38-40), this scribe is

introduced as one who approves of Jesus' teaching on the resurrection (v. 28). Mark formulates the two statements of approval almost identically: "seeing that he answered well" (καλῶς *kalōs,* v. 28), for the scribe's opinion of Jesus, and "seeing that he answered wisely" (νουνεχῶς *nounechōs,* v. 34), for Jesus' opinion of the scribe. Even though the scribe is not a disciple, he is able to affirm the truth of Jesus' teaching.[517]

The comment that love of God and love of neighbor take precedence over the sacrificial cult echoes prophetic complaints against those who pay careful attention to ritual while ignoring justice (cf. Ps 51:16-17; Isa 1:10-17). Since this passage is juxtaposed with earlier episodes in this section of Mark—the symbolic declaration that the Temple and its authority will soon come to an end and the statement that God will give the vineyard to others—Mark's readers might understand the scribe as doing more than establishing the order of priorities. He acknowledges that the Christian community can fulfill the will of God as expressed in the commandments without participating in the Jewish cult. This emphasis on the priority of the love command over sacrifices parallels Jesus' earlier insistence that purity is determined by what is in a person's heart, not by external ritual (7:1-16). Pharisees and scribes from Jerusalem had challenged Jesus on the question of purity. The controversies between Jesus and the religious authorities conclude with this unusual instance of the scribe who is near the kingdom of God.

512. He belongs to a series of Jewish characters who step out of the usual stereotype in the Gospel. See Malbon, "Jewish Leaders," 276.

513. See Donahue, "Neglected Factor," 579-80.

514. See, e.g., *Testament of Issachar* 5:2; 7:6; *Testament of Daniel* 5:4; *Testament of Benjamin* 3:3-5.

515. The entire episode builds up to this saying, so Karl Kertelge, "Das Doppelgebot der Liebe im Markusevangelium," *Trierer Theologische Zeitschrift* 103 (1994) 40. This statement also reminds the reader that Jesus is the one through whom the kingdom of God becomes present (1:15).

516. The variants in Luke 10:25-28 and Matt 22:34-40 adopt a more concise form of the story which may be dependent on Q. See Kertelge, "Doppelgebot," 42-43.

517. Donahue, "Neglected Factor," 579-81, sees this pericope as the conclusion of a section in which Mark presents the positive theology concerning God and piety, which replaces the Jewish institutions that have been displaced. He sees the setting of this theology in the mission to the Gentiles (Mark 13:9).

REFLECTIONS

1. Throughout this section of the Gospel, Mark has emphasized the importance of single-hearted devotion to what God intends for humanity. Mark contains much less teaching about specific obligations to others than do Matthew and Luke. The list of virtues that constitute individual holiness, a commitment to serving others rather than seeking one's own exaltation, and the love command sum up the main lines of the ethic that emerges in Mark's Gospel. Other cases, such as sabbath obligations, the permanence of marriage, and civic obligations, refer to the understanding of God as the beneficent creator, who seeks healing and blessing for humanity.

2. When Christians today read this passage, they sometimes think that Christianity differs from other religions in its moral superiority. But summaries of the Law that emphasize the duty to love God and neighbor were not unique to Jesus. Devotion to the supremacy of one

God over all creatures has been admirably expressed in Islam. Judaism has struggled consistently with the need to understand what it means to be a people set apart from the other nations by God. Compassion for all living beings has been radically formulated in Buddhism. Christianity's faith is not in a moral system that is absent from or surpasses that of other religions. In fact, other religions may teach Christians how to live out their own moral insights with greater consistency. Christianity's faith lies in the unique manifestation of God in Jesus, a manifestation that the scribe in this story recognizes.

3. The Great Commandment contains three key elements in Christian faith: (a) belief in one God, (b) whole-hearted devotion to God, and (c) love of neighbor. What does it mean for Christians today to say "the Lord our God, the Lord is one"? Most of us do not live surrounded by temples and images of polytheism. Yet we might ask whether we have not given in to another kind of polytheism, a casual pluralism that accepts whatever anyone believes as "okay." Or again, we allow good things that are not ultimate to become the ultimate and defining forces in our lives—nation, occupation, family, race, political cause, or theological system.

The exchange between Jesus and the scribe becomes itself something of an illustration of the Great Commandment. Even though the exchange occurs in the middle of a dispute (12:28), a running argument between Jesus and representatives of the parties and leaders of the religious establishment, Jesus and the scribe are able to transcend the party strife and cross the dividing line of hostility to confess a common faith. Because they join together in the conviction that there is no commandment greater than love of God and neighbor, they are able to treat each other as neighbors. Both the scribe and Jesus have stepped away from the "us" versus "them" categories. Their mutual affirmation is an island of reconciliation in a sea of hostility. The scribe recognizes Jesus as the great Teacher; Jesus recognizes the scribe as a pilgrim moving toward the kingdom. Their lived out common devotion to God and neighbor silences the debate (12:34).

Mark 12:35-37, The Son of David Is Lord

NIV

[35]While Jesus was teaching in the temple courts, he asked, "How is it that the teachers of the law say that the Christ[a] is the son of David? [36]David himself, speaking by the Holy Spirit, declared:

"'The Lord said to my Lord:
"Sit at my right hand
until I put your enemies
under your feet."'[b]

[37]David himself calls him 'Lord.' How then can he be his son?"

The large crowd listened to him with delight.

[a]35 Or Messiah   [b]36 Psalm 110:1

NRSV

[35]While Jesus was teaching in the temple, he said, "How can the scribes say that the Messiah[a] is the son of David? [36]David himself, by the Holy Spirit, declared,

'The Lord said to my Lord,
"Sit at my right hand,
until I put your enemies under your feet."'
[37]David himself calls him Lord; so how can he be his son?" And the large crowd was listening to him with delight.

[a]Or the Christ

COMMENTARY

The wise scribe of the previous episode is the last Jewish teacher to question Jesus in the Temple. Mark concludes that episode with the comment that no one dared question Jesus any longer. The rest of his teaching is addressed to either those in the crowd (vv. 35, 38) or his disciples (v. 43; 13:1, 3). Having defeated his opponents, Jesus poses a question to the crowd concerning the teaching of the scribes. Although the title "Son of David" was used by others as Jesus approached Jerusalem (10:47; 11:10), its royal overtones have been carefully controlled, because Mark does not think that the political overtones of an anointed successor to David are appropriate for Jesus.[518] Jesus will be crucified by the Roman governor on the false charge that he is "king of the Jews" (15:26). This episode, however, indicates that the charge is false because the Messiah is more than a claimant to David's throne.

Mark uses an early Christian proof text that depicted the exaltation of the risen Jesus (Ps 110:1; 1 Cor 15:25-27; Eph 1:20-23; 1 Pet 3:21*b*-22) to form the centerpiece of a comment on the question of Davidic sonship. The early Christian use of "Son of God" for Jesus derived from another Davidic psalm (Ps 2:7). Both psalms describe God's establishing the Davidic monarchy on Zion

and delivering the king's enemies to crushing defeat. In the first century CE, these images were used for the final, end-time victory of God's anointed king. Seated in the divine throne room, the messianic king will witness the destruction of his enemies. Thus his rule participates in God's power over the nations.[519]

This pericope invests the psalm with a somewhat different significance. Jesus is not announcing his appearance in Jerusalem to witness the destruction of God's enemies. Instead, Jesus points out that David, the inspired author of the psalm, describes the one who receives God's promise as "my Lord."[520] Such an address indicates that David is not speaking to one who is simply his biological descendant, since the "Lord" must be superior to David.[521]

---

518. See Joel Marcus, "The Jewish War and the *Sitz im Leben* of Mark," *JBL* III (1992) 456.

519. See Marcus, *Way of the Lord,* 132-37. Marcus underscores the apocalyptic dimensions of the reference by arguing that the central figure in 11QMelch has been drawn from Ps 110:4.

520. The psalms scroll at Qumran attributes 4,050 psalms and songs to David, all of them inspired by a prophetic spirit received from God (11QPs^a 27:2-11). See Fitzmyer, *Luke X–XXIV,* 1314.

521. This formulation leaves the question of whether this incident was used in early Christian circles that did not have a tradition of Jesus' Davidic descent to explain how a Galilean could claim to fulfill the Davidic promises. Since there is no clear evidence for a pre-Christian interpretation of Psalm 110 in reference to a Davidic messiah the messianic use of the psalm in that sense was probably developed in early Palestinian Christian circles. Perhaps that development was rooted in some use of the psalm by Jesus. See Fitzmyer, *Luke X–XXIV,* 1311-13.

REFLECTIONS

The caveat that this pericope expresses about referring to Jesus as "Son of David" reminds readers that Jesus' identity cannot be defined by the expectations that had clustered around traditional titles and expectations for those who would be the agent of salvation for the people. We should apply a similar caution to other names and roles attributed to Jesus. Jesus consistently points back to God as the origin of his message and ministry. Classical theology teaches that human names and images for God are only imperfect analogies. A negative qualification that acknowledges the fact that God cannot be determined by human concepts should accompany the use of such terms. This pericope suggests that a similar form of "negative theology" should apply to our images of Jesus. He is always more, or "other," than our christological language suggests.

Mark 12:38-40, Warning About the Scribes

NIV

NRSV

[38]As he taught, Jesus said, "Watch out for the teachers of the law. They like to walk around in flowing robes and be greeted in the marketplaces, [39]and have the most important seats in the synagogues and the places of honor at banquets. [40]They devour widows' houses and for a show make lengthy prayers. Such men will be punished most severely."

[38]As he taught, he said, "Beware of the scribes, who like to walk around in long robes, and to be greeted with respect in the marketplaces, [39]and to have the best seats in the synagogues and places of honor at banquets! [40]They devour widows' houses and for the sake of appearance say long prayers. They will receive the greater condemnation."

COMMENTARY

The previous pericope demonstrated that the scribes failed to understand David's prophecy about the Messiah. Jesus has also warned his disciples to watch out for the yeast of the Pharisees and Herod (8:15). Now he warns the crowd to watch out for the scribes. Although the reference to Jesus' "teaching" (v. 38) suggests that the warning will apply to their teaching, the sayings that follow describe the scribes' practices instead. The description of the scribes lists what could be seen as normal privileges of the aristocracy in a traditional society: wearing long, ornate robes; being greeted by others when they go out in public; having the best seats in public gatherings; and indulging in elaborate banquets (vv. 38-39; cf. the rich man in Luke 16:19; Jas 2:2-3). In this section of the Gospel, Mark frequently associates scribes with the high priests (11:27). Although not all scribes would be in the position to indulge in ostentatious display of this sort, those who were retainers of the wealthy high priestly families around Jerusalem might have taken on the trappings of wealth and power.[522]

The charge that the scribes "devour widows' houses" (v. 40) also seems more characteristic of prophetic charges against the rich than of a particular role played by scribes. Some interpreters

have hypothesized that scribes might have acted as guardians for widows who lacked male relatives.[523] Others suggest that they may have accepted hospitality from widows under the pretense of piety in order to support their tastes for wealth and power.[524] When he sent them out to preach, Jesus prohibited his own disciples from accumulating wealth or moving from the first household to take them in (6:8-10). Jesus also constantly warned his own disciples against seeking honor rather than serving others (9:33-35; 10:42-45). Mark's Gentile readers were not likely to have had dealings with scribes, but they could recognize the same characteristics among others. The wandering Cynic philosophers who frequented Greco-Roman cities often castigated other philosophers whose wealthy patrons provided luxurious clothes, sumptuous food, and social honor.[525]

With the exception of the wise scribe (vv. 28-34), the controversies with the scribes and other religious authorities have demonstrated that they did not care about God's truth. This ad hominem attack undermines the authority of the scribes by linking them with their patrons, a posturing, wealthy aristocracy that had no concern for the people.

---

522. While scribes in Galilee appear to be somewhere in the middle of the social scale, those in Jerusalem, which appears to have been their center of influence, may have attained increased status and influence through association with the priestly aristocracy. See Sean Freyne, *Galilee, Jesus and the Gospels: Literary Approaches and Historical Investigations* (Philadelphia: Fortress, 1988) 172, 200-202.

523. See J. D. M. Derrett, " 'Eating Up the Homes of Widows': Jesus' Comment on Lawyers?" *NovT* 14 (1972) 1-9.

524. See Elizabeth Struthers Malbon, "The Poor Widow in Mark and Her Poor Rich Readers," *CBQ* 53 (1991) 595.

525. For the influence of this tradition on the sayings material in Q, see Gerald Downing, *Cynics and Christian Origins* (Edinburgh: T. & T. Clark, 1992) 115-49.

REFLECTIONS

The story of the wise scribe (12:28-34) makes it clear that this description of the scribes should not be treated as being stereotypical of all scribes in the Jewish community. It describes the rich and powerful at their worst, much as the sharp social commentary that one finds in newspaper columnists. Every debater knows that if one can use a strong image to make opponents look ridiculous, the audience will have a hard time believing anything the opponents say. Of course, such comments must point to a real evil or social problem in order to be effective. Jesus insisted that his disciples not adopt social standards of power and influence. This depiction of the scribes applies to any religious authorities who treat their position as access to the influence and power of the wealthy, making those who should be defenders of the widow, the orphaned, and the poor the agents of their destruction. The condemnation for those who engage in such practices will be even worse than that for others, since they use the name of God to mask what they are doing.

Mark 12:41-44, The Widow's Offering

NIV

⁴¹Jesus sat down opposite the place where the offerings were put and watched the crowd putting their money into the temple treasury. Many rich people threw in large amounts. ⁴²But a poor widow came and put in two very small copper coins,ᵃ worth only a fraction of a penny.ᵇ

⁴³Calling his disciples to him, Jesus said, "I tell you the truth, this poor widow has put more into the treasury than all the others. ⁴⁴They all gave out of their wealth; but she, out of her poverty, put in everything—all she had to live on."

ᵃ42 Greek *two lepta*   ᵇ42 Greek *kodrantes*

NRSV

⁴¹He sat down opposite the treasury, and watched the crowd putting money into the treasury. Many rich people put in large sums. ⁴²A poor widow came and put in two small copper coins, which are worth a penny. ⁴³Then he called his disciples and said to them, "Truly I tell you, this poor widow has put in more than all those who are contributing to the treasury. ⁴⁴For all of them have contributed out of their abundance; but she out of her poverty has put in everything she had, all she had to live on."

COMMENTARY

The catchword *widow* links this pericope with the condemnation of the scribes in the previous section. Jesus has moved to the Temple treasury, marking the third case in which coins play a role in Jesus' teaching. (The "treasury" may not refer to the actual building but to the receptacles for collecting the Temple taxes and freewill offerings.[526]) By first describing the event (vv. 41-42) and then having Jesus repeat what has happened in commenting on the widow's action (vv. 43-44),[527] Mark underlines

the gap between a wealthy person's offering and the widow's gift of her whole livelihood. The large amounts contributed by the wealthy were probably visible to all. Jesus summons his disciples (cf. 6:7; 8:1, 34; 10:42) and points out the widow's offering, two of the smallest copper coins. Whereas the widow gives her whole livelihood, the wealthy give from their surplus. Thus the great amounts that gain them honor as benefactors are nothing compared with the offering made by the widow.[528] Some interpreters point out that the exem-

---

526. See Josephus *The Jewish War* 5.5.2; sec. 200; *m. š eqal* 6:5; Joseph A. Fitzmyer, *The Gospel According to Luke X–XXIV*, AB 28A (Garden City, N.Y.: Doubleday, 1985) 1322.

527. Luke's shorter version (Luke 21:1-4) does not highlight the contrast between the ostentatious "large sums" of the rich and the widow's coins; contra Fitzmyer, *Luke X–XXIV*, 1320.

528. The motif of the poor widow or of the poor couple who please the gods by giving all they have is common in folklore. Mark's readers might have been familiar with the widow who gives the last food in the house to Elijah (1 Kgs 17:9-20). However, this episode is not a folk tale. The woman does not discover a magic supply of coins when she leaves the Temple.

plary character of the widow's offering lies in her willingness to give everything to God (cf. 10:28-31). Unlike the rich man who would not give up his wealth to become a disciple (10:17-22), the widow belongs to the kingdom.

Praise for the widow does not imply that Jesus approves of the social conditions that have created her poverty. The condemnation of scribes whose taste for wealth and ostentation is linked to "devouring the houses of widows" (12:38-40) must not be forgotten in reading this passage. On the other hand, some interpreters find the meaning of the story in the contrast between the widow and the scribes of the previous story. They suggest that Jesus is attacking both the scribes and the religious system that taught this woman to offer her tiny coins, as though God would demand such sacrifices of the poor of the world.[529] Jesus has already castigated the Pharisees and some scribes from Jerusalem (7:1) for permitting wealth dedicated to the Temple to be exempt from the command to care for one's parents.

529. See Addison G. Wright, "The Widow's Mites: Praise or Lament?—A Matter of Context," *CBQ* 44 (1982) 256-65.

REFLECTIONS

1. This story poses the same challenge to readers today as it did in Jesus' time. People usually think of giving to the church and to charities as an option. The money for charitable giving comes out of the surplus after personal expenses have been met. Those "necessary" expenses usually include many extras in terms of entertainment, clothes, food, and toys.

2. This story can be linked with prophetic condemnations of the rich who provide for a luxurious cult at the sanctuary while fostering injustice that reduces others in the society to poverty (cf. Amos 4:4-5; 5:11-12, 21-24). Jesus intensifies the disparity between the two types of giving. The woman has two small coins and gives both, all that she had to live. The image of an impoverished widow giving all that she has forms a remote parallel to the story of the poor widow and the prophet Elijah, who asks for her last bit of food (1 Kgs 17:8-16). In that case, the widow, her son, and the prophet are provided for during the famine.[530] Jesus does not offer this widow any such reassurance. The contrast between her offering and all the others who are tossing in what they can spare exhibits the false values of a society that does not really offer sacrifice to God. Jesus has already told his disciples that persons must be willing to renounce their own desires, take up the cross, and become slaves of all in order to follow him (8:34; 9:35; 10:42-45). The widow's story can be read as an anticipation of Jesus' own sacrifice of his life.[531]

530. Unlike the situation described in 12:40, where the scribes are said to "eat up the houses of widows."
531. See Malbon, "Poor Widow," 600.

Mark 13:1-37, The Apocalyptic Discourse

OVERVIEW

Mark 13:1-37 contains the Gospel's longest discourse of Jesus outside the treatment of the parables in chap. 4. The discourse shifts attention from the actions of Jesus and his disciples to events that will follow Jesus' death, and finally to the end time. We have already turned to this chapter for clues about the experiences of Christians in Mark's day. Its references bear the marks of the social upheaval and the associated civil strife that engulfed Judea during the revolt against Rome: war (v. 7), social turmoil (v. 12), flight from Jerusalem (v. 14*b*), false prophets (vv. 5-6, 21), desecration of the Temple (v. 14), and the Temple's destruction (v. 2). Consequently, chap.

13 has become the primary source of evidence for those who think that Mark was composed in Palestine during or shortly after the Jewish war, although Mark's apparent use of traditional material in composing the discourse makes it difficult to determine whether such parallels ought to be associated with the evangelist or his source.[532] Other scholars highlight discrepancies between Mark's account and information derived from Josephus.[533] Josephus, writing in Rome at the end of the century, could presume an interest in a history of the Jewish war. Therefore, a gospel written earlier in the century might use general information about the revolt in Judea.[534]

Gerd Theissen has proposed that a different crisis forms the background to the eschatological discourse.[535] During the years 35–41 CE the Temple was threatened with desecration by Roman Emperor Caligula's demand that the Jews set up a statue of him in the Temple precincts. According to Philo, this demand was punishment for the Jews' in Jamnia tearing down a newly erected altar to the emperor.[536] Resistance to the erection of imperial images in the synagogues of Alexandria a year or so earlier had led to violent outbursts between Jews and non-Jews in that city.[537]

Several legions moved into Palestine to enforce Caligula's order (c. 39–40).[538] This movement of troops indicates that the Romans thought there would be war. Tacitus asserts that they had to put down an armed uprising.[539] Since these events also involved embassies to plead the Jewish case in Rome, the Jewish community in Rome may have been aware of the proceedings. At this time, Christians belonged to the Jewish community.

If the oracles in Mark 13 originated in conflicts during the first decade of Christian history, then they are not direct evidence for the situation facing Markan Christians. Instead, as in other historical apocalypses, the correlation between events that are in the future from the point of view of the speaker, but past from the reader's perspective establishes the validity of the ensuing prophecy or the certainty that all history is under divine control.[540] The apocalyptic predictions in Mark 13:5-27 are introduced by two brief exchanges between Jesus and his disciples concerning the fate of the Temple: Jesus warns that the Temple will not endure (vv. 1-2); Peter, James, and John ask privately when these things will be accomplished (vv. 3-4). The request for an explanation in private, accompanied by a change in location, fits the pattern already established in the Gospel of giving the disciples a private explanation of a public statement (e.g., 4:10, 34; 7:17; 9:28; 10:10). Yet the only reference to the Temple in the apocalyptic section of the discourse concerns its defilement (v. 14), not its destruction—at least not prior to the end-time destruction of all things. Some interpreters have equated the two events, but the possibility that the oracle about the abomination in the Temple originated during the crisis over setting up imperial images makes that hypothesis less likely.

The question of whether Mark's reader knows that the Temple has been destroyed by the Romans is more difficult to answer. On the one hand, its complete destruction corresponds to the historical facts. On the other hand, Mark makes no mention of the fire or the general devastation of the city as a whole. It is possible, therefore, to conclude that the Temple had not yet been destroyed.[541] However, the question cannot be decided with reference to this single passage. The fate of the Temple is entwined with Jesus' death. He is falsely accused of claiming that he will

532. So Joel Marcus, "The Jewish War and the *Sitz im Leben* of Mark," *JBL* 111 (1992) 446-48. See also Lars Hartman, *Prophecy Interpreted: The Formation of Some Jewish Apocalyptic Texts and of the Eschatological Discourse Mark 13 par.*, Coniectanea biblica NT Series 1 (Lund: Gleerup, 1966); Egon Brandenburger, *Markus 13 und die Apokalyptik* (Göttingen: FRLANT, 1984). Brandenburger thinks that the apocalyptic source must have been formulated among Jewish Christians in Jerusalem (*Apokalyptik, 69*).

533. *Such differences should not be overemphasized, since we have seen that Mark and Josephus also differ in their accounts of the death of John the Baptist.*

534. *See Robert H. Gundry, Mark: A Commentary on His Apology for the Cross* (Grand Rapids: Eerdmans, 1993) 755.

535. Gerd Theissen, *The Gospels in Context: Social and Political History in the Synoptic Tradition* (Minneapolis: Fortress, 1993) 125-65.

536. See Philo *Legatio* 200-207. Theissen (*Gospels in Context,* 141) accepts Philo's account as the real reason for the initial demand. Philo participated in a mission to plead with the emperor. Josephus, writing about the incident in Rome after the Jewish revolt, would have reason to remain silent about this part of the conflict, since it would suggest consistent opposition to Roman rule among Jews rather than the misguided fervor of the zealots. If Mark's readers were aware of the cause of the Caligula incident, the earlier discussion of Caesar's image on the coin presented to Jesus in the Temple (12:13-17) takes on added significance. Jesus appears to distance himself from those who wish to tear down imperial altars.

537. Philo *Flaccus* 41-43. E. Schürer, *A History of the Jewish People in the Time of Jesus Christ,* rev. ed. (Edinburgh: T. & T. Clark, 1986) 1:390-91.

538. Josephus *The Jewish War* 92.186; Philo *Legatio* 207.

539. Tacitus *Histories* 5.9.2. See the detailed reconstruction of these events in Theissen, *Gospels in Context,* 137-51.

540. Cf. John J. Collins, *The Apocalyptic Imagination* (New York: Crossroad, 1984) 22, 50; *Daniel* (Minneapolis: Fortress, 1993) 54-56.

541. So Gundry, *Mark,* 754.

destroy the Temple and rebuild it in three days (14:58; 15:29). At the time of Jesus' death, the sanctuary veil is torn from top to bottom (15:38). The irony of the false accusation and the symbolic power of the torn veil are both considerably enhanced if the Roman destruction of the Temple is familiar to Mark's audience.[542]

542. So Raymond E. Brown, *The Death of the Messiah: From Gethsemane to the Grave. A Commentary on the Passion Narratives in the Four Gospels*, vol. 2 (Garden City, N.Y.: Doubleday, 1994) 451-53; 1135.

Mark 13:1-2, The Temple Will Be Destroyed

NIV

13 As he was leaving the temple, one of his disciples said to him, "Look, Teacher! What massive stones! What magnificent buildings!"

²"Do you see all these great buildings?" replied Jesus. "Not one stone here will be left on another; every one will be thrown down."

NRSV

13 As he came out of the temple, one of his disciples said to him, "Look, Teacher, what large stones and what large buildings!" ²Then Jesus asked him, "Do you see these great buildings? Not one stone will be left here upon another; all will be thrown down."

COMMENTARY

Despite Jesus' warnings not to be taken in by appearances of wealth, the disciples are awed by the massive Herodian masonry and the extensive buildings that were part of the Temple complex. Jesus predicts that the whole place will be completely destroyed. This prediction differs from the false charges brought against him at his trial, since Jesus does not claim to be the agent of its destruction. The various forms of this saying and its role in the passion narrative suggest that it goes back to Jesus.[543] Prophets had made similar predictions about the first temple (Jer 26:18; Mic 3:12). Josephus reports that a prophetic figure went around Jerusalem predicting the city's destruction for several years prior to the outbreak of the rebellion against Rome. Religious authorities attempted to silence the man, but the Roman governor concluded that he was merely insane.[544] These examples show that Jesus may have made such a prophecy. As the conclusion to the activity of Jesus in the Temple area, the announcement of doom shows that the so-called cleansing (11:15-17) should also be read as an oracle of judgment.

543. Ibid., 450.
544. Josephus *The Jewish Wars* 6.5; sec. 300-309.

The Temple was not purified or restored to the function for which God had intended it.

The prophecy itself does not serve to date Mark's Gospel, even though the sum total of its references to the Temple suggest familiarity with the fact that it has been destroyed. By locating that prediction outside the apocalyptic prophecies concerning the end time, and even the survey of divinely orchestrated events, Mark may have intended to defuse speculation that the Temple's destruction meant that the judgment was near. The temporal perspective of the discourse in Mark 13 looks beyond the immediate turmoil to preaching among the nations (v. 10). Therefore, the destruction of the Temple does not appear to be the turning point that introduces the events of the end time.

Even if Mark's Gospel was composed prior to the destruction of the Temple, most readers come to the text knowing that the prophecy was indeed fulfilled. The oracle joins a number of passages in the passion narrative that demonstrate that Jesus is a true prophet. The certainty with which he foresaw events that are now past should encourage readers to have confidence in his words about the future.

REFLECTIONS

1. Today's readers have difficulty with prophetic oracles, because they think of them solely in terms of predicting the future. We demand that experts give us predictions about the future, even when we know that the phenomena in question are subject to wide variation. Experts and pundits happily offer their opinions. Old Testament prophecy, however, provides a different framework for statements about the future. They are diagnoses of the moral or spiritual health of the people. A prophetic word of judgment intends to promote repentance and reform, even though many of the people reject the prophet's word. Destruction occurs only because the words of warning go unheeded. Thus prophetic speech is a form of instruction, not fortune telling.

2. After the fact, it is easy to forget that prophetic words of judgment must have seemed unbelievable at the time. The large blocks of stone that make up the lower part of the Wailing Wall provide visual evidence of the massive architecture that inspired the original expressions of awe. Jesus looks beyond the appearance to reality. No matter how secure buildings or institutions may appear, they can all be overthrown.

Mark 13:3-13, Evil Times Are Not the End Time

NIV

³As Jesus was sitting on the Mount of Olives opposite the temple, Peter, James, John and Andrew asked him privately, ⁴"Tell us, when will these things happen? And what will be the sign that they are all about to be fulfilled?"

⁵Jesus said to them: "Watch out that no one deceives you. ⁶Many will come in my name, claiming, 'I am he,' and will deceive many. ⁷When you hear of wars and rumors of wars, do not be alarmed. Such things must happen, but the end is still to come. ⁸Nation will rise against nation, and kingdom against kingdom. There will be earthquakes in various places, and famines. These are the beginning of birth pains.

⁹"You must be on your guard. You will be handed over to the local councils and flogged in the synagogues. On account of me you will stand before governors and kings as witnesses to them. ¹⁰And the gospel must first be preached to all nations. ¹¹Whenever you are arrested and brought to trial, do not worry beforehand about what to say. Just say whatever is given you at the time, for it is not you speaking, but the Holy Spirit.

¹²"Brother will betray brother to death, and a father his child. Children will rebel against their

NRSV

3When he was sitting on the Mount of Olives opposite the temple, Peter, James, John, and Andrew asked him privately, ⁴"Tell us, when will this be, and what will be the sign that all these things are about to be accomplished?" ⁵Then Jesus began to say to them, "Beware that no one leads you astray. ⁶Many will come in my name and say, 'I am he!'ᵃ and they will lead many astray. ⁷When you hear of wars and rumors of wars, do not be alarmed; this must take place, but the end is still to come. ⁸For nation will rise against nation, and kingdom against kingdom; there will be earthquakes in various places; there will be famines. This is but the beginning of the birth pangs.

9"As for yourselves, beware; for they will hand you over to councils; and you will be beaten in synagogues; and you will stand before governors and kings because of me, as a testimony to them. ¹⁰And the good newsᵇ must first be proclaimed to all nations. ¹¹When they bring you to trial and hand you over, do not worry beforehand about what you are to say; but say whatever is given you at that time, for it is not you who speak, but the Holy Spirit. ¹²Brother will betray brother to

ᵃGk I am   ᵇGk gospel

NIV	NRSV
parents and have them put to death. [13]All men will hate you because of me, but he who stands firm to the end will be saved."	death, and a father his child, and children will rise against parents and have them put to death; [13]and you will be hated by all because of my name. But the one who endures to the end will be saved."

COMMENTARY

Although Mark 13 is often referred to as an apocalypse, it does not follow the usual pattern of apocalypses, in which symbolic visions are interpreted by a heavenly revealer.[545] Attempts to delineate a written apocalypse as the source for the chapter have not been generally persuasive.[546] The traditional material in Mark 13 appears to depend on smaller units that embody sayings of the Lord and oracles from early Christian prophets. The chapter follows a literary pattern that Mark has used frequently in the Gospel. Jesus makes a public statement (v. 2), then disciples question him privately (vv. 3-4). In this case, the four disciples who were the first to be called (1:16-20) ask Jesus to give them a sign that will indicate when the destruction of the Temple will occur. Some interpreters treat Jesus' willingness to give a sign here as being contrary to his words to the Pharisees (8:11-12). This is probably not the case, since the Pharisees sought to "test" Jesus by demanding that he prove his authority. Jesus' initial reply (vv. 5-13) does not provide the disciples with the sign they seek. Instead, Jesus tells them how to conduct themselves in the midst of turmoil and persecution. Once again, Jesus' private instruction involves discipleship. Disciples must be willing to testify to the gospel, even though they will be persecuted. The social and political turmoil of the age is not to be mistaken for the end time (v. 8).

Apocalyptic writings often speak of the evil times to come before the end of the world as periods of turmoil during which the righteous may be led astray.[547] This form of prophecy appears to have flourished as "persecution literature" by which the righteous minority were able to affirm the truth of God's rule.[548] Mark 13, however, counsels both hope and patience. Christians should not engage in the rash apocalyptic fervor they see around them. But Mark does not deny that a crisis exists. Jesus' words warn of false prophets, political turmoil and natural disasters (vv. 5-8), and a church engaged in mission to the Gentiles and finds itself hated by both Jews and Gentiles (vv. 9-13).

13:5-8. Jesus' warning speaks of those who come in Jesus' name (v. 6), claiming, "I am" (see NRSV footnote). Since the referent is not supplied, the reader must decide who it is they claim to be. Since they are said to come in Jesus' name, they may be depicting themselves as the Lord's agents or inspired prophets. The expression "in my name" implies acting with an authority derived from Jesus, not claiming to be Jesus, himself, returned to earth.[549] The "name" in question may be "messiah" or "anointed" rather than Jesus. Several false prophets were reported to have been active during the Jewish revolt. The danger of false messiahs returns later in the discourse (vv. 21-23). The authority with which such false prophets interpret current events as evidence that the end is near is undermined by the catalogue of evils that are at best the prelude to the end time (vv. 7-8). The idea that wars and destruction in Jerusalem will be part of the initial events leading up to the end time is also found in Dan 9:26.[550]

13:9-13. Jesus then reminds the disciples of what their task is: to preach the gospel. Readers

---

545. See Christopher Bryan, *A Preface to Mark: Notes on the Gospel in Its Literary and Cultural Settings* (New York: Oxford, 1993) 109-11. However, the proposal to account for its form by appealing to the testament of a philosopher sage is equally unpersuasive; cf. Brandenburger, *Apokalyptik*, 13-15.

546. See the discussion of these attempts in Adela Yarbro Collins, *The Beginning of the Gospel* (Minneapolis: Fortress, 1992) 77-81.

547. Cf. 4 Ezra 5:9; 6:4; *Jub.* 23:19.

548. The book of Daniel, which provided striking images for early Christian prophets, reflects the persecution by Antiochus Epiphanes (cf. Collins, *Daniel,* 62-69).

549. See Collins, *Beginning of the Gospel,* 81.

550. See Rudolph Pesch, *Das Markusevangelium I. Teil,* HTKNT II (Freiburg: Herder, 1977) 2:280.

already know that the disciples can expect persecution and even death (4:17; 8:34-38; 10:30, 39). Divisions within families—which include brother betraying brother—are evident in the divisions in Jesus' own family (3:31; 6:1-6)—and even in Jesus' true family, the disciples, since one of them will betray Jesus. Disciples will be hauled into court, beaten, and executed just as Jesus will be. Micah 7:5-6 treats hostility and betrayal between friends and members of the same family as signs of an evil age that has forsaken God. The turmoil endured by Jesus and his disciples reflects the evils of such an age. As we have already seen, Christians were particularly vulnerable during the periods of political and social turmoil, which pitted Jews against Gentiles. Gentile Christians had converted to a "Jewish" movement but were not assimilated into the Jewish community. Either side might turn against the Christians in its midst (v. 9). This rather grim description of the fate of those who preach the gospel contains two words of hope: the Holy Spirit will provide the words for them to use in court (v. 11), and those who remain faithful will be saved (v. 13). Does "saved" imply that those brought into court will be freed without punishment (as in Acts 5:22-26; 12:6-19; 2 Cor 1:8-10)? Mark's earlier saying that persons who lose their lives for the gospel will instead save them (8:35) suggests that it does not necessarily promise rescue from the suffering imposed by persecutors. Rather, it promises salvation in the judgment before God (8:38).[551]

Disciples are told that being dragged into court is an opportunity to testify to the gospel (v. 9); Paul gives a similar interpretation of his imprisonment (Phil 1:12-14). Since the accused were not allowed to hire lawyers to speak for them, their fate depended on whatever eloquence an individual possessed. Only the wealthy and privileged were educated in rhetoric. Thus most of Jesus' followers would not have had such training. They must defend their preaching before a hostile judge, who would be likely to look down on such uneducated speech. They need to be assured that the Holy Spirit will assist in the defense! This scenario guarantees that the Son of Man will acknowledge such faithful witnesses before God (8:38).

By inserting v. 10 into the account of disciples before the courts, Mark makes such trials the vehicle for taking the message to all nations. The Greek word translated "nation" (ἔθνη *ethnē*) may refer to Gentiles when used in a Jewish context as well as its more common geographical meaning of nations. Jesus' trial and death serve as testimony to the Gentiles, since the Roman centurion acknowledges that Jesus is Son of God (15:39). "It is necessary" (δεῖ *dei*), used to formulate the various expressions of necessity in this chapter, carries the overtones of divine necessity. God's plan for the salvation of the nations is at stake. Combined with the earlier rejection of the signs of social and political turmoil as evidence for the end time, the geographical range of this phrase suggests that delay in the return of the Son of Man serves the process of salvation.[552]

The concluding verse generalizes the scope of persecution: "You will be hated by all for the sake of my name." Christians recognize this situation as the worst possible case. The new family of "brothers and sisters of the Lord" should provide a refuge from the hatred of friends and family. As long as disciples remain faithful to Jesus, they will be saved. Persecution and hatred are not to shake their faith.

---

551. So Gundry, *Mark*, 770-71.

552. See Pesch, *Das Markusevangelium*, 2:285.

REFLECTIONS

1. Every major world crisis brings its share of books describing the events as evidence that the signs in the book of Revelation are being fulfilled. The desire to use apocalyptic prophecies concerning the end time to make sense of traumatic upheavals in the world remains a significant temptation for many Christians. Jesus provides the fundamental response, even to those who "come in his name": The end time is not signaled by such events. Christians should remember that they have only one concern: giving testimony to the gospel. Apocalyptic prophecies do not constitute the testimony about which Jesus speaks.

2. With the legal protection of personal religious conviction we enjoy in this country, we find it difficult to imagine how terrifying it must have been for Jesus' followers to be dragged into court to answer their accusers before a judge. The Holy Spirit must have been a powerful presence in their lives.

Mark 13:14-23, Flee the End-time Turmoil

NIV

14"When you see 'the abomination that causes desolation'*ᵃ* standing where it*ᵇ* does not belong—let the reader understand—then let those who are in Judea flee to the mountains. ¹⁵Let no one on the roof of his house go down or enter the house to take anything out. ¹⁶Let no one in the field go back to get his cloak. ¹⁷How dreadful it will be in those days for pregnant women and nursing mothers! ¹⁸Pray that this will not take place in winter, ¹⁹because those will be days of distress unequaled from the beginning, when God created the world, until now—and never to be equaled again. ²⁰If the Lord had not cut short those days, no one would survive. But for the sake of the elect, whom he has chosen, he has shortened them. ²¹At that time if anyone says to you, 'Look, here is the Christ*ᶜ*!' or, 'Look, there he is!' do not believe it. ²²For false Christs and false prophets will appear and perform signs and miracles to deceive the elect—if that were possible. ²³So be on your guard; I have told you everything ahead of time."

ᵃ14 Daniel 9:27; 11:31; 12:11   ᵇ14 Or he; also in verse 29   ᶜ21 Or Messiah

NRSV

14"But when you see the desolating sacrilege set up where it ought not to be (let the reader understand), then those in Judea must flee to the mountains; ¹⁵the one on the housetop must not go down or enter the house to take anything away; ¹⁶the one in the field must not turn back to get a coat. ¹⁷Woe to those who are pregnant and to those who are nursing infants in those days! ¹⁸Pray that it may not be in winter. ¹⁹For in those days there will be suffering, such as has not been from the beginning of the creation that God created until now, no, and never will be. ²⁰And if the Lord had not cut short those days, no one would be saved; but for the sake of the elect, whom he chose, he has cut short those days. ²¹And if anyone says to you at that time, 'Look! Here is the Messiah!'*ᵃ* or 'Look! There he is!'—do not believe it. ²²False messiahs*ᵇ* and false prophets will appear and produce signs and omens, to lead astray, if possible, the elect. ²³But be alert; I have already told you everything."

ᵃOr the Christ   ᵇOr christs

COMMENTARY

The exhortation concerning testimony to the gospel is neatly framed by sections on false prophets and turmoil. The opening section moved from a warning against such prophets to a description of universal turmoil. This section opens with end-time turmoil (vv. 14-20) and concludes with the warning against false prophets (vv. 21-23). It is framed with solemn notices to the reader that the only true word of revelation concerning the end time is contained in these words.

13:14-20. The "desolating sacrilege" (v. 14) refers to either an object or a person that profanes the sanctuary. As we have seen, some interpreters thought that the original reference was to the statue of himself that Emperor Caligula ordered set up in the Temple. The phrase "standing where he ought not" makes it appear that the desolating sacrilege refers to a person. But since the imperial statue also had a human form, the expression does not exclude the possibility of that understanding of the image.[553] Some interpreters have proposed that another person is meant by the reference—namely, the zealot leader Eleazer.[554] On the other hand, Daniel, when referring to the desecration of the Temple by Antiochus IV (9:27; 11:31; 12:11), uses this phrase to describe an altar for pagan sacrifice (1 Macc 1:54-59).[555] In fact, the statement "let the reader understand" (v. 14) alludes to Dan 12:9-10. There the words of the prophecy are to be sealed up until the end time, and none of the wicked will understand their meaning. Although grammatically one would expect a neuter participle to designate the abomination as "standing," Mark uses a masculine form that appears to refer to Caligula's statue.[556] The phrase "abomination of desolation" suggests that the object or person in question will bring about the ruin of the Temple. If the saying originated during the earlier crisis, Christians had preserved the saying, despite the fact that in that case Caligula died before enforcing his order. If the Temple had already been destroyed by the time Mark wrote, the ambiguity about the prophecy would have been removed. The Jews desecrated the Temple by the revolutionary activities that took place during the revolt.[557] This passage suggests that readers should recognize the fulfillment of the prophecy.

The warnings to flee describe conditions in Judea (vv. 14-18). The urgency means that there will not be time for even the simplest preparations. The unprecedented severity of the end-time tribulation (v. 19) has been taken from Daniel (12:1). The horrors even threaten the elect, but God will shorten the apocalyptic timetable.[558] This promise shows that the end-time sufferings are qualitatively different from the persecutions the disciples can expect to undergo during routine testimony to the gospel. The latter can be endured to the end (v. 13b), but for the elect to endure the end time, God must shorten the time (v. 20).

13:21-23. This section concludes with another warning against false prophets. The false messiahs and prophets will use signs and omens to lead the elect astray. The command not to follow such persons is justified, because the elect do not need detailed signs or information to survive those days. Jesus' word has told the disciples all they need to know.

553. See Theissen, *Gospels in Context,* 157, 164.
554. See Marcus, "Jewish War," 454.
555. See Collins, *Daniel,* 109.
556. Josephus *Antiquities of the Jews* 18.8.4-9; secs. 277-304.

557. Josephus *The Jewish War* 4.3.10; secs 182-83; Marcus, "Jewish War," 455.
558. *1 Enoch* 80:2; *2 Baruch* 20:1-2; 83:1,6.

REFLECTIONS

The end-time flight will be like that of refuges during war or persons fleeing a sudden natural disaster. There is no way to prepare for the end time. Any stockpiled supplies would have to be abandoned. When the "abomination" appears, it is time to flee quickly. There will be no sign or advance warning. Christians who think that apocalyptic prophets give them evidence about the place of the present in the long-term schedule of salvation are turning away from the only task that faces disciples: preaching the gospel. Jesus would not give a sign to his own age (8:11-12). In this discourse, he indirectly refuses to give the disciples the kind of signs they are seeking. Instead, he suggests that they be faithful to preaching the gospel. God will ensure the survival of the elect.

Despite the carefully developed warnings about false prophecy in Mark, sectarian groups continue to preach that the end of the world is near. Survivalist sects stockpile arms, food, and other supplies so that members of the sect will be able to fight off the displaced humans created in the end-time turmoil. Instead of seeing that the wars, famines, disasters, and threats of conflict in today's world are no different from those in Mark's time, survivalists assume that the present age is the prelude to the end of all things.

Mark's account tells Christians that they have a very different responsibility. Like Jesus, they are to be suffering servants of the gospel. In order to carry the gospel message throughout the world, many faithful Christians go into the neighborhoods and countries where turmoil threatens to strip people of their humanity. Often the deaths of Christian missionaries provide the symbolic focus that draws world attention to the suffering of hundreds of victims in such areas of the world.

Mark 13:24-27, The Coming of the Son of Man

NIV	NRSV

²⁴"But in those days, following that distress,
 	
"'the sun will be darkened,
    and the moon will not give its light;
²⁵the stars will fall from the sky,
    and the heavenly bodies will be shaken.'^a
 	
²⁶"At that time men will see the Son of Man coming in clouds with great power and glory. ²⁷And he will send his angels and gather his elect from the four winds, from the ends of the earth to the ends of the heavens."
	²⁴"But in those days, after that suffering,
	the sun will be darkened,
	    and the moon will not give its light,
	²⁵ and the stars will be falling from heaven,
	    and the powers in the heavens will be
	        shaken.
	²⁶Then they will see 'the Son of Man coming in clouds' with great power and glory. ²⁷Then he will send out the angels, and gather his elect from the four winds, from the ends of the earth to the ends of heaven."

^a25 Isaiah 13:10; 34:4	

COMMENTARY

Both of the previous sections end with a note of warning to the elect: Persecution requires endurance (v. 13); the presence of false messiahs requires careful attention to the prophecies in the discourse (v. 23). Both sections also assure the faithful that they will be among the elect (vv. 13*b*, 20*b*). Thus each unit of prophetic discourse directs the reader's attention from the present or impending historical experiences of persecution to the culmination of all things at the end time.[559] The faithful testimony of Jesus' disciples before human courts will assure them that the Son of Man will testify on their behalf in the heavenly court (13:9-13 echoes 8:34-38). A prophecy concerning the coming of the Son of Man to gather the elect now makes explicit the expectations built up in the previous sections.

Sayings about the coming of the Son of Man circulated independently in early Christianity.[560] His appearance will follow the heavenly signs of the end of the world: The astronomical bodies will cease to perform the functions for which they were created (Gen 1:14-19). Such predictions draw from the imagery of the prophets (Isa 13:10; 34:4; Ezek 32:7-8; Joel 2:10-11; 3:4, 15), where a divine theophany causes the turmoil in nature. Here, the nations will see the Son of Man coming in the clouds with divine glory (v. 26). In Dan 7:13, the Son of Man comes with the clouds of heaven, but does so to ascend to the divine throne rather than to appear to those on earth. His ascent to the divine throne marks the end of the war being waged by the fourth beast against the "holy ones." God gives judgment on their behalf and bestows an everlasting dominion upon them (Dan 7:18, 26-27).[561]

559. In that sense, Mark's apocalyptic discourse is closer to the characteristic units of prophetic speech than to the surveys in historical apocalypses, which are laid out according to a symbolic sequence of years as in the section of Daniel from which Mark drew the image of the "abomination of desolation" (Dan 9:20-27). Daniel may have used the "seventy weeks of years" to correct the chronicler's historical interpretation of the restoration as the fulfillment of Jeremiah. Periodization is a standard feature of historical apocalypses (see John J. Collins, *Daniel* [Minneapolis: Fortress, 1993] 352-53).

560. See Barnabas Lindars, *Jesus Son of Man* (Grand Rapids: Eerdmans, 1984) 85-131.

561. Collins, *Daniel,* 299-324, argues that the vision describes a mythic scene in which the human figure who ascends the throne is the angel Michael, who will be the agent of Israel's deliverance, and the "holy ones" are angelic hosts. The kingdom that wages war against the "hosts" until the coming of the Son of Man reflects the true impiety of Antiochus, thinking he can challenge divine powers. Since the Qumran scrolls demonstrate a lively synergism between the human congregation of the righteous and their angelic counterparts (1QM 6:6; 10:11-12; 12), the "holy ones" also represent the faithful in Israel.

This scenario seems to be the primary source for the Markan understanding of the events of the end time.[562] In Dan 7:21-22, the holy ones are being defeated by the fourth beast until God comes to their rescue. Mark 13:20 indicates that God will shorten the time to rescue the elect. In Daniel's vision, the beast even attempts to change sacred seasons—i.e. the cultic calendar—while dominating the elect until condemned by the heavenly court (Dan 7:25-26). Then the elect enter into an everlasting rule (7:27). In Mark, the disturbance in the heavens attends the appearance of the Son of Man. Angels gather the persecuted elect from the entire cosmos (Mark 13:27).

Mark's readers know that the coming of the Son of Man will mean divine judgment (8:38). They might supply the missing judgment of their enemies, which should come between the appearance of the Son of Man and the gathering of the elect. However, this lack of an explicit description of the judgment of the wicked distinguishes Mark's apocalyptic prophecies from the usual apocalyptic scenario.[563] Readers are not encouraged to speculate about the fate of their enemies. Instead, they anticipate participating in the eternal rule of the Son. The formula by which the angels gather the elect emphasizes the fact that no one will be left out when the Son of Man comes, whether the person is dead or alive.

562. Collins, *Daniel*, 92-96, argues that since the Son of Man saying in Mark 13:26 does not identify Jesus with the Son of Man, it may reflect use of Dan 7:13-14 by Jesus himself. The imagery asserts that Jesus and his disciples will be vindicated by the appearance of Israel's heavenly liberator in judgment.

563. The imagery of Daniel 7 draws on traditions of Yahweh as the victorious divine warrior who defeats the chaos monster (Collins, *Daniel*, 277-93). Mark 13 mythologizes neither the Roman imperial powers nor those who persecute the faithful.

REFLECTIONS

Critics of Christians' hope for an end-time judgment have often accused Christians of fostering an ethic based on resentment. The lowly, unsuccessful have-nots of the world are encouraged to fantasize about the eventual destruction of the powerful or successful persons in society, critics argue. Resentment of the weak fuels a hatred of others, which is legitimized by being clothed in the religious guise of persecuted righteousness. Mark's end-time scenario provides no such opportunity. Its false prophets and messiahs arise within Christian circles. Disciples are to ignore them. The fate of those who persecute witnesses to the gospel is never described at all. These prophecies formulate a message of hope, which encourages the disciple to endure the hardships of testimony to the gospel. Those who do so will be gathered into the people of God, the elect.

Mark 13:28-31, Certainty of End-time Salvation

NIV	NRSV
28"Now learn this lesson from the fig tree: As soon as its twigs get tender and its leaves come out, you know that summer is near. 29Even so, when you see these things happening, you know that it is near, right at the door. 30I tell you the truth, this generation[a] will certainly not pass away until all these things have happened. 31Heaven and earth will pass away, but my words will never pass away."	28"From the fig tree learn its lesson: as soon as its branch becomes tender and puts forth its leaves, you know that summer is near. 29So also, when you see these things taking place, you know that he[a] is near, at the very gates. 30Truly I tell you, this generation will not pass away until all these things have taken place. 31Heaven and earth will pass away, but my words will not pass away."
a30 Or race	*a Or it*

COMMENTARY

A collection of short sayings leads to a confirmation formula that underlines the truth of Jesus' prophecy (v. 31). The image of the fig tree in bloom is a short parable or proverb. Its bloom is a certain sign of summer. Similarly, when readers see "these things" (ταῦτα *tauta*) they will know "he is near, at the gates" (vv. 28-29). In its present context, the saying about the fig tree creates several difficulties for the reader. Is the reader supposed to remember the fig tree with leaves and no fruit, which Jesus cursed (11:12-14, 20-22)? If so, then alleged "signs" must be carefully scrutinized. Who is "near"? God? A Son of Man other than Jesus? Jesus as Son of Man? What are "these things"? The previous section referred to cosmic signs that are clearly irrelevant to the kind of sign the disciples had originally requested (v. 4). When the heavenly bodies cease to perform their function, the world is near its end. The parable of the fig tree might have orginally referred to Jesus and his ministry as evidence for the in-breaking of God's kingdom.[564] Therefore, "these things" would appear to refer to vv. 14-23, the desolating sacrilege and the subsequent turmoil. Yet the advice to flee and to pay no attention to false messiahs might already have been fulfilled in the experience of the hearers. The earlier sections of the chapter appear to distance the destruction of the Temple and turmoil surrounding the Temple from the end time. The saying about the fig tree may have been intended by Mark to convey reassurance rather than information; as Christians begin to see events that conform to these predictions, they are assured that the day of salvation for the elect is near.

The promise that these events will occur before the present generation passes away (v. 30) appears to be a variant of the prophecy that some of Jesus' contemporaries would see the kingdom of God coming in power (9:1), and it fits uneasily into the larger discourse. Mark 13:9-13 suggests an extensive Christian mission, during which disciples can expect to suffer persecution from both Jews and Gentiles. It refers to "these things" being fulfilled before the speaker's generation has passed away. Since the referent of "these things" is no clearer in this saying than in v. 29, both sayings may have been used by the evangelist to highlight the truth of the earlier prophecies.[565] Unlike Mark 9:1, which speaks of those listening to Jesus, this saying refers only to "this generation."

The promise of an enduring validity for Jesus' words recasts the promise of eternal rule made in Dan 7:14, using prophetic sayings about the authority of God's Word as a model (Isa 40:8; 51:6). Jesus' word is identified with God's Word. Taken as an independent saying, the claim that Jesus' word is eternal also makes a christological assertion about Jesus: He is greater than the prophets who deliver God's word to the people.[566]

564. See Rudolph Pesch, *Das Markusevangelium I. Teil,* HTKNT II (Freiburg: Herder, 1977) 2:307.

565. Robert H. Gundry (*Mark: A Commentary on His Apology for the Cross* [Grand Rapids: Eerdmans, 1993] 790-91) argues that the wording of this saying does not support attempts to see it as Mark's variant of 9:1.

566. See Dieter Lührmann, *Das Markusevangelium, HNT* (Tübingen: J.C.B. Mohr [Paul Siebeck], 1987) 225. The eternity of Jesus' word also indicates the reason why other elements of an apocalyptic revelation are missing in this section of Mark. Heavenly journeys, symbolic visions, and angelic interpreters are not necessary for someone who can speak with the authority of Jesus.

Mark 13:32-37, Exhortation to Be Watchful

NIV

32"No one knows about that day or hour, not even the angels in heaven, nor the Son, but only the Father. 33Be on guard! Be alert[a]! You do not know when that time will come. 34It's like a man going away: He leaves his house and puts his

[a]33 Some manuscripts *alert and pray*

NRSV

32"But about that day or hour no one knows, neither the angels in heaven, nor the Son, but only the Father. 33Beware, keep alert;[a] for you do not know when the time will come. 34It is like a man going on a journey, when he leaves home and puts his slaves in charge, each with his work,

[a]Other ancient authorities add *and pray*

NIV	NRSV
servants in charge, each with his assigned task, and tells the one at the door to keep watch. 35"Therefore keep watch because you do not know when the owner of the house will come back—whether in the evening, or at midnight, or when the rooster crows, or at dawn. 36If he comes suddenly, do not let him find you sleeping. 37What I say to you, I say to everyone: 'Watch!'"	and commands the doorkeeper to be on the watch. 35Therefore, keep awake—for you do not know when the master of the house will come, in the evening, or at midnight, or at cockcrow, or at dawn, 36or else he may find you asleep when he comes suddenly. 37And what I say to you I say to all: Keep awake."

COMMENTARY

Verse 32 is an independent saying that also rejects the possibility that any human being knows God's plan for the coming of the end time.[567] Many interpreters attach it to the collection in vv. 28-31. The second-person plural imperative in v. 33, "look out" (βλέπετε *blepete*), fits the beginning of other sections (vv. 5, 9; "learn" [μάθετε *mathete*], v. 28). However, the exhortation to watchfulness, which follows, depends on this saying. Despite the assurance that Jesus' words will come true before the present generation has died, no one actually knows when God has decided that the end of the world will come. Jesus does not reveal signs of its approach, because he cannot.[568] Since God

has not made this time known to the angels either, apocalypses that claim to be based on angelic revelation are false as well.

If the time is unknown, then no one can expect a warning of its arrival. The only solution is constant watchfulness (v. 33). The chapter concludes with a parable concerning a master and his servants. The servants know the task that has been entrusted to them, but do not know when the master will return. The only way to be certain of the master's praise is to be faithful to the tasks assigned. Faithful servants do not need to know when the master will return. The conclusion brings the discourse back to the situation of Mark's readers; like the household servants, they must be prepared for the master's return.[569]

567. See Pesch, *Das Markusevangelium,* 2:310.
568. Adela Yarbro Collins (*The Beginning of the Gospel* [Minneapolis: Fortress, 1992] 87) suggests that the references to "day" and "hour," rather than the "weeks" and "years" of other apocalypses, indicates that the end is imminent.

569. See Pesch, *Das Markusevangelium,* 2:314-15.

REFLECTIONS

1. On the one hand, Mark underscores the certainty of Jesus' word. Readers know that the death of Jesus on the cross does not end the story of salvation. On the other hand, Christians need not concern themselves with apocalyptic speculation. Disciples should remember that "doing the will of God" (3:35) has no relationship to the timing of divine judgment. Neither should Christians concern themselves with the fate of those who persecute them or who reject the gospel. When Christians rush to judge others, they should remember this exhortation. The only question the master will ask is whether the servants have been faithful to their call as disciples.

2. Living some two millennia after these words were spoken, many Christians today assume that the word about watchfulness has no significance for them. Yet we all know that human life is fleeting. A young man was murdered on the streets of a large city merely for asking some youths why they were verbally tormenting an elderly man. The young man's fiancée discovers that her whole world has dissolved. Fortunately, the last words they had exchanged concerned love and their hopes for the future. A young woman went to pick up her infant from his nap and discovered that he had died of Sudden Infant Death Syndrome. Unfortunately, her last interaction with the baby had been one of anger and frustration over the child's fussing and crying. Both women are in terrible pain. They have been stripped of what they love most in the whole world. But the young mother has to face the nagging regret that she did not show her baby the love she feels for him in the last hours she spent with him. On a personal level, such stories remind us that we should be watchful as Christians. The early religious orders practiced a time of examining one's conscience, in which all members assessed how their behavior of the day just past reflected (or neglected) the conduct expected of members of their order. Being a faithful Christian does not just "happen" like crabgrass or dandelions popping up in the lawn. It requires the care, attention, and cultivation of an expert gardener.

MARK 14:1–15:47, THE PASSION AND DEATH OF JESUS

OVERVIEW

The discourse on the end time takes Mark's reader away from the narrative present, in which Jesus has powerful enemies who seek to destroy him, to the future, when a persecuted community of witnesses to the gospel await his return as the glorious Son of Man. Previous hints at the exaltation Jesus will enjoy were always matched with references to the necessity of his passion (8:27-33; 9:2-12). The Son of Man who is crucified (8:31) is also the one who will come in glory (13:26; 14:62). The earlier passion predictions have told the reader what will happen in outline: entry into Jerusalem; the Son of Man handed over to the chief priests and scribes; condemned to death; handed over to Gentiles; mocked, spit upon, scourged, and killed; and after three days risen from the dead (10:32-34).

This outline encompasses the passion narrative from the betrayal and arrest to the concluding announcement that Jesus has risen from the dead. It omits another narrative line that is woven into the story of Jesus and his enemies: the story of Jesus and his disciples. Readers know that the disciples find the passion harder to understand with each of the three predictions and that Judas Iscariot will betray Jesus (3:19). The betrayal and flight in the Gethsemane story complete those narrative foreshadowings.

Mark fills out the story of Jesus and his disciples with other traditional elements from the passion account: the anointing of Jesus (14:3-9); the last supper (14:12-31); the prayer in Gethsemane (14:32-42); Peter's denial (14:54, 66-72), and the burial of Jesus (15:42-47). In the first and last of these episodes, sympathetic outsiders highlight the failure of Jesus' disciples by doing what disciples should have done. In the first case, some of the disciples reproach the woman who anoints Jesus. That reaction fits a pattern typical of the disciples, who push others away from Jesus, a behavior established during Jesus' ministry (5:31 [indirectly]; 9:38; 10:13). Jesus always reverses the disciples' actions by making those persons whom the disciples scorn examples of faith.

Early creedal formulae like 1 Cor 15:3*b*-5 and the supper tradition in 1 Cor 11:23-25 indicate that accounts of the events to which they refer must have existed decades before Mark was written. Unique features of the passion narratives in Luke and John suggest that more than one version of events was in circulation by the last decades of the first century. Despite considerable scholarly discussion, there is no generally accepted view of what the pre-Markan passion tradition(s) was like. Since the needs of evangelization and of liturgical celebration of the eucharist would require very different accounts of the passion of Jesus, Mark probably used diverse passion traditions rather than one or two single narratives.[570]

570. See Ernest Best, *The Temptation and Passion: The Markan Soteriology,* 2nd ed., SNTSMS 2 (Cambridge: Cambridge University Press, 1990) xxvii-xxviii. A detailed analysis of the various proposals concerning the pre-Markan passion traditions may be found in Marion L. Soards, "The Question of a PreMarkan Passion Narrative," in Raymond E. Brown, *The Death of the Messiah: From Gethsemane to the Grave. A Commentary on the Passion Narratives in the Four Gospels,* vol. 2 (Garden City, N.Y.: Doubleday, 1994) 1492-1524.

Another early creedal formula (Rom 1:3) refers to Jesus as being descended from David; thus the kingship of Jesus is another theme Mark has linked to Jesus' presence in Jerusalem. Although Jesus has clearly indicated the inadequacy of the title "Son of David" (12:35-37), the passion tradition culminates with the crucifixion of Jesus, the "king of Israel" (15:32).[571] Pre-Markan traditions probably viewed the title positively, despite the fact that it occasions extensive mockery. It makes no sense to exalt a crucified person as "king of the Jews" when even Herod Antipas was not permitted to claim that title.[572] When the centurion, representing the converted enemy,[573] recognizes the truth about Jesus at his crucifixion, he confesses that Jesus is "Son of God" (15:39). As the apophthegm on the Son of David suggests, the only way to understand the crucified as "anointed king" is to understand that he is more than the descendant of David. Whatever traditions Mark took over have been reshaped to focus on the cross as the disclosure of Jesus, Son of God.[574]

571. See Frank Matera, *The Kingship of Jesus*, SBLDS 66 (Chico, Calif.: Scholars Press, 1982); J. D. Kingsbury, *The Christology of Mark's Gospel* (Philadelphia: Fortress, 1983) 124-29, argues that Jesus accepts the title "king of the Jews." His opponents, both the high priest and Pilate, do not believe that Jesus is in fact "king" in the sociopolitical sense in which they understand it.

572. Josephus (*Antiquities* 18.8.2 secs. 245-46) asserts that Antipas, although hesitant to do so, was persuaded by Herodias to petition Rome to bestow the title "king" upon him. However, he was denounced to the emperor by an agent of Agrippa for having a secret cache of weapons and was banished to Gaul (c. 39 CE). See E. Schürer, *A History of the Jewish People in the Time of Jesus Christ*, rev. ed. (Edinburgh: T. & T. Clark, 1986) 1:352-53.

573. Best, *Temptation*, xlvii, notes that the centurion fulfills the role of "converted torturer" in ancient martyr stories.

574. Mark may have composed the confession in 15:39 as the culminating confession of Jesus as Son of God (1:11; 9:7). Collins, Beginning of the Gospel, 117, suggests that Mark knew a tradition that concluded with the signs of a theophany in 15:38.

The juxtaposition of the Son of Man in glory with the crucified Son of Man plays out another important element in the passion narrative: Suffering replaces power.[575] Although readers have been told that Jesus came as servant to suffer for others (10:45), the Jesus they have met thus far is a man of extraordinary power.[576] The only limitations Jesus encounters are created by the lack of faith and hard heartedness characteristic of an evil age. The narrative has highlighted the authority of Jesus' word, whether in healing or in teaching. Jesus' word will endure as long as the Word of God itself (13:31). With the passion narrative, Jesus suddenly appears powerless. Only the power to prophesy remains. Jesus does not heal the severed ear of the high priest's slave (14:47; cf. Luke 22:51 *b*). The disciples have been promised that the Holy Spirit will tell them what to say in court (13:11); Jesus, however, remains largely silent before his accusers. Jesus, betrayed by friends and apparently helpless before his enemies, accepts the titles "Messiah" and "Son of God" and identifies himself as the coming Son of Man (14:61-62). Even if readers were tempted to take the paradox of the cross lightly in view of Jesus' future glory, Mark, the narrator, forces them to acknowledge the contradictions voiced by those who see Jesus crucified: "He saved others; he cannot save himself" (15:31). Mark's reader knows that there is a divine necessity to Jesus' death (10:45), but the passion narrative does not explain how to understand Jesus' death as a ransom.

575. See Dorothy A. Lee-Pollard, "Powerlessness as Power: A Key Emphasis in the Gospel of Mark," *SJT* 40 (1987) 183-84.

576. Ibid., 174-79.

Mark 14:1-2, Decision to Arrest Jesus

NIV	NRSV
14 Now the Passover and the Feast of Unleavened Bread were only two days away, and the chief priests and the teachers of the law were looking for some sly way to arrest Jesus and kill him. [2]"But not during the Feast," they said, "or the people may riot."	**14** It was two days before the Passover and the festival of Unleavened Bread. The chief priests and the scribes were looking for a way to arrest Jesus[a] by stealth and kill him; [2]for they said, "Not during the festival, or there may be a riot among the people." *a* Gk *him*

COMMENTARY

Mark returns to Jesus' enemies, who have decided that they cannot arrest Jesus during the Passover observance, since the crowds might riot (11:18; 12:12). The opportunity that they seek will be provided when one of Jesus' own disciples comes forward to betray him (vv. 10-11). By dividing the plot from the opportunity, Mark uses the certainty of Jesus' death to frame the story of Jesus' anointing by an unknown woman (vv. 3-9). Her gesture demonstrates a prophetic recognition of who Jesus is and highlights the horror of Jesus' betrayal by one of his own disciples.

This section of the Gospel opens with a precise designation of time, "two days before the Passover and the festival of Unleavened Bread" (v. 1). The next series of events is introduced as occurring on "the first day of Unleavened Bread, when the Passover lamb is sacrificed" (v. 12). These references cause some confusion. Mark presumably intends "Unleavened Bread" as an alternative designation for Passover (cf. Luke 22:1; 2 Chr 35:17).[577] Or Mark may have followed the older tradition in which "Unleavened Bread" was the designation for the seven-day period following the celebration of the Passover meal on 15 Nisan, during which nothing made with leaven could be eaten (Exod 12:8-20).[578] In either case, Mark's

assertion that the preparations for the meal were made on the first day of the feast of Unleavened Bread is inaccurate. The Preparation Day does not belong to the feast. The simplest solution is to assume that Mark considers days to begin in the morning, rather than in the evening, as was the custom. Hence the preparations during the day and the Passover meal eaten in the evening belong to the same day.[579] However, the hasty burial of Jesus on the afternoon of the crucifixion indicates that Mark does know that the sabbath begins at sundown. The confusion concerning when the feast began may have been heightened by Mark's use of the same Greek word (πάσχα pascha) to describe the festival, the slaughtering of the lamb, and the meal that followed. Mark's references to the pascha (vv. 12, 14, 16), however, all refer to the sacrifice or the meal. He reflects the confused usage typical of the first century but primarily thinks of the feast as Passover.[580]

If the anointing was an undated incident inserted by Mark into the episode concerning the plot against Jesus, then the date refers to the authorities' desire to seize Jesus and Judas' response to them; he knows of their desire to arrest Jesus.

577 See *Jub.* 49:22; Josephus *The Jewish Wars* 2.14. 3.
578. See Josephus *Antiquities of the Jews* 3.10.5, sec. 249. See also Pesch, *Das Markusevangelium,* 2:320.

579. See Adela Yarbro Collins, *The Beginning of the Gospel* (Minneapolis: Fortress, 1992) 101-2.
580. See Brown, *The Death of the Messiah,* 1353-57.

Mark 14:3-9, Jesus Is Anointed

NIV	NRSV
³While he was in Bethany, reclining at the table in the home of a man known as Simon the Leper, a woman came with an alabaster jar of very expensive perfume, made of pure nard. She broke the jar and poured the perfume on his head. ⁴Some of those present were saying indignantly to one another, "Why this waste of perfume? ⁵It could have been sold for more than a year's wages[a] and the money given to the poor." And they rebuked her harshly.	3While he was at Bethany in the house of Simon the leper,[a] as he sat at the table, a woman came with an alabaster jar of very costly ointment of nard, and she broke open the jar and poured the ointment on his head. ⁴But some were there who said to one another in anger, "Why was the ointment wasted in this way? ⁵For this ointment could have been sold for more than three hundred denarii,[b] and the money given to the poor." And

[a] 5 Greek *than three hundred denarii*

[a] The terms *leper* and *leprosy* can refer to several diseases
[b] The denarius was the usual day's wage for a laborer

NIV	NRSV
[6]"Leave her alone," said Jesus. "Why are you bothering her? She has done a beautiful thing to me. [7]The poor you will always have with you, and you can help them any time you want. But you will not always have me. [8]She did what she could. She poured perfume on my body beforehand to prepare for my burial. [9]I tell you the truth, wherever the gospel is preached throughout the world, what she has done will also be told, in memory of her."	they scolded her. [6]But Jesus said, "Let her alone; why do you trouble her? She has performed a good service for me. [7]For you always have the poor with you, and you can show kindness to them whenever you wish; but you will not always have me. [8]She has done what she could; she has anointed my body beforehand for its burial. [9]Truly I tell you, wherever the good news[a] is proclaimed in the whole world, what she has done will be told in remembrance of her."
	[a] Or gospel

COMMENTARY

The nameless woman's gesture shows that Jesus' followers still do not grasp the necessity of his passion.[581] Jesus defends the woman's prophetic action against those who denigrate her in the name of the poor.[582] The expansive gesture, breaking and pouring out the entire vial of expensive ointment rather than using a few drops, forms a foil to the cheapness of Jesus' life in the eyes of those who seek to destroy him. Since anointing the head belonged to the designation of kings (1 Sam 10:1; 2 Kgs 9:6), the woman's gesture has been seen as a symbolic recognition that Jesus is King of Israel. However, the interpretation that follows points not to messianic kingship but to Jesus' death.[583]

Jesus knows that some of the persons present at the dinner are indignant at the "waste" of the costly ointment.[584] Like Jesus' enemies in earlier controversy stories (2:23-28; 7:1-13), those at the dinner use a pious excuse to condemn the woman. The price of the ointment ought to have been given to the poor. This concern for the poor might have evoked the general sentiment that concern for the poor was appropriate to the Passover season (cf.

10:21).[585] Jesus' counterargument appeals to Scripture and to the specific time (Jesus is about to die). Although the complainers know that the Law requires that they support the poor, they do not recognize that the universality of poverty means that the righteous will always have to fulfill the responsibilities of charity (v. 7; Deut 15:11).

Jesus' rebuke accuses the complainers of harassing the woman. He designates what she has done a "good work" (καλὸν ἔργον kalon ergon; v. 6), a designation used for pious practices, like almsgiving. The virtue in her action surpasses the demand that her critics would have made on her to do a "good work" by giving the price of such ointment to the poor.[586] Her gesture of emptying out the entire contents of a very valuable vial of ointment might also be compared with that of the widow at the Temple treasury (12:41-44). The willingness of both women to give all of what they have raises doubts about the behavior of the others.

Jesus' praise for the woman for anointing his body for burial shows that he knows that the purpose of the journey to Jerusalem—his death (and resurrection)—will be accomplished as he has predicted (8:31; 9:31; 10:33-34). The disciples have failed to understand Jesus' words about his death. But now a woman has recognized the

581. This woman's story has become central in feminist interpretation.
582. See Elisabeth Schüssler Fiorenza, *In Memory of Her: A Feminist Theological Reconstruction of Christian Origins* (New York: Crossroad, 1983) 152-53.
583. See Joachim Gnilka, *Das Evangelium nach Markus. 1 Teilband Mk 1–8, 26*, EKKNT II (Zurich: Benziger, 1978) 2:223-24.
584. Mark's anonymous "they" indicates that those objecting are not among Jesus' disciples. See Gnilka, *Das Evangelium nach Markus*, 2:224. Matthew 26:8 makes the objection come from disciples. John personalizes the episode by having Jesus' friend Mary from Bethany anoint his feet, and Judas Iscariot protests the action (John 12:3-4).

585. See Gnilka, *Das Evangelium nach Markus*, 2:224.
586. See Pesch, *Das Markusevangelium*, 2:332. The NIV translates the Greek word καλός (*kalos*) by its aesthetic sense, "beautiful," rather than the common ethical meaning of the term, "noble" or "good," and consequently misses the point of Jesus' praise.

truth without such instruction. Just as Jesus promised that the kingdom belongs to the children whom the disciples tried to exclude (10:13-16), so also this woman's gesture makes her worthy of an unexpected reward. She will be remembered wherever the gospel is preached (14:9). This promise also provides Mark the opportunity to remind readers that the gospel will be preached throughout the world (cf. 13:10).

Jesus has been staying in Bethany throughout his visit to Jerusalem (11:11-12, 19-20, 27). It is unclear whether this incident is set in the house where Jesus has taken up residence or at a banquet in another house (as in the dinner with Levi, the tax collector). The host, "Simon, the leper," who plays no role in the narrative, may have been attached to the story in the tradition.

In any case, the woman belongs to the household. There is no indication that she had used all of her livelihood to buy the ointment, as some commentators suggest. Rather, the ointment's price suggests that she is a person of some means. Within Mark's Gospel, she is the antitype of Queen Herodias, who demanded the head of John the Baptist. In addition, Jesus promises that her deed, not her name, will be a permanent memorial to her wherever the gospel is preached.

Although some feminist exegetes look to her and the other women in the Markan account as evidence that women were included among Jesus' disciples, Mark maintains the cultural conventions of his time. Thus, like all of the women who encounter Jesus during his public ministry in Mark's Gospel, this woman is nameless. Women and children encounter Jesus only when Jesus is inside a household. The Syrophoenician woman, a Gentile, meets Jesus inside a house (7:24-25). Jesus is inside a house when women bring their children to him (10:10, 13); the hemorrhaging woman is clearly an exception, due to her desperate act. Mark has consistently structured his narrative around public events, which take place outside, and special instruction of the disciples, which often takes place indoors. Since Jesus is inside the household in this episode, the presence of women and children does not violate social conventions.[587] These women play a significant role in the narrative as foils to the male disciples, who are blind to much of Jesus' teaching.

587. See Winsome Munro, "Women Disciples in Mark?" *CBQ* 44 (1982) 227-29. Munro thinks that Mark envisages Jesus as a typical male teacher with his disciples and consequently suppresses the position of women as actual disciples during the ministry of Jesus (234-36).

REFLECTIONS

Just as Judas Iscariot is condemned to be the archetype of the "betrayer" wherever the gospel is preached, so also the anonymous woman is remembered as the one who recognizes the truth about Jesus. Anointing with costly ointment signals the burial of an important person, perhaps even a king. This gesture highlights the lack of faith that still remains among Jesus' followers. If they had been absolutely certain that Jesus was so important, would they have fled his accusers so readily?

The tension between those at the table with Jesus, who only see wasted ointment, and the woman's acknowledgment that Jesus is "the anointed" reminds us of the mystery of faith. Those at table with Jesus are so irritated by the woman's behavior that they do not even consider the honor that she is giving Jesus. Instead, they attempt to frame the woman as someone who wastes what is valuable rather than contributing the same amount to help the poor. Perhaps, that false religious excuse masks embarrassment over failure to treat Jesus with the respect he deserves, as a related story in Luke 7:36-50 suggests. Jesus points out that the Law (Deut 15:11) makes everyone responsible for helping the poor. If the poor are in desperate need, then this woman's failure to donate the cost of the ointment is neither the cause nor the cure. Jesus is not impressed by the false piety expressed in their excuses. This story raises in haunting fashion a question that perennially faces both individual believers and Christian congregations: How do we—by our actions and our disposal of resources—show honor to Jesus?

Mark 14:10-11, Judas Agrees to Betray Jesus

NIV	NRSV
[10]Then Judas Iscariot, one of the Twelve, went to the chief priests to betray Jesus to them. [11]They were delighted to hear this and promised to give him money. So he watched for an opportunity to hand him over.	10Then Judas Iscariot, who was one of the twelve, went to the chief priests in order to betray him to them. [11]When they heard it, they were greatly pleased, and promised to give him money. So he began to look for an opportunity to betray him.

COMMENTARY

Judas's desire to betray Jesus provides the opportunity sought by Jesus' enemies, who agree to pay Judas an indefinite sum for betraying Jesus (the amount is presumably trivial). By inserting the story of the woman who anoints Jesus between the authorities' quest for a means to arrest Jesus and Judas' response, Mark invites the reader to compare Judas with the woman. The unspecified sum that Judas is willing to accept forms a sharp contrast to the expensive ointment used by the woman. The brief notice is formulated to emphasize that Jesus is being betrayed by one of the Twelve. The betrayal of Jesus to the chief priests and scribes will mark the beginning of the passion (cf. 10:32-34).

It is impossible to ascertain from the narrative what might have led to Judas's action, since Mark never provides an explanation for the treachery. Jesus has defined his followers as a new family that will be devoted to doing the will of God (3:31-35).[588] The apocalyptic discourse, however, warns disciples that they might be turned in by "brothers, parents, or children" (13:12). Judas's action exemplifies such behavior. From this point on, the story refers to him only as "the betrayer."

588. See Richard Fenn, *The Death of Herod: An Essay in the Sociology of Religion* (Cambridge: Cambridge University Press, 1992) 59-63, 93-94.

REFLECTIONS

Mark has framed the anointing episode with the notice that Jesus will be betrayed into the hands of his enemies. Since the authorities were afraid to arrest him during the feast, Jesus would not have been killed without the participation of one of his disciples. Readers have been reminded that the same fate awaits them; disciples will be handed over to death by their own family members (13:12).

Christians who have lived under oppressive regimes know that fear of informants creeps into every corner of life. When the archives of the East German secret police were opened, some people discovered that close friends and family members had turned them in for offenses against the state. Pastors discovered that people who had come to them for counseling were really police agents. During the time of Jesus, intrigue and betrayal among family members was common in the Herodian court and the Roman imperial household. Mark's readers have seen the consequences of such scheming in the account of John the Baptist's death (6:17-29). In such evil times, prophets and others who witness to God's truth will not be welcome. They know the dangers awaiting them.

Mark 14:12-31, The Passover Meal

NIV

[12]On the first day of the Feast of Unleavened Bread, when it was customary to sacrifice the Passover lamb, Jesus' disciples asked him, "Where do you want us to go and make preparations for you to eat the Passover?"

[13]So he sent two of his disciples, telling them, "Go into the city, and a man carrying a jar of water will meet you. Follow him. [14]Say to the owner of the house he enters, 'The Teacher asks: Where is my guest room, where I may eat the Passover with my disciples?' [15]He will show you a large upper room, furnished and ready. Make preparations for us there."

[16]The disciples left, went into the city and found things just as Jesus had told them. So they prepared the Passover.

[17]When evening came, Jesus arrived with the Twelve. [18]While they were reclining at the table eating, he said, "I tell you the truth, one of you will betray me—one who is eating with me."

[19]They were saddened, and one by one they said to him, "Surely not I?"

[20]"It is one of the Twelve," he replied, "one who dips bread into the bowl with me. [21]The Son of Man will go just as it is written about him. But woe to that man who betrays the Son of Man! It would be better for him if he had not been born."

[22]While they were eating, Jesus took bread, gave thanks and broke it, and gave it to his disciples, saying, "Take it; this is my body."

[23]Then he took the cup, gave thanks and offered it to them, and they all drank from it.

[24]"This is my blood of the[a] covenant, which is poured out for many," he said to them. [25]"I tell you the truth, I will not drink again of the fruit of the vine until that day when I drink it anew in the kingdom of God."

[26]When they had sung a hymn, they went out to the Mount of Olives.

[27]"You will all fall away," Jesus told them, "for it is written:

[a]24 Some manuscripts the new   [b]27 Zech. 13:7

NRSV

12On the first day of Unleavened Bread, when the Passover lamb is sacrificed, his disciples said to him, "Where do you want us to go and make the preparations for you to eat the Passover?" [13]So he sent two of his disciples, saying to them, "Go into the city, and a man carrying a jar of water will meet you; follow him, [14]and wherever he enters, say to the owner of the house, 'The Teacher asks, Where is my guest room where I may eat the Passover with my disciples?' [15]He will show you a large room upstairs, furnished and ready. Make preparations for us there." [16]So the disciples set out and went to the city, and found everything as he had told them; and they prepared the Passover meal.

17When it was evening, he came with the twelve. [18]And when they had taken their places and were eating, Jesus said, "Truly I tell you, one of you will betray me, one who is eating with me." [19]They began to be distressed and to say to him one after another, "Surely, not I?" [20]He said to them, "It is one of the twelve, one who is dipping bread[a] into the bowl[b] with me. [21]For the Son of Man goes as it is written of him, but woe to that one by whom the Son of Man is betrayed! It would have been better for that one not to have been born."

22While they were eating, he took a loaf of bread, and after blessing it he broke it, gave it to them, and said, "Take; this is my body." [23]Then he took a cup, and after giving thanks he gave it to them, and all of them drank from it. [24]He said to them, "This is my blood of the[c] covenant, which is poured out for many. [25]Truly I tell you, I will never again drink of the fruit of the vine until that day when I drink it new in the kingdom of God."

26When they had sung the hymn, they went out to the Mount of Olives. [27]And Jesus said to them, "You will all become deserters; for it is written,

'I will strike the shepherd,
    and the sheep will be scattered.'

[28]But after I am raised up, I will go before you to

[a]Gk lacks bread   [b]Other ancient authorities read same bowl
[c]Other ancient authorities add new

NIV

" 'I will strike the shepherd,
  and the sheep will be scattered.'[b]

[28]But after I have risen, I will go ahead of you into Galilee."

[29]Peter declared, "Even if all fall away, I will not."

[30]"I tell you the truth," Jesus answered, "today—yes, tonight—before the rooster crows twice[a] you yourself will disown me three times."

[31]But Peter insisted emphatically, "Even if I have to die with you, I will never disown you." And all the others said the same.

[a]30 Some early manuscripts do not have twice.

NRSV

Galilee." [29]Peter said to him, "Even though all become deserters, I will not." [30]Jesus said to him, "Truly I tell you, this day, this very night, before the cock crows twice, you will deny me three times." [31]But he said vehemently, "Even though I must die with you, I will not deny you." And all of them said the same.

COMMENTARY

14:12-21. The confusing chronological notice that opens the section appears to identify the Day of Preparation (14 Nisan) with Passover (15 Nisan). Since John's Gospel suggests that Jesus died on 14 Nisan, various chronological theories have been developed, including divergent customs in Galilee and Judea or the possibility that a solar calendar, like that at Qumran, was being used by Jesus and his followers. However, since the lambs for the Passover meal were slaughtered in the Temple during the afternoon prior to the evening Passover meal, it would be difficult for anyone celebrating Passover in Jerusalem to do so prior to that time.[589] There is no question that the synoptic Gospels present Jesus' last meal as the Passover meal. However, it is possible to suggest that the last supper was not originally the Passover meal but came to be associated with that meal because of the early identification of Jesus as the paschal lamb. Paul's first letter to the Corinthians reflects both traditions separately: Jesus is the paschal sacrifice (1 Cor 5:6-7, also in the metaphorical context of unleavened bread), and the Lord's supper commemorates the meal that Jesus celebrated with his disciples on the night he was betrayed (1 Cor 11:23).

Since we have no reliable information prior to the Mishna (c. 200 CE) about the ritual for celebrating a Passover meal, it is impossible to say whether details in the Markan narrative reflect early Passover meal customs.[590] Mark has probably received a tradition in which the last supper had been identified as a Passover meal. The Fourth Gospel shows that there were other chronological traditions in early Christianity. In addition, confusion about the designations "Passover" and "Feast of Unleavened Bread" in the first century made it possible to think that 14 Nisan was Passover. Therefore, a strong case can be made for concluding that the last supper took place on the eve of the Passover.[591]

Just as Jesus had done with the donkey (11:1-2), so also now he demonstrates his foresight in giving the disciples signs by which they are to find a house in Jerusalem for the Passover celebration. The unusual sight of a man carrying a water jar directs them to the house (vv. 13-14).[592] The request that they are to make of its owner underlines the fact that Jesus will celebrate the meal as a teacher with his disciples (v. 14), not among a family group as might be expected for a Passover meal.[593] Other details in Mark's account also diverge from later Pass-

589. See Raymond E. Brown, *The Death of the Messiah: From Gethsemane to the Grave. A Commentary on the Passion Narratives in the Four Gospels,* vol. 2 (Garden City, N.Y.: Doubleday, 1994) 1364.

590. Ibid., 1369-71.

591. See ibid., 1373-76. Since the day following Jesus' death was a sabbath, the most plausible year(s) for his death are either 30 or 33 CE.

592. This task was commonly performed by women; cf. Gen 24:11; John 4:7.

593. See Robert H. Gundry, *Mark: A Commentary on His Apology for the Cross* (Grand Rapids: Eerdmans, 1993) 821.

over traditions. The shared bread is immediately followed by each person's drinking from a common cup rather than from individual cups later in the meal or at its conclusion.[594] The words concerning the cup are spoken after everyone has drunk from it. Paul's version identifies the cup with the one that is blessed after the Passover meal (1 Cor 11:25). Even if we knew the actual first-century CE Passover ritual, we should not make too many conclusions, since Mark's church is unlikely to have been concerned with the observance of the external details of Jewish Passover ritual (cf. 7:1-23).

The entire focus of the meal is on Jesus' death. Mark highlights that fact by framing it with the predictions of betrayal (vv. 17-21) and denial (vv. 26-31). Mark's reader knows that the first prediction has already been fulfilled, leaving no doubt that Jesus' second prediction will come true.[595]

As the passion narrative develops, citations from or allusions to the Prophets and the book of Psalms shape many of the details. The psalms concerning righteous sufferers are particularly frequent.[596] When the disciples protest that none of them will betray Jesus, he alludes to Ps 41:9, which speaks of a friend who has eaten bread with the speaker becoming an enemy. Jesus' be-

trayal by a friend has been predicted (v. 21a), and the agent of that betrayal is cursed (v. 21b). The curse serves as part of the divine vindication in which God "raises up" the sufferer. Mark's readers already know that Jesus anticipates deliverance from his enemies and exaltation.[597]

Since Jesus has told his disciples that his death is imminent, betrayal makes the person responsible an agent in the crucifixion. Jesus emphasizes that the betrayer is one of the Twelve who is dipping his bread into the common dish (v. 20). He never identifies the betrayer, but readers know that Judas has already agreed to hand Jesus over to his enemies (vv. 10-11).

14:22-25. While they are eating, Jesus speaks the words about his death over the bread and wine. There is considerable diversity in the formulation of the words over both the bread and the cup in the Synoptics and in Paul's writings. The word for "bread" appears in variations of two forms: Luke/1 Corinthians and Mark/Matthew (see Fig. 14).[598] The variants of the word for "cup" show more expansion in the formula than do the words used for "bread" (see Fig. 15).

594. Ibid., 840-41. Luke 22:15-20 includes two cups, one before the bread and one at the conclusion of the meal, which appears closer to later Passover traditions. However, the participants still share a single cup (cf. Joseph A. Fitzmyer, *The Gospel According to Luke X–XXIV*, AB28 (Garden City, N.Y.: Doubleday, 1981) 1396-1402). The cup of blessing at the conclusion of the meal would be the third cup in later Passover meal traditions.

595. See Rudolph Pesch, *Das Markusevangelium I. Teil,* HTKNT II (Freiburg: Herder, 1977) 2:346.

596. Joel Marcus, *The Way of the Lord: Christological Exegesis of the Old Testament in the Gospel of Mark* (Minneapolis: Fortress, 1992) 174-75, provides the following list of parallels between the passion narrative and psalms about righteous sufferers: Mark 14:1/Ps 10:7-8,

by cunning, to kill; Mark 14:18/Ps 41:9, on eating with me; Mark 14:34/Pss 42:5, 11; 43:5, very sad; Mark 14:41/Ps 140:8, delivered over to sinners; Mark 14:55/Ps 37:32, sought to put him to death; Mark 14:57/Pss 27:12; 35:11, false witnesses rising up; Mark 14:61; 15:4-5/Ps 35:13-15, silence before accusers; Mark 15:24/Ps 22:18, division of garments; Mark 15:29/Ps 22:7, mockery, head shaking; Mark 15:30-31/Ps 22:8, save yourself!; Mark 15:32/Ps 22:6, reviling; Mark 15:34/Ps 22:1, cry of dereliction; Mark 15:36/Ps 69:21, gave him vinegar to drink; Mark 15:40/Ps 38:11, looking on at a distance.

597. Ibid., 183.

598. The Luke/1 Corinthians form may reflect liturgical practice at Antioch, and that in Mark/Matthew the Jerusalem practice. See Fitzmyer, *Luke X–XXIV*, 1392-93.

Figure 14: Variants of the Word for "Bread"

a. τοῦτό μού ἐστιν τὸ σῶμα τὸ ὑπὲρ ὑμῶν *Touto mou estin to sōma to hyper hymōn* (1 Cor 11:24, "This is my body that is for you.")

b. τοῦτό ἐστιν τὸ σῶμά μου τὸ ὑπὲρ ὑμῶν διδόμενον *Touto estin to sōma mou to hyper hymōn didomenon* (Luke 22:19, "This is my body, which is given for you.")

c. λάβετε· τοῦτό ἐστιν τὸ σῶμά μου *labete, touto estin to sōma mou* (Mark 14:22, "Take; this is my body.")

d. λάβετε φάγετε· τοῦτό ἐστιν τὸ σῶμά μου *labete, phagete, touto estin to sōma mou* (Matt 26:26, "Take, eat; this is my body.")[599]

599. All Scripture quotations in this figure and the following one are from the NRSV.

Figure 15: Variants of the Word for "Cup"

a. τοῦτο τὸ ποτήριον ἡ καινὴ διαθήκη ἐστὶν ἐν τῷ ἐμῷ αἵματι *touto to potērion hē kainē diathēkē estin en tō emō haimati* (1 Cor 11:25, "This cup is the new covenant in my blood.")

b. τοῦτο τὸ ποτήριον ἡ καινὴ διαθήκη ἐν τῷ αἵματί μου, τὸ ὑπὲρ ὑμῶν ἐκχυννόμενον *touto to potērion hē kainē diathēkē en tō haimati mou to hyper hymōn ekchynnomenon* (Luke 22:20, "This cup that is poured out for you is the new covenant in my blood.")

c. τοῦτό ἐστιν τὸ αἷμά μου τῆς διαθήκης τὸ ἐκχυννόμενον ὑπὲρ πολλῶν *touto estin to haima mou tēs diathēkēs to ekchynnomenon hyper pollōn* (Mark 14:24, "This is my blood of the covenant, which is poured out for many.")

d. πίετε ἐξ αὐτοῦ πάντες· τοῦτο γάρ ἐστιν τὸ αἷμά μου τῆς διαθήκης τὸ περὶ πολλῶν ἐκχυννόμενον εἰς ἄφεσιν ἁμαρτιῶν *piete ex autou pantes, touto gar estin to haima mou tēs diathēkēs to peri pollōn ekchynnomenon eis aphesin hamartiōn* (Matt 26:27-28, "Drink from it, all of you; for this is my blood of the covenant, which is poured out for many for the forgiveness of sins.")

The soteriological significance of the eucharist is bound to the words associated with the cup in the Mark/Matthew tradition. The blood of Jesus, shed in death, is the foundation of the new covenant between God and humanity. (Matthew 26:28 spells out the significance of "poured out for many" by including the reference to forgiveness of sins.) It is possible to formulate the Markan words in Aramaic.[600] Hence, the original formula could have originated in Palestine. Since in Mark the two sayings are not symmetrical and the word about the cup is deferred until after the disciples have drunk from it (cf. Matthew's command to "drink"), some exegetes think that a liturgical tradition similar to that in 1 Cor 11:23-26 and Luke 22:15-20 has been modified in the Markan community. However, the versions need not be forced back to a single form. The formula itself did not have to remain fixed in order to express the significance of Jesus' gesture.

The brief formula associated with the bread looks back to the betrayer's dipping his bread in the common dish. The gesture of handing the bread/body to the disciples may be an invitation to participate in Jesus' suffering (8:34). Jesus' word about the cup looks away from the betrayal to the divine necessity that brings him to make this sacrifice. The association between wine and the blood of a covenant sacrifice shed for the people (Exod 24:8; Zech 9:11) makes the symbolism of the cup more significant than that of the bread.

The apocalyptic section of Zechariah 9–14 provides the symbolism for a number of details in the passion. Zechariah 14:4 asserts that when Yahweh comes to defeat Israel's enemies, Yahweh will stand on the Mount of Olives; Jesus' destination after the supper is the Mount of Olives.[601] In Zech 9:11, Yahweh speaks to the daughter of Zion/Jerusalem, promising to liberate her captives "by the blood of your covenant." The existence of the covenant between Yahweh and Israel grounds the promise of eschatological liberation in Zechariah.[602] In Mark, Jesus' blood establishes a "new covenant" with the Lord (cf. 12:1-12), which is the basis for the experience of salvation.

The cup symbolism takes on a further eschatological meaning by anticipating the wine of the banquet that Jesus will celebrate with his followers in the kingdom of God (v. 25; cf. Isa 25:6-8; 55:1-2; 65:13-14[603]). Like the earlier resurrection and parousia predictions, this notice reminds the reader that the death of Jesus is not the end of the story. Jesus' sacrificial death is part of the divine plan that brings the kingdom into existence. The Essene sect also celebrated a meal in which blessings of bread and wine played a prominent role. This celebration anticipates the meal that will take place when the messianic king and priest come to establish God's rule over the elect.[604] Although the Christian meal looks forward to the heavenly banquet with the Lord, it

---

600. Luke 22:19b-20 can also be retroverted into Aramaic. See Fitzmyer, *Luke X–XXIV*, 1394-95.

601. Marcus, *Way of the Lord*, 156, presses the eschatological imagery to support his claim that Mark sees the death of Jesus as the victory in a cosmological battle.

602. See Carol L. Meyers and Eric M. Meyers, *Zechariah 9–14*, AB 25C (New York: Doubleday, 1993) 140-41.

603. See *1 Enoch* 62:14; 1QSa 2:17-22.

604. See Joachim Gnilka, *Das Evangelium nach Markus. 1 Teilband Mk 1–8, 26*, EKKNT II (Zurich: Benziger, 1978) 2:246-47.

---

remains focused on the sacrificial death of Jesus. Paul tells the Corinthians that the celebration, "proclaim[s] the Lord's death until he comes" (1 Cor 11:26 NRSV).[605]

14:26-31. The meal concludes with a hymn before Jesus and the disciples leave for the Mount of Olives.[606] As they depart, Jesus warns the disciples that they will desert him (v. 27). Like the prediction about betrayal, this warning takes the form of a citation from Scripture (Zech 13:7). Desertion is not the last word, however, as Jesus immediately promises to "go before" the disciples to Galilee after his resurrection (v. 28). The verb used for "go before" (προάγω *proagō)* figured prominently in the introduction to the final passion prediction, "They were on the road, going up to Jerusalem, and Jesus was *going before* [NRSV: "walking ahead"] them . . . and those who followed were afraid" (10:32). Although the expression is ambiguous, the parallel to the earlier description makes it clear that restoration of

the relationship between Jesus and the disciples is intended. The fear that takes hold of them during the passion will be overcome. Once again, the events surrounding the crucifixion are not the last word.

Peter insists that even if everyone else deserts Jesus, he will not, paralleling his response to the first passion prediction (8:31-33). Indeed, Peter will not run away with the others in Gethsemane, but his attempt to follow Jesus will lead to something worse: denial that he even knows Jesus (v. 30). When Jesus predicts Peter's denial (v. 30), Peter again protests, this time insisting that he will die with Jesus rather than deny him (v. 31). The other disciples agree. Mark's readers probably knew that Peter had been martyred by the time of their reading, and Mark has already told them that James and John would drink the cup that Jesus is about to drink (10:39). Looking beyond the context of the story, therefore, one finds some truth in their words. The disciples should know by now that when Jesus makes a statement about what is to happen, it will come about. Attempts to challenge the truth of Jesus' word are futile.

605. Fitzmyer, *Luke X–XXIV,* 1398, contrasts the eschatological orientation of the saying about drinking wine in the kingdom with the Pauline focus on the Second Coming of Jesus.

606. The Hallel psalms sung at the end of a Passover meal (Psalms 114–118) may be the referent of this expression. See Gnilka, *Das Evangelium nach Markus,* 2:247.

REFLECTIONS

1. The drama of the Last Supper draws the reader into the paradox of what is about to happen. One who has been closest to Jesus will be involved in the plot to destroy him, and Jesus' own disciples are too weak and frightened to suffer with him. But Mark does not let readers forget that the story continues beyond the cross. The death of Jesus is a covenant sacrifice that establishes a new community, and the risen Lord will gather the disciples. When the kingdom of God comes in its fullness, they will all celebrate with new wine.

2. Peter responds to the predictions of suffering the way most people do: He tries to deny them. Knowing the horror of friends or disciples deserting their teacher, he tries to deny that he would ever do such a thing. Yet Jesus has continually reminded the disciples that denial of suffering is not the route to life. Only those who deny *themselves* find eternal life (8:34-38). Peter's adamant denials are triggered by another misperception as well. He thinks that Jesus' death will mean the end of the road and that his own denial of Jesus would be the end of their relationship. Given Jesus' predictions, however, we know that neither perception is true.

3. It is easy to think that the disciples should have believed what Jesus told them. They had plenty of evidence that whatever Jesus said was true. If we step back from the story into our own human experience, we recognize how difficult it is to accept the fact that a loved one is going to die. It is difficult enough when the person is already very sick, but when he or she appears to be healthy it is almost impossible to accept. Also, we do not like being reminded by the illness of a loved one of our own weaknesses as well. The situation is even more incomprehensible when the ailing person has always been in charge, always the strong member of a family or team who could be counted on to solve other people's problems.

4. Moving from these human experiences to the case of Jesus demonstrates the personal and emotional paradox of the cross. Dying was not something that people hoped the Messiah would do. The power Jesus exhibited in healing and teaching should have led directly to glory, not to the cross. Jesus keeps insisting that the disciples take a different stance. The cross is an offering for others, not the brutal victory of Jesus' enemies. God's power is greater than death. God will bring Jesus and the disciples through the horrible experiences of the passion to form the basis of a new people. The future mission of the disciples will spread the gospel to all the nations.

Mark 14:32-42, Prayer in Gethsemane

NIV

32They went to a place called Gethsemane, and Jesus said to his disciples, "Sit here while I pray." 33He took Peter, James and John along with him, and he began to be deeply distressed and troubled. 34"My soul is overwhelmed with sorrow to the point of death," he said to them. "Stay here and keep watch."

35Going a little farther, he fell to the ground and prayed that if possible the hour might pass from him. 36"*Abba*,*a* Father," he said, "everything is possible for you. Take this cup from me. Yet not what I will, but what you will."

37Then he returned to his disciples and found them sleeping. "Simon," he said to Peter, "are you asleep? Could you not keep watch for one hour? 38Watch and pray so that you will not fall into temptation. The spirit is willing, but the body is weak."

39Once more he went away and prayed the same thing. 40When he came back, he again found them sleeping, because their eyes were heavy. They did not know what to say to him.

41Returning the third time, he said to them, "Are you still sleeping and resting? Enough! The hour has come. Look, the Son of Man is betrayed into the hands of sinners. 42Rise! Let us go! Here comes my betrayer!"

a36 Aramaic for *Father*

NRSV

32They went to a place called Gethsemane; and he said to his disciples, "Sit here while I pray." 33He took with him Peter and James and John, and began to be distressed and agitated. 34And he said to them, "I am deeply grieved, even to death; remain here, and keep awake." 35And going a little farther, he threw himself on the ground and prayed that, if it were possible, the hour might pass from him. 36He said, "Abba,*a* Father, for you all things are possible; remove this cup from me; yet, not what I want, but what you want." 37He came and found them sleeping; and he said to Peter, "Simon, are you asleep? Could you not keep awake one hour? 38Keep awake and pray that you may not come into the time of trial;*b* the spirit indeed is willing, but the flesh is weak." 39And again he went away and prayed, saying the same words. 40And once more he came and found them sleeping, for their eyes were very heavy; and they did not know what to say to him. 41He came a third time and said to them, "Are you still sleeping and taking your rest? Enough! The hour has come; the Son of Man is betrayed into the hands of sinners. 42Get up, let us be going. See, my betrayer is at hand."

*a*Aramaic for *Father*   *b*Or *into temptation*

COMMENTARY

The eucharistic words and the promise of a banquet in the kingdom have demonstrated that God is not about to establish the kingdom by appearing on the Mount of Olives as a divine warrior. The kingdom will be established through the blood of a new covenant. Now Jesus' prayer in Gethsemane prepares readers for the fact that he will not exercise his power during the passion.[607] Everything will happen as though Jesus were an ordinary human victim, like John the Baptist. Jesus begins to isolate himself from his followers, commanding them to remain while he prays; this is the last time the group will be referred to as "the disciples" until after the resurrection (16:7).[608]

Mark may have adapted an earlier account of Jesus' prayer in Gethsemane in which Jesus goes to pray alone once (as he prays alone in 1:35; 6:46), discovers the disciples sleeping, reproves Peter, and announces the presence of the betrayer. Two references to Jesus' prayer in indirect speech (vv. 35, 39) frame the words of that prayer (v. 36). In contrast to the brief notices that Jesus withdrew to pray alone earlier in the Gospel, the repetition of this prayer scene fixes the solemnity of the moment in the reader's mind. The extended period of prayer in which the disciples are sleeping also provides time for Judas to leave the group and return with the crowd.

Separating himself from the other disciples, Jesus takes Peter, James, and John with him as he did when he restored Jairus's daughter to life (5:37) and at the transfiguration (9:2). Mark probably intends readers to recall the latter scene, in which Moses and Elijah appear from heaven and the divine voice pronounces that Jesus is God's beloved Son, as they witness Jesus' prayer to his Father. The prayer binds Jesus to other figures of the suffering righteous.[609] Readers who remember the transfiguration know that God will not aban-

don Jesus but will exalt him to a position of heavenly glory greater than that of Elijah and Moses.

The failure of the three disciples to obey the command to stay awake and watch (v. 34) recalls the general warning at the end of the discourse on the end time: "Keep awake!" (13:37). Earlier in the narrative, Peter, James, and John play a particular role in scenes concerning the passion. Peter has denied Jesus' prediction about the passion (8:31-33), a denial followed by Jesus' teaching on discipleship as taking up one's cross (8:34-38). On the way to the Mount of Olives, Peter again denies another prediction by insisting that he will never desert Jesus, even if the others do (14:29), prompting Jesus to reply that Peter will deny him three times that very night. James and John have requested the highest places of honor when Jesus comes into his kingdom (10:37). Jesus' warning that they will indeed "share the cup" that he is about to drink (10:39) again evokes an image of suffering. When the rest of the disciples become indignant, Jesus reminds them that the Son of Man came as a suffering servant to give his life as ransom "for many" (10:45; in the eucharistic formula, Jesus an-nounces that his blood is poured out "for many" [14:24]). Now, by being brought close enough to witness how Jesus prays, the three disciples have the opportunity to participate in Jesus' "cup." Instead, despite their earlier boasting, they fall asleep and fail to watch with Jesus—not just once, but three times (vv. 37, 40, 41). This scene is a stunning portrayal of the failure of Jesus' most prominent disciples to understand his suffering and glory.[610]

The earlier instruction on prayer assured disciples that God could and would answer the prayer of those who believe. There is no obstacle to God's power (11:23-24). The picture of Jesus praying evokes the model of a psalm of lament by a righteous person suffering affliction: expression of deep anguish (v. 34); acknowledgment of God's power to save (v. 36a); and acceptance of what comes from the hand of God (v. 36b). Typical of laments, which often include reference to abandonment by friends, the sleeping disciples effectively abandon Jesus in his suffering. But

---

607. Mark must continually subvert human expectations for a kingdom that rests upon human expectations about power. Gethsemane is the beginning of Jesus' experience of powerlessness in the narrative. See Lee-Pollard, "Powerlessness," 178-79.

608. See Brown, *The Death of the Messiah,* 147.

609. Gnilka, *Das Evangelium nach Markus,* 2:257, suggests a combination of the transfiguration and the *Testament of Job.* The anguished prayer defuses any elements of apocalyptic expectation that might be associated with Jesus' move to the Mount of Olives. God will not establish the kingdom by appearing as a mighty divine warrior.

610. See Brown, *The Death of the Messiah,* 151-52.

unlike many laments, which conclude with words of praise for God's deliverance, in this case both Jesus and Mark's readers know that God will not deliver Jesus by taking away the cup of suffering. The conclusion of the prayer—"Not what I want, but what you want" (v. 36b)—reminds readers that Jesus has been devoted to doing the will of God from the beginning. Those who belong to Jesus' new family must have a similar commitment to doing the will of God (3:35).[611]

Jesus' prayer in Gethsemane underlines the divine necessity of his passion and his own willingness to suffer. These notices make it clear that the death of Jesus will not be the victory that his enemies are anticipating. God will deliver the righteous sufferer from his enemies, even though they appear to have succeeded in killing him and scattering his followers.

After the prayer, Jesus finds the disciples sleeping. He rebukes Peter for not being strong enough to stay awake even for an hour (v. 37). Peter's boast that he would even die with Jesus (v. 31) suddenly seems very distant. Jesus commands all three disciples (v. 38 uses the plural "you") to pray lest they enter into the "time of trial" (πει-ρασμός *peirasmos*), recalling the account of Jesus' testing by Satan (1:13), which used the corresponding verb. The exhortation also parallels the final petition of the Lord's Prayer (Matt 6:13; Luke 11:4).[612] Hebrews 5:7-10 indicates that there was an early Christian tradition of Jesus' struggle to accept the Father's will.[613]

Jesus' warning to Peter recasts the flight and denial as a satanic testing of the disciples. The observation that Jesus attaches to the exhortation, "the spirit indeed is willing, but the flesh is weak" (v. 38b) appears to be proverbial, although it has no OT parallels. The antithesis appears in paraenetic texts in the Pauline epistles (e.g., Gal 5:16-17). In that context, "spirit" refers to God's Spirit or to the Christian's spirit renewed by the reception of God's Spirit. The reference to a "willing" or "eager" spirit might have been a variant of the "upright" spirit for which the psalmist prays (Ps 51:12). The function of this proverbial generalization is unclear. It may imply that individuals should acknowledge the constant need for prayer because the weakness of the flesh works against the spirit's commitment to the will of God. Or it may be an explanation for the failures of the disciples, which seeks to diffuse some of the blame readers would be tempted to attribute to their failures.[614]

Earlier in the narrative, Jesus' disciples were unable to cast out a demon, which required prayer (9:29). Now they again fail to pray. Jesus goes to pray for the third time without waking the disciples (vv. 39-40), rousing them from sleep only when the betrayer arrives. Their separation from Jesus is evident when they have nothing to say in reply to him (vv. 41-42). Jesus announces the hour of the passion, "The hour has come; the Son of Man is betrayed into the hands of sinners" (14:41).

611. See Sharyn Echols Dowd, *Prayer, Power and the Problem of Suffering: Mark 11:22-25 in the Context of Markan Theology,* SBLDS 105 (Atlanta: Scholars Press, 1988) 151-62. Dowd's claim that Mark never offers a solution to the theodicy problem seems extreme. Jesus as suffering righteous dies "for many." The disciples suffer "for the sake of the gospel" and share in Jesus' "cup," denying their lives to take up the cross. The solution to the theodicy problem lies in the recognition that God establishes the kingdom through the suffering servant, not a divine warrior.
612. Although Mark's Gospel does not contain a version of the Lord's Prayer, several passages suggest that the prayer may have been familiar to Mark's readers. Mark 11:25 echoes the petition for forgiveness and describes God as "your Father who is in heaven." Jesus also prays to do "the will" of the Father (14:36).

613. See the extensive discussion of the Gethsemane prayer tradition in Brown, *The Death of the Messiah,* 154-78, 223-34.
614. See ibid., 198-99.

REFLECTIONS

Jesus' prayer in Gethsemane presents two strong models for readers: both Jesus and the three disciples. Jesus demonstrates that the powerful Son of Man will submit to the will of God and offer his life for others. By presenting himself as the righteous sufferer of the psalms of lament, Jesus shows his followers that his suffering is real. Neither the extraordinary relationship to God that Jesus enjoys nor his ability to heal the sufferings of others will isolate Jesus from the suffering of the cross.

At the same time, the story of the disciples provides encouragement to believers. If even the disciples, who fell asleep and failed to pray, could become stronger in the faith, then surely other Christians can pick themselves up and start again even if they have lapsed for a while. Guilt and self-blame are out. Jesus calls the disciples to task and reminds them of what is necessary to do God's will in an evil age, but he does not blame them for their weaknesses. Frequently, Christians fall into the trap of thinking that prayer is only for times of suffering, trial, or weakness. They may even be shocked by the words Jesus uses to address God, because they associate prayer with weakness. However, the example of Peter, James, and John reminds us that confidence in our own power and success can fail when it is put to the test. Christians who pray regularly acknowledge their dependence on God's Spirit to sustain them at all times.

Mark 14:43-52, Jesus Is Arrested

NIV

43Just as he was speaking, Judas, one of the Twelve, appeared. With him was a crowd armed with swords and clubs, sent from the chief priests, the teachers of the law, and the elders.

44Now the betrayer had arranged a signal with them: "The one I kiss is the man; arrest him and lead him away under guard." 45Going at once to Jesus, Judas said, "Rabbi!" and kissed him. 46The men seized Jesus and arrested him. 47Then one of those standing near drew his sword and struck the servant of the high priest, cutting off his ear.

48"Am I leading a rebellion," said Jesus, "that you have come out with swords and clubs to capture me? 49Every day I was with you, teaching in the temple courts, and you did not arrest me. But the Scriptures must be fulfilled." 50Then everyone deserted him and fled.

51A young man, wearing nothing but a linen garment, was following Jesus. When they seized him, 52he fled naked, leaving his garment behind.

NRSV

43Immediately, while he was still speaking, Judas, one of the twelve, arrived; and with him there was a crowd with swords and clubs, from the chief priests, the scribes, and the elders.

44Now the betrayer had given them a sign, saying, "The one I will kiss is the man; arrest him and lead him away under guard." 45So when he came, he went up to him at once and said, "Rabbi!" and kissed him. 46Then they laid hands on him and arrested him. 47But one of those who stood near drew his sword and struck the slave of the high priest, cutting off his ear. 48Then Jesus said to them, "Have you come out with swords and clubs to arrest me as though I were a bandit? 49Day after day I was with you in the temple teaching, and you did not arrest me. But let the scriptures be fulfilled." 50All of them deserted him and fled.

51A certain young man was following him, wearing nothing but a linen cloth. They caught hold of him, 52but he left the linen cloth and ran off naked.

COMMENTARY

Judas violates all the conventions of friendship. He has just shared a meal with Jesus and now greets him with a kiss, a sign of friendship.[615] He has perverted that sign into a signal for the armed posse to seize Jesus (vv. 43-46). The inherent violence of the scene becomes evident when a bystander draws his sword

and cuts off the ear of the high priest's slave (v. 47). The other Gospels' account of the arrest assume that one of Jesus' disciples was responsible for striking the man, and they have Jesus heal the man and instruct his followers not to use such violence (cf. Matt 26:51-52; Luke 22:50; the Gospel of John attributes the deed to Peter, John 18:10-11). Mark's version has no such connection with the disciples. The episode is the type of

615. Rabbinic sources depict the kiss of Esau in Gen 33:4 as a false sign of brotherly love (*Gen. Rab.* 5.71*b*). See Gnilka, *Das Evangelium nach Markus*, 2:269.

random violence that breaks out among an armed, angry crowd.[616]

Jesus describes the crowd as a kind of posse that might go in search of "bandits" (v. 48). The term translated "bandit" (ληστής *lēstēs*) refers to violent, armed men who prey on others or who form the nucleus of armed resistance to Roman policies. Josephus describes bands of robbers ravaging the Syrian frontier prior to Herod the Great's rise to power.[617] Jesus has charged the religious leaders with making the Temple a den of "bandits" (11:17). The term will appear again in the passion narrative, describing those crucified with Jesus (15:27).[618] The absurdity of treating Jesus as though he belonged to this class of person is immediately evident. Jesus is no bandit. People know that they can find him in the Temple teaching (v. 49). Readers know that the authorities are arresting him in secret because they fear the response of the crowds who had listened to him with enthusiasm. The reaction of the bystander indicates that the authorities' fears were not entirely unfounded.

Jesus' remark, "But let the scriptures be fulfilled" (v. 49), indicates that his arrest by a crowd as though he were a bandit is part of the divine plan, although Mark does not indicate which passage of Scripture he has in mind. Isaiah 53:12 describes the suffering servant as one who "was numbered with the transgressors."[619] Some inter-

preters take the reference to apply to the flight of the disciples (v. 50), which Jesus has already predicted by alluding to Scripture (Zech 13:7, cited in v. 27).[620]

The Gethsemane scene ends with the account of a young man who flees naked (vv. 51-52). This peculiar episode has generated many fanciful explanations, including the legend in an apocryphal fragment known as the *Secret Gospel of Mark*, in which Jesus raises a young man from the dead and is in the process of initiating him into the mysteries of the kingdom when he is arrested,[621] or the view that the young man represents a "cameo" appearance of the author. Others have noted a parallel to Joseph's flight from Potiphar's wife, leaving his garments in her hand (Gen 39:12-13; later tradition presumed that he had fled naked).[622] Since Mark has used the detail about the sword to illustrate the violence of the situation (v. 47), this episode probably continues that motif: The disciples have all fled, so when the young man attempts to follow Jesus, he is in danger of being dragged off by the mob, and he escapes only because he is wearing a linen toga-like garment, which comes off in their hands as he flees. His flight shows that the disciples are in grave danger as well. The crowd is so excited that they will seize anyone who appears to be a follower of Jesus.[623]

---

616. The swordsman must have belonged to a group other than the disciples or the arresting party. See Brown, *The Death of the Messiah*, 266-67.

617. Josephus *The Jewish War* 1.10.5; sec. 205. When Herod died, Simon of Perea took a crown for himself, collected such a band, and burned the palace in Jericho (ibid., 2.42.2; sec. 57).

618. See Brown, *The Death of the Messiah*, 283-84. For a general discussion of attempts to use the passion narrative to imply that Jesus was associated with the revolutionary ideology of some groups of peasant rebels, see ibid., 679-93.

619. For other allusions to Isaiah 53 in the passion narrative, see Marcus, *Way of the Lord*, 189.

620. Ibid., 153.

621. See H. Merkel, "The Secret Gospel of Mark," in Wilhelm Schneemelcher, ed., *Gospels and Related Writings*, volume 1 of *The New Testament Apocrypha*, rev. ed., trans. R. McL. Wilson (Louisville: Westminster/John Knox, 1991) 106-9.

622. See *Testament of Joseph* 8:3. See also Gundry, *Mark*, 881.

623. See the detailed survey of all the hypotheses for a symbolic reference in Brown, *The Death of the Messiah*, 294-303. Brown emphasizes the biting irony implied in using this story to highlight the flight of Jesus' disciples. The disciples once left everything to follow Jesus (10:28). Now they must leave everything to escape arrest.

REFLECTIONS

Mark emphasizes the injustice and violence of the arrest in Gethsemane. An armed posse, led by one of the Twelve, is sent by the chief priest, the scribes, and the elders to arrest Jesus. The story illustrates the random violence that breaks out when an angry mob apprehends a criminal. Although Jesus points out the absurdity of treating him as though he were a robber, the crowd follows its own logic, which does not perceive the difference between chasing a criminal and someone who teaches God's Word in the Temple. The crowd will reappear during the trial before Pilate to clamor for Jesus' death. The random violence that breaks out, regardless of the victim, first against the high priest's slave, then against a young follower of Jesus, shows that the danger of crowds' turning hostile is always a reality.

Jesus has renounced entirely exercising power on his own behalf. The random violence and injustice of crowds who have been incited against a person or group are pressing realities in urban settings. Jesus displays an important role for the churches in riot-torn areas. They must speak out publicly against the violence and injustice. They must speak for the innocent victims of this violence. The churches should challenge their own members whenever they claim that crowd demonstrations and threats of violence are the way to social reform.

Mark 14:53-65, Trial Before the Sanhedrin

NIV

53They took Jesus to the high priest, and all the chief priests, elders and teachers of the law came together. 54Peter followed him at a distance, right into the courtyard of the high priest. There he sat with the guards and warmed himself at the fire.

55The chief priests and the whole Sanhedrin were looking for evidence against Jesus so that they could put him to death, but they did not find any. 56Many testified falsely against him, but their statements did not agree.

57Then some stood up and gave this false testimony against him: 58"We heard him say, 'I will destroy this man-made temple and in three days will build another, not made by man.'" 59Yet even then their testimony did not agree.

60Then the high priest stood up before them and asked Jesus, "Are you not going to answer? What is this testimony that these men are bringing against you?" 61But Jesus remained silent and gave no answer.

Again the high priest asked him, "Are you the Christ,*a* the Son of the Blessed One?"

62"I am," said Jesus. "And you will see the Son of Man sitting at the right hand of the Mighty One and coming on the clouds of heaven."

63The high priest tore his clothes. "Why do we need any more witnesses?" he asked. 64"You have heard the blasphemy. What do you think?"

They all condemned him as worthy of death. 65Then some began to spit at him; they blindfolded him, struck him with their fists, and said, "Prophesy!" And the guards took him and beat him.

a61 Or Messiah

NRSV

53They took Jesus to the high priest; and all the chief priests, the elders, and the scribes were assembled. 54Peter had followed him at a distance, right into the courtyard of the high priest; and he was sitting with the guards, warming himself at the fire. 55Now the chief priests and the whole council were looking for testimony against Jesus to put him to death; but they found none. 56For many gave false testimony against him, and their testimony did not agree. 57Some stood up and gave false testimony against him, saying, 58"We heard him say, 'I will destroy this temple that is made with hands, and in three days I will build another, not made with hands.'" 59But even on this point their testimony did not agree. 60Then the high priest stood up before them and asked Jesus, "Have you no answer? What is it that they testify against you?" 61But he was silent and did not answer. Again the high priest asked him, "Are you the Messiah,*a* the Son of the Blessed One?" 62Jesus said, "I am; and

'you will see the Son of Man
   seated at the right hand of the Power,'
   and 'coming with the clouds of heaven.'"

63Then the high priest tore his clothes and said, "Why do we still need witnesses? 64You have heard his blasphemy! What is your decision?" All of them condemned him as deserving death. 65Some began to spit on him, to blindfold him, and to strike him, saying to him, "Prophesy!" The guards also took him over and beat him.

aOr the Christ

COMMENTARY

A notice that Peter has managed to follow Jesus into the high priest's courtyard where he is with the guards warming his hands sets the stage for the denial episode (v. 54). Mark follows his customary narrative pattern by inserting another story before returning to Peter, so that Jesus' testimony before the Sanhedrin has been concluded before Peter's denial takes place. Mark imagines that the room in which the trial takes place is above the courtyard (v. 66). However, there is no contact between those in the courtyard and those involved in the trial.[624]

The Sanhedrin proceedings pose a number of legal problems.[625] One problem lies in the lack of evidence for the procedures that might have governed the Sanhedrin in this period. Although the descriptions of Jesus' trial do not conform to legal practice in the Mishnah,[626] one cannot assume that the first-century Sanhedrin was governed by rabbinic law. Josephus concurs with the impression given in the Gospels that the Sanhedrin functioned as a court in death-penalty cases (Matt 26:59; Mark 15:1; Luke 22:66; John 11:47[627]). Since the province of Judea was under direct Roman rule, however, many scholars do not think that Jews would have been permitted to execute anyone without permission of the Roman prefect (as John 18:31 asserts). For example, Herod the Great needed to obtain the emperor's permission to execute his own sons on charges of treason,[628] whereas when Herod Antipas executed John the Baptist no formal charges were filed against him, since that judgment was under Antipas's jurisdiction. Thus many historians think that there

was never a formal trial of Jesus before the Sanhedrin. Rather, as John (18:12-14, 19-24) suggests, a group of the high priest's friends and advisors gathered to collect possible evidence against Jesus and prepare to turn him over to the Roman prefect. Even if the Sanhedrin could execute persons guilty of violating the Temple sanctuary or some other capital offense, they might not have done so in Jesus' case. From the reader's perspective, Mark has already identified Jesus as "Son of David." Trials that involve actual or alleged kingship must involve Caesar or his representative. In sum, the assertion that some members or even the Sanhedrin as a body were responsible for arresting, interrogating, and charging Jesus of Nazareth before Pilate remains the most plausible interpretation of the facts.[629]

Mark's version of the Sanhedrin proceedings has been formulated to demonstrate the injustice of the entire trial. Readers know that the chief priests, elders, and scribes have been determined to destroy Jesus for some time. They are responsible for interrogating Jesus during the night of his arrest and for formulating the charges against him (vv. 53-65) before a morning session with the Sanhedrin, which precedes the delivery of Jesus to Pilate (15:1).

Several witnesses give conflicting testimony concerning Jesus' sayings about the Temple. Some allege that Jesus claimed that he would destroy the Temple and miraculously replace it with the heavenly Temple (vv. 56-61 a). The contrast between "made with hands" and "not made with hands" was commonplace in ancient discussions of temples as sacred places. The gods and goddesses were said not to require places made with hands. Jews distinguished God's dwelling in heaven from pagan idols, which were "made with hands" (cf. Acts 17:24-25). The Gospel of John interprets this saying as an allusion to the risen Christ as the Temple (John 2:19-22), attributing the saying to Jesus himself. Mark's version, presented as the testimony of false witnesses, fits the mold of the claims of messianic pretenders, around the time of the Jewish revolt, who told

---

624. Robert H. Gundry, *Mark: A Commentary on His Apology for the Cross* (Grand Rapids: Eerdmans, 1993) 887-88, resolves this problem by suggesting that the conclusion of v. 65, "the guards received him with blows," implies that Jesus was brought down into the courtyard where Peter was warming himself with the guards and that Jesus' reappearance provoked the questions put to Peter.

625. Raymond E. Brown, *The Death of the Messiah: From Gethsemane to the Grave. A Commentary on the Passion Narratives in the Four Gospels*, vol. 2 (Garden City, N.Y.: Doubleday, 1994) 328-97, provides a thorough survey and discussion of the evidence.

626. Ibid., 343-63.

627. See also Josephus *Antiquities of the Jews* 14.9.3; sec. 167.

628. Their deaths were part of a complex struggle over succession among the wives and sons of Herod the Great. An earlier trial of two of Herod's sons before the emperor concluded with dramatic pleas for reconciliation. Josephus notes the feigned pleasure of another brother, Antipater, when the accused were spared. See ibid., 16.4.5; sec. 257. See also Richard Fenn, *The Death of Herod: An Essay in the Sociology of Religion* (Cambridge: Cambridge University Press, 1992) 58-70.

629. So Brown, *The Death of the Messiah*, 371-72, who suggests that the Jews probably could have executed Jesus on allegations of religious impropriety but made a prudent judgment to turn him over to the Romans, so that if the crowds did protest, the Sanhedrin would not be responsible.

the crowds that they would repeat some ancient miracle. Both destroying the existing Temple and bringing in the heavenly Temple would have to be accomplished by God's power.[630] According to 2 Esdr 10:54, no building constructed by human hands can stand in the city of the Most High. First-century Jews apparently did not expect that the Messiah would be responsible for either destroying the old Temple or for establishing the new one. God will provide the Temple in the last days,[631] which, unlike its predecessors, will never be destroyed. Even in their confused form, such charges do not constitute serious evidence against Jesus.

The question of how Mark understood the accusation to be false is more complex.[632] Lack of agreement among witnesses (v. 59) should have led to dismissal of all the testimony (Deut 17:6).[633] When the crowd mocks Jesus with this saying, they understand it as his claim to destroy and rebuild the Temple in three days (15:29), and they make no reference to the heavenly Temple. Mark's readers know that Jesus has predicted that the Temple will be destroyed (13:2). If the Gospel was written after 70 CE, readers also know that Titus had destroyed the Temple and that it was not rebuilt.[634] Insofar as Mark has a positive understanding of "I will build . . . " it must refer to the community that comes into being through Jesus' death.[635]

Jesus refuses to answer his accusers. Since their testimony is false and conflicting, an answer from him would hardly seem possible. Silence before accusers also belongs to the general description of the suffering righteous (Isa 53:7). "Answer nothing at all" indicates that Jesus will not cooperate with his accusers in any way. He adopts the same posture in the trial before Pilate (15:5).[636]

The high priest formulates a charge that uses christological affirmations about Jesus as evidence for blasphemy (vv. 61b-64), a charge that did carry the death penalty in the Jewish Law. Historians are quick to point out that it is not blasphemous for a person to claim to be "anointed by God" or to be "son of God" even if the individual is wrong in saying that he is God's agent or "son of David" as a human claimant to royal authority. Mark certainly expects his readers to recognize the Christian meaning of "messiah" and "Son of God" (i.e., "Son of the Blessed One"). They know that the Messiah is greater than David (12:35-37)[637] and that God has testified that this is God's Son (1:11; 9:7). This passage exhibits Mark's tendency to use a series of titles to describe the identity of Jesus. Since Jesus openly admits to being Son of God, the reserve attached to that confession during his ministry no longer remains. By allowing himself to be crucified, the Son of God exhibits the paradox of suffering powerlessness. None of the titles can be used appropriately for Jesus in isolation from the cross. God is named in an allusive way in both the high priest's question and Jesus' response (v. 62) in the mention of the divine attributes of God, "blessed" and "power." Since these expressions are not usually surrogates for the divine name, Brown suggests that Mark or his source created them to represent the linguistic convention of pious Jewish speech.[638]

The OT pattern of the psalms of lament and the portrayal of the suffering righteous requires the eventual exaltation of the sufferer. Mark has not let the reader forget that the story does not end on the cross. True to form, Jesus points beyond the present to the future appearance of the Son of Man in glory (v. 62; Dan 7:13). Readers know that for Jesus' enemies the coming of the Son of Man heralds divine judgment (Mark 8:38). By not answering the false accusers, Jesus turns the trial into the evidence to be presented against his enemies when the Son of Man appears at the right hand of God.[639]

Christian readers who identify the mysterious figure at God's right hand as Jesus and who

---

630. See *Jub.* 1:17-29; *1 Enoch* 90:28-29.

631. See Brown, *The Death of the Messiah,* 441-42.

632. See ibid., 444-60.

633. See 11QTemple 61:9; Gundry, *Mark,* 903.

634. The apocalyptic discourse in 13:5-23 separated the profanation of the Temple (v. 14) from the coming of the Son of Man. A saying that reported in Mark 14:58, if it was understood as being from Jesus, might have played into the hands of the false prophets against whom Jesus spoke. See Brown, *The Death of the Messiah,* 452-53.

635. Since all references to the Temple are depicted in the light of the events surrounding it, which occurred after Jesus' death until its destruction, Brown suggests a modest historical element in this tradition: Some prophetic word or deed that referred to the destruction of the Temple was part of the decision that Jesus deserved death (ibid., 460).

636. See ibid., 464. Since Mark does not cite any of the possible OT allusions to the sufferer who is silent before his accusers, Brown suggests that the historical memory of Jesus' silence existed before psalm texts were found to explain its significance.

637. See ibid., 467.

638. Ibid., 470.

639. See Rudolph Pesch, *Das Markusevangelium I. Teil,* HTKNT II (Freiburg: Herder, 1977) 2:437-39.

understand the title "Son of God" to be a claim to divine authority later found themselves accused of blasphemy. The Gospel of John retrojects the charge of "making himself equal to God" into the ministry of Jesus (e.g., John 5:18-30).

Proleptic reminders of the Son of Man in glory always lead back to the passion in Mark. The high priest tears his garments, a gesture of extreme grief (Gen 37:34; 2 Sam 1:11-12), before inciting the group to render their judgment against Jesus by claiming that he has just uttered blasphemy (vv. 63-64a). If Jesus' words are taken in their most prosaic sense, he cannot be accused of blasphemy. At best, he would appear to be a misguided prophet or rabble-rouser who thinks that he is God's agent to restore the Davidic kingship. The prophecy concerning the Son of Man's coming with the clouds would then indicate that he expects angelic forces from heaven to come and install him on the throne. However, Christian readers recognize that Jesus *is* the heavenly Son of Man who will come with God's power and authority. They understand "Messiah" and "Son of God" not as designations for charismatic political leaders but as expressions of Jesus' role in God's plan of salvation. When Jesus is confessed by believers as the exalted Messiah, Son of God, and Son of Man, then such words appear blasphemous to unbelieving Jews.[640]

After condemning Jesus to death (v. 64b), members of the group subject him to torture. Spitting and scourging continue the affliction of Jesus as righteous sufferer (Isa 50:6-7).[641] An ironic challenge to Jesus to prophesy (v. 65) mocks the judgment oracle that he has just spoken against his enemies (v. 62b). At the same time, the behavior of Jesus' enemies shows the reader that Jesus' own predictions of what would happen to him during the passion are true. He has been delivered to the chief priests and scribes, condemned to death, mocked, and spat upon (cf. 10:32). The Roman trial of Jesus will conclude with a similar scene of mockery, focusing on the charge against Jesus at that proceeding: "king of the Jews" (15:16-20). John 18:22 has an attendant slap Jesus when he responds to the high priest's question in an insolent way, a detail that fits the context of this episode. It may have been transformed into a mockery scene by Mark in order to bring out the theological significance of the Sanhedrin trial.[642]

640. See Brown, *The Death of the Messiah,* 526-47. The overall impact of Jesus' ministry provides examples of actions that border on blasphemy, if blasphemy is understood as claiming for oneself power that properly belongs only to God (546-47).

641. See Joel Marcus, *The Way of the Lord: Christological Exegesis of the Old Testament in the Gospel of Mark* (Minneapolis: Fortress, 1992) 189.

642. See Brown, *The Death of the Messiah,* 573-85.

REFLECTIONS

1. Mark uses the Sanhedrin trial to exhibit the malice and disregard for justice on the part of Jesus' enemies. Since Jesus has accepted the fact that they will condemn him, he does not offer a response to the false accusers. He does not attempt to save his life.

Yet Jesus cannot let the trial go on without some word. He accepts the statement that he claims to be Messiah and Son of God. The judgment oracle that follows (v. 62) names the evil of condemning an innocent person to death. Those who participate in this charade of justice and concern to protect God against blasphemy have sealed their own condemnation before the Son of Man.

2. Justice can be as difficult to obtain today as it was in Jesus' time. Jesus faces the hostile court alone. To them he is an outsider, a Galilean prophet with a dangerous popularity among the people, but someone of no significance. His death will end the business. Christians should be concerned whether outsiders, poor people, and the like receive justice in their societies. In too many places, false arrest, imprisonment, or execution of innocent persons or of persons who have not had a fair hearing are still dreadful realities. As rising crime rates lead people to demand mandatory, swift sentencing, Christians should ask themselves whether such a situation serves justice or increases the risk to innocent victims.

Mark 14:66-72, Peter Denies Jesus

NIV

66While Peter was below in the courtyard, one of the servant girls of the high priest came by. 67When she saw Peter warming himself, she looked closely at him.

"You also were with that Nazarene, Jesus," she said.

68But he denied it. "I don't know or understand what you're talking about," he said, and went out into the entryway.[a]

69When the servant girl saw him there, she said again to those standing around, "This fellow is one of them." 70Again he denied it.

After a little while, those standing near said to Peter, "Surely you are one of them, for you are a Galilean."

71He began to call down curses on himself, and he swore to them, "I don't know this man you're talking about."

72Immediately the rooster crowed the second time.[b] Then Peter remembered the word Jesus had spoken to him: "Before the rooster crows twice[c] you will disown me three times." And he broke down and wept.

[a]68 Some early manuscripts entryway and the rooster crowed
[b]72 Some early manuscripts do not have the second time.
[c]72 Some early manuscripts do not have twice.

NRSV

66While Peter was below in the courtyard, one of the servant-girls of the high priest came by. 67When she saw Peter warming himself, she stared at him and said, "You also were with Jesus, the man from Nazareth." 68But he denied it, saying, "I do not know or understand what you are talking about." And he went out into the forecourt.[a] Then the cock crowed.[b] 69And the servant-girl, on seeing him, began again to say to the bystanders, "This man is one of them." 70But again he denied it. Then after a little while the bystanders again said to Peter, "Certainly you are one of them; for you are a Galilean." 71But he began to curse, and he swore an oath, "I do not know this man you are talking about." 72At that moment the cock crowed for the second time. Then Peter remembered that Jesus had said to him, "Before the cock crows twice, you will deny me three times." And he broke down and wept.

[a]Or gateway [b]Other ancient authorities lack Then the cock crowed

COMMENTARY

Peter's three denials before the cock crows twice demonstrate that another of Jesus' prophetic statements have come true (v. 30). Each accusation of being one of Jesus' followers brings a more vehement denial: Peter claims not to understand what the servant girl is talking about (v. 68); denies being one of Jesus' followers (v. 70); swears an oath that he does not know the person they are talking about (v. 71). The oath, a curse against himself if he is lying, introduces the explicit denial that he does not know Jesus.[643] In Mark's version of the events, Peter leaves

the "inner hall" ($\alpha\dot{\upsilon}\lambda\acute{\eta}$ aulē) for the "forecourt" ($\pi\rho o\alpha\dot{\upsilon}\lambda\iota o\nu$ proaulion) after the first confrontation and denial. The movement indicates his desire to escape. Yet he does not immediately leave the area.[644] The second denial is reported indirectly. The same servant girl makes the accusation to others standing around. By using the imperfect tense of the verb for "deny," Mark indicates that Peter now repeatedly denies being a follower of Jesus. The first denial is followed by the cock's crowing (v. 68; cf. NIV footnote). Some time passes between the denials to the maidservant and the charge by one of the bystanders that Peter must be one of Jesus' disciples because he is a

643. See Pesch, Das Markusevangelium, 2:450-51. Brown, The Death of the Messiah, 604, denies that an oath/curse formula is intended. Joachim Gnilka, Das Evangelium nach Markus. 1 Teilband Mk 1–8, 26, EKKNT II (Zurich: Benziger, 1978) 2:293, favors supplying Jesus as the object of the verb translated "to curse."

644. See Brown, The Death of the Messiah, 601-2.

Galilean (v. 70). Peter apparently does not notice the first crowing, but the second reminds him of what Jesus had said. "And he broke down and wept" (v. 72).

REFLECTIONS

1. When Peter breaks down weeping, he illustrates that he recognizes what he has done.[645] Although Jesus' prophetic word and his warning to pray have not prevented Peter from denying Jesus, they do provide the basis for insight and repentance. Unlike Jesus' enemies, who have become hardened in their determination to see him dead, disciples can still be redeemed.

2. Peter's denials exhibit the ability of repeated interrogation and fear to overwhelm a person. Mark tells the reader that Peter is standing with the guards (v. 54). When Mark's readers are subjected to persecution, they may face similar questions. Faced with a barrage of hostile questions, they, like Peter, may deny any knowledge of Jesus.

Most Christians today face the problem of denial in very different circumstances. Religious toleration seems to mean that religion is something one does not bring up unless asked and then only reluctantly. Or Christians may stand by and let others be subject to the verbal abuse of racism, sexism, or other forms of injustice. They may let others mock religious belief in their presence without responding. Such polite silences may do more to destroy the possibility of faith for others than Peter's denials in the high priest's courtyard.

645. Mary Ann Tolbert, *Sowing the Gospel: Mark's World in Literary-Historical Perspective* (Minneapolis: Fortress, 1989) 218, argues that there is no indication in Mark that Peter has had a change of heart. She suggests that his sorrow should be compared to that of the rich young man who walks away from Jesus (10:22).

Mark 15:1-20, Jesus Before Pilate

NIV

15 Very early in the morning, the chief priests, with the elders, the teachers of the law and the whole Sanhedrin, reached a decision. They bound Jesus, led him away and handed him over to Pilate.

²"Are you the king of the Jews?" asked Pilate.

"Yes, it is as you say," Jesus replied.

³The chief priests accused him of many things. ⁴So again Pilate asked him, "Aren't you going to answer? See how many things they are accusing you of."

⁵But Jesus still made no reply, and Pilate was amazed.

⁶Now it was the custom at the Feast to release a prisoner whom the people requested. ⁷A man called Barabbas was in prison with the insurrectionists who had committed murder in the uprising. ⁸The crowd came up and asked Pilate to do for them what he usually did.

⁹"Do you want me to release to you the king of the Jews?" asked Pilate, ¹⁰knowing it was out

NRSV

15 As soon as it was morning, the chief priests held a consultation with the elders and scribes and the whole council. They bound Jesus, led him away, and handed him over to Pilate. ²Pilate asked him, "Are you the King of the Jews?" He answered him, "You say so." ³Then the chief priests accused him of many things. ⁴Pilate asked him again, "Have you no answer? See how many charges they bring against you." ⁵But Jesus made no further reply, so that Pilate was amazed.

6Now at the festival he used to release a prisoner for them, anyone for whom they asked. ⁷Now a man called Barabbas was in prison with the rebels who had committed murder during the insurrection. ⁸So the crowd came and began to ask Pilate to do for them according to his custom. ⁹Then he answered them, "Do you want me to release for you the King of the Jews?" ¹⁰For he realized that it was out of jealousy that the chief priests had handed him over. ¹¹But the chief priests stirred up the crowd to have him release

NIV

of envy that the chief priests had handed Jesus over to him. [11]But the chief priests stirred up the crowd to have Pilate release Barabbas instead.

[12]"What shall I do, then, with the one you call the king of the Jews?" Pilate asked them.

[13]"Crucify him!" they shouted.

[14]"Why? What crime has he committed?" asked Pilate.

But they shouted all the louder, "Crucify him!" [15]Wanting to satisfy the crowd, Pilate released Barabbas to them. He had Jesus flogged, and handed him over to be crucified.

[16]The soldiers led Jesus away into the palace (that is, the Praetorium) and called together the whole company of soldiers. [17]They put a purple robe on him, then twisted together a crown of thorns and set it on him. [18]And they began to call out to him, "Hail, king of the Jews!" [19]Again and again they struck him on the head with a staff and spit on him. Falling on their knees, they paid homage to him. [20]And when they had mocked him, they took off the purple robe and put his own clothes on him. Then they led him out to crucify him.

NRSV

Barabbas for them instead. [12]Pilate spoke to them again, "Then what do you wish me to do[a] with the man you call[b] the King of the Jews?" [13]They shouted back, "Crucify him!" [14]Pilate asked them, "Why, what evil has he done?" But they shouted all the more, "Crucify him!" [15]So Pilate, wishing to satisfy the crowd, released Barabbas for them; and after flogging Jesus, he handed him over to be crucified.

16Then the soldiers led him into the courtyard of the palace (that is, the governor's headquarters[c]); and they called together the whole cohort. [17]And they clothed him in a purple cloak; and after twisting some thorns into a crown, they put it on him. [18]And they began saluting him, "Hail, King of the Jews!" [19]They struck his head with a reed, spat upon him, and knelt down in homage to him. [20]After mocking him, they stripped him of the purple cloak and put his own clothes on him. Then they led him out to crucify him.

[a]Other ancient authorities read *what should I do*
[b]Other ancient authorities lack *the man you call*
[c]Gk *the praetorium*

COMMENTARY

The trial before Pilate is as complex as the earlier trial by the Sanhedrin. Historical details, legend, and imagery drawn from lament psalms and from the suffering servant passages in Isaiah have been worked together in the narrative. The proceedings against Jesus were initiated by others, but he could be crucified only by order of the Roman prefect, Pontius Pilate. When Judea was established as a Roman province after the removal of Herod the Great's son Archaeleus in 6 CE, a prefect (a governor of equestrian rank) was sent to administer its affairs. The governor possessed the *imperium* from Caesar, including the right to pass the death sentence on criminals.[646] Pilate was accustomed to dealing with Caiaphas and other members of the Jewish aristocracy who made up

the Sanhedrin.[647] As prefect, Pilate was free to dispose of such a case in any way he chose, but would have been unlikely to bother with investigating charges against an obscure Galilean. Those who formed the governing council of Jerusalem were important persons whose judgment he would have every reason to accept.

As Jewish writers describe him, Pilate was not sympathetic to the Jews whom he governed.[648] When his troops brought Roman standards into Jerusalem in violation of Jewish Law, crowds gathered to protest before Pilate's palace at Caesarea and sat there for five days. The standards were removed only after the crowds, when threat-

---

646. See Josephus *The Jewish War* 2.8.1; sec. 117; *Antiquities of the Jews* 18.1. See also Brown, *The Death of the Messiah*, 336.

647. Caiaphas remained high priest during the entire time that Pilate was prefect, which suggests that he had informal working ties with Pilate. See Brown, *The Death of the Messiah*, 372.

648. Philo *Legatio* 38, quotes a letter by Agrippa I, who describes Pilate as "a man of inflexible disposition, harsh and obdurate."

ened by Roman troops, displayed a willingness to be slaughtered rather than abandon their protest.[649] On another occasion, when the wealthy aristocrats in Jerusalem would not pay for building the city's aqueduct, Pilate seized the money needed from the Temple treasury. When the crowds there rioted, Pilate sent disguised troops into the crowd to beat the rioters with clubs. Many people died from the beatings, while others were trampled in the ensuing rush to escape.[650] Pilate was also said to be friendly with Sejanus, an adviser to the emperor Tiberias, who was known to be hostile to the Jews.

These accounts give historians no reason to think that Pilate would have been at all hesitant to execute Jesus. Pilate, who condemned Jesus, was more likely to have exhibited contempt than concern. Nor would the charge "king of the Jews" have been a matter of serious concern. Technically, after the death of Herod the Great, the Jews had no king. When the Romans installed his sons over parts of Herod's old kingdom, they explicitly refused to confer Herod's title "king" on any of them.

Mark presents Pilate in a more positive light than does Josephus by placing the Barabbas episode at the center of the trial before Pilate (vv. 6-15). Mark creates the impression that Pilate considers Jesus innocent. When Jesus' enemies hand him over to Pilate, they are required to state some charge against him. Although the charge that Jesus claimed to be "king of the Jews" was not made during the Sanhedrin trial, Mark's readers know that this title was used by the crowds when they welcomed Jesus' arrival in Jerusalem as the advent of the kingdom of David (11:10); readers also know that Jesus does not consider "Son of David" an appropriate description of who he is (12:35-37). However, when charged by the high priest, accepts the titles "Messiah" and "Son of God," both of which can be understood as designations for someone claiming to restore the Davidic kingship (Ps 2:7).

In the earlier trial Jesus refused to answer the false accusations made against him (14:60-61a). He continues to do so when charged before Pilate (15:4-5). This detail again evokes the image of Jesus as the suffering servant (Isa 38:13-15; 53:7). Jesus' refusal to offer a defense makes Pilate's presumption that Jesus is innocent all the more surprising, since he already has the judgment of guilty from persons who usually speak for the Jewish people as a whole. The social dynamics of the time would make Jesus' execution by the prefect a foregone conclusion.[651]

Mark never has Pilate pronounce a verdict in the case, although the offer to exchange Jesus for Barabbas suggests that Jesus has been found guilty. (Some historians point out that Roman legal procedure automatically proclaimed guilty a defendant who offered no defense to the charges brought against him or her.) Barabbas is guilty of inciting the same type of rebellious violence of which Jesus stands accused (v. 7). Thus the episode results in the exchange of an innocent man for a guilty one. Writing in Rome at the end of the first century, Josephus tells his readers that the Jewish rebellion was fomented by bandits, like Barabbas, who gained control of Judea and Jerusalem. The internal struggles for power between factional leaders, however, further weakened the city's defenses.[652] The Roman historian Tacitus also describes the internal strife in the city.[653] Whether or not Mark's Gospel was written in Syro-palestine during the Jewish war, readers were probably familiar with the divisive struggles between such revolutionary leaders. It was as a result of these struggles that the Jewish aristocracy lost control of the city and the Temple. So by inciting the crowds to demand the release of Barabbas, the Jewish authorities are ironically contributing to their own downfall.[654]

Since Barabbas was part of a bandit group and not a populist leader, Jesus' accusers have to incite

651. This observation does not mean that Pilate is being "whitewashed" by Mark, but those who hold that Mark paints a negative portrait of the governor because he does not release a person he states is innocent fail to recognize the asymmetry between Jesus and his accusers. Legal proceedings in the ancient world generally favored the wealthy and well born.

652. Josephus *The Jewish War* 5.1,1-5 secs. 2-35.

653. Tacitus *Histories* 5.12.

654. Gundry's suggestion that the high priests incited the crowd to ask for Barabbas rather than Jesus by pointing out Barabbas's proven reputation as a freedom fighter in contrast to Jesus' ambiguous position on imperial rule (12:13-17) imports the political climate of the decade before the Jewish revolt back into the time of Jesus. See Gundry, *Mark,* 937.

649. Josephus *The Jewish War* 2.9.2-3; secs. 169-74; *Antiquities of the Jews* 18.3.1; secs. 55-59. Some historians suggest that he did so only because members of the Jewish aristocracy were concerned about loss of crops if the people remained away from the fields during a key agricultural season. See also Martin Goodman, *The Ruling Class of Judea: The Origins of the Jewish Revolt Against Rome A.D. 66–70* (Cambridge: Cambridge University Press, 1987) 174.

650. Josephus *The Jewish War* 2.9, 2-4; secs. 169-71; *Antiquities of the Jews* 18.3. 1-3; secs. 55-64; Philo *Legatio* secs. 299-305.

the crowd to demand Barabbas's release (v. 11). Mark's suggestion that the crowd took their cue from the high priests (v. 11) does strike a note of realism. The Jewish crowds were notoriously fickle. After Herod the Great had put a symbol of an eagle above the gate of the Temple, some young men, promised beatitude by their teachers if they died as martyrs, and with popular support, tore down and destroyed the offensive symbol. Close to forty of them were caught, however, and when Herod called for their execution, the crowds, fearing a greater slaughter, quickly withdrew their support. Thus the young men and their teachers were executed.[655]

There is no evidence of the granting of amnesty as a general custom outside the New Testament (v. 8).[656] Pilate's legal powers, which permitted him to determine how he would dispose of subjects who were not Roman citizens, would permit him to release any prisoner as well. Mark or his source may have converted a story about a unique incident or an occasional instance into such a custom.[657] Nor is there any reason to think that Pilate would choose to cater to the wishes of the crowd if they had not reflected those of the Jewish leaders. Since Mark wishes to make it clear that the Roman prefect thought Jesus innocent (v. 14), he needs a reason to explain why Pilate handed Jesus over to be crucified (v. 15). Since Pilate is acting as a prefect charged with keeping order in a small province, there is no reason to present the case against Jesus as though it conformed to a full imperial trial on charges of treason, such as the accusations Herod the Great brought against his sons, for example. Pilate may not have acted with much concern for Jesus, hardly surprising given other reports about the governor, but neither has he acted illegally in condemning Jesus to death.[658]

It is difficult to determine what Jesus' exchange with Pilate is intended to convey to Mark's reader. His silence in the face of many charges (vv. 4-5) continues Jesus' earlier action before the Sanhedrin (14:60-61a). Jesus' answer to Pilate's ques-

tion, which contains a possible christological title "King of the Jews," is more ambiguous than that given in the earlier trial (v. 62a). Jesus has neither denied nor accepted the assertion outright. Nor does Mark explain what amazed Pilate about Jesus' conduct at the proceedings (v. 5).[659] Readers may be intended to associate Jesus' conduct with Pilate's conclusion that the case was brought out of envy (v. 10).[660] No one would expect the Roman governor to consider anything but Roman interests in dealing with such a case.

Being scourged, spat upon, and mocked fulfill Jesus' prediction (10:33-34) as well as echo the sufferings of the righteous servant (Isa 50:6-7). Just as the Sanhedrin trial concluded with mockery of Jesus as prophet (14:65), so also the Roman trial concludes with mockery of the "king of the Jews." Jesus had predicted that he would be mocked by the Gentiles (10:34). Either Mark or his source has elaborated the story of mockery by soldiers to highlight the irony of the royal theme (clearly, a whole cohort of six hundred or more men was probably not involved [v. 16]). They dress Jesus as a mock king (v. 17). Beating, spitting, and sarcastic homage show the reader the disdain the soldiers have for this Jew (vv. 18-19). They pretend to hail him as though he were Caesar.[661] He is no threat to imperial power.[662]

The location of the Praetorium in first-century Jerusalem is unclear.[663] Normally, the term applied to the residence of the Roman governor, which was where he passed judgment. Since Pilate's official residence was in Caesarea, Philo and Josephus assumed that he took up residence in Herod's royal place near the modern Jaffa gate when in Jerusalem, and Josephus depicts him as going into the theater to give judgment. Some archaeologists have identified an area of stone

---

655. See Josephus *The Jewish Wars* 1.33.3. See also Fenn, *Death of Herod,* 122.

656. See E. Schürer, *A History of the Jewish People in the Time of Jesus Christ,* rev. ed. (Edinburgh: T. & T. Clark, 1986) 1:385.

657. See Gundry, *Mark,* 935.

658. See Brown, *The Death of the Messiah,* 711-22.

659. See ibid., 733-34. Brown suggests that Pilate was amazed by Jesus' detachment from the proceedings. Elsewhere in the Gospel the verb *thaumazō* (θαυμάζω) designates uncomprehending amazement (5:20; 6:6)—i.e., Pilate will be "amazed" by the rapidity of Jesus' death (15:44).

660. Although this motivation hardly fits the immediate circumstances of Jesus' trial, it does fit the complexity of dynastic struggles in both Herodian and Roman imperial circles. First-century readers were certainly aware of the perilous situation created by envy among those who aspired to rule.

661. See Brown, *The Death of the Messiah,* 868.

662. The governor of Judea did not have legions at his disposal. Instead, they were stationed in Syria. The soldiers of Pilate's guard were local, non-Jewish recruits, possibly from Samaria. Consequently, in some of the episodes in which Pilate commands his troops to attack a Jewish crowd, the violence may reflect local hatred between the non-Jewish and Jewish inhabitants of the region.

663. See Brown, *The Death of the Messiah,* 705-10.

paving in the Fortress Antonia in the northwest corner of the Temple Mount as the location Josephus intended, and thus as the site of Jesus' trial as well. However, this pavement is from a later date.

REFLECTIONS

1. Because the charge of having killed Jesus became the basis for centuries of Christian persecution of Jews, many modern historians focus on Pilate's responsibility for the death of Jesus, going so far as to assert that the Jews were never involved in the death of Jesus. This claim would be plausible only if the movement around Jesus was considerably more incendiary than any of the evidence suggests. Mark's narrative never claims that the Jews were responsible. Mark's readers would recognize that jealousies and struggles for power made the imperial court and other governing circles dangerous for anyone. They knew what later readers forgot: that Jesus was the victim of local struggles for power. Mark has made it clear that a particular group orchestrated the death of Jesus much as the death of John the Baptist was orchestrated by Herodias.

2. Responsibility for the death of Jesus lies at the feet of those who participate in the deceit and power politics that permit the casual sacrifice of innocent persons. Such phenomena have not vanished from our world. The mocking cynicism of the Roman soldiers shows how depersonalizing the victim increases the violence in a society. The Barabbas incident suggests another severe consequence of the corruption introduced by power politics: People can no longer distinguish the guilty and dangerous person from the innocent. They may not even care whether a person is innocent or guilty.

3. In a symbolic sense, the Barabbas episode depicts the soteriology associated with Jesus' death. The Son of Man gives his life as a "ransom" (10:45). In this case, his life is exchanged for that of a sinner.

The two images used for the way in which Jesus' death has brought salvation in Mark (paying a ransom [10:45] and the blood of a covenant offering [14:24] are difficult for Christians today. When we think of "ransom," we think of kidnapped executives, diplomats, travelers, and the like. The question of "paying ransom" is tangled up with the issue of dealing with criminals. That context makes it appear that Jesus' death would be a kind of extortion. Mark 10:45 speaks of Jesus coming to serve and to offer his life as a ransom. He is not being compelled to pay because someone close to him has been kidnapped. Of course, ransom was a more common transaction in ancient societies. One was expected to rescue relatives from debt slavery or from captivity in war. Likewise, outside help is necessary to break the power of sin. Jesus' death provides that ransom for all human beings. Even before he was crucified, his life replaced that of a condemned man. The image of covenant sacrifice reminds us of another facet of salvation, a new relationship with God. On the human level, ransom is not permanent. Someone could fall into debt or be captured again. Jesus' self-offering on the cross will never be repeated. It has established a permanent covenant between humanity and God that can never be broken.

Mark 15:21-41, Jesus Is Crucified

NIV	NRSV
[21]A certain man from Cyrene, Simon, the father of Alexander and Rufus, was passing by on his	21They compelled a passer-by, who was coming in from the country, to carry his cross; it was

NIV

way in from the country, and they forced him to carry the cross. ²²They brought Jesus to the place called Golgotha (which means The Place of the Skull). ²³Then they offered him wine mixed with myrrh, but he did not take it. ²⁴And they crucified him. Dividing up his clothes, they cast lots to see what each would get.

²⁵It was the third hour when they crucified him. ²⁶The written notice of the charge against him read: THE KING OF THE JEWS. ²⁷They crucified two robbers with him, one on his right and one on his left.ᵃ ²⁹Those who passed by hurled insults at him, shaking their heads and saying, "So! You who are going to destroy the temple and build it in three days, ³⁰come down from the cross and save yourself!"

³¹In the same way the chief priests and the teachers of the law mocked him among themselves. "He saved others," they said, "but he can't save himself! ³²Let this Christ,ᵇ this King of Israel, come down now from the cross, that we may see and believe." Those crucified with him also heaped insults on him.

³³At the sixth hour darkness came over the whole land until the ninth hour. ³⁴And at the ninth hour Jesus cried out in a loud voice, *"Eloi, Eloi, lama sabachthani?"*—which means, "My God, my God, why have you forsaken me?"ᶜ

³⁵When some of those standing near heard this, they said, "Listen, he's calling Elijah."

³⁶One man ran, filled a sponge with wine vinegar, put it on a stick, and offered it to Jesus to drink. "Now leave him alone. Let's see if Elijah comes to take him down," he said.

³⁷With a loud cry, Jesus breathed his last.

³⁸The curtain of the temple was torn in two from top to bottom. ³⁹And when the centurion, who stood there in front of Jesus, heard his cry andᵈ saw how he died, he said, "Surely this man was the Sonᵉ of God!"

⁴⁰Some women were watching from a distance. Among them were Mary Magdalene, Mary the mother of James the younger and of Joses, and Salome. ⁴¹In Galilee these women had followed

ᵃ27 Some manuscripts *left, ²⁸and the scripture was fulfilled which says, "He was counted with the lawless ones"* (Isaiah 53:12) ᵇ32 Or *Messiah* ᶜ34 Psalm 22:1 ᵈ39 Some manuscripts do not have *heard his cry and* ᵉ39 Or *a son*

NRSV

Simon of Cyrene, the father of Alexander and Rufus. ²²Then they brought Jesusᵃ to the place called Golgotha (which means the place of a skull). ²³And they offered him wine mixed with myrrh; but he did not take it. ²⁴And they crucified him, and divided his clothes among them, casting lots to decide what each should take.

25It was nine o'clock in the morning when they crucified him. ²⁶The inscription of the charge against him read, "The King of the Jews." ²⁷And with him they crucified two bandits, one on his right and one on his left.ᵇ ²⁹Those who passed by derivedᶜ him, shaking their heads and saying, "Aha! You who would destroy the temple and build it in three days, ³⁰save yourself, and come down from the cross!" ³¹In the same way the chief priests, along with the scribes, were also mocking him among themselves and saying, "He saved others; he cannot save himself. ³²Let the Messiah,ᵈ the King of Israel, come down from the cross now, so that we may see and believe." Those who were crucified with him also taunted him.

33When it was noon, darkness came over the whole landᵉ until three in the afternoon. ³⁴At three o'clock Jesus cried out with a loud voice, "Eloi, Eloi, lema sabachthani?" which means, "My God, my God, why have you forsaken me?"ᶠ ³⁵When some of the bystanders heard it, they said, "Listen, he is calling for Elijah." ³⁶And someone ran, filled a sponge with sour wine, put it on a stick, and gave it to him to drink, saying, "Wait, let us see whether Elijah will come to take him down." ³⁷Then Jesus gave a loud cry and breathed his last. ³⁸And the curtain of the temple was torn in two, from top to bottom. ³⁹Now when the centurion, who stood facing him, saw that in this way heᵍ breathed his last, he said, "Truly this man was God's Son!"ʰ

40There were also women looking on from a distance; among them were Mary Magdalene, and Mary the mother of James the younger and of Joses, and Salome. ⁴¹These used to follow him and

ᵃGk *him* ᵇOther ancient authorities add verse 28, *And the scripture was fulfilled that says, "And he was counted among the lawless."* ᶜOr *blasphemed* ᵈOr *the Christ* ᵉOr *earth* ᶠOther ancient authorities read *made me a reproach* ᵍOther ancient authorities add *cried out and* ʰOr *a son of God*

NIV

him and cared for his needs. Many other women who had come up with him to Jerusalem were also there.

NRSV

provided for him when he was in Galilee; and there were many other women who had come up with him to Jerusalem.

COMMENTARY

The crucifixion of Jesus highlights the suffering and abandonment of the Son. The onlookers emphasize the powerlessness of Jesus by challenging him to liberate himself from the cross (vv. 30-32). At the same time, they remind Christian readers that the cross is the source of salvation. Stories of the persecuted righteous usually end with a scene of vindication, wherein their enemies are forced to recognize that the ones whom they persecuted are now exalted and that they, themselves, stand condemned by God (cf. Wis 5:1-16).[664] Mark's readers know that when the Son of Man is revealed as judge, his enemies will be condemned (14:62). The death of Jesus also brings an acknowledgment from another enemy, the centurion. He sees that Jesus is God's Son (v. 39).

15:21. The reference to Simon of Cyrene suggests that he is familiar to the reader, who would be expected to recognize Alexander and Rufus as well (v. 21).[665] Mark may have used this reference to Simon's sons to provide a reliable witness to the events that occur at the crucifixion, since Jesus' male disciples have all fled.[666] Although disciples were enjoined to "take up their cross" (8:34), Jesus does not do so (cf. John 19:17). Tradition often depicts Jesus as dragging the whole cross and falling under its weight. In fact, those sentenced to crucifixion carried only the cross bar.[667] Since Simon is said to have come into the city from the countryside, he is not associated with the crowds that had been present at the trial before Pilate or with those who had followed Jesus into the city. He has merely

been conscripted by the soldiers to carry the cross beam. How are readers to understand this detail? Is it an indication of how severely the abuse suffered during his trials has weakened Jesus?[668] Or is it an indication that Jesus is being accorded respect that would not have been shown to common criminals, like the bandits crucified with him?[669]

15:22. *Golgotha* is the Aramaic term for "skull." The more popular name, "Calvary," comes from the Latin term *calvaria.*

15:23. Wine mixed with myrrh was probably used as a narcotic (Prov 31:6 recommends strong drink for those who are dying). Jesus' refusal to drink the wine indicates that he is fully conscious throughout the crucifixion. He will not fall asleep at the crucial hour, as his disciples had done in Gethsemane. The detail may also be intended to underline the fact that Jesus dies in full possession of his powers, not as someone semiconscious and drugged.[670]

15:24. The soldiers cast lots for Jesus' clothing, echoing Ps 22:19. Several details in the crucifixion story, including Jesus' final words, are taken from that lament psalm.

15:25-32. Mark has filled in the narrative time between the nailing of Jesus to the cross and his death with an expanded account of Jesus' being mocked by onlookers. Their taunting reminds the reader of earlier events in the Gospel. Mark has used references to time to situate events throughout the passion account: The trial before Pilate takes place after dawn at an unspecified time; the crucifixion takes place at the third hour (9:00 A.M.); the mockery by the soldiers, the march to the place of execution, and the crucifixion of the condemned occupies most of the time be-

---

664. See the detailed treatment of this motif as a structural pattern for the whole Markan passion narrative by George E. Nickelsburg, "The Genre and Function of the Markan Passion Narrative," *HTR* 73 (1980) 153-84.

665. Robert H. Gundry, *Mark: A Commentary on His Apology for the Cross* (Grand Rapids: Eerdmans, 1993) 953, argues that identifying the father by the sons' names implies that he is not known to the audience.

666. See Joachim Gnilka, *Das Evangelium nach Markus. 1 Teilband Mk 1-8, 26,* EKKNT II (Zurich: Benziger, 1978) 2:314.

667. See Artemidorus *Interpretation of Dreams* 2.56.

668. So Raymond E. Brown, *The Death of the Messiah: From Gethsemane to the Grave. A Commentary on the Passion Narratives in the Four Gospels,* vol. 2 (Garden City, N.Y.: Doubleday, 1994) 914-15.

669. The suggestion that a gesture of respect, distinguishing Jesus from the common criminal, is intended need not imply ascribing royal dignity to Jesus, as Gnilka has proposed (*Das Evangelium nach Markus,* 2:311).

670. Cf. Gundry, *Mark,* 954-56.

tween the trial before Pilate and 9:00 A.M. (v. 25).[671] Jesus will die after hanging something over six hours on the cross.[672] Since prisoners often survived more than twenty-four hours, Jesus' death came an unusually short time into his crucifixion (v. 44). Mark repeats that they "crucified him" three times in vv. 24-27. Each repetition introduces another element of the scene surrounding Jesus as the righteous sufferer: The soldiers divide his garments (v. 24); the charge on the cross specifies his crime, "king of the Jews" (vv. 25-26); he is crucified between two "bandits" (λῃσταί lēstai, cf. 14:48).

Mark has arranged the taunting so that everyone rejects Jesus. Those who happen to pass by shake their heads at him (cf. Ps 22:8) and repeat the false charge that Jesus had promised to destroy the Temple and rebuild it in three days (v. 29), echoing the testimony of false witnesses in the Sanhedrin trial (14:58). Members of the Sanhedrin participate in the mockery by renewing the challenge to Jesus to save himself and adding the peculiar charges that they had formulated to serve as grounds for execution, "Messiah, King of Israel" (v. 32a). They actually taunt Jesus with the challenge to save himself from the cross by claiming that if he did so they "would see and believe" (v. 32b). Mark's reader, knowing that even Jesus' disciples had difficulty "seeing and believing," cannot consider that remark anything other than vicious sarcasm. Finally, Mark adds the note that the men crucified with Jesus also mock him (v. 32c).[673]

15:33. Three hours of darkness begin at noon. Mark may intend readers to recognize the darkness as a divine sign of judgment against those persons who mocked Jesus (cf. Amos 5:18). In the ancient Near East, cosmological signs were thought to accompany the death of great persons. Mark's readers probably knew the story that the sun had grown dark when Julius Caesar died as well.[674]

15:34. As his death approaches, Jesus prays the opening words of Ps 22:2. Scholars disagree over whether readers are intended to supply the entire lament, including the words of confidence in divine vindication (Ps 22:23-32)[675] or whether they are to consider only the words quoted. In the latter case, Jesus appears to be abandoned even by God. He is not depicted as a heroic martyr with his eyes firmly focused on heaven (cf. Stephen in Acts 7:54-60). Instead, Jesus has identified completely with the suffering righteous of the lament psalms, who cry out against God's apparent indifference to their plight. In quoting the psalm, Mark distinguishes Jesus' cry of despair from the anguished cries of pain that crucifixion was designed to elicit from its victims.[676]

15:35-36. The crowd, still looking for a miraculous rescue, misinterprets Jesus' words as a cry to Elijah. Someone offers Jesus sour wine (cf. Ps 69:21); although such wine was a common peasant drink, probably brought to the execution site by the soldiers who would have to watch over the dying men for hours, the psalm text suggests that the gesture was not intended as an act of kindness.[677] The person who offers the wine also wonders whether Elijah will rescue Jesus. Mark's reader knows that Elijah will not save Jesus from suffering, since Elijah has already returned in the person of John the Baptist and has been executed (9:11-13). However, the question is formulated in a way that suggests a miraculous sign at Jesus' death: "Let us see if Elijah will come and take him down." The challenge suggests that even if Jesus dies, a miraculous rescue, an ascent into heaven like that of Elijah, would be evidence of Jesus' claims. Instead, a human being comes to take Jesus' dead body down from the cross (v. 46).

15:37-39. A loud cry signals Jesus' death (v. 37). Mark's juxtaposition of the loud cry with the notice that the Temple veil is torn leads some interpreters to treat the cry as an apocalyptic sign that causes the veil to tear. The text does not make clear what is symbolized by this event or which veil was torn. The inner veil separating the holy of holies from the rest of the sanctuary might

---

671. See Brown, *The Death of the Messiah*, 958.

672. The traditions do not agree about when Jesus was crucified. In John 19:14 the trial before Pilate continues until noon. Brown (ibid., 958-61) suggests that Mark created the intervening time references to divide the time between the trial (near dawn) and Jesus' death (about 3:00 P.M.). If the tradition stated that Jesus was on the cross for six hours before Joseph removed the body (about 6:00 P.M.), the conclusion may drawn that he was crucified six hours prior to his death.

673. See Brown, *The Death of the Messiah*, 984-1000.

674. See Pliny *Naturalis Historia* 2.30 sec. 98; Virgil *Georgics* 1.466-68. See also Rudolph Pesch, *Das Markusevangelium I. Teil*, HTKNT II (Freiburg: Herder, 1977) 2:493.

675. Joel Marcus, *The Way of the Lord: Christological Exegesis of the Old Testament in the Gospel of Mark* (Minneapolis: Fortress, 1992) 177-82, emphasizes the tradition of interpreting the psalm in an eschatological context. Its triumphant conclusion and worship by the nations (v. 27) suits the centurion's confession. Although Mark does not cite this section of the psalm in the passion narrative, his allusions to it throughout the narrative remind readers of the later verses.

676. See Brown, *The Death of the Messiah*, 1044.

677. See ibid., 1059-64.

be intended to reveal that God is no longer present there or that now there is open access to God's presence. Other interpreters think that for Mark the torn veil foreshadowed the destruction of the Temple. The *Gospel of the Nazarenes* replaced the torn veil with the collapse of a large lintel, evidently an alternative symbol of the Temple's destruction.[678] Still other exegetes think that the torn Temple veil is a cosmological sign. If the outer veil, embroidered with signs of the zodiac,[679] is meant, then the torn zodiac and the darkened sun remind Mark's readers of the cosmic signs that will herald the coming of the Son of Man (13:24-26); darkened sun, stars falling, and disturbed heavenly powers were traditionally associated with the prelude to a divine theophany.

The centurion's confession is likewise appropriate to such a divine manifestation: "Truly this man was God's Son!" (v. 39). This centurion's confession recalls the two earlier examples of that identification, both spoken by the divine voice (1:10; 9:7). At Jesus' baptism, the heavens were "opened" (σχιζομένους *schizomenous*) just as the veil of the Temple is now "torn" (ἐσχίσθη *eschisthē*). Both Moses and Elijah were present at the transfiguration, a clear sign to Mark's reader that Jesus will be taken up into heavenly glory. In this case, a human being speaks the words of the heavenly voice. The centurion's confession has led scholars to ponder what it was that he saw that evoked this response. Since the soldiers had previously mocked Jesus' apparent claims of royalty (15:16-24), it cannot be said that the centurion was sympathetic to Jesus. Martyrdom traditions include elements of vindication in which the torturers recognize what they have done (cf. Wis 5:1-8).[680] The only "sign" of Jesus' vindication in the narrative is the torn veil of the Temple.[681]

15:40-41. The journey to the cross began with Simon of Cyrene, who is identified by reference to his two sons. The witness of others to what happened is critical to understanding the authenticity of the traditions about Jesus' death, since his male disciples had fled. Now, Mark appends a list of Galilean women as witnesses to the crucifixion.[682] The three women named—Mary Magdalene, Mary the mother of James and Joses, and Salome—are identified as women who followed and provided for Jesus in Galilee (v. 41). Mark has never mentioned them before; their names were probably taken from the empty tomb and burial traditions. Mark inserts this notice to provide a link between the crucifixion and the traditions associated with Jesus' tomb. Other Galilean women are also said to be present. This group of Galilean women highlights the absence of Jesus' male disciples. It is the only time that women followers of Jesus appear publicly in Mark's Gospel.

---

678. See ibid., 1099-1101.

679. Josephus *The Jewish War* 5.5.4; sec. 213; *Antiquities of the Jews* 3.6.4; sec. 132. See also David Ulansey, "The Heavenly Veil Torn: Mark's Cosmic *Inclusio*," *JBL* 110 (1991) 123-25.

680. See Ernest Best, *The Temptation and Passion: The Markan Soteriology*, 2nd ed., SNTSMS 2 (Cambridge: Cambridge University Press, 1990) xlvii; George Nickesburg, "The Genre and Function of the Markan Passion Narrative," *HTR* 73 (1980) 161-65.

681. Of course, the "apocalyptic sign" of the torn veil cannot be used to construct a geographical location for Golgotha that would make it actually possible for the centurion to see the event. See Brown, *The Death of the Messiah*, 1144-45.

682. The evangelist does not automatically represent as disciples the persons introduced into the story at this juncture. See ibid., 1157-59.

REFLECTIONS

1. The only surprise in the crucifixion scene is the dramatic confession by the centurion. All of the other characters in the episode continue to act as they have from the beginning of the passion account. The mockery scene appears especially cruel, as every disappointed hope is thrown back in Jesus' face. Yet the story is not without its hints of God's presence. The lament psalms move through suffering to confidence in God's saving power. Darkness silences those who are looking at the cross and taunting Jesus by making it impossible for them to see. Signs in the heaven herald the approach of God. Although the centurion represents the enemy who is forced to acknowledge the superiority of the oppressed, his confession supplies the real title that should be written on the cross: "Son of God." The fact that the centurion's confession stands at the end of Mark suggests that the whole story of Jesus must be heard, the crucifixion must be seen, before one knows what it means to confess "This is the Son of God."

---

2. The cross demonstrates divine power identified with the weak. Those who expect God to come and physically throw out the enemy are mistaken. Suffering, cruelty, wars, and their cost in innocent lives remain realities of human life. Disciples learn to find God at work in the sufferings of the present. They are not deterred by the mockery of those who think they have a false hope in God's saving power.

Mark 15:42-47, The Burial of Jesus

[42]It was Preparation Day (that is, the day before the Sabbath). So as evening approached, [43]Joseph of Arimathea, a prominent member of the Council, who was himself waiting for the kingdom of God, went boldly to Pilate and asked for Jesus' body. [44]Pilate was surprised to hear that he was already dead. Summoning the centurion, he asked him if Jesus had already died. [45]When he learned from the centurion that it was so, he gave the body to Joseph. [46]So Joseph bought some linen cloth, took down the body, wrapped it in the linen, and placed it in a tomb cut out of rock. Then he rolled a stone against the entrance of the tomb. [47]Mary Magdalene and Mary the mother of Joses saw where he was laid.

42When evening had come, and since it was the day of Preparation, that is, the day before the sabbath, [43]Joseph of Arimathea, a respected member of the council, who was also himself waiting expectantly for the kingdom of God, went boldly to Pilate and asked for the body of Jesus. [44]Then Pilate wondered if he were already dead; and summoning the centurion, he asked him whether he had been dead for some time. [45]When he learned from the centurion that he was dead, he granted the body to Joseph. [46]Then Joseph[a] bought a linen cloth, and taking down the body,[b] wrapped it in the linen cloth, and laid it in a tomb that had been hewn out of the rock. He then rolled a stone against the door of the tomb. [47]Mary Magdalene and Mary the mother of Joses saw where the body[b] was laid.

a Gk *he*   *b* Gk *it*

COMMENTARY

The notice that it is near evening, just before the sabbath begins, introduces the burial.[683] Unlike the disciples of John the Baptist (6:29), Jesus' disciples do not appear to claim the body.[684] Even if they had not fled, Jesus' disciples might have had difficulty in obtaining the body from Pilate without a patron from the Jewish aristocracy in Jerusalem who could make the request.[685] Instead, Joseph of Arimathea, another sympathizer, emerges from the ranks of Jesus' enemies. Just as earlier a scribe had shown that he was not far from the kingdom of God (12:34), so also now a member of the group that had condemned Jesus claims the body for burial (vv. 43-45). Joseph had probably not participated in the proceedings against Jesus,

683. Although "preparation day" appears to designate the day before Passover, the term could also be used for Friday (Josephus *Antiquities of the Jews* 16.6.2; sec. 163). Deuteronomy 21:23*a* directs that bodies of those "hung on a tree" are to be removed before sundown (cf. Philo *On the Special Law* 3,28; sec. 152; Josephus *The Jewish Wars* 4.5.2; sec. 317; see also Pesch, *Das Markusevangelium*, 2:511-12). John 19:31 makes this concern the motive for the request.

684. The discovery of the skeleton of a first-century crucifixion victim in a family tomb indicates that retrieval of the body by friends or relatives was not impossible. See Joe Zias and James H. Charlesworth, "CRUCIFIXION: Archaeology, Jesus and the Dead Sea Scrolls,"

in *Jesus and the Dead Sea Scrolls*, J. H. Charlesworth, ed. (New York: Doubleday, 1992) 279-85.

685. In a traditional, hierarchical society, all requests to persons of superior rank must be mediated through patrons known to the person from whom the favor is being sought. Since this request is unusual—Pilate has no reason to think that Jesus is dead yet, and is not a normal petition to take the body for burial—the need for a patron trusted by Pilate would be even greater. For an extensive discussion of the disposal of bodies of such victims, see Brown, *The Death of the Messiah,* 1207-11.

since, like the earlier scribe, he awaits the coming of the kingdom.[686]

Rock tombs that are sealed by rolling a stone across the opening are common in the vicinity of the traditional site of Golgotha.[687] The purchase of a new linen shroud to bury Jesus may also be a sign of respect, just as the anonymous woman's extraordinary anointing had been (14:3-9). However, Joseph engages in only minimal preparations: tying the body in the shroud needed to place it in the

tomb.[688] To ensure that the tomb was correctly identified by the women when the sabbath was over, Mark adds the notice that two of the women who had been present at the crucifixion—Mary Magdalene and Mary the mother of Joses—observe Jesus' burial. Since Joseph is not one of Jesus' disciples, the women do not participate in the burial or lament as they normally would during a funeral. One must imagine that they had remained watching the body of Jesus and followed Joseph when he removed it to see what would happen.[689] The two Marys, along with Salome, return to the tomb on what we now call Easter morning.

686. Joseph was probably a sympathizer who acted out of piety, and not an actual follower of Jesus (so Pesch, *Das Markusevangelium,* 2:513). But tradition turns Joseph into a disciple of Jesus (Matt 27:57; John 19:38). Luke 23:51 assumes that he must have been present at the Sanhedrin but did not agree with its actions.

687. See Brown, *The Death of the Messiah,* 1271-83, for a discussion of the details of the burial. The first-century cave tombs in the area make the site on which the church of the Holy Sepulchre stands the most likely place for the cave tomb in which Joseph placed Jesus' body.

688. This detail indicates that Joseph is acting out of piety, not as a disciple of Jesus. See ibid., 1246.

689. Ibid., 1251.

REFLECTIONS

1. The decision for or against Jesus is not determined by the group to which a person belongs. Although Jesus had warned that rich persons find entering the kingdom difficult, Levi, the tax collector, became one of his disciples. Although scribes from Jerusalem are among Jesus' enemies from the beginning of the story, one scribe is near the kingdom of God. Although the Roman execution squad mock their prisoner, the officer in charge comes to recognize that he is Son of God. Although the wealthy chief priests and aristocrats who make up the Sanhedrin engineer Jesus' death, one of them steps forward to honor him with burial. These mediating characters make it clear that no individual can be judged because of his or her membership in a particular class. Sympathetic outsiders, and even potential believers, can be found everywhere. Such people will receive their reward (Mark 8:37, 41).

2. The dramatic story of Jesus' conflict with his enemies and the misunderstanding and fear among the disciples makes it appear that Jesus was a failure. Those who reach that conclusion have adopted the perspective of the hostile onlookers. Mark uses the tradition about Jesus' burial to demonstrate once again that Jesus' ministry touched many people who did not join the immediate circle of disciples. Joseph is such a person. One can only wonder what his next encounter with fellow members of the Sanhedrin was like. Jesus' disciples owe Joseph a debt of gratitude, because they failed to do what the Baptist's followers did for their teacher (6:29).

MARK 16:1-20, JESUS IS RISEN

NIV	NRSV
16 When the Sabbath was over, Mary Magdalene, Mary the mother of James, and Salome bought spices so that they might go to anoint Jesus' body. ²Very early on the first day of	**16** When the sabbath was over, Mary Magdalene, and Mary the mother of James, and Salome bought spices, so that they might go and anoint him. ²And very early on the first

NIV

the week, just after sunrise, they were on their way to the tomb ³and they asked each other, "Who will roll the stone away from the entrance of the tomb?"

⁴But when they looked up, they saw that the stone, which was very large, had been rolled away. ⁵As they entered the tomb, they saw a young man dressed in a white robe sitting on the right side, and they were alarmed.

⁶"Don't be alarmed," he said. "You are looking for Jesus the Nazarene, who was crucified. He has risen! He is not here. See the place where they laid him. ⁷But go, tell his disciples and Peter, 'He is going ahead of you into Galilee. There you will see him, just as he told you.'"

⁸Trembling and bewildered, the women went out and fled from the tomb. They said nothing to anyone, because they were afraid.

[The earliest manuscripts and some other ancient witnesses do not have Mark 16:9-20.]

⁹When Jesus rose early on the first day of the week, he appeared first to Mary Magdalene, out of whom he had driven seven demons. ¹⁰She went and told those who had been with him and who were mourning and weeping. ¹¹When they heard that Jesus was alive and that she had seen him, they did not believe it.

¹²Afterward Jesus appeared in a different form to two of them while they were walking in the country. ¹³These returned and reported it to the rest; but they did not believe them either.

¹⁴Later Jesus appeared to the Eleven as they were eating; he rebuked them for their lack of faith and their stubborn refusal to believe those who had seen him after he had risen.

¹⁵He said to them, "Go into all the world and preach the good news to all creation. ¹⁶Whoever believes and is baptized will be saved, but whoever does not believe will be condemned. ¹⁷And these signs will accompany those who believe: In my name they will drive out demons; they will speak in new tongues; ¹⁸they will pick up snakes with their hands; and when they drink deadly poison, it will not hurt them at all; they will place their hands on sick people, and they will get well."

¹⁹After the Lord Jesus had spoken to them, he

NRSV

day of the week, when the sun had risen, they went to the tomb. ³They had been saying to one another, "Who will roll away the stone for us from the entrance to the tomb?" ⁴When they looked up, they saw that the stone, which was very large, had already been rolled back. ⁵As they entered the tomb, they saw a young man, dressed in a white robe, sitting on the right side; and they were alarmed. ⁶But he said to them, "Do not be alarmed; you are looking for Jesus of Nazareth, who was crucified. He has been raised; he is not here. Look, there is the place they laid him. ⁷But go, tell his disciples and Peter that he is going ahead of you to Galilee; there you will see him, just as he told you." ⁸So they went out and fled from the tomb, for terror and amazement had seized them; and they said nothing to anyone, for they were afraid.ᵃ

THE SHORTER ENDING OF MARK

[[And all that had been commanded them they told briefly to those around Peter. And afterward Jesus himself sent out through them, from east to west, the sacred and imperishable proclamation of eternal salvation.ᵇ]]

THE LONGER ENDING OF MARK

9 [[Now after he rose early on the first day of the week, he appeared first to Mary Magdalene, from whom he had cast out seven demons. ¹⁰She went out and told those who had been with him, while they were mourning and weeping. ¹¹But when they heard that he was alive and had been seen by her, they would not believe it.

12After this he appeared in another form to two of them, as they were walking into the country. ¹³And they went back and told the rest, but they did not believe them.

14Later he appeared to the eleven themselves as they were sitting at the table; and he upbraided them for their lack of faith and stubbornness, because they had not believed those who saw him

---

ᵃSome of the most ancient authorities bring the book to a close at the end of verse 8. One authority concludes the book with the shorter ending; others include the shorter ending and then continue with verses 9-20. In most authorities verses 9-20 follow immediately after verse 8, though in some of these authorities the passage is marked as being doubtful.   ᵇOther ancient authorities add *Amen*

NIV

was taken up into heaven and he sat at the right hand of God. ²⁰Then the disciples went out and preached everywhere, and the Lord worked with them and confirmed his word by the signs that accompanied it.

NRSV

after he had risen.ᵃ ¹⁵And he said to them, "Go into all the world and proclaim the good newsᵇ to the whole creation. ¹⁶The one who believes and is baptized will be saved; but the one who does not believe will be condemned. ¹⁷And these signs will accompany those who believe: by using my name they will cast out demons; they will speak in new tongues; ¹⁸they will pick up snakes in their hands,ᶜ and if they drink any deadly thing, it will not hurt them; they will lay their hands on the sick, and they will recover."

19So then the Lord Jesus, after he had spoken to them, was taken up into heaven and sat down at the right hand of God. ²⁰And they went out and proclaimed the good news everywhere, while the Lord worked with them and confirmed the message by the signs that accompanied it.ᵈ]]

ᵃOther ancient authorities add, in whole or in part, And they excused themselves, saying, "This age of lawlessness and unbelief is under Satan, who does not allow the truth and power of God to prevail over the unclean things of the spirits. Therefore reveal your righteousness now"—thus they spoke to Christ. And Christ replied to them, "The term of years of Satan's power has been fulfilled, but other terrible things draw near. And for those who have sinned I was handed over to death, that they may return to the truth and sin no more, that they may inherit the spiritual and imperishable glory of righteousness that is in heaven."   ᵇOr gospel
ᶜOther ancient authorities lack in their hands
ᵈOther ancient authorities add Amen

COMMENTARY

The passion predictions (Mark 8:31; 9:31; 10:34) and Jesus' promise to go before the disciples to Galilee after his resurrection (Mark 14:28) have led the reader to assume that the story cannot end with the death and burial of Jesus. The references to the coming of the Son of Man in judgment (13:24-27) in Jesus' discourse on the end time make it clear that the parousia lies in the future.[690] It cannot be the occasion on which Jesus reassembles the scattered disciples. The passion predictions include the notice that Jesus will rise from the dead three days after his death. Readers asked to state what they think should come next might supply a story about

the risen Jesus and the disciples, probably in Galilee. The fact that such a story is never told has led to extensive debate over the conclusion of the Gospel.

In antiquity, scribes supplemented the Gospel with two endings. Some manuscripts add a brief summary affirming that Jesus sent the disciples out on a mission to the world.[691] A longer ending (16:9-20), already known in the early second century, combines elements from the resurrection appearance stories in the other Gospels or their traditions: (a) an appearance to Mary Magdalene (vv. 9-11; cf. John 20:1-2); (b) an appearance to two disciples on the road (vv. 12-13; cf. Luke 24:13-27); (c) an appearance to the disciples dur-

690. Adela Yarbro Collins (The Beginning of the Gospel [Minneapolis: Fortress, 1992] 22) emphasizes the importance of the open eschatological horizon in Mark. Jesus' life and death have made new possibilities available that are fulfilled only when the righteous are gathered from the ends of the earth at the end time (13:27).

691. This ending combines the command to the women to tell Peter and the disciples about the resurrection (Mark 16:7) with the general notice about the disciples' commissioning in second-century Christianity. Cf. 1 Clem. 5-6ff.; Pesch, Das Markusevangelium, 2:557-559.

ing a meal in which Jesus castigates them for refusing to believe witnesses to his resurrection and sends them on a worldwide mission (vv. 14-18; Luke 24:36-43; John 20:19-20), and (d) the ascension of Jesus (vv. 19-20; Luke 24:50-51; Acts 1:9-11). Elements of the apostolic tradition in Acts are also included in the longer ending: the ability to perform miracles, to speak in tongues, to handle deadly serpents, and to heal the sick, and Jesus' ascension into heaven after instructing his disciples.[692]

The oldest manuscripts of Mark's Gospel do not end that way. Instead, the angel[693] tells the women at the tomb that Jesus has been raised and sends them to remind the disciples of Jesus' earlier promise: "But go, tell his disciples and Peter that he is going ahead of you to Galilee; there you will see him, just as he told you" (v. 7). The angel's words add "there you will see him" to the earlier prediction. This addition solidifies the reader's anticipation of a further episode in Galilee. But the women flee and tell no one because they are afraid (v. 8).

Some scholars continue to hold that the original ending of Mark has been lost but might be reconstructed from elements in the endings of Matthew and Luke.[694] Such proposals represent a contemporary version of the efforts made by ancient readers. Most interpreters take 16:8 as the original conclusion of the Gospel. The challenge lies in finding a literary account of the relationship between this ending and the narrative structures of the Gospel as a whole.[695]

The fearful silence of the women repeats the flight and denial shown by the disciples earlier.[696] If the pre-Markan tomb story describes an angelo-

phany at the tomb, then fear as awe at the angelic presence is an expected response (cf. Luke 1:29-30).[697] Ordinarily, such fear is overcome by angelic reassurance. It does not result in flight and silence as in Mark 16:8.[698] Yet the reader knows that the disciples did go on to proclaim the gospel, that some of them were even martyred, and that Jesus did rise on the third day; so the rest of his promise must also come to pass.[699]

The dispute over resurrection between Jesus and the Sadducee skeptics (12:18-27) and the presence of Elijah and Moses in the transfiguration vision (9:2-4) provide the reader with information about what "resurrection" means. It implies that persons so described are with God in heavenly glory, not dead. Resurrection does not imply return to the conditions of bodily existence, such as the revival of Jairus's daughter (Mark 5:43). It means becoming like the angels (12:25). From the imagery of Dan 12:2-3, reflected in Mark 12:18-27, readers know that resurrection of the righteous represents the end-time renewal of all creation.[700] To announce that Jesus has been raised might suggest that the time of salvation has been initiated. The silence command following the transfiguration applied "until after the Son of Man should have risen from the dead" (9:9).[701] Therefore, Mark's readers will recognize that the angelic proclamation "he has been raised" indicates Jesus' special, heavenly status. In the Jewish tradition, Enoch, Moses, and Elijah all had been translated into heavenly glory.[702] The clues Mark provides for his readers do not apply to the women at the tomb. Rather Mark 9:10 indicates that Peter, James, and John kept the affair to themselves.

692. Cf. Pesch, *Das Evangelium nach Markus*, 2:544-55. Although not part of the original Gospel of Mark, this ending was declared canonical by the Council of Trent and is the Gospel reading for the feast of St. Mark in the Roman Catholic lectionary.

693. The Greek "young man" (v. 5, νεανίσκος *neaniskos*) has generated a number of theories that link this figure with the young man who flees in Gethsemane (14:51). The flight of that young man, like that of the disciples, means no return. The only possible connection between the two passages might lie in the contrast. By describing the angel as a "young man" Mark reminds readers of the missing disciples. Cf. Brown, *Death*, 297-305.

694. Gundry, *Mark*, 1009-21.

695. Cf. Norman R. Petersen, "When Is the End Not the End? Literary Reflections on the Ending of Mark's Narrative," *Int* 34 (1980) 151-66; Andrew T. Lincoln, "The Promise and the Failure—Mark 16:7, 8," *JBL* 106 (1989) 283-300.

696. Some readings of this ending suggest that it anticipates the suffering of Jesus' disciples in the time between the resurrection and Jesus' glorious return as Son of Man. Jesus' public vindication, the normal conclusion to a tale of the suffering righteous, did not take place on Easter. Disciples still await his coming (13:33-37; cf. Nickelsburg, "Genre," 182).

697. Cf. Hubert Ritt, "Die Frauen und die Osterbotschaft. Synopse der Grabesgeschichten (Mk 16, 1-8; Mt 26, 62-28, 15; Kj 24ml-121 Joh 20, 1-18), "*Auferstehung Jesu—Auferstehung der Christen,* G. Dautzenberg; H. Merklein; K. K. Müller (Freiburg: Herder, 1983) 122-23; Pheme Perkins, " 'I Have Seen the Lord' (John 20:18): Women Witnesses to the Resurrection," *Int* 46 (1992) 38-41.

698. Therefore, it is impossible to read the flight of the women in Mark 16:8 in a positive light. Cf. Lincoln, "Promise," 284-87.

699. Lincoln, "Promise," 297.

700. Collins, *Beginning of the Gospel*, 144.

701. The reader may also recall that the command to secrecy in Mark 1:44 was "see that you say nothing to anyone." It was broken by speech. Here the command to tell is broken by silence. See Lincoln, "Promise," 290-91. Jesus' identity remains a mystery at the end of the Gospel. The reader must construct the insight into who Jesus is from the clues in the narrative that point toward the Christian experience of Jesus as Lord.

702. See Collins, *Beginning of the Gospel,* 138-43; James D. Tabor, " 'Returning to the Divinity': Josephus' Portrayal of the Disappearance of Enoch, Elijah and Moses," *JBL* 108 (1989) 225-38.

Readers have also learned that fear demonstrates lack of faith among Jesus' followers. Their fear during the storms at sea indicates a hardhearted misunderstanding: The disciples do not recognize that Jesus exercises God's saving power over the waters of chaos (4:40-41; 6:50-52). Peter's inappropriate response to the transfiguration vision is motivated by fear (9:6). The passion predictions elicit fear and misunderstanding (9:32; 10:32). In all of these cases, fear isolates the disciples from Jesus. Jesus is not present at the tomb. The women's flight, like that of the disciples before them, illustrates the effect of such isolation.

Creedal formulae describing the resurrection do not associate the empty tomb with resurrection (1 Cor 15:3-5). Many scholars think that the empty tomb story was a legend that developed around a cult associated with the tomb in Jerusalem. But such a cult legend would have little significance for Gentile Christians. Mark 13:14-15 warns those in Judea to flee when the desolating sacrilege appears. Those who argue for a cult legend presume that pointing to the place in the angel's word, "Look, there is the place they laid him" (v. 6), reflects the high point of such a rite. An alternate reading that emphasized the preceding sentence, "He has been raised; he is not here," forms the center of the episode. It argues against attachment to any physical place. Attention to where Jesus was laid serves to emphasize the emptiness of the tomb, not its suitability to cultic celebration.[703]

If the picture of Jesus' talking with Moses and Elijah at the transfiguration provides the key to this episode, then emphasis on the fact that Jesus is not in the tomb indicates that Jesus has been translated into heaven just as they were. (Mark's Gentile readers may have been familiar with the imagery of the emperor being translated into heaven from the funeral pyre.) Jesus would not appear on earth, but he might appear in his heavenly reality. Nevertheless, the angel's words

point to a promise that the disciples and Peter would "see him as he told you" in Galilee, suggesting a reunion that is more than an ecstatic vision of Jesus exalted in heaven, identified with an angelic figure at God's right hand.[704] Since the message is directed to the disciples who had fled and particularly to Peter who had denied Jesus, "see again" does not appear to refer to the public manifestation of the Son of Man in judgment (13:26-27; 14:62). It must refer to the resurrection appearances of the Lord that were known to Mark's readers in early creedal formulae (e.g., 1 Cor 15:3-5).[705]

The opening of the pericope contains two time references (vv. 1-2). Verse 1 links the episode to the previous section, both in time ("the day before the Sabbath," 15:42), and by the list of names (15:40, 47). Verse 1 also gives the reason for the women's visit to the tomb. Although Jesus was anointed with costly, pure myrrh prior to his death (14:3), Joseph did not anoint the body prior to burying it. The second temporal notice (v. 2) may have been in part taken from the source that Mark used for this episode. The phrase "early in the morning" takes the reader back to the consultation just before Jesus is turned over to Pilate (15:1). Mark may have arranged the matching notices to emphasize that the "third day" of resurrection has arrived.[706]

The women's concern with the way the stone will be removed (v. 3) reminds the reader that they witnessed Joseph rolling it across the entrance (15:46). They are presumed to have witnessed the minimal burial preparations as well. Hence, the women know that the body was not anointed. In order to indicate that their finding the tomb open is unusual, Mark adds the notice that the stone was very large (v. 4). It also emphasizes the need for a helper if the women are to accomplish their task of anointing the body.[707]

When they enter the tomb, the women see an angel (v. 5). Some interpreters have claimed that

---

703. On the historicity of the empty tomb traditions, see W. L. Craig, "The Historicity of the Empty Tomb of Jesus," *NTS* 31 (1985) 39-67. Even if the empty-tomb tradition was formulated after the fact on the basis of an understanding of resurrection as restoration of the physical body, more like 2 Macc than Dan 12, as Collins suggests (*Beginning of the Gospel*, 144-47), there is no basis in the Markan narrative for interest in venerating the tomb. Tombs that were venerated in antiquity contain the remains of a prophet, a sage, or a saint. The empty tomb—like the empty Temple—points the reader's attention to the presence of Jesus with God in heaven.

704. For this type of identification as the basis for early Christian belief in the divine status of the risen Jesus, see Alan Segal, "The Risen Christ and the Angelic Mediator Figures," in Charlesworth, *Jesus and the Dead Sea Scrolls*, 302-38.

705. See Lincoln, "Promise," 285.

706. See Gundry, *Mark*, 988-90.

707. Pesch, *Das Markusevangelium*, 2:531. The need for a helper reminds readers of the missing disciples. Joseph of Arimathea is not a disciple of Jesus in Mark's account.

the young man in a white robe should not be interpreted as an angel but as the youth who fled in Gethsemane (14:51-52). This view ignores the women's reaction, the fear appropriate to an angelic appearance (cf. Luke 1:11-12, 29), and the fact that the reader has already learned from the transfiguration that shining, white garments designate a heavenly being (9:3). The angel already knows what the women are seeking.[708] Perhaps, the fact that the angel is seated on the right side is intended to remind the reader that as the exalted Son of Man, Jesus now sits at the right hand of God (14:62).

Angelophanies typically include reassurance, a statement about what the individual witnesses, and a command concerning what the person is to do in the future. Verses 6-7 have expanded these features with summary statements that relate the resurrection announcement to the earlier narrative. Even if Mark took over the earlier story of an angelic appearance to some women, he has reformulated its content to refer to his own narrative. The concrete identification of the person being sought, "Jesus of Nazareth, who was crucified" (v. 6), serves an apologetic function. It wards off the possible objection that the women had gone into the wrong tomb. (Mark 15:47 also indicated that the women knew where Jesus had been laid.) The expression "has been raised" reflects the early kerygma of the church (1 Cor 15:4) rather than the passion predictions in the Gospel.[709] The traditional phrase has been framed with references to the tomb: (a) you are seeking . . . Jesus; and (b) see . . . the place. This concentric composition uses the traditional resurrection kerygma to interpret the empty tomb. Since resurrection was depicted as God's end-time vindication of the righteous, the emptiness of the tomb would not initially lead to the conclusion that Jesus had been raised.[710]

Mark has formulated the commission the angel gives to the women in v. 7 to underline the failure of Jesus' disciples. Although modern commentators usually speak of the women *disciples* replacing the men at the cross, the evangelist never speaks of women as "disciples." They are among Jesus' true family (3:35) and are said to have followed and provided for him (15:40-41). However, the title *disciples* refers to those male followers of the teacher who participated directly in his activities.[711] Their failures to comprehend who Jesus is and to stand by him in his passion have already been underlined.

The angel's words are formulated to do so once again. The phrase "his disciples and Peter" singles out Peter, because he had boasted that he would die with Jesus even if all the rest fled (14:31); instead, he denied even knowing who Jesus was (14:71).[712] When the reader last saw Peter, he was weeping as he recalled Jesus' words. This message contains a note of promise for the apostle: He will be reunited with Jesus. The tradition that Mark reworked may have contained a special reference to Peter, because he was the first disciple to see the risen Lord (cf. 1 Cor 15:5, "he appeared to Cephas, then to the twelve").

The women are told to remind the disciples of the promise that Jesus had already made. After his resurrection, he would go before them to Galilee (14:28). As we have seen, this promise recalls the earlier picture of Jesus "going before" his frightened disciples on the road up to Jerusalem (10:32). The angel adds a clause to the earlier promise, "there you will see him." Although some exegetes hold that "you will see" refers to the coming of the Son of Man in glory (14:62), the context suggests a resurrection appearance in which the disciples are commissioned to finally undertake the mission for which Jesus has prepared them. The silence command that followed the transfiguration was limited to the time before the resurrection (9:9).

Readers may construct the future mission of Jesus' disciples based on their own experience of the early Christian mission (13:9-13). "Go before" indicated the relationship between Jesus and the disciples on the journey to Jerusalem (10:32). Now the disciples are to proclaim that the crucified Jesus of Nazareth is the beloved Son of God. By following Jesus back to Galilee, the disciples

---

708. Ibid., 532.

709. Ibid., 533.

710. See Joachim Gnilka, *Das Evangelium nach Markus. 1 Teilband Mk 1–8, 26*, EKKNT II (Zurich: Benziger, 1978) 2:342. The Fourth Gospel makes this fact evident. Mary Magdalene assumes that "they" (probably "the Jews") have taken the body of Jesus away (John 20:2, 13-15).

711. See Winsome Munro, "Women Disciples in Mark?" *CBQ* 44 (1982) 255-41; Elizabeth S. Malbon, "Fallible Followers: Women and Men in the Gospel of Mark," *Semeia* 28 (1983) 29-48.

712. Or perhaps even cursed Jesus; so Andrew T. Lincoln, "The Promise and the Failure—Mark 16:7, 8," *JBL* 106 (1989) 289.

begin their mission where Jesus had begun his.[713] Matthew clearly understood the angel's words as a reference to such a commissioning vision in Galilee. Thus he concludes his Gospel with the account of a vision on the mountain in Galilee (Matt 28:16-20).

Mark's narrative ends at the tomb in Jerusalem. The "terror and amazement" that seize the women remind the reader that the women have just experienced a divine revelation (cf. 9:6). The second half of v. 8 poses the problem of an apparently incomplete ending, which has perplexed readers from Matthew to the present. This abrupt ending forces the reader to reassemble the rest of the story out of clues given earlier in the Gospel. As we have seen, these clues point to a more extensive story that is shared, by the evangelist and his readers. It must have included at least one resurrection appearance in Galilee; the subsequent missionary activity by the disciples, the martyrdom of James and John, and the future coming of Jesus as Son of Man, have all been clearly indicated.[714] Nothing in the narrative tells the reader whether the women broke their silence except for the presence of the tomb story itself. Since they are the only witnesses to the location of the tomb and to the angelophany, they must have told someone eventually. However, human testimony did not overcome the scandal of the cross. Jesus' words have always been fulfilled. Therefore, his promise that the failure of the disciples would be overcome can also be trusted. No intermediaries can reverse the situation. Only the word and presence of Jesus restores faith among the disciples.[715]

The fulfilled promise to which the angelic message points remains off stage. Mark has insisted that the cross is the way to life for those who wish to follow Jesus. He does not compromise the paradox of suffering service by producing a glorious triumph in the end. Instead, the reader must learn that the powerlessness of Jesus on the cross has broken apart the old order of evil and initiated the rule of God.[716]

713. Mark's formulation of the command given the women indicates that the disciples' Easter faith was not mediated by their testimony. It can emerge only when they see the Lord.

714. Collins (*Beginning of the Gospel,* 137) points out that it was common practice in ancient literature to refer to events that would occur after the time of the narrative without actually recounting those events. Therefore, the fact that Mark does not narrate appearances of Jesus to Peter and the others does not mean that Mark did not think that such resurrection appearances actually occurred.

715. Lincoln ("Promise," 298-300) thinks that Mark's narrative does leave the reader with an unanswered question. Mark and his readers live in a present between the cross/resurrection and the parousia that is marked by mission and suffering discipleship. The gospel anticipates an end to that situation when the Son of Man returns in glory. The public vindication of the gospel's claims about Jesus and discipleship are associated with the parousia. Therefore, the question remains: What happens to the ethos of the gospel if the parousia promise appears to have failed?

716. Dorothy A. Lee-Pollard, "Powerlessness as Power: A Key Emphasis in the Gospel of Mark," *SJT* 40 (1987) 186-87.

REFLECTIONS

Matthew shifted the ending of his Gospel so that it conforms to the expectations created by the narrative: Jesus appears twice, to the women at the tomb (Matt 28:8-10) and to the disciples in Galilee (Matt 28:16-20). The women rush to tell the disciples (v. 8). The risen Jesus sends the eleven remaining disciples to gather a new people by preaching to the nations (vv. 19-20). The Gospels of Luke and John conclude with even more expansive stories of Jesus appearing and commissioning his disciples. Subsequent generations of Christians bring their knowledge of these stories to the ending of Mark. It is not clear whether Mark's readers were familiar with actual narratives about Jesus' appearances. Despite the fact that Jesus' appearances to Peter, to the Twelve, and to other followers were well-known (1 Cor 15:3-10), narrative accounts of such events were not necessarily widely circulated. Even when the apostle Paul discusses resurrection in 1 Corinthians, he does not refer to details of his own experience of the risen Lord.

It is possible to believe in the death and resurrection of Jesus without appearance stories. Early christological hymns speak of the self-emptying of Jesus on the cross and his exaltation at the right hand of God over all the powers in the cosmos (cf. Phil 2:6-11; Heb 1:2-4). The vision of the Son of Man in Dan 7:13-14 described a human figure ascending to God's throne in heaven. When Paul experienced the reality of the risen Jesus as God's Son (Gal 1:16), he apparently did so in the context of a vision of Jesus' heavenly exaltation (2 Cor 12:1-6).[717] The transfiguration story in Mark's Gospel is a vision of heavenly figures along with the presence and voice of God. According to this tradition, the resurrection of Jesus cannot be confirmed by appearances of Jesus on earth. Matthew resolves that difficulty by having Jesus tell the disciples that he has been invested with cosmic authority (Matt 28:18). Despite the appearance story, resurrection faith remains dependent upon the word of Jesus and the disciples' experience of the power of God that is active through Jesus.

Mark's ending reminds Christians that resurrection is exaltation to God's glory, not another event in the sequence of events that we catalogue as history. The women's response also brings readers face to face with the mystery of faith. There are no heroes among Jesus' followers. The hostility that puts Jesus on the cross has reduced them all to flight and fearful silence. Nevertheless, God brings faith out of just such weakness and failure. Jesus did not need to come once again and choose a new team in some grand lottery for better disciples. Despite all the appearances, Jesus did accomplish the will of God through suffering on the cross. However imperfect our faith and however many times we remain silent when we should testify to the gospel, we can always return to the Lord. None of us can get so far away from Jesus that we cannot be touched by God's healing presence.

717. See Segal, "Angelic Mediator Figures," 314-18.

TRANSLITERATION SCHEMA

HEBREW AND ARAMAIC TRANSLITERATION

Consonants:

א	=	'	ט	=	t	פ or ף	=	p	
ב	=	b	י	=	y	צ or ץ	=	$ṣ$	
ג	=	g	כ or ך	=	k	ק	=	q	
ד	=	d	ל	=	l	ר	=	r	
ה	=	h	מ or ם	=	m	שׂ	=	$ś$	
ו	=	w	נ or ן	=	n	שׁ	=	$š$	
ז	=	z	ס	=	s	ת	=	t	
ח	=	$ḥ$	ע	=	'				

Masoretic Pointing:

Pure-long			Tone-long			Short			Composite *shewa*		
הָ	=	$â$		=	$ā$		=	a		=	$ă$
ִי	=	$ê$		=	$ē$		=	e	or	=	$ĕ$
or ִי	=	$î$					=	i			
or וֹ	=	$ô$		=	$ō$		=	o		=	$ŏ$
or וּ	=	$û$					=	u			

GREEK TRANSLITERATION

α	=	a	ι	=	i	ρ	=	r
β	=	b	κ	=	k	σ or ς	=	s
γ	=	g	λ	=	l	τ	=	t
δ	=	d	μ	=	m	υ	=	y
ε	=	e	ν	=	n	φ	=	ph
ζ	=	z	ξ	=	x	χ	=	ch
η	=	$ē$	ο	=	o	ψ	=	ps
θ	=	th	π	=	p	ω	=	$ō$

INDEX OF MAPS, CHARTS, AND ILLUSTRATIONS

Index of Excursuses

ABBREVIATIONS

Ep. Arist.	*Epistle of Aristeas*
Jub.	*Jubilees*
Pss. Sol.	*Psalms of Solomon*
Sib. Or.	*Sibylline Oracles*
T. Levi	Testament of Levi
Gos. Pet.	Gospel of Peter
1 Clem.	1 Clement
Did.	Didache
Ign. *Eph.*	Ignatius, *Letter to the Ephesians*
Ign. *Magn.*	Ignatius, *Letter to the Magnesians*
Ign. *Phld.*	Ignatius, *Letter to the Philadelphians*
Ign. *Pol.*	Ignatius, *Letter to Polycarp*
Ign. *Rom.*	Ignatius, *Letter to the Romans*
Ign. *Smyrn.*	Ignatius, *Letter to the Smyrnaeans*

Names of Dead Sea Scrolls and Related Texts

CD	Cairo (Genizah text of the) *Damascus (Document)*
1Q, 2Q, 3Q, 4Q, etc.	Numbered caves of Qumran, yielding written material; followed by abbreviation of biblical or apocryphal book
1QH	*Hôdāayôt* (*Thanksgiving Hymns*) from Qumran Cave 1
1QpHab	*Pesher on Habakkuk* from Qumran Cave 1
1QM	*Milhāmāh* (*War Scroll*)
1QS	*Serek hayyahad* (*Rule of the Community, Manual of Discipline*)
1QSa	Appendix A (*Rule of the Congregation*) to 1QS
4QFlor	*Florilegium* (or *Eschatological Midrashim*) from Qumran Cave 4
4QpNah	*Nahum Pesher* from Qumran Cave 4
4QpPss^a	*Psalm Pesher A* from Qumran Cave 4
4QPs37	*Psalm Scroll* from Qumran Cave 4
4QTestim	*Testimonia* text from Qumran Cave 4
11QMelch	*Melchizedek* text from Qumran Cave 11
11QPs^a	*Psalm Scroll* from Qumran Cave 11
11QTemple	*Temple Scroll* from Qumran Cave 11

Orders and Tractates in Mishnaic and Related Literature

To distinguish the same-named tractates in the Mishna, Tosepta, Babylonian Talmud, and Jerusalem Talmud, *m., t., b.,* or *y.* precedes the title of the tractate.

ʾAbot	*ʾAbot*
B. Bat.	Baba Batra
Ber.	Berakot
Git.	Gittin
Menah.	Menahot
Pesah.	Pesahim
Šabb.	Šabbat
Sanh.	Sanhedrin
Sota	Sota
Taʿan.	Taʿanit
Yoma	Yoma (= Kippurim)

Other Rabbinic Works

ʾAbot R. Nat.	*ʾAbot de Rabbi Nathan*
Rab.	*Rabbah* (following abbreviation for biblical book)

Greek Manuscripts and Ancient Versions

Papyrus Manuscripts

$\mathfrak{P}^1$	Third-century Greek Papyrus manuscript of the Gospels
$\mathfrak{P}^{29}$	Third- or fourth-century Greek Papyrus manuscript
$\mathfrak{P}^{33}$	Sixth-century Greek Papyrus manuscript of Acts
$\mathfrak{P}^{37}$	Third- or fourth-century Greek Papyrus manuscript of the Gospels
$\mathfrak{P}^{38}$	Fourth-century Greek Papyrus manuscript of Acts
$\mathfrak{P}^{45}$	Third-century Greek Papyrus manuscript of the Gospels
$\mathfrak{P}^{48}$	Third-century Greek Papyrus manuscript of Acts
$\mathfrak{P}^{52}$	Second-century Greek Papyrus manuscript of John 18:31-33, 37-38
$\mathfrak{P}^{58}$	Sixth-century Greek Papyrus manuscript of Acts
$\mathfrak{P}^{64}$	Third-century Greek Papyrus fragment of Matthew
$\mathfrak{P}^{66}$	Third-century Greek Papyrus manuscript of the Gospels
$\mathfrak{P}^{67}$	Third-century Greek Papyrus fragment of Matthew
$\mathfrak{P}^{75}$	Third-century Greek Papyrus manuscript of the Gospels

Lettered Uncials

ℵ	Codex Sinaiticus, fourth-century manuscript of LXX, NT, *Epistle of Barnabas,* and *Shepherd of Hermas*
A	Codex Alexandrinus, fifth-century manuscript of LXX, NT, 1 & 2 Clement, and Psalms of Solomon
B	Codex Vaticanus, fourth-century manuscript of LXX and parts of the NT
C	Codex Ephraemi, fifth-century manuscript of parts of LXX and NT
D	Codex Bezae, fifth-century bilingual (Greek and Latin) manuscript of the Gospels and Acts
G	Ninth-century manuscript of the Gospels
K	Ninth-century manuscript of the Gospels
L	Eighth-century manuscript of the Gospels
W	Washington Codex, fifth-century manuscript of the Gospels
Z	Sixth-century manuscript of Matthew
Θ	Koridethi Codex, ninth-century manuscript of the Gospels

Numbered Uncials

058	Fourth-century fragment of Matthew 18
074	Sixth-century fragment of Matthew
078	Sixth-century fragment of Matthew, Luke, and John
0170	Fifth- or sixth-century uncial manuscript of Matthew

Numbered Minuscules

33	Tenth-century manuscript of the Gospels
565	Ninth-century miniscule manuscript of the Gospels
700	An eleventh-century miniscule manuscript of the Gospels
892	Ninth-century miniscule manuscript of the Gospels

Ancient Versions

bo	The Bohairic (Memphitic) Coptic Version
bo^{mss}	Some manuscripts in the Bohairic tradition
bo^{pt}	Some manuscripts in the Bohairic tradition
ff^{2}	Old Latin manuscript, fifth-century translation of the Gospels
Ir^{lat}	The Latin translation of Iraneaus
latt	The whole Latin tradition (including the Vulgate)
mae	Middle Egyptian
sa	The Sahidic (Thebaic) Coptic Version
sy	The Syriac Version
sy^{s}	The Sinaitic Syriac Version

Other Abbreviations

pc	A few other manuscripts
f^{1}	Family 1: miniscule manuscripts belonging to the Lake Group (1, 118, 131, 209, 1582)
f^{13}	Family 13: miniscule manuscripts belonging to the Ferrar Group (13, 69, 124, 174, 230, 346, 543, 788, 826, 828, 983, 1689, 1709)
𝔐	The Majority text (the mass of later manuscripts)
C^{2}	The corrected text of Codex Ephraemi
700*	The original reading of manuscript 700

Commonly Used Periodicals, Reference Works, and Serials

AB	Anchor Bible
ABD	Anchor Bible Dictionary
AnBib	Analecta biblica
ANRW	*Aufstieg und Niedergang der römischen Welt*
ANTJ	Arbeiten zum Neuen Testament und Judentum
ASNU	Acta seminarii neotestamentici upsaliensis
BAR	*Biblical Archaeologist Reader*
BETL	Bibliotheca ephemeridum theologicarum lovaniensium
BZNW	BeiheRe *ZNW*
CB	*Cultura biblica*
CBQ	*Catholic Biblical Quarterly*
CBQMS	Catholic Biblical Quarterly—Monograph Series
CRINT	Compendia rerum iudaicarum ad novum testamentum
EKKNT	Evangelisch-katholischer Kommentar zum Neuen Testament
ExpTim	*Expository Times*
FRLANT	Forschungen zur Religion und Literatur des Alten und Neuen Testaments
GCS	Griechischen christlichen Schriftsteller
HDB	*Hastings Dictionary of the Bible*

HNT	Handbuch zum Neuen Testament
HTKNT	Herders theologischer Kommentar zum Neuen Testament
HTR	*Harvard Theological Review*
HTS	Harvard Theological Studies
IBS	*Irish Biblical Studies*
ICC	International Critical Commentary
IDB	G. A. Buttrick (ed.), *Interpreter's Dictionary of the Bible*
IDBSup	Supplementary volume to *IDB*
Int	*Interpretation*
IRT	Issues in Religion and Theology
JBL	*Journal of Biblical Literature*
JR	*Journal of Religion*
JSNT	*Journal for the Study of the New Testament*
JSNTSup	Journal for the Study of the New Testament—Supplement Series
JSOT	*Journal for the Study of the Old Testament*
JSP	*Journal for the Study of the Pseudepigrapha*
JTC	*Journal for Theology and the Church*
JTS	*Journal of Theological Studies*
NHS	Nag Hammadi Studies
NovT	*Novum Testamentum*
NovTSup	Novum Testamentum, Supplements
NTS	*New Testament Studies*
OTP	J. H. Charlesworth (ed.), *The Old Testament Pseudepigrapha*
RB	*Revue biblique*
SBB	Stuttgarter biblische Beiträge
SBL	Society of Biblical Literature
SBLDS	SBL Dissertation Series
SBLSP	SBL Seminar Papers
SBT	Studies in Biblical Theology
SJT	*Scottish Journal of Theology*
SNTSMS	Society for New Testament Studies Monograph Series
SVTP	Studia in Veteris Testamenti pseudepigrapha
TDNT	G. Kittel and G. Friedrich (eds.), *Theological Dictionary of the New Testament*
TS	*Theological Studies*
UBSGNT	United Bible Societies *Greek New Testament*
WBC	Word Biblical Commentary
ZNW	*Zeitschrift für die neutestamentliche Wissenschaft*